# a multilingual
# commercial dictionary

English (including American English)
German Spanish French Italian Portuguese

**Pan Books** London and Sydney

First published 1978 by Pan Books Ltd
Cavaye Place, London SW10 9PG
© Laurence Urdang Associates Ltd 1978
ISBN 0 330 25436 7
Prepared for automatic typesetting by
Laurence Urdang Associates Ltd Aylesbury
Typesetting by Oriel Computer Services Ltd, Oxford
Printed in Great Britain by Richard Clay
(The Chaucer Press) Ltd, Bungay, Suffolk.

# preface

Businessmen are finding that now, more than ever before, they are dealing at an international level ; this has meant that a knowledge of basic commercial terminology in several languages is not merely a convenience, it is essential. In business, the difference between a profit and a loss may rest on a correct interpretation of the terms on which a particular deal has been negotiated ; certainly the deal will be more easily negotiated if the terms are clear to all parties ! This dictionary provides a selection of the most commonly used terms in international business in six languages, with the addition of American English where it differs from British English. A particularly useful feature of the dictionary is that all the terms from all the languages are arranged alphabetically in the same list under the first letter of the term in the source language. Thus, the Englishman who wants to know the French for *bill of lading* will look under *b*. The Frenchman who wants to know the German for *bill of lading* will look in the same list under *c* for his native word *connaissement*. Both the Englishman and the Frenchman will find the equivalents of *bill of lading/ connaissement* in all the other languages.

The dictionary is designed to be useful to exporters and importers, bankers, accountants, and those concerned with finance, commodity and stock markets, insurance, shipping, manufacturing, wholesaling, and retailing. It will be indispensable to anyone doing business in or with the Common Market, Spain, Portugal and the countries of South America.

This book has been prepared for Pan Books Ltd
by Laurence Urdang Associates Ltd, Aylesbury
Series Editor: Dr Alan Isaacs

Contributors
Hans Smith, MA, FCII, Dip. Leg. Tr. (French, German)
F. García (Spanish)
A. Lauria Ll D (Italian)
Manolo B. R. Santos, BA, MIL (Portuguese)

# A

**abandon** *(m) n* Fr
De  Abandon *(m)*
En  abandonment
Es  abandono *(m)*
It  abbandono *(m)*
Pt  abandono *(m)*

**Abandon** *(m) n* De
En  abandonment
Es  abandono *(m)*
Fr  abandon *(m)*
It  abbandono *(m)*
Pt  abandono *(m)*

**abandonment** *n* En
De  Abandon *(m)*
Es  abandono *(m)*
Fr  abandon *(m)*
It  abbandono *(m)*
Pt  abandono *(m)*

**abandono** *(m) n* Es, Pt
De  Abandon *(m)*
En  abandonment
Fr  abandon *(m)*
It  abbandono *(m)*

**abbandono** *(m) n* It
De  Abandon *(m)*
En  abandonment
Es  abandono *(m)*
Fr  abandon *(m)*
Pt  abandono *(m)*

**abbonamento** *(m) n* It
De  Abonnement *(n)*
En  subscription (to a journal, etc.)
Es  abono *(m)*
Fr  abonnement *(m)*
Pt  assinatura *(f)*

**abbuono** *(m) n* It
De  Rabatt *(m)*
En  allowance
Es  bonificación *(f)*
Fr  rabais *(m)*
Pt  provisão *(f)*

**Abfallprodukt** *(n) n* De
En  waste products
Es  desperdicios *(m pl)*
Fr  déchets *(m pl)*
It  produtto di rifiuto *(m)*
Pt  desperdicios *(m pl)*

**abgabenfrei** *adj* De
En  duty-free
Es  exento de impuestos
Fr  exempt de douane
It  esente da dazio
Pt  isento de impostos

**abgabenpflichtig** *adj* De
En  dutiable
Es  tasable
Fr  taxable
It  tassabile
Pt  tributável

**Abgangstag** *(m) n* De
En  sailing date
Es  día de salida *(m)*
Fr  date de départ *(f)*
It  data di partenza *(f)*
Pt  dia de saída *(m)*

**ab Kai** De
En  ex quay
Es  en muelle
Fr  à prendre sur quai
It  sulla banchina
Pt  ex-cais

**Abkommen** *(n) n* De
En  agreement; covenant
Es  contrato; pacto *(m)*
Fr  convention *(f)*
It  accordo; convenzione *(m f)*
Pt  acordo; pacto *(m)*

**Ablauf** *(m) n* De
En  expiry
Es  expiración *(f)*

Fr  expiration *(f)*
It  termine *(m)*
Pt  expiração *(f)*

**Ablehnung** *(f) n* De
En  disclaimer; rejection
Es  renuncia rechazo *(f m)*
Fr  déni; refus *(m)*
It  rinunzia; rifiuto *(f m)*
Pt  descarte; rejeição *(m f)*

**ablösbare Vorzugsaktien** *(f pl)* De
En  redeemable preference shares
Es  acciónes preferentes amortizables *(f pl)*
Fr  actions privilégiées amortissables *(f pl)*
It  azioni preferenziali redimibili *(f pl)*
Pt  acções redimíveis preferenciais *(f pl)*

**abnehmend** *adj* De
En  diminishing
Es  decreciente
Fr  décroissant
It  decrescente
Pt  decrescente

**abnehmender Ertrag** *(m)* De
En  diminishing returns
Es  rendimientos decrecientes *(m pl)*
Fr  rendements décroissants *(m pl)*
It  proventi decrescenti *(m pl)*
Pt  rendimentos decrescentes *(m pl)*

**Abnehmerverein** *(m) n* De
En  consumer group
Es  grupo de consumidores *(m)*
Fr  groupe consommateur *(m)*
It  gruppo di consumatori *(m)*
Pt  grupo de consumidores *(m)*

**aboard** *adv* En
De  an Bord
Es  a bordo
Fr  à bord

It a bordo
Pt a bordo

**abogado** *(m) n* Es
De Anwalt *(m)*
En lawyer; barrister; counsel
Am attorney
Fr avocat *(m)*
It avvocato *(m)*
Pt advogado *(m)*

**abonnement** *(m) n* Fr
De Abonnement *(n)*
En subscription (to a journal, etc.)
Es abono *(m)*
It abbonamento *(m)*
Pt assinatura *(f)*

**Abonnement** *(n) n* De
En subscription (to a journal, etc.)
Es abono *(m)*
Fr abonnement *(m)*
It abbonamento *(m)*
Pt assinatura *(f)*

**abono** *(m) n* Es
De Abonnement *(n)*
En subscription (to a journal, etc.)
Fr abonnement *(m)*
It abbonamento *(m)*
Pt assinatura *(f)*

**à bord** Fr
De an Bord
En aboard
Es a bordo
It a bordo
Pt a bordo

**a bordo** Es, It, Pt
De an Bord
En aboard
Fr à bord

**above-mentioned** *adj* En
De obenerwähnt
Es susodicho
Fr susmentionné
It suddetto
Pt supracitado

**above par** En
De über Pari
Es a premio
Fr au-dessus du pair

It sopra la pari
Pt a prémio

**Abrechnung** *(f) n* De
En settlement (of accounts)
Es ajuste *(m)*
Fr règlement *(m)*
It quietanza *(f)*
Pt ajuste *(m)*

**Abrechnungstag** *(m) n* De
En settlement day; account day
Am due date
Es día de liquidación *(m)*
Fr jour de règlement *(m)*
It giorno della liquidazione *(m)*
Pt dia de liquidação *(m)*

**Abrechnungszeitraum** *(m) n* De
En accounting period
Es ejercicio *(m)*
Fr exercice *(f)*
It esercizio *(m)*
Pt exercício *(m)*

**a breve scadenza** It
De kurzfristig
En short-dated
Es a corto plazo
Fr à courte échéance
Pt a curto prazo

**a breve termine** It
De kurzfristig
En short-term
Es a corto plazo
Fr à court terme
Pt a curto prazo

**Abriss** *(m) n* De
En abstract
Es resumen *(m)*
Fr résumé *(m)*
It riassunto *(m)*
Pt resumo *(m)*

**abroad** *adv* En
De im Ausland
Es en el extranjero
Fr à l'étranger
It all'estero
Pt no estrangeiro

**Absatzdirektor** *(m) n* De
En marketing director
Es director mercantil *(m)*
Fr administrateur chef d'écoulement *(m)*
It direttore di mercato *(m)*
Pt director de comercialização *(m)*

**Absatzübereinkommen** *(n) n* De
En marketing agreement
Es acuerdo mercantil *(m)*
Fr accord de commercialisation *(m)*
It accordo di mercato *(m)*
Pt acordo sobre comercialização *(m)*

**Abschätzung** *(f) n* De
En appraisal
Es evaluación *(f)*
Fr évaluation *(f)*
It valutazione *(f)*
Pt avaliação *(f)*

**ab Schiff** De
En ex ship
Es en el buque
Fr ex ship
It ex ship
Pt ex-navio

**Abschluss** *(m) n* De
En deal
Es negocio *(m)*
Fr affaire *(f)*
It affare *(f)*
Pt negócio *(m)*

**Abschreibtypistin** *(f) n* De
En copy typist
Am transcriber
Es mecanógrafa *(f)*
Fr dactylo copiste *(f)*
It dattilografa *(f)*
Pt dactilógrafa *(f)*

**Abschreibung für Abnützung (AfA)** *(f)* De
En depreciation allowance
Es provisión para amortización *(f)*
Fr provision pour amortissement *(f)*
It quota di ammortamento *(f)*
Pt provisão para amortização *(f)*

**Abschrift** (f) n De
En copy
Es copia (f)
Fr copie (f)
It copia (f)
Pt cópia (f)

**abscond** vb En
De sich heimlich davonmachen
Es esconderse
Fr s'enfuir; décamper
It nascondersi
Pt ausentar-se para parte incerta

**absenden** vb De
En dispatch
Es expedir
Fr expédier
It spedire
Pt expedir

**Absender** (m) n De
En consignor
Es consignador (m)
Fr expéditeur (m)
It speditore (m)
Pt consignante (m)

**(zur) Absendung empfangen** De
En received for shipment
Es recibido para envio
Fr reçu pour envoi
It ricevuto per caricazione
Pt recebido para carregamento

**Absendungserklärung** (f) n De
En declaration of shipment
Es declaración de expedición (f)
Fr déclaration d'expédition (f)
It dichiarazione d'imbarco (f)
Pt declaração de expedição (f)

**absentee** n En
De Abwesende(r) (m)
Es ausente (m)
Fr manquant (m)
It assente (m)
Pt ausente (m)

**absenteeism** n En
De unerlaubte Abwesenheit (f)
Es ausentismo (m)
Fr absentéisme (m)

It assenteismo (m)
Pt absentismo (m)

**absentéisme** (m) n Fr
De unerlaubte Abwesenheit (f)
En absenteeism
Es ausentismo (m)
It assenteismo (m)
Pt absentismo (m)

**absentismo** (m) n Pt
De unerlaubte Abwesenheit (f)
En absenteeism
Es ausentismo (m)
Fr absentéisme (m)
It assenteismo (m)

**abstain** vb En
De seine Stimme enthalten
Es abstenerse
Fr s'abstenir
It astenersi
Pt abster-se

**abstenerse** vb Es
De seine Stimme enthalten
En abstain
Fr s'abstenir
It astenersi
Pt abster-se

**s'abstenir** vb Fr
De seine Stimme enthalten
En abstain
Es abstenerse
It astenersi
Pt abster-se

**abster-se** vb Pt
De seine Stimme enthalten
En abstain
Es abstenerse
Fr s'abstenir
It astenersi

**abstract** n En
De Abriss (m)
Es resumen (m)
Fr résumé (m)
It riassunto (m)
Pt resumo (m)

**Abteilung** (f) n De
En department; division
Es departamento; sección (m f)
Fr département; service (m)

It dipartimento; divisione (m f)
Pt departamento; secção (m f)

**Abteilungsleiter** (m) n De
En head of department
Es jefe de departamento (m)
Fr chef de service (m)
It capo reparto (m)
Pt chefe de departamento (m)

**Abtretungsvertrag** (m) n De
En deed of assignment
Es titulo de asignación (m)
Fr acte attributif (m)
It atto di cessione (m)
Pt titulo de consignação (m)

**a buon mercato** It
De billig
En cheap
Es barato
Fr bon marché
Pt barato

**abuso di influenza** (m) It
De unzulässige Beeinflussung (f)
En undue influence
Es abuso de influencia (m)
Fr influence illégitime (f)
Pt influência imprópria (f)

**abweichend** adj De
En dissenting
Es disidente
Fr dissident
It dissidente
Pt dissidente

**Abweichung** (f) n De
En discrepancy
Es desacuerdo (m)
Fr écart (m)
It divergenza (f)
Pt discrepância (f)

**ab Werk** De
En ex works
Es de fábrica
Fr prise usine
It franco fabbrica
Pt na fábrica

**Abwesende(r)** (m) n De
En absentee
Es ausente (m)

Fr manquant *(m)*
It assente *(m)*
Pt ausente *(m)*

**abwickeln** *vb* De
En wind up (a business)
Es liquidar (un negocio)
Fr liquider (une entreprise)
It liquidare (una azienda)
Pt liquidar (um negócio)

**abziehbare Unkosten** *(pl)* De
En allowable expense
Es gastos deducibles *(m pl)*
Fr dépense déductible *(f)*
It spesa permessa *(f)*
Pt despesas deduzíveis *(f)*

**abziehen** *vb* De
En deduct
Es deducir
Fr déduire
It dedurre
Pt deduzir

**acaparador** *(m) n* Es
De Gewinnler *(m)*
En profiteer
Fr profiteur *(m)*
It profittatore *(m)*
Pt especulador *(m)*

**acaparar el mercado** Es
De den Markt beherrschen
En corner a market
Fr accaparer le marché
It accaparrare il mercato
Pt cerrar um mercado

**acção** *(f) n* Pt
De Aktie *(f)*
En share
Es acción *(f)*
Fr action *(f)*
It azione *(f)*

**acção judicial** *(f)* Pt
De Prozess; Klage *(m f)*
En legal action
Es pleito *(m)*
Fr action juridique *(f)*
It processo *(m)*

**acção ordinária** *(f)* Pt
De Stammaktie *(f)*
En ordinary share
Es acción ordinaria *(f)*

Fr action ordinaire *(f)*
It azione ordinaria *(f)*

**acção preferencial** *(f)* Pt
De Vorzugsaktie *(f)*
En preference share
Es acción preferente *(f)*
Fr action privilégiée *(f)*
It azione privilegiata *(f)*

**accaparer le marché** Fr
De den Markt beherrschen
En corner a market
Es acaparar el mercado
It accaparrare il mercato
Pt cerrar um mercado

**accaparrare il mercato** It
De den Markt beherrschen
En corner a market
Es acaparar el mercado
Fr accaparer le marché
Pt cerrar um mercado

**accattatore** *(m) n* It
De Kreditnehmer *(m)*
En borrower
Es prestatario *(m)*
Fr emprunteur *(m)*
Pt beneficiário de empréstimo *(m)*

**accelerated depreciation** En
De beschleunigte Abschreibung *(f)*
Es depreciación acelerada *(f)*
Fr amortissement accéléré *(m)*
It deprezzamento accelerato *(m)*
Pt depreciação acelerada *(f)*

**accept** *vb* En
De annehmen
Es aceptar
Fr accepter
It accettare
Pt aceitar

**aceptación comercial** *(f)* Es
De Handelsakzept *(n)*
En trade acceptance
Fr acceptation de commerce *(f)*
It accettazione commerciale *(f)*
Pt aceitação comercial *(f)*

**acceptance** *n* En
De Akzept *(n)*
Es aceptación *(f)*
Fr acceptation *(f)*
It accettazione *(f)*
Pt aceitação *(f)*

**acceptance credit** En
De Akzeptkredit *(m)*
Es crédito de aceptación *(m)*
Fr crédit par acceptation *(m)*
It credito d'accettazione *(m)*
Pt crédito de aceitação *(m)*

**acceptance for honour** En
De Intervention (bei Wechselakzept) *(f)*
Es aceptación por intervención *(f)*
Fr acceptation par intervention *(f)*
It accettazione per intervento *(f)*
Pt aceitação por intervenção *(f)*

**acceptance interval** En
De Akzeptfrist *(f)*
Es intervalo de aceptación *(m)*
Fr intervalle d'acceptation *(f)*
It intervallo dell'accettazione *(m)*
Pt intervalo de aceitação *(m)*

**accept an offer** En
De ein Angebot annehmen
Es aceptar una oferta
Fr accepter une offre
It accettare una offerta
Pt aceitar uma oferta

**acceptation** *(f) n* Fr
De Akzept *(n)*
En acceptance
Es aceptación *(f)*
It accettazione *(f)*
Pt aceitação *(f)*

**acceptation conditionnelle** *(f)* Fr
De Annahme unter Vorbehalt *(f)*
En qualified acceptance
Es aceptación condicionada *(f)*
It accettazione con riserva *(f)*
Pt aceitação com reservas *(f)*

**acceptation de commerce** *(f)*
Fr
De Handelsakzept *(n)*
En trade acceptance
Es aceptación comercial *(f)*
It accettazione commerciale
*(f)*
Pt aceitação comercial *(f)*


**acceptation par intervention**
*(f)* Fr
De Intervention (bei Wechselakzept) *(f)*
En acceptance for honour
Es aceptación por intervención
*(f)*
It accettazione per intervento
*(f)*
Pt aceitação por intervenção
*(f)*


**accepter** *vb* Fr
De annehmen
En accept
Es aceptar
It accettare
Pt aceitar


**accepter une offre** Fr
De ein Angebot annehmen
En accept an offer
Es aceptar una oferta
It accettare una offerta
Pt aceitar uma oferta


**accettare** *vb* It
De annehmen
En accept
Es aceptar
Fr accepter
Pt aceitar


**accettare una offerta** It
De ein Angebot annehmen
En accept an offer
Es aceptar una oferta
Fr accepter une offre
Pt aceitar uma oferta


**accettazione** *(f)* n It
De Akzept *(n)*
En acceptance
Es aceptación *(f)*
Fr acceptation *(f)*
Pt aceitação *(f)*


**accettazione commerciale** *(f)*
It
De Handelsakzept *(n)*
En trade acceptance
Es aceptación comercial *(f)*
Fr acceptation de commerce
*(f)*
Pt aceitação comercial *(f)*


**accettazione con riserva** *(f)* It
De Annahme unter Vorbehalt
*(f)*
En qualified acceptance
Es aceptación condicionada *(f)*
Fr acceptation conditionnelle
*(f)*
Pt aceitação com reservas *(f)*


**accettazione per intervento**
*(f)* It
De Intervention (bei Wechselakzept) *(f)*
En acceptance for honour
Es aceptación por intervención
*(f)*
Fr acceptation par intervention *(f)*
Pt aceitação por intervenção
*(f)*


**accident du travail** *(m)* Fr
De Arbeitsunfall *(m)*
En industrial accident
Es accidente de trabajo *(m)*
It infortunio sul lavoro *(m)*
Pt acidente de trabalho *(m)*


**accidente de trabajo** *(m)* Es
De Arbeitsunfall *(m)*
En industrial accident
Fr accident du travail *(m)*
It infortunio sul lavoro *(m)*
Pt acidente de trabalho *(m)*


**acción** *(f)* n Es
De Aktie *(f)*
En share
Fr action *(f)*
It azione *(f)*
Pt acção *(f)*


**acciones aplazadas** *(f pl)* Es
De Nachzugsaktien *(f pl)*
En deferred shares
Fr actions différées *(f pl)*
It azioni postergate *(f pl)*
Pt acções diferidas *(f pl)*


**acciones auríferas** *(f pl)* Es
De Aktien von Goldbergwerken
*(f pl)*
En gold shares
Fr valeurs aurifères *(f pl)*
It azioni aurifere *(f pl)*
Pt acções de ouro *(f pl)*


**acciones con derecho de voto**
*(f pl)* Es
De stimmberechtigte Aktien *(f
pl)*
En voting shares
Fr actions avec droit de vote
*(f pl)*
It azioni con diritto a voto *(f
pl)*
Pt acçoes com direito a voto
*(f pl)*


**acciones dadas como primas**
*(f pl)* Es
De Gratisaktien *(f pl)*
En bonus shares
Am stock dividend
Fr actions d'attribution *(f pl)*
It azioni di godimento *(f pl)*
Pt acções de prémio *(f pl)*


**acciones del fundador** *(f pl)* Es
De Gründeraktien *(f pl)*
En founder's shares
Fr actions de fondateur *(f pl)*
It azioni del fondatore *(f pl)*
Pt acções de fundador *(f pl)*


**acciónes preferentes amor-
tizables** *(f pl)* Es
De ablösbare Vorzugsaktien *(f
pl)*
En redeemable     preference
shares
Fr actions privilégiées amortissables *(f pl)*
It azioni preferenziali redimibili *(f pl)*
Pt acções redimíveis preferenciais *(f pl)*


**acciones sin derecho de voto**
*(f pl)* Es
De Aktien ohne Stimmrecht *(f
pl)*
En non-voting shares
Fr actions sans droit de vote
*(f pl)*
It azioni senza diritto a voto *(f
pl)*

Pt acçoes sem direito a voto
*(f pl)*

**accionista** *(m) n* Es, Pt
De Aktionär *(m)*
En shareholder; stockholder
Fr actionnaire *(m)*
It azionista *(m)*

**acción ordinaria** *(f)* Es
De Stammaktie *(f)*
En ordinary share
Fr action ordinaire *(f)*
It azione ordinaria *(f)*
Pt acção ordinaria *(f)*

**acción preferente** *(f)* Es
De Vorzugsaktie *(f)*
En preference share
Fr action privilégiée *(f)*
It azione privilegiata *(f)*
Pt acção preferencial *(f)*

**acción por daños** *(f)* Es
De Schadenersatzklage *(f)*
En action for damages
Fr action en dommages et
intérêts *(f)*
It processo per risarcimento
*(m)*
Pt processamento por danos
*(m)*

**accluso** *adj* It
De beiliegend
En enclosed
Es adjunto
Fr ci-joint; ci-inclus
Pt incluso

**acçoes com direito a voto** *(f
pl)* Pt
De stimmberechtigte Aktien *(f
pl)*
En voting shares
Es acciones con derecho de
voto *(f pl)*
Fr actions avec droit de vote
*(f pl)*
It azioni con diritto a voto *(f
pl)*

**acçôes de fundador** *(f pl)* Pt
De Gründeraktien *(f pl)*
En founder's shares
Es acciones del fundador *(f pl)*
Fr actions de fondateur *(f pl)*
It azioni del fondatore *(f pl)*

**acçôes de ouro** *(f pl)* Pt
De Aktien von Goldbergwerken
*(f pl)*
En gold shares
Es acciones auríferas *(f pl)*
Fr valeurs aurifères *(f pl)*
It azioni aurifere *(f pl)*

**acçôes de prémio** *(f pl)* Pt
De Gratisaktien *(f pl)*
En bonus shares
Am stock dividend
Es acciones dadas como pri-
mas *(f pl)*
Fr actions d'attribution *(f pl)*
It azioni di godimento *(f pl)*

**acçôes diferidas** *(f pl)* Pt
De Nachzugsaktien *(f pl)*
En deferred shares
Es acciones aplazadas *(f pl)*
Fr actions différées *(f pl)*
It azioni postergate *(f pl)*

**acçôes preferenciais cumula-
tivas** *(f pl)* Pt
De kumulative Vorzugsaktien *(f
pl)*
En cumulative preference
shares
Es valores privilegiados cumulativos *(m pl)*
Fr actions de priorité cumulatives *(f pl)*
It azioni preferenziali cumulative *(f pl)*

**acçôes redimíveis preferen-
ciais** *(f pl)* Pt
De ablösbare Vorzugsaktien *(f
pl)*
En redeemable preference
shares
Es acciónes preferentes amortizables *(f pl)*
Fr actions privilégiées amortissables *(f pl)*
It azioni preferenziali redimibili *(f pl)*

**acçoes sem direito a voto** *(f
pl)* Pt
De Aktien ohne Stimmrecht *(f
pl)*
En non-voting shares
Es acciones sin derecho de
voto *(f pl)*

Fr actions sans droit de vote
*(f pl)*
It azioni senza diritto a voto *(f
pl)*

**accommodation bill** En
De Gefälligkeitswechsel *(m)*
Es pagaré de favor *(m)*
Fr billet de complaisance *(m)*
It cambiale di favore *(f)*
Pt letra de favor *(f)*

**accomplissement** *(m) n* Fr
De Erfüllung *(f)*
En fulfilment
Es cumplimiento *(m)*
It adempimento *(m)*
Pt cumprimento *(m)*

**acconto** *(m) n* It
De Sofortzahlung *(f)*
En down-payment
Es pago de entrada *(m)*
Fr acompte *(m)*
Pt pagamento inicial *(m)*

**acconto di dividendo** *(m)* It
De vorläufige Dividende *(f)*
En interim dividend
Es dividendo provisional *(m)*
Fr dividende intérimaire *(m)*
Pt dividendo interino *(m)*

**accord** *(m) n* Fr
De Vereinbarung *(f)*
En settlement (agreement)
Es acuerdo *(m)*
It accordo *(m)*
Pt acordo *(m)*

**accord de commerce bilatéral**
*(m)* Fr
De bilateraler Handelsvertrag
*(m)*
En bilateral trade agreement
Es contrato comercial bilateral
*(m)*
It accordo di commercio
bilaterale *(m)*
Pt acordo comercial bilateral
*(m)*

**accord de commercialisation**
*(m)* Fr
De Absatzübereinkommen *(n)*
En marketing agreement
Es acuerdo mercantil *(m)*
It accordo di mercato *(m)*

Pt acordo sobre comercia-
   lização *(m)*

**accord en réserve** *(m)* Fr
De Notvereinbarung *(f)*
En stand-by agreement
Es contrato de reserva *(m)*
It accordo di riserva *(m)*
Pt acordo a postos *(m)*

**Accord Général sur les Tarifs
Douaniers et le Com-
merce** *(m)* Fr
De Allgemeines Zoll- und Han-
   delsabkommen *(n)*
En General Agreement on
   Tariffs and Trade (GATT)
Es Acuerdo General sobre
   Tarifas Aduaneras y Comer-
   cio *(m)*
It Accordo Generale sulle
   Tariffe Doganali e sul
   Commercio *(m)*
Pt Acordo geral de Tarifas e
   Comércio *(m)*

**Accord Monétaire Européen
(AME)** *(m)* Fr
De Europäisches Währungs-
   abkommen (EWA) *(n)*
En European Monetáry Agree-
   ment
Es Acuerdo Monetario Euro-
   peo (AME) *(m)*
It Accordo Monetario Euro-
   peo (AME) *(m)*
Pt Acuerdo Monetário Euro-
   peu (AME) *(m)*

**accord mutuel** *(m)* Fr
De gegenseitiges Einverneh-
   men *(n)*
En mutual agreement
Es acuerdo común *(m)*
It comune accordo *(m)*
Pt acordo mútuo *(m)*

**accordo** *(m) n* It
De Abkommen *(n)*
En agreement
Es contrato *(m)*
Fr convention *(f)*
Pt acordo *(m)*

**accordo** *(m) n* It
De Vereinbarung *(f)*
En settlement (agreement)

Es acuerdo *(m)*
Fr accord *(m)*
Pt acordo *(m)*

**accord occulte** *(m)* Fr
De Geheimvertrag *(m)*
En secret agreement
Es acuerdo secreto *(m)*
It accordo segreto *(m)*
Pt acordo secreto *(m)*

**accordo di commercio bila-
terale** *(m)* It
De bilateraler Handelsvertrag
   *(m)*
En bilateral trade agreement
Es contrato comercial bilateral
   *(m)*
Fr accord de commerce bilatéral *(m)*
Pt acordo comercial bilateral
   *(m)*

**accordo di mercato** *(m)* It
De Absatzübereinkommen *(n)*
En marketing agreement
Es acuerdo mercantil *(m)*
Fr accord de commerciali-
   sation *(m)*
Pt acordo sobre comercia-
   lização *(m)*

**accordo di riserva** *(m)* It
De Notvereinbarung *(f)*
En stand-by agreement
Es contrato de reserva *(m)*
Fr accord en réserve *(m)*
Pt acordo a postos *(m)*

**accordo di servizio** *(m)* It
De Dienstvertrag *(m)*
En service agreement
Es contrato de servicio *(m)*
Fr contrat de service *(m)*
Pt contrato de serviço *(m)*

**Accordo Generale sulle Ta-
riffe Doganali e sul
Commercio** *(m)* It
De Allgemeines Zoll- und Han-
   delsabkommen *(n)*
En General Agreement on
   Tariffs and Trade (GATT)
Es Acuerdo General sobre
   Tarifas Aduaneras y Comer-
   cio *(m)*

Fr Accord Général sur les
   Tarifs Douaniers et le
   Commerce *(m)*
Pt Acordo geral de Tarifas e
   Comércio *(m)*

**Accordo Monetario Europeo
(AME)** *(m)* It
De Europäisches Währungs-
   abkommen (EWA) *(n)*
En European Monetary Agree-
   ment
Es Acuerdo Monetario Euro-
   peo (AME) *(m)*
Fr Accord Monétaire Euro-
   péen (AME) *(m)*
Pt Acuerdo Monetário Euro-
   peu (AME) *(m)*

**accordo restrittivo** *(m)* It
De einschränkende Bestimm-
   ung *(f)*
En restrictive covenant
Es convenio restrictivo *(m)*
Fr accord restrictif *(m)*
Pt obrigação restritiva *(f)*

**accordo segreto** *(m)* It
De Geheimvertrag *(m)*
En secret agreement
Es acuerdo secreto *(m)*
Fr accord occulte *(m)*
Pt acordo secreto *(m)*

**accordo sui salari** *(m)* It
De Lohnvereinbarung *(f)*
En wages agreement
Es acuerdo sobre salarios *(m)*
Fr convention des salaires *(f)*
Pt acordo sobre salários *(m)*

**accordo sulla parola** *(m)* It
De Kavaliersabkommen *(n)*
En gentleman´s agreement
Es acuerdo sobre palabra *(m)*
Fr convention verbale *(f)*
Pt pacto de honra *(m)*

**accordo tacito** *(m)* It
De stillschweigendes Überein-
   kommen *(n)*
En tacit agreement
Es acuerdo tácito *(m)*
Fr convention tacite *(f)*
Pt acordo tácito *(m)*

**accordo tariffario** *(m)* It
De Zollabkommen *(n)*
En tariff agreement
Es acuerdo tarifario *(m)*
Fr accord tarifaire *(m)*
Pt acordo de tarifas *(m)*

**accord restrictif** *(m)* Fr
De einschränkende Bestimmung *(f)*
En restrictive covenant
Es convenio restrictivo *(m)*
It accordo restrittivo *(m)*
Pt obrigação restritiva *(f)*

**accord tarifaire** *(m)* Fr
De Zollabkommen *(n)*
En tariff agreement
Es acuerdo tarifario *(m)*
It accordo tariffario *(m)*
Pt acordo de tarifas *(m)*

**account** *n* En
De Konto *(n)*
Es cuenta *(f)*
Fr compte *(m)*
It conto *(m)*
Pt conta *(f)*

**accountability** *n* En
De Verantwortlichkeit *(f)*
Es responsabilidad *(f)*
Fr responsabilité *(f)*
It responsabilità *(f)*
Pt responsabilidade *(f)*

**accountancy** *n* En
De Buchhaltung *(f)*
Es contabilidad *(f)*
Fr comptabilité *(f)*
It contabilità *(f)*
Pt contabilidade *(f)*

**accountant** *n* En
De Buchhalter *(m)*
Es contador *(m)*
Fr comptable *(m)*
It contabile *(m)*
Pt contabilista *(m)*

**account book** En
De Kontobuch *(n)*
Es libro de cuentas *(m)*
Fr livre de compte *(m)*
It libro di conti *(m)*
Pt livro de contas *(m)*

**account day** En
Am settlement date
De Abrechnungstag *(m)*
Es día de liquidación *(m)*
Fr jour de liquidation *(m)*
It giorno di liquidazione *(m)*
Pt dia de liquidação *(m)*

**account executive** En
De Kontaktgruppenleiter *(m)*
Es ejecutivo de cuenta *(m)*
Fr chef de comptes client *(m)*
It direttore conto cliente *(m)*
Pt chefe de conta de cliente *(m)*

**accounting department** Am
En accounts department
De Buchhaltung *(f)*
Es departamento de contabilidad *(m)*
Fr service de la comptabilité *(m)*
It ufficio contabilità *(m)*
Pt departamento de contabilidade *(m)*

**accounting period** En
De Abrechnungszeitraum *(m)*
Es ejercicio *(m)*
Fr exercice *(f)*
It esercizio *(m)*
Pt exercício *(m)*

**account overdrawn** En
De Konto überzogen *(n)*
Es cuenta en descubierto *(m)*
Fr compte découvert *(m)*
It conto scoperto *(m)*
Pt conta a descoberto *(f)*

**account rendered** En
De zur Begleichung vorgelegte Rechnung *(f)*
Es cuenta rendida *(f)*
Fr compte rendu *(m)*
It conto reso *(m)*
Pt conta remetida *(f)*

**accounts department** En
Am accounting department
De Buchhaltung *(f)*
Es departamento de contabilidad *(m)*
Fr service de la comptabilité *(m)*
It ufficio contabilità *(m)*

Pt departamento de contabilidade *(m)*

**accounts payable** En
De Kreditoren *(m pl)*
Es cuentas a pagar *(f pl)*
Fr comptes à payer *(m pl)*
It conti passivi *(m pl)*
Pt contas a pagar *(f pl)*

**accounts receivable** En
De Debitoren *(m pl)*
Es cuentas a recibir *(f pl)*
Fr créances *(f pl)*
It conti attivi *(m pl)*
Pt contas a receber *(f pl)*

**accredited agent** En
De Handelsbevollmächtigte(r) *(m)*
Es agente acreditudo *(m)*
Fr agent accrédité *(m)*
It agente accreditato *(m)*
Pt agente acreditado *(m)*

**accréditif automatiquement renouvelable** *(m)* Fr
De automatisch sich erneuendes Akkreditiv *(n)*
En revolving credit
Es crédito reponible *(m)*
It credito rotativo *(m)*
Pt crédito renovável *(m)*

**accroissement** *(m) n* Fr
De Erhöhung; Wertzuwachs *(f m)*
En increase; increment
Es aumento; incremento *(m)*
It aumento; incremento *(m)*
Pt aumento; incremento *(m)*

**accroissement des coûts** *(m)* Fr
De erhöhte Kosten *(pl)*
En increased costs
Es costes incrementados *(m pl)*
It costi aumentati *(m pl)*
Pt custos aumentados *(m pl)*

**accrual** (to an account) *n* En
De Zugang *(m)*
Es incremento *(m)*
Fr augmentation *(f)*
It incremento *(m)*
Pt acréscimo *(m)*

**accrual** (of interest) *n* En
De Auflaufen *(n)*
Es acumulación *(f)*
Fr accumulation *(f)*
It maturazione *(f)*
Pt acumulação *(f)*

**accrue** *vb* En
De auflaufen
Es acumular
Fr accumuler
It accumularsi
Pt acumular

**accrued interest** En
De aufgelaufene Zinsen *(m pl)*
Es interés acumulado *(m)*
Fr intérêts accumulés *(m pl)*
It interesse maturato *(m)*
Pt juro acumulado *(m)*

**accumular** *vb* Pt
De auflaufen
En accrue
Es acumular
Fr accumuler
It accumularsi

**accumularsi** *vb* It
De auflaufen
En accrue
Es acumular
Fr accumuler
Pt acumular

**accumulation** *(f) n* Fr
De Auflaufen *(n)*
En accrual
Es acumulación *(f)*
It maturazione *(f)*
Pt acumulação *(f)*

**accumuler** *vb* Fr
De auflaufen
En accrue
Es acumular
It accumularsi
Pt acumular

**accusare ricevuta di** It
De Empfang bestätigen
En acknowledge receipt of
Es acusar recibo de
Fr accuser réception de
Pt acusar a recepção de

**accusé de réception** *(m)* Fr
De Empfangsbestätigung *(f)*
En acknowledgment of receipt
Es aviso de recepción *(m)*
It avviso di recezione *(m)*
Pt aviso de recepção *(m)*

**accuser réception de** Fr
De Empfang bestätigen
En acknowledge receipt of
Es acusar recibo de
It accusare ricevuta di
Pt acusar a recepção de

**aceitação** *(f) n* Pt
De Akzept *(n)*
En acceptance
Es aceptación *(f)*
Fr acceptation *(f)*
It accettazione *(f)*

**aceitação comercial** *(f)* Pt
De Handelsakzept *(n)*
En trade acceptance
Es aceptación comercial *(f)*
Fr acceptation de commerce *(f)*
It accettazione commerciale *(f)*

**aceitação com reservas** *(f)* Pt
De Annahme unter Vorbehalt *(f)*
En qualified acceptance
Es aceptación condicionada *(f)*
Fr acceptation conditionnelle *(f)*
It accettazione con riserva *(f)*

**aceitação por intervenção** *(f)* Pt
De Intervention (bei Wechselakzept) *(f)*
En acceptance for honour
Es aceptación por intervención *(f)*
Fr acceptation par intervention *(f)*
It accettazione per intervento *(f)*

**aceitar** *vb* Pt
De annehmen
En accept
Es aceptar
Fr accepter
It accettare

**aceitar uma oferta** Pt
De ein Angebot annehmen
En accept an offer
Es aceptar una oferta
Fr accepter une offre
It accettare una offerta

**aceptación** *(f) n* Es
De Akzept *(n)*
En acceptance
Fr acceptation *(f)*
It accettazione *(f)*
Pt aceitação *(f)*

**aceptación condicionada** *(f)* Es
De Annahme unter Vorbehalt *(f)*
En qualified acceptance
Fr acceptation conditionnelle *(f)*
It accettazione con riserva *(f)*
Pt aceitação com reservas *(f)*

**aceptación por intervención** *(f)* Es
De Intervention (bei Wechselakzept) *(f)*
En acceptance for honour
Fr acceptation par intervention *(f)*
It accettazione per intervento *(f)*
Pt aceitação por intervenção *(f)*

**aceptar** *vb* Es
De annehmen
En accept
Fr accepter
It accettare
Pt aceitar

**aceptar una oferta** Es
De ein Angebot annehmen
En accept an offer
Fr accepter une offre
It accettare una offerta
Pt aceitar uma oferta

**achat** *(m) n* Fr
De Kauf; Einkauf *(m)*
En purchase
Es compra *(f)*
It cómpra *(f)*
Pt compra *(f)*

**achats** *(m pl)* Fr
De Einkäufe *(m pl)*
En purchases
Es adquisiciones *(f pl)*
It acquisti *(m pl)*
Pt aquisições *(f pl)*

**achat sur l'entrainement du moment** *(m)* Fr
De Impulskaufen *(n)*
En impulse buying
Es compra espontánea *(f)*
It compra sullo stimolo del momento *(f)*
Pt compra impulsiva *(f)*

**acheter** *vb* Fr
De kaufen
En buy
Es comprar
It comprare
Pt comprar

**acheteur** *(m)* n Fr
De Käufer *(m)*
En buyer
Es comprador *(m)*
It compratore *(m)*
Pt comprador *(m)*

**acidente de trabalho** *(m)* Pt
De Arbeitsunfall *(m)*
En industrial accident
Es accidente de trabajo *(m)*
Fr accident du travail *(m)*
It infortunio sul lavoro *(m)*

**acknowledge receipt of** En
De Empfang bestätigen
Es acusar recibo de
Fr accuser réception de
It accusare ricevuta di
Pt acusar a recepção de

**acknowledgment of receipt** En
De Empfangsbestätigung *(f)*
Es aviso de recepción *(m)*
Fr accusé de réception *(m)*
It avviso di recezione *(m)*
Pt aviso de recepção *(m)*

**a cobrar** Pt
De anrechenbar
En chargeable
Es imputable; a cobrar
Fr imputable; imposable
It imputabile; imponibile

**acompte** *(m)* n Fr
De Sofortzahlung *(f)*
En down-payment
Es pago de entrada *(m)*
It acconto *(m)*
Pt pagamento inicial *(m)*

**acompte** *(m)* n Fr
De Rate *(f)*
En instalment
Es plazo *(m)*
It rata *(f)*
Pt prestação *(f)*

**à concurrence de** Fr
De hinauslaufend auf
En amounting to
Es ascendiendo a
It ammontante a
Pt no montante de

**a condición** Es
De vorausgesetzt
En on condition
Fr sous réserve
It a condizione
Pt sob condição de

**acondicionamiento de aire** *(m)* Es
De Klimatisierung *(f)*
En air-conditioning
Fr climatisation *(f)*
It condizionamento dell'aria *(m)*
Pt condicionamento do ar *(m)*

**a condizione** It
De vorausgesetzt
En on condition
Es a condición
Fr sous réserve
Pt sob condição de

**à consignação** Pt
De in Kommission
En on consignment
Es en consignación
Fr en consignation
It in conto deposito

**a conto** De
En on account
Es a cuenta
Fr à valoir
It in acconto
Pt por conta

**acordo** *(m)* n Pt
De Abkommen; Vereinbarung *(n f)*
En agreement; settlement
Es contrato; acuerdo *(m)*
Fr convention; accord *(f m)*
It accordo; concordato *(m)*

**acordo a postos** *(m)* Pt
De Notvereinbarung *(f)*
En stand-by agreement
Es contrato de reserva *(m)*
Fr accord en réserve *(m)*
It accordo di riserva *(m)*

**acordo comercial bilateral** *(m)* Pt
De bilateraler Handelsvertrag *(m)*
En bilateral trade agreement
Es contrato comercial bilateral *(m)*
Fr accord de commerce bilatéral *(m)*
It accordo di commercio bilaterale *(m)*

**acordo de tarifas** *(m)* Pt
De Zollabkommen *(n)*
En tariff agreement
Es acuerdo tarifario *(m)*
Fr accord tarifaire *(m)*
It accordo tariffario *(m)*

**Acordo geral de Tarifas e Comércio** *(m)* Pt
De Allgemeines Zoll- und Handelsabkommen *(n)*
En General Agreement on Tariffs and Trade (GATT)
Es Acuerdo General sobre Tarifas Aduaneras y Comercio *(m)*
Fr Accord Général sur les Tarifs Douaniers et le Commerce *(m)*
It Accordo Generale sulle Tariffe Doganali e sul Commercio *(m)*

**acordo irrevogavel** *(m)* Pt
De bindender Vertrag *(m)*
En binding agreement
Es obligación irrevocable *(f)*
Fr convention irrévocable *(f)*
It contratto vincolante *(m)*

**acordo mútuo** *(m)* Pt
De gegenseitiges Einvernehmen *(n)*
En mutual agreement
Es acuerdo común *(m)*
Fr accord mutuel *(m)*
It comune accordo *(m)*

**acordo secreto** *(m)* Pt
De Geheimvertrag *(m)*
En secret agreement
Es acuerdo secreto *(m)*
Fr accord occulte *(m)*
It accordo segreto *(m)*

**acordo sobre salários** *(m)* Pt
De Lohnvereinbarung *(f)*
En wages agreement
Es acuerdo sobre salarios *(m)*
Fr convention des salaires *(f)*
It accordo sui salari *(m)*

**acordo tácito** *(m)* Pt
De stillschweigendes Übereinkommen *(n)*
En tacit agreement
Es acuerdo tácito *(m)*
Fr convention tacite *(f)*
It accordo tacito *(m)*

**a corto plazo** Es
De kurzfristig
En short-term; short dated
Fr à court terme; à courte échéance
It a breve termine; a breve scadenza
Pt a curto prazo

**à courte échéance** Fr
De kurzfristig
En short-dated
Es a corto plazo
It a breve scadenza
Pt a curto prazo

**à court terme** Fr
De kurzfristig
En short-term
Es a corto plazo
It a breve termine
Pt a curto prazo

**acque territoriali** *(f pl)* It
De Hoheitsgewässer *(n pl)*
En territorial waters
Es aguas territoriales *(f pl)*

Fr eaux territoriales *(f pl)*
Pt águas territoriais *(f pl)*

**acquisition** *n* En, Fr *(f)*
De Erwerb *(m)*
Es adquisición *(f)*
It acquisizione *(f)*
Pt aquisição *(f)*

**acquisizione** *(f)* n It
De Erwerb *(m)*
En acquisition
Es adquisición *(f)*
Fr acquisition *(f)*
Pt aquisição *(f)*

**acquisti** *(m pl)* It
De Einkäufe *(m pl)*
En purchases
Es adquisiciones *(f pl)*
Fr achats *(m pl)*
Pt aquisições *(f pl)*

**acquitté** *adj* Fr
De verzollt
En duty-paid
Es derechos pagados
It dazio pagato
Pt direitos pagos

**acquitter une dette** Fr
De eine Schuld begleichen
En discharge a debt
Es descargar una deuda
It estinguere un debito
Pt cancelar uma dívida

**acreedor** *(m)* n Es
De Gläubiger *(m)*
En creditor
Fr créancier; créditeur *(m)*
It creditore *(m)*
Pt credor *(m)*

**acreedores varios** *(m pl)* Es
De Kreditoren *(m pl)*
En sundry creditors
Fr créditeurs divers *(m pl)*
It creditori diversi *(m pl)*
Pt créditos diversos *(m pl)*

**acreedor no garantizado** *(m)* Es
De nicht gesicherter Gläubiger *(m)*
En unsecured creditor
Fr créancier chirographaire *(m)*

It creditore non garantito *(m)*
Pt credor sem garantia *(m)*

**acreedor privilegiado** *(m)* Es
De bevorrechtigter Gläubiger *(m)*
En preferential creditor
Fr créancier privilégié *(m)*
It creditore privilegiato *(m)*
Pt credor preferencial *(m)*

**acréscimo** *(m)* n Pt
De Zugang *(m)*
En accrual
Es incremento *(m)*
Fr augmentation *(f)*
It incremento *(m)*

**acta de disposición** *(f)* Es
De Vergleichsabkommen *(n)*
En deed of arrangement
Fr contrat d'arrangement *(m)*
It atto di accordo *(m)*
Pt escritura de acordo *(f)*

**actas** *(f pl)* n Es
De Protokoll *(n)*
En minutes (of a meeting)
Fr procès-verbal *(m)*
It verbale *(m)*
Pt minutas de acta *(f pl)*

**acte** *(m)* n Fr
De Urkunde *(f)*
En deed; document
Es título; escritura *(m f)*
It atto *(m)*
Pt título; escritura *(m f)*

**acte attributif** *(m)* Fr
De Abtretungsvertrag *(m)*
En deed of assignment
Es título de asignación *(f)*
It atto di cessione *(m)*
Pt título de consignação *(m)*

**acte de cession** *(m)* Fr
De Übertragungsvertrag *(m)*
En transfer deed
Es escritura de transferencia *(f)*
It atto di trapasso *(m)*
Pt título de transferência *(m)*

**acte de vente** *(f)* Fr
De Kaufvertrag *(m)*
En bill of sale
Es escritura de venta *(f)*

It contratto di vendita *(m)*
Pt escritura de venda *(f)*

**acte dommageable** *(m)* Fr
De unerlaubte Handlung *(f)*
En tort
Es agravio *(m)*
It torto *(m)*
Pt agravo *(m)*

**actif** *(m) n* Fr
De Aktivposten *(m)*
En asset
Es activo *(m)*
It attivo *(m)*
Pt valor *(m)*

**actif** *adj* Fr
De wirksam
En operative
Es operativo; activo
It attivo; operativo
Pt efectivo; em vigor

**actif courant** *(m)* Fr
De Umlaufsvermögen *(n)*
En current assets
Es activo realizable *(m)*
It attivo liquido *(m)*
Pt bens no activo actual *(m pl)*

**actif et passif** *(m)* Fr
De Aktiva und Passiva *(n pl)*
En assets and liabilities
Es activo y pasivo *(m)*
It attivo e passivo *(m)*
Pt activo e passivo *(m)*

**actif immobilisé** *(m)* Fr
De Vermögensanlage *(f)*
En capital asset
Am fixed asset
Es activo fijo *(m)*
It capitale fisso *(m)*
Pt bens de capital *(m pl)*

**actif incorporel** *(m)* Fr
De nicht greifbare Aktiven *(n pl)*
En intangible assets
Es activo intangible *(m)*
It beni incorporali *(m pl)*
Pt bens intocáveis *(m pl)*

**actif liquide** *(m)* Fr
De flüssige Aktiven *(n pl)*
En liquid assets

Es activo líquido *(m)*
It disponibilità; attività liquida *(f)*
Pt bens de activo líquidos *(m pl)*

**actif net** *(m)* Fr
De Reinvermögen *(n)*
En net assets
Es activo neto *(m)*
It attivo netto *(m)*
Pt bens líquidos *(m)*

**actifs défectibles** *(m pl)* Fr
De kurzlebige Aktiva *(n pl)*
En wasting assets
Am depleting assets
Es activo gastable *(m)*
It attività in esaurimento *(f pl)*
Pt bens em uso ou deteriora-ção *(m pl)*

**action** *(f) n* Fr
De Aktie *(f)*
En share
Es acción *(f)*
It azione *(f)*
Pt acção *(f)*

**action for damages** En
De Schadenersatzklage *(f)*
Es acción por daños *(f)*
Fr action en dommages et intérêts *(f)*
It processo per risarcimento *(m)*
Pt processamento por danos *(m)*

**action juridique** *(f)* Fr
De Prozess; Klage *(m f)*.
En legal action
Es pleito *(m)*
It processo *(m)*
Pt acção judicial *(f)*

**actionnaire** *(m) n* Fr
De Aktionär *(m)*
En shareholder
Am stockholder
Es accionista *(m)*
It azionista *(m)*
Pt titular de acções; accionista *(m)*

**action ordinaire** *(f)* Fr
De Stammaktie *(f)*
En ordinary share

Es acción ordinaria *(f)*
It azione ordinaria *(f)*
Pt acção ordinária *(f)*

**action privilégiée** *(f)* Fr
De Vorzugsaktie *(f)*
En preference share
Es acción preferente *(f)*
It azione privilegiata *(f)*
Pt acção preferencial *(f)*

**actions avec droit de vote** *(f pl)* Fr
De stimmberechtigte Aktien *(f pl)*
En voting shares
Es acciones con derecho de voto *(f pl)*
It azioni con diritto a voto *(f pl)*
Pt acçoes com direito a voto *(f pl)*

**actions d'attribution** *(f pl)* Fr
De Gratisaktien *(f pl)*
En bonus shares
Am stock dividend
Es acciones dadas como primas *(f pl)*
It azioni di godimento *(f pl)*
Pt acções de prémio *(f pl)*

**actions de fondateur** *(f pl)* Fr
De Gründeraktien *(f pl)*
En founder's shares
Es acciones del fundador *(f pl)*
It azioni del fondatore *(f pl)*
Pt acções de fundador *(f pl)*

**actions de priorité cumulatives** *(f pl)* Fr
De kumulative Vorzugsaktien *(f pl)*
En cumulative preference shares
Es valores privilegiados cumulativos *(m pl)*
It azioni preferenziali cumulative *(f pl)*
Pt acções preferenciais cumulativas *(f pl)*

**actions différées** *(f pl)* Fr
De Nachzugsaktien *(f pl)*
En deferred shares
Es acciones aplazadas *(f pl)*
It azioni postergate *(f pl)*
Pt acções diferidas *(f pl)*

**actions privilégiées amortissables** *(f pl)* Fr
De ablösbare Vorzugsaktien *(f pl)*
En redeemable preference shares
Es acciónes preferentes amortizables *(f pl)*
It azioni preferenziali redimibili *(f pl)*
Pt acções redimíveis preferenciais *(f pl)*

**actions sans droit de vote** *(f pl)* Fr
De Aktien ohne Stimmrecht *(f pl)*
En non-voting shares
Es acciones sin derecho de voto *(f pl)*
It azioni senza diritto a voto *(f pl)*
Pt acçoes sem direito a voto *(f pl)*

**active balance** En
De Aktivsaldo *(m)*
Es saldo acreedor *(m)*
Fr balance excédentaire *(f)*
It saldo attivo *(m)*
Pt saldo credor *(m)*

**active partner** En
De aktiver Teilhaber *(m)*
Es socio activo *(m)*
Fr associé en nom *(m)*
It socio attivo *(m)*
Pt sócio activo *(m)*

**activo** *(m)* n Es
De Aktivposten *(m)*
En asset
Fr actif *(m)*
It attivo *(m)*
Pt valor *(m)*

**activo e passivo** *(m)* Pt
De Aktiva und Passiva *(n pl)*
En assets and liabilities
Es activo y pasivo *(m)*
Fr actif et passif *(m)*
It attivo e passivo *(m)*

**activo fijo** *(m)* Es
De Vermögensanlage; Anlagevermögen *(f; n)*
En capital asset; fixed assets

**activo gastable** *(m)* Es
De kurzlebige Aktiva *(n pl)*
En wasting assets
Am depleting assets
Fr actifs défectibles *(m pl)*
It attività in esaurimento *(f pl)*
Pt bens em uso ou deterioração *(m pl)*

**activo intangible** *(m)* Es
De nicht greifbare Aktiven *(n pl)*
En intangible assets
Fr actif incorporel *(m)*
It beni incorporali *(m pl)*
Pt bens intocáveis *(m pl)*

**activo líquido** *(m)* Es
De flüssige Aktiven *(n pl)*
En liquid assets
Fr actif liquide *(m)*
It disponibilità; attività liquida *(f)*
Pt bens de activo líquidos *(m pl)*

**activo neto** *(m)* Es
De Reinvermögen *(n)*
En net assets
Fr actif net *(m)*
It attivo netto *(m)*
Pt bens líquidos *(m)*

**activo realizable** *(m)* Es
De Umlaufsvermögen *(n)*
En current assets
Fr actif courant *(m)*
It attivo liquido *(m)*
Pt bens no activo actual *(m pl)*

**activos congelados** *(m pl)* Es
De eingefrorene Guthaben *(n pl)*
En frozen assets
Fr fonds bioqués *(m pl)*
It attivo congelato *(m)*
Pt bens do activo congelados *(m pl)*

**actif immobilisé; immobilisations** *(m; f pl)*
It capitale fisso; immobilizzazioni *(m; f pl)*
Pt bens de capital; bens fixos *(m pl)*

**activo tangible** *(m)* Es
De greifbare Aktiven *(n pl)*
En tangible assets
Fr biens immobiliers *(m pl)*
It beni materiali *(m pl)*
Pt bens visíveis *(m pl)*

**activo y pasivo** *(m)* Es
De Aktiva und Passiva *(n pl)*
En assets and liabilities
Fr actif et passif *(m)*
It attivo e passivo *(m)*
Pt activo e passivo *(m)*

**actuaire** *(m)* n Fr
De Aktuar *(m)*
En actuary
Es actuario *(m)*
It attuario *(m)*
Pt actuário *(m)*

**actual cost** En
De Gestehungskosten *(m pl)*
Es precio verdadero *(m)*
Fr prix de revient effectif *(m)*
It costo effettivo *(m)*
Pt custo verdadeiro *(m)*

**actual total loss** En
De wirklicher Totalverlust *(m)*
Es pérdida total efectiva *(f)*
Fr perte totale effective *(f)*
It perdita totale assoluta *(f)*
Pt perda total efectiva *(f)*

**actuarial** *adj* En, Es, Pt
De versicherungsmathematisch
Fr actuariel
It attuariale

**actuariel** *adj* Fr
De versicherungsmathematisch
En actuarial
Es actuarial
It attuariale
Pt actuarial

**actuario** *(m)* n Es
De Aktuar *(m)*
En actuary
Fr actuaire *(m)*
It attuario *(m)*
Pt actuário *(m)*

**actuário** *(m)* n Pt
De Aktuar *(m)*
En actuary
Es actuario *(m)*
Fr actuaire *(m)*
It attuario *(m)*

**actuary** n En
De Aktuar *(m)*
Es actuario *(m)*
Fr actuaire *(m)*
It attuario *(m)*
Pt actuário *(m)*

**a cuenta** Es
De a conto; auf Abschlag
En on account
Fr à valoir
It in acconto
Pt por conta

**acuerdo** *(m)* n Es
De Vereinbarung *(f)*
En settlement (agreement)
Fr accord *(m)*
It accordo *(m)*
Pt acordo *(m)*

**acuerdo común** *(m)* Es
De gegenseitiges Einvernehmen *(n)*
En mutual agreement
Fr accord mutuel *(m)*
It comune accordo *(m)*
Pt acordo mútuo *(m)*

**Acuerdo General sobre Tarifas Aduaneras y Comercio** *(m)* Es
De Allgemeines Zoll- und Handelsabkommen *(n)*
En General Agreement on Tariffs and Trade (GATT)
Fr Accord Général sur les Tarifs Douaniers et le Commerce *(m)*
It Accordo Generale sulle Tariffe Doganali e sul Commercio *(m)*
Pt Acordo geral de Tarifas e Comércio *(m)*

**acuerdo mercantil** *(m)* Es
De Absatzübereinkommen *(n)*
En marketing agreement
Fr accord de commercialisation *(m)*
It accordo di mercato *(m)*

Pt acordo sobre comercialização *(m)*

**Acuerdo Monetario Europeo (AME)** *(m)* Es
De Europäisches Währungsabkommen (EWA) *(n)*
En European Monetary Agreement
Fr Accord Monétaire Européen (AME) *(m)*
It Accordo Monetario Europeo (AME) *(m)*
Pt Acuerdo Monetário Europeu (AME) *(m)*

**Acuerdo Monetário Europeu (AME)** *(m)* Pt
De Europäisches Währungsabkommen (EWA) *(n)*
En European Monetary Agreement
Es Acuerdo Monetario Europeo (AME) *(m)*
Fr Accord Monétaire Européen (AME) *(m)*
It Accordo Monetario Europeo (AME) *(m)*

**acuerdo secreto** *(m)* Es
De Geheimvertrag *(m)*
En secret agreement
Fr accord occulte *(m)*
It accordo segreto *(m)*
Pt acordo secreto *(m)*

**acuerdo sobre palabra** *(m)* Es
De Kavaliersabkommen *(n)*
En gentleman's agreement
Fr convention verbale *(f)*
It accordo sulla parola *(m)*
Pt pacto de honra *(m)*

**acuerdo sobre salarios** *(m)* Es
De Lohnvereinbarung *(f)*
En wages agreement
Fr convention des salaires *(f)*
It accordo sui salari *(m)*
Pt acordo sobre salários *(m)*

**acuerdo tácito** *(m)* Es
De stillschweigendes Übereinkommen *(n)*
En tacit agreement
Fr convention tacite *(f)*
It accordo tacito *(m)*
Pt acordo tácito *(m)*

**acuerdo tarifario** *(m)* Es
De Zollabkommen *(n)*
En tariff agreement
Fr accord tarifaire *(m)*
It accordo tariffario *(m)*
Pt acordo de tarifas *(m)*

**acumulação** *(f)* n Pt
De Auflaufen; Hort *(n m)*
En accrual; hoard
Es acumulación; atesoramiento *(f m)*
Fr accumulation; thésaurisation *(f)*
It maturazione; ammasso *(f m)*

**acumulación** *(f)* n Es
De Auflaufen *(n)*
En accrual
Fr accumulation *(f)*
It maturazione *(f)*
Pt acumulação *(f)*

**acumular** vb Es
De auflaufen
En accrue
Fr accumuler
It accumularsi
Pt accumular

**acumular existencias** Es
De Vorratslager anlegen
En stockpile
Fr stocker
It ammassare
Pt acumular existências

**acumular existências** Pt
De Vorratslager anlegen
En stockpile
Es acumular existencias
Fr stocker
It ammassare

**acumulativo** adj Es
De kumulativ
En cumulative
Fr cumulatif
It cumulativo
Pt cumulativo

**a curto prazo** Pt
De kurzfristig
En short-term; short-dated
Es a corto plazo
Fr à court terme; à courte échéance

It   a breve termine; a breve
     scadenza

**acusar a recepção de** Pt
De   Empfang bestätigen
En   acknowledge receipt of
Es   acusar recibo de
Fr   accuser réception de
It   accusare ricevuta di

**acusar recibo de** Es
De   Empfang bestätigen
En   acknowledge receipt of
Fr   accuser réception de
It   accusare ricevuta di
Pt   acusar a recepção de

**add** vb En
De   hinzufügen
Es   añadir
Fr   ajouter
It   aggiungere
Pt   adicionar

**added value** En
De   Mehrwert (f)
Es   valor agregado (m)
Fr   valeur ajoutée (f)
It   valore aggiunto (m)
Pt   valor adicionado (m)

**addieren** vb De
En   add up
Es   sumar
Fr   totaliser; additioner
It   sommare
Pt   somar

**Addiermaschine** (f) n De
En   adding machine
Es   máquina de sumar (f)
Fr   machine à additionner (f)
It   addizionatrice (f)
Pt   máquina de somar (f)

**adding machine** En
De   Addiermaschine (f)
Es   máquina de sumar (f)
Fr   machine à additionner (f)
It   addizionatrice (f)
Pt   máquina de somar (f)

**addition** n En, Fr (f)
De   Aufschlag (m)
Es   adición (f)
It   addizione (f)
Pt   adição (f)

**addizionatrice** (f) n It
De   Addiermaschine (f)
En   adding machine
Es   máquina de sumar (f)
Fr   machine à additionner (f)
Pt   máquina de somar (f)

**addizione** (f) n It
De   Aufschlag (m)
En   addition
Es   adición (f)
Fr   addition (f)
Pt   adição (f)

**address** n En
De   Adresse (f)
Es   dirección (f)
Fr   adresse (f)
It   indirizzo (m)
Pt   endereço (m)

**addressee** n En
De   Adressat (m)
Es   destinatario (m)
Fr   destinataire (m)
It   destinatario (m)
Pt   destinatário (m)

**addressing machine** En
De   Adressiermaschine (f)
Es   máquina de imprimir direc-
     ciones (f)
Fr   machine à imprimer les
     adresses (f)
It   macchina per stampare
     indirizzi (f)
Pt   máquina de endereços (m)

**add up** En
De   addieren
Es   sumar
Fr   totaliser; additioner
It   sommare
Pt   somar

**adelanto** (m) n Es
De   Vorschuss (m)
En   advance
Fr   avance (f)
It   anticipazione (f)
Pt   adiantamento (m)

**adempiere** vb It
De   erfüllen
En   fulfil
Es   cumplir
Fr   remplir
Pt   comprir

**adempimento** (m) n It
De   Erfüllung (f)
En   fulfilment
Es   cumplimiento (m)
Fr   accomplissement (m)
Pt   cumprimento (m)

**adiamento** (m) n Pt
De   Vertagung (f)
En   adjournment
Es   aplazamiento (m)
Fr   ajournement (m)
It   aggiornamento (m)

**adiantamento** (m) n Pt
De   Vorschuss (m)
En   advance
Es   adelanto (m)
Fr   avance (f)
It   anticipazione (f)

**adiantar** vb Pt
De   vorschiessen
En   advance
Am   prepay
Es   anticipar
Fr   avancer
It   anticipare

**adiante** adj Pt
De   Termin-
En   forward
Es   a término
Fr   en avant; à terme
It   a termine

**adiar** vb Pt
De   vertagen; zurückstellen
En   adjourn; defer
Es   aplazar
Fr   ajourner; différer
It   aggiornare; differire

**adição** (f) n Pt
De   Aufschlag (m)
En   addition
Es   adición (f)
Fr   addition (f)
It   addizione (f)

**adición** (f) n Es
De   Aufschlag (m)
En   addition
Fr   addition (f)
It   addizione (f)
Pt   adição (f)

**adicionar** vb Pt
De hinzufügen
En add
Es añadir
Fr ajouter
It aggiungere

**adjourn** vb En
De vertagen
Es aplazar
Fr ajourner
It aggiornare
Pt adiar

**adjournment** n En
De Vertagung (f)
Es aplazamiento (m)
Fr ajournement (m)
It aggiornamento (m)
Pt adiamento (m)

**adjudicación** (f) n Es
De Verteilung (f)
En allotment
Fr attribution (f)
It ripartizione (f)
Pt aporcionamento (m)

**adjudicar** vb Es, Pt
De gerichtlich entscheiden
En adjudicate
Fr juger
It aggiudicare

**adjudicate** vb En
De gerichtlich entscheiden
Es adjudicar
Fr juger
It aggiudicare
Pt adjudicar

**adjuger des dommages-intér-êts** Fr
De Schadenersatz zugestehen
En award damages
Es conceder daños
It concedere i danni
Pt conceder compensação

**adjunto** adj Es
De beiliegend
En enclosed
Fr ci-joint; ci-inclus
It accluso
Pt incluso

**adjustment** (insurance) En
De Regulierung (f)
Es reglamento (m)
Fr règlement (m)
It regolamento (m)
Pt ajuste (m)

**admettre une caution** Fr
De gegen Haftkaution freige-ben
En grant bail
Es conceder fianza
It concedere la libertà provvi-soria su cauzione
Pt autorizar caução

**administer** vb En
De verwalten
Es administrar
Fr administrer
It amministrare
Pt administrar

**administração** (f) n Pt
De Verwaltung (f)
En administration
Es ministerio (m)
Fr gouvernement (m)
It governo (m)

**administración** (f) n Es
De Verwaltung (f)
En administration
Fr gestion (f)
It gestione (f)
Pt gestão (f)

**administrador** (m) n Es; Pt
De Verwalter (m)
En administrator
Fr administrateur (m)
It amministratore (m)

**administrar** vb Es, Pt
De verwalten
En administer
Fr administrer
It amministrare

**administrateur** (m) n Fr
De Direktor; Verwalter (m)
En director; administrator
Es director; administrador (m)
It amministratore (m)
Pt director; administrador (m)

**administrateur chef d'écoule-ment** (m) Fr
De Absatzdirektor (m)
En marketing director
Es director mercantil (m)
It direttore di mercato (m)
Pt director de comercialização (m)

**administrateur délégué** (m) Fr
De geschäftsleitender Direktor (m)
En managing director
Am president
Es director gerente (m)
It amministratore delegato (m)
Pt director geral (m)

**administrateur dirigeant** (m) Fr
De geschäftsführender Direktor (m)
En executive director
Am corporate officer
Es director ejecutivo (m)
It amministratore dirigente (m)
Pt director administrativo (m)

**administration** (business) n En
De Verwaltung (f)
Es administración (f)
Fr gestion (f)
It gestione (f)
Pt gestão (f)

**administration** (government) n En
De Staatsverwaltung (f)
Es ministerio (m)
Fr gouvernement (m)
It governo (m)
Pt administração (f)

**administration** (f) n Fr
De Vorstand (m)
En management
Es dirección (f)
It direzione; amministrazione (f)
Pt gerência; direcção (f)

**administrative assistant** Am
En personal assistant (PA)
De persönlicher Assistent (m)
Es asistente privado (m)
Fr fonctionnel (m)

It assistente privato *(m)*
Pt secretário *(m)*

**administrator** (of an estate) *n*
En
De Nachlassverwalter *(m)*
Es administrador *(m)*
Fr curateur *(m)*
It curatore *(m)*
Pt curador *(m)*

**administrator** (business) *n* En
De Verwalter *(m)*
Es administrador *(m)*
Fr administrateur *(m)*
It amministratore *(m)*
Pt administrador *(m)*

**administrer** *vb* Fr
De verwalten
En administer
Es administrar
It amministrare
Pt administrar

**admisión libre de impuestos**
*(f)* Es
De zollfreie Einfuhr *(f)*
En duty-free admission
Fr admission en franchise *(f)*
It ammissione in franchigia
doganale *(f)*
Pt admissão livre de impostos
*(f)*

**admissão** *(f)* n Pt
De Eintritt *(m)*
En entry
Es entrada *(f)*
Fr entrée *(f)*
It entrata *(f)*

**admissão livre de impostos** *(f)*
Pt
De zollfreie Einfuhr *(f)*
En duty-free admission
Es admisión libre de impues-
tos *(f)*
Fr admission en franchise *(f)*
It ammissione in franchigia
doganale *(f)*

**admission en franchise** *(f)* Fr
De zollfreie Einfuhr *(f)*
En duty-free admission
Es admisión libre de impues-
tos *(f)*

It ammissione in franchigia
doganale *(f)*
Pt admissão livre de impostos
*(f)*

**admission free** En
De Eintritt frei *(m)*
Es entrada gratuita *(f)*
Fr entrée gratuite *(f)*
It ingresso gratuito *(m)*
Pt entrada gratis *(f)*

**adquisición** *(f)* n Es
De Erwerb *(m)*
En acquisition
Fr acquisition *(f)*
It acquisizione *(f)*
Pt aquisição *(f)*

**adquisiciones** *(f pl)* Es
De Einkäufe *(m pl)*
En purchases
Fr achats *(m pl)*
It acquisti *(m pl)*
Pt aquisições *(f pl)*

**Adressat** *(m)* n De
En addressee
Es destinatario *(m)*
Fr destinataire *(m)*
It destinatario *(m)*
Pt destinatário *(m)*

**Adressbuch** *(n)* n De
En directory
Es guía *(f)*
Fr répertoire *(m)*
It guida *(f)*
Pt guia *(m)*

**adresse** *(f)* n Fr
De Adresse *(f)*
En address
Es dirección *(f)*
It indirizzo *(m)*
Pt endereço *(m)*

**Adresse** *(f)* n De
En address
Es dirección *(f)*
Fr adresse *(f)*
It indirizzo *(m)*
Pt endereço *(m)*

**adresse télégraphique** *(f)* Fr
De Telegrammadresse *(f)*
En telegraphic address
Es dirección telegráfica *(f)*

It indirizzo telegrafico *(m)*
Pt endereço telegráfico *(m)*

**Adressiermaschine** *(f)* n De
En addressing machine
Es r. áquina de imprimir direc-
ciones *(f)*
Fr machine à imprimer les
adresses *(f)*
It macchina per stampare
indirizzi *(f)*
Pt máquina de endereços *(m)*

**aduana** *(f)* n Es
De Zoll *(m)*
En customs
Fr douane *(f)*
It dogana *(f)*
Pt alfândega *(f)*

**advance** (money) *vb* En
Am prepay
De vorschiessen
Es anticipar
Fr avancer
It anticipare
Pt adiantar

**advance** (of money) *n* En
Am prepayment
De Vorschuss *(m)*
Es adelanto *(m)*
Fr avance *(f)*
It anticipazione *(f)*
Pt adiantamento *(m)*

**advance account** En
De Darlehenskonto *(n)*
Es cuenta de anticipos *(f)*
Fr compte d'avances *(m)*
It conto anticipo *(m)*
Pt conta de adiantamentos *(f)*

**advance in price** *vb* En
De teurer werden; steigen
Es encarecer
Fr renchérir
It aumentare di prezzo
Pt encarecer

**advance in price** *n* En
De Preiserhöhung *(f)*
Es encarecimiento *(m)*
Fr renchérissement *(m)*
It rialzo *(m)*
Pt encarecimento *(m)*

**advance payment** En
De Vorauszahlung (f)
Es anticipo (m)
Fr paiement par anticipation (m)
It pagamento anticipato (m)
Pt pagamento adiantado (m)

**adverse balance** En
Am negative balance
De Passivsaldo (m)
Es saldo adverso (m)
Fr balance déficitaire (f)
It saldo passivo (m)
Pt saldo negativo (m)

**advertisement** n En
De Anzeige (f)
Es anuncio (m)
Fr annonce (f)
It annunzio (m)
Pt anúncio (m)

**advertiser** n En
De Anzeiger (m)
Es anunciante (m)
Fr annonceur (m)
It inserzionista (m)
Pt anunciante (m)

**advertising** n En
De Reklame; Werbung (f)
Es publicidad (f)
Fr publicité (f)
It pubblicità (f)
Pt publicidade (f)

**advertising agency** En
De Werbebüro (n)
Es agencia de publicidad (f)
Fr agence de publicité (f)
It agenzia pubblicitaria (f)
Pt agência de publicidade (f)

**advertising brochure** En
De Werbeschrift (f)
Es folleto publicitario (m)
Fr prospectus publicitaire (m)
It opuscolo pubblicitario (m)
Pt folheto publicitário (m)

**advertising campaign** En
De Werbefeldzug (m)
Es campaña publicitaria (f)
Fr campagne de publicité (f)
It campagna pubblicitaria (f)
Pt campanha publicitária (f)

**advertising consultant** En
De Werbeberater (m)
Es consultor de publicidad (m)
Fr conseil en publicité (m)
It consulente di pubblicità (m)
Pt perito de publicidade (m)

**advertising copy** En
De Werbetext (m)
Es material publicitario (m)
Fr copie publicitaire (f)
It testo pubblicitario (m)
Pt texto de publicidade (m)

**advertising expenditure** En
De Werbekosten (pl)
Es gastos publicitarios (m pl)
Fr dépenses de publicité (f pl)
It spese di pubblicità (f pl)
Pt despesa com publicidade (f)

**advertising medium** En
De Werbemittel (n)
Es medio de publicidad (m)
Fr support publicitaire (m)
It mezzo pubblicitario (m)
Pt meio publicitário (m)

**advertising rates** En
De Werbetarif (m)
Es tarifa para anuncios (f)
Fr tarifs de publicité (m pl)
It tariffa delle inserzioni (f)
Pt taxas de publicidade (f)

**advertising schedule** En
De Werbeplan (m)
Es plan de propaganda (m)
Fr programme des annonces (m)
It programma delle inserzioni (m)
Pt plano de campanha publicitária (m)

**advice note** En
De Anzeige (f)
Es aviso (m)
Fr lettre d'avis (f)
It lettera d'avviso (f)
Pt guia de remessa (f)

**advisory** adj En
De Beratungs-
Es consultivo
Fr consultatif

It consultivo
Pt consultivo

**advisory board** En
De Beratungsausschuss (m)
Es consejo consultivo (m)
Fr comité consultatif (m)
It consiglio consultivo (m)
Pt comité consultivo (m)

**advogado** (m) n Pt
De Anwalt (m)
En barrister; counsel
Am attorney
Es abogado (m)
Fr avocat (m)
It avvocato (m)

**aérogare** (f) n Fr
De Luftterminal (n)
En air terminal
Es terminal de aeropuerto (f)
It aerostazione (f)
Pt estação terminal aérea (f)

**aérogramme** (m) Fr
De Luftpostbrief (m)
En air letter
Es carta por avión (f)
It lettera aerea (f)
Pt carta de avião (f)

**aéroport** (m) n Fr
De Lufthafen (m)
En airport
Es aeropuerto (m)
It aeroporto (m)
Pt aeroporto (m)

**aeroporto** (m) n It, Pt
De Lufthafen (m)
En airport
Es aeropuerto (m)
Fr aéroport (m)

**aeropuerto** (m) n Es
De Lufthafen (m)
En airport
Fr aéroport (m)
It aeroporto (m)
Pt aeroporto (m)

**aerostazione** (f) n It
De Luftterminal (n)
En air terminal
Es terminal de aeropuerto (f)
Fr aérogare (f)
Pt estação terminal aérea (f)

**affaire** *(f)* n Fr
De Abschluss *(m)*
En deal
Es negocio *(m)*
It affare *(f)*
Pt negócio *(m)*

**affaire équitable** *(f)* Fr
De anständige Abmachung *(f)*
En fair deal
Es trato equitativo *(m)*
It affare giusto *(m)*
Pt transacção razoável *(f)*

**affaire qui marche** *(f)* Fr
De gewinnbringendes Unternehmen *(n)*
En going concern
Es negocio en marcha *(m)*
It azienda in piena attività *(f)*
Pt negócio que vinga *(m)*

**affaires** *(f pl)* n Fr
De Geschäft *(n)*
En business
Es negocios *(m pl)*
It affari *(m pl)*
Pt negócios *(m pl)*

**affare** *(m)* n It
De Handel; Abschluss *(m)*
En bargain; deal
Es negocio *(m)*
Fr marché; affaire *(m f)*
Pt negócio *(m)*

**affare giusto** *(m)* It
De anständige Abmachung *(f)*
En fair deal
Es trato equitativo *(m)*
Fr affaire équitable *(f)*
Pt transacção razoável *(f)*

**affari** *(m pl)* n It
De Geschäft *(n)*
En business
Es negocios *(m pl)*
Fr affaires *(f pl)*
Pt negócios *(m pl)*

**affectation** *(f)* n Fr
De Zuführung *(f)*
En appropriation
Es apropiación *(f)*
It stanziamento *(m)*
Pt apropriação *(f)*

**affidare** *vb* It
De anvertrauen
En entrust
Es confiar
Fr confier
Pt confiar

**affidavit** n En
De beeidigte Erklärung *(f)*
Es declaración jurada *(f)*
Fr déclaration sous serment *(f)*
It dichiarazione giurata *(f)*
Pt declaração sob juramento *(f)*

**affiliated company** En
De Schwestergesellschaft *(f)*
Es compañía afiliada *(f)*
Fr société sœur *(f)*
It società affiliata *(f)*
Pt companhia subsidiária *(f)*

**affittare** *vb* It
De vermieten
En rent
Es alquilar
Fr louer; affermer
Pt alugar

**affitto** *(m)* n It
De Verpachtung *(f)*
En lease
Es alquiler *(m)*
Fr bail *(m)*
Pt aluguer; arrendamento *(m)*

**affitto di terreno** *(m)* It
De Grundpacht *(f)*
En ground-rent
Es renta del terreno *(f)*
Fr rente foncière *(f)*
Pt renda sobre o terreno *(f)*

**affittuario** *(m)* n It
De Mieter *(m)*
En tenant
Es inquilino *(m)*
Fr locataire *(m)*
Pt inquilino *(m)*

**affrancatrice postale** *(f)* It
De Frankiermaschine *(f)*
En franking machine
Es máquina de franquear *(f)*
Fr machine à affranchir *(f)*
Pt máquina de franquear *(f)*

**affrètement** *(m)* n Fr
De Befrachtung *(f)*
En chartering
Es fletamento *(m)*
It noleggio *(m)*
Pt fretamento *(m)*

**affrètement à temps** *(m)* Fr
De Zeitcharter *(f)*
En time charter
Es fletamento de tiempo *(m)*
It contratto di noleggio a tempo *(m)*
Pt fretamento de tempo *(m)*

**affréteur** *(m)* n Fr
De Befrachter *(m)*
En charterer
Es fletador *(m)*
It noleggiatore *(m)*
Pt fretador *(m)*

**afloat** *adv* En
De flott
Es a flote
Fr à flot
It flottante
Pt flutuante

**à flot** Fr
De flott
En afloat
Es a flote
It flottante
Pt flutuante

**a flote** Es
De flott
En afloat
Fr à flot
It flottante
Pt flutuante

**agence** *(f)* n Fr
De Agentur *(f)*
En agency
Es agencia *(f)*
It agenzia *(f)*
Pt agência *(f)*

**agence de placement** *(f)* Fr
De Stellenvermittlungsbüro *(n)*
En employment agency
Es agencia de colocaciones *(f)*
It agenzia di collocamento *(f)*
Pt agência de emprego *(f)*

**agence de presse** (f) Fr
De Nachrichtenbüro (n)
En news agency
Es agencia de prensa (f)
It agenzia d'informazioni (f)
Pt agência de notícias (f)

**agence de publicité** (f) Fr
De Werbebüro (n)
En advertising agency
Es agencia de publicidad (f)
It agenzia pubblicitaria (f)
Pt agência de publicidade (f)

**agence de voyages** (f) Fr
De Reisebüro (n)
En travel agent
Es agencia de viajes (f)
It agenzia di viaggi (f)
Pt agente de viagens (m)

**agence immobilière** (f) Fr
De Immobilienbüro (n)
En estate agency
Am real estate agency
Es correduría de fincas (f)
It agenzia immobiliare (f)
Pt agência de propriedades (f)

**agencia** (f) n Es
De Agentur (f)
En agency
Fr agence (f)
It agenzia (f)
Pt agência (f)

**agência** (f) n Pt
De Agentur (f)
En agency
Es agencia (f)
Fr agence (f)
It agenzia (f)

**agência corretora de descontos** (f) Pt
De Diskontbank (f)
En discount house
Es casa de descuentos (f)
Fr maison d'escompte (f)
It banca di sconto (f)

**agencia de colocaciones** (f) Es
De Stellenvermittlungsbüro (n)
En employment agency
Fr agence de placement (f)
It agenzia di collocamento (f)
Pt agência de emprego (f)

**agência de emprego** (f) Pt
De Stellenvermittlungsbüro (n)
En employment agency
Es agencia de colocaciones (f)
Fr agence de placement (f)
It agenzia di collocamento (f)

**agência de notícias** (f) Pt
De Nachrichtenbüro (n)
En news agency
Es agencia de prensa (f)
Fr agence de presse (f)
It agenzia d'informazioni (f)

**agencia de prensa** (f) Es
De Nachrichtenbüro (n)
En news agency
Fr agence de presse (f)
It agenzia d'informazioni (f)
Pt agência de notícias (f)

**agência de propriedades** (f) Pt
De Immobilienbüro (n)
En estate agency
Am real estate agency
Es correduría de fincas (f)
Fr agence immobilière (f)
It agenzia immobiliare (f)

**agencia de publicidad** (f) Es
De Werbebüro (n)
En advertising agency
Fr agence de publicité (f)
It agenzia pubblicitaria (f)
Pt agência de publicidade (f)

**agência de publicidade** (f) Pt
De Werbebüro (n)
En advertising agency
Es agencia de publicidad (f)
Fr agence de publicité (f)
It agenzia pubblicitaria (f)

**agencia de viajes** (f) Es
De Reisebüro (n)
En travel agent
Fr agence de voyages (f)
It agenzia di viaggi (f)
Pt agente de viagens (m)

**agency** (commercial) n En
De Agentur (f)
Es agencia (f)
Fr agence (f)
It agenzia (f)
Pt agência (f)

**agency** (legal) n En
De Vertretung (f)
Es mandato (m)
Fr mandat (m)
It mandato (m)
Pt mandato (m)

**agenda** n En
De Tagesordnung (f)
Es orden del día (m)
Fr ordre du jour (m)
It ordine del giorno (m)
Pt agenda (f)

**agenda** (f) n Pt
De Tagesordnung (f)
En agenda
Es orden del día (m)
Fr ordre du jour (m)
It ordine del giorno (m)

**agenda da reunião** (f) Pt
De Tagesordnung (f)
En business before the meeting
Am agenda
Es orden del día (f)
Fr ordre du jour (m)
It scopo dell'assemblea (m)

**agent** n En, Fr (m)
De Agent (m)
Es agente (m)
It agente (m)
Pt agente (m)

**Agent** (m) n De
En agent
Es agente (m)
Fr agent (m)
It agente (m)
Pt agente (m)

**agent accrédité** (m) Fr
De Handelsbevollmächtigte(r) (m)
En accredited agent
Es agente acreditudo (m)
It agente accreditato (m)
Pt agente acreditado (m)

**agent attitré** (m) Fr
De Handelsvertreter (m)
En appointed agent
Es agente nombrado (m)
It agente ufficiale (m)
Pt agente oficial (m)

**agent d'assurances** *(m)* Fr
De  Versicherungsvertreter *(m)*
En  insurance agent
Es  agente de seguros *(m)*
It  agenzia di assicurazioni *(f)*
Pt  agente de seguros *(m)*

**agent de commerce** *(m)* Fr
De  Handelsvertreter *(m)*
En  mercantile agent
Am sales agent
Es  agente mercantil *(m)*
It  agente di commercio *(m)*
Pt  agente comercial *(m)*

**agent de recouvrement** *(m)* Fr
De  Inkassobeauftragte(r) *(m)*
En  debt collector
Es  agente recaudador *(m)*
It  agente di ricupero crediti *(m)*
Pt  cobrador *(m)*

**agent ducroire** *(m)* Fr
De  Delkrederevertreter *(m)*
En  del credere agent
Es  agente del crédere *(m)*
It  agente con del credere *(m)*
Pt  agente del credere *(m)*

**agente** *(m) n* Es, It, Pt
De  Agent *(m)*
En  agent (commercial)
Fr  agent *(m)*

**agente accreditato** *(m)* It
De  Handelsbevollmächtigte(r) *(m)*
En  accredited agent
Es  agente acreditudo *(m)*
Fr  agent accrédité *(m)*
Pt  agente acreditado *(m)*

**agente acreditado** *(m)* Pt
De  Handelsbevollmächtigte(r) *(m)*
En  accredited agent
Es  agente acreditudo *(m)*
Fr  agent accrédité *(m)*
It  agente accreditato *(m)*

**agente acreditudo** *(m)* Es
De  Handelsbevollmächtigte(r) *(m)*
En  accredited agent
Fr  agent accrédité *(m)*
It  agente accreditato *(m)*
Pt  agente acreditado *(m)*

**agente comercial** *(m)* Pt
De  Handelsvertreter *(m)*
En  mercantile agent
Am sales agent
Es  agente mercantil *(m)*
Fr  agent de commerce *(m)*
It  agente di commercio *(m)*

**agente con del credere** *(m)* It
De  Delkrederevertreter *(m)*
En  del credere agent
Es  agente del crédere *(m)*
Fr  agent ducroire *(m)*
Pt  agente del credere *(m)*

**agente de cargas e despachos** *(m)* Pt
De  Spediteur *(m)*
En  shipping and forwarding agent
Es  agente de embarques *(m)*
Fr  agent metteur à bord *(m)*
It  agente marittimo e di spedizione *(m)*

**agente de embarques** *(m)* Es
De  Spediteur *(m)*
En  shipping and forwarding agent
Fr  agent metteur à bord *(m)*
It  agente marittimo e di spedizione *(m)*
Pt  agente de cargas e despachos *(m)*

**agente del crédere** *(m)* Es
De  Delkrederevertreter *(m)*
En  del credere agent
Fr  agent ducroire *(m)*
It  agente con del credere *(m)*
Pt  agente del credere *(m)*

**agente del credere** *(m)* Pt
De  Delkrederevertreter *(m)*
En  del credere agent
Es  agente del crédere *(m)*
Fr  agent ducroire *(m)*
It  agente con del credere *(m)*

**agente delle imposte** *(m)* It
De  Schätzer *(m)*
En  assessor
Es  asesor *(m)*
Fr  appréciateur *(m)*
Pt  avaliador *(rn)*

**agente de patentes** *(m)* Es, Pt
De  Patentanwalt *(m)*
En  patent agent
Fr  conseil en brevets *(m)*
It  agente di brevetti *(m)*

**agente de seguros** *(m)* Es, Pt
De  Versicherungsvertreter *(m)*
En  insurance agent
Fr  agent d'assurances *(m)*
It  agenzia di assicurazioni *(f)*

**agente de viagems** *(m)* Pt
De  Reisebüro *(n)*
En  travel agent
Es  agencia de viajes *(f)*
Fr  agence de voyages *(f)*
It  agenzia di viaggi *(f)*

**agente di assicurazioni marittime** *(m)* It
De  Seetransportversicherungsmakler *(m)*
En  marine insurance broker
Es  corredor de seguro marítimo *(m)*
Fr  courtier d'assurances maritimes *(m)*
Pt  corretor de seguros marítimos *(m)*

**agente di borsa** *(m)* It
De  Börsenmakler *(m)*
En  stockbroker
Es  corredor de bolsa *(m)*
Fr  courtier en bourse *(m)*
Pt  corretor da bolsa *(m)*

**agente di brevetti** *(m)* It
De  Patentanwalt *(m)*
En  patent agent
Es  agente de patentes *(m)*
Fr  conseil en brevets *(m)*
Pt  agente de patentes *(m)*

**agente di commercio** *(m)* It
De  Handelsvertreter *(m)*
En  mercantile agent
Am sales agent
Es  agente mercantil *(m)*
Fr  agent de commerce *(m)*
Pt  agente comercial *(m)*

**agente di ricupero crediti** *(m)* It
De  Inkassobeauftragte(r) *(m)*
En  debt collector
Es  agente recaudador *(m)*

Fr  agent de recouvrement *(m)*
Pt  cobrador *(m)*

**agente di sconto** *(m)* It
De  Wechselmakler *(m)*
En  bill broker
Es  corredor de cambios *(m)*
Fr  courtier de bons *(m)*
Pt  corretor de câmbios *(m)*

**agente exclusivo** *(m)* Es, Pt
De  Alleinvertreter *(m)*
En  sole agent
Fr  agent exclusif *(m)*
It  rappresentante esclusivo *(m)*

**agente expedidor** *(m)* Es, Pt
De  Spediteur *(m)*
En  forwarding agent
Fr  transitaire *(m)*
It  spedizioniere *(m)*

**agente marittimo e di spedizione** *(m)* It
De  Spediteur *(m)*
En  shipping and forwarding agent
Es  agente de embarques *(m)*
Fr  agent metteur à bord *(m)*
Pt  agente de cargas e despachos *(m)*

**agente mercantil** *(m)* Es
De  Handelsvertreter *(m)*
En  mercantile agent
Am  sales agent
Fr  agent de commerce *(m)*
It  agente di commercio *(m)*
Pt  agente comercial *(m)*

**agente nombrado** *(m)* Es
De  Handelsvertreter *(m)*
En  appointed agent
Fr  agent attitré *(m)*
It  agente ufficiale *(m)*
Pt  agente oficial *(m)*

**agente oficial** *(m)* Pt
De  Handelsvertreter *(m)*
En  appointed agent
Es  agente nombrado *(m)*
Fr  agent attitré *(m)*
It  agente ufficiale *(m)*

**agente recaudador** *(m)* Es
De  Inkassobeauftragte(r) *(m)*
En  debt collector

Fr  agent de recouvrement *(m)*
It  agente di ricupero crediti *(m)*
Pt  cobrador *(m)*

**agente sob comissão** *(m)* Pt
De  Kommissionär *(m)*
En  commission agent
Es  comisionista *(m)*
Fr  commissionnaire en marchandises *(m)*
It  commissionario *(m)*

**agente ufficiale** *(m)* It
De  Handelsvertreter *(m)*
En  appointed agent
Es  agente nombrado *(m)*
Fr  agent attitré *(m)*
Pt  agente oficial *(m)*

**agent exclusif** *(m)* Fr
De  Alleinvertreter *(m)*
En  sole agent
Es  agente exclusivo *(m)*
It  rappresentante esclusivo *(m)*
Pt  agente exclusivo *(m)*

**agent metteur à bord** *(m)* Fr
De  Spediteur *(m)*
En  shipping and forwarding agent
Es  agente de embarques *(m)*
It  agente marittimo e di spedizione *(m)*
Pt  agente de cargas e despachos *(m)*

**Agentur** *(f)* n De
En  agency
Es  agencia *(f)*
Fr  agence *(f)*
It  agenzia *(f)*
Pt  agência *(f)*

**agenzia** *(f)* n It
De  Agentur *(f)*
En  agency
Es  agencia *(f)*
Fr  agence *(f)*
Pt  agência *(f)*

**agenzia di assicurazioni** *(f)* It
De  Versicherungsvertreter *(m)*
En  insurance agent
Es  agente de seguros *(m)*
Fr  agent d'assurances *(m)*
Pt  agente de seguros *(m)*

**agenzia di collocamento** *(f)* It
De  Stellenvermittlungsbüro *(n)*
En  employment agency
Es  agencia de colocaciones *(f)*
Fr  agence de placement *(f)*
Pt  agência de emprego *(f)*

**agenzia d'informazioni** *(f)* It
De  Nachrichtenbüro *(n)*
En  news agency
Es  agencia de prensa *(f)*
Fr  agence de presse *(f)*
Pt  agência de notícias *(f)*

**agenzia di viaggi** *(f)* It
De  Reisebüro *(n)*
En  travel agent
Es  agencia de viajes *(f)*
Fr  agence de voyages *(f)*
Pt  agente de viagems *(m)*

**agenzia immobiliare** *(f)* It
De  Immobilienbüro *(n)*
En  estate agency
Am  real estate agency
Es  corredería de fincas *(f)*
Fr  agence immobilière *(f)*
Pt  agência de propriedades *(f)*

**agenzia pubblicitaria** *(f)* It
De  Werbebüro *(n)*
En  advertising agency
Es  agencia de publicidad *(f)*
Fr  agence de publicité *(f)*
Pt  agência de publicidade *(f)*

**aggiornamento** *(m)* n It
De  Vertagung *(f)*
En  adjournment
Es  aplazamiento *(m)*
Fr  ajournement *(m)*
Pt  adiamento *(m)*

**aggiornare** *vb* It
De  vertagen
En  adjourn
Es  aplazar
Fr  ajourner
Pt  adiar

**aggiotatore** *(m)* n It
De  Börsenhändler *(m)*
En  stockjobber
Es  agiotista *(m)*
Fr  marchand de titres *(m)*
Pt  agiota *(m)*

**aggiudicare** *vb* It
De gerichtlich entscheiden
En adjudicate
Es adjudicar
Fr juger
Pt adjudicar

**aggiungere** *vb* It
De hinzufügen
En add
Es añadir
Fr ajouter
Pt adicionar

**aggregate** *adj* En
De gesamt
Es total
Fr global
It complessivo
Pt total

**agio account** En
De Agiokonto *(n)*
Es cuenta de agio *(f)*
Fr compte d'agio *(m)*
It conto d'aggio *(m)*
Pt conta de ágio *(f)*

**Agiokonto** *(n) n* De
En agio account
Es cuenta de agio *(f)*
Fr compte d'agio *(m)*
It conto d'aggio *(m)*
Pt conta de ágio *(f)*

**agiota** *(m) n* Pt
De Börsenhändler *(m)*
En stockjobber
Es agiotista *(m)*
Fr marchand de titres *(m)*
It aggiotatore *(m)*

**agiotista** *(m) n* Es
De Börsenhändler *(m)*
En stockjobber
Fr marchand de titres *(m)*
It aggiotatore *(m)*
Pt agiota *(m)*

**agotado** *adj* Es
De ausverkauft
En sold out
Fr tout vendu
It tutto venduto
Pt esgotado

**a granel** Es, Pt
De in grosser Menge
En in bulk
Fr en vrac
It alla rinfusa

**agravio** *(m) n* Es
De Beschwerde; unerlaubte Handlung *(f)*
En grievance; tort
Fr grief; acte dommageable *(m)*
It lagnanza; torto *(f m)*
Pt agravo *(m)*

**agravo** *(m) n* Pt
De Beschwerde; unerlaubte Handlung *(f)*
En grievance; tort
Es agravio *(m)*
Fr grief; acte dommageable *(m)*
It lagnanza; torto *(f m)*

**agreement** (written) *n* En
De Abkommen *(n)*
Es contrato *(m)*
Fr convention (par écrit) *(f)*
It accordo *(m)*
Pt acordo *(m)*

**agricoltura** *(f) n* It
De Landwirtschaft *(f)*
En agriculture
Es agricultura *(f)*
Fr agriculture *(f)*
Pt agricultura *(f)*

**agricultura** *(f) n* Es, Pt
De Landwirtschaft *(f)*
En agriculture
Fr agriculture *(f)*
It agricoltura *(f)*

**agriculture** *n* En, Fr *(f)*
De Landwirtschaft *(f)*
Es agricultura *(f)*
It agricoltura *(f)*
Pt agricultura *(f)*

**aguarde** Pt
De am Apparat bleiben
En hold the line
Es espere al aparato
Fr ne quittez pas
It resta in linea

**águas territoriais** *(f pl)* Pt
De Hoheitsgewässer *(n pl)*
En territorial waters
Es aguas territoriales *(f pl)*
Fr eaux territoriales *(f pl)*
It acque territoriali *(f pl)*

**à haute teneur** Fr
De erstklassig
En high-grade
Es alta calidad
It di qualità superiore
Pt alto-nível

**ahorrar** *vb* Es
De aufsparen
En save
Fr épargner; économiser
It risparmiare; economizzare
Pt poupar; economizar

**ainto** *(m) n* It
De Hilfe *(f)*
En help
Es ayuda *(f)*
Fr secours *(m)*
Pt ajuda *(f)*

**air-conditioning** *n* En
De Klimatisierung *(f)*
Es acondicionamiento de aire *(m)*
Fr climatisation *(f)*
It condizionamento dell'aria *(m)*
Pt condicionamento do ar *(m)*

**air freight** En
De Luftfracht *(f)*
Es flete aéreo *(m)*
Fr fret aérien *(m)*
It trasporto aereo *(m)*
Pt frete aéreo *(m)*

**air letter** En
De Luftpostbrief *(m)*
Es carta por avión *(f)*
Fr aérogramme *(m)*
It lettera aerea *(f)*
Pt carta de avião *(f)*

**air line** En
De Fluggesellschaft *(f)*
Es línea aérea *(f)*
Fr compagnie aérienne *(f)*
It linea aerea *(f)*
Pt companhia de aviação *(f)*

**airmail** n En
De Luftpost (f)
Es correo aéreo (m)
Fr poste aérienne (f)
It posta aerea (f)
Pt correio aéreo (m)

**airmail receipt** En
De Luftpostempfangsbescheinigung (f)
Es recibo aeropostal (m)
Fr récépissé de poste aérienne (m)
It ricevimento per posta aerea (m)
Pt recibo de via aérea (m)

**airport** n En
De Lufthafen (m)
Es aeropuerto (m)
Fr aéroport (m)
It aeroporto (m)
Pt aeroporto (m)

**air terminal** En
De Luftterminal (n)
Es terminal de aeropuerto (f)
Fr aérogare (f)
It aerostazione (f)
Pt estação terminal aérea (f)

**air traffic** En
De Luftverkehr (m)
Es tráfico aéreo (m)
Fr trafic aérien (m)
It traffico aereo (m)
Pt tráfego aéreo (m)

**air transport** En
De Lufttransport (m)
Es transporte aéreo (m)
Fr transport aérien (m)
It trasporto aereo (m)
Pt transporte aéreo (m)

**air waybill** En
De Luftfrachtbrief (m)
Es carta de porte aéreo (f)
Fr lettre de transport aérien (f)
It nota di spedizione aerea (f)
Pt guia de porte aéreo (m)

**ajournement** (m) n Fr
De Vertagung (f)
En adjournment
Es aplazamiento (m)

It aggiornamento (m)
Pt adiamento (m)

**ajourner** vb Fr
De vertagen
En adjourn
Es aplazar
It aggiornare
Pt adiar

**ajouter** vb Fr
De hinzufügen
En add
Es añadir
It aggiungere
Pt adicionar

**ajuda** (f) n Pt
De Hilfe (f)
En help
Es ayuda (f)
Fr secours (m)
It ainto (m)

**ajuste** (m) n Es, Pt
De Abrechnung (f)
En settlement
Fr règlement (m)
It quietanza (f)

**Akkordarbeit** (f) n De
En piecework
Es trabajo a destajo (m)
Fr travail à la tâche (m)
It lavoro a cottimo (m)
Pt trabalho por peça (m)

**Akte** (f) n De
En file
Es archivo (m)
Fr dossier (m)
It archivio (m)
Pt ficheiro (m)

**Aktenschrank** (m) n De
En filing cabinet
Es fichero (m)
Fr classeur (m)
It schedario (m)
Pt móvel ficheiro (m)

**Aktie** (f) n De
En share
Es acción (f)
Fr action (f)
It azione (f)
Pt acção (f)

**Aktiengesellschaft (AG)** (f) De
En public limited company
Es Sociedad anónima (SA) (f)
Fr Société anonyme (SA) (f)
It Società anonima (SA) (f)
Pt Sociedade anónima (SA) (f)

**Aktienindex** (m) n De
En share index
Es índice de las acciones (m)
Fr indice des actions (m)
It indice delle azioni (m)
Pt índice das acções (m)

**Aktieninhaber** (m) n De
En stockholder
Es accionista (m)
Fr détenteur de titres (m)
It azionista (m)
Pt accionista (m)

**Aktienkapital** (n) n De
En share capital
Am stock capital
Es capital en acciones (m)
Fr capital social (m)
It capitale azionario (m)
Pt capital em acções (m)

**Aktienmarkt** (m) n De
En share market
Am stock market
Es mercado de valores (m)
Fr marché des valeurs (m)
It mercato azionario (m)
Pt mercado de acções (m)

**Aktien ohne Stimmrecht** (f pl) De
En non-voting shares
Es acciones sin derecho de voto (f pl)
Fr actions sans droit de vote (f pl)
It azioni senza diritto a voto (f pl)
Pt acçoes sem direito a voto (f pl)

**Aktien von Goldbergwerken** (f pl) De
En gold shares
Es acciones auríferas (f pl)
Fr valeurs aurifères (f pl)
It azioni aurifere (f pl)
Pt acções de ouro (f pl)

**Aktienzertifikat** (n) n De
En share certificate
Am certificate of stock
Es título de acción (m)
Fr certificat d'actions (m)
It certificato azionario (m)
Pt título de acções (m)

**Aktionär** (m) n De
En shareholder
Am stockholder
Es accionista (m)
Fr actionnaire (m)
It azionista (m)
Pt titular de acções; accio-
nista (m)

**Aktiva und Passiva** (n pl) De
En assets and liabilities
Es activo y pasivo (m)
Fr actif et passif (m)
It attivo e passivo (m)
Pt activo e passivo (m)

**aktiver Teilhaber** (m) De
En working partner; active
partner
Es socio activo (m)
Fr associé actif; associé en
nom (m)
It socio attivo (m)
Pt sócio actuante; sócio activo
(m)

**Aktivposten** (m) n De
En asset
Es activo (m)
Fr actif (m)
It attivo (m)
Pt valor (m)

**Aktivsaldo** (m) n De
En active balance
Es saldo acreedor (m)
Fr balance excédentaire (f)
It saldo attivo (m)
Pt saldo credor (m)

**Aktivwert** (m) n De
En asset value
Es valor en activo (m)
Fr valeur de l'actif (f)
It valore in attivo (m)
Pt valor do activo (m)

**Aktuar** (m) n De
En actuary
Es actuario (m)

Fr actuaire (m)
It attuario (m)
Pt actuário (m)

**Akzept** (n) n De
En acceptance
Es aceptación (f)
Fr acceptation (f)
It accettazione (f)
Pt aceitação (f)

**Akzeptfrist** (f) n De
En acceptance interval
Es intervalo de aceptación (m)
Fr intervalle d'acceptation (f)
It intervallo dell'accettazione
(m)
Pt intervalo de aceitação (m)

**Akzeptkredit** (m) n De
En acceptance credit
Es crédito de aceptación (m)
Fr crédit par acceptation (m)
It credito d'accettazione (m)
Pt crédito de aceitação (m)

**à l'acquitté** Fr
De verzollt
En ex bond
Es fuera de aduanas
It sdoganato
Pt livre de alfândega

**a largo plazo** Es
De langfristig
En long-term; long term
Fr à long terme; à longue
échéance
It a lunga scadenza
Pt a longo prazo

**a la vista** Es
De bei Sicht
En at sight
Fr à vue
It a vista
Pt à vista

**albacea** (m) n Es
De Vollstrecker (m)
En executor
Fr exécuteur (m)
It esecutore (m)
Pt executor (m)

**albergo** (m) n It
De Hotel (n)
En hotel

Es hotel (m)
Fr hôtel (m)
Pt hotel (m)

**alcista** (m) n Es
De Haussespekulant (m)
En bull
Fr haussier (m)
It rialzista (m)
Pt altista (f)

**alcista** adj Es
De steigend
En bullish
Fr haussier
It rialzista
Pt altista

**al contado contra documen-
tos** Es
De bar gegen Versandpapiere
En cash against documents
(c.a.d.)
Fr comptant contre docu-
ments
It contanti contro documenti
Pt em dinheiro contra docu-
mentação

**à l'étranger** Fr
De im Ausland
En abroad
Es en el extranjero
It all'estero
Pt no estrangeiro

**alfândega** (f) n Pt
De Zoll (m)
En customs
Es aduana (f)
Fr douane (f)
It dogana (f)

**algorithm** n En
De Algorithmus (m)
Es algoritmo (m)
Fr algorithme (m)
It algoritmo (m)
Pt algorítmo (m)

**algorithme** (m) n Fr
De Algorithmus (m)
En algorithm
Es algoritmo (m)
It algoritmo (m)
Pt algorítmo (m)

**Algorithmus** *(m)* n De
En algorithm
Es algoritmo *(m)*
Fr algorithme *(m)*
It algoritmo *(m)*
Pt algorítmo *(m)*

**algoritmo** *(m)* n Es, It
De Algorithmus *(m)*
En algorithm
Fr algorithme *(m)*
Pt algorítmo *(m)*

**algorítmo** *(m)* n Pt
De Algorithmus *(m)*
En algorithm
Es algoritmo *(m)*
Fr algorithme *(m)*
It algoritmo *(m)*

**alien** *adj* En
De ausländisch
Es extranjero
Fr étranger
It straniero
Pt estrangeiro

**alijar** *vb* Pt
De über Bord werfen
En jettison
Es echar al mar
Fr jeter à la mer
It fare gettito

**alimentation** *(f)* n Fr
De Esswaren *(f pl)*
En foodstuffs
Es comestibles *(m pl)*
It generi alimentari *(m pl)*
Pt géneros alimentícios *(m pl)*

**alla pari** It
De al Pari
En at par
Es al par
Fr au pair
Pt ao par

**alla rinfusa** It
De in grosser Menge
En in bulk
Es a granel
Fr en vrac
Pt a granel

**allegato** *(m)* n It
De Beilage *(f)*
En enclosure

Es anexo *(m)*
Fr annexe *(f)*
Pt anexo *(m)*

**allège** *(f)* n Fr
De Leichter *(m)*
En lighter (boat)
Es barcaza; gabarra *(f)*
It chiatta *(f)*
Pt barcaça *(f)*

**alle Gefahren** *(f pl)* De
En all risks
Es todos los riesgos *(m pl)*
Fr tous risques *(m pl)*
It tutti i rischi *(m pl)*
Pt todos os riscos *(m pl)*

**Alleinvertreter** *(m)* n De
En sole agent
Es agente exclusivo *(m)*
Fr agent exclusif *(m)*
It rappresentante esclusivo *(m)*
Pt agente exclusivo *(m)*

**all'estero** *adv* It
De im Ausland
En abroad
Es en el extranjero
Fr à l'étranger
Pt no estrangeiro

**allestimento delle vetrine** *(m)* It
De Schaufensterdekoration *(f)*
En window-dressing
Es preparación de escaparates *(f)*
Fr art de l'étalage *(m)*
Pt preparação de montras *(f)*

**allgemeines Hauptbuch** *(n)* De
En general ledger
Es libro mayor general *(m)*
Fr journal général *(m)*
It libro mastro generale *(m)*
Pt livro-mestre geral *(m)*

**allgemeines Pfandrecht** *(n)* De
En general lien
Es privilegio general *(m)*
Fr privilège général *(m)*
It privilegio generale *(m)*
Pt privilégio geral *(m)*

**Allgemeines Zoll- und Handelsabkommen** *(n)* De
En General Agreement on Tariffs and Trade (GATT)
Es Acuerdo General sobre Tarifas Aduaneras y Comercio *(m)*
Fr Accord Général sur les Tarifs Douaniers et le Commerce *(m)*
It Accordo Generale sulle Tariffe Doganali e sul Commercio *(m)*
Pt Acordo geral de Tarifas e Comércio *(m)*

**allgemeine Unkosten** *(pl)* De
En general expenses
Es gastos generales *(m pl)*
Fr frais généraux *(m pl)*
It spese generali *(f pl)*
Pt despesas gerais *(f pl)*

**allot** (shares, etc.) *vb* En
De verteilen
Es asignar
Fr attribuer
It assegnare
Pt atribuir

**allotment** (of shares) *n* En
De Verteilung *(f)*
Es adjudicación *(f)*
Fr attribution *(f)*
It ripartizione *(f)*
Pt aporcionamento *(m)*

**allotment letter** En
De Verteilungsbrief *(m)*
Es letra de adjudicación *(f)*
Fr avis d'attribution *(m)*
It lettera da ripartizione *(f)*
Pt aviso de aporcionamento *(m)*

**allow** (a discount) *vb* En
De gewähren (einen Rabatt)
Es conceder (un descuento)
Fr consentir (une remise)
It concedere (uno sconto)
Pt conceder (um desconto)

**allowable expense** En
De abziehbare Unkosten *(pl)*
Es gastos deducibles *(m pl)*
Fr dépense déductible *(f)*
It spesa permessa *(f)*
Pt despesas deduzíveis *(f)*

**allowance** n En
De Rabatt (m)
Es bonificación (f)
Fr rabais (m)
It abbuono (m)
Pt provisão (f)

**all risks** En
De alle Gefahren (f pl)
Es todos los riesgos (m pl)
Fr tous risques (m pl)
It tutti i rischi (m pl)
Pt todos os riscos (m pl)

**almacén** (m) n Es
De Lager; Warenlager (n)
En store; warehouse
Fr magasin; entrepôt (m)
It magazzino (m)
Pt armazém (m)

**almacenamiento** (m) n Es
De Lagerung (f)
En storage
Fr emmagasinage (m)
It maggazzinaggio (m)
Pt armazenamento (m)

**almacenar** vb Es
De lagern
En store
Fr emmagasiner
It immagazzinare
Pt armazenar

**almacén de aduanas** (m) Es
De Lager unter Zollverschluss (n)
En bonded warehouse
Fr entrepôt (m)
It magazzino doganale (m)
Pt armazém alfandegário (m)

**a longo prazo** Pt
De langfristig
En long-term; long-dated
Es a largo plazo
Fr à long terme; à longue échéance
It a lunga scadenza

**à long terme** Fr
De langfristig
En long-term
Es a largo plazo
It a lunga scadenza
Pt a longo prazo

**à longue échéance** Fr
De langfristig
En long-dated
Es a largo plazo
It a lunga scadenza
Pt a longo prazo

**al par** Es
De al Pari
En at par
Fr au pair
It alla pari
Pt ao par

**al Pari** De
En at par
Es al par
Fr au pair
It alla pari
Pt ao par

**alquilador** (m) n Es
De Mieter (m)
En hirer
Fr locataire (m)
It noleggiatore (m)
Pt alugador (m)

**alquilar** vb Es
De mieten; vermieten
En hire; rent
Fr louer; affermer
It noleggiare; affittare
Pt alugar

**alquiler** (m) n Es
De Verpachtung; Miete (f)
En lease; rent
Fr bail; loyer (m)
It affitto; pigione (m)
Pt aluguer; renda (m f)

**als Gegenrechnung** De
En per contra
Es en contrapartida
Fr en contrepartie; par contre
It in contropartita
Pt em contrapartida

**alta calidad** Es
De erstklassig
En high-grade
Fr à haute teneur
It di qualità superiore
Pt alto-nível

**alta mar** (f) Es
De hohe See (f)
En high seas
Fr hautes mers (f pl)
It alto mare (m)
Pt alto-mar (m)

**alteingeführtes Geschäft** (n) De
En old-established business
Es casa sólida (f)
Fr maison solide (f)
It casa di vecchia fondazione (f)
Pt empresa de há muito estabelecida (f)

**alterations** (to a building) n pl En
De Umbau (m)
Es reformas (f pl)
Fr travaux de transformation (m pl)
It modifiche (f pl)
Pt modificações (f pl)

**alterations and renewals** En
De Änderungen und Erneuerungen
Es reformas y renovaciones
Fr réfections et améliorations
It modifiche e rinnovamenti
Pt modificações e renovações

**alterations and repairs** En
De Änderungen und Reparaturen
Es reformas y reparaciones
Fr transformations et réparations
It modifiche e riparazioni
Pt modificações e reparações

**Altersversorgung** (f) De
En old-age pension
Es retiro de vejez (m)
Fr pension de retraite (f)
It pensione per la vecchiaia (f)
Pt pensão (f)

**altista** (f) n Pt
De Haussespekulant (m)
En bull
Es alcista (m)
Fr haussier (m)
It rialzista (m)

**altista** *adj* Pt
De steigend
En bullish
Es alcista
Fr haussier
It rialzista

**alto** *adj* Es, It
De hoch
En high
Fr haut; élevé
Pt elevado

**alto-mar** *(m)* Pt
De hohe See *(f)*
En high seas
Es alta mar *(f)*
Fr hautes mers *(f pl)*
It alto mare *(m)*

**alto mare** *(m)* It
De hohe See *(f)*
En high seas
Es alta mar *(f)*
Fr hautes mers *(f pl)*
Pt alto-mar *(m)*

**alto-nível** *adj* Pt
De erstklassig
En high-grade
Es alta calidad
Fr à haute teneur
It di qualità superiore

**alugador** *(m) n* Pt
De Mieter *(m)*
En hirer
Es alquilador; arrendador *(m)*
Fr locataire *(m)*
It noleggiatore *(m)*

**alugar** *vb* Pt
De mieten; vermieten
En hire; rent
Es alquilar
Fr louer; affermer
It noleggiare; affittare

**aluguer** *(m) n* Pt
De Verpachtung *(f)*
En lease
Es alquiler *(m)*
Fr bail *(m)*
It affitto *(m)*

**a lunga scadenza** It
De langfristig
En long-term; long-dated

Es a largo plazo
Fr à long terme; à longue
échéance
Pt a longo prazo

**ama de casa** *(f)* Es
De Hausfrau *(f)*
En housewife
Fr ménagère *(f)*
It massaia *(f)*
Pt dona de casa *(f)*

**amalgamación** *(f) n* Es
De Fusion *(f)*
En amalgamation
Am merger
Fr fusion *(f)*
It fusione *(f)*
Pt amalgamento *(m)*

**amalgamar** *vb* Es, Pt
De fusionieren
En amalgamate
Am merge
Fr fusionner
It fondersi

**amalgamate** *vb* En
Am merge
De fusionieren
Es amalgamar
Fr fusionner
It fondersi
Pt amalgamar

**amalgamation** *n* En
Am merger
De Fusion *(f)*
Es amalgamación *(f)*
Fr fusion *(f)*
It fusione *(f)*
Pt amalgamento *(m)*

**amalgamento** *(m) n* Pt
De Fusion *(f)*
En amalgamation
Am merger
Es amalgamación *(f)*
Fr fusion *(f)*
It fusione *(f)*

**amanhã** *adv* Pt
De morgen
En tomorrow
Es mañana
Fr demain
It domani

**à mão** Pt
De vorrätig
En on hand
Es disponible
Fr disponible
It disponibile

**am Apparat bleiben** De
En hold the line
Es espere al aparato
Fr ne quittez pas
It resta in linea
Pt aguarde

**amélioration** *(f) n* Fr
De Verbesserung *(f)*
En improvement
Es mejora *(f)*
It miglioramento *(m)*
Pt melhoramento *(m)*

**amende** *(f) n* Fr
De Geldstrafe *(f)*
En fine
Es sanción; multa *(f)*
It multa *(f)*
Pt multa *(f)*

**a mitad de precio** Es
De zum halben Preise
En half price
Fr à moitié prix
It metà prezzo
Pt metade do preço

**ammanco** *(m) n* It
De Mangel; Fehlbetrag *(m)*
En deficiency
Es deficiencia *(f)*
Fr manque; insuffisance *(m f)*
Pt deficiência; defeito *(f m)*

**ammassare** *vb* It
De Vorratslager anlegen
En stockpile
Es acumular existencias
Fr stocker
Pt acumular existências

**ammasso** *(m) n* It
De Hort *(m)*
En hoard
Es atesoramiento *(m)*
Fr thésaurisation *(f)*
Pt acumulação *(f)*

**amministrare** *vb* It
De verwalten
En administer
Es administrar
Fr administrer
Pt administrar

**amministratore** *(m) n* It
De Verwalter; Direktor *(m)*
En administrator; director
Es administrador; director *(m)*
Fr administrateur *(m)*
Pt administrador; director *(m)*

**amministratore delegato** *(m)* It
De geschäftsleitender Direktor *(m)*
En managing director
Am president
Es director gerente *(m)*
Fr administrateur délégué *(m)*
Pt director geral *(m)*

**amministratore dirigente** *(m)* It
De geschäftsführender Direktor *(m)*
En executive director
Am corporate officer
Es director ejecutivo *(m)*
Fr administrateur dirigeant *(m)*
Pt director administrativo *(m)*

**ammissione in franchigia doganale** *(f)* It
De zollfreie Einfuhr *(f)*
En duty-free admission
Es admisión libre de impuestos *(f)*
Fr admission en franchise *(f)*
Pt admissão livre de impostos *(f)*

**ammontante a** It
De hinauslaufend auf
En amounting to
Es ascendiendo a
Fr à concurrence de
Pt no montante de

**ammontare** *(m) n* It
De Betrag *(m)*
En amount
Es suma *(f)*
Fr somme *(f)*
Pt quantia *(f)*

**ammontare da riportare** *(m)* It
De Übertrag *(m)*
En amount carried forward
Am carry forward amount
Es suma y sigue *(f)*
Fr report à nouveau *(m)*
Pt importância transportada *(f)*

**ammortamento** *(m) n* It
De Amortisation; Entwertung *(f)*
En amortization; depreciation; redemption
Es amortización; depreciación *(f)*
Fr amortissement; dépréciation *(m)*
Pt amortização; depreciação *(f)*

**à moitié** Fr
De halb
En half
Es medio
It mezzo
Pt meio

**à moitié prix** Fr
De zum halben Preise
En half price
Es a mitad de precio
It metà prezzo
Pt metade do preço

**amortir une créance** Fr
De eine Schuld erlassen
En write off a debt
Es cancelar una deuda
It cancellare un credito
Pt cancelar um débito

**amortir une perte** Fr
De einen Verlust abschreiben
En write off a loss
Es cancelar una pérdida
It cancellare una perdita
Pt anular um prejuízo

**Amortisation** *(f) n* De
En amortization
Es amortización *(f)*
Fr amortissement *(m)*
It ammortamento *(m)*
Pt amortização *(f)*

**amortissement** *(m) n* Fr
De Tilgung; Amortisation *(f)*
En redemption; amortization

Es amortización *(f)*
It ammortamento *(m)*
Pt amortização *(f)*

**amortissement accéléré** *(m)* Fr
De beschleunigte Abschreibung *(f)*
En accelerated depreciation
Es depreciación acelerada *(f)*
It deprezzamento accelerato *(m)*
Pt depreciação acelerada *(f)*

**amortização** *(f) n* Pt
De Tilgung; Amortisation *(f)*
En redemption; amortization
Es amortización *(f)*
Fr amortissement; remboursement *(m)*
It ammortamento *(m)*

**amortización** *(f) n* Es
De Tilgung; Amortisation *(f)*
En redemption; amortization
Fr amortissement; remboursement *(m)*
It ammortamento *(m)*
Pt amortização *(f)*

**amortization** *n* En
De Amortisation
Es amortización *(f)*
Fr amortissement *(m)*
It ammortamento *(m)*
Pt amortização *(f)*

**amostra** *(f) n* Pt
De Probe; Muster *(f n)*
En sample
Es muestra *(f)*
Fr échantillon *(m)*
It campione *(m)*

**amostra avulso** *(f)* Pt
De Stichprobe *(f)*
En random sample
Es muestra aleatoria *(f)*
Fr épreuve au hasard *(f)*
It campione a casaccio *(m)*

**amostra gratis** *(f)* Pt
De kostenlose Probe *(f)*
En free sample
Es muestra gratuita *(f)*
Fr échantillon gratuit *(m)*
It campione gratuito *(m)*

**amostra sem valor** (f) Pt
De Muster ohne Wert (n)
En sample of no value
Es muestra sin valor (f)
Fr échantillon sans valeur (m)
It campione senza valore (m)

**amount** n En
De Betrag (m)
Es suma (f)
Fr somme (f)
It ammontare (m)
Pt quantia (f)

**amount carried forward** En
Am carry forward amount
De Übertrag (m)
Es suma y sigue (f)
Fr report à nouveau (m)
It ammontare da riportare (m)
Pt importância transportada (f)

**amounting to** En
De hinauslaufend auf
Es ascendiendo a
Fr à concurrence de
It ammontante a
Pt no montante de

**amtlich** adj De
En official
Es oficial
Fr officiel
It ufficiale
Pt oficial

**añadir** vb Es
De hinzufügen
En add
Fr ajouter
It aggiungere
Pt adicionar

**análise** (f) n Pt
De Analyse (f)
En analysis
Es análisis (m)
Fr analyse (f)
It analisi (f)

**análise de custo** (f) Pt
De Kostenanalyse (f)
En cost analysis
Es análisis de costes (m)
Fr analyse des coûts (f)
It analisi dei costi (f)

**análise de custo e benefício**
(f) Pt
De Gewinnanalyse (f)
En cost benefit analysis
Es análisis de costes y bene-
ficios (m)
Fr analyse des coûts et rende-
ments (f)
It analisi dei costi e benefici
(f)

**análise de sistemas** (f) Pt
De Systemanalyse (f)
En systems analysis
Es análisis de sistemas (m)
Fr analyse de systèmes (f)
It analisi di sistemi (f)

**análise de variação** (f) Pt
De Varianzanalyse (f)
En variance analysis
Es análisis de variaciones (m)
Fr analyse de la variance (f)
It analisi della variazione (f)

**análise de vendas** (f) Pt
De Verkaufsanalyse (f)
En sales analysis
Es análisis de ventas (m)
Fr analyse des ventes (f)
It analisi delle vendite (f)

**análise do tempo e progresso**
(f) Pt
De Arbeitszeit- und Ablaufstudie (f)
En time and motion study
Es estudio de tiempo y progreso (m)
Fr étude du temps et mouvements (f)
It studio dei tempi e dei
movimenti (m)

**análise marginal** (f) Pt
De Randanalyse (f)
En marginal analysis
Es análisis marginal (m)
Fr analyse marginale (f)
It analisi marginale (f)

**analisi** (f) n It
De Analyse (f)
En analysis
Es análisis (m)
Fr analyse (f)
Pt análise (f)

**analisi dei costi** (f) It
De Kostenanalyse (f)
En cost analysis
Es análisis de costes (m)
Fr analyse des coûts (f)
Pt análise de custo (f)

**analisi dei costi e benefici** (f)
It
De Gewinnanalyse (f)
En cost benefit analysis
Es análisis de costes y bene-
ficios (m)
Fr analyse des coûts et rende-
ments (f)
Pt análise de custo e bene-
fício (f)

**analisi della linea critica** (f) It
De Netzplantechnik (f)
En critical path analysis
(c.p.a.)
Es análisis de recorrido crítico
(m)
Fr analyse du chemin critique
(m)
Pt análise de transcurso crí-
tico (f)

**analisi della variazione** (f) It
De Varianzanalyse (f)
En variance analysis
Es análisis de variaciones (m)
Fr analyse de la variance (f)
Pt análise de variação (f)

**analisi delle vendite** (f) It
De Verkaufsanalyse (f)
En sales analysis
Es análisis de ventas (m)
Fr analyse des ventes (f)
Pt análise de vendas (f)

**analisi di sistemi** (f) It
De Systemanalyse (f)
En systems analysis
Es análisis de sistemas (m)
Fr analyse de systèmes (f)
Pt análise de sistemas (f)

**analisi marginale** (f) It
De Randanalyse (f)
En marginal analysis
Es análisis marginal (m)
Fr analyse marginale (f)
Pt análise marginal (f)

**análisis** *(m)* n Es
  De Analyse *(f)*
  En analysis
  Fr analyse *(f)*
  It analisi *(f)*
  Pt análise *(f)*

**análisis de costes** *(m)* Es
  De Kostenanalyse *(f)*
  En cost analysis
  Fr analyse des coûts *(f)*
  It analisi dei costi *(f)*
  Pt análise de custo *(f)*

**análisis de costes y beneficios** *(m)* Es
  De Gewinnanalyse *(f)*
  En cost benefit analysis
  Fr analyse des coûts et rendements *(f)*
  It analisi dei costi e benefici *(f)*
  Pt análise de custo e benefício *(f)*

**análisis de sistemas** *(m)* Es
  De Systemanalyse *(f)*
  En systems analysis
  Fr analyse de systèmes *(f)*
  It analisi di sistemi *(f)*
  Pt análise de sistemas *(f)*

**análisis de variaciones** *(m)* Es
  De Varianzanalyse *(f)*
  En variance analysis
  Fr analyse de la variance *(f)*
  It analisi della variazione *(f)*
  Pt análise de variaçåo *(f)*

**análisis de ventas** *(m)* Es
  De Verkaufsanalyse *(f)*
  En sales analysis
  Fr analyse des ventes *(f)*
  It analisi delle vendite *(f)*
  Pt análise de vendas *(f)*

**análisis marginal** *(m)* Es
  De Randanalyse *(f)*
  En marginal analysis
  Fr analyse marginale *(f)*
  It analisi marginale *(f)*
  Pt análise marginal *(f)*

**analizador de inversiones** *(m)* Es
  De Investitionsanalyst *(m)*
  En investment analyst

Fr analyste d'investissements *(m)*
It analizzatore d'investimenti *(m)*
Pt analizador de investimentos *(m)*

**analizador de investimentos** *(m)* Pt
  De Investitionsanalyst *(m)*
  En investment analyst
  Es analizador de inversiones *(m)*
  Fr analyste d'investissements *(m)*
  It analizzatore d'investimenti *(m)*

**an alle, die es angeht** De
  En to whom it may concern
  Es a quien concierna
  Fr à qui de droit
  It a tutti gli interessati
  Pt a quem disser respeito

**Analogrechner** *(m)* n De
  En analogue computer
  Am analog computer
  Es computadora analógica *(f)*
  Fr calculateur analogique *(m)*
  It calcolatore analogico *(m)*
  Pt computador analógico *(m)*

**analogue computer** En
  Am analog computer
  De Analogrechner *(m)*
  Es computadora analógica *(f)*
  Fr calculateur analogique *(m)*
  It calcolatore analogico *(m)*
  Pt computador analógico *(m)*

**analyse** *(f)* n Fr
  De Analyse *(f)*
  En analysis
  Es análisis *(m)*
  It analisi *(f)*
  Pt análise *(f)*

**Analyse** *(f)* n De
  En analysis
  Es análisis *(m)*
  Fr analyse *(f)*
  It analisi *(f)*
  Pt análise *(f)*

**analyse de la variance** *(f)* Fr
  De Varianzanalyse *(f)*
  En variance analysis

Es análisis de variaciones *(m)*
It analisi della variazione *(f)*
Pt análise de variação *(f)*

**analyse des coûts** *(f)* Fr
  De Kostenanalyse *(f)*
  En cost analysis
  Es análisis de costes *(m)*
  It analisi dei costi *(f)*
  Pt análise de custo *(f)*

**analyse des coûts et rendements** *(f)* Fr
  De Gewinnanalyse *(f)*
  En cost benefit analysis
  Es análisis de costes y beneficios *(m)*
  It analisi dei costi e benefici *(f)*
  Pt análise de custo e benefício *(f)*

**analyse des ventes** *(f)* Fr
  De Verkaufsanalyse *(f)*
  En sales analysis
  Es análisis de ventas *(m)*
  It analisi delle vendite *(f)*
  Pt análise de vendas *(f)*

**analyse de systèmes** *(f)* Fr
  De Systemanalyse *(f)*
  En systems analysis
  Es análisis de sistemas *(m)*
  It analisi di sistemi *(f)*
  Pt análise de sistemas *(f)*

**analyse du chemin critique** *(m)* Fr
  De Netzplantechnik *(f)*
  En critical path analysis (c.p.a.)
  Es análisis de recorrido crítico *(m)*
  It analisi della linea critica *(f)*
  Pt análise de transcurso crítico *(f)*

**analyse marginale** *(f)* Fr
  De Randanalyse *(f)*
  En marginal analysis
  Es análisis marginal *(m)*
  It analisi marginale *(f)*
  Pt análise marginal *(f)*

**Analysenwerkzeug** *(n)* n De
  En analytical tool
  Es instrumento de análisis *(m)*
  Fr instrument d'analyse *(m)*

It strumento d´analisi *(m)*
Pt instrumento de análise *(m)*

**analysis** *n* En
De Analyse *(f)*
Es análisis *(m)*
Fr analyse *(f)*
It analisi *(f)*
Pt análise *(f)*

**analyste d´investissements**
*(m)* Fr
De Investitionsanalyst *(m)*
En investment analyst
Es analizador de inversiones
*(m)*
It analizzatore d´investimenti
*(m)*
Pt analizador de investimen-
tos *(m)*

**analytical tool** En
De Analysenwerkzeug *(n)*
Es instrumento de análisis *(m)*
Fr instrument d´analyse *(m)*
It strumento d´analisi *(m)*
Pt instrumento de análise *(m)*

**anbieten** *vb* De
En offer
Es ofrecer
Fr offrir
It offrire
Pt oferecer

**an Bord** De
En aboard
Es a bordo
Fr à bord
It a bordo
Pt a bordo

**anchorage** *n* En
De Ankerplatz *(m)*
Es anclaje *(m)*
Fr ancrage *(m)*
It ancoraggio *(m)*
Pt ancoragem *(f)*

**anclaje** *(m)* *n* Es
De Ankerplatz *(m)*
En anchorage
Fr ancrage *(m)*
It ancoraggio *(m)*
Pt ancoragem *(f)*

**ancoragem** *(f)* *n* Pt
De Ankerplatz *(m)*
En anchorage
Es anclaje *(m)*
Fr ancrage *(m)*
It ancoraggio *(m)*

**ancoraggio** *(m)* *n* It
De Ankerplatz *(m)*
En anchorage
Es anclaje *(m)*
Fr ancrage *(m)*
Pt ancoragem *(f)*

**ancrage** *(m)* *n* Fr
De Ankerplatz *(m)*
En anchorage
Es anclaje *(m)*
It ancoraggio *(m)*
Pt ancoragem *(f)*

**andar com serviço incluido**
*(m)* Pt
De Etagenwohnung mit Bedienung *(f)*
En service flat
Es piso con servicio incluido
*(m)*
Fr appartement avec service
*(m)*
It appartamento con servizio
*(m)*

**andar independente** *(m)* Pt
De Einfamilienwohnung *(f)*
En self-contained flat
Es piso independiente com-
pleto *(m)*
Fr appartement indépendant
*(m)*
It appartamento indipendente
*(m)*

**andar mobilado** *(m)* Pt
De möblierte Mietwohnung *(f)*
En furnished flat
Am furnished apartment
Es piso amueblado *(m)*
Fr appartement meublé *(m)*
It appartamento ammobigli-
ato *(m)*

**Änderungen und Erneuerun-
gen** De
En alterations and renewals
Es reformas y renovaciones
Fr réfections et améliorations

It modifiche e rinnovamenti
Pt modificações e renovações

**Änderungen und Reparaturen**
De
En alterations and repairs
Es reformas y reparaciones
Fr transformations et répara-
tions
It modifiche e riparazioni
Pt modificações e reparações

**andeuten** *vb* De
En imply
Es implicar
Fr impliquer
It implicare
Pt significar

**anerkannter Streik** *(m)* De
En official strike
Es huelga oficial *(f)*
Fr grève officielle *(f)*
It sciopero ufficiale *(m)*
Pt greve oficial *(f)*

**anexo** *(m)* *n* Es
De Beilage *(f)*
En enclosure
Fr annexe *(f)*
It allegato *(m)*
Pt anexo *(m)*

**anexo** *(m)* *n* Pt
De Beilage *(f)*
En enclosure
Es anexo *(m)*
Fr annexe *(f)*
It allegato *(m)*

**Anfangs-** De
En initial
Es inicial; primario
Fr initial; premier
It iniziale
Pt inicial

**Anforderung** *(f)* *n* De
En requisition
Es pedido; solicitud *(m f)*
Fr demande *(f)*
It richiesta; requisizione *(f)*
Pt pedido *(m)*

**angeben** (den Preis) De
En quote
Es cotizar
Fr coter

It    quotare
Pt    cotizar

**Angebot** *(n)* n De
En    bid; tender
Es    oferta *(f)*
Fr    offre; soumission *(f)*
It    offerta *(f)*
Pt    oferta; proposta *(f)*

**(ein) Angebot annehmen** De
En    accept an offer
Es    aceptar una oferta
Fr    accepter une offre
It    accettare una offerta
Pt    aceitar uma oferta

**Angebot und Nachfrage** De
En    supply and demand
Es    oferta y demanda
Fr    offre et demande
It    offerta e domanda
Pt    oferta e procura

**angegebener Preis** *(m)* De
En    quoted price
Es    precio cotizado *(m)*
Fr    prix coté *(m)*
It    prezzo quotato *(m)*
Pt    preço cotizado *(m)*

**angegebener Zollwert** *(m)* De
En    declared value
Es    valor declarado *(m)*
Fr    valeur déclarée *(f)*
It    valore dichiarato *(m)*
Pt    valor declarado *(m)*

**angelernt** *adj* De
En    semi-skilled
Es    semidiestro
Fr    semi-qualifié
It    semiprovetto
Pt    semi-especializado

**angemessener Ertrag** *(m)* De
En    fair return
Es    beneficio razonable *(m)*
Fr    rendement équitable *(m)*
It    discreto profitto *(m)*
Pt    rendimento justo *(m)*

**angemessener Preis** *(m)* De
En    fair price
Es    precio razonable *(m)*
Fr    prix raisonnable *(m)*
It    prezzo equo *(m)*
Pt    preço razoável *(m)*

**angenommener Totalverlust**
      *(m)* De
En    constructive total loss
Es    pérdida total constructiva
      *(f)*
Fr    perte réputée totale *(f)*
It    perdita presunta totale *(f)*
Pt    perda total construtiva *(f)*

**Angestellte(r)** *(m)* n De
En    (salaried) employee; clerk
Es    empleado (a sueldo); ofici-
      nista *(m)*
Fr    appointé; employé; commis
      *(m)*
It    stipendiato; impiegato *(m)*
Pt    assalariado; empregado (de
      escritório) *(m)*

**Ankerplatz** *(m)* n De
En    anchorage
Es    anclaje *(m)*
Fr    ancrage *(m)*
It    ancoraggio *(m)*
Pt    ancoragem *(f)*

**Ankunft** *(f)* n De
En    arrival
Es    llegada *(f)*
Fr    arrivée *(f)*
It    arrivo *(m)*
Pt    chegada *(f)*

**Anlage** *(f)* n De
En    installation; plant
Es    planta; instalación *(f)*
Fr    appareil; installation *(m f)*
It    impianto; macchinario *(m)*
Pt    instalação (fabril) *(f)*

**Anlagegüter** *(n pl)* n De
En    capital goods
Es    bienes de producción *(m
      pl)*
Fr    biens d'équipement *(m pl)*
It    beni strumentali *(m pl)*
Pt    mercadorias de capital *(f
      pl)*

**Anlagevermögen** *(n)* n De
En    fixed assets
Es    activo fijo *(m)*
Fr    immobilisations *(f pl)*
It    immobilizzazioni;      attivo
      fisso *(f pl; m)*
Pt    bens fixos *(m pl)*

**Anlaufhafen** *(m)* n De
En    port of call
Es    puerto de escala *(m)*
Fr    port d'escale *(m)*
It    porto di scalo *(m)*
Pt    porto de escala *(m)*

**anlegen** *vb* De
En    invest
Es    invertir
Fr    investir; placer
It    investire
Pt    investir

**Anleihe** *(f)* n De
En    loan
Es    empréstito *(m)*
Fr    emprunt *(m)*
It    prestito *(m)*
Pt    empréstime *(m)*

**(eine) Anleihe begeben** De
En    float a loan
Am    raise a loan
Es    emitir un empréstito
Fr    émettre un emprunt
It    lanciare un prestito
Pt    lançar um empréstimo

**Anleihekonto** *(n)* n De
En    loan account
Es    cuenta de préstamos *(f)*
Fr    compte des prêts *(m)*
It    conto anticipazioni *(m)*
Pt    conta de empréstimos *(f)*

**Anleihewerte** *(m pl)* n De
En    loan stock
Es    títulos de préstamo *(m pl)*
Fr    titres d'emprunt *(m pl)*
It    titoli di prestito *(m pl)*
Pt    títulos de empréstimo *(m
      pl)*

**Anleitung** *(f)* n De
En    instruction
Es    instrucción *(f)*
Fr    instruction *(f)*
It    istruzione *(f)*
Pt    instrução *(f)*

**Anmeldegebühr** *(f)* n De
En    registration fee
Es    derechos de registro *(m pl)*
Fr    droit d'enregistrement *(m)*
It    tassa di registrazione *(f)*
Pt    custas de registo *(f pl)*

**Annahme unter Vorbehalt** (f)
De
En qualified acceptance
Es aceptación condicionada (f)
Fr acceptation conditionnelle
(f)
It accettazione con riserva (f)
Pt aceitação com reservas (f)

**année civile** (f) Fr
De Kalenderjahr (n)
En calendar year
Es año civil (m)
It anno solare (m)
Pt ano civil (m)

**année de base** (f) Fr
De Grundjahr (n)
En base year
Es año de base (m)
It anno di base (m)
Pt ano base (m)

**année en cours** (f) Fr
De laufendes Jahr (n)
En current year
Es año en curso (m)
It anno in corso (m)
Pt ano corrente (m)

**annehmen** vb De
En accept
Es aceptar
Fr accepter
It accettare
Pt aceitar

**annexe** (f) n Fr
De Beilage (f)
En enclosure
Es anexo (m)
It allegato (m)
Pt anexo (m)

**anno di base** (m) It
De Grundjahr (n)
En base year
Es año de base (m)
Fr année de base (f)
Pt ano base (m)

**anno fiscale** (m) It
De Steuerjahr; Einkommens-
teuerjahr (n)
En tax year; fiscal year; in-
come-tax year
Es año fiscal (m)

Fr exercice fiscal; exercice
budgétaire (m)
Pt ano fiscal (m)

**anno in corso** (m) It
De laufendes Jahr (n)
En current year
Es año en curso (m)
Fr année en cours (f)
Pt ano corrente (m)

**annonce** (f) n Fr
De Anzeige (f)
En advertisement
Es anuncio (m)
It annunzio (m)
Pt anúncio (m)

**annonceur** (m) n Fr
De Anzeiger (m)
En advertiser
Es anunciante (m)
It inserzionista (m)
Pt anunciante (m)

**anno solare** (m) It
De Kalenderjahr (n)
En calendar year
Es año civil (m)
Fr année civile (f)
Pt ano civil (m)

**annuaire des téléphones** (m)
Fr
De Fernsprechbuch (n)
En telephone directory
Es guía de teléfonos (f)
It elenco telefonico (m)
Pt lista telefónica (f)

**annual** adj En
De jährlich
Es anual
Fr annuel
It annuale
Pt anual

**annual accounts** En
De Jahresabschluss (m)
Es balance anual (m)
Fr bilan annuel (m)
It bilancio annuale (m)
Pt balancete anual (m)

**annuale** adj It
De jährlich
En annual
Es anual

Fr annuel
Pt anual

**annual general meeting** En
Am stockholders' meeting
De Jahreshauptversammlung
(f)
Es asamblea general anual
(f)
Fr assemblée d'actionnaires
annuelle (f)
It assemblea generale annu-
ale (f)
Pt assembleia geral anual (f)

**annualitá** (f) n It
De Annuität (f)
En annuity
Es anualidad (f)
Fr annuité (f)
Pt anuidade (f)

**annual rate** En
De Jahreskurs (m)
Es tasa anual (f)
Fr taux annuel (m)
It tasso annuale (m)
Pt taxa anual (f)

**annual report** En
De Jahresbericht (m)
Es memoria anual (f)
Fr rapport annuel (m)
It relazione annuale (f)
Pt relatório anual (m)

**annuel** adj Fr
De jährlich
En annual
Es anual
It annuale
Pt anual

**Annuität** (f) n De
En annuity
Es anualidad (f)
Fr annuité (f)
It annualitá (f)
Pt anuidade (f)

**annuité** (f) n Fr
De Annuität (f)
En annuity
Es anualidad (f)
It annualitá (f)
Pt anuidade (f)

**annuité différée** *(f)* Fr
De Anwartschaft auf Leibrente
*(f)*
En deferred annuity
Es anualidad aplazada *(f)*
It rendita vitalizia differita *(f)*
Pt anuidade diferida *(f)*

**annuity** *n* En
De Annuität *(f)*
Es anualidad *(f)*
Fr annuité *(f)*
It annualitá *(f)*
Pt anuidade *(f)*

**annulation** *(f)* *n* Fr
De Annullierung *(f)*
En annulment; cancellation
Es anulación; cancelación *(f)*
It annullamento *(m)*
Pt anulação; cancelamento *(f m)*

**annuler** *vb* Fr
De annullieren
En cancel
Es cancelar
It cancellare
Pt cancelar

**annuler un chèque** Fr
De einen Scheck rückgängig
machen
En cancel a cheque
Am cancel a check
Es anular un cheque
It annullare un assegno
Pt cancelar um cheque

**annullamento** *(m)* *n* It
De Annullierung *(f)*
En annulment; cancellation
Es anulación; cancelación *(f)*
Fr annulation *(f)*
Pt anulação; cancelamento *(f m)*

**annullare un assegno** It
De einen Scheck rückgängig
machen
En cancel a cheque
Am cancel a check
Es anular un cheque
Fr annuler un chèque
Pt cancelar um cheque

**annullieren** *vb* De
En cancel
Es cancelar
Fr annuler
It cancellare
Pt cancelar

**Annullierung** *(f)* *n* De
En annulment; cancellation
Es anulación; cancelación *(f)*
Fr annulation *(f)*
It annullamento *(m)*
Pt anulação; cancelamento *(f m)*

**annunzio** *(m)* *n* It
De Anzeige *(f)*
En advertisement
Es anuncio *(m)*
Fr annonce *(f)*
Pt anúncio *(m)*

**ano base** *(m)* Pt
De Grundjahr *(n)*
En base year
Es año de base *(m)*
Fr année de base *(f)*
It anno di base *(m)*

**año civil** *(m)* Es
De Kalenderjahr *(n)*
En calendar year
Fr année civile *(f)*
It anno solare *(m)*
Pt ano civil *(m)*

**ano civil** *(m)* Pt
De Kalenderjahr *(n)*
En calendar year
Es año civil *(m)*
Fr année civile *(f)*
It anno solare *(m)*

**ano corrente** *(m)* Pt
De laufendes Jahr *(n)*
En current year
Es año en curso *(m)*
Fr année en cours *(f)*
It anno in corso *(m)*

**año de base** *(m)* Es
De Grundjahr *(n)*
En base year
Fr année de base *(f)*
It anno di base *(m)*
Pt ano base *(m)*

**año económico** *(m)* Es
De Geschäftsjahr *(n)*
En financial year
Fr exercice *(m)*
It esercizio *(m)*
Pt ano financeiro *(m)*

**año en curso** *(m)* Es
De laufendes Jahr *(n)*
En current year
Fr année en cours *(f)*
It anno in corso *(m)*
Pt ano corrente *(m)*

**ano financeiro** *(m)* Pt
De Geschäftsjahr *(n)*
En financial year
Es año económico *(m)*
Fr exercice *(m)*
It esercizio *(m)*

**año fiscal** *(m)* Es
De Steuerjahr; Einkommen-
steuerjahr *(n)*
En fiscal year; tax year; income-
tax year
Fr exercice budgétaire; exer-
cice fiscal *(m)*
It anno fiscale *(m)*
Pt ano fiscal *(m)*

**ano fiscal** *(m)* Pt
De Steuerjahr; Einkommen-
steuerjahr *(n)*
En fiscal year; tax year; income-
tax year
Es año fiscal *(m)*
Fr exercice budgétaire; exer-
cice fiscal *(m)*
It anno fiscale *(m)*

**anotação de diário** *(f)* Pt
De Tagebuchsposten *(m)*
En journal-entry
Es asiento en el libro diario
*(m)*
Fr article d'un livre journal *(m)*
It registrazione a giornale *(f)*

**anpassungsfähig** adj De
En flexible
Es flexible
Fr flexible
It flessibile
Pt flexível

**anrechenbar** adj De
En chargeable
Es imputable; a cobrar
Fr imputable; imposable
It imputabile; imponibile
Pt a cobrar

**Anreiz** (m) n De
En incentive
Es estímulo; incentivo (m)
Fr incitation; stimulant (f m)
It incentivo (m)
Pt incentivo (m)

**Anruf** (m) n De
En telephone call
Es llamada telefónica (f)
Fr appel téléphonique (m)
It chiamata telefonica (f)
Pt chamada telefónica (f)

**Anschaffungskosten** (pl) De
En historic cost
Es coste primitivo (m)
Fr coût d'acquisition primitif (m)
It costo primitivo (m)
Pt custo original (m)

**Anspruch** (m) n De
En claim; (legal) title
Es reclamación; título (f m)
Fr réclamation; titre; droit (f m m)
It reclamo; titolo; diritto (m)
Pt reclamação; título (f m)

**anständige Abmachung** (f) De
En fair deal
Es trato equitativo (m)
Fr affaire équitable (f)
It affare giusto (m)
Pt transacção razoável (f)

**anständige Handlungsweise** (f) De
En fair play
Es juego limpio (m)
Fr traitement juste (m)
It condotta leale (f)
Pt jogo limpo (m)

**anstellen** vb De
En engage; appoint
Am hire
Es apalabrar
Fr engager
It fissare
Pt empregar

**anstiften** vb De
En instigate
Es instigar; provocar
Fr provoquer
It provocare; istigare
Pt instigar

**answer** n En
De Antwort (f)
Es respuesta (f)
Fr réponse (f)
It risposta (f)
Pt resposta (f)

**anteayer** Es
De vorgestern
En day before yesterday
Fr avant-hier
It avantieri
Pt anteontem

**antecipado** adj Pt
De vorzeitig (bezahlt)
En anticipated
Es anticipado
Fr anticipé
It anticipato

**anteontem** Pt
De vorgestern
En day before yesterday
Es anteayer
Fr avant-hier
It avantieri

**anteporto** (m) n Pt
De Aussenhafen (m)
En outer harbour
Es antepuerto (m)
Fr avant-port (m)
It avamporto (m)

**antepuerto** (m) n Es
De Aussenhafen (m)
En outer harbour
Fr avant-port (m)
It avamporto (m)
Pt anteporto (m)

**anticipado** adj Es
De vorzeitig (bezahlt)
En anticipated
Fr anticipé
It anticipato
Pt antecipado

**anticipar** vb Es
De vorschiessen
En advance (money)
Am prepay
Fr avancer (de l'argent)
It anticipare
Pt adiantar

**anticipare** vb It
De vorschiessen
En advance (money)
Am prepay
Es anticipar
Fr avancer (de l'argent)
Pt adiantar

**anticipated** adj En
De vorzeitig (bezahlt)
Es anticipado
Fr anticipé
It anticipato
Pt antecipado

**anticipato** adj It
De vorzeitig (bezahlt)
En anticipated
Es anticipado
Fr anticipé
Pt antecipado

**anticipazione** (f) n It
De Vorschuss (m)
En advance (of money)
Am prepayment
Es adelanto (m)
Fr avance (f)
Pt adiantamento (m)

**anticipé** adj Fr
De vorzeitig (bezahlt)
En anticipated
Es anticipado
It anticipato
Pt antecipado

**anticipo** (m) n Es
De Vorauszahlung (f)
En advance payment
Fr paiement par anticipation (m)

It pagamento anticipato *(m)*
Pt pagamento adiantado *(m)*

**Antrag** *(m) n* De
En application; motion
Es solicitud; moción *(f)*
Fr demande; motion *(f)*
It domanda; mozione *(f)*
Pt requisição; moção *(f)*

**Antragsformular** *(n) n* De
En application form; entry form
Es formulario de solicitud; solicitud de inscripción *(m f)*
Fr formulaire de demande; feuille d'inscription *(m f)*
It modulo di domanda; bolletta d'entrata *(m f)*
Pt formulário de requisição; impresso de admissão *(m)*

**Antwort** *(f) n* De
En answer
Es respuesta *(f)*
Fr réponse *(f)*
It risposta *(f)*
Pt resposta *(f)*

**anual** *adj* Es, Pt
De jährlich
En annual
Fr annuel
It annuale

**anualidad** *(f) n* Es
De Annuität *(f)*
En annuity
Fr annuité *(f)*
It annualitá *(f)*
Pt anuidade *(f)*

**anualidad aplazada** *(f)* Es
De Anwartschaft auf Leibrente *(f)*
En deferred annuity
Fr annuité différée *(f)*
It rendita vitalizia differita *(f)*
Pt anuidade diferida *(f)*

**anuidade** *(f) n* Pt
De Annuität *(f)*
En annuity
Es anualidad *(f)*
Fr annuité *(f)*
It annualitá *(f)*

**anuidade diferida** *(f)* Pt
De Anwartschaft auf Leibrente *(f)*
En deferred annuity
Es anualidad aplazada *(f)*
Fr annuité différée *(f)*
It rendita vitalizia differita *(f)*

**anulação** *(f) n* Pt
De Annullierung *(f)*
En annulment
Es anulación *(f)*
Fr annulation *(f)*
It annullamento *(m)*

**anulación** *(f) n* Es
De Annullierung *(f)*
En annulment
Fr annulation *(f)*
It annullamento *(m)*
Pt anulação *(f)*

**anular um prejuízo** Pt
De einen Verlust abschreiben
En write off a loss
Es cancelar una pérdida
Fr amortir une perte
It cancellare una perdita

**anular un cheque** Es
De einen Scheck rückgängig machen
En cancel a cheque
Am cancel a check
Fr annuler un chèque
It annullare un assegno
Pt cancelar um cheque

**anunciante** *(m) n* Es, Pt
De Anzeiger *(m)*
En advertiser
Fr annonceur *(m)*
It inserzionista *(m)*

**anuncio** *(m) n* Es
De Anzeige *(f)*
En advertisement
Fr annonce *(f)*
It annunzio *(m)*
Pt anúncio *(m)*

**anúncio** *(m) n* Pt
De Anzeige *(f)*
En advertisement
Es anuncio *(m)*
Fr annonce *(f)*
It annunzio *(m)*

**anúncios classificados** *(m pl)* Pt
De Kleinanzeige *(f)*
En classified advertisement
Es anuncio por palabras *(m pl)*
Fr petite annonce *(f)*
It piccola pubblicità *(f)*

**anuncio por palabras** *(m)* Es
De Kleinanzeige *(f)*
En classified advertisement
Fr petite annonce *(f)*
It piccola pubblicità *(f)*
Pt anúncios classificados *(m pl)*

**anvertrauen** *vb* De
En entrust
Es confiar
Fr confier
It affidare
Pt confiar

**Anwalt** *(m) n* De
En lawyer; barrister
Am attorney
Es abogado *(m)*
Fr avocat *(m)*
It avvocato *(m)*
Pt advogado *(m)*

**Anwartschaft auf Leibrente** *(f)* De
En deferred annuity
Es anualidad aplazada *(f)*
Fr annuité différée *(f)*
It rendita vitalizia differita *(f)*
Pt anuidade diferida *(f)*

**Anzahlung** *(f) n* De
En deposit; payment on account
Es desembolso inicial; pago a cuenta *(m)*
Fr arrhes; versement à compte *(f pl; m)*
It caparra; pagamento in conto *(f m)*
Pt sinal; anúncio *(m)*

**Anzeige** *(f) n* De
En advertisement; advice note
Es anuncio; aviso *(m)*
Fr annonce; lettre d'avis *(f)*
It annunzio; lettera d'avviso *(m f)*
Pt anúncio; guia de remessa *(m f)*

**Anzeiger** *(m)* n De
En advertiser
Es anunciante *(m)*
Fr annonceur *(m)*
It inserzionista *(m)*
Pt anunciante *(m)*

**an Zollfreilager** De
En ex warehouse
Es puesto en almacén
Fr à prendre en entrepôt
It franco magazzino
Pt no armazzém

**ao par** Pt
De al Pari
En at par
Es al par
Fr au pair
It alla pari

**à ordem da alfândega** Pt
De unter Zollverschluss
En in bond
Es en aduanas
Fr en entrepôt
It sotto vincolo doganale

**apalabrar** *vb* Es
De anstellen
En engage; appoint
Am hire
Fr engager
It fissare
Pt empregar

**aparatos eléctricos de casa**
 *(m pl)* Es
De elektrische Haushaltsgüter
 *(n pl)*
En household electrical goods
Fr electro-ménager *(m)*
It elettrodomestici *(m pl)*
Pt electro-domésticos *(m pl)*

**apartamento** *(m)* n Es, Pt
De Etagenwohnung *(f)*
En flat
Am apartment
Fr appartement *(m)*
It appartamento *(m)*

**apartment** n Am
En flat
De Etagenwohnung *(f)*
Es apartamento *(m)*
Fr appartement *(m)*

It appartamento *(m)*
Pt apartamento *(m)*

**apartment house** Am
En block of flats
De Wohnungsgebäude *(n)*
Es bloque de pisos *(m)*
Fr immeuble *(m)*
It fabbricato di appartamenti
 *(m)*
Pt edifício de andares *(m)*

**aplazamiento** *(m)* n Es
De Vertagung *(f)*
En adjournment
Fr ajournement *(m)*
It aggiornamento *(m)*
Pt adiamento *(m)*

**aplazar** *vb* Es
De vertagen;    zurückstellen;
 aufschieben
En adjourn; defer; hold over
Fr ajourner; différer
It aggiornare; differire
Pt adiar

**apoderado** *(m)* n Es
De Bevollmächtigte(r); Stellver-
 treter *(m)*
En attorney; proxy
Fr mandataire *(m)*
It mandatario;    procuratore
 *(m)*
Pt procurador *(m)*

**apólice** (de seguro) *(f)* n Pt
De Police *(f)*
En policy
Es poliza *(f)*
Fr police *(f)*
It polizza *(f)*

**apólice com participação nos**
 **lucros** *(f)* Pt
De Police mit Gewinnberech-
 tigung *(f)*
En with-profits policy
Am participating policy
Es póliza con beneficios *(f)*
Fr police avec participation
 aux bénéfices *(f)*
It polizza con profitti *(f)*

**apólice de seguro de incêndio**
 *(f)* Pt
De Feuerversicherungsschein
 *(m)*

En fire insurance policy
Es póliza de seguro de incen-
 dios *(f)*
Fr police incendie *(f)*
It polizza    d'assicurazione
 incendio *(f)*

**apólice de seguros** *(f)* Pt
De Versicherungspolice *(f)*
En insurance policy
Es póliza de seguro *(f)*
Fr police d'assurance *(f)*
It polizza di assicurazione *(f)*

**apólice flutuante** *(f)* Pt
De laufende Polizze *(f)*
En floating policy
Es póliza flotante *(f)*
Fr police flottante *(f)*
It polizza flottante *(f)*

**apólice liquidada** *(f)* Pt
De beitragsfreie Police *(f)*
En paid-up policy
Es póliza liberada *(f)*
Fr assurance libérée *(f)*
It polizza interamente pagata
 *(f)*

**aporcionamento** *(m)* n Pt
De Verteilung *(f)*
En allotment
Es adjudicación *(f)*
Fr attribution *(f)*
It ripartizione *(f)*

**a porte debido** Es
De Portonachnahme
En carriage forward
Am F.O.B. shipping point
Fr en port dû
It porto assegnato
Pt transporte a pagar

**a porte pagado** Es
De franko
En carriage paid
Am freight charges paid
Fr port payé
It franco di porto
Pt porte pago

**aposentação** *(f)* n Pt
De Rücktritt; Pensionierung *(m*
 *f)*
En retirement
Es retiro *(m)*

Fr  retraite (f)
It  ritiro (m)

**apostilla** (f) n Es
De  Fussnote (f)
En  footnote
Fr  apostille (f)
It  postilla (f)
Pt  nota de rodapé (f)

**apostille** (f) n Fr
De  Fussnote (f)
En  footnote
Es  apostilla (f)
It  postilla (f)
Pt  nota de rodapé (f)

**appareil** (m) n Fr
De  Gerät; Anlage (n f)
En  appliance; plant (industrial)
Es  aparato; planta (m f)
It  apparecchio; impianto (m)
Pt  aparelho; instalação (m f)

**appartamento** (m) n It
De  Etagenwohnung (f)
En  flat
Am  apartment
Es  apartamento (m)
Fr  appartement (m)
Pt  apartamento (m)

**appartamento ammobigliato**
    (m) It
De  möblierte Mietwohnung (f)
En  furnished flat
Am  furnished apartment
Es  piso amueblado (m)
Fr  appartement meublé (m)
Pt  andar mobilado (m)

**appartamento con servizio** (m)
    It
De  Etagenwohnung mit Bedie-
    nung (f)
En  service flat
Es  piso con servicio incluido
    (m)
Fr  appartement avec service
    (m)
Pt  andar com serviço incluido
    (m)

**appartamento indipendente**
    (m) It
De  Einfamilienwohnung (f)
En  self-contained flat

Es  piso independiente comple-
    to (m)
Fr  appartement indépendant
    (m)
Pt  andar independente (m)

**appartement** (m) n Fr
De  Etagenwohnung (f)
En  flat
Am  apartment
Es  apartamento (m)
It  appartamento (m)
Pt  apartamento (m)

**appartement avec service** (m)
    Fr
De  Etagenwohnung mit Bedie-
    nung (f)
En  service flat
Es  piso con servicio incluido
    (m)
It  appartamento con servizio
    (m)
Pt  andar com serviço incluido
    (m)

**appartement indépendant** (m)
    Fr
De  Einfamilienwohnung (f)
En  self-contained flat
Es  piso independiente comple-
    to (m)
It  appartamento indipendente
    (m)
Pt  andar independente (m)

**appartement meublé** (m) Fr
De  möblierte Mietwohnung (f)
En  furnished flat
Am  furnished apartment
Es  piso amueblado (m)
It  appartamento ammobigli-
    ato (m)
Pt  andar mobilado (m)

**appel (de fonds)** (m) Fr
De  Kündigung (von Geldern) (f)
En  call (for funds)
Es  llamada (de fondos) (f)
It  richiesta (di fondi) (f)
Pt  chamada (de fundos) (f)

**appel téléphonique** (m) Fr
De  Anruf (m)
En  telephone call
Es  llamada telefónica (f)
It  chiamata telefonica (f)
Pt  chamada telefónica (f)

**appel téléphonique interur-
bain** (m) Fr
De  Ferngespräch (n)
En  trunk call
Am  long distance call
Es  llamada interurbana (f)
It  comunicazione interurbana
    (f)
Pt  chamada inter-urbana (tro-
    ncas) (f)

**applicant** (for a post) n En
De  Bewerber (m)
Es  candidato (m)
Fr  candidat (m)
It  candidato (m)
Pt  candidato (m)

**application** n En
De  Antrag (m)
Es  solicitud (f)
Fr  demande (f)
It  domanda (f)
Pt  requisição (f)

**application form** En
De  Antragsformular (n)
Es  formulario de solicitud (m)
Fr  formulaire de demande (m)
It  modulo di domanda (m)
Pt  formulário de requisição
    (m)

**appoint** vb En
De  ernennen
Es  nombrar
Fr  nommer
It  nominare
Pt  nomear

**appointé** (m) Fr
De  Angestellte(r) (m)
En  salaried employee
Es  empleado a sueldo (m)
It  stipendiato (m)
Pt  assalariado (m)

**appointed agent** En
De  Handelsvertreter (m)
Es  agente nombrado (m)
Fr  agent attitré (m)
It  agente ufficiale (m)
Pt  agente oficial (m)

**appointment** (meeting) n En
De  Verabredung (f)
Es  entrevista (f)
Fr  entrevue (f)

It appuntamento *(m)*
Pt encontro *(m)*

**apportion** *vb* En
De zuteilen
Es repartir
Fr répartir
It ripartire
Pt atribuir

**appraisal** *n* En
De Abschätzung *(f)*
Es evaluación *(f)*
Fr évaluation *(f)*
It valutazione *(f)*
Pt avaliação *(f)*

**appreciate** (in value) *vb* En
De im Wert steigen
Es subir (en valor)
Fr apprécier
It aumentare (di valore)
Pt aumentar; subir

**appréciateur** *(m)* *n* Fr
De Schätzer *(m)*
En assessor
Es asesor *(m)*
It agente delle imposte *(m)*
Pt avaliador *(m)*

**appreciation** (in value) *n* En
De Wertsteigerung *(f)*
Es subida (en valor) *(f)*
Fr appréciation *(f)*
It aumento *(m)*
Pt aumento *(m)*

**appréciation** *(f)* *n* Fr
De Wertsteigerung; Planungs-
gewinn *(f m)*
En appreciation; betterment
Es subida (en valor); plusvalía
*(f)*
It aumento; plus-valore *(m)*
Pt aumento; melhoria *(f)*

**apprécier** *vb* Fr
De im Wert steigen
En appreciate (in value)
Es subir (en valor)
It aumentare (di valore)
Pt aumentar; subir

**apprendista** *(m)* *n* It
De Lehrling *(m)*
En apprentice
Am trainee

Es aprendiz *(m)*
Fr apprenti *(m)*
Pt aprendiz *(m)*

**apprenti** *(m)* *n* Fr
De Lehrling *(m)*
En apprentice
Am trainee
Es aprendiz *(m)*
It apprendista *(m)*
Pt aprendiz *(m)*

**apprentice** *n* En
Am trainee
De Lehrling *(m)*
Es aprendiz *(m)*
Fr apprenti *(m)*
It apprendista *(m)*
Pt aprendiz *(m)*

**apprenticeship** *n* En
Am trainee period
De Lehre *(f)*
Es aprendizaje *(m)*
Fr apprentissage *(m)*
It tirocinio *(m)*
Pt aprendizagem *(f)*

**apprentissage** *(m)* *n* Fr
De Lehre *(f)*
En apprenticeship
Am trainee period
Es aprendizaje *(m)*
It tirocinio *(m)*
Pt aprendizagem *(f)*

**appropriarsi indebitamente** It
De unterschlagen
En embezzle
Es defalcar
Fr détourner
Pt desfalcar

**appropriation** *n* En
De Zuführung *(f)*
Es apropiación *(f)*
Fr affectation *(f)*
It stanziamento *(m)*
Pt apropriação *(f)*

**appropriation account** En
De Rückstellungskonto *(n)*
Es cuenta de apropiación *(f)*
Fr compte d'affectation *(m)*
It conto di stanziamento *(m)*
Pt conta de apropriação *(f)*

**appropriazione indebita** *(f)* It
De Unterschlagung *(f)*
En embezzlement
Es defalco *(m)*
Fr détournement de fonds *(m)*
Pt desfalque *(m)*

**appuntamento** *(m)* *n* It
De Verabredung *(f)*
En appointment
Es entrevista *(f)*
Fr entrevue *(f)*
Pt encontro *(m)*

**a premio** Es
De über Pari
En above par
Fr au-dessus du pair
It sopra la pari
Pt a prémio

**a prémio** Pt
De über Pari
En above par
Es a premio
Fr au-dessus du pair
It sopra la pari

**aprendiz** *(m)* *n* Es, Pt
De Lehrling *(m)*
En apprentice
Am trainee
Fr apprenti *(m)*
It apprendista *(m)*

**aprendizagem** *(f)* *n* Pt
De Lehre *(f)*
En apprenticeship
Am trainee period
Es aprendizaje *(m)*
Fr apprentissage *(m)*
It tirocinio *(m)*

**aprendizaje** *(m)* *n* Es
De Lehre *(f)*
En apprenticeship
Am trainee period
Fr apprentissage *(m)*
It tirocinio *(m)*
Pt aprendizagem *(f)*

**à prendre en entrepôt** Fr
De an Zollfreilager
En ex warehouse
Es puesto en almacén
It franco magazzino
Pt no armazzém

**à prendre sur quai** Fr
De  ab Kai
En  ex quay
Es  en muelle
It  sulla banchina
Pt  ex-cais

**après demain** Fr
De  übermorgen
En  day after tomorrow
Es  pasado mañana
It  dopodomani
Pt  depois de amanhã

**apresentar demissão** Pt
De  den Rücktritt einreichen
En  hand in one's resignation
Es  presentar la dimisión
Fr  remettre sa démission
It  rassegnare le dimissioni

**apresentar letra para aceite** Pt
De  einen Wechsel vorlegen
En  present a bill for acceptance
Es  presentar una letra para aceptación
Fr  présenter une traite à l'acceptation
It  presentare una cambiale per accettazione

**apropiación** (f) n Es
De  Zuführung (f)
En  appropriation
Fr  affectation (f)
It  stanziamento (m)
Pt  apropriação (f)

**apropriação** (f) n Pt
De  Zuführung (f)
En  appropriation
Es  apropiación (f)
Fr  affectation (f)
It  stanziamento (m)

**aguas territoriales** (f pl) Es
De  Hoheitsgewässer (n pl)
En  territorial waters
Fr  eaux territoriales (f pl)
It  acque territoriali (f pl)
Pt  águas territoriais (f pl)

**aquecimento central** (m) Pt
De  Zentralheizung (f)
En  central heating
Es  calefacción central (f)

Fr  chauffage central (m)
It  riscaldamento centrale (m)

**a quem disser respeito** Pt
De  an alle, die es angeht
En  to whom it may concern
Es  a quien concierna
Fr  à qui de droit
It  a tutti gli interessati

**à qui de droit** Fr
De  an·alle, die es angeht
En  to whom it may concern
Es  a quien concierna
It  a tutti gli interessati
Pt  a quem disser respeito

**a quien concierna** Es
De  an alle, die es angeht
En  to whom it may concern
Fr  à qui de droit
It  a tutti gli interessati
Pt  a quem disser respeito

**aquisição** (f) n Pt
De  Erwerb (m)
En  acquisition
Es  adquisición (f)
Fr  acquisition (f)
It  acquisizione (f)

**aquisições** (f pl) Pt
De  Einkäufe (m pl)
En  purchases pl n
Es  adquisiciones (f pl)
Fr  achats (m pl)
It  acquisti (m pl)

**Arbeit** (f) n De
En  work
Es  trabajo (m)
Fr  travail (m)
It  lavoro (m)
Pt  trabalho (m)

**Arbeiter** (m) n De
En  worker
Es  trabajador (m)
Fr  ouvrier (m)
It  lavoratore (m)
Pt  trabalhador (m)

**Arbeitgeber** (m) n De
En  employer
Es  patrono (m)
Fr  employeur (m)
It  datore di lavoro (m)
Pt  patrão (m)

**Arbeit in der Ausführung** (f)
De
En  work-in-progress
Am  work in process
Es  trabajo en curso (m)
Fr  travaux en cours (m pl)
It  lavoro in corso (m)
Pt  trabalho em curso (m)

**Arbeitsaufgabe** (f) n De
En  job specification
Es  especificación del trabajo (f)
Fr  donnée d'exécution (f)
It  specifica del lavoro (f)
Pt  especificação de obra (f)

**Arbeitsbedingungen** (f pl) n De
En  working conditions
Es  condiciones de trabajo (f pl) .
Fr  conditions de travail (f pl)
It  condizioni di lavoro (f pl)
Pt  condições de trabalho (f pl)

**Arbeitsbeschreibung** (f) n De
En  job description
Es  descripción del trabajo (f)
Fr  description du travail (f)
It  descrizione del lavoro (f)
Pt  descrição da tarefa (f)

**Arbeitsbewertung** (f) n De
En  job evaluation
Es  valoracion del trabajo (f)
Fr  évaluation du travail (f)
It  valutazione del lavoro (f)
Pt  avaliação de tarefa (f)

**Arbeitsbeziehungen** (f pl) n De
En  industrial relations
Es  relaciones humanas industriales (f pl)
Fr  relations humaines dans l'entreprise (f pl)
It  relazioni nell'industria (f pl)
Pt  relações industriais (f pl)

**Arbeitseinkommen** (n) n De
En  earned income
Es  renta del trabajo (f)
Fr  revenu du travail (m)
It  reddito di lavoro (m)
Pt  receita de trabalho (f)

**Arbeitserlaubnis** *(n)* n De
En work permit
Es permiso de trabajo *(m)*
Fr permis de travail *(m)*
It permesso di lavoro *(m)*
Pt carta de trabalho *(f)*

**Arbeitskonflikt** *(m)* n De
En industrial dispute
Es conflicto laboral *(m)*
Fr conflit ouvrier *(m)*
It vertenza operaia *(f)*
Pt conflito de trabalho *(m)*

**Arbeitskräfte** *(f pl)* n De
En labour force
Es mano de obra *(f)*
Fr main d'œuvre *(m)*
It mano d'opera *(f)*
Pt trabalhadores; mão de obra *(m f)*

**arbeitslos** *adj* De
En out of work
Es parado; sin trabajo
Fr en chômage
It disoccupato
Pt desempregado

**Arbeitslosenunterstützung** *(f)* n De
En unemployment benefit
Es subsidio de paro *(m)*
Fr secours de chômage *(m)*
It indennità di disoccupazione *(f)*
Pt subsidio de desemprego *(m)*

**Arbeitslosigkeit** *(f)* n De
En unemployment
Es desempleo *(m)*
Fr chômage *(m)*
It disoccupazione *(f)*
Pt desemprego *(m)*

**Arbeitsmarkt** *(m)* n De
En labour market
Es mercado de mano de obra *(m)*
Fr marché du travail *(m)*
It mercato della mano d'opera *(m)*
Pt mercado de mão de obra *(m)*

**Arbeitsnachweisstelle** *(f)* n De
En employment exchange
Am state employment agency
Es bolsa de trabajo *(f)*
Fr bureau de placement *(m)*
It ufficio di collocamento *(m)*
Pt centro de serviços de emprego *(m)*

**Arbeitspsychologie** *(f)* n De
En industrial psychology
Es psicología industrial *(f)*
Fr psychotechnique *(f)*
It psicologia industriale *(f)*
Pt psicologia industrial *(f)*

**Arbeitsschicht** *(f)* n De
En shiftwork
Es trabajo por torno *(m)*
Fr travail par équipes *(m)*
It lavoro a turno *(m)*
Pt trabalho por turno *(m)*

**Arbeitsstreitigkeit** *(f)* n De
En trade dispute
Es conflicto laboral *(m)*
Fr conflit du travail *(m)*
It vertenza di lavoro *(f)*
Pt conflito comercial *(m)*

**Arbeitsstudium** *(n)* n De
En work study
Es estudio del trabajo *(m)*
Fr étude du travail *(f)*
It studio di lavoro *(m)*
Pt estudo sobre trabalho *(m)*

**Arbeitsstunde pro Mann** *(f)* De
En man-hours
Es horas-hombre *(f pl)*
Fr heures-homme *(f pl)*
It ore-uomo *(f pl)*
Pt horas-homem *(f pl)*

**Arbeitstag** *(m)* n De
En working day
Es día laborable *(m)*
Fr jour ouvrable *(m)*
It giornata lavorativa *(f)*
Pt dia de trabalho *(m)*

**Arbeitsteilung** *(f)* n De
En division of labour
Es división del trabajo *(f)*
Fr division du travail *(f)*
It divisione del lavoro *(f)*
Pt divisão do trabalho *(f)*

**Arbeitsumsatz** *(m)* n De
En labour turnover
Es movimiento de la mano de obra *(m)*
Fr fluctuations de personnel *(f pl)*
It movimento della mano d'opera *(m)*
Pt movimento de trabalhadores *(m)*

**Arbeitsunfall** *(m)* n De
En industrial accident
Es accidente de trabajo *(m)*
Fr accident du travail *(m)*
It infortunio sul lavoro *(m)*
Pt acidente de trabalho *(m)*

**Arbeitsverhältnisse** *(npl)* De
En labour relations
Es relaciones patrón-obrero *(f pl)*
Fr rapports du travail *(m pl)*
It relazioni con la mano d'opera *(f pl)*
Pt relações de trabalho *(f pl)*

**Arbeitswoche** *(f)* n De
En working week
Es semana laboral *(f)* .
Fr semaine de travail *(f)*
It settimana lavorativa *(f)*
Pt semana de trabalho *(f)*

**Arbeitszeit** *(f)* n De
En hours of work
Es jornada laboral *(f)*
Fr durée du travail *(f)*
It ore lavorative *(f pl)*
Pt horas de trabalho *(f pl)*

**Arbeitszeit- und Ablaufstudie** *(f)* De
En time and motion study
Es estudio de tiempo y progreso *(m)*
Fr étude du temps et mouvements *(f)*
It studio dei tempi e dei movimenti *(m)*
Pt análise do tempo e progresso *(f)*

**arbitrador** *(m)* n Es
De Schiedsrichter *(m)*
En arbitrator
Fr arbitre *(m)*

It   arbitro *(m)*
Pt   árbitro *(m)*

**arbitrage** *n* En
De   Kursvergleich *(m)*
Es   arbitraje *(m)*
Fr   arbitrage *(m)*
It   arbitraggio *(m)*
Pt   arbitragem *(f)*

**arbitrage** *(m) n* Fr
De   Kursvergleich;   Schieds-
     gerichtverfahren *(m n)*
En   arbitrage; arbitration
Es   arbitraje; arbitramento *(m)*
It   arbitraggio; arbitrato *(m)*
Pt   arbitragem *(f)*

**arbitragem** *(f) n* Pt
De   Kursvergleich;   Schieds-
     gerichtverfahren *(m n)*
En   arbitrage; arbitration
Es   arbitraje; arbitramento *(m)*
Fr   arbitrage *(m)*
It   arbitraggio; arbitrato *(m)*

**arbitrager** *vb* Fr
De   sich decken
En   hedge
Es   cubrirse
It   coprirsi
Pt   cobrir-se

**arbitraggio** *(m) n* It
De   Kursvergleich *(m)*
En   arbitrage
Es   arbitraje *(m)*
Fr   arbitrage *(m)*
Pt   arbitragem *(f)*

**arbitraje** *(m) n* Es
De   Kursvergleich *(m)*
En   arbitrage
Fr   arbitrage *(m)*
It   arbitraggio *(m)*
Pt   arbitragem *(f)*

**arbitramento** *(m) n* Es
De   Schiedsgerichtverfahren *(n)*
En   arbitration
Fr   arbitrage *(m)*
It   arbitrato *(m)*
Pt   arbitragem *(f)*

**arbitration** *n* En
De   Schiedsgerichtverfahren *(n)*
Es   arbitramento *(m)*
Fr   arbitrage *(m)*

It   arbitrato *(m)*
Pt   arbitragem *(f)*

**arbitration award** En
De   Schiedsspruch *(m)*
Es   sentencia arbitral *(f)*
Fr   sentence arbitrale *(f)*
It   lodo arbitrale *(m)*
Pt   decisão de arbitragem *(f)*

**arbitration board (court)** En
De   Schiedsgericht *(n)*
Es   tribunal arbitral *(m)*
Fr   cour d'arbitrage *(m)*
It   tribunale arbitrale *(m)*
Pt   tribunal de arbitragem *(m)*

**arbitrato** *(m) n* It
De   Schiedsgerichtverfahren *(n)*
En   arbitration
Es   arbitramento *(m)*
Fr   arbitrage *(m)*
Pt   arbitragem *(f)*

**arbitrator** *n* En
De   Schiedsrichter *(m)*
Es   arbitrador *(m)*
Fr   arbitre *(m)*
It   arbitro *(m)*
Pt   árbitro *(m)*

**arbitre** *(m) n* Fr
De   Schiedsrichter *(m)*
En   arbitrator
Es   arbitrador *(m)*
It   arbitro *(m)*
Pt   árbitro *(m)*

**arbitro** *(m) n* It
De   Schiedsrichter *(m)*
En   arbitrator
Es   arbitrador *(m)*
Fr   arbitre *(m)*
Pt   árbitro *(m)*

**árbitro** *(m) n* Pt
De   Schiedsrichter *(m)*
En   arbitrator
Es   arbitrador *(m)*
Fr   arbitre *(m)*
It   arbitro *(m)*

**architect** *n* En
De   Architekt *(m)*
Es   arquitecto *(m)*
Fr   architecte *(m)*
It   architetto *(m)*
Pt   arquitecto *(m)*

**architecte** *(m) n* Fr
De   Architekt *(m)*
En   architect
Es   arquitecto *(m)*
It   architetto *(m)*
Pt   arquitecto *(m)*

**Architekt** *(m) n* De
En   architect
Es   arquitecto *(m)*
Fr   architecte *(m)*
It   architetto *(m)*
Pt   arquitecto *(m)*

**architetto** *(m) n* It
De   Architekt *(m)*
En   architect
Es   arquitecto *(m)*
Fr   architecte *(m)*
Pt   arquitecto *(m)*

**archivar** *vb* Es
De   aufreihen
En   file
Fr   classer
It   archiviare
Pt   arquivar

**archiviare** *vb* It
De   aufreihen
En   file
Es   archivar
Fr   classer
Pt   arquivar

**archivio** *(m) n* It
De   Akte *(f)*
En   file
Es   archivo *(m)*
Fr   dossier *(m)*
Pt   ficheiro *(m)*

**archivo** *(m) n* Es
De   Akte *(f)*
En   file
Fr   dossier *(m)*
It   archivio *(m)*
Pt   ficheiro *(m)*

**archivo de fichas** *(m)* Es
De   Kartei *(f)*
En   card-index file
Fr   fichier *(m)*
It   schedario *(m)*
Pt   ficheiro com indice *(m)*

**área de chão** (f) Pt
De Bodenfläche (f)
En floor space
Es superficie de piso (f)
Fr surface de plancher (f)
It superficie di pavimento (f)

**area indigente** (f) It
De Notstandsgebiet (n)
En distressed area
Es región deprimida (f)
Fr région déprimée (f)
Pt zona deprimida (f)

**argent** (m) n Fr
De Geld (n)
En money
Es dinero (m)
It denaro (m)
Pt dinheiro (m)

**argent à vue** (m) Fr
De Sichtgelder (n pl)
En money on call
Es dinero a la vista (m)
It denaro a vista (m)
Pt dinheiro à ordem (m)

**argent bon marché** (m) Fr
De billiges Geld (n)
En cheap money
Es dinero barato (m)
It denaro a basso interesse (m)
Pt dinheiro barato (m)

**argent cher** (m) Fr
De teueres Geld (n)
En dear money
Es dinero caro (m)
It denaro ad alto interesse (m)
Pt dinheiro caro (m)

**argent comptant** (m) Fr
De Bargeld (n)
En cash
Es dinero contante (m)
It denaro contante (m)
Pt dinheiro de contado (m)

**arithmetic mean** En
De arithmetisches Mittel (n)
Es media aritmética (f)
Fr moyenne arithmétique (f)
It media aritmetica (f)
Pt média aritmética (f)

**arithmetisches Mittel** (n) De
En arithmetic mean
Es media aritmética (f)
Fr moyenne arithmétique (f)
It media aritmetica (f)
Pt média aritmética (f)

**armazém** (m) Pt
De Warenhaus; Warenlager (n)
En department store; warehouse; store
Es grandes almacenes; almacén (m pl; m)
Fr grand magasin; magasin; entrepôt (m)
It grande magazzino; magazzino (m)

**armazém alfandegário** (m) Pt
De Lager unter Zollverschluss (n)
En bonded warehouse
Es almacén de aduanas (m)
Fr entrepôt (m)
It magazzino doganale (m)

**armazenamento** (m) n Pt
De Lagerung (f)
En storage
Es almacenamiento (m)
Fr emmagasinage (m)
It maggazzinaggio (m)

**armazenar** vb Pt
De lagern
En store
Es almacenar
Fr emmagasiner
It immagazzinare

**armed forces** En
De Streitkräfte (f pl)
Es fuerzas armadas (f pl)
Fr forces armées (f pl)
It forze armate (f pl)
Pt forças armadas (f pl)

**arquitecto** (m) n Es, Pt
De Architekt (m)
En architect
Fr architecte (m)
It architetto (m)

**arquivar** vb Pt
De aufreihen
En file
Es archivar

Fr classer
It archiviare

**arrears** pl n En
De Rückstand (m)
Es atrasos (m pl)
Fr arrérages (m pl)
It arretrati (m pl)
Pt atrasos (m pl)

**arrendador** (m) n Es
De Vermieter (m)
En lessor
Fr bailleur (m)
It locatore (m)
Pt senhorio; arrendador (m)

**arrendatario** (m) n Es
De Mieter (m)
En lessee
Fr locataire (m)
It locatario (m)
Pt locatário; arrendatário (m)

**arrérages** (m pl) Fr
De Rückstand (m)
En arrears
Es atrasos (m pl)
It arretrati (m pl)
Pt atrasos (m pl)

**arretrati** (m pl) It
De Rückstand (m)
En arrears
Es atrasos (m pl)
Fr arrérages (m pl)
Pt atrasos (m pl)

**arretrati di paga** (m pl) It
De Lohnnachzahlung (f)
En back pay
Es pago atrasado (m)
Fr rappel de traitement (m)
Pt vencimento atrasado (m)

**arrhes** (f pl) n Fr
De Anzahlung (f)
En deposit
Es desembolso inicial (m)
It caparra (f)
Pt sinal (m)

**arriéré** adj Fr
De rückständig
En overdue
Es vencido
It scaduto
Pt vencido

**arriesgar** *vb* Es
De  wagen
En  hazard
Fr  hasarder
It  arrischiare
Pt  arriscar

**arrimage** *(m)* *n* Fr
De  Verstauung *(f)*
En  stowage
Es  estiba *(f)*
It  stivaggio *(m)*
Pt  estiva *(f)*

**arrimer** *vb* Fr
De  verstauen
En  stow
Es  estibar
It  stivare
Pt  estivar

**arriscar** *vb* Pt
De  wagen
En  hazard
Es  arriesgar
Fr  hasarder
It  arrischiare

**arrischiare** *vb* It
De  wagen
En  hazard
Es  arriesgar
Fr  hasarder
Pt  arriscar

**arrival** *n* En
De  Ankunft *(f)*
Es  llegada *(f)*
Fr  arrivée *(f)*
It  arrivo *(m)*
Pt  chegada *(f)*

**arrivée** *(f)* *n* Fr
De  Ankunft *(f)*
En  arrival
Es  llegada *(f)*
It  arrivo *(m)*
Pt  chegada *(f)*

**arrivo** *(m)* *n* It
De  Ankunft *(f)*
En  arrival
Es  llegada *(f)*
Fr  arrivée *(f)*
Pt  chegada *(f)*

**art de l'étalage** *(m)* Fr
De  Schaufensterdekoration *(f)*
En  window-dressing
Es  preparación de escaparates *(f)*
It  allestimento delle vetrine *(m)*
Pt  preparação de montras *(f)*

**art de vendre** *(m)* Fr
De  Verkaufsgewandtheit *(f)*
En  salesmanship
Es  arte de vender *(m)*
It  arte della vendita *(f)*
Pt  ciência de vender *(f)*

**arte della vendita** *(f)* It
De  Verkaufsgewandtheit *(f)*
En  salesmanship
Es  arte de vender *(m)*
Fr  art de vendre *(m)*
Pt  ciência de vender *(f)*

**arte de vender** *(m)* Es
De  Verkaufsgewandtheit *(f)*
En  salesmanship
Fr  art de vendre *(m)*
It  arte della vendita *(f)*
Pt  ciência de vender *(f)*

**article d'un livre journal** *(m)* Fr
De  Tagebuchsposten *(m)*
En  journal-entry
Es  asiento en el libro diario *(m)*
It  registrazione a giornale *(f)*
Pt  anotação de diário *(f)*

**articles de luxe** *(m pl)* Fr
De  Luxuswaren *(f pl)*
En  luxury goods
Es  artículos de lujo *(m pl)*
It  articoli di lusso *(m pl)*
Pt  artigos de luxo *(m pl)*

**articles de marque** *(m pl)* Fr
De  Markenwaren *(f pl)*
En  branded goods
Es  artículos de marca *(m pl)*
It  articoli di marca *(m pl)*
Pt  artigos de marca *(m pl)*

**articles of association** En
Am  articles of incorporation
De  Gesellschaftsvertrag *(m)*
Es  artículos de asociación *(m pl)*
Fr  contrat de société *(m)*

It  statuto sociale *(m)*
Pt  escritura de sociedade *(f)*

**articles of incorporation** Am
En  articles of association
De  Gesellschaftsvertrag *(m)*
Es  artículos de asociación *(m pl)*
Fr  contrat de société *(m)*
It  statuto sociale *(m)*
Pt  escritura de sociedade *(f)*

**articoli di lusso** *(m pl)* It
De  Luxuswaren *(f pl)*
En  luxury goods
Es  artículos de lujo *(m pl)*
Fr  articles de luxe *(m pl)*
Pt  artigos de luxo *(m pl)*

**articoli di marca** *(m pl)* It
De  Markenwaren *(f pl)*
En  branded goods
Es  artículos de marca *(m pl)*
Fr  articles de marque *(m pl)*
Pt  artigos de marca *(m pl)*

**articoli di spesa** *(m pl)* It
De  Aufwendungsposten *(f pl)*
En  items of expenditure
Es  artículos de gasto *(m pl)*
Fr  postes de dépense *(m pl)*
Pt  itens de despesa *(m pl)*

**articoli fantasia** *(m pl)* It
De  Modeartikel *(m pl)*
En  fancy goods
Es  artículos de fantasía *(m pl)*
Fr  nouveautés *(f pl)*
Pt  artigos de fantasia *(m pl)*

**artículos de asociación** *(m pl)* Es
De  Gesellschaftsvertrag *(m)*
En  articles of association
Am  articles of incorporation
Fr  contrat de société *(m)*
It  statuto sociale *(m)*
Pt  escritura de sociedade *(f)*

**artículos de fantasía** *(m pl)* Es
De  Modeartikel *(m pl)*
En  fancy goods
Fr  nouveautés *(f pl)*
It  articoli fantasia *(m pl)*
Pt  artigos de fantasia *(m pl)*

**artículos de gasto** *(m pl)* Es
De Aufwendungsposten *(f pl)*
En items of expenditure
Fr postes de dépense *(m pl)*
It articoli di spesa *(m pl)*
Pt itens de despesa *(m pl)*

**artículos de lujo** *(m pl)* Es
De Luxuswaren *(f pl)*
En luxury goods
Fr articles de luxe *(m pl)*
It articoli di lusso *(m pl)*
Pt artigos de luxo *(m pl)*

**artículos de marca** *(m pl)* Es
De Markenwaren *(f pl)*
En branded goods
Fr articles de marque *(m pl)*
It articoli di marca *(m pl)*
Pt artigos de marca *(m pl)*

**artigos à consignação** *(m pl)*
Pt
De Kommissionsgüter *(n pl)*
En goods on consignment
Es mercancías en consignación *(f pl)*
Fr marchandises en consignation *(f pl)*
It merce in conto deposito *(f)*

**artigos de cabedal** *(m pl)* Pt
De Lederwaren *(f pl)*
En leather goods
Es marroquinería *(f)*
Fr maroquinerie *(f)*
It pelletterie *(f pl)*

**artigos de consumo perduraveis** *(m pl)* Pt
De dauerhafte Konsumgüter *(n pl)*
En consumer durables
Es bienes de consumo duraderos *(m pl)*
Fr biens de consommation durables *(m pl)*
It beni di consumo durabili *(m pl)*

**artigos de fantasia** *(m pl)* Pt
De Modeartikel *(m pl)*
En fancy goods
Es artículos de fantasía *(m pl)*
Fr nouveautés *(f pl)*
It articoli fantasia *(m pl)*

**artigos de luxo** *(m pl)* Pt
De Luxuswaren *(f pl)*
En luxury goods
Es artículos de lujo *(m pl)*
Fr articles de luxe *(m pl)*
It articoli di lusso *(m pl)*

**artigos de malha de lã** *(m pl)*
Pt
De Strickwaren *(f pl)*
En knitted goods
Es géneros de punto *(m pl)*
Fr bonneterie *(f)*
It maglieria *(f)*

**artigos de marca** *(m pl)* Pt
De Markenwaren *(f pl)*
En branded goods
Es artículos de marca *(m pl)*
Fr articles de marque *(m pl)*
It articoli di marca *(m pl)*

**artigos sujeitos a aprovação**
*(m pl)* Pt
De Probegüter *(n pl)*
En goods on approval
Es mercancías sujetas a aprobación *(f pl)*
Fr marchandises à condition *(f pl)*
It merce soggetta ad approvazione *(f)*

**ärztliche Untersuchung** *(f)* De
En medical examination
Es examen médico *(m)*
Fr examen médical *(m)*
It visita medica *(f)*
Pt inspecção médica *(f)*

**asalariado** *(m)* Es
De Lohnempfänger *(m)*
En wage earner
Fr salarié *(m)*
It salariato *(m)*
Pt assalariado *(m)*

**asamblea general** *(f)* Es
De Hauptversammlung; ordentliche Versammlung *(f)*
En general meeting; statutory meeting
Fr assemblée générale; assemblée ordinaire *(f)*
It assemblea generale *(f)*
Pt assembleia geral; assembleia estatutária *(f)*

**asamblea general anual** *(f)* Es
De Jahreshauptversammlung *(f)*
En annual general meeting
Am stockholders' meeting
Fr assemblée d'actionnaires annuelle *(f)*
It assemblea generale annuale *(f)*
Pt assembleia geral anual *(f)*

**asamblea general extraordinaria** *(f)* Es
De ausserordentliche Generalversammlung *(f)*
En extraordinary general meeting
Fr assemblée générale extraordinaire *(f)*
It assemblea generale straordinaria *(f)*
Pt assembleia geral extraordinária *(f)*

**asamblea general ordinaria** *(f)*
Es
De ordentliche Generalversammlung *(f)*
En ordinary general meeting
Am stockholders' meeting
Fr assemblée générale *(f)*
It assemblea generale ordinaria *(f)*
Pt assembleia geral ordinária *(f)*

**ascender** *vb* Es
De befördern
En promote
Fr donner de l'avancement à
It promuovere
Pt promover

**ascendiendo a** Es
De hinauslaufend auf
En amounting to
Fr à concurrence de
It ammontante a
Pt no montante de

**ascenseur** *(m)* n Fr
De Aufzug *(m)*
En lift
Am elevator
Es ascensor *(m)*
It ascensore *(m)*
Pt ascensor *(m)*

**ascenso** *(m)* n Es
De Beförderung *(f)*
En promotion
Fr avancement; promotion *(m f)*
It avanzamento; promozione *(m f)*
Pt promoção *(f)*

**ascensor** *(m)* n Es, Pt
De Aufzug *(m)*
En lift
Am elevator
Fr ascenseur *(m)*
It ascensore *(m)*

**ascensore** *(m)* n It
De Aufzug *(m)*
En lift
Am elevator
Es ascensor *(m)*
Fr ascenseur *(m)*
Pt ascensor *(m)*

**asegurable** *adj* Es
De versicherbar
En insurable
Fr assurable
It assicurabile
Pt susceptível de ser objecto de seguro

**asegurado** *(m)* n Es
De Versicherte(r) *(m)*
En insured
Fr assuré *(m)*
It assicurato *(m)*
Pt titular de seguro *(m)*

**asegurador** *(m)* n Es
De Versicherer *(m)*
En insurer; underwriter
Fr assureur *(m)*
It assicuratore *(m)*
Pt segurador *(m)*

**asegurar** *vb* Es
De versichern
En insure
Fr assurer
It assicurare
Pt segurar

**asesor** *(m)* n Es
De Schätzer *(m)*
En assessor
Fr appréciateur *(m)*

It agente delle imposte *(m)*
Pt avaliador *(m)*

**asesor administrativo** *(m)* Es
De Geschäftsführungsberater *(m)*
En management consultant
Fr ingénieur-conseil en organisation *(m)*
It consulente di direzione aziendale *(m)*
Pt perito de administração *(m)*

**asiento** *(m)* n Es
De Eintragung *(f)*
En entry
Fr inscription *(f)*
It registrazione *(f)*
Pt lançamento *(m)*

**asiento en el libro diario** *(m)* Es
De Tagebuchsposten *(m)*
En journal-entry
Fr article d'un livre journal *(m)*
It registrazione a giornale *(f)*
Pt anotação de diário *(f)*

**asientos saldados** *(m pl)* Es
De Ausgleichsposten *(m pl)*
En balancing items
Fr postes rééquilibrants *(m pl)*
It voci di pareggio *(f pl)*
Pt valores de equilíbrio *(m pl)*

**asignar** *vb* Es
De verteilen
En allot
Fr attribuer
It assegnare
Pt atribuir

**asistente** *(m)* n Es
De Assistent *(m)*
En assistant
Fr commis *(m)*
It assistente *(m)*
Pt assistente *(m)*

**asistente privado** *(m)* Es
De persönlicher Assistent *(m)*
En personal assistant (PA)
Am administrative assistant
Fr fonctionnel *(m)*
It assistente privato *(m)*
Pt secretário *(m)*

**asociación** *(f)* n Es
De Verband *(m)*
En association
Fr association *(f)*
It associazione *(f)*
Pt associação *(f)*

**asociación comercial** *(f)* Es
De Unternehmerverband *(m)*
En trade association
Fr association professionnelle *(f)*
It associazione commerciale *(f)*
Pt associação comercial *(f)*

**Asociación de Mercado Libre de América Latina** *(f)* Es
De Lateinamerikanische Freihandelszone *(f)*
En Latin American Free Trade Association (LAFTA)
Fr Association Latine-Américaine de Libre-Échange *(f)*
It Associazione di Libero Scambio dell'America Latine *(f)*
Pt Associação do Comércio Livre da América Latina *(f)*

**assalariado** *(m)* n Pt
De Lohnempfänger *(m)*
En wage earner
Es asalariado *(m)*
Fr salarié *(m)*
It salariato *(m)*

**assay** n En
De Probe *(f)*
Es ensayo *(m)*
Fr essai *(m)*
It saggio *(m)*
Pt verificação *(f)*

**assegnare** *vb* It
De verteilen
En allot
Es asignar
Fr attribuer
Pt atribuir

**assegnatario** *(m)* n It
De Zessionär *(m)*
En assignee
Es cesionario *(m)*
Fr cessionnaire *(m)*
Pt cessionário *(m)*

**assegno** *(m)* n It
De Scheck *(m)*
En cheque
Am check
Es cheque *(m)*
Fr chèque *(m)*
Pt cheque *(m)*

**assegno al portatore** *(m)* It
De Inhaberscheck *(m)*
En cheque payable to bearer
Am check payable to bearer
Es cheque al portador *(m)*
Fr chèque payable au porteur *(m)*
Pt cheque ao portador *(m)*

**assegno aperto** *(m)* It
De Inhaberscheck *(m)*
En open cheque
Es cheque abierto *(m)*
Fr chèque ouvert *(m)*
Pt cheque em branco *(m)*

**assegno falsificato** *(m)* It
De gefälschter Scheck *(m)*
En forged cheque
Es cheque falsificado *(m)*
Fr faux chèque *(m)*
Pt cheque falsificado *(m)*

**assegno garantito** *(m)* It
De bestätigter Scheck *(m)*
En certified cheque
Am certified check
Es cheque certificado *(m)*
Fr chèque certifié *(m)*
Pt cheque certificado *(m)*

**assegno in bianco** *(m)* It
De Blankoscheck *(m)*
En blank cheque
Am blank check
Es cheque en blanco *(m)*
Fr chèque en blanc *(m)*
Pt cheque em branco *(m)*

**assegno postdatato** *(m)* It
De nachdatierter Scheck *(m)*
En postdated cheque
Es cheque a fecha retrasada *(m)*
Fr chèque postdaté *(m)*
Pt cheque post-datado *(m)*

**assegno sbarrato** *(m)* It
De Verrechnungsscheck *(m)*
En crossed cheque

Es cheque cruzado *(m)*
Fr chèque barré *(m)*
Pt cheque cruzado *(m)*

**assegno turistico** *(m)* It
De Reisescheck *(m)*
En traveller's cheque
Am traveler's check
Es cheque de viajero *(m)*
Fr chèque de voyage *(m)*
Pt cheque de viajante *(m)*

**assemblea dei creditori** *(f)* It
De Gläubigerversammlung *(f)*
En meeting of creditors
Es reunión de acreedores *(f)*
Fr assemblée de créanciers *(f)*
Pt assembleia de credores *(f)*

**assemblea generale** *(f)* It
De Hauptversammlung; ordentliche Versammlung *(f)*
En general meeting; statutory meeting
Es asamblea general *(f)*
Fr assemblée générale; assemblée ordinaire *(f)*
Pt assembleia geral; assembleia estatutária *(f)*

**assemblea generale annuale** *(f)* It
De Jahreshauptversammlung *(f)*
En annual general meeting
Am stockholders' meeting
Es asamblea general anual *(f)*
Fr assemblée d'actionnaires annuelle *(f)*
Pt assembleia geral anual *(f)*

**assemblea generale straordinaria** *(f)* It
De ausserordentliche Generalversammlung *(f)*
En extraordinary general meeting
Es asamblea general extraordinaria *(f)*
Fr assemblée générale extraordinaire *(f)*
Pt assembleia geral extraordinária *(f)*

**assemblée d'actionnaires annuelle** *(f)* Fr

De Jahreshauptversammlung *(f)*
En annual general meeting
Am stockholders' meeting
Es asamblea general anual *(f)*
It assemblea generale annuale *(f)*
Pt assembleia geral anual *(f)*

**assemblée de créanciers** *(f)* Fr
De Gläubigerversammlung *(f)*
En meeting of creditors
Es concurso de acreedores *(m)*
It convocazione dei creditori *(f)*
Pt reunião de credores *(f)*

**assemblée générale** *(f)* Fr
De Hauptversammlung; ordentliche Generalversammlung *(f)*
En general meeting; ordinary general meeting
Es asamblea general; asamblea general ordinaria *(f)*
It assemblea generale; assemblea generale ordinaria *(f)*
Pt assembleia geral; assembleia geral ordinária *(f)*

**assemblée générale extraordinaire** *(f)* Fr
De ausserordentliche Generalversammlung *(f)*
En extraordinary general meeting
Es asamblea general extraordinaria *(f)*
It assemblea generale straordinaria *(f)*
Pt assembleia geral extraordinária *(f)*

**assemblée ordinaire** *(f)* Fr
De ordentliche Versammlung *(f)*
En statutory meeting
Es asamblea general *(f)*
It assemblea generale *(f)*
Pt assembleia estatutária *(f)*

**assembleia de credores** *(f)* Pt
De Gläubigerversammlung *(f)*
En meeting of creditors
Es reunión de acreedores *(f)*

Fr assemblée de créanciers *(f)*
It assemblea dei creditori *(f)*

**assembleia estatutária** *(f)* Pt
De ordentliche Versammlung *(f)*
En statutory meeting
Es asamblea general *(f)*
Fr assemblée ordinaire *(f)*
It assemblea generale *(f)*

**assembleia geral** *(f)* Pt
De Hauptversammlung *(f)*
En general meeting
Es asamblea general *(f)*
Fr assemblée générale *(f)*
It assemblea generale *(f)*

**assembleia geral anual** *(f)* Pt
De Jahreshauptversammlung *(f)*
En annual general meeting
Am stockholders' meeting
Es asamblea general anual *(f)*
Fr assemblée d'actionnaires annuelle *(f)*
It assemblea generale annuale *(f)*

**assembleia geral extraordinária** *(f)* Pt
De ausserordentliche Generalversammlung *(f)*
En extraordinary general meeting
Es asamblea general extraordinaria *(f)*
Fr assemblée générale extraordinaire *(f)*
It assemblea generale straordinaria *(f)*

**assembleia geral ordinária** *(f)* Pt
De ordentliche Generalversammlung *(f)*
En ordinary general meeting
Am stockholders' meeting
Es asamblea general ordinaria *(f)*
Fr assemblée générale *(f)*
It assemblea generale ordinaria *(f)*

**assembly line** En
De Montageband *(n)*
Es línea de montaje *(f)*
Fr chaîne de montage *(f)*

It catena di montaggio *(f)*
Pt cadeia de montagem *(f)*

**assente** *(m)* n It
De Abwesende(r) *(m)*
En absentee
Es ausente *(m)*
Fr manquant *(m)*
Pt ausente *(m)*

**assenteismo** *(m)* n It
De unerlaubte Abwesenheit *(f)*
En absenteeism
Es ausentismo *(m)*
Fr absentéisme *(m)*
Pt absentismo *(m)*

**assess damages** En
De den Schadenersatzbetrag feststellen
Es evaluar daños
Fr fixer des dommages-intérêts
It valutare i danni
Pt avaliar os danos

**assessment** n En
De Besteuerung *(f)*
Es evaluación *(f)*
Fr imposition *(f)*
It imposta *(f)*
Pt balanço fiscal *(m)*

**assessor** n En
De Schätzer *(m)*
Es asesor *(m)*
Fr appréciateur *(m)*
It agente delle imposte *(m)*
Pt avaliador *(m)*

**asset** n En
De Aktivposten *(m)*
Es activo *(m)*
Fr actif *(m)*
It attivo *(m)*
Pt valor *(m)*

**assets and liabilities** En
De Aktiva und Passiva *(n pl)*
Es activo y pasivo *(m)*
Fr actif et passif *(m)*
It attivo e passivo *(m)*
Pt activo e passivo *(m)*

**asset value** En
De Aktivwert *(m)*
Es valor en activo *(m)*
Fr valeur de l'actif *(f)*

It valore in attivo *(m)*
Pt valor do activo *(m)*

**assicurabile** adj It
De versicherbar
En insurable
Es asegurable
Fr assurable
Pt susceptível de ser objecto de seguro

**assicurare** vb It
De versichern
En insure
Es asegurar
Fr assurer
Pt segurar

**assicurato** *(m)* n It
De Versicherte(r) *(m)*
En insured
Es asegurado *(m)*
Fr assuré *(m)*
Pt titular de seguro *(m)*

**assicuratore** *(m)* n It
De Versicherer *(m)*
En insurer; underwriter
Es asegurador *(m)*
Fr assureur *(m)*
Pt segurador *(m)*

**assicurazione** *(f)* n It
De Versicherung *(f)*
En assurance
Es seguro *(m)*
Fr assurance *(f)*
Pt seguro *(m)*

**assicurazione contro i rischi di guerra** *(f)* It
De Kriegsrisikoversicherung *(f)*
En war-risk insurance
Es seguro contra riesgo de guerra *(f)*
Fr assurance du risque de guerre *(f)*
Pt seguro contra risco de guerra *(m)*

**assicurazione contro terzi** *(f)* It
De Haftpflichtversicherung *(f)*
En third-party insurance
Es seguro contra responsabilidad civil *(m)*

Fr assurance responsabilité civile (RC) (f)
Pt seguro contra terceiros (m)

**assicurazione corpo** (m) It
De Kaskoversicherung (f)
En hull insurance
Es seguro del casco (m)
Fr assurance sur le corps (f)
Pt seguro do casco (m)

**assicurazione credito** (f) It
De Kreditversicherung (f)
En credit insurance
Es seguro crediticio (m)
Fr assurance crédit (f)
Pt seguro de crédito (m)

**assicurazione di gruppo** (f) It
De Gruppenversicherung (f)
En group insurance
Es seguro de grupo (m)
Fr assurance de groupe (f)
Pt seguro de grupo (m)

**assicurazione domestica** (f) It
De Wohnungsversicherung (f)
En household insurance
Es seguro de casa (m)
Fr assurance ménagère (f)
Pt seguro de casa (m)

**assicurazione dotale** (f) It
De Erlebensversicherung (f)
En endowment policy
Es póliza dotal (f)
Fr assurance à terme fixe (f)
Pt título de doação (m)

**assicurazione incendio** (f) It
De Feuerversicherung (f)
En fire insurance
Es seguro de incendios (m)
Fr assurance incendie (f)
Pt seguro de incêndio (m)

**assicurazione malattia** (f) It
De Krankenversicherung (f)
En health insurance
Es seguro de enfermedad (m)
Fr assurance maladie (f)
Pt seguro de obença (m)

**assicurazione mista** (f) It
De kombinierte Versicherung (f)
En comprehensive insurance
Es seguro combinado (m)

Fr assurance combinée (f)
Pt seguro compreensivo (m)

**assicurazione sulla vita** (f) It
De Lebensversicherung (f)
En life assurance
Am life insurance
Es seguro de vida (m)
Fr assurance sur la vie (f)
Pt seguro de vida (m)

**assiette de l'impôt** (f) Fr
De Bemessungsgrundlage (f)
En tax base
Es base contributiva (f)
It ripartizione della tassazione (f)
Pt base de imposto (f)

**assignation** (f) n Fr
De Vorladung (f)
En writ
Es auto; orden (m f)
It citazione (f)
Pt citação; ordem (f m)

**assignee** n En
De Zessionär (m)
Es cesionario (m)
Fr cessionnaire (m)
It assegnatario (m)
Pt cessionário (m)

**assignment** n En
De Übertragung (f)
Es cesión (f)
Fr cession (f)
It cessione (f)
Pt consignação (f)

**assignor** n En
De Übertrager (m)
Es cesionista (m)
Fr cédant (m)
It cedente (m)
Pt cessionista (m)

**assinatura** (f) n Pt
De Unterschrift; Abonnement (f n)
En signature; subscription
Es firma; abono (f m)
Fr signature; abonnement (f m)
It firma; abbonamento (f m)

**assinatura em branco** (f) Pt
De Blankounterschrift (f)
En blank signature
Es firma en blanco (f)
Fr blanc-seing (m)
It firma in bianco (f)

**assistant** n En
De Assistent (m)
Es asistente (m)
Fr commis (m)
It assistente (m)
Pt assistente (m)

**assistant manager** En
De Unterdirektor (m)
Es sub-director (m)
Fr sous-directeur (m)
It vice-direttore (m)
Pt sub-director (m)

**Assistent** (m) n De
En assistant
Es asistente (m)
Fr commis (m)
It assistente (m)
Pt assistente (m)

**assistente** (m) n It, Pt
De Assistent (m)
En assistant
Es asistente (m)
Fr commis (m)

**assistente privato** (m) It
De persönlicher Assistent (m)
En personal assistant (PA)
Am administrative assistant
Es asistente privado (m)
Fr fonctionnel (m)
Pt secretário (m)

**associação** (f) n Pt
De Verband (m)
En association
Es asociación (f)
Fr association (f)
It associazione (f)

**associação comercial** (f) Pt
De Unternehmerverband (m)
En trade association
Es asociación comercial (f)
Fr association professionnelle (f)
It associazione commerciale (f)

**Associação do Comércio Livre da América Latina** *(f)* Pt
De Lateinamerikanische Freihandelszone *(f)*
En Latin American Free Trade Association (LAFTA)
Es Asociación de Mercado Libre de América Latina *(f)*
Fr Association Latine-Américaine de Libre-Échange *(f)*
It Associazione di Libero Scambio dell'America Latine *(f)*

**association** *n* En, Fr *(f)*
De Verband *(m)*
Es asociación *(f)*
It associazione *(f)*
Pt associação *(f)*

**Association Latine-Américaine de Libre-Échange** *(f)* Fr
De Lateinamerikanische Freihandelszone *(f)*
En Latin American Free Trade Association (LAFTA)
Es Asociación de Mercado Libre de América Latina *(f)*
It Associazione di Libero Scambio dell'America Latine *(f)*
Pt Associação do Comércio Livre da América Latina *(f)*

**associazione commerciale** *(f)* It
De Unternehmerverband *(m)*
En trade association
Es asociación comercial *(f)*
Fr association professionnelle *(f)*
Pt associação comercial *(f)*

**Associazione di Libero Scambio dell'America Latine** *(f)* It
De Lateinamerikanische Freihandelszone *(f)*
En Latin American Free Trade Association (LAFTA)
Es Asociación de Mercado Libre de América Latina *(f)*
Fr Association Latine-Américaine de Libre-Échange *(f)*
Pt Associação do Comércio Livre da América Latina *(f)*

**associé** *(m)* n Fr
De Teilhaber *(m)*
En partner
Es socio *(m)*
It socio *(m)*
Pt sócio *(m)*

**associé actif** *(m)* Fr
De aktiver Teilhaber *(m)*
En working partner
Es socio activo *(m)*
It socio attivo *(m)*
Pt sócio actuante *(m)*

**associé en second** *(m)* Fr
De jüngerer Teilhaber *(m)*
En junior partner
Es segundo asociado *(m)*
It socio giovane *(m)*
Pt sócio junior *(m)*

**assurable** *adj* Fr
De versicherbar
En insurable
Es asegurable
It assicurabile
Pt susceptível de ser objecto de seguro

**assurance** *n* En
De Versicherung *(f)*
Es seguro *(m)*
Fr assurance *(f)*
It assicurazione *(f)*
Pt seguro *(m)*

**assurance** *(f)* n Fr
De Versicherung *(f)*
En insurance; assurance
Es seguro *(m)*
It assicurazione *(f)*
Pt seguro *(m)*

**assurance à terme fixe** *(f)* Fr
De Erlebensversicherung *(f)*
En endowment policy
Es póliza dotal *(f)*
It assicurazione dotale *(f)*
Pt título de doação *(m)*

**assurance combinée** *(f)* Fr
De kombinierte Versicherung *(f)*
En comprehensive insurance
Es seguro combinado *(m)*
It assicurazione mista *(f)*
Pt seguro compreensivo *(m)*

**assurance crédit** *(f)* Fr
De Kreditversicherung *(f)*
En credit insurance
Es seguro crediticio *(m)*
It assicurazione credito *(f)*
Pt seguro de crédito *(m)*

**assurance de groupe** *(f)* Fr
De Gruppenversicherung *(f)*
En group insurance
Es seguro de grupo *(m)*
It assicurazione di gruppo *(f)*
Pt seguro de grupo *(m)*

**assurance du risque de guerre** *(f)* Fr
De Kriegsrisikoversicherung *(f)*
En war-risk insurance
Es seguro contra riesgo de guerra *(m)*
It assicurazione contro i rischi di guerra *(f)*
Pt seguro contra risco de guerra *(m)*

**assurance incendie** *(f)* Fr
De Feuerversicherung *(f)*
En fire insurance
Es seguro de incendios *(m)*
It assicurazione incendio *(f)*
Pt seguro de incêndio *(m)*

**assurance libérée** *(f)* Fr
De beitragsfreie Police *(f)*
En paid-up policy
Es póliza liberada *(f)*
It polizza interamente pagata *(f)*
Pt apólice liquidada *(f)*

**assurance maladie** *(f)* Fr
De Krankenversicherung *(f)*
En health insurance
Es seguro de enfermedad *(m)*
It assicurazione malattia *(f)*
Pt seguro de obença *(m)*

**assurance ménagère** *(f)* Fr
De Wohnungsversicherung *(f)*
En household insurance
Es seguro de casa *(m)*
It assicurazione domestica *(f)*
Pt seguro de casa *(m)*

**assurance mutuelle** *(f)* Fr
De Versicherung auf Gegenseitigkeit *(f)*
En mutual insurance

Es coaseguro *(m)*
It mutua assicurazione *(f)*
Pt seguro mútuo *(m)*

**assurance responsabilité civile (RC)** *(f)* Fr
De Haftpflichtversicherung *(f)*
En third-party insurance
Es seguro contra responsabilidad civil *(m)*
It assicurazione contro terzi *(f)*
Pt seguro contra terceiros *(m)*

**assurance sur la vie** *(f)* Fr
De Lebensversicherung *(f)*
En life assurance
Am life insurance
Es seguro de vida *(m)*
It assicurazione sulla vita *(f)*
Pt seguro de vida *(m)*

**assurance sur le corps** *(f)* Fr
De Kaskoversicherung *(f)*
En hull insurance
Es seguro del casco *(m)*
It assicurazione corpo *(m)*
Pt seguro do casco *(m)*

**assuré** *(m)* n Fr
De Versicherte(r) *(m)*
En insured
Es asegurado *(m)*
It assicurato *(m)*
Pt titular de seguro *(m)*

**assurer** *vb* Fr
De versichern
En insure
Es asegurar
It assicurare
Pt segurar

**assureur** *(m)* n Fr
De Versicherer *(m)*
En insurer; underwriter
Es asegurador *(m)*
It assicuratore *(m)*
Pt segurador *(m)*

**asta** *(f)* n It
De Versteigerung *(f)*
En auction
Es subasta *(f)*
Fr vente aux enchères *(f)*
Pt leilão *(m)*

**astenersi** *vb* It
De seine Stimme enthalten
En abstain
Es abstenerse
Fr s'abstenir
Pt abster-se

**astillero** *(m)* n Es
De Schiffswerft *(f)*
En dockyard
Fr chantier de construction de navires *(m)*
It cantiere *(m)*
Pt estaleiro *(m)*

**a termine** It
De Termin-
En forward
Es a término
Fr en avant; à terme
Pt adiante

**a término** Es
De Termin-
En forward
Fr en avant; à terme
It a termine
Pt adiante

**atesoramiento** *(m)* n Es
De Hort *(m)*
En hoard
Fr thésaurisation *(f)*
It ammasso *(m)*
Pt acumulação *(f)*

**at par** En
De al Pari
Es al par
Fr au pair
It alla pari
Pt ao par

**atracagem** *(m)* n Pt
De Kaigeld *(n)*
En wharfage
Es muellaje *(m)*
Fr quayage *(m)*
It diritto di sosta *(m)*

**atrasos** *(m pl)* n Es, Pt
De Rückstand *(m)*
En arrears *pl n*
Fr arrérages *(m pl)*
It arretrati *(m pl)*

**atrazo** *(m)* n Pt
De Verzug *(m)*
En delay
Es retraso *(m)*
Fr retard; délai *(m)*
It ritardo *(m)*

**atribuir** *vb* Pt
De verteilen; zuteilen
En allot; apportion
Es asignar; repartir
Fr attribuer; répartir
It assegnare; ripartire

**at sight** En
De bei Sicht
Es a la vista
Fr à vue
It a vista
Pt à vista

**attache-papiers** *(m)* n Fr
De Büroklammer *(f)*
En paper clip
Es sujetapapeles *(m)*
It fermacarte *(m)*
Pt grampo *(m)*

**attività in esaurimento** *(f pl)* It
De kurzlebige Aktiva *(n pl)*
En wasting assets
Am depleting assets
Es activo gastable *(m)*
Fr actifs défectibles *(m pl)*
Pt bens em uso ou deterioração *(m pl)*

**attivo** *(m)* n It
De Aktivposten *(m)*
En asset
Es activo *(m)*
Fr actif *(m)*
Pt valor *(m)*

**attivo** *adj* It
De wirksam
En operative
Es operativo; activo
Fr actif
Pt efectivo; em vigor

**attivo congelato** *(m)* It
De eingefrorene Guthaben *(n pl)*
En frozen assets
Es activos congelados *(m pl)*
Fr fonds bloqués *(m pl)*

Pt  bens do activo congelados
    *(m pl)*

**attivo e passivo** *(m)* It
De  Aktiva und Passiva *(n pl)*
En  assets and liabilities
Es  activo y pasivo *(m)*
Fr  actif et passif *(m)*
Pt  activo e passivo *(m)*

**attivo liquido** *(m)* It
De  Umlaufsvermögen *(n)*
En  current assets
Es  activo realizable *(m)*
Fr  actif courant *(m)*
Pt  bens no activo actual *(m pl)*

**attivo netto** *(m)* It
De  Reinvermögen *(n)*
En  net assets
Es  activo neto *(m)*
Fr  actif net *(m)*
Pt  bens líquidos *(m pl)*

**atto** *(m) n* It
De  Urkunde *(f)*
En  deed; document
Es  título; escritura *(m f)*
Fr  acte; titre *(m)*
Pt  título; escritura *(m f)*

**atto a tenere il mare** It
De  seefest
En  seaworthy
Es  marinero
Fr  en état de navigabilité
Pt  em condições de nave-
    gação

**atto costitutivo e statuto
sociale** *(m)* It
De  Statuten *(f pl)*
En  Memorandum and Articles
    of Association
Am  articles of incorporation
Es  estatutos; carta orgánica
    *(m pl; f)*
Fr  statuts; acte constitutif *(m
    pl; m)*
Pt  estatuto de associação *(m)*

**atto di accordo** *(m)* It
De  Vergleichsabkommen *(n)*
En  deed of arrangement
Es  acta de disposición *(f)*
Fr  contrat d'arrangement *(m)*
Pt  escritura de acordo *(f)*

**atto di cessione** *(m)* It
De  Abtretungsvertrag *(m)*
En  deed of assignment
Es  titulo de asignación *(m)*
Fr  acte attributif *(m)*
Pt  titulo de consignação *(m)*

**atto di concordato** *(m)* It
De  Vergleichsabkommen *(n)*
En  deed of composition
Es  concordato *(m)*
Fr  concordat *(m)*
Pt  concordata (por escrito) *(f)*

**atto di nazionalita** *(m)* It
De  Schiffsregister *(n)*
En  ship's register
Es  registro del barco *(m)*
Fr  certificat d'immatriculation
    *(m)*
Pt  registo do navio *(m)*

**atto di trapasso** *(m)* It
De  Übertragungsvertrag *(m)*
En  transfer deed
Es  escritura de transferencia
    *(f)*
Fr  acte de cession *(m)*
Pt  título de transferência *(m)*

**atto ipotecario** *(m)* It
De  Verpfändungsurkunde *(f)*
En  letter of hypothecation
Es  carta de hipoteca *(f)*
Fr  lettre hypothécaire *(f)*
Pt  carta de hipoteca *(f)*

**attorney** *n* En
De  Bevollmächtigte(r) *(m)*
Es  apoderado *(m)*
Fr  mandataire *(m)*
It  mandatario *(m)*
Pt  procurador *(m)*

**attorney** *n* Am
En  barrister
De  Anwalt *(m)*
Es  abogado *(m)*
Fr  avocat *(m)*
It  avvocato *(m)*
Pt  advogado *(m)*

**attribuer** *vb* Fr
De  verteilen
En  allot
Es  asignar
It  assegnare
Pt  atribuir

**attribution** *(f) n* Fr
De  Verteilung *(f)*
En  allotment
Es  adjudicación *(f)*
It  ripartizione *(f)*
Pt  aporcionamento *(m)*

**attuare** *vb* It
De  bewerkstelligen; ausführen
En  implement
Es  hacer efectivo; ejecutar
Fr  exécuter
Pt  executar

**attuariale** *adj* It
De  versicherungsmathema-
    tisch
En  actuarial
Es  actuarial
Fr  actuariel
Pt  actuarial

**attuario** *(m) n* It
De  Aktuar *(m)*
En  actuary
Es  actuario *(m)*
Fr  actuaire *(m)*
Pt  actuário *(m)*

**a tutti gli interessati** It
De  an alle, die es angeht
En  to whom it may concern
Es  a quien concierna
Fr  à qui de droit
Pt  a quem disser respeito

**at warehouse** En
De  auf Lager
Es  en almacén
Fr  en dépôt
It  in deposito
Pt  em armazém

**au-dessus du pair** Fr
De  über Pari
En  above par
Es  a premio
It  sopra la pari
Pt  a prémio

**auction** *n* En
De  Versteigerung *(f)*
Es  subasta *(f)*
Fr  vente aux enchères *(f)*
It  asta *(f)*
Pt  leilão *(m)*

**auctioneer** n En
De Versteigerer (m)
Es subastador (m)
Fr commissaire-priseur (m)
It venditore all'asta (m)
Pt leiloeiro (m)

**audio-dactilógrafa** (f) n Pt
De Audio-typistin (f)
En audio-typist
Am dictaphone operator
Es audio-mecanógrafa (f)
Fr dictaphoniste (f)
It dittafonista (f)

**audio-mecanógrafa** (f) n Es
De Audio-typistin (f)
En audio-typist
Am dictaphone operator
Fr dictaphoniste (f)
It dittafonista (f)
Pt audio-dactilógrafa (f)

**audio-typist** n En
Am dictaphone operator
De Audio-typistin (f)
Es audio-mecanógrafa (f)
Fr dictaphoniste (f)
It dittafonista (f)
Pt audio-dactilógrafa (f)

**Audio-typistin** (f) n De
En audio-typist
Am dictaphone operator
Es audio-mecanógrafa (f)
Fr dictaphoniste (f)
It dittafonista (f)
Pt audio-dáctilógrafa (f)

**audio-visivo** adj It
De audiovisuell
En audio-visual
Es audio-visual
Fr audio-visuel
Pt audio-visual

**audio-visual** adj En, Es, Pt
De audiovisuell
Fr audio-visuel
It audio-visivo

**audio-visuel** adj Fr
De audiovisuell
En audio-visual
Es audio-visual
It audio-visivo
Pt audio-visual

**audiovisuell** adj De
En audio-visual
Es audio-visual
Fr audio-visuel
It audio-visivo
Pt audio-visual

**audit** n En
De Bücherrevision (f)
Es revisión (examen) de cuentas (f)
Fr vérification comptable (f)
It revisione dei conti (f)
Pt fiscalização de contas (f)

**audit** vb En
De prüfen
Es revisar
Fr vérifier et certifier
It rivedere
Pt fiscalizar as contas

**audited accounts** En
De geprüfte Geschäftsbücher (n pl)
Es cuentas revisadas (f pl)
Fr comptes vérifiés et certifiés (m pl)
It conti verificati e certificati (m pl)
Pt contas fiscalizadas (f pl)

**auditor** n En
De Bücherrevisor (m)
Es revisor de conti (m)
Fr réviseur des comptes (m)
It sindaco (m)
Pt fiscal de contas (m)

**auditor's report** En
De Bericht des Abschlussprüfers (m)
Es informe de los interventores (m)
Fr rapport des vérificateurs des comptes (m)
It relazione dei sindaci (f)
Pt relatório do fiscal de contas (m)

**auf den Markt bringen** De
En launch (a product)
Es lanzar (un producto)
Fr lancer sur le marché
It lanciare (un prodotto)
Pt lançar (um produto)

**aufdrängliches Verkaufen** (n) De
En hard sell
Es venta insistente (f)
Fr vente débrouillarde (f)
It vendita facendo sforzo (f)
Pt venda insistente (f)

**aufgeben** vb De
En give up
Es renunciar
Fr céder
It cedere
Pt desistir

**aufgelaufene Zinsen** (m pl) De
En accrued interest
Es interés acumulado (m)
Fr intérêts accumulés (m pl)
It interesse maturato (m)
Pt juro acumulado (m)

**aufgeschobene Schulden** (f pl) De
En deferred liabilities
Es pasivo transitorio (m)
Fr passif différé (m)
It passività differite (f pl)
Pt passivo adiado (m)

**auf Lager** De
En at warehouse
Es en almacén
Fr en dépôt
It in deposito
Pt em armazém

**auflaufen** vb De
En accrue
Es acumular
Fr accumuler
It accumularsi
Pt acumular

**Auflaufen** (n) n De
En accrual
Es acumulación (f)
Fr accumulation (f)
It maturazione (f)
Pt acumulação (f)

**auflegen** (ein Schiff) vb De
En lay-up
Es desarmar
Fr désarmer
It disamare
Pt desarmar

**Auflösung** (f) n De
En dissolution
Es disolución (f)
Fr dissolution (f)
It scioglimento (m)
Pt dissolução (f)

**aufreihen** vb De
En file
Es archivar
Fr classer
It archiviare
Pt arquivar

**Aufruhr und innere Unruhen**
De
En riot and civil commotion
Es revueltas y conmociones
  civiles
Fr émeutes et désordres
It rivolte e moti civili
Pt motins e perturbações civis

**aufschieben** vb De
En hold over
Es aplazar; diferir
Fr différer
It differire
Pt conservar; adiar

**aufschiebende Bedingung** (f)
De
En condition precedent
Es previa condición (f)
Fr condition suspensive (f)
It condizione sospensiva (f)
Pt condição prévia (f)

**Aufschlag** (m) n De
En addition
Es adición (f)
Fr addition (f)
It addizione (f)
Pt adição (f)

**Aufseher** (m) n De
En supervisor
Es supervisor (m)
Fr surveillant (m)
It supervisore (m)
Pt supervisor (m)

**Aufsicht** (f) n De
En control
Es control (m)
Fr contrôle (m)
It controllo (m)
Pt controlo (m)

**Aufsichtsbeamte(r)** (m) n De
En inspector
Es inspector (m)
Fr inspecteur; vérificateur (m)
It ispettore (m)
Pt inspector (m)

**aufsparen** vb De
En save
Es ahorrar; economizar
Fr épargner; économiser
It risparmiare; economizzare
Pt poupar; economizar

**Auftrag durch die Post** (m) De
En mail order
Es pedido por correo (m)
Fr commande par lettre (f)
It ordine per corrispondenza
  (f)
Pt venda pelo correio (f)

**Auftragsbuch** (n) n De
En order book
Es libro de pedidos (m)
Fr livre de commandes (m)
It libro degli ordini (m)
Pt livro de encomendas (m)

**auf Treu und Glauben** De
En in good faith
Es de buena fé
Fr de bonne foi
It in buona fede
Pt de boa fé

**auf Verlangen** De
En on demand
Es a vista
Fr sur demande
It a vista
Pt à vista; sob demanda

**Aufwendungsposten** (f pl) n
De
En items of expenditure
Es artículos de gasto (m pl)
Fr postes de dépense (m pl)
It articoli di spesa (m pl)
Pt itens de despesa (m pl)

**Aufwertung** (f) n De
En revaluation
Es revalorización (f)
Fr revalorisation (f)
It rivalutazione (f)
Pt revalorização (f)

**Aufzug** (m) n De
En lift
Am elevator
Es ascensor (m)
Fr ascenseur (m)
It ascensore (m)
Pt ascensor (m)

**augmentation** (f) n Fr
De Zugang (m)
En accrual
Es incremento (m)
It incremento (m)
Pt acréscimo (m)

**augmentation de capital** (f) Fr
De Kapitalerhöhung (f)
En increase of capital
Es aumento de capital (m)
It aumento di capitale (m)
Pt aumento de capital (m)

**augmenter** vb Fr
De steigen; zunehmen
En increase; rise
Es aumentar; encarecer
It aumentare; crescere
Pt aumentar

**au jour le jour** Fr
De täglich
En day-to-day
Es día a día
It di giorno in giorno
Pt dia a dia

**aumentar** vb Es, Pt
De steigen; zunehmen
En increase; rise
Fr augmenter; hausser
It aumentare; crescere

**aumentare** vb It
De steigen; zunehmen
En increase; rise
Es aumentar; alzar
Fr augmenter; hausser
Pt aumentar

**aumentare di prezzo** It
De teurer werden; steigen
En advance in price; go up
Es encarecer
Fr renchérir
Pt encarecer

**aumentato costo della vita**
(m) It
- De erhöhte Lebenshaltungskosten (pl)
- En increased cost of living
- Es coste de vida más alto (m)
- Fr renchérissement du coût de la vie (m)
- Pt custo de vida mais elevado (m)

**aumento** (m) n Es, It, Pt
- De Erhöhung; Zunahme (f)
- En increase; rise
- Fr hausse; accroissement (f)

**aumento de capital** (m) Es, Pt
- De Kapitalerhöhung (f)
- En increase of capital
- Fr augmentation de capital (f)
- It aumento di capitale (m)

**aumento di capitale** (m) It
- De Kapitalerhöhung (f)
- En increase of capital
- Es aumento de capital (m)
- Fr augmentation de capital (f)
- Pt aumento de capital (m)

**au pair** Fr
- De al Pari
- En at par
- Es al par
- It alla pari
- Pt ao par

**ausbeuten** vb De
- En exploit
- Es explotar
- Fr exploiter
- It sfruttare
- Pt explorar

**ausente** (m) n Es, Pt
- De Abwesende(r) (m)
- En absentee
- Fr manquant (m)
- It assente (m)

**ausentismo** (m) n Es
- De unerlaubte Abwesenheit (f)
- En absenteeism
- Fr absentéisme (m)
- It assenteismo (m)
- Pt absentismo (m)

**Ausfallbürgschaft** (f) n De
- En letter of indemnity
- Es carta de indemnización (f)
- Fr cautionnement (m)
- It lettera di garanzia (f)
- Pt documento de garantia (m)

**Ausfuhranreiz** (m) n De
- En export incentive
- Es estímulo de exportación (m)
- Fr motif d'exportation (m)
- It incentivo alla esportazione (m)
- Pt incentivo para a exportação (m)

**ausführen** vb De
- En export
- Es exportar
- Fr exporter
- It esportare
- Pt exportar

**Ausfuhrgenehmigung** (f) n De
- En export permit
- Es permiso de exportación (m)
- Fr autorisation d'exporter (f)
- It permesso d'esportazione (m)
- Pt licença de exportação (f)

**Ausfuhrprämie** (f) n De
- En export bonus
- Es subsidio a las exportaciones (m)
- Fr prime à l'exportation (f)
- It premio d'esportazione (m)
- Pt subsídio de exportação (m)

**Ausführsonderrabatt** (m) n De
- En export rebate
- Es descuento por exportación (m)
- Fr remise sur les exports (f)
- It sconto d'esportazione (m)
- Pt desconto de exportação (m)

**Ausfuhrverkäufe** (m pl) n De
- En export sales
- Es ventas de exportación (f pl)
- Fr ventes d'exportation (f pl)
- It vendite per esportazione (f pl)
- Pt vendas de exportação (f pl)

**Ausgabedruck** (m) n De
- En computer printout
- Es impresión (f)
- Fr sortie sur imprimante (f)
- It stampato d'uscita dell'elaboratore (m)
- Pt informe impresso pelo computador (m)

**Ausgabe junger Aktien** (f) De
- En new issue
- Es nueva emisión (f)
- Fr émission d'actions nouvelles (f)
- It nuova emissione (f)
- Pt emissão nova (f)

**Ausgaben** (f pl) n De
- En expenditure
- Es desembolso (m)
- Fr frais (m pl)
- It spesa (f)
- Pt despesas (f pl)

**Ausgaben- und Ertragskonto**
(n) De
- En income and expenditure account
- Es cuenta de ingresos y gastos (f)
- Fr compte de revenus et dépenses (m)
- It conto proventi e spese (m)
- Pt conta de receitas e despesas (f)

**ausgeben** vb De
- En issue
- Es emitir
- Fr émettre
- It emettere
- Pt emitir

**ausgegebenes Kapital** (n) De
- En issued capital
- Es capital emitido (m)
- Fr capital versé (m)
- It capitale emesso (m)
- Pt capital emitido (m)

**Ausgleich** (m) n De
- En settlement
- Es satisfacción (f)
- Fr règlement (m)
- It regolamento (m)
- Pt satisfação (f)

**ausgleichen (eine Rechnung)**
De
En balance an account
Es saldar una cuenta
Fr balancer un compte
It pareggiare un conto
Pt equilibrar uma conta

**Ausgleichsfonds** (m) n De
En equalization fund
Es fondo de compensación (m)
Fr fonds de régularisation (m)
It cassa di compensazione (f)
Pt fundo de compensação (m)

**Ausgleichsposten** (m pl) n De
En balancing items
Es asientos saldados (m pl)
Fr postes rééquilibrants (m pl)
It voci di pareggio (f pl)
Pt valores de equilíbrio (m pl)

**Ausgleichssaldo** (m) n De
En balance due
Es balance vencido (m)
Fr solde dû (m)
It saldo dovuto (m)
Pt saldo em dívida (m)

**Auskunft** (f) n De
En information
Es información (f)
Fr information; renseignement (f m)
It informazione (f)
Pt informação (f)

**Ausländer** (m) n De
En foreigner
Es extranjero (m)
Fr étranger (m)
It straniero (m)
Pt estrangeiro (m)

**ausländisch** adj De
En foreign; alien
Es extranjero
Fr étranger
It straniero; estero
Pt estrangeiro

**Auslandsanleihe** (f) n De
En external loan
Es préstamo exterior (m)
Fr emprunt extérieur (m)
It prestito esterno (m)
Pt empréstimo externo (m)

**Auslandskonto** (n) n De
En external account
Am foreign currency account
Es cuenta exterior (f)
Fr compte transférable (m)
It conto estero (m)
Pt conta externa (f)

**Auslandswechsel** (m) n De
En foreign bill
Es letra sobre el exterior (f)
Fr lettre de change sur l'étranger (f)
It cambiale sull' estero (f)
Pt letra de país a país (cambial) (f)

**Auslassung** (f) n De
En omission
Es omisión (f)
Fr omission (f)
It omissione (f)
Pt omissão (f)

**Auslegung** (f) n De
En interpretation
Es interpretación (f)
Fr interprétation (f)
It interpretazione (f)
Pt interpretação (f)

**Ausrüstung** (f) n De
En equipment
Es equipo (m)
Fr équipement (m)
It equipaggiamento (m)
Pt equipamento (m)

**ausschliessen** vb De
En exclude
Es excluir
Fr exclure
It escludere
Pt excluir

**ausschliesslicher Markt** (m) De
En exclusive market
Es mercado exclusivo (m)
Fr marché exclusif (m)
It mercato esclusivo (m)
Pt mercado exclusivo (m)

**Ausschluss** (m) n De
En exclusion
Es exclusión (f)
Fr exclusion (f)

It esclusione (f)
Pt exclusão (f)

**Aussenhafen** (m) n De
En outer harbour
Es antepuerto (m)
Fr avant-port (m)
It avamporto (m)
Pt anteporto (m)

**Aussenhandel** (m) n De
En foreign trade
Es comercio exterior (m)
Fr commerce extérieur (m)
It commercio estero (m)
Pt comércio externo (m)

**Aussenhandelsdefizit** (n) n De
En trade gap
Es vacío comercial (m)
Fr déficit du commerce extérieur (m)
It disavanzo della bilancia commerciale (m)
Pt vazio comercial (m)

**ausserordentliche Generalversammlung** (f) De
En extraordinary general meeting
Es asamblea general extraordinaria (f)
Fr assemblée générale extraordinaire (f)
It assemblea generale straordinaria (f)
Pt assembleia geral extraordinária (f)

**ausser Steuer** De
En excluding tax
Es impuesto no incluido
Fr hors taxe (HT)
It tassa esclusa
Pt impostos excluidos

**äusserst guter Glaube** (m) De
En utmost good faith
Es máxima buena fé (f)
Fr plus grande bonne foie (f)
It massima buona fede (f)
Pt máxima boa-fé (f)

**Aussperrung** (f) n De
En lock-out
Es cierre (m)
Fr lock-out (m)

It   serrata *(f)*
Pt   lockout *(m)*

**ausstatten** *vb* De
En   equip; endow
Es   equipar; dotar
Fr   équiper; doter
It   equipaggiare; dotare
Pt   equipar; dotar

**ausstehende Schulden** *(m pl)*
   De
En   outstanding accounts
Es   cuentas pendientes *(f pl)*
Fr   comptes à percevoir *(m pl)*
It   conti aperti *(m pl)*
Pt   contas por saldar *(f pl)*

**Aussteller** *(m)* *n* De
En   drawer; exhibitor
Es   librador; exhibidor *(m)*
Fr   tireur; exposant *(m)*
It   traente; espositore *(m)*
Pt   sacador; expositor *(m)*

**Ausstellung** *(f)* *n* De
En   exhibition
Es   exposicion *(f)*
Fr   exposition *(f)*
It   esposizione *(f)*
Pt   exposicão *(f)*

**ausverkauft** *adj* De
En   sold out; out of stock
Es   agotado
Fr   tout vendu
It   tutto venduto; esaurito
Pt   esgotado

**Auszahlung** *(f)* *n* De
En   disbursement
Es   desembolso *(m)*
Fr   déboursement *(m)*
It   esborso *(m)*
Pt   desembolso *(m)*

**aus zweiter Hand** De
En   second-hand
Es   de segunda mano
Fr   d'occasion
It   di seconda mano
Pt   de segunda mão

**authority** *n* En
De   Vollmacht *(f)*
Es   autoridad *(f)*
Fr   mandat *(m)*

It   autorità *(f)*
Pt   autoridade *(f)*

**authorized capital** En
De   genehmigtes Kapital *(n)*
Es   capital autorizado *(m)*
Fr   capital autorisé *(m)*
It   capitale autorizzato *(m)*
Pt   capital autorizado *(m)*

**auto** *(m)* *n* Es
De   Vorladung *(f)*
En   writ
Fr   assignation *(f)*
It   citazione *(f)*
Pt   citação; ordem *(f m)*

**Auto** *(n)* *n* De
En   car
Es   coche *(m)*
Fr   voiture; automobile *(f)*
It   automobile; macchina *(f)*
Pt   carro; automóvel *(m)*

**auto-servicio** *(m)* *n* Es
De   Selbstbedienung *(f)*
En   self-service
Fr   libre service *(m)*
It   servirsi da sè *(m)*
Pt   self-service *(m)*

**automation** *n* En, Fr *(f)*
De   Automation *(f)*
Es   automatización *(f)*
It   automazione *(f)*
Pt   automatização *(m)*

**Automation** *(f)* *n* De
En   automation
Es   automatización *(f)*
Fr   automation *(f)*
It   automazione *(f)*
Pt   automatização *(m)*

**automatisch sich erneuendes**
   **Akkreditiv** *(n)* De
En   revolving credit
Es   crédito reponible *(m)*
Fr   accréditif automatiquement
   renouvelable *(m)*
It   credito rotativo *(m)*
Pt   crédito renovável *(m)*

**automatização** *(m)* *n* Pt
De   Automation *(f)*
En   automation
Es   automatización *(f)*

Fr   automation *(f)*
It   automazione *(f)*

**automatización** *(f)* *n* Es
De   Automation *(f)*
En   automation
Fr   automation *(f)*
It   automazione *(f)*
Pt   automatização *(m)*

**automazione** *(f)* *n* It
De   Automation *(f)*
En   automation
Es   automatización *(f)*
Fr   automation *(f)*
Pt   automatização *(m)*

**automobile** *(f)* *n* It
De   Auto; Wagen *(n m)*
En   car
Es   coche *(m)*
Fr   voiture; automobile *(f)*
Pt   carro; automóvel *(m)*

**autoridad** *(f)* *n* Es
De   Vollmacht *(f)*
En   authority
Fr   mandat *(m)*
It   autorità *(f)*
Pt   autoridade *(f)*

**autoridade** *(f)* *n* Pt
De   Vollmacht *(f)*
En   authority
Es   autoridad *(f)*
Fr   mandat *(m)*
It   autorità *(f)*

**autorimessa** *(f)* *n* It
De   Garage *(f)*
En   garage
Es   garaje *(m)*
Fr   garage *(m)*
Pt   garagem *(f)*

**autorità** *(f)* *n* It
De   Vollmacht *(f)*
En   authority
Es   autoridad *(f)*
Fr   mandat *(m)*
Pt   autoridade *(f)*

**autorização** *(f)* *n* Pt
De   Erlaubnis; Erlaubnisschein
   *(f m)*
En   permit
Es   permiso *(m)*

Fr permis (m)
It permesso (m)

**autorizar caução** Pt
De gegen Haftkaution freige-
ben
En grant bail
Es conceder fianza
Fr admettre une caution
It concedere la libertà provvi-
soria su cauzione

**autorisation d'exporter** (f) Fr
De Ausfuhrgenehmigung (f)
En export permit
Es permiso de exportación (m)
It permesso d'esportazione
(m)
Pt licença de exportação (f)

**available** adj En
De verfügbar
Es disponible
Fr disponible
It disponibile
Pt disponível

**avalar** vb Es
De gegenzeichnen
En back
Fr avaliser
It avallare
Pt avalizar

**avaliação** (f) n Pt
De Abschätzung; Wertbestim-
mung (f)
En appraisal; valuation
Es valuación; evaluación (f)
Fr évaluation (f)
It valutazione (f)

**avaliação aproximada** (f) Pt
De rohe Schätzung (f)
En rough estimate
Es presupuesto aproximado
(m)
Fr estimation approximative (f)
It valutazione approssimativa
(f)

**avaliação cautelosa** (f) Pt
De vorsichtige Schätzung (f)
En conservative estimate
Es presupuesto prudente (m)
Fr évaluation prudente (f)
It valutazione prudente (f)

**avaliação de tarefa** (f) Pt
De Arbeitsbewertung (f)
En job evaluation
Es valoracion del trabajo (f)
Fr évaluation du travail (f)
It valutazione del lavoro (f)

**avaliação excessiva** (f) Pt
De Überschätzung (f)
En over-estimate
Es presupuesto por exceso (m)
Fr surestimation (f)
It valutazione eccessiva (f)

**avaliação insuficiente** (f) Pt
De Unterschätzung (f)
En under-estimate
Es presupuesto por defecto
(m)
Fr sous-estimation (f)
It sottovalutazione (f)

**avaliador** (m) n Pt
De Schätzer (m)
En assessor
Es asesor (m)
Fr appréciateur (m)
It agente delle imposte (m)

**avaliar** vb Pt
De einschätzen; bewerten
En estimate; evaluate
Es estimar; evaluar
Fr estimer; évaluer
It stimare; valutare

**avaliar os danos** Pt
De den Schadenersatzbetrag
feststellen
En assess damages
Es evaluar daños
Fr fixer des dommages-intér-
êts
It valutare i danni

**avaliser** vb Fr
De gegenzeichnen
En back
Es avalar
It avallare
Pt avalizar

**avalista** (m) n Es, Pt
De Gegenzeichner (m)
En backer
Fr avaliste (m)
It avallante (m)

**avaliste** (m) n Fr
De Gegenzeichner (m)
En backer
Es avalista (m)
It avallante (m)
Pt avalista (m)

**avalizar** vb Pt
De gegenzeichnen
En back
Es avalar
Fr avaliser
It avallare

**avallante** (m) n It
De Gegenzeichner (m)
En backer
Es avalista (m)
Fr avaliste (m)
Pt avalista (m)

**avallare** vb It
De gegenzeichnen
En back
Es avalar
Fr avaliser
Pt avalizar

**à valoir** Fr
De a conto; auf Abschlag
En on account
Es a cuenta
It in acconto
Pt por conta

**avamporto** (m) n It
De Aussenhafen (m)
En outer harbour
Es antepuerto (m)
Fr avant-port (m)
Pt anteporto (m)

**avance** (f) n Fr
De Vorschuss (m)
En advance
Am prepayment
Es adelanto (m)
It anticipazione (f)
Pt adiantamento (m)

**avancement** (m) n Fr
De Beförderung (f)
En promotion
Es ascenso; promoción (m f)
It avanzamento; promozione
(m f)
Pt promoção (f)

**avancer** (de l'argent) *vb* Fr
De vorschiessen
En advance
Am prepay
Es anticipar
It anticipare
Pt adiantar

**avantages accessoires** (*m pl*)
    Fr
De Sozialleistungen (*f pl*)
En fringe benefits
Es beneficios suplementarios
    (*m pl*)
It vantaggi accessori (*m pl*)
Pt benefícios extras (*m pl*)

**avant-hier** *adv* Fr
De vorgestern
En day before yesterday
Es anteayer
It avantieri
Pt anteontem

**avantieri** *adv* It
De vorgestern
En day before yesterday
Es anteayer
Fr avant-hier
Pt anteontem

**avant-port** (*m*) *n* Fr
De Aussenhafen (*m*)
En outer harbour
Es antepuerto (*m*)
It avamporto (*m*)
Pt anteporto (*m*)

**avanzamento** (*m*) *n* It
De Beförderung (*f*)
En promotion
Es ascenso; promoción (*m f*)
Fr avancement; promotion (*m
    f*)
Pt promoção (*f*)

**avaria** (*f*) *n* It, Pt
De Havarie (*f*)
En average (marine insurance)
Es avería (*f*)
Fr avarie (*f*)

**avaria generale** (*f*) It
De grosse Havarie (*f*)
En general average (G.A.)
Es avería general (*f*)
Fr avaries communes (*f pl*)
Pt avaria grossa (*f*)

**avaria grossa** (*f*) Pt
De grosse Havarie (*f*)
En general average (G.A.)
Es avería general (*f*)
Fr avaries communes (*f pl*)
It avarie generale (*f*)

**avaria particolare** (*f*) It
De besondere Havarie (*f*)
En particular average
Es avería particular (*f*)
Fr avarie particulière (*f*)
Pt avaria particular (*f*)

**avaria particular** (*f*) Pt
De besondere Havarie (*f*)
En particular average
Es avería particular (*f*)
Fr avarie particulière (*f*)
It avaria particolare (*f*)

**avarie** (*f*) *n* Fr
De Havarie (*f*)
En average (marine insurance)
Es avería (*f*)
It avaria (*f*)
Pt avaria (*f*)

**avarié** *adj* Fr
De havariert
En with average (WA)
Es con avería
It con avaria
Pt com avaria

**avarie particulière** (*f*) Fr
De besondere Havarie (*f*)
En particular average
Es avería particular (*f*)
It avaria particolare (*f*)
Pt avaria particular (*f*)

**avaries communes** (*f pl*) Fr
De grosse Havarie (*f*)
En general average (G.A.)
Es avería general (*f*)
It avaria generale (*f*)
Pt avaria grossa (*f*)

**avaries de route** (*f pl*) Fr
De Beschädigung beim Transport (*f*)
En damage in transit
Es daños en ruta (*m pl*)
It danno durante trasporto (*m*)
Pt danos em trânsito (*m pl*)

**avec droit de recours** Fr
De mit Rückgriff
En with recourse
Es con recurso
It con ricorso
Pt com recurso

**average** *n* En
De Durchschnitt (*m*)
Es promedio (*m*)
Fr moyenne (*f*)
It media (*f*)
Pt média (*f*)

**average** (marine insurance) *n*
    En
De Havarie (*f*)
Es avería (*f*)
Fr avarie (*f*)
It avaria (*f*)
Pt avaria (*f*)

**average bond** En
De Havarieschein (*m*)
Es fianza de avería (*f*)
Fr compromis d'avarie (*m*)
It compromesso d'avaria (*m*)
Pt fiança de avaria (*f*)

**average cost** En
De Durchschnittskosten (*m pl*)
Es coste promedio (*m*)
Fr coût moyen (*m*)
It costo medio (*m*)
Pt custo médio (*m*)

**avería** (*f*) *n* Es
De Havarie (*f*)
En average (marine insurance)
Fr avarie (*f*)
It avaria (*f*)
Pt avaria (*f*)

**avería general** (*f*) Es
De grosse Havarie (*f*)
En general average (G.A.)
Fr avaries communes (*f pl*)
It avaria generale (*f*)
Pt avaria grossa (*f*)

**avería particular** (*f*) Es
De besondere Havarie (*f*)
En particular average
Fr avarie particulière (*f*)
It avaria particolare (*f*)
Pt avaria particular (*f*)

**avião a jacto** *(m)* Pt
De Düsenflugzeug *(n)*
En jet aircraft
Es avión jet *(m)*
Fr avion à réaction *(m)*
It aviogetto *(m)*

**aviogetto** *(m)* n It
De Düsenflugzeug *(n)*
En jet aircraft
Es avión jet *(m)*
Fr avion à réaction *(m)*
Pt avião a jacto *(m)*

**avion à réaction** *(m)* Fr
De Düsenflugzeug *(n)*
En jet aircraft
Es avión jet *(m)*
It aviogetto *(m)*
Pt avião a jacto *(m)*

**avión jet** *(m)* Es
De Düsenflugzeug *(n)*
En jet aircraft
Fr avion à réaction *(m)*
It aviogetto *(m)*
Pt avião a jacto *(m)*

**avis** *(m)* n Fr
De Benachrichtung *(f)*
En notice
Es aviso *(m)*
It avviso; preavviso *(m)*
Pt aviso *(m)*

**avis d'attribution** *(m)* Fr
De Verteilungsbrief *(m)*
En allotment letter
Es letra de adjudicación *(f)*
It lettera da ripartizione *(f)*
Pt aviso de aporcionamento *(m)*

**avis de crédit** *(m)* Fr
De Gutschriftanzeige *(f)*
En credit note
Es nota de crédito *(f)*
It nota di credito *(f)*
Pt aviso de crédito *(m)*

**avis de débit** *(m)* Fr
De Lastschrift *(f)*
En debit note
Es nota de débito *(f)*
It nota di addebito *(f)*
Pt aviso de débito *(m)*

**aviso** *(m)* n Es, Pt
De Anzeige; Benachrichtigung *(f)*
En advice note; notice
Fr avis; lettre d'avis *(m f)*
It avviso; lettera d'avviso *(m f)*

**aviso de aporcionamento** *(m)* Pt
De Verteilungsbrief *(m)*
En allotment letter
Es letra de adjudicación *(f)*
Fr avis d'attribution *(m)*
It lettera da ripartizione *(f)*

**aviso de crédito** *(m)* Pt
De Gutschriftanzeige *(f)*
En credit note
Es nota de crédito *(f)*
Fr avis de crédit *(m)*
It nota di credito *(f)*

**aviso de débito** *(m)* Pt
De Lastschrift *(f)*
En debit note
Es nota de débito *(f)*
Fr avis de débit *(m)*
It nota di addebito *(f)*

**aviso de despacho** *(m)* Pt
De Versandschein *(m)*
En despatch note
Es aviso de expedición *(m)*
Fr bordereau d'expédition; bulletin d'envoi *(m)*
It bollettino di spedizione *(m)*

**aviso de entrega** *(m)* Es
De Lieferschein *(m)*
En delivery note
Fr bordereau de livraison *(m)*
It nota di consegna *(f)*
Pt guia de entrega *(f)*

**aviso de expedición** *(m)* Es
De Versandschein *(m)*
En despatch note
Fr bordereau d'expédition; bulletin d'envoi *(m)*
It bollettino di spedizione *(m)*
Pt aviso de despacho *(m)*

**aviso de recepção** *(m)* Pt
De Empfangsbestätigung *(f)*
En acknowledgment of receipt
Es aviso de recepción *(m)*

Fr accusé de réception *(m)*
It avviso di recezione *(m)*

**aviso de recepción** *(m)* Es
De Empfangsbestätigung *(f)*
En acknowledgment of receipt
Fr accusé de réception *(m)*
It avviso di recezione *(m)*
Pt aviso de recepção *(m)*

**aviso de seguro del riesgo** *(m)* Es
De Deckungszusage *(f)*
En cover note
Fr lettre de couverture *(f)*
It nota di copertura *(f)*
Pt nota de cobertura *(f)*

**aviso oficial** *(m)* Es
De Inverzugsetzung *(f)*
En formal notice
Fr mise en demeure *(f)*
It intimazione *(f)*
Pt notificação formal *(f)*

**a vista** It
De bei Sicht
En at sight
Es a la vista
Fr à vue
Pt à vista

**à vista** Pt
De bei Sicht
En at sight
Es a la vista
Fr à vue
It a vista

**avocat** *(m)* n Fr
De Anwalt *(m)*
En lawyer; barrister; counsel
Am attorney
Es abogado *(m)*
It avvocato *(m)*
Pt advogado *(m)*

**à vue** Fr
De bei Sicht
En at sight
Es a la vista
It a vista
Pt à vista

**avviamento** *(m)* n It
De Geschäftswert *(m)*
En goodwill
Es valor de la clientela *(m)*

avviso                                                                62

Fr  bon vouloir *(m)*
Pt  boa vontade *(f)*

**avviso** *(m) n* It
De  Benachrichtung *(f)*
En  notice
Es  aviso *(m)*
Fr  avis; préavis *(m)*
Pt  aviso *(m)*

**avviso di recezione** *(m)* It
De  Empfangsbestätigung *(f)*
En  acknowledgment of receipt
Es  aviso de recepción *(m)*
Fr  accusé de réception *(m)*
Pt  aviso de recepção *(m)*

**avvocato** *(m) n* It
De  Anwalt *(m)*
En  lawyer; barrister; counsel
Am  attorney
Es  abogado *(m)*
Fr  avocat *(m)*
Pt  advogado *(m)*

**award damages** En
De  Schadenersatz zugestehen
Es  conceder daños
Fr  adjuger des dommages-intérêts
It  concedere i danni
Pt  conceder compensação

**ayer** *adv* Es
De  gestern
En  yesterday
Fr  hier
It  ieri
Pt  ontem

**ayuda** *(f) n* Es
De  Hilfe *(f)*
En  help
Fr  secours *(m)*
It  ainto *(m)*
Pt  ajuda *(f)*

**azar** *(m) n* Es
De  Wagnis *(n)*
En  hazard
Fr  hasard; risque *(m)*
It  rischio *(m)*
Pt  risco; azar *(m)*

**azione** *(f) n* It
De  Aktie *(f)*
En  share
Es  acción *(f)*

Fr  action *(f)*
Pt  acção *(f)*

**azione ordinaria** *(f)* It
De  Stammaktie *(f)*
En  ordinary share
Es  acción ordinaria *(f)*
Fr  action ordinaire *(f)*
Pt  acção ordinária *(f)*

**azione privilegiata** *(f)* It
De  Vorzugsaktie *(f)*
En  preference share
Es  acción preferente *(f)*
Fr  action privilégiée *(f)*
Pt  acção preferencial *(f)*

**azioni aurifere** *(f pl)* It
De  Aktien von Goldbergwerken *(f pl)*
En  gold shares
Es  acciones auríferas *(f pl)*
Fr  valeurs aurifères *(f pl)*
Pt  acções de ouro *(f pl)*

**azioni con diritto a voto** *(f pl)* It
De  stimmberechtigte Aktien *(f pl)*
En  voting shares
Es  acciones con derecho de voto *(f pl)*
Fr  actions avec droit de vote *(f pl)*
Pt  acçoes com direito a voto *(f pl)*

**azioni del fondatore** *(f pl)* It
De  Gründeraktien *(f pl)*
En  founder's shares
Es  acciones del fundador *(f pl)*
Fr  actions de fondateur *(f pl)*
Pt  acções de fundador *(f pl)*

**azioni di godimento** *(f pl)* It
De  Gratisaktien *(f pl)*
En  bonus shares
Am  stock dividend
Es  acciones dadas como primas *(f pl)*
Fr  actions d'attribution *(f pl)*
Pt  acções de prémio *(f pl)*

**azioni postergate** *(f pl)* It
De  Nachzugsaktien *(f pl)*
En  deferred shares
Es  acciones aplazadas *(f pl)*

Fr  actions différées *(f pl)*
Pt  acções diferidas *(f pl)*

**azioni preferenziali cumulative** *(f pl)* It
De  kumulative Vorzugsaktien *(f pl)*
En  cumulative preference shares
Es  valores privilegiados cumulativos *(m pl)*
Fr  actions de priorité cumulatives *(f pl)*
Pt  acções preferenciais cumulativas *(f pl)*

**azioni preferenziali redimibili** *(f pl)* It
De  ablösbare Vorzugsaktien *(f pl)*
En  redeemable preference shares
Es  acciónes preferentes amortizables *(f pl)*
Fr  actions privilégiées amortissables *(f pl)*
Pt  acções redimíveis preferenciais *(f pl)*

**azioni senza diritto a voto** *(f pl)* It
De  Aktien ohne Stimmrecht *(f pl)*
En  non-voting shares
Es  acciones sin derecho de voto *(f pl)*
Fr  actions sans droit de vote *(f pl)*
Pt  acçoes sem direito a voto *(f pl)*

**azionista** *(m) n* It
De  Aktionär *(m)*
En  shareholder
Am  stockholder
Es  accionista *(m)*
Fr  actionnaire *(m)*
Pt  accionista *(m)*

**B**

**bac** *(m) n* Fr
De  Fährboot *(n)*
En  ferry-boat
Es  transbordador *(m)*

It   nave traghetto (f)
Pt   barco de travessia (m)

**bacino carbonifero** (m) It
De   Kohlenrevier (n)
En   coal field
Es   yacimiento de carbón (m)
Fr   bassin houiller (m)
Pt   jazigo de carvão (m)

**bacino di carenaggio** (m) It
De   Trockendock (n)
En   dry dock
Es   dique seco (m)
Fr   cale sèche (f)
Pt   doca-seca (f)

**bacino di raddobbo** (m) It
De   Trockendock (n)
En   graving dock
Es   dique de carenas (m)
Fr   bassin de radoub (m)
Pt   doca de querenas (f)

**back** vb En
De   gegenzeichnen
Es   avalar
Fr   avaliser
It   avallare
Pt   avalizar

**backer** n En
De   Gegenzeichner (m)
Es   avalista (m)
Fr   avaliste (m)
It   avallante (m)
Pt   avalista (m)

**back pay** En
De   Lohnnachzahlung (f)
Es   pago atrasado (m)
Fr   rappel de traitement (m)
It   arretrati di paga (m pl)
Pt   vencimento atrasado (m)

**backwardation** n En
De   Kursabschlag (m)
Es   prima de aplazamiento (f)
Fr   déport (m)
It   deporto (m)
Pt   juro de mora (m)

**bad debt** En
De   uneinbringliche Schuld (f)
Es   deuda incobrable (f)
Fr   créance irrécouvrable (f)
It   credito inesigibile (m)
Pt   dívida incobrável (f)

**bad debt reserve** En
De   Dubiosenreserve (f)
Es   reserva para deudas inco-
     brables (f)
Fr   provision pour créances
     douteuses (f)
It   riserva per crediti inesigibili
     (f)
Pt   reserva para dividas inco-
     bráveis (f)

**bagagem de mão** (f) Pt
De   Handgepäck (n)
En   hand-luggage
Es   equipaje de mano (m)
Fr   bagages à main (m pl)
It   bagaglio a mano (m)

**bagages à main** (m pl) Fr
De   Handgepäck (n)
En   hand-luggage
Es   equipaje de mano (m)
It   bagaglio a mano (m)
Pt   bagagem de mão (f)

**bagagliaio** (m) n It
De   Packwagen (m)
En   guard's van
Es   furgón (m)
Fr   fourgon (m)
Pt   carruagem do guarda (f)

**bagaglio a mano** (m) It
De   Handgepäck (n)
En   hand-luggage
Es   equipaje de mano (m)
Fr   bagages à main (m pl)
Pt   bagagem de mão (f)

**bagaglio eccedente** (m) It
De   Ubergepäck (n)
En   excess luggage
Es   exceso de equipaje (m)
Fr   excédent de bagages (m)
Pt   excesso de bagagem (m)

**Bahnfrachtbrief** (m) n De
En   railway receipt
Es   recibo ferroviario (m)
Fr   bulletin de chargement (m)
It   ricevuta ferroviaria (f)
Pt   recibo ferroviário (m)

**bail** n En
De   Haftkaution (f)
Es   fianza (f)
Fr   caution (f)

It   cauzione (f)
Pt   caução (f)

**bail** (m) n Fr
De   Verpachtung (f)
En   lease
Es   alquiler (m)
It   affitto (m)
Pt   aluguer; arrendamento (m)

**bailee** n En
De   Gewahrsaminhaber (m)
Es   depositario (m)
Fr   dépositaire (m)
It   depositario (m)
Pt   caucionado (m)

**bailleur** (m) n Fr
De   Vermieter (m)
En   lessor
Es   arrendador (m)
It   locatore (m)
Pt   senhorio; arrendador (m)

**baisse** (f) n Fr
De   Sturz (m)
En   fall
Es   baja; caida (f)
It   caduta; ribasso (f; m)
Pt   baixa; gueda (f)

**Baissekonto** (n) n De
En   bear account
Es   cuenta de especulaciones
     a la baja (f)
Fr   compte des speculations à
     la baisse (m)
It   conto di speculazioni al
     ribasso (m)
Pt   conta de especulações
     baixistas (f)

**Baissemarkt** (m) n De
En   bear market
Es   mercado bajista (m)
Fr   marché orienté à la baisse
     (m)
It   mercato tendente al ri-
     basso (m)
Pt   mercado de tendência
     baixista (m)

**baisser** vb Fr
De   stürzen
En   fall
Es   caer; bajar
It   cadere; ribassare
Pt   cair; baixar

**Baissespekulant** (m) n De
En bear
Es bajista (m)
Fr baissier (m)
It ribassista (m)
Pt baixista (m)

**baissier** (m) n Fr
De Baissespekulant; Baissier (m)
En bear
Es bajista (m)
It ribassista (m)
Pt baixista (m)

**baixa** (f) n Pt
De Sturz (m)
En fall
Es baja; caida (f)
Fr baisse; chute (f)
It caduta; ribasso (f; m)

**baixista** (m) n Pt
De Baissespekulant; Baissier (m)
En bear
Es bajista (m)
Fr baissier (m)
It ribassista (m)

**baixista** adj Pt
De flau
En bearish
Es bajista
Fr orienté à la baisse
It ribassista

**baixo-nível** adj Pt
De minderwertig
En low-grade
Es baja calidad
Fr de qualité inférieure
It di qualità inferiore

**baja** (f) n Es
De Sturz (m)
En fall
Fr baisse; chute (f)
It caduta; ribasso (f; m)
Pt baixa; gueda (f)

**baja calidad** Es
De minderwertig
En low-grade
Fr de qualité inférieure
It di qualità inferiore
Pt baixo-nível

**bajar de valor** Es
De nachlassen
En fall off
Fr ralentir; baisser de valeur
It diminuire
Pt diminuir; decrescer

**bajista** (m) n Es
De Baissespekulant; Baissier (m)
En bear
Fr baissier (m)
It ribassista (m)
Pt baixista (m)

**bajista** adj Es
De flau
En bearish
Fr orienté à la baisse
It ribassista
Pt baixista

**balança** (f) n Pt
De Waage (f)
En scales
Es balanza (f)
Fr balance (f)
It bilancia (f)

**balança comercial** (f) Pt
De Handelsbilanz (f)
En trade balance
Es balanza comercial (f)
Fr balance commerciale (f)
It bilancia commerciale (f)

**balança de pagamentos** (f) Pt
De Zahlungsbilanz (f)
En balance of payments
Es balanza de pagos (f)
Fr balance des paiements (f)
It bilancia dei pagamenti (f)

**balance** n En
De Saldo (m)
Es balance; saldo (m)
Fr balance; solde (f m)
It bilancio; saldo (m)
Pt saldo (m)

**balance** (m) n Es
De Saldo; Bilanz (f)
En balance; balance sheet
Fr balance; solde; bilan (f m m)
It bilancio; saldo (m)
Pt saldo; balancete (m)

**balance** (f) n Fr
De Saldo; Waage (m f)
En balance; scales
Es balance; saldo; balanza (m m f)
It bilancio; saldo; bilancia (m m f)
Pt saldo; balança (m f)

**balance a budget** En
De einen Haushaltsplan ins Gleichgewicht bringen
Es balancear el presupuesto
Fr équilibrer un budget
It pareggiare un bilancio
Pt equilibrar um orçamento

**balance a cuenta nueva** (m) Es
De Übertrag (m)
En balance brought down
Am balance carried forward
Fr solde à reporter (m)
It bilancio riportato (m)
Pt saldo transportado (m)

**balance an account** En
De eine Rechnung ausgleichen
Es saldar una cuenta
Fr balancer un compte
It pareggiare un conto
Pt equilibrar uma conta

**balance anual** (m) Es
De Jahresabschluss (m)
En annual accounts
Fr bilan annuel (m)
It bilancio annuale (m)
Pt balancete anual (m)

**balancear el presupuesto** Es
De einen Haushaltsplan ins Gleichgewicht bringen
En balance a budget
Fr équilibrer un budget
It pareggiare un bilancio
Pt equilibrar um orçamento

**balance brought down** En
Am balance carried forward
De Übertrag (m)
Es balance a cuenta nueva (m)
Fr solde à reporter (m)
It bilancio riportato (m)
Pt saldo transportado (m)

**balance carried forward** En
De Saldovortrag *(m)*
Es saldo de entrada *(m)*
Fr report à nouveau *(m)*
It saldo da riportare *(m)*
Pt saldo transportado *(m)*

**balance commerciale** *(f)* Fr
De Handelsbilanz *(f)*
En trade balance
Es balanza comercial *(f)*
It bilancia commerciale *(f)*
Pt balança comercial *(f)*

**balance de comprobación de saldos** *(m)* Es
De Probebilanz *(f)*
En trial balance
Fr bilan de vérification *(m)*
It bilancio di verifica *(m)*
Pt balancete de verificação *(m)*

**balance déficitaire** *(f)* Fr
De Passivsaldo *(m)*
En adverse balance
Am negative balance
Es saldo adverso *(m)*
It saldo passivo *(m)*
Pt saldo negativo *(m)*

**balance des paiements** *(f)* Fr
De Zahlungsbilanz *(f)*
En balance of payments
Es balanza de pagos *(m)*
It bilancia dei pagamenti *(f)*
Pt balança de pagamentos *(f)*

**balance due** En
De Ausgleichssaldo *(m)*
Es balance vencido *(m)*
Fr solde dû *(m)*
It saldo dovuto *(m)*
Pt saldo em dívida *(m)*

**balance excédentaire** *(f)* Fr
De Aktivsaldo *(m)*
En active balance
Es saldo acreedor *(m)*
It saldo attivo *(m)*
Pt saldo credor *(m)*

**balance in hand** En
De verfügbarer Saldo *(m)*
Es sobrante *(m)*
Fr solde en caisse *(m)*
It saldo in cassa *(m)*
Pt saldo em poder *(m)*

**balance of payments** En
De Zahlungsbilanz *(f)*
Es balanza de pagos *(f)*
Fr balance des paiements *(f)*
It bilancia dei pagamenti *(f)*
Pt balança de pagamentos *(f)*

**balance of trade** En
De Handelsbilanz *(f)*
Es balanza comercial *(f)*
Fr balance commerciale *(f)*
It bilancia commerciale *(f)*
Pt balança comercial *(f)*

**balancer un compte** Fr
De eine Rechnung ausgleichen
En balance an account
Es saldar una cuenta
It pareggiare un conto
Pt equilibrar uma conta

**balance sheet** En
De Bilanz *(f)*
Es balance *(m)*
Fr bilan *(m)*
It bilancio *(m)*
Pt balancete *(m)*

**balancete** *(m)* n Pt
De Bilanz *(f)*
En balance sheet
Es balance *(m)*
Fr bilan *(m)*
It bilancio *(m)*

**balancete de verificação** *(m)* Pt
De Probebilanz *(f)*
En trial balance
Es balance de comprobación de saldos
Fr bilan de vérification *(m)*
It bilancio di verifica *(m)*

**balance vencido** *(m)* Es
De Ausgleichssaldo *(m)*
En balance due
Fr solde dû *(m)*
It saldo dovuto *(m)*
Pt saldo em dívida *(m)*

**balancing items** En
De Ausgleichsposten *(m pl)*
Es asientos saldados *(m pl)*
Fr postes rééquilibrants *(m pl)*
It voci di pareggio *(f pl)*
Pt valores de equilíbrio *(m pl)*

**balanço final** *(m)* Pt
De Schlussbilanz *(f)*
En final balance
Es saldo final *(m)*
Fr solde net *(m)*
It saldo finale *(m)*

**balanço fiscal** *(m)* Pt
De Besteuerung *(f)*
En assessment
Es evaluación *(f)*
Fr imposition *(f)*
It imposta *(f)*

**balanza** *(f)* n Es
De Waage *(f)*
En scales
Fr balance *(f)*
It bilancia *(f)*
Pt balança *(f)*

**balanza comercial** *(f)* Es
De Handelsbilanz *(f)*
En trade balance
Fr balance commerciale *(f)*
It bilancia commerciale *(f)*
Pt balança comercial *(f)*

**balanza de pagos** *(f)* Es
De Zahlungsbilanz *(f)*
En balance of payments
Fr balance des paiements *(f)*
It bilancia dei pagamenti *(f)*
Pt balança de pagamentos *(f)*

**ballast** (marine) n En
De Ballast *(m)*
Es lastre *(m)*
Fr lest *(m)*
It zavorra *(f)*
Pt lastro *(m)*

**Ballast** *(m)* n De
En ballast
Es lastre *(m)*
Fr lest *(m)*
It zavorra *(f)*
Pt lastro *(m)*

**banca** *(f)* n It
De Bank *(f)*
En bank
Es banco *(m)*
Fr banque *(f)*
Pt banco *(m)*

**banca agricola** *(f)* It
De Landbank *(f)*
En land bank
Es banco agrícola *(m)*
Fr banque agricole *(f)*
Pt banca d'agricultura *(f)*

**banca associata alla stanza di compensazione** *(f)* It
De Girobank *(f)*
En clearing bank
Es banco de compensación *(m)*
Fr banque de virement *(f)*
Pt banco de compensação e rateio *(m)*

**banca commerciale** *(f)* It
De Handelsbank *(f)*
En merchant bank
Es banco mercantil *(m)*
Fr banque commerciale *(f)*
Pt banco comercial *(m)*

**banca d'agricultura** *(f)* Pt
De Landbank *(f)*
En land bank
Es banco agrícola *(m)*
Fr banque agricole *(f)*
It banca agricola *(f)*

**banca di emissione** *(f)* It
De Notenbank *(f)*
En issuing bank
Es banco emisor *(m)*
Fr banque d'émission *(f)*
Pt banco emissor *(m)*

**banca d'investimenti** *(f)* It
De Finanzbank *(f)*
En investment bank
Es banco de inversiones *(m)*
Fr banque d'affaires *(f)*
Pt banco de investimentos *(m)*

**banca di prestiti** *(f)* It
De Kreditbank *(f)*
En lending bank
Es banco de préstamos *(m)*
Fr banque de prêts *(f)*
Pt banco de empréstimos *(m)*

**banca di sconto** *(f)* It
De Diskontbank *(f)*
En discount house
Es casa de descuentos *(f)*
Fr maison d'escompte *(f)*

Pt agência corretora de descontos *(f)*

**Banca Europea d'Investimenti** *(f)* It
De Europäische Investitionsbank *(f)*
En European Investment Bank
Es Banco Europeo de Inversiones *(m)*
Fr Banque Européenne d'Investissement *(f)*
Pt Banco Europeu de Investimentos *(m)*

**Banca Internazionale per la Ricostruzione e lo Sviluppo** *(f)* It
De Internationale Bank für Wiederaufbau und Wirtschaftsförderung *(f)*
En International Bank for Reconstruction and Development
Es Banco Internacional para Reconstrucción y Desarrollo *(m)*
Fr Banque Internationale pour la reconstruction et le développement *(f)*
Pt Banco Internacional de Reconstrução e Desenvolvimento *(m)*

**banca privata** *(f)* It
De Privatbank *(f)*
En private bank
Es banco privado *(m)*
Fr banque privée *(f)*
Pt banco privado *(m)*

**bancarotta** *(f)* n It
De Bankrott *(m)*
En bankruptcy
Es bancarrota *(f)*
Fr faillite *(f)*
Pt bancarrota *(f)*

**bancarrota** *(f)* n Es, Pt
De Bankrott *(m)*
En bankruptcy
Fr faillite *(f)*
It bancarotta *(f)*

**banca succursale** *(f)* It
De Filialbank; Zweigbank *(f)*
En branch bank
Es sucursal del banco *(f)*

Fr banque succursale *(f)*
Pt filial de banco *(f)*

**banchiere** *(m)* n It
De Bankier *(m)*
En banker
Es banquero *(m)*
Fr banquier *(m)*
Pt banqueiro *(m)*

**banchina** *(f)* n It
De Kai *(m)*
En quay
Am pier
Es muelle *(m)*
Fr quai *(m)*
Pt cais *(m)*

**banco** *(m)* n Es, Pt
De Bank *(f)*
En bank
Fr banque *(f)*
It banca *(f)*

**banco agrícola** *(m)* Es
De Landbank *(f)*
En land bank
Fr banque agricole *(f)*
It banca agricola *(f)*
Pt banca d'agricultura *(f)*

**banco comercial** *(m)* Pt
De Handelsbank *(f)*
En merchant bank
Es banco mercantil *(m)*
Fr banque commerciale *(f)*
It banca commerciale *(f)*

**banco de compensação e rateio** *(m)* Pt
De Girobank *(f)*
En clearing bank
Es banco de compensación *(m)*
Fr banque de virement *(f)*
It banca associata alla stanza di compensazione *(f)*

**banco de compensación** *(m)* Es
De Girobank *(f)*
En clearing bank
Fr banque de virement *(f)*
It banca associata alla stanza di compensazione *(f)*
Pt banco de compensação e rateio *(m)*

**banco de empréstimos** *(m)* Pt
De Kreditbank *(f)*
En lending bank
Es banco de préstamos *(m)*
Fr banque de prêts *(f)*
It banca di prestiti *(f)*

**banco de inversiones** *(m)* Es
De Finanzbank *(f)*
En investment bank
Fr banque d´affaires *(f)*
It banca d´investimenti *(f)*
Pt banco de investimentos *(m)*

**banco de investimentos** *(m)* Pt
De Finanzbank *(f)*
En investment bank
Es banco de inversiones *(m)*
Fr banque d´affaires *(f)*
It banca d´investimenti *(f)*

**banco de préstamos** *(m)* Es
De Kreditbank *(f)*
En lending bank
Fr banque de prêts *(f)*
It banca di prestiti *(f)*
Pt banco de empréstimos *(m)*

**banco emisor** *(m)* Es
De Notenbank *(f)*
En issuing bank
Fr banque d´émission *(f)*
It banca di emissione *(f)*
Pt banco emissor *(m)*

**banco emissor** *(m)* Pt
De Notenbank *(f)*
En issuing bank
Es banco emisor *(m)*
Fr banque d´émission *(f)*
It banca di emissione *(f)*

**Banco Europeo de Inversiones** *(m)* Es
De Europäische Investitionsbank *(f)*
En European Investment Bank
Fr Banque Européenne d´Investissement *(f)*
It Banca Europea d´Investimenti *(f)*
Pt Banco Europeu de Investimentos *(m)*

**Banco Europeu de Investimentos** *(m)* Pt

De Europäische Investitionsbank *(f)*
En European Investment Bank
Es Banco Europeo de Inversiones *(m)*
Fr Banque Européenne d´Investissement *(f)*
It Banca Europea d´Investimenti *(f)*

**banco fideicomisario** *(m)* Es
De Treuhandgesellschaft *(f)*
En trust company
Fr société fiduciaire *(f)*
It società fiduciaria *(f)*
Pt empresa de investimentos *(f)*

**Banco Internacional de Reconstrução e Desenvolvimento** *(m)* Pt
De Internationale Bank für Wiederaufbau und Wirtschaftsförderung *(f)*
En International Bank for Reconstruction and Development
Es Banco Internacional para Reconstrucción y Desarrollo *(m)*
Fr Banque Internationale pour la reconstruction et le développement *(f)*
It Banca Internazionale per la Ricostruzione e lo Sviluppo *(f)*

**Banco Internacional para Reconstrucción y Desarrollo** *(m)* Es
De Internationale Bank für Wiederaufbau und Wirtschaftsförderung *(f)*
En International Bank for Reconstruction and Development
Fr Banque Internationale pour la reconstruction et le développement *(f)*
It Banca Internazionale per la Ricostruzione e lo Sviluppo *(f)*
Pt Banco Internacional de Reconstrução e Desenvolvimento *(m)*

**banco mercantil** *(m)* Es
De Handelsbank *(f)*
En merchant bank
Fr banque commerciale *(f)*
It banca commerciale *(f)*
Pt banco comercial *(m)*

**banco privado** *(m)* Es, Pt
De Privatbank *(f)*
En private bank
Fr banque privée *(f)*
It banca privata *(f)*

**bandeira** *(f)* n Pt
De Flagge *(f)*
En flag
Es bandera *(f)*
Fr pavillon; drapeau *(m)*
It bandiera *(f)*

**bandeira de conveniência** *(f)* Pt
De billige Flagge *(f)*
En flag of convenience
Es bandera de conveniencia *(f)*
Fr enseigne de convenance *(f)*
It bandiera di convenienza *(f)*

**bandeja** *(f)* Es
De Palette *(f)*
En pallet
Fr palette *(f)*
It paletta *(f)*
Pt paleta *(f)*

**bande magnétique** *(f)* Fr
De Magnetband *(n)*
En magnetic tape
Es cinta magnética *(f)*
It nastro magnetico *(m)*
Pt fita magnética *(f)*

**bandera** *(f)* n Es
De Flagge *(f)*
En flag
Fr pavillon; drapeau *(m)*
It bandiera *(f)*
Pt bandeira *(f)*

**bandera de conveniencia** *(f)* Es
De billige Flagge *(f)*
En flag of convenience
Fr enseigne de convenance *(f)*
It bandiera di convenienza *(f)*
Pt bandeira de conveniência *(f)*

**bandiera** *(f)* n It
De Flagge *(f)*
En flag
Es bandera *(f)*
Fr pavillon; drapeau *(m)*
Pt bandeira *(f)*

**bandiera di convenienza** *(f)* It
De billige Flagge *(f)*
En flag of convenience
Es bandera de conveniencia *(f)*
Fr enseigne de convenance *(f)*
Pt bandeira de conveniência *(f)*

**bank** n En
De Bank *(f)*
Es banco *(m)*
Fr banque *(f)*
It banca *(f)*
Pt banco *(m)*

**bank** vb En
De einlegen
Es depositar (en el banco)
Fr déposer à banque
It depositare in una banca
Pt depositar (no banco)

**Bank** *(f)* n De
En bank
Es banco *(m)*
Fr banque *(f)*
It banca *(f)*
Pt banco *(m)*

**bankable bills** En
De diskontierbare Wechsel *(m pl)*
Es efectos negociables *(m pl)*
Fr papier bancable *(m)*
It effetti scontabili *(m pl)*
Pt valores transaccionáveis pelo banco *(m pl)*

**bank account** En
De Bankkonto *(n)*
Es cuenta bancaria *(f)*
Fr compte en banque *(m)*
It conto in banca *(m)*
Pt conta bancária *(f)*

**Bankauftrag** *(m)* De
En banker's order
Es orden bancaria *(f)*
Fr ordre bancaire *(m)*

It ordine bancario *(m)*
Pt ordem bancária *(f)*

**bank balance** En
De Bankguthaben *(n)*
Es saldo de banco *(m)*
Fr solde en banque *(m)*
It saldo in banca *(m)*
Pt saldo no banco *(m)*

**bankbook** n Am
En passbook
De Bankbuch; Sparbuch *(n)*
Es libreta de banco *(f)*
Fr carnet de compte *(m)*
It libretto di conto *(m)*
Pt livrete de conta *(f)*

**Bankbuch** *(n)* n De
En passbook
Am bankbook
Es libreta de banco *(f)*
Fr carnet de compte *(m)*
It libretto di conto *(m)*
Pt livrete de conta *(f)*

**bank charges** En
De Bankspesen *(f pl)*
Es gastos de banco *(m pl)*
Fr frais bancaires *(m pl)*
It spese di banca *(f pl)*
Pt taxas bancárias *(f pl)*

**bank crash** En
De Bankkrach *(m)*
Es quiebra de banco *(f)*
Fr krach d'une banque *(m)*
It crollo di banca *(m)*
Pt falência bancária *(f)*

**bank credit** En
De Bankkredit *(m)*
Es crédito bancario *(m)*
Fr crédit bancaire *(m)*
It credito bancario *(m)*
Pt crédito bancário *(m)*

**bank credit card** Am
En cheque card
De Scheckkarte *(f)*
Es tarjeta de cheque *(f)*
Fr carte de chèque *(f)*
It scheda per assegni *(f)*
Pt cartão de validação de cheques *(m)*

**Bankdarlehen** *(n)* n De
En bank loan
Es préstamo bancario *(m)*
Fr prêt bancaire *(m)*
It prestito bancario *(m)*
Pt empréstimo bancário *(m)*

**bank deposit** En
De Bankeinlage *(f)*
Es depósito bancario *(m)*
Fr dépôt bancaire *(m)*
It deposito bancario *(m)*
Pt depósito bancário *(m)*

**bank discount** En
De Diskont *(m)*
Es descuento bancario *(m)*
Fr escompte en dehors *(m)*
It sconto di banca *(m)*
Pt desconto bancário *(m)*

**Bankeinlage** *(f)* n De
En bank deposit
Es depósito bancario *(m)*
Fr dépôt bancaire *(m)*
It deposito bancario *(m)*
Pt depósito bancário *(m)*

**banker** n En
De Bankier *(m)*
Es banquero *(m)*
Fr banquier *(m)*
It banchiere *(m)*
Pt banqueiro *(m)*

**banker's draft** En
De Banktratte *(f)*
Es giro bancario *(m)*
Fr traite bancaire *(f)*
It tratta bancaria *(f)*
Pt letra de banco *(f)*

**banker's indemnity** En
Am banker's guarantee
De Bankgarantie *(f)*
Es garantía bancaria *(f)*
Fr garantie de banque *(f)*
It garanzia bancaria *(f)*
Pt garantia bancária *(f)*

**banker's order** En
De Bankauftrag *(m)*
Es orden bancaria *(f)*
Fr ordre bancaire *(m)*
It ordine bancario *(m)*
Pt ordem bancária *(f)*

**banker's reference** En
De Bankzeugnis (n)
Es referencia bancaria (f)
Fr référence de banquier (f)
It riferenza bancaria (f)
Pt referência bancária (f)

**Bankgarantie** (f) n De
En banker's indemnity
Am banker's guarantee
Es garantía bancaria (f)
Fr garantie de banque (f)
It garanzia bancaria (f)
Pt garantia bancária (f)

**Bankguthaben** (n) n De
En bank balance
Es saldo de banco (m)
Fr solde en banque (m)
It saldo in banca (m)
Pt saldo no banco (m)

**Bank Holiday** En
Am legal holiday
De gesetzlicher Feiertag (m)
Es día de fiesta (m)
Fr jour férié (m)
It festività legali (f)
Pt feriado (m)

**Bankier** (m) n De
En banker
Es banquero (m)
Fr banquier (m)
It banchiere (m)
Pt banqueiro (m)

**Bankkonto** (n) n De
En bank account
Es cuenta bancaria (f)
Fr compte en banque (m)
It conto in banca (m)
Pt conta bancária (f)

**Bankkrach** (m) n De
En bank crash
Es quiebra de banco (f)
Fr krach d'une banque (m)
It crollo di banca (m)
Pt falência bancária (f)

**Bankkredit** (m) n De
En bank credit
Es crédito bancario (m)
Fr crédit bancaire (m)
It credito bancario (m)
Pt crédito bancário (m)

**bank loan** En
De Bankdarlehen (n)
Es préstamo bancario (m)
Fr prêt bancaire (m)
It prestito bancario (m)
Pt empréstimo bancário (m)

**banknote** n En
Am bill
De Banknote (f)
Es billete de banco (m)
Fr billet de banque (m)
It biglietto di banca (m)
Pt nota de banco (f)

**Banknote** (f) n De
En banknote
Am bill
Es billete de banco (m)
Fr billet de banque (m)
It biglietto di banca (m)
Pt nota de banco (f)

**bank rate** En
De Diskontsatz; Banksatz (m)
Es tasa de descuento (f)
Fr taux d'escompte (m)
It tasso di sconto (m)
Pt taxa de desconto (f)

**Bankrott** (m) n De
En bankruptcy; failure
Es quiebra; insolvencia (f)
Fr faillite (f)
It bancarotta; fallimento (f m)
Pt falência (f)

**bankrupt** n En
De Gemeinschuldner (m)
Es quebrado (m)
Fr failli (m)
It fallito (m)
Pt falido (m)

**bankruptcy** n En
De Konkurs; Bankrott (m)
Es quiebra (f)
Fr faillite (f)
It fallimento; bancarotta (m f)
Pt falência (f)

**Banksatz** (f) n De
En bank rate
Es tasa de descuento (f)
Fr taux d'escompte (m)
It tasso di sconto (m)
Pt taxa de desconto (f)

**Bankspesen** (f pl) n De
En bank charges
Es gastos de banco (m pl)
Fr frais bancaires (m pl)
It spese di banca (f pl)
Pt taxas bancárias (f pl)

**bank statement** En
De Kontoauszug (m)
Es extracto de cuenta (m)
Fr relevé de compte (m)
It estratto conto (m)
Pt extracto de conta bancária (m)

**bank transfer** En
De Banküberweisung (f)
Es transferencia bancaria (f)
Fr virement bancaire (m)
It trasferimento bancario (m)
Pt transferência bancária (f)

**Banktratte** (f) n De
En banker's draft
Es giro bancario (m)
Fr traite bancaire (f)
It tratta bancaria (f)
Pt letra de banco (f)

**Banküberweisung** (f) n De
En bank transfer
Es transferencia bancaria (f)
Fr virement bancaire (m)
It trasferimento bancario (m)
Pt transferência bancária (f)

**Bankzeugnis** (n) n De
En banker's reference
Es referencia bancaria (f)
Fr référence de banquier (f)
It riferenza bancaria (f)
Pt referência bancária (f)

**banque** (f) n Fr
De Bank (f)
En bank
Es banco (m)
It banca (f)
Pt banco (m)

**banque agricole** (f) Fr
De Landbank (f)
En land bank
Es banco agrícola (m)
It banca agricola (f)
Pt banca d'agricultura (f)

**banque commerciale** (f) Fr
De Handelsbank (f)
En merchant bank
Es banco mercantil (m)
It banca commerciale (f)
Pt banco comercial (m)

**banque d'affaires** (f) Fr
De Finanzbank (f)
En investment bank
Es banco de inversiones (m)
It banca d'investimenti (f)
Pt banco de investimentos (m)

**banque d'émission** (f) Fr
De Notenbank (f)
En issuing bank
Es banco emisor (m)
It banca di emissione (f)
Pt banco emissor (m)

**banque de prêts** (f) Fr
De Kreditbank (f)
En lending bank
Es banco de préstamos (m)
It banca di prestiti (f)
Pt banco de empréstimos (m)

**banque de virement** (f) Fr
De Girobank (f)
En clearing-bank
Es banco de compensación (m)
It banca associata alla stanza di compensazione (f)
Pt banco de compensação e rateio (m)

**Banque Européenne d'Investissement** (f) Fr
De Europäische Investitionsbank (f)
En European Investment Bank
Es Banco Europeo de Inversiones (m)
It Banca Europea d'Investimenti (f)
Pt Banco Europeu de Investimentos (m)

**Banque Internationale pour la reconstruction et le développement** (f) Fr
De Internationale Bank für Wiederaufbau und Wirtschaftsförderung (f)
En International Bank for Reconstruction and Development
Es Banco Internacional para Reconstrucción y Desarrollo (m)
It Banca Internazionale per la Ricostruzione e lo Sviluppo (f)
Pt Banco Internacional de Reconstrução e Desenvolvimento (m)

**banqueiro** (m) n Pt
De Bankier (m)
En banker
Es banquero (m)
Fr banquier (m)
It banchiere (m)

**banque privée** (f) Fr
De Privatbank (f)
En private bank
Es banco privado (m)
It banca privata (f)
Pt banco privado (m)

**banquero** (m) n Es
De Bankier (m)
En banker
Fr banquier (m)
It banchiere (m)
Pt banqueiro (m)

**banque succursale** (f) Fr
De Filialbank; Zweigbank (f)
En branch bank
Es sucursal del banco (f)
It banca succursale (f)
Pt filial de banco (f)

**banquier** (m) n Fr
De Bankier (m)
En banker
Es banquero (m)
It banchiere (m)
Pt banqueiro (m)

**barataria** (f) n Pt
De Baratterie (f)
En barratry
Es baratería (f)
Fr baraterie (f)
It baratteria (f)

**baratería** (f) n Es
De Baratterie (f)
En barratry
Fr baraterie (f)
It baratteria (f)
Pt barataria (f)

**baraterie** (f) n Fr
De Baratterie (f)
En barratry
Es baratería (f)
It baratteria (f)
Pt barataria (f)

**barato** adj Es, Pt
De billig
En cheap
Fr bon marché
It a buon mercato

**barattare** vb It
De Tauschhandel treiben
En barter
Es trocar
Fr troquer
Pt trocar

**baratteria** (f) n It
De Baratterie (f)
En barratry
Es baratería (f)
Fr baraterie (f)
Pt barataria (f)

**Baratterie** (f) n De
En barratry
Es baratería (f)
Fr baraterie (f)
It baratteria (f)
Pt barataria (f)

**Barbestand** (m) n De
En cash in hand
Es efectivo en caja (m)
Fr espèces en caisse (f pl)
It pronti contanti (m pl)
Pt fundos à ordem (m pl)

**barcaça** (f) n Pt
De Lastkahn; Leichter (m)
En barge; lighter
Es barcaza; gabarra (f)
Fr péniche; allège (f)
It chiatta (f)

**barcaza** (f) n Es
De Lastkahn; Leichter (m)
En barge; lighter
Fr péniche; allège (f)
It chiatta (f)
Pt barcaça (f)

**barco** *(m) n* Es
De Schiff *(n)*
En ship
Fr navire *(m)*
It nave *(f)*
Pt navio *(m)*

**barco de carga** *(m)* Pt
De Frachtschiff *(n)*
En cargo boat
Es buque de carga *(m)*
Fr cargo *(m)*
It nave da carico *(f)*

**barco de contenedores** *(m)* Es
De Containerschiff *(n)*
En container ship
Fr navire porte-containers *(m)*
It nave da contenitori *(f)*
Pt navio de contentres *(m)*

**barco de travessia** *(m)* Pt
De Fährboot *(n)*
En ferry-boat
Es transbordador *(m)*
Fr bac *(m)*
It nave traghetto *(f)*

**barco mercante** *(m)* Es
De Handelsschiff *(n)*
En merchant ship
Fr navire marchand *(m)*
It nave mercantile *(f)*
Pt navio mercante *(m)*

**barème** *(m) n* Fr
De Tarif *(m)*
En scale (of fees, charges, etc.)
Es tarifa *(f)*
It tariffa *(f)*
Pt tarifa *(f)*

**bargain** (deal) *n* En
De Handel *(m)*
Es negocio *(m)*
Fr marché; affaire *(m f)*
It affare *(m)*
Pt negócio *(m)*

**bargain** (cheap purchase) *n* En
De Gelegenheitskauf *(m)*
Es ganga *(f)*
Fr occasion *(f)*
It occasione *(f)*
Pt pechincha *(f)*

**bargain** *vb* Am
En haggle
De feilschen
Es regatear
Fr marchander; chipoter
It mercanteggiare; cavillare
Pt regatear

**bargain-hunting** *n* En
De Sucht nach Sonderangeboten *(f)*
Es caza de rebajas *(f)*
Fr chasse aux soldes *(f)*
It caccia alle occasioni *(f)*
Pt caça aos saldos *(f)*

**bargaining position** En
De Verhandlungslage *(f)*
Es situación de negociar *(f)*
Fr situation permettant de négocier *(f)*
It situazione permettente di trattare *(f)*
Pt situação de regatear *(f)*

**bargaining power** En
De Verhandlungsposition *(f)*
Es poder de negociación *(m)*
Fr pouvoir de négociation *(m)*
It potere di contrattare *(m)*
Pt poder de regateio *(m)*

**bargain offer** En
De Sonderangebot *(n)*
Es oferta de ocasión *(f)*
Fr offre exceptionelle *(f)*
It offerta d'occasione *(f)*
Pt oferta a preço excepcional *(f)*

**bargain price** En
De Spottpreis *(m)*
Es precio de ocasión *(m)*
Fr prix de solde *(m)*
It prezzo d'occasione *(m)*
Pt preço excepcional *(m)*

**barge** *n* En
De Lastkahn *(m)*
Es barcaza *(f)*
Fr péniche *(f)*
It chiatta *(f)*
Pt barcaça *(f)*

**bar gegen Versandpapiere** De
En cash against documents (c.a.d.)

Es al contado contra documentos
Fr comptant contre documents
It contanti contro documenti
Pt em dinheiro contra documentação

**Bargeld** *(n) n* De
En cash
Es dinero efectivo *(m)*
Fr espèces *(f pl)*
It denaro *(m)*
Pt dinheiro *(m)*

**Bargeldauszahlungsautomat** *(m) n* De
En cash dispenser
Es caja automática *(f)*
Fr distributeur d'argent comptant *(m)*
It cassa automatica *(f)*
Pt caixa automática *(f)*

**Bargeldvoraussage** *(f) n* De
En cash forecast
Es previsión de fondos *(f)*
Fr prévision comptant *(f)*
It previsione contanti *(f)*
Pt previsão de fundos (em dinheiro) *(f)*

**Bargeschäft** *(n) n* De
En cash deal
Es trato al contado *(m)*
Fr transaction au comptant *(f)*
It operazione a contanti *(f)*
Pt negócio em dinheiro *(m)*

**Barrabatt** *(m) n* De
En cash discount
Es descuento de caja *(m)*
Fr escompte de caisse *(m)*
It sconto per pagamento a contanti *(m)*
Pt desconto de contado *(m)*

**barratry** *n* En
De Baratterie *(f)*
Es baratería *(f)*
Fr baraterie *(f)*
It baratteria *(f)*
Pt barataria *(f)*

**barreira alfandegária** *(f)* Pt
De Zollschranke *(f)*
En customs barrier
Es barrera aduanera *(f)*

Fr  barrière douanière *(f)*
It  barriera doganale *(f)*

**barreira comercial** *(f)* Pt
De  Handelsschranke *(f)*
En  trade barrier
Es  barrera comercial *(f)*
Fr  barrière commerciale *(f)*
It  barriera commerciale *(f)*

**barrel** *n* En
De  Fass *(n)*
Es  barril *(m)*
Fr  tonneau *(m)*
It  botte *(f)*
Pt  barril *(m)*

**Barren** *(m) n* De
En  ingot
Es  lingote *(m)*
Fr  lingot; barre *(m f)*
It  lingotto *(m)*
Pt  lingote *(m)*

**barrera aduanera** *(f)* Es
De  Zollschranke *(f)*
En  customs barrier
Fr  barrière douanière *(f)*
It  barriera doganale *(f)*
Pt  barreira alfandegária *(f)*

**barrera comercial** *(f)* Es
De  Handelsschranke *(f)*
En  trade barrier
Fr  barrière commerciale *(f)*
It  barriera commerciale *(f)*
Pt  barreira comercial *(f)*

**barriera commerciale** *(f)* It
De  Handelsschranke *(f)*
En  trade barrier
Es  barrera comercial *(f)*
Fr  barrière commerciale *(f)*
Pt  barreira comercial *(f)*

**barriera doganale** *(f)* It
De  Zollschranke *(f)*
En  customs barrier
Es  barrera aduanera *(f)*
Fr  barrière douanière *(f)*
Pt  barreira alfandegária *(f)*

**barrière commerciale** *(f)* Fr
De  Handelsschranke *(f)*
En  trade barrier
Es  barrera comercial *(f)*
It  barriera commerciale *(f)*
Pt  barreira comercial *(f)*

**barrière douanière** *(f)* Fr
De  Zollschranke *(f)*
En  customs barrier
Es  barrera aduanera *(f)*
It  barriera doganale *(f)*
Pt  barreira alfandegária *(f)*

**barril** *(m) n* Es, Pt
De  Fass *(n)*
En  barrel
Fr  tonneau *(m)*
It  botte *(f)*

**barrister** *n* En
Am  attorney
De  Anwalt *(m)*
Es  abogado *(m)*
Fr  avocat *(m)*
It  avvocato *(m)*
Pt  advogado *(m)*

**barter** *vb* En
De  Tauschhandel treiben
Es  trocar
Fr  troquer
It  barattare
Pt  trocar

**base aurea** *(f)* It
De  Goldobligation *(f)*
En  gold standard
Es  patrón oro *(m)*
Fr  étalon or *(m)*
Pt  ouro-padrão *(m)*

**base contributiva** *(f)* Es
De  Bemessungsgrundlage *(f)*
En  tax base
Fr  assiette de l'impôt *(f)*
It  ripartizione della tassazione *(f)*
Pt  base de imposto *(f)*

**base de imposto** *(f)* Pt
De  Bemessungsgrundlage *(f)*
En  tax base
Es  base contributiva *(f)*
Fr  assiette de l'impôt *(f)*
It  ripartizione della tassazione *(f)*

**base metal** En
De  unedles Metall *(n)*
Es  metal no noble *(m)*
Fr  métal vil *(m)*
It  basso metallo *(m)*
Pt  metal pobre *(m)*

**base salarial** *(f)* Pt
De  Lohnsatz *(m)*
En  wage rate
Es  tarifa de salarios *(f)*
Fr  taux des salaires *(m)*
It  tariffa salariale *(f)*

**base year** En
De  Grundjahr *(n)*
Es  año de base *(m)*
Fr  année de base *(f)*
It  anno di base *(m)*
Pt  ano base *(m)*

**basic pay** En
Am  base pay
De  Grundlohn *(m)*
Es  salario-base *(m)*
Fr  salaire de base *(f)*
It  salario fondamentale *(m)*
Pt  salário-base *(m)*

**bassin de radoub** *(m)* Fr
De  Trockendock *(n)*
En  graving dock
Es  dique de carenas *(m)*
It  bacino di raddobbo *(m)*
Pt  doca de querenas *(f)*

**bassin houiller** *(m)* Fr
De  Kohlenrevier *(n)*
En  coal field
Es  yacimiento de carbón *(m)*
It  bacino carbonifero *(m)*
Pt  jazigo de carvão *(m)*

**basso metallo** *(m)* It
De  unedles Metall *(n)*
En  base metal
Es  metal no noble *(m)*
Fr  métal vil *(m)*
Pt  metal pobre *(m)*

**batch** *n* En
De  Stoss *(m)*
Es  lote *(m)*
Fr  lot *(m)*
It  lotto *(m)*
Pt  lote *(m)*

**batch costing** En
De  Stapelkostenberechnung *(f)*
Es  fijación de precio por lotes *(f)*
Fr  évaluation du coût des lots *(f)*
It  valutazione del costo per partita *(f)*

Pt fixação do preço por lote
   (f)

**bateau à vapeur** (m) Fr
De Dampfer (m)
En steamer
Es buque de vapor (m)
It vapore (m)
Pt vapor (m)

**Baukostenvoranschlag** (m) n
   De
En bill of quantities
Es cubicación de obra (f)
Fr devis (m)
It preventivo (m)
Pt relação de quantidades (f)

**Baukredit** (m) n De
En building loan
Es crédito de construcción (m)
Fr crédit de construction (m)
It prestito immobiliare (m)
Pt empréstimo para constru-
   ção (m)

**Bauland** (n) n De
En building land
Es solares (m pl)
Fr terrain à bâtir (m)
It terreno edile (m)
Pt terreno para construção
   (m)

**Bauunternehmer** (m) n De
En building contractor
Es contratista de obras (m)
Fr entrepreneur de bâtiment
   (m)
It impresa edile (f)
Pt constructor de obras (m)

**Beamte(r)** (m) n De
En civil servant
Am government employee
Es funcionario del gobierno
   (m)
Fr fonctionnaire (m)
It impiegato statale (m)
Pt foncionário público (m)

**bear** n En
De Baissespekulant; Baissier
   (m)
Es bajista (m)
Fr baissier (m)
It ribassista (m)
Pt baixista (m)

**bear account** En
De Baissekonto (n)
Es cuenta de especulaciones
   a la baja (f)
Fr compte des speculations à
   la baisse (m)
It conto di speculazioni al
   ribasso (m)
Pt conta de especulações
   baixistas (f)

**bearer bond** En
De Inhaberobligation (f)
Es título al portador (m)
Fr bon au porteur (m)
· It titolo al portatore (m)
Pt título ao portador (m)

**bearer debenture** En
De Inhaberobligation (f)
Es obligación al portador (f)
Fr obligation au porteur (f)
It obbligazione al portatore (f)
Pt obrigação ao portador (f)

**bearer security** En
De Inhabereffekten (n pl)
Es valor al portador (m)
Fr valeur au porteur (f)
It valore al portatore (f)
Pt título ao portador (m)

**bearish** adj En
De flau
Es bajista
Fr orienté à la baisse
It ribassista
Pt baixista

**bear market** En
De Baissemarkt (m)
Es mercado bajista (m)
Fr marché orienté à la baisse
   (m)
It mercato tendente al ri-
   basso (m)
Pt mercado de tendência
   baixista (m)

**become operative** En
De wirksam werden
Es entrar en vigor
Fr entrer en vigueur
It entrare in vigore
Pt entrar em vigor

**bedingt** adj De
En conditional
Es condicional
Fr conditionnel
It condizionale
Pt condicional

**Bedingung** (f) n De
En condition
Es condición (f)
Fr condition (f)
It condizione (f)
Pt condição (f)

**Bedingungen** (f pl) n De
En terms
Es condiciones (f pl)
Fr conditions (f pl)
It condizioni (f pl)
Pt condições (f pl)

**beeidigte Erklärung** (f) De
En affidavit
Es declaración jurada (f)
Fr déclaration sous serment
   (f)
It dichiarazione giurata (f)
Pt declaração sob juramento
   (f)

**befördern** vb De
En promote
Es ascender
Fr donner de l'avancement à
It promuovere
Pt promover

**Beförderung** (eines Ange-
   stellten) (f) n De
En promotion
Es ascenso; promoción (m f)
Fr avancement; promotion (m
   f)
It avanzamento; promozione
   (m f)
Pt promoção (f)

**Beförderung** (Transport) (f) n
   De
En transport
Es transporte (m)
Fr transport (m)
It trasporto (m)
Pt transporte (m)

**Befrachter** (m) n De
En charterer
Es fletador (m)

Fr affréteur *(m)*
It noleggiatore *(m)*
Pt fretador *(m)*

**Befrachtung** *(f)* n De
En chartering
Es fletamento *(m)*
Fr affrètement *(m)*
It noleggio *(m)*
Pt fretamento *(m)*

**Befragte(r)** *(m)* n De
En interviewee
Es persona entrevistada *(f)*
Fr personne interrogée *(f)*
It intervistato *(m)*
Pt entrevistado *(m)*

**befreien** *vb* De
En free
Es liberar
Fr libérer; affranchir
It liberare
Pt libertar; livrar

**Befreiung** *(f)* n De
En exemption
Es exención *(f)*
Fr exemption *(f)*
It esenzione *(f)*
Pt isenção *(f)*

**Befugnis** *(f)* n De
En warrant
Es mandato *(m)*
Fr ordonnance *(f)*
It mandato *(m)*
Pt mandato *(m)*

**begebbar** *adj* De
En negotiable
Es negociable
Fr négotiable
It negoziabile
Pt negociável

**begebbares Wertpapier** *(n)* De
En negotiable instrument
Es titulo negociable *(m)*
Fr effet de commerce *(m)*
It titolo negoziabile *(m)*
Pt título negociável *(m)*

**beglaubigte Abschrift** *(f)* De
En certified true copy
Es copia auténtica *(f)*
Fr copie certifiée *(f)*

It copia conforme *(f)*
Pt cópia autenticada *(f)*

**(zur) Begleichung vorgelegte Rechnung** *(f)* De
En account rendered
Es cuenta rendida *(f)*
Fr compte rendu *(m)*
It conto reso *(m)*
Pt conta remetida *(f)*

**Begünstigte(r)** *(m)* n De
En beneficiary
Es beneficiario *(m)*
Fr bénéficiaire *(m)*
It beneficiario *(m)*
Pt beneficiário *(m)*

**behalten** *vb* De
En keep
Es tener; conservar
Fr tenir; maintenir
It tenere; mantenere
Pt manter; reter

**Beilage** *(f)* n De
En enclosure
Es anexo *(m)*
Fr annexe *(f)*
It allegato *(m)*
Pt anexo *(m)*

**beiliegend** *adj* De
En enclosed
Es adjunto
Fr ci-joint; ci-inclus
It accluso
Pt incluso

**bei Nichterfüllung** De
En in case of default
Es en caso de incumplimiento
Fr en cas de défaillance
It in caso di inadempienza
Pt em caso de não cumprimento

**bei Sicht** De
En at sight
Es a la vista
Fr à vue
It à vista
Pt à vista

**Beitrag** *(m)* n De
En contribution
Es contribución *(f)*
Fr contribution *(f)*

It contributo *(m)*
Pt contribuição *(f)*

**beitragen** *vb* De
En contribute
Es contribuir
Fr contribuer
It contribuire
Pt contribuir

**beitragsfreie Police** *(f)* De
En paid-up policy
Es póliza liberada *(f)*
Fr assurance libérée *(f)*
It polizza interamente pagata *(f)*
Pt apólice liquidada *(f)*

**Belegschaft** *(f)* n De
En work force
Es masa obrera *(f)*
Fr effectifs *(m pl)*
It massa lavoratrice *(f)*
Pt massa trabalhadora *(f)*

**Belegstück** *(n)* n De
En voucher
Es pieza justificativa *(f)*
Fr pièce justificative; fiche *(f)*
It pezza d'appoggio *(f)*
Pt vale *(m)*

**beliefern** *vb* De
En supply
Es surtir
Fr fournir
It fornire
Pt fornecer

**Bemessungsgrundlage** *(f)* n De
En tax base
Es base contributiva *(f)*
Fr assiette de l'impôt *(f)*
It ripartizione della tassazione *(f)*
Pt base de imposto *(f)*

**benachrichtigen** *vb* De
En inform
Es informar; avisar
Fr informer; renseigner
It informare
Pt informar

**Benachrichtigung** *(f)* n De
En notice; communication
Es aviso; comunicación *(m f)*
Fr avis; communication *(m f)*

It  avviso; comunicazione *(m f)*

Pt  aviso; comunicação *(m f)*


**Benannte(r)** *(m) n* De

En  nominee

Es  nominatario *(m)*

Fr  personne dénommée *(f)*

It  persona nominata *(f)*

Pt  nomeado *(m)*


**bénéfice** *(m) n* Fr

De  Gewinn *(m)*

En  profit

Es  ganancia; beneficio *(f m)*

It  utile; profitto *(m)*

Pt  lucro; benefício *(m)*


**bénéfice brut** *(m)* Fr

De  Bruttogewinn *(m)*

En  gross profit

Es  ganancia bruta *(f)*

It  utile lordo *(m)*

Pt  lucro bruto *(m)*


**bénéfice net** *(m)* Fr

De  Reingewinn *(m)*

En  net profit

Es  ganancia neta *(f)*

It  utile netto *(m)*

Pt  lucro líquido *(m)*


**bénéfice par titre** *(m)* Fr

De  Gewinn pro Aktie *(n)*

En  earnings per share

Es  beneficios por acción *(m pl)*

It  profitti per azione *(m pl)*

Pt  proventos por acção *(m pl)*


**bénéfices non répartis** *(m pl)* Fr

De  unverteilte Gewinne *(n pl)*

En  undistributed profits

Es  beneficios no distribuidos *(m pl)*

It  profitti non distribuiti *(m pl)*

Pt  lucros não distribuidos *(m pl)*


**bénéficiaire** *(m) n* Fr

De  Begünstigte(r); Zahlungs-
    berechtigte(r) *(m)*

En  beneficiary; payee

Es  beneficiario *(m)*

It  beneficiario *(m)*

Pt  beneficiário *(m)*


**beneficial interest** En

De  Niessbrauchsrecht *(n)*

Es  usufructo *(m)*

Fr  usufruit *(m)*

It  usufrutto *(m)*

Pt  usufruto *(m)*


**beneficial owner** En

De  Niessbrauchnutzer *(m)*

Es  usufructuario *(m)*

Fr  usufruitier *(m)*

It  usufruttuario *(m)*

Pt  usufrutuário *(m)*


**beneficiario** *(m) n* Es, It

De  Begünstigte(r); Zahlungs-
    berechtigte(r) *(m)*

En  beneficiary; payee

Fr  bénéficiaire *(m)*

Pt  beneficiário *(m)*


**beneficiário** *(m) n* Pt

De  Begünstigte(r); Zahlungs-
    berechtigte(r) *(m)*

En  beneficiary; payee

Es  beneficiario *(m)*

Fr  bénéficiaire *(m)*

It  beneficiario *(m)*


**beneficiário de empréstimo** *(m)* Pt

De  Kreditnehmer *(m)*

En  borrower

Es  prestatario *(m)*

Fr  emprunteur *(m)*

It  accattatore *(m)*


**beneficiary** *n* En

De  Begünstigte(r) *(m)*

Es  beneficiario *(m)*

Fr  bénéficiaire *(m)*

It  beneficiario *(m)*

Pt  beneficiário *(m)*


**beneficio** *(m) n* Es

De  Gewinn *(m)*

En  profit

Fr  bénéfice *(m)*

It  utile *(m)*

Pt  benefício *(m)*


**benefício** *(m) n* Pt

De  Gewinn *(m)*

En  profit

Es  beneficio *(m)*

Fr  bénéfice *(m)*

It  utile *(m)*


**beneficio razonable** *(m)* Es

De  angemessener Ertrag *(m)*

En  fair return

Fr  rendement équitable *(m)*

It  discreto profitto *(m)*

Pt  rendimento justo *(m)*


**benefícios extras** *(m pl)* Pt

De  Sozialleistungen *(f pl)*

En  fringe benefits

Es  beneficios suplementarios *(m pl)*

Fr  avantages accessoires *(m pl)*

It  vantaggi accessori *(m pl)*


**beneficios no distribuidos** *(m pl)* Es

De  unverteilte Gewinne *(n pl)*

En  undistributed profits

Fr  bénéfices non répartis *(m pl)*

It  profitti non distribuiti *(m pl)*

Pt  lucros não distribuidos *(m pl)*


**beneficio sobre capital** *(m)* Es

De  Kapitalertrag *(m)*

En  return on capital

Fr  rémunération du capital *(f)*

It  reddito del capitale *(m)*

Pt  juro sobre o capital *(m)*


**beneficios por acción** *(m pl)* Es

De  Gewinn pro Aktie *(n)*

En  earnings per share

Fr  bénéfice par titre *(m)*

It  profitti per azione *(m pl)*

Pt  proventos por acção *(m pl)*


**beneficios sobre capital** *(m pl)* Es

De  Kapitalgewinn *(n)*

En  capital gains

Fr  gains en capital *(m pl)*

It  plusvalore di capitale *(m pl)*

Pt  lucros de capital *(m pl)*


**beneficios suplementarios** *(m pl)* Es

De  Sozialleistungen *(f pl)*

En  fringe benefits

Fr  avantages accessoires *(m pl)*

It  vantaggi accessori *(m pl)*

Pt  benefícios extras *(m pl)*

**Benennung des Bestimmungshafen** *(f)* De
En port mark
Es marca de destino *(f)*
Fr marque de destination *(f)*
It marche di destinazione *(f pl)*
Pt marca de porto *(f)*

**beni di consumo** *(m pl)* It
De Konsumgüter *(n pl)*
En consumer goods
Es bienes de consumo *(m pl)*
Fr biens de consommation *(m pl)*
Pt bens de consumo *(m pl)*

**beni di consumo durabili** *(m pl)* It
De dauerhafte Konsumgüter *(n pl)*
En consumer durables
Es bienes de consumo duraderos *(m pl)*
Fr biens de consommation durables *(m pl)*
Pt artigos de consumo perduraveis *(m pl)*.

**beni di consumo non durevoli** *(m pl)* It
De nicht-dauerhafte Verbrauchsgüter *(n pl)*
En consumer non-durables
Es bienes de consumo perecederos *(m pl)*
Fr biens de consommation non-durables *(m pl)*
Pt bens de consumo não duráveis *(m pl)*

**beni durevoli** *(m pl)* It
De langlebige Güter *(n pl)*
En durable goods
Es mercancías no perecederas *(f pl)*
Fr biens durables *(m pl)*
Pt mercadorias imperecíveis *(f pl)*

**beni immobili** *(m pl)* It
De unbewegliches Vermögen; Immobilien *(n; f pl)*
En real estate
Es bienes inmuebles *(m pl)*
Fr biens immeubles *(m pl)*
Pt propriedade imobiliária *(f)*

**beni incorporali** *(m pl)* It
De nicht greifbare Aktiven *(n pl)*
En intangible assets
Es activo intangible *(m)*
Fr actif incorporel *(m)*
Pt bens intocáveis *(m pl)*

**beni materiali** *(m pl)* It
De greifbare Aktiven *(n pl)*
En tangible assets
Es activo tangible *(m)*
Fr biens immobiliers *(m pl)*
Pt bens visíveis *(m pl)*

**beni strumentali** *(m pl)* It
De Anlagegüter *(n pl)*
En capital goods
Es bienes de producción *(m pl)*
Fr biens d'équipement *(m pl)*
Pt mercadorias de capital *(f pl)*

**bens** *(m pl)* n Pt
De Vermögen *(n)*
En estate; property
Es finca *(f)*
Fr bien; propriété *(m; f)*
It proprietà *(f)*

**bens de activo líquidos** *(m pl)* Pt
De flüssige Aktiven *(n pl)*
En liquid assets
Es activo líquido *(m)*
Fr actif liquide *(m)*
It disponibilità; attività liquida *(f)*

**bens de capital** *(m pl)* Pt
De Vermögensanlage *(f)*
En capital asset
Am fixed asset
Es activo fijo *(m)*
Fr actif immobilisé *(m)*
It capitale fisso *(m)*

**bens de consumo** *(m pl)* Pt
De Konsumgüter *(n pl)*
En consumer goods
Es bienes de consumo *(m pl)*
Fr biens de consommation *(m pl)*
It beni di consumo *(m pl)*

**bens de consumo não duráveis** *(m pl)* Pt
De nicht-dauerhafte Verbrauchsgüter *(n pl)*
En consumer non-durables
Es bienes de consumo perecederos *(m pl)*
Fr biens de consommation non-durables *(m pl)*
It beni di consumo non durevoli *(m pl)*

**bens do activo congelados** *(m pl)* Pt
De eingefrorene Guthaben *(n pl)*
En frozen assets
Es activos congelados *(m pl)*
Fr fonds bloqués *(m pl)*
It attivo congelato *(m)*

**bens fixos** *(m pl)* Pt
De Anlagevermögen *(n)*
En fixed assets
Es activo fijo *(m)*
Fr immobilisations *(f pl)*
It immobilizzazioni; attivo fisso *(f pl; m)*

**bens intocáveis** *(m pl)* Pt
De nicht greifbare Aktiven *(n pl)*
En intangible assets
Es activo intangible *(m)*
Fr actif incorporel *(m)*
It beni incorporali *(m pl)*

**bens líquidos** *(m pl)* Pt
De Reinvermögen *(n)*
En net assets
Es activo neto *(m)*
Fr actif net *(m)*
It attivo netto *(m)*

**bens mobiliários** *(m pl)* Pt
De bewegliche Güter *(n pl)*
En movable assets
Es mobiliario *(m)*
Fr biens mobiliers *(m pl)*
It proprietà mobiliare *(f)*

**bens no activo actual** *(m pl)* Pt
De Umlaufsvermögen *(n)*
En current assets
Es activo realizable *(m)*
Fr actif courant *(m)*
It attivo liquido *(m)*

**bens visíveis** *(m pl)* Pt
De greifbare Aktiven *(n pl)*
En tangible assets
Es activo tangible *(m)*
Fr biens immobiliers *(m pl)*
It beni materiali *(m pl)*

**Berater** *(m)* n De
En consultant
Es consultor *(m)*
Fr conseil *(m)*
It consulente *(m)*
Pt consultor *(m)*

**Beratungs-** De
En advisory
Es consultivo
Fr consultatif
It consultivo
Pt consultivo

**Beratungsausschuss** *(m)* n De
En advisory board
Es consejo consultivo *(m)*
Fr comité consultatif *(m)*
It consiglio consultivo *(m)*
Pt comité consultivo *(m)*

**berechnen** *vb* De
En calculate
Es calcular
Fr calculer
It calcolare
Pt calcular

**Berechnung** *(f)* n De
En calculation
Es cálculo *(m)*
Fr calcul *(m)*
It calcolazione *(f)*
Pt cálculo *(m)*

**Bergegeld** *(n)* n De
En salvage charges
Es cargos de salvamento *(m pl)*
Fr indemnité de sauvetage *(f)*
It spese di salvataggio *(f pl)*
Pt encargos de salvamento *(m pl)*

**Bergung** *(f)* n De
En salvage
Es salvamento *(m)*
Fr sauvetage *(m)*
It salvataggio *(m)*
Pt salvamento *(m)*

**Bergwerk** *(n)* n De
En mine
Es mina *(f)*
Fr mine *(f)*
It miniera *(f)*
Pt mina *(f)*

**Bergwerkskonzession** *(f)* n De
En mineral concession
Es concesión minera *(f)*
Fr concession minière *(f)*
It concessione mineraria *(f)*
Pt concessão mineira *(f)*

**Bericht** *(m)* n De
En report
Es informe; reportaje *(m)*
Fr rapport; compte-rendu *(m)*
It relazione; rapporto *(f m)*
Pt relatório *(m)*

**Berichtigung** *(f)* n De
En correction
Es corrección *(f)*
Fr correction *(f)*
It correzione *(f)*
Pt correcção *(f)*

**bersaglio** *(m)* n It
De Ziel *(n)*
En target
Es objetivo *(m)*
Fr but *(m)*
Pt objectivo *(m)*

**Beruf** *(m)* n De
En job; occupation
Es trabajo *(m)*
Fr occupation *(f)*
It lavoro; occupazione *(m f)*
Pt ocupação *(f)*

**Berufsausbildung** *(f)* n De
En vocational training
Es formación profesional *(f)*
Fr formation professionnelle *(f)*
It addestramento professionale *(m)*
Pt treino vocacional *(m)*

**Berufsrisiko** *(n)* n De
En occupational hazard
Es riesgo profesional *(m)*
Fr risque professionnel *(m)*
It rischio del lavoro *(m)*
Pt acidente próprio da profissão *(m)*

**Berufungsgericht** *(n)* n De
En court of appeal
Es tribunal de apelación *(m)*
Fr cour d'appel *(m)*
It corte d'appello *(f)*
Pt tribunal de apelação *(m)*

**beschädigte Waren** *(f pl)* De
En damaged goods
Es mercancías averiadas *(f pl)*
Fr marchandises avariées *(f pl)*
It merce avariata *(f)*
Pt mercadorias danificadas *(f pl)*

**Beschädigung** *(f)* n De
En damage
Es daño *(m)*
Fr dommage *(m)*
It danno *(m)*
Pt dano *(m)*

**Beschädigung beim Transport** *(f)* De
En damage in transit
Es daños en ruta *(m pl)*
Fr avaries de route *(f pl)*
It danno durante trasporto *(m)*
Pt danos em trânsito *(m pl)*

**beschäftigen** *vb* De
En employ
Es emplear
Fr employer
It impiegare
Pt empregar

**Beschäftigung** *(f)* n De
En occupation; employment
Es ocupación; empleo *(f m)*
Fr occupation; emploi *(f m)*
It occupazione; impiego *(f m)*
Pt ocupação; emprego *(f m)*

**bescheinigen** *vb* De
En certify
Es certificar
Fr certifier
It certificare
Pt certificar

**Bescheinigung** *(f)* n De
En certificate
Es certificado *(m)*
Fr certificat *(m)*

It    certificato *(m)*
Pt    certificado *(m)*

**Beschlagnahme** *(f)* n De
En    embargo
Es    embargo *(m)*
Fr    embargo *(m)*
It    embargo *(m)*
Pt    embargo *(m)*

**beschleunigte Abschreibung**
*(f)* De
En    accelerated depreciation
Es    depreciación acelerada *(f)*
Fr    amortissement accéléré *(m)*
It    deprezzamento accelerato
      *(m)*
Pt    depreciação acelerada *(f)*

**Beschluss** *(m)* n De
En    resolution; decision
Es    resolución *(f)*
Fr    resolution *(f)*
It    deliberazione *(f)*
Pt    resolução; proposta *(f)*

**beschlussfähige Anzahl** *(f)* De
En    quorum
Es    quórum *(m)*
Fr    quorum *(m)*
It    quorum *(m)*
Pt    quorum *(m)*

**beschränkt** adj De
En    limited
Es    limitado
Fr    limité
It    limitato
Pt    limitado

**Beschreibung** *(f)* n De
En    description
Es    descripción *(f)*
Fr    description *(f)*
It    descrizione *(f)*
Pt    descrição *(f)*

**Beschwerde** *(f)* n De
En    complaint; grievance
Es    queja; agravio *(f m)*
Fr    plainte; grief *(f m)*
It    lagnanza *(f)*
Pt    queixa; agravo *(f m)*

**besondere Havarie** *(f)* De
En    particular average
Es    avería particular *(f)*
Fr    avarie particulière *(f)*

It    avaria particolare *(f)*
Pt    avaria particular *(f)*

**Bestandaufnahme** *(f)* n De
En    stocktaking
Es    inventario; balance *(m)*
Fr    levée d'inventaire *(f)*
It    compilazione dell'inventario
      *(f)*
Pt    inventário de existências
      *(m)*

**bestätigen** vb De
En    confirm
Es    confirmar
Fr    confirmer
It    confermare
Pt    confirmar

**bestätigter Kreditbrief** *(m)* De
En    confirmed letter of credit
Es    carta de crédito confirmada
      *(f)*
Fr    lettre de crédit confirmée
      *(f)*
It    lettera di credito confer-
      mata *(f)*
Pt    carta de crédito confirmada
      *(f)*

**bestätigter Scheck** *(m)* De
En    certified cheque
Am    certified check
Es    cheque certificado *(m)*
Fr    chèque certifié *(m)*
It    assegno garantito *(m)*
Pt    cheque certificado *(m)*

**bestätigter unwiderruflicher**
**Kreditbrief** *(m)* De
En    confirmed irrevocable letter
      of credit
Es    carta de crédito irrevocable
      confirmada *(f)*
Fr    lettre de crédit irrévocable
      confirmée *(f)*
It    lettera di credito confer-
      mata e irrevocabile *(f)*
Pt    carta de crédito irrevogável
      confirmada *(f)*

**Bestätigung** *(f)* n De
En    confirmation
Es    confirmación *(f)*
Fr    confirmation *(f)*
It    conferma *(f)*
Pt    confirmação *(f)*

**bestechen** vb De
En    bribe
Es    sobornar
Fr    corrompre
It    corrompere
Pt    sobornar

**Bestechung** *(f)* n De
En    bribery
Es    soborno *(m)*
Fr    corruption *(f)*
It    corruzione *(f)*
Pt    soborno *(m)*

**Bestechungsgeld** *(n)* n De
En    bribe
Es    soborno *(m)*
Fr    pot-de-vin *(m)*
It    dono per corrompere *(m)*
Pt    soborno *(m)*

**bestellen** vb De
En    order
Es    hacer un pedido
Fr    commander; passer une
      commande
It    ordinare
Pt    encomendar

**Bestellformular** *(n)* n De
En    order-form
Es    solicitud de pedido *(f)*
Fr    bulletin de commande *(m)*
It    foglio d'ordinazione *(m)*
Pt    impresso de encomenda
      *(m)*

**Bestellung** *(f)* n De
En    order
Es    pedido *(m)*
Fr    commande *(f)*
It    ordine *(m)*
Pt    encomenda *(f)*

**Besteuerung** *(f)* n De
En    taxation; assessment
Es    tributación; evaluación *(f)*
Fr    imposition *(f)*
It    tassazione; imposta *(f)*
Pt    tributação; balanço fiscal *(f
      m)*

**Bestimmungshafen** *(m)* n De
En    port of destination
Es    puerto de destino *(m)*
Fr    port de destination *(m)*
It    porto di destinazione *(m)*
Pt    porto de destino *(m)*

**Bestimmungsort** *(m)* n De
En destination
Es destino *(m)*
Fr destination *(f)*
It destinazione *(f)*
Pt destino *(m)*

**beteiligen** *vb* De
En participate
Es participar
Fr participer
It partecipare
Pt participar

**beteiligt sein** De
En hold shares
Es tener acciones
Fr détenir des actions
It tenere azioni
Pt reter acções

**Betrag** *(m)* n De
En amount
Es suma *(f)*
Fr somme; montant *(f m)*
It ammontare *(m)*
Pt quantia *(f)*

**Betriebsausgaben** *(f pl)* n De
En operating costs
Es costes operacionales *(m pl)*
Fr frais d'exploitation *(m pl)*
It spese di gestione *(f pl)*
Pt custos de exercício *(m pl)*

**Betriebsgeheimnis** *(n)* n De
En trade secret
Es secreto comercial *(m)*
Fr secret industriel *(m)*
It segreto commerciale *(m)*
Pt segredo comercial *(m)*

**Betriebskapital** *(n)* n De
En trading capital; working capital
Es capital de explotación; capital circulante *(m)*
Fr fonds de roulement *(m)*
It capitale d'esercizio *(m)*
Pt capital de exploração *(m)*

**Betrug** *(m)* n De
En fraud
Es fraude *(m)*
Fr fraude *(f)*
It frode *(f)*
Pt fraude *(f)*

**betrügen** *vb* De
En cheat
Es engañar
Fr tricher
It truffare
Pt enganar

**betrügerisch** *adj* De
En fraudulent
Es fraudulento
Fr frauduleux
It fraudolento
Pt fraudulento

**betterment** n En
De Planungsgewinn *(m)*
Es plusvalía *(f)*
Fr appréciation *(f)*
It plus-valore *(m)*
Pt melhoria *(f)*

**Bevölkerung** *(f)* n De
En population
Es población *(f)*
Fr population *(f)*
It popolazione *(f)*
Pt população *(f)*

**Bevollmächtigte(r)** *(m)* n De
En attorney
Es apoderado *(m)*
Fr mandataire *(m)*
It mandatario *(m)*
Pt procurador *(m)*

**bevorrechtigter Gläubiger** *(m)* De
En preferential creditor
Es acreedor privilegiado *(m)*
Fr créancier privilégié *(m)*
It creditore privilegiato *(m)*
Pt credor preferencial *(m)*

**bewegliche Güter** *(n pl)* De
En movable assets
Es mobiliario *(m)*
Fr biens mobiliers *(m pl)*
It proprietà mobiliare *(f)*
Pt bens mobiliários *(m pl)*

**Beweglichkeit** *(f)* n De
En mobility
Es movilidad *(f)*
Fr mobilité *(f)*
It mobilità *(f)*
Pt mobilidade *(f)*

**Beweis** *(m)* n De
En evidence
Es evidencia *(f)*
Fr preuve *(f)*
It prova *(f)*
Pt prova *(f)*

**beweisen** *vb* De
En establish; prove
Es demostrar; probar
Fr démontrer; prouver
It dimostrare; provare
Pt demonstrar; provar

**Bewerber** *(m)* n De
En applicant
Es candidato *(m)*
Fr candidat *(m)*
It candidato *(m)*
Pt candidato *(m)*

**bewerkstelligen** *vb* De
En implement; bring about
Es hacer efectivo; ejecutar
Fr exécuter
It attuare; effettuare
Pt executar

**bewerten** *vb* De
En evaluate
Es evaluar
Fr évaluer
It valutare
Pt avaliar

**bezahlter Urlaub** *(m)* De
En holidays with pay
Es vacaciones retribuidas *(f pl)*
Fr congés payés *(m pl)*
It vacanze retribuite *(f pl)*
Pt férias pagas *(f pl)*

**Bezogene(r)** *(m)* n De
En drawee
Es librado *(m)*
Fr tiré *(m)*
It trattario *(m)*
Pt sacado *(m)*

**Bezüge** *(m pl)* n De
En emolument
Es emolumento *(m)*
Fr émoluments *(m pl)*
It rimunerazione *(f)*
Pt emolumento *(m)*

**bid** *n* En
De Angebot *(n)*
Es oferta *(f)*
Fr offre *(f)*
It offerta *(f)*
Pt oferta *(f)*

**bidder** *n* En
De Bietende(r) *(m)*
Es ofertante *(m)*
Fr enchérisseur *(m)*
It offerente *(m)*
Pt proponente *(m)*

**bien** *(m) n* Fr
De Vermögen *(n)*
En estate; property
Es finca *(f)*
It proprietà *(f)*
Pt bens; propriedade *(m pl; m)*

**bienes de consumo** *(m pl)* Es
De Konsumgüter *(n pl)*
En consumer goods
Fr biens de consommation *(m pl)*
It beni di consumo *(m pl)*
Pt bens de consumo *(m pl)*

**bienes de consumo duraderos** *(m pl)* Es
De dauerhafte Konsumgüter *(n pl)*
En consumer durables
Fr biens de consommation durables *(m pl)*
It beni di consumo durabili *(m pl)*
Pt artigos de consumo perduraveis *(m pl)*

**bienes de producción** *(m pl)* Es
De Anlagegüter *(n pl)*
En capital goods
Fr biens d'équipement *(m pl)*
It beni strumentali *(m pl)*
Pt mercadorias de capital *(f pl)*

**bienes inmuebles** *(m pl)* Es
De unbewegliches Vermögen; Immobilien *(n; f pl)*
En real estate
Fr biens immeubles *(m pl)*
It beni immobili *(m pl)*
Pt propriedade imobiliária *(f)*

**biens d'équipement** *(m pl)* Fr
De Anlagegüter *(n pl)*
En capital goods
Es bienes de producción *(m pl)*
It beni strumentali *(m pl)*
Pt mercadorias de capital *(f pl)*

**biens de consommation** *(m pl)* Fr
De Konsumgüter *(n pl)*
En consumer goods
Es bienes de consumo *(m pl)*
It beni di consumo *(m pl)*
Pt bens de consumo *(m pl)*

**biens de consommation durables** *(m pl)* Fr
De dauerhafte Konsumgüter *(n pl)*
En consumer durables
Es bienes de consumo duraderos *(m pl)*
It beni di consumo durabili *(m pl)*
Pt artigos de consumo perduraveis *(m pl)*

**biens de consommation non-durables** *(m pl)* Fr
De nicht-dauerhafte Verbrauchsgüter *(n pl)*
En consumer non-durables
Es bienes de consumo perecederos *(m pl)*
It beni di consumo non durevoli *(m pl)*
Pt bens de consumo não duráveis *(m pl)*

**biens durables** *(m pl)* Fr
De langlebige Güter *(n pl)*
En durable goods
Es mercancías no perecederas *(f pl)*
It beni durevoli *(m pl)*
Pt mercadorias imperecíveis *(f pl)*

**biens immeubles** *(m pl)* Fr
De unbewegliches Vermögen; Immobilien *(n; f pl)*
En real estate; tangible assets
Es bienes inmuebles *(m pl)*
It beni immobili *(m pl)*
Pt propriedade imobiliária *(f)*

**biens mobiliers** *(m pl)* Fr
De bewegliche Güter *(n pl)*
En movable assets
Es mobiliario *(m)*
It proprietà mobiliare *(f)*
Pt bens mobiliários *(m pl)*

**biens saisis** *(m pl)* Fr
De gepfändete Güter *(n pl)*
En distressed goods
Es mercancías embargadas *(f pl)*
It merce sequestrata *(f)*
Pt mercadorias embargadas *(f)*

**Bietende(r)** *(m) n* De
En bidder
Es ofertante *(m)*
Fr enchérisseur *(m)*
It offerente *(m)*
Pt proponente *(m)*

**biglietto d'andata** *(m)* It
De einfache Fahrkarte *(f)*
En single fare; single ticket
Am one way fare
Es pasaje de ida *(m)*
Fr billet d'aller *(m)*
Pt passagem de ida *(f)*

**biglietto di andata e ritorno** *(m)* It
De Rückfahrkarte *(f)*
En return fare; return ticket
Am roundtrip fare
Es pasaje de ida y vuelta *(m)*
Fr billet d'aller et retour *(m)*
Pt passagem de ida e volta *(f)*

**biglietto di banca** *(m)* It
De Banknote *(f)*
En banknote
Am bill
Es billete de banco *(m)*
Fr billet de banque *(m)*
Pt nota de banco *(f)*

**biglietto gratuito** *(m)* It
De Freikarte *(f)*
En free ticket
Es billete gratuito *(m)*
Fr billet de faveur *(m)*
Pt bilhete gratuito *(m)*

**bilan** *(m)* Fr
De Bilanz *(f)*
En balance sheet

Es balance *(m)*
It bilancio *(m)*
Pt balancete *(m)*

**bilan annuel** *(m)* Fr
De Jahresabschluss *(m)*
En annual accounts
Es balance anual *(m)*
It bilancio annuale *(m)*
Pt balancete anual *(m)*

**bilancia** *(f)* n It
De Waage *(f)*
En scales
Es balanza *(f)*
Fr balance *(f)*
Pt balança *(f)*

**bilancia commerciale** *(f)* It
De Handelsbilanz *(f)*
En trade balance
Es balanza comercial *(f)*
Fr balance commerciale *(f)*
Pt balança comercial *(f)*

**bilancia dei pagamenti** *(f)* It
De Zahlungsbilanz *(f)*
En balance of payments
Es balanza de pagos *(f)*
Fr balance des paiements *(f)*
Pt balança de pagamentos *(f)*

**bilancio** *(m)* n It
De Saldo; Bilanz *(m f)*
En balance; balance sheet
Es balance; saldo *(m)*
Fr balance; solde; bilan *(f m m)*
Pt saldo; balancete *(m)*

**bilancio annuale** *(m)* It
De Jahresabschluss *(m)*
En annual accounts
Es balance anual *(m)*
Fr bilan annuel *(m)*
Pt balancete anual *(m)*

**bilancio di verifica** *(m)* It
De Probebilanz *(f)*
En trial balance
Es balance de comprobación de saldos *(m)*
Fr bilan de vérification *(m)*
Pt balancete de verificação *(m)*

**bilancio preventivo** *(m)* It
De Haushaltsplan *(m)*
En budget
Es presupuesto *(m)*
Fr budget *(m)*
Pt orçamento *(m)*

**bilancio riportato** *(m)* It
De Übertrag *(m)*
En balance brought down
Am balance carried forward
Es balance a cuenta nueva *(m)*
Fr solde à reporter *(m)*
Pt saldo transportado *(m)*

**bilan consolidé** *(m)* Fr
De konsolidierte Bilanz *(f)*
En consolidated balance sheet
Es hoja de balance consolidado *(f)*
It bilancio consolidato *(m)*
Pt folha de balanço consolidado *(f)*

**bilan de vérification** *(m)* Fr
De Probebilanz *(f)*
En trial balance
Es balance de comprobación de saldos *(m)*
It bilancio di verifica *(m)*
Pt balancete de verificação *(m)*

**bilan intérimaire** *(m)* Fr
De Zwischenbilanz *(f)*
En interim financial statement
Es extracto financiero provisional *(m)*
It rendiconto finanziario provvisorio *(m)*
Pt extracto financeiro interino *(m)*

**Bilanz** *(f)* De
En balance sheet
Es balance *(m)*
Fr bilan *(m)*
It bilancio *(m)*
Pt balancete *(m)*

**bilateraler Handelsvertrag** *(m)* De
En bilateral trade agreement
Es contrato comercial bilateral *(m)*
Fr accord de commerce bilatéral *(m)*

It accordo di commercio bilaterale *(m)*
Pt acordo comercial bilateral *(m)*

**bilateral trade agreement** En
De bilateraler Handelsvertrag *(m)*
Es contrato comercial bilateral *(m)*
Fr accord de commerce bilatéral *(m)*
It accordo di commercio bilaterale *(m)*
Pt acordo comercial bilateral *(m)*

**bilden** *vb* De
En form; constitute
Es constituir
Fr constituer
It constituire
Pt constituir

**Bildschirmeinheit** *(f)* n De
En visual-display unit (vdu)
Es unidad de visualización *(f)*
Fr unité de visualisation *(f)*
It unità di visualizzazione *(f)*
Pt móvel-montra de exposição de visuais *(f)*

**bilhete de identidade** *(m)* Pt
De Personalausweis *(m)*
En identity card
Es carnet de identidad *(m)*
Fr carte d'identité *(f)*
It carta d'identità *(f)*

**bilhete gratuito** *(m)* Pt
De Freikarte *(f)*
En free ticket
Es billete gratuito *(m)*
Fr billet de faveur *(m)*
It biglietto gratuito *(m)*

**bill** (account) n En
De Rechnung *(f)*
Es cuenta. nota *(f)*
Fr compte; note *(m f)*
It conto; nota *(m f)*
Pt conta *(f)*

**bill** (paper money) Am
En banknote
De Banknote *(f)*
Es billete de banco *(m)*
Fr billet de banque *(m)*

It    biglietto di banca *(m)*
Pt   nota de banco *(f)*

**bill broker** En
De   Wechselmakler *(m)*
Es   corredor de cambios *(m)*
Fr   courtier de bons *(m)*
It    agente di sconto *(m)*
Pt   corretor de câmbios *(m)*

**billet à ordre** *(m)* Fr
De   Schuldschein *(m)*
En   promissory note
Es   pagaré *(m)*
It    pagherò *(m)*
Pt   promissória *(f)*

**billet d'aller** *(m)* Fr
De   einfache Fahrkarte *(f)*
En   single fare; single ticket
Am  one way fare
Es   pasaje de ida *(m)*
It    biglietto d'andata *(m)*
Pt   passagem de ida *(f)*

**billet d'aller et retour** *(m)* Fr
De   Rückfahrkarte *(f)*
En   return fare; return ticket
Am  roundtrip fare
Es   pasaje de ida y vuelta *(m)*
It    biglietto di andata e ritorno
       *(m)*
Pt   passagem de ida e volta *(f)*

**billet de banque** *(m)* Fr
De   Banknote *(f)*
En   banknote
Am  bill
Es   billete de banco *(m)*
It    biglietto di banca *(m)*
Pt   nota de banco *(f)*

**billet de bord** *(m)* Fr
De   Übernahmebescheini-
       gung *(f)*
En   mate's receipt
Es   recibo de embarco *(m)*
It    ricevuta d'imbarco *(f)*
Pt   recibo de embarque *(m)*

**billet de complaisance** *(m)* Fr
De   Gefälligkeitswechsel *(m)*
En   accommodation bill
Es   pagaré de favor *(m)*
It    cambiale di favore *(f)*
Pt   letra de favor *(f)*

**billet de faveur** *(m)* Fr
De   Freikarte *(f)*
En   free ticket
Es   billete gratuito *(m)*
It    biglietto gratuito *(m)*
Pt   bilhete gratuito *(m)*

**billete de banco** *(m)* Es
De   Banknote *(f)*
En   banknote
Am  bill
Fr   billet de banque *(m)*
It    biglietto di banca *(m)*
Pt   nota de banco *(f)*

**billete gratuito** *(m)* Es
De   Freikarte *(f)*
En   free ticket
Fr   billet de faveur *(m)*
It    biglietto gratuito *(m)*
Pt   bilhete gratuito *(m)*

**billig** *adj* De
En   cheap; equitable
Es   barato; equitativo
Fr   bon marché; équitable
It    a buon mercato; equo
Pt   barato; equitativo

**billige Flagge** *(f)* De
En   flag of convenience
Es   bandera de conveniencia
       *(f)*
Fr   enseigne de convenance *(f)*
It    bandiera di convenienza *(f)*
Pt   bandeira de conveniência
       *(f)*

**billiger** *adj* De
En   cheaper
Es   más barato
Fr   meilleur marché
It    meno caro
Pt   mais barato

**billiges Geld** *(n)* De
En   cheap money
Es   dinero barato *(m)*
Fr   argent bon marché *(m)*
It    denaro a basso interesse
       *(m)*
Pt   dinheiro barato *(m)*

**bill of entry** En
De   Zolleinfuhrschein *(m)*
Es   declaración de aduana *(f)*
Fr   déclaration en douane *(f)*

It    bolletta di entrata *(f)*
Pt   declaração alfandegária *(f)*

**bill of exchange** En
De   Wechsel; Tratte *(m f)*
Es   letra de cambio *(f)*
Fr   lettre de change *(f)*
It    tratta cambiale *(f)*
Pt   letra de câmbio *(f)*

**bill of lading** En
De   Konnossement *(n)*
Es   conocimiento (de embar-
       que) *(m)*
Fr   connaissement *(m)*
It    polizza de carico *(f)*
Pt   conhecimento *(m)*

**bill of quantities** En
De   Baukostenvoranschlag *(m)*
Es   cubicación de obra *(f)*
Fr   devis *(m)*
It    preventivo *(m)*
Pt   relação de quantidades *(f)*

**bill of sale** En
De   Kaufvertrag *(m)*
Es   escritura de venta *(f)*
Fr   acte de vente *(f)*
It    contratto di vendita *(m)*
Pt   escritura de venda *(f)*

**bill payable at sight** En
De   Sichttratte *(f)*
Es   letra a la vista *(f)*
Fr   effet exigible à vue *(m)*
It    effetto pagabile a vista *(m)*
Pt   letra à vista *(f)*

**bill rate** En
De   Diskontsatz *(m)*
Es   tasa de descuento (efectos)
       *(m)*
Fr   taux d'escompte (traites)
       *(m)*
It    tasso di sconto (cambiale)
       *(m)*
Pt   taxa de desconto (letras) *(f)*

**bills discounted** En
De   diskontierte Wechsel *(m pl)*
Es   efectos descontados *(m pl)*
Fr   effets escomptés *(m pl)*
It    effetti scontati *(m pl)*
Pt   letras descontadas *(f pl)*

**bills for collection** En
De fällige Wechsel *(m pl)*
Es efectos a cobrar *(m pl)*
Fr effets en recouvrement *(m pl)*
It effetti all'incasso *(m pl)*
Pt letras a descontar *(f pl)*

**bills payable** En
De Wechselschulden *(f pl)*
Es letras pagaderas *(f pl)*
Fr effets à payer *(m pl)*
It effetti passivi *(m pl)*
Pt letras a pagar *(f pl)*

**bills receivable** En
De Wechselforderungen *(f pl)*
Es letras a cobrar *(f pl)*
Fr effets à recevoir *(m pl)*
It effetti attivi *(m pl)*
Pt letras a cobrar *(f pl)*

**bindender Vertrag** *(m)* De
En binding agreement
Es obligación irrevocable *(f)*
Fr convention irrévocable *(f)*
It contratto vincolante *(m)*
Pt acordo irrevogavel *(m)*

**binding agreement** En
De bindender Vertrag *(m)*
Es obligación irrevocable *(f)*
Fr convention irrévocable *(f)*
It contratto vincolante *(m)*
Pt acordo irrevogavel *(m)*

**Binnenhandel** *(m) n* De
En home trade
Am domestic sales
Es comercio interior *(m)*
Fr commerce intérieur *(m)*
It commercio interno *(m)*
Pt comércio interno *(m)*

**bitte nachsenden** De
En please forward
Es se ruega hacer seguir
Fr prière de faire suivre
It far proseguire
Pt é favor enviar

**blacking** *n* En
Am boycott
De Boykott *(m)*
Es boicoteo *(m)*
Fr boycottage *(m)*
It ostracismo *(m)*
Pt boicote *(m)*

**black list** En
De schwarze Liste *(f)*
Es lista negra *(f)*
Fr liste noire *(f)*
It lista nera *(f)*
Pt lista negra *(f)*

**black market** (securities) En
De schwarze Börse *(f)*
Es bolsa negra *(f)*
Fr bourse noire *(f)*
It borsa nera *(f)*
Pt bolsa negra *(f)*

**black market** (goods) En
De schwarzer Markt *(m)*
Es mercado negro *(m)*
Fr marché noir *(m)*
It mercato nero *(m)*
Pt mercado negro *(m)*

**blanc-seing** *(m) n* Fr
De Blankounterschrift *(f)*
En blank signature
Es firma en blanco *(f)*
It firma in bianco *(f)*
Pt assinatura em branco *(f)*

**blank bill** En
De Blankowechsel *(m)*
Es letra en blanco *(f)*
Fr traite en blanc *(f)*
It effetto in bianco *(m)*
Pt letra em branco *(f)*

**blank cheque** En
De Blankoscheck *(m)*
Es cheque en blanco *(m)*
Fr chèque en blanc *(m)*
It assegno in bianco *(m)*
Pt cheque em branco *(m)*

**blank credit** En
De offener Kredit *(m)*
Es crédito en blanco *(m)*
Fr crédit à découvert *(m)*
It credito in bianco *(m)*
Pt crédito em branco *(m)*

**blank endorsement** En
De Blankoindossament *(n)*
Es endoso en blanco *(m)*
Fr endossement en blanc *(m)*
It girata in bianco *(f)*
Pt endosse em branco *(m)*

**blank form** En
De Blankoformular *(n)*
Es formulario en blanco *(m)*
Fr formulaire en blanc *(m)*
It modulo in bianco *(m)*
Pt impresso em branco *(m)*

**Blankoformular** *(n) n* De
En blank form
Es formulario en blanco *(m)*
Fr formulaire en blanc *(m)*
It modulo in bianco *(m)*
Pt impresso em branco *(m)*

**Blankoindossament** *(n) n* De
En blank endorsement
Es endoso en blanco *(m)*
Fr endossement en blanc *(m)*
It girata in bianco *(f)*
Pt endosse em branco *(m)*

**Blankoscheck** *(m) n* De
En blank cheque
Am blank check
Es cheque en blanco *(m)*
Fr chèque en blanc *(m)*
It assegno in bianco *(m)*
Pt cheque em branco *(m)*

**Blankounterschrift** *(f) n* De
En blank signature
Es firma en blanco *(f)*
Fr blanc-seing *(m)*
It firma in bianco *(f)*
Pt assinatura em branco *(f)*

**Blankowechsel** *(m) n* De
En blank bill
Es letra en blanco *(f)*
Fr traite en blanc *(f)*
It effetto in bianco *(m)*
Pt letra em branco *(f)*

**blank signature** En
De Blankounterschrift *(f)*
Es firma en blanco *(f)*
Fr blanc-seing *(m)*
It firma in bianco *(f)*
Pt assinatura em branco *(f)*

**Blitz** *(m) n* De
En lightning
Es relámpago *(m)*
Fr foudre *(f)*
It fulmine *(m)*
Pt relâmpago *(m)*

**blocage des dividendes** (m) Fr
De Dividendenstop (m)
En dividend limitation
Es bloqueo de dividendos (m)
It blocco dei dividendi (m)
Pt limitação de dividendos (f)

**blocage des salaires** (m) Fr
De Lohnstopp (m)
En wage-freeze
Es bloqueo de salarios (m)
It blocco dei salari (m)
Pt congelação de salários (f)

**blocco** (m) n It
De Blockade (f)
En blockade
Es bloqueo (m)
Fr blocus (m)
Pt bloqueio (m)

**blocco degli affitti** (m) It
De Mietzinskontrolle (f)
En rent control
Es control de alquileres (m)
Fr contrôle des loyers (m)
Pt controlo de rendas (m)

**blocco dei dividendi** (m) It
De Dividendenstop (m)
En dividend limitation
Es bloqueo de dividendos (m)
Fr blocage des dividendes (m)
Pt limitação de dividendos (f)

**blocco dei salari** (m) It
De Lohnstopp (m)
En wage-freeze
Es bloqueo de salarios (m)
Fr blocage des salaires (m)
Pt congelação de salários (f)

**bloc commercial** (m) Fr
De Handelsblock (m)
En trade bloc
Es bloque comercial (m)
It unione commerciale (f)
Pt bloque comercial (m)

**blockade** n En
De Blockade (f)
Es bloqueo (m)
Fr blocus (m)
It blocco (m)
Pt bloqueio (m)

**Blockade** (f) n De
En blockade
Es bloqueo (m)
Fr blocus (m)
It blocco (m)
Pt bloqueio (m)

**block diagram** En
De Säulendiagramm (m)
Es diagrama de bloque (m)
Fr ordinogramme (m)
It schema a blocchi (m)
Pt organigrama (m)

**blocked account** En
De gesperrtes Konto (n)
Es cuenta bloqueada (f)
Fr compte bloqué (m)
It conto bloccato (m)
Pt conta bloqueada (f)

**blocked deposits** En
De gesperrte Einlagen (f pl)
Es depósitos bloqueados (m pl)
Fr dépôts bloqués (m pl)
It deposito con vincolo bloccato (m)
Pt depósitos bloqueados (m pl)

**blocked exchange** En
De blockierte Devisen (f pl)
Es divisas bloqueadas (f pl)
Fr devises bloquées (f pl)
It valute bloccate (f pl)
Pt câmbio bloqueado (m)

**blockierte Devisen** (f pl) De
En blocked exchange
Es divisas bloqueadas (f pl)
Fr devises bloquées (f pl)
It valute bloccate (f pl)
Pt câmbio bloqueado (m)

**block of flats** En
Am apartment house
De Wohnungsgebäude (n)
Es bloque de pisos (m)
Fr immeuble (m)
It fabbricato di appartamenti (m)
Pt edifício de andares (m)

**blocus** (m) n Fr
De Blockade (f)
En blockade
Es bloqueo (m)

It blocco (m)
Pt bloqueio (m)

**bloque comercial** (m) Es, Pt
De Handelsblock (m)
En trade bloc
Fr bloc commercial (m)
It unione commerciale (f)

**bloque de pisos** (m) Es
De Wohnungsgebäude (n)
En block of flats
Am apartment house
Fr immeuble (m)
It fabbricato di appartamenti (m)
Pt edifício de andares (m)

**bloqueio** (m) n Pt
De Blockade (f)
En blockade
Es bloqueo (m)
Fr blocus (m)
It blocco (m)

**bloqueo** (m) n Es
De Blockade (f)
En blockade
Fr blocus (m)
It blocco (m)
Pt bloqueio (m)

**bloqueo de dividendos** (m) Es
De Dividendenstop (m)
En dividend limitation
Fr blocage des dividendes (m)
It blocco dei dividendi (m)
Pt limitação de dividendos (f)

**bloqueo de salarios** (m) Es
De Lohnstopp (m)
En wage-freeze
Fr blocage des salaires (m)
It blocco dei salari (m)
Pt congelação de salários (f)

**bloquer un chèque** Fr
De einen Scheck sperren
En stop a cheque
Am stop a check
Es suspender el pago de un cheque
It fermare un assegno
Pt suspender o pagamento de um cheque

85 bon

**blotting paper** En
  De Löschpapier *(n)*
  Es papel secante *(m)*
  Fr papier buvard *(m)*
  It carta assorbente *(f)*
  Pt papel mata-borrão *(m)*

**board meeting** En
  De Vorstandssitzung *(f)*
  Es reunión del consejo de
    administración *(f)*
  Fr réunion du conseil d'admi-
    nistration *(f)*
  It riunione del consiglio
    d'amministrazione *(f)*
  Pt reunião da administração
    *(f)*

**board of directors** En
  De Vorstand *(m)*
  Es consejo de administración
    *(m)*
  Fr conseil d'administration
    *(m)*
  It consiglio d'amministrazione
    *(m)*
  Pt direcção *(f)*

**boa vontade** *(f)* Pt
  De Geschäftswert *(m)*
  En goodwill
  Es valor de la clientela *(m)*
  Fr bon vouloir *(m)*
  It avviamento *(m)*

**bodega** *(f)* n Es
  De Laderaum *(m)*
  En hold
  Fr cale *(f)*
  It stiva *(f)*
  Pt porão *(m)*

**Bodenfläche** *(f)* n De
  En floor space
  Es superficie de piso *(f)*
  Fr surface de plancher *(f)*
  It superficie di pavimento *(f)*
  Pt área de chão *(f)*

**Bodmereibrief** *(m)* n De
  En bottomry bond
  Es contrato de préstamo a la
    gruesa *(m)*
  Fr contrat à la grosse aven-
    ture *(m)*
  It contratto di prestito a
    cambio marittimo *(m)*
  Pt título de bodemeria *(m)*

**Bodmereidarlehenszinsen** *(m
  pl)* n De
  En bottomry interest
  Es interés de préstamo a la
    gruesa *(m)*
  Fr profit maritime *(m)*
  It interessenza a cambio ma-
    rittimo *(f)*
  Pt juro de bodemeria *(m)*

**bogus** *adj* En
  De falsch
  Es falso
  Fr faux
  It falso
  Pt falso

**bogus company** En
  Am phantom operation
  De Schwindelgesellschaft *(f)*
  Es sociedad fantasma *(f)*
  Fr société fantôme *(f)*
  It società fasulla *(f)*
  Pt sociedade fantasma *(f)*

**boicote** *(m)* n Pt
  De Boykott *(m)*
  En boycott; blacking
  Es boicoteo *(m)*
  Fr boycottage *(m)*
  It boicottaggio; ostracismo
    *(m)*

**boicoteo** *(m)* n Es
  De Boykott *(m)*
  En boycott; blacking
  Fr boycottage *(m)*
  It boicottaggio; ostracismo
    *(m)*
  Pt boicote *(m)*

**boicottaggio** *(m)* n It
  De Boykott *(m)*
  En boycott
  Es boicoteo *(m)*
  Fr boycottage *(m)*
  Pt boicote *(m)*

**boîte aux lettres** *(f)* Fr
  De Briefkasten *(m)*
  En letter-box
  Am mail-box
  Es buzón *(m)*
  It cassetta postale *(f)*
  Pt caixa do correio *(f)*

**bolletta di entrata** *(f)* It
  De Zolleinfuhrschein; Antrags-
    formular *(m n)*
  En bill of entry; entry-form
  Es declaración de aduana;
    solicitud de inscripción *(f)*
  Fr déclaration en douane;
    feuille d'inscription *(f)*
  Pt declaração alfandegária;
    impresso de admissão *(f
    m)*

**bollettino di spedizione** *(m)* It
  De Versandschein *(m)*
  En despatch note
  Es aviso de expedición *(m)*
  Fr bordereau d'expédition;
    bulletin d'envoi *(m)*
  Pt aviso de despacho *(m)*

**bollo** *(m)* n It
  De Stempel *(m)*
  En stamp
  Es sello *(m)*
  Fr timbre *(m)*
  Pt selo *(m)*

**bolsa** *(f)* n Es, Pt
  De Börse *(f)*
  En stock exchange
  Fr bourse *(f)*
  It borsa *(f)*

**bolsa de trabajo** *(f)* Es
  De Arbeitsnachweisstelle *(f)*
  En employment exchange
  Am state employment agency
  Fr bureau de placement *(m)*
  It ufficio di collocamento *(m)*
  Pt centro de serviços de
    emprego *(m)*

**bolsa negra** *(f)* Es, Pt
  De schwarze Börse *(f)*
  En black market (securities)
  Fr bourse noire *(f)*
  It borsa nera *(f)*

**bom** *adj* Pt
  De gut
  En good
  Es bueno
  Fr bon
  It buono

**bon** *(m)* n Fr
  De Obligation; Gutschein *(f m)*
  En bond; voucher

Es bono; obligación *(m f)*
It buono; obbligazione *(m f)*
Pt titulo; obrigação *(m f)*

**bon** *adj* Fr
De gut
En good
Es bueno
It buono
Pt bom

**bonança** *(f)* n Pt
De Hausse *(f)*
En boom
Es bonanza *(f)*
Fr haute conjoncture *(f)*
It rialzo *(m)*

**bonanza** *(f)* n Es
De Hausse *(f)*
En boom
Fr haute conjoncture *(f)*
It rialzo *(m)*
Pt bonança *(f)*

**bon au porteur** *(m)* Fr
De Inhaberobligation *(f)*
En bearer bond
Es título al portador *(m)*
It titolo al portatore *(m)*
Pt título ao portador *(m)*

**bond** n En
De Obligation; Pfandbrief *(f m)*
Es bono; obligación *(m f)*
Fr bon; obligation *(m f)*
It buono; obbligazione *(m f)*
Pt titulo; obrigação *(m f)*

**bonded goods** En
De Waren unter Zollverschluss
   *(f pl)*
Es mercancías en aduana *(f pl)*
Fr marchandises en douane *(f pl)*
It merci sotto vincolo doganale *(f pl)*
Pt mercadorias à ordem da alfândega *(f pl)*

**bonded warehouse** En
De Lager unter Zollverschluss *(n)*
Es almacén de aduanas *(m)*
Fr entrepôt *(m)*
It magazzino doganale *(m)*
Pt armazém alfandegário *(m)*

**bondholder** n En
De Obligationär *(m)*
Es obligacionista *(m)*
Fr obligataire *(m)*
It portatore di obbligazioni *(m)*
Pt titular de obrigações *(m)*

**bon du trésor** *(m)* Fr
De Schatzwechsel *(m)*
En exchequer bond
Am treasury bond
Es bono de tesorería *(m)*
It buono del tesoro *(m)*
Pt título do tesouro *(m)*

**bonificación** *(f)* n Es
De Rabatt *(m)*
En allowance
Fr rabais *(m)*
It abbuono *(m)*
Pt provisão *(f)*

**bonificación por no-recla-
mación** *(f)* Es
De Schadenfreiheitsrabatt *(m)*
En no-claims discount or bonus
Fr bonification pour non sinistre *(f)*
It sconto per assenza di sinistri *(m)*
Pt disconto por ausência de reclamações *(m)*

**bonification pour non sinistre**
*(f)* Fr
De Schadenfreiheitsrabatt *(m)*
En no-claims discount or bonus
Es bonificación por no-reclamación *(f)*
It sconto per assenza di sinistri *(m)*
Pt disconto por ausência de reclamações *(m)*

**bon marché** Fr
De billig
En cheap
Es barato
It a buon mercato
Pt barato

**bonne garde** *(f)* Fr
De sichere Verwahrung *(f)*
En safe custody
Es custodia *(f)*

It custodia *(f)*
Pt custódia segura *(f)*

**bonneterie** *(f)* n Fr
De Strickwaren *(f pl)*
En knitted goods
Es géneros de punto *(m pl)*
It maglieria *(f)*
Pt artigos de malha de lã *(m pl)*

**bono** *(m)* n Es
De Obligation; Gutschein *(f m)*
En bond; voucher
Fr bon; obligation *(m f)*
It buono; obbligazione *(m f)*
Pt titulo; obrigação *(m f)*

**bono de tesorería** *(m)* Es
De Schatzwechsel *(m)*
En exchequer bond
Am treasury bond
Fr bon du trésor *(m)*
It buono del tesoro *(m)*
Pt título do tesouro *(m)*

**bons offices** *(m pl)* Fr
De Liebesdienste *(m pl)*
En good offices
Es buenos servicios *(m pl)*
It buoni uffici *(m pl)*
Pt bons serviços *(m pl)*

**bons serviços** *(m pl)* Pt
De Liebesdienste *(m pl)*
En good offices
Es buenos servicios *(m pl)*
Fr bons offices *(m pl)*
It buoni uffici *(m pl)*

**bonus** n En
De Prämie *(f)*
Es prima; gratificación *(f)*
Fr prime; gratification *(f)*
It gratificazione *(f)*
Pt bonus; gratificação *(m f)*

**bonus** *(m)* n Pt
De Prämie *(f)*
En bonus
Es prima; gratificación *(f)*
Fr prime; gratification *(f)*
It gratificazione *(f)*

**bonus shares** En
Am stock dividend
De Gratisaktien *(f pl)*

Es acciones dadas como pri-
mas *(f pl)*
Fr actions d'attribution *(f pl)*
It azioni di godimento *(f pl)*
Pt acções de prémio *(f pl)*

**bon vouloir** *(m)* Fr
De Geschäftswert *(m)*
En goodwill
Es valor de la clientela *(m)*
It avviamento *(m)*
Pt boa vontade *(f)*

**book cost** En
De Buchwert der Einkäufe *(m)*
Es coste contable *(m)*
Fr prix de revient comptable
*(m)*
It costo contabile *(m)*
Pt custo contabilizado *(m)*

**book debt** En
De Buchschuld *(f)*
Es deuda contabilizada *(f)*
Fr dette comptable *(f)*
It debito attivo *(m)*
Pt débito contabilizado *(m)*

**bookkeeper** *n* En
De Buchhalter *(m)*
Es contable *(m)*
Fr commis-contable *(m)*
It contabile *(m)*
Pt empregado de contabili-
dade *(m)*

**book-keeping** *n* En
De Buchhaltung *(f)*
Es contabilidad *(f)*
Fr comptabilité *(f)*
It contabilità *(f)*
Pt contabilidade *(f)*

**books of account** En
De Geschäftsbücher *(n pl)*
Es libros de cuentas *(m pl)*
Fr livres comptables *(m pl)*
It libri contabili *(m pl)*
Pt livros de contabilidade *(m
pl)*

**book value** En
De Buchwert *(m)*
Es valor contable *(m)*
Fr valeur comptable *(f)*
It valore d'inventario *(m)*
Pt valor contabilizado *(m)*

**boom** *n* En
De Hausse *(f)*
Es bonanza *(f)*
Fr haute conjoncture *(f)*
It rialzo *(m)*
Pt bonança *(f)*

**bordereau d'achat** *(m)* Fr
De Schlusschein *(m)*
En contract note
Es nota de contrato *(f)*
It nota di contratto *(f)*
Pt nota-contrato *(f)*

**bordereau d'expédition** *(m)* Fr
De Versandschein *(m)*
En despatch note
Es aviso de expedición *(m)*
It bollettino di spedizione *(m)*
Pt aviso de despacho *(m)*

**bordereau de livraison** *(m)* Fr
De Lieferschein *(m)*
En delivery note
Es aviso de entrega *(m)*
It nota di consegna *(f)*
Pt guia de entrega *(f)*

**borrador** *(m)* *n* Es
De Konzept; Entwurf *(m n)*
En draft; rough copy
Fr projet; brouillon *(m)*
It bozza *(f)*
Pt rascunho *(m)*

**borrow** *vb* En
De entleihen
Es pedir un préstamo
Fr emprunter
It prestire
Pt contrair empréstimo

**borrowed capital** En
De Fremdkapital *(n)*
Es capital a préstamo *(m)*
Fr capitaux empruntés *(m pl)*
It capitale preso a prestito
*(m)*
Pt capital por empréstimo *(m)*

**borrower** *n* En
De Kreditnehmer *(m)*
Es prestatario *(m)*
Fr emprunteur *(m)*
It accattatore *(m)*
Pt beneficiário de empréstimo
*(m)*

**borrowing power** En
De Kreditfähigkeit *(f)*
Es facultad de crédito *(f)*
Fr capacité à avoir du crédit
*(f)*
It capacità creditizia *(f)*
Pt potencial de obtenção de
crédito *(m)*

**borsa** *(f)* *n* It
De Börse *(f)*
En stock exchange
Es bolsa *(f)*
Fr bourse *(f)*
Pt bolsa *(f)*

**borsa nera** *(f)* It
De schwarze Börse *(f)*
En black market (securities)
Es bolsa negra *(f)*
Fr bourse noire *(f)*
Pt bolsa negra *(f)*

**Börse** *(f)* *n* De
En stock exchange
Es bolsa *(f)*
Fr bourse *(f)*
It borsa *(f)*
Pt bolsa *(f)*

**(an der) Börse notierte Wert-**
**papiere** *(n pl)* De
En listed security
Es valores cotizables *(m pl)*
Fr valeurs admises à la Bourse
*(f pl)*
It titoli quotati (in Borsa) *(m
pl)*
Pt valor de Bolsa com cotação
oficial *(m)*

**(die) Börse spielen** De
En gamble on the stock
exchange
Es jugar a la Bolsa
Fr jouer à la Bourse
It giocare in Borsa
Pt jogar na Bolsa

**Börsenhändler** *(m)* *n* De
En stockjobber
Es agiotista *(m)*
Fr marchand de titres *(m)*
It aggiotatore *(m)*
Pt agiota *(m)*

**Börsenkurs** (m) n De
En  stock-exchange quotation
Es  curso de bolsa (m)
Fr  cours de bourse (m)
It  quotation di borsa (f)
Pt  cotação da bolsa (f)

**Börsenmakler** (m) n De
En  stockbroker
Es  corredor de bolsa (m)
Fr  courtier en bourse (m)
It  agente di borsa (m)
Pt  corretor da bolsa (m)

**Börsentag** (m) n De
En  market day
Es  día de bolsa (m)
Fr  jour de bourse (m)
It  giorno di borsa (m)
Pt  dia de bolsa (m)

**botte** (f) n It
De  Fass (n)
En  barrel
Es  barril (m)
Fr  tonneau (m)
Pt  barril (m)

**bottega** (f) n It
De  Laden (m)
En  shop
Es  tienda (f)
Fr  magasin (m)
Pt  loja (f)

**bottle-neck** n En
De  Engpass (m)
Es  embotellamiento (m)
Fr  goulot d'étranglement (m)
It  strozzatura (f)
Pt  engarrafamento (m)

**bottomry bond** En
De  Bodmereibrief (m)
Es  contrato de préstamo a la
    gruesa (m)
Fr  contrat à la grosse aven-
    ture (m)
It  contratto di prestito a
    cambio marittimo (m)
Pt  titulo de bodemeria (m)

**bottomry interest** En
De  Bodmereidarlehenszinsen
    (m pl)
Es  interés de préstamo a la
    gruesa (m)
Fr  profit maritime (m)

It  interessenza a cambio ma-
    rittimo (f)
Pt  juro de bodemeria (m)

**bouche-trou** (m) n Fr
De  Überbrückung (f)
En  stop-gap
Es  recurso provisional (m)
It  provvedimento temporaneo
    (m)
Pt  tapa-buracos (m)

**bought ledger** En
Am  purchase book
De  Einkaufsbuch (n)
Es  libro mayor de compras
    (m)
Fr  grand livre d'achats (m)
It  mastro acquisti (m)
Pt  livro-mestre de compras
    (m)

**bourse** (f) n Fr
De  Börse (f)
En  stock exchange
Es  bolsa (f)
It  borsa (f)
Pt  bolsa (f)

**bourse noire** (f) Fr
De  schwarze Börse (f)
En  black market (securities)
Es  bolsa negra (f)
It  borsa nera (f)
Pt  bolsa negra (f)

**bout** (m) n Fr
De  Ziel (n)
En  goal
Es  meta; objetivo (f m)
It  scopo; traguardo (m)
Pt  meta; objectivo (f m)

**boycott** n En
De  Boykott (m)
Es  boicoteo (m)
Fr  boycottage (m)
It  boicottaggio (m)
Pt  boicote (m)

**boycottage** (m) n Fr
De  Boykott (m)
En  boycott; blacking
Es  boicoteo (m)
It  boicottaggio (m)
Pt  boicote (m)

**Boykott** (m) n De
En  boycott; blacking
Es  boicoteo (m)
Fr  boycottage (m)
It  boicottaggio (m)
Pt  boicote (m)

**bozza** (f) n It
De  Konzept (n)
En  draft; copy
Es  borrador (m)
Fr  projet (m)
Pt  rascunho (m)

**branch** n En
De  Filiale; Zweigstelle (f)
Es  sucursal; filial (f)
Fr  succursale; filiale (f)
It  succursale; filiale (f)
Pt  filial (f)

**branch bank** En
De  Filialbank; Zweigbank (f)
Es  sucursal del banco (f)
Fr  banque succursale (f)
It  banca succursale (f)
Pt  filial de banco (f)

**branch office** En
De  Zweigbüro (n)
Es  sucursal (f)
Fr  succursale (f)
It  succursale (f)
Pt  sucursal (f)

**brand** n En
De  Handelsmarke (f)
Es  marca (de fábrica) (f)
Fr  marque (f)
It  marca (di fabbrica) (f)
Pt  marca de fabrico (f)

**Brand** (m) n De
En  fire
Es  fuego; incendio (m)
Fr  incendie (f)
It  incendio (m)
Pt  fogo; incêndio (m)

**branded goods** En
De  Markenwaren (f pl)
Es  artículos de marca (m pl)
Fr  articles de marque (m pl)
It  articoli di marca (m pl)
Pt  artigos de marca (m pl)

**brand image** En
De Warenimage (n)
Es imagen de marca (f)
Fr image de marque (f)
It immagine di marca (f)
Pt imagem apresentada pela marca (f)

**brand leader** En
De führende Marke (f)
Es marca directriz (f)
Fr marque de point (f)
It marca di punta (f)
Pt marca mais cotada (f)

**brand name** En
De Markenbezeichnung (f)
Es nombre comercial (m)
Fr marque de fabrique (f)
It marca (f)
Pt marca (f)

**breach of contract** En
De Vertragsverletzung (f)
Es incumplimiento del contrato (m)
Fr rupture de contrat (f)
It rottura di contratto (f)
Pt rotura de contrato (f)

**breach of warranty** En
De Verletzung der Gewährleistungspflicht (f)
Es incumplimiento de la garantía (m)
Fr rupture de garantie (f)
It violazione di garanzia (f)
Pt violação de garantia (f)

**break-even point** En
De Rentabilitätsgrenze (f)
Es punto de igualdad de ingresos y gastos (m)
Fr point de seuil (m)
It punto di pareggio (m)
Pt ponto de acerto (m)

**breaking bulk** En
De Löschen der Ladung (n)
Es fraccionamiento de la carga (m)
Fr rupture de charge (f)
It inizio scarico (m)
Pt retalhar a carga (f)

**Brennerei** (f) n De
En distillery
Es destilería (f)

Fr distillerie (f)
It distilleria (f)
Pt distilaria (f)

**brevet** (m) n Fr
De Patenturkunde (f)
En letters patent
Am patent
Es patente de invención (f)
It brevetto (m)
Pt patente de invenção (m)

**brevet d'invention** (m) Fr
De Erfindungspatent (n)
En patent
Es patente (f)
It brevetto (m)
Pt patente (f)

**brevetto** (m) n It
De Erfindungspatent; Patenturkunde (n f)
En patent; letters patent
Es patente; patente de invención (f)
Fr brevet; brevet d'invention (m)
Pt patente; patente de invenção

**bribe** n En
De Bestechungsgeld (n)
Es soborno (m)
Fr pot-de-vin (f)
It dono per corrompere (m)
Pt soborno (m)

**bribe** vb En
De bestechen
Es sobornar
Fr corrompre
It corrompere
Pt sobornar

**bribery** n En
De Bestechung (f)
Es soborno (m)
Fr corruption (f)
It corruzione (f)
Pt soborno (m)

**bridging loan** En
Am bridge-over
De Vorschusskredit (m)
Es crédito provisional (m)
Fr crédit provisoire (m)
It credito provvisorio (m)
Pt crédito provisório (m)

**Brief** (m) n De
En letter
Es carta; letra (f)
Fr lettre (f)
It lettera (f)
Pt carta (f)

**Briefkasten** (m) n De
En letter-box
Am mail-box
Es buzón (m)
Fr boîte aux lettres (f)
It cassetta postale (f)
Pt caixa do correio (f)

**Briefkopf** (m) n De
En letterhead
Es membrete (m)
Fr en-tête (m)
It intestazione (f)
Pt cabeçalho (m)

**Briefmarke** (f) n De
En postage stamp
Es sello de correos (m)
Fr timbre-poste (m)
It francobollo (m)
Pt selo postal (m)

**Briefwechsel** (m) n De
En correspondence
Es correspondencia (f)
Fr correspondance (f)
It corrispondenza (f)
Pt correspondência (f)

**broker** n En
De Makler (m)
Es corredor (m)
Fr courtier (m)
It sensale (m)
Pt corretor (m)

**brokerage** n En
De Maklergebühr (f)
Es corretaje (m)
Fr courtage (m)
It senseria (f)
Pt corretagem (f)

**brouillon** (m) n Fr
De Entwurf (m)
En rough copy
Am draft
Es borrador (m)
It brutta copia (f)
Pt cópia rascunho (f)

**Bruchteil** (n) n De
En fraction
Es fracción (f)
Fr fraction (f)
It frazione (f)
Pt fracção (f)

**Brüsseler Verzeichnis** (n) De
En Brussels Nomenclature
Es Nomenclatura de Bruselas (f)
Fr Nomenclature de Bruxelles (N.D.B.) (f)
It Nomenclatura di Bruxelles (f)
Pt Nomenclatura de Bruxelas (f)

**Brussels Nomenclature** En
De Brüsseler Verzeichnis (n)
Es Nomenclatura de Bruselas (f)
Fr Nomenclature de Bruxelles (N.D.B.) (f)
It Nomenclatura di Bruxelles (f)
Pt Nomenclatura de Bruxelas (f)

**brut** adj Fr
De brutto
En gross
Es bruto
It lordo
Pt bruto

**bruto** adj Es, Pt
De brutto
En gross
Fr brut; gros
It lordo

**brutto** adj De
En gross
Es bruto
Fr brut; gros
It lordo
Pt bruto

**Bruttobetrag** (m) n De
En gross amount
Es importe bruto (m)
Fr montant brut (m)
It importo lordo (m)
Pt importância total (m)

**Bruttoeinkommen** (n) n De
En gross income
Es ingreso bruto (m)
Fr rendement brut (m)
It reddito lordo (m)
Pt receita bruta (f)

**Bruttogewicht** (n) n De
En gross weight
Es peso bruto (m)
Fr poids brut (m)
It peso lordo (m)
Pt peso bruto (m)

**Bruttogewinn** (m) n De
En gross profit
Es ganancia bruta (f)
Fr bénéfice brut (m)
It utile lordo (m)
Pt lucro bruto (m)

**Bruttoinlandprodukt** (n) n De
En gross domestic product (GDP)
Es producto interior bruto (m)
Fr produit intérieur brut (m)
It prodotto interno lordo (m)
Pt produto interno bruto (m)

**Bruttoprämie** (f) n De
En gross premium
Es prima bruta (f)
Fr prime brute (f)
It premio lordo (m)
Pt prémio bruto (m)

**Brutto-Registertonne** (f) n De
En gross register ton
Es tonelada de registro brutto (f)
Fr tonneau de jauge brute (m)
It tonnellaggio lordo di registro (m)
Pt tonelada de registo bruto (f)

**Bruttosozialprodukt** (n) n De
En gross national product (GNP)
Es producto nacional bruto (m)
Fr produit national brut (m)
It prodotto nazionale lordo (m)
Pt produto nacional bruto (m)

**Brutto-Tonnage** (f) n De
En gross tonnage
Es tonelaje brutto (m)
Fr tonnage brut (m)
It tonnellaggio lordo (m)
Pt tonelagem de peso bruto (f)

**Brutto-Tonne** (f) n De
En gross ton
Es tonelada bruta (f)
Fr tonne forte (f)
It tonnellata lorda (f)
Pt tonelada de peso bruto (f)

**Bruttoverdienstspanne** (f) n De
En gross margin
Es márgen bruto (m)
Fr marge brute de bénéfices (f)
It margine lordo (m)
Pt margem bruta (f)

**Bruttozins** (m) n De
En gross interest
Es interés bruto (m)
Fr intérêts bruts (m pl)
It interesse lordo (m)
Pt juro bruto (m)

**Bücherrevision** (f) n De
En audit
Es revisión de cuentas (f)
Fr vérification comptable (f)
It revisione dei conti (f)
Pt fiscalização de contas (f)

**Bücherrevisor** (m) n De
En auditor
Es revisor de cuentas (m)
Fr réviseur des comptes (m)
It sindaco (m)
Pt fiscal de contas (m)

**Buchhalter** (m) n De
En accountant; bookkeeper
Es contador (m)
Fr comptable (m)
It contabile (m)
Pt contabilista (m)

**Buchhaltung** (f) n De
En book-keeping; accountancy; accounts department
Es contabilidad; departamento de contabilidad (f m)

Fr comptabilité; service de la comptabilité *(f m)*
It contabilità; ufficio contabilità *(f m)*
Pt contabilidade; departamento de contabilidade *(f m)*

**Buchschuld** *(f) n* De
En book debt
Es deuda contabilizada *(f)*
Fr dette comptable *(f)*
It debito attivo *(m)*
Pt débito contabilizado *(m)*

**Buchwert** *(m) n* De
En book value
Es valor contable *(m)*
Fr valeur comptable *(f)*
It valore d'inventario *(m)*
Pt valor contabilizado *(m)*

**Buchwert der Einkäufe** *(m)* De
En book cost
Es coste contable *(m)*
Fr prix de revient comptable *(m)*
It costo contabile *(m)*
Pt custo contabilizado *(m)*

**budget** *n* En, Fr *(m)*
De Haushaltsplan *(m)*
Es presupuesto *(m)*
It bilancio preventivo *(m)*
Pt orçamento *(m)*

**budgetary control** En
De Haushaltskontrolle *(f)*
Es control presupuestario *(m)*
Fr contrôle budgétaire *(m)*
It controllo a bilancio preventivo *(m)*
Pt controlo orçamental *(m)*

**bueno** *adj* Es
De gut
En good
Fr bon
It buono
Pt bom

**buenos servicios** *(m pl)* Es
De Liebesdienste *(m pl)*
En good offices
Fr bons offices *(m pl)*
It buoni uffici *(m pl)*
Pt bons serviços *(m pl)*

**Buffer-stocks** *(m pl) n* De
En buffer stocks
Es existencias de regularización *(f pl)*
Fr stocks de régularisation *(m pl)*
It scorte di equilibrio *(f pl)*
Pt existências de regularização *(f pl)*

**buffer stocks** En
De Buffer-stocks *(m pl)*
Es existencias de regularización *(f pl)*
Fr stocks de régularisation *(m pl)*
It scorte di equilibrio *(f pl)*
Pt existências de regularização *(f pl)*

**building contractor** En
De Bauunternehmer *(m)*
Es contratista de obras *(m)*
Fr entrepreneur de bâtiment *(m)*
It impresa edile *(f)*
Pt constructor de obras *(m)*

**building land** En
De Bauland *(n)*
Es solares *(m pl)*
Fr terrain à bâtir *(m)*
It terreno edile *(m)*
Pt terreno para construção *(m)*

**building loan** En
De Baukredit *(m)*
Es crédito de construcción *(m)*
Fr crédit de construction *(m)*
It prestito immobiliare *(m)*
Pt empréstimo para construção *(m)*

**built-in obsolescence** En
De eingebautes Veralten *(n)*
Es decaimiento incorporado *(m)*
Fr désuétude incorporée *(f)*
It decadimento incorporato *(m)*
Pt obsolência pre-incorporada *(f)*

**bulk cargo** En
De Schüttgut *(n)*
Es carga en granel *(f)*
Fr cargaison en vrac *(f)*
It carico alla rinfusa *(m)*
Pt carga a granel *(f)*

**bulk carrier** En
De Massenfrachtführer *(m)*
Es transportador a grand *(m)*
Fr transporteur de marchandises en vrac *(m)*
It trasportatore di merce alla rinfusa *(m)*
Pt transportador de carga geral *(m)*

**bull** *n* En
De Haussespekulant *(m)*
Es alcista *(m)*
Fr haussier *(m)*
It rialzista *(m)*
Pt altista *(f)*

**bulletin de chargement** *(m)* Fr
De Bahnfrachtbrief *(m)*
En railway receipt
Es recibo ferroviario *(m)*
It ricevuta ferroviaria *(f)*
Pt recibo ferroviário *(m)*

**bulletin de commande** *(m)* Fr
De Bestellformular *(n)*
En order-form
Es solicitud de pedido *(f)*
It foglio d'ordinazione *(m)*
Pt impresso de encomenda *(m)*

**bullion** *n* En
De Gold und Silberbarren
Es oro y plata sin acuñar
Fr barres d'or ou d'argent
It oro ed argento in verghe
Pt ouro ou prata em barra

**bullish** *adj* En
De steigend
Es alcista
Fr haussier
It rialzista
Pt altista

**bull market** En
De Haussemarkt *(m)*
Es mercado alcista *(m)*
Fr marché orienté à la hausse *(m)*
It mercato tendente al rialzo *(m)*
Pt mercado de tendência altista *(m)*

**Bummelstreik** *(m)* n De
En go-slow strike
Am slow down
Es huelga de producción lenta *(f)*
Fr grève perlée *(f)*
It sciopero a singhiozzo *(m)*
Pt greve de abrandamento do ritmo de produção *(f)*

**Bundes-** De
En federal
Es federal
Fr fédéral
It federale
Pt federal

**bunker** n En
De Bunker *(m)*
Es carbonera *(f)*
Fr soute *(f)*
It carbonile *(m)*
Pt carvoeira *(f)*

**Bunker** *(m)* n De
En bunker
Es carbonera *(f)*
Fr soute *(f)*
It carbonile *(m)*
Pt carvoeira *(f)*

**buona qualità media** *(f)* It
De gute Durchschnittsqualität *(f)*
En fair average quality (faq)
Es calidad media razonable *(f)*
Fr qualité commerciale moyenne *(f)*
Pt qualidade media razoável *(f)*

**buoni uffici** *(m pl)* It
De Liebesdienste *(m pl)*
En good offices
Es buenos servicios *(m pl)*
Fr bons offices *(m pl)*
Pt bons serviços *(m pl)*

**buono** *(m)* n It
De Obligation; Gutschein *(f m)*
En bond; voucher
Es bono; obligación *(m f)*
Fr bon; obligation *(m f)*
Pt título; obrigação *(m f)*

**buono** adj It
De gut
En good

Es bueno
Fr bon
Pt bom

**buono del tesoro** *(m)* It
De Schatzwechsel *(m)*
En exchequer bond
Am treasury bond
Es bono de tesorería *(m)*
Fr bon du trésor *(m)*
Pt título do tesouro *(m)*

**buque de carga** *(m)* Es
De Frachtschiff *(n)*
En cargo boat
Fr cargo *(m)*
It nave da carico *(f)*
Pt barco de carga *(m)*

**buque de vapor** *(m)* Es
De Dampfer *(m)*
En steamer
Fr bateau à vapeur *(m)*
It vapore *(m)*
Pt vapor *(m)*

**bureau** *(m)* n Fr
De Büro; Schreibtisch *(n m)*
En office; desk
Es oficina; mesa *(f)*
It ufficio; scrittoio *(m)*
Pt escritório; secretária *(m f)*

**bureau de placement** *(m)* Fr
De Arbeitsnachweisstelle *(f)*
En employment exchange
Am state employment agency
Es bolsa de trabajo *(f)*
It ufficio di collocamento *(m)*
Pt centro de serviços de emprego *(m)*

**bureau de poste** *(m)* Fr
De Postamt *(n)*
En post office
Es oficina de correos *(f)*
It ufficio postale *(m)*
Pt estação de correios *(f)*

**bureau sans cloisons** *(m)* Fr
De Grossraumbüro *(n)*
En open-plan office
Es oficina sin particiones *(f)*
It ufficio senza divisioni *(m)*
Pt escritório sem divisões *(m)*

**Bürge** *(m)* n De
En surety; guarantor
Es fianza; garante *(f m)*
Fr cautionnement; garant *(m)*
It cauzione; garante *(f m)*
Pt fiança; fiador *(f m)*

**burglary** n En
De Einbruchdiebstahl *(m)*
Es robo *(m)*
Fr vol avec effraction *(m)*
It furto con scasso *(m)*
Pt roubo *(m)*

**Bürgschaft** *(f)* n De
En surety
Es fiador *(m)*
Fr caution *(f)*
It garante *(m)*
Pt fiador *(m)*

**Bürgschaft leisten** De
En guarantee
Es garantizar; avalar
Fr garantir; avaliser
It garantire; avallare
Pt garantir; assegurar

**Büro** *(n)* n De
En office
Es oficina *(f)*
Fr bureau *(m)*
It ufficio *(m)*
Pt escritório *(m)*

**Büroklammer** *(f)* n De
En paper clip
Es sujetapapeles *(m)*
Fr attache-papiers *(m)*
It fermacarte *(m)*
Pt grampo *(m)*

**Bürovorsteher** *(m)* n De
En office manager
Es jefe de oficina *(m)*
Fr chef de bureau *(m)*
It capo ufficio *(m)*
Pt chefe de escritório *(m)*

**business** (the occupation) n En
De Geschäft *(n)*
Es negocios *(m pl)*
Fr affaires *(f pl)*
It affari *(m pl)*
Pt negócios *(m pl)*

**business** (firm) *n* En
 De Firma *(f)*
 Es casa de comercio *(f)*
 Fr maison de commerce *(f)*
 It casa commerciale *(f)*
 Pt casa de comércio *(f)*

**business before the meeting**
 En
 Am agenda
 De Tagesordnung *(f)*
 Es orden del día *(f)*
 Fr ordre du jour *(m)*
 It scopo dell'assemblea *(m)*
 Pt agenda da reunião *(f)*

**business cycle** En
 De Konjunkturzyklus *(m)*
 Es ciclo económico *(m)*
 Fr cycle économique *(m)*
 It ciclo d'affari *(m)*
 Pt ciclo económico *(m)*

**business expenses** En
 De Geschäftskosten *(pl)*
 Es gastos de los negocios *(m pl)*
 Fr frais commerciaux *(m pl)*
 It spese generali *(f pl)*
 Pt despesas do exercício *(f pl)*

**business hours** En
 De Geschäftszeit *(f)*
 Es horario de comercio *(m)*
 Fr heures d'ouverture *(f pl)*
 It orario d'apertura *(m)*
 Pt horas de funcionamento *(f pl)*

**businessman** *n* En
 De Geschäftsmann *(m)*
 Es hombre de negocios *(m)*
 Fr homme d'affaires *(m)*
 It uomo d'affari *(m)*
 Pt homem de negócios *(m)*

**business manager** En
 De Geschäftsführer *(m)*
 Es gerente de negocios *(m)*
 Fr gérant d'affaires *(m)*
 It direttore commerciale *(m)*
 Pt gerente de negócios *(m)*

**Bussklausel** *(f) n* De
 En forfeit clause
 Es cláusula de decomiso *(f)*
 Fr clause de dédit *(f)*

It clausola di penalità per inandempienza *(f)*
 Pt cláusula de cedência *(f)*

**busta** *(f) n* It
 De Umschlag *(m)*
 En envelope
 Es sobre *(m)*
 Fr enveloppe *(f)*
 Pt envelope *(m)*

**busta con finestra** *(f)* It
 De Fensterbriefumschlag *(m)*
 En window-envelope
 Es sobre de ventanilla *(m)*
 Fr enveloppe à fenêtre *(f)*
 Pt envelope de endereço exposto *(m)*

**but** *(m) n* Fr
 De Ziel; Zweck *(m)*
 En target; purpose
 Es objetivo *(m)*
 It bersaglio; scopo *(m)*
 Pt objectivo *(m)*

**buy** *vb* En
 De kaufen
 Es comprar
 Fr acheter
 It comprare
 Pt comprar

**buyer** *n* En
 De Käufer *(m)*
 Es comprador *(m)*
 Fr acheteur *(m)*
 It compratore *(m)*
 Pt comprador *(m)*

**buzón** *(m) n* Es
 De Briefkasten *(m)*
 En letter-box
 Am mail-box
 Fr boîte aux lettres *(f)*
 It cassetta postale *(f)*
 Pt caixa do correio *(f)*

**by air** En
 De per Flugpost
 Es por avión
 Fr par avion
 It per via aerea
 Pt por avião

**by-product** *n* En
 De Nebenprodukt *(n)*
 Es producto derivado *(m)*

Fr sous-produit *(m)*
 It sottoprodotto *(m)*
 Pt produto derivado *(m)*

# C

**caballo de vapor (cv)** *(m)* Es
 De Pferdestärke (PS) *(f)*
 En horse-power (hp)
 Fr cheval-vapeur (ch-v) *(m)*
 It cavallo *(m)*
 Pt cavalo-vapor *(m)*

**cabeçalho** *(m) n* Pt
 De Briefkopf *(m)*
 En letterhead
 Es membrete *(m)*
 Fr en-tête *(m)*
 It intestazione *(f)*

**cabedal de imitação** *(m)* Pt
 De Kunstleder *(n)*
 En imitation leather
 Es piel de imitación *(f)*
 Fr similicuir *(m)*
 It finta pelle *(f)*

**cable** *n* En, Es *(m)*
 De Telegramm *(n)*
 Fr câble *(m)*
 It cablogramma *(m)*
 Pt telegrama *(m)*

**câble** *(m) n* Fr
 De Telegramm *(n)*
 En cable
 Es cable *(m)*
 It cablogramma *(m)*
 Pt telegrama *(m)*

**cablogramma** *(m) n* It
 De Telegramm *(n)*
 En cable
 Es cable *(m)*
 Fr câble *(m)*
 Pt telegrama *(m)*

**cabotage** *n* En, Fr *(m)*
 De Küstenschiffahrt *(f)*
 Es cabotaje *(m)*
 It cabotaggio *(m)*
 Pt cabotagem *(f)*

**cabotagem** (f) n Pt
De  Küstenschiffahrt (f)
En  cabotage
Es  cabotaje (m)
Fr  cabotage (m)
It  cabotaggio (m)

**cabotaggio** (m) n It
De  Küstenschiffahrt (f)
En  cabotage
Es  cabotaje (m)
Fr  cabotage (m)
Pt  cabotagem (f)

**cabotaje** (m) n Es
De  Küstenschiffahrt (f)
En  cabotage
Fr  cabotage (m)
It  cabotaggio (m)
Pt  cabotagem (f)

**caça aos saldos** (f) Pt
De  Sucht nach Sonderange-
    boten (f)
En  bargain-hunting
Es  caza de rebajas (f)
Fr  chasse aux soldes (f)
It  caccia alle occasioni (f)

**caccia alle occasioni** (f) It
De  Sucht nach Sonderange-
    boten (f)
En  bargain-hunting
Es  caza de rebajas (f)
Fr  chasse aux soldes (f)
Pt  caça aos saldos (f)

**cadeia de montagem** (f) Pt
De  Montageband (n)
En  assembly line
Es  línea de montaje (f)
Fr  chaîne de montage (f)
It  catena di montaggio (f)

**cadere** vb It
De  stürzen
En  fall
Es  caer; bajar
Fr  baisser; tomber
Pt  cair; baixar

**caduta** (f) n It
De  Sturz (m)
En  fall
Es  baja; caida (f)
Fr  baisse; chute (f)
Pt  baixa; gueda (f)

**caer** vb Es
De  stürzen
En  fall
Fr  baisser; tomber
It  cadere; ribassare
Pt  cair; baixar

**caer en quiebra** Es
De  Konkurs anmelden
En  go bankrupt
Fr  faire faillite
It  fallire
Pt  falir

**café** (m) n Es, Fr, Pt
De  Kaffee (m)
En  coffee
It  caffè (m)

**caffè** (m) n It
De  Kaffee (m)
En  coffee
Es  café (m)
Fr  café (m)
Pt  café (m)

**cair** vb Pt
De  stürzen
En  fall
Es  caer; bajar
Fr  baisser; tomber
It  cadere; ribassare

**cais** (m) n Pt
De  Kai (m)
En  quay; wharf
Am  pier
Es  muelle (m)
Fr  quai (m)
It  banchina; scalo (f m)

**caisse** (f) n Fr
De  Kasse; Geldkassette (f)
En  cash-desk; cash-box
Es  caja (f)
It  cassa; cassetta (f)
Pt  caixa (f)

**caisse d'épargne** (f) Fr
De  Sparkasse (f)
En  savings bank
Es  caja de ahorros (f)
It  cassa di risparmio (f)
Pt  caixa económica (f)

**caisse d'épargne postale** (f) Fr
De  Postsparkasse (f)
En  Post Office Savings Bank

Es  caja postal de ahorros (f)
It  cassa di risparmio postale
    (f)
Pt  caixa económica postal (f)

**caissier** (m) n Fr
De  Kassierer (m)
En  cashier
Am  teller
Es  cajero (m)
It  cassiere (m)
Pt  caixa (m)

**caixa** (f) n Pt
De  Kasse; Geldkassette (f)
En  cash-desk; cash-box
Es  caja (f)
Fr  caisse (f)
It  cassa; cassetta (f)

**caixa** (m) n Pt
De  Kassierer (m)
En  cashier
Am  teller
Es  cajero (m)
Fr  caissier (m)
It  cassiere (m)

**caixa automática** (f) Pt
De  Bargeldauszahlungsautomat
    (m)
En  cash dispenser
Es  caja automática (f)
Fr  distributeur d'argent com-
    ptant (m)
It  cassa automatica (f)

**caixa de cartão** (f) Pt
De  Karton (m)
En  carton
Es  cartón (m)
Fr  carton (m)
It  cartone (m)

**caixa do correio** (f) Pt
De  Briefkasten (m)
En  letter-box
Am  mail-box
Es  buzón (m)
Fr  boîte aux lettres (f)
It  cassetta postale (f)

**caixa económica** (f) Pt
De  Sparkasse (f)
En  savings bank
Es  caja de ahorros (f)
Fr  caisse d'épargne (f)
It  cassa di risparmio (f)

**caixa económica postal** *(f)* Pt
De Postsparkasse *(f)*
En Post Office Savings Bank
Es caja postal de ahorros *(f)*
Fr caisse d'épargne postale *(f)*
It cassa di risparmio postale *(f)*

**caixeiro viajante** *(m)* Pt
De Handelsvertreter; Geschäftsreisende(r) *(m)*
En commercial traveller
Am salesman
Es viajante de comercio *(m)*
Fr commis-voyageur *(m)*
It viaggiatore di commercio *(m)*

**caja** *(f)* n Es
De Geldkassette *(f)*
En cash-box
Fr caisse *(f)*
It cassetta *(f)*
Pt caixa *(f)*

**caja** *(f)* n Es
De Kasse; Geldkassette *(f)*
En cash-desk; cash-box
Fr caisse *(f)*
It cassa; cassetta *(f)*
Pt caixa *(f)*

**caja automática** *(f)* Es
De Bargeldauszahlungsautomat *(m)*
En cash dispenser
Fr distributeur d'argent comptant *(m)*
It cassa automatica *(f)*
Pt caixa automática *(f)*

**caja de ahorros** *(f)* Es
De Sparkasse *(f)*
En savings bank
Fr caisse d'épargne *(f)*
It cassa di risparmio *(f)*
Pt caixa económica *(f)*

**caja de seguridad nocturna** *(f)* Es
De Nachttresor *(m)*
En night safe
Fr coffre de nuit *(m)*
It deposito notturno *(m)*
Pt cofre nocturno *(m)*

**caja fuerte** *(f)* Es
De Geldschrank *(m)*
En safe
Fr coffre-fort *(m)*
It cassaforte *(f)*
Pt cofre *(m)*

**caja menor** *(f)* Es
De kleine Kasse *(f)*
En petty cash
Fr petite caisse *(f)*
It piccola cassa *(f)*
Pt despesas de caixa *(f pl)*

**caja postal de ahorros** *(f)* Es
De Postsparkasse *(f)*
En Post Office Savings Bank
Fr caisse d'épargne postale *(f)*
It cassa di risparmio postale *(f)*
Pt caixa económica postal *(f)*

**cajero** *(m)* n Es
De Kassierer *(m)*
En cashier
Am teller
Fr caissier *(m)*
It cassiere *(m)*
Pt caixa *(m)*

**calado** *(m)* n Es, Pt
De Tiefgang *(m)*
En draught (of a ship)
Fr tirant d'eau *(m)*
It pescaggio *(m)*

**calcolare** *vb* It
De berechnen
En calculate
Es calcular
Fr calculer
Pt calcular

**calcolatore** *(m)* n It
De Rechner; Computer *(m)*
En computer
Es computadora *(f)*
Fr ordinateur *(m)*
Pt computador *(m)*

**calcolatore analogico** *(m)* It
De Analogrechner *(m)*
En analogue computer
Am analog computer
Es computadora analógica *(f)*
Fr calculateur analogique *(m)*
Pt computador analógico *(m)*

**calcolatrice** *(f)* n It
De Rechenmaschine *(f)*
En calculator
Es calculadora *(f)*
Fr machine à calculer *(f)*
Pt máquina de calcular *(f)*

**calcolazione** *(f)* n It
De Berechnung *(f)*
En calculation
Es cálculo *(m)*
Fr calcul *(m)*
Pt cálculo *(m)*

**calcolo errato** *(m)* It
De Rechenfehler *(m)*
En miscalculation
Es cálculo erróneo *(m)*
Fr erreur de calcul *(f)*
Pt erro de cálculo *(m)*

**calcul** *(m)* n Fr
De Berechnung *(f)*
En calculation
Es cálculo *(m)*
It calcolazione *(f)*
Pt cálculo *(m)*

**calculadora** *(f)* n Es
De Rechenmaschine *(f)*
En calculator
Fr machine à calculer *(f)*
It calcolatrice *(f)*
Pt máquina de calcular *(f)*

**calculador de custos** *(m)* Pt
De Kalkulator *(m)*
En cost accountant
Es contable de costes *(m)*
Fr comptable de prix de revient *(m)*
It contabile dei costi di produzione *(m)*

**calcular** *vb* Es, Pt
De berechnen
En calculate
Fr calculer
It calcolare

**calculate** *vb* En
De berechnen
Es calcular
Fr calculer
It calcolare
Pt calcular

**calculateur analogique** (m) Fr
De Analogrechner (m)
En analogue computer
Am analog computer
Es computadora analógica (f)
It calcolatore analogico (m)
Pt computador analógico (m)

**calculateur digital** (m) Fr
De Digitalrechner (m)
En digital computer
Es computadora numérica (f)
It elaboratore numerico (m)
Pt computador de dígitos (m)

**calculation** n En
De Berechnung (f)
Es cálculo (m)
Fr calcul (m)
It calcolazione (f)
Pt cálculo (m)

**calculator** n En
De Rechenmaschine (f)
Es calculadora (f)
Fr machine à calculer (f)
It calcolatrice (f)
Pt máquina de calcular (f)

**calculer** vb Fr
De berechnen
En calculate
Es calcular
It calcolare
Pt calcular

**cálculo** (m) n Es, Pt
De Berechnung (f)
En calculation
Fr calcul (m)
It calcolazione (f)

**cálculo erróneo** (m) Es
De Rechenfehler (m)
En miscalculation
Fr erreur de calcul (f)
It calcolo errato (m)
Pt erro de cálculo (m)

**cálculo revisado** (m) Es
De überarbeitete Schätzung (f)
En revised estimate
Fr devis rectifié (m)
It preventivo riveduto (m)
Pt estimativa revista (f)

**cálculo suplementario** (m) Es
De Nachschätzung (f)
En supplementary estimate
Fr devis supplémentaire (f)
It preventivo supplementare (m)
Pt estimativa suplementar (f)

**cale** (f) n Fr
De Laderaum (m)
En hold
Es bodega (f)
It stiva (f)
Pt porão (m)

**calefacción central** (f) Es
De Zentralheizung (f)
En central heating
Fr chauffage central (m)
It riscaldamento centrale (m)
Pt aquecimento central (m)

**calendar** n En
De Kalender (m)
Es calendario (m)
Fr calendrier (m)
It calendario (m)
Pt calendário (m)

**calendario** (m) n Es, It
De Kalender (m)
En calendar
Fr calendrier (m)
Pt calendário (m)

**calendário** (m) n Pt
De Kalender (m)
En calendar
Es calendario (m)
Fr calendrier (m)
It calendario (m)

**calendar year** En
De Kalenderjahr (n)
Es año civil (m)
Fr année civile (f)
It anno solare (m)
Pt ano civil (m)

**calendrier** (m) n Fr
De Kalender (m)
En calendar
Es calendario (m)
It calendario (m)
Pt calendário (m)

**cale sèche** (f) Fr
De Trockendock (n)
En dry dock
Es dique seco (m)
It bacino di carenaggio (m)
Pt doca-seca (f)

**calibre padrão** (m) Pt
De Normalmass (n)
En standard gauge
Es calibre patrón (m)
Fr écartement normal (m)
It scartamento normale (m)

**calibre patrón** (m) Es
De Normalmass (n)
En standard gauge
Fr écartement normal (m)
It scartamento normale (m)
Pt calibre padrão (m)

**calidad** (f) n Es
De Qualität (f)
En quality
Fr qualité (f)
It qualità (f)
Pt qualidade (f)

**calidad comerciable** (f) Es
De marktgängige Qualität (f)
En merchantable quality
Fr qualité vendable (f)
It qualità commerciabile (f)
Pt qualidade comerciável (f)

**calidad del contenido desconocida** Es
De Qualität und Inhalt nicht bekannt
En quality and contents unknown
Fr qualité et contenu inconnus
It qualità e contenuto sconosciuti
Pt qualidade e conteúdo desconhecidos

**calidad media razonable** (f) Es
De gute Durchschnittsqualität (f)
En fair average quality (faq)
Fr qualité commerciale moyenne (f)
It buona qualità media (f)
Pt qualidade media razoável (f)

**call** (for funds) n En
De Kündigung (von Geldern) (f)
Es llamada (de fondos) (f)
Fr appel (de fonds) (m)
It richiesta (di fondi) (f)
Pt chamada (de fundos) (f)

**call a strike** En
De zum Streik auffordern
Es declararse en huelga
Fr ordonner une grève
It proclamare uno sciopero
Pt declarar greve

**call off** (a deal) En
De rückgängig machen
Es anular
Fr annuler
It annullare
Pt anular

**call option** En
De Kaufoption (f)
Es opción de compras (f)
Fr option (f)
It premio d'acquisto (m)
Pt opção de compra (f)

**cámara de comercio** (f) Es
De Handelskammer (f)
En chamber of commerce
Fr chambre de commerce (f)
It camera di commercio (f)
Pt câmara de comércio (f)

**câmara de comércio** (f) Pt
De Handelskammer (f)
En chamber of commerce
Es cámara de comercio (f)
Fr chambre de commerce (f)
It camera di commercio (f)

**cámara de compensaciones** (f) Es
De Verrechnungsstelle (f)
En clearing house
Fr chambre de compensation (f)
It stanza di compensazione (f)
Pt câmara de compensações e rateio (f)

**câmara de compensações e rateio** (f) Pt
De Verrechnungsstelle (f)
En clearing house
Es cámara de compensaciones (f)

Fr chambre de compensation (f)
It stanza di compensazione (f)

**Cámara Internacional de Comercio** (f) Es
De Internationale Handelskammer (f)
En International Chamber of Commerce
Fr Chambre de Commerce Internationale (f)
It Camera di Commercio Internazionale (f)
Pt Câmara Internacional do Comércio (f)

**Câmara Internacional do Comércio** (f) Pt
De Internationale Handelskammer (f)
En International Chamber of Commerce
Es Cámara Internacional de Comercio (f)
Fr Chambre de Commerce Internationale (f)
It Camera di Commercio Internazionale (f)

**cambiale di favore** (f) It
De Gefälligkeitswechsel (m)
En accommodation bill
Es pagaré de favor (m)
Fr billet de complaisance (m)
Pt letra de favor (f)

**cambiale scontata** (f) It
De Diskontwechsel (m)
En discounted bill
Es efecto descontado (m)
Fr effet escompté (m)
Pt letra descontada (f)

**cambiale sull' estero** (f) It
De Auslandswechsel (m)
En foreign bill
Es letra sobre el exterior (f)
Fr lettre de change sur l'étranger (f)
Pt letra de país a país (cambial) (f)

**cambio** (m) n Es, It
De Tausch (m)
En exchange
Fr échange (m)
Pt câmbio (m)

**câmbio** (m) n Pt
De Tausch; Wechselkurs (m)
En exchange; rate of exchange
Es cambio; tipo de cambio (m)
Fr échange; taux de change (m)
It cambio; corso del cambio (m)

**cambio a termine** (m) It
De Termindevisen (f pl)
En forward exchange
Es divisas a término (f pl)
Fr change à terme (m)
Pt divisas adiantada (f pl)

**câmbio bloqueado** (m) Pt
De blockierte Devisen (f pl)
En blocked exchange
Es divisas bloqueadas (f pl)
Fr devises bloquées (f pl)
It valute bloccate (f pl)

**cambio fluttuante** (m) It
De flexibler Wechselkurs (m)
En floating exchange rate
Es tipo de cambio flotante (m)
Fr taux de change flottant (m)
Pt taxa de câmbio flutuante (f)

**camera di commercio** (f) It
De Handelskammer (f)
En chamber of commerce
Es cámara de comercio (f)
Fr chambre de commerce (f)
Pt câmara de comércio (f)

**Camera di Commercio Internazionale** (f) It
De Internationale Handelskammer (f)
En International Chamber of Commerce
Es Cámara Internacional de Comercio (f)
Fr Chambre de Commerce Internationale (f)
Pt Câmara Internacional do Comércio (f)

**caminho de ferro** (m) Pt
De Eisenbahn (f)
En railway
Es ferrocarril (m)
Fr chemin de fer (m)
It ferrovia (f)

**camionnage** *(m)* n Fr
De Transport *(m)*
En haulage
Am trucking
Es transporte *(m)*
It trasporto *(m)*
Pt transporte *(m)*

**campagna** *(f)* n It
De Kampagne *(f)*
En campaign
Es campaña *(f)*
Fr campagne *(f)*
Pt campanha *(f)*

**campagna pubblicitaria** *(f)* It
De Werbefeldzug *(m)*
En advertising campaign; publicity campaign
Es campaña publicitaria *(f)*
Fr campagne de publicité *(f)*
Pt campanha publicitária *(f)*

**campagne** *(f)* n Fr
De Kampagne *(f)*
En campaign
Es campaña *(f)*
It campagna *(f)*
Pt campanha *(f)*

**campagne de publicité** *(f)* Fr
De Werbefeldzug *(m)*
En advertising campaign; publicity campaign
Es campaña publicitaria *(f)*
It campagna pubblicitaria *(f)*
Pt campanha publicitária *(f)*

**campaign** n En
De Kampagne *(f)*
Es campaña *(f)*
Fr campagne *(f)*
It campagna *(f)*
Pt campanha *(f)*

**campaña** *(f)* n Es
De Kampagne *(f)*
En campaign
Fr campagne *(f)*
It campagna *(f)*
Pt campanha *(f)*

**campaña publicitaria** *(f)* Es
De Werbefeldzug *(m)*
En advertising campaign; publicity campaign
Fr campagne de publicité *(f)*

It campagna pubblicitaria *(f)*
Pt campanha publicitária *(f)*

**campanha** *(f)* n Pt
De Kampagne *(f)*
En campaign
Es campaña *(f)*
Fr campagne *(f)*
It campagna *(f)*

**campanha publicitária** *(f)* Pt
De Werbefeldzug *(m)*
En advertising campaign; publicity campaign
Es campaña publicitaria *(f)*
Fr campagne de publicité *(f)*
It campagna pubblicitaria *(f)*

**campione** *(m)* n It
De Probe; Muster *(f n)*
En sample
Es muestra *(f)*
Fr échantillon *(m)*
Pt amostra *(f)*

**campione a casaccio** *(m)* It
De Stichprobe *(f)*
En random sample
Es muestra aleatoria *(f)*
Fr épreuve au hasard *(f)*
Pt amostra avulso *(f)*

**campione gratuito** *(m)* It
De kostenlose Probe *(f)*
En free sample
Es muestra gratuita *(f)*
Fr échantillon gratuit *(m)*
Pt amostra gratis *(f)*

**campione senza valore** *(m)* It
De Muster ohne Wert *(n)*
En sample of no value
Es muestra sin valor *(f)*
Fr échantillon sans valeur *(m)*
Pt amostra sem valor *(f)*

**canal** n En; Es, Fr, Pt *(m)*
De Kanal *(m)*
It canale *(m)*

**canale** *(m)* n It
De Kanal *(m)*
En canal
Es canal *(m)*
Fr canal *(m)*
Pt canal *(m)*

**canali d'informazione** *(m pl)* It
De Werbeträger *(m pl)*
En media
Es medios de información *(m pl)*
Fr supports *(m pl)*
Pt meios de informação *(m pl)*

**cancel** *vb* En
De annullieren
Es cancelar
Fr annuler
It cancellare
Pt cancelar

**cancel a cheque** En
Am cancel a check
De einen Scheck rückgängig machen
Es anular un cheque
Fr annuler un chèque
It annullare un assegno
Pt cancelar um cheque

**cancelación** *(f)* n Es
De Annullierung *(f)*
En cancellation
Fr annulation *(f)*
It annullamento *(m)*
Pt cancelamento *(m)*

**cancelamento** *(m)* n Pt
De Annullierung *(f)*
En cancellation
Es cancelación *(f)*
Fr annulation *(f)*
It annullamento *(m)*

**cancelar** *vb* Es, Pt
De annullieren
En cancel
Fr annuler
It cancellare

**cancelar uma dívida** Pt
De eine Schuld begleichen
En discharge a debt
Es descargar una deuda
Fr acquitter une dette
It estinguere un debito

**cancelar um cheque** Pt
De einen Scheck rückgängig machen
En cancel a cheque
Am cancel a check
Es anular un cheque

Fr  annuler un chèque
It  annullare un assegno

**cancelar um débito** Pt
De  eine Schuld erlassen
En  write off a debt
Es  cancelar una deuda
Fr  amortir une créance
It  cancellare un credito

**cancelar una deuda** Es
De  eine Schuld erlassen
En  write off a debt
Fr  amortir une créance
It  cancellare un credito
Pt  cancelar um débito

**cancelar una pérdida** Es
De  einen Verlust abschreiben
En  write off a loss
Fr  amortir une perte
It  cancellare una perdita
Pt  anular um prejuízo

**cancellare** vb It
De  annullieren; streichen
En  cancel; delete
Es  cancelar; tachar
Fr  annuler; rayer
Pt  cancelar; cortar

**cancellare una perdita** It
De  einen Verlust abschreiben
En  write off a loss
Es  cancelar una pérdida
Fr  amortir une perte
Pt  anular um prejuízo

**cancellare un credito** It
De  eine Schuld erlassen
En  write off a debt
Es  cancelar una deuda
Fr  amortir une créance
Pt  cancelar um débito

**cancellation** n En
De  Annullierung (f)
Es  cancelación (f)
Fr  annulation (f)
It  annullamento (m)
Pt  cancelamento (m)

**candidat** (m) n Fr
De  Bewerber (m)
En  applicant
Es  candidato (m)
It  candidato (m)
Pt  candidato (m)

**candidato** (m) n Es, It, Pt
De  Bewerber (m)
En  applicant
Fr  candidat (m)

**cantidad** (f) n Es
De  Menge (f)
En  quantity
Fr  quantité (f)
It  quantità (f)
Pt  quantidade (f)

**cantiere** (m) n It
De  Schiffswerft (f)
En  dockyard
Es  astillero (m)
Fr  chantier de construction de
    navires (m)
Pt  estaleiro (m)

**capacidad** (f) n Es
De  Fähigkeit; Inhalt (f m)
En  capacity
Fr  capacité (f)
It  capacità (f)
Pt  capacidade (f)

**capacidad cúbica** (f) Es
De  Kubikinhalt (m)
En  cubic capacity
Fr  volume (m)
It  volume (m)
Pt  capacidade cúbica (f)

**capacidade** (f) n Pt
De  Fähigkeit; Inhalt (f m)
En  capacity
Es  capacidad (f)
Fr  capacité (f)
It  capacità (f)

**capacidade cúbica** (f) Pt
De  Kubikinhalt (m)
En  cubic capacity
Es  capacidad cúbica (f)
Fr  volume (m)
It  volume (m)

**capacidade excessiva** (f) Pt
De  Überkapazität (f)
En  overcapacity
Es  exceso de capacidad (m)
Fr  surcapacité (f)
It  capacità in eccedenza (f)

**capacità** (f) n It
De  Fähigkeit (f)
En  capacity

Es  capacidad (f)
Fr  capacité (f)
Pt  capacidade (f)

**capacità creditizia** (f) It
De  Kreditfähigkeit (f)
En  borrowing power
Es  facultad de crédito (f)
Fr  capacité à avoir du crédit
    (f)
Pt  potencial de obtenção de
    crédito (m)

**capacità in eccedenza** (f) It
De  Überkapazität (f)
En  overcapacity
Es  exceso de capacidad (m)
Fr  surcapacité (f)
Pt  capacidade excessiva (f)

**capacité** (f) n Fr
De  Fähigkeit; Inhalt (f m)
En  capacity
Es  capacidad (f)
It  capacità (f)
Pt  capacidade (f)

**capacité excédentaire** (f) Fr
De  übrige Ladefähigkeit (f)
En  excess capacity
Es  capacidad en exceso (f)
It  capacità in eccesso (f)
Pt  capacidade em excesso (f)

**capacity** n En
De  Fähigkeit; Inhalt (f m)
Es  capacidad (f)
Fr  capacité (f)
It  capacità (f)
Pt  capacidade (f)

**caparra** (f) n It
De  Anzahlung (f)
En  deposit; first payment
Es  desembolso inicial (m)
Fr  arrhes (f pl)
Pt  sinal (m)

**capataz** (m) n Es, Pt
De  Vorarbeiter (m)
En  foreman
Fr  contremaître; chef d'équipe
    (m)
It  capo operaio; capo squa-
    dra (m)

**capataz jefe** *(m)* Es
De Werkmeister *(m)*
En head foreman
Fr chef d'atelier *(m)*
It capo officina *(m)*
Pt encarregado-chefe *(m)*

**capitaine** *(m)* n Fr
De Kapitän *(m)*
En master of a ship
Es capitán de navío *(m)*
It capitano di nave *(m)*
Pt capitão de navio *(m)*

**capitaine de port** *(m)* Fr
De Hafenmeister *(m)*
En harbour-master
Es capitán de puerto *(m)*
It capitano di porto *(m)*
Pt capitão de porto *(m)*

**capital** n En; Es, Fr, Pt *(m)*
De Kapital *(n)*
It capitale *(m)*

**capital account** En
De Kapitalkonto *(n)*
Es cuenta de capital *(f)*
Fr compte capital *(m)*
It conto capitale *(m)*
Pt conta de capital *(f)*

**capital a corto plazo** *(m)* Es
De kurzfristiges Kapital *(n)*
En short-term capital
Fr capitaux à court terme *(m pl)*
It capitale a breve termine *(m)*
Pt capital a curto prazo *(m)*

**capital a curto prazo** *(m)* Pt
De kurzfristiges Kapital *(n)*
En short-term capital
Es capital a corto plazo *(m)*
Fr capitaux à court terme *(m pl)*
It capitale a breve termine *(m)*

**capital a largo plazo** *(m)* Es
De langfristiges Kapital *(n)*
En long-term capital
Fr capitaux à long terme *(m pl)*
It capitale consolidato a lunga scadenza *(m)*
Pt capital a longo prazo *(m)*

**capital allowances** En
De Steuerbegünstigung auf Anlagen *(f)*
Es deducciones fiscales sobre inversiones *(f pl)*
Fr déductions fiscales sur les investissements *(f pl)*
It deduzioni fiscali sugli investimenti *(f pl)*
Pt concessões sobre capital *(f pl)*

**capital a longo prazo** *(m)* Pt
De langfristiges Kapital *(n)*
En long-term capital
Es capital a largo plazo *(m)*
Fr capitaux à long terme *(m pl)*
It capitale consolidato a lunga scadenza *(m)*

**capital a préstamo** *(m)* Es
De Fremdkapital *(n)*
En borrowed capital
Fr capitaux empruntés *(m pl)*
It capitale preso a prestito *(m)*
Pt capital por empréstimo *(m)*

**capital asset** En
Am fixed asset
De Vermögensanlage *(f)*
Es activo fijo *(m)*
Fr actif immobilisé *(m)*
It capitale fisso *(m)*
Pt bens de capital *(m pl)*

**capital autorisé** *(m)* Fr
De genehmigtes Kapital *(n)*
En authorized capital
Es capital autorizado *(m)*
It capitale autorizzato *(m)*
Pt capital autorizado *(m)*

**capital autorizado** *(m)* Es, Pt
De genehmigtes Kapital *(n)*
En authorized capital
Fr capital autorisé *(m)*
It capitale autorizzato *(m)*

**capital circulante** *(m)* Es
De Betriebskapital *(n)*
En working capital
Fr fonds de roulement *(m pl)*
It capitale d'esercizio *(m)*
Pt capital para movimentação *(m)*

**capital de especulação** *(m)* Pt
De Spekulationskapital *(n)*
En risk capital
Es capital de especulación *(m)*
Fr capitaux spéculatifs *(m pl)*
It capitale di speculazione *(m)*

**capital de especulación** *(m)* Es
De Spekulationskapital *(n)*
En risk capital
Fr capitaux spéculatifs *(m pl)*
It capitale di speculazione *(m)*
Pt capital de especulação *(m)*

**capital de exploração** *(m)* Pt
De Betriebskapital *(n)*
En trading capital
Es capital de explotación *(m)*
Fr fonds de roulement *(m)*
It capitale d'esercizio *(m)*

**capital de explotación** *(m)* Es
De Betriebskapital *(n)*
En trading capital
Fr fonds de roulement *(m)*
It capitale d'esercizio *(m)*
Pt capital de exploração *(m)*

**capital de reserva** *(m)* Es
De nicht eingerufenes Kapital *(n)*
En uncalled capital
Fr capital non appelé *(m)*
It capitale non richiamato *(m)*
Pt capital irrealizado *(m)*

**capital desembolsado** *(m)* Es
De eingezahltes Kapital *(n)*
En paid-up capital
Fr capital versé *(m)*
It capitale versato *(m)*
Pt capital realizado *(m)*

**capitale** *(m)* n It
De Kapital *(n)*
En capital
Es capital *(m)*
Fr capital *(m)*
Pt capital *(m)*

**capitale a breve termine** *(m)* It
De kurzfristiges Kapital *(n)*
En short-term capital
Es capital a corto plazo *(m)*
Fr capitaux à court terme *(m pl)*
Pt capital a curto prazo *(m)*

**capitale autorizzato** (m) It
De genehmigtes Kapital (n)
En authorized capital
Es capital autorizado (m)
Fr capital autorisé (m)
Pt capital autorizado (m)

**capitale azionario** (m) It
De Aktienkapital (n)
En share capital
Am stock capital
Es capital en acciones (m)
Fr capital social (m)
Pt capital em acções (m)

**capitale consolidato a lunga
scadenza** (m) It
De langfristiges Kapital (n)
En long-term capital
Es capital a largo plazo (m)
Fr capitaux à long terme (m
pl)
Pt capital a longo prazo (m)
Es capital circulante (m)

**capitale d'esercizio** (m) It
De Betriebskapital (n)
En trading capital; working
capital
Es capital de explotación;
capital circulante (m)
Fr fonds de roulement (m)
Pt capital de exploração (m)

**capitale di speculazione** (m) It
De Spekulationskapital (n)
En risk capital
Es capital de especulación (m)
Fr capitaux spéculatifs (m pl)
Pt capital de especulação (m)

**capitale emesso** (m) It
De ausgegebenes Kapital (n)
En issued capital
Es capital emitido (m)
Fr capital versé (m)
Pt capital emitido (m)

**capitale fisso** (m) It
De feste Kapitalanlagen; Ver-
mögensanlage (f pl; f)
En fixed capital; capital asset
Es capital fijo; activo fijo (m)
Fr capital fixe; actif immobilisé
(m)
Pt capital fixado; bens de
capital (m; m pl)

**capital em acções** (m) Pt
De Aktienkapital (n)
En share capital
Am stock capital
Es capital en acciones (m)
Fr capital social (m)
It capitale azionario (m)

**capital emitido** (m) Es, Pt
De ausgegebenes Kapital (n)
En issued capital
Fr capital versé (m)
It capitale emesso (m)

**capital en acciones** (m) Es
De Aktienkapital (n)
En share capital
Am stock capital
Fr capital social (m)
It capitale azionario (m)
Pt capital em acções (m)

**capitale nominale** (m) It
De Nennkapital (m)
En nominal capital
Es capital nominal (m)
Fr capital nominal (m)
Pt capital nominal (m)

**capitale non emesso** (m) It
De nicht ausgegebenes Kapital
(n)
En unissued capital
Es capital no emitido (m)
Fr capitaux pas encore émis
(m pl)
Pt capital não emitido (m)

**capitale non richiamato** (m) It
De nicht eingerufenes Kapital
(n)
En uncalled capital
Es capital de reserva (m)
Fr capital non appelé (m)
Pt capital irrealizado (m)

**capitale preso a prestito** (m) It
De Fremdkapital (n)
En borrowed capital
Es capital a préstamo (m)
Fr capitaux empruntés (m pl)
Pt capital por empréstimo (m)

**capitale sottoscritto** (m) It
De gezeichnetes Kapital (n)
En subscribed capital
Es capital subscrito (m)

Fr capital souscrit (m)
Pt capital subscrito (m)

**capitale versato** (m) It
De eingezahltes Kapital (n)
En paid-up capital
Es capital desembolsado (m)
Fr capital versé (m)
Pt capital realizado (m)

**capital expenditure** En
De Kapitalauslagen (f pl)
Es inmovilizaciones (f pl)
Fr immobilisations (f pl)
It immobilizzazioni (f pl)
Pt despesas em termos de
capital (f pl)

**capital fijo** (m) Es
De feste Kapitalanlagen (f pl)
En fixed capital
Fr capital fixe (m)
It capitale fisso (m)
Pt capital fixado (m)

**capital fixado** (m) Pt
De feste Kapitalanlagen (f pl)
En fixed capital
Es capital fijo (m)
Fr capital fixe (m)
It capitale fisso (m)

**capital fixe** (m) Fr
De feste Kapitalanlagen (f pl)
En fixed capital
Es capital fijo (m)
It capitale fisso (m)
Pt capital fixado (m)

**capital gains** En
De Kapitalgewinn (m)
Es beneficios sobre capital (m
pl)
Fr gains en capital (m pl)
It plusvalore di capitale (m pl)
Pt lucros de capital (m pl)

**capital gains tax** En
De Kapitalertragsteuer (f)
Es impuesto sobre las ganan-
cias de capital (m)
Fr impôt sur les plus-values
en capital (m)
It imposta sul plusvalore di
capitale (f)
Pt imposto sobre lucros de
capital (m)

**capital goods** En
De Anlagegüter *(n pl)*
Es bienes de producción *(m pl)*
Fr biens d'équipement *(m pl)*
It beni strumentali *(m pl)*
Pt mercadorias de capital *(f pl)*

**capital grants** En
De Kapitalhilfe *(f)*
Es subvención de capital *(f)*
Fr subventions en capital *(f pl)*
It sovvenzioni di capitale *(f pl)*
Pt subvenções de capital *(f pl)*

**capital-intensive** *adj* En
De kapitalintensiv
Es intensivo de capital
Fr intensif de capital
It concentrato sul capitale
Pt intensivo em termos de capital

**capital irrealizado** *(m)* Pt
De nicht eingerufenes Kapital *(n)*
En uncalled capital
Es capital de reserva *(m)*
Fr capital non appelé *(m)*
It capitale non richiamato *(m)*

**capitalisation** *(f)* n Fr
De Kapitalisierung *(f)*
En capitalization
Es capitalización *(f)*
It capitalizzazione *(f)*
Pt capitalização *(f)*

**capitaliser** *vb* Fr
De kapitalisieren
En capitalize
Es capitalizar
It capitalizzare
Pt capitalizar

**capitalism** *n* En
De Kapitalismus *(m)*
Es capitalismo *(m)*
Fr capitalisme *(m)*
It capitalismo *(m)*
Pt capitalismo *(m)*

**capitalisme** *(m)* n Fr
De Kapitalismus *(m)*
En capitalism
Es capitalismo *(m)*

It capitalismo *(m)*
Pt capitalismo *(m)*

**capitalismo** *(m)* n Es, It, Pt
De Kapitalismus *(m)*
En capitalism
Fr capitalisme *(m)*

**capitalista** *(m)* n It, Pt
De Geldgeber *(m)*
En investor
Es inversionista *(m)*
Fr investisseur *(m)*

**capitalização** *(f)* n Pt
De Kapitalisierung *(f)*
En capitalization
Es capitalización *(f)*
Fr capitalisation *(f)*
It capitalizzazione *(f)*

**capitalización** *(f)* n Es
De Kapitalisierung *(f)*
En capitalization
Fr capitalisation *(f)*
It capitalizzazione *(f)*
Pt capitalização *(f)*

**capitalizar** *vb* Es, Pt
De kapitalisieren
En capitalize
Fr capitaliser
It capitalizzare

**capitalization** *n* En
De Kapitalisierung *(f)*
Es capitalización *(f)*
Fr capitalisation *(f)*
It capitalizzazione *(f)*
Pt capitalização *(f)*

**capitalize** *vb* En
De kapitalisieren
Es capitalizar
Fr capitaliser
It capitalizzare
Pt capitalizar

**capitalized value** En
De kapitalisierter Wert *(m)*
Es valor capitalizado *(m)*
Fr valeur capitalisée *(f)*
It valore capitalizzato *(m)*
Pt valor capitalizado *(m)*

**capitalizzare** *vb* It
De kapitalisieren
En capitalize

It capitalismo *(m)*
Pt capitalismo *(m)*

Es capitalizar
Fr capitaliser
Pt capitalizar

**capitalizzazione** *(f)* n It
De Kapitalisierung *(f)*
En capitalization
Es capitalización *(f)*
Fr capitalisation *(f)*
Pt capitalização *(f)*

**capital loss** En
De Kapitalverlust *(m)*
Es pérdida de capital *(f)*
Fr perte de capital *(f)*
It perdita di capitale *(f)*
Pt perdas de capital *(f pl)*

**capital não emitido** *(m)* Pt
De nicht ausgegebenes Kapital *(n)*
En unissued capital
Es capital no emitido *(m)*
Fr capitaux pas encore émis *(m pl)*
It capitale non emesso *(m)*

**capital no emitido** *(m)* Es
De nicht ausgegebenes Kapital *(n)*
En unissued capital
Fr capitaux pas encore émis *(m pl)*
It capitale non emesso *(m)*
Pt capital não emitido *(m)*

**capital nominal** *(m)* Es, Fr, Pt
De Nennkapital *(m)*
En nominal capital
It capitale nominale *(m)*

**capital non appelé** *(m)* Fr
De nicht eingerufenes Kapital *(n)*
En uncalled capital
Es capital de reserva *(m)*
It capitale non richiamato *(m)*
Pt capital irrealizado *(m)*

**capital oisif** *(m)* Fr
De totes Kapital *(n)*
En idle money
Es dinero sin invertir *(m)*
It denaro inattivo *(m)*
Pt dinheiro paralisado *(m)*

**capital por empréstimo** *(m)* Pt
De Fremdkapital *(n)*
En borrowed capital
Es capital a préstamo *(m)*
Fr capitaux empruntés *(m pl)*
It capitale preso a prestito *(m)*

**capital realizado** *(m)* Pt
De eingezahltes Kapital *(n)*
En paid-up capital
Es capital desembolsado *(m)*
Fr capital versé *(m)*
It capitale versato *(m)*

**capital reserves** En
De Kapitalreserve *(f)*
Es reserva de capital *(f)*
Fr réserve de capitaux *(f)*
It riserva di capitale *(f)*
Pt reservas de capital *(f pl)*

**capital social** *(m)* Fr
De Aktienkapital *(n)*
En share capital
Am stock capital
Es capital en acciones *(m)*
It capitale azionario *(m)*
Pt capital em acções *(m)*

**capital souscrit** *(m)* Fr
De gezeichnetes Kapital *(n)*
En subscribed capital
Es capital subscrito *(m)*
It capitale sottoscritto *(m)*
Pt capital subscrito *(m)*

**capital subscrito** *(m)* Es, Pt
De gezeichnetes Kapital *(n)*
En subscribed capital
Fr capital souscrit *(m)*
It capitale sottoscritto *(m)*

**capital versé** *(m)* Fr
De ausgegebenes Kapital; eingezahltes Kapital *(n)*
En issued capital; paid-up capital
Es capital emitido; capital desembolsado *(m)*
It capitale emesso; capitale versato *(m)*
Pt capital emitido; capital realizado *(m)*

**capitán de navío** *(m)* Es
De Kapitän *(m)*
En master of a ship

Fr capitaine *(m)*
It capitano di nave *(m)*
Pt capitão de navio *(m)*

**capitán de puerto** *(m)* Es
De Hafenmeister *(m)*
En harbour-master
Fr capitaine de port *(m)*
It capitano di porto *(m)*
Pt capitão de porto *(m)*

**capitano di nave** *(m)* It
De Kapitän *(m)*
En master of a ship
Es capitán de navío *(m)*
Fr capitaine *(m)*
Pt capitão de navio *(m)*

**capitano di porto** *(m)* It
De Hafenmeister *(m)*
En harbour-master
Es capitán de puerto *(m)*
Fr capitaine de port *(m)*
Pt capitão de porto *(m)*

**capitão de navio** *(m)* Pt
De Kapitän *(m)*
En master of a ship
Es capitán de navío *(m)*
Fr capitaine *(m)*
It capitano di nave *(m)*

**capitão de porto** *(m)* Pt
De Hafenmeister *(m)*
En harbour-master
Es capitán de puerto *(m)*
Fr capitaine de port *(m)*
It capitano di porto *(m)*

**capitaux à court terme** *(m pl)* Fr
De kurzfristiges Kapital *(n)*
En short-term capital
Es capital a corto plazo *(m)*
It capitale a breve termine *(m)*
Pt capital a curto prazo *(m)*

**capitaux à long terme** *(m pl)* Fr
De langfristiges Kapital *(n)*
En long-term capital
Es capital a largo plazo *(m)*
It capitale consolidato a lunga scadenza *(m)*
Pt capital a longo prazo *(m)*

**capitaux empruntés** *(m pl)* Fr
De Fremdkapital *(n)*
En borrowed capital
Es capital a préstamo *(m)*
It capitale preso a prestito *(m)*
Pt capital por empréstimo *(m)*

**capitaux pas encore émis** *(m pl)* Fr
De nicht ausgegebenes Kapital *(n)*
En unissued capital
Es capital no emitido *(m)*
It capitale non emesso *(m)*
Pt capital não emitido *(m)*

**capitaux spéculatifs** *(m pl)* Fr
De Spekulationskapital *(n)*
En risk capital
Es capital de especulación *(m)*
It capitale di speculazione *(m)*
Pt capital de especulação *(m)*

**capo-famiglia** *(m)* n It
De Hausherr *(m)*
En householder
Es jefe de familia *(m)*
Fr chef de famille *(m)*
Pt dono da casa *(m)*

**capo officina** *(m)* It
De Werkmeister *(m)*
En head foreman
Es capataz jefe *(m)*
Fr chef d'atelier *(m)*
Pt encarregado-chefe *(m)*

**capo operaio** *(m)* It
De Vorarbeiter *(m)*
En foreman
Es capataz *(m)*
Fr contremaître; chef d'équipe *(m)*
Pt encarregado; capataz *(m)*

**capo reparto** *(m)* It
De Abteilungsleiter *(m)*
En head of department
Es jefe de departamento *(m)*
Fr chef de service *(m)*
Pt chefe de departamento *(m)*

**capo servizio acquisti** *(m)* It
De Haupteinkäufer *(m)*
En head buyer
Es jefe del departamento de compras *(m)*

Fr chef du service des achats
(m)
Pt chefe de compras (m)

**capo ufficio** (m) It
De Bürovorsteher (m)
En office manager
Es jefe de oficina (m)
Fr chef de bureau (m)
Pt chefe de escritório (m)

**car** n En
De Auto; Wagen (n m)
Es coche (m)
Fr voiture; automobile (f)
It automobile; macchina (f)
Pt carro; automóvel (m)

**característica** (f) n Es, Pt
De Merkmal (n)
En feature
Fr particularité (f)
It caratteristica (f)

**caratteristica** (f) n It
De Merkmal (n)
En feature
Es característica (f)
Fr particularité (f)
Pt característica (f)

**carbón** (m) n Es
De Kohle (f)
En coal
Fr houille; charbon (f m)
It carbone (m)
Pt carvão (m)

**carbon copy** En
De Durchschlag (m)
Es copia en papel carbón (f)
Fr copie au carbone (f)
It copia carbone (f)
Pt copia a químico (f)

**carbone** (m) n It
De Kohle (f)
En coal
Es carbón (m)
Fr charbon (m)
Pt carvão (m)

**carbonera** (f) n Es
De Bunker (m)
En bunker
Fr soute (f)
It carbonile (m)
Pt carvoeira (f)

**carbonile** (m) n It
De Bunker (m)
En bunker
Es carbonera (f)
Fr soute (f)
Pt carvoeira (f)

**carbon paper** En
De Kohlepapier (n)
Es papel carbón (m)
Fr papier carbone (m)
It carta carbone (f)
Pt papel químico (m)

**card** n En
De Karte (f)
Es tarjeta (f)
Fr carte (f)
It scheda (f)
Pt cartão (m)

**card index** En
De Kartothek (f)
Es fichero (m)
Fr fichier (m)
It schedario (m)
Pt ficheiro (m)

**card-index file** En
De Kartei (f)
Es archivo de fichas (m)
Fr fichier (m)
It schedario (m)
Pt ficheiro com indice (m)

**carga** (f) n Es, Pt
De Ladung (f)
En cargo; loading
Fr cargaison; chargement (f m)
It carico; caricamento (m)

**carga de convés** (f) Pt
De Deckladung (f)
En deck cargo
Es carga en cubierta (f)
Fr cargaison de pont (f)
It carico in coperta (m)

**cargador de muelle** (m) Es
De Hafenàrbeiter (m)
En docker
Am longshoreman
Fr docker (m)

It lavoratore del porto (m)
Pt trabalhador das docas (m)

**carga en cubierta** (f) Es
De Deckladung (f)
En deck cargo
Fr cargaison de pont (f)
It carico in coperta (m)
Pt carga de convés (f)

**carga en granel** (f) Es
De Schüttgut (n)
En bulk cargo
Fr cargaison en vrac (f)
It carico alla rinfusa (m)
Pt carga geral (f)

**carga geral** (f) Pt
De Schüttgut (n)
En bulk cargo
Es carga en granel (f)
Fr cargaison en vrac (f)
It carico alla rinfusa (m)

**cargaison** (f) n Fr
De Ladung (f)
En cargo
Es carga (f)
It carico (m)
Pt carga (f)

**cargaison de pont** (f) Fr
De Deckladung (f)
En deck cargo
Es carga en cubierta (f)
It carico in coperta (m)
Pt carga de convés (f)

**cargaison en vrac** (f) Fr
De Schüttgut (n)
En bulk cargo
Es carga en granel (f)
It carico alla rinfusa (m)
Pt carga geral (f)

**cargo** n En
De Ladung (f)
Es carga (f)
Fr cargaison; chargement (f m)
It carico (m)
Pt carga (f)

**cargo** (m) n Fr
De Frachtschiff (n)
En cargo boat

Es  buque de carga *(m)*
It  nave da carico *(f)*
Pt  barco de carga *(m)*

**cargo boat** En
De  Frachtschiff *(n)*
Es  buque de carga *(m)*
Fr  cargo *(m)*
It  nave da carico *(f)*
Pt  barco de carga *(m)*

**cargos de salvamento** *(m pl)*
    Es
De  Bergegeld *(n)*
En  salvage charges
Fr  indemnité de sauvetage *(f)*
It  spese di salvataggio *(f pl)*
Pt  encargos de salvamento *(m pl)*

**cargos imprevistos** *(m pl)* Es
De  Nebenkosten *(pl)*
En  incidental charges
Fr  charges annexes *(f pl)*
It  spese accessorie *(f pl)*
Pt  encargos ocasionais *(m pl)*

**carico** *(m)* n It
De  Ladung *(f)*
En  cargo; loading
Es  carga *(f)*
Fr  cargaison; chargement *(f m)*
Pt  carga; carregamento *(f m)*

**carico alla rinfusa** *(m)* It
De  Schüttgut *(n)*
En  bulk cargo
Es  carga en granel *(f)*
Fr  cargaison en vrac *(f)*
Pt  carga geral *(f)*

**carico in coperta** *(m)* It
De  Deckladung *(f)*
En  deck cargo
Es  carga en cubierta *(f)*
Fr  cargaison de pont *(f)*
Pt  carga de convés *(f)*

**carimbo** *(m)* n Pt
De  Stempel *(m)*
En  (rubber) stamp
Es  estampilla *(f)*
Fr  tampon; timbre *(m)*
It  stampiglia *(f)*

**carimbo de datas** *(m)* Pt
De  Tagesstempel *(m)*
En  date-stamp
Es  sello de fecha *(m)*
Fr  dateur *(m)*
It  timbro a data *(m)*

**carnet de chèques** *(m)* Fr
De  Scheckheft *(n)*
En  cheque book
Am  check book
Es  libro de cheques *(m)*
It  libretto assegni *(m)*
Pt  livro de cheques *(m)*

**carnet de compte** *(m)* Fr
De  Bankbuch; Sparbuch *(n)*
En  passbook
Am  bankbook
Es  libreta de banco *(f)*
It  libretto di conto *(m)*
Pt  livrete de conta *(f)*

**carnet de identidad** *(m)* Es
De  Personalausweis *(m)*
En  identity card
Fr  carte d'identité *(f)*
It  carta d'identità *(f)*
Pt  bilhete de identidade *(m)*

**caro** adj Es, It, Pt
De  kostspielig; teuer
En  expensive
Fr  cher

**carpeta** *(f)* n Es
De  Mappe *(f)*
En  folder
Fr  chemise *(f)*
It  cartella *(f)*
Pt  pasta *(f)*

**carregamento** *(m)* n Pt
De  Ladung *(f)*
En  loading
Es  carga *(f)*
Fr  chargement *(m)*
It  carico; caricamento *(m)*

**carretta** *(f)* n It
De  Trampschiff *(n)*
En  tramp steamer
Es  vapor volandero *(m)*
Fr  navire de tramping *(m)*
Pt  vapor de serviço autónomo *(m)*

**carriage forward** En
Am  F.O.B. shipping point
De  Portonachnahme
Es  a porte debido
Fr  en port dû
It  porto assegnato
Pt  transporte a pagar

**carriage free** En
Am  F.O.B. destination
De  frachtfrei
Es  franco de porte
Fr  franco
It  porto franco
Pt  porte gratis

**carriage paid** En
Am  freight charges paid
De  franko
Es  a porte pagado
Fr  port payé
It  franco di porto
Pt  porte pago

**carrier** n En
Am  conveyer
De  Spediteur *(m)*
Es  transportador *(m)*
Fr  expéditeur *(m)*
It  vettore *(m)*
Pt  transportador *(m)*

**carro** *(m)* n Pt
De  Auto; Wagen *(n m)*
En  car
Es  coche *(m)*
Fr  voiture; automobile *(f)*
It  automobile; macchina *(f)*

**carrozza ferroviaria** *(f)* It
De  Eisenbahnwagen *(m)*
En  railway carriage
Am  railroad car
Es  vagón de ferrocarril *(m)*
Fr  wagon de chemin de fer *(m)*
Pt  vagão de caminhos de ferro *(m)*

**carruagem do guarda** *(f)* Pt
De  Packwagen *(m)*
En  guard's van
Es  furgón *(m)*
Fr  fourgon *(m)*
It  bagagliaio *(m)*

**carry forward amount** Am
En amount carried forward
De Übertrag *(m)*
Es suma y sigue *(f)*
Fr report à nouveau *(m)*
It ammontare da riportare *(m)*
Pt importância transportada *(f)*

**carry out** En
De durchführen
Es ejecutar
Fr exécuter
It eseguire
Pt executar

**carta** *(f)* n Es, Pt
De Brief *(m)*
En letter
Fr lettre *(f)*
It lettera *(f)*

**carta assorbente** *(f)* It
De Löschpapier *(n)*
En blotting paper
Es papel secante *(m)*
Fr papier buvard *(m)*
Pt papel mata-borrão *(m)*

**carta carbone** *(f)* It
De Kohlepapier *(n)*
En carbon paper
Es papel carbón *(m)*
Fr papier carbone *(m)*
Pt papel químico *(m)*

**carta certificada** *(f)* Es
De eingeschriebener Brief *(m)*
En registered letter
Fr lettre recommandée *(f)*
It lettera raccomandata *(f)*
Pt carta registada *(f)*

**carta comercial de primera orden** *(f)* Es
De erstklassiger Handelswechsel *(m)*
En prime trade bill
Fr papier de haut commerce *(m)*
It carta commerciale di primo ordine *(f)*
Pt estatuto de comercialização de primeira ordem *(m)*

**carta commerciale di primo ordine** *(f)* It
De erstklassiger Handelswechsel *(m)*

En prime trade bill
Es carta comercial de primera orden *(f)*
Fr papier de haut commerce *(m)*
Pt estatuto de comercialização de primeira ordem *(m)*

**carta de avião** *(f)* Pt
De Luftpostbrief *(m)*
En air letter
Es carta por avión *(f)*
Fr aérogramme *(m)*
It lettera aerea *(f)*

**carta de crédito** *(f)* Es, Pt
De Kreditbrief *(m)*
En letter of credit
Fr lettre de crédit *(f)*
It lettera di credito *(f)*

**carta de crédito confirmada** *(f)* Es, Pt
De bestätigter Kreditbrief *(m)*
En confirmed letter of credit
Fr lettre de crédit confirmée *(f)*
It lettera di credito confermata *(f)*

**carta de crédito irrevocable** *(f)* Es
De unwiderruflicher Kreditbrief *(m)*
En irrevocable letter of credit
Fr lettre de crédit irrévocable *(f)*
It lettera di credito irrevocabile *(f)*
Pt carta de crédito irrevogável *(f)*

**carta de crédito irrevocable confirmada** *(f)* Es
De bestätigter unwiderruflicher Kreditbrief *(m)*
En confirmed irrevocable letter of credit
Fr lettre de crédit irrévocable confirmée *(f)*
It lettera di credito confermata e irrevocabile *(f)*
Pt carta de crédito irrevogável confirmada *(f)*

**carta de crédito irrevogável** *(f)* Pt

De unwiderruflicher Kreditbrief *(m)*
En irrevocable letter of credit
Es carta de crédito irrevocable *(f)*
Fr lettre de crédit irrévocable *(f)*
It lettera di credito irrevocabile *(f)*

**carta de crédito irrevogável confirmada** *(f)* Pt
De bestätigter unwiderruflicher Kreditbrief *(m)*
En confirmed irrevocable letter of credit
Es carta de crédito irrevocable confirmada *(f)*
Fr lettre de crédit irrévocable confirmée *(f)*
It lettera di credito confermata e irrevocabile *(f)*

**carta de hipoteca** *(f)* Es, Pt
De Verpfändungsurkunde *(f)*
En letter of hypothecation
Fr lettre hypothécaire *(f)*
It atto ipotecario *(m)*

**carta de indemnización** *(f)* Es
De Ausfallbürgschaft *(f)*
En letter of indemnity
Fr cautionnement *(m)*
It lettera di garanzia *(f)*
Pt documento de garantia *(m)*

**carta de porte aéreo** *(f)* Es
De Luftfrachtbrief *(m)*
En air waybill
Fr lettre de transport aérien *(f)*
It nota di spedizione aerea *(f)*
Pt guia de porte aéreo *(m)*

**carta de publicidad de ventas** *(f)* Es
De Werbebrief *(m)*
En publicity letter; sales letter
Fr lettre de publicité ventes *(f)*
It lettera di pubblicità vendite *(f)*
Pt carta de publicidade de vendas *(f)*

**carta de trabalho** *(f)* Pt
De Arbeitserlaubnis *(n)*
En work permit
Es permiso de trabajo *(m)*

Fr  permis de travail *(m)*
It  permesso di lavoro *(m)*

**carta di credito** *(f)* It
De  Kreditkarte *(f)*
En  credit card
Es  tarjeta de crédito *(f)*
Fr  carte de crédit *(f)*
Pt  cartão de crédito *(m)*

**carta d'identità** *(f)* It
De  Personalausweis *(m)*
En  identity card
Es  carnet de identidad *(m)*
Fr  carte d'identité *(f)*
Pt  bilhete de identidade *(m)*

**carta expresso** *(f)* Pt
De  Eilbrief *(m)*
En  express letter
Am  special delivery
Es  carta urgente *(f)*
Fr  lettre par exprès *(f)*
It  lettera espresso *(f)*

**carta millimetrata** *(f)* It
De  Millimeterpapier *(n)*
En  graph paper
Es  papel milimetrado *(m)*
Fr  papier quadrillé *(m)*
Pt  papel milimétrico *(m)*

**carta moneta** *(f)* It
De  Papiergeld *(n)*
En  paper money
Es  papel monetario *(m)*
Fr  papier-monnaie *(m)*
Pt  papel-moeda *(m)*

**cartão** *(m)* n Pt
De  Karte *(f)*
En  card
Es  tarjeta *(f)*
Fr  carte *(f)*
It  scheda *(f)*

**cartão de crédito** *(m)* Pt
De  Kreditkarte *(f)*
En  credit card
Es  tarjeta de crédito *(f)*
Fr  carte de crédit *(f)*
It  carta di credito *(f)*

**carta por avión** *(f)* Es
De  Luftpostbrief *(m)*
En  air letter
Fr  aérogramme *(m)*

It  lettera aerea *(f)*
Pt  carta de avião *(f)*

**carta registada** *(f)* Pt
De  eingeschriebener Brief *(m)*
En  registered letter
Es  carta certificada *(f)*
Fr  lettre recommandée *(f)*
It  lettera raccomandata *(f)*

**carta urgente** *(f)* Es
De  Eilbrief *(m)*
En  express letter
Am  special delivery
Fr  lettre par exprès *(f)*
It  lettera espresso *(f)*
Pt  carta expresso *(f)*

**carte** *(f)* n Fr
De  Karte *(f)*
En  card
Es  tarjeta *(f)*
It  scheda *(f)*
Pt  cartão *(m)*

**carte d'identité** *(f)* Fr
De  Personalausweis *(m)*
En  identity card
Es  carnet de identidad *(m)*
It  carta d'identità *(f)*
Pt  bilhete de identidade *(m)*

**carte de chèque** *(f)* Fr
De  Scheckkarte *(f)*
En  cheque card
Am  bank credit card
Es  tarjeta de cheque *(f)*
It  scheda per assegni *(f)*
Pt  cartão de validação de
    cheques *(m)*

**carte de crédit** *(f)* Fr
De  Kreditkarte *(f)*
En  credit card
Es  tarjeta de crédito *(f)*
It  carta di credito *(f)*
Pt  cartão de crédito *(m)*

**carte di bordo** *(f pl)* It
De  Schiffspapiere *(n pl)*
En  ship's papers
Es  documentación marítima *(f)*
Fr  papiers de bord *(m pl)*
Pt  documentação do navio *(f)*

**carteira de investimentos** *(m)*
    Pt
De  Investitionsportefeuille *(n)*

En  investment portfolio
Es  cartera de inversiones *(f)*
Fr  portefeuille d'investisse-
    ments *(m)*
It  portafoglio titoli *(m)*

**cartel** n En; Es, Fr, Pt *(m)*
De  Kartell *(n)*
It  cartello *(m)*

**cartella** *(f)* n It
De  Mappe *(f)*
En  folder
Es  carpeta *(f)*
Fr  chemise *(f)*
Pt  pasta *(f)*

**cartello** *(m)* n It
De  Kartell *(n)*
En  cartel
Es  cartel *(m)*
Fr  cartel *(m)*
Pt  cartel *(m)*

**carte perforée** Fr
De  Lochkarte *(f)*
En  punched card
Es  tarjeta perforada *(f)*
It  scheda perforata *(f)*
Pt  ficha perforada *(f)*

**cartera** (ministerial) *(f)* n Es
De  Portefeuille;
    Geschäftsbereich *(n m)*
En  portfolio
Fr  portefeuille *(f)*
It  portafoglio *(m)*
Pt  pasta *(f)*

**cartera de inversiones** *(f)* Es
De  Investitionsportefeuille *(n)*
En  investment portfolio
Fr  portefeuille d'investisse-
    ments *(m)*
It  portafoglio titoli *(m)*
Pt  carteira de investimentos
    *(m)*

**carton** n En, Fr *(m)*
De  Karton *(m)*
Es  cartón *(m)*
It  cartone *(m)*
Pt  caixa de cartão *(f)*

**cartón** *(m)* n Es
De  Karton *(m)*
En  carton
Fr  carton *(m)*

It   cartone *(m)*
Pt  caixa de cartão *(f)*

**cartone** *(m)* n It
De  Karton *(m)*
En  carton
Es  cartón *(m)*
Fr  carton *(m)*
Pt  caixa de cartão *(f)*

**carvão** *(m)* n Pt
De  Kohle *(f)*
En  coal
Es  carbón *(m)*
Fr  houille; charbon *(f m)*
It   carbone

**carvoeira** *(f)* n Pt
De  Bunker *(m)*
En  bunker
Es  carbonera *(f)*
Fr  soute *(f)*
It   carbonile *(m)*

**casa** *(f)* n Es, It, Pt
De  Haus; Haushalt *(n m)*
En  house; household
Fr  maison; ménage *(f m)*

**casa commerciale** *(f)* It
De  Firma *(f)*
En  business; firm
Es  casa de comercio *(f)*
Fr  maison de commerce *(f)*
Pt  casa de comércio *(f)*

**casa da moeda** *(f)* Pt
De  Münze *(f)*
En  mint
Es  casa de la moneda *(f)*
Fr  la Monnaie
It   zecca *(f)*

**casa de comercio** *(f)* Es
De  Firma *(f)*
En  business; firm
Fr  maison de commerce *(f)*
It   casa commerciale *(f)*
Pt  casa de comércio *(f)*

**casa de comércio** *(f)* Pt
De  Firma *(f)*
En  business; firm
Es  casa de comercio *(f)*
Fr  maison de commerce *(f)*
It   casa commerciale *(f)*

**casa de descuentos** *(f)* Es
De  Diskontbank *(f)*
En  discount house
Fr  maison d'escompte *(f)*
It   banca di sconto *(f)*
Pt  agência corretora de descontos *(f)*

**casa de la moneda** *(f)* Es
De  Münze *(f)*
En  mint
Fr  la Monnaie
It   zecca *(f)*
Pt  casa da moeda *(f)*

**casa di vecchia fondazione** *(f)* It
De  alteingeführtes Geschäft *(n)*
En  old-established business
Es  casa sólida *(f)*
Fr  maison solide *(f)*
Pt  empresa de há muito estabelecida *(f)*

**casa editora** *(f)* Pt
De  Verlag *(m)*
En  publishing house
Es  casa editorial *(f)*
Fr  maison d'édition *(f)*
It   casa editrice *(f)*

**casa editorial** *(f)* Es
De  Verlag *(m)*
En  publishing house
Fr  maison d'édition *(f)*
It   casa editrice *(f)*
Pt  casa editora *(f)*

**casa editrice** *(f)* It
De  Verlag *(m)*
En  publishing house
Es  casa editorial *(f)*
Fr  maison d'édition *(f)*
Pt  casa editora *(f)*

**casa sólida** *(f)* Es
De  alteingeführtes Geschäft *(n)*
En  old-established business
Fr  maison solide *(f)*
It   casa di vecchia fondazione *(f)*
Pt  empresa de há muito estabelecida *(f)*

**case** (legal) n En
De  Rechtsfall *(m)*
Es  causa *(f)*
Fr  procès *(m)*

It   causa *(f)*
Pt  causa *(f)*

**cash** n En
De  Bargeld *(n)*
Es  dinero efectivo *(m)*
Fr  espèces *(f pl)*
It   denaro contante *(m)*
Pt  dinheiro de contado *(m)*

**cash** vb En
De  einkassieren
Es  cobrar
Fr  encaisser
It   incassare
Pt  cobrar

**cash a cheque** En
Am cash a check
De  einen Scheck einlösen
Es  cobrar un cheque
Fr  toucher un chèque
It   incassare un assegno
Pt  cobrar um cheque

**cash against documents** (c.a.d.) En
De  bar gegen Versandpapiere
Es  al contado contra documentos
Fr  comptant contre documents
It   contanti contro documenti
Pt  em dinheiro contra documentação

**cash balance** En
De  Kassensaldo *(m)*
Es  resto en efectivo *(m)*
Fr  solde de caisse *(m)*
It   residuo di cassa *(m)*
Pt  saldo em dinheiro *(m)*

**cash book** En
De  Kassenbuch *(n)*
Es  libro de caja *(m)*
Fr  livre de caisse *(m)*
It   libro cassa *(m)*
Pt  livro de caixa *(m)*

**cash-box** n En
De  Geldkassette *(f)*
Es  caja *(f)*
Fr  caisse *(f)*
It   cassetta *(f)*
Pt  caixa *(f)*

**cash deal** En
De Bargeschäft (n)
Es trato al contado (m)
Fr transaction au comptant (f)
It operazione a contanti (f)
Pt negócio em dinheiro (m)

**cash-desk** n En
De Kasse (f)
Es caja (f)
Fr caisse (f)
It cassa (f)
Pt caixa (f)

**cash discount** En
De Barrabatt (m)
Es descuento de caja (m)
Fr escompte de caisse (m)
It sconto per pagamento a
   contanti (m)
Pt desconto de contado (m)

**cash dispenser** En
De Bargeldauszahlungsautomat
   (m)
Es caja automática (f)
Fr distributeur d'argent com-
   ptant (m)
It cassa automatica (f)
Pt caixa automática (f)

**cash flow** En
De Cash-flow (n)
Es flujo de caja (m)
Fr cash flow (m)
It flusso di cassa (m)
Pt movimento em dinheiro (m)

**cash forecast** En
De Bargeldvoraussage (f)
Es previsión de fondos (f)
Fr prévision comptant (f)
It previsione contanti (f)
Pt previsão de fundos (em
   dinheiro) (f)

**cashier** n En
Am teller
De Kassierer (m)
Es cajero (m)
Fr caissier (m)
It cassiere (m)
Pt caixa (m)

**cash in hand** En
De Barbestand (m)

Es efectivo en caja (m)
Fr espèces en caisse (f pl)
It pronti contanti (m pl)
Pt fundos à ordem (m pl)

**cash on delivery** (c.o.d.) En
De Lieferung gegen Nach-
   nahme
Es entrega contra reembolso
Fr paiement à la livraison
It pagamento alla consegna
Pt entrega contra reembolso

**cash reserve** En
De Kassenreserve (f)
Es reserva en efectivo (f)
Fr réserve en espèces (f)
It riserva in contanti (f)
Pt reserva em dinheiro (f)

**cash sale** En
De Kassageschäft (n)
Es venta al conta (f)
Fr vente au comptant (f)
It vendita a contanti (f)
Pt venda a dinheiro (f)

**cash with order** En
De gegen Barzahlung
Es pagadero con el pedido
Fr payable à la commande
It pagamento con l'ordine
Pt pagamento no acto de
   requisição

**casilla de equipaje** (f) Es
De Gepäckschliessfach (n)
En luggage locker
Fr coffre de bagages (m)
It cassetta bagaglio (f)
Pt depósito de bagagem indi-
   vidualizado (m)

**cassa** (f) n It
De Kasse (f)
En cash-desk
Es caja (f)
Fr caisse (f)
Pt caixa (f)

**cassa automatica** (f) It
De Bargeldauszahlungsautomat
   (m)
En cash dispenser
Es caja automática (f)

Fr distributeur d'argent comptant (m)
Pt caixa automática (f)

**cassa di compensazione** (f) It
De Ausgleichsfonds (m)
En equalization fund
Es fondo de compensación
   (m)
Fr fonds de régularisation (m
   pl)
Pt fundo de compensação (m)

**cassa di risparmio** (f) It
De Sparkasse (f)
En savings bank
Es caja de ahorros (f)
Fr caisse d'épargne (f)
Pt caixa económica (f)

**cassa di risparmio postale** (f)
   It
De Postsparkasse (f)
En Post Office Savings Bank
Es caja postal de ahorros (f)
Fr caisse d'épargne postale
   (f)
Pt caixa económica postal (f)

**cassaforte** (f) n It
De Geldschrank (m)
En safe
Es caja fuerte (f)
Fr coffre-fort (m)
Pt cofre (m)

**cassetta** (f) n It
De Geldkassette (f)
En cash-box
Es caja (f)
Fr caisse (f)
Pt caixa (f)

**cassetta bagaglio** (f) It
De Gepäckschliessfach (n)
En luggage locker
Es casilla de equipaje (f)
Fr coffre de bagages (m)
Pt depósito de bagagem indi-
   vidualizado (m)

**cassetta postale** (f) It
De Briefkasten (m)
En letter-box
Am mail-box
Es buzón (m)
Fr boîte aux lettres (f)
Pt caixa do correio (f)

**cassiere** *(m)* n It
De Kassierer *(m)*
En cashier
Am teller
Es cajero *(m)*
Fr caissier *(m)*
Pt caixa *(m)*

**casting vote** En
De entscheidende Stimme *(f)*
Es voto decisivo *(m)*
Fr voix prépondérante *(f)*
It voto decisivo *(m)*
Pt voto decisivo *(m)*

**cast iron** En
De Gusseisen *(n)*
Es hierro colado *(m)*
Fr fonte de fer *(f)*
It ghisa *(f)*
Pt ferro fundido *(m)*

**catálogo** *(m)* n Es, Pt
De Katalog *(m)*
En catalogue
Fr catalogue *(m)*
It catalogo *(m)*

**catalogo** *(m)* n It
De Katalog *(m)*
En catalogue
Es catálogo *(m)*
Fr catalogue *(m)*
Pt catálogo *(m)*

**catálogo comercial** *(m)* Es, Pt
De Preiskatalog *(m)*
En trade catalogue
Fr tarif-album *(m)*
It catalogo commerciale *(m)*

**catalogo commerciale** *(m)* It
De Preiskatalog *(m)*
En trade catalogue
Es catálogo comercial *(m)*
Fr tarif-album *(m)*
Pt catálogo comercial *(m)*

**catalogue** n En, Fr *(m)*
De Katalog *(m)*
Es catálogo *(m)*
It catalogo *(m)*
Pt catálogo *(m)*

**catalogue price** En
De Listenpreis *(m)*
Es precio de catálogo *(m)*
Fr prix de catalogue *(m)*

It prezzo di catalogo *(m)*
Pt preço de catálogo *(m)*

**catena di montaggio** *(f)* It
De Montageband *(n)*
En assembly line
Es línea de montaje *(f)*
Fr chaîne de montage *(f)*
Pt cadeia de montagem *(f)*

**cattivo pagatore** *(m)* It
De schlechter Zahler *(m)*
En slow payer
Es deudor moroso *(m)*
Fr mauvais payeur *(m)*
Pt mau-pagador *(m)*

**caução** *(f)* n Pt
De Haftkaution *(f)*
En bail
Es fianza *(f)*
Fr caution *(f)*
It cauzione *(f)*

**caucionado** *(m)* n Pt
De Gewahrsaminhaber *(m)*
En bailee
Es depositario *(m)*
Fr dépositaire *(m)*
It depositario *(m)*

**causa** *(f)* n Es, It, Pt
De Rechtsfall *(m)*
En (legal) case
Fr procès *(m)*

**caution** *(f)* n Fr
De Haftkaution; Bürgschaft *(f)*
En bail; surety
Es fianza; fiador *(f m)*
It cauzione; garante *(f m)*
Pt caução; fiador *(f m)*

**cautionnement** *(m)* n Fr
De Bürge;      Ausfallbürgschaft
*(m f)*
En surety; letter of indemnity
Es fianza; carta de indem-
nización *(f)*
It cauzione; lettera di garanzia
*(f)*
Pt fiança;     documento    de
garantia *(f m)*

**cauzione** *(f)* n It
De Haftkaution; Bürge *(f m)*
En bail; surety
Es fianza *(f)*

Fr caution; cautionnement *(f*
*m)*
Pt caução; fiança *(f)*

**cavallo** *(m)* n It
De Pferdestärke (PS) *(f)*
En horse-power (hp)
Es caballo de vapor (cv) *(m)*
Fr cheval-vapeur (ch-v) *(m)*
Pt cavalo-vapor *(m)*

**cavalo-vapor** *(m)* n Pt
De Pferdestärke (PS) *(f)*
En horse-power (hp)
Es caballo de vapor (cv) *(m)*
Fr cheval-vapeur (ch-v) *(m)*
It cavallo *(m)*

**caza de rebajas** *(f)* Es
De Sucht nach Sonderange-
boten *(f)*
En bargain-hunting
Fr chasse aux soldes *(f)*
It caccia alle occasioni *(f)*
Pt caça aos saldos *(f)*

**cédant** *(m)* n Fr
De Übertrager; Zedent *(m)*
En assignor; transferor
Es cesionista *(m)*
It cedente *(m)*
Pt cessionista *(m)*

**cedente** *(m)* n It
De Übertrager; Zedent *(m)*
En assignor; transferor
Es cesionista *(m)*
Fr cédant *(m)*
Pt cessionista *(m)*

**céder** Fr
De aufgeben; überweisen
En give up; transfer
Es renunciar; transferir
It cedere; trasferire
Pt desistir; transferir

**cedere** It
De aufgeben
En give up
Es renunciar
Fr céder
Pt desistir

**cedola** *(f)* n It
De Kupon *(m)*
En coupon
Es cupón *(m)*

Fr  coupon *(m)*
Pt  cupão *(m)*

**cedola di dividendo** *(f)* It
De  Gewinnanteilschein *(m)*
En  dividend warrant
Es  cupón de dividendos *(m)*
Fr  dividende-warrant *(m)*
Pt  cédula de dividendo *(f)*

**cédula de dividendo** *(f)* Pt
De  Gewinnanteilschein *(m)*
En  dividend warrant
Es  cupón de dividendos *(m)*
Fr  dividende-warrant *(m)*
It  cedola di dividendo *(f)*

**cédula hipotecaria** *(f)* Es
De  Grund- und Gebäudeobli-
     gation *(f)*
En  property bond
Fr  obligation foncière *(f)*
It  obbligazione fondiaria *(f)*
Pt  título de investimento imo-
     biliário *(m)*

**celebrar una reunión** Es
De  eine Versammlung abhal-
     ten
En  hold a meeting
Fr  tenir une assemblée
It  tenere una riunione
Pt  fazer uma reunião

**censimento** *(m)* n It
De  Volkszählung *(f)*
En  census
Es  censo *(m)*
Fr  recensement *(m)*
Pt  censo *(m)*

**censo** *(m)* n Es, Pt
De  Volkszählung *(f)*
En  census
Fr  recensement *(m)*
It  censimento *(m)*

**census** n En
De  Volkszählung *(f)*
Es  censo *(m)*
Fr  recensement *(m)*
It  censimento *(m)*
Pt  censo *(m)*

**center** n Am
En  centre
De  Mitte *(f)*
Es  centro *(m)*

Fr  centre *(m)*
It  centro *(m)*
Pt  centro *(m)*

**central buying office** En
De  Einkaufszentrale *(f)*
Es  oficina central de compras
     *(f)*
Fr  centrale d'achats *(f)*
It  ufficio centrale d'acquisti
     *(m)*
Pt  escritório central de com-
     pras *(m)*

**centrale d'achats** *(f)* Fr
De  Einkaufszentrale *(f)*
En  central buying office
Es  oficina central de compras
     *(f)*
It  ufficio centrale d'acquisti
     *(m)*
Pt  escritório central de com-
     pras *(m)*

**centrale telefonica** *(f)* It
De  Fernsprechamt *(n)*
En  telephone exchange
Es  central telefónica *(f)*
Fr  central téléphonique *(m)*
Pt  central telefónica *(f)*

**central heating** En
De  Zentralheizung *(f)*
Es  calefacción central *(f)*
Fr  chauffage central *(m)*
It  riscaldamento centrale *(m)*
Pt  aquecimento central *(m)*

**centralisation** *(f)* n Fr
De  Zentralisierung *(f)*
En  centralization
Es  centralización *(f)*
It  centralizzazione *(f)*
Pt  centralização *(f)*

**centralização** *(f)* n Pt
De  Zentralisierung *(f)*
En  centralization
Es  centralización *(f)*
Fr  centralisation *(f)*
It  centralizzazione *(f)*

**centralización** *(f)* n Es
De  Zentralisierung *(f)*
En  centralization
Fr  centralisation *(f)*
It  centralizzazione *(f)*
Pt  centralização *(f)*

**centralization** n En
De  Zentralisierung *(f)*
Es  centralización *(f)*
Fr  centralisation *(f)*
It  centralizzazione *(f)*
Pt  centralização *(f)*

**centralizzazione** *(f)* n It
De  Zentralisierung *(f)*
En  centralization
Es  centralización *(f)*
Fr  centralisation *(f)*
Pt  centralização *(f)*

**central telefónica** *(f)* Es, Pt
De  Fernsprechamt *(n)*
En  telephone exchange
Fr  central téléphonique *(m)*
It  centrale telefonica *(f)*

**central téléphonique** *(m)* Fr
De  Fernsprechamt *(n)*
En  telephone exchange
Es  central telefónica *(f)*
It  centrale telefonica *(f)*
Pt  central telefónica *(f)*

**centre** n En, Fr *(m)*
Am  center
De  Mitte *(f)*
Es  centro *(m)*
It  centro *(m)*
Pt  centro *(m)*

**centre commercial** *(m)* Fr
De  Geschäftszentrum *(n)*
En  shopping centre
Es  centro de negocios *(m)*
It  zona degli acquisti *(f)*
Pt  centro de comércio *(m)*

**centro** *(m)* n Es, It, Pt
De  Mitte *(f)*
En  centre
Am  center
Fr  centre *(m)*

**centro de comércio** *(m)* Pt
De  Geschäftszentrum *(n)*
En  shopping centre
Es  centro de negocios *(m)*
Fr  centre commercial *(m)*
It  zona degli acquisti *(f)*

**centro de negocios** *(m)* Es
De  Geschäftszentrum *(n)*
En  shopping centre
Fr  centre commercial *(m)*

It   zona degli acquisti *(f)*
Pt  centro de comércio *(m)*

**centro de serviços de em-
prego** *(m)* Pt
De  Arbeitsnachweisstelle *(f)*
En  employment exchange
Am  state employment agency
Es  bolsa de trabajo *(f)*
Fr  bureau de placement *(m)*
It   ufficio di collocamento *(m)*

**centro fabril** *(m)* Pt
De  Industriegebiet *(n)*
En  industrial estate
Am  industrial park
Es  precinto industrial *(m)*
Fr  domaine industriel *(m)*
It   centro industriale *(m)*

**centro industriale** *(m)* It
De  Industriegebiet *(n)*
En  industrial estate
Am  industrial park
Es  precinto industrial *(m)*
Fr  domaine industriel *(m)*
Pt  centro fabril *(m)*

**cerrar um mercado** Pt
De  den Markt beherrschen
En  corner a market
Es  acaparar el mercado
Fr  accaparer le marché
It   accaparrare il mercato

**certidão de óbito** *(f)* Pt
De  Totenschein *(m)*
En  death certificate
Es  partida de defunción *(f)*
Fr  extrait d'acte de décès *(m)*
It   certificato di morte *(m)*

**certidão de peso** *(f)* Pt
De  Wiegeschein *(m)*
En  weight note
Es  certificado de pesaje *(m)*
Fr  note de poids *(f)*
It   distinta pesi *(f)*

**certificado** *(m)* n Es, Pt
De  Bescheinigung *(f)*
En  certificate; warrant
Fr  certificat *(m)*
It   certificato *(m)*

**certificado de acción** *(m)* Es
De  Aktie *(f)*
En  ordinary share certificate

Am  stock certificate
Fr  certificat d'action *(m)*
It   certificato azionario *(m)*
Pt  título de acções ordinárias
     *(m)*

**certificado de declaración de
entrada** *(m)* Es
De  Eintrittsdeklarationsschein
     *(m)*
En  jerque note
Fr  certificat d'entrée autorisée
     *(m)*
It   certificato di dichiarazione
     d'entrata *(m)*
Pt  certificado de verificação
     alfandegária *(m)*

**certificado de origem** *(m)* Pt
De  Ursprungszeugnis *(n)*
En  certificate of origin
Es  certificado de origen *(m)*
Fr  certificat d'origine *(m)*
It   certificato d'origine *(m)*

**certificado de origen** *(m)* Es
De  Ursprungszeugnis *(n)*
En  certificate of origin
Fr  certificat d'origine *(m)*
It   certificato d'origine *(m)*
Pt  certificado de origem *(m)*

**certificado de pesaje** *(m)* Es
De  Wiegeschein *(m)*
En  weight note
Fr  note de poids *(f)*
It   distinta pesi *(f)*
Pt  certidão de peso *(f)*

**certificado de seguro** *(m)* Es,
Pt
De  Versicherungsschein *(m)*
En  insurance certificate
Fr  certificat d'assurance *(m)*
It   certificato di assicurazione
     *(m)*

**certificado de verificação
alfandegária** *(m)* Pt
De  Eintrittsdeklarationsschein
     *(m)*
En  jerque note
Es  certificado de declaración
     de entrada *(m)*
Fr  certificat d'entrée autorisée
     *(m)*
It   certificato di dichiarazione
     d'entrata *(m)*

**certificar** *vb* Es, Pt
De  bescheinigen
En  certify
Fr  certifier
It   certificare

**certificare** *vb* It
De  bescheinigen
En  certify
Es  certificar
Fr  certifier
Pt  certificar

**certificat** *(m)* n Fr
De  Bescheinigung *(f)*
En  certificate; warrant
Es  certificado *(m)*
It   certificato *(m)*
Pt  certificado *(m)*

**certificat d'actions** *(m)* Fr
De  Aktienzertifikat *(n)*
En  share certificate
Am  certificate of stock
Es  título de acción *(m)*
It   certificato azionario *(m)*
Pt  título de acções *(m)*

**certificat d'assurance** *(m)* Fr
De  Versicherungsschein *(m)*
En  insurance certificate
Es  certificado de seguro *(m)*
It   certificato di assicurazione
     *(m)*
Pt  certificado de seguro *(m)*

**certificat d'entrée autorisée**
*(m)* Fr
De  Eintrittsdeklarationsschein
     *(m)*
En  jerque note
Es  certificado de declaración
     de entrada *(m)*
It   certificato di dichiarazione
     d'entrata *(m)*
Pt  certificado de verificação
     alfandegária *(m)*

**certificat d'immatriculation**
(d'un navire) *(m)* Fr
De  Schiffsregister *(n)*
En  ship's register
Es  registro del barco *(m)*
It   atto di nazionalità *(m)*
Pt  registo do navio *(m)*

cessione

**certificat d'origine** *(m)* Fr
De Ursprungszeugnis *(n)*
En certificate of origin
Es certificado de origen *(m)*
It certificato d'origine *(m)*
Pt certificado de origem *(m)*

**certificate** *n* En
De Bescheinigung *(f)*
Es certificado *(m)*
Fr certificat *(m)*
It certificato *(m)*
Pt certificado *(m)*

**certificate of insurance** En
De Versicherungsurkunde *(f)*
Es certificado de seguro *(m)*
Fr certificat d'assurance *(m)*
It certificato di assicurazione *(m)*
Pt certificado de seguro *(m)*

**certificate of origin** En
De Ursprungszeugnis *(n)*
Es certificado de origen *(m)*
Fr certificat d'origine *(m)*
It certificato d'origine *(m)*
Pt certificado de origem *(m)*

**certificate of stock** Am
En share certificate
De Aktienzertifikat; Anteilschein *(n m)*
Es título de acción *(m)*
Fr certificat d'actions *(m)*
It certificato azionario *(m)*
Pt título de acções *(m)*

**certificato** *(m)* n It
De Bescheinigung *(f)*
En certificate; warrant
Es certificado *(m)*
Fr certificat *(m)*
Pt certificado *(m)*

**certificato azionario** *(m)* It
De Aktienzertifikat; Aktie *(n f)*
En share certificate
Am certificate of stock
Es título de acción *(m)*
Fr certificat d'actions *(m)*
Pt título de acções *(m)*

**certificato di assicurazione** *(m)* It
De Versicherungsurkunde *(f)*
En insurance certificate
Es certificado de seguro *(m)*

Fr certificat d'assurance *(m)*
Pt certificado de seguro *(m)*

**certificato di deposito** *(m)* It
De Depositenschein *(m)*
En deposit receipt
Es recibo de depósito *(m)*
Fr récépissé de dépôt *(m)*
Pt recibo de depósito *(m)*

**certificato di dichiarazione d'entrata** *(m)* It
De Eintrittsdeklarationsschein *(m)*
En jerque note
Es certificado de declaración de entrada *(m)*
Fr certificat d'entrée autorisée *(m)*
Pt certificado de verificação alfandegária *(m)*

**certificato di morte** *(m)* It
De Totenschein *(m)*
En death certificate
Es partida de defunción *(f)*
Fr extrait d'acte de décès *(m)*
Pt certidão de óbito *(f)*

**certificato d'origine** *(m)* It
De Ursprungszeugnis *(n)*
En certificate of origin
Es certificado de origen *(m)*
Fr certificat d'origine *(m)*
Pt certificado de origem *(m)*

**certified cheque** En
Am certified check
De bestätigter Scheck *(m)*
Es cheque certificado *(m)*
Fr chèque certifié *(m)*
It assegno garantito *(m)*
Pt cheque certificado *(m)*

**certified true copy** En
De beglaubigte Abschrift *(f)*
Es copia auténtica *(f)*
Fr copie certifiée *(f)*
It copia conforme *(f)*
Pt cópia autenticada *(f)*

**certifier** *vb* Fr
De bescheinigen
En certify
Es certificar
It certificare
Pt certificar

**certify** *vb* En
De bescheinigen
Es certificar
Fr certifier
It certificare
Pt certificar

**cesión** *(f)* n Es
De Überweisung; Ubertragung *(f)*
En transfer; assignment
Fr transfert; cession *(m f)*
It cessione *(f)*
Pt trespasse; consignação *(m f)*

**cesionario** *(m)* n Es
De Zessionär *(m)*
En assignee; transferee
Fr cessionnaire *(m)*
It assegnatario; cessionario *(m)*
Pt cessionário *(m)*

**cesionista** *(m)* n Es
De Übertrager; Zedent *(m)*
En assignor; transferor
Fr cédant *(m)*
It cedente *(m)*
Pt cessionista *(m)*

**cession** *(f)* n Fr
De Übertragung *(f)*
En assignment
Es cesión *(f)*
It cessione *(f)*
Pt consignação *(f)*
En transferee

**cessionario** *(m)* n It
De Zessionär *(m)*
En transferee
Es cesionario *(m)*
Fr cessionnaire *(m)*
Pt cessionário *(m)*

**cessionário** *(m)* n Pt
De Zessionär *(m)*
En transferee
Es cesionario *(m)*
Fr cessionnaire *(m)*
It cessionario *(m)*

**cessione** *(f)* n It
De Übertragung *(f)*
En assignment
Es cesión *(f)*

Fr cession (f)
Pt consignação (f)

**cessione** (f) n It
De Überweisung: Übertragung (f)
En transfer; assignment
Es cesión (f)
Fr transfert; cession (m f)
Pt trespasse; consignação (m f)

**cessionista** (m) n Pt
De Übertrager
En assignor; transferor
Es cesionista (m)
Fr cédant (m)
It cedente (m)

**cessionnaire** (m) n Fr
De Zessionär (m)
En assignee; transferee
Es cesionario (m)
It assegnatario; cessionario (m)
Pt cessionário (m)

**chaîne de montage** (f) Fr
De Montageband (n)
En assembly line
Es línea de montaje (f)
It catena di montaggio (f)
Pt cadeia de montagem (f)

**chain store** En
De Kettengeschäft (n)
Es sucursal de cadena de almacenes (f)
Fr magasin à succursales multiples (m)
It negozio a catena (m)
Pt sucursal de cadeia de armazéns (f)

**chairman** n En
De Vorsitzende(r) (m)
Es presidente (m)
Fr président (m)
It presidente (m)
Pt presidente (m)

**chamada (de fundos)** (f) Pt
De Kündigung (von Geldern) (f)
En call (for funds)
Es llamada (de fondos) (f)
Fr appel (de fonds) (m)
It richiesta (di fondi) (f)

**chamada inter-urbana (troncas)** (f) Pt
De Ferngespräch (n)
En trunk call
Am long distance call
Es llamada interurbana (f)
Fr appel téléphonique interurbain (m)
It comunicazione interurbana (f)

**chamada telefónica** (f) Pt
De Anruf (m)
En telephone call
Es llamada telefónica (f)
Fr appel téléphonique (m)
It chiamata telefonica (f)

**chamber of commerce** En
De Handelskammer (f)
Es cámara de comercio (f)
Fr chambre de commerce (f)
It camera di commercio (f)
Pt câmara de comércio (f)

**chambre de commerce** (f) Fr
De Handelskammer (f)
En chamber of commerce
Es cámara de comercio (f)
It camera di commercio (f)
Pt câmara de comércio (f)

**Chambre de Commerce Internationale** (f) Fr
De Internationale Handelskammer (f)
En International Chamber of Commerce
Es Cámara Internacional de Comercio (f)
It Camera di Commercio Internazionale (f)
Pt Câmara Internacional do Comércio (f)

**chambre de compensation** (f) Fr
De Verrechnungsstelle (f)
En clearing house
Es cámara de compensaciones (f)
It stanza di compensazione (f)
Pt câmara de compensações e rateio (f)

**change à terme** (m) Fr
De Termindevisen (f pl)
En forward exchange

Es divisas a término (f pl)
It cambio a termine (m)
Pt divisas adiantada (f pl)

**chantier de construction de navires** (m) Fr
De Schiffswerft (f)
En dockyard
Es astillero (m)
It cantiere (m)
Pt estaleiro (m)

**chapa de vidro** (f) Pt
De Spiegelglas (n)
En plate glass
Es vidrio plano pulido (m)
Fr verre à glaces; glace de vitrage (m f)
It cristallo (m)

**chapado en oro** Es
De vergoldet
En gold-plated
Fr plaqué d'or
It placcato in oro
Pt laminado a ouro

**charbon** (m) n Fr
De Kohle; Holzkohle (f)
En coal; charcoal
Es carbón; carbón de leña (m)
It carbone (m)
Pt carvão; carvão de lenha (m)

**chargeable** adj En
De anrechenbar
Es imputable; a cobrar
Fr imputable; imposable
It imputabile; imponibile
Pt a cobrar

**charge account** En
De Kundenkonto (n)
Es cuenta personal (f)
Fr compte personnel (m)
It conto personale (m)
Pt conta pessoal (f)

**chargement** (m) n Fr
De Ladung (f)
En loading
Es carga (f)
It carico; caricamento (m)
Pt carregamento (m)

**charges** *n pl* En
De Kosten *(pl)*
Es costes *(m pl)*
Fr frais *(m pl)*
It spese *(f pl)*
Pt despesas *(f pl)*

**charges annexes** *(f pl)* Fr
De Nebenkosten *(pl)*
En incidental charges
Es cargos imprevistos *(m pl)*
It spese accessorie *(f pl)*
Pt encargos ocasionais *(m pl)*

**charges forward** En
De per Nachnahme
Es costes a reembolso
Fr frais à percevoir à la livraison
It spese assegnate
Pt entrega contra reembolso

**charges lourdes** *(f pl)* Fr
De drückende Spesen *(f pl)*
En heavy charges
Es gastos fuertes *(m pl)*
It forti spese *(f pl)*
Pt encargos pesados *(m pl)*

**chart** *n* En
De Tabelle *(f)*
Es gráfico *(m)*
Fr graphique *(m)*
It grafico *(m)*
Pt tabela *(f)*

**charterer** *n* En
De Befrachter *(m)*
Es fletador *(m)*
Fr affréteur *(m)*
It noleggiatore *(m)*
Pt fretador *(m)*

**chartering** *n* En
De Befrachtung *(f)*
Es fletamento *(m)*
Fr affrètement *(m)*
It noleggio *(m)*
Pt fretamento *(m)*

**chasse aux soldes** *(f)* Fr
De Sucht nach Sonderangeboten *(f)*
En bargain-hunting
Es caza de rebajas *(f)*
It caccia alle occasioni *(f)*
Pt caça aos saldos *(f)*

**chauffage central** *(m)* Fr
De Zentralheizung *(f)*
En central heating
Es calefacción central *(f)*
It riscaldamento centrale *(m)*
Pt aquecimento central *(m)*

**chave** *(f)* *n* Pt
De Schlüssel *(m)*
En key
Es llave *(f)*
Fr clef *(f)*
It chiave *(f)*

**cheap** *adj* En
De billig
Es barato
Fr bon marché
It a buon mercato
Pt barato

**cheaper** *adj* En
De billiger
Es más barato
Fr meilleur marché
It meno caro
Pt mais barato

**cheap money** En
De billiges Geld *(n)*
Es dinero barato *(m)*
Fr argent bon marché *(m)*
It denaro a basso interesse *(m)*
Pt dinheiro barato *(m)*

**cheat** *vb* En
De betrügen
Es engañar
Fr tricher
It truffare
Pt enganar

**check** *n* Am
En cheque
De Scheck *(m)*
Es cheque *(m)*
Fr chèque *(m)*
It assegno *(m)*
Pt cheque *(m)*

**check book** Am
En cheque book
De Scheckheft *(n)*
Es libro de cheques *(m)*
Fr carnet de chèques; chéquier *(m)*

It libretto assegni *(m)*
Pt livro de cheques *(m)*

**check digit** En
De Kontrollziffer *(f)*
Es número de control *(m)*
Fr digit de contrôle *(m)*
It cifra di controllo *(f)*
Pt dígito de controle *(m)*

**checking account** Am
En current account
De Kontokorrent *(n)*
Es cuenta corriente *(f)*
Fr compte courant *(m)*
It conto corrente *(m)*
Pt conta corrente *(f)*

**check payable to bearer** Am
En cheque payable to bearer
De Inhaberscheck *(m)*
Es cheque al portador *(m)*
Fr chèque payable au porteur *(m)*
It assegno al portatore *(m)*
Pt cheque ao portador *(m)*

**chef comptable** *(m)* Fr
De Oberbuchhalter *(m)*
En chief accountant
Es jefe de contabilidad *(m)*
It ragioniere capo *(m)*
Pt chefe contabilista *(m)*

**chef d'atelier** *(m)* Fr
De Werkmeister *(m)*
En head foreman
Es capataz jefe *(m)*
It capo officina *(m)*
Pt encarregado-chefe *(m)*

**chef de bureau** *(m)* Fr
De Bürovorsteher *(m)*
En office manager
Es jefe de oficina *(m)*
It capo ufficio *(m)*
Pt chefe de escritório *(m)*

**chef de comptes client** *(m)* Fr
De Kontaktgruppenleiter *(m)*
En account executive
Es ejecutivo de cuenta *(m)*
It direttore conto cliente *(m)*
Pt chefe de conta de cliente *(m)*

**chef de famille** (m) Fr
De Hausherr (m)
En householder
Es jefe de familia (m)
It capo-famiglia (m)
Pt dono da casa (m)

**chef de service** (m) Fr
De Abteilungsleiter (m)
En head of department
Es jefe de departamento (m)
It capo reparto (m)
Pt chefe de departamento (m)

**chef du personnel** (m) Fr
De Personalchef (m)
En personnel manager
Es jefe de personal (m)
It direttore del personale (m)
Pt chefe do pessoal (m)

**chef du service des achats** (m) Fr
De Haupteinkäufer (m)
En head buyer
Es jefe del departamento de compras (m)
It capo servizio acquisti (m)
Pt chefe de compras (m)

**chef du service exportation** (m) Fr
De Exportabteilungsleiter (m)
En export manager
Es jefe de exportación (m)
It direttore esportazione (m)
Pt gerente de exportações (m)

**chefe contabilista** (m) Pt
De Oberbuchhalter (m)
En chief accountant
Es jefe de contabilidad (m)
Fr chef comptable (m)
It ragioniere capo (m)

**chefe de compras** (m) Pt
De Haupteinkäufer (m)
En head buyer
Es jefe del departamento de compras (m)
Fr chef du service des achats (m)
It capo servizio acquisti (m)

**chefe de conta de cliente** (m) Pt
De Kontaktgruppenleiter (m)
En account executive

Es ejecutivo de cuenta (m)
Fr chef de comptes client (m)
It direttore conto cliente (m)

**chefe de departamento** (m) Pt
De Abteilungsleiter (m)
En head of department
Es jefe de departamento (m)
Fr chef de service (m)
It capo reparto (m)

**chefe de escritório** (m) Pt
De Bürovorsteher (m)
En office manager
Es jefe de oficina (m)
Fr chef de bureau (m)
It capo ufficio (m)

**chefe de gerência** (m) Pt
De Geschäftsführer (m)
En chief executive
Es jefe ejecutivo (m)
Fr directeur général (m)
It direttore generale (m)

**chefe de vendas** (m) Pt
De Verkaufsleiter (m)
En sales manager
Es jefe de ventas (m)
Fr directeur commercial (m)
It direttore commerciale (m)

**chefe do pessoal** (m) Pt
De Personalchef (m)
En personnel manager
Es jefe de personal (m)
Fr chef du personnel (m)
It direttore del personale (m)

**chegada** (f) n Pt
De Ankunft (f)
En arrival
Es llegada (f)
Fr arrivée (f)
It arrivo (m)

**cheio** adj Pt
De voll
En full
Es lleno
Fr plein
It pieno

**chemical engineering** En
De Industriechemie (f)
Es ingeniería química (f)
Fr génie chimique (f)

It ingegneria chimica (f)
Pt engenharia química (f)

**chemin de fer** (m) Fr
De Eisenbahn (f)
En railway
Es ferrocarril (m)
It ferrovia (f)
Pt caminho de ferro (m)

**chemise** (f) n Fr
De Mappe (f)
En folder
Es carpeta (f)
It cartella (f)
Pt pasta (f)

**cheque** n En; Es, Pt (m)
Am check
De Scheck (m)
Fr chèque (m)
It assegno (m)

**chèque** (m) n Fr
De Scheck (m)
En cheque
Am check
Es cheque (m)
It assegno (m)
Pt cheque (m)

**cheque abierto** (m) Es
De Inhaberscheck (m)
En open cheque
Fr chèque ouvert (m)
It assegno aperto (m)
Pt cheque em branco (m)

**cheque a fecha retrasada** (m) Es
De nachdatierter Scheck (m)
En postdated cheque
Fr chèque postdaté (m)
It assegno postdatato (m)
Pt cheque post-datado (m)

**cheque al portador** (m) Es
De Inhaberscheck (m)
En cheque payable to bearer
Fr chèque payable au porteur (m)
It assegno al portatore (m)
Pt cheque ao portador (m)

**cheque ao portador** (m) Pt
De Inhaberscheck (m)
En cheque payable to bearer
Es cheque al portador (m)

Fr chèque payable au porteur *(m)*
It assegno al portatore *(m)*

**chèque barré** *(m)* Fr
De Verrechnungsscheck *(m)*
En crossed cheque
Es cheque cruzado *(m)*
It assegno sbarrato *(m)*
Pt cheque cruzado *(m)*

**cheque book** En
Am check book
De Scheckheft *(n)*
Es libro de cheques *(m)*
Fr carnet de chèques: chéquier *(m)*
It libretto assegni *(m)*
Pt livro de cheques *(m)*

**cheque card** En
Am bank credit card
De Scheckkarte *(f)*
Es tarjeta de cheque *(f)*
Fr carte de chèque *(f)*
It scheda per assegni *(f)*
Pt cartão de validação de cheques *(m)*

**cheque certificado** *(m)* Es, Pt
De bestätigter Scheck *(m)*
En certified cheque
Fr chèque certifié *(m)*
It assegno garantito *(m)*

**chèque certifié** *(m)* Fr
De bestätigter Scheck *(m)*
En certified cheque
Es cheque certificado *(m)*
It assegno garantito *(m)*
Pt cheque certificado *(m)*

**cheque cruzado** *(m)* Es, Pt
De Verrechnungsscheck *(m)*
En crossed cheque
Fr chèque barré *(m)*
It assegno sbarrato *(m)*

**cheque de viajante** *(m)* Pt
De Reisescheck *(m)*
En traveller's cheque
Es cheque de viajero *(m)*
Fr chèque de voyage *(m)*
It assegno turistico *(m)*

**cheque de viajero** *(m)* Es
De Reisescheck *(m)*
En traveller's cheque

Fr chèque de voyage *(m)*
It assegno turistico *(m)*
Pt cheque de viajante *(m)*

**chèque de voyage** *(m)* Fr
De Reisescheck *(m)*
En traveller's cheque
Es cheque de viajero *(m)*
It assegno turistico *(m)*
Pt cheque de viajante *(m)*

**cheque em branco** *(m)* Pt
De Blankoscheck *(m)*
En blank cheque; open cheque
Es cheque en blanco; cheque abierto *(m)*
Fr chèque en blanc; chèque ouvert *(m)*
It assegno in bianco; assegno aperto *(m)*

**chèque en blanc** *(m)* Fr
De Blankoscheck *(m)*
En blank cheque
Es cheque en blanco *(m)*
It assegno in bianco *(m)*
Pt cheque em branco *(m)*

**cheque en blanco** *(m)* Es
De Blankoscheck *(m)*
En blank cheque
Fr chèque en blanc *(m)*
It assegno in bianco *(m)*
Pt cheque em branco *(m)*

**cheque falsificado** *(m)* Es, Pt
De gefälschter Scheck *(m)*
En forged cheque
Fr faux chèque *(m)*
It assegno falsificato *(m)*

**chèque ouvert** *(m)* Fr
De Inhaberscheck *(m)*
En open cheque
Es cheque abierto *(m)*
It assegno aperto *(m)*
Pt cheque em branco *(m)*

**chèque payable au porteur** *(m)* Fr
De Inhaberscheck *(m)*
En cheque payable to bearer
Es cheque al portador *(m)*
It assegno al portatore *(m)*
Pt cheque ao portador *(m)*

**cheque payable to bearer** En
De Inhaberscheck *(m)*
Es cheque al portador *(m)*
Fr chèque payable au porteur *(m)*
It assegno al portatore *(m)*
Pt cheque ao portador *(m)*

**cheque post-datado** *(m)* Pt
De nachdatierter Scheck *(m)*
En postdated cheque
Es cheque a fecha retrasada *(m)*
Fr chèque postdaté *(m)*
It assegno postdatato *(m)*

**chèque postdaté** *(m)* Fr
De nachdatierter Scheck *(m)*
En postdated cheque
Es cheque a fecha retrasada *(m)*
It assegno postdatato *(m)*
Pt cheque post-datado *(m)*

**cher** *adj* Fr
De kostspielig; teuer
En expensive
Es caro
It caro
Pt caro

**cheval-vapeur (ch-v)** *(m)* Fr
De Pferdestärke (PS) *(f)*
En horse-power (hp)
Es caballo de vapor (cv) *(m)*
It cavallo *(m)*
Pt cavalo-vapor *(m)*

**chiamata telefonica** *(f)* It
De Anruf *(m)*
En telephone call
Es llamada telefónica *(f)*
Fr appel téléphonique *(m)*
Pt chamada telefónica *(f)*

**chiatta** *(f)* n It
De Lastkahn; Leichter *(m)*
En barge; lighter
Es barcaza; gabarra *(f)*
Fr péniche; allège *(f)*
Pt barcaça *(f)*

**chiave** *(f)* n It
De Schlüssel *(m)*
En key
Es llave *(f)*
Fr clef *(f)*
Pt chave *(f)*

**chief accountant** En
De Oberbuchhalter *(m)*
Es jefe de contabilidad *(m)*
Fr chef comptable *(m)*
It ragioniere capo *(m)*
Pt chefe contabilista *(m)*

**chief executive** En
De Geschäftsführer *(m)*
Es jefe ejecutivo *(m)*
Fr directeur général *(m)*
It direttore generale *(m)*
Pt chefe de gerência *(m)*

**chiffre** *(m)* n Fr
De Zahl *(f)*
En figure
Es cifra *(f)*
It cifra *(f)*
Pt número *(m)*

**chiffre d'affaires** *(m)* Fr
De Umsatz *(m)*
En turnover
Es volumen de ventas *(m)*
It giro d'affari *(m)*
Pt movimento de dinheiro *(m)*

**chômage** *(m)* n Fr
De Arbeitslosigkeit *(f)*
En unemployment
Es desempleo *(m)*
It disoccupazione *(f)*
Pt desemprego *(m)*

**chômage saisonnier** *(m)* Fr
De jahreszeitlich bedingte Arb-
eitslosigkeit *(f)*
En seasonal unemployment
Es paro de temporada *(m)*
It disoccupazione stagionale
*(f)*
Pt desemprego de estação
*(m)*

**cibernética** *(f)* n Es, Pt
De Kybernetik *(f)*
En cybernetics
Fr cybernétique *(f)*
It cibernetica *(f)*

**cibernetica** *(f)* n It
De Kybernetik *(f)*
En cybernetics
Es cibernética *(f)*
Fr cybernétique *(f)*
Pt cibernética *(f)*

**ciclo comercial** *(m)* Pt
De Handelszyklus *(m)*
En trade cycle
Es ciclo del negocio *(m)*
Fr cycle de commerce *(m)*
It cyclo degli affari *(m)*

**ciclo d'affari** *(m)* It
De Konjunkturzyklus *(m)*
En business cycle
Es ciclo económico *(m)*
Fr cycle économique *(m)*
Pt ciclo económico *(m)*

**ciclo del negocio** *(m)* Es
De Handelszyklus *(m)*
En trade cycle
Fr cycle de commerce *(m)*
It cyclo degli affari *(m)*
Pt ciclo comercial *(m)*

**ciclo económico** *(m)* Es, Pt
De Konjunkturzyklus *(m)*
En business cycle
Fr cycle économique *(m)*
It ciclo d'affari *(m)*

**ciência de vender** *(f)* Pt
De Verkaufsgewandtheit *(f)*
En salesmanship
Es arte de vender *(m)*
Fr art de vendre *(m)*
It arte della vendita *(f)*

**cierre** *(m)* n Es
De Aussperrung *(f)*
En lock-out
Fr lock-out *(m)*
It serrata *(f)*
Pt lockout *(m)*

**cifra** *(f)* n Es, It
De Zahl *(f)*
En figure
Fr chiffre *(m)*
Pt número *(m)*

**cifra de ventas** *(f)* Es
De Umsatz *(m)*
En sales figure
Fr chiffre d'affaires *(f)*
It cifra di vendite *(f)*
Pt número de vendas *(m)*

**cifra di controllo** *(f)* It
De Kontrollziffer *(f)*
En check digit
Es número de control *(m)*

Fr digit de contrôle *(m)*
Pt dígito de controle *(m)*

**cifra di vendite** *(f)* It
De Umsatz *(m)*
En sales figure
Es cifra de ventas *(f)*
Fr chiffre d'affaires *(f)*
Pt número de vendas *(m)*

**ci-joint** adj Fr
De beiliegend
En enclosed
Es adjunto
It accluso
Pt incluso

**cilindrada** *(f)* n Es, Pt
De Hubraum *(m)*
En cubic capacity
Fr cylindrée *(f)*
It cilindrata *(f)*

**cilindrata** *(f)* n It
De Hubraum *(m)*
En cubic capacity
Es cilindrada *(f)*
Fr cylindrée *(f)*
Pt cilindrada *(f)*

**cinta magnética** *(f)* Es
De Magnetband *(n)*
En magnetic tape
Fr bande magnétique *(f)*
It nastro magnetico *(m)*
Pt fita magnética *(f)*

**circulação** *(f)* n Pt
De Strom *(m)*
En flow
Es flujo *(m)*
Fr flux *(m)*
It flusso *(m)*

**citação** *(f)* n Pt
De Vorladung *(f)*
En writ
Es auto; orden *(m f)*
Fr assignation *(f)*
It citazione *(f)*

**citazione** *(f)* n It
De Vorladung *(f)*
En writ
Es auto; orden *(m f)*
Fr assignation *(f)*
Pt citação; ordem *(f m)*

**civil engineering** En
De Ingenieurbau *(m)*
Es ingeniería civil *(f)*
Fr génie civil *(m)*
It ingegneria civile *(f)*
Pt engenharia civil *(f)*

**civil servant** En
Am government employee
De Beamte(r) *(m)*
Es funcionario del gobierno *(m)*
Fr fonctionnaire *(m)*
It impiegato statale *(m)*
Pt foncionário público *(m)*

**claim** n En
De Anspruch *(m)*
Es reclamación *(f)*
Fr réclamation; créance *(f)*
It reclamo *(m)*
Pt demanda; requerimento *(f m)*

**classer** vb Fr
De aufreihen
En file
Es archivar
It archiviare
Pt arquivar

**classeur** *(m)* n Fr
De Aktenschrank *(m)*
En filing cabinet
Es fichero *(m)*
It schedario *(m)*
Pt móvel ficheiro *(m)*

**classified advertisement** En
De Kleinanzeige *(f)*
Es anuncio por palabras *(m)*
Fr petite annonce *(f)*
It piccola pubblicità *(f)*
Pt anúncios classificados *(m pl)*

**clause** n En; Fr *(f)*
De Klausel *(f)*
Es cláusula *(f)*
It clausola *(f)*
Pt cláusula *(f)*

**clause de dédit** *(f)* Fr
De Bussklausel *(f)*
En forfeit clause
Es cláusula de decomiso *(f)*

It clausola di penalità per inandempienza *(f)*
Pt cláusula de cedência *(f)*

**clause de résiliation** *(f)* Fr
De Rücktrittsklausel *(f)*
En escape clause
Es cláusula evasiva *(f)*
It clausola risolutiva *(f)*
Pt cláusula de evasão *(f)*

**clause pénale** *(f)* Fr
De Strafklausel *(f)*
En penalty clause
Es cláusula de multa *(f)*
It clausola penale *(f)*
Pt cláusula de penalidade *(f)*

**clause résolutoire** *(f)* Fr
De Rücktrittsklausel *(f)*
En determination clause
Es cláusula resolutiva *(f)*
It clausola risolutiva *(f)*
Pt cláusula de rescisão *(f)*

**clausola** *(f)* n It
De Klausel *(f)*
En clause
Es cláusula *(f)*
Fr clause *(f)*
Pt cláusula *(f)*

**clausola di penalità per inandempienza** *(f)* It
De Bussklausel *(f)*
En forfeit clause
Es cláusula de decomiso *(f)*
Fr clause de dédit *(f)*
Pt cláusula de cedência *(f)*

**clausola penale** *(f)* It
De Strafklausel *(f)*
En penalty clause
Es cláusula de multa *(f)*
Fr clause pénale *(f)*
Pt cláusula de penalidade *(f)*

**clausola risolutiva** *(f)* It
De Rücktrittsklausel *(f)*
En determination clause
Es cláusula resolutiva *(f)*
Fr clause résolutoire *(f)*
Pt cláusula de rescisão *(f)*

**cláusula** *(f)* n Es, Pt
De Klausel *(f)*
En clause

Fr clause *(f)*
It clausola *(f)*

**cláusula de actualização de preços** *(f)* Pt
De Gleitklausel *(f)*
En escalator clause
Es cláusula de revisión de precios *(f)*
Fr échelle mobile *(f)*
It scala mobile *(f)*

**cláusula de cedência** *(f)* Pt
De Bussklausel *(f)*
En forfeit clause
Es cláusula de decomiso *(f)*
Fr clause de dédit *(f)*
It clausola di penalità per inandempienza *(f)*

**cláusula de decomiso** *(f)* Es
De Bussklausel *(f)*
En forfeit clause
Fr clause de dédit *(f)*
It clausola di penalità per inandempienza *(f)*
Pt cláusula de cedência *(f)*

**cláusula de evasão** *(f)* Pt
De Rücktrittsklausel *(f)*
En escape clause
Es cláusula evasiva *(f)*
Fr clause de résiliation *(f)*
It clausola risolutiva *(f)*

**cláusula de multa** *(f)* Es
De Strafklausel *(f)*
En penalty clause
Fr clause pénale *(f)*
It clausola penale *(f)*
Pt cláusula de penalidade *(f)*

**cláusula de penalidade** *(f)* Pt
De Strafklausel *(f)*
En penalty clause
Es cláusula de multa *(f)*
Fr clause pénale *(f)*
It clausola penale *(f)*

**cláusula de rescisão** *(f)* Pt
De Rücktrittsklausel *(f)*
En determination clause
Es cláusula resolutiva *(f)*
Fr clause résolutoire *(f)*
It clausola risolutiva *(f)*

**cláusula de revisión de precios** *(f)* Es
De Gleitklausel *(f)*
En escalator clause
Fr échelle mobile *(f)*
It scala mobile *(f)*
Pt cláusula de actualização de preços *(f)*

**cláusula evasiva** *(f)* Es
De Rücktrittsklausel *(f)*
En escape clause
Fr clause de résiliation *(f)*
It clausola risolutiva *(f)*
Pt cláusula de evasão *(f)*

**cláusula resolutiva** *(f)* Es
De Rücktrittsklausel *(f)*
En determination clause
Fr clause résolutoire *(f)*
It clausola risolutiva *(f)*
Pt cláusula de rescisão *(f)*

**clave** *(f)* n Es
De Schlüssel *(m)*
En code
Fr clef *(f)*
It codice *(m)*
Pt código *(m)*

**clean bill of lading** En
De echtes Konnossement *(n)*
Es conocimiento de embarque sin objecciones *(m)*
Fr connaissement sans réserve *(m)*
It polizza di carico senza riserve *(f)*
Pt conhecimento sem embargos *(m)*

**clearing-bank** n En
De Girobank *(f)*
Es banco de compensación *(m)*
Fr banque de virement *(f)*
It banca associata alla stanza di compensazione *(f)*
Pt banco de compensação e rateio *(m)*

**clearing house** En
De Verrechnungsstelle *(f)*
Es cámara de compensaciones *(f)*
Fr chambre de compensation *(f)*
It stanza di compensazione *(f)*

Pt câmara de compensações e rateio *(f)*

**clear through customs** En
De verzollen
Es retirar de aduanas
Fr dédouaner
It sdoganare
Pt despachar na alfândega

**clef** *(f)* n Fr
De Schlüssel *(m)*
En key; code
Es llave; clave *(f)*
It chiave; codice *(f m)*
Pt chave; código *(f m)*

**clerk** n En
De Angestellte(r) *(m)*
Es oficinista *(m)*
Fr commis *(m)*
It impiegato *(m)*
Pt empregado de escritório *(m)*

**client** n En, Fr, *(m)*
De Kunde *(m)*
Es cliente *(m)*
It cliente *(m)*
Pt cliente *(m)*

**cliente** *(m)* n Es, It, Pt
De Kunde *(m)*
En customer
Fr client *(m)*

**clientela** *(f)* n Es, It, Pt
De Kundschaft *(f)*
En custom; clientele
Fr clientèle *(f)*

**clientèle** *(f)* n Fr
De Kundschaft *(f)*
En custom; clientele
Es clientela *(f)*
It clientela *(f)*
Pt clientela *(f)*

**climatisation** *(f)* n Fr
De Klimatisierung *(f)*
En air-conditioning
Es acondicionamiento de aire *(m)*
It condizionamento dell'aria *(m)*
Pt condicionamento do ar *(m)*

**closed market** En
De gesperrter Markt *(m)*
Es mercado cerrado *(m)*
Fr marché fermé *(m)*
It mercato chiuso *(m)*
Pt mercado fechado *(m)*

**closing date** En
De Schlusstermin *(m)*
Es último día *(m)*
Fr dernier jour *(m)*
It ultima data *(f)*
Pt último dia *(m)*

**closing price** En
De Schlussnotierung *(f)*
Es precio de cierre *(m)*
Fr cours de clôture *(m)*
It prezzo di chiusura *(f)*
Pt último preço *(m)*

**coal** n En
De Kohle *(f)*
Es carbón *(m)*
Fr houille; charbon *(f m)*
It carbone *(m)*
Pt carvão *(m)*

**coal field** En
De Kohlenrevier *(n)*
Es yacimiento de carbón *(m)*
Fr bassin houiller *(m)*
It bacino carbonifero *(m)*
Pt jazigo de carvão *(m)*

**coalición de vendedores** *(f)* Es
De Preisabsprache *(f)*
En price ring
Fr coalition de vendeurs *(f)*
It sindacato dei prezzi *(m)*
Pt convénio de preços *(m)*

**coalition de vendeurs** *(f)* Fr
De Preisabsprache *(f)*
En price ring
Es coalición de vendedores *(f)*
It sindacato dei prezzi *(m)*
Pt convénio de preços *(m)*

**coaseguro** *(m)* n Es
De Versicherung auf Gegenseitigkeit *(f)*
En mutual insurance
Fr assurance mutuelle *(f)*
It mutua assicurazione *(f)*
Pt seguro mútuo *(m)*

**cobertura** *(f)* *n* Es, Pt
De Deckung *(f)*
En cover
Fr couverture *(f)*
It copertura *(f)*

**cobertura de la póliza de seguro** *(f)* Es
De Versicherungsdeckung *(f)*
En insurance cover
Fr garantie d'assurance *(f)*
It copertura assicurativa *(f)*
Pt cobertura de seguro *(f)*

**cobertura de seguro** *(f)* Pt
De Versicherungsdeckung *(f)*
En insurance cover
Es cobertura de la póliza de seguro *(f)*
Fr garantie d'assurance *(f)*
It copertura assicurativa *(f)*

**cobertura flotante** *(f)* Es
De offene Versicherung *(f)*
En open cover
Fr police à aliment *(f)*
It polizza flottante *(f)*
Pt cobertura ilimitada *(f)*

**cobertura ilimitada** *(f)* Pt
De offene Versicherung *(f)*
En open cover
Es cobertura flotante *(f)*
Fr police à aliment *(f)*
It polizza flottante *(f)*

**cobertura provisional** *(f)* Es
De temporäre Deckung *(f)*
En temporary cover
Fr couverture temporaire *(m)*
It copertura provvisoria *(f)*
Pt cobertura provisória *(f)*

**cobertura provisória** *(f)* Pt
De temporäre Deckung *(f)*
En temporary cover
Es cobertura provisional *(f)*
Fr couverture temporaire *(m)*
It copertura provvisoria *(f)*

**cobertura total** *(f)* Pt
De Vollwertdeckung *(f)*
En full cover
Es garantía total *(f)*
Fr garantie totale *(f)*
It garanzia totale *(f)*

**cobrador** *(m)* *n* Pt
De Inkassobeauftragte(r) *(m)*
En debt collector
Es agente recaudador *(m)*
Fr agent de recouvrement *(m)*
It agente di ricupero crediti *(m)*

**cobrador de impostos** *(m)* Pt
De Steuereinnehmer *(m)*
En tax collector
Es recaudador de impuestos *(m)*
Fr percepteur des impôts *(m)*
It esattore delle imposte *(m)*

**cobrar** *vb* Es, Pt
De einkassieren
En cash
Fr encaisser
It incassare

**cobrar uma dívida** Pt
De Schulden eintreiben
En collect a debt
Es recaudar una deuda
Fr recouvrer une créance
It incassare un credito

**cobrar um cheque** Pt
De einen Scheck einlösen
En cash a cheque
Es cobrar un cheque
Fr toucher un chèque
It incassare un assegno

**cobrar un cheque** Es
De einen Scheck einlösen
En cash a cheque
Fr toucher un chèque
It incassare un assegno
Pt cobrar um cheque

**cobrir-se** *vb* Pt
De sich decken
En hedge
Es cubrirse
Fr arbitrager
It coprirsi

**coche** *(m)* *n* Es
De Auto; Wagen *(n m)*
En car
Fr voiture; automobile *(f)*
It automobile; macchina *(f)*
Pt carro; automóvel *(m)*

**code** (legal) *n* En
De Ordnung *(f)*
Es código *(m)*
Fr code *(m)*
It codice *(m)*
Pt código *(m)*

**code** (telegraphic) *n* En
De Schlüssel *(m)*
Es clave *(f)*
Fr clef *(f)*
It codice *(m)*
Pt código *(m)*

**code** *(m)* *n* Fr
De Ordnung *(f)*
En code
Es código *(m)*
It codice *(m)*
Pt código *(m)*

**codice** *(m)* *n* It
De Ordnung; Schlüssel *(f m)*
En code
Es código; clave *(m f)*
Fr code; clef *(m f)*
Pt código *(m)*

**codice postale** *(m)* It
De Postleitzahl *(f)*
En postcode
Am zip code
Es designación postal *(f)*
Fr indicatif postal *(m)*
Pt designação postal *(f)*

**código** *(m)* *n* Es
De Ordnung; Schlüssel *(f m)*
En code
Fr code; clef *(m f)*
It codice *(m)*
Pt código *(m)*

**coefficiente di sicurezza** *(m)* It
De Sicherheitskoeffizient *(m)*
En safety factor
Es factor de seguridad *(m)*
Fr facteur de sécurité *(m)*
Pt factor de segurança *(m)*

**coerção** *(f)* *n* Pt
De Zwang *(m)*
En duress
Es compulsión *(f)*
Fr contrainte *(f)*
It costrizione *(f)*

**coffee** n En
De Kaffee (m)
Es café (m)
Fr café (m)
It caffè (m)
Pt café (m)

**coffre-fort** (m) n Fr
De Geldschrank (m)
En safe
Es caja fuerte (f)
It cassaforte (f)
Pt cofre (m)

**coffre de bagages** (m) Fr
De Gepäckschliessfach (n)
En luggage locker
Es casilla de equipaje (f)
It cassetta bagaglio (f)
Pt depósito de bagagem indi-
   vidualizado (m)

**coffre de nuit** (m) Fr
De Nachttresor (m)
En night safe
Es caja de seguridad nocturna
   (f)
It deposito notturno (m)
Pt cofre nocturno (m)

**cofre** (m) n Pt
De Geldschrank (m)
En safe
Es caja fuerte (f)
Fr coffre-fort (m)
It cassaforte (f)

**cofre nocturno** (m) Pt
De Nachttresor (m)
En night safe
Es caja de seguridad nocturna
   (f)
Fr coffre de nuit (m)
It deposito notturno (m)

**coin** n En
De Münze (f)
Es moneda (f)
Fr pièce (de monnaie) (f)
It moneta (f)
Pt moeda (f)

**colaborar** vb Es, Pt
De mitarbeiten
En collaborate
Fr collaborer
It collaborare

**colaggio** (m) n It
De Lecken (n)
En leakage
Es escape (m)
Fr fuite (f)
Pt escape; fuga (m f)

**colateral** (f) n Pt
De Sicherheit (f)
En collateral
Es garantía colateral (f)
Fr nantissement (m)
It garanzia collaterale (f)

**colheita** (f) n Pt
De Ernte (f)
En harvest
Es cosecha (f)
Fr moisson; récolte (f)
It raccolto (m)

**collaborare** vb It
De mitarbeiten
En collaborate
Es colaborar
Fr collaborer
Pt colaborar

**collaborate** vb En
De mitarbeiten
Es colaborar
Fr collaborer
It collaborare
Pt colaborar

**collaborer** vb Fr
De mitarbeiten
En collaborate
Es colaborar
It collaborare
Pt colaborar

**collateral** (security) n En
De Sicherheit (f)
Es garantía colateral (f)
Fr nantissement (m)
It garanzia collaterale (f)
Pt colateral (f)

**collect a debt** En
De Schulden eintreiben
Es recaudar una deuda
Fr recouvrer une créance
It incassare un credito
Pt cobrar uma dívida

**collection charges** En
De Einzugskosten (pl)
Es gastos de cobranza (m pl)
Fr frais d'encaissement (m pl)
It spese di riscossione (f pl)
Pt gastos de cobrança (m pl)

**collective bargaining** En
De Tarifvertragsverhandlung (f)
Es contratación collectiva (f)
Fr négociations de conven-
   tions collectives (f pl)
It contrattazione collettiva (f)
Pt regateio colectivo (m)

**colonna** (f) n It
De Spalte (f)
En column
Es columna (f)
Fr colonne (f)
Pt coluna (f)

**colonne** (f) n Fr
De Spalte (f)
En column
Es columna (f)
It colonna (f)
Pt coluna (f)

**col presente** It
De hiermit
En hereby
Es por esto
Fr par la présente
Pt pelo presente

**column** n En
De Spalte (f)
Es columna (f)
Fr colonne (f)
It colonna (f)
Pt coluna (f)

**columna** (f) n Es
De Spalte (f)
En column
Fr colonne (f)
It colonna (f)
Pt coluna (f)

**coluna** (f) n Pt
De Spalte (f)
En column
Es columna (f)
Fr colonne (f)
It colonna (f)

**com avaria** Pt
De havariert
En with average (WA)
Es con avería
Fr avarié
It con avaria

**comboio de mercadorías** (m) Pt
De Güterzug (m)
En goods train
Am freight train
Es tren de mercancías (m)
Fr train de marchandises (m)
It treno merci (m)

**comboio rápido** (m) Pt
De D-Zug; Schnellzug (m)
En express train
Es tren expreso (m)
Fr train express (m)
It direttissimo; rapido (m)

**com dividendo** Pt
De mit Dividende
En cum dividend
Es con dividendo
Fr droit attaché
It con dividendo

**comercializável** adj Pt
De marktfähig
En marketable
Es vendible
Fr vendable
It vendibile

**comerciante** (m) n Es, Pt
De Händler; Kaufmann (m)
En dealer; merchant
Fr négociant (m)
It negoziante; commerciante (m)

**comerciante al por menor** (m) Es
De Einzelhändler; Kleinhändler (m)
En retailer
Fr commerçant au détail (m)
It commerciante al minuto (m)
Pt comerciante a retalho; retalhista (m)

**comerciante a retalho** (m) Pt
De Einzelhändler; Kleinhändler (m)
En retailer
Es comerciante al por menor (m)
Fr commerçant au détail (m)
It commerciante al minuto (m)

**comercio** (m) n Es
De Handel (m)
En commerce; trade
Fr commerce (m)
It commercio (m)
Pt comércio (m)

**comércio** (m) n Pt
De Handel (m)
En commerce; trade
Es comercio (m)
Fr commerce (m)
It commercio (m)

**comercio al por mayor** (m) Es
De Grosshandel (m)
En wholesale trade
Fr commerce en gros (m)
It commercio all'ingrosso (m)
Pt comércio por atacado (m)

**comercio al por menor** (m) Es
De Einzelhandel (m)
En retail trade
Fr commerce en détail (m)
It commercio al minuto (m)
Pt comércio a retalho (m)

**comércio a retalho** (m) Pt
De Einzelhandel (m)
En retail trade
Es comercio al por menor (m)
Fr commerce en détail (m)
It commercio al minuto (m)

**comercio exterior** (m) Es
De Aussenhandel (m)
En foreign trade
Fr commerce extérieur (m)
It commercio estero (m)
Pt comércio externo (m)

**comércio externo** (m) Pt
De Aussenhandel (m)
En foreign trade
Es comercio exterior (m)
Fr commerce extérieur (m)
It commercio estero (m)

**comércio franco** (m) Pt
De Freihandel (m)
En free trade
Es comercio libre (m)
Fr libre-échange (m)
It libero scambio (m)

**comercio interior** (m) Es
De Binnenhandel (m)
En home trade
Am domestic sales
Fr commerce intérieur (m)
It commercio interno (m)
Pt comércio interno (m)

**comércio interno** (m) Pt
De Binnenhandel (m)
En home trade
Am domestic sales
Es comercio interior (m)
Fr commerce intérieur (m)
It commercio interno (m)

**comercio libre** (m) Es
De Freihandel (m)
En free trade
Fr libre-échange (m)
It libero scambio (m)
Pt comércio franco (m)

**comercio multilateral** (m) Es
De mehrseitiges Handeln (n)
En multilateral trade
Fr commerce multilatéral (m)
It commercio multilaterale (m)
Pt comércio multilateral (m)

**comércio multilateral** (m) Pt
De mehrseitiges Handeln (n)
En multilateral trade
Es comercio multilateral (m)
Fr commerce multilatéral (m)
It commercio multilaterale (m)

**comércio por atacado** (m) Pt
De Grosshandel (m)
En wholesale trade
Es comercio al por mayor (m)
Fr commerce engros (m)
It commercio all'ingrosso (m)

**comestibles** (m pl) n Es
De Esswaren (f pl)
En foodstuffs
Fr alimentation (f)

It   generi alimentari *(m pl)*
Pt   géneros alimentícios *(m pl)*

**comisión** *(f) n* Es
De   Provision *(f)*
En   commission
Fr   commission *(f)*
It   provvigione *(f)*
Pt   comissão *(f)*

**Comisión Europea** *(f)* Es
De   Europäische Kommission *(f)*
En   European Commission
Fr   Commission des Communautés Européennes *(f)*
It   Commissione Europea *(f)*
Pt   Comissão Europeia *(f)*

**comisionista** *(m) n* Es
De   Kommissionär *(m)*
En   commission agent
Fr   commissionnaire en marchandises *(m)*
It   commissionario *(m)*
Pt   comissionista *(m)*

**comissão** *(f) n* Pt
De   Provision *(f)*
En   commission
Es   comisión *(f)*
Fr   commission *(f)*
It   provvigione *(f)*

**Comissão Europeia** *(f)* Pt
De   Europäische Kommission *(f)*
En   European Commission
Es   Comisión Europea *(f)*
Fr   Commission des Communautés Européennes *(f)*
It   Commissione Europea *(f)*

**comissionista** *(m) n* Pt
De   Kommissionär *(m)*
En   commission agent
Es   comisionista *(m)*
Fr   commissionnaire en marchandises *(m)*
It   commissionario *(m)*

**comitato** *(m) n* It
De   Kommission *(f)*
En   committee
Es   comité *(m)*
Fr   comité *(f)*
Pt   comité *(m)*

**comité** *(m) n* Es, Fr, Pt
De   Kommission; Ausschuss *(f m)*
En   committee
It   comitato *(m)*

**comité consultatif** *(m)* Fr
De   Beratungsausschuss *(m)*
En   advisory board
Es   consejo consultivo *(m)*
It   consiglio consultivo *(m)*
Pt   comité consultivo *(m)*

**comité consultivo** *(m)* Pt
De   Beratungsausschuss *(m)*
En   advisory board
Es   consejo consultivo *(m)*
Fr   comité consultatif *(m)*
It   consiglio consultivo *(m)*

**commande** *(f) n* Fr
De   Bestellung *(f)*
En   order
Es   pedido *(m)*
It   ordine *(m)*
Pt   encomenda *(f)*

**commande d'exportation** *(f)* Fr
De   Exportauftrag *(m)*
En   export order
Es   pedido de exportación *(m)*
It   ordine per esportazione *(m)*
Pt   encomenda de exportação *(f)*

**commande par lettre** *(f)* Fr
De   Auftrag durch die Post *(m)*
En   mail order
Es   pedido por correo *(m)*
It   ordine per corrispondenza *(f)*
Pt   venda pelo correio *(f)*

**commanditaire** *(m) n* Fr
De   stiller Gesellschafter *(m)*
En   sleeping partner
Am   silent partner
Es   socio comanditario *(m)*
It   socio accomandante *(m)*
Pt   sócio comanditário *(m)*

**commerçant au détail** *(m)* Fr
De   Einzelhändler; Kleinhändler *(m)*
En   retailer
Es   comerciante al por menor *(m)*

It   commerciante al minuto *(m)*
Pt   comerciante a retalho; retalhista *(m)*

**commerce** *n* En, Fr *(m)*
De   Handel *(m)*
Es   comercio *(m)*
It   commercio *(m)*
Pt   comércio *(m)*

**commerce de tourisme** *(m)* Fr
De   Reisegewerbe *(n)*
En   tourist trade
Es   industria del turismo *(f)*
It   commercio turistico *(m)*
Pt   indústria do turismo *(f)*

**commerce en détail** *(m)* Fr
De   Einzelhandel *(m)*
En   retail trade
Es   comercio al por menor *(m)*
It   commercio al minuto *(m)*
Pt   comércio a retalho *(m)*

**commerce en gros** *(m)* Fr
De   Grosshandel *(m)*
En   wholesale trade
Es   comercio al por mayor *(m)*
It   commercio all'ingrosso *(m)*
Pt   comércio por atacado *(m)*

**commerce extérieur** *(m)* Fr
De   Aussenhandel *(m)*
En   foreign trade
Es   comercio exterior *(m)*
It   commercio estero *(m)*
Pt   comércio externo *(m)*

**commerce intérieur** *(m)* Fr
De   Binnenhandel *(m)*
En   home trade
Am   domestic sales
Es   comercio interior *(m)*
It   commercio interno *(m)*
Pt   comércio interno *(m)*

**commerce multilatéral** *(m)* Fr
De   mehrseitiges Handeln *(n)*
En   multilateral trade
Es   comercio multilateral *(m)*
It   commercio multilaterale *(m)*
Pt   comércio multilateral *(m)*

**commercial invoice** En
De   Geschäftsfaktur *(f)*
Es   factura comercial *(f)*

Fr  facture commerciale (f)
It  fattura commerciale (f)
Pt  factura comercial (f)

**commercial traveller** En
Am salesman
De Handelsvertreter; Geschäftsreisende(r) (m)
Es  viajante de comercio (m)
Fr  commis-voyageur (m)
It  viaggiatore di commercio (m)
Pt  caixeiro viajante (m)

**commercial vehicle** En
De Nutzfahrzeug (n)
Es  vehículo comercial (m)
Fr  véhicule commerciale (f)
It  veicolo commerciale (m)
Pt  veículo comercial (m)

**commerciante** (m) n It
De Kaufmann (m)
En merchant
Es  comerciante (m)
Fr  négociant (m)
Pt  comerciante (m)

**commerciante al minuto** (m) It
De Einzelhändler; Kleinhändler (m)
En retailer
Es  comerciante al por menor (m)
Fr  commerçant au détail (m)
Pt  comerciante a retalho; retalhista (m)

**commercio** (m) n It
De Handel (m)
En commerce; trade
Es  comercio (m)
Fr  commerce (m)
Pt  comércio (m)

**commercio all'ingrosso** (m) It
De Grosshandel (m)
En wholesale trade
Es  comercio al por mayor (m)
Fr  commerce en gros (m)
Pt  comércio por atacado (m)

**commercio al minuto** (m) It
De Einzelhandel (m)
En retail trade
Es  comercio al por menor (m)
Fr  commerce en détail (m)
Pt  comércio a retalho (m)

**commercio estero** (m) It
De Aussenhandel (m)
En foreign trade
Es  comercio exterior (m)
Fr  commerce extérieur (m)
Pt  comércio externo (m)

**commercio interno** (m) It
De Binnenhandel (m)
En home trade
Am domestic sales
Es  comercio interior (m)
Fr  commerce intérieur (m)
Pt  comércio interno (m)

**commercio multilaterale** (m) It
De mehrseitiges Handeln (n)
En multilateral trade
Es  comercio multilateral (m)
Fr  commerce multilatéral (m)
Pt  comércio multilateral (m)

**commercio turistico** (m) It
De Reisegewerbe (n)
En tourist trade
Es  industria del turismo (f)
Fr  commerce de tourisme (f)
Pt  indústria do turismo (f)

**commesso di spedizioniere** (m) It
De Expedient (m)
En shipping clerk
Es  dependiente de muelle (m)
Fr  expéditionnaire (m)
Pt  despachante (m)

**commis** (m) n Fr
De Angestellte(r); Assistent (m)
En clerk; assistant
Es  oficinista; asistente (m)
It  impiegato; assistente (m)
Pt  empregado de escritório; assistente (m)

**commis-contable** (m) n Fr
De Buchhalter (m)
En ledger clerk
Am bookkeeper
Es  contable (m)
It  contabile (m)
Pt  empregado de contabilidade (m)

**commis-voyageur** (m) n Fr
De Geschäftsreisende(r) (m)
En (commercial) traveller
Es  viajante (m)

It  viaggiatore di commercio (m)
Pt  viajante (m)

**commissaire-priseur** (m) n Fr
De Versteigerer (m)
En auctioneer
Es  subastador (m)
It  venditore all'asta (m)
Pt  leiloeiro (m)

**commissaire de la marine** (m) Fr
De Zahlmeister (m)
En purser
Es  contador de navio (m)
It  commissario di bordo (m)
Pt  commissário de bordo (m)

**commissário de bordo** (m) Pt
De Zahlmeister (m)
En purser
Es  contador de navio (m)
Fr  commissaire de la marine (m)
It  commissario di bordo (m)

**commissario di bordo** (m) It
De Zahlmeister (m)
En purser
Es  contador de navio (m)
Fr  commissaire de la marine (m)
Pt  commissário de bordo (m)

**commission** n En, Fr (f)
De Provision (f)
Es  comisión (f)
It  provvigione (f)
Pt  comissão (f)

**commission agent** En
De Kommissionär (m)
Es  comisionista (m)
Fr  commissionnaire en marchandises (m)
It  commissionario (m)
Pt  comissionista (m)

**commissionario** (m) n It
De Kommissionär (m)
En commission agent
Es  comisionista (m)
Fr  commissionnaire en marchandises (m)
Pt  comissionista (m)

**Commission des Communautés Européennes** (f) Fr
De Europäische Kommission (f)
En European Commission
Es Comisión Europea (f)
It Commissione Europea (f)
Pt Comissão Europeia (f)

**Commissione Europea** (f) It
De Europäische Kommission (f)
En European Commission
Es Comisión Europea (f)
Fr Commission des Communautés Européennes (f)
Pt Comissão Europeia (f)

**commissionnaire en marchandises** (m) Fr
De Kommissionär (m)
En commission agent
Es comisionista (m)
It commissionario (m)
Pt comissionista (m)

**committee** n En
De Kommission; Ausschuss (f m)
Es comité (m)
Fr comité (f)
It comitato (m)
Pt comité (m)

**commodity** n En
De Gut; Ware (n f)
Es mercadería (f)
Fr marchandise; produit (f m)
It merce; prodotto (f m)
Pt mercadoria; produto (f m)

**commodity broker** En
De Makler für Verbrauchsgüter (m)
Es corredor de mercaderías (m)
Fr courtier en marchandises (m)
It sensale di merci (m)
Pt corretor de mercadorias (m)

**commodity market** En
De Rohstoffmarkt (m)
Es mercado de materias primas (m)
Fr marché de matières premières (m)

It mercato di materie prime (m)
Pt mercado de matérias primas (m)

**Common Agricultural Policy** En
De gemeinsame Agrarpolitik (f)
Es política agrícola común (f)
Fr politique agricole commune (f)
It politica agricola comune (f)
Pt política agrícola comum (f)

**common carrier** En
De Güterbeförderer (m)
Es empresa de transportes (f)
Fr voiturier public (m)
It vettore (m)
Pt empresa de transportes (f)

**Common Commercial Policy** En
De gemeinsame Handelspolitik (f)
Es política comercial común (f)
Fr politique commerciale commune (f)
It politica commerciale comune (f)
Pt política comercial comum (f)

**common external tariff** En
De gemeinsamer Aussentariff (m)
Es tarifa exterior común (f)
Fr tarif extérieur commun (m)
It tariffa estera comune (f)
Pt tarifa externa comum (f)

**Common Fisheries Policy** En
De gemeinsame Fischereipolitik (f)
Es política común de la pesca (f)
Fr politique commune de la pêche (f)
It politica comune della pesca (f)
Pt política comum da pesca (f)

**Common Market** En
De gemeinsamer Markt (m)
Es mercado común (m)
Fr marché commun (m)

It mercato comune (m)
Pt mercado comum (m)

**communal** adj Fr
De Kommunal-
En municipal
Es municipal
It municipale
Pt municipal

**communauté** (f) n Fr
De Gemeinschaft (f)
En community
Es comunidad (f)
It comunità (f)
Pt comunidade (f)

**Communauté Économique Européenne** (f) Fr
De Europäische Wirtschaftsgemeinschaft (f)
En European Economic Community
Es Comunidad Económica Europea (f)
It Comunità Economica Europea (f)
Pt Comunidade Económica Europeia (f)

**Communauté Européenne de l'Energie Atomique** (f) Fr
De Europäische Atomgemeinschaft (f)
En European Atomic Energy Community
Es Comunidad Europea de Energía Atómica (f)
It Comunità Europea dell'Energia Atomica (f)
Pt Comunidade Europeia de Energia Atómica (f)

**Communauté Européenne du Charbon et de l'Acier** (f) Fr
De Europäische Gemeinschaft für Kohle und Stahl (f)
En European Coal and Steel Community
Es Comunidad Europea de Carbón y Acero (f)
It Comunità Europea del Carbone e Acciaio (f)
Pt Comunidade Europeia do Carrão e do Aço (f)

**communication** n En, Fr *(f)*
De Benachrichtigung *(f)*
Es comunicación *(f)*
It comunicazione *(f)*
Pt comunicação *(f)*

**community** n En
De Gemeinschaft *(f)*
Es comunidad *(f)*
Fr communauté *(f)*
It comunità *(f)*
Pt comunidade *(f)*

**compagnia di assicurazione**
*(f)* It
De Versicherungsgesellschaft *(f)*
En insurance company
Es compañía de seguros *(f)*
Fr compagnie d'assurance *(f)*
Pt companhia de seguros *(f)*

**compagnie aérienne** *(f)* Fr
De Fluggesellschaft *(f)*
En air line
Es línea aérea *(f)*
It linea aerea *(f)*
Pt companhia de aviação *(f)*

**compagnie d'assurance** *(f)* Fr
De Versicherungsgesellschaft *(f)*
En insurance company
Es compañía de seguros *(f)*
It compagnia di assicurazione *(f)*
Pt companhia de seguros *(f)*

**compagnie de navigation** *(f)* Fr
De Reederei *(f)*
En shipping line
Es compañia navièra *(f)*
It società di navigazione *(f)*
Pt companhia de navegação *(f)*

**companhia** *(f)* n Pt
De Gesellschaft *(f)*
En company
Es compañía; empresa *(f)*
Fr société; entreprise *(f)*
It società *(f)*

**companhia arrendatária** *(f)* Pt
De Leasinggesellschaft *(f)*
En leasing company
Es compañía arrendataria *(f)*
Fr société de leasing *(f)*
It società di leasing *(f)*

**companhia controladora** *(f)* Pt
De Gesellschaft mit Kontrollbefugnis *(f)*
En controlling company
Es compañía directriz *(f)*
Fr société directrice *(f)*
It società direttrice *(f)*

**companhia cotizada** *(f)* Pt
De Gesellschaft notiert an der Börse *(f)*
En quoted company
Es compañía cotizada en bolsa *(f)*
Fr société cotée à la Bourse *(f)*
It società quotata in borsa *(f)*

**companhia de aviação** *(f)* Pt
De Fluggesellschaft *(f)*
En air line
Es línea aérea *(f)*
Fr compagnie aérienne *(f)*
It linea aerea *(f)*

**companhia de investimentos** *(f)* Pt
De Investierungsgesellschaft *(f)*
En investment company
Es compañía inversionista *(f)*
Fr société de placement *(f)*
It società per investimenti *(f)*

**companhia de navegação** *(f)* Pt
De Reederei *(f)*
En shipping line
Es compañia navièra *(f)*
Fr compagnie de navigation *(f)*
It società di navigazione *(f)*

**companhia de seguros** *(f)* Pt
De Versicherungsgesellschaft *(f)*
En insurance company
Es compañía de seguros *(f)*
Fr compagnie d'assurance *(f)*
It compagnia di assicurazione *(f)*

**companhia proprietária** *(f)* Pt
De Dachgesellschaft *(f)*
En holding company
Es compañía tenedora *(f)*
Fr société holding *(f)*
It società holding *(f)*

**companhia subsidiária** *(f)* Pt
De Tochtergesellschaft *(f)*
En subsidiary company
Es filial; empresa subsidiaría *(f)*
Fr filiale *(f)*
It filiale *(f)*

**compañía** *(f)* n Es
De Gesellschaft *(f)*
En company
Fr société; entreprise *(f)*
It società *(f)*
Pt companhia *(f)*

**compañía afiliada** *(f)* Es
De Schwestergesellschaft *(f)*
En affiliated company
Fr société sœur *(f)*
It società affiliata *(f)*
Pt companhia subsidiária *(f)*

**compañía arrendataria** *(f)* Es
De Leasinggesellschaft *(f)*
En leasing company
Fr société de leasing *(f)*
It società di leasing *(f)*
Pt companhia arrendatária *(f)*

**compañía asociada** *(f)* Es
De Schwestergesellschaft *(f)*
En sister company
Fr société sœur *(f)*
It società sorella *(f)*
Pt empresa gémea *(f)*

**compañía cotizada en bolsa** *(f)* Es
De Gesellschaft notiert an der Börse *(f)*
En quoted company
Fr société cotée à la Bourse *(f)*
It società quotata in borsa *(f)*
Pt companhia cotizada *(f)*

**compañía de explotación** *(f)* Es
De Erschliessungsgesellschaft *(f)*
En development company
Fr société d'exploitation *(f)*
It società d'imprese *(f)*
Pt empresa de exploração *(f)*

**compañía de seguros** *(f)* Es
De Versicherungsgesellschaft *(f)*
En insurance company
Fr compagnie d'assurance *(f)*
It compagnia di assicurazione *(f)*
Pt companhia de seguros *(f)*

**compañía directriz** *(f)* Es
De Gesellschaft mit Kontrollbefugnis *(f)*
En controlling company
Fr société directrice *(f)*
It società direttrice *(f)*
Pt companhia controladora *(f)*

**compañía inversionista** *(f)* Es
De Investierungsgesellschaft *(f)*
En investment company
Fr société de placement *(f)*
It società per investimenti *(f)*
Pt companhia de investimentos *(f)*

**compañía matriz** *(f)* Es
De Muttergesellschaft *(f)*
En parent company
Fr société mère *(f)*
It società madre *(f)*
Pt empresa matriz *(f)*

**compañía navièra** *(f)* Es
De Reederei *(f)*
En shipping line
Fr compagnie de navigation *(f)*
It società di navigazione *(f)*
Pt companhia de navegação *(f)*

**Compañía privada de responsabilidad limitada** *(f)* Es
De Gesellschaft mit beschränkter Haftung (GmbH) *(f)*
En private limited company
Fr Société à responsabilité limitée (SARL) *(f)*
It Società a responsabilità limitata (Sarl) *(f)*
Pt Sociedade por quotas de responsabilidade limitada *(f)*

**compañía tenedora** *(f)* Es
De Dachgesellschaft *(f)*
En holding company
Fr société holding *(f)*

It società holding *(f)*
Pt companhia proprietária *(f)*

**company** *n* En
De Gesellschaft *(f)*
Es compañía; empresa *(f)*
Fr société; entreprise *(f)*
It società *(f)*
Pt companhia *(f)*

**compensação** *(f)* *n* Pt
De Entschädigung *(f)*
En compensation
Es compensación *(f)*
Fr compensation *(f)*
It compenso *(m)*

**compensación** *(f)* *n* Es
De Entschädigung *(f)*
En compensation
Fr compensation *(f)*
It compenso *(m)*
Pt compensação *(f)*

**compensar** *vb* Es, Pt
De vergüten
En compensate
Fr compenser
It compensare

**compensare** *vb* It
De vergüten
En compensate
Es compensar
Fr compenser
Pt compensar

**compensate** *vb* En
De vergüten
Es compensar
Fr compenser
It compensare
Pt compensar

**compensation** *n* En, Fr *(f)*
De Entschädigung *(f)*
Es compensación *(f)*
It compenso *(m)*
Pt compensação *(f)*

**compenser** *vb* Fr
De vergüten
En compensate
Es compensar
It compensare
Pt compensar

**compenso** *(m)* *n* It
De Entschädigung *(f)*
En compensation
Es compensación *(f)*
Fr compensation *(f)*
Pt compensação *(f)*

**compenso per il rischio** *(m)* It
De Gefahrenzulage *(f)*
En danger money
Es suma para riesgos *(f)*
Fr prime de risque *(f)*
Pt prémio de risco *(m)*

**compete** *vb* En
De Konkurrenz machen
Es competir
Fr concurrencer
It competere
Pt competir

**competere** *vb* It
De Konkurrenz machen
En compete
Es competir
Fr concurrencer
Pt competir

**competição** *(f)* *n* Pt
De Wettbewerb *(m)*
En competition
Es competición *(f)*
Fr concurrence *(f)*
It concorrenza *(f)*

**competición** *(f)* *n* Es
De Wettbewerb *(m)*
En competition
Fr concurrence *(f)*
It concorrenza *(f)*
Pt competição *(f)*

**competidor** *adj* Es
De wetteifernd
En competitive
Fr compétitif
It in concorrenza
Pt competitivo

**competir** *vb* Es, Pt
De Konkurrenz machen
En compete
Fr concurrencer
It competere

**compétitif** *adj* Fr
De wetteifernd
En competitive

comprir

Es competidor
It in concorrenza
Pt competitivo

**competition** n En
De Wettbewerb (m)
Es competición (f)
Fr concurrence (f)
It concorrenza (f)
Pt competição (f)

**competitive** adj En
De wetteifernd
Es competidor
Fr compétitif
It in concorrenza
Pt competitivo

**competitivo** adj Pt
De wetteifernd
En competitive
Es competidor
Fr compétitif
It in concorrenza

**compilazione dell'inventario**
(f) It
De Bestandaufnahme (f)
En stocktaking
Es inventario; balance (m)
Fr levée d'inventaire (f)
Pt inventário de existências
(m)

**complessivo** adj It
De gesamt
En aggregate
Es total
Fr global
Pt total

**completo** adj Es
De umfassend
En comprehensive
Fr exhaustif; complet
It comprensivo
Pt compreensivo

**comportamento precedente**
(m) It
De Leistung in der Vergangen-
heit (f)
En past performance
Es operación anterior (f)
Fr comportement antérieur
(m)
Pt desempenho anterior (m)

**comportement antérieur** (m)
Fr
De Leistung in der Vergangen-
heit (f)
En past performance
Es operación anterior (f)
It comportamento preceden-
te (m)
Pt desempenho anterior (m)

**compound interest** En
De Zinsezinsen (m pl)
Es interés compuesto (m)
Fr intérêts composés (m pl)
It interesse composto (m)
Pt juro composto (m)

**compra** (f) n Es, It, Pt
De Einkauf; Anschaffung (m f)
En purchase
Fr achat (m)

**compra a plazos** (f) Es
De Ratenkauf (m)
En hire-purchase
Fr location-vente (f)
It vendita a rate (f)
Pt venda a prestações (f)

**comprador** (m) n Es, Pt
De Käufer (m)
En buyer
Fr acheteur (m)
It compratore (m)

**compra espontánea** (f) Es
De Impulskaufen (n)
En impulse buying
Fr achat sur l'entrainement
du moment (m)
It compra sullo stimolo del
momento (f)
Pt compra impulsiva (f)

**compra impulsiva** (f) Pt
De Impulskaufen (n)
En impulse buying
Es compra espontánea (f)
Fr achat sur l'entrainement
du moment (m)
It compra sullo stimolo del
momento (f)

**comprar** vb Es, Pt
De kaufen
En buy
Fr acheter
It comprare

**comprare** vb It
De kaufen
En buy
Es comprar
Fr acheter
Pt comprar

**compra sullo stimolo del
momento** (f) It
De Impulskaufen (n)
En impulse buying
Es compra espontánea (f)
Fr achat sur l'entrainement
du moment (m)
Pt compra impulsiva (f)

**compratore** (m) n It
De Käufer (m)
En buyer
Es comprador (m)
Fr acheteur (m)
Pt comprador (m)

**compreensivo** adj Pt
De umfassend
En comprehensive
Es completo
Fr exhaustif; complet
It comprensivo

**comprehensive** adj En
De umfassend
Es completo
Fr exhaustif; complet
It comprensivo
Pt compreensivo

**comprehensive insurance** En
De kombinierte Versicherung
(f)
Es seguro combinado (m)
Fr assurance combinée (f)
It assicurazione mista (f)
Pt seguro compreensivo (m)

**comprensivo** adj It
De umfassend
En comprehensive
Es completo
Fr exhaustif; complet
Pt compreensivo

**comprir** vb Pt
De erfüllen
En fulfil
Es cumplir
Fr remplir
It adempiere

**compromesso d'avaria** (m) It
De  Havarieschein (m)
En  average bond
Es  fianza de avería (f)
Fr  compromis d'avarie (m)
Pt  fiança de avaria (f)

**compromis d'avarie** (m) Fr
De  Havarieschein (m)
En  average bond
Es  fianza de avería (f)
It  compromesso d'avaria (m)
Pt  fiança de avaria (f)

**comproprietà** (f) It
De  Miteigentum (n)
En  joint ownership
Es  copropiedad (f)
Fr  copropriété (f)
Pt  copropriedade (f)

**comptabilité** (f) n Fr
De  Buchhaltung (f)
En  book-keeping; accountancy
Es  contabilidad (f)
It  contabilità (f)
Pt  contabilidade (f)

**comptable** (m) n Fr
De  Buchhalter (m)
En  accountant
Es  contador (m)
It  contabile (m)
Pt  contabilista (m)

**comptable de prix de revient**
  (m) Fr
De  Kalkulator (m)
En  cost accountant
Es  contable de costes (m)
It  contabile dei costi di
    produzione (m)
Pt  calculador de custos (m)

**comptant contre documents**
  Fr
De  bar gegen Versandpapiere
En  cash against documents
    (c.a.d.)
Es  al contado contra docu-
    mentos
It  contanti contro documenti
Pt  em dinheiro contra docu-
    mentação

**compte** (en banque) (m) n Fr
De  Konto (n)
En  account

Es  cuenta (f)
It  conto (m)
Pt  conta (f)

**compte** (note) (m) n Fr
De  Rechnung (f)
En  bill; account
Es  cuenta; nota (f)
It  conto; nota (m f)
Pt  conta; nota (f)

**compte bloqué** (m) Fr
De  gesperrtes Konto (n)
En  blocked account
Es  cuenta bloqueada (f)
It  conto bloccato (m)
Pt  conta bloqueada (f)

**compte capital** (m) Fr
De  Kapitalkonto (n)
En  capital account
Es  cuenta de capital (f)
It  conto capitale (m)
Pt  conta de capital (f)

**compte commercial** (m) Fr
De  Handelskonto (n)
En  trade account
Es  cuenta comercial (f)
It  conto commerciale (m)
Pt  conta comercial (f)

**compte contrepartie** (m) Fr
De  Gegenkonto (n)
En  contra account
Es  contracuenta (f)
It  conto d'ordine (m)
Pt  contra-conta (f)

**compte courant** (m) Fr
De  Kontokorrent (n)
En  current account
Am  checking account
Es  cuenta corriente (f)
It  conto corrente (m)
Pt  conta corrente (f)

**compte d'affectation** (m) Fr
De  Rückstellungskonto (n)
En  appropriation account
Es  cuenta de apropiación (f)
It  conto di stanziamento (m)
Pt  conta de apropriação (f)

**compte d'agio** (m) Fr
De  Agiokonto (n)
En  agio account
Es  cuenta de agio (f)

It  conto d'aggio (m)
Pt  conta de ágio (f)

**compte d'avances** (m) Fr
De  Darlehenskonto (n)
En  advance account
Es  cuenta de anticipos (f)
It  conto anticipo (m)
Pt  conta de adiantamentos (f)

**compte d'ordre** (m) Fr
De  Übergangskonto (n)
En  suspense account
Es  cuenta suspensa (f)
It  conto sospeso (m)
Pt  conta pendente (m)

**compte de contrôle** (m) Fr
De  Kontrollkonto (n)
En  control account
Es  cuenta de control (f)
It  conto di controllo (m)
Pt  conta de controlo (f)

**compte découvert** (m) Fr
De  Konto überzogen (n)
En  account overdrawn
Es  cuenta en descubierto (f)
It  conto scoperto (m)
Pt  conta a descoberto (f)

**compte de dépôt** (m) Fr
De  Depositenkonto (n)
En  deposit account
Am  interest-bearing account
Es  cuenta de ahorras (f)
It  conto di deposito (m)
Pt  conta de depósito (f)

**compte de mise à terre** (m) Fr
De  Löschungskonto (n)
En  landing account
Es  cuenta de desembarque (f)
It  conto di sbarco (m)
Pt  conta de descargas (f)

**compte de revenus et dépen-
  ses** (m) Fr
De  Ausgaben- und Ertrags-
    konto (n)
En  income and expenditure
    account
Es  cuenta de ingresos y gastos
    (f)
It  conto proventi e spese (m)
Pt  conta de receitas e des-
    pesas (f)

**compte des prêts** *(m)* Fr
De Anleihekonto *(n)*
En loan account
Es cuenta de préstamos *(f)*
It conto anticipazioni *(m)*
Pt conta de empréstimos *(f)*

**compte des speculations à la baisse** *(m)* Fr
De Baissekonto *(n)*
En bear account
Es cuenta de especulaciones a la baja *(f)*
It conto di speculazioni al ribasso *(m)*
Pt conta de especulações baixistas *(f)*

**compte en banque** *(m)* Fr
De Bankkonto *(n)*
En bank account
Es cuenta bancaria *(f)*
It conto in banca *(m)*
Pt conta bancária *(f)*

**compte identifié par numéro** *(m)* Fr
De numeriertes Konto *(n)*
En numbered account
Es cuenta identificada con número *(f)*
It conto identificato da numero *(m)*
Pt conta numerada *(f)*

**compte impersonnel** *(m)* Fr
De Firmenkonto *(n)*
En impersonal account
Es cuenta simulada *(f)*
It conto d'ordine *(m)*
Pt conta impessoal *(f)*

**compte joint** *(m)* Fr
De Gemeinschaftskonto *(n)*
En joint account
Es cuenta común *(f)*
It conto in comune *(m)*
Pt conta conjunta *(f)*

**compte nominal** *(m)* Fr
De Firmenkonto *(n)*
En nominal account
Es cuenta de resultado *(f)*
It conto d'ordine *(m)*
Pt conta nominal *(f)*

**compte personnel** *(m)* Fr
De Kundenkonto *(n)*
En charge account
Es cuenta personal *(f)*
It conto personale *(m)*
Pt conta pessoal *(f)*

**compte profits et pertes** *(m)* Fr
De Gewinn- und Verlustkonto *(n)*
En profit and loss account
Es cuenta de ganancias y pérdidas *(f)*
It conto profitti e perdite *(m)*
Pt conta de lucros e perdas *(f)*

**compte rendu** *(m)* Fr
De zur Begleichung vorgelegte Rechnung *(f)*
En account rendered
Es cuenta rendida *(f)*
It conto reso *(m)*
Pt conta remetida *(f)*

**comptes à payer** *(m pl)* Fr
De Kreditoren *(m pl)*
En accounts payable
Es cuentas a pagar *(f pl)*
It conti passivi *(m pl)*
Pt contas a pagar *(f pl)*

**comptes à percevoir** *(m pl)* Fr
De ausstehende Schulden *(m pl)*
En outstanding accounts
Es cuentas pendientes *(f pl)*
It conti aperti *(m pl)*
Pt contas por saldar *(f pl)*

**comptes consolidés** *(m pl)* Fr
De konsolidierter Kontenabschluss *(m)*
En consolidated accounts
Es cuentas consolidadas *(f pl)*
It conti consolidati *(m pl)*
Pt contas consolidadas *(f pl)*

**compte transférable** *(m)* Fr
De Auslandskonto *(n)*
En external account
Am foreign currency account
Es cuenta exterior *(f)*
It conto estero *(m)*
Pt conta externa *(f)*

**comptroller** *n* En
De Rechnungsprüfer *(m)*
Es interventor *(m)*
Fr vérificateur des comptes *(m)*
It controllore *(m)*
Pt controlador *(m)*

**compulsión** *(f)* *n* Es
De Zwang *(m)*
En duress
Fr contrainte *(f)*
It costrizione *(f)*
Pt coerção *(f)*

**compulsory** *adj* En
De verbindlich
Es obligatorio
Fr obligatoire
It obbligatorio
Pt obrigatório

**compulsory purchase** En
De Enteignung *(f)*
Es expropiación *(f)*
Fr expropriation *(f)*
It espropriazione *(f)*
Pt expropriação *(f)*

**compulsory winding-up** En
Am forced liquidation
De Zwangsliquidation *(f)*
Es liquidación forzosa *(f)*
Fr liquidation forcée *(f)*
It liquidazione forzata *(f)*
Pt liquidação forçada *(f)*

**computador** *(m)* *n* Pt
De Rechner; Computer *(m)*
En computer
Es computadora *(f)*
Fr ordinateur *(m)*
It elaboratore; calcolatore *(m)*

**computadora** *(f)* *n* Es
De Rechner; Computer *(m)*
En computer
Fr ordinateur *(m)*
It elaboratore; calcolatore *(m)*
Pt computador *(m)*

**computadora analógica** *(f)* Es
De Analogrechner *(m)*
En analogue computer
Fr calculateur analogique *(m)*
It calcolatore analogico *(m)*
Pt computador analógico *(m)*

**computador analógico** (m) Pt
De Analogrechner (m)
En analogue computer
Es computadora analógica (f)
Fr calculateur analogique (m)
It calcolatore analogico (m)

**computadora numérica** (f) Es
De Digitalrechner (m)
En digital computer
Fr calculateur digital (m)
It elaboratore numerico (m)
Pt computador de dígitos (m)

**computador de dígitos** (m) Pt
De Digitalrechner (m)
En digital computer
Es computadora numérica (f)
Fr calculateur digital (m)
It elaboratore numerico (m)

**computer** n En
De Rechner; Computer (m)
Es computadora (f)
Fr ordinateur (m)
It elaboratore; calcolatore (m)
Pt computador (m)

**Computer** (m) n De
En computer
Es computadora (f)
Fr ordinateur (m)
It elaboratore; calcolatore (m)
Pt computador (m)

**computer language** En
De Rechnersprache (f)
Es lenguaje de computadoras (m)
Fr langage-machine (m)
It linguaggio macchina (m)
Pt linguagem de computador (f)

**computer printout** En
De Ausgabedruck (m)
Es impresión (f)
Fr sortie sur imprimante (f)
It stampato d'uscita dell'elaboratore (m)
Pt informe impresso pelo computador (m)

**computer program** En
De Computerprogramm (n)
Es programa de computadora (m)

Fr programme d'ordinateur (m)
It programma di elaboratore (m)
Pt programa de computador (m)

**Computerprogramm** (n) n De
En computer program
Es programa de computadora (m)
Fr programme d'ordinateur (m)
It programma di elaboratore (m)
Pt programa de computador (m)

**com recurso** Pt
De mit Rückgriff
En with recourse
Es con recurso
Fr avec droit de recours
It con ricorso

**comune accordo** (m) It
De gegenseitiges Einvernehmen (n)
En mutual agreement
Es acuerdo común (m)
Fr accord mutuel (m)
Pt acordo mútuo (m)

**comunicação** (f) n Pt
De Benachrichtigung (f)
En communication
Es comunicación (f)
Fr communication (f)
It comunicazione (f)

**comunicación** (f) n Es
De Benachrichtigung (f)
En communication
Fr communication (f)
It comunicazione (f)
Pt comunicação (f)

**comunicazione** (f) n It
De Benachrichtigung (f)
En communication
Es comunicación (f)
Fr communication (f)
Pt comunicação (f)

**comunicazione interurbana** (f) It
De Ferngespräch (n)
En trunk call

Am long distance call
Es llamada interurbana (f)
Fr appel téléphonique interurbain (m)
Pt chamada inter-urbana (troncas) (f)

**comunidad** (f) n Es
De Gemeinschaft (f)
En community
Fr communauté (f)
It comunità (f)
Pt comunidade (f)

**comunidade** (f) n Pt
De Gemeinschaft (f)
En community
Es comunidad (f)
Fr communauté (f)
It comunità (f)

**Comunidad Económica Europea** (f) Es
De Europäische Wirtschaftsgemeinschaft (f)
En European Economic Community
Fr Communauté Économique Européenne (f)
It Comunità Economica Europea (f)
Pt Comunidade Económica Europeia (f)

**Comunidade Económica Europeia** (f) Pt
De Europäische Wirtschaftsgemeinschaft (f)
En European Economic Community
Es Comunidad Económica Europea (f)
Fr Communauté Économique Européenne (f)
It Comunità Economica Europea (f)

**Comunidade Europeia de Energia Atómica** (f) Pt
De Europäische Atomgemeinschaft (f)
En European Atomic Energy Community
Es Comunidad Europea de Energía Atómica (f)
Fr Communauté Européenne de l'Energie Atomique (f)

It Comunità Europea del-
l'Energia Atomica *(f)*

**Comunidade Europeia do
Carrão e do Aço** *(f)* Pt
De Europäische Gemeinschaft
für Kohle und Stahl *(f)*
En European Coal and Steel
Community
Es Comunidad Europea de
Carbón y Acero *(f)*
Fr Communauté Européenne
du Charbon et de l'Acier *(f)*
It Comunità Europea del Car-
bone e Acciaio *(f)*

**Comunidad Europea de Car-
bón y Acero** *(f)* Es
De Europäische Gemeinschaft
für Kohle und Stahl *(f)*
En European Coal and Steel
Community
Fr Communauté Européenne
du Charbon et de l'Acier *(f)*
It Comunità Europea del Car-
bone e Acciaio *(f)*
Pt Comunidade Europeia do
Carrão e do Aço *(f)*

**Comunidad Europea de Ener-
gía Atómica** *(f)* Es
De Europäische Atomgemein-
schaft *(f)*
En European Atomic Energy
Community
Fr Communauté Européenne
de l'Energie Atomique *(f)*
It Comunità Europea del-
l'Energia Atomica *(f)*
Pt Comunidade Europeia de
Energia Atómica *(f)*

**comunità** *(f) n* It
De Gemeinschaft *(f)*
En community
Es comunidad *(f)*
Fr communauté *(f)*
Pt comunidade *(f)*

**Comunità Economica Europea**
*(f)* It
De Europäische Wirtschafts-
gemeinschaft *(f)*
En European Economic Com-
munity
Es Comunidad Económica
Europea *(f)*

Fr Communauté Économique
Européenne *(f)*
Pt Comunidade Económica
Europeia *(f)*

**Comunità Europea del Car-
bone e Acciaio** *(f)* It
De Europäische Gemeinschaft
für Kohle und Stahl *(f)*
En European Coal and Steel
Community
Es Comunidad Europea de
Carbón y Acero *(f)*
Fr Communauté Européenne
du Charbon et de l'Acier *(f)*
Pt Comunidade Europeia do
Carrão e do Aço *(f)*

**Comunità Europea dell'Ener-
gia Atomica** *(f)* It
De Europäische Atomgemein-
schaft *(f)*
En European Atomic Energy
Community
Es Comunidad Europea de
Energía Atómica *(f)*
Fr Communauté Européenne
de l'Energie Atomique *(f)*
Pt Comunidade Europeia de
Energia Atómica *(f)*

**con avaria** It
De havariert
En with average (WA)
Es con avería
Fr avarié
Pt com avaria

**con avería** Es
De havariert
En with average (WA)
Fr avarié
It con avaria
Pt com avaria

**conceder (um desconto)** Pt
De gewähren (einen Rabatt)
En allow (a discount)
Es conceder (un descuento)
Fr consentir (une remise)
It concedere (uno sconto)

**conceder (un descuento)** Es
De gewähren (einen Rabatt)
En allow (a discount)
Fr consentir (une remise)
It concedere (uno sconto)
Pt conceder (um desconto)

**conceder compensação** Pt
De Schadenersatz zugestehen
En award damages
Es conceder daños
Fr adjuger des dommages-
intérêts
It concedere i danni

**conceder daños** Es
De Schadenersatz zugestehen
En award damages
Fr adjuger des dommages-
intérêts
It concedere i danni
Pt conceder compensação

**concedere (uno sconto)** It
De gewähren (einen Rabatt)
En allow (a discount)
Es conceder (un descuento)
Fr consentir (une remise)
Pt conceder (um desconto)

**concedere i danni** It
De Schadenersatz zugestehen
En award damages
Es conceder daños
Fr adjuger des dommages-
intérêts
Pt conceder compensação

**concedere la libertà provvi-
soria su cauzione** It
De gegen Haftkaution freige-
ben
En grant bail
Es conceder fianza
Fr admettre une caution
Pt autorizar caução

**conceder fianza** Es
De gegen Haftkaution freige-
ben
En grant bail
Fr admettre une caution
It concedere la libertà provvi-
soria su cauzione
Pt autorizar caução

**concentrato sul capitale** It
De kapitalintensiv
En capital-intensive
Es intensivo de capital
Fr intensif de capital
Pt intensivo em termos de
capital

**concepteur-rédacteur** *(m)* n Fr
De Textverfasser *(m)*
En copywriter
Es redactor *(m)*
It redattore publicitario *(m)*
Pt redactor de publicidade *(m)*

**concesión** *(f)* n Es
De Konzession *(f)*
En franchise; concession
Fr concession *(f)*
It concessione *(f)*
Pt concessão *(f)*

**concesión (de una patente)** *(f)*
Es
De Erteilung (eines Patentes) *(f)*
En grant (of a patent)
Fr délivrance (d'un brevet) *(f)*
It concessione (di brevetto) *(f)*
Pt concessão (de uma patente) *(f)*

**concesión minera** *(f)* Es
De Bergwerkskonzession *(f)*
En mineral concession
Fr concession minière *(f)*
It concessione mineraria *(f)*
Pt concessão mineira *(f)*

**concesión recíproca** *(f)* Es
De Geben und Nehmen *(n)*
En give and take
Fr concessions mutuelles *(f pl)*
It concessione reciproca *(f)*
Pt concessão mútua *(f)*

**concessão** *(f)* n Pt
De Konzession *(f)*
En franchise; concession
Es concesión *(f)*
Fr concession *(f)*
It concessione *(f)*

**concessão (de uma patente)** *(f)* Pt
De Erteilung (eines Patentes) *(f)*
En grant (of a patent)
Es concesión (de una patente) *(f)*
Fr délivrance (d'un brevet) *(f)*
It concessione (di brevetto) *(f)*

**concessão mineira** *(f)* Pt
De Bergwerkskonzession *(f)*
En mineral concession
Es concesión minera *(f)*
Fr concession minière *(f)*
It concessione mineraria *(f)*

**concessão mútua** *(f)* Pt
De Geben und Nehmen *(n)*
En give and take
Es concesión recíproca *(f)*
Fr concessions mutuelles *(f pl)*
It concessione reciproca *(f)*

**concession** n En, Fr *(f)*
De Konzession *(f)*
Es concesión *(f)*
It concessione *(f)*
Pt concessão *(f)*

**concessione** *(f)* n It
De Konzession *(f)*
En concession; franchise
Es concesión *(f)*
Fr concession *(f)*
Pt concessão *(f)*

**concessione (di brevetto)** *(f)* It
De Erteilung (eines Patentes) *(f)*
En grant (of a patent)
Es concesión (de una patente) *(f)*
Fr délivrance (d'un brevet) *(f)*
Pt concessão (de uma patente) *(f)*

**concessione mineraria** *(f)* It
De Bergwerkskonzession *(f)*
En mineral concession
Es concesión minera *(f)*
Fr concession minière *(f)*
Pt concessão mineira *(f)*

**concessione reciproca** *(f)* It
De Geben und Nehmen *(n)*
En give and take
Es concesión recíproca *(f)*
Fr concessions mutuelles *(f pl)*
Pt concessão mútua *(f)*

**concession minière** *(f)* Fr
De Bergwerkskonzession *(f)*
En mineral concession
Es concesión minera *(f)*

It concessione mineraria *(f)*
Pt concessão mineira *(f)*

**concessions mutuelles** *(f pl)* Fr
De Geben und Nehmen *(n)*
En give and take
Es concesión recíproca *(f)*
It concessione reciproca *(f)*
Pt concessão mútua *(f)*

**concessões sobre capital** *(f pl)* Pt
De Steuerbegünstigung auf Anlagen *(f)*
En capital allowances
Es deducciones fiscales sobre inversiones *(f pl)*
Fr déductions fiscales sur les investissements *(f pl)*
It deduzioni fiscali sugli investimenti *(f pl)*

**concezione difettosa** *(f)* It
De schlechte Ausführung *(f)*
En faulty design
Es diseño defectuoso *(m)*
Fr construction fautive *(f)*
Pt desenho defeituoso *(m)*

**concierge** *(m)* n Fr
De Hausmeister *(m)*
En hall-porter
Es conserje *(m)*
It portiere *(m)*
Pt porteiro *(m)*

**conciliação** *(f)* n Pt
De Schlichtung *(f)*
En conciliation
Es conciliación *(f)*
Fr conciliation *(f)*
It conciliazione *(f)*

**conciliación** *(f)* n Es
De Schlichtung *(f)*
En conciliation
Fr conciliation *(f)*
It conciliazione *(f)*
Pt conciliação *(f)*

**conciliation** n En, Fr *(f)*
De Schlichtung *(f)*
Es conciliación *(f)*
It conciliazione *(f)*
Pt conciliação *(f)*

**conciliazione** (f) n It
 De Schlichtung (f)
 En conciliation
 Es conciliación (f)
 Fr conciliation (f)
 Pt conciliação (f)

**concordat** (m) n Fr
 De Vergleichsabkommen (n)
 En deed of composition
 Es concordato (m)
 It atto di concordato (m)
 Pt concordata (por escrito) (f)

**concordata** (por escrito) (f) Pt
 De Vergleichsabkommen (n)
 En deed of composition
 Es concordato (m)
 Fr concordat (m)
 It atto di concordato (m)

**concordato** (m) n Es
 De Vergleichsabkommen (n)
 En deed of composition
 Fr concordat (m)
 It atto di concordato (m)
 Pt concordata (por escrito) (f)

**concorrenza** (f) n It
 De Wettbewerb (m)
 En competition
 Es competición (f)
 Fr concurrence (f)
 Pt competição (f)

**concurrence** (f) n Fr
 De Wettbewerb (m)
 En competition
 Es competición (f)
 It concorrenza (f)
 Pt competição (f)

**concurrencer** vb Fr
 De Konkurrenz machen
 En compete
 Es competir
 It competere
 Pt competir

**concurso de acreedores** (m)
  Es
 De Gläubigerversammlung (f)
 En meeting of creditors
 Fr assemblée de créanciers (f)
 It convocazione dei creditori
  (f)
 Pt reunião de credores (f)

**condição** (f) n Pt
 De Bedingung (f)
 En condition
 Es condición (f)
 Fr condition (f)
 It condizione (f)

**condição prévia** (f) Pt
 De aufschiebende Bedingung
  (f)
 En condition precedent
 Es previa condición (f)
 Fr condition suspensive (f)
 It condizione sospensiva (f)

**condición** (f) n Es
 De Bedingung (f)
 En condition
 Fr condition (f)
 It condizione (f)
 Pt condição (f)

**condicional** adj Es, Pt
 De bedingt
 En conditional
 Fr conditionnel
 It condizionale

**condicionamento do ar** (m) Pt
 De Klimatisierung (f)
 En air-conditioning
 Es acondicionamiento de aire
  (m)
 Fr climatisation (f)
 It condizionamento dell'aria
  (m)

**condiciones** (f pl) n Es
 De Bedingungen (f pl)
 En terms
 Fr conditions (f pl)
 It condizioni (f pl)
 Pt condições (f pl)

**condiciones del mercado** (f pl)
  Es
 De Marktumständen (m pl)
 En state of the market
 Fr état du marché (m)
 It condizioni del mercato (f
  pl)
 Pt situação do mercado (f)

**condiciones de pago** (f pl) Es
 De Zahlungsbedingungen (f pl)
 En payment terms
 Fr conditions de paiement (f
  pl)

 It condizioni di pagamento (f
  pl)
 Pt condições de pagamento (f
  pl)

**condiciones de trabajo** (f pl)
  Es
 De Arbeitsbedingungen (f pl)
 En working conditions
 Fr conditions de travail (f pl)
 It condizioni di lavoro (f pl)
 Pt condições de trabalho (f pl)

**condiciones implícitas** (f pl) Es
 De stillschweigende Bedingun-
  gen (f pl)
 En implied terms
 Fr conditions implicites (f pl)
 It condizioni implicite (f pl)
 Pt condições implícitas (f pl)

**condiciones normales** (f pl) Es
 De Standardbedingungen (f pl)
 En standard conditions
 Fr conditions courantes (f pl)
 It condizioni normali (f pl)
 Pt condições normais (f pl)

**condições** (f pl) n Pt
 De Bedingungen (f pl)
 En terms
 Es condiciones (f pl)
 Fr conditions (f pl)
 It condizioni (f pl)

**condições de pagamento** (f pl)
  Pt
 De Zahlungsbedingungen (f pl)
 En payment terms
 Es condiciones de pago (f pl)
 Fr conditions de paiement (f
  pl)
 It condizioni di pagamento (f
  pl)

**condições de trabalho** (f pl) Pt
 De Arbeitsbedingungen (f pl)
 En working conditions
 Es condiciones de trabajo (f
  pl)
 Fr conditions de travail (f pl)
 It condizioni di lavoro (f pl)

**condições implícitas** (f pl) Pt
 De stillschweigende Bedingun-
  gen (f pl)
 En implied terms
 Es condiciones implícitas (f pl)

Fr conditions implicites *(f pl)*
It condizioni implicite *(f pl)*

**condições normais** *(f pl)* Pt
De Standardbedingungen *(f pl)*
En standard conditions
Es condiciones normales *(f pl)*
Fr conditions courantes *(f pl)*
It condizioni normali *(f pl)*

**condition** *n* En, Fr *(f)*
De Bedingung *(f)*
Es condición *(f)*
It condizione *(f)*
Pt condição *(f)*

**conditional** *adj* En
De bedingt
Es condicional
Fr conditionnel
It condizionale
Pt condicional

**conditionnel** *adj* Fr
De bedingt
En conditional
Es condicional
It condizionale
Pt condicional

**condition precedent** En
De aufschiebende Bedingung *(f)*
Es previa condición *(f)*
Fr condition suspensive *(f)*
It condizione sospensiva *(f)*
Pt condição prévia *(f)*

**conditions** *(f pl)* *n* Fr
De Bedingungen *(f pl)*
En terms
Es condiciones *(f pl)*
It condizioni *(f pl)*
Pt condições *(f pl)*

**conditions courantes** *(f pl)* Fr
De Standardbedingungen *(f pl)*
En standard conditions
Es condiciones normales *(f pl)*
It condizioni normali *(f pl)*
Pt condições normais *(f pl)*

**conditions de paiement** *(f pl)* Fr
De Zahlungsbedingungen *(f pl)*
En payment terms
Es condiciones de pago *(f pl)*

It condizioni di pagamento *(f pl)*
Pt condições de pagamento *(f pl)*

**conditions de travail** *(f pl)* Fr
De Arbeitsbedingungen *(f pl)*
En working conditions
Es condiciones de trabajo *(f pl)*
It condizioni di lavoro *(f pl)*
Pt condições de trabalho *(f pl)*

**conditions implicites** *(f pl)* Fr
De stillschweigende Bedingungen *(f pl)*
En implied terms
Es condiciones implícitas *(f pl)*
It condizioni implicite *(f pl)*
Pt condições implícitas *(f pl)*

**condition suspensive** *(f)* Fr
De aufschiebende Bedingung *(f)*
En condition precedent
Es previa condición *(f)*
It condizione sospensiva *(f)*
Pt condição prévia *(f)*

**con dividendo** Es, It
De mit Dividende
En cum dividend
Fr droit attaché
Pt com dividendo

**condizionale** *adj* It
De bedingt
En conditional
Es condicional
Fr conditionnel
Pt condicional

**condizionamento dell'aria** *(m)* It
De Klimatisierung *(f)*
En air-conditioning
Es acondicionamiento de aire *(m)*
Fr climatisation *(f)*
Pt condicionamento do ar *(m)*

**condizione** *(f)* *n* It
De Bedingung *(f)*
En condition
Es condición *(f)*
Fr condition *(f)*
Pt condição *(f)*

**condizione sospensiva** *(f)* It
De aufschiebende Bedingung *(f)*
En condition precedent
Es previa condición *(f)*
Fr condition suspensive *(f)*
Pt condição prévia *(f)*

**condizioni** *(f pl)* *n* It
De Bedingungen *(f pl)*
En terms
Es condiciones *(f pl)*
Fr conditions *(f pl)*
Pt condições *(f pl)*

**condizioni del mercato** *(f pl)* It
De Marktumständen *(m pl)*
En state of the market
Es condiciones del mercado *(f pl)*
Fr état du marché *(m)*
Pt situação do mercado *(f)*

**condizioni di lavoro** *(f pl)* It
De Arbeitsbedingungen *(f pl)*
En working conditions
Es condiciones de trabajo *(f pl)*
Fr conditions de travail *(f pl)*
Pt condições de trabalho *(f pl)*

**condizioni di pagamento** *(f pl)* It
De Zahlungsbedingungen *(f pl)*
En payment terms
Es condiciones de pago *(f pl)*
Fr conditions de paiement *(f pl)*
Pt condições de pagamento *(f pl)*

**condizioni implicite** *(f pl)* It
De stillschweigende Bedingungen *(f pl)*
En implied terms
Es condiciones implícitas *(f pl)*
Fr conditions implicites *(f pl)*
Pt condições implícitas *(f pl)*

**condizioni normali** *(f pl)* It
De Standardbedingungen *(f pl)*
En standard conditions
Es condiciones normales *(f pl)*
Fr conditions courantes *(f pl)*
Pt condições normais *(f pl)*

**condominio** *(m)* n It
De Miteigentum *(n)*
En co-ownership
Es copropiedad *(f)*
Fr copropriété *(f)*
Pt copropriedade *(f)*

**condotta leale** *(f)* It
De anständige Handlungs–
   weise *(f)*
En fair play
Es juego limpio *(m)*
Fr traitement juste *(m)*
Pt jogo limpo *(m)*

**con esto** Es
De hiermit
En herewith
Fr ci-joint; sous ce pli
It qui unito; con la presente
Pt incluso; junto

**conference** n En
De Kongress *(m)*
Es conferencia *(f)*
Fr conférence *(f)*
It conferenza *(f)*
Pt conferência *(f)*

**conférence** *(f)* n Fr
De Kongress *(m)*
En conference
Es conferencia *(f)*
It conferenza *(f)*
Pt conferência *(f)*

**conferencia** *(f)* n Es
De Kongress *(m)*
En conference
Fr conférence *(f)*
It conferenza *(f)*
Pt conferência *(f)*

**conferência** *(f)* n Pt
De Kongress *(m)*
En conference
Es conferencia *(f)*
Fr conférence *(f)*
It conferenza *(f)*

**conferenza** *(f)* n It
De Kongress *(m)*
En conference
Es conferencia *(f)*
Fr conférence *(f)*
Pt conferência *(f)*

**conférer des pleins pouvoirs**
   Fr
De eine Vollmacht erteilen
En execute a power of attor-
   ney
Es otorgar poder notarial
It conferire una procura
Pt dar execução a poderes de
   procuração

**conferire una procura** It
De eine Vollmacht erteilen
En execute a power of attor-
   ney
Es otorgar poder notarial
Fr conférer des pleins pou-
   voirs
Pt dar execução a poderes de
   procuração

**conferma** *(f)* n It
De Bestätigung *(f)*
En confirmation
Es confirmación *(f)*
Fr confirmation *(f)*
Pt confirmação *(f)*

**confermare** *vb* It
De bestätigen
En confirm
Es confirmar
Fr confirmer
Pt confirmar

**confermare per iscritto** It
De schriftlich bestätigen
En confirm in writing
Es confirmar por escrito
Fr confirmer par écrit
Pt confirmar por escrito

**confiar** *vb* Es, Pt
De anvertrauen
En entrust
Fr confier
It affidare

**confidence trick** En
Am confidence game
De Schwindlertrick *(m)*
Es timo *(m)*
Fr escroquerie *(f)*
It truffa all'americana *(f)*
Pt conto do vigário *(m)*

**confier** *vb* Fr
De anvertrauen
En entrust

Es confiar
It affidare
Pt confiar

**confirm** *vb* En
De bestätigen
Es confirmar
Fr confirmer
It confermare
Pt confirmar

**confirmação** *(f)* n Pt
De Bestätigung *(f)*
En confirmation
Es confirmación *(f)*
Fr confirmation *(f)*
It conferma *(f)*

**confirmación** *(f)* n Es
De Bestätigung *(f)*
En confirmation
Fr confirmation *(f)*
It conferma *(f)*
Pt confirmação *(f)*

**confirmar** *vb* Es, Pt
De bestätigen
En confirm
Fr confirmer
It confermare

**confirmar por escrito** Es, Pt
De schriftlich bestätigen
En confirm in writing
Fr confirmer par écrit
It confermare per iscritto

**confirmation** n En, Fr *(f)*
De Bestätigung *(f)*
Es confirmación *(f)*
It conferma *(f)*
Pt confirmação *(f)*

**confirmed irrevocable letter**
   **of credit** En
De bestätigter unwiderruflicher
   Kreditbrief *(m)*
Es carta de crédito irrevocable
   confirmada *(f)*
Fr lettre de crédit irrévocable
   confirmée *(f)*
It lettera di credito confer-
   mata e irrevocabile *(f)*
Pt carta de crédito irrevogável
   confirmada *(f)*

**confirmed letter of credit** En
De bestätigter Kreditbrief (m)
Es carta de crédito confirmada (f)
Fr lettre de crédit confirmée (f)
It lettera di credito confermata (f)
Pt carta de crédito confirmada (f)

**confirmer** vb Fr
De bestätigen
En confirm
Es confirmar
It confermare
Pt confirmar

**confirmer par écrit** Fr
De schriftlich bestätigen
En confirm in writing
Es confirmar por escrito
It confermare per iscritto
Pt confirmar por escrito

**confirm in writing** En
De schriftlich bestätigen
Es confirmar por escrito
Fr confirmer par écrit
It confermare per iscritto
Pt confirmar por escrito

**conflict** n En
De Konflikt (m)
Es conflicto (m)
Fr conflit (m)
It conflitto (m)
Pt conflito (m)

**conflicto** (m) n Es
De Konflikt (m)
En conflict
Fr conflit (m)
It conflitto (m)
Pt conflito (m)

**conflict of interest** En
De widerstreitende Interessen (n pl)
Es pugna de intereses (f)
Fr opposition d'intérêts (f)
It conflitto d'interessi (m)
Pt conflito de interesses (m)

**conflicto laboral** (m) Es
De Arbeitskonflikt (m)
En industrial dispute
Fr conflit ouvrier (m)

It vertenza operaia (f)
Pt conflito de trabalho (m)

**conflit** (m) n Fr
De Konflikt (m)
En conflict
Es conflicto (m)
It conflitto (m)
Pt conflito (m)

**conflit du travail** (m) Fr
De Arbeitsstreitigkeit (f)
En trade dispute
Es conflicto laboral (m)
It vertenza di lavoro (f)
Pt conflito comercial (m)

**conflito** (m) n Pt
De Konflikt (m)
En conflict
Es conflicto (m)
Fr conflit (m)
It conflitto (m)

**conflito comercial** (m) Pt
De Arbeitsstreitigkeit (f)
En trade dispute
Es conflicto laboral (m)
Fr conflit du travail (m)
It vertenza di lavoro (f)

**conflito de interesses** (m) Pt
De widerstreitende Interessen (n pl)
En conflict of interest
Es pugna de intereses (f)
Fr opposition d'intérêts (f)
It conflitto d'interessi (m)

**conflito de trabalho** (m) Pt
De Arbeitskonflikt (m)
En industrial dispute
Es conflicto laboral (m)
Fr conflit ouvrier (m)
It vertenza operaia (f)

**conflit ouvrier** (m) Fr
De Arbeitskonflikt (m)
En industrial dispute
Es conflicto laboral (m)
It vertenza operaia (f)
Pt conflito de trabalho (m)

**conflitto** (m) n It
De Konflikt (m)
En conflict
Es conflicto (m)

Fr conflit (m)
Pt conflito (m)

**conflitto d'interessi** (m) It
De widerstreitende Interessen (n pl)
En conflict of interest
Es pugna de intereses (f)
Fr opposition d'intérêts (f)
Pt conflito de interesses (m)

**conforme à** Fr
De in Übereinstimmung mit
En in accordance with
Es en conformidad con
It in conformità con
Pt em conformidade com

**congedare** vb It
De entlassen
En dismiss
Am fire
Es despedir
Fr congédier
Pt despedir

**congédiement** (m) n Fr
De Entlassung (f)
En dismissal
Am firing
Es despido (m)
It licenziamento (m)
Pt despedimento (m)

**congédier** vb Fr
De entlassen
En dismiss
Am fire
Es despedir
It congedare
Pt despedir

**congédier un employé** Fr
De einen Arbeitnehmer entlassen
En discharge an employee
Am fire an employee
Es despedir a un empleado
It licenziare un impiegato
Pt despedir um empregado

**congelação de salários** (f) Pt
De Lohnstopp (m)
En wage-freeze
Es bloqueo de salarios (m)
Fr blocage des salaires (m)
It blocco dei salari (m)

**congés payés** *(m pl)* Fr
De bezahlter Urlaub *(m)*
En holidays with pay
Es vacaciones retribuidas *(f pl)*
It vacanze retribuite *(f pl)*
Pt férias pagas *(f pl)*

**congettura** *(f) n* It
De Mutmassung *(f)*
En guess-work
Es conjetura *(f)*
Fr conjecture *(f)*
Pt conjectura *(f)*

**conhecimento** *(m) n* Pt
De Kenntnis *(f)*
En knowledge
Es conocimientos *(m pl)*
Fr connaissance *(f)*
It conoscenza *(f)*

**conhecimento** (de embarque)
*(m)* Pt
De Konnossement *(n)*
En bill of lading
Es conocimiento (de embar-
que) *(m)*
Fr connaissement *(m)*
It polizza de carico *(f)*

**conhecimento com embargos**
*(m)* Pt
De einschränkendes Konnossement *(n)*
En foul (dirty) bill of lading
Es conocimiento de embarque
con objecciones *(m)*
Fr connaissement avec ré-
serve *(m)*
It polizza di carico con riserve
*(f)*

**conhecimento de carga
embarcada** *(m)* Pt
De Hafenkonnossement *(n)*
En shipped bill of lading
Es conocimiento de embarque
a bordo *(m)*
Fr connaissement de mar-
chandises à bord *(m)*
It polizza di carico con merce
a bordo *(f)*

**conhecimento sem embargos**
*(m)* Pt
De echtes Konnossement *(n)*
En clean bill of lading

Es conocimiento de embarque
sin objeciones *(m)*
Fr connaissement sans ré-
serve *(m)*
It polizza di carico senza
riserve *(f)*

**conjectura** *(f) n* Pt
De Mutmassung *(f)*
En guess-work
Es conjetura *(f)*
Fr conjecture *(f)*
It congettura *(f)*

**conjecture** *(f) n* Fr
De Mutmassung *(f)*
En guess-work
Es conjetura *(f)*
It congettura *(f)*
Pt conjectura *(f)*

**conjetura** *(f) n* Es
De Mutmassung *(f)*
En guess-work
Fr conjecture *(f)*
It congettura *(f)*
Pt conjectura *(f)*

**conjointement et solidaire-
ment** Fr
De gesamtschuldnerisch
En jointly and severally
Es en conjunto y separada-
mente
It solidalmente e individual-
mente
Pt em conjunto e por vários

**conjunto de rutinas** *(m)* Es
De Programmausrüstung *(f)*
En (computer) software
Fr software *(m)*
It programmatura; software *(f
m)*
Pt sistema lógico; software
*(m)*

**connaissance** *(f) n* Fr
De Kenntnis *(f)*
En knowledge
Es conocimientos *(m pl)*
It conoscenza *(f)*
Pt conhecimento *(m)*

**connaissement** *(m)* Fr
De Konnossement *(n)*
En bill of lading

Es conocimiento (de embar-
que) *(m)*
It polizza de carico *(f)*
Pt conhecimento *(m)*

**connaissement avec réserve**
*(m)* Fr
De einschränkendes Konnossement *(n)*
En foul (dirty) bill of lading
Es conocimiento de embarque
con objecciones *(m)*
It polizza di carico con riserve
*(f)*
Pt conhecimento com embargos *(m)*

**connaissement de marchan-
dises à bord** *(m)* Fr
De Hafenkonnossement *(n)*
En shipped bill of lading
Es conocimiento de embarque
a bordo *(m)*
It polizza di carico con merce
a bordo *(f)*
Pt conhecimento de carga
embarcada *(m)*

**connaissement sans réserve**
*(m)* Fr
De echtes Konnossement *(n)*
En clean bill of lading
Es conocimiento de embarque
sin objeciones *(m)*
It polizza di carico senza
riserve *(f)*
Pt conhecimento sem embar-
gos *(m)*

**conocimiento (de embarque)**
*(m)* Es
De Konnossement *(n)*
En bill of lading
Fr connaissement *(m)*
It polizza de carico *(f)*
Pt conhecimento *(m)*

**conocimiento de embarque a
bordo** *(m)* Es
De Hafenkonnossement *(n)*
En shipped bill of lading
Fr connaissement de mar-
chandises à bord *(m)*
It polizza di carico con merce
a bordo *(f)*
Pt conhecimento de carga
embarcada *(m)*

**conocimiento de embarque con objecciones** *(m)* Es
De einschränkendes Konnossement *(n)*
En foul (dirty) bill of lading
Fr connaissement avec réserve *(m)*
It polizza di carico con riserve *(f)*
Pt conhecimento com embargos *(m)*

**conocimiento de embarque sin objecciones** *(m)* Es
De echtes Konnossement *(n)*
En clean bill of lading
Fr connaissement sans réserve *(m)*
It polizza di carico senza riserve *(f)*
Pt conhecimento sem embargos *(m)*

**conocimientos** *(m pl)* n Es
De Kenntnis *(f)*
En knowledge
Fr connaissance *(f)*
It conoscenza *(f)*
Pt conhecimento *(m)*

**conoscenza** *(f)* n It
De Kenntnis *(f)*
En knowledge
Es conocimientos *(m pl)*
Fr connaissance *(f)*
Pt conhecimento *(m)*

**con plico a parte** It
De getrennt
En under separate cover
Es por separado
Fr sous pli séparé
Pt em separado

**con recurso** Es
De mit Rückgriff
En with recourse
Fr avec droit de recours
It con ricorso
Pt com recurso

**con ricorso** It
De mit Rückgriff
En with recourse
Es con recurso
Fr avec droit de recours
Pt com recurso

**consegna** *(f)* n It
De Lieferung; Versendung *(f)*
En delivery; consignment
Es entrega; consignación *(f)*
Fr livraison; envoi *(f m)*
Pt entrega; consignação *(f)*

**consegna a termine** *(f)* It
De Terminlieferung *(f)*
En forward delivery
Es entrega futura *(f)*
Fr livraison à terme *(f)*
Pt entrega futura *(f)*

**consegna deficiente** *(f)* It
De mangelhafte Lieferung *(f)*
En short delivery
Es entrega deficiente *(f)*
Fr livraison incomplète *(f)*
Pt entrega insuficiente *(f)*

**consegna franco** It
De portofreie Lieferung
En delivery free
Es libre entrega
Fr livré franco
Pt remessa gratuita

**consegnare** *vb* It
De konsignieren; übersenden
En consign
Es consignar
Fr consigner
Pt consignar

**consegnatario** *(m)* n It
De Empfänger *(m)*
En consignee
Es consignatario *(m)*
Fr destinataire *(m)*
Pt consignatário *(m)*

**conseil** *(m)* n Fr
De Rat; Berater *(m)*
En council; consultant
Es consejo; consultor *(m)*
It consiglio; consulente *(m)*
Pt conselho; consultor *(m)*

**conseil d'administration** *(m)* Fr
De Vorstand *(m)*
En board of directors
Es consejo de administración *(m)*
It consiglio d'amministrazione *(m)*
Pt direcção *(f)*

**conseil en brevets** *(m)* Fr
De Patentanwalt *(m)*
En patent agent
Es agente de patentes *(m)*
It agente di brevetti *(m)*
Pt agente de patentes *(m)*

**conseil en publicité** *(m)* Fr
De Werbeberater *(m)*
En advertising consultant
Es consultor de publicidad *(m)*
It consulente di pubblicità *(m)*
Pt perito de publicidade *(m)*

**consejo** *(m)* n Es
De Rat *(m)*
En council
Fr conseil *(m)*
It consiglio *(m)*
Pt conselho *(m)*

**consejo consultivo** *(m)* Es
De Beratungsausschuss *(m)*
En advisory board
Fr comité consultatif *(m)*
It consiglio consultivo *(m)*
Pt comité consultivo *(m)*

**consejo de administración** *(m)* Es
De Vorstand *(m)*
En board of directors
Fr conseil d'administration *(m)*
It consiglio d'amministrazione *(m)*
Pt direcção *(f)*

**conselho** *(m)* n Pt
De Rat *(m)*
En council
Es consejo *(m)*
Fr conseil *(m)*
It consiglio *(m)*

**consentir (une remise)** Fr
De gewähren (einen Rabatt)
En allow (a discount)
Es conceder (un descuento)
It concedere (uno sconto)
Pt conceder (um desconto)

**consequential damages** En
De immaterieller Schaden *(m)*
Es daños indirectos *(m pl)*
Fr dommages indirects *(m pl)*
It danni indiretti *(m pl)*
Pt danos decorrentes *(m pl)*

**consequential loss** En
De Folgeschaden *(m)*
Es pérdida indirecta *(f)*
Fr perte indirect *(f)*
It perdita indiretta *(f)*
Pt perda por consequência *(f)*

**conserje** *(m)* n Es
De Hausmeister *(m)*
En hall-porter
Fr concierge *(m)*
It portiere *(m)*
Pt porteiro *(m)*

**consertar** *vb* Pt
De reparieren
En repair
Es reparar; componer
Fr réparer; réfectionner
It riparare; rifare

**conservative estimate** En
De vorsichtige Schätzung *(f)*
Es presupuesto prudente *(m)*
Fr évaluation prudente *(f)*
It valutazione prudente *(f)*
Pt avaliação cautelosa *(f)*

**consiglio** *(m)* n It
De Rat *(m)*
En council
Es consejo *(m)*
Fr conseil *(m)*
Pt conselho *(m)*

**consiglio consultivo** *(m)* It
De Beratungsausschuss *(m)*
En advisory board
Es consejo consultivo *(m)*
Fr comité consultatif *(m)*
Pt comité consultivo *(m)*

**consignação** *(f)* n Pt
De Versendung; Übertragung *(f)*
En consignment; assignment
Es consignación; cesión *(f)*
Fr expédition; cession *(f)*
It consegna; cessione *(f)*

**consignación** *(f)* n Es
De Versendung *(f)*
En consignment
Fr envoi; expédition *(m f)*
It consegna; spedizione *(f)*
Pt consignação *(f)*

**consignador** *(m)* n Es, Pt
De Absender *(m)*
En consignor
Fr expéditeur *(m)*
It speditore *(m)*

**consignar** *vb* Es, Pt
De konsignieren; übersenden
En consign
Fr consigner
It consegnare

**consignatario** *(m)* n Es
De Empfänger *(m)*
En consignee
Fr destinataire *(m)*
It consegnatario *(m)*
Pt consignatário *(m)*

**consignatário** *(m)* n Pt
De Empfänger *(m)*
En consignee
Es consignatario *(m)*
Fr destinataire *(m)*
It consegnatario *(m)*

**consignee** n En
De Empfänger *(m)*
Es consignatario *(m)*
Fr destinataire *(m)*
It consegnatario *(m)*
Pt consignatário *(m)*

**consigner** *vb* Fr
De konsignieren; übersenden
En consign
Es consignar
It consegnare
Pt consignar

**consignment** n En
De Versendung *(f)*
Es consignación *(f)*
Fr envoi; expédition *(m f)*
It consegna; spedizione *(f)*
Pt consignação *(f)*

**consignment note** En
De Frachtbrief *(m)*
Es nota de consignación *(f)*
Fr lettre de voiture *(f)*
It nota di spedizione *(f)*
Pt guia de consignação *(f)*

**consignor** n En
De Absender *(m)*
Es consignador *(m)*
Fr expéditeur *(m)*

It speditore *(m)*
Pt consignante *(m)*

**consolato** *(m)* n It
De Konsulat *(n)*
En consulate
Es consulado *(m)*
Fr consulat *(m)*
Pt consulado *(m)*

**console** *(m)* n It
De Konsul *(m)*
En consul
Es cónsul *(m)*
Fr consul *(m)*
Pt cônsul *(m)*

**consolidado** *adj* Es, Pt
De konsolidiert
En consolidated
Fr consolidé
It consolidato

**consolidare** *vb* It
De fundieren
En fund
Es fundar; consolidar
Fr fonder; consolider
Pt dotar de fundos

**consolidated** *adj* En
De konsolidiert
Es consolidado
Fr consolidé
It consolidato
Pt consolidado

**consolidated accounts** En
De konsolidierter Kontenabschluss *(m)*
Es cuentas consolidadas *(f pl)*
Fr comptes consolidés *(m pl)*
It conti consolidati *(m pl)*
Pt contas consolidadas *(f pl)*

**consolidato** *adj* It
De konsolidiert
En consolidated
Es consolidado
Fr consolidé
Pt consolidado

**consolidé** *adj* Fr
De konsolidiert
En consolidated
Es consolidado
It consolidato
Pt consolidado

**consommateur** *(m)* n Fr
De Verbraucher; Konsument *(m)*
En consumer
Es consumidor *(m)*
It consumatore *(m)*
Pt consumidor *(m)*

**consommation** *(f)* n Fr
De Verbrauch *(m)*
En consumption
Es consumición *(f)*
It consumo *(m)*
Pt consumo *(m)*

**consorcio** *(m)* n Es
De Konsortium *(n)*
En consortium
Fr consortium *(m)*
It consorzio *(m)*
Pt consórcio *(m)*

**consórcio** *(m)* n Pt
De Konsortium *(n)*
En consortium
Es consorcio *(m)*
Fr consortium *(m)*
It consorzio *(m)*

**consórcio de seguradores** *(m)* Pt
De Versicherungssyndikat *(n)*
En underwriting syndicate (insurance)
Es sindicato de seguros *(m)*
Fr syndicat d'assureurs *(m)*
It sindacato di assicuratori *(m)*

**consórcio de subscritores** *(m)* Pt
De Emissionssyndikat *(n)*
En underwriting syndicate (new issues)
Es grupo de suscriptores *(m)*
Fr syndicat de garantie *(m)*
It consorzio finanziario *(m)*

**consortium** n En, Fr *(m)*
De Konsortium *(n)*
Es consorcio *(m)*
It consorzio *(m)*
Pt consórcio *(m)*

**consorzio** *(m)* n It
De Konsortium *(n)*
En consortium
Es consorcio *(m)*

Fr consortium *(m)*
Pt consórcio *(m)*

**consorzio finanziario** *(m)* It
De Syndikat *(n)*
En syndicate
Es sindicato *(m)*
Fr syndicat *(m)*
Pt sindicato *(m)*

**consorzio per investimenti** *(m)* It
De Investment-Trust *(m)*
En investment trust
Es fideicomiso de inversiones *(m)*
Fr société fiduciaire de placements *(f)*
Pt instituição de investimentos *(f)*

**constituer** *vb* Fr
De bilden
En form; constitute
Es constituir
It constituire
Pt constituir

**constituir** *vb* Es, Pt
De bilden
En form; constitute
Fr constituer
It constituire

**constituire** *vb* It
De bilden
En form; constitute
Es constituir
Fr constituer
Pt constituir

**construction électrique** *(f)* Fr
De Elektrotechnik *(f)*
En electrical engineering
Es ingeniería eléctrica *(f)*
It elettrotecnica *(f)*
Pt engenharia electrotécnica *(f)*

**construction fautive** *(f)* Fr
De schlechte Ausführung *(f)*
En faulty design
Es diseño defectuoso *(m)*
It concezione difettosa *(f)*
Pt desenho defeituoso *(m)*

**construction mécanique** *(f)* Fr
De Maschinenbau *(m)*
En mechanical engineering
Es ingeniería mecánica *(f)*
It ingegneria meccanica *(f)*
Pt engenharia mecânica *(f)*

**constructive total loss** En
De angenommener Totalverlust *(m)*
Es pérdida total constructiva *(f)*
Fr perte réputée totale *(f)*
It perdita presunta totale *(f)*
Pt perda total construtiva *(f)*

**constructor de obras** *(m)* Pt
De Bauunternehmer *(m)*
En building contractor
Es contratista de obras *(m)*
Fr entrepreneur de bâtiment *(m)*
It impresa edile *(f)*

**consul** n En, Fr *(m)*
De Konsul *(m)*
Es cónsul *(m)*
It console *(m)*
Pt cônsul *(m)*

**cónsul** *(m)* n Es
De Konsul *(m)*
En consul
Fr consul *(m)*
It console *(m)*
Pt cônsul *(m)*

**cônsul** *(m)* n Pt
De Konsul *(m)*
En consul
Es cónsul *(m)*
Fr consul *(m)*
It console *(m)*

**consulado** *(m)* n Es, Pt
De Konsulat *(n)*
En consulate
Fr consulat *(m)*
It consolato *(m)*

**consular invoice** En
De Konsulatsfaktura *(f)*
Es factura consular *(f)*
Fr facture consulaire *(f)*
It fattura consolare *(f)*
Pt factura consular *(f)*

**consulat** (m) n Fr
De Konsulat (n)
En consulate
Es consulado (m)
It consolato (m)
Pt consulado (m)

**consulate** n En
De Konsulat (n)
Es consulado (m)
Fr consulat (m)
It consolato (m)
Pt consulado (m)

**consulente** (m) n It
De Berater (m)
En consultant
Es consultor (m)
Fr conseil (m)
Pt consultor (m)

**consulente di direzione azien-
    dale** (m) It
De Geschäftsführungsberater
    (m)
En management consultant
Es asesor administrativo (m)
Fr ingénieur-conseil en org-
    anisation (m)
Pt perito de administração (m)

**consulente di pubblicità** (m) It
De Werbeberater (m)
En advertising consultant
Es consultor de publicidad (m)
Fr conseil en publicité (m)
Pt perito de publicidade (m)

**consultant** n En
De Berater (m)
Es consultor (m)
Fr conseil (m)
It consulente (m)
Pt consultor (m)

**consultatif** adj Fr
De Beratungs-
En advisory
Es consultivo
It consultivo
Pt consultivo

**consultivo** adj Es, It, Pt
De Beratungs-
En advisory
Fr consultatif

**consultor** (m) n Es, Pt
De Berater (m)
En consultant
Fr conseil (m)
It consulente (m)

**consultor de publicidad** (m) Es
De Werbeberater (m)
En advertising consultant
Fr conseil en publicité (m)
It consulente di pubblicità (m)
Pt perito de publicidade (m)

**consumatore** (m) n It
De Verbraucher; Konsument
    (m)
En consumer
Es consumidor (m)
Fr consommateur (m)
Pt consumidor (m)

**consumer** n En
De Verbraucher; Konsument
    (m)
Es consumidor (m)
Fr consommateur (m)
It consumatore (m)
Pt consumidor (m)

**consumer durables** En
De dauerhafte Konsumgüter (n
    pl)
Es bienes de consumo dura-
    deros (m pl)
Fr biens de consommation
    durables (m pl)
It beni di consumo durabili
    (m pl)
Pt artigos de consumo per-
    duraveis (m pl)

**consumer goods** En
De Konsumgüter (n pl)
Es bienes de consumo (m pl)
Fr biens de consommation (m
    pl)
It beni di consumo (m pl)
Pt bens de consumo (m pl)

**consumer group** En
De Abnehmerverein (m)
Es grupo de consumidores (m)
Fr groupe consommateur (m)
It gruppo di consumatori (m)
Pt grupo de consumidores (m)

**consumer non-durables** En
De nicht-dauerhafte Ver-
    brauchsgüter (n pl)
Es bienes de consumo pere-
    cederos (m pl)
Fr biens de consommation
    non-durables (m pl)
It beni di consumo non dure-
    voli (m pl)
Pt bens de consumo não
    duráveis (m pl)

**consumición** (f) n Es
De Verbrauch (m)
En consumption
Fr consommation (f)
It consumo (m)
Pt consumo (m)

**consumidor** (m) n Es, Pt
De Verbraucher; Konsument
    (m)
En consumer
Fr consommateur (m)
It consumatore (m)

**consumo** (m) n It, Pt
De Verbrauch (m)
En consumption
Es consumición (f)
Fr consommation (f)

**consumo naturale** (m) It
De natürlicher Abgang (m)
En natural wastage
Es merma natural (f)
Fr déperdition naturelle (f)
Pt desperdício natural (m)

**consumption** n En
De Verbrauch (m)
Es consumición (f)
Fr consommation (f)
It consumo (m)
Pt consumo (m)

**conta** (bancária) (f) n Pt
De Konto (n)
En account
Es cuenta (f)
Fr compte (m)
It conto (m)

**conta** (nota) (f) n Pt
De Rechnung (f)
En bill; account
Es cuenta, nota (f)

Fr compte; note *(m f)*
It conto; nota *(m f)*

**conta a descoberto** *(f)* Pt
De Überziehung *(f)*
En overdraft
Es sobregiro; saldo deudor *(m)*
Fr découvert; solde débiteur *(m)*
It scoperto *(m)*

**conta bancária** *(f)* Pt
De Bankkonto *(n)*
En bank account
Es cuenta bancaria *(f)*
Fr compte en banque *(m)*
It conto in banca *(m)*

**contabile** *(m)* n It
De Buchhalter *(m)*
En accountant
Es contador *(m)*
Fr comptable *(m)*
Pt contabilista *(m)*

**contabile dei costi di pro-
duzione** *(m)* It
De Kalkulator *(m)*
En cost accountant
Es contable de costes *(m)*
Fr comptable de prix de
revient *(m)*
Pt calculador de custos *(m)*

**contabilidad** *(f)* n Es
De Buchhaltung *(f)*
En accountancy; book-keeping
Fr comptabilité *(f)*
It contabilità *(f)*
Pt contabilidade *(f)*

**contabilidade** *(f)* n Pt
De Buchhaltung *(f)*
En accountancy; book-keeping
Es contabilidad *(f)*
Fr comptabilité *(f)*
It contabilità *(f)*

**contabilidad por partida sen-
cilla** *(f)* Es
De einfache Buchführung *(f)*
En single-entry book-keeping
Fr comptabilité en partie sim-
ple *(f)*
It contabilità in partita sem-
plice *(f)*
Pt contabilização por lan-
çamento simples *(f)*

**contabilista** *(m)* n Pt
De Buchhalter *(m)*
En accountant
Es contador *(m)*
Fr comptable *(m)*
It contabile *(m)*

**contabilità** *(f)* n It
De Buchhaltung *(f)*
En accountancy; book-keeping
Es contabilidad *(f)*
Fr comptabilité *(f)*
Pt contabilidade *(f)*

**contabilità in partita semplice**
*(f)* It
De einfache Buchführung *(f)*
En single-entry book-keeping
Es contabilidad por partida
sencilla *(f)*
Fr comptabilité en partie sim-
ple *(f)*
Pt contabilização por lan-
çamento simples *(f)*

**contabilização por lançam-
ento simples** *(f)* Pt
De einfache Buchführung *(f)*
En single-entry book-keeping
Es contabilidad por partida
sencilla *(f)*
Fr comptabilité en partie sim-
ple *(f)*
It contabilità in partita sem-
plice *(f)*

**contable** *(m)* Es
De Buchhalter *(m)*
En ledger clerk
Am book-keeper
Fr commis-contable *(m)*
It contabile *(m)*
Pt empregado de contabili-
dade *(m)*

**contable de costes** *(m)* Es
De Kalkulator *(m)*
En cost accountant
Fr comptable de prix de
revient *(m)*
It contabile dei costi di
produzione *(m)*
Pt calculador de custos *(m)*

**conta bloqueada** *(f)* Pt
De gesperrtes Konto *(n)*
En blocked account
Es cuenta bloqueada *(f)*

Fr compte bloqué *(m)*
It conto bloccato *(m)*

**conta comercial** *(f)* Pt
De Handelskonto *(n)*
En trade account
Es cuenta comercial *(f)*
Fr compte commercial *(m)*
It conto commerciale *(m)*

**conta conjunta** *(f)* Pt
De Gemeinschaftskonto *(n)*
En joint account
Es cuenta común *(f)*
Fr compte joint *(m)*
It conto in comune *(m)*

**conta corrente** *(f)* Pt
De Kontokorrent *(n)*
En current account
Am checking account
Es cuenta corriente *(f)*
Fr compte courant *(m)*
It conto corrente *(m)*

**conta de adiantamentos** *(f)* Pt
De Darlehenskonto *(n)*
En advance account
Es cuenta de anticipos *(f)*
Fr compte d'avances *(m)*
It conto anticipo *(m)*

**conta de ágio** *(f)* Pt
De Agiokonto *(n)*
En agio account
Es cuenta de agio *(f)*
Fr compte d'agio *(m)*
It conto d'aggio *(m)*

**conta de apropriação** *(f)* Pt
De Rückstellungskonto *(n)*
En appropriation account
Es cuenta de apropiación *(f)*
Fr compte d'affectation *(m)*
It conto di stanziamento *(m)*

**conta de capital** *(f)* Pt
De Kapitalkonto *(n)*
En capital account
Es cuenta de capital *(f)*
Fr compte capital *(m)*
It conto capitale *(m)*

**conta de compensação de
transacções** *(f)* Pt
De Währungsausgleichsfonds
*(m)*

En exchange equalization account
Es cuenta de compensación de cambio (f)
Fr fonds de stabilisation des changes (m pl)
It conto per la stabilizzazione dei cambi (m)

**conta de controlo** (f) Pt
De Kontrollkonto (n)
En control account
Es cuenta de control (f)
Fr compte de contrôle (m)
It conto di controllo (m)

**conta de depósito** (m) Pt
De Depositenkonto (n)
En deposit account
Am interest-bearing account
Es cuenta de ahorras (f)
Fr compte de dépôt (m)
It conto di deposito (m)

**conta de descargas** (f) Pt
De Löschungskonto (n)
En landing account
Es cuenta de desembarque (f)
Fr compte de mise à terre (m)
It conto di sbarco (m)

**conta de empréstimos** (f) Pt
De Anleihekonto (n)
En loan account
Es cuenta de préstamos (f)
Fr compte des prêts (m)
It conto anticipazioni (m)

**conta de especulações bai-**
**xistas** (f) Pt
De Baissekonto (n)
En bear account
Es cuenta de especulaciones a la baja (f)
Fr compte des speculations à la baisse (m)
It conto di speculazioni al ribasso (m)

**conta de lucros e perdas** (f) Pt
De Gewinn- und Verlustkonto (n)
En profit and loss account
Es cuenta de ganancias y pérdidas (f)
Fr compte profits et pertes (m)
It conto profitti e perdite (m)

**conta de receitas e despesas**
(f) Pt
De Ausgaben- und Ertrags-konto (n)
En income and expenditure account
Es cuenta de ingresos y gastos (f)
Fr compte de revenus et dépenses (m)
It conto proventi e spese (m)

**contador** (m) n Es
De Buchhalter (m)
En accountant
Fr comptable (m)
It contabile (m)
Pt contabilista (m)

**contador de navio** (m) Es
De Zahlmeister (m)
En purser
Fr commissaire de la marine (m)
It commissario di bordo (m)
Pt commissário de bordo (m)

**contador habilitado** (m) Es
De Wirtschaftsprüfer (m)
En qualified accountant
Fr expert comptable (m)
It ragioniere diplomato (m)
Pt guarda-livros diplomado (m)

**conta externa** (f) Pt
De Auslandskonto (n)
En external account
Am foreign currency account
Es cuenta exterior (f)
Fr compte transférable (m)
It conto estero (m)

**conta impessoal** (f) Pt
De Firmenkonto (n)
En impersonal account
Es cuenta simulada (f)
Fr compte impersonnel (m)
It conto d'ordine (m)

**containerisation** (f) n Fr
De Containerisation (f)
En containerization
Es contenedorización (f)
It containerization (f)
Pt containerização (f)

**Containerisation** (f) n De
En containerization
Es contenedorización (f)
Fr containerisation (f)
It containerization (f)
Pt containerização (f)

**containerização** (f) n Pt
De Containerisation (f)
En containerization
Es contenedorización (f)
Fr containerisation (f)
It containerization (f)

**containerization** n En, It (f)
De Containerisation (f)
Es contenedorización (f)
Fr containerisation (f)
Pt containerização (f)

**Containerschiff** (n) n De
En container ship
Es barco de contenedores (m)
Fr navire porte-containers (m)
It nave da contenitori (f)
Pt navio de contentres (m)

**container ship** En
De Containerschiff (n)
Es barco de contenedores (m)
Fr navire porte-containers (m)
It nave da contenitori (f)
Pt navio de contentres (m)

**conta nominal** (f) Pt
De Firmenkonto (n)
En nominal account
Es cuenta de resultado (f)
Fr compte nominal (m)
It conto d'ordine (m)

**contanti contro documenti** It
De bar gegen Versandpapiere
En cash against documents (c.a.d.)
Es al contado contra documen-tos
Fr comptant contre docum-ents
Pt em dinheiro contra docu-mentação

**conta numerada** (f) Pt
De numeriertes Konto (n)
En numbered account
Es cuenta identificada con número (f)

Fr compte identifié par numéro (m)
It conto identificato da numero (m)

**conta pendente** (m) Pt
De Ubergangskonto (n)
En suspense account
Es cuenta suspensa (f)
Fr compte d'ordre (m)
It conto sospeso (m)

**conta pessoal** (f) Pt
De Kundenkonto (n)
En charge account
Es cuenta personal (f)
Fr compte personnel (m)
It conto personale (m)

**conta remetida** (f) Pt
De zur Begleichung vorgelegte Rechnung (f)
En account rendered
Es cuenta rendida (f)
Fr compte rendu (m)
It conto reso (m)

**contas anuais** (f) Pt
De Jahresabschluss (m)
En annual accounts
Es balance anual (m)
Fr bilan annuel (m)
It bilancio annuale (m)

**contas a pagar** (f pl) Pt
De Kreditoren (m pl)
En accounts payable
Es cuentas a pagar (f pl)
Fr comptes à payer (m pl)
It conti passivi (m pl)

**contas a receber** (f pl) Pt
De Debitoren (m pl)
En accounts receivable
Es cuentas a recibir (f pl)
Fr créances (f pl)
It conti attivi (m pl)

**contas consolidadas** (f pl) Pt
De konsolidierter Kontenabschluss (m)
En consolidated accounts
Es cuentas consolidadas (f pl)
Fr comptes consolidés (m pl)
It conti consolidati (m pl)

**contas fiscalizadas** (f pl) Pt
De geprüfte Geschäftsbücher (n pl)
En audited accounts
Es cuentas revisadas (f pl)
Fr comptes vérifiés et certifiés (m pl)
It conti verificati e certificati (m pl)

**contas por saldar** (f pl) Pt
De ausstehende Schulden (m pl)
En outstanding accounts
Es cuentas pendientes (f pl)
Fr comptes à percevoir (m pl)
It conti aperti (m pl)

**contenedorización** (f) n Es
De Containerisation (f)
En containerization
Fr containerisation (f)
It containerization (f)
Pt containerização (f)

**contenido** (m) n Es
De Inhalt (m)
En contents
Fr contenu (m)
It contenuto (m)
Pt conteúdo (m)

**contents** n pl En
De Inhalt (m)
Es contenido (m)
Fr contenu (m)
It contenuto (m)
Pt conteúdo (m)

**contenu** (m) n Fr
De Inhalt (m)
En contents
Es contenido (m)
It contenuto (m)
Pt conteúdo (m)

**contenuto** (m) n It
De Inhalt (m)
En contents
Es contenido (m)
Fr contenu (m)
Pt conteúdo (m)

**contestation** (f) n Fr
De Streit (m)
En dispute
Es disputa (f)

It disputa (f)
Pt disputa (f)

**contestation syndicale des compétences** (f) Fr
De Fähigkeitsstreitigkeit (f)
En demarcation dispute
Es disputa sobre demarcación (f)
It disputa di competenza (f)
Pt disputa sobre demarcação (f)

**conteúdo** (m) n Pt
De Inhalt (m)
En contents
Es contenido (m)
Fr contenu (m)
It contenuto (m)

**conti aperti** (m pl) It
De ausstehende Schulden (m pl)
En outstanding accounts
Es cuentas pendientes (f pl)
Fr comptes à percevoir (m pl)
Pt contas por saldar (f pl)

**conti attivi** (m pl) It
De Debitoren (m pl)
En accounts receivable
Es cuentas a recibir (f pl)
Fr créances (f pl)
Pt contas a receber (f pl)

**conti consolidati** (m pl) It
De konsolidierter Kontenabschluss (m)
En consolidated accounts
Es cuentas consolidadas (f pl)
Fr comptes consolidés (m pl)
Pt contas consolidadas (f pl)

**contingence** (f) n Fr
De Eventualität (f)
En contingency
Es contingencia (f)
It contingenza (f)
Pt contingência (f)·

**contingencia** (f) n Es
De Eventualität (f)
En contingency
Fr contingence (f)
It contingenza (f)
Pt contingência (f)

**contingência** *(f)* n Pt
De Eventualität *(f)*
En contingency
Es contingencia *(f)*
Fr contingence *(f)*
It contingenza *(f)*

**contingency** n En
De Eventualität *(f)*
Es contingencia *(f)*
Fr contingence *(f)*
It contingenza *(f)*
Pt contingência *(f)*

**contingency reserve** En
De Rückstellung für Eventual-
  verbindlichkeiten *(f)*
Es reserva para imprevistos *(f)*
Fr réserve de prévoyance *(f)*
It riserva di previdenza *(f)*
Pt reserva para as contingên-
  cias *(f)*

**contingent d'importation** *(m)*
  Fr
De Einfuhrkontingent *(n)*
En import quota
Es cupo de importación *(m)*
It contingente d'importazione
  *(m)*
Pt quota de importação *(f)*

**contingente d'importazione**
  *(m)* It
De Einfuhrkontingent *(n)*
En import quota
Es cupo de importación *(m)*
Fr contingent d'importation
  *(m)*
Pt quota de importação *(f)*

**contingent liability** En
De Eventualverpflichtung *(f)*
Es responsabilidad continge-
  nte *(f)*
Fr obligation éventuelle *(f)*
It sopravvenienza passiva *(f)*
Pt responsabilidade conting-
  ente *(f)*

**contingenza** *(f)* n It
De Eventualität *(f)*
En contingency
Es contingencia *(f)*
Fr contingence *(f)*
Pt contingência *(f)*

**conti passivi** *(m pl)* It
De Kreditoren *(m pl)*
En accounts payable
Es cuentas a pagar *(f pl)*
Fr comptes à payer *(m pl)*
Pt contas a pagar *(f pl)*

**conti verificati e certificati** *(m
  pl)* It
De geprüfte Geschäftsbücher
  *(n pl)*
En audited accounts
Es cuentas revisadas *(f pl)*
Fr comptes vérifiés et certifiés
  *(m pl)*
Pt contas fiscalizadas *(f pl)*

**conto** (in banca) *(m)* n It
De Konto *(n)*
En account
Es cuenta *(f)*
Fr compte *(m)*
Pt conta *(f)*

**conto** (nota) *(m)* n It
De Rechnung *(f)*
En bill; account
Es cuenta; nota *(f)*
Fr compte; note *(m f)*
Pt conta *(f)*

**conto anticipazioni** *(m)* It
De Anleihekonto *(n)*
En loan account
Es cuenta de préstamos *(f)*
Fr compte des prêts *(m)*
Pt conta de empréstimos *(f)*

**conto bloccato** *(m)* It
De gesperrtes Konto *(n)*
En blocked account
Es cuenta bloqueada *(f)*
Fr compte bloqué *(m)*
Pt conta bloqueada *(f)*

**conto capitale** *(m)* It
De Kapitalkonto *(n)*
En capital account
Es cuenta de capital *(f)*
Fr compte capital *(m)*
Pt conta de capital *(f)*

**conto commerciale** *(m)* It
De Handelskonto *(n)*
En trade account
Es cuenta comercial *(f)*
Fr compte commercial *(m)*
Pt conta comercial *(f)*

**conto corrente** *(m)* It
De Kontokorrent *(n)*
En current account
Am checking account
Es cuenta corriente *(f)*
Fr compte courant *(m)*
Pt conta corrente *(f)*

**conto d'aggio** *(m)* It
De Agiokonto *(n)*
En agio account
Es cuenta de agio *(f)*
Fr compte d'agio *(m)*
Pt conta de ágio *(f)*

**conto di controllo** *(m)* It
De Kontrollkonto *(n)*
En control account
Es cuenta de control *(f)*
Fr compte de contrôle *(m)*
Pt conta de controlo *(f)*

**conto di deposito** *(m)* It
De Depositenkonto *(n)*
En deposit account
Am interest-bearing account
Es cuenta de ahorras *(f)*
Fr compte de dépôt *(m)*
Pt conta de depósito *(m)*

**conto di sbarco** *(m)* It
De Löschungskonto *(n)*
En landing account
Es cuenta de desembarque *(f)*
Fr compte de mise à terre *(m)*
Pt conta de descargas *(f)*

**conto di speculazioni al
  ribasso** *(m)* It
De Baissekonto *(n)*
En bear account
Es cuenta de especulaciones
  a la baja *(f)*
Fr compte des speculations à
  la baisse *(m)*
Pt conta de especulações
  baixistas *(f)*

**conto di stanziamento** *(m)* It
De Rückstellungskonto *(n)*
En appropriation account
Es cuenta de apropiación *(f)*
Fr compte d'affectation *(m)*
Pt conta de apropriação *(f)*

**conto do vigário** *(m)* Pt
De Schwindlertrick
En confidence trick

148

Am confidence game
Es timo *(m)*
Fr escroquerie *(f)*
It truffa all´americana *(f)*

**conto estero** *(m)* It
De Auslandskonto *(n)*
En external account
Am foreign currency account
Es cuenta exterior *(f)*
Fr compte transférable *(m)*
Pt conta externa *(f)*

**conto identificato da numero**
*(m)* It
De numeriertes Konto *(n)*
En numbered account
Es cuenta identificada con nú-
mero *(f)*
Fr compte identifié par nu-
méro *(m)*
Pt conta numerada *(f)*

**conto in banca** *(m)* It
De Bankkonto *(n)*
En bank account
Es cuenta bancaria *(f)*
Fr compte en banque *(m)*
Pt conta bancária *(f)*

**conto in comune** *(m)* It
De Gemeinschaftskonto *(n)*
En joint account
Es cuenta común *(f)*
Fr compte joint *(m)*
Pt conta conjunta *(f)*

**conto per la stabilizzazione
dei cambi** *(m)* It
De Währungsausgleichsfonds
*(m pl)*
En exchange equalization account
Es cuenta de compensación
de cambio *(f)*
Fr fonds de stabilisation des
changes *(m pl)*
Pt conta de compensação de
transacções *(f)*

**conto personale** *(m)* It
De Kundenkonto *(n)*
En charge account
Es cuenta personal *(f)*
Fr compte personnel *(m)*
Pt conta pessoal *(f)*

**conto profitti e perdite** *(m)* It
De Gewinn- und Verlustkonto
*(n)*
En profit and loss account
Es cuenta de ganancias y
pérdidas *(f)*
Fr compte profits et pertes
*(m)*
Pt conta de lucros e perdas *(f)*

**conto proventi e spese** *(m)* It
De Ausgaben- und Ertrags-
konto *(n)*
En income and expenditure
account
Es cuenta de ingresos y gastos
*(f)*
Fr compte de revenus et
dépenses *(m)*
Pt conta de receitas e despesas *(f)*

**conto reso** *(m)* It
- De zur Begleichung vorgelegte
Rechnung *(f)*
En account rendered
Es cuenta rendida *(f)*
Fr compte rendu *(m)*
Pt conta remetida *(f)*

**conto scoperto** *(m)* It
De Konto überzogen *(n)*
En account overdrawn
Es cuenta en descubierto *(f)*
Fr compte découvert *(m)*
Pt conta a descoberto *(f)*

**conto sospeso** *(m)* It
De Übergangskonto *(n)*
En suspense account
Es cuenta suspensa *(f)*
Fr compte d´ordre *(m)*
Pt conta pendente *(m)*

**contra account** En
De Gegenkonto *(n)*
Es contracuenta *(f)*
Fr compte contrepartie *(m)*
It conto d´ordine *(m)*
Pt contra-conta *(f)*

**contraband** *n* En
De Schmuggelware *(f)*
Es contrabando *(m)*
Fr contrebande *(f)*
It contrabbando *(m)*
Pt contrabando *(m)*

**contrabando** *(m)* *n* Es, Pt
De Schmuggelware *(f)*
En contraband
Fr contrebande *(f)*
It contrabbando *(m)*

**contrabbandare** *vb* It
De schmuggeln
En smuggle
Es pasar de contrabando
Fr faire la contrebande
Pt passar por contrabando

**contrabbando** *(m)* *n* It
De Schmuggelware *(f)*
En contraband
Es contrabando *(m)*
Fr contrebande *(f)*
Pt contrabando *(m)*

**contra-conta** *(f)* *n* Pt
De Gegenkonto *(n)*
En contra account
Es contracuenta *(f)*
Fr compte contrepartie *(m)*
It conto d´ordine *(m)*

**contract** *n* En
De Vertrag *(m)*
Es contrato *(m)*
Fr contrat *(m)*
It contratto *(m)*
Pt contrato *(m)*

**contractador** *(m)* *n* Pt
De Unternehmer *(m)*
En contractor
Es contratista *(m)*
Fr entrepreneur *(m)*
It impresario *(m)*

**contract note** En
De Schlusschein *(m)*
Es nota de contrato *(f)*
Fr bordereau d´achat *(m)*
It nota di contratto *(m)*
Pt nota-contrato *(f)*

**contractor** *n* En
De Unternehmer *(m)*
Es contratista *(m)*
Fr entrepreneur *(m)*
It impresario *(m)*
Pt contractador *(m)*

**contract price** En
De Vertragspreis *(m)*
Es precio contractual *(m)*

Fr prix contractuel *(m)*
It prezzo contrattuale *(m)*
Pt preço contractual *(m)*

**contractual** *adj* En, Es, Pt
De vertraglich
Fr contractuel
It contrattuale

**contractuel** *adj* Fr
De vertraglich
En contractual
Es contractual
It contrattuale
Pt contractual

**contracuenta** *(f) n* Es
De Gegenkonto *(n)*
En contra account
Fr compte contrepartie *(m)*
It conto d'ordine *(m)*
Pt contra-conta *(f)*

**contraffare** *vb* It
De fälschen
En forge
Es falsificar
Fr contrefaire
Pt falsificar

**contrainte** *(f) n* Fr
De Zwang *(m)*
En duress
Es compulsión *(f)*
It costrizione *(f)*
Pt coerção *(f)*

**contrainte sur les salaires** *(f)*
   Fr
De Lohnbeschränkung *(f)*
En wage restraint
Es restricción de salario *(f)*
It restrizioni sui salari *(f pl)*
Pt restrição de salários *(f)*

**contrair empréstimo** Pt
De entleihen
En borrow
Es pedir un préstamo
Fr emprunter
It prestire

**contrat** *(m) n* Fr
De Vertrag *(m)*
En contract
Es contrato *(m)*
It contratto *(m)*
Pt contrato *(m)*

**contratación collectiva** *(f)* Es
De Tarifvertragsverhandlung *(f)*
En collective bargaining
Fr négociations de conven-
   tions collectives *(f pl)*
It contrattazione collettiva *(f)*
Pt regateio colectivo *(m)*

**contrat à la grosse aventure**
   *(m)* Fr
De Bodmereibrief *(m)*
En bottomry bond
Es contrato de préstamo a la
   gruesa *(m)*
It contratto di prestito a
   cambio marittimo *(m)*
Pt titulo de bodemeria *(m)*

**contrat d'arrangement** *(m)* Fr
De Vergleichsabkommen *(n)*
En deed of arrangement
Es acta de disposición *(f)*
It atto di accordo *(m)*
Pt escritura de acordo *(f)*

**contrat de service** *(m)* Fr
De Dienstvertrag *(m)*
En service agreement
Es contrato de servicio *(m)*
It accordo di servizio *(m)* '
Pt contrato de serviço *(m)*

**contrat de société** *(m)* Fr
De Gesellschaftsvertrag *(m)*
En articles of association
Am articles of incorporation
Es artículos de asociación *(m
   pl)*
It statuto sociale *(m)*
Pt escritura de sociedade *(f)*

**contrat en régie** *(m)* Fr
De Kosten und Vertrag
En cost-plus contract
Es contrato al costo más
   beneficio *(m)*
It contratto in economia *(m)*
Pt contrato de custo e adi-
   cionais *(m)*

**contratista** *(m) n* Es
De Unternehmer *(m)*
En contractor
Fr entrepreneur *(m)*
It impresario *(m)*
Pt contractador *(m)*

**contratista de obras** *(m)* Es
De Bauunternehmer *(m)*
En building contractor
Fr entrepreneur de bâtiment
   *(m)*
It impresa edile *(f)*
Pt constructor de obras *(m)*

**contratista de transportes** *(m)*
   Es
De Transportunternehmer *(m)*
En haulage contractor
Am trucking company
Fr entrepreneur de camion-
   nage *(m)*
It imprenditore di trasporti
   *(m)*
Pt empreiteiro de transportes
   *(m)*

**contrato** *(m) n* Es, Pt
De Vertrag *(m)*
En contract
Fr contrat *(m)*
It contratto *(m)*

**contrato al costo más bene-
   ficio** *(m)* Es
De Kosten und Vertrag
En cost-plus contract
Fr contrat en régie *(m)*
It contratto in economia *(m)*
Pt contrato de custo e adi-
   cionais *(m)*

**contrato de préstamo a la
   gruesa** *(m)* Es
De Bodmereibrief *(m)*
En bottomry bond
Fr contrat à la grosse aven-
   ture *(m)*
It contratto di prestito a
   cambio marittimo *(m)*
Pt título de bodemeria *(m)*

**contrato de reserva** *(m)* Es
De Notvereinbarung *(f)*
En stand-by agreement
Fr accord en réserve *(m)*
It accordo di riserva *(m)*
Pt acordo a postos *(m)*

**contrato de servicio** *(m)* Es
De Dienstvertrag *(m)*
En service agreement
Fr contrat de service *(m)*
It accordo di servizio *(m)*
Pt contrato de serviço *(m)*

**contrato de servicio** (m) Pt
De Dienstvertrag (m)
En service agreement
Es contrato de servicio (m)
Fr contrat de service (m)
It accordo di servizio (m)

**contrato global** (m) Es, Pt
De Globalgeschäft (n)
En package deal
Fr marché global (m)
It contratto globale (m)

**contrattazione collettiva** (f) It
De Tarifvertragsverhandlung (f)
En collective bargaining
Es contratación collectiva (f)
Fr négociations de conventions collectives (f pl)
Pt regateio colectivo (m)

**contratto** (m) n It
De Vertrag (m)
En contract
Es contrato (m)
Fr contrat (m)
Pt contrato (m)

**contratto di noleggio a tempo** (m) It
De Zeitcharter (f)
En time charter
Es fletamento de tiempo (m)
Fr affrètement à temps (m)
Pt fretamento de tempo (m)

**contratto di prestito a cambio marittimo** (m) It
De Bodmereibrief (m)
En bottomry bond
Es contrato de préstamo a la gruesa (m)
Fr contrat à la grosse aventure (m)
Pt titulo de bodemeria (m)

**contratto di vendita** (m) It
De Kaufvertrag (m)
En bill of sale
Es escritura de venta (f)
Fr acte de vente (f)
Pt escritura de venda (f)

**contratto globale** (m) It
De Globalgeschäft (n)
En package deal
Es contrato global (m)

Fr marché global (m)
Pt contrato global (m)

**contratto in economia** (m) It
De Kosten und Vertrag
En cost-plus contract
Es contrato al costo más beneficio (m)
Fr contrat en régie (f)
Pt contrato de custo e adicionais (m)

**contratto vincolante** (m) It
De bindender Vertrag (m)
En binding agreement
Es obligación irrevocable (f)
Fr convention irrévocable (f)
Pt acordo irrevogavel (m)

**contrattuale** adj It
De vertraglich
En contractual
Es contractual
Fr contractuel
Pt contractual

**contrebande** (f) n Fr
De Schmuggelware (f)
En contraband
Es contrabando (m)
It contrabbando (m)
Pt contrabando (m)

**contrefaçon** (f) n Fr
De Fälschung (f)
En forgery
Es falsificación (f)
It falsificazione (f)
Pt falsificação (f)

**contrefaçon littéraire** (f) Fr
De Urheberrechtsverletzung (f)
En infringement of copyright
Es infracción de los derechos de autor (f)
It infrazione dei diritti d'autore (f)
Pt infracção de direitos de autor (f)

**contrefaire** vb Fr
De fälschen
En forge
Es falsificar
It contraffare
Pt falsificar

**contremaitre** (m) n Fr
De Vorarbeiter (m)
En foreman
Es capataz (m)
It capo operaio; capo squadra (m)
Pt encarregado; capataz (m)

**contresigner** vb Fr
De gegenzeichnen
En countersign
Es refrendar
It controfirmare
Pt validar por assinatura

**contribuable** (m) n Fr
De Steuerzahler (m)
En tax payer
Es contribuyente (m)
It contribuente fiscale (m)
Pt contribuinte (m)

**contribución** (f) n Es
De Beitrag (m)
En contribution
Fr contribution (f)
It contributo (m)
Pt contribuição (f)

**contribuciones directas** (f pl) Es
De direkte Steuern (f pl)
En direct taxation
Fr contributions directes (f pl)
It imposte dirette (f pl)
Pt tributação directa (f)

**contribuciones indirectas** (f pl) Es
De indirekte Steuern (f pl)
En indirect taxation
Fr contributions indirectes (f pl)
It imposte indirette (f pl)
Pt tributação indirecta (f)

**contribución municipal** (f) Es
De Gemeindesteuer (f)
En rates
Am realty tax
Fr taxes municipales (f pl)
It tassa comunale (f)
Pt contribuições (f pl)

**contribuente fiscale** (m) It
De Steuerzahler (m)
En tax payer
Es contribuyente (m)

Fr  contribuable *(m)*
Pt  contribuinte *(m)*

**contribuer** *vb* Fr
De  beitragen
En  contribute
Es  contribuir
It  contribuire
Pt  contribuir

**contribuição** *(f) n* Pt
De  Beitrag *(m)*
En  contribution
Es  contribución *(f)*
Fr  contribution *(f)*
It  contributo *(m)*

**contribuição indirecta** *(f)* Pt
De  indirekte Steuern *(f pl)*
En  indirect taxation
Es  contribuciones indirectas *(f pl)*
Fr  contributions indirectes *(f pl)*
It  imposte indirette *(f pl)*

**contribuições** *(f pl)* Pt
De  Gemeindesteuer *(f)*
En  rates
Am  realty tax
Es  contribución municipal *(f)*
Fr  taxes municipales *(f pl)*
It  tassa comunale *(f)*

**contribuinte** *(m) n* Pt
De  Steuerzahler *(m)*
En  tax payer
Es  contribuyente *(m)*
Fr  contribuable *(m)*
It  contribuente fiscale *(m)*

**contribuir** *vb* Es, Pt
De  beitragen
En  contribute
Fr  contribuer
It  contribuire

**contribuire** *vb* It
De  beitragen
En  contribute
Es  contribuir
Fr  contribuer
Pt  contribuir

**contribute** *vb* En
De  beitragen
Es  contribuir
Fr  contribuer

It  contribuire
Pt  contribuir

**contribution** *n* En, Fr *(f)*
De  Beitrag *(m)*
Es  contribución *(f)*
It  contributo *(m)*
Pt  contribuição *(f)*

**contributions directes** *(f pl)* Fr
De  direkte Steuern *(f pl)*
En  direct taxation
Es  contribuciones directas *(f pl)*
It  imposte dirette *(f pl)*
Pt  tributação directa *(f)*

**contributions indirectes** *(f pl)* Fr
De  indirekte Steuern *(f pl)*
En  indirect taxation
Es  contribuciones indirectas *(f pl)*
It  imposte indirette *(f pl)*
Pt  tributação indirecta *(f)*

**contributo** *(m) n* It
De  Beitrag *(m)*
En  contribution
Es  contribución *(f)*
Fr  contribution *(f)*
Pt  contribuição *(f)*

**contributory pension** En
De  Kassenpension *(f)*
Es  retiro contributivo *(m)*
Fr  retraite de régime à cotisations *(f)*
It  pensione a contributi *(f)*
Pt  reforma de contribuição prévia *(f)*

**contribuyente** *(m) n* Es
De  Steuerzahler *(m)*
En  tax payer
Fr  contribuable *(m)*
It  contribuente fiscale *(m)*
Pt  contribuinte *(m)*

**controfirmare** *vb* It
De  gegenzeichnen
En  countersign
Es  refrendar
Fr  contresigner
Pt  validar por assinatura

**control** *n* En, Es *(m)*
De  Aufsicht *(f)*
Fr  contrôle *(m)*
It  controllo *(m)*
Pt  controlo *(m)*

**control account** En
De  Kontrollkonto *(n)*
Es  cuenta de control *(f)*
Fr  compte de contrôle *(m)*
It  conto di controllo *(m)*
Pt  conta de controlo *(f)*

**controlador** *(m) n* Pt
De  Kontrolleur; Rechnungsprüfer *(m)*
En  controller; comptroller
Es  interventor *(m)*
Fr  contrôleur; vérificateur des comptes *(m)*
It  controllore *(m)*

**control al azar** *(m)* Es
De  Stichprobe *(f)*
En  spot check
Fr  contrôle par sondage *(m)*
It  controllo saltuario *(m)*
Pt  controlo de ocasião *(m)*

**control de aduanas** *(m)* Es
De  zollamtliche Untersuchung *(f)*
En  customs examination
Fr  visite douanière *(f)*
It  visita doganale *(f)*
Pt  verificação alfandegária *(f)*

**control de alquileres** *(m)* Es
De  Mietzinskontrolle *(f)*
En  rent control
Fr  contrôle des loyers *(m)*
It  blocco degli affitti *(m)*
Pt  controlo de rendas *(m)*

**control de calidad** *(m)* Es
De  Qualitätskontrolle *(f)*
En  quality control
Fr  contrôle de qualité *(m)*
It  controllo di qualità *(m)*
Pt  controlo de qualidade *(m)*

**control de precios** *(m)* Es
De  Preiskontrolle *(f)*
En  price control
Fr  contrôle des prix *(m)*
It  controllo sui prezzi *(m)*
Pt  controlo de preços *(m)*

**control de producción** (m) Es
De Produktionskontrolle (f)
En production control
Fr contrôle de production (m)
It controllo della produzione (m)
Pt controlo da produção (m)

**contrôle** (m) n Fr
De Aufsicht (f)
En control
Es control (m)
It controllo (m)
Pt controlo (m)

**contrôle budgétaire** (m) Fr
De Haushaltskontrolle (f)
En budgetary control
Es control presupuestario (m)
It controllo a bilancio preventivo (m)
Pt controlo orçamental (m)

**contrôle de production** (m) Fr
De Produktionskontrolle (f)
En production control
Es control de producción (m)
It controllo della produzione (m)
Pt controle da produção (m)

**contrôle de qualité** (m) Fr
De Qualitätskontrolle (f)
En quality control
Es control de calidad (m)
It controllo di qualità (m)
Pt controlo de qualidade (m)

**contrôle des changes** (m) Fr
De Devisenkontrolle (f)
En exchange control
Am currency control
Es fiscalización de cambios (f)
It controllo sui cambi (m)
Pt controlo de câmbios (m)

**contrôle des loyers** (m) Fr
De Mietzinskontrolle (f)
En rent control
Es control de alquileres (m)
It blocco degli affitti (m)
Pt controlo de rendas (m)

**contrôle des prix** (m) Fr
De Preiskontrolle (f)
En price control
Es control de precios (m)

It controllo sui prezzi (m)
Pt controlo de preços (m)

**contrôle des stocks** (m) Fr
De Lagerverwaltung (f)
En stock control
Es fiscalización de las existencias (f)
It controllo delle scorte (m)
Pt controlo de existências (m)

**contrôle par sondage** (m) Fr
De Stichprobe (f)
En spot check
Es control al azar (m)
It controllo saltuario (m)
Pt controlo de ocasião (m)

**contrôleur** (m) n Fr
De Kontrolleur (m)
En controller
Es interventor (m)
It controllore (m)
Pt controlador (m)

**controller** n En
De Kontrolleur (m)
Es interventor (m)
Fr contrôleur (m)
It controllore (m)
Pt controlador (m)

**controlling company** En
De Gesellschaft mit Kontrollbefugnis (f)
Es compañía directriz (f)
Fr société directrice (f)
It società direttrice (f)
Pt companhia controladora (f)

**controlling interest** En
De Mehrheitsbeteiligung (f)
Es interés mayoritario (m)
Fr participation donnant le contrôle (f)
It interesse della parte maggioritaria (m)
Pt interesse maioritário (m)

**controllo** (m) n It
De Aufsicht (f)
En control
Es control (m)
Fr contrôle (m)
Pt controlo (m)

**controllo a bilancio preventivo** (m) It
De Haushaltskontrolle (f)
En budgetary control
Es control presupuestario (m)
Fr contrôle budgétaire (m)
Pt controlo orçamental (m)

**controllo della produzione** (m) It
De Produktionskontrolle (f)
En production control
Es control de producción (m)
Fr contrôle de production (m)
Pt controlo da produção (m)

**controllo delle scorte** (m) It
De Lagerverwaltung (f)
En stock control
Es fiscalización de las existencias (f)
Fr contrôle des stocks (m)
Pt controlo de existências (m)

**controllo di qualità** (m) It
De Qualitätskontrolle (f)
En quality control
Es control de calidad (m)
Fr contrôle de qualité (m)
Pt controlo de qualidade (m)

**controllore** (m) n It
De Kontrolleur; Rechnungsprüfer (m)
En controller; comptroller
Es interventor (m)
Fr contrôleur; vérificateur des comptes (m)
Pt controlador (m)

**controllo saltuario** (m) It
De Stichprobe (f)
En spot check
Es control al azar (m)
Fr contrôle par sondage (m)
Pt controlo de ocasião (m)

**controllo sui cambi** (m) It
De Devisenkontrolle (f)
En exchange control
Am currency control
Es fiscalización de cambios (f)
Fr contrôle des changes (m)
Pt controlo de câmbios (m)

**controllo sui prezzi** (m) It
De Preiskontrolle (f)
En price control

Es control de precios (m)
Fr contrôle des prix (m)
Pt controlo de preços (m)

**controlo** (m) n Pt
De Aufsicht (f)
En control
Es control (m)
Fr contrôle (m)
It controllo (m)

**controlo da produção** (m) Pt
De Produktionskontrolle (f)
En production control
Es control de producción (m)
Fr contrôle de production (m)
It controllo della produzione (m)

**controlo de câmbios** (m) Pt
De Devisenkontrolle (f)
En exchange control
Am currency control
Es fiscalización de cambios (f)
Fr contrôle des changes (m)
It controllo sui cambi (m)

**controlo de existências** (m) Pt
De Lagerverwaltung (f)
En stock control
Es fiscalización de las existencias (f)
Fr contrôle des stocks (m)
It controllo delle scorte (m)

**controlo de ocasião** (m) Pt
De Stichprobe (f)
En spot check
Es control al azar (m)
Fr contrôle par sondage (m)
It controllo saltuario (m)

**controlo de preços** (m) Pt
De Preiskontrolle (f)
En price control
Es control de precios (m)
Fr contrôle des prix (m)
It controllo sui prezzi (m)

**controlo de qualidade** (m) Pt
De Qualitätskontrolle (f)
En quality control
Es control de calidad (m)
Fr contrôle de qualité (m)
It controllo di qualità (m)

**controlo de rendas** (m) Pt
De Mietzinskontrolle (f)
En rent control
Es control de alquileres (m)
Fr contrôle des loyers (m)
It blocco degli affitti (m)

**controlo orçamental** (m) Pt
De Haushaltskontrolle (f)
En budgetary control
Es control presupuestario (m)
Fr contrôle budgétaire (m)
It controllo a bilancio preventivo (m)

**control presupuestario** (m) Es
De Haushaltskontrolle (f)
En budgetary control
Fr contrôle budgétaire (m)
It controllo a bilancio preventivo (m)
Pt controlo orçamental (m)

**controstallia** (f) n It
De Überliegezeit (f)
En demurrage
Es sobreestadía (f)
Fr surestarie (f)
Pt sobreestadía (f)

**convene** vb En
De einberufen
Es convenir
Fr convoquer
It convocare
Pt convocar

**convénio de preços** (m) Pt
De Preisabsprache (f)
En price ring
Es coalición de vendedores (f)
Fr coalition de vendeurs (f)
It sindacato dei prezzi (m)

**convenio restrictivo** (m) Es
De einschränkende Bestimmung (f)
En restrictive covenant
Fr accord restrictif (m)
It accordo restrittivo (m)
Pt obrigação restritiva (f)

**convenir** vb Es
De einberufen
En convene
Fr convoquer
It convocare
Pt convocar

**convention** (f) n Fr
De Abkommen (n)
En agreement
Es acuerdo (m)
It accordo (m)
Pt acordo (m)

**convention des salaires** (f) Fr
De Lohnvereinbarung (f)
En wages agreement
Es acuerdo sobre salarios (m)
It accordo sui salari (m)
Pt acordo sobre salários (m)

**convention irrévocable** (f) Fr
De bindender Vertrag (m)
En binding agreement
Es obligación irrevocable (f)
It contratto vincolante (m)
Pt acordo irrevogavel (m)

**convention tacite** (f) Fr
De stillschweigendes Übereinkommen (n)
En tacit agreement
Es acuerdo tácito (m)
It accordo tacito (m)
Pt acordo tácito (m)

**convention verbale** (f) Fr
De Kavaliersabkommen (n)
En gentleman's agreement
Es acuerdo sobre palabra (m)
It accordo sulla parola (m)
Pt pacto de honra (m)

**convenzione** (f) n It
De Abkommen (n)
En covenant
Es pacto (m)
Fr convention (f)
Pt pacto (m)

**conversão** (f) n Pt
De Konversion (f)
En conversion
Es conversión (f)
Fr conversion (f)
It conversione (f)

**conversion** n En, Fr (f)
De Konversion (f)
Es conversión (f)
It conversione (f)
Pt conversão (f)

**conversión** (f) n Es
De Konversion (f)
En conversion
Fr conversion (f)
It conversione (f)
Pt conversão (f)

**conversione** (f) n It
De Konversion (f)
En conversion
Es conversión (f)
Fr conversion (f)
Pt conversão (f)

**conversion factor** En
De Umrechnungskoeffizient (m)
Es factor de conversión (m)
Fr facteur de conversion (m)
It fattore di conversion (m)
Pt factor de conversão (m)

**convert** vb En
De konvertieren
Es convertir
Fr convertir
It convertire
Pt convertir

**convertibile** adj It
De konvertierbar
En convertible
Es convertible
Fr convertible
Pt convertível

**convertible** adj En, Es, Fr
De konvertierbar
It convertibile
Pt convertível

**convertir** vb Es, Fr, Pt
De konvertieren
En convert
It convertire

**convertire** vb It
De konvertieren
En convert
Es convertir
Fr convertir
Pt convertir

**convertível** adj Pt
De konvertierbar
En convertible
Es convertible

Fr convertible
It convertibile

**convés** (m) n Pt
De Deck (n)
En deck
Es cubierta (f)
Fr pont (m)
It coperta; ponte (f m)

**conveyance of property** En
De Übertragung (f)
Es traspaso de propiedad (m)
Fr transmission de biens (f)
It trasferimento di beni (m)
Pt trespasse de propriedade (m)

**conveyer** n Am
En carrier
De Spediteur (m)
Es transportador (m)
Fr expéditeur (m)
It vettore (m)
Pt transportador (m)

**convidar** vb Pt
De einladen; auffordern
En invite
Es invitar
Fr inviter
It invitare

**convite** (m) n Pt
De Einladung; Aufforderung (f)
En invitation
Es invitación (f)
Fr invitation; appel (f m)
It invito (m)

**convocar** vb Pt
De einberufen
En convene
Es convenir
Fr convoquer
It convocare

**convocare** vb It
De einberufen
En convene
Es convenir
Fr convoquer
Pt convocar

**convocazione dei creditori** (f) It
De Gläubigerversammlung (f)
En meeting of creditors

Es concurso de acreedores (m)
Fr assemblée de créanciers (f)
Pt reunião de credores (f)

**convoquer** vb Fr
De einberufen
En convene
Es convenir
It convocare
Pt convocar

**cooperação** (f) n Pt
De Zusammenarbeit (f)
En cooperation
Es cooperación (f)
Fr coopération (f)
It cooperazione (f)

**cooperación** (f) n Es
De Zusammenarbeit (f)
En cooperation
Fr coopération (f)
It cooperazione (f)
Pt cooperação (f)

**cooperation** n En
De Zusammenarbeit (f)
Es cooperación (f)
Fr coopération (f)
It cooperazione (f)
Pt cooperação (f)

**coopération** (f) n Fr
De Zusammenarbeit (f)
En cooperation
Es cooperación (f)
It cooperazione (f)
Pt cooperação (f)

**cooperativa** (f) n Es, It, Pt
De Genossenschaft (f)
En cooperative
Fr société coopérative (f)

**cooperative** n En
De Genossenschaft (f)
Es cooperativa (f)
Fr société coopérative (f)
It cooperativa (f)
Pt cooperativa (f)

**cooperazione** (f) n It
De Zusammenarbeit (f)
En cooperation
Es cooperación (f)
Fr coopération (f)
Pt cooperação (f)

**co-opt** *vb* En
De hinzuwählen
Es cooptar
Fr coopter
It cooptare
Pt cooptar

**cooptar** *vb* Es, Pt
De hinzuwählen
En co-opt
Fr coopter
It cooptare

**cooptare** *vb* It
De hinzuwählen
En co-opt
Es cooptar
Fr coopter
Pt cooptar

**coopter** *vb* Fr
De hinzuwählen
En co-opt
Es cooptar
It cooptare
Pt cooptar

**coordenação** *(f) n* Pt
De Gleichordnung *(f)*
En coordination
Es coordinación *(f)*
Fr coordination *(f)*
It coordinamento *(m)*

**coordinación** *(f) n* Es
De Gleichordnung *(f)*
En coordination
Fr coordination *(f)*
It coordinamento *(m)*
Pt coordenação *(f)*

**coordinamento** *(m) n* It
De Gleichordnung *(f)*
En coordination
Es coordinación *(f)*
Fr coordination *(f)*
Pt coordenação *(f)*

**coordination** *n* En, Fr *(f)*
De Gleichordnung *(f)*
Es coordinación *(f)*
It coordinamento *(m)*
Pt coordenação *(f)*

**co-ownership** *n* En
De Miteigentum *(n)*
Es copropiedad *(f)*
Fr copropriété *(f)*

It comproprietà *(f)*
Pt copropriedade *(f)*

**coperta** *(f) n* It
De Deck *(n)*
En deck
Es cubierta *(f)*
Fr pont *(m)*
Pt convés *(m)*

**copertura** *(f) n* It
De Deckung *(f)*
En cover
Es cobertura *(f)*
Fr couverture *(f)*
Pt cobertura *(f)*

**copertura assicurativa** *(f)* It
De Versicherungsdeckung *(f)*
En insurance cover
Es cobertura de la póliza de seguro *(f)*
Fr garantie d'assurance *(f)*
Pt cobertura de seguro *(f)*

**copertura provvisoria** *(f)* It
De temporäre Deckung *(f)*
En temporary cover
Es cobertura provisional *(f)*
Fr couverture temporaire *(m)*
Pt cobertura provisória *(f)*

**copia** *(f) n* Es, It
De Abschrift; Kopie *(f)*
En copy
Fr copie *(f)*
Pt cópia *(f)*

**cópia** *(f) n* Pt
De Abschrift; Kopie *(f)*
En copy
Es copia *(f)*
Fr copie *(f)*
It copia *(f)*

**copia a químico** *(f)* Pt
De Durchschlag *(m)*
En carbon copy
Es copia en papel carbón *(f)*
Fr copie au carbone *(f)*
It copia carbone *(f)*

**copia auténtica** *(f)* Es
De beglaubigte Abschrift *(f)*
En certified true copy
Fr copie certifiée *(f)*
It copia conforme *(f)*
Pt cópia autenticada *(f)*

**cópia autenticada** *(f)* Pt
De beglaubigte Abschrift *(f)*
En certified true copy
Es copia auténtica *(f)*
Fr copie certifiée *(f)*
It copia conforme *(f)*

**copia carbone** *(f)* It
De Durchschlag *(m)*
En carbon copy
Es copia en papel carbón *(f)*
Fr copie au carbone *(f)*
Pt copia a químico *(f)*

**copia conforme** *(f)* It
De beglaubigte Abschrift *(f)*
En certified true copy
Es copia auténtica *(f)*
Fr copie certifiée *(f)*
Pt cópia autenticada *(f)*

**copia en papel carbón** *(f)* Es
De Durchschlag *(m)*
En carbon copy
Fr copie au carbone *(f)*
It copia carbone *(f)*
Pt copia a químico *(f)*

**copiar** *vb* Es, Pt
De kopieren
En copy
Fr transcrire
It copiare

**cópia rascunho** *(f)* Pt
De Entwurf *(m)*
En rough copy
Am draft
Es borrador *(m)*
Fr brouillon *(m)*
It brutta copia *(f)*

**copiare** *vb* It
De kopieren
En copy
Es copiar
Fr transcrire
Pt copiar

**copie** *(f) n* Fr
De Abschrift; Kopie *(f)*
En copy
Es copia *(f)*
It copia *(f)*
Pt cópia *(f)*

**copie au carbone** *(f)* Fr
De Durchschlag *(m)*
En carbon copy
Es copia en papel carbón *(f)*
It copia carbone *(f)*
Pt copia a químico *(f)*

**copie certifiée** *(f)* Fr
De beglaubigte Abschrift *(f)*
En certified true copy
Es copia auténtica *(f)*
It copia conforme *(f)*
Pt cópia autenticada *(f)*

**copie publicitaire** *(f)* Fr
De Werbetext *(m)*
En advertising copy
Es material publicitario *(m)*
It testo pubblicitario *(m)*
Pt texto de publicidade *(m)*

**coprirsi** *vb* It
De sich decken
En hedge
Es cubrirse
Fr arbitrager
Pt cobrir-se

**copropiedad** *(f)* *n* Es
De Miteigentum *(n)*
En joint ownership
Fr copropriété *(f)*
It comproprietà *(f)*
Pt copropriedade *(f)*

**copropriedade** *(f)* *n* Pt
De Miteigentum *(n)*
En joint ownership
Es copropiedad *(f)*
Fr copropriété *(f)*
It comproprietà *(f)*

**copropriété** *(f)* *n* Fr
De Miteigentum *(n)*
En joint ownership
Es copropiedad *(f)*
It comproprietà *(f)*
Pt copropriedade *(f)*

**copy** *vb* En
De kopieren
Es copiar
Fr transcrire
It copiare
Pt copiar

**copy** *n* En
De Abschrift; Kopie *(f)*
Es copia *(f)*
Fr copie *(f)*
It copia *(f)*
Pt cópia *(f)*

**copyright** *n* En
De Urheberrecht *(n)*
Es derechos de autor *(m pl)*
Fr droit d'auteur *(m)*
It diritto d'autore *(m)*
Pt direitos de autor *(m pl)*

**copy typist** En
Am transcriber
De Abschreibtypistin *(f)*
Es mecanógrafa *(f)*
Fr dactylo copiste *(f)*
It dattilografa *(f)*
Pt dactilógrafa *(f)*

**copywriter** *n* En
De Textverfasser *(m)*
Es redactor *(m)*
Fr concepteur-rédacteur *(m)*
It redattore pubblicitario *(m)*
Pt redactor de publicidade *(m)*

**corner a market** En
De den Markt beherrschen
Es acaparar el mercado
Fr accaparer le marché
It accaparrare il mercato
Pt sender um mercado

**corporação** *(f)* *n* Pt
De Körperschaft *(f)*
En corporation
Es corporación *(f)*
Fr corporation *(f)*
It corporazione *(f)*

**Corporação Internacional de Finanças** *(f)* Pt
De Internationale Finanzkorporation *(f)*
En International Finance Corporation
Es Corporación Internacional de Finanzas *(f)*
Fr Société Financière Internationale *(f)*
It Corporazione Finanziaria Internazionale *(f)*

**corporación** *(f)* *n* Es
De Körperschaft *(f)*
En corporation
Fr corporation *(f)*
It corporazione *(f)*
Pt corporação *(f)*

**Corporación Internacional de Finanzas** *(f)* Es
De Internationale Finanzkorporation *(f)*
En International Finance Corporation
Fr Société Financière Internationale *(f)*
It Corporazione Finanziaria Internazionale *(f)*
Pt Corporação Internacional de Finanças *(f)*

**corporate** *adj* En
De körperschaftlich
Es corporativo
Fr corporatif
It corporativo
Pt corporativo

**corporate officer** Am
En executive director
De geschäftsführender Direktor *(m)*
Es director ejecutivo *(m)*
Fr administrateur dirigeant *(m)*
It amministratore dirigente *(m)*
Pt director administrativo *(m)*

**corporatif** *adj* Fr
De körperschaftlich
En corporate
Es corporativo
It corporativo
Pt corporativo

**corporation** *n* En, Fr *(f)*
De Körperschaft *(f)*
Es corporación *(f)*
It corporazione *(f)*
Pt corporação *(f)*

**corporation tax** En
De Körperschaftsteuer *(f)*
Es impuesto sobre renta de la sociedad *(m)*
Fr impôt sur le revenu des sociétés *(m)*
It imposta sui proventi delle società *(f)*

Pt imposto sobre corporação
(m)

**corporativo** adj Es, It, Pt
De körperschaftlich
En corporate
Fr corporatif

**corporazione** (f) n It
De Körperschaft (f)
En corporation
Es corporación (f)
Fr corporation (f)
Pt corporação (f)

**Corporazione Finanziaria Int-
ernazionale** (f) It
De Internationale Finanzkorporation (f)
En International Finance Corporation
Es Corporación Internacional
de Finanzas (f)
Fr Société Financière. Internationale (f)
Pt Corporação Internacional
de Finanças (f)

**correcção** (f) n Pt
De Berichtigung (f)
En correction
Es corrección (f)
Fr correction (f)
It correzione (f)

**corrección** (f) n Es
De Berichtigung (f)
En correction
Fr correction (f)
It correzione (f)
Pt correcção (f)

**correct** vb En
De korrigieren
Es corregir
Fr corriger
It correggere
Pt corrigir

**correction** n En, Fr (f)
De Berichtigung (f)
Es corrección (f)
It correzione (f)
Pt correcção (f)

**corredor** (m) n Es
De Makler (m)
En broker

Fr courtier (m)
It sensale (m)
Pt corretor (m)

**corredor de bolsa** (m) Es
De Börsenmakler (m)
En stockbroker
Fr courtier en bourse (m)
It agente di borsa (m)
Pt corretor da bolsa (m)

**corredor de cambios** (m) Es
De Wechselmakler (m)
En bill broker
Fr courtier de bons (m)
It agente di sconto (m)
Pt corretor de câmbios (m)

**corredor de mercaderías** (m)
Es
De Makler für Verbrauchsgüter
(m)
En commodity broker
Fr courtier en marchandises
(m)
It sensale di merci (m)
Pt corretor de mercadorias
(m)

**corredor de seguro marítimo**
(m) Es
De Seetransportversicherungsmakler (m)
En marine insurance broker
Fr courtier d'assurances maritimes (m)
It agente d'assicurazioni marittime (m)
Pt corretor de seguros marítimos (m)

**corredor de seguros** (m) Es
De Versicherungsmakler (m)
En insurance broker
Fr courtier d'assurance (m)
It mediatore di assicurazioni
(m)
Pt corretor de seguros (m)

**corredor marítimo** (m) Es
De Schiffsmakler (m)
En shipbroker
Fr courtier maritime (m)
It sensale marittimo (m)
Pt corretor marítimo (m)

**correduría de fincas** (f) Es
De Immobilienbüro (n)
En estate agency
Am real estate agency
Fr agence immobilière (f)
It agenzia immobiliare (f)
Pt agência de propriedades (f)

**correggere** vb It
De korrigieren
En correct
Es corregir
Fr corriger
Pt corrigir

**corregir** vb Es
De korrigieren
En correct
Fr corriger
It correggere
Pt corrigir

**correio** (m) n Pt
De Post (f)
En mail
Es correo (m)
Fr poste (f)
It posta (f)

**correio aéreo** (m) Pt
De Luftpost (f)
En airmail
Es correo aéreo (m)
Fr poste aérienne (f)
It posta aerea (f)

**corrente** adj It, Pt
De laufend
En current
Es corriente
Fr courant; en cours

**corrente continua** (f) It, Pt
De Gleichstrom (m)
En direct current (d.c.)
Es corriente continua (f)
Fr courant continu (m)

**correo** (m) n Es
De Post (f)
En mail
Fr poste (f)
It posta (f)
Pt correio (m)

**correo aéreo** (m) Es
De Luftpost (f)
En airmail

Fr   poste aérienne *(f)*
It   posta aerea *(f)*
Pt   correio aéreo *(m)*


**correspondance** *(f) n* Fr
De   Briefwechsel *(m)*
En   correspondence
Es   correspondencia *(f)*
It   corrispondenza *(f)*
Pt   correspondência *(f)*


**correspondence** *n* En
De   Briefwechsel *(m)*
Es   correspondencia *(f)*
Fr   correspondance *(f)*
It   corrispondenza *(f)*
Pt   correspondência *(f)*


**correspondencia** *(f) n* Es
De   Briefwechsel *(m)*
En   correspondence
Fr   correspondance *(f)*
It   corrispondenza *(f)*
Pt   correspondência *(f)*


**correspondência** *(f) n* Pt
De   Briefwechsel *(m)*
En   correspondence
Es   correspondencia *(f)*
Fr   correspondance *(f)*
It   corrispondenza *(f)*


**corretagem** *(f) n* Pt
De   Maklergebühr *(f)*
En   brokerage
Es   corretaje *(m)*
Fr   courtage *(m)*
It   senseria *(f)*


**corretaje** *(m) n* Es
De   Maklergebühr *(f)*
En   brokerage
Fr   courtage *(m)*
It   senseria *(f)*
Pt   corretagem *(f)*


**corretor** *(m) n* Pt
De   Makler *(m)*
En   broker
Es   corredor *(m)*
Fr   courtier *(m)*
It   sensale *(m)*


**corretor da bolsa** *(m)* Pt
De   Börsenmakler *(m)*
En   stockbroker
Es   corredor de bolsa *(m)*


Fr   courtier en bourse *(m)*
It   agente di borsa *(m)*


**corretor de câmbios** *(m)* Pt
De   Wechselmakler *(m)*
En   bill broker
Es   corredor de cambios *(m)*
Fr   courtier de bons *(m)*
It   agente di sconto *(m)*


**corretor de mercadorias** *(m)*
     Pt
De   Makler für Verbrauchsgüter
     *(m)*
En   commodity broker
Es   corredor de mercaderías
     *(m)*
Fr   courtier en marchandises
     *(m)*
It   sensale di merci *(m)*


**corretor de opções** *(m)* Pt
De   Terminmakler *(m)*
En   option dealer
Es   operador a prima *(m)*
Fr   opérateur à prime *(m)*
It   operatore in contratti a
     premio *(m)*


**corretor de seguros** *(m)* Pt
De   Versicherungsmakler *(m)*
En   insurance broker
Es   corredor de seguros *(m)*
Fr   courtier d'assurance *(m)*
It   mediatore di assicurazioni
     *(m)*


**corretor marítimo** *(m)* Pt
De   Schiffsmakler *(m)*
En   shipbroker
Es   corredor marítimo *(m)*
Fr   courtier maritime *(m)*
It   sensale marittimo *(m)*


**correzione** *(f) n* It
De   Berichtigung *(f)*
En   correction
Es   corrección *(f)*
Fr   correction *(f)*
Pt   correcção *(f)*


**corriente** *adj* Es
De   laufend
En   current
Fr   courant; en cours
It   corrente
Pt   corrente


**corriente continua** *(f)* Es
De   Gleichstrom *(m)*
En   direct current (d.c.)
Fr   courant continu *(m)*
It   corrente continua *(f)*
Pt   corrente continua *(f)*


**corriger** *vb* Fr
De   korrigieren
En   correct
Es   corregir
It   correggere
Pt   corrigir


**corrigir** *vb* Pt
De   korrigieren
En   correct
Es   corregir
Fr   corriger
It   correggere


**corrispondenza** *(f) n* It
De   Briefwechsel *(m)*
En   correspondence
Es   correspondencia *(f)*
Fr   correspondance *(f)*
Pt   correspondência *(f)*


**corrompere** *vb* It
De   bestechen
En   bribe
Es   sobornar
Fr   corrompre
Pt   sobornar


**corrompre** *vb* Fr
De   bestechen
En   bribe
Es   sobornar
It   corrompere
Pt   sobornar


**corruption** *(f) n* Fr
De   Bestechung *(f)*
En   bribery; corruption
Es   soborno *(m)*
It   corruzione *(f)*
Pt   soborno *(m)*


**corruzione** *(f) n* It
De   Bestechung *(f)*
En   bribery; corruption
Es   soborno *(m)*
Fr   corruption *(f)*
Pt   soborno *(m)*

**corso del cambio** *(m)* It
De Umrechnungskurs *(m)*
En rate of exchange
Es tipo de cambio *(m)*
Fr cours de change *(m)*
Pt taxa de câmbio *(f)*

**cortar** *vb* Pt
De streichen
En delete
Es tachar; anular
Fr rayer; effacer
It cancellare

**corte arbitrale** *(f)* It
De Schiedsgericht *(n)*
En court of arbitration
Es tribunal arbitral *(m)*
Fr cour d'arbitrage *(m)*
Pt tribunal de arbitragem *(m)*

**corte d'appello** *(f)* It
De Berufungsgericht *(n)*
En court of appeal
Es tribunal de apelación *(m)*
Fr cour d'appel *(m)*
Pt tribunal de apelação *(m)*

**cosecha** *(f)* *n* Es
De Ernte *(f)*
En harvest
Fr moisson; récolte *(f)*
It raccolto *(m)*
Pt colheita *(f)*

**cost** *n* En
De Kosten *(pl)*
Es coste *(m)*
Fr coût *(m)*
It costo *(m)*
Pt custo *(m)*

**cost** *vb* En
De kosten
Es costar
Fr coûter
It costare
Pt custear

**cost accountant** En
De Kalkulator *(m)*
Es contable de costes *(m)*
Fr comptable de prix de revient *(m)*
It contabile dei costi di produzione *(m)*
Pt calculador de custos *(m)*

**costa marginale** *(m)* It
De Randkosten *(pl)*
En marginal cost
Es coste marginal *(m)*
Fr coût marginal *(m)*
Pt custo marginal *(m)*

**cost analysis** En
De Kostenanalyse *(f)*
Es análisis de costes *(m)*
Fr analyse des coûts *(f)*
It analisi dei costi *(f)*
Pt análise de custo *(f)*

**cost and freight** (c. & f.) En
De Kosten und Fracht
Es coste y flete
Fr coût et fret
It costo e nolo
Pt custo e frete

**costar** *vb* Es
De kosten
En cost
Fr coûter
It costare
Pt custear

**costare** *vb* It
De kosten
En cost
Es costar
Fr coûter
Pt custear

**cost benefit analysis** En
De Gewinnanalyse *(f)*
Es análisis de costes y beneficios *(m)*
Fr analyse des coûts et rendements *(f)*
It analisi dei costi e benefici *(f)*
Pt análise de custo e benefício *(f)*

**coste** *(m)* *n* Es
De Kosten *(pl)*
En cost
Fr coût *(m)*
It costo *(m)*
Pt custo *(m)*

**coste contable** *(m)* Es
De Buchwert der Einkäufe *(m)*
En book cost
Fr prix de revient comptable *(m)*

It costo contabile *(m)*
Pt custo contabilizado *(m)*

**coste de la mano de obra** *(m)* Es
De Lohnkosten *(pl)*
En cost of labour
Fr coût de la main-d'œuvre *(m)*
It costo di mano d'opera *(m)*
Pt custo da mão de obra *(m)*

**coste de repuesto** *(m)* Es
De Wiederanschaffungskosten *(pl)*
En replacement cost
Fr coût de remplacement *(m)*
It costo di rimpiazzo *(m)*
Pt custo de substituição *(m)*

**coste de venta** *(m)* Es
De Verkaufskosten *(pl)*
En selling cost
Fr frais de vente *(m)*
It costo di vendita *(m)*
Pt custo de venda *(m)*

**coste de vida** *(m)* Es
De Lebenshaltungskosten *(pl)*
En cost of living
Fr coût de la vie *(m)*
It costo della vita *(m)*
Pt custo de vida *(m)*

**coste de vida más alto** *(m)* Es
De erhöhe Lebenshaltungskosten *(pl)*
En increased cost of living
Fr renchérissement du coût de la vie *(m)*
It aumentato costo della vita *(m)*
Pt custo de vida mais elevado *(m)*

**coste directo** *(m)* Es
De direkte Kosten *(pl)*
En direct cost
Fr prix direct de revient *(m)*
It costo diretto *(m)*
Pt custo directo *(m)*

**cost-effectiveness** *n* En
De Wirtschaftlichkeit *(f)*
Es efectividad de coste *(f)*
Fr coût et efficacité
It rendimento della spesa *(m)*

Pt eficiência relativa ao custo
(f)

**coste marginal** (m) Es
De Randkosten (pl)
En marginal cost
Fr coût marginal (m)
It costa marginale (m)
Pt custo marginal (m)

**coste por unidad** (m) Es
De Einheitskosten (pl)
En unit cost
Fr coût de l'unité (m)
It costo unitario (m)
Pt custo por unidade (m)

**coste primitivo** (m) Es
De Anschaffungskosten (pl)
En historic cost
Fr coût d'acquisition primitif
(m)
It costo primitivo (m)
Pt custo original (m)

**coste promedio** (m) Es
De Durchschnittskosten (pl)
En average cost
Fr coût moyen (m)
It costo medio (m)
Pt custo médio (m)

**costes** (m pl) Es
De Kosten (pl)
En charges
Fr frais (m pl)
It spese (f pl)
Pt despesas (f pl)

**costes a reembolso** Es
De per Nachnahme
En charges forward
Fr frais à percevoir à la
livraison
It spese assegnate
Pt entrega contra reembolso

**coste, seguro, y flete** Es
De Kosten, Versicherung,
Fracht
En cost, insurance, and freight
(c.i.f.)
Fr coût, assurance, fret
It costo, assicurazione, nolo
Pt custo, seguro, e frete

**costes incrementados** (m pl)
Es
De erhöhte Kosten (pl)
En increased costs
Fr accroissement des coûts
(m)
It costi aumentati (m pl)
Pt custos aumentados (m pl)

**costes indirectos** (m pl) Es
De Gemeinkosten (pl)
En indirect costs
Fr frais indirects (m pl)
It costi indiretti (m pl)
Pt custos indirectos (m pl)

**coste social** (m) Es
De Sozialkosten (pl)
En social cost
Fr coût social (m)
It costo sociale (m)
Pt custo social (m)

**costes operacionales** (m pl) Es
De Betriebsausgaben (f pl)
En operating costs
Fr frais d'exploitation (m pl)
It spese di gestione (f pl)
Pt custos de exercício (m pl)

**coste unitario** (m) Es
De Einheitskosten (pl)
En unit cost
Fr prix coûtant unitaire (m)
It costo unitario (m)
Pt custo por unidade (m)

**coste variable** (m) Es
De variable Kosten (pl)
En variable cost
Fr coût variable (m)
It costo variabile (m)
Pt custo variavel (m)

**coste y flete** Es
De Kosten und Fracht
En cost and freight (c. & f.)
Fr coût et fret
It costo e nolo
Pt custo e frete

**costi aumentati** (m pl) It
De erhöhte Kosten (pl)
En increased costs
Es costes incrementados (m
pl)

Fr accroissement des coûts
(m)
Pt custos aumentados (m pl)

**costi indiretti** (m pl) It
De Gemeinkosten (pl)
En indirect costs
Es costes indirectos (m pl)
Fr frais indirects (m pl)
Pt custos indirectos (m pl)

**cost, insurance, and freight**
(c.i.f.) En
De Kosten, Versicherung,
Fracht
Es coste, seguro, y flete
Fr coût, assurance, fret
It costo, assicurazione, nolo
Pt custo, seguro, e frete

**costituzione** (di una società) (f)
n It
De Eintragung (einer Gesell-
schaft) (f)
En incorporation
Es incorporación (f)
Fr incorporation (f)
Pt incorporação (f)

**costo** (m) n It
De Kosten (pl)
En cost
Es coste (m)
Fr coût (m)
Pt custo (m)

**costo, assicurazione, nolo** It
De Kosten, Versicherung,
Fracht
En cost, insurance, and freight
(c.i.f.)
Es coste, seguro, y flete
Fr coût, assurance, fret
Pt custo, seguro, e frete

**costo contabile** (m) It
De Buchwert der Einkäufe (m)
En book cost
Es coste contable (m)
Fr prix de revient comptable
(m)
Pt custo contabilizado (m)

**costo della vita** (m) It
De Lebenshaltungskosten (pl)
En cost of living
Es coste de vida (m)

Fr coût de la vie *(m)*
Pt custo de vida *(m)*


**costo di mano d'opera** *(m)* It
De Lohnkosten *(pl)*
En cost of labour
Es coste de la mano de obra
   *(m)*
Fr coût de la main-d'œuvre
   *(m)*
Pt custo da mão de obra *(m)*


**costo diretto** *(m)* It
De direkte Kosten *(pl)*
En direct cost
Es coste directo *(m)*
Fr prix direct de revient *(m)*
Pt custo directo *(m)*


**costo di rimpiazzo** *(m)* It
De Wiederanschaffungskosten
   *(pl)*
En replacement cost
Es coste de repuesto *(m)*
Fr coût de remplacement *(m)*
Pt custo de substituição *(m)*


**costo di vendita** *(m)* It
De Verkaufskosten *(pl)*
En selling cost
Es coste de venta *(m)*
Fr frais de vente *(m)*
Pt custo de venda *(m)*


**costo effettivo** *(m)* It
De Gestehungskosten *(pl)*
En actual cost
Es precio verdadero *(m)*
Fr prix de revient effectif *(m)*
Pt custo verdadeiro *(m)*


**costo e nolo** It
De Kosten und Fracht
En cost and freight (c. & f.)
Es coste y flete
Fr coût et fret
Pt custo e frete


**cost of labour** En
De Lohnkosten *(pl)*
Es coste de la mano de obra
   *(m)*
Fr coût de la main-d'œuvre
   *(m)*
It costo di mano d'opera *(m)*
Pt custo da mão de obra *(m)*


**cost of living** En
De Lebenshaltungskosten *(pl)*
Es coste de vida *(m)*
Fr coût de la vie *(m)*
It costo della vita *(m)*
Pt custo de vida *(m)*


**costo medio** *(m)* It
De Durchschnittskosten *(pl)*
En average cost
Es coste promedio *(m)*
Fr coût moyen *(m)*
Pt custo médio *(m)*


**costo primitivo** *(m)* It
De Anschaffungskosten *(pl)*
En historic cost
Es coste primitivo *(m)*
Fr coût d'acquisition primitif
   *(m)*
Pt custo original *(m)*


**costo sociale** *(m)* It
De Sozialkosten *(pl)*
En social cost
Es coste social *(m)*
Fr coût social *(m)*
Pt custo social *(m)*


**costo unitario** *(m)* It
De Einheitskosten *(pl)*
En unit cost
Es coste unitario *(m)*
Fr prix coûtant unitaire *(m)*
Pt custo por unidade *(m)*


**costo variabile** *(m)* It
De variable Kosten *(pl)*
En variable cost
Es coste variable *(m)*
Fr coût variable *(m)*
Pt custo variavel *(m)*


**cost-plus contract** En
De Kosten und Vertrag
Es contrato al costo más
   beneficio *(m)*
Fr contrat en régie *(m)*
It contratto in economia *(m)*
Pt contrato de custo e adi-
   cionais *(m)*


**cost price** En
De Einstandspreis *(m)*
Es precio de coste *(m)*
Fr prix de revient *(m)*
It prezzo di costo *(m)*
Pt preço de custo *(m)*


**costrizione** *(f)* n It
De Zwang *(m)*
En duress
Es compulsión *(f)*
Fr contrainte *(f)*
Pt c erção *(f)*


**cota** *(f)* n Pt
De Quote; Beteiligung *(f)*
En quota
Es cuota *(f)*
Fr quote-part *(f)*
It quota *(f)*


**cotação** *(f)* n Pt
De Kostenanschlag *(m)*
En quotation
Es cotización *(f)*
Fr cotation *(f)*
It quotazione *(f)*


**cotação da bolsa** *(f)* Pt
De Börsenkurs *(m)*
En stock-exchange quotation
Es curso de bolsa *(m)*
Fr cours de bourse *(m)*
It quotation di borsa *(f)*


**cotation** *(f)* n Fr
De Kostenanschlag *(m)*
En quotation
Es cotización *(f)*
It quotazione *(f)*
Pt cotação *(f)*


**coter** *vb* Fr
De (den Preis) angeben
En quote
Es cotizar
It quotare
Pt cotizar


**coter sans obligation** Fr
De nicht fest anbieten
En quote not firm
Es cotizar sin compromiso
It quotare senza impegno
Pt cotizar sem fixação de valor


**cotización** *(f)* n Es
De Kostenanschlag *(m)*
En quotation
Fr cotation *(f)*
It quotazione *(f)*
Pt cotação *(f)*

**cotizar** vb Es, Pt
De (den Preis) angeben
En quote
Fr coter
It quotare

**cotizar sem fixação de valor** Pt
De nicht fest anbieten
En quote not firm
Es cotizar sin compromiso
Fr coter sans obligation
It quotare senza impegno

**cotizar sin compromiso** Es
De nicht fest anbieten
En quote not firm
Fr coter sans obligation
It quotare senza impegno
Pt cotizar sem fixação de valor

**counsel** n En
De Anwalt (m)
Es abogado (m)
Fr avocat
It avvocato (m)
Pt advogado (m)

**counterfeit** adj En
De falsch; verfälscht
Es falso; falsificado
Fr faux; contrefait
It falso; contraffatto
Pt falsificado

**counterfoil** n En
Am stub
De Talon (m)
Es talón (m)
Fr talon (m)
It matrice (f)
Pt talão (m)

**countersign** vb En
De gegenzeichnen
Es refrendar
Fr contresigner
It controfirmare
Pt validar por assinatura

**country** n En
De Land (n)
Es país (m)
Fr pays (m)
It paese (m)
Pt país (m)

**country of origin** En
De Herkunftsland (n)
Es pais de origen (m)
Fr pays de provenance (m)
It paese di origine (m)
Pt país de origem (m)

**coupon** n En, Fr (m)
De Kupon (m)
Es cupón (m)
It cedola (f)
Pt cupão (m)

**courant** adj Fr
De laufend
En current
Es corriente
It corrente
Pt corrente

**courant continu** (m) Fr
De Gleichstrom (m)
En direct current (d.c.)
Es corriente continua (f)
It corrente continua (f)
Pt corrente continua (f)

**courbe de la demande** (f) Fr
De Nachfragekurve (f)
En demand curve
Es curva de relación demanda (f)
It curva della domanda (f)
Pt curva de procura (f)

**cour d'appel** (m) Fr
De Berufungsgericht (n)
En court of appeal
Es tribunal de apelación (m)
It corte d'appello (f)
Pt tribunal de apelação (m)

**cour d'arbitrage** (m) Fr
De Schiedsgericht (n)
En court of arbitration
Es tribunal arbitral (m)
It corte arbitrale (f)
Pt tribunal de arbitragem (m)

**cours à terme** (m) Fr
De Terminnotierung (f)
En forward price
Es precio a término (m)
It prezzo per futura consegna (m)
Pt preço adiantado (m)

**cours de bourse** (m) Fr
De Börsenkurs (m)
En stock-exchange quotation
Es curso de bolsa (m)
It quotation di borsa (f)
Pt cotação da bolsa (f)

**cours de change** (m) Fr
De Umrechnungskurs (m)
En rate of exchange
Es tipo de cambio (m)
It corso del cambio (m)
Pt taxa de câmbio (f)

**cours de clôture** (m) Fr
De Schlussnotierung (f)
En closing price
Es precio de cierre (m)
It prezzo di chiusura (m)
Pt último preço (m)

**cours du marché** (m) Fr
De Marktpreis (m)
En market price
Es precio de mercado (m)
It prezzo del mercato (m)
Pt preço de mercado (m)

**cours moyen** (m) Fr
De Mittelpreis; Mittelkurs (m)
En middle price
Es precio medio (m)
It prezzo medio (m)
Pt preço médio (m)

**courtage** (m) n Fr
De Maklergebühr (f)
En brokerage
Es corretaje (m)
It senseria (f)
Pt corretagem (f)

**courtier** (m) n Fr
De Makler (m)
En broker
Es corredor (m)
It sensale (m)
Pt corretor (m)

**courtier d'assurance** (m) Fr
De Versicherungsmakler (m)
En insurance broker
Es corredor de seguros (m)
It mediatore di assicurazioni (m)
Pt corretor de seguros (m)

**courtier d'assurances maritimes** *(m)* Fr
De Seetransportversicherungsmakler *(m)*
En marine insurance broker
Es corredor de seguro marítimo *(m)*
It agente d'assicurazioni marittime *(m)*
Pt corretor de seguros marítimos *(m)*

**courtier de bons** *(m)* Fr
De Wechselmakler *(m)*
En bill broker
Es corredor de cambios *(m)*
It agente di sconto *(m)*
Pt corretor de câmbios *(m)*

**courtier en bourse** *(m)* Fr
De Börsenmakler *(m)*
En stockbroker
Es corredor de bolsa *(m)*
It agente di borsa *(m)*
Pt corretor da bolsa *(m)*

**courtier en marchandises** *(m)* Fr
De Makler für Verbrauchsgüter *(m)*
En commodity broker
Es corredor de mercaderías *(m)*
It sensale di merci *(m)*
Pt corretor de mercadorias *(m)*

**courtier maritime** *(m)* Fr
De Schiffsmakler *(m)*
En shipbroker
Es corredor marítimo *(m)*
It sensale marittimo *(m)*
Pt corretor marítimo *(m)*

**court of appeal** En
De Berufungsgericht *(n)*
Es tribunal de apelación *(m)*
Fr cour d'appel *(m)*
It corte d'appello *(f)*
Pt tribunal de apelação *(m)*

**court of arbitration** En
De Schiedsgericht *(n)*
Es tribunal arbitral *(m)*
Fr cour d'arbitrage *(m)*
It corte arbitrale *(f)*
Pt tribunal de arbitragem *(m)*

**court of law** En
De Gericht *(n)*
Es tribunal *(m)*
Fr tribunal *(m)*
It tribunale *(m)*
Pt tribunal *(m)*

**coût** *(m)* n Fr
De Kosten *(pl)*
En cost
Es coste *(m)*
It costo *(m)*
Pt custo *(m)*

**coût, assurance, fret** Fr
De Kosten, Versicherung, Fracht
En cost, insurance, and freight (c.i.f.)
Es coste, seguro, y flete
It costo, assicurazione, nolo
Pt custo, seguro, e frete

**coût d'acquisition primitif** *(m)* Fr
De Anschaffungskosten *(pl)*
En historic cost
Es coste primitivo *(m)*
It costo primitivo *(m)*
Pt custo original *(m)*

**coût de la main-d'œuvre** *(m)* Fr
De Lohnkosten *(pl)*
En cost of labour
Es coste de la mano de obra *(m)*
It costo di mano d'opera *(m)*
Pt custo da mão de obra *(m)*

**coût de la vie** *(m)* Fr
De Lebenshaltungskosten *(pl)*
En cost of living
Es coste de vida *(m)*
It costo della vita *(m)*
Pt custo de vida *(m)*

**coût de l'unité** *(m)* Fr
De Einheitskosten *(pl)*
En unit cost
Es coste por unidad *(m)*
It costo unitario *(m)*
Pt custo por unidade *(m)*

**coût de remplacement** *(m)* Fr
De Wiederanschaffungskosten *(pl)*
En replacement cost
Es coste de repuesto *(m)*

It costo di rimpiazzo *(m)*
Pt custo de substituição *(m)*

**coûter** *vb* Fr
De kosten
En cost
Es costar
It costare
Pt custear

**coût et efficacité** Fr
De Wirtschaftlichkeit *(f)*
En cost-effectiveness
Es efectividad de coste *(f)*
It rendimento della spesa *(m)*
Pt eficiência relativa ao custo *(f)*

**coût et fret** Fr
De Kosten und Fracht
En cost and freight (c. & f.)
Es coste y flete
It costo e nolo
Pt custo e frete

**coût marginal** *(m)* Fr
De Randkosten *(pl)*
En marginal cost
Es coste marginal *(m)*
It costa marginale *(m)*
Pt custo marginal *(m)*

**coût moyen** *(m)* Fr
De Durchschnittskosten *(pl)*
En average cost
Es coste promedio *(m)*
It costo medio *(m)*
Pt custo médio *(m)*

**coût social** *(m)* Fr
De Sozialkosten *(pl)*
En social cost
Es coste social *(m)*
It costo sociale *(m)*
Pt custo social *(m)*

**coût variable** *(m)* Fr
De variable Kosten *(pl)*
En variable cost
Es coste variable *(m)*
It costo variabile *(m)*
Pt custo variavel *(m)*

**couverture** *(f)* n Fr
De Deckung *(f)*
En cover
Es cobertura *(f)*

It copertura (f)
Pt cobertura (f)

**couverture temporaire** (m) Fr
De temporäre Deckung (f)
En temporary cover
Es cobertura provisional (f)
It copertura provvisoria (f)
Pt cobertura provisória (f)

**covenant** n En
De Abkommen (n)
Es pacto (m)
Fr convention (f)
It convenzione (f)
Pt pacto (m)

**cover** n En
De Deckung (f)
Es cobertura (f)
Fr couverture (f)
It copertura (f)
Pt cobertura (f)

**cover note** En
De Deckungszusage (f)
Es aviso de seguro del riesgo (m)
Fr lettre de couverture (f)
It nota di copertura (f)
Pt nota de cobertura (f)

**crane** n En
De Kran (m)
Es grúa (f)
Fr grue (f)
It gru (f)
Pt grúa (f)

**créance** (f) n Fr
De Schuld (f)
En debt
Es deuda (f)
It debito (m)
Pt dívida (f)

**créance douteuse** (f) Fr
De zweifelhafte Forderung (f)
En doubtful debt
Es deuda de pago dudoso (f)
It credito dubbio (m)
Pt dívida duvidosa (f)

**créance irrécouvrable** (f) Fr
De uneinbringliche Schuld (f)
En bad debt
Es deuda incobrable (f)

It credito inesigibile (m)
Pt dívida incobrável (f)

**créances** (f pl) n Fr
De Debitoren (m pl)
En accounts receivable
Es cuentas a recibir (f pl)
It conti attivi (m pl)
Pt contas a receber (f pl)

**créancier** (m) n Fr
De Gläubiger (m)
En creditor
Es acreedor (m)
It creditore (m)
Pt credor (m)

**créancier chirographaire** (m) Fr
De nicht gesicherter Gläubiger (m)
En unsecured creditor
Es acreedor no garantizado (m)
It creditore non garantito (m)
Pt credor sem garantia (m)

**créancier privilégié** (m) Fr
De bevorrechtigter Gläubiger (m)
En preferential creditor
Es acreedor privilegiado (m)
It creditore privilegiato (m)
Pt credor preferencial (m)

**crecimiento** (m) n Es
De Entwicklung (f)
En growth
Fr croissance (f)
It crescita; sviluppo (f m)
Pt crescimento (m)

**crecimiento económico** (m) Es
De Wirtschaftswachstum (m)
En economic growth
Fr croissance économique (f)
It sviluppo economico (m)
Pt crescimento económico (m)

**credit** n En
De Kredit (m)
Es crédito (m)
Fr crédit (m)
It credito (m)
Pt crédito (m)

**crédit** (m) n Fr
De Kredit (m)
En credit
Es crédito (m)
It credito (m)
Pt crédito (m)

**crédit à découvert** (m) Fr
De offener Kredit (m)
En open credit
Es crédito en descubierto (m)
It credito allo scoperto (m)
Pt crédito em aberto (m)

**credit balance** En
De Kreditsaldo (m)
Es saldo acreedor (m)
Fr solde créditeur (m)
It saldo creditore (m)
Pt saldo credor (m)

**crédit bancaire** (m) Fr
De Bankkredit (m)
En bank credit
Es crédito bancario (m)
It credito bancario (m)
Pt crédito bancário (m)

**credit card** En
De Kreditkarte (f)
Es tarjeta de crédito (f)
Fr carte de crédit (f)
It carta di credito (f)
Pt cartão de crédito (m)

**crédit de construction** (m) Fr
De Baukredit (m)
En building loan
Es crédito de construcción (m)
It prestito immobiliare (m)
Pt empréstimo para construção (m)

**crédit documentaire** (m) Fr
De Dokumenten-Akkreditiv (n)
En documentary credit
Es crédito documentario (m)
It credito documentario (m)
Pt crédito contra documentação (m)

**créditeur** (m) n Fr
De Gläubiger (m)
En creditor
Es acreedor (m)
It creditore (m)
Pt credor (m)

**créditeurs divers** *(m pl)* Fr
De Kreditoren *(m pl)*
En sundry creditors
Es acreedores varios *(m pl)*
It creditori diversi *(m pl)*
Pt créditos diversos *(m pl)*

**crediti bloccati** *(m pl)* It
De eingefrorene Kredite *(m pl)*
En frozen credits
Es créditos congelados *(m pl)*
Fr crédits bloqués *(m pl)*
Pt créditos congelados *(m pl)*

**credit insurance** En
De Kreditversicherung *(f)*
Es seguro crediticio *(m)*
Fr assurance crédit *(f)*
It assicurazione credito *(f)*
Pt seguro de crédito *(m)*

**credit note** En
De Gutschriftanzeige *(f)*
Es nota de crédito *(f)*
Fr avis de crédit *(m)*
It nota di credito *(f)*
Pt aviso de crédito *(m)*

**crédito** *(m)* n Es, Pt
De Kredit *(m)*
En credit
Fr crédit *(m)*
It credito *(m)*

**credito** *(m)* n It
De Kredit *(m)*
En credit
Es crédito *(m)*
Fr crédit *(m)*
Pt crédito *(m)*

**credito allo scoperto** *(m)* It
De offener Kredit *(m)*
En open credit
Es crédito en descubierto *(m)*
Fr crédit à découvert *(m)*
Pt crédito em aberto *(m)*

**crédito bancario** *(m)* Es
De Bankkredit *(m)*
En bank credit
Fr crédit bancaire *(m)*
It credito bancario *(m)*
Pt crédito bancário *(m)*

**credito bancario** *(m)* It
De Bankkredit *(m)*
En bank credit

Es crédito bancario *(m)*
Fr crédit bancaire *(m)*
Pt crédito bancário *(m)*

**crédito bancário** *(m)* Pt
De Bankkredit *(m)*
En bank credit
Es crédito bancario *(m)*
Fr crédit bancaire *(m)*
It credito bancario *(m)*

**crédito contra documentação**
*(m)* Pt
De Dokumenten-Akkreditiv *(n)*
En documentary credit
Es crédito documentario *(m)*
Fr crédit documentaire *(m)*
It credito documentario *(m)*

**credito d'accettazione** *(m)* It
De Akzeptkredit *(m)*
En acceptance credit
Es crédito de aceptación *(m)*
Fr crédit par acceptation *(m)*
Pt crédito de aceitação *(m)*

**crédito de aceitação** *(m)* Pt
De Akzeptkredit *(m)*
En acceptance credit
Es crédito de aceptación *(m)*
Fr crédit par acceptation *(m)*
It credito d'accettazione *(m)*

**crédito de aceptación** *(m)* Es
De Akzeptkredit *(m)*
En acceptance credit
Fr crédit par acceptation *(m)*
It credito d'accettazione *(m)*
Pt crédito de aceitação *(m)*

**crédito de construcción** *(m)*
Es
De Baukredit *(m)*
En building loan
Fr crédit de construction *(m)*
It prestito immobiliare *(m)*
Pt empréstimo para constru-
ção *(m)*

**crédito documentario** *(m)* Es
De Dokumenten-Akkreditiv *(n)*
En documentary credit
Fr crédit documentaire *(m)*
It credito documentario *(m)*
Pt crédito contra documen-
tação *(m)*

**credito documentario** *(m)* It
De Dokumenten-Akkreditiv *(n)*
En documentary credit
Es crédito documentario *(m)*
Fr crédit documentaire *(m)*
Pt crédito contra documen-
tação *(m)*

**credito dubbio** *(m)* It
De zweifelhafte Forderung *(f)*
En doubtful debt
Es deuda de pago dudoso *(f)*
Fr créance douteuse *(f)*
Pt dívida duvidosa *(f)*

**crédito em aberto** *(m)* Pt
De offener Kredit *(m)*
En open credit
Es crédito en descubierto *(m)*
Fr crédit à découvert *(m)*
It credito allo scoperto *(m)*

**crédito em branco** *(m)* Pt
De offener Kredit *(m)*
En blank credit
Es crédito en blanco *(m)*
Fr crédit à découvert *(m)*
It credito in bianco *(m)*

**crédito en blanco** *(m)* Es
De offener Kredit *(m)*
En blank credit
Fr crédit à découvert *(m)*
It credito in bianco *(m)*
Pt crédito em branco *(m)*

**crédito en descubierto** *(m)* Es
De offener Kredit *(m)*
En open credit
Fr crédit à découvert *(m)*
It credito allo scoperto *(m)*
Pt crédito em aberto *(m)*

**credito in bianco** *(m)* It
De offener Kredit *(m)*
En blank credit
Es crédito en blanco *(m)*
Fr crédit à découvert *(m)*
Pt crédito em branco *(m)*

**credito inesigibile** *(m)* It
De uneinbringliche Schuld *(f)*
En bad debt
Es deuda incobrable *(f)*
Fr créance irrécouvrable *(f)*
Pt dívida incobrável *(f)*

**crédito provisional** *(m)* Es
De Vorschusskredit *(m)*
En bridging loan
Am bridge-over
Fr crédit provisoire *(m)*
It credito provvisorio *(m)*
Pt crédito provisório *(m)*

**crédito provisório** *(m)* Pt
De Vorschusskredit *(m)*
En bridging loan
Am bridge-over
Es crédito provisional *(m)*
Fr crédit provisoire *(m)*
It credito provvisorio *(m)*

**credito provvisorio** *(m)* It
De Vorschusskredit *(m)*
En bridging loan
Am bridge-over
Es crédito provisional *(m)*
Fr crédit provisoire *(m)*
Pt crédito provisório *(m)*

**creditor** *n* En
De Gläubiger *(m)*
Es acreedor *(m)*
Fr créancier; créditeur *(m)*
It creditore *(m)*
Pt credor *(m)*

**creditore** *(m)* *n* It
De Gläubiger *(m)*
En creditor
Es acreedor *(m)*
Fr créancier; créditeur *(m)*
Pt credor *(m)*

**creditore non garantito** *(m)* It
De nicht gesicherter Gläubiger *(m)*
En unsecured creditor
Es acreedor no garantizado *(m)*
Fr créancier chirographaire *(m)*
Pt credor sem garantia *(m)*

**crédito renovável** *(m)* Pt
De automatisch sich erneuen-des Akkreditiv *(n)*
En revolving credit
Es crédito reponible *(m)*
Fr accréditif automatiquement renouvelable *(m)*
It credito rotativo *(m)*

**crédito reponible** *(m)* Es
De automatisch sich erneuen-des Akkreditiv *(n)*
En revolving credit
Fr accréditif automatiquement renouvelable *(m)*
It credito rotativo *(m)*
Pt crédito renovável *(m)*

**creditore privilegiato** *(m)* It
De bevorrechtigter Gläubiger *(m)*
En preferential creditor
Es acreedor privilegiado *(m)*
Fr créancier privilégié *(m)*
Pt credor preferencial *(m)*

**creditori diversi** *(m pl)* It
De Kreditoren *(m pl)*
En sundry creditors
Es acreedores varios *(m pl)*
Fr créditeurs divers *(m pl)*
Pt créditos diversos *(m pl)*

**credito rotativo** *(m)* It
De automatisch sich erneuen-des Akkreditiv *(n)*
En revolving credit
Es crédito reponible *(m)*
Fr accréditif automatiquement renouvelable *(m)*
Pt crédito renovável *(m)*

**créditos congelados** *(m pl)* Es, Pt
De eingefrorene Kredite *(m pl)*
En frozen credits
Fr crédits bloqués *(m pl)*
It crediti bloccati *(m pl)*

**créditos diversos** *(m pl)* Pt
De Kreditoren *(m pl)*
En sundry creditors
Es acreedores varios *(m pl)*
Fr créditeurs divers *(m pl)*
It creditori diversi *(m pl)*

**crédit par acceptation** *(m)* Fr
De Akzeptkredit *(m)*
En acceptance credit
Es crédito de aceptación *(m)*
It credito d'accettazione *(m)*
Pt crédito de aceitação *(m)*

**crédit provisoire** *(m)* Fr
De Vorschusskredit *(m)*
En bridging loan
Am bridge-over

Es crédito provisional *(m)*
It credito provvisorio *(m)*
Pt crédito provisório *(m)*

**credit rating** En
De Kreditwürdigkeit *(f)*
Es límite de crédito *(m)*
Fr degré de solvabilité *(m)*
It stima del credito *(f)*
Pt nível de crédito *(m)*

**crédits bloqués** *(m pl)* Fr
De eingefrorene Kredite *(m pl)*
En frozen credits
Es creditos congelados *(m pl)*
It crediti bloccati *(m pl)*
Pt créditos congelados *(m pl)*

**credit squeeze** En
De Kreditklemme *(f)*
Es escasez de créditos *(f)*
Fr resserrement de crédit *(m)*
It restrizione di credito *(f)*
Pt restrição de crédito *(f)*

**credor** *(m)* *n* Pt
De Gläubiger *(m)*
En creditor
Es acreedor *(m)*
Fr créancier; créditeur *(m)*
It creditore *(m)*

**credor sem garantia** *(m)* Pt
De nicht gesicherter Gläubiger *(m)*
En unsecured creditor
Es acreedor no garantizado *(m)*
Fr créancier chirographaire *(m)*
It creditore non garantito *(m)*

**crescimento** *(m)* *n* Pt
De Entwicklung *(f)*
En growth
Es crecimiento *(m)*
Fr croissance *(f)*
It crescita; sviluppo *(f; m)*

**crescimento económico** *(m)* Pt
De Wirtschaftswachstum *(m)*
En economic growth
Es crecimiento económico *(m)*
Fr croissance économique *(f)*
It sviluppo economico *(m)*

**crescita** *(f)* *n* It
　De Entwicklung *(f)*
　En growth
　Es crecimiento *(m)*
　Fr croissance *(f)*
　Pt crescimento *(m)*

**crew** *n* En
　De Mannschaft *(f)*
　Es tripulación *(f)*
　Fr équipage *(m)*
　It equipaggio *(m)*
　Pt tripulação *(f)*

**crise économique** *(f)* Fr
　De Wirtschaftskrise *(f)*
　En depression
　Es crisis económica *(f)*
　It crisi *(f)*
　Pt depressão *(f)*

**crisi** *(f)* *n* It
　De Wirtschaftskrise *(f)*
　En depression
　Es crisis económica *(f)*
　Fr crise économique *(f)*
　Pt depressão *(f)*

**crisis económica** *(f)* Es
　De Wirtschaftskrise *(f)*
　En depression
　Fr crise économique *(f)*
　It crisi *(f)*
　Pt depressão *(f)*

**cristal deslustrado** *(m)* Es
　De Mattscheibe *(f)*
　En ground glass
　Fr verre dépoli *(m)*
　It vetro smerigliato *(m)*
　Pt vidro esmerilado *(m)*

**cristal de ventana** *(m)* Es
　De Fensterglas *(n)*
　En window glass
　Fr verre à vitres *(m)*
　It vetro da finestre *(m)*
　Pt vidro de montra *(m)*

**cristallo** *(m)* *n* It
　De Spiegelglas *(n)*
　En plate glass
　Es vidrio plano pulido *(m)*
　Fr verre à glaces; glace de vitrage *(m f)*
　Pt chapa de vidro *(f)*

**critical path analysis** (c.p.a.) En
　De Netzplantechnik *(f)*
　Es análisis de recorrido crítico *(m)*
　Fr analyse du chemin critique *(m)*
　It analisi della linea critica *(f)*
　Pt análise de transcurso crítico *(f)*

**croissance** *(f)* *n* Fr
　De Entwicklung *(f)*
　En growth
　Es crecimiento *(m)*
　It crescita; sviluppo *(f; m)*
　Pt crescimento *(m)*

**croissance économique** *(f)* Fr
　De Wirtschaftswachstum *(m)*
　En economic growth
　Es crecimiento económico *(m)*
　It sviluppo economico *(m)*
　Pt crescimento económico *(m)*

**crollo di banca** *(m)* It
　De Bankkrach *(m)*
　En bank crash
　Es quiebra de banco *(f)*
　Fr krach d'une banque *(m)*
　Pt falência bancária *(f)*

**crossed cheque** En
　De Verrechnungsscheck *(m)*
　Es cheque cruzado *(m)*
　Fr chèque barré *(m)*
　It assegno sbarrato *(m)*
　Pt cheque cruzado *(m)*

**cuadro de conexión** *(m)* Es
　De Schalttafel *(f)*
　En switchboard
　Fr tableau de distribution *(m)*
　It quadro di comando *(m)*
　Pt quadro de distribuição *(m)*

**cuarentena** *(f)* *n* Es
　De Quarantäne *(f)*
　En quarantine
　Fr quarantaine *(f)*
　It quarantena *(f)*
　Pt quarantena *(f)*

**cubicación de obra** *(f)* Es
　De Baukostenvoranschlag *(m)*
　En bill of quantities
　Fr devis *(m)*

It preventivo *(m)*
　Pt relação de quantidades *(f)*

**cubic capacity** (cargo, bunker, etc.) En
　De Kubikinhalt *(m)*
　Es capacidad cúbica *(f)*
　Fr volume *(m)*
　It volume *(m)*
　Pt capacidade cúbica *(f)*

**cubic capacity** (engine) En
　De Hubraum *(m)*
　Es cilindrada *(f)*
　Fr cylindrée *(f)*
　It cilindrata *(f)*
　Pt cilindrada *(f)*

**cubierta** *(f)* *n* Es
　De Deck *(n)*
　En deck
　Fr pont *(m)*
　It coperta; ponte *(f m)*
　Pt convés *(m)*

**cubrirse** *vb* Es
　De sich decken
　En hedge
　Fr arbitrager
　It coprirsi
　Pt cobrir-se

**cuenta** (bancaria) *(f)* *n* Es
　De Konto *(n)*
　En account
　Fr compte *(m)*
　It conto *(m)*
　Pt conta *(f)*

**cuenta** (nota) *(f)* Es
　De Rechnung *(f)*
　En bill; account
　Fr compte; note *(m f)*
　It conto; nota *(m f)*
　Pt conta *(f)*

**cuenta bancaria** *(f)* Es
　De Bankkonto *(n)*
　En bank account
　Fr compte en banque *(m)*
　It conto in banca *(m)*
　Pt conta bancária *(f)*

**cuenta bloqueada** *(f)* Es
　De gesperrtes Konto *(n)*
　En blocked account
　Fr compte bloqué *(m)*

It conto bloccato *(m)*
Pt conta bloqueada *(f)*

**cuenta comercial** *(f)* Es
De Handelskonto *(n)*
En trade account
Fr compte commercial *(m)*
It conto commerciale *(m)*
Pt conta comercial *(f)*

**cuenta común** *(f)* Es
De Gemeinschaftskonto *(n)*
En joint account
Fr compte joint *(m)*
It conto in comune *(m)*
Pt conta conjunta *(f)*

**cuenta corriente** *(f)* Es
De Kontokorrent *(n)*
En current account
Am checking account
Fr compte courant *(m)*
It conto corrente *(m)*
Pt conta corrente *(f)*

**cuenta de agio** *(f)* Es
De Agiokonto *(n)*
En agio account
Fr compte d'agio *(m)*
It conto d'aggio *(m)*
Pt conta de ágio *(f)*

**cuenta de ahorras** *(f)* Es
De Depositenkonto *(n)*
En deposit account
Am interest-bearing-account
Fr compte de dépôt *(m)*
It conto di deposito *(m)*
Pt conta de depósito *(m)*

**cuenta de anticipos** *(f)* Es
De Darlehenskonto *(n)*
En advance account
Fr compte d'avances *(m)*
It conto anticipo *(m)*
Pt conta de adiantamentos *(f)*

**cuenta de apropiación** *(f)* Es
De Rückstellungskonto *(n)*
En appropriation account
Fr compte d'affectation *(m)*
It conto di stanziamento *(m)*
Pt conta de apropriação *(f)*

**cuenta de capital** *(f)* Es
De Kapitalkonto *(n)*
En capital account
Fr compte capital *(m)*

It conto capitale *(m)*
Pt conta de capital *(f)*

**cuenta de compensación de cambio** *(f)* Es
De Währungsausgleichsfonds *(m)**
En exchange equalization account
Fr fonds de stabilisation des changes *(m pl)*
It conto per la stabilizzazione dei cambi *(m)*
Pt conta de compensação de transacções *(f)*

**cuenta de control** *(f)* Es
De Kontrollkonto *(n)*
En control account
Fr compte de contrôle *(m)*
It conto di controllo *(m)*
Pt conta de controlo *(f)*

**cuenta de desembarque** *(f)* Es
De Löschungskonto *(n)*
En landing account
Fr compte de mise à terre *(m)*
It conto di sbarco *(m)*
Pt conta de descargas *(f)*

**cuenta de especulaciones a la baja** *(f)* Es
De Baissekonto *(n)*
En bear account
Fr compte des speculations à la baisse *(m)*
It conto di speculazioni al ribasso *(m)*
Pt conta de especulações baixistas *(f)*

**cuenta de ingresos y gastos** *(f)* Es
De Ausgaben- und Ertragskonto *(n)*
En income and expenditure account
Fr compte de revenus et dépenses *(m)*
It conto proventi e spese *(m)*
Pt conta de receitas e despesas *(f)*

**cuenta de préstamos** *(f)* Es
De Anleihekonto *(n)*
En loan account
Fr compte des prêts *(m)*

It conto anticipazioni *(m)*
Pt conta de empréstimos *(f)*

**cuenta de resultado** *(f)* Es
De Firmenkonto *(n)*
En nominal account
Fr compte nominal *(m)*
It conto d'ordine *(m)*
Pt conta nominal *(f)*

**cuenta en descubierto** *(f)* Es
De Konto überzogen *(n)*
En account overdrawn
Fr compte découvert *(m)*
It conto scoperto *(m)*
Pt conta a descoberto *(f)*

**cuenta exterior** *(f)* Es
De Auslandskonto *(n)*
En external account
Am foreign currency account
Fr compte transférable *(m)*
It conto estero *(m)*
Pt conta externa *(f)*

**cuenta identificada con número** *(f)* Es
De numeriertes Konto *(n)*
En numbered account
Fr compte identifié par numéro *(m)*
It conto identificato da numero *(m)*
Pt conta numerada *(f)*

**cuenta personal** *(f)* Es
De Kundenkonto *(n)*
En charge account
Fr compte personnel *(m)*
It conto personale *(m)*
Pt conta pessoal *(f)*

**cuenta rendida** *(f)* Es
De zur Begleichung vorgelegte Rechnung *(f)*
En account rendered
Fr compte rendu *(m)*
It conto reso *(m)*
Pt conta remetida *(f)*

**cuentas a pagar** *(f pl)* Es
De Kreditoren *(m pl)*
En accounts payable
Fr comptes à payer *(m pl)*
It conti passivi *(m pl)*
Pt contas a pagar *(f pl)*

**cuentas a recibir** (f pl) Es
De Debitoren (m pl)
En accounts receivable
Fr créances (f pl)
It conti attivi (m pl)
Pt contas a receber (f pl)

**cuentas consolidadas** (f pl) Es
De konsolidierter Kontenab-
    schluss (m)
En consolidated accounts
Fr comptes consolidés (m pl)
It conti consolidati (m pl)
Pt contas consolidadas (f pl)

**cuenta simulada** (f) Es
De Firmenkonto (n)
En impersonal account
Fr compte impersonnel (m)
It conto d'ordine (m)
Pt conta impessoal (f)

**cuentas pendientes** (f pl) Es
De ausstehende Schulden (m
    pl)
En outstanding accounts
Fr comptes à percevoir (m pl)
It conti aperti (m pl)
Pt contas por saldar (f pl)

**cuentas revisadas** (f pl) Es
De geprüfte Geschäftsbücher
    (n pl)
En audited accounts
Fr comptes vérifiés et certifiés
    (m pl)
It conti verificati e certificati
    (m pl)
Pt contas fiscalizadas (f pl)

**cuenta suspensa** (f) Es
De Übergangskonto (n)
En suspense account
Fr compte d'ordre (m)
It conto sospeso (m)
Pt conta pendente (m)

**cuestionario** (m) n Es
De Fragebogen (m)
En questionnaire
Fr questionnaire (m)
It questionario (m)
Pt questionário (m)

**cum dividend** En
De mit Dividende
Es con dividendo
Fr droit attaché

It con dividendo
Pt com dividendo

**cumplimiento** (m) n Es
De Erfüllung (f)
En fulfilment
Fr accomplissement (m)
It adempimento (m)
Pt cumprimento (m)

**cumplir** vb Es
De erfüllen
En fulfil
Fr remplir
It adempiere
Pt comprir

**cumprimento** (m) n Pt
De Erfüllung (f)
En fulfilment
Es cumplimiento (m)
Fr accomplissement (m)
It adempimento (m)

**cumprimento final** (m) Pt
De Rechnungsentlastung (f)
En final discharge
Es finiquito (m)
Fr quitus (m)
It quietanza finale (f)

**cumulatif** adj Fr
De kumulativ
En cumulative
Es acumulativo
It cumulativo
Pt cumulativo

**cumulative** adj En
De kumulativ
Es acumulativo
Fr cumulatif
It cumulativo
Pt cumulativo

**cumulativo** adj Es, It, Pt
De kumulativ
En cumulative
Fr cumulatif

**cuota** (f) n Es
De Quote; Beteiligung (f)
En quota
Fr quote-part (f)
It quota (f)
Pt cota; quota-parte (f)

**cupão** (m) n Pt
De Kupon (m)
En coupon
Es cupón (m)
Fr coupon (m)
It cedola (f)

**cupo de importación** (m) Es
De Einfuhrkontingent (n)
En import quota
Fr contingent d'importation
    (m)
It contingente d'importazione
    (m)
Pt quota de importação (f)

**cupón** (m) n Es
De Kupon (m)
En coupon
Fr coupon (m)
It cedola (f)
Pt cupão (m)

**cupón de dividendos** (m) Es
De Gewinnanteilschein (m)
En dividend warrant
Fr dividende-warrant (m)
It cedola di dividendo (f)
Pt cédula de dividendo (f)

**curador** (m) n Pt
De Nachlassverwalter (m)
En administrator (of an estate)
Es administrador (m)
Fr curateur (m)
It curatore (m)

**curateur** (m) n Fr
De Nachlassverwalter (m)
En administrator (of an estate)
Es administrador (m)
It curatore (m)
Pt curador (m)

**curatore** (m) n It
De Konkursverwalter; Nach-
    lassverwalter (m)
En (official) receiver; admin-
    istrator
Es sindico; administrador (m)
Fr syndic de faillite; curateur
    (m)
Pt sindico; curador (m)

**currency** n En
De Währung (f)
Es moneda (f)
Fr monnaie (f)

It    valuta *(f)*
Pt   moeda *(f)*

**currency area** En
De  Währungsgebiet *(n)*
Es  zona monetaria *(f)*
Fr  zone monétaire *(f)*
It   zona monetaria *(f)*
Pt  zona monetária *(f)*

**currency control** Am
En  exchange control
De  Devisenkontrolle *(f)*
Es  fiscalización de cambios *(f)*
Fr  contrôle des changes *(m)*
It   controllo sui cambi *(m)*
Pt  controlo de câmbios *(m)*

**current** *adj* En
De  laufend
Es  corriente
Fr  courant; en cours
It   corrente
Pt  corrente

**current account** En
Am checking account
De  Kontokorrent *(n)*
Es  cuenta corriente *(f)*
Fr  compte courant *(m)*
It   conto corrente *(m)*
Pt  conta corrente *(f)*

**current assets** En
De  Umlaufsvermögen *(n)*
Es  activo realizable *(m)*
Fr  actif courant *(m)*
It   attivo liquido *(m)*
Pt  bens no activo actual *(m pl)*

**current liabilities** En
De  laufende Verbindlichkeiten *(f pl)*
Es  pasivo exigible *(m)*
Fr  passif exigible *(m)*
It   passività esigibili *(f pl)*
Pt  passivo actual *(m)*

**current year** En
De  laufendes Jahr *(n)*
Es  año en curso *(m)*
Fr  année en cours *(f)*
It   anno in corso *(m)*
Pt  ano corrente *(m)*

**curso de bolsa** *(m)* Es
De  Börsenkurs *(m)*
En  stock-exchange quotation
Fr  cours de bourse *(m)*
It   quotation di borsa *(f)*
Pt  cotação da bolsa *(f)*

**curva della domanda** *(f)* It
De  Nachfragekurve *(f)*
En  demand curve
Es  curva de relación demanda *(f)*
Fr  courbe de la demande *(f)*
Pt  curva de procura *(f)*

**curva de procura** *(f)* Pt
De  Nachfragekurve *(f)*
En  demand curve
Es  curva de relación demanda *(f)*
Fr  courbe de la demande *(f)*
It   curva della domanda *(f)*

**curva de relación demanda** *(f)* Es
De  Nachfragekurve *(f)*
En  demand curve
Fr  courbe de la demande *(f)*
It   curva della domanda *(f)*
Pt  curva de procura *(f)*

**custas de manejo** *(f pl)* Pt
De  Manipulationsgebühr *(f)*
En  handling charges
Es  gastos de manutención *(m pl)*
Fr  frais de manutention *(m pl)*
It   spese di gestione *(f pl)*

**custas de registo** *(f pl)* Pt
De  Anmeldegebühr *(f)*
En  registration fee
Es  derechos de registro *(m pl)*
Fr  droit d'enregistrement *(m)*
It   tassa di registrazione *(f)*

**custear** *vb* Pt
De  kosten
En  cost
Es  costar
Fr  coûter
It   costare

**custo** *(m)* n Pt
De  Kosten *(pl)*
En  cost
Es  coste *(m)*

Fr  coût *(m)*
It   costo *(m)*

**custo contabilizado** *(m)* Pt
De  Buchwert der Einkäufe *(m)*
En  book cost
Es  coste contable *(m)*
Fr  prix de revient comptable *(m)*
It   costo contabile *(m)*

**custo da mão de obra** *(m)* Pt
De  Lohnkosten *(pl)*
En  cost of labour
Es  coste de la mano de obra *(m)*
Fr  coût de la main-d'œuvre *(m)*
It   costo di mano d'opera *(m)*

**custo de substituição** *(m)* Pt
De  Wiederanschaffungskosten *(pl)*
En  replacement cost
Es  coste de repuesto *(m)*
Fr  coût de remplacement *(m)*
It   costo di rimpiazzo *(m)*

**custo de venda** *(m)* Pt
De  Verkaufskosten *(pl)*
En  selling cost
Es  coste de venta *(m)*
Fr  frais de vente *(m)*
It   costo di vendita *(m)*

**custo de vida** *(m)* Pt
De  Lebenshaltungskosten *(pl)*
En  cost of living
Es  coste de vida *(m)*
Fr  coût de la vie *(m)*
It   costo della vita *(m)*

**custo de vida mais elevado** *(m)* Pt
De  erhöhte Lebenshaltungskosten *(pl)*
En  increased cost of living
Es  coste de vida más alto *(m)*
Fr  renchérissement du coût de la vie *(m)*
It   aumentato costo della vita *(m)*

**custodia** *(f)* Es, It
De  sichere Verwaltung *(f)*
En  safe custody
Fr  bonne garde *(f)*
Pt  custódia segura *(f)*

**custódia segura** (f) Pt
  De sichere Verwahrung (f)
  En safe custody
  Es custodia (f)
  Fr bonne garde (f)
  It custodia (f)

**custo directo** (m) Pt
  De direkte Kosten (pl)
  En direct cost
  Es coste directo (m)
  Fr prix direct de revient (m)
  It costo diretto (m)

**custo e frete** Pt
  De Kosten und Fracht
  En cost and freight (c. & f.)
  Es coste y flete
  Fr coût et fret
  It costo e nolo

**custom** (clientele) n En
  De Kundschaft (f)
  Es clientela (f)
  Fr clientèle (f)
  It clientela (f)
  Pt clientela (f)

**custo marginal** (m) Pt
  De Randkosten (pl)
  En marginal cost
  Es coste marginal (m)
  Fr coût marginal (m)
  It costa marginale (m)

**custo médio** (m) Pt
  De Durchschnittskosten (pl)
  En average cost
  Es coste promedio (m)
  Fr coût moyen (m)
  It costo medio (m)

**customer** n En
  De Kunde (m)
  Es cliente (m)
  Fr client (m)
  It cliente (m)
  Pt cliente (m)

**custom of the trade** En
  De Handelsgebrauch (m)
  Es uso comercial (m)
  Fr usage commercial (m)
  It uso commerciale (m)
  Pt uso comercial (m)

**customs** pl n En
  De Zoll (n)
  Es aduana (f)
  Fr douane (f)
  It dogana (f)
  Pt alfândega (f)

**customs barrier** En
  De Zollschranke (f)
  Es barrera aduanera (f)
  Fr barrière douanière (f)
  It barriera doganale (f)
  Pt barreira alfandegária (f)

**customs clearance** En
  De Zollabfertigung (f)
  Es paso de aduanas (f)
  Fr dédouanement (m)
  It sdoganamento (m)
  Pt despacho alfandegário (m)

**customs declaration** En
  De Zollerklärung (f)
  Es declaración de aduana (f)
  Fr déclaration en douane (f)
  It dichiarazione doganale (f)
  Pt declaração alfandegária (f)

**customs duty** En
  De Zoll (m)
  Es derechos de aduanas (m pl)
  Fr droit de douane (m)
  It diritto doganale (m)
  Pt direitos alfandegários (m pl)

**customs examination** En
  De zollamtliche Untersuchung (f)
  Es control de aduanas (m)
  Fr visite douanière (f)
  It visita doganale (f)
  Pt verificação alfandegária (f)

**customs union** En
  De Zollunion (f)
  Es unión aduanera (f)
  Fr union douanière (f)
  It unione doganale (f)
  Pt união aduaneira (f)

**custo original** (m) Pt
  De Anschaffungskosten (pl)
  En historic cost
  Es coste primitivo (m)

  Fr coût d'acquisition primitif (m)
  It costo primitivo (m)

**custo por unidade** (m) Pt
  De Einheitskosten (pl)
  En unit cost
  Es coste por unidad (m)
  Fr coût de l'unité (m)
  It costo unitario (m)

**custos aumentados** (m pl) Pt
  De erhöhte Kosten (pl)
  En increased costs
  Es costes incrementados (m pl)
  Fr accroissement des coûts (m)
  It costi aumentati (m pl)

**custos de exercício** (m pl) Pt
  De Betriebsausgaben (f pl)
  En operating costs
  Es costes operacionales (m pl)
  Fr frais d'exploitation (m pl)
  It spese di gestione (f pl)

**custo, seguro, e frete** Pt
  De Kosten, Versicherung, Fracht
  En cost, insurance, and freight (c.i.f.)
  Es coste, seguro, y flete
  Fr coût, assurance, fret
  It costo, assicurazione, nolo

**custos indirectos** (m pl) Pt
  De Gemeinkosten (pl)
  En indirect costs
  Es costes indirectos (m pl)
  Fr frais indirects (m pl)
  It costi indiretti (m pl)

**custo social** (m) Pt
  De Sozialkosten (pl)
  En social cost
  Es coste social (m)
  Fr coût social (m)
  It costo sociale (m)

**custo variavel** (m) Pt
  De variable Kosten (pl)
  En variable cost
  Es coste variable (m)
  Fr coût variable (m)
  It costo variabile (m)

**custo verdadeiro** *(m)* Pt
De Gestehungskosten *(pl)*
En actual cost
Es precio verdadero *(m)*
Fr prix de revient effectif *(m)*
It costo effettivo *(m)*

**cybernetics** *n* En
De Kybernetik *(f)*
Es cibernética *(f)*
Fr cybernétique *(f)*
It cibernetica *(f)*
Pt cibernética *(f)*

**cybernétique** *(f) n* Fr
De Kybernetik *(f)*
En cybernetics
Es cibernética *(f)*
It cibernetica *(f)*
Pt cibernética *(f)*

**cycle de commerce** *(m)* Fr
De Handelszyklus *(m)*
En trade cycle
Es ciclo del negocio *(m)*
It cyclo degli affari *(m)*
Pt ciclo comercial *(m)*

**cycle économique** *(m)* Fr
De Konjunkturzyklus *(m)*
En business cycle
Es ciclo económico *(m)*
It ciclo d'affari *(m)*
Pt ciclo económico *(m)*

**cyclo degli affari** *(m)* It
De Handelszyklus *(m)*
En trade cycle
Es ciclo del negocio *(m)*
Fr cycle de commerce *(m)*
Pt ciclo comercial *(m)*

**cylindrée** *(f)* Fr
De Hubraum *(m)*
En cubic capacity
Es cilindrada *(f)*
It cilindrata *(f)*
Pt cilindrada *(f)*

# D

**d'accord avec** Fr
De im Einvernehmen mit
En in agreement with
Es de acuerdo con

It d'accordo con
Pt de acordo com

**d'accordo con** It
De im Einvernehmen mit
En in agreement with
Es de acuerdo con
Fr d'accord avec
Pt de acordo com

**Dachgesellschaft** *(f) n* De
En holding company
Es compañía tenedora *(f)*
Fr société holding *(f)*
It società holding *(f)*
Pt companhia proprietária *(f)*

**dactilógrafa** *(f) n* Pt
De Abschreibtypistin *(f)*
En copy typist
Am transcriber
Es mecanógrafa *(f)*
Fr dactylo copiste *(f)*
It dattilografa *(f)*

**dactylo copiste** *(f)* Fr
De Abschreibtypistin *(f)*
En copy typist
Am transcriber
Es mecanógrafa *(f)*
It dattilografa *(f)*
Pt dactilógrafa *(f)*

**dados** *(m pl) n* Pt
De Daten *(n pl)*
En data
Es datos *(m pl)*
Fr données *(f pl)*
It dati *(m pl)*

**damage** *n* En
De Beschädigung; Schaden *(f m)*
Es daño *(m)*
Fr dommage *(m)*
It danno *(m)*
Pt dano *(m)*

**damaged goods** En
De beschädigte Waren *(f pl)*
Es mercancías averiadas *(f pl)*
Fr marchandises avariées *(f pl)*
It merce avariata *(f)*
Pt mercadorias danificadas *(f pl)*

**damage in transit** En
De Beschädigung beim Transport *(f)*
Es daños en ruta *(m pl)*
Fr avaries de route *(f pl)*
It danno durante trasporto *(m)*
Pt danos em trânsito *(m pl)*

**damages** *n pl* En
De Schadenersatz *(m)*
Es daños *(m pl)*
Fr dommages-intérêts *(m pl)*
It danni *(m pl)*
Pt danos *(m pl)*

**Dampfer** *(m) n* De
En steamer
Es buque de vapor *(m)*
Fr bateau à vapeur *(m)*
It vapore *(m)*
Pt vapor *(m)*

**danger money** En
De Gefahrenzulage *(f)*
Es suma para riesgos *(f)*
Fr prime de risque *(f)*
It compenso per il rischio *(m)*
Pt prémio de risco *(m)*

**dangerous goods** En
De gefährliche Waren *(f pl)*
Es mercancías peligrosas *(f pl)*
Fr marchandises dangereuses *(f pl)*
It merce pericolosa *(f)*
Pt mercadorias perigosas *(f pl)*

**danni** *(m pl) n* It
De Schadenersatz *(m)*
En damages
Es daños *(m pl)*
Fr dommages-intérêts *(m pl)*
Pt danos *(m pl)*

**danni indiretti** *(m pl)* It
De immaterieller Schaden *(m)*
En consequential damages
Es daños indirectos *(m pl)*
Fr dommages indirects *(m pl)*
Pt danos decorrentes *(m pl)*

**danni liquidati** *(m pl)* It
De Konventionalstrafe *(f)*
En liquidated damages
Es daños liquidados *(m pl)*

Fr dommages-intérêts fixés en argent *(m pl)*
Pt danos liquidados *(m pl)*

**danni nominali** *(m pl)* It
De Ordnungsentschädigung *(f)*
En nominal damages
Es daños nominales *(m pl)*
Fr indemnité de principe *(f)*
Pt danos nominais *(m pl)*

**danni particolari** *(m pl)* It
De Ersatz immateriellen Schadens *(m)*
En special damages
Es daños especiales *(m pl)*
Fr dommages indirects *(m pl)*
Pt indemnização especial *(f)*

**danno** *(m)* n It
De Beschädigung; Schaden *(f m)*
En damage; injury
Es daño *(m)*
Fr dommage; avarie *(m f)*
Pt dano; injúria *(m f)*

**danno causato dall'acqua** *(m)* It
De Wasserschaden *(m)*
En water damage
Es daño causado por el agua *(m)*
Fr dégâts des eaux *(m pl)*
Pt dano causado por água *(m)*

**danno d'acqua di mare** *(m)* It
De Seewasserschaden *(m)*
En sea-water damage
Es daño de agua de mar *(m)*
Fr dégâts d'eau de mer *(m pl)*
Pt dano causado por água do mar *(m)*

**danno d'acqua dolce** *(m)* It
De Süsswasserschaden *(m)*
En fresh-water damage
Es daño de agua dulce *(m)*
Fr dégâts d'eau douce *(m pl)*
Pt dano causado por água doce *(m)*

**danno durante trasporto** *(m)* It
De Beschädigung beim Transport *(f)*
En damage in transit
Es daños en ruta *(m pl)*

Fr avaries de route *(f pl)*
Pt danos em trânsito *(m pl)*

**danno indiretti** *(m)* It
De indirekter Schaden *(m)*
En consequential damage
Es daños indirectos *(m pl)*
Fr dommage indirect *(m)*
Pt dano por consequência *(m)*

**daño** *(m)* n Es
De Beschädigung; Schaden *(f m)*
En damage; injury
Fr dommage; avarie *(m f)*
It danno *(m)*
Pt dano; injúria *(m f)*

**dano** *(m)* n Pt
De Beschädigung; Schaden *(f m)*
En damage; injury
Es daño *(m)*
Fr dommage; avarie *(m f)*
It danno *(m)*

**dano causado por água** *(m)* Pt
De Wasserschaden *(m)*
En water damage
Es daño causado por el agua *(m)*
Fr dégâts des eaux *(m pl)*
It danno causato dall'acqua *(m)*

**dano causado por água doce** *(m)* Pt
De Süsswasserschaden *(m)*
En fresh-water damage
Es daño de agua dulce *(m)*
Fr dégâts d'eau douce *(m pl)*
It danno d'acqua dolce *(m)*

**dano causado por água do mar** *(m)* Pt
De Seewasserschaden *(m)*
En sea-water damage
Es daño de agua de mar *(m)*
Fr dégâts d'eau de mer *(m pl)*
It danno d'acqua di mare *(m)*

**daño causado por el agua** *(m)* Es
De Wasserschaden *(m)*
En water damage
Fr dégâts des eaux *(m pl)*

It danno causato dall'acqua *(m)*
Pt dano causado por água *(m)*

**daño de agua de mar** *(m)* Es
De Seewasserschaden *(m)*
En sea-water damage
Fr dégâts d'eau de mer *(m pl)*
It danno d'acqua di mare *(m)*
Pt dano causado pela água do mar *(m)*

**daño de agua dulce** *(m)* Es
De Süsswasserschaden *(m)*
En fresh-water damage
Fr dégâts d'eau douce *(m pl)*
It danno d'acqua dolce *(m)*
Pt dano causado por água doce *(m)*

**dano por consequência** *(m)* Pt
De indirekter Schaden *(m)*
En consequential damage
Es daños indirectos *(m pl)*
Fr dommage indirect *(m)*
It danno indiretti *(m)*

**daños** *(m pl)* n Es
De Schadenersatz *(m)*
En damages
Fr dommages-intérêts *(m pl)*
It danni *(m pl)*
Pt danos *(m pl)*

**danos** *(m pl)* n Pt
De Schadenersatz *(m)*
En damages
Es daños *(m pl)*
Fr dommages-intérêts *(m pl)*
It danni *(m pl)*

**danos decorrentes** *(m pl)* Pt
De immaterieller Schaden *(m)*
En consequential damages
Es daños indirectos *(m pl)*
Fr dommages indirects *(m pl)*
It danni indiretti *(m pl)*

**danos em trânsito** *(m pl)* Pt
De Beschädigung beim Transport *(f)*
En damage in transit
Es daños en ruta *(m pl)*
Fr avaries de route *(f pl)*
It danno durante trasporto *(m)*

**daños en ruta** *(m pl)* Es
De Beschädigung beim Trans—
    port *(f)*
En damage in transit
Fr avaries de route *(f pl)*
It danno durante trasporto
    *(m)*
Pt danos em trânsito *(m pl)*

**daños especiales** *(m pl)* Es
De Ersatz immateriellen Scha-
    dens *(m)*
En special damages
Fr dommages indirects *(m pl)*
It danni particolari *(m pl)*
Pt indemnização especial *(f)*

**daños indirectos** *(m pl)* Es
De immaterieller Schaden *(m)*
En consequential damages
Fr dommages indirects *(m pl)*
It danni indiretti *(m pl)*
Pt danos decorrentes *(m pl)*

**daños liquidados** *(m pl)* Es
De Konventionalstrafe *(f)*
En liquidated damages
Fr dommages-intérêts fixés en
    argent *(m pl)*
It danni liquidati *(m pl)*
Pt danos liquidados *(m pl)*

**danos liquidados** *(m pl)* Pt
De Konventionalstrafe *(f)*
En liquidated damages
Es daños liquidados *(m pl)*
Fr dommages-intérêts fixés en
    argent *(m pl)*
It danni liquidati *(m pl)*

**danos nominais** *(m pl)* Pt
De Ordnungsentschädigung *(f)*
En nominal damages
Es daños nominales *(m pl)*
Fr indemnité de principe *(f)*
It danni nominali *(m pl)*

**daños nominales** *(m pl)* Es
De Ordnungsentschädigung *(f)*
En nominal damages
Fr indemnité de principe *(f)*
It danni nominali *(m pl)*
Pt danos nominais *(m pl)*

**dare impulso a** It
De fördern
En promote (a product)
Es promover

Fr chauffer
Pt promover

**dare una settimana di preav-
viso** It
De einwöchig kündigen
En give a week´s notice
Es dar una semana de aviso
Fr donner ses huit jours
Pt dar um prazo de uma
    semana para despedimento

**dar execução a um testa-
mento** Pt
De ein Testament vollstrecken
En execute a will
Es ejecutar un testamento
Fr exécuter un testament
It eseguire un testamento

**dar execução a um título legal**
    Pt
De eine Urkunde unterzeichnen
En execute a deed
Es firmar una escritura
Fr passer un acte
It perfezionare un atto

**dar execução a poderes de
procuração** Pt
De eine Vollmacht erteilen
En execute a power of attor-
    ney
Es otorgar poder notarial
Fr conférer des pleins pou-
    voirs
It conferire una procura

**Darlehenskonto** *(n)* n De
En advance account
Es cuenta de anticipos *(f)*
Fr compte d´avances *(m)*
It conto anticipo *(m)*
Pt conta de adiantamentos *(f)*

**darlehensweise** De
En on loan
Es en préstamo
Fr sous forme de prêt
It in prestito
Pt por empréstimo

**dar um prazo de uma semana**
    (para despedimento) Pt
De einwöchig kündigen
En give a week´s notice
Es dar una semana de aviso
Fr donner ses huit jours

**dar una semana de aviso** Es
De einwöchig kündigen
En give a week´s notice
Fr donner ses huit jours
It dare una settimana di
    preavviso
Pt dar um prazo de uma
    semana para despedimento

**data** pl n En
De Daten *(n pl)*
Es datos *(m pl)*
Fr données *(f pl)*
It dati *(m pl)*
Pt dados *(m pl)*

**data** *(f)* n It, Pt
De Datum *(n)*
En date
Es fecha *(f)*
Fr date *(f)*

**data capture** En
De Datenerfassung *(f)*
Es recogida de datos *(f)*
Fr saisie des données *(f)*
It raccolta dati *(f)*
Pt recolha de dados *(f)*

**data de entrega** *(f)* Pt
De Liefertermin *(m)*
En delivery date
Es fecha de entrega *(f)*
Fr date de livraison *(f)*
It data di consegna *(f)*

**data de resgate** *(f)* Pt
De Einlösungstag *(m)*
En redemption date
Es fecha de reembolso *(f)*
Fr date du remboursement *(f)*
It data di rimborso *(f)*

**data de vencimento** *(f)* Pt
De Fälligkeittag *(m)*
En date of maturity; due date
Es fecha de vencimiento *(f)*
Fr date d´échéance *(f)*
It data di scadenza *(f)*

**data di consegna** *(f)* It
De Liefertermin *(m)*
En delivery date
Es fecha de entrega *(f)*

Fr  date de livraison *(f)*
Pt  data de entrega *(f)*

**data di partenza** *(f)* It
De  Abgangstag *(m)*
En  sailing date
Es  día de salida *(m)*
Fr  date de départ *(f)*
Pt  dia de saída *(m)*

**data di rimborso** *(f)* It
De  Einlösungstag *(m)*
En  redemption date
Es  fecha de reembolso *(f)*
Fr  date du remboursement *(f)*
Pt  data de resgate *(f)*

**data di scadenza** *(f)* It
De  Fälligkeitstag *(m)*
En  date of maturity; due date
Es  fecha de vencimiento *(f)*
Fr  date d'échéance *(f)*
Pt  data de vencimento *(f)*

**data processing** En
De  Datenverarbeitung *(f)*
Es  tratamiento de datos *(m)*
Fr  traitement d'informatique *(m)*
It  elaborazione dei dati *(f)*
Pt  processamento de dados *(m)*

**date** *n* En, Fr *(f)*
De  Datum *(n)*
Es  fecha *(f)*
It  data *(f)*
Pt  data *(f)*

**date d'échéance** *(f)* Fr
De  Fälligkeitstag *(m)*
En  date of maturity
Es  fecha de vencimiento *(f)*
– It  data di scadenza *(f)*
Pt  data de vencimento *(f)*

**date de départ** *(f)* Fr
De  Abgangstag *(m)*
En  sailing date
Es  día de salida *(m)*
It  data di partenza *(f)*
Pt  dia de saída *(m)*

**date de livraison** *(f)* Fr
De  Liefertermin *(m)*
En  delivery date
Es  fecha de entrega *(f)*
It  data di consegna *(f)*

Pt  data de entrega ou remessa *(f)*

**date du remboursement** *(f)* Fr
De  Einlösungstag *(m)*
En  redemption date
Es  fecha de reembolso *(f)*
It  data di rimborso *(f)*
Pt  data de resgate *(f)*

**date limite** *(f)* Fr
De  Verfalltermin *(m)*
En  deadline
Es  fecha tope *(f)*
It  ultima data o ora possibile *(f)*
Pt  data de vencimento *(f)*

**Daten** *(n pl)* n De
En  data
Es  datos *(m pl)*
Fr  données *(f pl)*
It  dati *(m pl)*
Pt  dados *(m pl)*

**Datenerfassung** *(f)* n De
En  data capture
Es  recogida de datos *(f)*
Fr  saisie des données *(f)*
It  raccolta dati *(f)*
Pt  recolha de dados *(f)*

**Datenverarbeitung** *(f)* n De
En  data processing
Es  tratamiento de datos *(m)*
Fr  traitement d'informatique *(m)*
It  elaborazione dei dati *(f)*
Pt  processamento de dados *(m)*

**date of maturity** En
De  Fälligkeitstag *(m)*
Es  fecha de vencimiento *(f)*
Fr  date d'échéance *(f)*
It  data di scadenza *(f)*
Pt  data de vencimento *(f)*

**date-stamp** n En
De  Tagesstempel *(m)*
Es  sello de fecha *(m)*
Fr  dateur *(m)*
It  timbro a data *(m)*
Pt  carimbo de datas *(m)*

**dateur** *(m)* n Fr
De  Tagesstempel *(m)*
En  date-stamp

Es  sello de fecha *(m)*
It  timbro a data *(m)*
Pt  carimbo de datas *(m)*

**dati** *(m pl)* n It
De  Daten *(n pl)*
En  data
Es  datos *(m pl)*
Fr  données *(f pl)*
Pt  dados *(m pl)*

**datore di lavoro** *(m)* It
De  Arbeitgeber *(m)*
En  employer
Es  patrono *(m)*
Fr  employeur *(m)*
Pt  patrão *(m)*

**datos** *(m pl)* n Es
De  Daten *(n pl)*
En  data
Fr  données *(f pl)*
It  dati *(m pl)*
Pt  dados *(m pl)*

**dattilografa** *(f)* n It
De  Abschreibtypistin *(f)*
En  copy typist
Am  transcriber
Es  mecanógrafa *(f)*
Fr  dactylo copiste *(f)*
Pt  dactilógrafa *(f)*

**dattiloscritto** *(m)* n It
De  Maschinenschrift *(f)*
En  typescript
Es  texto mecanografiado *(m)*
Fr  manuscrit dactylographié *(m)*
Pt  texto dactilografado *(m)*

**Datum** *(n)* n De
En  date
Es  fecha *(f)*
Fr  date *(f)*
It  data *(f)*
Pt  data *(f)*

**Dauer** *(f)* n De
En  duration
Es  duración *(f)*
Fr  durée *(f)*
It  durata *(f)*
Pt  duração *(f)*

**dauerhafte  Konsumgüter** *(n pl)* De
En  consumer durables

Es bienes de consumo duraderos *(m pl)*
Fr biens de consommation
durables *(m pl)*
It beni di consumo durabili
*(m pl)*
Pt artigos de consumo perduraveis *(m pl)*

**Dauerschuldverschreibung** *(f)*
*n* De
En perpetual debenture
Es obligación a perpetuidad *(f)*
Fr obligation perpétuelle *(f)*
It obbligazione perpetua *(f)*
Pt obrigação de perenidade *(f)*

**da vendere o rimandare** It
De Rücksendung wenn unver-
kauft
En sale or return
Es venta o devolución
Fr vente avec faculté de retour
Pt venda ou devolução

**day** *n* En
De Tag *(m)*
Es día *(m)*
Fr jour *(m)*
It giorno *(m)*
Pt dia *(m)*

**day after tomorrow** En
De übermorgen
Es pasado mañana
Fr après demain
It dopodomani
Pt depois de amanhã

**day before yesterday** En
De vorgestern
Es anteayer
Fr avant-hier
It avantieri
Pt anteontem

**day-book** *n* En
De Tagebuch *(n)*
Es diario *(m)*
Fr journal *(m)*
It giornale *(m)*
Pt diário *(m)*

**day off** En
De dienstfreier Tag *(m)*
Es día libre *(m)*
Fr jour de congé *(m)*

It giorno di riposo *(m)*
Pt dia de folga *(m)*

**day-shift** *n* En
De Tagschicht *(f)*
Es turno de día *(m)*
Fr équipe du jour *(f)*
It turno di giorno *(m)*
Pt turno de dia *(m)*

**days of grace** En
De Nachfrist *(f)*
Es días de gracia *(f pl)*
Fr délai supplémentaire *(m)*
It giorni di grazia *(m pl)*
Pt dias de tolerância *(m pl)*

**day-to-day** En
De täglich
Es día a día
Fr au jour le jour
It di giorno in giorno
Pt dia a dia

**dazio d'importazione** *(m)* It
De Einfuhrzoll *(m)*
En import duty
Es derechos de importación
*(m pl)*
Fr droits d'entrée *(m pl)*
Pt direitos de importação *(m)*

**dazio pagato** It
De verzollt
En duty-paid
Es derechos pagados
Fr acquitté
Pt direitos pagos

**de acordo com** Pt
De im Einvernehmen mit
En in agreement with
Es de acuerdo con
Fr d'accord avec
It d'accordo con

**de acuerdo con** Es
De im Einvernehmen mit
En in agreement with
Fr d'accord avec
It d'accordo con
Pt de acordo com

**deadline** *n* En
De Verfalltermin *(m)*
Es fecha tope *(f)*
Fr date limite *(f)*

It ultima data o ora possibile
*(f)*
Pt data de vencimento *(f)*

**deadweight** *n* En
De Tragfähigkeit *(f)*
Es peso muerto *(m)*
Fr port en lourd *(m)*
It peso morto *(m)*
Pt peso morto *(m)*

**deal** *n* En
De Abschluss *(m)*
Es negocio *(m)*
Fr affaire *(f)*
It affare *(f)*
Pt negócio *(m)*

**dealer** *n* En
De Händler *(m)*
Es comerciante *(m)*
Fr négociant *(m)*
It negoziante: commerciante
*(m)*
Pt negociante *(m)*

**dear money** En
De teueres Geld *(n)*
Es dinero caro *(m)*
Fr argent cher *(m)*
It denaro ad alto interesse
*(m)*
Pt dinheiro caro *(m)*

**death** *n* En
De Tod *(m)*
Es muerte *(m)*
Fr mort *(f)*
It morte *(f)*
Pt morte *(f)*

**death certificate** En
De Totenschein *(m)*
Es partida de defunción *(f)*
Fr extrait d'acte de décès *(m)*
It certificato di morte *(m)*
Pt certidão de óbito *(f)*

**death duties** En
Am estate taxes
De Erbschaftssteuern *(f pl)*
Es derechos sucesorios *(m pl)*
Fr droits de succession *(m pl)*
It diritti di successione *(m pl)*
Pt impostos de sucessão *(m pl)*

**death rate** En
   De Sterblichkeitsziffer *(f)*
   Es mortalidad *(f)*
   Fr taux de mortalité *(m)*
   It tasso di mortalità *(m)*
   Pt taxa de mortalidade *(f)*

**debenture** *n* En
   De Obligation; Schuldversch-
      reibung *(f)*
   Es obligación *(f)*
   Fr obligation *(f)*
   It obbligazione *(f)*
   Pt obrigação *(f)*

**debenture holder** En
   De Obligationsinhaber *(m)*
   Es obligacionista *(m)*
   Fr porteur d'obligations; obli-
      gataire *(m)*
   It obbligazionista *(m)*
   Pt titular de obrigação *(m)*

**Debet** *(n) n* De
   En debit
   Es débito *(m)*
   Fr doit; débit *(m)*
   It debito; dare *(m)*
   Pt débito *(m)*

**debit** *n* En
   De Debet; Soll *(n)*
   Es débito *(m)*
   Fr doit; débit *(m)*
   It debito; dare *(m)*
   Pt débito *(m)*

**débit** *(m) n* Fr
   De Debet; Soll *(n)*
   En debit
   Es débito *(m)*
   It debito; dare *(m)*
   Pt débito *(m)*

**debit balance** En
   De Sollsaldo *(m)*
   Es saldo en débito *(m)*
   Fr solde débiteur *(m)*
   It saldo debitore *(m)*
   Pt saldo devedor *(m)*

**débit direct** *(m)* Fr
   De direkte Belastung *(f)*
   En direct debit
   Es débito directo *(m)*
   It debito diretto *(m)*
   Pt débito directo *(m)*

**débiteur** *(m) n* Fr
   De Schuldner *(m)*
   En debtor
   Es deudor *(m)*
   It debitore *(m)*
   Pt devedor *(m)*

**debit note** En
   De Lastschrift *(f)*
   Es nota de débito *(f)*
   Fr avis de débit *(m)*
   It nota di addebito *(f)*
   Pt aviso de débito *(m)*

**débito** *(m) n* Es, Pt
   De Debet; Soll *(n)*
   En debit
   Fr doit; débit *(m)*
   It debito; dare *(m)*

**debito** *(m) n* It
   De Debet; Schuld *(n f)*
   En debit; debt
   Es débito; deuda *(m f)*
   Fr débit; créance *(m f)*
   Pt débito; dívida *(m f)*

**debito attivo** *(m)* It
   De Buchschuld *(f)*
   En book debt
   Es deuda contabilizada *(f)*
   Fr dette comptable *(f)*
   Pt débito contabilizado *(m)*

**débito contabilizado** *(m)* Pt
   De Buchschuld *(f)*
   En book debt
   Es deuda contabilizada *(f)*
   Fr dette comptable *(f)*
   It debito attivo *(m)*

**débito directo** *(m)* Es, Pt
   De direkte Belastung *(f)*
   En direct debit
   Fr débit direct *(m)*
   It debito diretto *(m)*

**debito diretto** *(m)* It
   De direkte Belastung *(f)*
   En direct debit
   Es débito directo *(m)*
   Fr débit direct *(m)*
   Pt débito directo *(m)*

**debito pubblico** *(m)* It
   De Staatsschuld *(f)*
   En national debt
   Es deuda pública *(f)*

   Fr dette publique *(f)*
   Pt dívida pública *(f)*

**debitore** *(m) n* It
   De Schuldner *(m)*
   En debtor
   Es deudor *(m)*
   Fr débiteur *(m)*
   Pt devedor *(m)*

**Debitoren** *(m pl) n* De
   En accounts receivable
   Es cuentas a recibir *(f pl)*
   Fr créances *(f pl)*
   It conti attivi *(m pl)*
   Pt contas a receber *(f pl)*

**de boa fé** Pt
   De auf Treu und Glauben
   En in good faith
   Es de buena fé
   Fr de bonne foi
   It in buona fede

**de bonne foi** Fr
   De auf Treu und Glauben
   En in good faith
   Es de buena fé
   It in buona fede
   Pt de boa fé

**déboursement** *(m) n* Fr
   De Auszahlung *(f)*
   En disbursement
   Es desembolso *(m)*
   It esborso *(m)*
   Pt desembolso *(m)*

**debt** *n* En
   De Schuld *(f)*
   Es deuda *(f)*
   Fr créance *(f)*
   It debito *(m)*
   Pt dívida *(f)*

**debt collector** En
   De Inkassobeauftragte(r) *(m)*
   Es agente recaudador *(m)*
   Fr agent de recouvrement *(m)*
   It agente di ricupero crediti
      *(m)*
   Pt cobrador *(m)*

**debtor** *n* En
   De Schuldner *(m)*
   Es deudor *(m)*
   Fr débiteur *(m)*

It debitore (m)
Pt devedor (m)

**de buena fé** Es
De auf Treu und Glauben
En in good faith
Fr de bonne foi
It in buona fede
Pt de boa fé

**decadimento incorporato** (m)
It
De eingebautes Veralten (n)
En built-in obsolescence
Es decaimiento incorporado (m)
Fr désuétude incorporée (f)
Pt obsolência pre-incorporada (f)

**decaimiento incorporado** (m)
Es
De eingebautes Veralten (n)
En built-in obsolescence
Fr désuétude incorporée (f)
It decadimento incorporato (m)
Pt obsolência pre-incorporada (f)

**décentraliser** vb Fr
De dezentralisieren
En decentralize
Es decentralizar
It decentralizzare
Pt descentralizar

**decentralizar** vb Es
De dezentralisieren
En decentralize
Fr décentraliser
It decentralizzare
Pt descentralizar

**decentralize** vb En
De dezentralisieren
Es decentralizar
Fr décentraliser
It decentralizzare
Pt descentralizar

**decentralizzare** vb It
De dezentralisieren
En decentralize
Es decentralizar
Fr décentraliser
Pt descentralizar

**déchets** (m pl) n Fr
De Abfallprodukt (n)
En waste products
Es desperdicios (m pl)
It produtto di rifiuto (m)
Pt desperdicios (m pl)

**déchets toxiques** (m pl) Fr
De giftiger Abfall (m)
En toxic waste
Es efluentes tóxicos (m pl)
It rifiuti tossici (m pl)
Pt despejos tóxicos (m pl)

**decide** vb En
De entscheiden
Es decidir
Fr décider
It decidere
Pt decidir

**décider** vb Fr
De entscheiden
En decide
Es decidir
It decidere
Pt decidir

**decidere** vb It
De entscheiden
En decide
Es decidir
Fr décider
Pt decidir

**decidir** vb Es, Pt
De entscheiden
En decide
Fr décider
It decidere

**decimal** adj En, Es, Pt
De dezimal
Fr décimal
It decimale

**décimal** adj Fr
De dezimal
En decimal
Es decimal
It decimale
Pt decimal

**decimale** adj It
De dezimal
En decimal
Es decimal

Fr décimal
Pt decimal

**decisão** (f) n Pt
De Entscheidung (f)
En decision
Es decisión (f)
Fr décision (f)
It decisione (f)

**decisão de arbitragem** (f) Pt
De Schiedsspruch (m)
En arbitration award
Es sentencia arbitral (f)
Fr sentence arbitrale (f)
It lodo arbitrale (m)

**decision** n En
De Entscheidung (f)
Es decisión (f)
Fr décision (f)
It decisione (f)
Pt decisão (f)

**decisión** (f) n Es
De Entscheidung (f)
En decision
Fr décision (f)
It decisione (f)
Pt decisão (f)

**décision** (f) n Fr
De Entscheidung (f)
En decision
Es decisión (f)
It decisione (f)
Pt decisão (f)

**decisione** (f) n It
De Entscheidung (f)
En decision
Es decisión (f)
Fr décision (f)
Pt decisão (f)

**decision theory** En
De Entscheidungslehre (f)
Es teoría de la decisión (f)
Fr théorie de la décision (f)
It teoria della decisione (f)
Pt teoria de decisão (f)

**deck** (of a ship) n En
De Deck (n)
Es cubierta (f)
Fr pont (m)
It coperta; ponte (f m)
Pt convés (m)

**Deck** *(n)* n De
En  deck
Es  cubierta *(f)*
Fr  pont *(m)*
It  coperta; ponte *(f m)*
Pt  convés *(m)*

**deck cargo** En
De  Deckladung *(f)*
Es  carga en cubierta *(f)*
Fr  cargaison de pont *(f)*
It  carico in coperta *(m)*
Pt  carga de convés *(f)*

**Deckladung** *(f)* n De
En  deck cargo
Es  carga en cubierta *(f)*
Fr  cargaison de pont *(f)*
It  carico in coperta *(m)*
Pt  carga de convés *(f)*

**Deckung** *(f)* n De
En  cover
Es  cobertura *(f)*
Fr  couverture *(f)*
It  copertura *(f)*
Pt  cobertura *(f)*

**Deckungszusage** *(f)* n De
En  cover note
Es  aviso de seguro del riesgo
    *(m)*
Fr  lettre de couverture *(f)*
It  nota di copertura *(f)*
Pt  nota de cobertura *(f)*

**declaração** *(f)* n Pt
De  Erklärung *(f)*
En  declaration
Es  declaración *(f)*
Fr  déclaration *(f)*
It  dichiarazione *(f)*

**declaração alfandegária** *(f)* Pt
De  Zollerklärung *(f)*
En  customs declaration
Es  declaración de aduana *(f)*
Fr  déclaration en douane *(f)*
It  dichiarazione doganale *(f)*

**declaração de expedição** *(f)* Pt
De  Absendungserklärung *(f)*
En  declaration of shipment
Es  declaración de expedición
    *(f)*
Fr  déclaration d'expédition *(f)*
It  dichiarazione d'imbarco *(f)*

**declaração de propósito** *(f)* Pt
De  Willenserklärung *(f)*
En  declaration of intent
Es  declaración de intención *(f)*
Fr  déclaration d'intention *(f)*
It  dichiarazione d'intenzione
    *(f)*

**declaração fiscal** *(f)* Pt
De  Einkommensteuererklärung
    *(f)*
En  income-tax return
Es  declaración fiscal *(f)*
Fr  déclaration de revenu *(f)*
It  dichiarazione del reddito *(f)*

**declaração para efeitos de
tributação** *(f)* Pt
De  Steuererklärung *(f)*
En  tax return
Es  declaración de ingresos *(f)*
Fr  déclaration de l'impôt *(f)*
It  dichiarazione fiscale *(f)*

**declaração sob juramento** *(f)*
Pt
De  beeidigte Erklärung *(f)*
En  affidavit
Es  declaración jurada *(f)*
Fr  déclaration sous serment
    *(f)*
It  dichiarazione giurata *(f)*

**declaración** *(f)* n Es
De  Erklärung *(f)*
En  declaration
Fr  déclaration *(f)*
It  dichiarazione *(f)*
Pt  declaração *(f)*

**declaración de aduana** *(f)* Es
De  Zollerklärung *(f)*
En  customs declaration
Fr  déclaration en douane *(f)*
It  dichiarazione doganale *(f)*
Pt  declaração alfandegária *(f)*

**declaración de expedición** *(f)*
Es
De  Absendungserklärung *(f)*
En  declaration of shipment
Fr  déclaration d'expédition *(f)*
It  dichiarazione d'imbarco *(f)*
Pt  declaração de expedição *(f)*

**declaración de ingresos** *(f)* Es
De  Steuererklärung *(f)*
En  tax return

Fr  déclaration de l'impôt *(f)*
It  dichiarazione fiscale *(f)*
Pt  declaração para efeitos de
    tributação *(f)*

**declaración de intención** *(f)* Es
De  Willenserklärung *(f)*
En  declaration of intent
Fr  déclaration d'intention *(f)*
It  dichiarazione d'intenzione
    *(f)*
Pt  declaração de propósito *(f)*

**declaración falsa** *(f)* Es
De  Verdrehung *(f)*
En  misrepresentation
Fr  déclaration inexacte *(f)*
It  dichiarazione falsa *(f)*
Pt  deturpação *(f)*

**declaración fiscal** *(f)* Es
De  Einkommensteuererklärung
    *(f)*
En  income-tax return
Fr  déclaration de revenu *(f)*
It  dichiarazione del reddito *(f)*
Pt  declaração fiscal *(f)*

**declaración jurada** *(f)* Es
De  beeidigte Erklärung *(f)*
En  affidavit
Fr  déclaration sous serment
    *(f)*
It  dichiarazione giurata *(f)*
Pt  declaração sob juramento
    *(f)*

**declarar** *vb* Es, Pt
De  erklären
En  declare
Fr  déclarer
It  dichiarare

**declarar greve** Pt
De  zum Streik auffordern
En  call a strike
Es  declararse en huelga
Fr  ordonner une grève
It  proclamare uno sciopero

**declarar huelga** Es
De  streiken
En  strike
Fr  faire la grève
It  scioperare
Pt  fazer greve

**declararse en huelga** Es
De zum Streik auffordern
En call a strike
Fr ordonner une grève
It proclamare uno sciopero
Pt declarar greve

**declaration** n En
De Erklärung (f)
Es declaración (f)
Fr déclaration (f)
It dichiarazione (f)
Pt declaração (f)

**déclaration** (f) n Fr
De Erklärung (f)
En declaration
Es declaración (f)
It dichiarazione (f)
Pt declaração (f)

**déclaration de l'impôt** (f) Fr
De Steuererklärung (f)
En tax return
Es declaración de ingresos (f)
It dichiarazione fiscale (f)
Pt declaração para efeitos de
   tributação (f)

**déclaration de revenu** (f) Fr
De Einkommensteuererklärung
   (f)
En income-tax return
Es declaración fiscal (f)
It dichiarazione del reddito (f)
Pt declaração fiscal (f)

**déclaration d'expédition** (f) Fr
De Absendungserklärung (f)
En declaration of shipment
Es declaración de expedición
   (f)
It dichiarazione d'imbarco (f)
Pt declaração de expedição (f)

**déclaration d'intention** (f) Fr
De Willenserklärung (f)
En declaration of intent
Es declaración de intención (f)
It dichiarazione d'intenzione
   (f)
Pt declaração de propósito (f)

**déclaration en douane** (f) Fr
De Zollerklärung (f)
En customs declaration
Es declaración de aduana (f)

It dichiarazione doganale (f)
Pt declaração alfandegária (f)

**déclaration inexacte** (f) Fr
De Verdrehung (f)
En misrepresentation
Es declaración falsa (f)
It dichiarazione falsa (f)
Pt deturpação (f)

**declaration of intent** En
De Willenserklärung (f)
Es declaración de intención (f)
Fr déclaration d'intention (f)
It dichiarazione d'intenzione
   (f)
Pt declaração de propósito (f)

**declaration of shipment** En
De Absendungserklärung (f)
Es declaración de expedición
   (f)
Fr déclaration d'expédition (f)
It dichiarazione d'imbarco (f)
Pt declaração de expedição (f)

**déclaration sous serment** (f)
   Fr
De beeidigte Erklärung (f)
En affidavit
Es declaración jurada (f)
It dichiarazione giurata (f)
Pt declaração sob juramento
   (f)

**declare** vb En
De erklären
Es declarar
Fr déclarer
It dichiarare
Pt declarar

**declared value** En
De angegebener Zollwert (m)
Es valor declarado (m)
Fr valeur déclarée (f)
It valore dichiarato (m)
Pt valor declarado (m)

**déclarer** vb Fr
De erklären
En declare
Es declarar
It dichiarare
Pt declarar

**de classe superior** Pt
De hochwertig
En top quality
Es de primera calidad
Fr de première qualité
It di qualità superiore

**découvert** (m) n Fr
De Überziehung (f)
En overdraft
Es sobregiro; saldo deudor (m)
It scoperto (m)
Pt conta a descoberto (f)

**decreciente** adj Es
De abnehmend
En diminishing
Fr décroissant
It decrescente
Pt decrescente

**decrescente** adj It, Pt
De abnehmend
En diminishing
Es decreciente
Fr décroissant

**décroissant** adj Fr
De abnehmend
En diminishing
Es decreciente
It decrescente
Pt decrescente

**dédommager** vb Fr
De entschädigen
En indemnify
Es indemnizar; resarcir
It indennizzare; risarcire
Pt indemnizar

**dédouané** Fr
De verzollt
En out of bond
Es despachado de aduanas
It sdoganato
Pt despachado alfândega

**dédouanement** (m) n Fr
De Zollabfertigung (f)
En customs clearance
Es paso de aduanas (f)
It sdoganamento (m)
Pt despacho alfandegário (m)

**dédouaner** Fr
De verzollen
En clear through customs

Es retirar de aduanas
It sdoganare
Pt despachar na alfândega

**dedução adiada** (f) Pt
De nachträglicher Umsatzbonus (m)
En deferred rebate
Es descuento diferido (m)
Fr rabais différé (m)
It sconto differito (m)

**deducciones fiscales sobre inversiones** (f pl) Es
De Steuerbegünstigung auf Anlagen (f)
En capital allowances
Fr déductions fiscales sur les investissements (f pl)
It deduzioni fiscali sugli investimenti (f pl)
Pt concessões sobre capital (f pl)

**deducibile da tassa** It
De steuerabsetzbar
En tax deductible
Es deducible de impuestos
Fr déductible à l'impôt
Pt impostos a deduzir

**deducible de impuestos** Es
De steuerabsetzbar
En tax deductible
Fr déductible à l'impôt
It deducibile da tassa
Pt ilíquido de impostos

**deducir** vb Es
De abziehen
En deduct
Fr déduire
It dedurre
Pt deduzir

**deduct** vb En
De abziehen
Es deducir
Fr déduire
It dedurre
Pt deduzir

**déductible à l'impôt** Fr
De steuerabsetzbar
En tax deductible
Es deducible de impuestos
It deducibile da tassa
Pt ilíquido de impostos

**déductions fiscales sur les investissements** (f pl) Fr
De Steuerbegünstigung auf Anlagen (f)
En capital allowances
Es deducciones fiscales sobre inversiones (f pl)
It deduzioni fiscali sugli estimenti (f pl)
Pt concessões sobre capital (f pl)

**déduire** vb Fr
De abziehen
En deduct
Es deducir
It dedurre
Pt deduzir

**dedurre** vb It
De abziehen
En deduct
Es deducir
Fr déduire
Pt deduzir

**deduzioni fiscali sugli investimenti** (f pl) It
De Steuerbegünstigung auf Anlagen (f)
En capital allowances
Es deducciones fiscales sobre inversiones (f pl)
Fr déductions fiscales sur les investissements (f pl)
Pt concessões sobre capital (f pl)

**deduzir** vb Pt
De abziehen
En deduct
Es deducir
Fr déduire
It dedurre

**deed** (document) n En
De Urkunde (f)
Es título; escritura (m f)
Fr acte; titre (m)
It atto (m)
Pt título; escritura (m f)

**deed of arrangement** En
De Vergleichsabkommen (n)
Es acta de disposición (f)
Fr contrat d'arrangement (m)
It atto di accordo (m)
Pt escritura de acordo (f)

**deed of assignment** En
De Abtretungsvertrag (m)
Es título de asignación (m)
Fr acte attributif (m)
It atto di cessione (m)
Pt título de consignação (m)

**deed of composition** En
De Vergleichsabkommen (n)
Es concordato (m)
Fr concordat (m)
It atto di concordato (m)
Pt concordata (por escrito) (f)

**deed of covenant** En
De Pakt (m)
Es pacto (m)
Fr pacte (m)
It patto (m)
Pt escritura de compromisso (m)

**de fábrica** Es
De ab Werk
En ex works
Fr prise usine
It franco fabbrica
Pt na fábrica

**défaillance** (f) n Fr
De Nichteinhaltung (f)
En default
Es falta (f)
It mancanza (f)
Pt falta (f)

**defalcador** (m) n Es
De Veruntreuer (m)
En embezzler
Fr détourneur (m)
It malversatore (m)
Pt desfalcador (m)

**defalcar** vb Es
De unterschlagen
En embezzle
Fr détourner
It appropriarsi indebitamente
Pt desfalcar

**defalco** (m) n Es
De Unterschlagung (f)
En embezzlement
Fr détournement de fonds (m)
It appropriazione indebita (f)
Pt desfalque (m)

**default** n En
De Nichteinhaltung (f)
Es falta (f)
Fr défaillance; défaut (f m)
It mancanza (f)
Pt falta (f)

**défaut** (m) n Fr
De Nichteinhaltung; Mangel (f m)
En default; defect
Es falta; defecto (f m)
It mancanza; difetto (f m)
Pt falta; defeito (f m)

**défaut de paiement** (m) Fr
De Nichtzahlung (f)
En failure to pay
Es falta de pago (f)
It mancato pagamento (m)
Pt falta de pagamento (f)

**defect** n En
De Mangel (m)
Es defecto (m)
Fr défaut (m)
It difetto (m)
Pt defeito (m)

**defecto** (m) n Es
De Mangel (m)
En defect
Fr défaut (m)
It difetto (m)
Pt defeito (m)

**defecto latente** (m) Es
De versteckter Mangel (m)
En latent defect
Fr vice caché (m)
It difetto latente (m)
Pt defeito latente (m)

**défectueux** adj Fr
De fehlerhaft
En faulty
Es defectuoso
It difettoso
Pt defeituoso

**defectuoso** adj Es
De fehlerhaft
En faulty
Fr défectueux
It difettoso
Pt defeituoso

**defeito** (m) n Pt
De Mangel (m)
En defect
Es defecto (m)
Fr défaut (m)
It difetto (m)

**defeito latente** (m) Pt
De versteckter Mangel (m)
En latent defect
Es defecto latente (m)
Fr vice caché (m)
It difetto latente (m)

**defeituoso** adj Pt
De fehlerhaft
En faulty
Es defectuoso
Fr défectueux
It difettoso

**defer** vb En
De zurückstellen
Es aplazar
Fr différer; ajourner
It differire
Pt adiar

**deferred annuity** En
De Anwartschaft auf Leibrente (f)
Es anualidad aplazada (f)
Fr annuité différée (f)
It rendita vitalizia differita (f)
Pt anuidade diferida (f)

**deferred liabilities** En
De aufgeschobene Schulden (f pl)
Es pasivo transitorio (m)
Fr passif différé (m)
It passività differite (f pl)
Pt passivo adiado (m)

**deferred payment** En
De gestundete Zahlung (f)
Es pago aplazado (m)
Fr paiement différé
It pagamento differito (m)
Pt pagamento adiado (m)

**deferred rebate** En
De nachträglicher Umsatzbonus (m)
Es descuento diferido (m)
Fr rabais différé (m)
It sconto differito (m)
Pt dedução adiada (f)

**deferred shares** En
De Nachzugsaktien (f pl)
Es acciones aplazadas (f pl)
Fr actions différées (f pl)
It azioni postergate (f pl)
Pt acções diferidas (f pl)

**deferred taxation** En
De latente Steuerpflicht (f)
Es tasación diferida (f)
Fr imposition différée (f)
It tassazione differita (f)
Pt tributação diferida (f)

**deficiencia** (f) n Es
De Mangel; Fehlbetrag (m)
En deficiency
Fr manque; insuffisance (m f)
It ammanco; insufficienza (m f)
Pt deficiência; defeito (f m)

**deficiência** (f) n Pt
De Mangel; Fehlbetrag (m)
En deficiency
Es deficiencia (f)
Fr manque; insuffisance (m f)
It ammanco; insufficienza (m f)

**deficiency** n En
De Mangel; Fehlbetrag (m)
Es deficiencia (f)
Fr manque; insuffisance (m f)
It ammanco; insufficienza (m f)
Pt deficiência; defeito (f m)

**deficit** n En, It (m)
De Defizit (n)
Es déficit (m)
Fr déficit (m)
Pt déficit (m)

**déficit** (m) n Es, Fr, Pt
De Defizit (n)
En deficit
It deficit (m)

**Defizit** (n) n De
En deficit
Es déficit (m)
Fr déficit (m)
It deficit (m)
Pt déficit (m)

**deflação** *(f) n* Pt
De Deflation *(f)*
En deflation
Es deflación *(f)*
Fr déflation *(f)*
It deflazione *(f)*

**deflación** *(f) n* Es
De Deflation *(f)*
En deflation
Fr déflation *(f)*
It deflazione *(f)*
Pt deflação *(f)*

**deflation** *n* En
De Deflation *(f)*
Es deflación *(f)*
Fr déflation *(f)*
It deflazione *(f)*
Pt deflação *(f)*

**déflation** *(f) n* Fr
De Deflation *(f)*
En deflation
Es deflación *(f)*
It deflazione *(f)*
Pt deflação *(f)*

**Deflation** *(f) n* De
En deflation
Es deflación *(f)*
Fr déflation *(f)*
It deflazione *(f)*
Pt deflação *(f)*

**deflazione** *(f) n* It
De Deflation *(f)*
En deflation
Es deflación *(f)*
Fr déflation *(f)*
Pt deflação *(f)*

**defunct company** En
De erloschene Gesellschaft *(f)*
Es sociedad extinta *(f)*
Fr société liquidée *(f)*
It società estinta *(f)*
Pt empresa extinta *(f)*

**dégâts d'eau de mer** *(m pl)* Fr
De Seewasserschaden *(m)*
En sea-water damage
Es daño de agua de mar *(m)*
It danno d'acqua di mare *(m)*
Pt dano causado por água do mar *(m)*

**dégâts d'eau douce** *(m pl)* Fr
De Süsswasserschaden *(m)*
En fresh-water damage
Es daño de agua dulce *(m)*
It danno d'acqua dolce *(m)*
Pt dano causado por água doce *(m)*

**dégâts des eaux** *(m pl)* Fr
De Wasserschaden *(m)*
En water damage
Es daño causado por el agua *(m)*
It danno causato dall'acqua *(m)*
Pt dano causado por água *(m)*

**degré de solvabilité** *(m)* Fr
De Kreditwürdigkeit *(f)*
En credit rating
Es límite de crédito *(m)*
It stima del credito *(f)*
Pt nível de crédito *(m)*

**dégrèvement** *(m)* Fr
De Steuerbefreiung *(f)*
En tax relief
Es desgravación *(f)*
It sgravio fiscale *(m)*
Pt isenção de imposto *(f)*

**dégrèvement de charges fiscales doubles** *(m)* Fr
De Doppelbesteuerungserleichterung *(f)*
En double taxation relief
Es desgravación de tributación doble *(f)*
It sgravio per doppia tassazione *(m)*
Pt isenção de tributação dupla *(f)*

**délai de paiement** *(m)* Fr
De Verlängerungszeitraum *(m)*
En extension of payment time
Es prórroga de pago *(f)*
It proroga di pagamento *(f)*
Pt prorrogação de pagamento *(f)*

**délai supplémentaire** *(m)* Fr
De Nachfrist *(f)*
En days of grace
Es días de gracia *(f pl)*
It giorni di grazia *(m pl)*
Pt dias de tolerância *(m pl)*

**delay** *n* En
De Verzug *(m)*
Es retraso *(m)*
Fr retard; délai *(m)*
It ritardo *(m)*
Pt atrazo *(m)*

**del credere agent** En
De Delkrederevertreter *(m)*
Es agente del crédere *(m)*
Fr agent ducroire *(m)*
It agente con del credere *(m)*
Pt agente del credere *(m)*

**delegação** *(f) n* Pt
De Delegierung *(f)*
En delegation
Es delegación *(f)*
Fr délégation *(f)*
It delegazione *(f)*

**delegación** *(f) n* Es
De Delegierung *(f)*
En delegation
Fr délégation *(f)*
It delegazione *(f)*
Pt delegação *(f)*

**delegado** *(m) n* Es, Pt
De Delegierte(r) *(m)*
En delegate
Fr délégué *(m)*
It delegato *(m)*

**delegate** *n* En
De Delegierte(r) *(m)*
Es delegado *(m)*
Fr délégué *(m)*
It delegato *(m)*
Pt delegado *(m)*

**delegation** *n* En
De Delegierung *(f)*
Es delegación *(f)*
Fr délégation *(f)*
It delegazione *(f)*
Pt delegação *(f)*

**délégation** *(f) n* Fr
De Delegierung *(f)*
En delegation
Es delegación *(f)*
It delegazione *(f)*
Pt delegação *(f)*

**delegato** *(m) n* It
De Delegierte(r) *(m)*
En delegate

Es delegado *(m)*
Fr délégué *(m)*
Pt delegado *(m)*

**delegazione** *(f)* n It
De Delegierung *(f)*
En delegation
Es delegación *(f)*
Fr délégation *(f)*
Pt delegação *(f)*

**Delegierte(r)** *(m)* n De
En delegate
Es delegado *(m)*
Fr délégué *(m)*
It delegato *(m)*
Pt delegado *(m)*

**Delegierung** *(f)* n De
En delegation
Es delegación *(f)*
Fr délégation *(f)*
It delegazione *(f)*
Pt delegação *(f)*

**délégué** *(m)* n Fr
De Delegierte(r) *(m)*
En delegate
Es delegado *(m)*
It delegato *(m)*
Pt delegado *(m)*

**delete** vb En
De streichen
Es tachar; anular
Fr rayer; effacer
It cancellare
Pt cortar; riscar

**deliberazione** *(f)* n It
De Beschluss *(m)*
En resolution
Es resolución *(f)*
Fr resolution *(f)*
Pt resolução; proposta *(f)*

**delivered price** En
De Lieferpreis *(m)*
Es precio incluida entrega *(m)*
Fr prix livraison inclus *(m)*
It prezzo incluso consegna *(m)*
Pt preço incluindo portes *(m)*

**delivery** n En
De Lieferung *(f)*
Es entrega *(f)*
Fr livraison *(f)*

It consegna *(f)*
Pt entrega *(f)*

**delivery date** En
De Liefertermin *(m)*
Es fecha de entrega *(f)*
Fr date de livraison *(f)*
It data di consegna *(f)*
Pt data de entrega ou remessa *(f)*

**delivery free** En
De portofreie Lieferung
Es libre entrega
Fr livré franco
It consegna franco
Pt remessa gratuita

**delivery note** En
De Lieferschein *(m)*
Es aviso de entrega *(m)*
Fr bordereau de livraison *(m)*
It nota di consegna *(f)*
Pt guia de entrega *(f)*

**délivrance (d'un brevet)** *(f)* Fr
De Erteilung (eines Patentes) *(f)*
En grant (of a patent)
Es concesión (de una patente) *(f)*
It concessione (di brevetto) *(f)*
Pt concessão (de uma patente) *(f)*

**Delkrederevertreter** *(m)* n De
En del credere agent
Es agente del crédere *(m)*
Fr agent ducroire *(m)*
It agente con del credere *(m)*
Pt agente del credere *(m)*

**demain** adv Fr
De morgen
En tomorrow
Es mañana
It domani
Pt amanhã

**demanda** *(f)* n Pt
De Anspruch *(m)*
En claim
Es reclamación *(f)*
Fr réclamation; créance *(f)*
It reclamo *(m)*

**demanda** *(f)* n Es
De Nachfrage *(f)*
En inquiry
Fr demande *(f)*
It domanda *(f)*
Pt pergunta *(f)*

**demanda de salário** *(f)* Pt
De Lohnforderung *(f)*
En wage claim
Es reclamación de salario *(f)*
Fr revendication de salaire *(f)*
It rivendicazione salariale *(f)*

**demand curve** En
De Nachfragekurve *(f)*
Es curva de relación demanda *(f)*
Fr courbe de la demande *(f)*
It curva della domanda *(f)*
Pt curva de procura *(f)*

**demande** *(f)* n Fr
De Nachfrage; Antrag *(f m)*
En inquiry; application
Es demanda; solicitud *(f)*
It domanda *(f)*
Pt pergunta; requisição *(f)*

**demandé** Fr
De gefragt
En in demand
Es solicitado
It ricercato
Pt procurado

**demarcation dispute** En
De Fähigkeitsstreitigkeit *(f)*
Es disputa sobre demarcación *(f)*
Fr contestation syndicale des compétences *(f)*
It disputa di competenza *(f)*
Pt disputa sobre demarcação *(f)*

**se démettre** vb Fr
De zurücktreten
En resign
Es dimitir
It dimettersi
Pt demitir-se

**demi-salaire** *(m)* n Fr
De Halbsold *(m)*
En half-pay
Es medio salario *(m)*

It    mezza paga (f)
Pt    meio-salário (m)

**demitir-se** vb Pt
De    zurücktreten
En    resign
Es    dimitir
Fr    se démettre
It    dimettersi

**demonstrar** vb Pt
De    beweisen
En    establish; prove
Es    demostrar; probar
Fr    démontrer
It    dimostrare; provare

**démontrer** vb Fr
De    beweisen
En    establish; prove
Es    demostrar; probar
It    dimostrare; provare
Pt    demonstrar; provar

**demostrar** vb Es
De    beweisen
En    establish; prove
Fr    démontrer
It    dimostrare; provare
Pt    demonstrar; provar

**demurrage** n En
De    Überliegezeit (f)
Es    sobreestadía (f)
Fr    surestarie (f)
It    controstallia (f)
Pt    sobreestadía (f)

**denaro** (m) n It
De    Geld (n)
En    money
Es    dinero (m)
Fr    argent (m)
Pt    dinheiro (m)

**denaro a basso interesse** (m)
      It
De    billiges Geld (n)
En    cheap money
Es    dinero barato (m)
Fr    argent bon marché (m)
Pt    dinheiro barato (m)

**denaro a corso legale** (m) It
De    gesetzliches Zahlungsmittel
      (n)
En    legal tender
Es    moneda legal (f)

Fr    monnaie légale (f)
Pt    moeda legal (m)

**denaro ad alto interesse** (m) It
De    teueres Geld (n)
En    dear money
Es    dinero caro (m)
Fr    argent cher (m)
Pt    dinheiro caro (m)

**denaro a vista** (m) It
De    Sichtgelder (n pl)
En    money on call
Es    dinero a la vista (m)
Fr    argent à vue (m)
Pt    dinheiro à ordem (m)

**denaro contante** (m) It
De    Bargeld (n)
En    cash
Es    dinero efectivo (m)
Fr    espèces; argent comptant
      (f pl; m)
Pt    dinheiro de contado (m)

**denaro inattivo** (m) It
De    totes Kapital (n)
En    idle money
Es    dinero sin invertir (m)
Fr    capital oisif (m)
Pt    dinheiro paralizado (m)

**déni** (m) n Fr
De    Ablehnung (f)
En    disclaimer
Es    renuncia (f)
It    rinunzia (f)
Pt    descarte (f)

**den Markt beherrschen** De
En    corner a market
Es    acaparar el mercado
Fr    accaparer le marché
It    accaparrare il mercato
Pt    cerrar um mercado

**denomination** (of shares) n En
De    Stückelung (f)
Es    valor (m)
Fr    valeur nominale (f)
It    taglio (m)
Pt    valor nominal (m)

**denominazione commerciale**
      (f) It
De    Firmenname (m)
En    trade name
Es    razón social (f)

Fr    raison sociale (f)
Pt    razão comercial (f)

**departamento** (m) n Es, Pt
De    Abteilung (f)
En    department
Fr    département (m)
It    dipartimento (m)

**departamento de contabili-
      dade** (m) Pt
De    Buchhaltung (f)
En    accounts department
Am    accounting department
Es    departamento de contabili-
      dad (m)
Fr    service de la comptabilité
      (m)
It    ufficio contabilità (m)

**departamento de vendas** (m)
      Pt
De    Verkaufsabteilung (f)
En    sales department
Es    departamento de ventas
      (m)
Fr    service ventes (m)
It    ufficio vendite (m)

**departamento de ventas** (m)
      Es
De    Verkaufsabteilung (f)
En    sales department
Fr    service ventes (m)
It    ufficio vendite (m)
Pt    departamento de vendas
      (m)

**département** (m) n Fr
De    Abteilung (f)
En    department
Es    departamento (m)
It    dipartimento (m)
Pt    departamento (m)

**department** n En
De    Abteilung (f)
Es    departamento (m)
Fr    département (m)
It    dipartimento (m)
Pt    departamento (m)

**department store** En
De    Warenhaus (n)
Es    grandes almacenes (m pl)
Fr    grand magasin (m)
It    grande magazzino (m)
Pt    armazém (m)

**dependiente de muelle** *(m)* Es
De Expedient *(m)*
En shipping clerk
Fr expéditionnaire *(m)*
It commesso di spedizioniere *(m)*
Pt despachante *(m)*

**dépense déductible** *(f)* Fr
De abziehbare Unkosten *(f pl)*
En allowable expense
Es gastos deducibles *(m pl)*
It spesa permessa *(f)*
Pt despesas deduzíveis *(f)*

**dépenses de publicité** *(f pl)* Fr
De Werbekosten *(pl)*
En advertising expenditure
Es gastos publicitarios *(m pl)*
It spese di pubblicità *(f pl)*
Pt despesa com publicidade *(f)*

**déperdition naturelle** *(f)* Fr
De natürlicher Abgang *(m)*
En natural wastage
Es merma natural *(f)*
It consumo naturale *(m)*
Pt desperdício natural *(m)*

**déplacement** *(m)* n Fr
De Tonnengehalt *(m)*
En displacement
Es desplazamiento *(m)*
It dislocamento *(m)*
Pt deslocação *(f)*

**depleting assets** Am
En wasting assets
De kurzlebige Aktiva *(n pl)*
Es activo gastable *(m)*
Fr actifs défectibles *(m pl)*
It attività in esaurimento *(f pl)*
Pt bens em uso ou deteriora-ção *(m pl)*

**depois de amanhã** Pt
De übermorgen
En day after tomorrow
Es pasado mañana
Fr après demain
It dopodomani

**déport** *(m)* n Fr
De Kursabschlag *(m)*
En backwardation
Es prima de aplazamiento *(f)*

It deporto *(m)*
Pt juro de mora *(m)*

**deporto** *(m)* n It
De Kursabschlag *(m)*
En backwardation
Es prima de aplazamiento *(f)*
Fr déport *(m)*
Pt juro de mora *(m)*

**déposant** *(m)* n Fr
De Einzahler *(m)*
En depositor
Es depositante *(m)*
It depositante *(m)*
Pt depositante *(m)*

**déposer** *vb* Fr
De einlegen
En file
Es interponer
It depositare
Pt registar

**déposer** (à banque) Fr
De einlegen
En bank
Es depositar (en el banco)
It depositare (in una banca)
Pt depositar (no banco)

**deposit** (in bank) n En
De Depot *(n)*
En depósito *(m)*
Fr dépôt *(m)*
It deposito *(m)*
Pt depósito *(m)*

**deposit** (first payment) n En
De Anzahlung *(f)*
Es desembolso inicial *(m)*
Fr arrhes *(f pl)*
It caparra *(f)*
Pt sinal *(m)*

**deposit account** En
Am interest-bearing account
De Depositenkonto *(n)*
Es cuenta de ahorras *(f)*
Fr compte de dépôt *(m)*
It conto di deposito *(m)*
Pt conta de depósito *(m)*

**dépositaire** *(m)* n Fr
De Verwahrer; Gewahrsamin-haber *(m)*
En depositary; bailee
Es depositario *(m)*

It depositario *(m)*
Pt depositário; caucionado *(m)*

**depositante** *(m)* n Es, It, Pt
De Einzahler *(m)*
En depositor
Fr déposant *(m)*

**depositar** (en el banco) Es
De einlegen
En bank
Fr déposer (à banque)
It depositare (in una banca)
Pt depositar (no banco)

**depositar** (no banco) Pt
De einlegen
En bank
Es depositar (en el banco)
Fr déposer (à banque)
It depositare (in una banca)

**depositare** *vb* It
De einlegen
En file
Es interponer
Fr déposer
Pt registar

**depositare** (in una banca) It
De einlegen
En bank
Es depositar (en el banco)
Fr déposer (à banque)
Pt depositar (no banco)

**depositario** *(m)* n Es, It
De Verwahrer; Gewahrsamin-haber *(m)*
En depositary; bailee
Fr dépositaire *(m)*
Pt depositário; caucionado *(m)*

**depositário** *(m)* n Pt
De Verwahrer *(m)*
En depositary
Es depositario *(m)*
Fr dépositaire *(m)*
It depositario *(m)*

**depositary** n En
De Verwahrer *(m)*
Es depositario *(m)*
Fr dépositaire *(m)*
It depositario *(m)*
Pt depositário *(m)*

**Depositeneinlage** *(f)* n De
En fixed deposit
Es depósito a plazo fijo *(m)*
Fr dépôt à terme (fixe) *(m)*
It deposito a termine fisso *(m)*
Pt depósito a prazo *(m)*

**Depositenkonto** *(n)* n De
En deposit account
Am interest-bearing account
Es cuenta de ahorras *(f)*
Fr compte de dépôt *(m)*
It conto di deposito *(m)*
Pt conta de depósito *(m)*

**Depositenschein** *(m)* n De
En deposit receipt
Es recibo de depósito *(m)*
Fr récépissé de dépôt *(m)*
It certificato di deposito *(m)*
Pt recibo de depósito *(m)*

**depósito** *(m)* n Es, Pt
De Depot *(n)*
En deposit
Fr dépôt *(m)*
It deposito *(m)*

**deposito** *(m)* n It
De Depot *(n)*
En deposit
Es depósito *(m)*
Fr dépôt *(m)*
Pt depósito *(m)*

**depósito a plazo fijo** *(m)* Es
De Depositeneinlage *(f)*
En fixed deposit
Fr dépôt à terme (fixe) *(m)*
It deposito a termine fisso *(m)*
Pt depósito a prazo *(m)*

**depósito a prazo** *(m)* Pt
De Depositeneinlage *(f)*
En fixed deposit
Es depósito a plazo fijo *(m)*
Fr dépôt à terme (fixe) *(m)*
It deposito a termine fisso *(m)*
Pt depósito a prazo *(m)*

**deposito a termine fisso** *(m)* It
De Depositeneinlage *(f)*
En fixed deposit
Es depósito a plazo fijo *(m)*
Fr dépôt à terme (fixe) *(m)*
Pt depósito a prazo *(m)*

**depósito bancario** *(m)* Es
De Bankeinlage *(f)*
En bank deposit
Fr dépôt bancaire *(m)*
It deposito bancario *(m)*
Pt depósito bancário *(m)*

**deposito bancario** *(m)* It
De Bankeinlage *(f)*
En bank deposit
Es depósito bancario *(m)*
Fr dépôt bancaire *(m)*
Pt depósito bancário *(m)*

**depósito bancário** *(m)* Pt
De Bankeinlage *(f)*
En bank deposit
Es depósito bancario *(m)*
Fr dépôt bancaire *(m)*
It deposito bancario *(m)*

**depósito em cofre forte** *(m)* Pt
De Verwahrung in Stahlfach *(f)*
En safe deposit
Es depósito en caja fuerte *(m)*
Fr dépôt en coffre-fort *(m)*
It servizio di cassette di sicurezza *(m)*

**depósito en caja fuerte** *(m)* Es
De Verwahrung in Stahlfach *(f)*
En safe deposit
Fr dépôt en coffre-fort *(m)*
It servizio di cassette di sicurezza *(m)*
Pt depósito em cofre forte *(m)*

**deposito notturno** *(m)* It
De Nachttresor *(m)*
En night safe
Es caja de seguridad nocturna *(f)*
Fr coffre de nuit *(m)*
Pt cofre nocturno *(m)*

**depositor** n En
De Einzahler *(m)*
Es depositante *(m)*
Fr déposant *(m)*
It depositante *(m)*
Pt depositante *(m)*

**depósitos bloqueados** *(m pl)* Es, Pt
De gesperrte Einlagen *(f pl)*
En blocked deposits
Fr dépôts bloqués *(m pl)*

It deposito con vincolo bloccato *(m)*

**deposit receipt** En
De Depositenschein *(m)*
Es recibo de depósito *(m)*
Fr récépissé de dépôt *(m)*
It certificato di deposito *(m)*
Pt recibo de depósito *(m)*

**dépôt** *(m)* n Fr
De Depot *(n)*
En deposit
Es depósito *(m)*
It deposito *(m)*
Pt depósito *(m)*

**Depot** *(n)* n De
En deposit
Es depósito *(m)*
Fr dépôt *(m)*
It deposito *(m)*
Pt depósito *(m)*

**dépôt à terme (fixe)** *(m)* Fr
De Depositeneinlage *(f)*
En fixed deposit
Es depósito a plazo fijo *(m)*
It deposito a termine fisso *(m)*
Pt depósito a prazo *(m)*

**dépôt bancaire** *(m)* Fr
De Bankeinlage *(f)*
En bank deposit
Es depósito bancario *(m)*
It deposito bancario *(m)*
Pt depósito bancário *(m)*

**dépôt en coffre-fort** *(m)* Fr
De Verwahrung in Stahlfach *(f)*
En safe deposit
Es depósito en caja fuerte *(m)*
It servizio di cassette di sicurezza *(m)*
Pt depósito em cofre forte *(m)*

**dépôts bloqués** *(m pl)* Fr
De gesperrte Einlagen *(f pl)*
En blocked deposits
Es depósitos bloqueados *(m pl)*
It deposito con vincolo bloccato *(m)*
Pt depósitos bloqueados *(m pl)*

**depreciação** *(f) n* Pt
De Entwertung; Abschreibung *(f)*
En depreciation
Es depreciación *(f)*
Fr dépréciation; amortissement *(f m)*
It ammortamento *(m)*

**depreciação acelerada** *(f)* Pt
De beschleunigte Abschreibung *(f)*
En accelerated depreciation
Es depreciación acelerada *(f)*
Fr amortissement accéléré *(m)*
It deprezzamento accelerato *(m)*

**depreciación** *(f) n* Es
De Entwertung; Abschreibung *(f)*
En depreciation
Fr dépréciation; amortissement *(f m)*
It ammortamento *(m)*
Pt depreciação; amortização *(f)*

**depreciación acelerada** *(f)* Es
De beschleunigte Abschreibung *(f)*
En accelerated depreciation
Fr amortissement accéléré *(m)*
It deprezzamento accelerato *(m)*
Pt depreciação acelerada *(f)*

**depreciar** *vb* Es, Pt
De entwerten
En depreciate
Fr déprécier
It deprezzare

**depreciate** *vb* En
De entwerten
Es depreciar
Fr déprécier
It deprezzare
Pt depreciar

**depreciation** *n* En
De Entwertung; Abschreibung *(f)*
Es depreciación *(f)*
Fr dépréciation; amortissement *(f m)*
It ammortamento *(m)*

Pt depreciação; amortização *(f)*

**dépréciation** *(f) n* Fr
De Entwertung; Abschreibung *(f)*
En depreciation
Es depreciación *(f)*
It ammortamento *(m)*
Pt depreciação; amortização *(f)*

**depreciation allowance** En
De Abschreibung für Abnützung (AfA) *(f)*
Es provisión para amortización *(f)*
Fr provision pour amortissement *(f)*
It quota di ammortamento *(f)*
Pt provisão para amortização *(f)*

**dépréciation de la monnaie** *(f)* Fr
De Geldabwertung *(f)*
En depreciation of money
Es desvalorización de la moneda *(f)*
It svalutazione della moneta *(f)*
Pt desvalorização da moeda *(f)*

**depreciation of money** En
De Geldabwertung *(f)*
Es desvalorización de la moneda *(f)*
Fr dépréciation de la monnaie *(f)*
It svalutazione della moneta *(f)*
Pt desvalorização da moeda *(f)*

**déprécier** *vb* Fr
De entwerten
En depreciate
Es depreciar
It deprezzare
Pt depreciar

**de première qualité** Fr
De hochwertig
En top quality
Es de primera calidad
It di qualità superiore
Pt de classe superior

**depressão** *(f) n* Pt
De Wirtschaftskrise *(f)*
En depression
Es crisis económica *(f)*
Fr crise économique *(f)*
It crisi *(f)*

**depression** *n* En
De Wirtschaftskrise *(f)*
Es crisis económica *(f)*
Fr crise économique *(f)*
It crisi *(f)*
Pt depressão *(f)*

**deprezzamento accelerato** *(m)* It
De beschleunigte Abschreibung *(f)*
En accelerated depreciation
Es depreciación acelerada *(f)*
Fr amortissement accéléré *(m)*
Pt depreciação acelerada *(f)*

**deprezzare** *vb* It
De entwerten
En depreciate
Es depreciar
Fr déprécier
Pt depreciar

**de primera calidad** Es
De hochwertig
En top quality
Fr de première qualité
It di qualità superiore
Pt de classe superior

**de qualité inférieure** Fr
De minderwertig
En low-grade
Es baja calidad
It di qualità inferiore
Pt baixo-nível

**derecho de entrada** *(m)* Es
De Eintrittsgebühr *(f)*
En entrance fee
Fr droit d'entrée *(m)*
It tassa d'entrata *(f)*
Pt taxa de admissão *(f)*

**derecho de retencíon** *(m)* Es
De Pfandrecht *(n)*
En lien
Fr droit de retention *(m)*
It diritto di sequestro *(m)*
Pt direito de retenção *(m)*

**derechos** *(m pl)* n Es
De Rechte; Gebühr *(n pl; f)*
En rights; duty
Fr droits; taxe *(m pl; f)*
It diritti; tassa *(m pl; f)*
Pt direitos; taxa *(m pl; f)*

**derechos de aduanas** *(m pl)* Es
De Zoll *(m)*
En customs duty
Fr droit de douane *(m)*
It diritto doganale *(m)*
Pt direitos alfandegários *(m pl)*

**derechos de autor** *(m pl)* Es
De Urheberrecht *(n)*
En copyright
Fr droit d'auteur *(m)*
It diritto d'autore *(m)*
Pt direitos de autor *(m pl)*

**derechos de importación** *(m pl)* Es
De Einfuhrzoll *(m)*
En import duty
Fr droits d'entrée *(m pl)*
It dazio d'importazione *(m)*
Pt direitos de importação *(m)*

**derechos de muelle** *(m pl)* Es
De Dockgebühr *(f)*
En dock dues
Fr droits de dock *(m pl)*
It diritti di dock *(m pl)*
Pt encargos de doca *(m pl)*

**derechos de registro** *(m pl)* Es
De Anmeldegebühr *(f)*
En registration fee
Fr droit d'enregistrement *(m)*
It tassa di registrazione *(f)*
Pt custas de registo *(f pl)*

**derechos de sucesión** *(m pl)* Es
De Nachlassteuer *(f)*
En estate duty
Am estate tax
Fr droits de succession *(m pl)*
It diritti di successione *(m pl)*
Pt direitos de sucessão *(m pl)*

**derechos mineros** *(m pl)* Es
De Mineralgewinnungsrechte *(n pl)*
En mineral rights
Fr droits miniers *(m pl)*

It diritti minerari *(m pl)*
Pt direitos mineiros *(m pl)*

**derechos pagados** Es
De verzollt
En duty-paid
Fr acquitté
It dazio pagato
Pt direitos pagos

**derechos portuarios** *(m pl)* Es
De Hafengebühren *(f pl)*
En port charges
Fr droits de port *(m pl)*
It diritti portuali *(m pl)*
Pt direitos portuários *(m pl)*

**derechos preferenciales** *(m pl)* Es
De Vorzugssatz *(m)*
En preferential duty
Fr tarif de faveur *(m)*
It tariffa preferenziale *(f)*
Pt direito preferencial *(m)*

**dernier jour** *(m)* Fr
De Schlusstermin *(m)*
En closing date
Es último día *(m)*
It ultima data *(f)*
Pt último dia *(m)*

**dernier versement** *(m)* Fr
De letzte Rate *(f)*
En final instalment
Es último plazo *(m)*
It ultima rata *(f)*
Pt última prestação *(f)*

**desacuerdo** *(m)* n Es
De Abweichung *(f)*
En discrepancy
Fr écart *(m)*
It divergenza *(f)*
Pt discrepância *(f)*

**desalojar um inquilino** Pt
De einen Mieter entfernen
En evict a tenant
Es desalojar un inquilino
Fr expulser un locataire
It sfrattare un locatario

**desalojar un inquilino** Es
De einen Mieter entfernen
En evict a tenant
Fr expulser un locataire

It sfrattare un locatario
Pt desalojar um inquilino

**desarmar** *vb* Es, Pt
De auflegen
En lay up
Fr désarmer
It disamare

**désarmer** *vb* Fr
De auflegen
En lay up
Es desarmar
It disamare
Pt desarmar

**descanso** *(m)* n Es
De Freizeit *(f)*
En leisure
Fr loisir *(m)*
It svago *(m)*
Pt lazer *(m)*

**descargar una deuda** Es
De eine Schuld begleichen
En discharge a debt
Fr acquitter une dette
It estinguere un debito
Pt cancelar uma dívida

**descarte** *(m)* n Pt
De Ablehnung *(f)*
En disclaimer
Es renuncia *(f)*
Fr déni *(m)*
It rinunzia *(f)*

**descentralizar** *vb* Pt
De dezentralisieren
En decentralize
Es decentralizar
Fr décentraliser
It decentralizzare

**desconto** *(m)* n Pt
De Skonto; Nachlass *(m)*
En discount; rebate
Es descuento; rebaja *(m f)*
Fr escompte; rabais *(m)*
It sconto; ribasso *(m)*

**desconto à praça** *(m)* Pt
De Händlerrabatt *(m)*
En trade discount
Es descuento comercial *(m)*
Fr rabais de demi-gros *(m)*
It sconto di revendita *(m)*

**desconto bancário** (m) Pt
De Diskont (m)
En bank discount
Es descuento bancario (m)
Fr escompte en dehors (m)
It sconto di banca (m)

**desconto de contado** (m) Pt
De Barrabatt (m)
En cash discount
Es descuento de caja (m)
Fr escompte de caisse (m)
It sconto per pagamento a
    contanti (m)

**desconto de exportação** (m)
Pt
De Ausführsonderrabatt (m)
En export rebate
Es descuento por exportación
    (m)
Fr remise sur les exports (f)
It sconto d'esportazione (m)

**descrição** (f) n Pt
De Beschreibung (f)
En description
Es descripción (f)
Fr description (f)
It descrizione (f)

**descrição da tarefa** (f) Pt
De Arbeitsbeschreibung (f)
En job description
Es descripción del trabajo (f)
Fr description du travail (f)
It descrizione del lavoro (f)

**descripción** (f) n Es
De Beschreibung (f)
En description
Fr description (f)
It descrizione (f)
Pt descrição (f)

**descripción del trabajo** (f) Es
De Arbeitsbeschreibung (f)
En job description
Fr description du travail (f)
It descrizione del lavoro (f)
Pt descrição da tarefa (f)

**description** n En, Fr (f)
De Beschreibung (f)
Es descripción (f)
It descrizione (f)
Pt descrição (f)

**description du travail** (f) Fr
De Arbeitsbeschreibung (f)
En job description
Es descripción del trabajo (f)
It descrizione del lavoro (f)
Pt descrição da tarefa (f)

**descrizione** (f) n It
De Beschreibung (f)
En description
Es descripción (f)
Fr description (f)
Pt dèscrição (f)

**descrizione del lavoro** (f) It
De Arbeitsbeschreibung (f)
En job description
Es descripción del trabajo (f)
Fr description du travail (f)
Pt descrição da tarefa (f)

**descuento** (m) n Es
De Skonto (m)
En discount
Fr escompte (m)
It sconto; ribasso (m)
Pt desconto (m)

**descuento bancario** (m) Es
De Diskont (m)
En bank discount
Fr escompte en dehors (m)
It sconto di banca (m)
Pt desconto bancário (m)

**descuento comercial** (m) Es
De Händlerrabatt (m)
En trade discount
Fr rabais de demi-gros (m)
It sconto di revendita (m)
Pt desconto à praça (m)

**descuento de caja** (m) Es
De Barrabatt (m)
En cash discount
Fr escompte de caisse (m)
It sconto per pagamento a
    contanti (m)
Pt desconto de contado (m)

**descuento diferido** (m) Es
De nachträglicher Umsatzbo-
    nus (m)
En deferred rebate
Fr rabais différé (f)
It sconto differito (m)
Pt dedução adiada (f)

**descuento por exportación**
    (m) Es
De Ausführsonderrabatt (m)
En export rebate
Fr remise sur les exports (f)
It sconto d'esportazione (m)
Pt desconto de exportação
    (m)

**de segunda mano** Es
De aus zweiter Hand; Ge-
    braucht-
En second-hand
Fr d'occasion
It di seconda mano
Pt de segunda mão

**de segunda mão** Pt
De aus zweiter Hand; Ge-
    braucht-
En second-hand
Es de segunda mano
Fr d'occasion
It di seconda mano

**desembolso** (m) n Es, Pt
De Ausgaben; Auszahlung (f
    pl; f)
En expenditure; disbursement
Fr frais; déboursement (m pl;
    m)
It spesa; esborso (f m)

**desembolso inicial** (m) Es
De Anzahlung (f)
En deposit; first payment
Fr arrhes (f pl)
It caparra (f)
Pt sinal (m)

**desempenho** (m) n Pt
De Erfüllung (f)
En performance
Es ejecución (f)
Fr exécution (f)
It esecuzione (f)

**desempenho anterior** (m) Pt
De Leistung in der Vergangen-
    heit (f)
En past performance
Es operación anterior (f)
Fr comportement antérieur
    (m)
It comportamento precede-
    nte (m)

**desempleo** (m) n Es
De Arbeitslosigkeit (f)
En unemployment
Fr chômage (m)
It disoccupazione (f)
Pt desemprego (m)

**desempregado** adj Pt
De arbeitslos
En out of work
Es parado; sin trabajo
Fr en chômage
It disoccupato

**desemprego** (m) n Pt
De Arbeitslosigkeit (f)
En unemployment
Es desempleo (m)
Fr chômage (m)
It disoccupazione (f)

**desemprego de estação** (m) Pt
De jahreszeitlich bedingte Arbeitslosigkeit (f)
En seasonal unemployment
Es paro de temporada (m)
Fr chômage saisonnier (m)
It disoccupazione stagionale (f)

**desenhador** (m) n Pt
De Entwerfer (m)
En draughtsman
Es dibujante (m)
Fr dessinateur (m)
It disegnatore (m)

**desenho** (f) n Pt
De Zeichnung (f)
En design
Es diseño (m)
Fr dessein (m)
It disegno (m)

**desfalcador** (m) n Pt
De Veruntreuer (m)
En embezzler
Es defalcador (m)
Fr détourneur (m)
It malversatore (m)

**desfalcar** vb Pt
De unterschlagen
En embezzle
Es defalcar
Fr détourner
It appropriarsi indebitamente

**desfalque** (m) n Pt
De Unterschlagung (f)
En embezzlement
Es defalco (m)
Fr détournement de fonds (m)
It appropriazione indebita (f)

**desgaste** (m) n Es, Pt
De natürliche Abnützung (f)
En wear and tear
Fr usure normale (f)
It logorio naturale (m)

**desgravación** (f) n Es
De Steuerbefreiung (f)
En tax relief
Fr dégrèvement (m)
It sgravio fiscale (m)
Pt redução de imposto (f)

**desgravación de tributación doble** (f) Es
De Doppelbesteuerungserleichterung (f)
En double taxation relief
Fr dégrèvement de charges fiscales doubles (m)
It sgravio per doppia tassazione (m)
Pt isenção de tributação dupla (f)

**deshipotecado** Es
De von Hypothek befreit
En free from mortgage
Fr déshypothéqué
It libero d'ipoteca
Pt livre de hipoteca

**deshonesto** adj Es, Pt
De unehrlich
En dishonest
Fr malhonnête
It disonesto

**déshypothéqué** Fr
De von Hypothek befreit
En free from mortgage
Es deshipotecado
It libero d'ipoteca
Pt livre de hipoteca

**design** n En
De Zeichnung (f)
Es diseño (m)
Fr dessein (m)
It disegno (m)
Pt desenho (f)

**designação postal** (f) Pt
De Postleitzahl (f)
En postcode
Am zip code
Es designación postal (f)
Fr indicatif postal (m)
It codice postale (m)

**designación postal** (f) Es
De Postleitzahl (f)
En postcode
Am zip code
Fr indicatif postal (m)
It codice postale (m)
Pt designação postal (f)

**designer** n En
De Zeichner (m)
Es diseñador (m)
Fr dessinateur (m)
It disegnatore (m)
Pt desenhador (m)

**desistir** Pt
De aufgeben
En give up
Es renunciar
Fr céder
It cedere

**desk** n En
De Schreibtisch (m)
Es mesa (f)
Fr bureau (m)
It scrittoio (m)
Pt secretária (f)

**deslocação** (f) n Pt
De Tonnengehalt (m)
En displacement
Es desplazamiento (m)
Fr déplacement (m)
It dislocamento (m)

**despachado alfândega** Pt
De verzollt
En out of bond
Es despachado de aduanas
Fr dédouané
It sdoganato

**despachado de aduanas** Es
De verzollt
En out of bond
Fr dédouané
It sdoganato
Pt despachado alfândega

**despachante** *(m)* Pt
De Expedient *(m)*
En shipping clerk
Es dependiente de muelle *(m)*
Fr expéditionnaire *(m)*
It commesso di spedizioniere *(m)*

**despachar na alfândega** Pt
De verzollen
En clear through customs
Es retirar de aduanas
Fr dédouaner
It sdoganare

**despacho** *(m)* n Es
De Versand *(m)*
En despatch; dispatch
Fr envoi *(m)*
It spedizione; dispaccio *(f m)*
Pt despacho; remessa *(m f)*

**despacho de aduana** *(m)* Es
De Verzollung *(f)*
En customs clearance
Fr formalités douanières *(f pl)*
It sdoganamento *(m)*
Pt despacho de alfândega *(m)*

**despacho de alfândega** *(m)* Pt
De Verzollung *(f)*
En customs clearance
Es despacho de aduana *(m)*
Fr formalités douanières *(f pl)*
It sdoganamento *(m)*

**despedimento** *(m)* n Pt
De Entlassung *(f)*
En dismissal
Am firing
Es despido *(m)*
Fr congédiement *(m)*
It licenziamento *(m)*

**despedir** vb Es, Pt
De entlassen
En dismiss
Am fire
Fr congédier
It congedare

**despejos tóxicos** *(m pl)* Pt
De giftiger Abfall *(m)*
En toxic waste
Es efluentes tóxicos *(m pl)*
Fr déchets toxiques *(m pl)*
It rifiuti tossici *(m pl)*

**desperdício natural** *(m)* Pt
De natürlicher Abgang *(m)*
En natural wastage
Es merma natural *(f)*
Fr déperdition naturelle *(f)*
It consumo naturale *(m)*

**desperdicios** *(m pl)* n Es
De Abfallprodukt *(n)*
En waste products
Fr déchets *(m pl)*
It produtto di rifiuto *(m)*
Pt desperdícios *(m pl)*

**desperdícios** *(m pl)* n Pt
De Abfallprodukt *(n)*
En waste products
Es desperdicios *(m pl)*
Fr déchets *(m pl)*
It produtto di rifiuto *(m)*

**despesa** *(f)* n Pt
De Kosten *(pl)*
En expense
Es gasto *(m)*
Fr frais *(m pl)*
It spesa *(f)*

**despesa com publicidade** *(f)* Pt
De Werbekosten *(pl)*
En advertising expenditure
Es gastos publicitarios *(m pl)*
Fr dépenses de publicité *(f pl)*
It spese di pubblicità *(f pl)*

**despesas** *(f pl)* n Pt
De Ausgaben; Kosten *(f pl; pl)*
En expenditure; charges
Es desembolso; costes *(m; m pl)*
Fr frais *(m pl)*
It spesa; spese *(f; f pl)*

**despesas deduzíveis** *(f)* Pt
De abziehbare Unkosten *(f pl)*
En allowable expense
Es gastos deducibles *(m pl)*
Fr dépense déductible *(f)*
It spesa permessa *(f)*

**despesas de representação** *(f pl)* Pt
De Repräsentationskosten *(pl)*
En entertainment expenses
Es gastos de representación *(m pl)*

Fr frais de représentation *(m pl)*
It spese di rappresentanza *(f pl)*

**despesas de viagem** *(f pl)* Pt
De Reisekosten *(pl)*
En travelling expenses
Es dietas de viajes *(f pl)*
Fr frais de voyage *(m pl)*
It spese di viaggio *(f pl)*

**despesas directas** *(f pl)* Pt
De Einzelkosten *(pl)*
En direct expenses
Es gastos directos *(m pl)*
Fr frais directs *(m pl)*
It spese dirette *(f pl)*

**despesas diversas** *(f pl)* Pt
De verschiedene Ausgaben *(f pl)*
En sundry expenses
Es gastos varios *(m pl)*
Fr frais divers *(m pl)*
It spese varie *(f pl)*

**despesas do exercício** *(f pl)* Pt
De Geschäftskosten *(pl)*
En business expenses
Es gastos de los negocios *(m pl)*
Fr frais commerciaux *(m pl)*
It spese generali *(f pl)*

**despesas em termos de capital** *(f pl)* Pt
De Kapitalauslagen *(f pl)*
En capital expenditure
Es inmovilizaciones *(f pl)*
Fr immobilisations *(f pl)*
It immobilizzazioni *(f pl)*

**despesas gerais** *(f pl)* Pt
De allgemeine Unkosten *(pl)*
En general expenses
Es gastos generales *(m pl)*
Fr frais généraux *(m pl)*
It spese generali *(f pl)*

**despesas ocasionais** *(f pl)* Pt
De Nebenkosten *(f pl)*
En incidental expenses
Es gastos imprevistos *(m pl)*
Fr faux frais *(m pl)*
It spese impreviste *(f pl)*

**despido** (m) n Es
De Entlassung (f)
En dismissal
Am firing
Fr congédiement (m)
It licenziamento (m)
Pt despedimento (m)

**desplazamiento** (m) n Es
De Tonnengehalt (m)
En displacement
Fr déplacement (m)
It dislocamento (m)
Pt deslocação (f)

**dessein** (m) n Fr
De Zeichnung (f)
En design
Es diseño (m)
It disegno (m)
Pt desenho (f)

**dessinateur** (m) n Fr
De Entwerfer (m)
En draughtsman
Es dibujante (m)
It disegnatore (m)
Pt desenhador (m)

**destilería** (f) n Es
De Brennerei (f)
En distillery
Fr distillerie (f)
It distilleria (f)
Pt distilaria (f)

**destinataire** (m) n Fr
De Adressat; Empfänger (m)
En addressee; consignee
Es destinatario; consignatario (m)
It destinatario; consegnatario (m)
Pt destinatário; consignatário (m)

**destinatario** (m) n Es, It
De Adressat (m)
En addressee
Fr destinataire (m)
Pt destinatário (m)

**destinatário** (m) n Pt
De Adressat (m)
En addressee
Es destinatario (m)
Fr destinataire (m)
It destinatario (m)

**destination** n En, Fr (f)
De Bestimmungsort (m)
Es destino (m)
It destinazione (f)
Pt destino (m)

**destinazione** (f) n It
De Bestimmungsort (m)
En destination
Es destino (m)
Fr destination (f)
Pt destino (m)

**destino** (m) n Es, Pt
De Bestimmungsort (m)
En destination
Fr destination (f)
It destinazione (f)

**désuétude incorporée** (f) Fr
De eingebautes Veralten (n)
En built-in obsolescence
Es decaimiento incorporado (m)
It decadimento incorporato (m)
Pt obsolência pre-incorporada (f)

**desvalorização** (f) n Pt
De Währungsabwertung (f)
En devaluation
Es devaluación (f)
Fr dévaluation (f)
It svalutazione (f)

**desvalorização da moeda** (f) Pt
De Geldabwertung (f)
En depreciation of money
Es desvalorización de la moneda (f)
Fr dépréciation de la monnaie (f)
It svalutazione della moneta (f)

**desvalorización de la moneda** (f) Es
De Geldabwertung (f)
En depreciation of money
Fr dépréciation de la monnaie (f)
It svalutazione della moneta (f)
Pt desvalorização da moeda (f)

**desviación normal** (f) Es
De normale Abweichung (f)
En standard deviation
Fr déviation normale (f)
It deviazione normale (f)
Pt desvio normal (m)

**desvio normal** (m) Pt
De normale Abweichung (f)
En standard deviation
Es desviación normal (f)
Fr déviation normale (f)
It deviazione normale (f)

**détaillé** adj Fr
De postenmässig dargestellt
En itemized
Es detallado
It dettagliato
Pt pormenorizado

**détails** (m pl) n Fr
De Einzelheiten; Angaben (f pl)
En particulars
Es detalles (m pl)
It particolari (m pl)
Pt pormenores (m pl)

**detallado** adj Es
De postenmässig dargestellt
En itemized
Fr détaillé
It dettagliato
Pt pormenorizado

**detalles** (m pl) Es
De Einzelheiten; Angaben (f pl)
En particulars
Fr détails (m pl)
It particolari (m pl)
Pt pormenores (m pl)

**détenir des actions** Fr
De beteiligt sein; Aktien besitzen
En hold shares
Es tener acciones
It tenere azioni
Pt reter acções

**détenteur** (m) n Fr
De Inhaber (m)
En holder
Es titular (m)
It titolare (m)
Pt titular (m)

**détenteur de titres** *(m)* Fr
De Aktieninhaber *(m)*
En stockholder
Es accionista *(m)*
It azionista *(m)*
Pt accionista *(m)*

**detentore legittimo** *(m)* It
De entgeltigter Besitzer *(m)*
En holder for value
Es tenedor legítimo *(m)*
Fr porteur à titre onéreux *(m)*
Pt proprietário legítimo *(m)*

**determination clause** En
De Rücktrittsklausel *(f)*
Es cláusula resolutiva *(f)*
Fr clause résolutoire *(f)*
It clausola risolutiva *(f)*
Pt cláusula de rescisão *(f)*

**determination of a contract**
En
De Vertragsbeendigung *(f)*
Es rescisión de un contrato *(f)*
Fr résolution d'un contrat *(f)*
It risoluzione di un contratto *(f)*
Pt rescisão de contrato *(f)*

**détournement de fonds** *(m)* Fr
De Unterschlagung *(f)*
En embezzlement
Es defalco *(m)*
It appropriazione indebita *(f)*
Pt desfalque *(m)*

**détourner** *vb* Fr
De unterschlagen
En embezzle
Es defalcar
It appropriarsi indebitamente
Pt desfalcar

**détourneur** *(m)* *n* Fr
De Veruntreuer *(m)*
En embezzler
Es defalcador *(m)*
It malversatore *(m)*
Pt desfalcador *(m)*

**dettagliato** *adj* It
De postenmässig dargestellt
En itemized
Es detallado
Fr détaillé
Pt pormenorizado

**dettare** *vb* It
De diktieren
En dictate
Es dictar
Fr dicter
Pt ditar

**dettato** *(m)* *n* It
De Diktat *(n)*
En dictation
Es dictado *(m)*
Fr dictée *(f)*
Pt ditado *(m)*

**dette comptable** *(f)* Fr
De Buchschuld *(f)*
En book debt
Es deuda contabilizada *(f)*
It debito attivo *(m)*
Pt débito contabilizado *(m)*

**dette publique** *(f)* Fr
De Staatsschuld *(f)*
En national debt
Es deuda pública *(f)*
It debito pubblico *(m)*
Pt dívida pública *(f)*

**deturpação** *(f)* *n* Pt
De Verdrehung *(f)*
En misrepresentation
Es declaración falsa *(f)*
Fr déclaration inexacte *(f)*
It dichiarazione falsa *(f)*

**deuda** *(f)* *n* Es
De Schuld *(f)*
En debt
Fr créance *(f)*
It debito *(m)*
Pt dívida *(f)*

**deuda contabilizada** *(f)* Es
De Buchschuld *(f)*
En book debt
Fr dette comptable *(f)*
It debito attivo *(m)*
Pt débito contabilizado *(m)*

**deuda de pago dudoso** *(f)* Es
De zweifelhafte Forderung *(f)*
En doubtful debt
Fr créance douteuse *(f)*
It credito dubbio *(m)*
Pt dívida duvidosa *(f)*

**deuda incobrable** *(f)* Es
De uneinbringliche Schuld *(f)*
En bad debt
Fr créance irrécouvrable *(f)*
It credito inesigibile *(m)*
Pt dívida incobrável *(f)*

**deuda pública** *(f)* Es
De Staatsschuld *(f)*
En national debt
Fr dette publique *(f)*
It debito pubblico *(m)*
Pt dívida pública *(f)*

**deudor** *(m)* *n* Es
De Schuldner *(m)*
En debtor
Fr débiteur *(m)*
It debitore *(m)*
Pt devedor *(m)*

**deudor moroso** *(m)* Es
De schlechter Zahler *(m)*
En slow payer
Fr mauvais payeur *(m)*
It cattivo pagatore *(m)*
Pt mau-pagador *(m)*

**de valeur** Fr
De wertvoll
En valuable
Es valioso
It di valore
Pt valioso

**devaluación** *(f)* *n* Es
De Währungsabwertung *(f)*
En devaluation
Fr dévaluation *(f)*
It svalutazione *(f)*
Pt desvalorização *(f)*

**devaluation** *n* En
De Währungsabwertung *(f)*
Es devaluación *(f)*
Fr dévaluation *(f)*
It svalutazione *(f)*
Pt desvalorização *(f)*

**dévaluation** *(f)* *n* Fr
De Währungsabwertung *(f)*
En devaluation
Es devaluación *(f)*
It svalutazione *(f)*
Pt desvalorização *(f)*

**devedor** *(m)* *n* Pt
De Schuldner *(m)*
En debtor
Es deudor *(m)*
Fr débiteur *(m)*
It debitore *(m)*

**developing country** En
De Entwicklungsland *(n)*
Es pais en desarrollo *(m)*
Fr pays en voie de dévelop-
pement *(m)*
It paese in via di sviluppo *(m)*
Pt país em desenvolvimento
*(m)*

**development** (of property, etc.)
*n* En
De Erschliessung *(f)*
Es explotación *(f)*
Fr exploitation; lotissement *(f
m)*
It valorizzazione *(f)*
Pt exploração *(f)*

**development area** En
De Ortsplanungsgebiet *(n)*
Es zona de desarrollo *(f)*
Fr zone de développement *(f)*
It zona di sviluppo *(f)*
Pt zona de desenvolvimento
*(f)*

**development company** En
De Erschliessungsgesellschaft
*(f)*
Es compañía de explotación
*(f)*
Fr société d'exploitation *(f)*
It società d'imprese *(f)*
Pt empresa de exploração *(f)*

**déviation normale** *(f)* Fr
De normale Abweichung *(f)*
En standard deviation
Es desviación normal *(f)*
It deviazione normale *(f)*
Pt desvio normal *(m)*

**deviazione normale** *(f)* It
De normale Abweichung *(f)*
En standard deviation
Es desviación normal *(f)*
Fr déviation normale *(f)*
Pt desvio normal *(m)*

**devis** *(m)* *n* Fr
De Voranschlag *(m)*
En estimate
Es presupuesto *(m)*
It preventivo *(m)*
Pt previsão *(f)*

**devise** *(f)* *n* Fr
De Devisen *(f pl)*
En foreign currency
Es divisas extranjeras *(f pl)*
It valuta estera *(f)*
Pt moeda estrangeira *(f)*

**Devisen** *(f pl)* *n* De
En foreign currency; foreign
exchange
Es divisas extranjeras *(f pl)*
Fr devise; devises *(f; f pl)*
It valuta estera *(f)*
Pt moeda estrangeira *(f)*

**Devisenkontrolle** *(f)* *n* De
En exchange control
Am currency control
Es fiscalización de cambios *(f)*
Fr contrôle des changes *(m)*
It controllo sui cambi *(m)*
Pt controlo de câmbios *(m)*

**Devisenkurs** *(m)* *n* De
En foreign exchange rates
Es tasas de cambio exterior *(f
pl)*
Fr cours des changes *(m)*
It corso dei cambi *(m)*
Pt taxas de câmbio *(f pl)*

**devises** *(f pl)* *n* Fr
De Devisen *(f pl)*
En foreign exchange
Es divisas extranjeras *(f pl)*
It valuta estera *(f)*
Pt moeda estrangeira *(f)*

**devises bloquées** *(f pl)* Fr
De blockierte Devisen *(f pl)*
En blocked exchange
Es divisas bloqueadas *(f pl)*
It valute bloccate *(f pl)*
Pt câmbio bloqueado *(m)*

**devis rectifié** *(m)* Fr
De überarbeitete Schätzung *(f)*
En revised estimate
Es cálculo revisado *(m)*
It preventivo riveduto *(m)*
Pt estimativa revista *(f)*

**devis supplémentaire** *(m)* Fr
De Nachschätzung *(f)*
En supplementary estimate
Es cálculo suplementario *(m)*
It preventivo supplementare
*(m)*
Pt estimativa suplementar *(f)*

**devolver um cheque ao
sacado** Pt
De einen Scheck uneingelöst
lassen
En refer a cheque to drawer
Es rehusar pago de un cheque
Fr refuser d'honorer un
chèque
It rifiutare di pagare un
assegno

**dezentralisieren** *vb* De
En decentralize
Es decentralizar
Fr décentraliser
It decentralizzare
Pt descentralizar

**dezimal** *adj* De
En decimal
Es decimal
Fr décimal
It decimale
Pt decimal

**día** *(m)* *n* Es
De Tag *(m)*
En day
Fr jour *(m)*
It giorno *(m)*
Pt dia *(m)*

**dia** *(m)* *n* Pt
De Tag *(m)*
En day
Es día *(m)*
Fr jour *(m)*
It giorno *(m)*

**día a día** Es
De täglich
En day-to-day
Fr au jour le jour
It di giorno in giorno
Pt dia a dia

**dia a dia** Pt
De täglich
En day-to-day
Es día a día

Fr   au jour le jour
It   di giorno in giorno

**día de bolsa** *(m)* Es
De   Börsentag *(m)*
En   (financial) market day
Fr   jour de bourse *(m)*
It   giorno di borsa *(m)*
Pt   dia de bolsa *(m)*

**dia de bolsa** *(m)* Pt
De   Börsentag *(m)*
En   (financial) market day
Es   día de bolsa *(m)*
Fr   jour de bourse *(m)*
It   giorno di borsa *(m)*

**día de fiesta** *(m)* Es
De   gesetzlicher Feiertag *(m)*
En   public holiday
Fr   jour férié *(m)*
It   giorno di festa *(m)*
Pt   feriado *(m)*

**dia de folga** *(m)* Pt
De   dienstfreier Tag *(m)*
En   day off
Es   día libre *(m)*
Fr   jour de congé *(m)*
It   giorno di riposo *(m)*

**dia de liquidação** *(m)* Pt
De   Abrechnungstag *(m)*
En   settlement day; account
     day
Es   día de liquidación *(m)*
Fr   jour de règlement *(m)*
It   giorno della liquidazione
     *(m)*

**día de liquidación** *(m)* Es
De   Abrechnungstag *(m)*
En   settlement day; · account
     day
Fr   jour de règlement *(m)*
It   giorno della liquidazione
     *(m)*
Pt   dia de liquidação *(m)*

**día de mercado** *(m)* Es
De   Markttag *(m)*
En   (local) market day
Fr   jour de place *(m)*
It   giorno di mercato *(m)*
Pt   dia de mercado *(m)*

**dia de mercado** *(m)* Pt
De   Markttag *(m)*
En   (local) market day
Es   día de mercado *(m)*
Fr   jour de place *(m)*
It   giorno di mercato *(m)*

**día de pago** *(m)* Es
De   Zahltag *(m)*
En   pay day
Fr   jour de paiement *(m)*
It   giorno di paga *(m)*
Pt   dia de recebimento *(m)*

**dia de recebimento** *(m)* Pt
De   Zahltag *(m)*
En   pay day
Es   día de pago *(m)*
Fr   jour de paiement *(m)*
It   giorno di paga *(m)*

**dia de saída** *(m)* Pt
De   Abgangstag *(m)*
En   sailing date
Es   día de salida *(m)*
Fr   date de départ *(f)*
It   data di partenza *(f)*

**día de salida** *(m)* Es
De   Abgangstag *(m)*
En   sailing date
Fr   date de départ *(f)*
It   data di partenza *(f)*
Pt   dia de saída *(m)*

**dia de trabalho** *(m)* Pt
De   Arbeitstag *(m)*
En   working day
Es   día laborable *(m)*
Fr   jour ouvrable *(m)*
It   giornata lavorativa *(f)*

**dia de vencimento trimestral**
*(m)* Pt
De   Quartalstag *(m)*
En   quarter day
Es   primer día del trimestre *(m)*
Fr   jour du terme *(m)*
It   giorno della pigione *(m)*

**diagram** *n* En
De   graphische Darstellung *(f)*
Es   diagrama *(m)*
Fr   diagramme *(m)*
It   diagramma *(m)*
Pt   diagrama *(m)*

**diagrama** *(m)* *n* Es, Pt
De   graphische Darstellung *(f)*
En   diagram
Fr   diagramme *(m)*
It   diagramma *(m)*

**diagrama de flujo** *(m)* Es
De   Flussplan *(m)*
En   flow chart
Fr   ordinogramme *(m)*
It   diagramma di flusso *(m)*
Pt   gráfico de operação *(m)*

**diagrama de bloque** *(m)* Es
De   Säulendiagramm *(m)*
En   block diagram
Fr   ordinogramme *(m)*
It   schema a blocchi *(m)*
Pt   organigrama *(m)*

**diagramma** *(m)* *n* It
De   graphische Darstellung *(f)*
En   diagram
Es   diagrama *(m)*
Fr   diagramme *(m)*
Pt   diagrama *(m)*

**diagramma di flusso** *(m)* It
De   Flussplan *(m)*
En   flow chart
Es   diagrama de flujo *(m)*
Fr   ordinogramme *(m)*
Pt   gráfico de operação *(m)*

**diagramme** *(m)* *n* Fr
De   graphische Darstellung *(f)*
En   diagram
Es   diagrama *(m)*
It   diagramma *(m)*
Pt   diagrama *(m)*

**día laborable** *(m)* Es
De   Arbeitstag *(m)*
En   working day
Fr   jour ouvrable *(m)*
It   giornata lavorativa *(f)*
Pt   dia de trabalho *(m)*

**día libre** *(m)* Es
De   dienstfreier Tag *(m)*
En   day off
Fr   jour de congé *(m)*
It   giorno di riposo *(m)*
Pt   dia de folga *(m)*

**diario** *(m)* *n* Es
De   Tagebuch *(n)*
En   day-book

Fr journal *(m)*
It giornale *(m)*
Pt diário *(m)*

**diário** *(m)* n Pt
De Tagebuch *(n)*
En journal; day-book
Es (libro) diario *(m)*
Fr journal *(m)*
It (libro) giornale *(m)*

**diário de bordo** *(m)* Pt
De Log *(n)*
En (ship's) log
Es diario de navegación *(m)*
Fr journal de navigation *(m)*
It solcometro *(m)*

**diario de navegación** *(m)* Es
De Log *(n)*
En (ship's) log
Fr journal de navigation *(m)*
It solcometro *(m)*
Pt diário de bordo *(m)*

**días de gracia** *(f pl)* Es
De Nachfrist *(f)*
En days of grace
Fr délai supplémentaire *(m)*
It giorni di grazia *(m pl)*
Pt dias de tolerância *(m pl)*

**dias de tolerância** *(m pl)* Pt
De Nachfrist *(f)*
En days of grace
Es días de gracia *(f pl)*
Fr délai supplémentaire *(m)*
It giorni di grazia *(m pl)*

**dibujante** *(m)* n Es
De Entwerfer *(m)*
En draughtsman
Fr dessinateur *(m)*
It disegnatore *(m)*
Pt desenhador *(m)*

**dichiarare** vb It
De erklären
En declare
Es declarar
Fr déclarer
Pt declarar

**dichiarazione** *(f)* n It
De Erklärung *(f)*
En declaration
Es declaración *(f)*

Fr déclaration *(f)*
Pt declaração *(f)*

**dichiarazione del reddito** *(f)* It
De Einkommensteuererklärung *(f)*
En income-tax return
Es declaración fiscal *(f)*
Fr déclaration de revenu *(f)*
Pt declaração fiscal *(f)*

**dichiarazione d'imbarco** *(f)* It
De Absendungserklärung *(f)*
En declaration of shipment
Es declaración de expedición *(f)*
Fr déclaration d'expédition *(f)*
Pt declaração de expedição *(f)*

**dichiarazione d'intenzione** *(f)* It
De Willenserklärung *(f)*
En declaration of intent
Es declaración de intención *(f)*
Fr déclaration d'intention *(f)*
Pt declaração de propósito *(f)*

**dichiarazione doganale** *(f)* It
De Zollerklärung *(f)*
En customs declaration
Es declaración de aduana *(f)*
Fr déclaration en douane *(f)*
Pt declaração alfandegária *(f)*

**dichiarazione falsa** *(f)* It
De Verdrehung *(f)*
En misrepresentation
Es declaración falsa *(f)*
Fr déclaration inexacte *(f)*
Pt deturpação *(f)*

**dichiarazione fiscale** *(f)* It
De Steuererklärung *(f)*
En tax return
Es declaración de ingresos *(f)*
Fr déclaration de l'impôt *(f)*
Pt declaração para efeitos de tributação *(f)*

**dichiarazione giurata** *(f)* It
De beeidigte Erklärung *(f)*
En affidavit
Es declaración jurada *(f)*
Fr déclaration sous serment *(f)*
Pt declaração sob juramento *(f)*

**dictado** *(m)* n Es
De Diktat *(n)*
En dictation
Fr dictée *(f)*
It dettato; dettatura *(m f)*
Pt ditado *(m)*

**dictáfono** *(m)* n Es
De Diktaphon *(n)*
En dictating machine
Fr machine à dictée *(f)*
It dittafono *(m)*
Pt máquina de dictar *(f)*

**dictaphone operator** Am
En audio-typist
De Audio-typistin *(f)*
Es audio-mecanógrafa *(f)*
Fr dictaphoniste *(f)*
It dittafonista *(f)*
Pt audio-dactilógrafa *(f)*

**dictaphoniste** *(f)* n Fr
De Audio-typistin *(f)*
En audio-typist
Am dictaphone operator
Es audio-mecanógrafa *(f)*
It dittafonista *(f)*
Pt audio-dactilógrafa *(f)*

**dictar** vb Es
De diktieren
En dictate
Fr dicter
It dettare
Pt ditar

**dictate** vb En
De diktieren
Es dictar
Fr dicter
It dettare
Pt ditar

**dictating machine** En
De Diktaphon *(n)*
Es dictáfono *(m)*
Fr machine à dictée *(f)*
It dittafono *(m)*
Pt máquina de dictar *(f)*

**dictation** n En
De Diktat *(n)*
Es dictado *(m)*
Fr dictée *(f)*
It dettato; dettatura *(m f)*
Pt ditado *(m)*

**dictée** *(f)* n Fr
De Diktat *(n)*
En dictation
Es dictado *(m)*
It dettato; dettatura *(m f)*
Pt ditado *(m)*

**dicter** *vb* Fr
De diktieren
En dictate
Es dictar
It dettare
Pt ditar

**Diebstahl** *(m)* n De
En theft
Es robo *(m)*
Fr vol *(m)*
It furto *(m)*
Pt furto *(m)*

**dienstfreier Tag** *(m)* De
En day off
Es día libre *(m)*
Fr jour de congé *(m)*
It giorno di riposo *(m)*
Pt dia de folga *(m)*

**Dienstvertrag** *(m)* n De
En service agreement
Es contrato de servicio *(m)*
Fr contrat de service *(m)*
It accordo di servizio *(m)*
Pt contrato de serviço *(m)*

**dietas de viajes** *(f pl)* Es
De Reisekosten *(pl)*
En travelling expenses
Fr frais de voyage *(m pl)*
It spese di viaggio *(f pl)*
Pt despesas de viagem *(f pl)*

**diferença** *(f)* n Pt
De Unterschied *(m)*
En difference
Es diferencia *(f)*
Fr différence *(f)*
It differenza *(f)*

**diferença de preço** *(f)* Pt
De Preisunterschied *(m)*
En difference in price
Es diferencia de precio *(f)*
Fr écart de prix *(m)*
It differenza di prezzo *(f)*

**diferencia** *(f)* n Es
De Unterschied *(m)*
En difference
Fr différence *(f)*
It differenza *(f)*
Pt diferença *(f)*

**diferencia de precio** *(f)* Es
De Preisunterschied *(m)*
En difference in price
Fr écart de prix *(m)*
It differenza di prezzo *(f)*
Pt diferença de preço *(f)*

**diferencial** *(m)* n Es, Pt
De Differenz *(f)*
En differential
Fr différentiel *(m)*
It differenziale *(m)*

**difetto** *(m)* n It
De Mangel *(m)*
En defect
Es defecto *(m)*
Fr défaut *(m)*
Pt defeito *(m)*

**difetto latente** *(m)* It
De versteckter Mangel *(m)*
En latent defect
Es defecto latente *(m)*
Fr vice caché *(m)*
Pt defeito latente *(m)*

**difettoso** *adj* It
De fehlerhaft
En faulty
Es defectuoso
Fr défectueux
Pt defeituoso

**difference** n En
De Unterschied *(m)*
Es diferencia *(f)*
Fr différence *(f)*
It differenza *(f)*
Pt diferença *(f)*

**différence** *(f)* n Fr
De Unterschied *(m)*
En difference
Es diferencia *(f)*
It differenza *(f)*
Pt diferença *(f)*

**difference in price** En
De Preisunterschied *(m)*
Es diferencia de precio *(f)*

Fr écart de prix *(m)*
It differenza di prezzo *(f)*
Pt diferença de preço *(f)*

**differential** n En
De Differenz *(f)*
Es diferencial *(m)*
Fr différentiel *(m)*
It differenziale *(m)*
Pt diferencial *(m)*

**différentiel** *(m)* n Fr
De Differenz *(f)*
En differential
Es diferencial *(m)*
It differenziale *(m)*
Pt diferencial *(m)*

**Differenz** *(f)* n De
En differential
Es diferencial *(m)*
Fr différentiel *(m)*
It differenziale *(m)*
Pt diferencial *(m)*

**differenza** *(f)* n It
De Unterschied *(m)*
En difference
Es diferencia *(f)*
Fr différence *(f)*
Pt diferença *(f)*

**differenza di prezzo** *(f)* It
De Preisunterschied *(m)*
En difference in price
Es diferencia de precio *(f)*
Fr écart de prix *(m)*
Pt diferença de preço *(f)*

**differenziale** *(m)* n It
De Differenz *(f)*
En differential
Es diferencial *(m)*
Fr différentiel *(m)*
Pt diferencial *(m)*

**différer** *vb* Fr
De aufschieben; zurückstellen
En hold over; defer
Es aplazar; diferir
It differire
Pt conservar; adiar

**differire** *vb* It
De aufschieben; zurückstellen
En hold over; defer
Es aplazar; diferir

Fr  différer; ajourner
Pt  conservar; adiar

**difficile** adj Fr, It
De  schwierig
En  difficult
Es  difícil
Pt  difícil

**difficoltà di vendita** (f) It
De  Kaufabneigung (f)
En  sales resistance
Es  dificultades de ventas (f pl)
Fr  résistance à la vente (f)
Pt  resistência contra vendas (f)

**difficult** adj En
De  schwierig
Es  difícil
Fr  difficile
It  difficile
Pt  difícil

**difícil** adj Es
De  schwierig
En  difficult
Fr  difficile
It  difficile
Pt  difícil

**difícil** adj Pt
De  schwierig
En  difficult
Es  difícil
Fr  difficile
It  difficile

**dificultades de ventas** (f pl) Es
De  Kaufabneigung (f)
En  sales resistance
Fr  résistance à la vente (f)
It  difficoltà di vendita (f)
Pt  resistência contra vendas (f)

**di giorno in giorno** It
De  täglich
En  day-to-day
Es  día a día
Fr  au jour le jour
Pt  dia a dia

**digital computer** En
De  Digitalrechner (m)
Es  computadora numérica (f)
Fr  calculateur digital (m)

It  elaboratore numerico (m)
Pt  computador de dígitos (m)

**Digitalrechner** (m) n De
En  digital computer
Es  computadora numérica (f)
Fr  calculateur digital (m)
It  elaboratore numerico (m)
Pt  computador de dígitos (m)

**digit de contrôle** (m) Fr
De  Kontrollziffer (f)
En  check digit
Es  número de control (m)
It  cifra di controllo (f)
Pt  dígito de controle (m)

**dígito de controle** (m) Pt
De  Kontrollziffer (f)
En  check digit
Es  número de control (m)
Fr  digit de contrôle (m)
It  cifra di controllo (f)

**digne de confiance** Fr
De  zuverlässig
En  reliable
Es  digno de confianza
It  fidato; attendibile
Pt  digno de confiança

**digno de confiança** Pt
De  zuverlässig
En  reliable
Es  digno de confianza
Fr  digne de confiance
It  fidato; attendibile

**digno de confianza** Es
De  zuverlässig
En  reliable
Fr  digne de confiance
It  fidato; attendibile
Pt  digno de confiança

**digue** (m) n Es
De  Mole (f)
En  jetty
Fr  jetée; digue (f)
It  molo (m)
Pt  pontão; cais (m)

**Diktaphon** (n) n De
En  dictating machine
Es  dictáfono (m)
Fr  machine à dictée (f)
It  dittafono (m)
Pt  máquina de dictar (f)

**Diktat** (n) n De
En  dictation
Es  dictado (m)
Fr  dictée (f)
It  dettato; dettatura (m f)
Pt  ditado (m)

**diktieren** vb De
En  dictate
Es  dictar
Fr  dicter
It  dettare
Pt  ditar

**dimettersi** vb It
De  zurücktreten
En  resign
Es  dimitir
Fr  se démettre
Pt  demitir-se

**diminishing** adj En
De  abnehmend
Es  decreciente
Fr  décroissant
It  decrescente
Pt  decrescente

**diminishing returns** En
De  abnehmender Ertrag (m)
Es  rendimientos decrecientes (m pl)
Fr  rendements décroissants (m pl)
It  proventi decrescenti (m pl)
Pt  rendimentos decrescentes (m pl)

**diminuir** vb Pt
De  nachlassen
En  fall off
Es  disminuir
Fr  ralentir
It  diminuire

**diminuire** It
De  nachlassen
En  fall off
Es  disminuir
Fr  ralentir
Pt  diminuir; decrescer

**dimitir** vb Es
De  zurücktreten
En  resign
Fr  se démettre
It  dimettersi
Pt  demitir-se

**dimostrare** vb It
De beweisen
En establish; prove
Es demostrar; probar
Fr démontrer
Pt demonstrar; provar

**dinero** (m) n Es
De Geld (n)
En money
Fr argent (m)
It denaro (m)
Pt dinheiro (m)

**dinero a la vista** (m) Es
De Sichtgelder (n pl)
En money on call
Fr argent à vue (m)
It denaro a vista (m)
Pt dinheiro à ordem (m)

**dinero barato** (m) Es
De billiges Geld (n)
En cheap money
Fr argent bon marché (m)
It denaro a basso interesse (m)
Pt dinheiro barato (m)

**dinero caro** (m) Es
De teueres Geld (n)
En dear money
Fr argent cher (m)
It denaro ad alto interesse (m)
Pt dinheiro caro (m)

**dinero efectivo** (m) Es
De Bargeld (n)
En cash
Fr espèces (f pl)
It denaro (m)
Pt dinheiro (m)

**dinero sin invertir** (m) Es
De totes Kapital (n)
En idle money
Fr capital oisif (m)
It denaro inattivo (m)
Pt dinheiro paralizado (m)

**dinheiro** (m) n Pt
De Geld (n)
En money
Es dinero (m)
Fr argent (m)
It denaro (m)

**dinheiro à ordem** (m) Pt
De Sichtgelder (n pl)
En money on call
Es dinero a la vista (m)
Fr argent à vue (m)
It denaro a vista (m)

**dinheiro barato** (m) Pt
De billiges Geld (n)
En cheap money
Es dinero barato (m)
Fr argent bon marché (m)
It denaro a basso interesse (m)

**dinheiro caro** (m) Pt
De teueres Geld (n)
En dear money
Es dinero caro (m)
Fr argent cher (m)
It denaro ad alto interesse (m)

**dinheiro de contado** (m) Pt
De Bargeld (n)
En cash
Es dinero efectivo (m)
Fr espèces; argent comptant (f pl; m)
It denaro contante (m)

**dinheiro paralizado** (m) Pt
De totes Kapital (n)
En idle money
Es dinero sin invertir (m)
Fr capital oisif (m)
It denaro inattivo (m)

**dipartimento** (m) n It
De Abteilung (f)
En department
Es departamento (m)
Fr département (m)
Pt departamento (m)

**Diplom** (n) n De
En diploma
Es diploma (m)
Fr diplôme; brevet (m)
It diploma (m)
Pt diploma (m)

**diploma** n En; Es, It, Pt (m)
De Diplom (n)
Fr diplôme; brevet (m)

**diplôme** (m) n Fr
De Diplom (n)
En diploma
Es diploma (m)
It diploma (m)
Pt diploma (m)

**di qualità inferiore** It
De minderwertig
En low-grade
Es baja calidad
Fr de qualité inférieure
Pt baixo-nível

**di qualità superiore** It
De erstklassig
En high-grade
Es alta calidad
Fr de qualité supérieure
Pt alto-nível

**dique de carenas** (m) Es
De Trockendock (n)
En graving dock
Fr bassin de radoub (m)
It bacino di raddobbo (m)
Pt doca de querenas (f)

**dique seco** (m) Es
De Trockendock (n)
En dry dock
Fr cale sèche (f)
It bacino di carenaggio (m)
Pt doca-seca (f)

**direcção** (f) Pt
De Vorstand (m)
En management; board of directors
Es dirección; consejo de administración (f m)
Fr direction; conseil d'administration (f m)
It direzione; consiglio d'amministrazione (f m)

**dirección** (correo) (f) n Es
De Adresse (f)
En address
Fr adresse (f)
It indirizzo (m)
Pt endereço (m)

**dirección** (de una sociedad) (f) n Es
De Vorstand (m)
En management
Fr direction (f)

It direzione (f)
Pt gerência; direcção (f)

**dirección superior** (f) Es
De Direktion (f)
En top management
Fr haute direction (f)
It direzione superiore (f)
Pt gerência superior (f)

**dirección telegráfica** (f) Es
De Telegrammadresse (f)
En telegraphic address
Fr adresse télégraphique (f)
It indirizzo telegrafico (m)
Pt endereço telegráfico (m)

**direct cost** En
De direkte Kosten (pl)
Es coste directo (m)
Fr prix direct de revient (m)
It costo diretto (m)
Pt custo directo (m)

**direct current** (d.c.) En
De Gleichstrom (m)
Es corriente continua (f)
Fr courant continu (m)
It corrente continua (f)
Pt corrente continua (f)

**direct debit** En
De direkte Belastung (f)
Es débito directo (m)
Fr débit direct (m)
It debito diretto (m)
Pt débito directo (m)

**directeur** (m) n Fr
De Geschäftsleiter; Direktor (m)
En manager; director
Es director (m)
It direttore (m)
Pt gerente; director (m)

**directeur commercial** (m) Fr
De Verkaufsleiter (m)
En sales manager
Es jefe de ventas (m)
It direttore commerciale (m)
Pt chefe de vendas (m)

**directeur général** (m) Fr
De Geschäftsführer (m)
En chief executive
Es jefe ejecutivo (m)

It direttore generale (m)
Pt chefe de gerência (m)

**direct expenses** En
De Einzelkosten (pl)
Es gastos directos (m pl)
Fr frais directs (m pl)
It spese dirette (f pl)
Pt despesas directas (f pl)

**directions for use** En
De Gebrauchsanweisung (f)
Es modo de empleo (m)
Fr mode d'emploi (f)
It istruzioni per l'uso (f pl)
Pt instruções para uso (f pl)

**directiva** (f) n Es
De Verordnung (f)
En directive
Fr directive (f)
It direttivo (m)
Pt ordem de serviço (f)

**directive** n En, Fr (f)
De Verordnung (f)
Es directiva (f)
It direttivo (m)
Pt ordem de serviço (f)

**directivo** (m) n Es
De Geschäftsleiter (m)
En executive
Fr dirigeant (m)
It dirigente (m)
Pt dirigente (m)

**direct labour** En
De produktive Arbeitskräfte (f pl)
Es jornales directos (m pl)
Fr travail en régie (m)
It lavoro in economia (m)
Pt trabalho directamente produtivo (m)

**direct mail** En
De Postversandwerbung (f)
Es propaganda directa por correo (f)
Fr publicité directe (f)
It pubblicità diretta (f)
Pt publicidade por correio ao domicílio (f)

**director** n En
De Verwaltungsrat; Direktor (m)

Es director (m)
Fr directeur; administrateur (m)
It direttore; amministratore (m)
Pt director (m)

**director** (m) n Es
De Direktor; Geschäftsleiter (m)
En director; manager
Fr directeur; administrateur (m)
It direttore; amministratore (m)
Pt director; gerente (m)

**director** (m) n Pt
De Direktor; Prinzipal (m)
En director; principal
Es director; principal (m)
Fr directeur; principal (m)
It direttore; principale (m)

**director administrativo** (m) Pt
De geschäftsführender Direktor (m)
En executive director
Am corporate officer
Es director ejecutivo (m)
Fr administrateur dirigeant (m)
It amministratore dirigente (m)

**director de comercialização** (m) Pt
De Absatzdirektor (m)
En marketing director
Es director mercantil (m)
Fr administrateur chef d'écoulement (m)
It direttore di mercato (m)

**director ejecutivo** (m) Es
De geschäftsführender Direktor (m)
En executive director
Am corporate officer
Fr administrateur dirigeant (m)
It amministratore dirigente (m)
Pt director administrativo (m)

**director geral** (m) Pt
De geschäftsleitender Direktor (m)
En managing director
Am president

Es director gerente *(m)*
Fr administrateur délégué *(m)*
It amministratore delegato *(m)*

**director gerente** *(m)* Es
De geschäftsleitender Direktor *(m)*
En managing director
Am president
Fr administrateur délégué *(m)*
It amministratore delegato *(m)*
Pt director geral *(m)*

**director mercantil** *(m)* Es
De Absatzdirektor *(m)*
En marketing director
Fr administrateur chef d'écoulement *(m)*
It direttore di mercato *(m)*
Pt director de comercialização *(m)*

**directors' emoluments** En
De Direktorenbezüge *(m pl)*
Es emolumentos de directores *(m pl)*
Fr émoluments des administrateurs *(m pl)*
It emolumenti degli amministratori *(m pl)*
Pt emolumentos de directores *(m pl)*

**directors' report** En
De Vorstandsbericht *(m)*
Es informe de la administración *(m)*
Fr rapport des administrateurs *(m)*
It relazione degli amministratori *(f)*
Pt relatório de directores *(m)*

**directory** *n* En
De Adressbuch *(n)*
Es guía *(f)*
Fr répertoire *(m)*
It guida *(f)*
Pt guia *(m)*

**direct selling** En
De Direktverkauf *(m)*
Es venta directa *(f)*
Fr vente directe *(f)*
It vendita diretta *(f)*

Pt venda directa ao consumidor *(f)*

**direct taxation** En
De direkte Steuern *(f pl)*
Es contribuciones directas *(f pl)*
Fr contributions directes *(f pl)*
It imposte dirette *(f pl)*
Pt tributação directa *(f)*

**direito de retenção** *(m)* Pt
De Pfandrecht *(n)*
En lien
Es derecho de retencíon *(m)*
Fr droit de retention *(m)*
It diritto de sequestro *(m)*

**direito preferencial** *(m)* Pt
De Vorzugssatz *(m)*
En preferential duty
Es derechos preferenciales *(m pl)*
Fr tarif de faveur *(m)*
It tariffa preferenziale *(f)*

**direitos** *(m pl)* Pt
De Rechte; Gewinnanteil *(n pl; m)*
En rights; royalty
Es derechos *(m pl)*
Fr droits; redevance *(m pl; f)*
It diritti *(m pl)*

**direitos alfandegários** *(m pl)* Pt
De Zoll *(m)*
En customs duty
Es derechos de aduanas *(m pl)*
Fr droit de douane *(m)*
It diritto doganale *(m)*

**direitos de autor** *(m pl)* Pt
De Urheberrecht *(n)*
En copyright
Es derechos de autor *(m pl)*
Fr droits d'auteur *(m pl)*
It diritto d'autore *(m)*

**direitos de importação** *(m)* Pt
De Einfuhrzoll *(m)*
En import duty
Es derechos de importación *(m pl)*
Fr droits d'entrée *(m pl)*
It dazio d'importazione *(m)*

**direitos de sucessão** *(m pl)* Pt
De Nachlassteuer *(f)*
En estate duty
Am estate tax
Es derechos de sucesión *(m pl)*
Fr droits de succession *(m pl)*
It diritti di successione *(m pl)*

**direitos mineiros** *(m pl)* Pt
De Mineralgewinnungsrechte *(n pl)*
En mineral rights
Es derechos mineros *(m pl)*
Fr droits miniers *(m pl)*
It diritti minerari *(m pl)*

**direitos pagos** Pt
De verzollt
En duty-paid
Es derechos pagados
Fr acquitté
It dazio pagato

**direitos portuários** *(m pl)* Pt
De Hafengebühren *(f pl)*
En port charges
Es derechos portuarios *(m pl)*
Fr droits de port *(m pl)*
It diritti portuali *(m pl)*

**direkte Belastung** *(f)* De
En direct debit
Es débito directo *(m)*
Fr débit direct *(m)*
It debito diretto *(m)*
Pt débito directo *(m)*

**direkte Kosten** *(pl)* De
En direct cost
Es coste directo *(m)*
Fr prix direct de revient *(m)*
It costo diretto *(m)*
Pt custo directo *(m)*

**direkte Steuern** *(f pl)* De
En direct taxation
Es contribuciones directas *(f pl)*
Fr contributions directes *(f pl)*
It imposte dirette *(f pl)*
Pt tributação directa *(f)*

**Direktion** *(f)* *n* De
En top management
Es dirección superior *(f)*
Fr haute direction *(f)*

It   direzione superiore *(f)*
Pt   gerência superior *(f)*

**Direktor** *(m)* n De
En   director
Es   director *(m)*
Fr   directeur; administrateur *(m)*
It   direttore; amministratore *(m)*
Pt   director *(m)*

**Direktorenbezüge** *(m pl)* n De
En   directors' emoluments
Es   emolumentos de directores *(m pl)*
Fr   émoluments des administrateurs *(m pl)*
It   emolumenti degli amministratori *(m pl)*
Pt   emolumentos de directores *(m pl)*

**Direktverkauf** *(m)* n De
En   direct selling
Es   venta directa *(f)*
Fr   vente directe *(f)*
It   vendita diretta *(f)*
Pt   venda directa ao consumidor *(f)*

**direttissimo** *(m)* n It
De   D-Zug; Schnellzug *(m)*
En   express train
Es   tren expreso *(m)*
Fr   train express *(m)*
Pt   comboio rápido *(m)*

**direttivo** *(m)* n It
De   Verordnung *(f)*
En   directive
Es   directiva *(f)*
Fr   directive *(f)*
Pt   ordem de serviço *(f)*

**direttore** *(m)* n It
De   Geschäftsleiter *(m)*
En   manager
Es   director *(m)*
Fr   directeur *(m)*
Pt   gerente; director *(m)*

**direttore commerciale** *(m)* It
De   Verkaufsleiter *(m)*
En   sales manager
Es   jefe de ventas *(m)*
Fr   directeur commercial *(m)*
Pt   chefe de vendas *(m)*

**direttore conto cliente** *(m)* It
De   Kontaktgruppenleiter *(m)*
En   account executive
Es   ejecutivo de cuenta *(m)*
Fr   chef de comptes client *(m)*
Pt   chefe de conta de cliente *(m)*

**direttore del personale** *(m)* It
De   Personalchef *(m)*
En   personnel manager
Es   jefe de personal *(m)*
Fr   chef du personnel *(m)*
Pt   chefe do pessoal *(m)*

**direttore di mercato** *(m)* It
De   Absatzdirektor *(m)*
En   marketing director
Es   director mercantil *(m)*
Fr   administrateur chef d'écoulement *(m)*
Pt   director de comercialização *(m)*

**direttore esportazione** *(m)* It
De   Exportabteilungsleiter *(m)*
En   export manager
Es   jefe de exportación *(m)*
Fr   chef du service exportation *(m)*
Pt   gerente de exportações *(m)*

**direttore generale** *(m)* It
De   Geschäftsführer *(m)*
En   chief executive
Es   jefe ejecutivo *(m)*
Fr   directeur général *(m)*
Pt   chefe de gerência *(m)*

**direzione** *(f)* n It
De   Vorstand *(m)*
En   management
Es   dirección *(f)*
Fr   administration *(f)*
Pt   gerência; direcção *(f)*

**direzione superiore** *(f)* It
De   Direktion *(f)*
En   top management
Es   dirección superior *(f)*
Fr   haute direction *(f)*
Pt   gerência superior *(f)*

**dirigeant** *(m)* n Fr
De   Geschäftsleiter *(m)*
En   executive
Es   directivo *(m)*

It   dirigente *(m)*
Pt   dirigente *(m)*

**dirigente** *(m)* n It, Pt
De   Geschäftsleiter *(m)*
En   executive
Es   directivo *(m)*
Fr   dirigeant *(m)*

**diritto de sequestro** *(m)* It
De   Pfandrecht *(n)*
En   lien
Es   derecho de retencíon *(m)*
Fr   droit de retention *(m)*
Pt   direito de retenção *(m)*

**diritti** *(m pl)* n It
De   Rechte; Gewinnanteil *(n pl; m)*
En   rights; royalties
Es   derechos *(m pl)*
Fr   droits; redevance *(m pl; f)*
Pt   direitos *(m pl)*

**diritti di dock** *(m pl)* It
De   Dockgebühr *(f)*
En   dock dues
Es   derechos de muelle *(m pl)*
Fr   droits de dock *(m pl)*
Pt   encargos de doca *(m pl)*

**diritti di successione** *(m pl)* It
De   Erbschaftssteuern *(f pl)*
En   death duties
Am   estate taxes
Es   derechos sucesorios *(m pl)*
Fr   droits de succession *(m pl)*
Pt   impostos de sucessão *(m pl)*

**diritti minerari** *(m pl)* It
De   Mineralgewinnungsrechte *(n pl)*
En   mineral rights
Es   derechos mineros *(m pl)*
Fr   droits miniers *(m pl)*
Pt   direitos mineiros *(m pl)*

**diritti portuali** *(m pl)* It
De   Hafengebühren *(f pl)*
En   port charges
Es   derechos portuarios *(m pl)*
Fr   droits de port *(m pl)*
Pt   direitos portuários *(m pl)*

**diritto acquisito** *(m)* It
De   festbegründetes Recht *(n)*
En   vested interest

**diritto**

Es interés creado *(m)*
Fr droit acquis *(m)*
Pt interesse adquirido *(m)*

**diritto d'autore** *(m)* It
De Urheberrecht *(n)*
En copyright
Es derechos de autor *(m pl)*
Fr droits d'auteur *(m pl)*
Pt direitos de autor *(m pl)*

**diritto di sosta** *(m)* It
De Kaigeld *(n)*
En wharfage
Es muellaje *(m)*
Fr quayage *(m)*
Pt atracagem *(m)*

**diritto doganale** *(m)* It
De Zoll *(m)*
En customs duty
Es derechos de aduanas *(m pl)*
Fr droit de douane *(m)*
Pt direitos alfandegários *(m pl)*

**disagree** *vb* En
De nicht übereinstimmen
Es no estar de acuerdo
Fr être en désaccord
It essere in disaccordo
Pt discordar

**disamare** *vb* It
De auflegen
En lay up
Es desarmar
Fr désarmer
Pt desarmar

**disavanzo della bilancia commerciale** *(m)* It
De Aussenhandelsdefizit *(n)*
En trade gap
Es vacío comercial *(m)*
Fr déficit du commerce extérieur *(m)*
Pt vazio comercial *(m)*

**disbursement** *n* En
De Auszahlung *(f)*
Es desembolso *(m)*
Fr déboursement *(m)*
It esborso *(m)*
Pt desembolso *(m)*

**discharge a debt** En
De eine Schuld begleichen
Es descargar una deuda
Fr acquitter une dette
It estinguere un debito
Pt cancelar uma dívida

**discharge an employee** En
Am fire an employee
De einen Arbeitnehmer entlassen
Es despedir a un empleado
Fr congédier un employé
It licenziare un impiegato
Pt despedir um empregado

**discharged bankrupt** En
De entlasteter Gemeinschuldner *(m)*
Es fallido rehabilitado *(m)*
Fr failli réhabilité *(m)*
It fallito riabilitato *(m)*
Pt falido rehabilitado *(m)*

**disclaimer** *n* En
De Ablehnung *(f)*
Es renuncia *(f)*
Fr déni *(m)*
It rinunzia *(f)*
Pt descarte *(m)*

**disclosure** *n* En
De Offenlegung *(f)*
Es revelación *(f)*
Fr révélation; divulgation *(f)*
It rivelazione *(f)*
Pt revelação; divulgação *(f)*

**disconto por ausência de reclamações** *(m)* Pt
De Schadenfreiheitsrabatt *(m)*
En no-claims discount
Es bonificación por no-reclamación *(f)*
Fr bonification pour non sinistre *(f)*
It sconto per assenza di sinistri *(m)*

**discordar** *vb* Pt
De nicht übereinstimmen
En disagree
Es no estar de acuerdo
Fr être en désaccord
It essere in disaccordo

**discount** *n* En
De Skonto *(m)*
Es descuento *(m)*
Fr escompte *(m)*
It sconto; ribasso *(m)*
Pt desconto *(m)*

**discounted bill** En
De Diskontwechsel *(m)*
Es efecto descontado *(m)*
Fr effet escompté *(m)*
It cambiale scontata *(f)*
Pt letra descontada *(f)*

**discounted cash flow** (d.c.f.) En
De diskontiertes Cash-flow *(n)*
Es flujo de caja descontado *(m)*
Fr flux monétaire actualisé *(m)*
It flusso di cassa scontato *(m)*
Pt movimento em dinheiro descontado *(m)*

**discount house** En
De Diskontbank *(f)*
Es casa de descuentos *(f)*
Fr maison d'escompte *(f)*
It banca di sconto *(f)*
Pt agência corretora de descontos *(f)*

**discount market** En
De Diskontmarkt *(m)*
Es mercado de descuentos *(m)*
Fr marché de l'escompte *(m)*
It mercato di sconto *(m)*
Pt mercado de desconto *(m)*

**discount rate** En
De Diskontsatz *(m)*
Es tasa de descuento *(f)*
Fr taux d'escompte *(m)*
It tasso di sconto *(m)*
Pt taxa de desconto *(f)*

**discrepância** *(f)* *n* Pt
De Abweichung *(f)*
En discrepancy
Es desacuerdo *(m)*
Fr écart *(m)*
It divergenza *(f)*

**discrepancy** *n* En
De Abweichung *(f)*
Es desacuerdo *(m)*

Fr  écart *(m)*
It  divergenza *(f)*
Pt  discrepância *(f)*

**discretionary trust** En
De  unumschränkte Treuhand *(f)*
Es  fideicomiso discrecional *(m)*
Fr  fidéicommis à appréciation *(m)*
It  fondo fiduciario discrezionale *(m)*
Pt  fundação discricionária *(f)*

**discreto profitto** *(m)* It
De  angemessener Ertrag *(m)*
En  fair return
Es  beneficio razonable *(m)*
Fr  rendement équitable *(m)*
Pt  rendimento justo *(m)*

**discriminating tariff** En
De  diskriminierender Tarif *(m)*
Es  tarifa diferencial *(f)*
Fr  tarif discriminatoire *(m)*
It  tariffa discriminante *(f)*
Pt  tarifa discriminatória *(f)*

**discriminatoire** *adj* Fr
De  unterschiedlich
En  discriminatory
Es  discriminatorio
It  discriminatorio
Pt  discriminatório

**discriminatorio** *adj* Es, It
De  unterschiedlich
En  discriminatory
Fr  discriminatoire
Pt  discriminatório

**discriminatório** *adj* Pt
De  unterschiedlich
En  discriminatory
Es  discriminatorio
Fr  discriminatoire
It  discriminatorio

**discriminatory** *adj* En
De  unterschiedlich
Es  discriminatorio
Fr  discriminatoire
It  discriminatorio
Pt  discriminatório

**di seconda mano** It
De  aus zweiter Hand; Gebraucht

En  second-hand
Es  de segunda mano
Fr  d'occasion
Pt  de segunda mão

**disegnatore** *(m)* n It
De  Zeichner; Entwerfer *(m)*
En  designer; draughtsman
Es  diseñador; dibujante *(m)*
Fr  dessinateur *(m)*
Pt  desenhador *(m)*

**disegno** *(m)* n It
De  Zeichnung *(f)*
En  design
Es  diseño *(m)*
Fr  dessein *(m)*
Pt  desenho *(f)*

**diseñador** *(m)* n Es
De  Zeichner *(m)*
En  designer
Fr  dessinateur *(m)*
It  disegnatore *(m)*
Pt  desenhador *(m)*

**diseño** *(m)* n Es
De  Zeichnung *(f)*
En  design
Fr  dessein *(m)*
It  disegno *(m)*
Pt  desenho *(f)*

**disette** *(f)* n Fr
De  Knappheit *(f)*
En  short supply
Es  escasez *(f)*
It  scarsezza *(f)*
Pt  escassez *(f)*

**dishonest** *adj* En
De  unehrlich
Es  deshonesto
Fr  malhonnête
It  disonesto
Pt  desonesto

**dishonour a bill** En
De  einen Wechsel nicht akzeptieren
Es  protestar una letra
Fr  ne pas honorer un effet
It  non onorare un effetto
Pt  protestar uma letra

**disidente** *adj* Es
De  abweichend
En  dissenting

Fr  dissident
It  dissidente
Pt  dissidente

**Diskont** *(m)* n De
En  bank discount
Es  descuento bancario *(m)*
Fr  escompte en dehors *(m)*
It  sconto di banca *(m)*
Pt  desconto bancário *(m)*

**Diskontbank** *(f)* n De
En  discount house
Es  casa de descuentos *(f)*
Fr  maison d'escompte *(f)*
It  banca di sconto *(f)*
Pt  agência corretora de descontos *(f)*

**diskontierbare Wechsel** *(m pl)* De
En  bankable bills
Es  efectos negociables *(m pl)*
Fr  papier bancable *(m)*
It  effetti scontabili *(m pl)*
Pt  valores transaccionáveis pelo banco *(m pl)*

**diskontiertes Cash-flow** *(n)* De
En  discounted cash flow (d.c.f.)
Es  flujo de caja descontado *(m)*
Fr  flux monétaire actualisé *(m)*
It  flusso di cassa scontato *(m)*
Pt  movimento em dinheiro descontado *(m)*

**diskontierte Wechsel** *(m pl)* De
En  bills discounted
Es  efectos descontados *(m pl)*
Fr  effets escomptés *(m pl)*
It  effetti scontati *(m pl)*
Pt  letras descontadas *(f pl)*

**Diskontmarkt** *(m)* n De
En  discount market
Es  mercado de descuentos *(m)*
Fr  marché de l'escompte *(m)*
It  mercato di sconto *(m)*
Pt  mercado de desconto *(m)*

**Diskontsatz** *(m)* n De
En discount rate
Es tasa de descuento *(f)*
Fr taux d'escompte *(m)*
It tasso di sconto *(m)*
Pt taxa de desconto *(f)*

**Diskontwechsel** *(m)* n De
En discounted bill
Es efecto descontado *(m)*
Fr effet escompté *(m)*
It cambiale scontata *(f)*
Pt letra descontada *(f)*

**diskriminierender Tarif** *(m)* De
En discriminating tariff
Es tarifa diferencial *(f)*
Fr tarif discriminatoire *(m)*
It tariffa discriminante *(f)*
Pt tarifa discriminatória *(f)*

**dislocamento** *(m)* n It
De Tonnengehalt *(m)*
En displacement
Es desplazamiento *(m)*
Fr déplacement *(m)*
Pt deslocação *(f)*

**dismiss** *vb* En
Am fire
De entlassen
Es despedir
Fr congédier
It congedare
Pt despedir

**dismissal** n En
Am firing
De Entlassung *(f)*
Es despido *(m)*
Fr congédiement *(m)*
It licenziamento *(m)*
Pt despedimento *(m)*

**disoccupato** *adj* It
De arbeitslos
En out of work; unemployed
Es parado; sin trabajo
Fr en chômage
Pt desempregado

**disoccupazione** *(f)* n It
De Arbeitslosigkeit *(f)*
En unemployment
Es desempleo *(m)*
Fr chômage *(m)*
Pt desemprego *(m)*

**disoccupazione stagionale** *(f)* It
De jahreszeitlich bedingte Arbeitslosigkeit *(f)*
En seasonal unemployment
Es paro de temporada *(m)*
Fr chômage saisonnier *(m)*
Pt desemprego de estação *(m)*

**disolución** *(f)* n Es
De Auflösung *(f)*
En dissolution
Fr dissolution *(f)*
It scioglimento *(m)*
Pt dissolução *(f)*

**disonesto** *adj* It
De unehrlich
En dishonest
Es deshonesto
Fr malhonnête
Pt deshonesto

**dispatch** *vb* En
De absenden
Es expedir
Fr expédier
It spedire
Pt expedir

**dispatch** n En
De Versand *(m)*
Es despacho; expedición *(m f)*
Fr envoi *(m)*
It spedizione; dispaccio *(f m)*
Pt despacho; remessa *(m f)*

**dispatch note** En
De Versandschein *(m)*
Es aviso de expedición *(m)*
Fr bordereau d'expedition *(m)*
It bollettino di spedizione *(m)*
Pt aviso de despacho *(m)*

**displacement** n En
De Tonnengehalt *(m)*
Es desplazamiento *(m)*
Fr déplacement *(m)*
It dislocamento *(m)*
Pt deslocação *(f)*

**displacement-ton** n En
De Verdrängungstonne *(f)*
Es tonelada de desplazamiento *(f)*
Fr tonneau de déplacement *(m)*

It tonnellata di dislocamento *(f)*
Pt tonelada de deslocação *(f)*

**display** n En
De Schaustellung *(f)*
Es presentación *(f)*
Fr présentation *(f)*
It mostra *(f)*
Pt exposição *(f)*

**display unit** En
De Schaukasten *(m)*
Es presentación *(f)*
Fr présentoir *(m)*
It mostra *(f)*
Pt montra *(f)*

**disponibile** *adj* It
De verfügbar
En available
Es disponible
Fr disponible
Pt disponível

**disponibilidades de crédito sem cabertura** *(f pl)* Pt
De Überziehungsdisposition *(f)*
En overdraft facilities
Am overdraw facility
Es facilidades de descubierto *(f pl)*
Fr facilités de caisse *(f pl)*
It facilitazione di scoperto *(f)*

**disponibilità** *(f)* n It
De flüssige Mittel *(n pl)*
En funds available
Es fondos disponibles *(m pl)*
Fr disponibilités *(f pl)*
Pt fundos disponíveis *(m pl)*

**disponibilités** *(f pl)* n Fr
De flüssige Mittel *(n pl)*
En funds available
Es fondos disponibles *(m pl)*
It fondi disponibili; disponibilità *(m pl; f)*
Pt fundos disponíveis *(m pl)*

**disponible** *adj* Es, Fr
De verfügbar
En available
It disponibile
Pt disponível

**disponível** adj Pt
De verfügbar
En available
Es disponible
Fr disponible
It disponibile

**disposable income** En
De verfügbares Einkommen (n)
Es renta disponible (f)
Fr revenu disponible (m)
It reddito disponibile (m)
Pt receita disponível (f)

**disposable wrapping** En
De wegwerfbare Verpackung (f)
Es envoltura desechable (f)
Fr emballage perdu (m)
It imballaggio a perdere (m)
Pt embalagem a destruir (f)

**disposal** n En
De Verfügung (f)
Es disposición (f)
Fr disposition (f)
It disposizione (f)
Pt disposição (f)

**disposição** (f) n Pt
De Verfügung (f)
En disposal
Es disposición (f)
Fr disposition (f)
It disposizione (f)

**disposición** (f) n Es
De Verfügung (f)
En disposal
Fr disposition (f)
It disposizione (f)
Pt disposição (f)

**disposition** (f) n Fr
De Verfügung (f)
En disposal
Es disposición (f)
It disposizione (f)
Pt disposição (f)

**disposizione** (f) n It
De Verfügung (f)
En disposal
Es disposición (f)
Fr disposition (f)
Pt disposição (f)

**disputa** (f) n Es, It, Pt
De Streit (m)
En dispute
Fr contestation (f)

**disputa di competenza** (f) It
De Fähigkeitsstreitigkeit (f)
En demarcation dispute
Es disputa sobre demarcación (f)
Fr contestation syndicale des compétences (f)
Pt disputa sobre demarcação (f)

**disputa sobre demarcação** (f) Pt
De Fähigkeitsstreitigkeit (f)
En demarcation dispute
Es disputa sobre demarcación (f)
Fr contestation syndicale des compétences (f)
It disputa di competenza (f)

**disputa sobre demarcación** (f) Es
De Fähigkeitsstreitigkeit (f)
En demarcation dispute
Fr contestation syndicale des compétences (f)
It disputa di competenza (f)
Pt disputa sobre demarcação (f)

**dispute** n En
De Streit (m)
Es disputa (f)
Fr contestation (f)
It disputa (f)
Pt disputa (f)

**dissenting** adj En
De abweichend
Es disidente
Fr dissident
It dissidente
Pt dissidente

**dissident** adj Fr
De abweichend
En dissenting
Es disidente
It dissidente
Pt dissidente

**dissidente** adj It, Pt
De abweichend
En dissenting
Es disidente
Fr dissident

**dissolução** (f) n Pt
De Auflösung (f)
En dissolution
Es disolución (f)
Fr dissolution (f)
It scioglimento (m)

**dissolution** n En, Fr (f)
De Auflösung (f)
Es disolución (f)
It scioglimento (m)
Pt dissolução (f)

**distance** n En, Fr (f)
De Entfernung (f)
Es distancia (f)
It distanza (f)
Pt distância (f)

**distancia** (f) n Es
De Entfernung (f)
En distance
Fr distance (f)
It distanza (f)
Pt distância (f)

**distância** (f) n Pt
De Entfernung (f)
En distance
Es distancia (f)
Fr distance (f)
It distanza (f)

**distanza** (f) n It
De Entfernung (f)
En distance
Es distancia (f)
Fr distance (f)
Pt distância (f)

**distilaria** (f) n Pt
De Brennerei (f)
En distillery
Es destilería (f)
Fr distillerie (f)
It distilleria (f)

**distilleria** (f) n It
De Brennerei (f)
En distillery
Es destilería (f)

Fr  distillerie *(f)*
Pt  distilaria *(f)*


**distillerie** *(f)* n Fr
De  Brennerei *(f)*
En  distillery
Es  destilería *(f)*
It  distilleria *(f)*
Pt  distilaria *(f)*


**distillery** n En
De  Brennerei *(f)*
Es  destilería *(f)*
Fr  distillerie *(f)*
It  distilleria *(f)*
Pt  distilaria *(f)*


**distinta pesi** *(f)* It
De  Wiegeschein *(m)*
En  weight note
Es  certificado de pesaje *(m)*
Fr  note de poids *(f)*
Pt  certidão de peso *(f)*


**distressed area** En
De  Notstandsgebiet *(n)*
Es  región deprimida *(f)*
Fr  région déprimée *(f)*
It  area indigente *(f)*
Pt  zona deprimida *(f)*


**distressed goods** En
De  gepfändete Güter *(n pl)*
Es  mercancías embargadas *(f pl)*
Fr  biens saisis *(m pl)*
It  merce sequestrata *(f)*
Pt  mercadorias embargadas *(f)*


**distribución** *(f)* n Es
De  Vertrieb *(m)*
En  distribution
Fr  distribution *(f)*
It  distribuzione *(f)*
Pt  distribuição *(f)*


**distribución de las frecuencias** *(f)* Es
De  Häufigkeitsverteilung *(f)*
En  frequency distribution
Fr  distribution de fréquences *(f)*
It  distribuzione delle frequenze *(f)*
Pt  distribuição de frequência *(f)*


**distribuer** *vb* Fr
De  vertreiben
En  distribute
Es  distribuir
It  distribuire
Pt  distribuir


**distribuição** *(f)* n Pt
De  Vertrieb *(m)*
En  distribution (of goods)
Es  distribución *(f)*
Fr  distribution *(f)*
It  distribuzione *(f)*


**distribuição de frequência** *(f)* Pt
De  Häufigkeitsverteilung *(f)*
En  frequency distribution
Es  distribución de las frecuencias *(f)*
Fr  distribution de fréquences *(f)*
It  distribuzione delle frequenze *(f)*


**distribuidor** *(m)* n Es, Pt
De  Verkaufsagent; Konzessionär *(m)*
En  distributor
Fr  distributeur; concessionnaire *(m)*
It  distributore; concessionario *(m)*


**distribuir** *vb* Es, Pt.
De  vertreiben
En  distribute
Fr  distribuer
It  distribuire


**distribuire** *vb* It
De  vertreiben
En  distribute
Es  distribuir
Fr  distribuer
Pt  distribuir


**distribute** (profits, dividends, etc.) *vb* En
De  verteilen
Es  repartir
Fr  répartir
It  repartire
Pt  repartir


**distribute** (goods) *vb* En
De  vertreiben
Es  distribuir


Fr  distribuer
It  distribuire
Pt  distribuir


**distributeur** *(m)* n Fr
De  Verkaufsagent; Konzessionär *(m)*
En  distributor
Es  distribuidor; concesionario *(m)*
It  distributore; concessionario *(m)*
Pt  distribuidor; concessionário *(m)*


**distributeur automatique** *(m)* Fr
De  Verkaufsautomat *(m)*
En  vending machine
Es  máquina expendedora *(f)*
It  macchina venditrice automatica *(f)*
Pt  máquina de vendas *(f)*


**distributeur d'argent comptant** *(m)* Fr
De  Bargeldauszahlungsautomat *(m)*
En  cash dispenser
Es  caja automática *(f)*
It  cassa automatica *(f)*
Pt  caixa automática *(f)*


**distribution** n En, Fr *(f)*
De  Verteilung; Vertrieb *(f m)*
Es  reparto; distribución *(m f)*
It  ripartizione; distribuzione *(f)*
Pt  distribuição *(f)*


**distribution de fréquences** *(f)* Fr
De  Häufigkeitsverteilung *(f)*
En  frequency distribution
Es  distribución de las frecuencias *(f)*
It  distribuzione delle frequenze *(f)*
Pt  distribuição de frequência *(f)*


**distributor** n En
De  Verkaufsagent; Konzessionär *(m)*
Es  distribuidor; concesionario *(m)*
Fr  distributeur; concessionnaire *(m)*

It distributore; concessionario
(m)
Pt distribuidor; concessionário
(m)

**distributore** (m) n It
De Verkaufsagent; Konzessio-
när (m)
En distributor
Es distribuidor; concesionario
(m)
Fr distributeur; concession-
naire (m)
Pt distribuidor; concessionário
(m)

**distribuzione** (f) n It
De Vertrieb (m)
En distribution
Es distribución (f)
Fr distribution (f)
Pt distribuição (f)

**distribuzione delle frequenze**
(f) It
De Häufigkeitsverteilung (f)
En frequency distribution
Es distribución de las frecuen-
cias (f)
Fr distribution de fréquences
(f)
Pt distribuição de frequência
(f)

**ditado** (m) n Pt
De Diktat (n)
En dictation
Es dictado (m)
Fr dictée (f)
It dettato; dettatura (m f)

**ditar** vb Pt
De diktieren
En dictate
Es dictar
Fr dicter
It dettare

**ditta** (f) n It
De Firma (f)
En firm; company
Es casa; casa (f)
Fr firme; maison (f)
Pt empresa; firma (f)

**dittafonista** (f) n It
De Audio-typistin (f)
En audio-typist

Am dictaphone operator
Es audio-mecanógrafa (f)
Fr dictaphoniste (f)
Pt audio-dactilógrafa (f)

**dittafono** (m) n It
De Diktaphon (n)
En dictating machine
Es dictáfono (m)
Fr machine à dictée (f)
Pt máquina de dictar (f)

**di valore** It
De wertvoll
En valuable
Es valioso
Fr de valeur
Pt valioso

**divergenza** (f) n It
De Abweichung (f)
En discrepancy
Es desacuerdo (m)
Fr écart (m)
Pt discrepância (f)

**diversificação** (f) n Pt
De Vervielfältigung der Pro-
dukte (f)
En diversification
Es diversificación (f)
Fr diversification (f)
It diversificazione (f)

**diversificación** (f) n Es
De Vervielfältigung der Pro-
dukte (f)
En diversification
Fr diversification (f)
It diversificazione (f)
Pt diversificação (f)

**diversification** n En, Fr (f)
De Vervielfältigung der Pro-
dukte (f)
Es diversificación (f)
It diversificazione (f)
Pt diversificação (f)

**diversificazione** (f) n It
De Vervielfältigung der Pro-
dukte (f)
En diversification
Es diversificación (f)
Fr diversification (f)
Pt diversificação (f)

**dívida** (f) n Pt
De Schuld (f)
En debt
Es deuda (f)
Fr créance (f)
It debito (m)

**dívida duvidosa** (f) Pt
De zweifelhafte Forderung (f)
En doubtful debt
Es deuda de pago dudoso (f)
Fr créance douteuse (f)
It credito dubbio (m)

**dívida incobrável** (f) Pt
De uneinbringliche Schuld (f)
En bad debt
Es deuda incobrable (f)
Fr créance irrécouvrable (f)
It credito inesigibile (m)

**dívida pública** (f) Pt
De Staatsschuld (f)
En national debt
Es deuda pública (f)
Fr dette publique (f)
It debito pubblico (m)

**dividend** n En
De Dividende (f)
Es dividendo (m)
Fr dividende (m)
It dividendo (m)
Pt dividendo (m)

**dividende** (m) n Fr
De Dividende (f)
En dividend
Es dividendo (m)
It dividendo (m)
Pt dividendo (m)

**Dividende** (f) n De
En dividend
Es dividendo (m)
Fr dividende (m)
It dividendo (m)
Pt dividendo (m)

**dividende intérimaire** (m) Fr
De vorläufige Dividende (f)
En interim dividend
Es dividendo provisional (m)
It acconto di dividendo (m)
Pt dividendo interino (m)

**Dividendenstop** *(m)* n De
En dividend limitation
Es bloqueo de dividendos *(m)*
Fr blocage des dividendes *(m)*
It blocco dei dividendi *(m)*
Pt limitação de dividendos *(f)*

**dividende semestrielle** *(f)* Fr
De halbjährliche Dividende *(f)*
En half-yearly dividend
Es dividendo semestral *(m)*
It dividendo semestrale *(m)*
Pt dividendo semi-anual *(m)*

**dividende-warrant** *(m)* Fr
De Gewinnanteilschein *(m)*
En dividend warrant
Es cupón de dividendos *(m)*
It cedola di dividendo *(f)*
Pt cédula de dividendo *(f)*

**dividend limitation** En
De Dividendenstop *(m)*
Es bloqueo de dividendos *(m)*
Fr blocage des dividendes *(m)*
It blocco dei dividendi *(m)*
Pt limitação de dividendos *(f)*

**dividendo** *(m)* n Es, It, Pt
De Dividende *(f)*
En dividend
Fr dividende *(m)*

**dividendo excluido** Pt
De ohne Dividende
En ex dividend
Es sin dividendo
Fr ex-dividende
It senza dividendo

**dividendo final** *(m)* Pt
De Schlussdividende *(f)*
En final dividend
Es saldo del dividendo *(m)*
Fr solde de dividende *(m)*
It saldo del dividendo *(m)*

**dividendo interino** *(m)* Pt
De vorläufige Dividende *(f)*
En interim dividend
Es dividendo provisional *(m)*
Fr dividende intérimaire *(m)*
It acconto di dividendo *(m)*

**dividendo provisional** *(m)* Es
De vorläufige Dividende *(f)*
En interim dividend
Fr dividende intérimaire *(m)*

It acconto di dividendo *(m)*
Pt dividendo interino *(m)*

**dividendo semestral** *(m)* Es
De halbjährliche Dividende *(f)*
En half-yearly dividend
Fr dividende semestrielle *(f)*
It dividendo semestrale *(m)*
Pt dividendo semi-anual *(m)*

**dividendo semestrale** *(m)* It
De halbjährliche Dividende *(f)*
En half-yearly dividend
Es dividendo semestral *(m)*
Fr dividende semestrielle *(f)*
Pt dividendo semi-anual *(m)*

**dividendo semi-anual** *(m)* Pt
De halbjährliche Dividende *(f)*
En half-yearly dividend
Es dividendo semestral *(m)*
Fr dividende semestrielle *(f)*
It dividendo semestrale *(m)*

**dividend warrant** En
De Gewinnanteilschein *(m)*
Es cupón de dividendos *(m)*
Fr dividende-warrant *(m)*
It cedola di dividendo *(f)*
Pt cédula de dividendo *(f)*

**dividere** vb It
De teilen
En share
Es repartir
Fr partager
Pt repartir

**dividere a metà la differenza**
It
De einen strittigen Preisunter-
    schied teilen
En split the difference
Es repartir la diferencia
Fr partager la différence
Pt dividir a meio a diferença

**dividir a meio a diferença** Pt
De einen strittigen Preisunter-
    schied teilen
En split the difference
Es repartir la diferencia
Fr partager la différence
It dividere a metà la differenza

**divieto d'importazione** *(m)* It
De Einfuhrverbot *(n)*
En import ban

Es prohibición de importación
    *(f)*
Fr prohibition d'entrée *(f)*
Pt proibição de importação *(f)*

**divisão** *(f)* n Pt
De Teilung *(f)*
En division
Es división *(f)*
Fr division *(f)*
It divisione *(f)*

**divisão do trabalho** *(f)* Pt
De Arbeitsteilung *(f)*
En division of labour
Es división del trabajo *(f)*
Fr division du travail *(f)*
It divisione del lavoro *(f)*

**divisas adiantada** *(f pl)* Pt
De Termindevisen *(f pl)*
En forward exchange
Es divisas a término *(f pl)*
Fr change à terme *(m)*
It cambio a termine *(m)*

**divisas a término** *(f pl)* Es
De Termindevisen *(f pl)*
En forward exchange
Fr change à terme *(f)*
It cambio a termine *(m)*
Pt divisas adiantada *(f pl)*

**divisas bloqueadas** *(f pl)* Es
De blockierte Devisen *(f pl)*
En blocked exchange
Fr devises bloquées *(f pl)*
It valute bloccate *(f pl)*
Pt câmbio bloqueado *(m)*

**divisas extranjeras** *(f pl)* Es
De Devisen *(f pl)*
En foreign currency
Fr devises *(f pl)*
It valuta estera *(f)*
Pt moeda estrangeira *(f)*

**division** n En, Fr *(f)*
De Teilung; Abteilung *(f)*
Es división; sección *(f)*
It divisione *(f)*
Pt divisão; secção *(f)*

**división** *(f)* n Es
De Teilung *(f)*
En division
Fr division *(f)*

It    divisione *(f)*
Pt    divisão *(f)*

**división del trabajo** *(f)* Es
De    Arbeitsteilung *(f)*
En    division of labour
Fr    division du travail *(f)*
It    divisione del lavoro *(f)*
Pt    divisão do trabalho *(f)*

**division du travail** *(f)* Fr
De    Arbeitsteilung *(f)*
En    division of labour
Es    división del trabajo *(f)*
It    divisione del lavoro *(f)*
Pt    divisão do trabalho *(f)*

**divisione** *(f)* n It
De    Teilung; Abteilung *(f)*
En    division
Es    división; sección *(f)*
Fr    division *(f)*
Pt    divisão; secção *(f)*

**divisione del lavoro** *(f)* It
De    Arbeitsteilung *(f)*
En    division of labour
Es    división del trabajo *(f)*
Fr    division du travail *(f)*
Pt    divisão do trabalho *(f)*

**division of labour** En
De    Arbeitsteilung *(f)*
Es    división del trabajo *(f)*
Fr    division du travail *(f)*
It    divisione del lavoro *(f)*
Pt    divisão do trabalho *(f)*

**doca** *(f)* n Pt
De    Dock *(n)*
En    dock
Es    muelle *(m)*
Fr    dock; bassin *(m)*
It    dock; bacino *(m)*

**doca de querenas** *(f)* Pt
De    Trockendock *(n)*
En    graving dock
Es    dique de carenas *(m)*
Fr    bassin de radoub *(m)*
It    bacino di raddobbo *(m)*

**doca-seca** *(f)* n Pt
De    Trockendock *(n)*
En    dry dock
Es    dique seco *(m)*
Fr    cale sèche *(f)*
It    bacino di carenaggio *(m)*

**docas francas** Pt
De    frei Docklager
En    delivered docks
Es    franco en muelle
Fr    franco dock
It    franco dock

**d'occasion** Fr
De    aus zweiter Hand; Ge-
        braucht-
En    second-hand
Es    de segunda mano
It    di seconda mano
Pt    de segunda mão

**dock** n En, Fr, It
De    Dock *(n)*
Es    muelle *(m)*
Pt    doca *(f)*

**Dock** *(n)* n De
En    dock
Es    muelle *(m)*
Fr    dock; bassin *(m)*
It    dock; bacino *(m)*
Pt    doca *(f)*

**dock dues** En
De    Dockgebühr *(f)*
Es    derechos de muelle *(m pl)*
Fr    droits de dock *(m pl)*
It    diritti di dock *(m pl)*
Pt    encargos de doca *(m pl)*

**Dockempfangsschein** *(m)* n De
En    dock receipt
Es    recibo de entrega en muelle
        *(m)*
Fr    quittance de dock *(f)*
It    quietanza di darsena *(f)*
Pt    recibo de doca *(m)*

**docker** n En, Fr *(m)*
Am  longshoreman
De    Hafenarbeiter *(m)*
Es    cargador de muelle *(m)*
It    lavoratore del porto *(m)*
Pt    trabalhador das docas *(m)*

**Dockgebühr** *(f)* n De
En    dock dues
Es    derechos de muelle *(m pl)*
Fr    droits de dock *(m pl)*
It    diritti di dock *(m pl)*
Pt    encargos de doca *(m pl)*

**dock receipt** En
De    Dockempfangsschein *(m)*
Es    recibo de entrega en muelle
        *(m)*
Fr    quittance de dock *(f)*
It    quietanza di darsena *(f)*
Pt    recibo de doca *(m)*

**dock strike** En
De    Hafenarbeiterstreik *(m)*
Es    huelga de obreros de
        muelle *(f)*
Fr    grève des dockers *(f)*
It    sciopero portuale *(m)*
Pt    greve na doca *(f)*

**dockyard** n En
De    Schiffswerft *(f)*
Es    astillero *(m)*
Fr    chantier de construction de
        navires *(m)*
It    cantiere *(m)*
Pt    estaleiro *(m)*

**document** n En, Fr *(m)*
De    Urkunde *(f)*
Es    documento *(m)*
It    documento *(m)*
Pt    documento *(m)*

**documentação do navio** *(f)* Pt
De    Schiffspapiere *(n pl)*
En    ship's papers
Es    documentación marítima *(f)*
Fr    papiers de bord *(m pl)*
It    carte di bordo *(f pl)*

**documentación marítima** *(f)* Es
De    Schiffspapiere *(n pl)*
En    ship's papers
Fr    papiers de bord *(m pl)*
It    carte di bordo *(f pl)*
Pt    documentação do navio *(f)*

**documentary bill** En
De    Dokumentenwechsel *(m)*
Es    efecto documentario *(m)*
Fr    traite documentaire *(f)*
It    tratta documentaria *(f)*
Pt    titulo documental *(m)*

**documentary credit** En
De    Dokumenten-Akkreditiv *(n)*
Es    crédito documentario *(m)*
Fr    crédit documentaire *(m)*
It    credito documentario *(m)*
Pt    crédito contra documen-
        tação *(m)*

**documentary evidence** En
De Urkundenbeweis *(m)*
Es prueba documental *(f)*
Fr preuve écrite *(f)*
It prova scritta *(f)*
Pt prova documental *(f)*

**documenti contro accetta-zione** *(m pl)* It
De Dokumente gegen Akzept *(n pl)*
En documents against accep-tance *(d/a)*
Es documentos contra accep-tación *(m pl)*
Fr documents contre accepta-tion *(m pl)*
Pt documentos contra aceita-ção *(m pl)*

**documenti contro pagamento** *(m pl)* It
De Dokumente gegen Einlö-sung *(n pl)*
En documents against pay-ment *(d/p)*
Es documentos contra pago *(m pl)*
Fr documents contre paie-ment *(m pl)*
Pt documentos contra paga-mento *(m pl)*

**documento** *(m)* n Es, It, Pt
De Urkunde *(f)*
En document
Fr document *(m)*

**documento de garantia** *(m)* Pt
De Ausfallbürgschaft *(f)*
En letter of indemnity
Es carta de indemnización *(f)*
Fr cautionnement *(m)*
It lettera di garanzia *(f)*

**document of title** En
De Eigentumstitel *(m)*
Es título de propiedad *(m)*
Fr titre de propriété *(m)*
It titolo di proprietà *(m)*
Pt título de propriedade *(m)*

**documentos contra accep-tación** *(m pl)* Es
De Dokumente gegen Akzept *(n pl)*
En documents against accep-tance *(d/a)*

Fr documents contre accepta-tion *(m pl)*
It documenti contro accet-tazione *(m pl)*
Pt documentos contra aceita-ção *(m pl)*

**documentos contra aceitação** *(m pl)* Pt
De Dokumente gegen Akzept *(n pl)*
En documents against accep-tance *(d/a)*
Es documentos contra accep-tación *(m pl)*
Fr documents contre accepta-tion *(m pl)*
It documenti contro accet-tazione *(m pl)*

**documentos contra paga-mento** *(m pl)* Pt
De Dokumente gegen Einlö-sung *(n pl)*
En documents against pay-ment *(d/p)*
Es documentos contra pago *(m pl)*
Fr documents contre paie-ment *(m pl)*
It documenti contro paga-mento *(m pl)*
Pt documentos contra paga-mento *(m pl)*

**documentos contra pago** *(m pl)* Es
De Dokumente gegen Einlö-sung *(n pl)*
En documents against pay-ment *(d/p)*
Fr documents contre paie-ment *(m pl)*
It documenti contro paga-mento *(m pl)*
Pt documentos contra paga-mento *(m pl)*

**documents against payment** *(d/p)* En
De Dokumente gegen Einlö-sung *(n pl)*
Es documentos contra pago *(m pl)*
Fr documents contre paie-ment *(m pl)*
It documenti contro paga-mento *(m pl)*
Pt documentos contra paga-mento *(m pl)*

**documents contre paiement** *(m pl)* Fr
De Dokumente gegen Einlö-sung *(n pl)*
En documents against pay-ment *(d/p)*
Es documentos contra pago *(m pl)*
It documenti contro paga-mento *(m pl)*
Pt documentos contra paga-mento *(m pl)*

**dogana** *(f)* n It
De Zoll *(m)*
En customs
Es aduana *(f)*
Fr douane *(f)*
Pt alfândega *(f)*

**doit** *(m)* n Fr
De Debet; Soll *(n)*
En debit
Es débito *(m)*
It debito; dare *(m)*
Pt débito *(m)*

**Dokumente gegen Akzept** *(n pl)* De
En documents against accep-tance *(d/a)*
Es documentos contra accep-tación *(m pl)*
Fr documents contre accepta-tion *(m pl)*
It documenti contro accet-tazione *(m pl)*
Pt documentos contra aceita-ção *(m pl)*

**Dokumente gegen Einlösung** *(n pl)* De
En documents against pay-ment *(d/p)*
Es documentos contra pago *(m pl)*
Fr documents contre paie-ment *(m pl)*
It documenti contro paga-mento *(m pl)*
Pt documentos contra paga-mento *(m pl)*

**Dokumenten-Akkreditiv** *(n)* n De
En documentary credit
Es crédito documentario *(m)*
Fr crédit documentaire *(m)*

It   credito documentario (m)
Pt   crédito contra documen-
     tação (m)


**Dokumentenwechsel** (m) n De
En   documentary bill
Es   efecto documentario (m)
Fr   traite documentaire (f)
It   tratta documentaria (f)
Pt   titulo documental (m)


**dollars pétroliers** (m pl) Fr
De   Öldollar (m pl)
En   petrodollars
Es   petrodólares (m pl)
It   petrodollari (m pl)
Pt   petrodólares (m pl)


**domaine industriel** (m) Fr
De   Industriegebiet (n)
En   industrial estate
Am   industrial park
Es   precinto industrial (m)
It   centro industriale (m)
Pt   centro fabril (m)


**domanda** (f) n It
De   Antraq; Nachfrage (m f)
En   application; inquiry
Es   solicitud; demanda (f)
Fr   demande (f)
Pt   requisição; pergunta (f)


**domani** adv It
De   morgen
En   tomorrow
Es   mañana
Fr   demain
Pt   amanhã


**domestic sales** Am
En   home trade
De   Binnenhandel (m)
Es   comercio interior (m)
Fr   commerce intérieur (m)
It   commercio interno (m)
Pt   comércio interno (m)


**dommage** (m) n Fr
De   Beschädigung; Schaden (f
     m)
En   damage; injury
Es   daño (m)
It   danno (m)
Pt   dano; injúria (m f)


**dommage indirect** (m) Fr
De   indirekter Schaden (m)
En   consequential damage
Es   daños indirectos (m pl)
It   danno indiretti (m)
Pt   dano por consequência (m)


**dommages indirects** (m pl) Fr
De   immaterieller Schaden (m)
En   consequential damages
Es   daños indirectos (m pl)
It   danni indiretti (m pl)
Pt   danos decorrentes (m pl)


**dommages indirects** (m pl) Fr
De   Ersatz immateriellen Scha-
     dens (m)
En   special damages
Es   daños especiales (m pl)
It   danni particolari (m pl)
Pt   indemnização especial (f)


**dommages-intérêts** (m pl) n Fr
De   Schadenersatz (m)
En   damages
Es   daños (m pl)
It   danni (m pl)
Pt   danos (m pl)


**dommages-intérêts fixés en
argent** (m pl) Fr
De   Konventionalstrafe (f)
En   liquidated damages
Es   daños liquidados (m pl)
It   danni liquidati (m pl)
Pt   danos liquidados (m pl)


**don** (m) n Fr
De   Geschenk (n)
En   gift
Es   regalo (m)
It   dono; donazione (m f)
Pt   prenda; presente (f m)


**dona de casa** (f) Pt
De   Hausfrau (f)
En   housewife
Es   ama de casa (f)
Fr   ménagère (f)
It   massaia (f)


**donnée d'exécution** (f) Fr
De   Arbeitsaufgabe (f)
En   job specification
Es   especificación del trabajo
     (f)
It   specifica del lavoro (f)
Pt   especificação de obra (f)


**données** (f pl) n Fr
De   Daten (n pl)
En   data
Es   datos (m pl)
It   dati (m pl)
Pt   dados (m pl)


**donner de l'avancement à** Fr
De   befördern
En   promote
Es   ascender
It   promuovere
Pt   promover


**donner des arrhès** Fr
De   hinterlegen
En   pay a deposit
Es   hacer un depósito
It   versare un deposito
Pt   pagar depósito


**donner ses huit jours** Fr
De   einwöchig kündigen
En   give a week's notice
Es   dar una semana de aviso
It   dare una settimana di
     preavviso
Pt   dar um prazo de uma
     semana para despedimento


**dono** (m) n It
De   Geschenk (n)
En   gift
Es   regalo (m)
Fr   don; cadeau (m)
Pt   prenda; presente (f m)


**dono da casa** (m) Pt
De   Hausherr (m)
En   householder
Es   jefe de familia (m)
Fr   chef de famille (m)
It   capo-famiglia (m)


**dono per corrompere** (m) It
De   Bestechungsgeld (n)
En   bribe
Es   soborno (m)
Fr   pot-de-vin (m)
Pt   soborno (m)


**door-to-door selling** En
De   Haus-zu-Hausverkauf (m)
Es   venta a domicilio (f)
Fr   vente à domicile (f)
It   vendita a domicilio (f)
Pt   venda de porta-a-porta (f)

**dopodomani** *adv* It
De übermorgen
En day after tomorrow
Es pasado mañana
Fr après demain
Pt depois de amanhã

**Doppelbesteuerungserleichterung** *(f) n* De
En double taxation relief
Es desgravación de tributación doble *(f)*
Fr dégrèvement de charges fiscales doubles *(m)*
It sgravio per doppia tassazione *(m)*
Pt isenção de tributação dupla *(f)*

**doppelte Buchführung** *(f)* De
En double entry book-keeping
Es partida doble *(f)*
Fr partie double *(f)*
It partita doppia *(f)*
Pt lançamento duplo *(m)*

**dossier** *(m) n* Fr
De Akte *(f)*
En file
Es archivo *(m)*
It archivio *(m)*
Pt ficheiro *(m)*

**dotar** *vb* Es, Pt
De ausstatten
En endow
Fr doter
It dotare

**dotar de fundos** Pt
De fundieren
En fund
Es fundar; consolidar
Fr fonder; consolider
It consolidare

**dotare** *vb* It
De ausstatten
En endow
Es dotar
Fr doter
Pt dotar

**doter** *vb* Fr
De ausstatten
En endow
Es dotar

It dotare
Pt dotar

**douane** *(f) n* Fr
De Zoll *(m)*
En customs
Es aduana *(f)*
It dogana *(f)*
Pt alfândega *(f)*

**double** *(m) n* Fr
De Duplikat *(n)*
En duplicate
Es duplicado *(m)*
It duplicato *(m)*
Pt duplicado *(m)*

**double entry book-keeping** En
De doppelte Buchführung *(f)*
Es partida doble *(f)*
Fr partie double *(f)*
It partita doppia *(f)*
Pt lançamento duplo *(m)*

**double option** En, Fr *(f)*
De Stellgeschäft *(n)*
Es opción doble *(f)*
It opzione doppia *(f)*
Pt opção dupla *(f)*

**double taxation relief** En
De Doppelbesteuerungserleichterung *(f)*
Es desgravación de tributación doble *(f)*
Fr dégrèvement de charges fiscales doubles *(m)*
It sgravio per doppia tassazione *(m)*
Pt isenção de tributação dupla *(f)*

**doubtful debt** En
De zweifelhafte Forderung *(f)*
Es deuda de pago dudoso *(f)*
Fr créance douteuse *(f)*
It credito dubbio *(m)*
Pt dívida duvidosa *(f)*

**down-payment** *n* En
De Sofortzahlung *(f)*
Es pago de entrada *(m)*
Fr acompte *(m)*
It acconto *(m)*
Pt pagamento inicial *(m)*

**down time** En
De Leerlaufzeit *(f)*
Es tiempo improductivo *(m)*
Fr temps d´arrêt *(m)*
It tempo improduttivo *(m)*
Pt tempo improdutivo *(m)*

**draft** (bank) *n* En
De Tratte *(f)*
Es letra *(f)*
Fr traite *(f)*
It tratta *(f)*
Pt letra *(f)*

**draft** (preliminary version) *n* En
De Konzept *(n)*
Es borrador *(m)*
Fr projet *(m)*
It bozza *(f)*
Pt rascunho *(m)*

**draft agreement** En
De Entwurf eines Übereinkommens *(m)*
Es proyecto de convenio *(m)*
Fr projet de convention *(m)*
It schema di contratto *(m)*
Pt pró-forma de accordo *(m)*

**draft contract** En
De Vertragsentwurf *(m)*
Es proyecto de contrato *(m)*
Fr projet de contrat *(m)*
It progetto di contratto *(m)*
Pt minuta de contrato *(f)*

**draught** (of a ship) *n* En
De Tiefgang *(m)*
Es calado *(m)*
Fr tirant d´eau *(m)*
It pescaggio *(m)*
Pt calado *(m)*

**draughtsman** *n* En
De Entwerfer *(m)*
Es dibujante *(m)*
Fr dessinateur *(m)*
It disegnatore *(m)*
Pt desenhador *(m)*

**draw a cheque** En
De einen Scheck ausstellen
Es extender un cheque
Fr tirer un chèque
It emettere un assegno
Pt passar um cheque

**drawback** (customs) n En
De Zollrückvergütung (f)
Es reembolso de derechos de aduana (m)
Fr remboursement des droits d'importation (m)
It rimborso d'esportazione (m)
Pt reimbolso de direitos alfandegários (m)

**drawee** n En
De Bezogene(r) (m)
Es librado (m)
Fr tiré (m)
It trattario (m)
Pt sacado (m)

**drawer** n En
De Aussteller (m)
Es librador (m)
Fr tireur (m)
It traente (m)
Pt sacador (m)

**drawing account** En
De Scheckkonto (n)
Es cuenta corrienta (f)
Fr compte courant (m)
It conto corrente (m)
Pt conta corrente (f)

**draw on reserves** En
De die Reserven angreifen
Es sacar reservas
Fr prélever sur les réserves
It prelevare dalle riserve
Pt recorrer a reservas

**draw up a contract** En
De einen Vertrag formulieren
Es redactar un contrato
Fr rédiger un contrat
It redigere un contratto
Pt redigir um contrato

**dresser un plan** Fr
De planen
En schedule
Es programar
It programmare
Pt programar

**Dritte(r)** (m) n De
En third party
Es tercero (m)
Fr tiers (m)

It terzi (m pl)
Pt terceiros (m pl)

**droit acquis** (m) Fr
De festbegründetes Recht (n)
En vested interest
Es interés creado (m)
It diritto acquisito (m)
Pt interesse adquirido (m)

**droit attaché** Fr
De mit Dividende
En cum dividend
Es con dividendo
It con dividendo
Pt com dividendo

**droits d'auteur** (m pl) Fr
De Urheberrecht (n)
En copyright
Es derechos de autor (m pl)
It diritto d'autore (m)
Pt direitos de autor (m pl)

**droit de douane** (m) Fr
De Zoll (m)
En customs duty
Es derechos de aduanas (m pl)
It diritto doganale (m)
Pt direitos alfandegários (m pl)

**droit d'enregistrement** (m) Fr
De Anmeldegebühr (f)
En registration fee
Es derechos de registro (m pl)
It tassa di registrazione (f)
Pt custas de registo (f pl)

**droit d'entrée** (m) Fr
De Eintrittsgebühr (f)
En entrance fee
Es derecho de entrada (m)
It tassa d'entrata (f)
Pt taxa de admissão (f)

**droit de retention** (m) Fr
De Pfandrecht (n)
En lien
Es derecho de retención (m)
It diritto di sequestro (m)
Pt embargo direito de retenção (m)

**droit de timbre** (m) Fr
De Stempelgebühr (f)
En stamp duty

Es impuesto del timbre (m)
It tassa di bollo (f)
Pt imposto de selo (m)

**droits** (m pl) n Fr
De Rechte (n pl)
En rights
Es derechos (m pl)
It diritti (m pl)
Pt direitos (m pl)

**droits d'entrée** (m pl) Fr
De Einfuhrzoll (m)
En import duty
Es derechos de importación (m pl)
It dazio d'importazione (m)
Pt direitos de importação (m pl)

**droits de dock** (m pl) Fr
De Dockgebühr (f)
En dock dues
Es derechos de muelle (m pl)
It diritti di dock (m pl)
Pt encargos de doca (m pl)

**droits de port** (m pl) Fr
De Hafengebühren (f pl)
En port charges
Es derechos portuarios (m pl)
It diritti portuali (m pl)
Pt direitos portuários (m pl)

**droits de succession** (m pl) Fr
De Nachlasssteuer (f)
En estate duty
Am estate tax
Es derechos de sucesión (m pl)
It diritti di successione (m pl)
Pt direitos de sucessão (m pl)

**droits miniers** (m pl) Fr
De Mineralgewinnungsrechte (n pl)
En mineral rights
Es derechos mineros (m pl)
It diritti minerari (m pl)
Pt direitos mineiros (m pl)

**droit sur la consommation** (m) Fr
De Verbrauchsabgabe (f)
En excise duty
Es impuesto de consumos (m)
It imposta sul consumo (f)
Pt imposto indirecto (m)

**drückende Spesen** (f pl) De
En heavy charges
Es gastos fuertes (m pl)
Fr charges lourdes (f pl)
It forti spese (f pl)
Pt encargos pesados (m pl)

**Druckmesser** (m) n De
En pressure gauge
Es manómetro (m)
Fr manomètre: jauge de pression (m f)
It manometro (m)
Pt manómetro (m)

**dry dock** En
De Trockendock (n)
Es dique seco (m)
Fr cale sèche (f)
It bacino di carenaggio (m)
Pt doca-seca (f)

**Dubiosenreserve** (f) n De
En bad debt reserve
Es reserva para deudas incobrables (f)
Fr provision pour créances douteuses (f)
It riserva per crediti inesigibili (f)
Pt reserva para dividas incobráveis (f)

**due date** En
De Fälligkeitstag (m)
Es fecha de vencimiento (f)
Fr échéance (f)
It data di scadenza (f)
Pt data de vencimento (f)

**due date** Am
En settlement day
De Abrechnungstag (m)
Es día de liquidación (m)
Fr jour de règlement (m)
It giorno della liquidazione (m)
Pt dia de liquidação (m)

**dumping** n En; Fr, It (m)
De Dumping (n)
Es inundación de mercancía barata (f)
Pt saturação (de mercadorias baratas); descarga (f)

**Dumping** (n) n De
En dumping
Es inundación de mercancía barata (f)
Fr dumping (m)
It dumping (m)
Pt saturação (de mercadorias baratas); descarga (f)

**duplicado** (m) n Es, Pt
De Duplikat (n)
En duplicate
Fr double; duplicata (m)
It duplicato (m)

**duplicate** n En
De Duplikat (n)
Es duplicado (m)
Fr double; duplicata (m)
It duplicato (m)
Pt duplicado (m)

**duplicata** (m) n Fr
De Duplikat (n)
En duplicate
Es duplicado (m)
It duplicato (m)
Pt duplicado (m)

**duplicato** (m) n It
De Duplikat (n)
En duplicate
Es duplicado (m)
Fr double; duplicata (m)
Pt duplicado (m)

**Duplikat** (n) n De
En duplicate
Es duplicado (m)
Fr double; duplicata (m)
It duplicato (m)
Pt duplicado (m)

**durable goods** En
De langlebige Güter (n pl)
Es mercancías no perecederas (f pl)
Fr biens durables (m pl)
It beni durevoli (m pl)
Pt mercadorias imperecíveis (f pl)

**duração** (f) n Pt
De Dauer (f)
En duration
Es duración (f)
Fr durée (f)
It durata (f)

**duración** (f) n Es
De Dauer (f)
En duration
Fr durée (f)
It durata (f)
Pt duração (f)

**durata** (f) n It
De Dauer (f)
En duration
Es duración (f)
Fr durée (f)
Pt duração (f)

**duration** n En
De Dauer (f)
Es duración (f)
Fr durée (f)
It durata (f)
Pt duração (f)

**Durchfallquote** (f) n De
En failure rate
Es proporción de fracasos (f)
Fr taux de défaillance (m)
It indice dei fallimenti (m)
Pt proporção de fracassos (f)

**Durchführbarkeit** (f) n De
En feasibility
Es practicabilidad (f)
Fr practicabilité (f)
It fattibilità (f)
Pt viabilidade (f)

**Durchführbarkeitanalyse** (f) n De
En feasibility study
Es estudio de viabilidad (m)
Fr étude probatoire (f)
It studio delle possibilità (m)
Pt estudo de viabilidade (m)

**durchführen** De
En carry out
Es ejecutar
Fr exécuter
It eseguire
Pt executar

**Durchschlag** (m) n De
En carbon copy
Es copia en papel carbón (f)
Fr copie au carbone (f)
It copia carbone (f)
Pt copia a químico (f)

**Durchschnitt** *(m)* n De
En average
Es promedio *(m)*
Fr moyenne *(f)*
It media *(f)*
Pt média *(f)*

**Durchschnittskosten** *(m pl)* n
De
En average cost
Es coste promedio *(m)*
Fr coût moyen *(m)*
It costo medio *(m)*
Pt custo médio *(m)*

**durée** *(f)* n Fr
De Dauer *(f)*
En duration
Es duración *(f)*
It durata *(f)*
Pt duração *(f)*

**durée du travail** *(f)* Fr
De Arbeitszeit *(f)*
En hours of work
Es jornada laboral *(f)*
It ore lavorative *(f pl)*
Pt horas de trabalho *(f pl)*

**duress** n En
De Zwang *(m)*
Es compulsión *(f)*
Fr contrainte *(f)*
It costrizione *(f)*
Pt coerção *(f)*

**Düsenflugzeug** *(n)* n De
En jet aircraft
Es avión jet *(m)*
Fr avion à réaction *(m)*
It aviogetto *(m)*
Pt avião a jacto *(m)*

**Düsenmotor** *(m)* n De
En jet engine
Es motor de propulsión a
   chorro *(m)*
Fr réacteur *(m)*
It motore a reazione *(m)*
Pt motor a jacto

**dutiable** *adj* En
De abgabenpflichtig
Es tasable
Fr taxable
It tassabile
Pt tributável

**duty** n En
De Gebühr *(f)*
Es derechos; impuesto *(m)*
Fr taxe; impôt *(f m)*
It tassa; imposta *(f)*
Pt taxa; imposto *(f m)*

**duty-free** *adj* En
De abgabenfrei
Es exento de impuestos
Fr exempt de douane
It esente da dazio
Pt isento de impostos

**duty-free admission** En
De zollfreie Einfuhr *(f)*
Es admisión libre de impues-
   tos *(f)*
Fr admission en franchise *(f)*
It ammissione in franchigia
   doganale *(f)*
Pt admissão livre de impostos
   *(f)*

**duty-paid** *adj* En
De verzollt
Es derechos pagados
Fr acquitté
It dazio pagato
Pt direitos pagos

**D-Zug** *(m)* n De
En express train
Es tren expreso *(m)*
Fr train express *(m)*
It direttissimo; rapido *(m)*
Pt comboio rápido *(m)*


# E

**earn** *vb* En
De verdienen
Es ganar
Fr gagner
It guadagnare
Pt ganhar

**earned income** En
De Arbeitseinkommen *(n)*
Es renta del trabajo *(f)*
Fr revenu du travail *(m)*
It reddito di lavoro *(m)*
Pt receita de trabalho *(f)*

**earnings** (wages) n pl En
De Lohn *(m)*
Es salario *(m)*
Fr salaire *(m)*
It guadagni *(m pl)*
Pt salario *(m)*

**earnings per share** En
De Gewinn pro Aktie *(n)*
Es beneficios por acción *(m
   pl)*
Fr bénéfice par titre *(m)*
It profitti per azione *(m pl)*
Pt proventos por acção *(m pl)*

**eaux territoriales** *(f pl)* Fr
De Hoheitsgewässer *(n pl)*
En territorial waters
Es aguas territoriales *(f pl)*
It acque territoriali *(f pl)*
Pt águas territoriais *(f pl)*

**écart** *(m)* n Fr
De Abweichung *(f)*
En discrepancy
Es desacuerdo *(m)*
It divergenza *(f)*
Pt discrepância *(f)*

**écart de prix** *(m)* Fr
De Preisunterschied *(m)*
En difference in price
Es diferencia de precio *(f)*
It differenza di prezzo *(f)*
Pt diferença de preço *(f)*

**écartement normal** *(m)* Fr
De Normalmass *(n)*
En standard gauge
Es calibre patrón *(m)*
It scartamento normale *(m)*
Pt calibre padrão *(m)*

**eccedenza di peso** *(f)* It
De Übergewicht *(n)*
En excess weight
Es peso excedente *(m)*
Fr excédent de poids *(m)*
Pt excesso de peso *(m)*

**eccessivo** *adj* It
De übermässig
En excessive
Es excesivo
Fr excessif
Pt excessivo

**eccesso** (m) n It
De Überschuss (m)
En surplus
Es excedente (m)
Fr surplus; excédent (m)
Pt excedente (m)

**échange** (m) n Fr
De Tausch (m)
En exchange
Es cambio (m)
It cambio (m)
Pt câmbio (m)

**échantillon** (m) n Fr
De Probe; Muster (f n)
En sample
Es muestra (f)
It campione (m)
Pt amostra (f)

**échantillon gratuit** (m) Fr
De kostenlose Probe (f)
En free sample
Es muestra gratuita (f)
It campione gratuito (m)
Pt amostra gratis (f)

**échantillon sans valeur** (m) Fr
De Muster ohne Wert (n)
En sample of no value
Es muestra sin valor (f)
It campione senza valore (m)
Pt amostra sem valor (f)

**echar al mar** (carga) Es
De über Bord werfen
En jettison
Fr jeter à la mer
It fare gettito
Pt alijar

**échéance** (f) n Fr
De Fälligkeit (f)
En maturity
Es vencimiento (m)
It scadenza (f)
Pt vencimento (m)

**échelle** (f) n Fr
De Masstab (m)
En scale
Es escala (f)
It scala (f)
Pt escala (f)

**échelle mobile** (f) Fr
De gleitende Skala (f)
En sliding scale
Es escala móvil (f)
It scala mobile (f)
Pt escala móvel (f)

**échoir** vb Fr
De fällig sein
En fall due
Es vencer
It scadere; essere pagabile
Pt vencer-se

**échouer** vb Fr
De versagen; durchfallen
En fail
Es fallar; faltar
It mancare; fallire
Pt falhar; faltar

**echtes Konnossement** (n) De
En clean bill of lading
Es conocimiento de embarque sin objecciones (m)
Fr connaissement sans réserve (m)
It polizza di carico senza riserve (f)
Pt conhecimento sem embargos (m)

**econometría** (f) n Es
De Ökonometrik (f)
En econometrics
Fr économétrie (f)
It econometria (f)
Pt econometria (f)

**econometria** (f) n It, Pt
De Ökonometrik (f)
En econometrics n pl
Es econometría (f)
Fr économétrie (f)

**econometrics** n En
De Ökonometrik (f)
Es econometría (f)
Fr économétrie (f)
It econometria (f)
Pt econometria (f)

**économétrie** (f) n Fr
De Ökonometrik (f)
En econometrics
Es econometría (f)
It econometria (f)
Pt econometria (f)

**economía** (f) n Es
De Wirtschaft;Volkswirtschaftslehre (f)
En (the) economy; economics
Fr économie (f)
It economia (f)
Pt economia (f)

**economia** (f) n It, Pt
De Wirtschaft;Volkswirtschaftslehre (f)
En (the) economy; economics
Es economía (f)
Fr économie (f)

**economía del mercado libre** (f) Es
De freie Marktwirtschaft (f)
En free economy
Fr système économique du marché libre (m)
It economia di mercato libero (f)
Pt economia de mercado livre (f)

**economia de mercado livre** (f) Pt
De freie Marktwirtschaft (f)
En free economy
Es economía del mercado libre (f)
Fr système économique du marché libre (m)
It economia di mercato libero (f)

**economia di mercato libero** (f) It
De freie Marktwirtschaft (f)
En free economy
Es economía del mercado libre (f)
Fr système économique du marché libre (m)
Pt economia de mercado livre (f)

**economia mista** (f) It
De Gemischtwirtschaft (f)
En mixed economy
Es economía mixta (f)
Fr économie mixte (f)
Pt economia mixta (f)

**economía mixta** (f) Es
De Gemischtwirtschaft (f)
En mixed economy

Fr économie mixte *(f)*
It economia mista *(f)*
Pt economia mixta *(f)*

**economia mixta** *(f)* Pt
De Gemischtwirtschaft *(f)*
En mixed economy
Es economía mixta *(f)*
Fr économie mixte *(f)*
It economia mista *(f)*

**economia pianificata** *(f)* It
De Planwirtschaft *(f)*
En planned economy
Es economía planificada *(f)*
Fr économie planifiée *(f)*
Pt economia planeada *(f)*

**economia planeada** *(f)* Pt
De Planwirtschaft *(f)*
En planned economy
Es economía planificada *(f)*
Fr économie planifiée *(f)*
It economia pianificata *(f)*

**economía planificada** *(f)* Es
De Planwirtschaft *(f)*
En planned economy
Fr économie planifiée *(f)*
It economia pianificata *(f)*
Pt economia planeada *(f)*

**economias de amplitude** *(f pl)*
  Pt
De System der degressiven
  Kosten *(n)*
En economies of scale
Es economía en función de
  volumen *(f)*
Fr économies de grande
  échelle *(f pl)*
It economie in funzione della
  grandezza *(f pl)*

**economic** *adj* En
De wirtschaftlich
Es económico
Fr économique
It economico
Pt económico

**economic growth** En
De Wirtschaftswachstum *(m)*
Es crecimiento económico *(m)*
Fr croissance économique *(f)*
It sviluppo economico *(m)*
Pt crescimento económico
  *(m)*

**económico** *adj* Es, Pt
De wirtschaftlich
En economic
Fr économique
It economico

**economico** *adj* It
De wirtschaftlich
En economic
Es económico
Fr économique
Pt económico

**economics** *n* En
De Volkswirtschaftslehre *(f)*
Es economía *(f)*
Fr économie *(f)*
It economia *(f)*
Pt economia *(f)*

**economic sanctions** En
De wirtschaftliche Sanktionen
  *(f pl)*
Es sanciones económicas *(f
  pl)*
Fr sanctions économiques *(f
  pl)*
It sanzioni economiche *(f pl)*
Pt sanções económicas *(f pl)*

**économie** *(f)* *n* Fr
De Wirtschaft;Volkswirtschafts-
  lehre *(f)*
En (the) economy; economics
Es economía *(f)*
It economia *(f)*
Pt economia *(f)*

**economie in funzione della
  grandezza** *(f pl)* It
De System der degressiven
  Kosten *(n)*
En economies of scale
Es economía en función de
  volumen *(f)*
Fr économies de grande
  échelle *(f pl)*
Pt economias de amplitude *(f
  pl)*

**économie mixte** *(f)* Fr
De Gemischtwirtschaft *(f)*
En mixed economy
Es economía mixta *(f)*
It economia mista *(f)*
Pt economia mixta *(f)*

**économie planifiée** *(f)* Fr
De Planwirtschaft *(f)*
En planned economy
Es economía planificada *(f)*
It economia pianificata *(f)*
Pt economia planeada *(f)*

**économies de grande échelle**
  *(f pl)* Fr
De System der degressiven
  Kosten *(n)*
En economies of scale
Es economía en función de
  volumen *(f)*
It economie in funzione della
  grandezza *(f pl)*
Pt economias de amplitude *(f
  pl)*

**economies of scale** En
De System der degressiven
  Kosten *(n)*
Es economía en función de
  volumen *(f)*
Fr économies de grande
  échelle *(f pl)*
It economie in funzione della
  grandezza *(f pl)*
Pt economias de amplitude *(f
  pl)*

**économique** *adj* Fr
De wirtschaftlich
En economic
Es económico
It economico
Pt económico

**(the) economy** *n* En
De Wirtschaft *(f)*
Es economía *(f)*
Fr économie *(f)*
It economia *(f)*
Pt economia *(f)*

**écrire à la machine** Fr
De auf der Schreibmaschine
  schreiben
En type
Es escribir a máquina
It scrivere a macchina
Pt escrever à máquina

**edifício de andares** *(m)* Pt
De Wohnungsgebäude *(n)*
En block of flats
Am apartment house
Es bloque de pisos *(m)*

Fr immeuble *(m)*
It fabbricato di appartamenti *(m)*

**é favor enviar** Pt
De bitte nachsenden
En please forward
Es se ruega hacer seguir
Fr prière de faire suivre
It far proseguire

**efectividad de coste** *(f)* Es
De Wirtschaftlichkeit *(f)*
En cost-effectiveness
Fr coût et efficacité
It rendimento della spesa *(m)*
Pt eficiência relativa ao custo *(f)*

**efectivo** *adj* Es, Pt
De wirksam
En operative; effective
Fr actif; effectif
It attivo; operativo

**efectivo en caja** *(m)* Es
De Barbestand *(m)*
En cash in hand
Fr espèces en caisse *(f pl)*
It pronti contanti *(m pl)*
Pt fundos à ordem *(m pl)*

**efecto descontado** *(m)* Es
De Diskontwechsel *(m)*
En discounted bill
Fr effet escompté *(m)*
It cambiale scontata *(f)*
Pt letra descontada *(f)*

**efecto documentario** *(m)* Es
De Dokumentenwechsel *(m)*
En documentary bill
Fr traite documentaire *(f)*
It tratta documentaria *(f)*
Pt título documental *(m)*

**efectos** *(m pl) n* Es
De Effekten *(pl)*
En effects; securities
Fr effets *(m pl)*
It effetti *(m pl)*
Pt efeitos; títulos *(m pl)*

**efectos a cobrar** *(m pl)* Es
De fällige Wechsel *(m pl)*
En bills for collection
Fr effets en recouvrement *(m pl)*

It effetti all'incasso *(m pl)*
Pt letras a descontar *(f pl)*

**efectos a pagar** *(m pl)* Es
De fällige Wechsel; Wechselschulden *(m pl; f pl)*
En payables
Fr effets à payer *(m pl)*
It passività esigibili *(f)*
Pt contas a pagar *(f pl)*

**efectos descontados** *(m pl)* Es
De diskontierte Wechsel *(m pl)*
En bills discounted
Fr effets escomptés *(m pl)*
It effetti scontati *(m pl)*
Pt letras descontadas *(f pl)*

**efectos negociables** *(m pl)* Es
De diskontierbare Wechsel *(m pl)*
En bankable bills
Fr papier bancable *(m)*
It effetti scontabili *(m pl)*
Pt valores transaccionáveis pelo banco *(m pl)*

**effectifs** *(m pl) n* Fr
De Belegschaft *(f)*
En work force
Es masa obrera *(f)*
It massa lavoratrice *(f)*
Pt massa trabalhadora *(f)*

**effectiveness** *n* En
De Wirksamkeit *(f)*
Es eficacia *(f)*
Fr efficacité *(f)*
It efficacia *(f)*
Pt eficácia *(f)*

**effects** *pl n* En
De Effekten; Habe *(pl; f)*
Es efectos; bienes *(m pl)*
Fr effets; biens *(m pl)*
It effetti; beni *(m pl)*
Pt efeitos *(m pl)*

**efeitos** *(m pl) n* Pt
De Effekten; Habe *(pl; f)*
En effects
Es efectos; bienes *(m pl)*
Fr effets; biens *(m pl)*
It effetti; beni *(m pl)*

**Effekten** *(m pl) n* De
En effects; securities
Es efectos *(m pl)*

Fr effets *(m pl)*
It effetti *(m pl)*
Pt efeitos; títulos *(m pl)*

**effet de commerce** *(m)* Fr
De begebbares Wertpapier *(n)*
En negotiable instrument
Es título negociable *(m)*
It titolo negoziabile *(m)*
Pt título negociável *(m)*

**effet escompté** *(m)* Fr
De Diskontwechsel *(m)*
En discounted bill
Es efecto descontado *(m)*
It cambiale scontata *(f)*
Pt letra descontada *(f)*

**effet exigible à vue** *(m)* Fr
De Sichttratte *(f)*
En bill payable at sight
Es letra a la vista *(f)*
It effetto pagabile a vista *(m)*
Pt letra à vista *(f)*

**effets** *(m pl) n* Fr
De Effekten *(pl)*
En effects; securities
Es efectos *(m pl)*
It effetti *(m pl)*
Pt efeitos; títulos *(m pl)*

**effets à payer** *(m pl)* Fr
De Wechselschulden *(f pl)*
En bills payable
Es letras pagaderas *(f pl)*
It effetti passivi *(m pl)*
Pt letras a pagar *(f pl)*

**effets à recevoir** *(m pl)* Fr
De Wechselforderungen *(f pl)*
En bills receivable
Es letras a cobrar *(f pl)*
It effetti attivi *(m pl)*
Pt letras a cobrar *(f pl)*

**effets en recouvrement** *(m pl)* Fr
De fällige Wechsel *(m pl)*
En bills for collection
Es efectos a cobrar *(m pl)*
It effetti all'incasso *(m pl)*
Pt letras a descontar *(f pl)*

**effets escomptés** *(m pl)* Fr
De diskontierte Wechsel *(m pl)*
En bills discounted
Es efectos descontados *(m pl)*

It   effetti scontati *(m pl)*
Pt   letras descontadas *(f pl)*

**effetti** *(m pl)* n It
De   Effekten *(pl)*
En   effects; securities
Es   efectos *(m pl)*
Fr   effets *(m pl)*
Pt   efeitos; títulos *(m pl)*

**effetti all'incasso** *(m pl)* It
De   fällige Wechsel *(m pl)*
En   bills for collection
Es   efectos a cobrar *(m pl)*
Fr   effets en recouvrement *(m pl)*
Pt   letras a descontar *(f pl)*

**effetti attivi** *(m pl)* It
De   Wechselforderungen *(f pl)*
En   bills receivable
Es   letras a cobrar *(f pl)*
Fr   effets à recevoir *(m pl)*
Pt   letras a cobrar *(f pl)*

**effetti passivi** *(m pl)* It
De   Wechselschulden *(f pl)*
En   bills payable
Es   letras pagaderas *(f pl)*
Fr   effets à payer *(m pl)*
Pt   letras a pagar *(f pl)*

**effetti scontabili** *(m pl)* It
De   diskontierbare Wechsel *(m pl)*
En   bankable bills
Es   efectos negociables *(m pl)*
Fr   papier bancable *(m)*
Pt   valores transaccionáveis pelo banco *(m pl)*

**effetti scontati** *(m pl)* It
De   diskontierte Wechsel *(m pl)*
En   bills discounted
Es   efectos descontados *(m pl)*
Fr   effets escomptés *(m pl)*
Pt   letras descontadas *(f pl)*

**effetto in bianco** *(m)* It
De   Blankowechsel *(m)*
En   blank bill
Es   letra en blanco *(f)*
Fr   traite en blanc *(f)*
Pt   letra em branco *(f)*

**effetto pagabile a vista** *(m)* It
De   Sichttratte *(f)*
En   bill payable at sight

Es   letra a la vista *(f)*
Fr   effet exigible à vue *(m)*
Pt   letra à vista *(f)*

**efficacia** *(f)* n It
De   Wirksamkeit *(f)*
En   effectiveness
Es   eficacia *(f)*
Fr   efficacité *(f)*
Pt   eficácia *(f)*

**efficacité** *(f)* n Fr
De   Wirksamkeit; Leistungsfähigkeit *(f)*
En   effectiveness; efficiency
Es   eficacia; eficiencia *(f)*
It   efficacia; efficienza *(f)*
Pt   eficácia; eficiência *(f)*

**efficiency** n En
De   Leistungsfähigkeit *(f)*
Es   eficiencia *(f)*
Fr   efficacité *(f)*
It   efficienza *(f)*
Pt   eficiência *(f)*

**efficienza** *(f)* n It
De   Leistungsfähigkeit *(f)*
En   efficiency
Es   eficiencia *(f)*
Fr   efficacité *(f)*
Pt   eficiência *(f)*

**eficacia** *(f)* n Es
De   Wirksamkeit *(f)*
En   effectiveness
Fr   efficacité *(f)*
It   efficacia *(f)*
Pt   eficácia *(f)*

**eficácia** *(f)* n Pt
De   Wirksamkeit *(f)*
En   effectiveness
Es   eficacia *(f)*
Fr   efficacité *(f)*
It   efficacia *(f)*

**eficiencia** *(f)* n Es
De   Leistungsfähigkeit *(f)*
En   efficiency
Fr   efficacité *(f)*
It   efficienza *(f)*
Pt   eficiência *(f)*

**eficiência** *(f)* n Pt
De   Leistungsfähigkeit *(f)*
En   efficiency
Es   eficiencia *(f)*

Fr   efficacité *(f)*
It   efficienza *(f)*

**eficiência relativa ao custo** *(f)* Pt
De   Wirtschaftlichkeit *(f)*
En   cost-effectiveness
Es   efectividad de coste *(f)*
Fr   coût et efficacité
It   rendimento della spesa *(m)*

**efluentes tóxicos** *(m pl)* Es
De   giftiger Abfall *(m)*
En   toxic waste
Fr   déchets toxiques *(m pl)*
It   rifiuti tossici *(m pl)*
Pt   despejos tóxicos *(m pl)*

**Ehre** *(f)* n De
En   honour
Es   honor *(m)*
Fr   honneur *(f)*
It   onore *(m)*
Pt   honra *(f)*

**ehrenamtlich** *adj* De
En   honorary
Es   honorario
Fr   honoraire
It   onorario
Pt   honorário

**ehrlich** *adj* De
En   honest
Es   honesto
Fr   honnête
It   onesto
Pt   honesto

**Eigentum** *(n)* n De
En   property; ownership
Es   propiedad *(f)*
Fr   propriété *(f)*
It   proprietà; beni *(f; m pl)*
Pt   propriedade *(f)*

**Eigentümer** *(m)* n De
En   owner
Es   propietario; dueño *(m)*
Fr   propriétaire *(m)*
It   proprietario *(m)*
Pt   proprietário; dono *(m)*

**Eigentumstitel** *(m)* n De
En   title deed
Es   título de propiedad *(m)*
Fr   titre de propriété *(m)*

It   titolo di proprietà *(m)*
Pt  título de propriedade *(m)*

**Eilbrief** *(m) n* De
En  express letter
Am  special delivery
Es  carta urgente *(f)*
Fr  lettre par exprès *(f)*
It   lettera espresso *(f)*
Pt  carta expresso *(f)*

**einberufen** *vb* De
En  convene
Es  convenir
Fr  convoquer
It   convocare
Pt  convocar

**Einbruchdiebstahl** *(m) n* De
En  burglary
Es  robo *(m)*
Fr  vol avec effraction *(m)*
It   furto con scasso *(m)*
Pt  roubo *(m)*

**einfache Buchführung** *(f)* De
En  single-entry book-keeping
Es  contabilidad por partida
     sencilla *(f)*
Fr  comptabilité en partie si-
     mple *(f)*
It   contabilità in partita sem-
     plice *(f)*
Pt  contabilização por lan-
     çamento simples *(f)*

**einfache Fahrkarte** *(f)* De
En  single fare
Am  one way fare
Es  pasaje de ida *(m)*
Fr  billet d'aller *(m)*
It   biglietto d'andata *(m)*
Pt  passagem de ida *(f)*

**einfache Zinsen** *(m pl)* De
En  simple interest
Es  interés simple *(m)*
Fr  intérêts simples *(m pl)*
It   interesse semplice *(m)*
Pt  juro simples *(m)*

**Einfuhr** *(f) n* De
En  import
Es  importación *(f)*
Fr  importation *(f)*
It   importazione *(f)*
Pt  importação *(f)*

**Einfuhrbeschränkungen** *(f pl)*
     *n* De
En  import restrictions
Es  restricciones de impor-
     tación *(f pl)*
Fr  restrictions d'importation *(f
     pl)*
It   restrizioni delle importazioni
     *(f pl)*
Pt  restricções de importação
     *(f pl)*

**Einfuhrkontingent** *(n) n* De
En  import quota
Es  cupo de importación *(m)*
Fr  contingent d'importation
     *(m)*
It   contingente d'importazione
     *(m)*
Pt  quota de importação *(f)*

**Einfuhrverbot** *(n) n* De
En  import ban
Es  prohibición de importación
     *(f)*
Fr  prohibition d'entrée *(f)*
It   divieto d'importazione *(m)*
Pt  proibição de importação *(f)*

**Einfuhrzoll** *(m) n* De
En  import duty
Es  derechos de importación
     *(m pl)*
Fr  droits d'entrée *(m pl)*
It   dazio d'importazione *(m)*
Pt  direitos de importação *(m)*

**eingebautes Veralten** *(n)* De
En  built-in obsolescence
Es  decaimiento incorporado
     *(m)*
Fr  désuétude incorporée *(f)*
It   decadimento incorporato
     *(m)*
Pt  obsolência pre-incorporada
     *(f)*

**eingefrorene Guthaben** *(n pl)*
     De
En  frozen assets
Es  activos congelados *(m pl)*
Fr  fonds bloqués *(m pl)*
It   attivo congelato *(m)*
Pt  bens do activo congelados
     *(m pl)*

**eingefrorene Kredite** *(m pl)*
     De
En  frozen credits
Es  creditos congelados *(m pl)*
Fr  crédits bloqués *(m pl)*
It   crediti bloccati *(m pl)*
Pt  créditos congelados *(m pl)*

**eingeschriebener Brief** *(m)* De
En  registered letter
Es  carta certificada *(f)*
Fr  lettre recommandée *(f)*
It   lettera raccomandata *(f)*
Pt  carta registada *(f)*

**eingezahltes Kapital** *(n)* De
En  paid-up capital
Es  capital desembolsado *(m)*
Fr  capital versé *(m)*
It   capitale versato *(m)*
Pt  capital realizado *(m)*

**Eingliederung** *(f) n* De
En  integration
Es  integración *(f)*
Fr  intégration *(f)*
It   integrazione *(f)*
Pt  integração *(f)*

**Einheitskosten** *(pl) n* De
En  unit cost
Es  coste por unidad *(m)*
Fr  coût de l'unité *(m)*
It   costo unitario *(m)*
Pt  custo por unidade *(m)*

**Einheitssatz** *(m) n* De
En  flat rate
Es  tarifa unificada *(f)*
Fr  tarif uniforme *(f)*
It   tariffa uniforme *(f)*
Pt  tarifa de base *(f)*

**einkassieren** *vb* De
En  cash
Es  cobrar
Fr  encaisser
It   incassare
Pt  cobrar

**Einkauf** *(m) n* De
En  purchase
Es  compra *(f)*
Fr  achat *(m)*
It   compra *(f)*
Pt  compra *(f)*

**Einkäufe** *(m pl)* n De
En purchases
Es adquisiciones *(f pl)*
Fr achats *(m pl)*
It acquisti *(m pl)*
Pt aquisições *(f pl)*

**Einkaufsbuch** *(n)* n De
En bought ledger
Am purchase book
Es libro mayor de compras *(m)*
Fr grand livre d'achats *(m)*
It mastro acquisti *(m)*
Pt livro-mestre de compras *(m)*

**Einkaufszentrale** *(f)* n De
En central buying office
Es oficina central de compras *(f)*
Fr centrale d'achats *(f)*
It ufficio centrale d'acquisti *(m)*
Pt escritório central de compras *(m)*

**Einkommen** *(n)* n De
En revenue; income
Es ingresos; rédito *(m pl; m)*
Fr revenu; rentes *(m; f pl)*
It entrata; reddito *(f m)*
Pt rendimento; receita *(m f)*

**Einkommensteuererklärung** *(f)* n De
En income-tax return
Es declaración fiscal *(f)*
Fr déclaration de revenu *(f)*
It dichiarazione del reddito *(f)*
Pt declaração fiscal *(f)*

**Einkommensteuerjahr** *(n)* n De
En income-tax year
Es año fiscal *(m)*
Fr exercice fiscal *(m)*
It anno fiscale *(m)*
Pt ano fiscal *(m)*

**einladen** *vb* De
En invite
Es invitar
Fr inviter
It invitare
Pt convidar

**Einladung** *(f)* n De
En invitation
Es invitación *(f)*
Fr invitation *(f)*
It invito *(m)*
Pt convite *(m)*

**einlegen** (bei einer Bank) *vb* De
En bank
Es depositar (en el banco)
Fr déposer à banque
It depositare in una banca
Pt depositar (no banco)

**einlegen** (ein Patent) *vb* De
En file
Es interponer
Fr déposer
It depositare
Pt registar

**Einlösungsertrag** *(m)* n De
En redemption yield
Es rédito de reembolso *(m)*
Fr rendement sur remboursement *(m)*
It rendita di rimborso *(f)*
Pt rendimento de resgate *(m)*

**Einlösungstag** *(m)* n De
En redemption date
Es fecha de reembolso *(f)*
Fr date du remboursement *(f)*
It data di rimborso *(f)*
Pt data de resgate *(f)*

**Einrichtungen** *(f pl)* n De
En facilities
Es facilidades *(f pl)*
Fr facilités *(f pl)*
It facilitazione *(f)*
Pt facilidades *(f pl)*

**einschätzen** *vb* De
En estimate
Es estimar
Fr estimer
It stimare
Pt avaliar

**Einschiffung** *(f)* n De
En embarcation
Es embarco *(m)*
Fr embarquement *(m)*
It imbarco *(m)*
Pt embarcação *(f)*

**einschliesslich** *adj* De
En inclusive
Es incluido; inclusive
Fr inclus; compris
It incluso; compreso
Pt incluindo; incluso

**einschränkende Bestimmung** *(f)* De
En restrictive covenant
Es convenio restrictivo *(m)*
Fr accord restrictif *(m)*
It accordo restrittivo *(m)*
Pt obrigação restritiva *(f)*

**einschränkendes Konnossement** *(n)* De
En foul (dirty) bill of lading
Es conocimiento de embarque con objecciones *(m)*
Fr connaissement avec réserve *(m)*
It polizza di carico con riserve *(f)*
Pt conhecimento com embargos *(m)*

**einsetzen** *vb* De
En insert
Es insertar
Fr insérer
It inserire
Pt inserir

**Einsichtnahme** *(f)* n De
En inspection
Es inspección; examen *(f m)*
Fr inspection; vérification *(f)*
It ispezione *(f)*
Pt inspecção *(f)*

**Einstandspreis** *(m)* n De
En cost price
Es precio de coste *(m)*
Fr prix de revient *(m)*
It prezzo di costo *(m)*
Pt preço de custo *(m)*

**einstweilig** *adj* De
En temporary
Es temporal
Fr provisoire
It temporaneo
Pt temporário

**einträglich** *adj* De
En lucrative
Es lucrativo

Fr lucratif
It lucrativo
Pt lucrativo

**Eintragung** *(f)* n De
En entry
Es asiento *(m)*
Fr inscription *(f)*
It registrazione *(f)*
Pt lançamento *(m)*

**Eintragung** (einer Gesellschaft)
*(f)* n De
En incorporation
Es incorporación *(f)*
Fr incorporation *(f)*
It costituzione *(f)*
Pt incorporação *(f)*

**Eintritt** *(m)* n De
En entry
Es entrada *(f)*
Fr entrée *(f)*
It entrata *(f)*
Pt admissão *(f)*

**Eintritt frei** De
En admission free
Es entrada gratuita
Fr entrée gratuite
It ingresso gratuito
Pt entrada gratis

**Eintrittsdeklarationsschein**
*(m)* n De
En jerque note
Es certificado de declaración
   de entrada *(m)*
Fr certificat d'entrée autorisée
   *(m)*
It certificato di dichiarazione
   d'entrata *(m)*
Pt certificado de verificação
   alfandegária *(m)*

**Eintrittsgebühr** *(f)* n De
En entrance fee
Es derecho de entrada *(m)*
Fr droit d'entrée *(m)*
It tassa d'entrata *(f)*
Pt taxa de admissão *(f)*

**Einwanderung** *(f)* n De
En immigration
Es inmigración *(f)*
Fr immigration *(f)*
It immigrazione *(f)*
Pt imigração *(f)*

**einwöchig kündigen** De
En give a week's notice
Es dar una semana de aviso
Fr donner ses huit jours
It dare una settimana di
   preavviso
Pt dar um prazo de uma
   semana para despedimento

**Einzahler** *(m)* n De
En depositor
Es depositante *(m)*
Fr déposant *(m)*
It depositante *(m)*
Pt depositante *(m)*

**Einzelhandel** *(m)* n De
En retail trade
Es comercio al por menor *(m)*
Fr commerce en détail *(m)*
It commercio al minuto *(m)*
Pt comércio a retalho *(m)*

**Einzelhandelspreis** *(m)* n De
En retail price
Es precio al por menor *(m)*
Fr prix de détail *(m)*
It prezzo al minuto *(m)*
Pt preço a retalho *(m)*

**Einzelhändler** *(m)* n De
En retailer
Es comerciante al por menor
   *(m)*
Fr commerçant au détail *(m)*
It commerciante al minuto
   *(m)*
Pt comerciante a retalho;
   retalhista *(m)*

**Einzelheiten** *(f pl)* n De
En particulars
Es detalles *(m pl)*
Fr détails *(m pl)*
It particolari *(m pl)*
Pt pormenores *(m pl)*

**Einzelkosten** *(pl)* n De
En direct expenses
Es gastos directos *(m pl)*
Fr frais directs *(m pl)*
It spese dirette *(f pl)*
Pt despesas directas *(f pl)*

**Einzugskosten** *(pl)* n De
En collection charges
Es gastos de cobranza *(m pl)*
Fr frais d'encaissement *(m pl)*

It spese di riscossione *(f pl)*
Pt gastos de cobrança *(m pl)*

**Eisen** *(n)* n De
En iron
Es hierro *(m)*
Fr fer *(m)*
It ferro *(m)*
Pt ferro *(m)*

**Eisenbahn** *(f)* n De
En railway
Es ferrocarril *(m)*
Fr chemin de fer *(m)*
It ferrovia *(f)*
Pt caminho de ferro *(m)*

**Eisenbahnfahrplan** *(m)* n De
En railway timetable
Es horario de trenes *(m)*
Fr indicateur des chemins de
   fer *(m)*
It orario ferroviario *(m)*
Pt horário de caminhos de
   ferro *(m)*

**Eisenbahnwagen** *(m)* n De
En railway carriage
Am railroad car
Es vagón de ferrocarril *(m)*
Fr wagon de chemin de fer
   *(m)*
It carrozza ferroviaria *(f)*
Pt vagão de caminhos de ferro
   *(m)*

**Eisenerz** *(n)* n De
En iron ore
Es mineral de hierro *(m)*
Fr minerai de fer *(m)*
It minerale di ferro *(m)*
Pt minério de ferro *(m)*

**Eisenwaren** *(f pl)* n De
En hardware; ironmongery
Es ferretería; quincallería *(f)*
Fr quincaillerie *(f)*
It ferramenta *(f)*
Pt ferragens *(f pl)*

**ejecución** *(f)* n Es
De Vollstreckung; Erfüllung *(f)*
En performance
Fr exécution *(f)*
It esecuzione *(f)*
Pt desempenho *(m)*

**ejecutar** vb Es
  De vollstrecken; durchführen
  En execute; carry out
  Fr exécuter; réaliser
  It eseguire; effettuare
  Pt executar

**ejecutar un testamento** Es
  De ein Testament vollstrecken
  En execute a will
  Fr exécuter un testament
  It eseguire un testamento
  Pt dar execuçao a um testa-
     mento

**ejecutivo de cuenta** (m) Es
  De Kontaktgruppenleiter (m)
  En account executive
  Fr chef de comptes client (m)
  It direttore conto cliente (m)
  Pt chefe de conta de cliente
    (m)

**ejercicio** (m) n Es
  De Abrechnungszeitraum (m)
  En accounting period
  Fr exercice (f)
  It esercizio (m)
  Pt exercício (m)

**elaboratore** (m) n It
  De Rechner; Computer (m)
  En computer
  Es computadora (f)
  Fr ordinateur (m)
  Pt computador (m)

**elaboratore numerico** (m) It
  De Digitalrechner (m)
  En digital computer
  Es computadora numérica (f)
  Fr calculateur digital (m)
  Pt computador de dígitos (m)

**elaborazione dei dati** (f) It
  De Datenverarbeitung (f)
  En data processing
  Es tratamiento de datos (m)
  Fr traitement d'informatique
    (m)
  Pt processamento de dados
    (m)

**elasticidad de precio** (f) Es
  De Preisdehnbarkeit (f)
  En price elasticity
  Fr élasticité-prix (m)

It elasticità di prezzo (f)
Pt flexibilidade de preços (f)

**elasticità di prezzo** (f) It
  De Preisdehnbarkeit (f)
  En price elasticity
  Es elasticidad de precio (f)
  Fr élasticité-prix (m)
  Pt flexibilidade de preços (f)

**élasticité-prix** (m) n Fr
  De Preisdehnbarkeit (f)
  En price elasticity
  Es elasticidad de precio (f)
  It elasticità di prezzo (f)
  Pt flexibilidade de preços (f)

**electrical engineering** En
  De Elektrotechnik (f)
  Es ingeniería eléctrica (f)
  Fr construction électrique (f)
  It elettrotecnica (f)
  Pt engenharia electrotécnica
    (f)

**electricidad** (f) n Es
  De Elektrizität (f)
  En electricity
  Fr électricité (f)
  It elettricità (f)
  Pt electricidade (f)

**electricidade** (f) n Pt
  De Elektrizität (f)
  En electricity
  Es electricidad (f)
  Fr électricité (f)
  It elettricità (f)

**électricité** (f) n Fr
  De Elektrizität (f)
  En electricity
  Es electricidad (f)
  It elettricità (f)
  Pt electricidade (f)

**electricity** n En
  De Elektrizität (f)
  Es electricidad (f)
  Fr électricité (f)
  It elettricità (f)
  Pt electricidade (f)

**electro-domésticos** (m pl) n Pt
  De elektrische Haushaltsgüter
    (n pl)
  En household electrical goods

Es aparatos eléctricos de casa
  (m pl)
Fr electro-ménager (m)
It elettrodomestici (m pl)

**electro-ménager** (m) n Fr
  De elektrische Haushaltsgüter
    (n pl)
  En household electrical goods
  Es aparatos eléctricos de casa
    (m pl)
  It elettrodomestici (m pl)
  Pt electro-domésticos (m pl)

**electronic** adj En
  De elektronisch
  Es electrónico
  Fr électronique
  It elettronico
  Pt electrónico

**electrónica** (f) Es, Pt
  De Elektronik (f)
  En electronics
  Fr électronique (f)
  It elettronica (f)

**electrónico** adj Es, Pt
  De elektronisch
  En electronic
  Fr électronique
  It elettronico

**electronics** n En
  De Elektronik (f)
  Es electrónica (f)
  Fr électronique (f)
  It elettronica (f)
  Pt electrónica (f)

**électronique** adj Fr
  De elektronisch
  En electronic
  Es electrónico
  It elettronico
  Pt electrónico

**électronique** (f) Fr
  De Elektronik (f)
  En electronics
  Es electrónica (f)
  It elettronica (f)
  Pt electrónica (f)

**elektrische Haushaltsgüter** (n
pl) De
  En household electrical goods

Es aparatos eléctricos de casa
(m pl)
Fr electro-ménager (m)
It elettrodomestici (m pl)
Pt electro-domésticos (m pl)

**Elektrizität** (f) n De
En electricity
Es electricidad (f)
Fr électricité (f)
It elettricità (f)
Pt electricidade (f)

**Elektronik** (f) n De
En electronics
Es electrónica (f)
Fr électronique (f)
It elettronica (f)
Pt electrónica (f)

**elektronisch** adj De
En electronic
Es electrónico
Fr électronique
It elettronico
Pt electrónico

**Elektrotechnik** (f) n De
En electrical engineering
Es ingeniería eléctrica (f)
Fr construction électrique (f)
It elettrotecnica (f)
Pt engenharia electrotécnica
(f)

**elenco delle prenotazioni** (m)
It
De Warteliste (f)
En waiting list
Es lista de espera (f)
Fr liste d'attente (f)
Pt lista de espera (f)

**elenco telefonico** (m) It
De Fernsprechbuch (n)
En telephone directory
Es guía de teléfonos (f)
Fr annuaire des télephones
(m)
Pt lista telefónica (f)

**elettricità** (f) n It
De Elektrizität (f)
En electricity
Es electricidad (f)
Fr électricité (f)
Pt electricidade (f)

**elettrodomestici** (m pl) n It
De elektrische Haushaltsgüter
(n pl)
En household electrical goods
Es aparatos eléctricos de casa
(m pl)
Fr electro-ménager (m)
Pt electro-domésticos (m pl)

**elettronica** (f) n It
De Elektronik (f)
En electronics
Es electrónica (f)
Fr électronique (f)
Pt electrónica (f)

**elettronico** adj It
De elektronisch
En electronic
Es electrónico
Fr électronique
Pt electrónico

**elettrotecnica** (f) It
De Elektrotechnik (f)
En electrical engineering
Es ingeniería eléctrica (f)
Fr construction électrique (f)
Pt engenharia electrotécnica
(f)

**elevado** adj Pt
De hoch
En high
Es alto; elevado
Fr haut; élevé
It alto; elevato

**elevator** n Am
En lift
De Aufzug (m)
Es ascensor (m)
Fr ascenseur (m)
It ascensore (m)
Pt ascensor (m)

**em armazém** Pt
De auf Lager
En at warehouse
Es en almacén
Fr en dépôt
It in deposito

**embalagem** (m) n Pt
De Verpackung (f)
En packing
Es embalaje; envase (m)

Fr emballage (m)
It imballaggio (m)

**embalagem a destruir** (f) Pt
De wegwerfbare Verpackung
(f)
En disposable wrapping
Es envoltura desechable (f)
Fr emballage perdu (m)
It imballaggio a perdere (m)

**embalaje** (m) n Es
De Verpackung (f)
En packing
Fr emballage (m)
It imballaggio (m)
Pt embalagem; empacota-
mento (m)

**emballage** (m) n Fr
De Verpackung (f)
En packing
Es embalaje; envase (m)
It imballaggio (m)
Pt embalagem; empacota-
mento (m)

**emballage perdu** (m) Fr
De wegwerfbare Verpackung
(f)
En disposable wrapping
Es envoltura desechable (f)
It imballaggio a perdere (m)
Pt embalagem a destruir (f)

**embarcação** (f) n Pt
De Einschiffung (f)
En embarcation
Es embarco (m)
Fr embarquement (m)
It imbarco (m)

**embarcar** vb Es, Pt
De verschiffen; sich einschiffen
En ship; embark
Fr embarquer; s'embarquer
It imbarcare

**embarcation** n En
De Einschiffung (f)
Es embarco (m)
Fr embarquement (m)
It imbarco (m)
Pt embarcação (f)

**embarco** (m) n Es
De Einschiffung (f)
En embarcation

Fr embarquement *(m)*
It imbarco *(m)*
Pt embarcação *(f)*

**embark** *vb* En
De sich einschiffen
Es embarcar
Fr s'embarquer
It imbarcare
Pt embarcar

**embarque** *(m) n* Es, Pt
De Verladung *(f)*
En shipment
Fr embarquement *(m)*
It imbarco *(m)*

**embarquement** *(m) n* Fr
De Einschiffung; Verladung *(f)*
En embarcation; shipment
Es embarco; embarque *(m)*
It imbarco *(m)*
Pt embarcação; embarque *(f m)*

**embarquer** *vb* Fr
De verschiffen
En ship
Es embarcar
It imbarcare
Pt embarcar

**s'embarquer** *vb* Fr
De sich einschiffen
En embark
Es embarcar
It imbarcare
Pt embarcar

**embezzle** *vb* En
De unterschlagen
Es defalcar
Fr détourner
It appropriarsi indebitamente
Pt desfalcar

**embezzlement** *n* En
De Unterschlagung *(f)*
Es defalco *(m)*
Fr détournement de fonds *(m)*
It appropriazione indebita *(f)*
Pt desfalque *(m)*

**embezzler** *n* En
De Veruntreuer *(m)*
Es defalcador *(m)*
Fr détourneur *(m)*

It malversatore *(m)*
Pt desfalcador *(m)*

**em bom estado** Pt
De in gutem Zustand
En in good repair
Es en buen estado
Fr en bon état
It in buono stato

**embotellamiento** *(m) n* Es
De Engpass *(m)*
En bottle-neck
Fr goulot d'étranglement *(m)*
It strozzatura *(f)*
Pt engarrafamento *(m)*

**embotellamiento de tráfico** *(m)* Es
De Verkehrsstockung *(f)*
En traffic jam
Fr encombrement de circulation *(m)*
It ingorgo stradale *(m)*
Pt engarrafamento de tráfico *(m)*

**em caso de não comprimento** Pt
De bei Nichterfüllung
En in case of default
Es en caso de incumplimiento
Fr en cas de défaillance
It in caso di inadempienza

**em condições de navegação** Pt
De seefest
En seaworthy
Es marinero
Fr en état de navigabilité
It atto a tenere il mare

**em conformidade com** Pt
De in Übereinstimmung mit
En in accordance with
Es en conformidad con
Fr conforme à
It in conformità con

**em conjunto e por vários** Pt
De gesamtschuldnerisch
En jointly and severally
Es en conjunto y separadamente
Fr conjointement et solidairement

It solidalmente e individualmente

**em contrapartida** Pt
De als Gegenrechnung
En per contra
Es en contrapartida
Fr en contrepartie; par contre
It in contropartita

**em dinheiro contra documentação** Pt
De bar gegen Versandpapiere
En cash against documents (c.a.d.)
Es al contado contra documentos
Fr comptant contre documents
It contanti contro documenti

**em duplicado** Pt
De Duplikat-; zweifach
En in duplicate
Es par duplicado
Fr en double
It in duplice copia

**em espécie** Pt
De in Waren
En in kind
Es en especie
Fr en nature
It in natura

**emettere** *vb* It
De ausgeben
En issue
Es emitir
Fr émettre
Pt emitir

**emettere un assegno** It
De einen Scheck ausstellen
En draw a cheque
Es extender un cheque
Fr tirer un chèque
Pt passar um cheque

**émettre** *vb* Fr
De ausgeben
En issue
Es emitir
It emettere
Pt emitir

**émettre un emprunt** Fr
De eine Anleihe begeben
En float a loan
Am raise a loan
Es emitir un empréstito
It lanciare un prestito
Pt lançar um empréstimo

**émeutes et désordres** Fr
De Aufruhr und innere Unruhen
En riot and civil commotion
Es revueltas y conmociones civiles
It rivolte e moti civili
Pt motins e perturbações civis

**emisión de derechos** (f) Es
De Sonderemission gegen Bezugsrechte (f)
En rights issue
Fr émission sous droit de souscription (f)
It emissione di diritti (f)
Pt emissão de direitos (f)

**emisión fiduciaria** (f) Es
De ungedecktes Geld (n)
En fiduciary issue
Fr émission fiduciaire (f)
It emissione fiduciaria (f)
Pt emissão fiduciária (f)

**emisión no totalmente subscrita** (f) Es
De nicht in voller Höhe gezeichnete Emission (f)
En undersubscribed issue
Fr émission non couverte (f)
It emissione non interamente sottoscritta (f)
Pt emissão não subscrita na totalidade (f)

**emissão de direitos** (f) Pt
De Sonderemission gegen Bezugsrechte (f)
En rights issue
Es emisión de derechos (f)
Fr émission sous droit de souscription (f)
It emissione di diritti (f)

**emissão fiduciária** (f) Pt
De ungedecktes Geld (n)
En fiduciary issue
Es emisión fiduciaria (f)

Fr émission fiduciaire (f)
It emissione fiduciaria (f)

**emissão não subscrita na totalidade** (f) Pt
De nicht in voller Höhe gezeichnete Emission (f)
En undersubscribed issue
Es emisión no totalmente subscrita (f)
Fr émission non couverte (f)
It emissione non interamente sottoscritta (f)

**emissão nova** (f) Pt
De Ausgabe junger Aktien (f)
En new issue
Es nueva emisión (f)
Fr émission d'actions nouvelles (f)
It nuova emissione (f)

**emissione fiduciaria** (f) It
De ungedecktes Geld (n)
En fiduciary issue
Es emisión fiduciaria (f)
Fr émission fiduciaire (f)
Pt emissão fiduciária (f)

**emissione non interamente sottoscritta** (f) It
De nicht in voller Höhe gezeichnete Emission (f)
En undersubscribed issue
Es emisión no totalmente subscrita (f)
Fr émission non couverte (f)
Pt emissão não subscrita na totalidade (f)

**émission fiduciaire** (f) Fr
De ungedecktes Geld (n)
En fiduciary issue
Es emisión fiduciaria (f)
It emissione fiduciaria (f)
Pt emissão fiduciária (f)

**émission non couverte** (f) Fr
De nicht in voller Höhe gezeichnete Emission (f)
En undersubscribed issue
Es emisión no totalmente subscrita (f)
It emissione non interamente sottoscritta (f)
Pt emissão não subscrita na totalidade (f)

Fr émission fiduciaire (f)
It emissione fiduciaria (f)

**émission sous droit de souscription** (f) Fr
De Sonderemission gegen Bezugsrechte (f)
En rights issue
Es emisión de derechos (f)
It emissione di diritti (f)
Pt emissão de direitos (f)

**Emissionssyndikat** (n) n De
En underwriting syndicate
Es grupo de suscriptores (m)
Fr syndicat de garantie (m)
It consorzio finanziario (m)
Pt consórcio de subscritores (m)

**emitir** vb Es, Pt
De ausgeben
En issue
Fr émettre
It emettere

**emitir un empréstito** Es
De eine Anleihe begeben
En float a loan
Am raise a loan
Fr émettre un emprunt
It lanciare un prestito
Pt lançar um empréstimo

**emmagasinage** (m) n Fr
De Lagerung (f)
En storage
Es almacenamiento (m)
It maggazzinaggio (m)
Pt armazenamento (m)

**emmagasiner** (vb) Fr
De lagern
En store
Es almacenar
It immagazzinare
Pt armazenar

**emolument** n En
De Bezüge (m pl)
Es emolumento (m)
Fr émoluments (m pl)
It emolumento (m)
Pt emolumento (m)

**emolumenti degli amministratori** (m pl) It
De Direktorenbezüge (m pl)
En directors' emoluments
Es emolumentos de directores (m pl)

Fr émoluments des admini-
strateurs (m pl)
Pt emolumentos de directores
(m pl)

**emolumento** (m) n Es, It, Pt
De Bezüge (m pl)
En emolument
Fr émoluments (m pl)

**emolumentos de directores**
(m pl) Es, Pt
De Direktorenbezüge (m pl)
En directors' emoluments
Fr émoluments des admini-
strateurs (m pl)
It emolumenti degli ammini-
stratori (m pl)

**émoluments** (m pl) n Fr
De Bezüge (m pl)
En emolument
Es emolumento (m)
It emolumento (m)
Pt emolumento (m)

**émoluments des administra-
teurs** (m pl) Fr
De Direktorenbezüge (m pl)
En directors' emoluments
Es emolumentos de directores
(m pl)
It emolumenti degli ammini-
stratori (m pl)
Pt emolumentos de directores
(m pl)

**empacotamento para expor-
tação** (m) Pt
De Exportverpackung (f)
En export packing
Es embalaje para exportación
(m)
Fr emballage convenable à
l'exportation (m)
It imballaggio per esporta-
zione (m)

**empêchement** (m) n Fr
De Hinderung (f)
En hindrance
Es impedimento (m)
It impedimento (m)
Pt impedimento (m)

**Empfang bestätigen** De
En acknowledge receipt
Es acusar recibo

Fr accuser réception
It accusare ricevuta
Pt acusar a recepção

**Empfänger** (m) n De
En addressee; consignee
Es destinatario; consignatario
(m)
Fr destinataire (m)
It destinatario; consegnatario
(m)
Pt destinatário; consignatário
(m)

**Empfangsbestätigung** (f) n De
En acknowledgment of receipt
Es aviso de recepción (m)
Fr accusé de réception (m)
It avviso di recezione (m)
Pt aviso de recepção (m)

**empfohlener Ladenpreis** (m)
De
En recommended retail selling
price
Es precio detallista recomen-
dado (m)
Fr prix de détail racommandé
(m)
It prezzo al minuto indicativo
(m)
Pt preço de venda a retalho
recomendado (m)

**empleado** (m) n Es
De Angestellte(r); Arbeitneh-
mer (m)
En employee
Fr employé (m)
It impiegato (m)
Pt empregado (m)

**empleado a sueldo** (m) Es
De Angestellte(r) (m)
En salaried employee
Fr appointé (m)
It stipendiato (m)
Pt assalariado (m)

**emplear** vb Es
De beschäftigen
En employ
Fr employer
It impiegare
Pt empregar

**empleo** (m) n Es
De Beschäftigung; Stellung (f)
En employment; job
Fr emploi (m)
It impiego (m)
Pt emprego (m)

**emploi** (m) n Fr
De Beschäftigung; Stellung (f)
En employment; job
Es empleo (m)
It impiego (m)
Pt emprego (m)

**employ** vb En
De beschäftigen
Es emplear
Fr employer
It impiegare
Pt empregar

**employé** (m) n Fr
De Angestellte(r); Arbeitneh-
mer (m)
En employee
Es empleado (m)
It impiegato (m)
Pt empregado (m)

**employee** n En
De Angestellte(r); Arbeitneh-
mer (m)
Es empleado (m)
Fr employé (m)
It impiegato (m)
Pt empregado (m)

**employer** vb Fr
De beschäftigen
En employ
Es emplear
It impiegare
Pt empregar

**employer** n En
De Arbeitgeber (m)
Es patrono (m)
Fr employeur (m)
It datore di lavoro (m)
Pt patrão (m)

**employer's liability** En
De Haftpflicht des Arbeitge-
bers (f)
Es responsabilidad del patrono
(f)
Fr responsabilité patronale (f)

It responsabilità del datore di lavoro (f)

Pt responsabilidade do patrão (f)

**employeur** (m) n Fr
De Arbeitgeber (m)
En employer
Es patrono (m)
It datore di lavoro (m)
Pt patrão (m)

**employment** n En
De Beschäftigung (f)
Es empleo (m)
Fr emploi (m)
It impiego (m)
Pt emprego (m)

**employment agency** En
De Stellenvermittlungsbüro (n)
Es agencia de colocaciones (f)
Fr agence de placement (f)
It agenzia di collocamento (f)
Pt agência de emprego (f)

**employment exchange** En
Am state employment agency
De Arbeitsnachweisstelle (f)
Es bolsa de trabajo (f)
Fr bureau de placement (m)
It ufficio di collocamento (m)
Pt centro de serviços de emprego (m)

**employment tax** En
De Lohnsummensteuer (f)
Es impuesto por empleado (m)
Fr taxe sur l'emploi (f)
It imposta sull'impiego (f)
Pt imposto sobre emprego (m)

**empregado** (m) n Pt
De Angestellte(r); Arbeitnehmer (m)
En employee
Es empleado (m)
Fr employé (m)
It impiegato (m)

**empregado de contabilidade** (m) Pt
De Buchhalter (m)
En ledger clerk
Am bookkeeper
Es contable (m)
Fr commis-contable (m)
It contabile (m)

**empregado de escritório** (m) Pt
De Angestellte(r) (m)
En clerk
Es oficinista (m)
Fr commis (m)
It impiegato (m)

**empregado por conta-própria** (m) Pt
De selbständig Arbeitende(r) (m)
En self-employed person
Es trabajador por cuenta propia (m)
Fr travailleur indépendant (m)
It lavoratore indipendente (m)

**empregar** vb Pt
De beschäftigen; anstellen
En employ; engage
Es emplear; apalabrar
Fr employer; engager
It impiegare; fissare

**emprego** (m) n Pt
De Beschäftigung; Stellung (f)
En employment; job
Es empleo (m)
Fr emploi (m)
It impiego (m)

**empreiteiro de transportes** (m) Pt
De Transportunternehmer (m)
En haulage contractor
Am trucking company
Es contratista de transportes (m)
Fr entrepreneur de camionnage (m)
It imprenditore di trasporti (m)

**empresa** (f) n Es, Pt
De Unternehmen; Firma (n f)
En enterprise; firm
Fr entreprise; firme (f)
It impresa; ditta (f)

**empresa de exploração** (f) Pt
De Erschliessungsgesellschaft (f)
En development company
Es compañía de explotación (f)
Fr société d'exploitation (f)
It società d'imprese (f)

**empresa de há muito estabelecida** (f) Pt
De alteingeführtes Geschäft (n)
En old-established business
Es casa sólida (f)
Fr maison solide (f)
It casa di vecchia fondazione (f)

**empresa de transportes** (f) Es, Pt
De Güterbeförderer (m)
En common carrier
Fr voiturier public (m)
It vettore (m)

**empresa de utilidade pública** (f) Pt
De gemeinnütziges Unternehmen (n)
En utility company
Es empresa de servicios públicos (f)
Fr entreprise d'utilité publique (f)
It società di servizi pubblici (f)

**empresa en común** (f) Es
De Gemeinschaftsgründung (f)
En joint venture
Fr entreprise en participation (f)
It impresa in compartecipazione (f)
Pt iniciativa em comum (f)

**empresa extinta** (f) Pt
De erloschene Gesellschaft (f)
En defunct company
Es sociedad extinta (f)
Fr société liquidée (f)
It società estinta (f)

**empresa financeira** (f) Pt
De Finanzierungsgesellschaft (f)
En finance company
Es compañía de crédito comercial (f)
Fr société de financement (f)
It società finanziaria (f)

**empresa gémea** (f) Pt
De Schwestergesellschaft (f)
En sister company
Es compañía asociada (f)
Fr société sœur (f)
It società sorella (f)

**empresa matriz** *(f)* Pt
De Muttergesellschaft *(f)*
En parent company
Es compañía matriz *(f)*
Fr société mère *(f)*
It società madre *(f)*

**empresa privada** *(f)* Es, Pt
De Privatunternehmen *(n)*
En private enterprise
Fr entreprise privée *(f)*
It impresa privata *(f)*

**empresario** *(m)* n Es
De Unternehmer *(m)*
En entrepreneur
Fr entrepreneur *(m)*
It intraprenditore *(m)*
Pt empresário *(m)*

**empresário** *(m)* n Pt
De Unternehmer *(m)*
En entrepreneur
Es empresario *(m)*
Fr entrepreneur *(m)*
It intraprenditore *(m)*

**emprestar** *vb* Pt
De leihen
En lend
Es prestar
Fr prêter
It prestare

**empréstime** *(m)* n Pt
De Anleihe *(f)*
En loan
Es empréstito *(m)*
Fr emprunt *(m)*
It prestito *(m)*

**empréstimo bancário** *(m)* Pt
De Bankdarlehen *(n)*
En bank loan
Es préstamo bancario *(m)*
Fr prêt bancaire *(m)*
It prestito bancario *(m)*

**empréstimo do governo** *(m)* Pt
De Staatsanleihe *(f)*
En government loan
Es empréstito público *(m)*
Fr emprunt public *(m)*
It prestito pubblico *(m)*

**empréstimo externo** *(m)* Pt
De Auslandsanleihe *(f)*
En external loan
Es préstamo exterior *(m)*
Fr emprunt extérieur *(m)*
It prestito esterno *(m)*

**empréstimo para construção** *(m)* Pt
De Baukredit *(m)*
En building loan
Es crédito de construcción *(m)*
Fr crédit de construction *(m)*
It prestito immobiliare *(m)*

**empréstito** *(m)* n Es
De Anleihe *(f)*
En loan
Fr emprunt *(m)*
It prestito *(m)*
Pt empréstime *(m)*

**empréstito público** *(m)* Es
De Staatsanleihe *(f)*
En government loan
Fr emprunt public *(m)*
It prestito pubblico *(m)*
Pt empréstimo do governo *(m)*

**emprunt** *(m)* n Fr
De Anleihe *(f)*
En loan
Es empréstito *(m)*
It prestito *(m)*
Pt empréstime *(m)*

**emprunter** *vb* Fr
De entleihen
En borrow
Es pedir un préstamo
It prestire
Pt contrair empréstimo

**emprunteur** *(m)* n Fr
De Kreditnehmer *(m)*
En borrower
Es prestatario *(m)*
It accattatore *(m)*
Pt beneficiário de empréstimo *(m)*

**emprunt extérieur** *(m)* Fr
De Auslandsanleihe *(f)*
En external loan
Es préstamo exterior *(m)*
It prestito esterno *(m)*
Pt empréstimo externo *(m)*

**emprunt public** *(m)* Fr
De Staatsanleihe *(f)*
En government loan
Es empréstito público *(m)*
It prestito pubblico *(m)*
Pt empréstimo do governo *(m)*

**em reserva** Pt
De vorrätig
En in stock
Es en almacén
Fr en magasin
It in magazzino

**em separado** (correio) Pt
De getrennt
En under separate cover
Es por separado
Fr sous pli séparé
It con plico a parte

**em trânsito** Pt
De im Durchgangsverkehr
En in transit
Es en tránsito
Fr en transit
It in transito

**en aduanas** Es
De unter Zollverschluss
En in bond
Fr en entrepôt
It sotto vincolo doganale
Pt à ordem da alfândega

**en almacén** Es
De auf Lager
En at warehouse
Fr en dépôt
It in deposito
Pt em armazém

**en almacén** Es
De vorrätig
En in stock
Fr en magasin
It in magazzino
Pt em reserva

**en avant** Fr
De Termin-
En forward
Es a término
It a termine
Pt adiante

**en bon état** Fr
De in gutem Zustand
En in good repair
Es en buen estado
It in buono stato
Pt em bom estado

**en buen estado** Es
De in gutem Zustand
En in good repair
Fr en bon état
It in buono stato
Pt em bom estado

**encaisser** vb Fr
De einkassieren
En cash
Es cobrar
It incassare
Pt cobrar

**encarecer** vb Es, Pt
De teurer werden; steigen
En advance in price
Fr renchérir
It aumentare di prezzo

**encarecimento** (m) n Pt
De Preiserhöhung (f)
En advance in price
Es encarecimiento (m)
Fr renchérissement (m)
It rialzo (m)

**encarecimiento** (m) n Es
De Preiserhöhung (f)
En advance in price
Fr renchérissement (m)
It rialzo (m)
Pt encarecimento (m)

**encargos de armazenamento**
(m pl) Pt
De Lagergeld (n)
En storage charges
Es gastos de almacenaje (m
pl)
Fr frais de magasinage (m pl)
It spese di magazzinaggio (f
pl)

**encargos de doca** (m pl) Pt
De Dockgebühr (f)
En dock dues
Es derechos de muelle (m pl)
Fr droits de dock (m pl)
It diritti di dock (m pl)

**encargos de salvamento** (m
pl) Pt
De Bergegeld (n)
En salvage charges
Es cargos de salvamento (m
pl)
Fr indemnité de sauvetage (f)
It spese di salvataggio (f pl)

**encargos ocasionais** (m pl) Pt
De Nebenkosten (pl)
En incidental charges
Es cargos imprevistos (m pl)
Fr charges annexes (f pl)
It spese accessorie (f pl)

**encargos pesados** (m pl) Pt
De drückende Spesen (f pl)
En heavy charges
Es gastos fuertes (m pl)
Fr charges lourdes (f pl)
It forti spese (f pl)

**encargo suplementar** (m) Pt
De Zuschlagsgebühr (f)
En extra charge
Es suplemento (m)
Fr supplément (m)
It spesa supplementare (f)

**encarregado** (m) n Pt
De Vorarbeiter (m)
En foreman
Es capataz (m)
Fr contremaître; chef d'équipe
(m)
It capo operaio; capo squa-
dra (m)

**encarregado-chefe** (m) n Pt
De Werkmeister (m)
En head foreman
Es capataz jefe (m)
Fr chef d'atelier (m)
It capo officina (m)

**en cas de défaillance** Fr
De bei Nichterfüllung
En in case of default
Es en caso de incumplimiento
It in caso di inadempienza
Pt em caso de não compri-
mento

**en caso de incumplimiento** Es
De bei Nichterfüllung
En in case of default
Fr en cas de défaillance

It in caso di inadempienza
Pt em caso de não compri-
mento

**enchérisseur** (m) n Fr
De Bietende(r) (m)
En bidder
Es ofertante (m)
It offerente (m)
Pt proponente (m)

**en chômage** Fr
De arbeitslos
En unemployed
Es sin trabajo; parado
It senza lavoro
Pt desempregado

**enclosed** adj En
De beiliegend
Es adjunto
Fr ci-joint; ci-inclus
It accluso
Pt incluso

**enclosure** n En
De Beilage (f)
Es anexo (m)
Fr annexe (f)
It allegato (m)
Pt anexo (m)

**encombrement de circulation**
(m) Fr
De Verkehrsstockung (f)
En traffic jam
Es embotellamiento de tráfico
(m)
It ingorgo stradale (m)
Pt engarrafamento de tráfico
(m)

**encomenda** (f) n Pt
De Bestellung; Auftrag (f m)
En order
Es pedido (m)
Fr commande (f)
It ordine (m)

**encomenda** (postal) (f) n Pt
De Paket (n)
En parcel
Es paquete (m)
Fr colis (m)
It pacco (m)

**encomenda de exportação** *(f)*
  Pt
De Exportauftrag *(m)*
En export order
Es pedido de exportación *(m)*
Fr commande d'exportation *(f)*
It ordine per esportazione *(m)*

**encomendar** *vb* Pt
De bestellen
En order
Es hacer un pedido
Fr commander
It ordinare

**en conformidad con** Es
De in Übereinstimmung mit
En in accordance with
Fr conforme à
It in conformità con
Pt em conformidade com

**en conjunto y separadamente**
  Es
De gesamtschuldnerisch
En jointly and severally
Fr conjointement et solidaire-
  ment
It solidalmente e individual-
  mente
Pt em conjunto e por vários

**en consignación** Es
De in Kommission
En on consignment
Fr en consignation
It in conto deposito
Pt à consignação

**en consignation** Fr
De in Kommission
En on consignment
Es en consignación
It in conto deposito
Pt à consignação

**en contrapartida** Es
De als Gegenrechnung
En per contra
Fr en contrepartie; par contre
It in contropartita
Pt em contrapartida

**en contrepartie** Fr
De als Gegenrechnung
En per contra
Es en contrapartida

It in contropartita
Pt em contrapartida

**encontro** *(m)* n Pt
De Verabredung *(f)*
En appointment
Es entrevista *(f)*
Fr entrevue *(f)*
It appuntamento *(m)*

**encuesta** *(f)* n Es
De Untersuchung *(f)*
En inquiry
Fr enquête *(f)*
It inchiesta *(f)*
Pt inquérito *(m)*

**end** n En
De Ende *(n)*
Es fin *(m)*
Fr fin *(f)*
It fine *(f)*
Pt fim *(m)*

**Ende** *(n)* n De
En end
Es fin *(m)*
Fr fin *(f)*
It fine *(f)*
Pt fim *(m)*

**en dépôt** Fr
De auf Lager
En at warehouse
Es en almacén
It in deposito
Pt em armazém

**endereço** *(m)* n Pt
De Adresse *(f)*
En address
Es dirección *(f)*
Fr adresse *(f)*
It indirizzo *(m)*

**endereço telegráfico** *(m)* Pt
De Telegrammadresse *(f)*
En telegraphic address
Es dirección telegráfica *(f)*
Fr adresse télégraphique *(f)*
It indirizzo telegrafico *(m)*

**endeudado** *adj* Es
De verschuldet
En indebted
Fr redevable; endetté
It indebitato
Pt endividado; em dívida

**endgültig** *adj* De
En final
Es final
Fr final
It finale
Pt final

**endividado** *adj* Pt
De verschuldet
En indebted
Es endeudado
Fr redevable; endetté
It indebitato

**endorse** (a bill) *vb* En
De indossieren
Es endosar
Fr endosser
It girare
Pt endossar

**endorsement** n En
De Indossament *(n)*
Es endoso *(m)*
Fr endossement; endos *(m)*
It girata *(f)*
Pt endosse *(m)*

**endosar** *vb* Es
De indossieren
En endorse
Fr endosser
It girare
Pt endossar

**endoso** *(m)* n Es
De Indossament *(n)*
En endorsement
Fr endossement; endos *(m)*
It girata *(f)*
Pt endosse *(m)*

**endoso en blanco** *(m)* Es
De Blankoindossament *(n)*
En blank endorsement
Fr endossement en blanc *(m)*
It girata in bianco *(f)*
Pt endosse em branco *(m)*

**endoso restringido** *(m)* Es
De Rektaindossement *(n)*
En restrictive endorsement
Fr endossement restrictif *(m)*
It girata restrittiva *(f)*
Pt endosse restritivo *(m)*

**endossar** vb Pt
De indossieren
En endorse
Es endosar
Fr endosser
It girare

**endosse** (m) n Pt
De Indossament (n)
En endorsement
Es endoso (m)
Fr endossement; endos (m)
It girata (f)

**endosse em branco** (m) Pt
De Blankoindossament (n)
En blank endorsement
Es endoso en blanco (m)
Fr endossement en blanc (m)
It girata in bianco (f)

**endossement** (m) n Fr
De Indossament (n)
En endorsement
Es endoso (m)
It girata (f)
Pt endosse (m)

**endossement en blanc** (m) Fr
De Blankoindossament (n)
En blank endorsement
Es endoso en blanco (m)
It girata in bianco (f)
Pt endosse em branco (m)

**endossement restrictif** (m) Fr
De Rektaindossement (n)
En restrictive endorsement
Es endoso restringido (m)
It girata restrittiva (f)
Pt endosse restrivo (m)

**endosser** vb Fr
De indossieren
En endorse
Es endosar
It girare
Pt endossar

**endosse restritivo** (m) Pt
De Rektaindossement (n)
En restrictive endorsement
Es endoso restringido (m)
Fr endossement restrictif (m)
It girata restrittiva (f)

**en double** Fr
De Duplikat-; zweifach
En in duplicate
Es par duplicado
It in duplice copia
Pt em duplicado

**endow** vb En
De ausstatten
Es dotar
Fr doter
It dotare
Pt dotar

**endowment policy** En
De Erlebensversicherung (f)
Es póliza dotal (f)
Fr assurance à terme fixe (f)
It assicurazione dotale (f)
Pt título de doação (m)

**end-product** n En
De Endprodukt (n)
Es producto final (m)
Fr produit final (m)
It prodotto finale (m)
Pt produto final (m)

**Endprodukt** (n) n De
En end-product
Es producto final (m)
Fr produit final (m)
It prodotto finale (m)
Pt produto final (m)

**Endrechnung** (f) n De
En final invoice
Es factura final (f)
Fr facture finale (f)
It fattura finale (f)
Pt factura final (f)

**en el buque** Es
De ab Schiff
En ex ship
Fr ex ship
It ex ship
Pt ex-navio

**en el extranjero** Es
De im Ausland
En abroad
Fr à l'étranger
It all'estero
Pt no estrangeiro

**enemigo** (m) n Es
De Feind (m)
En enemy
Fr ennemi (m)
It nemico (m)
Pt inimigo (m)

**enemy** n En
De Feind (m)
Es enemigo (m)
Fr ennemi (m)
It nemico (m)
Pt inimigo (m)

**en entrepôt** Fr
De unter Zollverschluss
En in bond
Es en aduanas
It sotto vincolo doganale
Pt à ordem da alfândega

**en especie** Es
De in Waren
En in kind
Fr en nature
It in natura
Pt em espécie

**en état de navigabilité** Fr
De seefest
En seaworthy
Es marinero
It atto a tenere il mare
Pt em condições de nave-
  gação

**engage** (staff) vb En
Am hire
De anstellen
Es apalabrar
Fr engager
It fissare
Pt empregar

**engager** vb Fr
De anstellen
En engage
Am hire
Es apalabrar
It fissare
Pt empregar

**engañar** vb Es
De betrügen
En cheat
Fr tricher
It truffare
Pt enganar

**enganar** *vb* Pt
De betrügen
En cheat
Es engañar
Fr tricher
It truffare

**engarrafamento** *(m) n* Pt
De Engpass *(m)*
En bottle-neck
Es embotellamiento *(m)*
Fr goulot d'étranglement *(m)*
It strozzatura *(f)*

**engarrafamento de tráfico** *(m)*
Pt
De Verkehrsstockung *(f)*
En traffic jam
Es embotellamiento de tráfico
*(m)*
Fr encombrement de circu-
lation *(m)*
It ingorgo stradale *(m)*

**engenharia** *(f) n* Pt
De Maschinenbau *(m)*
En engineering
Es ingeniería *(f)*
Fr génie *(m)*
It ingegneria *(f)*

**engenharia civil** *(f)* Pt
De Ingenieurbau *(m)*
En civil engineering
Es ingeniería civil *(f)*
Fr génie civil *(m)*
It ingegneria civile *(f)*

**engenharia electrotécnica** *(f)*
Pt
De Elektrotechnik *(f)*
En electrical engineering
Es ingeniería eléctrica *(f)*
Fr construction électrique *(f)*
It elettrotecnica *(f)*

**engenharia mecânica** *(f)* Pt
De Maschinenbau *(m)*
En mechanical engineering
Es ingeniería mecánica *(f)*
Fr construction mécanique *(f)*
It ingegneria meccanica *(f)*

**engenharia química** *(f)* Pt
De Industriechemie *(f)*
En chemical engineering
Es ingeniería química *(f)*

Fr génie chimique *(m)*
It ingegneria chimica *(f)*

**engenheiro** *(m) n* Pt
De Ingenieur *(m)*
En engineer
Es ingeniero *(m)*
Fr ingénieur *(m)*
It ingegnere *(m)*

**engineer** *n* En
De Ingenieur *(m)*
Es ingeniero *(m)*
Fr ingénieur *(m)*
It ingegnere *(m)*
Pt engenheiro *(m)*

**engineering** *n* En
De Maschinenbau *(m)*
Es ingeniería *(f)*
Fr génie *(m)*
It ingegneria *(f)*
Pt engenharia *(f)*

**Engpass** *(m) n* De
En bottle-neck
Es embotellamiento *(m)*
Fr goulot d'étranglement *(m)*
It strozzatura *(f)*
Pt engarrafamento *(m)*

**engranaje** *(m) n* Es
De Getriebe *(n)*
En gearing
Fr engrenage *(m)*
It ingranaggio *(m)*
Pt engrenagem *(f)*

**engrenage** *(m) n* Fr
De Getriebe *(n)*
En gearing
Es engranaje *(m)*
It ingranaggio *(m)*
Pt engrenagem *(f)*

**engrenagem** *(f) n* Pt
De Getriebe *(n)*
En gearing
Es engranaje *(m)*
Fr engrenage *(m)*
It ingranaggio *(m)*

**en magasin** Fr
De vorrätig
En in stock
Es en almacén
It in magazzino
Pt em reserva

**en muelle** Es
De ab Kai
En ex quay
Fr à prendre sur quai
It sulla banchina
Pt ex-cais

**en nature** Fr
De in Waren
En in kind
Es en especie
It in natura
Pt em espécie

**ennemi** *(m) n* Fr
De Feind *(m)*
En enemy
Es enemigo *(m)*
It nemico *(m)*
Pt inimigo *(m)*

**en port dû** Fr
De Portonachnahme
En carriage forward
Am F.O.B. shipping point
Es a porte debido
It porto assegnato
Pt transporte a pagar

**en préstamo** Es
De darlehensweise
En on loan
Fr sous forme de prêt
It in prestito
Pt por empréstimo

**enquête** *(f) n* Fr
De Untersuchung *(f)*
En inquiry
Es encuesta *(f)*
It inchiesta *(f)*
Pt inquérito *(m)*

**enquête sur les lieux** *(f)* Fr
De Stellenüberblick *(m)*
En field study
Es estudio sobre el terreno
*(m)*
It studio sul terreno *(m)*
Pt estudo de campo *(m)*

**enregistrer** *vb* Fr
De registrieren
En register
Es registrar
It registrare
Pt registar

**ensaio** *(m)* n Pt
De Probe *(f)*
En test; trial
Es ensayo; prueba *(m f)*
Fr essai; épreuve *(m f)*
It saggio; prova *(m f)*

**ensayo** *(m)* n Es
De Probe *(f)*
En test; trial
Fr essai; épreuve *(m f)*
It saggio; prova *(m f)*
Pt ensaio; prova *(m f)*

**enseigne de convenance** *(f)* Fr
De billige Flagge *(f)*
En flag of convenience
Es bandera de conveniencia
*(f)*
It bandiera di convenienza *(f)*
Pt bandeira de conveniência
*(f)*

**enseignement supérieur** *(m)*
Fr
De Fortbildung *(f)*
En higher education
Es enseñanza superior *(f)*
It insegnamento superiore
*(m)*
Pt instrução superior *(f)*

**enseñanza superior** *(f)* Es
De Fortbildung *(f)*
En higher education
Fr enseignement supérieur
*(m)*
It insegnamento superiore
*(m)*
Pt instrução superior *(f)*

**en suspens** Fr
De in der Schwebe
En in abeyance
Es en suspenso
It in sospeso
Pt pendente

**en suspenso** Es
De in der Schwebe
En in abeyance
Fr en suspens
It in sospeso
Pt pendente

**Enteignung** *(f)* n De
En expropriation
Es expropiación *(f)*

Fr expropriation *(f)*
It espropriazione *(f)*
Pt expropriação *(f)*

**enterprise** n En
De Unternehmen *(n)*
Es negocio *(m)*
Fr entreprise *(f)*
It impresa *(f)*
Pt empresa *(f)*

**entertainment expenses** En
De Repräsentationskosten *(pl)*
Es gastos de representación
*(m pl)*
Fr frais de représentation *(m
pl)*
It spese di rappresentanza *(f
pl)*
Pt despesas de representação
*(f pl)*

**en-tête** *(m)* n Fr
De Briefkopf *(m)*
En letterhead
Es membrete *(m)*
It intestazione *(f)*
Pt cabeçalho *(m)*

**Entfernung** *(f)* n De
En distance
Es distancia *(f)*
Fr distance *(f)*
It distanza *(f)*
Pt distância *(f)*

**entgeltiger Besitzer** *(m)* De
En holder for value
Es tenedor legítimo *(m)*
Fr porteur à titre onéreux *(m)*
It detentore legittimo *(m)*
Pt proprietário legítimo *(m)*

**entlassen** *vb* De
En dismiss
Am fire
Es despedir
Fr congédier
It congedare
Pt despedir

**Entlassung** *(f)* n De
En dismissal
Am firing
Es despido *(m)*
Fr congédiement *(m)*
It licenziamento *(m)*
Pt despedimento *(m)*

**entlasteter Gemeinschuldner**
*(m)* De
En discharged bankrupt
Es fallido rehabilitado *(m)*
Fr failli réhabilité *(m)*
It fallito riabilitato *(m)*
Pt falido rehabilitado *(m)*

**entleihen** *vb* De
En borrow
Es pedir un préstamo
Fr emprunter
It prestire
Pt contrair empréstimo

**entrada** *(f)* n Es
De Eintritt *(m)*
En entry; admission
Fr entrée *(f)*
It entrata *(f)*
Pt admissão *(f)*

**entrada gratis** *(f)* Pt
De Eintritt frei *(m)*
En admission free
Es entrada gratuita *(f)*
Fr entrée gratuite *(f)*
It ingresso gratuito *(m)*

**entrada gratuita** *(f)* Es
De Eintritt frei *(m)*
En admission free
Fr entrée gratuite *(f)*
It ingresso gratuito *(m)*
Pt entrada gratis *(f)*

**entrance fee** En
De Eintrittsgebühr *(f)*
Es derecho de entrada *(m)*
Fr droit d'entrée *(m)*
It tassa d'entrata *(f)*
Pt taxa de admissão *(f)*

**en transit** Fr
De im Durchgangsverkehr
En in transit
Es en tránsito
It in transito
Pt em trânsito

**en tránsito** Es
De im Durchgangsverkehr
En in transit
Fr en transit
It in transito
Pt em trânsito

**entrare in vigore** It
De wirksam werden
En become operative
Es entrar en vigor
Fr entrer en vigueur
Pt entrar em vigor

**entrar em vigor** Pt
De wirksam werden
En become operative
Es entrar en vigor
Fr entrer en vigueur
It entrare in vigore

**entrar en vigor** Es
De wirksam werden
En become operative
Fr entrer en vigueur
It entrare in vigore
Pt entrar em vigor

**entrata** (ammissione) (f) n It
De Eintritt (m)
En entry; admission
Es entrada (f)
Fr entrée (f)
Pt admissão (f)

**entrata** (reddito) (f) n It
De Einkommen; Einkünfte (n; f pl)
En revenue
Es ingresos; rédito (m pl; m)
Fr revenu; rentes (m; f pl)
Pt rendimento (m)

**entrata netta** (f) It
De Nettoeinnahmen (f pl)
En net revenue
Es ingresos netos (m pl)
Fr recettes nettes (f pl)
Pt receita líquida (f)

**entredicho** (m) n Es
De gerichtliche Verfügung (f)
En injunction
Fr injonction; arrêt de suspension (f m)
It ingiunzione (f)
Pt interdição (f)

**entrée** (f) n Fr
De Eintritt (m)
En entry; admission
Es entrada (f)
It entrata (f)
Pt admissão (f)

**entrée gratuite** (f) Fr
De Eintritt frei (m)
En admission free
Es entrada gratuita (f)
It ingresso gratuito (m)
Pt entrada gratis (f)

**entrega** (f) n Es, Pt
De Lieferung (f)
En delivery
Fr livraison (f)
It consegna (f)

**entrega contra reembolso** Es, Pt
De Lieferung gegen Nachnahme
En cash on delivery (c.o.d.)
Fr paiement à la livraison
It pagamento alla consegna

**entrega deficiente** (f) Es
De mangelhafte Lieferung (f)
En short delivery
Fr livraison incomplète (f)
It consegna deficiente (f)
Pt entrega insuficiente (f)

**entrega futura** (f) Es, Pt
De Terminlieferung (f)
En forward delivery
Fr livraison à terme (f)
It consegna a termine (f)

**entrega imediata** (f) Pt
De sofortige Lieferung (f)
En prompt delivery
Es entrega inmediata (f)
Fr livraison immédiate (f)
It pronta consegna (f)

**entrega inmediata** (f) Es
De sofortige Lieferung (f)
En prompt delivery
Fr livraison immédiate (f)
It pronta consegna (f)
Pt entrega imediata (f)

**entrega insuficiente** (f) Pt
De mangelhafte Lieferung (f)
En short delivery
Es entrega deficiente (f)
Fr livraison incomplète (f)
It consegna deficiente (f)

**s'entremettre** vb Fr
De vermitteln
En mediate

Es intermediar
It fare da intermediario
Pt intermediar

**entrepôt** (m) n Fr
De Warenlager (n)
En warehouse
Es almacén (m)
It magazzino (m)
Pt armazém (m)

**entrepôt** (en douane) (m) n Fr
De Lager unter Zollverschluss (n)
En bonded warehouse
Es almacén de aduanas (m)
It magazzino doganale (m)
Pt armazém alfandegário (m)

**entrepreneur** n En
De Unternehmer (m)
Es empresario (m)
Fr entrepreneur (m)
It intraprenditore (m)
Pt empresário (m)

**entrepreneur** (m) n Fr
De Unternehmer (m)
En entrepreneur; contractor
Es empresario; contratista (m)
It intraprenditore; impresario (m)
Pt empresário; contractador (m)

**entrepreneur de bâtiment** (m) Fr
De Bauunternehmer (m)
En building contractor
Es contratista de obras (m)
It impresa edile (f)
Pt constructor de obras (m)

**entrepreneur de camionnage** (m) Fr
De Transportunternehmer (m)
En haulage contractor
Am trucking company
Es contratista de transportes (m)
It imprenditore di trasporti (m)
Pt empreiteiro de transportes (m)

**entreprise** (f) n Fr
De Unternehmen (n)
En enterprise

Es negocio (m)
It impresa (f)
Pt empresa (f)

**entreprise d'utilité publique**
(f) Fr
De gemeinnütziges Unternehmen (n)
En utility company
Es empresa de servicios públicos (f)
It società di servizi pubblici (f)
Pt empresa de utilidade pública (f)

**entreprise en participation** (f)
Fr
De Gemeinschaftsgründung (f)
En joint venture
Es empresa en común (f)
It impresa in compartecipazione (f)
Pt iniciativa em comum (f)

**entreprise privée** (f) Fr
De Privatunternehmen (n)
En private enterprise
Es empresa privada (f)
It impresa privata (f)
Pt empresa privada (f)

**entrer en vigueur** Fr
De wirksam werden
En become operative
Es entrar en vigor
It entrare in vigore
Pt entrar em vigor

**entretien** (m) n Fr
De Instandhaltung (f)
En maintenance
Es mantenimiento (m)
It manutenzione (f)
Pt manutenção (f)

**entrevista** (f) n Es, Pt
De Interview (n)
En interview
Fr interview; entrevue (f)
It intervista; abboccamento (f m)

**entrevistado** (m) n Pt
De Befragte(r) (m)
En interviewee
Es persona entrevistada (f)
Fr personne interrogée (f)
It intervistato (m)

**entrevistador** (m) n Es, Pt
De Interviewer (m)
En interviewer
Fr intervieweur; enquêteur (m)
It intervistatore (m)

**entrevue** (f) n Fr
De Verabredung; Interview (n)
En appointment; interview
Es entrevista (f)
It intervista (f)
Pt entrevista (f)

**entrust** vb En
De anvertrauen
Es confiar
Fr confier
It affidare
Pt confiar

**entry** (admission) n En
De Eintritt (m)
Es entrada (f)
Fr entrée (f)
It entrata (f)
Pt admissão (f)

**entry** (in book) n En
De Eintragung (f)
Es asiento (m)
Fr inscription (f)
It registrazione (f)
Pt lançamento (m)

**entry-form** n En
De Antragsformular (n)
Es solicitud de inscripción (f)
Fr feuille d'inscription (f)
It bolletta d'entrata (f)
Pt impresso de admissão (m)

**entschädigen** vb De
En indemnify
Es indemnizar; resarcir
Fr dédommager; indemniser
It indennizzare; risarcire
Pt indemnizar

**Entschädigung** (f) n De
En compensation; indemnity
Es compensación; indemnización (f)
Fr compensation; indemnité (f)
It compenso; indennità (m f)
Pt compensação; indemnização (f)

**entscheiden** vb De
En decide
Es decidir
Fr décider
It decidere
Pt decidir

**entscheidende Stimme** (f) De
En casting vote
Es voto decisivo (m)
Fr voix prépondérante (f)
It voto decisivo (m)
Pt voto decisivo (m)

**Entscheidung** (f) n De
En decision
Es decisión (f)
Fr décision (f)
It decisione (f)
Pt decisão (f)

**Entscheidungslehre** (f) De
En decision theory
Es teoría de la decisión (f)
Fr théorie de la décision (f)
It teoria della decisione (f)
Pt teoria de decisão (f)

**Entwerfer** (m) n De
En draughtsman
Es dibujante (m)
Fr dessinateur (m)
It disegnatore (m)
Pt desenhador (m)

**entwerten** vb De
En depreciate
Es depreciar
Fr déprécier
It deprezzare
Pt depreciar

**Entwertung** (f) n De
En depreciation
Es depreciación (f)
Fr dépréciation; amortissement (f m)
It ammortamento (m)
Pt depreciação; amortização (f)

**Entwicklung** (f) n De
En growth
Es crecimiento (m)
Fr croissance (f)
It crescita; sviluppo (f; m)
Pt crescimento (m)

**Entwicklungsland** *(n)* De
En developing country
Es pais en desarrollo *(m)*
Fr pays en voie de développement *(m)*
It paese in via di sviluppo *(m)*
Pt país em desenvolvimento *(m)*

**Entwurf** *(m) n* De
En plan
Es plan *(m)*
Fr projet *(m)*
It progetto *(m)*
Pt plano *(m)*

**envelope** *n* En, Pt *(m)*
De Umschlag *(m)*
Es sobre *(m)*
Fr enveloppe *(f)*
It busta *(f)*

**envelope de endereço exposto** *(m)* Pt
De Fensterbriefumschlag *(m)*
En window-envelope
Es sobre de ventanilla *(m)*
Fr enveloppe à fenêtre *(f)*
It busta con finestra *(f)*

**enveloppe** *(f) n* Fr
De Umschlag *(m)*
En envelope
Es sobre *(m)*
It busta *(f)*
Pt envelope *(m)*

**enveloppe à fenêtre** *(f)* Fr
De Fensterbriefumschlag *(m)*
En window-envelope
Es sobre de ventanilla *(m)*
It busta con finestra *(f)*
Pt envelope de endereço exposto *(m)*

**en vigor** Es
De in Kraft
En in force
Fr en vigueur
It in vigore
Pt vigente

**en vigueur** Fr
De in Kraft
En in force
Es en vigor
It in vigore
Pt vigente

**envío desde el punto de origen** *(m)* Es
De Versendung vom Ursprungsort *(f)*
En shipment from origin
Fr envoi du lieu de départ *(m)*
It spedizione dall´origine *(f)*
Pt carregamento desde a origem *(m)*

**envoi** *(m) n* Fr
De Versand; Versendung *(m f)*
En despatch; consignment
Es expedición; consignación *(f)*
It spedizione; consegna *(f)*
Pt remessa; consignação *(f)*

**envoi du lieu de départ** *(m)* Fr
De Versendung vom Ursprungsort *(f)*
En shipment from origin
Es envío desde el punto de origen *(m)*
It spedizione dall´origine *(f)*
Pt carregamento desde a origem *(m)*

**envoltura desechable** *(f)* Es
De wegwerfbare Verpackung *(f)*
En disposable wrapping
Fr emballage perdu *(m)*
It imballaggio a perdere *(m)*
Pt embalagem a destruir *(f)*

**envoyer** *vb* Fr
De expedieren; absenden
En send; forward
Es expedir; remitir
It spedire
Pt expedir; remeter

**en vrac** Fr
De in grosser Menge; unverpackt
En in bulk
Es a granel
It alla rinfusa
Pt a granel

**épargner** *vb* Fr
De aufsparen
En save
Es ahorrar; economizar
It risparmiare; economizzare
Pt poupar; economizar

**épreuve au hasard** *(f)* Fr
De Stichprobe *(f)*
En random sample
Es muestra aleatoria *(f)*
It campione a casaccio *(m)*
Pt amostra avulso *(f)*

**equalization fund** En
De Ausgleichsfonds *(m)*
Es fondo de compensación *(m)*
Fr fonds de régularisation *(m)*
It cassa di compensazione *(f)*
Pt fundo de compensação *(m)*

**equilibrar uma conta** Pt
De eine Rechnung ausgleichen
En balance an account
Es saldar una cuenta
Fr balancer un compte
It pareggiare un conto

**equilibrar um orçamento** Pt
De einen Haushaltsplan ins Gleichgewicht bringen
En balance a budget
Es balancear el presupuesto
Fr équilibrer un budget
It pareggiare un bilancio

**équilibre** *(m) n* Fr
De Gleichgewicht *(n)*
En equilibrium
Es equilibrio *(m)*
It equilibrio *(m)*
Pt equilíbrio *(m)*

**équilibrer un budget** Fr
De einen Haushaltsplan ins Gleichgewicht bringen
En balance a budget
Es balancear el presupuesto
It pareggiare un bilancio
Pt equilibrar um orçamento

**equilibrio** *(m) n* Es, It
De Gleichgewicht *(n)*
En equilibrium
Fr équilibre *(m)*
Pt equilíbrio *(m)*

**equilíbrio** *(m) n* Pt
De Gleichgewicht *(n)*
En equilibrium
Es equilibrio *(m)*
Fr équilibre *(m)*
It equilibrio *(m)*

**equilibrium** n En
De Gleichgewicht (n)
Es equilibrio (m)
Fr équilibre (m)
It equilibrio (m)
Pt equilíbrio (m)

**équipage** (m) n Fr
De Mannschaft (f)
En crew
Es tripulación (f)
It equipaggio (m)
Pt tripulação (f)

**equipaggiamento** (m) n It
De Ausrüstung (f)
En equipment
Es equipo (m)
Fr équipement (m)
Pt equipamento (m)

**equipaggio** (m) n It
De Mannschaft (f)
En crew
Es tripulación (f)
Fr équipage (m)
Pt tripulação (f)

**equipaje de mano** (m) Es
De Handgepäck (n)
En hand-luggage
Fr bagages à main (m pl)
It bagaglio a mano (m)
Pt bagagem de mão (f)

**equipamento** (m) n Pt
De Ausrüstung (f)
En equipment
Es equipo (m)
Fr équipement (m)
It equipaggiamento (m)

**équipe** (f) n Fr
De Schicht (f)
En shift
Es turno (m)
It turno (m)
Pt turno (m)

**équipe de nuit** (f) Fr
De Nachtschicht (f)
En night shift
Es turno de noche (m)
It turno di notte (m)
Pt turno da noite (m)

**équipe du jour** (f) Fr
De Tagschicht (f)
En day-shift
Es turno de día (m)
It turno di giorno (m)
Pt turno de dia (m)

**équipement** (m) n Fr
De Ausrüstung (f)
En equipment
Es equipo (m)
It equipaggiamento (m)
Pt equipamento (m)

**equipment** n En
De Ausrüstung (f)
Es equipo (m)
Fr équipement (m)
It equipaggiamento (m)
Pt equipamento (m)

**equipo** (m) n Es
De Ausrüstung (f)
En equipment
Fr équipement (m)
It equipaggiamento (m)
Pt equipamento (m)

**equitable** adj En
De billig
Es equitativo
Fr équitable
It equo
Pt equitativo

**équitable** adj Fr
De billig
En equitable
Es equitativo
It equo
Pt equitativo

**equitativo** adj Es, Pt
De billig
En equitable
Fr équitable
It equo

**equo** adj It
De billig
En equitable
Es equitativo
Fr équitable
Pt equitativo

**Erbe** (m) n De
En heir
Es heredero (m)

Fr héritier (m)
It erede (m)
Pt herdeiro (m)

**Erbschaft** (f) n De
En inheritance
Es herencia (f)
Fr succession (f)
It eredità (f)
Pt herança (f)

**Erbschaftssteuern** (f pl) n De
En death duties
Am estate taxes
Es derechos sucesorios (m pl)
Fr droits de succession (m pl)
It diritti di successione (m pl)
Pt impostos de sucessão (m pl)

**Erdgas** (n) n De
En natural gas
Es gas natural (m)
Fr gaz naturel (m)
It gas naturale (m)
Pt gás natural (m)

**Erdgeschoss** (n) n De
En ground floor
Es planta baja (f)
Fr rez-de-chaussée (m)
It pianterreno (m)
Pt rés-do-chão (m)

**erede** (m) n It
De Erbe (m)
En heir
Es heredero (m)
Fr héritier (m)
Pt herdeiro (m)

**eredità** (f) n It
De Erbschaft (f)
En inheritance
Es herencia (f)
Fr succession (f)
Pt herança (f)

**Erfindung** (f) n De
En invention
Es invento; invención (m f)
Fr invention (f)
It invenzione (f)
Pt invenção (f)

**Erfindungspatent** (n) n De
En patent
Es patente (f)

Fr  brevet d'invention *(m)*
It  brevetto *(m)*
Pt  patente *(f)*

**erfüllen** *vb* De
En  fulfil
Es  cumplir
Fr  remplir
It  adempiere
Pt  comprir

**Erfüllung** *(f)* n De
En  fulfilment
Es  cumplimiento *(m)*
Fr  accomplissement *(m)*
It  adempimento *(m)*
Pt  cumprimento *(m)*

**ergonomía** *(f)* n Es
De  Ergonomik *(f)*
En  ergonomics
Fr  ergonomie *(f)*
It  ergonomica *(f)*
Pt  ergonomia *(f)*

**ergonomia** *(f)* n Pt
De  Ergonomik *(f)*
En  ergonomics
Es  ergonomía *(f)*
Fr  ergonomie *(f)*
It  ergonomica *(f)*

**ergonomica** *(f)* n It
De  Ergonomik *(f)*
En  ergonomics
Es  ergonomía *(f)*
Fr  ergonomie *(f)*
Pt  ergonomia *(f)*

**ergonomics** n En
De  Ergonomik *(f)*
Es  ergonomía *(f)*
Fr  ergonomie *(f)*
It  ergonomica *(f)*
Pt  ergonomia *(f)*

**ergonomie** *(f)* n Fr
De  Ergonomik *(f)*
En  ergonomics
Es  ergonomía *(f)*
It  ergonomica *(f)*
Pt  ergonomia *(f)*

**Ergonomik** *(f)* n De
En  ergonomics
Es  ergonomía *(f)*
Fr  ergonomie *(f)*

It  ergonomica *(f)*
Pt  ergonomia *(f)*

**Erhebung** *(f)* n De
En  levy
Es  impuesto *(m)*
Fr  prélèvement *(m)*
It  imposta *(f)*
Pt  imposto *(m)*

**erhöhte Kosten** *(pl)* De
En  increased costs
Es  costes incrementados *(m pl)*
Fr  accroissement des coûts *(m)*
It  costi aumentati *(m pl)*
Pt  custos aumentados *(m pl)*

**Erhöhung** (Preise) *(f)* n De
En  advance in price
Es  encarecimiento *(m)*
Fr  renchérissement *(m)*
It  rialzo *(m)*
Pt  encarecimento *(m)*

**erklären** *vb* De
En  declare
Es  declarar
Fr  déclarer
It  dichiarare
Pt  declarar

**Erklärung** *(f)* n De
En  declaration
Es  declaración *(f)*
Fr  déclaration *(f)*
It  dichiarazione *(f)*
Pt  declaração *(f)*

**Erlaubnis** *(f)* n De
En  permit; licence
Es  permiso; licencia *(m f)*
Fr  permis; licence *(m f)*
It  permesso; licenza *(m f)*
Pt  autorização; licença *(f)*

**Erlebensversicherung** *(f)* n De
En  endowment policy
Es  póliza dotal *(f)*
Fr  assurance à terme fixe *(f)*
It  assicurazione dotale *(f)*
Pt  título de doação *(m)*

**erloschene Gesellschaft** *(f)* De
En  defunct company
Es  sociedad extinta *(f)*
Fr  société liquidée *(f)*

It  società estinta *(f)*
Pt  empresa extinta *(f)*

**ernennen** *vb* De
En  appoint
Es  nombrar
Fr  nommer
It  nominare
Pt  nomear

**Ernte** *(f)* n De
En  harvest
Es  cosecha *(f)*
Fr  moisson; récolte *(f)*
It  raccolto *(m)*
Pt  colheita *(f)*

**erreur** *(f)* n Fr
De  Fehler *(m)*
En  error
Es  error *(m)*
It  errore *(m)*
Pt  erro *(m)*

**erreur de calcul** *(f)* Fr
De  Rechenfehler *(m)*
En  miscalculation
Es  cálculo erróneo *(m)*
It  calcolo errato *(m)*
Pt  erro de cálculo *(m)*

**erro** *(m)* n Pt
De  Fehler *(m)*
En  error
Es  error *(m)*
Fr  erreur *(f)*
It  errore *(m)*

**erro de cálculo** *(m)* Pt
De  Rechenfehler *(m)*
En  miscalculation
Es  cálculo erróneo *(m)*
Fr  erreur de calcul *(f)*
It  calcolo errato *(m)*

**error** n En, Es *(m)*
De  Fehler *(m)*
Fr  erreur *(f)*
It  errore *(m)*
Pt  erró *(m)*

**errore** *(m)* n It
De  Fehler *(m)*
En  error
Es  error *(m)*
Fr  erreur *(f)*
Pt  erro *(m)*

**Ersatz immateriellen Schadens** *(m)* De
En special damages
Es daños especiales *(m pl)*
Fr dommages indirects *(m pl)*
It danni particolari *(m pl)*
Pt indemnização especial *(f)*

**Erschliessung** *(f)* n De
En development
Es explotación *(f)*
Fr exploitation; lotissement *(f m)*
It valorizzazione *(f)*
Pt exploração *(f)*

**Ersetzung** *(f)* n De
En subrogation
Es subrogación *(f)*
Fr subrogation *(f)*
It surrogazione *(f)*
Pt sub-rogação *(f)*

**erste Klasse** *(f)* De
En first class
Es primera clase *(f)*
Fr première classe *(f)*
It prima classe *(f)*
Pt primeira classe *(f)*

**erstklassig** *adj* De
En first-class
Es de primera orden
Fr de première qualité
It di qualità superiore
Pt de primeira ordem

**erstklassiger Handelswechsel** *(m)* De
En prime trade bill
Es carta comercial de primera orden *(f)*
Fr papier de haut commerce *(m)*
It carta commerciale di primo ordine *(f)*
Pt estatuto de comercialização de primeira ordem *(m)*

**Erteilung (eines Patentes)** *(f)* De
En grant (of a patent)
Es concesión (de una patente) *(f)*
Fr délivrance (d'un brevet) *(f)*
It concessione (di brevetto) *(f)*

Pt concessão (de uma patente) *(f)*

**Ertragsrate** *(f)* n De
En rate of return
Es tipo de rédito *(m)*
Fr taux de rendement *(m)*
It tasso di reddito *(m)*
Pt taxa de rendimento *(f)*

**Erwerb** *(m)* n De
En acquisition
Es adquisición *(f)*
Fr acquisition *(f)*
It acquisizione *(f)*
Pt aquisição *(f)*

**Erzeuger** *(m)* n De
En manufacturer
Es fabricante *(m)*
Fr fabricant *(m)*
It fabbricante *(m)*
Pt fabricante *(m)*

**Erzeugnis** *(f)* n De
En produce
Es producto *(m)*
Fr produit *(m)*
It prodotto *(m)*
Pt produto *(m)*

**Erzeugung** *(f)* n De
En production
Es producción *(f)*
Fr production *(f)*
It produzione *(f)*
Pt produção *(f)*

**esame più attento** *(m)* It
De Weiterüberlegung *(f)*
En further consideration
Es examen más detallado *(m)*
Fr examen plus attentif *(m)*
Pt consideração mais detalhada *(f)*

**esaminare** *vb* It
De untersuchen
En examine
Es examinar
Fr examiner
Pt examinar

**esattore delle imposte** *(m)* It
De Steuereinnehmer *(m)*
En tax collector
Es recaudador de impuestos *(m)*

Fr percepteur des impôts *(m)*
Pt cobrador de impostos *(m)*

**esaurito** *adj* It
De ausverkauft
En out of stock
Es stock agotado
Fr tout vendu
Pt esgotado

**esborso** *(m)* n It
De Auszahlung *(f)*
En disbursement
Es desembolso *(m)*
Fr déboursement *(m)*
Pt desembolso *(m)*

**escala** *(f)* n Es, Pt
De Masstab *(m)*
En scale
Fr échelle *(f)*
It scala *(f)*

**escala móvel** *(f)* Pt
De gleitende Skala *(f)*
En sliding scale
Es escala móvil *(f)*
Fr échelle mobile *(f)*
It scala mobile *(f)*

**escala móvil** *(f)* Es
De gleitende Skala *(f)*
En sliding scale
Fr échelle mobile *(f)*
It scala mobile *(f)*
Pt escala móvel *(f)*

**escalator clause** En
De Gleitklausel *(f)*
Es cláusula de revisión de precios *(f)*
Fr échelle mobile *(f)*
It scala mobile *(f)*
Pt cláusula de actualização de preços *(f)*

**escape** *(m)* n Es, Pt
De Lecken *(n)*
En leakage
Fr fuite *(f)*
It colaggio *(m)*

**escape clause** En
De Rücktrittsklausel *(f)*
Es cláusula evasiva *(f)*
Fr clause de résiliation *(f)*
It clausola risolutiva *(f)*
Pt cláusula de evasão *(f)*

**escasez** *(f) n* Es
De  Knappheit *(f)*
En  short supply
Fr  disette *(f)*
It  scarsezza *(f)*
Pt  escassez *(f)*

**escasez de créditos** *(f)* Es
De  Kreditklemme *(f)*
En  credit squeeze
Fr  resserrement de crédit *(m)*
It  restrizione di credito *(f)*
Pt  restrição de crédito *(f)*

**escassez** *(f) n* Pt
De  Knappheit *(f)*
En  short supply
Es  escasez *(f)*
Fr  disette *(f)*
It  scarsezza *(f)*

**escludere** *vb* It
De  ausschliessen
En  exclude
Es  excluir
Fr  exclure
Pt  excluir

**esclusione** *(f) n* It
De  Ausschluss *(m)*
En  exclusion
Es  exclusión *(f)*
Fr  exclusion *(f)*
Pt  exclusão *(f)*

**escompte** *(m) n* Fr
De  Skonto *(m)*
En  discount
Es  descuento *(m)*
It  sconto; ribasso *(m)*
Pt  desconto *(m)*

**escompte de caisse** *(m)* Fr
De  Barrabatt *(m)*
En  cash discount
Es  descuento de caja *(m)*
It  sconto per pagamento a
    contanti *(m)*
Pt  desconto de contado *(m)*

**escompte en dehors** *(m)* Fr
De  Diskont *(m)*
En  bank discount
Es  descuento bancario *(m)*
It  sconto di banca *(m)*
Pt  desconto bancário *(m)*

**esconderse** *vb* Es
De  sich heimlich davonmachen
En  abscond
Fr  s´enfuir; décamper
It  nascondersi
Pt  ausentar-se para parte
    incerta

**escrever à máquina** Pt
De  auf der Schreibmaschine
    schreiben
En  type
Es  escribir a máquina
Fr  écrire à la machine
It  scrivere a macchina

**escribir a máquina** Es
De  auf der Schreibmaschine
    schreiben
En  type
Fr  écrire à la machine
It  scrivere a macchina
Pt  escrever à máquina

**escritório** *(m) n* Pt
De  Büro *(n)*
En  office
Es  oficina *(f)*
Fr  bureau *(m)*
It  ufficio *(m)*

**escritório sem divisões** *(m)* Pt
De  Grossraumbüro *(n)*
En  open-plan office
Es  oficina sin particiones *(f)*
Fr  bureau sans cloisons *(m)*
It  ufficio senza divisioni *(m)*

**escritura de acordo** *(f)* Pt
De  Vergleichsabkommen *(n)*
En  deed of arrangement
Es  acta de disposición *(f)*
Fr  contrat d´arrangement *(m)*
It  atto di accordo *(m)*

**escritura de sociedade** *(f)* Pt
De  Gesellschaftsvertrag *(m)*
En  articles of association
Am  articles of incorporation
Es  artículos de asociación *(m
    pl)*
Fr  contrat de société *(m)*
It  statuto sociale *(m)*

**escritura de transferencia** *(f)*
    Es
De  Übertragungsvertrag *(m)*
En  transfer deed

Fr  acte de cession *(m)*
It  atto di trapasso *(m)*
Pt  título de transferência *(m)*

**escritura de venda** *(f)* Pt
De  Kaufvertrag *(m)*
En  bill of sale
Es  escritura de venta *(f)*
Fr  acte de vente *(f)*
It  contratto di vendita *(m)*

**escritura de venta** *(f)* Es
De  Kaufvertrag *(m)*
En  bill of sale
Fr  acte de vente *(f)*
It  contratto di vendita *(m)*
Pt  escritura de venda *(f)*

**esecutore** *(m) n* It
De  Vollstrecker *(m)*
En  executor
Es  albacea *(m)*
Fr  exécuteur *(m)*
Pt  executor *(m)*

**esecuzione** *(f) n* It
De  Vollstreckung *(f)*
En  execution
Es  ejecución *(f)*
Fr  exécution *(f)*
Pt  desempenho *(m)*

**eseguire** *vb* It
De  vollstrecken
En  execute
Es  ejecutar
Fr  exécuter
Pt  executar

**eseguire un testamento** It
De  ein Testament vollstrecken
En  execute a will
Es  ejecutar un testamento
Fr  exécuter un testament
Pt  dar execução a um testa-
    mento

**esente da dazio** It
De  abgabenfrei
En  duty-free
Es  exento de impuestos
Fr  exempt de douane
Pt  isento de impostos

**esente di tassa** It
De  steuerfrei
En  tax-free
Es  exento de impuestos

Fr exempt d'impôts
Pt isento de impostos

**esenzione** (f) n It
De Befreiung (f)
En exemption
Es exención (f)
Fr exemption (f)
Pt isenção (f)

**esercizio** (m) n It
De Geschäftsjahr (n)
En financial year
Es ejercicio (m)
Fr exercice (m)
Pt ano financeiro (m)

**esgotado** adj Pt
De ausverkauft
En sold out
Es agotado
Fr tout vendu
It tutto venduto

**esorbitante** adj It
De unmässig
En exorbitant
Es exorbitante
Fr exorbitant
Pt exorbitante

**espèces** (f pl) n Fr
De Bargeld (n)
En cash
Es dinero efectivo (m)
It denaro contante (m)
Pt dinheiro de contado (m)

**espèces en caisse** (f pl) Fr
De Barbestand (m)
En cash in hand
Es efectivo en caja (m)
It pronti contanti (m pl)
Pt fundos à ordem (m pl)

**especialista** (m) n Es, Pt
De Sachverständige(r) (m)
En specialist
Fr expert (m)
It specialista (m)

**especificação de obra** (f) Pt
De Arbeitsaufgabe (f)
En job specification
Es especificación del trabajo (f)
Fr donnée d'exécution (f)
It specifica del lavoro (f)

**especificación del trabajo** (f) Es
De Arbeitsaufgabe (f)
En job specification
Fr donnée d'exécution (f)
It specifica del lavoro (f)
Pt especificação de obra (f)

**especular** vb Es, Pt
De spekulieren
En speculate; job
Fr spéculer
It speculare

**espere al aparato** Es
De am Apparat bleiben
En hold the line
Fr ne quittez pas
It resta in linea
Pt aguarde

**espionage industriel** (m) Fr
De Wirtschaftsspionage (f)
En industrial espionage
Es espionaje industrial (m)
It spionaggio industriale (m)
Pt espionagem industrial (m)

**espionagem industrial** (m) Pt
De Wirtschaftsspionage (f)
En industrial espionage
Es espionaje industrial (m)
Fr espionage industriel (m)
It spionaggio industriale (m)

**espionaje industrial** (m) Es
De Wirtschaftsspionage (f)
En industrial espionage
Fr espionage industriel (m)
It spionaggio industriale (m)
Pt espionagem industrial (m)

**espiral de inflación** (f) Es
De Inflationsspirale (f)
En inflationary spiral
Fr spirale inflationniste (f)
It inflazione a spirale (f)
Pt espiral inflacionária (f)

**espiral inflacionária** (f) Pt
De Inflationsspirale (f)
En inflationary spiral
Es espiral de inflación (f)
Fr spirale inflationniste (f)
It inflazione a spirale (f)

**esponenziale** adj It
De Exponential-
En exponential
Es exponencial
Fr exponentiel
Pt exponencial

**esportare** vb It
De ausführen
En export
Es exportar
Fr exporter
Pt exportar

**esportatore** (m) n It
De Exporteur (m)
En exporter
Es exportador
Fr exportateur (m)
Pt exportador (m)

**esportazioni invisibili** (f pl) It
De unsichtbare Exporte (m pl)
En invisible exports
Es exportaciones invisibles (f pl)
Fr exportations invisibles (f pl)
Pt exportações invisíveis (f pl)

**espositore** (m) n It
De Aussteller (m)
En exhibitor
Es exhibidor (m)
Fr exposant (m)
Pt expositor (m)

**esposizione** (f) n It
De Ausstellung (f)
En exhibition
Es exposicion (f)
Fr exposition (f)
Pt exposição (f)

**espropriazione** (f) n It
De Enteignung (f)
En expropriation
Es expropiación (f)
Fr expropriation (f)
Pt expropriação (f)

**essai** (m) n Fr
De Probe (f)
En test; trial
Es ensayo; prueba (m f)
It saggio; prova (m f)
Pt ensaio; prova (m f)

**essai gratuit** *(m)* Fr
De kostenlose Probe *(f)*
En free trial
Es prueba gratuita *(f)*
It prova gratuita *(f)*
Pt prova gratuita *(f)*

**essentiel** *adj* Fr
De wesentlich
En material
Es material
It materiale
Pt material

**essere in disaccordo** It
De nicht übereinstimmen
En disagree
Es no estar de acuerdo
Fr être en désaccord
Pt discordar

**Esswaren** *(f pl)* n De
En foodstuffs
Es comestibles *(m pl)*
Fr alimentation *(f)*
It generi alimentari *(m pl)*
Pt géneros alimentícios *(m pl)*

**estabelecer** *vb* Pt
De gründen
En form; establish
Es establecer; formar
Fr former
It formare

**establecer** *vb* Es
De gründen
En form; establish
Fr former
It formare
Pt estabelecer

**establish** (a business, etc.) *vb*
En
De einrichten
Es fundar; establecer
Fr fonder; établir
It fondare; istituire
Pt fundar; estabelecer

**establish** (proof, etc.) *vb* En
De beweisen
Es demostrar; probar
Fr démontrer
It dimostrare; provare
Pt demonstrar; provar

**estação** *(f)* n Pt
De Jahreszeit *(f)*
En season
Es estación *(f)*
Fr saison *(f)*
It stagione *(f)*

**estação de correios** *(f)* Pt
De Postamt *(n)*
En post office
Es oficina de correos *(f)*
Fr bureau de poste *(m)*
It ufficio postale *(m)*

**estação terminal aérea** *(f)* Pt
De Luftterminal *(n)*
En air terminal
Es terminal de aeropuerto *(f)*
Fr aérogare *(f)*
It aerostazione *(f)*

**estación** *(f)* n Es
De Jahreszeit *(f)*
En season
Fr saison *(f)*
It stagione *(f)*
Pt estação *(f)*

**estadía** *(f)* n Es, Pt
De Liegezeit *(f)*
En lay days
Fr staries *(f pl)*
It stallie *(f pl)*

**estadística** *(f)* n Es
De Statistik *(f)*
En statistics
Fr statistique *(f)*
It statistica *(f)*
Pt estatística *(f)*

**estafar** *vb* Es
De schwindeln
En swindle
Fr filouter
It truffare
Pt enganar

**estaleiro** *(m)* n Pt
De Schiffswerft *(f)*
En dockyard
Es astillero *(m)*
Fr chantier de construction de navires *(m)*
It cantiere *(m)*

**estampilla** *(f)* n Es
De Stempel *(m)*
En (rubber) stamp
Fr tampon; timbre *(m)*
It stampiglia *(f)*
Pt carimbo *(m)*

**estate** (property) n En
De Vermögen *(n)*
Es finca *(f)*
Fr bien; propriété *(m; f)*
It proprietà *(f)*
Pt bens; propriedade *(m pl; m)*

**estate** (after death) n En
De Nachlass *(m)*
Es sucesión; herencia *(f)*
Fr succession *(f)*
It patrimonio; successione *(m f)*
Pt património; herança *(m f)*

**estate agency** En
Am real estate agency
De Immobilienbüro *(n)*
Es correduría de fincas *(f)*
Fr agence immobilière *(f)*
It agenzia immobiliare *(f)*
Pt agência de propriedades *(f)*

**estate duty** En
Am estate tax
De Nachlassteuer *(f)*
Es derechos de sucesión *(m pl)*
Fr droits de succession *(m pl)*
It diritti di successione *(m pl)*
Pt direitos de sucessão *(m pl)*

**estatística** *(f)* n Pt
De Statistik *(f)*
En statistics
Es estadística *(f)*
Fr statistique *(f)*
It statistica *(f)*

**estatutario** *adj* Es
De gesetzlich
En statutory
Fr statutaire
It statuario
Pt estatutário

**estatutário** *adj* Pt
De gesetzlich
En statutory
Es estatutario

Fr statutaire
It statuario

**estatuto** (m) n Es, Pt
De Gesetz (n)
En statute
Fr statut (m)
It statuto (m)

**estatuto de associação** (m) Pt
De Statuten (f pl)
En Memorandum and Articles
of Association
Am articles of incorporation
Es estatutos; carta orgánica
(m pl; f)
Fr statuts; acte constitutif (m
pl; m)
It atto costitutivo e statuto
sociale (m)

**estatuto de comercialização
de primeira ordem** (m) Pt
De erstklassiger Handelswechsel (m)
En prime trade bill
Es carta comercial de primera
orden (f)
Fr papier de haut commerce
(m)
It carta commerciale di primo
ordine (f)

**estatutos** (m pl) Es
De Statuten (f pl)
En Memorandum and Articles
of Association
Am articles of incorporation
Fr statuts; acte constitutif (m
pl; m)
It atto costitutivo e statuto
sociale (m)
Pt estatuto de associação (m)

**estenodactilógrafa** (f) n Pt
De Stenotypistin (f)
En shorthand typist
Es taquimecanógrafa (f)
Fr sténodactylographe (f)
It stenodattilografa (f)

**estenografia** (f) n Pt
De Kurzschrift (f)
En shorthand
Es taquigrafía (f)
Fr sténographie (f)
It stenografia (f)

**esterlina verde** (f) Es
De grünes Pfund (n)
En green pound
Fr livre sterling verte (f)
It sterlina verde (f)
Pt libra esterlina verde (f)

**estiba** (f) n Es
De Verstauung (f)
En stowage
Fr arrimage (m)
It stivaggio (m)
Pt estiva (f)

**estibar** vb Es
De verstauen
En stow
Fr arrimer
It stivare
Pt estivar

**estimar** vb Es
De einschätzen
En estimate
Fr estimer
It stimare
Pt avaliar

**estimate** vb En
De einschätzen
Es estimar
Fr estimer
It stimare
Pt avaliar

**estimate** n En
De Voranschlag (m)
Es presupuesto (m)
Fr devis (m)
It preventivo (m)
Pt previsão (f)

**estimation approximative** (f)
Fr
De rohe Schätzung (f)
En rough estimate
Es presupuesto aproximado
(m)
It valutazione approssimativa
(f)
Pt avaliação aproximada (f)

**estimativa revista** (f) Pt
De überarbeitete Schätzung (f)
En revised estimate
Es cálculo revisado (m)
Fr devis rectifié (m)
It preventivo riveduto (m)

**estimativa suplementar** (f) Pt
De Nachschätzung (f)
En supplementary estimate
Es cálculo suplementario (m)
Fr devis supplémentaire (f)
It preventivo supplementare
(m)

**estimer** vb Fr
De einschätzen
En estimate
Es estimar
It stimare
Pt avaliar

**estímulo** (m) n Es
De Anreiz (m)
En incentive
Fr incitation; stimulant (f m)
It incentivo (m)
Pt incentivo (m)

**estímulo de exportación** (m)
Es
De Ausfuhranreiz (m)
En export incentive
Fr motif d'exportation (m)
It incentivo alla esportazione
(m)
Pt incentivo para a exportação
(m)

**estinguere un debito** It
De eine Schuld begleichen
En discharge a debt
Es descargar una deuda
Fr acquitter une dette
Pt cancelar uma dívida

**estiva** (f) n Pt
De Verstauung (f)
En stowage
Es estiba (f)
Fr arrimage (m)
It stivaggio (m)

**estivar** vb Pt
De verstauen
En stow
Es estibar
Fr arrimer
It stivare

**estrangeiro** adj Pt
De ausländisch; fremd
En foreign; alien
Es extranjero

Fr étranger
It straniero; estero

**estrangeiro** *(m)* n Pt
De Ausländer *(m)*
En foreigner
Es extranjero *(m)*
Fr étranger *(m)*
It straniero *(m)*

**estrapolare** *vb* It
De extrapolieren
En extrapolate
Es extrapolar
Fr extrapoler
Pt extrapolar

**estratto conto** *(m)* It
De Kontoauszug *(m)*
En statement of account
Es extracto de cuenta *(m)*
Fr relevé de compte *(m)*
Pt extracto de conta *(m)*

**estudio del trabajo** *(m)* Es
De Arbeitsstudium *(n)*
En work study
Fr étude du travail *(f)*
It studio di lavoro *(m)*
Pt estudo sobre trabalho *(m)*

**estudio de tiempo y progreso**
*(m)* Es
De Arbeitszeit- und Ablaufstudie *(f)*
En time and motion study
Fr étude du temps et mouvements *(f)*
It studio dei tempi e dei
movimenti *(m)*
Pt análise do tempo e progresso *(f)*

**estudio de viabilidad** *(m)* Es
De Durchführbarkeitanalyse *(f)*
En feasibility study
Fr étude probatoire *(f)*
It studio delle possibilità *(m)*
Pt estudo de viabilidade *(m)*

**estudio sobre el terreno** *(m)*
Es
De Stellenüberblick *(m)*
En field study
Fr enquête sur les lieux *(f)*
It studio sul terreno *(m)*
Pt estudo de campo *(m)*

**estudo de campo** *(m)* Pt
De Stellenüberblick *(m)*
En field study
Es estudio sobre el terreno
*(m)*
Fr enquête sur les lieux *(f)*
It studio sul terreno *(m)*

**estudo de viabilidade** *(m)* Pt
De Durchführbarkeitanalyse *(f)*
En feasibility study
Es estudio de viabilidad *(m)*
Fr étude probatoire *(f)*
It studio delle possibilità *(m)*

**estudo sobre trabalho** *(m)* Pt
De Arbeitsstudium *(n)*
En work study
Es estudio del trabajo *(m)*
Fr étude du travail *(f)*
It studio di lavoro *(m)*

**Etagenwohnung** *(f)* n De
En flat
Am apartment
Es apartamento *(m)*
Fr appartement *(m)*
It appartamento *(m)*
Pt apartamento *(m)*

**Etagenwohnung mit Bedien-
ung** *(f)* De
En service flat
Es piso con servicio incluido
*(m)*
Fr appartement avec service
*(m)*
It appartamento con servizio
*(m)*
Pt andar com serviço incluido
*(m)*

**étalage** *(m)* n Fr
De Fensterauslegung *(f)*
En window-display
Es exhibición en vitrina *(f)*
It mostra in vetrina *(f)*
Pt exposição de montra *(f)*

**étalon or** *(m)* n Fr
De Goldobligation *(f)*
En gold standard
Es patrón oro *(m)*
It base aurea *(f)*
Pt ouro-padrão *(m)*

**état de finances** *(m)* Fr
De Finanzausweis *(m)*
En financial statement
Es extracto financiero *(m)*
It relazione finanziaria *(f)*
Pt extracto financeiro *(m)*

**état du marché** *(m)* Fr
De Marktumständen *(m pl)*
En state of the market
Es condiciones del mercado *(f
pl)*
It condizioni del mercato *(f
pl)*
Pt situação do mercado *(f)*

**etichetta** *(f)* n It
De Etikett *(n)*
En label
Es etiqueta *(f)*
Fr étiquette *(f)*
Pt rótulo; etiqueta *(m f)*

**Etikett** *(n)* n De
En label
Es etiqueta *(f)*
Fr étiquette *(f)*
It etichetta *(f)*
Pt rótulo; etiqueta *(m f)*

**etiqueta** *(f)* n Es, Pt
De Etikett *(n)*
En label
Fr étiquette *(f)*
It etichetta *(f)*

**étiquette** *(f)* n Fr
De Etikett *(n)*
En label
Es etiqueta *(f)*
It etichetta *(f)*
Pt rótulo; etiqueta *(m f)*

**étoffe** *(f)* n Fr
De Stoff *(m)*
En material; cloth
Es tejido *(m)*
It stoffa; tessuto *(f m)*
Pt tecido *(m)*

**étranger** *adj* Fr
De ausländisch; fremd
En foreign; alien
Es extranjero
It straniero; estero
Pt estrangeiro

**étranger** (m) n Fr
De Ausländer (m)
En foreigner
Es extranjero (m)
It straniero (m)
Pt estrangeiro (m)

**être en désaccord** Fr
De nicht übereinstimmen
En disagree
Es no estar de acuerdo
It essere in disaccordo
Pt discordar

**étude de motivation** (f) Fr
De Motivforschung (f)
En motivational research
Es investigación de motivación (f)
It indagine sulle motivazioni (f)
Pt investigação sobre motivação (f)

**étude du marché** (f) Fr
De Marktforschung (f)
En market research
Es investigación del mercado (f)
It indagine di mercato (f)
Pt pesquisa de mercado (f)

**.étude du temps et mouvements** (f) Fr
De Arbeitszeit- und Ablaufstudie (f)
En time and motion study
Es estudio de tiempo y progreso (m)
It studio dei tempi e dei movimenti (m)
Pt análise do tempo e progresso (f)

**étude du travail** (f) Fr
De Arbeitsstudium (n)
En work study
Es estudio del trabajo (m)
It studio di lavoro (m)
Pt estudo sobre trabalho (m)

**étude probatoire** (f) Fr
De Durchführbarkeitanalyse (f)
En feasibility study
Es estudio de viabilidad (m)
It studio delle possibilità (m)
Pt estudo de viabilidade (m)

**Europäische Atomgemeinschaft** (f) De
En European Atomic Energy Community
Es Comunidad Europea de Energía Atómica (f)
Fr Communauté Européenne de l'Energie Atomique (f)
It Comunità Europea dell'Energia Atomica (f)
Pt Comunidade Europeia de Energia Atómica (f)

**Europäischer Fonds** (m) De
En European Fund
Es Fondo Europeo (m)
Fr Fonds Européen (m)
It Fondo Europeo (m)
Pt Fundo Europeu (m)

**Europäische Gemeinschaft für Kohle und Stahl** (f) De
En European Coal & Steel Community
Es Comunidad Europea de Carbón y Acero (f)
Fr Communauté Européenne du Charbon et de l'Acier (f)
It Comunità Europea del Carbone e Acciaio (f)
Pt Comunidade Europeia do Carrão e do Aço (f)

**Europäische Investitionsbank** (f) De
En European Investment Bank
Es Banco Europeo de Inversiones (m)
Fr Banque Européenne d'Investissement (f)
It Banca Europea d'Investimenti (f)
Pt Banco Europeu de Investimentos (m)

**Europäische Kommission** (f) De
En European Commission
Es Comisión Europea (f)
Fr Commission des Communautés Européennes (f)
It Commissione Europea (f)
Pt Comissão Europeia (f)

**Europäisches Währungsabkommen (EWA)** (n) De
En European Monetary Agreement
Es Acuerdo Monetario Europeo (AME) (m)
Fr Accord Monétaire Européen (AME) (m)
It Accordo Monetario Europeo (AME) (m)
Pt Acuerdo Monetário Europeu (AME) (m)

**Europäische Wirtschaftsgemeinschaft** (f) De
En European Economic Community
Es Comunidad Económica Europea (f)
Fr Communauté Économique Européenne (f)
It Comunità Economica Europea (f)
Pt Comunidade Económica Europeia (f)

**European Atomic Energy Community** En
De Europäische Atomgemeinschaft (f)
Es Comunidad Europea de Energía Atómica (f)
Fr Communauté Européenne de l'Energie Atomique (f)
It Comunità Europea dell'Energia Atomica (f)
Pt Comunidade Europeia de Energia Atómica (f)

**European Commission** En
De Europäische Kommission (f)
Es Comisión Europea (f)
Fr Commission des Communautés Européennes (f)
It Commissione Europea (f)
Pt Comissão Europeia (f)

**European Economic Community** En
De Europäische Wirtschaftsgemeinschaft (f)
Es Comunidad Económica Europea (f)
Fr Communauté Économique Européenne (f)
It Comunità Economica Europea (f)

Pt Comunidade Económica
   Europeia (f)

**European Free Trade Area**
(EFTA) En
De Europäische Freihandels-
   zone (f)
Es Zona Europea de Comercio
   Libre (f)
Fr Zone Européenne de Libre
   Échange (f)
It Zona Europea di Libero
   Scambio (f)
Pt Zona Europeia de Comér-
   cio Livre (f)

**European Fund** En
De Europäischer Fonds (m)
Es Fondo Europeo (m)
Fr Fonds Européen (m)
It Fondo Europeo (m)
Pt Fundo Europeu (m)

**European Investment Bank**
En
De Europäische Investitions-
   bank (f)
Es Banco Europeo de Inver-
   siones (m)
Fr Banque Européenne d'Inve-
   stissement (f)
It Banca Europea d'Investi-
   menti (f)
Pt Banco Europeu de Investi-
   mentos (m)

**European Monetary Agree-
ment** En
De Europäisches Währungs-
   abkommen (EWA) (n)
Es Acuerdo Monetario Europeo (AME) (m)
Fr Accord Monétaire Euro-
   péen (AME) (m)
It Accordo Monetario Europeo (AME) (m)
Pt Acuerdo Monetário Europeu (AME) (m)

**evaluación** (f) n Es
De Abschätzung (f)
En appraisal
Fr évaluation (f)
It valutazione (f)
Pt avaliação (f)

**evaluar** vb Es
De bewerten
En evaluate
Fr évaluer
It valutare
Pt avaliar

**evaluar daños** Es
De den Schadenersatzbetrag
   feststellen
En assess damages
Fr fixer des dommages-intér-
   êts
It valutare i danni
Pt avaliar os danos

**evaluate** vb En
De bewerten
Es evaluar
Fr évaluer
It valutare
Pt avaliar

**évaluation** (f) n Fr
De Abschätzung; Wertbestim-
   mung (f)
En appraisal; valuation
Es evaluación (f)
It valutazione (f)
Pt avaliação (f)

**évaluation du coût des lots** (f)
Fr
De Stapelkostenberechnung (f)
En batch costing
Es fijación de precio por lotes
   (f)
It valutazione del costo per
   partida (f)
Pt fixação do preço por lote
   (f)

**évaluation du travail** (f) Fr
De Arbeitsbewertung (f)
En job evaluation
Es valoracion del trabajo (f)
It valutazione del lavoro (f)
Pt avaliação de tarefa (f)

**évaluation prudente** (f) Fr
De vorsichtige Schätzung (f)
En conservative estimate
Es presupuesto prudente (m)
It valutazione prudente (f)
Pt avaliação cautelosa (f)

**évaluer** vb Fr
De bewerten
En evaluate
Es evaluar
It valutare
Pt avaliar

**evasión de pago de impuestos**
(f) Es
De Steuerhinterziehung (f)
En evasion of tax
Fr fraude fiscale (f)
It evasione d'imposta (f)
Pt fuga a impostos (f)

**evasione d'imposta** (f) It
De Steuerhinterziehung (f)
En evasion of tax
Es evasión de pago de impue-
   stos (f)
Fr fraude fiscale (f)
Pt fuga a impostos (f)

**evasion of tax** En
De Steuerhinterziehung (f)
Es evasión de pago de impue-
   stos (f)
Fr fraude fiscale (f)
It evasione d'imposta (f)
Pt fuga a impostos (f)

**Eventualität** (f) n De
En contingency
Es contingencia (f)
Fr contingence (f)
It contingenza (f)
Pt contingência (f)

**Eventualverpflichtung** (f) De
En contingent liability
Es responsabilidad continge-
   nte (f)
Fr obligation éventuelle (f)
It sopravvenienza passiva (f)
Pt responsabilidade conting-
   ente (f)

**evict a tenant** En
De einen Mieter entfernen
Es desalojar un inquilino
Fr expulser un locataire
It sfrattare un locatario
Pt desalojar um inquilino

**evidence** n En
De Beweis (m)
Es evidencia (f)
Fr preuve (f)

It    prova *(f)*
Pt   prova *(f)*

**evidencia** *(f) n* Es
De  Beweis *(m)*
En  evidence
Fr   preuve *(f)*
It    prova *(f)*
Pt   prova *(f)*

**examen más detallado** *(m)* Es
De  Weiterüberlegung *(f)*
En  further consideration
Fr   examen plus attentif *(m)*
It    esame più attento *(m)*
Pt   consideração     posterior
     mais detalhada *(f)*

**examen médical** *(m)* Fr
De  ärztliche Untersuchung *(f)*
En  medical examination
Es  examen médico *(m)*
It    visita medica *(f)*
Pt   inspecção médica *(f)*

**examen médico** *(m)* Es
De  ärztliche Untersuchung *(f)*
En  medical examination
Fr   examen médical *(m)*
It    visita medica *(f)*
Pt   inspecção médica *(f)*

**examen plus attentif** *(m)* Fr
De  Weiterüberlegung *(f)*
En  further consideration
Es  examen más detallado *(m)*
It    esame più attento *(m)*
Pt   consideração     posterior
     mais detalhada *(f)*

**examinar** *vb* Es, Pt
De  untersuchen
En  examine
Fr   examiner
It    esaminare

**examine** *vb* En
De  untersuchen
Es  examinar
Fr   examiner
It    esaminare
Pt   examinar

**examiner** *vb* Fr
De  untersuchen
En  examine
Es  examinar

It    esaminare
Pt   examinar

**ex bond** En
De  verzollt
Es  fuera de aduanas
Fr   à l'acquitté
It    sdoganato
Pt   livre de alfândega

**ex-cais** Pt
De  ab Kai
En  ex quay
Es  en muelle
Fr   à prendre sur quai
It    sulla banchina

**excédent de bagages** *(m)* Fr
De  Übergepäck *(n)*
En  excess luggage
Es  exceso de equipaje *(m)*
It    bagaglio eccedente *(m)*
Pt   excesso de bagagem *(m)*

**excédent de poids** *(m)* Fr
De  Übergewicht *(n)*
En  excess weight
Es  peso excedente *(m)*
It    eccedenza di peso *(f)*
Pt   excesso de peso *(m)*

**excedente** *(m) n* Es, Pt
De  Überschuss *(m)*
En  surplus
Fr   surplus; excédent *(m)*
It    eccesso *(m)*

**excesivo** *adj* Es
De  übermässig
En  excessive
Fr   excessif
It    eccessivo
Pt   excessivo

**exceso de capacidad** *(m)* Es
De  Überkapazität *(f)*
En  overcapacity
Fr   surcapacité *(f)*
It    capacità in eccedenza *(f)*
Pt   capacidade excessiva *(f)*

**exceso de equipaje** *(m)* Es
De  Übergepäck *(n)*
En  excess luggage
Fr   excédent de bagages *(m)*
It    bagaglio eccedente *(m)*
Pt   excesso de bagagem *(m)*

**exceso de peso** *(m)* Es
De  Übergewicht *(n)*
En  overweight
Fr   excédent *(m)*
It    sovrappeso *(m)*
Pt   peso excessivo *(m)*

**exceso de producción** *(m)* Es
De  Überproduktion *(f)*
En  overproduction
Fr   surproduction *(f)*
It    sovraproduzione *(f)*
Pt   produção excessiva *(f)*

**excess** (of weight, etc.) *n* En
De  Überschuss *(m)*
Es  exceso *(m)*
Fr   excédent *(m)*
It    soprappeso *(m)*
Pt   excesso *(m)*

**excess capacity** En
De  übrige Ladefähigkeit *(f)*
Es  capacidad en exceso *(f)*
Fr   capacité excédentaire *(f)*
It    capacità in eccesso *(f)*
Pt   capacidade em excesso *(f)*

**excessif** *adj* Fr
De  übermässig
En  excessive
Es  excesivo
It    eccessivo
Pt   excessivo

**excessive** *adj* En
De  übermässig
Es  excesivo
Fr   excessif
It    eccessivo
Pt   excessivo

**excessivo** *adj* Pt
De  übermässig
En  excessive
Es  excesivo
Fr   excessif
It    eccessivo

**excess luggage** En
De  Übergepäck *(n)*
Es  exceso de equipaje *(m)*
Fr   excédent de bagages *(m)*
It    bagaglio eccedente *(m)*
Pt   excesso de bagagem *(m)*

**excesso** (m) n Pt
De Überschuss (m)
En excess
Es exceso (m)
Fr excédent (m)
It eccesso (m)

**excesso de bagagem** (m) Pt
De Übergepäck (n)
En excess luggage
Es exceso de equipaje (m)
Fr excédent de bagages (m)
It bagaglio eccedente (m)

**excesso de peso** (m) Pt
De Übergewicht (n)
En excess weight
Es peso excedente (m)
Fr excédent de poids (m)
It eccedenza di peso (f)

**excess profits tax** En
De Übergewinnsteuer (f)
Es impuesto sobre beneficios
   extraordinarios (m pl)
Fr impôts sur les superbéné-
   fices (m pl)
It imposta sui sopraprofitti (f)
Pt imposto sobre lucros exce-
   ssivos (m)

**excess weight** En
De Übergewicht (n)
Es peso excedente (m)
Fr excédent de poids (m)
It eccedenza di peso (f)
Pt excesso de peso (m)

**exchange** n En
De Tausch (m)
Es cambio (m)
Fr échange (m)
It cambio (m)
Pt câmbio (m)

**exchange control** En
Am currency control
De Devisenkontrolle (f)
Es fiscalización de cambios (f)
Fr contrôle des changes (m)
It controllo sui cambi (m)
Pt controlo de câmbios (m)

**exchange equalization ac-
   count** En
De Währungsausgleichsfonds
   (m)

Es cuenta de compensación
   de cambio (f)
Fr fonds de stabilisation des
   changes (m pl)
It conto per la stabilizzazione
   dei cambi (m)
Pt conta de compensação de
   transacções (f)

**exchange rate** En
De Wechselkurs (m)
Es tipo de cambio (m)
Fr taux de change (m)
It corso del cambio (m)
Pt câmbio (m)

**exchequer** n En
Am treasury
De Schatzamt (n)
Es hacienda (f)
Fr trésorerie (f)
It tesoro (m)
Pt tesouro (m)

**exchequer bond** (bill) En
Am treasury bond
De Schatzwechsel (m)
Es bono de tesorería (m)
Fr bon du trésor (m)
It buono del tesoro (m)
Pt título do tesouro (m)

**excise** n En
De indirekte Steuern (f pl)
Es contribuciones indirectas (f
   pl)
Fr contributions indirectes (f
   pl)
It imposte indirette (f pl)
Pt contribuição indirecta (f)

**excise duty** En
De Verbrauchsabgabe (f)
Es impuesto de consumos (m)
Fr droit sur la consommation
   (m)
It imposta sul consumo (f)
Pt imposto indirecto (m)

**exclude** vb En
De ausschliessen
Es excluir
Fr exclure
It escludere
Pt excluir

**excluding tax** En
De ausser Steuer
Es impuesto no incluido
Fr hors taxe (HT)
It tassa esclusa
Pt impostos excluidos

**excluir** vb Es, Pt
De ausschliessen
En exclude
Fr exclure
It escludere

**exclure** vb Fr
De ausschliessen
En exclude
Es excluir
It escludere
Pt excluir

**exclusão** (f) n Pt
De Ausschluss (m)
En exclusion
Es exclusión (f)
Fr exclusion (f)
It esclusione (f)

**exclusion** n En, Fr (f)
De Ausschluss (m)
Es exclusión (f)
It esclusione (f)
Pt exclusão (f)

**exclusión** (f) n Es
De Ausschluss (m)
En exclusion
Fr exclusion (f)
It esclusione (f)
Pt exclusão (f)

**exclusive market** En
De ausschliesslicher Markt (m)
Es mercado exclusivo (m)
Fr marché exclusif (m)
It mercato esclusivo (m)
Pt mercado exclusivo (m)

**ex coupon** En
De ohne Coupon
Es sin cupón
Fr ex-coupon
It senza cedola
Pt talão excluido

**ex-coupon** Fr
De ohne Coupon
En ex coupon
Es sin cupón

It   senza cedola
Pt   talão excluido

**ex dividend** En
De   ohne Dividende
Es   sin dividendo
Fr   ex-dividende
It   senza dividendo
Pt   dividendo excluido

**ex-dividende** Fr
De   ohne Dividende
En   ex dividend
Es   sin dividendo
It   senza dividendo
Pt   dividendo excluido

**ex-droits** Fr
De   ohne Bezugsrechte
En   ex rights
Es   sin privilegio
It   senza diritti
Pt   privilégios excluidos

**execução judicial a uma hipoteca** (f) Pt
De   Zwangsvollstreckung (f)
En   foreclosure
Es   venta por juicio hipotecario (f)
Fr   vente de l'immeuble hypothéqué (f)
It   vendita per giudizio ipotecario (f)

**executar** vb Pt
De   vollstrecken
En   execute
Es   ejecutar
Fr   exécuter
It   eseguire

**execute** vb En
De   vollstrecken
Es   ejecutar
Fr   exécuter
It   eseguire
Pt   executar

**execute a deed** En
De   eine Urkunde unterzeichnen
Es   firmar una escritura
Fr   passer un acte
It   perfezionare un atto
Pt   dar execução a um título legal

**execute a power of attorney** En
De   eine Vollmacht erteilen
Es   otorgar poder notarial
Fr   conférer des pleins pouvoirs
It   conferire una procura
Pt   dar execução a poderes de procuração

**execute a will** En
De   ein Testament vollstrecken
Es   ejecutar un testamento
Fr   exécuter un testament
It   eseguire un testamento
Pt   dar execução a um testamento

**exécuter** vb Fr
De   vollstrecken
En   execute
Es   ejecutar
It   eseguire
Pt   executar

**exécuter un testament** Fr
De   ein Testament vollstrecken
En   execute a will
Es   ejecutar un testamento
It   eseguire un testamento
Pt   dar execução a um testamento

**exécuteur** (m) n Fr
De   Vollstrecker (m)
En   executor
Es   albacea (m)
It   esecutore (m)
Pt   executor (m)

**exécution** (f) n Fr
De   Vollstreckung (f)
En   execution
Es   ejecución (f)
It   esecuzione (f)
Pt   execução (f)

**executive** n En
De   Geschäftsleiter (m)
Es   directivo (m)
Fr   dirigeant (m)
It   dirigente (m)
Pt   dirigente (m)

**executive director** En
Am   corporate officer
De   geschäftsführender Direktor (m)

Es   director ejecutivo (m)
Fr   administrateur dirigeant (m)
It   amministratore dirigente (m)
Pt   director administrativo (m)

**executor** n En, Pt (m)
De   Vollstrecker (m)
Es   albacea (m)
Fr   exécuteur (m)
It   esecutore (m)

**executor da liquidação** (m) Pt
De   Masseverwalter; Sachwalter (m)
En   liquidator
Es   liquidador (m)
Fr   liquidateur (m)
It   liquidatore (m)

**exempt de douane** Fr
De   abgabenfrei
En   duty-free
Es   exento de impuestos
It   esente da dazio
Pt   isento de impostos

**exempt d'impôts** Fr
De   steuerfrei
En   tax-free
Es   exento de impuestos
It   esente di tassa
Pt   isento de impostos

**exemption** n En, Fr (f)
De   Befreiung (f)
Es   exención (f)
It   esenzione (f)
Pt   isenção (f)

**exención** (f) n Es
De   Befreiung (f)
En   exemption
Fr   exemption (f)
It   esenzione (f)
Pt   isenção (f)

**exento de impuestos** Es
De   steuerfrei
En   tax-free
Fr   exempt d'impôts
It   esente di tassa
Pt   isento de impostos

**exercice** (m) n Fr
De   Abrechnungszeitraum; Geschäftsjahr (m n)

En accounting period; financial year
Es ejercicio *(m)*
It esercizio *(m)*
Pt exercício *(m)*

**exercice budgétaire** *(m)* Fr
De Steuerjahr *(n)*
En fiscal year
Es año fiscal *(m)*
It anno fiscale *(m)*
Pt ano fiscal *(m)*

**exercice fiscal** *(m)* Fr
De Steuerjahr *(n)*
En tax year
Es año fiscal *(m)*
It anno fiscale *(m)*
Pt ano fiscal *(m)*

**exercício** *(m)* n Pt
De Abrechnungszeitraum *(m)*
En accounting period
Es ejercicio *(m)*
Fr exercice *(f)*
It esercizio *(m)*

**exhaustif** *adj* Fr
De umfassend
En comprehensive
Es completo
It comprensivo
Pt compreensivo

**exhibidor** *(m)* n Es
De Aussteller *(m)*
En exhibitor
Fr exposant *(m)*
It espositore *(m)*
Pt expositor *(m)*

**exhibition** n En
De Ausstellung *(f)*
Es exposicion *(f)*
Fr exposition *(f)*
It esposizione *(f)*
Pt exposicão *(f)*

**exhibitor** n En
De Aussteller *(m)*
Es exhibidor *(m)*
Fr exposant *(m)*
It espositore *(m)*
Pt expositor *(m)*

**existencias** *(f pl)* n Es
De Vorrat *(m)*
En stock

Fr stock; marchandises *(m; f pl)*
It stock; scorta *(m f)*
Pt existências *(f pl)*

**existências** *(f pl)* n Pt
De Vorrat *(m)*
En stock
Es stock; existencias *(m; f pl)*
Fr stock; marchandises *(m; f pl)*
It stock; scorta *(m f)*

**ex-navio** Pt
De ab Schiff
En ex ship
Es en el buque
Fr. ex ship
It ex ship

**exorbitant** *adj* En, Fr
De unmässig
Es exorbitante
It esorbitante
Pt exorbitante

**exorbitante** *adj* Es, Pt
De unmässig
En exorbitant
Fr exorbitant
It esorbitante

**expedição** *vb* It
De absenden
En dispatch
Es expedir
Fr expédier
It spedire

**Expedient** *(m)* n De
En shipping clerk
Es dependiente de muelle *(m)*
Fr expéditionnaire *(m)*
It commesso di spedizioniere *(m)*
Pt despachante *(m)*

**expédier** *vb* Fr
De absenden; expedieren
En dispatch; forward
Es expedir; remitir
It spedire
Pt expedir; remeter

**expedieren** *vb* De
En forward; dispatch
Es expedir; remitir
Fr envoyer; expédier

It spedire
Pt expedir; remeter

**expedir** *vb* Es, Pt
De expedieren; absenden
En forward; dispatch
Fr envoyer; expédier
It spedire

**expéditeur** *(m)* n Fr
De Spediteur; Absender *(m)*
En carrier; consignor
Es transportador; consignador *(m)*
It vettore; speditore *(m)*
Pt transportador; consignante *(m)*

**expéditionnaire** *(m)* n Fr
De Expedient *(m)*
En shipping clerk
Es dependiente de muelle *(m)*
It commesso di spedizioniere *(m)*
Pt despachante *(m)*

**expenditure** n En
De Ausgaben *(f pl)*
Es desembolso *(m)*
Fr frais *(m pl)*
It spesa *(f)*
Pt despesas *(f pl)*

**expense** n En
De Kosten *(pl)*
Es gasto *(m)*
Fr frais *(m pl)*
It spesa *(f)*
Pt despesa *(f)*

**expensive** *adj* En
De teuer; kostspielig
Es caro
Fr cher
It caro
Pt caro

**experiente** *(m)* n Pt
De Sachkundige(r) *(m)*
En expert
Es experto *(m)*
Fr expert *(m)*
It competente *(m)*

**expert** n En, Fr *(m)*
De Sachkundige(r); Sachverständige(r) *(m)*
Es experto; especialista *(m)*

It  esperto; perito *(m)*
Pt  experiente; perito *(m)*

**expert's report** En
De  Sachverständigengutachten *(n)*
- Es  informe del especialista *(m)*
Fr  expertise *(f)*
It  perizia *(f)*
Pt  relatório do perito *(m)*

**expert comptable** *(m)* Fr
De  Wirtschaftsprüfer *(m)*
En  qualified accountant
Es  contador habilitado *(m)*
It  ragioniere diplomato *(m)*
Pt  guarda-livros diplomado *(m)*

**expertise** *(f)* n Fr
De  Sachverständigengutachten *(n)*
En  expert´s report
Es  informe del especialista *(m)*
It  perizia *(f)*
Pt  relatório do perito *(m)*

**experto** *(m)* n Es
De  Sachkundige(r) *(m)*
En  expert
Fr  expert *(m)*
It  competente *(m)*
Pt  experiente *(m)*

**expiração** *(f)* n Pt
De  Ablauf *(m)*
En  expiry
Es  expiración *(f)*
Fr  expiration *(f)*
It  termine *(m)*

**expiración** *(f)* n Es
De  Ablauf *(m)*
En  expiry
Fr  expiration *(f)*
It  termine *(m)*
Pt  expiração *(f)*

**expiration** *(f)* n Fr
De  Ablauf *(m)*
En  expiry
Es  expiración *(f)*
It  termine *(m)*
Pt  expiração *(f)*

**expiré** *adj* Fr
De  verfallen
En  expired

Es  vencido
It  scaduto
Pt  vencido

**expired** *adj* En
De  verfallen
Es  vencido
Fr  expiré
It  scaduto
Pt  vencido

**expiry** n En
De  Ablauf *(m)*
Es  expiración *(f)*
Fr  expiration *(f)*
It  termine *(m)*
Pt  expiração *(f)*

**exploit** *vb* En
De  ausbeuten
Es  explotar
Fr  exploiter
It  sfruttare
Pt  explorar

**exploitation** *(f)* n Fr
De  Erschliessung *(f)*
En  development
Es  explotación *(f)*
It  valorizzazione *(f)*
Pt  exploracão *(f)*

**exploiter** *vb* Fr
De  ausbeuten
En  exploit
Es  explotar
It  sfruttare
Pt  explorar

**exploracão** *(f)* n Pt
De  Erschliessung *(f)*
En  development
Es  explotación *(f)*
Fr  exploitation; lotissement *(f m)*
It  valorizzazione *(f)*

**explorar** *vb* Pt
De  ausbeuten
En  exploit
Es  explotar
Fr  exploiter
It  sfruttare

**explotación** *(f)* n Es
De  Erschliessung *(f)*
En  development

Fr  exploitation; lotissement *(f m)*
It  valorizzazione *(f)*
Pt  exploracão *(f)*

**explotar** *vb* Es
De  ausbeuten
En  exploit
Fr  exploiter
It  sfruttare
Pt  explorar

**exponencial** *adj* Es, Pt
De  Exponential-
En  exponential
Fr  exponentiel
It  esponenziale

**exponential** *adj* En
De  Exponential-
Es  exponencial
Fr  exponentiel
It  esponenziale
Pt  exponencial

**Exponential-** De
En  exponential
Es  exponencial
Fr  exponentiel
It  esponenziale
Pt  exponencial

**exponentiel** *adj* Fr
De  Exponential-
En  exponential
Es  exponencial
It  esponenziale
Pt  exponencial

**export** *vb* En
De  ausführen
Es  exportar
Fr  exporter
It  esportare
Pt  exportar

**Exportabteilungsleiter** *(m)* n De
En  export manager
Es  jefe de exportación *(m)*
Fr  chef du service exportation *(m)*
It  direttore esportazione *(m)*
Pt  gerente de exportações *(m)*

**exportaciones invisibles** *(f pl)* Es
De  unsichtbare Exporte *(m pl)*

En invisible exports
Fr exportations invisibles *(f pl)*
It esportazioni invisibili *(f pl)*
Pt exportações invisíveis *(f pl)*

**exportações invisíveis** *(f pl)* Pt
De unsichtbare Exporte *(m pl)*
En invisible exports
Es exportaciones invisibles *(f pl)*
Fr exportations invisibles *(f pl)*
It esportazioni invisibili *(f pl)*

**exportador** *n* Es, Pt
De Exporteur *(m)*
En exporter
Fr exportateur *(m)*
It esportatore *(m)*

**exportar** *vb* Es, Pt
De ausführen
En export
Fr exporter
It esportare

**exportateur** *(m) n* Fr
De Exporteur *(m)*
En exporter
Es exportador
It esportatore *(m)*
Pt exportador *(m)*

**exportations invisibles** *(f pl)* Fr
De unsichtbare Exporte *(m pl)*
En invisible exports
Es exportaciones invisibles *(f pl)*
It esportazioni invisibili *(f pl)*
Pt exportações invisíveis *(f pl)*

**Exportauftrag** *(m) n* De
En export order
Es pedido de exportación *(m)*
Fr commande d'exportation *(f)*
It ordine per esportazione *(m)*
Pt encomenda de exportação *(f)*

**export bonus** En
De Ausfuhrprämie *(f)*
Es subsidio a las exportaciones *(m)*
Fr prime à l'exportation *(f)*
It premio d'esportazione *(m)*
Pt subsídio de exportação *(m)*

**exporter** *vb* Fr
De ausführen
En export
Es exportar
It esportare
Pt exportar

**exporter** *n* En
De Exporteur *(m)*
Es exportador
Fr exportateur *(m)*
It esportatore *(m)*
Pt exportador *(m)*

**Exporteur** *(m) n* De
En exporter
Es exportador
Fr exportateur *(m)*
It esportatore *(m)*
Pt exportador *(m)*

**export incentive** En
De Ausfuhranreiz *(m)*
Es estímulo de exportación *(m)*
Fr motif d'exportation *(m)*
It incentivo alla esportazione *(m)*
Pt incentivo para a exportação *(m)*

**export manager** En
De Exportabteilungsleiter *(m)*
Es jefe de exportación *(m)*
Fr chef du service exportation *(m)*
It direttore esportazione *(m)*
Pt gerente de exportações *(m)*

**export order** En
De Exportauftrag *(m)*
Es pedido de exportación *(m)*
Fr commande d'exportation *(f)*
It ordine per esportazione *(m)*
Pt encomenda de exportação *(f)*

**export packing** En
De Exportverpackung *(f)*
Es embalaje para exportación *(m)*
Fr emballage convenable à l'exportation *(f)*
It imballaggio per esportazione *(m)*
Pt empacotamento para exportação *(m)*

**export permit** En
De Ausfuhrgenehmigung *(f)*
Es permiso de exportación *(m)*
Fr autorisation d'exporter *(f)*
It permesso d'esportazione *(m)*
Pt licença de exportação *(f)*

**export rebate** En
De Ausführsonderrabatt *(m)*
Es descuento por exportación *(m)*
Fr remise sur les exports *(f)*
It sconto d'esportazione *(m)*
Pt desconto de exportação *(m)*

**export sales** En
De Ausfuhrverkäufe *(m pl)*
Es ventas de exportación *(f pl)*
Fr ventes d'exportation *(f pl)*
It vendite per esportazione *(f pl)*
Pt vendas de exportação *(f pl)*

**Exportverpackung** *(f) n* De
En export packing
Es embalaje para exportación *(m)*
Fr emballage convénable à l'exportation *(f)*
It imballaggio per esportazione *(m)*
Pt empacotamento para exportação *(m)*

**exposant** *(m) n* Fr
De Aussteller *(m)*
En exhibitor
Es exhibidor *(m)*
It espositore *(m)*
Pt expositor *(m)*

**exposição** *(f) n* Pt
De Ausstellung *(f)*
En exhibition
Es exposicion *(f)*
Fr exposition *(f)*
It esposizione *(f)*

**exposição de montra** *(f)* Pt
De Fensterauslegung *(f)*
En window-display
Es exhibición en vitrina *(f)*
Fr étalage *(m)*
It mostra in vetrina *(f)*

**exposicion** (f) n Es
De Ausstellung (f)
En exhibition
Fr exposition (f)
It esposizione (f)
Pt exposicão (f)

**exposition** (f) n Fr
De Ausstellung (f)
En exhibition
Es exposicion (f)
It esposizione (f)
Pt exposicão (f)

**expositor** (m) n Pt
De Aussteller (m)
En exhibitor
Es exhibidor (m)
Fr exposant (m)
It espositore (m)

**express letter** En
Am special delivery
De Eilbrief (m)
Es carta urgente (f)
Fr lettre par exprès (f)
It lettera espresso (f)
Pt carta expresso (f)

**express train** En
De D-Zug; Schnellzug (m)
Es tren expreso (m)
Fr train express (m)
It direttissimo; rapido (m)
Pt comboio rápido (m)

**expropiación** (f) Es
De Enteignung (f)
En expropriation
Fr expropriation (f)
It espropriazione (f)
Pt expropriação (f)

**expropriação** (f) n Pt
De Enteignung (f)
En expropriation
Es expropiación (f)
Fr expropriation (f)
It espropriazione (f)

**expropriation** n En
De Enteignung (f)
Es expropiación (f)
Fr expropriation (f)
It espropriazione (f)
Pt expropriação (f)

**expropriation** (f) n Fr
De Enteignung (f)
En expropriation
Es expropiación (f)
It espropriazione (f)
Pt expropriação (f)

**expulser un locataire** Fr
De einen Mieter entfernen
En evict a tenant
Es desalojar un inquilino
It sfrattare un locatario
Pt desalojar um inquilino

**ex quay** En
De ab Kai
Es en muelle
Fr à prendre sur quai
It sulla banchina
Pt ex-cais

**ex rights** En
De ohne Bezugsrechte
Es sin privilegio
Fr ex-droits
It senza diritti
Pt privilégios excluidos

**ex ship** En, Fr, It
De ab Schiff
Es en el buque
Pt ex-navio

**extender un cheque** Es
De einen Scheck ausstellen
En draw a cheque
Fr tirer un chèque
It emettere un assegno
Pt passar um cheque

**extension of credit** En
De Verlängerung eines Kreditites (f)
Es prórroga de crédito (f)
Fr prolongation d'un crédit (f)
It proroga di credito (f)
Pt prorrogação de crédito

**extension of payment time** En
De Verlängerungszeitraum (m)
Es prórroga de pago (f)
Fr délai de paiement (m)
It proroga di pagamento (f)
Pt prorrogação de pagamento (f)

**external account** En
Am foreign currency account
De Auslandskonto (n)
Es cuenta exterior (f)
Fr compte transférable (m)
It conto estero (m)
Pt conta externa (f)

**external loan** En
De Auslandsanleihe (f)
Es préstamo exterior (m)
Fr emprunt extérieur (m)
It prestito esterno (m)
Pt empréstimo externo (m)

**extra** adj En, Es, It, Pt
De Sonder-
Fr supplémentaire

**extra charge** En
De Zuschlagsgebühr (f)
Es suplemento (m)
Fr supplément (m)
It spesa supplementare (f)
Pt encargo suplementar (m)

**extracto de conta** (m) Pt
De Kontoauszug (m)
En statement of account; bank statement
Es extracto de cuenta (m)
Fr relevé de compte (m)
It estratto conto (m)

**extracto de cuenta** (m) Es
De Kontoauszug (m)
En statement of account; bank statement
Fr relevé de compte (m)
It estratto conto (m)
Pt extracto de conta (m)

**extracto financeiro** (m) Pt
De Finanzausweis (m)
En financial statement
Es extracto financiero (m)
Fr état de finances (m)
It relazione finanziaria (f)

**extracto financiero** (m) Es
De Finanzausweis (m)
En financial statement
Fr état de finances (m)
It relazione finanziaria (f)
Pt extracto financeiro (m)

**extrait d'acte de décès** *(m)* Fr
De Totenschein *(m)*
En death certificate
Es partida de defunción *(f)*
It certificato di morte *(m)*
Pt certidão de óbito *(f)*

**extranjero** *adj* Es
De ausländisch; fremd
En foreign; alien
Fr étranger
It straniero; estero
Pt estrangeiro

**extranjero** *(m) n* Es
De Ausländer *(m)*
En foreigner
Fr étranger *(m)*
It straniero *(m)*
Pt estrangeiro *(m)*

**extraordinary general meeting**
En
De ausserordentliche General-
versammlung *(f)*
Es asamblea general extraor-
dinaria *(f)*
Fr assemblée générale extra-
ordinaire *(f)*
It assemblea generale straor-
dinaria *(f)*
Pt assembleia geral extraor-
dinária *(f)*

**extraordinary resolution** En
De Sonderentschluss *(m)*
Es resolución extraordinaria *(f)*
Fr résolution extraordinaire *(f)*
It deliberazione straordinaria
*(f)*
Pt resolução extraordinária *(f)*

**extrapolar** *vb* Es, Pt
De extrapolieren
En extrapolate
Fr extrapoler
It estrapolare

**extrapolate** *vb* En
De extrapolieren
Es extrapolar
Fr extrapoler
It estrapolare
Pt extrapolar

**extrapoler** *vb* Fr
De extrapolieren
En extrapolate

Es extrapolar
It estrapolare
Pt extrapolar

**extrapolieren** *vb* De
En extrapolate
Es extrapolar
Fr extrapoler
It estrapolare
Pt extrapolar

**ex warehouse** En
De an Zollfreilager
Es puesto en almacén
Fr à prendre en entrepôt
It franco magazzino
Pt no armazzém

**ex works** En
De ab Werk
Es de fábrica
Fr prise usine
It franco fabbrica
Pt na fábrica

# F

**f.a.s.** Pt
De frei Schiffseite
En free alongside ship (fas)
Es franco al costado del buque
Fr franco le long du bord
It franco lungobordo

**F.O.B. destination** Am
En carriage free
De frachtfrei
Es franco de porte
Fr franco
It porto franco
Pt porte gratis

**F.O.B. shipping point** Am
En carriage forward
De Portonachnahme
Es a porte debido
Fr en port dû
It porto assegnato
Pt transporte a pagar

**fabbrica** *(f) n* It
De Fabrik *(f)*
En factory
Es fábrica *(f)*

Fr fabrique; usine *(f)*
Pt fábrica *(f)*

**fabbricante** *(m) n* It
De Erzeuger; Hersteller *(m)*
En r anufacturer
Es fabricante *(m)*
Fr fabricant *(m)*
Pt fabricante *(m)*

**fabbricato di appartamenti** *(m)*
It
De Wohnungsgebäude *(n)*
En block of flats
Am apartment house
Es bloque de pisos *(m)*
Fr immeuble *(m)*
Pt edifício de andares *(m)*

**fabbricazione in massa** *(f)* It
De Massenherstellung *(f)*
En mass production
Es producción en masa *(f)*
Fr production en masse *(f)*
Pt produção em massa *(f)*

**fábrica** *(f) n* Es, Pt
De Fabrik *(f)*
En factory
Fr fabrique; usine *(f)*
It fabbrica *(f)*

**fabricant** *(m) n* Fr
De Erzeuger; Hersteller *(m)*
En manufacturer
Es fabricante *(m)*
It fabbricante *(m)*
Pt fabricante *(m)*

**fabricante** *(m) n* Es, Pt
De Erzeuger; Hersteller *(m)*
En manufacturer
Fr fabricant *(m)*
It fabbricante *(m)*

**Fabrik** *(f) n* De
En factory
Es fábrica *(f)*
Fr fabrique; usine *(f)*
It fabbrica *(f)*
Pt fábrica *(f)*

**fabrique** *(f) n* Fr
De Fabrik *(f)*
En factory
Es fábrica *(f)*
It fabbrica *(f)*
Pt fábrica *(f)*

**façade** (f) n Fr
De Vorderfront (f)
En frontage
Es fachada (f)
It facciata (f)
Pt fachada (f)

**facciata** (f) n It
De Vorderfront (f)
En frontage
Es fachada (f)
Fr façade (f)
Pt fachada (f)

**face value** En
De Nennwert (m)
Es valor nominal (m)
Fr valeur nominale (f)
It valore nominale (m)
Pt valor nominal (m)

**fachada** (f) n Es, Pt
De Vorderfront (f)
En frontage
Fr façade (f)
It facciata (f)

**facilidades** (f pl) n Es, Pt
De Einrichtungen (f pl)
En facilities
Fr facilités (f pl)
It facilitazione (f)

**facilidades de descubierto** (f pl) Es
De Überziehungsdisposition (f)
En overdraft facilities
Am overdraw facility
Fr facilités de caisse (f pl)
It facilitazione di scoperto (f)
Pt disponibilidades de crédito sem cabertura (f pl)

**facilitazione** (f) n It
De Einrichtungen (f pl)
En facilities
Es facilidades (f pl)
Fr facilités (f pl)
Pt facilidades (f pl)

**facilitazione di scoperto** (f) It
De Überziehungsdisposition (f)
En overdraft facilities
Am overdraw facility
Es facilidades de descubierto (f pl)
Fr facilités de caisse (f pl)

Pt disponibilidades de crédito sem cabertura (f pl)

**facilités** (f pl) n Fr
De Einrichtungen (f pl)
En facilities
Es facilidades (f pl)
It facilitazione (f)
Pt facilidades (f pl)

**facilités de caisse** (f pl) Fr
De Überziehungsdisposition (f)
En overdraft facilities
Am overdraw facility
Es facilidades de descubierto (f pl)
It facilitazione di scoperto (f)
Pt disponibilidades de crédito sem cabertura (f pl)

**facilities** n pl En
De Einrichtungen (f pl)
Es facilidades (f pl)
Fr facilités (f pl)
It facilitazione (f)
Pt facilidades (f pl)

**fact** n En
De Tatsache (f)
Es hecho (m)
Fr fait (m)
It fatto (m)
Pt facto (m)

**facteur** (m) n Fr
De Umstand (m)
En factor
Es factor (m)
It fattore (m)
Pt factor (m)

**facteur de conversion** (m) Fr
De Umrechnungskoeffizient (m)
En conversion factor
Es factor de conversión (m)
It fattore di conversion (m)
Pt factor de conversão (m)

**facteur de sécurité** (m) Fr
De Sicherheitskoeffizient (m)
En safety factor
Es factor de seguridad (m)
It coefficiente di sicurezza (m)
Pt factor de segurança (m)

**facto** (m) n Pt
De Tatsache (f)
En fact
Es hecho (m)
Fr fait (m)
It fatto (m)

**factor** n En; Es, Pt (m)
De Umstand (m)
Fr facteur (m)
It fattore (m)

**factor de conversão** (m) Pt
De Umrechnungskoeffizient (m)
En conversion factor
Es factor de conversión (m)
Fr facteur de conversion (m)
It fattore di conversion (m)

**factor de conversión** (m) Es
De Umrechnungskoeffizient (m)
En conversion factor
Fr facteur de conversion (m)
It fattore di conversion (m)
Pt factor de conversão (m)

**factor de segurança** (m) Pt
De Sicherheitskoeffizient (m)
En safety factor
Es factor de seguridad (m)
Fr facteur de sécurité (m)
It coefficiente di sicurezza (m)

**factor de seguridad** (m) Es
De Sicherheitskoeffizient (m)
En safety factor
Fr facteur de sécurité (m)
It coefficiente di sicurezza (m)
Pt factor de segurança (m)

**factory** n En
De Fabrik (f)
Es fábrica (f)
Fr fabrique: usine (f)
It fabbrica (f)
Pt fábrica (f)

**factory inspector** En
De Gewerbeaufsichtsbeamte(r) (m)
Es inspector de fábrica (m)
Fr inspecteur du travail (m)
It ispettore di fabbrica (m)
Pt inspector de fábrica (m)

**factory worker** En
De Gewerbearbeiter; Fabrikarbeiter *(m)*
Es obrero; operario *(m)*
Fr ouvrier *(m)*
It operaio *(m)*
Pt operário *(m)*

**factura** *(f)* n Es, Pt
De Faktura; Rechnung *(f)*
En invoice
Fr facture *(f)*
It fattura *(f)*

**factura comercial** *(f)* Es, Pt
De Geschäftsfaktur *(f)*
En commercial invoice
Fr facture commerciale *(f)*
It fattura commerciale *(f)*

**factura consular** *(f)* Es, Pt
De Konsulatsfaktura *(f)*
En consular invoice
Fr facture consulaire *(f)*
It fattura consolare *(f)*

**factura final** *(f)* Es, Pt
De Endrechnung *(f)*
En final invoice
Fr facture finale *(f)*
It fattura finale *(f)*

**factura proforma** *(f)* Es, Pt
De Proformarechnung *(f)*
En proforma invoice
Fr facture fictive *(f)*
It fattura proforma *(f)*

**facturar** *vb* Es, Pt
De fakturieren
En invoice
Fr facturer
It fatturare

**facture** *(f)* n Fr
De Faktura; Rechnung *(f)*
En invoice
Es factura *(f)*
It fattura *(f)*
Pt factura *(f)*

**facture commerciale** *(f)* Fr
De Geschäftsfaktur *(f)*
En commercial invoice
Es factura comercial *(f)*
It fattura commerciale *(f)*
Pt factura comercial *(f)*

**facture consulaire** *(f)* Fr
De Konsulatsfaktura *(f)*
En consular invoice
Es factura consular *(f)*
It fattura consolare *(f)*
Pt factura consular *(f)*

**facture fictive** *(f)* Fr
De Proformarechnung *(f)*
En proforma invoice
Es factura proforma *(f)*
It fattura proforma *(f)* ·
Pt factura proforma *(f)*

**facture finale** *(f)* Fr
De Endrechnung *(f)*
En final invoice
Es factura final *(f)*
It fattura finale *(f)*
Pt factura final *(f)*

**facturer** *vb* Fr
De fakturieren
En invoice
Es facturar
It fatturare
Pt facturar

**facultad de crédito** *(f)* Es
De Kreditfähigkeit *(f)*
En borrowing power
Fr capacité à avoir du crédit *(f)*
It capacità creditizia *(f)*
Pt potencial de obtenção de crédito *(m)*

**Fähigkeit** *(f)* n De
En capacity
Es capacidad *(f)*
Fr capacité *(f)*
It capacità *(f)*
Pt capacidade *(f)*

**Fähigkeitsstreitigkeit** *(f)* n De
En demarcation dispute
Es disputa sobre demarcación *(f)*
Fr contestation syndicale des compétences *(f)*
It disputa di competenza *(f)*
Pt disputa sobre demarcação *(f)*

**Fährboot** *(n)* n De
En ferry-boat
Es transbordador *(m)*
Fr bac *(m)*

It nave traghetto *(f)*
Pt barco de travessia *(m)*

**Fahrgeld** *(n)* n De
En fare
Es pasaje *(m)*
Fr prix du voyage *(m)*
It prezzo di viaggio *(m)*
Pt preço de passagem *(m)*

**Fahrlässigkeit** *(f)* n De
En negligence
Es negligencia *(f)*
Fr négligence *(f)*
It negligenza *(f)*
Pt negligência *(f)*

**fail** *vb* En
De versagen; durchfallen
Es fallar; faltar
Fr échouer; faillir
It mancare; fallire
Pt falhar; faltar

**failli** *(m)* n Fr
De Gemeinschuldner *(m)*
En bankrupt
Es quebrado *(m)*
It fallito *(m)*
Pt falido *(m)*

**failli non réhabilité** *(m)* Fr
De noch nicht entlasteter Gemeinschuldner *(m)*
En undischarged bankrupt
Es fallido no rehabilitado *(m)*
It fallito non riabilitato *(m)*
Pt falido insolvente *(m)*

**failli réhabilité** *(m)* Fr
De entlasteter Gemeinschuldner *(m)*
En discharged bankrupt
Es fallido rehabilitado *(m)*
It fallito riabilitato *(m)*
Pt falido rehabilitado *(m)*

**faillite** *(f)* n Fr
De Konkurs; Zahlungsunfähigkeit *(m f)*
En bankruptcy; insolvency
Es quiebra; insolvencia *(f)*
It fallimento; insolvenza *(m f)*
Pt falência; insolvência *(f)*

**failure** (of a business) n En
Am bankruptcy
De Bankrott *(m)*

**failure**

Es insolvencia (f)
Fr faillite (f)
It fallimento (m)
Pt falência (f)

**failure rate** En
De Durchfallquote (f)
Es proporción de fracasos (f)
Fr taux de défaillance (m)
It indice dei fallimenti (m)
Pt proporção de fracassos (f)

**failure to pay** En
De Nichtzahlung (f)
Es falta de pago (f)
Fr défaut de paiement (m)
It mancato pagamento (m)
Pt falta de pagamento (f)

**fair** n En
De Messe (f)
Es feria (f)
Fr foire (f)
It fiera (f)
Pt feira (f)

**fair** adj En
De recht und billig
Es razonable
Fr équitable
It equo
Pt razoável

**fair average quality** (faq) En
De gute Durchschnittsqualität (f)
Es calidad media razonable (f)
Fr qualité commerciale moyenne (f)
It buona qualità media (f)
Pt qualidade media razoável (f)

**fair deal** En
De anständige Abmachung (f)
Es trato equitativo (m)
Fr affaire équitable (f)
It affare giusto (m)
Pt transacção razoável (f)

**faire faillite** Fr
De Konkurs anmelden
En go bankrupt
Es caer en quiebra
It fallire
Pt falir

**faire la contrebande** Fr
De schmuggeln
En smuggle
Es pasar de contrabando
It contrabbandare
Pt fazer contrabando

**faire la grève** Fr
De streiken
En strike
Es declarar huelga
It scioperare
Pt fazer greve

**faire offre** Fr
De eine Offerte machen
En make an offer
Es hacer una oferta
It fare una offerta
Pt fazer uma oferta

**faire protester (une lettre de change)** Fr
De (einen Wechsel) protestieren
En protest (a bill)
Es protestar (una letra)
It protestare (una cambiale)
Pt protestar (uma letra)

**faire une contre-offre** Fr
De ein Gegenangebot abgeben
En make a counteroffer
Es hacer una contraoferta
It fare una controfferta
Pt fazer uma contra-proposta

**fair play** En
De anständige Handlungsweise (f)
Es juego limpio (m)
Fr traitement juste (m)
It condotta leale (f)
Pt jogo limpo (m)

**fair price** En
De angemessener Preis (m)
Es precio razonable (m)
Fr prix raisonnable (m)
It prezzo equo (m)
Pt preço razoável (m)

**fair return** En
De angemessener Ertrag (m)
Es beneficio razonable (m)
Fr rendement équitable (m)
It discreto profitto (m)
Pt rendimento justo (m)

**fair wear and tear** En
De übliche Abnützung (f)
Es uso y desgaste razonable (m)
Fr usure normale (f)
It usura normale (f)
Pt uso e desgaste razoável (m)

**fait** (m) n Fr
De Tatsache (f)
En fact
Es hecho (m)
It fatto (m)
Pt facto (m)

**fake** adj En
De gefälscht
Es falso
Fr truqué
It falso
Pt falsificado

**Faktura** (f) n De
En invoice
Es factura (f)
Fr facture (f)
It fattura (f)
Pt factura (f)

**fakturieren** vb De
En invoice
Es facturar
Fr facturer
It fatturare
Pt facturar

**fakturierter Preis** (m) De
En invoice price
Es precio facturado (m)
Fr prix facturé (m)
It prezzo di fattura (m)
Pt preço de factura (m)

**falência** (f) n Pt
De Konkurs; Bankrott (m)
En bankruptcy; failure
Es quiebra; bancarrota (f)
Fr faillite (f)
It fallimento; bancarotta (m f)

**falência bancária** (f) Pt
De Bankkrach (m)
En bank crash
Es quiebra de banco (f)
Fr krach d'une banque (m)
It crollo di banca (m)

**falhar** *vb* Pt
De versagen; durchfallen
En fail
Es fallar; faltar
Fr échouer; faillir
It mancare; fallire

**falido** *(m) n* Pt
De Gemeinschuldner *(m)*
En bankrupt
Es quebrado *(m)*
Fr failli *(m)*
It fallito *(m)*

**falido insolvente** *(m)* Pt
De noch nicht entlasteter Ge-
meinschuldner *(m)*
En undischarged bankrupt
Es fallido no rehabilitado *(m)*
Fr failli non réhabilité *(m)*
It fallito non riabilitato *(m)*

**falido rehabilitado** *(m)* Pt
De entlasteter Gemeinschuld-
ner *(m)*
En discharged bankrupt
Es fallido rehabilitado *(m)*
Fr failli réhabilité *(m)*
It fallito riabilitato *(m)*

**falir** *vb* Pt
De Konkurs anmelden
En go bankrupt
Es caer en quiebra
Fr faire faillite
It fallire

**fall** *n* En
De Sturz *(m)*
Es baja; caida *(f)*
Fr baisse; chute *(f)*
It caduta; ribasso *(f m)*
Pt baixa; gueda *(f)*

**fall** *vb* En
De stürzen
Es caer; bajar
Fr baisser; tomber
It cadere; ribassare
Pt cair; baixar

**fallar** *vb* Es
De versagen; durchfallen
En fail
Fr échouer; faillir
It mancare; fallire
Pt falhar; faltar

**fall due** En
De fällig sein
Es vencer
Fr échoir; venir à échéance
It scadere; essere pagabile
Pt vencer-se

**fallido no rehabilitado** *(m)* Es
De noch nicht entlasteter Ge-
meinschuldner *(m)*
En undischarged bankrupt
Fr failli non réhabilité *(m)*
It fallito non riabilitato *(m)*
Pt falido insolvente *(m)*

**fallido rehabilitado** *(m)* Es
De entlasteter Gemeinschuld-
ner *(m)*
En discharged bankrupt
Fr failli réhabilité *(m)*
It fallito riabilitato *(m)*
Pt falido rehabilitado *(m)*

**fällige Wechsel** *(m pl)* De
En bills for collection
Es efectos a cobrar *(m pl)*
Fr effets en recouvrement *(m
pl)*
It effetti all'incasso *(m pl)*
Pt letras a descontar *(f pl)*

**Fälligkeit** *(f) n* De
En maturity
Es vencimiento *(m)*
Fr échéance *(f)*
It scadenza *(f)*
Pt vencimento *(m)*

**Fälligkeitstag** *(m) n* De
En date of maturity; due date
Es fecha de vencimiento *(f)*
Fr date d'échéance *(f)*
It data di scadenza *(f)*
Pt data de vencimento *(f)*

**fällig sein** De
En fall due
Es vencer
Fr échoir; venir à échéance
It scadere; essere pagabile
Pt vencer-se

**fallimento** *(m) n* It
De Konkurs *(m)*
En bankruptcy
Es quiebra *(f)*
Fr faillite *(f)*
Pt falência *(f)*

**falling market** En
De Markt mit Baissetendenz
*(m)*
Es mercado en baja *(m)*
Fr marché orienté à la baisse
*(m)*
It mercato in declino *(m)*
Pt mercado em decréscimo
*(m)*

**fallire** *vb* It
De Konkurs anmelden
En go bankrupt
Es caer en quiebra
Fr faire faillite
Pt falir

**fallito** *(m) n* It
De Gemeinschuldner *(m)*
En bankrupt
Es quebrado *(m)*
Fr failli *(m)*
Pt falido *(m)*

**fallito non riabilitato** *(m)* It
De noch nicht entlasteter Ge-
meinschuldner *(m)*
En undischarged bankrupt
Es fallido no rehabilitado *(m)*
Fr failli non réhabilité *(m)*
Pt falido insolvente *(m)*

**fallito riabilitato** *(m)* It
De entlasteter Gemeinschuld-
ner *(m)*
En discharged bankrupt
Es fallido rehabilitado *(m)*
Fr failli réhabilité *(m)*
Pt falido rehabilitado *(m)*

**fall off** En
De nachlassen
Es bajar de valor; disminuir
Fr ralentir; baisser de valeur
It diminuire
Pt diminuir; decrescer

**falsch** *adj* De
En false; counterfeit
Es falso; falsificado
Fr faux; contrefait
It falso; contraffatto
Pt falso; falsificado

**fälschen** *vb* De
En forge
Es falsificar
Fr contrefaire

It  contraffare
Pt  falsificar

**Fälscher** *(m) n* De
En  forger
Es  falsificador *(m)*
Fr  faux-monnayeur; faussaire
*(m)*
It  falsificatore *(m)*
Pt  falsificador *(m)*

**Fälschung** *(f) n* De
En  forgery
Es  falsificación *(f)*
Fr  contrefaçon; faux *(f m)*
It  falsificazione *(f)*
Pt  falsificação *(f)*

**false** *adj* En
De  falsch
Es  falso
Fr  faux
It  falso
Pt  falso

**falsificação** *(f) n* Pt
De  Fälschung *(f)*
En  forgery
Es  falsificación *(f)*
Fr  contrefaçon; faux *(f m)*
It  falsificazione *(f)*

**falsificación** *(f) n* Es
De  Fälschung *(f)*
En  forgery
Fr  contrefaçon; faux *(f m)*
It  falsificazione *(f)*
Pt  falsificação *(f)*

**falsificado** Pt
De  falsch; verfälscht
En  counterfeit
Es  falso; falsificado
Fr  faux; contrefait
It  falso; contraffatto

**falsificador** *(m) n* Es, Pt
De  Fälscher *(m)*
En  forger
Fr  faux-monnayeur; faussaire
*(m)*
It  falsificatore *(m)*

**falsificar** *vb* Es, Pt
De  fälschen
En  forge
Fr  contrefaire
It  contraffare

**falsificatore** *(m) n* It
De  Fälscher *(m)*
En  forger
Es  falsificador *(m)*
Fr  faux-monnayeur; faussaire
*(m)*
Pt  falsificador *(m)*

**falsificazione** *(f) n* It
De  Fälschung *(f)*
En  forgery
Es  falsificación *(f)*
Fr  contrefaçon; faux *(f m)*
Pt  falsificação *(f)*

**falso** *adj* Es, It, Pt
De  falsch; verfälscht
En  false; counterfeit
Fr  faux; contrefait

**falta** *(f) n* Es, Pt
De  Nichteinhaltung *(f)*
En  default
Fr  défaillance; défaut *(f m)*
It  mancanza *(f)*

**falta de experiencia** *(f) n* Es
De  Unerfahrenheit *(f)*
En  inexperience
Fr  manque de pratique *(m)*
It  inesperienza *(f)*
Pt  inexperiência *(f)*

**falta de pagamento** *(f) n* Pt
De  Nichtzahlung *(f)*
En  failure to pay
Es  falta de pago *(f)*
Fr  défaut de paiement *(m)*
It  mancato pagamento *(m)*

**falta de pago** *(f) n* Es
De  Nichtzahlung *(f)*
En  failure to pay
Fr  défaut de paiement *(m)*
It  mancato pagamento *(m)*
Pt  falta de pagamento *(f)*

**fancy goods** En
De  Modeartikel *(m pl)*
Es  artículos de fantasía *(m pl)*
Fr  nouveautés *(f pl)*
It  articoli fantasia *(m pl)*
Pt  artigos de fantasia *(m pl)*

**fare** *n* En
De  Fahrgeld *(n)*
Es  pasaje *(m)*
Fr  prix du voyage *(m)*

It  prezzo di viaggio *(m)*
Pt  preço de passagem *(m)*

**fare da intermediario** It
De  vermitteln
En  mediate
Es  intermediar
Fr  s'entremettre
Pt  intermediar

**fare gettito** It
De  über Bord werfen
En  jettison
Es  echar al mar
Fr  jeter à la mer
Pt  alijar

**fare una controfferta** It
De  ein Gegenangebot abgeben
En  make a counteroffer
Es  hacer una contraoferta
Fr  faire une contre-offre
Pt  fazer uma contra-proposta

**fare una offerta** It
De  eine Offerte machen
En  make an offer
Es  hacer una oferta
Fr  faire offre

**far proseguire** It
De  bitte nachsenden
En  please forward
Es  se ruega hacer seguir
Fr  prière de faire suivre
Pt  é favor enviar

**Fass** *(n) n* De
En  barrel
Es  barril *(m)*
Fr  tonneau *(m)*
It  botte *(f)*
Pt  barril *(m)*

**fattibilità** *(f) n* It
De  Durchführbarkeit *(f)*
En  feasibility
Es  practicabilidad *(f)*
Fr  practicabilité *(f)*
Pt  viabilidade *(f)*

**fatto** *(m) n* It
De  Tatsache *(f)*
En  fact
Es  hecho *(m)*
Fr  fait *(m)*
Pt  facto *(m)*

**fattore** *(m)* *n* It
  De  Umstand *(m)*
  En  factor
  Es  factor *(m)*
  Fr  facteur *(m)*
  Pt  factor *(m)*

**fattore di conversion** *(m)* It
  De  Umrechnungskoeffizient
      *(m)*
  En  conversion factor
  Es  factor de conversión *(m)*
  Fr  facteur de conversion *(m)*
  Pt  factor de conversão *(m)*

**fattura** *(f)* *n* It
  De  Faktura; Rechnung *(f)*
  En  invoice
  Es  factura *(f)*
  Fr  facture *(f)*
  Pt  factura *(f)*

**fattura commerciale** *(f)* It
  De  Geschäftsfaktur *(f)*
  En  commercial invoice
  Es  factura comercial *(f)*
  Fr  facture commerciale *(f)*
  Pt  factura comercial *(f)*

**fattura consolare** *(f)* It
  De  Konsulatsfaktura *(f)*
  En  consular invoice
  Es  factura consular *(f)*
  Fr  facture consulaire *(f)*
  Pt  factura consular *(f)*

**fattura finale** *(f)* It
  De  Endrechnung *(f)*
  En  final invoice
  Es  factura final *(f)*
  Fr  facture finale *(f)*
  Pt  factura final *(f)*

**fattura proforma** *(f)* It
  De  Proformarechnung *(f)*
  En  proforma invoice
  Es  factura proforma *(f)*
  Fr  facture fictive *(f)*
  Pt  factura proforma *(f)*

**fatturare** *vb* It
  De  fakturieren
  En  invoice
  Es  facturar
  Fr  facturer
  Pt  facturar

**faulty** *adj* En
  De  fehlerhaft
  Es  defectuoso
  Fr  défectueux
  It  difettoso
  Pt  defeituoso

**faux** *adj* Fr
  De  falsch; verfälscht
  En  false; counterfeit
  Es  falso; falsificado
  It  falso; contraffatto
  Pt  falso; falsificado

**faux-monnayeur** *(m)* *n* Fr
  De  Fälscher *(m)*
  En  forger
  Es  falsificador *(m)*
  It  falsificatore *(m)*
  Pt  falsificador *(m)*

**faux chèque** *(m)* Fr
  De  gefälschter Scheck *(m)*
  En  forged cheque
  Es  cheque falsificado *(m)*
  It  assegno falsificato *(m)*
  Pt  cheque falsificado *(m)*

**faux frais** *(m pl)* Fr
  De  Nebenkosten *(pl)*
  En  incidental expenses
  Es  gastos imprevistos *(m pl)*
  It  spese impreviste *(f pl)*
  Pt  despesas ocasionais *(f pl)*

**fazer a contabilidade** Pt
  De  Konto führen
  En  keep the accounts
  Es  llevar la contabilidad
  Fr  tenir la comptabilité
  It  tenere la contabilità

**fazer greve** Pt
  De  streiken
  En  strike
  Es  declarar huelga
  Fr  faire la grève
  It  scioperare

**fazer uma contra-proposta** Pt
  De  ein Gegenangebot abgeben
  En  make a counteroffer
  Es  hacer una contraoferta
  Fr  faire une contre-offre
  It  fare una controfferta

**fazer uma oferta** Pt
  De  eine Offerte machen
  En  make an offer
  Es  hacer una oferta
  Fr  faire offre
  It  fare una offerta

**fazer uma reunião** Pt
  De  eine Versammlung abhalten
  En  hold a meeting
  Es  celebrar una reunión
  Fr  tenir une assemblée
  It  tenere una riunione

**feasibility** *n* En
  De  Durchführbarkeit *(f)*
  Es  practicabilidad *(f)*
  Fr  practicabilité *(f)*
  It  fattibilità *(f)*
  Pt  viabilidade *(f)*

**feasibility study** En
  De  Durchführbarkeitanalyse *(f)*
  Es  estudio de viabilidad *(m)*
  Fr  étude probatoire *(f)*
  It  studio delle possibilità *(m)*
  Pt  estudo de viabilidade *(m)*

**feature** *n* En
  De  Merkmal *(n)*
  Es  característica *(f)*
  Fr  particularité *(f)*
  It  caratteristica *(f)*
  Pt  característica *(f)*

**fecha** *(f)* *n* Es
  De  Datum *(n)*
  En  date
  Fr  date *(f)*
  It  data *(f)*
  Pt  data *(f)*

**fecha de entrega** *(f)* Es
  De  Liefertermin *(m)*
  En  delivery date
  Fr  date de livraison *(f)*
  It  data di consegna *(f)*
  Pt  data de entrega *(f)*

**fecha de reembolso** *(f)* Es
  De  Einlösungstag *(m)*
  En  redemption date
  Fr  date du remboursement *(f)*
  It  data di rimborso *(f)*
  Pt  data de resgate *(f)*

**fecha de vencimiento** (f) Es
De Fälligkeitstag (m)
En date of maturity; due date
Fr date d'échéance (f)
It data di scadenza (f)
Pt data de vencimento (f)

**fecha tope** (f) Es
De Verfalltermin (m)
En deadline
Fr date limite (f)
It ultima data o ora possibile (f)
Pt data de vencimento (f)

**fedeltà** (f) n It
De Treue (f)
En fidelity
Es fidelidad (f)
Fr fidélité (f)
Pt fidelidade (f)

**federal** adj En, Es, Pt
De Bundes-
Fr fédéral
It federale

**fédéral** adj Fr
De Bundes-
En federal
Es federal
It federale
Pt federal

**federale** adj It
De Bundes-
En federal
Es federal
Fr fédéral
Pt federal

**fee** n En
De Gebühr (f)
Es honorario; derecho (m)
Fr redevance; honoraires (f; m pl)
It onorario; diritto (m)
Pt honorários (m pl)

**feedback** n En
De Rückkoppelung (f)
Es retroacción (f)
Fr rétroaction (f)
It retroazione (f)
Pt reacção (f)

**Fehler** (m) n De
En error
Es error (m)
Fr erreur (f)
It errore (m)
Pt erro (m)

**fehlerhaft** adj De
En faulty
Es defectuoso
Fr défectueux
It difettoso
Pt defeituoso

**feilschen** vb De
En haggle
Am bargain
Es regatear
Fr marchander; chipoter
It mercanteggiare; cavillare
Pt regatear

**Feind** (m) n De
En enemy
Es enemigo (m)
Fr ennemi (m)
It nemico (m)
Pt inimigo (m)

**Feingehalt** (Gold, usw.) (m) n De
En fineness
Es ley (f)
Fr titre (m)
It finezza (f)
Pt pureza (f)

**Feingehaltsstempel** (m) n De
En hall-mark
Es punzón de garantía (m)
Fr poinçon (m)
It punzonatura di garanzia (f)
Pt marca de garantia (f)

**feira** (f) n Pt
De Messe (f)
En fair
Es feria (f)
Fr foire (f)
It fiera (f)

**feira comercial** (f) Pt
De Handelsmesse (f)
En trade fair
Es feria de muestras (f)
Fr foire commerciale (f)
It fiera commerciale (f)

**Fensterauslegung** (f) n De
En window-display
Es exhibición en vitrina (f)
Fr étalage (m)
It mostra in vetrina (f)
Pt exposição de montra (f)

**Fensterbriefumschlag** (m) n De
En window-envelope
Es sobre de ventanilla (m)
Fr enveloppe à fenêtre (f)
It busta con finestra (f)
Pt envelope de endereço exposto (m)

**Fensterglas** (n) n De
En window glass
Es cristal de ventana (f)
Fr verre à vitres (m)
It vetro da finestre (m)
Pt vidro de montra (m)

**fer** (m) n Fr
De Eisen (n)
En iron
Es hierro (m)
It ferro (m)
Pt ferro (m)

**fer de fonte** (m) Fr
De Gusseisen (n)
En cast iron
Es hierro colado (m)
It ghisa (f)
Pt ferro fundido (m)

**fer en gueuse** (m) Fr
De Roheisen (n)
En pig-iron
Es hierro bruto (m)
It pane di ghisa (m)
Pt ferro em bruto (m)

**feria** (f) n Es
De Messe (f)
En fair
Fr foire (f)
It fiera (f)
Pt feira (f)

**feria de muestras** (f) Es
De Handelsmesse (f)
En trade fair
Fr foire commerciale (f)
It fiera commerciale (f)
Pt feira comercial (f)

**feriado** (m) n Pt
De gesetzlicher Feiertag (m)
En public holiday
Es día de fiesta (m)
Fr jour férié (m)
It giorno di festa (m)

**férias** (f pl) n Pt
De Ferien; Urlaub (pl; m)
En vacation; holiday
Es vacación (f)
Fr vacances (f pl)
It vacanza (f)

**férias de verão** (f pl) Pt
De Sommerferien (pl)
En summer holidays
Es vacaciones de verano;
veraneo (f pl; m)
Fr vacances d'été (f pl)
It vacanze estive (f pl)

**férias pagas** (f pl) Pt
De bezahlter Urlaub (m)
En holidays with pay
Es vacaciones retribuidas (f pl)
Fr congés payés (m pl)
It vacanze retribuite (f pl)

**Ferien** (pl) n De
En vacation; holiday
Es vacación (f)
Fr vacances (f pl)
It vacanza (f)
Pt férias (f pl)

**fermacarte** (m) n It
De Büroklammer (f)
En paper clip
Es sujetapapeles (m)
Fr attache-papiers (m)
Pt grampo (m)

**fermare un assegno** It
De einen Scheck sperren
En stop a cheque
Es suspender el pago de un
cheque
Fr bloquer un chèque
Pt suspender o pagamento de
um cheque

**ferme** adj Fr
De fest
En firm
Es firme
It fermo
Pt firme

**ferme et non révisable** Fr
De fest und unveränderlich
En firm and not subject to
alteration
Es firme y no revisable
It fermo e non modificabile
Pt firme e irreversível

**fermo** adj It
De fest
En firm
Es firme
Fr ferme
Pt firme

**fermo e non modificabile** It
De fest und unveränderlich
En firm and not subject to
alteration
Es firme y no revisable
Fr ferme et non révisable
Pt firme e irreversível

**Ferngespräch** (n) n De
En trunk call
Am long distance call
Es llamada interurbana (f)
Fr appel téléphonique interur-
bain (m)
It comunicazione interurbana
(f)
Pt chamada inter-urbana (f)

**Fernschreiber** (m) n De
En Telex
Es télex (m)
Fr télex (m)
It telex (m)
Pt telex (m)

**Fernsprechamt** (n) n De
En telephone exchange
Es central telefónica (f)
Fr central téléphonique (m)
It centrale telefonica (f)
Pt central telefónica (f)

**Fernsprechbuch** (n) n De
En telephone directory
Es guía de teléfonos (f)
Fr annuaire des téléphones
(m)
It elenco telefonico (m)
Pt lista telefónica (f)

**Fernsprecher** (m) n De
En telephone
Es teléfono (m)

Fr téléphone (m)
It telefono (m)
Pt telefone (m)

**ferragens** (f pl) n Pt
De Eisenwaren (f pl)
En hardware; ironmongery
Es ferretería; quincallería (f)
Fr quincaillerie (f)
It ferramenta (f)

**ferramenta** (f) n It
De Eisenwaren (f pl)
En hardware; ironmongery
Es ferretería; quincallería (f)
Fr quincaillerie (f)
Pt ferragens (f pl)

**ferretería** (f) n Es
De Eisenwaren (f pl)
En hardware; ironmongery
Fr quincaillerie (f)
It ferramenta (f)
Pt ferragens (f pl)

**ferro** (m) n It, Pt
De Eisen (n)
En iron
Es hierro (m)
Fr fer (m)

**ferrocarril** (m) n Es
De Eisenbahn (f)
En railway
Fr chemin de fer (m)
It ferrovia (f)
Pt caminho de ferro (m)

**ferro em bruto** (m) Pt
De Roheisen (n)
En pig-iron
Es hierro bruto (m)
Fr fer en gueuse (m)
It pane di ghisa (m)

**ferro fundido** (m) Pt
De Gusseisen (n)
En cast iron
Es hierro colado (m)
Fr fer de fonte (m)
It ghisa (f)

**ferrovia** (f) n It
De Eisenbahn (f)
En railway
Es ferrocarril (m)
Fr chemin de fer (m)
Pt caminho de ferro (m)

**ferry-boat** n En
De Fährboot (n)
Es transbordador (m)
Fr bac (m)
It nave traghetto (f)
Pt barco de travessia (m)

**fest** adj De
En firm; fixed
Es firme; fijo
Fr ferme; fixe
It fermo; fisso
Pt firme; fixado

**festbegründetes Recht** (n) De
En vested interest
Es interés creado (m)
Fr droit acquis (m)
It diritto acquisito (m)
Pt interesse adquirido (m)

**feste Kapitalanlagen** (f pl) De
En fixed capital
Es capital fijo (m)
Fr capital fixe (m)
It capitale fisso (m)
Pt capital fixado (m)

**feste Parität** (f) De
En fixed parity
Es paridad fija (f)
Fr parité fixe (f)
It parità fissa (f)
Pt paridade fixa (f)

**festes Angebot** (n) De
En firm offer
Es oferta en firme (f)
Fr offre ferme (f)
It offerta ferma (f)
Pt oferta firme (f)

**festività legali** (f) It
De gesetzlicher Feiertag (m)
En Bank Holiday
Am legal holiday
Es día de fiesta (m)
Fr jour férié (m)
Pt feriado (m)

**fest und unveränderlich** De
En firm and not subject to alteration
Es firme y no revisable
Fr ferme et non révisable
It fermo e non modificabile
Pt firme e irreversível

**festverzinsliches Wertpapier** (n) De
En fixed-interest security
Es obligación a interés fijo (f)
Fr valeur à revenu fixe (f)
It titolo a interesse fisso (m)
Pt obrigação de juro fixo (f)

**Feuerversicherung** (f) n De
En fire insurance
Es seguro de incendios (m)
Fr assurance incendie (f)
It assicurazione incendio (f)
Pt seguro de incêndio (m)

**Feuerversicherungsschein** (m) n De
En fire insurance policy
Es póliza de seguro de incendios (f)
Fr police incendie (f)
It polizza d'assicurazione incendio (f)
Pt apólice de seguro de incêndio (f)

**feuille de paie** (f) Fr
De Lohnbuch (n)
En payroll
Es nómina de pago (f)
It libro paga (m)
Pt folha de salários (f)

**feuille d'inscription** (f) Fr
De Antragsformular (n)
En entry-form
Es solicitud de inscripción (f)
It bolletta d'entrata (f)
Pt impresso de admissão (m)

**fiador** (m) n Es, Pt
De Bürgschaft; Bürge (f m)
En surety; guarantor
Fr caution; garant (f m)
It garante; avallante (m)

**fiança** (f) n Pt
De Bürge; Nebenbürgschaft (m f)
En surety; security
Es fianza (f)
Fr cautionnement; nantissement (m)
It cauzione; pegno (f m)

**fiança de avaria** (f) Pt
De Havarieschein (m)
En average bond

Es fianza de avería (f)
Fr compromis d'avarie (m)
It compromesso d'avaria (m)

**fianza** (f) n Es `
De Bürge; Nebenbürgschaft (m f)
En surety; security
Fr cautionnement; nantissement (m)
It cauzione; pegno (f m)
Pt fiança (f)

**fianza de avería** (f) Es
De Havarieschein (m)
En average bond
Fr compromis d'avarie (m)
It compromesso d'avaria (m)
Pt fiança de avaria (f)

**ficha** (f) n Es, Pt
De Indexkarte (f)
En index card
Fr fiche (f)
It scheda (f)

**ficha perforada** (f) Pt
De Lochkarte (f)
En punched card
Es tarjeta perforada (f)
Fr carte perforée (f)
It scheda perforata (f)

**fiche** (f) n Fr
De Indexkarte (f)
En index card
Es ficha (f)
It scheda (f)
Pt ficha (f)

**ficheiro** (m) n Pt
De Akte (f)
En file
Es archivo (m)
Fr dossier (m)
It archivio (m)

**ficheiro com indice** (m) Pt
De Kartei (f)
En card-index file
Es archivo de fichas (m)
Fr fichier (m)
It schedario (m)

**fichero** (m) n Es
De Kartothek; Aktenschrank (f m)
En card index; filing cabinet

Fr fichier; classeur *(m)*
It schedario *(m)*
Pt ficheiro; móvel ficheiro *(m)*

**fichier** *(m)* n Fr
De Kartei *(f)*
En card-index file
Es archivo de fichas *(m)*
It schedario *(m)*
Pt ficheiro com indice *(m)*

**ficticio** *adj* Es
De unecht; Schein-
En fictitious
Fr fictif
It fittizio
Pt fictício

**fictício** *adj* Pt
De unecht; Schein-
En fictitious
Es ficticio
Fr fictif
It fittizio

**fictif** *adj* Fr
De unecht; Schein-
En fictitious
Es ficticio
It fittizio
Pt fictício

**fictitious** *adj* En
De unecht; Schein-
Es ficticio
Fr fictif
It fittizio
Pt fictício

**fidato** *adj* It
De zuverlässig
En reliable
Es digno de confianza
Fr digne de confiance
Pt digno de confiança

**fidecommissario** *(m)* n It
De Treuhänder *(m)*
En trustee
Es fideicomisario *(m)*
Fr fidéicommissaire *(m)*
Pt fiduciário *(m)*

**fideicomisario** *(m)* n Es
De Treuhänder *(m)*
En trustee
Fr fidéicommissaire *(m)*

It fidecommissario *(m)*
Pt fiduciário *(m)*

**fideicomiso de inversiones**
*(m)* Es
De Investment-Trust *(m)*
En investment trust
Fr société fiduciaire de place-
ments *(f)*
It consorzio per investimenti
*(m)*
Pt instituição de investimen-
tos *(f)*

**fideicomiso discrecional** *(m)*
Es
De unumschränkte Treuhand
*(f)*
En discretionary trust
Fr fidéicommis à appréciation
*(m)*
It fondo fiduciario discre-
zionale *(m)*
Pt fundação discricionária *(f)*

**fidéicommis à appréciation**
*(m)* Fr
De unumschränkte Treuhand
*(f)*
En discretionary trust
Es fideicomiso discrecional *(m)*
It fondo fiduciario discre-
zionale *(m)*
Pt fundação discricionária *(f)*

**fidéicommissaire** *(m)* n Fr
De Treuhänder *(m)*
En trustee
Es fideicomisario *(m)*
It fidecommissario *(m)*
Pt fiduciário *(m)*

**fidelidad** *(f)* n Es
De Treue *(f)*
En fidelity
Fr fidélité *(f)*
It fedeltà *(f)*
Pt fidelidade *(f)*

**fidelidade** *(f)* n Pt
De Treue *(f)*
En fidelity
Es fidelidad *(f)*
Fr fidélité *(f)*
It fedeltà *(f)*

**fidélité** *(f)* n Fr
De Treue *(f)*
En fidelity
Es fidelidad *(f)*
It fedeltà *(f)*
Pt fidelidade *(f)*

**fidelity** n En
De Treue *(f)*
Es fidelidad *(f)*
Fr fidélité *(f)*
It fedeltà *(f)*
Pt fidelidade *(f)*

**fiduciaire** *adj* Fr
De treuhänderisch
En fiduciary
Es fiduciario
It fiduciario
Pt fiduciário

**fiduciario** *adj* Es, It
De treuhänderisch
En fiduciary
Fr fiduciaire
Pt fiduciário

**fiduciário** *adj* Pt
De treuhänderisch
En fiduciary
Es fiduciario
Fr fiduciaire
It fiduciario

**fiduciário** *(m)* n Pt
De Treuhänder *(m)*
En trustee
Es fideicomisario *(m)*
Fr fidéicommissaire *(m)*
It fidecommissario *(m)*

**fiduciary** *adj* En
De treuhänderisch
Es fiduciario
Fr fiduciaire
It fiduciario
Pt fiduciário

**fiduciary issue** En
De ungedecktes Geld *(n)*
Es emisión fiduciaria *(f)*
Fr émission fiduciaire *(f)*
It emissione fiduciaria *(f)*
Pt emissão fiduciária *(f)*

**field study** En
De Stellenüberblick *(m)*

Es estudio sobre el terreno
(m)
Fr enquête sur les lieux (f)
It studio sul terreno (m)
Pt estudo de campo (m)

**fiera** (f) n It
De Messe (f)
En fair
Es feria (f)
Fr foire (f)
Pt feira (f)

**fiera commerciale** (f) It
De Handelsmesse (f)
En trade fair
Es feria de muestras (f)
Fr foire cómmerciale (f)
Pt feira comercial (f)

**figure** (number) n En
De Zahl (f)
Es cifra (f)
Fr chiffre (m)
It cifra (f)
Pt número (m)

**fijación de precio por lotes** (f)
Es
De Stapelkostenberechnung (f)
En batch costing
Fr évaluation du coût des lots
(f)
It valutazione del costo per
partita (f)
Pt fixação do preço por lote
(f)

**fijo** adj Es
De fest
En fixed
Fr fixe; fixé
It fisso; fissato
Pt fixado

**file** n En
De Akte (f)
Es archivo (m)
Fr dossier (m)
It archivio (m)
Pt ficheiro (m)

**file** (a patent) vb En
De einlegen
Es interponer
Fr déposer
It depositare
Pt registar

**file** (classify) vb En
De aufreihen
Es archivar
Fr classer
It archiviare
Pt arquivar

**filial** (f) n Pt
De Filiale; Zweigstelle (f)
En branch
Es sucursal (f)
Fr succursale; filiale (f)
It succursale; filiale (f)

**filial** (f) n Es
De Tochtergesellschaft (f)
En subsidiary company
Fr filiale (f)
It filiale (f)
Pt companhia subsidiária (f)

**Filialbank** (f) n De
En branch bank
Es sucursal del banco (f)
Fr banque succursale (f)
It banca succursale (f)
Pt filial de banco (f)

**filial de banco** (f) Pt
De Filialbank; Zweigbank (f)
En branch bank
Es sucursal del banco (f)
Fr banque succursale (f)
It banca succursale (f)

**filiale** (f) n Fr, It
De Tochtergesellschaft (f)
En subsidiary company
Es filial; empresa subsidiaría
(f)
Pt companhia subsidiária (f)

**Filiale** (f) n De
En branch
Es sucursal; filial (f)
Fr succursale; filiale (f)
It succursale; filiale (f)
Pt filial (f)

**filing cabinet** En
De Aktenschrank (m)
Es fichero (m)
Fr classeur (m)
It schedario (m)
Pt móvel ficheiro (m)

**filouter** vb Fr
De schwindeln
En swindle
Es estafar
It truffare
Pt enganar

**fim** (m) n Pt
De Ende (n)
En end
Es fin (m)
Fr fin (f)
It fine (f)

**fin** n Es (m), Fr (f)
De Ende (n)
En end
It fine (f)
Pt fim (m)

**final** adj En, Es, Fr, Pt
De endgültig
It finale

**final balance** En
De Schlussbilanz (f)
Es saldo final (m)
Fr solde net (m)
It saldo finale (m)
Pt balanço final (m)

**final discharge** En
De Rechnungsentlastung (f)
Es finiquito (m)
Fr quitus (m)
It quietanza finale (f)
Pt cumprimento final (m)

**final dividend** En
De Schlussdividende (f)
Es saldo del dividendo (m)
Fr solde de dividende (m)
It saldo del dividendo (m)
Pt dividendo final (m)

**finale** adj It
De endgültig
En final
Es final
Fr final
Pt final

**final instalment** En
De letzte Rate (f)
Es último plazo (m)
Fr dernier versement (m)
It ultima rata (f)
Pt última prestação (f)

**final invoice** En
   De Endrechnung *(f)*
   Es factura final *(f)*
   Fr facture finale *(f)*
   It fattura finale *(f)*
   Pt factura final *(f)*

**finança** *(f) n* Pt
   De Finanz *(f)*
   En finance
   Es finanza *(f)*
   Fr finance *(f)*
   It finanza *(f)*

**finance** *vb* En
   De finanzieren
   Es financiar
   Fr financer
   It finanziare
   Pt financiar

**finance** *n* En, Fr *(f)*
   De Finanz *(f)*
   Es finanza *(f)*
   It finanza *(f)*
   Pt finança *(f)*

**finance company** En
   De Finanzierungsgesellschaft
      *(f)*
   Es compañía de crédito co-
      mercial *(f)*
   Fr société de financement *(f)*
   'It società finanziaria *(f)*
   Pt empresa financeira *(f)*

**financeiro** *adj* Pt
   De finanziell
   En financial
   Es financiero
   Fr financier; fiscal
   It finanziario

**financer** *vb* Fr
   De finanzieren
   En finance
   Es financiar
   It finanziare
   Pt financiar

**financial** *adj* En
   De finanziell
   Es financiero
   Fr financier; fiscal
   It finanziario
   Pt financeiro

**financial statement** En
   De Finanzausweis *(m)*
   Es extracto financiero *(m)*
   Fr état de finances *(m)*
   It relazione finanziaria *(f)*
   Pt extracto financeiro *(m)*

**financial year** En
   De Geschäftsjahr *(n)*
   Es año económico *(m)*
   Fr exercice *(m)*
   It esercizio *(m)*
   Pt ano financeiro *(m)*

**financiar** *vb* Es, Pt
   De finanzieren
   En finance
   Fr financer
   It finanziare

**financier** *adj* Fr
   De finanziell
   En financial
   Es financiero
   It finanziario
   Pt financeiro

**financiero** *adj* Es
   De finanziell
   En financial
   Fr financier; fiscal
   It finanziario
   Pt financeiro

**Finanz** *(f) n* De
   En finance
   Es finanza *(f)*
   Fr finance *(f)*
   It finanza *(f)*
   Pt finança *(f)*

**Finanz-** De
   En fiscal
   Es fiscal
   Fr fiscal; budgétaire
   It fiscale
   Pt fiscal

**finanza** *(f) n* Es, It
   De Finanz *(f)*
   En finance
   Fr finance *(f)*
   Pt finança *(f)*

**Finanzausweis** *(m) n* De
   En financial statement
   Es extracto financiero *(m)*
   Fr état de finances *(m)*

   It relazione finanziaria *(f)*
   Pt extracto financeiro *(m)*

**Finanzbank** *(f) n* De
   En investment bank
   Es banco de inversiones *(m)*
   Fr banque d'affaires *(f)*
   It banca d'investimenti *(f)*
   Pt banco de investimentos *(m)*

**finanziare** *vb* It
   De finanzieren
   En finance
   Es financiar
   Fr financer
   Pt financiar

**finanziario** *adj* It
   De finanziell
   En financial
   Es financiero
   Fr financier; fiscal
   Pt financeiro

**finanziell** *adj* De
   En financial
   Es financiero
   Fr financier; fiscal
   It finanziario
   Pt financeiro

**finanzieren** *vb* De
   En finance
   Es financiar
   Fr financer
   It finanziare
   Pt financiar

**Finanzierungsgesellschaft** *(f)*
      *n* De
   En finance company
   Es compañía de crédito co-
      mercial *(f)*
   Fr société de financement *(f)*
   It società finanziaria *(f)*
   Pt empresa financeira *(f)*

**finca** *(f) n* Es
   De Vermögen *(n)*
   En estate; property
   Fr bien; propriété *(m f)*
   It proprietà *(f)*
   Pt bens; propriedade *(m pl;
      m)*

**fine** *(f) n* It
   De Ende *(n)*
   En end

Es  fin (m)
Fr  fin (f)
Pt  fim (m)

**fine** n En
De  Geldstrafe (f)
Es  sanción; multa (f)
Fr  amende (f)
It  multa (f)
Pt  multa (f)

**fineness** (of gold, etc.) n En
De  Feingehalt (m)
Es  ley (f)
Fr  titre (m)
It  finezza (f)
Pt  pureza (f)

**finezza** (d'oro, ecc.) (f) n It
De  Feingehalt (m)
En  fineness
Es  ley (f)
Fr  titre (m)
Pt  pureza (f)

**finiquito** (m) n Es
De  Rechnungsentlastung (f)
En  final discharge
Fr  quitus (m)
It  quietanza finale (f)
Pt  cumprimento final (m)

**finta pelle** (f) It
De  Kunstleder (n)
En  imitation leather
Es  piel de imitación (f)
Fr  similicuir (m)
Pt  cabedal de imitação (m)

**fire** vb En
De  entlassen
Es  despedir
Fr  congédier
It  congedare
Pt  despedir

**fire** n En
De  Brand (m)
Es  fuego; incendio (m)
Fr  incendie (f)
It  incendio (m)
Pt  fogo; incêndio (m)

**fire insurance** En
De  Feuerversicherung (f)
Es  seguro de incendios (m)
Fr  assurance incendie (f)

It  assicurazione incendio (f)
Pt  seguro de incêndio (m)

**fire insurance policy** En
De  Feuerversicherungsschein
    (m)
Es  póliza de seguro de incen-
    dios (f)
Fr  police incendie (f)
It  polizza    d'assicurazione
    incendio (f)
Pt  apólice de seguro de incê-
    ndio (f)

**firing** (dismissal) n En
De  Entlassung (f)
Es  despido (m)
Fr  congédiement (m)
It  licenziamento (m)
Pt  despedimento (m)

**firm** adj En
De  fest
Es  firme
Fr  ferme
It  fermo
Pt  firme

**firm** n En
Am  company
De  Firma (f)
Es  firma; casa (f)
Fr  firme; maison (f)
It  ditta (f)
Pt  empresa; firma (f)

**firma** (f) n Es, Pt
De  Firma (f)
En  firm
Fr  firme; maison (f)
It  ditta (f)

**firma** (f) n Es, It, Pt
De  Unterschrift (f)
En  signature
Fr  signature (f)

**Firma** (f) n De
En  firm; company
Es  firma; casa (f)
Fr  firme; maison (f)
It  ditta (f)
Pt  empresa; firma (f)

**firma en blanco** (f) Es
De  Blankounterschrift (f)
En  blank signature
Fr  blanc-seing (m)

**firma in bianco** (f) It
De  Blankounterschrift (f)
En  blank signature
Es  firma en blanco (f)
Fr  blanc-seing (m)
Pt  assinatura em branco (f)

**firm and not subject to altera-
tion** En
De  fest und unveränderlich
Es  firme y no revisable
Fr  ferme et non révisable
It  fermo e non modificabile
Pt  firme e irreversível

**firmar una escritura** Es
De  eine Urkunde unterzeichnen
En  execute a deed
Fr  passer un acte
It  perfezionare un atto
Pt  dar execução a um título
    legal

**firme** adj Es, Pt
De  fest
En  firm
Fr  ferme
It  fermo

**firme** (f) n Fr
De  Firma (f)
En  firm; company
Es  firma; casa (f)
It  ditta (f)
Pt  empresa; firma (f)

**firme e irreversível** Pt
De  fest und unveränderlich
En  firm and not subject to
    alteration
Es  firme y no revisable
Fr  ferme et non révisable
It  fermo e non modificabile

**Firmenkonto** (n) n De
En  impersonal account
Es  cuenta simulada (f)
Fr  compte impersonnel (m)
It  conto d'ordine (m)
Pt  conta impessoal (f)

**Firmenname** (m) n De
En  trade name
Es  razón social (f)
Fr  raison sociale (f)
It  denominazione
    commerciale (f)
Pt  razão comercial (f)

**firme y no revisable** Es
De fest und unveränderlich
En firm and not subject to
　alteration
Fr ferme et non révisable
It fermo e non modificabile
Pt firme e irreversível

**firm offer** En
De festes Angebot (n)
Es oferta en firme (f)
Fr offre ferme (f)
It offerta ferma (f)
Pt oferta firme (f)

**first class** En
De erste Klasse (f)
Es primera clase (f)
Fr première classe (f)
It prima classe (f)
Pt primeira classe (f)

**first of exchange** En
De Primawechsel (m)
Es primera de cambio (f)
Fr première de change (f)
It prima di cambio (f)
Pt primeira de câmbio (f)

**fiscal** adj En, Es, Fr, Pt
De Finanz-
It fiscale

**fiscal de contas** (m) Pt
De Bücherrevisor (m)
En auditor
Es revisor de conti (m)
Fr réviseur des comptes (m)
It sindaco (m)

**fiscale** adj It
De Finanz-
En fiscal
Es fiscal
Fr fiscal; budgétaire
Pt fiscal

**fiscalização contabilística interna** (f) Pt
De interne Revision (f)
En internal audit
Es verificación contable interna (f)
Fr vérification interne (f)
It verifica contabile interna (f)

**fiscalização de contas** (f) Pt
De Bücherrevision (f)
En audit
Es revisión de cuentas (f)
Fr vérification comptable (f)
It revisione dei conti (f)

**fiscalización de cambios** (f) Es
De Devisenkontrolle (f)
En exchange control
Am currency control
Fr contrôle des changes (m)
It controllo sui cambi (m)
Pt controlo de câmbios (m)

**fiscalización de las existencias** (f) Es
De Lagerverwaltung (f)
En stock control
Fr contrôle des stocks (m)
It controllo delle scorte (m)
Pt controlo de existências (m)

**fiscalizar** (as contas) vb Pt
De prüfen
En audit
Es revisar
Fr vérifier et certifier
It rivedere

**fiscal year** En
De Steuerjahr (n)
Es año fiscal (m)
Fr exercice budgétaire (m)
It anno fiscale (m)
Pt ano fiscal (m)

**Fischerflotte** (f) n De
En fishing fleet
Es flota pesquera (f)
Fr flottille de pêche (f)
It flotta peschereccia (f)
Pt frota de pesca (f)

**fishing fleet** En
De Fischerflotte (f)
Es flota pesquera (f)
Fr flottille de pêche (f)
It flotta peschereccia (f)
Pt frota de pesca (f)

**fissare** vb It
De anstellen
En engage
Am hire
Es apalabrar
Fr engager
Pt empregar

**fissare un appuntamento** It
De eine Verabredung treffen
En make an appointment
Es hacer una cita
Fr prendre un rendez-vous
Pt marcar um encontro

**fisso** adj It
De fest
En fixed
Es fijo
Fr fixe; fixé
Pt fixado

**fita magnética** (f) Pt
De Magnetband (n)
En magnetic tape
Es cinta magnética (f)
Fr bande magnétique (f)
It nastro magnetico (m)

**fittizio** adj It
De unecht; Schein-
En fictitious
Es ficticio
Fr fictif
Pt fictício

**fixação do preço por lote** (f) Pt
De Stapelkostenberechnung (f)
En batch costing
Es fijación de precio por lotes (f)
Fr évaluation du coût des lots (f)
It valutazione del costo per partita (f)

**fixado** adj Pt
De fest
En fixed
Es fijo
Fr fixe; fixé
It fisso; fissato

**fixe** adj Fr
De fest
En fixed
Es fijo
It fisso; fissato
Pt fixado

**fixed** adj En
De fest
Es fijo
Fr fixe; fixé

It fisso; fissato
Pt fixado

**fixed assets** En
De Anlagevermögen (n)
Es activo fijo (m)
Fr immobilisations (f pl)
It immobilizzazioni; attivo fisso (f pl; m)
Pt bens fixos (m pl)

**fixed capital** En
De feste Kapitalanlagen (f pl)
Es capital fijo (m)
Fr capital fixe (m)
It capitale fisso (m)
Pt capital fixado (m)

**fixed deposit** En
De Depositeneinlage (f)
Es depósito a plazo fijo (m)
Fr dépôt à terme (fixe) (m)
It deposito a termine fisso (m)
Pt depósito a prazo (m)

**fixed-interest security** En
De festverzinsliches Wertpapier (n)
Es obligación a interés fijo (f)
Fr valeur à revenu fixe (f)
It titolo a interesse fisso (m)
Pt obrigação de juro fixo (f)

**fixed parity** En
De feste Parität (f)
Es paridad fija (f)
Fr parité fixe (f)
It parità fissa (f)
Pt paridade fixa (f)

**fixer des dommages-intérêts** Fr
De den Schadenersatzbetrag feststellen
En assess damages
Es evaluar daños
It valutare i danni
Pt avaliar os danos

**flach** adj De
En flat
Es llano; plano
Fr plat; uniforme
It piatto
Pt plano; liso

**flag** n En
De Flagge (f)
Es bandera (f)
Fr pavillon; drapeau (m)
It bandiera (f)
Pt bandeira (f)

**Flagge** (f) n De
En flag
Es bandera (f)
Fr pavillon; drapeau (m)
It bandiera (f)
Pt bandeira (f)

**flag of convenience** En
De billige Flagge (f)
Es bandera de conveniencia (f)
Fr enseigne de convenance (f)
It bandiera di convenienza (f)
Pt bandeira de conveniência (f)

**flat** n En
Am apartment
De Etagenwohnung (f)
Es apartamento (m)
Fr appartement (m)
It appartamento (m)
Pt apartamento (m)

**flat** adj En
De flach
Es llano; plano
Fr plat; uniforme
It piatto
Pt plano; liso

**flat rate** En
De Einheitssatz (m)
Es tarifa unificada (f)
Fr tarif uniforme (m)
It tariffa uniforme (f)
Pt tarifa de base (f)

**flau** adj De
En bearish
Es bajista
Fr orienté à la baisse
It ribassista
Pt baixista

**fleet** n En
De Flotte (f)
Es flota (f)
Fr flotte (f)
It flotta (f)
Pt frota (f)

**flessibile** adj It
De flexibel; anpassungsfähig
En flexible
Es flexible
Fr flexible
Pt flexível

**fletador** (m) n Es
De Befrachter (m)
En charterer
Fr affréteur (m)
It noleggiatore (m)
Pt fretador (m)

**fletamento** (m) n Es
De Befrachtung (f)
En chartering
Fr affrètement (m)
It noleggio (m)
Pt fretamento (m)

**fletamento de tiempo** (m) Es
De Zeitcharter (f)
En time charter
Fr affrètement à temps (m)
It contratto di noleggio a tempo (m)
Pt fretamento de tempo (m)

**flete** (m) n Es
De Fracht (f)
En freight
Fr fret (m)
It nolo (m)
Pt frete (m)

**flete aéreo** (m) Es
De Luftfracht (f)
En air freight
Fr fret aérien (m)
It trasporto aereo (m)
Pt frete aéreo (m)

**flete pagado** Es
De Fracht vorausbezahlt
En freight pre-paid
Fr fret payé d'avance
It nolo prepagato
Pt frete pago

**flexibilidade de preços** (f) Pt
De Preisdehnbarkeit (f)
En price-elasticity
Es elasticidad de precio (f)
Fr élasticité-prix (m)
It elasticità di prezzo (f)

**flexibel** *adj* De
En flexible
Es flexible
Fr flexible
It flessibile
Pt flexível

**flexible** *adj* En, Es, Fr
De flexibel; anpassungsfähig
It flessibile
Pt flexível

**flexibler Wechselkurs** *(m)* De
En floating exchange rate
Es tipo de cambio flotante *(m)*
Fr taux de change flottant *(m)*
It cambio fluttuante *(m)*
Pt taxa de câmbio flutuante *(f)*

**flexível** *adj* Pt
De flexibel; anpassungsfähig
En flexible
Es flexible
Fr flexible
It flessibile

**flight** *n* En
De Flucht *(f)*
Es vuelo *(m)*
Fr vol *(m)*
It volo *(m)*
Pt voo *(m)*

**float a company** En
De eine Gesellschaft gründen
Es lanzar una compañía
Fr lancer une entreprise
It lanciare una società
Pt lançar uma empresa

**float a loan** En
Am raise a loan
De eine Anleihe begeben
Es emitir un empréstito
Fr émettre un emprunt
It lanciare un prestito
Pt lançar um empréstimo

**floating crane** En
De Pontonkran *(m)*
Es grúa flotante *(f)*
Fr ponton-grue *(m)*
It grue galleggiante *(f)*
Pt guindaste flutuante *(m)*

**floating exchange rate** En
De flexibler Wechselkurs *(m)*
Es tipo de cambio flotante *(m)*

Fr taux de change flottant *(m)*
It cambio fluttuante *(m)*
Pt taxa de câmbio flutuante *(f)*

**floating policy** En
De laufende Polizze *(f)*
Es póliza flotante *(f)*
Fr police flottante *(f)*
It polizza flottante *(f)*
Pt apólice flutuante *(f)*

**floor space** En
De Bodenfläche *(f)*
Es superficie de piso *(f)*
Fr surface de plancher *(f)*
It superficie di pavimento *(f)*
Pt área de chão *(f)*

**flota** *(f)* n Es
De Flotte *(f)*
En fleet
Fr flotte *(f)*
It flotta *(f)*
Pt frota *(f)*

**flota mercanto** *(f)* Es
De Handelsflotte *(f)*
En merchant fleet
Fr flotte marchande *(f)*
It flotta mercantile *(f)*
Pt frota mercante *(f)*

**flota pesquera** *(f)* Es
De Fischerflotte *(f)*
En fishing fleet
Fr flottille de pêche *(f)*
It flotta peschereccia *(f)*
Pt frota de pesca *(f)*

**flott** *adv* De
En afloat
Es a flote
Fr à flot
It flottante
Pt flutuante

**flotta** *(f)* n It
De Flotte *(f)*
En fleet
Es flota *(f)*
Fr flotte *(f)*
Pt frota *(f)*

**flotta mercantile** *(f)* It
De Handelsflotte *(f)*
En merchant fleet
Es flota mercanto *(f)*

Fr flotte marchande *(f)*
Pt frota mercante *(f)*

**flottante** *adv* It
De flott
En afloat
Es a flote
Fr à flot
Pt flutuante

**flotta peschereccia** *(f)* It
De Fischerflotte *(f)*
En fishing fleet
Es flota pesquera *(f)*
Fr flottille de pêche *(f)*
Pt frota de pesca *(f)*

**flotte** *(f)* n Fr
De Flotte *(f)*
En fleet
Es flota *(f)*
It flotta *(f)*
Pt frota *(f)*

**Flotte** *(f)* n De
En fleet
Es flota *(f)*
Fr flotte *(f)*
It flotta *(f)*
Pt frota *(f)*

**flotte marchande** *(f)* Fr
De Handelsflotte *(f)*
En merchant fleet
Es flota mercanto *(f)*
It flotta mercantile *(f)*
Pt frota mercante *(f)*

**flottille de pêche** *(f)* Fr
De Fischerflotte *(f)*
En fishing fleet
Es flota pesquera *(f)*
It flotta peschereccia *(f)*
Pt frota de pesca *(f)*

**flow** *n* En
De Strom *(m)*
Es flujo *(m)*
Fr flux *(m)*
It flusso *(m)*
Pt circulação; fluxo *(f m)*

**flow chart** En
De Flussplan *(m)*
Es diagrama de flujo *(m)*
Fr ordinogramme *(m)*
It diagramma di flusso *(m)*
Pt gráfico de operação *(m)*

**Flucht** (f) n De
En flight
Es vuelo (m)
Fr vol (m)
It volo (m)
Pt voo (m)

**fluctuación** (f) n Es
De Schwankung (f)
En fluctuation
Fr fluctuation (f)
It fluttuazione (f)
Pt flutuação (f)

**fluctuaciones estacionales** (f pl) Es
De saisonbedingte Schwankungen (f pl)
En seasonal fluctuations
Fr variations saisonnières (f pl)
It fluttuazioni stagionali (f pl)
Pt flutuações de época (f pl)

**fluctuando** adj Es
De schwankend
En fluctuating
Fr fluctuant
It fluttuante
Pt flutuando

**fluctuant** adj Fr
De schwankend
En fluctuating
Es fluctuando
It fluttuante
Pt flutuando

**fluctuar** vb Es
De schwanken
En fluctuate
Fr fluctuer
It fluttuare
Pt flutuar

**fluctuate** vb En
De schwanken
Es fluctuar
Fr fluctuer
It fluttuare
Pt flutuar

**fluctuating** adj En
De schwankend
Es fluctuando
Fr fluctuant
It fluttuante
Pt flutuando

**fluctuating rate** En
De schwankender Kurs (m)
Es tipo oscilante (m)
Fr taux variable (m)
It tasso variabile (m)
Pt taxa variável (f)

**fluctuation** n En, Fr (f)
De Schwankung (f)
Es fluctuación (f)
It fluttuazione (f)
Pt flutuação (f)

**fluctuations de personnel** (f pl) Fr
De Arbeitsumsatz (m)
En labour turnover
Es movimiento de la mano de obra (m)
It movimento della mano d'opera (m)
Pt movimento de trabalhadores (m)

**fluctuer** vb Fr
De schwanken
En fluctuate
Es fluctuar
It fluttuare
Pt flutuar

**Fluggesellschaft** (f) n De
En air line
Es línea aérea (f)
Fr compagnie aérienne (f)
It linea aerea (f)
Pt companhia de aviação (f)

**fluidez** (f) n Es, Pt
De Flüssigkeit (f)
En fluidity
Fr fluidité (f)
It fluidità (f)

**fluidità** (f) n It
De Flüssigkeit (f)
En fluidity
Es fluidez (f)
Fr fluidité (f)
Pt fluidez (f)

**fluidité** (f) n Fr
De Flüssigkeit (f)
En fluidity
Es fluidez (f)
It fluidità (f)
Pt fluidez (f)

**fluidity** n En
De Flüssigkeit (f)
Es fluidez (f)
Fr fluidité (f)
It fluidità (f)
Pt fluidez (f)

**flujo** (m) n Es
De Strom (m)
En flow
Fr flux (m)
It flusso (m)
Pt circulação; fluxo (f m)

**flujo de caja** (m) Es
De Cash-flow (n)
En cash flow
Fr cash flow (m)
It flusso di cassa (m)
Pt movimento em dinheiro (m)

**flujo de caja descontado** (m) Es
De diskontiertes Cash-flow (n)
En discounted cash flow (d.c.f.)
Fr flux monétaire actualisé (m)
It flusso di cassa scontato (m)
Pt movimento em dinheiro descontado (m)

**flüssige Aktiven** (n pl) De
En liquid assets
Es activo líquido (m)
Fr actif liquide (m)
It disponibilità; attività liquida (f)
Pt bens de activo líquidos (m pl)

**flüssige Mittel** (n pl) De
En funds available
Es fondos disponibles (m pl)
Fr disponibilités (f pl)
It fondi disponibili (m pl)
Pt fundos disponíveis (m pl)

**Flüssigkeit** (f) n De
En fluidity
Es fluidez (f)
Fr fluidité (f)
It fluidità (f)
Pt fluidez (f)

**flusso** (m) n It
De Strom (m)
En flow

Es flujo (m)
Fr flux (m)
Pt circulação; fluxo (f m)

**flusso di cassa** (m) It
De Cash-flow (n)
En cash flow
Es flujo de caja (m)
Fr cash flow (m)
Pt movimento em dinheiro (m)

**flusso di cassa scontato** (m) It
De diskontiertes Cash-flow (n)
En discounted cash flow (d.c.f.)
Es flujo de caja descontado (m)
Fr flux monétaire actualisé (m)
Pt movimento em dinheiro descontado (m)

**Flussplan** (m) n De
En flow chart
Es diagrama de flujo (m)
Fr ordinogramme (m)
It diagramma di flusso (m)
Pt gráfico de operação (m)

**fluttuante** adj It
De schwankend
En fluctuating
Es fluctuando
Fr fluctuant
Pt flutuando

**fluttuare** vb It
De schwanken
En fluctuate
Es fluctuar
Fr fluctuer
Pt flutuar

**fluttuazione** (f) n It
De Schwankung (f)
En fluctuation
Es fluctuación (f)
Fr fluctuation (f)
Pt flutuação (f)

**fluttuazioni stagionali** (f pl) It
De saisonbedingte Schwankungen (f pl)
En seasonal fluctuations
Es fluctuaciones estacionales (f pl)
Fr variations saisonnières (f pl)
Pt flutuações de época (f pl)

**flutuação** (f) n Pt
De Schwankung (f)
En fluctuation
Es fluctuación (f)
Fr fluctuation (f)
It fluttuazione (f)

**flutuações de época** (f pl) Pt
De saisonbedingte Schwankungen (f pl)
En seasonal fluctuations
Es fluctuaciones estacionales (f pl)
Fr variations saisonnières (f pl)
It fluttuazioni stagionali (f pl)

**flutuando** adj Pt
De schwankend
En fluctuating
Es fluctuando
Fr fluctuant
It fluttuante

**flutuante** adv Pt
De flott
En afloat
Es a flote
Fr à flot
It flottante

**flutuar** vb Pt
De schwanken
En fluctuate
Es fluctuar
Fr fluctuer
It fluttuare

**flux** (m) n Fr
De Strom (m)
En flow
Es flujo (m)
It flusso (m)
Pt circulação; fluxo (f m)

**flux monétaire actualisé** (m) Fr
De diskontiertes Cash-flow (n)
En discounted cash flow (d.c.f.)
Es flujo de caja descontado (m)
It flusso di cassa scontato (m)
Pt movimento em dinheiro descontado (m)

**fluxo** (m) n Pt
De Strom (m)
En flow
Es flujo (m)
Fr flux (m)
It flusso (m)

**foglio d'ordinazione** (m) It
De Bestellformular (n)
En order-form
Es solicitud de pedido (f)
Fr bulletin de commande (m)
Pt impresso de encomenda (m)

**fogo** (m) n Pt
De Brand (m)
En fire
Es fuego; incendio (m)
Fr incendie (f)
It incendio (m)

**foire** (f) n Fr
De Messe (f)
En fair
Es feria (f)
It fiera (f)
Pt feira (f)

**foire commerciale** (f) Fr
De Handelsmesse (f)
En trade fair
Es feria de muestras (f)
It fiera commerciale (f)
Pt feira comercial (f)

**folder** n En
De Mappe (f)
Es carpeta (f)
Fr chemise (f)
It cartella (f)
Pt pasta (f)

**Folgeschaden** (m) n De
En consequential loss
Es pérdida indirecta (f)
Fr perte indirect (f)
It perdita indiretta (f)
Pt perda por consequência (f)

**folha de salários** (f) Pt
De Lohnbuch (n)
En payroll
Es nómina de pago (f)
Fr feuille de paie (f)
It libro paga (m)

**folheto publicitário** *(m)* Pt
De Werbeschrift *(f)*
En advertising brochure
Es folleto publicitario *(m)*
Fr prospectus publicitaire *(m)*
It opuscolo pubblicitario *(m)*

**folleto publicitario** *(m)* Es
De Werbeschrift *(f)*
En advertising brochure
Fr prospectus publicitaire *(m)*
It opuscolo pubblicitario *(m)*
Pt folheto publicitário *(m)*

**follow up** En
De weiterverfolgen
Es perseguir
Fr poursuivre
It seguitare
Pt perseguir

**fomento** *(m)* *n* Pt
De Förderung *(f)*
En promotion
Es promoción *(f)*
Fr promotion *(f)*
It promozione *(f)*

**foncionário público** *(m)* Pt
De Beamte(r) *(m)*
En civil servant
Am government employee
Es funcionario del gobierno *(m)*
Fr fonctionnaire *(m)*
It impiegato statale *(m)*

**fonction** *(f)* *n* Fr
De Aufgabe *(f)*
En function
Es función *(f)*
It funzione *(f)*
Pt função *(f)*

**fonctionnaire** *(m)* *n* Fr
De Beamte(r) *(m)*
En civil servant
Am government employee
Es funcionario del gobierno *(m)*
It impiegato statale *(m)*
Pt foncionário público *(m)*

**fonctionnel** *adj* Fr
De sachlich; praktisch
En functional
Es funcional

It funzionale
Pt funcional

**fonctionnel** *(m)* *n* Fr
De persönlicher Assistent *(m)*
En personal assistant (PA)
Am administrative assistant
Es asistente privado *(m)*
It assistente privato *(m)*
Pt secretário *(m)*

**fondare** *vb* It
De einrichten; gründen
En establish; found
Es fundar; establecer
Fr fonder; établir
Pt fundar; estabelecer

**fondateur** *(m)* *n* Fr
De Gründer *(m)*
En founder
Es fundador *(m)*
It fondatore *(m)*
Pt fundador *(m)*

**fondatore** *(m)* *n* It
De Gründer *(m)*
En founder
Es fundador *(m)*
Fr fondateur *(m)*
Pt fundador *(m)*

**fonder** (établir) *vb* Fr
De einrichten; gründen
En establish; found
Es fundar; establecer
It fondare; istituire
Pt fundar; estabelecer

**fonder** (une créance) *vb* Fr
De fundieren
En fund
Es fundar; consolidar
It consolidare
Pt dotar de fundos

**fondersi** *vb* It
De fusionieren
En amalgamate
Am merge
Es amalgamar
Fr fusionner
Pt amalgamar

**fondi disponibili** *(m pl)* It
De flüssige Mittel *(n pl)*
En funds available
Es fondos disponibles *(m pl)*

Fr disponibilités *(f pl)*
Pt fundos disponíveis *(m pl)*

**fondo** *(m)* *n* Es, It
De Fonds *(m)*
En fund
Fr fonds *(m)*
Pt fundos *(m pl)*

**fondo circulante** *(m)* Es
De Umlaufkapital *(n)*
En revolving fund
Fr fonds renouvelable *(m)*
It fondo rotativo *(m)*
Pt fundos renováveis *(m pl)*

**fondo de amortización** *(m)* Es
De Tilgungsfonds *(m)*
En sinking fund
Fr fonds d'amortissement *(m)*
It fondo di ammortamento *(m)*
Pt fundo de amortização *(m)*

**fondo de compensación** *(m)* Es
De Ausgleichsfonds *(m)*
En equalization fund
Fr fonds de régularisation *(m)*
It cassa di compensazione *(f)*
Pt fundo de compensação *(m)*

**fondo de reserva** *(m)* Es
De Reservefonds *(m)*
En reserve fund
Fr fonds de réserve *(m)*
It fondo di riserva *(m)*
Pt fundo de reserva *(m)*

**fondo di ammortamento** *(m)* It
De Tilgungsfonds *(m)*
En sinking fund
Es fondo de amortización *(m)*
Fr fonds d'amortissement *(m)*
Pt fundo de amortização *(m)*

**fondo di riserva** *(m)* It
De Reservefonds *(m)*
En reserve fund
Es fondo de reserva *(m)*
Fr fonds de réserve *(m)*
Pt fundo de reserva *(m)*

**Fondo Europeo** *(m)* Es, It
De Europäische Fonds *(m)*
En European Fund
Fr Fonds Européen *(m)*
Pt Fundo Europeu *(m)*

**fondo fiduciario** *(m)* Es, It
De Treuhandfonds *(m)*
En trust fund
Fr fonds fiduciaire *(m)*
Pt fundação fiduciária *(f)*

**fondo fiduciario discrezionale**
*(m)* It
De unumschränkte Treuhand
*(f)*
En discretionary trust
Es fideicomiso discrecional *(m)*
Fr fidéicommis à appréciation
*(m)*
Pt fundação discricionária *(f)*

**Fondo Monetario Interna-**
**cional** *(m)* Es
De Internationaler Währungs-
fonds *(m)*
En International Monetary
Fund (IMF)
Fr Fonds Monétaire Interna-
tional *(m)*
It Fondo Monetario Inter-
nazionale *(m)*
Pt Fundo Monetário Inter-
nacional *(m)*

**Fondo Monetario Internazio-**
**nale** *(m)* It
De Internationaler Währungs-
fonds *(m)*
En International Monetary
Fund (IMF)
Es Fondo Monetario Inter-
nacional *(m)*
Fr Fonds Monétaire Interna-
tional *(m)*
Pt Fundo Monetário Inter-
nacional *(m)*

**fondo rotativo** *(m)* It
De Umlaufkapital *(n)*
En revolving fund
Es fondo circulante *(m)*
Fr fonds renouvelable *(m)*
Pt fundos renováveis *(m pl)*

**fondos disponibles** *(m pl)* Es
De flüssige Mittel *(n pl)*
En funds available
Fr disponibilités *(f pl)*
It fondi disponibili *(m pl)*
Pt fundos disponíveis *(m pl)*

**fonds** *(m)* n Fr
De Fonds *(m)*
En fund
Es fondo *(m)*
It fondo *(m)*
Pt fundos *(m pl)*

**Fonds** *(m)* n De
En fund
Es fondo *(m)*
Fr fonds *(m)*
It fondo *(m)*
Pt fundos *(m pl)*

**fonds bloqués** *(m pl)* Fr
De eingefrorene Guthaben *(n
pl)*
En frozen assets
Es activos congelados *(m pl)*
It attivo congelato *(m)*
Pt bens do activo congelados
*(m pl)*

**fonds d'amortissement** *(m)* Fr
De Tilgungsfonds *(m)*
En sinking fund
Es fondo de amortización *(m)*
It fondo di ammortamento
*(m)*
Pt fundo de amortização *(m)*

**fonds de régularisation** *(m)* Fr
De Ausgleichsfonds *(m)*
En equalization fund
Es fondo de compensación
*(m)*
It cassa di compensazione *(f)*
Pt fundo de compensação *(m)*

**fonds de réserve** *(m)* Fr
De Reservefonds *(m)*
En reserve fund
Es fondo de reserva *(m)*
It fondo di riserva *(m)*
Pt fundo de reserva *(m)*

**fonds de roulement** *(m)* Fr
De Betriebskapital *(n)*
En trading capital
Es capital de explotación *(m)*
It capitale d'esercizio *(m)*
Pt capital de exploração *(m)*

**fonds de stabilisation des**
**changes** *(m pl)* Fr
De Währungsausgleichsfonds
*(m)*

En exchange equalization account
Es cuenta de compensación
de cambio *(f)*
It conto per la stabilizzazione
dei cambi *(m)*
Pt conta de compensação de
transacções *(f)*

**Fonds Européen** *(m)* Fr
De Europäische Fonds *(m)*
En European Fund
Es Fondo Europeo *(m)*
It Fondo Europeo *(m)*
Pt Fundo Europeu *(m)*

**fonds fiduciaire** *(m)* Fr
De Treuhandfonds *(m)*
En trust fund
Es fondo fiduciario *(m)*
It fondo fiduciario *(m)*
Pt fundação fiduciária *(f)*

**Fonds Monétaire Interna-**
**tional** *(m)* Fr
De Internationaler Währungs-
fonds *(m)*
En International Monetary
Fund (IMF)
Es Fondo Monetario Inter-
nacional *(m)*
It Fondo Monetario Inter-
nazionale *(m)*
Pt Fundo Monetário Inter-
nacional *(m)*

**fonds renouvelable** *(m)* Fr
De Umlaufkapital *(n)*
En revolving fund
Es fondo circulante *(m)*
It fondo rotativo *(m)*
Pt fundos renováveis *(m pl)*

**foodstuffs** *pl* n En
De Esswaren *(f pl)*
Es comestibles *(m pl)*
Fr alimentation *(f)*
It generi alimentari *(m pl)*
Pt géneros alimentícios *(m pl)*

**footnote** n En
De Fussnote *(f)*
Es apostilla *(f)*
Fr apostille *(f)*
It postilla *(f)*
Pt nota de rodapé *(f)*

**força** (f) n Pt
De Gewalt (f)
En force
Es fuerza (f)
Fr force (f)
It forza (f)

**forçado** adj Pt
De Zwangs-
En forced
Es forzado
Fr forcé
It forzato

**forças armadas** (f pl) Pt
De Streitkräfte (f pl)
En armed forces
Es fuerzas armadas (f pl)
Fr forces armées (f pl)
It forze armate (f pl)

**forças de mercado** (f pl) Pt
De Marktkräfte (f pl)
En market forces
Es fuerzas del mercado (f pl)
Fr forces du marché (f pl)
It forze di mercato (f pl)

**force** n En, Fr (f)
De Gewalt (f)
Es fuerza (f)
It forza (f)
Pt força (f)

**forcé** adj Fr
De Zwangs-
En forced
Es forzado
It forzato
Pt forçado

**forced** adj En
De Zwangs-
Es forzado
Fr forcé
It forzato
Pt forçado

**forced liquidation** Am
En compulsory winding-up
De Zwangsliquidation (f)
Es liquidación forzosa (f)
Fr liquidation forcée (f)
It liquidazione forzata (f)
Pt liquidação forçada (f)

**forced sale** En
De Zwangsverkauf (m)
Es venta forzosa (f)
Fr vente forcée (f)
It vendita sforzosa (f)
Pt venda forçada (f)

**forces armées** (f pl) Fr
De Streitkräfte (f pl)
En armed forces
Es fuerzas armadas (f pl)
It forze armate (f pl)
Pt forças armadas (f pl)

**forces du marché** (f pl) Fr
De Marktkräfte (f pl)
En market forces
Es fuerzas del mercado (f pl)
It forze di mercato (f pl)
Pt forças de mercado (f pl)

**fördern** vb De
En promote
Es promover
Fr chauffer
It dare impulso a
Pt promover

**Forderung** (f) n De
En claim; demand
Es reclamación (f)
Fr demande (f)
It domanda (f)
Pt reclamação (f)

**Förderung** (f) n De
En promotion
Es promoción (f)
Fr promotion (f)
It promozione (f)
Pt fomento (m)

**forecast** vb En
De vorhersehen
Es pronosticar
Fr prévoir
It pronosticare
Pt prognosticar

**forecasting** n En
De Voraussagen (n)
Es pronóstico (m)
Fr prévision (f)
It previsione (f)
Pt previsão (f)

**foreclosure** n En
De Zwangsvollstreckung (f)
Es venta por juicio hipotecario (f)
Fr vente de l'immeuble hypothéqué (f)
It vendita per giudizio ipotecario (f)
Pt execução judicial a uma hipoteca (f)

**foreign** adj En
De ausländisch; fremd
Es extranjero
Fr étranger
It straniero; estero
Pt estrangeiro

**foreign bill** En
De Auslandswechsel (m)
Es letra sobre el exterior (f)
Fr lettre de change sur l'étranger (f)
It cambiale sull' estero (f)
Pt letra de país a país (cambial) (f)

**foreign currency** En
De Devisen (f pl)
Es divisas extranjeras (f pl)
Fr devises (f pl)
It valuta estera (f)
Pt moeda estrangeira (f)

**foreign currency account** Am
En external account
De Auslandskonto (n)
Es cuenta exterior (f)
Fr compte transférable (m)
It conto estero (m)
Pt conta externa (f)

**foreigner** n En
De Ausländer (m)
Es extranjero (m)
Fr étranger (m)
It straniero (m)
Pt estrangeiro (m)

**foreign exchange** En
De Devisen (f pl)
Es divisas extranjeras (f pl)
Fr devises (f pl)
It valuta estera (f)
Pt moeda estrangeira (f)

279

formality

**foreign exchange rates** En
De Devisenkurs (m)
Es tasas de cambio exterior (f pl)
Fr cours des changes (m)
It corso dei cambi (m)
Pt taxas de câmbio (f pl)

**foreign labour** En
De Fremdarbeiterschaft (f)
Es mano de obra extranjera (f)
Fr main-d'œuvre étrangère (f)
It mano d'opera straniera (f)
Pt mão-de-obra estrangeira (f)

**foreign trade** En
De Aussenhandel (m)
Es comercio exterior (m)
Fr commerce extérieur (m)
It commercio estero (m)
Pt comércio externo (m)

**foreman** n En
De Vorarbeiter (m)
Es capataz (m)
Fr contremaître; chef d'équipe (m)
It capo operaio; capo squadra (m)
Pt encarregado; capataz (m)

**forfeit clause** En
De Bussklausel (f)
Es cláusula de decomiso (f)
Fr clause de dédit (f)
It clausola di penalità per inandempienza (f)
Pt cláusula de cedência (f)

**forge** vb En
De fälschen
Es falsificar
Fr contrefaire
It contraffare
Pt falsificar

**forged cheque** En
De gefälschter Scheck (m)
Es cheque falsificado (m)
Fr faux chèque (m)
It assegno falsificato (m)
Pt cheque falsificado (m)

**forger** n En
De Fälscher (m)
Es falsificador (m)
Fr faux-monnayeur; faussaire (m)

It falsificatore (m)
Pt falsificador (m)

**forgery** n En
De Fälschung (f)
Es falsificación (f)
Fr contrefaçon; faux (f m)
It falsificazione (f)
Pt falsificação (f)

**form** (printed sheet) n En
De Formular (n)
Es formulario (m)
Fr formule (f)
It modulo (m)
Pt formulário (m)

**form** (shape) En
De Form (f)
Es forma (f)
Fr forme (f)
It forma (f)
Pt forma (f)

**form** (constitute) vb En
De bilden
Es constituir
Fr constituer
It constituire
Pt constituir

**form** (establish) vb En
De gründen
Es establecer; formar
Fr former
It formare
Pt estabelecer

**Form** (f) De
En form
Es forma (f)
Fr forme (f)
It forma (f)
Pt forma (f)

**forma** (f) Es, It, Pt
De Form (f)
En form
Fr forme (f)

**formación profesional** (f) Es
De Berufsausbildung (f)
En vocational training
Fr formation professionnelle (f)
It addestramento professionale (m)
Pt treino vocacional (m)

**formal** adj En, Es, Pt
De formell
Fr formel
It formale

**formale** adj It
De formell
En formal
Es formal
Fr formel
Pt formal

**formalidad** (f) n Es
De Formalität (f)
En formality
Fr formalité (f)
It formalità (f)
Pt formalidade (f)

**formalidade** (f) n Pt
De Formalität (f)
En formality
Es formalidad (f)
Fr formalité (f)
It formalità (f)

**formalità** (f) n It
De Formalität (f)
En formality
Es formalidad (f)
Fr formalité (f)
Pt formalidade (f)

**Formalität** (f) n De
En formality
Es formalidad (f)
Fr formalité (f)
It formalità (f)
Pt formalidade (f)

**formalité** (f) n Fr
De Formalität (f)
En formality
Es formalidad (f)
It formalità (f)
Pt formalidade (f)

**formalités douanières** (f pl) Fr
De Verzollung (f)
En customs clearance
Es despacho de aduana (m)
It sdoganamento (m)
Pt despacho de alfândega (m)

**formality** n En
De Formalität (f)
Es formalidad (f)
Fr formalité (f)

It formalità (f)
Pt formalidade (f)

**formal notice** En
De Inverzugsetzung (f)
Es aviso oficial (m)
Fr mise en demeure (f)
It intimazione (f)
Pt notificação formal (f)

**formare** vb It
De gründen
En form
Es establecer; formar
Fr former
Pt estabelecer

**formation professionnelle** (f) Fr
De Berufsausbildung (f)
En vocational training
Es formación profesional (f)
It addestramento professionale (m)
Pt treino vocacional (m)

**forme** (f) Fr
De Form (f)
En form
Es forma (f)
It forma (f)
Pt forma (f)

**formel** adj Fr
De formell
En formal
Es formal
It formale
Pt formal

**Formel** (f) n De
En formula
Es fórmula (f)
Fr formule (f)
It formula (f)
Pt fórmula (f)

**formell** adj De
En formal
Es formal
Fr formel
It formale
Pt formal

**former** vb Fr
De gründen
En form
Es establecer; formar

It formare
Pt estabelecer

**formlos** (nicht formell) adj De
En informal
Es sin ceremonia
Fr sans formalités
It senza formalità
Pt sem formalidade

**formula** n En, It (f)
De Formel (f)
Es fórmula (f)
Fr formule (f)
Pt fórmula (f)

**fórmula** (f) n Es, Pt
De Formel (f)
En formula
Fr formule (f)
It formula (f)

**formulaire** (m) n Fr
De Vordruck (m)
En printed form
Es formulario; impreso (m)
It modulo stampato (m)
Pt impresso (m)

**formulaire de demande** (m) Fr
De Antragsformular (n)
En application form
Es formulario de solicitud (m)
It modulo di domanda (m)
Pt formulário de requisição (m)

**formulaire en blanc** (m) Fr
De Blankoformular (n)
En blank form
Es formulario en blanco (m)
It modulo in bianco (m)
Pt impresso em branco (m)

**Formular** (n) n De
En form
Es formulario (m)
Fr formule (f)
It modulo (m)
Pt formulário (m)

**formulario** (m) n Es
De Formular (n)
En form
Fr formule (f)
It modulo (m)
Pt formulário (m)

**formulário** (m) n Pt
De Formular (n)
En form
Es formulario (m)
Fr formule (f)
It modulo (m)

**formulário de requisição** (m) Pt
De Antragsformular (n)
En application form
Es formulario de solicitud (m)
Fr formulaire de demande (m)
It modulo di domanda (m)

**formulario de solicitud** (m) Es
De Antragsformular (n)
En application form
Fr formulaire de demande (m)
It modulo di domanda (m)
Pt formulário de requisição (m)

**formulario en blanco** (m) Es
De Blankoformular (n)
En blank form
Fr formulaire en blanc (m)
It modulo in bianco (m)
Pt impresso em branco (m)

**formule** (f) n Fr
De Formel (f)
En formula
Es fórmula (f)
It formula (f)
Pt fórmula (f)

**formule** (imprimée) (f) n Fr
De Formular (n)
En form
Es formulario (m)
It modulo (m)
Pt formulário (m)

**fornecedor** (m) n Pt
De Lieferant (m)
En supplier
Es proveedor (m)
Fr fournisseur (m)
It fornitore (m)

**fornecer** vb Pt
De beliefern
En supply
Es surtir
Fr fournir
It fornire

**fornecimentos em existência** *(m pl)* Pt
De lieferfertiges Angebot *(n)*
En supplies on hand
Es provisiones existentes *(f pl)*
Fr ressources existantes *(f pl)*
It forniture esistenti *(f pl)*

**fornire** *vb* It
De beliefern
En supply
Es surtir
Fr fournir
Pt fornecer

**fornitore** *(m)* *n* It
De Lieferant *(m)*
En supplier
Es proveedor *(m)*
Fr fournisseur *(m)*
Pt fornecedor *(m)*

**forniture esistenti** *(f pl)* It
De lieferfertiges Angebot *(n)*
En supplies on hand
Es provisiones existentes *(f pl)*
Fr ressources existantes *(f pl)*
Pt fornecimentos em existên-cia *(m pl)*

**Forschung** *(f)* *n* De
En research
Es investigación *(f)*
Fr recherche *(f)*
It ricerca *(f)*
Pt investigação *(f)*

**Fortbildung** *(f)* *n* De
En higher education
Es enseñanza superior *(f)*
Fr enseignement supérieur *(m)*
It insegnamento superiore *(m)*
Pt instrução superior *(f)*

**forte amende** *(f)* Fr
De schwere Busse *(f)*
En heavy fine
Es sanción elevada *(f)*
It forte multa *(f)*
Pt multa pesada *(f)*

**forte multa** *(f)* It
De schwere Busse *(f)*
En heavy fine
Es sanción elevada *(f)*

Fr forte amende *(f)*
Pt multa pesada *(f)*

**forte perdita** *(f)* It
De schwere Verluste *(m pl)*
En heavy loss
Es fuerte pérdida; pérdida sensible *(f)*
Fr lourde perte *(f)*
Pt perda avultada *(f)*

**Fortfall der Geschäftsgrund-lage** *(m)* De
En frustration
Es frustración *(f)*
Fr frustration *(f)*
It frustrazione *(f)*
Pt frustração *(f)*

**forthcoming** *adj* En
De bevorstehend
Es próximo
Fr prochain
It prossimo
Pt próximo

**forti spese** *(f pl)* It
De drückende Spesen *(f pl)*
En heavy charges
Es gastos fuertes *(m pl)*
Fr charges lourdes *(f pl)*
Pt encargos pesados *(m pl)*

**forward** *adj* En
De Termin-
Es a término
Fr en avant; à terme
It a termine
Pt adiante

**forward** *vb* En
De expedieren; absenden
Es expedir; remitir
Fr envoyer; expédier
It spedire
Pt expedir; remeter

**forward dealings** En
De Zeitgeschäfte *(n pl)*
Es negociaciones a término *(f pl)*
Fr opérations à terme *(f pl)*
It operazioni a termine *(f pl)*
Pt transacções adiantadas *(f pl)*

**forward delivery** En
De Terminlieferung *(f)*
Es entrega futura *(f)*
Fr livraison à terme *(f)*
It consegna a termine *(f)*
Pt entrega futura *(f)*

**forward exchange** En
De Termindevisen *(f pl)*
Es divisas a término *(f pl)*
Fr change à terme *(m)*
It cambio a termine *(m)*
Pt divisas adiantada *(f pl)*

**forwarding agent** En
De Spediteur *(m)*
Es agente expedidor *(m)*
Fr transitaire *(m)*
It spedizioniere *(m)*
Pt agente expedidor *(m)*

**forward price** En
De Terminnotierung *(f)*
Es precio a término *(m)*
Fr cours à terme *(m)*
It prezzo per futura consegna *(m)*
Pt preço adiantado *(m)*

**forza** *(f)* *n* It
De Gewalt *(f)*
En force
Es fuerza *(f)*
Fr force *(f)*
Pt força *(f)*

**forzado** *adj* Es
De Zwangs-
En forced
Fr forcé
It forzato
Pt forçado

**forzato** *adj* It
De Zwangs-
En forced
Es forzado
Fr forcé
Pt forçado

**forze armate** *(f pl)* It
De Streitkräfte *(f pl)*
En armed forces
Es fuerzas armadas *(f pl)*
Fr forces armées *(f pl)*
Pt forças armadas *(f pl)*

**forze di mercato** *(f pl)* It
De Marktkräfte *(f pl)*
En market forces
Es fuerzas del mercado *(f pl)*
Fr forces du marché *(f pl)*
Pt forças de mercado *(f pl)*

**forze di vendita** *(f pl)* It
De Verkaufspersonal *(n)*
En sales force
Es personal de ventas *(m)*
Fr personnel de vente *(m)*
Pt pessoal de vendas *(m)*

**foudre** *(f)* n Fr
De Blitz *m*
En lightning
Es relámpago *(m)*
It fulmine *(m)*
Pt relâmpago *(m)*

**foul (dirty) bill of lading** En
De einschränkendes Konnossement *(n)*
Es conocimiento de embarque con objecciones *(m)*
Fr connaissement avec réserve *(m)*
It polizza di carico con riserve *(f)*
Pt conhecimento com embargos *(m)*

**found** *vb* En
De gründen
Es fundar
Fr fonder
It fondare
Pt fundar

**founder** n En
De Gründer *(m)*
Es fundador *(m)*
Fr fondateur *(m)*
It fondatore *(m)*
Pt fundador *(m)*

**founder member** En
De Gründermitglied *(m)*
Es miembro fundador *(m)*
Fr membre fondateur *(m)*
It socio fondatore *(m)*
Pt membro fondador *(m)*

**founder's shares** En
De Gründeraktien *(f pl)*
Es acciones del fundador *(f pl)*
Fr actions de fondateur *(f pl)*

It azioni del fondatore *(f pl)*
Pt acções de fundador *(f pl)*

**fourgon** *(m)* n Fr
De Packwagen *(m)*
En guard's van
Es furgón *(m)*
It bagagliaio *(m)*
Pt carruagem do guarda *(f)*

**fournir** *vb* Fr
De beliefern
En supply
Es surtir
It fornire
Pt fornecer

**fournisseur** *(m)* n Fr
De Lieferant *(m)*
En supplier
Es proveedor *(m)*
It fornitore *(m)*
Pt fornecedor *(m)*

**fracção** *(f)* n Pt
De Bruchteil *(n)*
En fraction
Es fracción *(f)*
Fr fraction *(f)*
It frazione *(f)*

**fracción** *(f)* n Es
De Bruchteil *(n)*
En fraction
Fr fraction *(f)*
It frazione *(f)*
Pt fracção *(f)*

**fraccionamiento de la carga** *(m)* Es
De Löschen der Ladung *(n)*
En breaking bulk
Fr rupture de charge *(f)*
It inizio scarico *(m)*
Pt retalhar a carga *(f)*

**Fracht** *(f)* n De
En freight
Es flete *(m)*
Fr fret *(m)*
It nolo *(m)*
Pt frete *(m)*

**Frachtbrief** *(m)* n De
En consignment note
Es nota de consignación *(f)*
Fr lettre de voiture *(f)*

It nota di spedizione *(f)*
Pt guia de consignação *(f)*

**frachtfrei** *adv* De
En carriage free
Am F.O.B. destination
Es franco de porte
Fr franco
It porto franco
Pt porte gratis

**Frachtschiff** *(n)* n De
En cargo boat
Es buque de carga *(m)*
Fr cargo *(m)*
It nave da carico *(f)*
Pt barco de carga *(m)*

**Fracht vorausbezahlt** De
En freight pre-paid
Es flete pagado
Fr fret payé d'avance
It nolo prepagato
Pt frete pago

**fraction** n En, Fr *(f)*
De Bruchteil *(n)*
Es fracción *(f)*
It frazione *(f)*
Pt fracção *(f)*

**Fragebogen** *(m)* n De
En questionnaire
Es cuestionario *(m)*
Fr questionnaire *(m)*
It questionario *(m)*
Pt questionário *(m)*

**frágil** *adj* Es, Pt
De zerbrechlich
En fragile
Fr fragile
It fragile

**fragile** *adj* En, Fr, It
De zerbrechlich
Es frágil
Pt frágil

**frais** *(m pl)* n Fr
De Kosten; Ausgaben *(pl; f pl)*
En charges; expenditure
Es costes; desembolso *(m pl; m)*
It spesa; spese *(f; f pl)*
Pt despesa; despesas *(f; f pl)*

**frais à percevoir à la livraison**
Fr
De  per Nachnahme
En  charges forward
Es  costes a reembolso
It  spese assegnate
Pt  entrega contra reembolso

**frais bancaires** (m pl) Fr
De  Bankspesen (f pl)
En  bank charges
Es  gastos de banco (m pl)
It  spese di banca (f pl)
Pt  taxas bancárias (f pl)

**frais commerciaux** (m pl) Fr
De  Geschäftskosten (pl)
En  business expenses
Es  gastos de los negocios (m pl)
It  spese generali (f pl)
Pt  despesas do exercício (f pl)

**frais de magasinage** (m pl) Fr
De  Lagergeld (n)
En  storage charges
Es  gastos de almacenaje (m pl)
It  spese di magazzinaggio (f pl)
Pt  encargos de armazenamento (m pl)

**frais de manutention** (m pl) Fr
De  Manipulationsgebühr (f)
En  handling charges
Es  gastos de manutención (m pl)
It  spese di gestione (f pl)
Pt  custas de manejo (f pl)

**frais d'encaissement** (m pl) Fr
De  Einzugskosten (pl)
En  collection charges
Es  gastos de cobranza (m pl)
It  spese di riscossione (f pl)
Pt  gastos de cobrança (m pl)

**frais de poste** (m pl) Fr
De  Postspesen (f pl)
En  postage; postal charges
Es  gastos de correo (m pl)
It  spese postali (f pl)
Pt  despesas de franquia (f pl)

**frais de représentation** (m pl) Fr
De  Repräsentationskosten (pl)
En  entertainment expenses
Es  gastos de representación (m pl)
It  spese di rappresentanza (f pl)
Pt  despesas de representação (f pl)

**frais de vente** (m) Fr
De  Verkaufskosten (pl)
En  selling cost
Es  coste de venta (m)
It  costo di vendita (m)
Pt  custo de venda (m)

**frais de voyage** (m pl) Fr
De  Reisekosten (pl)
En  travelling expenses
Es  dietas de viajes (f pl)
It  spese di viaggio (f pl)
Pt  despesas de viagem (f pl)

**frais d'exploitation** (m pl) Fr
De  Betriebsausgaben (f pl)
En  operating costs
Es  costes operacionales (m pl)
It  spese di gestione (f pl)
Pt  custos de exercício (m pl)

**frais directs** (m pl) Fr
De  Einzelkosten (pl)
En  direct expenses
Es  gastos directos (m pl)
It  spese dirette (f pl)
Pt  despesas directas (f pl)

**frais divers** (m pl) Fr
De  verschiedene Ausgaben (f pl)
En  sundry expenses
Es  gastos varios (m pl)
It  spese varie (f pl)
Pt  despesas diversas (f pl)

**frais généraux** (m pl) Fr
De  allgemeine Unkosten; Generalunkosten (pl)
En  general expenses; overheads
Es  gastos generales (m pl)
It  spese generali (f pl)
Pt  despesas gerais (f pl)

**frais indirects** (m pl) Fr
De  Gemeinkosten (pl)
En  indirect costs
Es  costes indirectos (m pl)
It  costi indiretti (m pl)
Pt  custos indirectos (m pl)

**franc d'avarie particulière** Fr
De  frei von besonderer Havarie
En  free of particular average (fpa)
Es  franco de avería particular
It  franco di avaria particolare
Pt  franco de avaria particular

**franc de toutes avaries** Fr
De  ganz havariefrei
En  free of all averages
Es  franco de toda avería
It  franco d'ogni avaria
Pt  franco de todas as avarías

**franchigia** (f) n It
De  Franchise (f)
En  exemption
Es  franquicia (f)
Fr  franchise (f)
Pt  franquia (f)

**franchise** (concession) n En
De  Konzession (f)
Es  concesión (f)
Fr  concession (f)
It  concessione (f)
Pt  concessão (f)

**franchise** (f) n Fr
De  Franchise (f)
En  exemption
Es  franquicia (f)
It  franchigia (f)
Pt  franquia (f)

**Franchise** (f) n De
En  exemption
Es  franquicia (f)
Fr  franchise (f)
It  franchigia (f)
Pt  franquia (f)

**franco** adv Fr
De  frachtfrei
En  carriage free
Am  F.O.B. destination
Es  franco de porte
It  porto franco
Pt  porte gratis

**franco à bord** Fr
De  frei an Bord
En  free on board (fob)
Es  franco a bordo

It franco a bordo
Pt franco a bordo

**franco a bordo** Es, It, Pt
De frei an Bord
En free on board (fob)
Fr franco à bord

**franco al costado del buque**
    Es
De frei Schiffseite
En free alongside ship (fas)
Fr franco le long du bord
It franco lungobordo
Pt f.a.s.

**franco banchina** It
De frei Kai
En free on quay (foq)
Es franco sobre muelle
Fr franco quai
Pt franco sobre cais (foq)

**francobollo** (m) n It
De Briefmarke (f)
En postage stamp
Es sello de correos (m)
Fr timbre-poste (m)
Pt selo postal (m)

**franco-comisión** Es
De maklergebührenfrei
En free of commission
Fr franco courtage
It franco mediazione
Pt isento de comissão

**franco courtage** Fr
De maklergebührenfrei
En free of commission
Es franco-comisión
It franco mediazione
Pt isento de comissão

**franco de avaria particular** Pt
De frei von besonderer Havarie
En free of particular average
    (fpa)
Es franco de avería particular
Fr franc d'avarie particulière
It franco di avaria particolare

**franco de avería particular** Es
De frei von besonderer Havarie
En free of particular average
    (fpa)
Fr franc d'avarie particulière

It franco di avaria particolare
Pt franco de avaria particular

**franco d'emballage** Fr
De Verpackung einbegriffen
En including packing
Es franco embalaje
It imballaggio incluso
Pt incluindo embalagem

**franco de·porte** Es
De portofrei; frachtfrei
En postage paid; carriage free
Fr port-payé; franco
It porto pagato; franco di
    porto
Pt porte pago; porte gratis

**franco de toda avería** Es
De ganz havariefrei
En free of all averages
Fr franc de toutes avaries
It franco d'ogni avaria
Pt franco de todas as avarías

**franco de todas as avarías** Pt
De ganz havariefrei
En free of all averages
Es franco de toda avería
Fr franc de toutes avaries
It franco d'ogni avaria

**franco di avaria particolare** It
De frei von besonderer Havarie
En free of particular average
    (fpa)
Es franco de avería particular
Fr franc d'avarie particulière
Pt franco de avaria particular

**franco di porto** It
De franko; portofrei
En carriage paid; carriage free
Am freight    charges    paid;
    F.O.B. destination
Es a porte pagado; franco de
    porte
Fr port-payé; franco
Pt porte pago; porte gratis

**franco dock** Fr, It
De frei Docklager
En delivered docks
Es franco en muelle
Pt docas francas

**franco d'ogni avaria** It
De ganz havariefrei
En free of all averages
Es franco de toda avería
Fr franc de toutes avaries
Pt franco de todas as avarías

**franco embalaje** Es
De Verpackung einbegriffen
En including packing
Fr franco d'emballage
It imballaggio incluso
Pt incluindo embalagem

**franco en muelle** Es
De frei Docklager
En delivered docks
Fr franco dock
It franco dock
Pt docas francas

**franco fabbrica** It
De ab Fabrik
En ex factory
Es de fábrica
Fr prise usine
Pt na fábrica

**franco le long du bord** Fr
De frei Schiffseite
En free alongside ship (fas)
Es franco al costado del buque
It franco lungobordo
Pt f.a.s.

**franco lungobordo** It
De frei Schiffseite
En free alongside ship (fas)
Es franco al costado del buque
Fr franco le long du bord
Pt f.a.s.

**franco magazzino** It
De an Zollfreilager
En ex warehouse
Es puesto en almacén
Fr à prendre en entrepôt
Pt no armazzém

**franco mediazione** It
De maklergebührenfrei
En free of commission
Es franco-comisión
Fr franco courtage
Pt isento de comissão

**franco quai** Fr
De frei Kai
En free on quay (foq)
Es franco sobre muelle
It franco banchina
Pt franco sobre cais (foq)

**franco sobre cais (foq)** Pt
De frei Kai
En free on quay (foq)
Es franco sobre muelle
Fr franco quai
It franco banchina

**franco sobre muelle** Es
De frei Kai
En free on quay (foq)
Fr franco quai
It franco banchina
Pt franco sobre cais (foq)

**franco sobre vagão** Pt
De frei Waggon
En free on rail (for)
Es franco sobre vagón
Fr franco wagon
It franco vagone

**franco sobre vagón** Es
De frei Waggon
En free on rail (for)
Fr franco wagon
It franco vagone
Pt franco sobre vagão

**franco vagone** It
De frei Waggon
En free on rail (for)
Es franco sobre vagón
Fr franco wagon
Pt franco sobre vagão

**franco wagon** Fr
De frei Waggon
En free on rail (for)
Es franco sobre vagón
It franco vagone
Pt franco sobre vagão

**Frankiermaschine** (f) n De
En franking machine
Es máquina de franquear (f)
Fr machine à affranchir (f)
It affrancatrice postale (f)
Pt máquina de franquear (f)

**franking machine** En
De Frankiermaschine (f)
Es máquina de franquear (f)
Fr machine à affranchir (f)
It affrancatrice postale (f)
Pt máquina de franquear (f)

**franko** adv De
En carriage paid
Am freight charges paid
Es a porte pagado
Fr port-payé; franco
It franco di porto
Pt porte pago

**franquia** (f) n Pt
De Franchise (f)
En exemption
Es franquicia (f)
Fr franchise (f)
It franchigia (f)

**franquicia** (f) n Es
De Franchise (f)
En exemption
Fr franchise (f)
It franchigia (f)
Pt franquia (f)

**fraud** n En
De Betrug (m)
Es fraude (m)
Fr fraude (f)
It frode (f)
Pt fraude (f)

**fraude** n Es (m); Fr, Pt (f)
De Betrug (m)
En fraud
It frode (f)

**fraude fiscale** (f) Fr
De Steuerhinterziehung (f)
En evasion of tax
Es evasión de pago de impuestos (f)
It evasione d'imposta (f)
Pt fuga a impostos (f)

**fraudolento** adj It
De betrügerisch
En fraudulent
Es fraudulento
Fr frauduleux
Pt fraudulento

**fraudulent** adj En
De betrügerisch
Es fraudulento
Fr frauduleux
It fraudolento
Pt fraudulento

**fraudulento** adj Es, Pt
De betrügerisch
En fraudulent
Fr frauduleux
It fraudolento

**frauduleux** adj Fr
De betrügerisch
En fraudulent
Es fraudulento
It fraudolento
Pt fraudulento

**frazione** (f) n It
De Bruchteil (n)
En fraction
Es fracción (f)
Fr fraction (f)
Pt fracção (f)

**frecuencia** (f) n Es
De Häufigkeit (f)
En frequency
Fr fréquence (f)
It frequenza (f)
Pt frequência (f)

**free** vb En
De befreien
Es liberar
Fr libérer; affranchir
It liberare
Pt libertar; livrar

**free** adj En
De frei; franko
Es libre; franco
Fr libre; franco
It libero; franco
Pt livre; franco

**free alongside ship** (fas) En
De freie Schiffseite
Es franco al costado del buque
Fr franco le long du bord
It franco lungobordo
Pt f.a.s.

**free economy** En
De freie Marktwirtschaft (f)

Es economía del mercado libre *(f)*
Fr système économique du marché libre *(m)*
It economia di mercato libero *(f)*
Pt economia de mercado livre *(f)*

**free enterprise** En
De freie Wirtschaft *(f)*
Es libre empresa *(f)*
Fr libre entreprise *(f)*
It libertà d´iniziativa *(f)*
Pt livre-empreendimento *(m)*

**free from mortgage** En
De von Hypothek befreit
Es deshipotecado
Fr déshypothéqué
It libero d´ipoteca
Pt livre de hipoteca

**freehold** *n* En
De uneingeschränkter Grundbesitz *(m)*
Es propiedad absoluta *(f)*
Fr propriété foncière perpetuelle *(f)*
It proprietà allodiale *(f)*
Pt propriedade absoluta *(f)*

**freeholder** *n* En
De uneingeschränkter Eigentümer *(m)*
Es propietario absoluto *(m)*
Fr propriétaire foncier *(m)*
It proprietario allodiale *(m)*
Pt proprietário absoluto *(m)*

**free of all averages** En
De ganz havariefrei
Es franco de toda avería
Fr franc de toutes avaries
It franco d´ogni avaria
Pt franco de todas as avarías

**free of commission** En
De maklergebührenfrei
Es franco-comisión
Fr franco courtage
It franco mediazione
Pt isento de comissão

**free of particular average** (fpa) En
De frei von besonderer Havarie
Es franco de avería particular

Fr franc d´avarie particulière
It franco di avaria particolare
Pt franco de avaria particular

**free on board** (fob) En
De frei an Bord
Es franco a bordo
Fr franco à bord
It franco a bordo
Pt franco a bordo

**free on quay** (foq) En
De frei Kai
Es franco sobre muelle
Fr franco quai
It franco banchina
Pt franco sobre cais

**free on rail** (for) En
De frei Waggon
Es franco sobre vagón
Fr franco wagon
It franco vagone
Pt franco sobre vagão

**free port** En
De Freihafen *(m)*
Es puerto libre *(m)*
Fr port franc *(m)*
It porto franco *(m)*
Pt porto franco *(m)*

**free sample** En
De kostenlose Probe *(f)*
Es muestra gratuita *(f)*
Fr échantillon gratuit *(m)*
It campione gratuito *(m)*
Pt amostra gratis *(f)*

**free ticket** En
De Freikarte *(f)*
Es billete gratuito *(m)*
Fr billet de faveur *(m)*
It biglietto gratuito *(m)*
Pt bilhete gratuito *(m)*

**free trade** En
De Freihandel *(m)*
Es comercio libre *(m)*
Fr libre-échange *(m)*
It libero scambio *(m)*
Pt comércio franco *(m)*

**free trial** En
De kostenlose Probe *(f)*
Es prueba gratuita *(f)*
Fr essai gratuit *(m)*

It prova gratuita *(f)*
Pt prova gratuita *(f)*

**frei** *adj* De
En free
Es libre; franco
Fr libre; franco
It libero; franco
Pt livre; franco

**frei an Bord** De
En free on board (fob)
Es franco a bordo
Fr franco à bord
It franco a bordo
Pt franco a bordo

**frei Docklager** De
En delivered docks
Es franco en muelle
Fr franco dock
It franco dock
Pt docas francas

**freie Marktwirtschaft** *(f)* De
En free economy
Es economía del mercado libre *(f)*
Fr système économique du marché libre *(m)*
It economia di mercato libero *(f)*
Pt economia de mercado livre *(f)*

**freier Markt** *(m)* De
En open market
Es mercado libre *(m)*
Fr marché libre *(m)*
It mercato libero *(m)*
Pt mercado livre *(m)*

**freie Wirtschaft** *(f)* De
En free enterprise
Es libre empresa *(f)*
Fr libre entreprise *(f)*
It libertà d´iniziativa *(f)*
Pt livre-empreendimento *(m)*

**freight** *n* En
De Fracht *(f)*
Es flete *(m)*
Fr fret *(m)*
It nolo *(m)*
Pt frete *(m)*

**freight charges paid** En
De franko
Es a porte pagado
Fr port-payé
It franco di porto
Pt porte pago

**freight pre-paid** En
De Fracht vorausbezahlt
Es flete pagado
Fr fret payé d'avance
It nolo prepagato
Pt frete pago

**freight ton** En
De Handelstonne (f)
Es tonelada de flete (f)
Fr tonneau de fret (m)
It tonnellata di nolo (f)
Pt tonelada de frete (f)

**freight train** Am
En goods train
De Güterzug (m)
Es tren de mercancías (m)
Fr train de marchandises (m)
It treno merci (m)
Pt comboio de mercadorías (m)

**Freihafen** (m) n De
En free port
Es puerto libre (m)
Fr port franc (m)
It porto franco (m)
Pt porto franco (m)

**Freihandel** (m) n De
En free trade
Es comercio libre (m)
Fr libre-échange (m)
It libero scambio (m)
Pt comércio franco (m)

**frei Kai** De
En free on quay (foq)
Es franco sobre muelle
Fr franco quai
It franco banchina
Pt franco sobre cais

**Freikarte** (f) n De
En free ticket
Es billete gratuito (m)
Fr billet de faveur (m)
It biglietto gratuito (m)
Pt bilhete gratuito (m)

**frei Schiffseite** De
En free alongside ship (fas)
Es franco al costado del buque
Fr franco le long du bord
It franco lungobordo
Pt f.a.s.

**frei von besonderer Havarie** De
En free of particular average (fpa)
Es franco de avería particular
Fr franc d'avarie particulière
It franco di avaria particolare
Pt franco de avaria particular

**frei Waggon** De
En free on rail (for)
Es franco sobre vagón
Fr franco wagon
It franco vagone
Pt franco sobre vagão

**freiwillig** adj De
En voluntary
Es voluntario
Fr volontaire
It volontario
Pt voluntário

**Freizeit** (f) n De
En leisure
Es descanso (m)
Fr loisir (m)
It svago (m)
Pt lazer (m)

**Fremdarbeiterschaft** (f) n De
En foreign labour
Es mano de obra extranjera (f)
Fr main-d'œuvre étrangère (f)
It mano d'opera straniera (f)
Pt mão-de-obra estrangeira (f)

**Fremdkapital** (n) n De
En borrowed capital
Es capital a préstamo (m)
Fr capitaux empruntés (m pl)
It capitale preso a prestito (m)
Pt capital por empréstimo (m)

**fréquence** (f) n Fr
De Häufigkeit (f)
En frequency
Es frecuencia (f)
It frequenza (f)
Pt frequência (f)

**frequência** (f) n Pt
De Häufigkeit (f)
En frequency
Es frecuencia (f)
Fr fréquence (f)
It frequenza (f)

**frequency** n En
De Häufigkeit (f)
Es frecuencia (f)
Fr fréquence (f)
It frequenza (f)
Pt frequência (f)

**frequency distribution** En
De Häufigkeitsverteilung (f)
Es distribución de las frecuencias (f)
Fr distribution de fréquences (f)
It distribuzione delle frequenze (f)
Pt distribuição de frequência (f)

**frequenza** (f) n It
De Häufigkeit (f)
En frequency
Es frecuencia (f)
Fr fréquence (f)
Pt frequência (f)

**fresh-water damage** En
De Süsswasserschaden (m)
Es daño de agua dulce (m)
Fr dégâts d'eau douce (m pl)
It danno d'acqua dolce (m)
Pt dano causado por água doce (m)

**fret** (m) n Fr
De Fracht (f)
En freight
Es flete (m)
It nolo (m)
Pt frete (m)

**fretador** (m) n Pt
De Befrachter (m)
En charterer
Es fletador (m)
Fr affréteur (m)
It noleggiatore (m)

**fret aérien** (m) Fr
De Luftfracht (f)
En air freight
Es flete aéreo (m)

It   trasporto aereo *(m)*
Pt   frete aéreo *(m)*

**fretamento** *(m) n* Pt
De   Befrachtung *(f)*
En   chartering
Es   fletamento *(m)*
Fr   affrètement *(m)*
It   noleggio *(m)*

**fretamento de tempo** *(m)* Pt
De   Zeitcharter *(f)*
En   time charter
Es   fletamento de tiempo *(m)*
Fr   affrètement à temps *(m)*
It   contratto di noleggio a tempo *(m)*

**frete** *(m) n* Pt
De   Fracht *(f)*
En   freight
Es   flete *(m)*
Fr   fret *(m)*
It   nolo *(m)*

**frete aéreo** *(m)* Pt
De   Luftfracht *(f)*
En   air freight
Es   flete aéreo *(m)*
Fr   fret aérien *(m)*
It   trasporto aereo *(m)*

**frete pago** Pt
De   Fracht vorausbezahlt
En   freight pre-paid
Es   flete pagado
Fr   fret payé d'avance
It   nolo prepagato

**fret payé d'avance** Fr
De   Fracht vorausbezahlt
En   freight pre-paid
Es   flete pagado
It   nolo prepagato
Pt   frete pago

**friendly society** En
Am  lodge
De   Versicherungsverein auf Gegenseitigkeit *(m)*
Es   sociedad de socorro mutuo *(f)*
Fr   société de secours mutuel *(f)*
It   società di mutuo soccorso *(f)*
Pt   mutualidade *(f)*

**fringe benefits** En
De   Sozialleistungen *(f pl)*
Es   beneficios suplementarios *(m pl)*
Fr   avantages accessoires *(m pl)*
It   vantaggi accessori *(m pl)*
Pt   benefícios extras *(m pl)*

**frode** *(f) n* It
De   Betrug *(m)*
En   fraud
Es   fraude *(m)*
Fr   fraude *(f)*
Pt   fraude *(f)*

**frontage** *n* En
De   Vorderfront *(f)*
Es   fachada *(f)*
Fr   façade *(f)*
It   facciata *(f)*
Pt   fachada *(f)*

**fronteira** *(f) n* Pt
De   Grenze *(f)*
En   frontier
Es   frontera *(f)*
Fr   frontière *(f)*
It   frontiera *(f)*

**frontera** *(f) n* Es
De   Grenze *(f)*
En   frontier
Fr   frontière *(f)*
It   frontiera *(f)*
Pt   fronteira *(f)*

**frontier** *n* En
De   Grenze *(f)*
Es   frontera *(f)*
Fr   frontière *(f)*
It   frontiera *(f)*
Pt   fronteira *(f)*

**frontiera** *(f) n* It
De   Grenze *(f)*
En   frontier
Es   frontera *(f)*
Fr   frontière *(f)*
Pt   fronteira *(f)*

**frontière** *(f) n* Fr
De   Grenze *(f)*
En   frontier
Es   frontera *(f)*
It   frontiera *(f)*
Pt   fronteira *(f)*

**frota** *(f) n* Pt
De   Flotte *(f)*
En   fleet
Es   flota *(f)*
Fr   flotte *(f)*
It   flotta *(f)*

**frota de pesca** *(f)* Pt
De   Fischerflotte *(f)*
En   fishing fleet
Es   flota pesquera *(f)*
Fr   flottille de pêche *(f)*
It   flotta peschereccia *(f)*

**frota mercante** *(f)* Pt
De   Handelsflotte *(f)*
En   merchant fleet
Es   flota mercanto *(f)*
Fr   flotte marchande *(f)*
It   flotta mercantile *(f)*

**frozen assets** En
De   eingefrorene Guthaben *(n pl)*
Es   activos congelados *(m pl)*
Fr   fonds bloqués *(m pl)*
It   attivo congelato *(m)*
Pt   bens do activo congelados *(m pl)*

**frozen credits** En
De   eingefrorene Kredite *(m pl)*
Es   creditos congelados *(m pl)*
Fr   crédits bloqués *(m pl)*
It   crediti bloccati *(m pl)*
Pt   créditos congelados *(m pl)*

**Fruchtwechsel** *(m) n* De
En   rotation of crops
Es   rotación de cultivos *(f)*
Fr   rotation des cultures *(f)*
It   rotazione delle coltivazioni *(f)*
Pt   rotação de culturas *(f)*

**frustração** *(f) n* Pt
De   Fortfall der Geschäftsgrundlage *(m)*
En   frustration
Es   frustración *(f)*
Fr   frustration *(f)*
It   frustrazione *(f)*

**frustración** *(f) n* Es
De   Fortfall der Geschäftsgrundlage *(m)*
En   frustration
Fr   frustration *(f)*

It frustrazione *(f)*
Pt frustração *(f)*

**frustration** *n* En, Fr *(f)*
De Fortfall der Geschäfts-
   grundlage *(m)*
Es frustración *(f)*
It frustrazione *(f)*
Pt frustração *(f)*

**frustrazione** *(f)* *n* It
De Fortfall der Geschäfts-
   grundlage *(m)*
En frustration
Es frustración *(f)*
Fr frustration *(f)*
Pt frustração *(f)*

**fuego** *(m)* *n* Es
De Brand *(m)*
En fire
Fr incendie *(f)*
It incendio *(m)*
Pt fogo; incêndio *(m)*

**fuel-oil** *(m)* Es
De Heizöl *(n)*
En fuel oil
Fr mazout *(m)*
It petrolio da ardere *(m)*
Pt petróleo combustível *(m)*

**fuel oil** *n* En
De Heizöl *(n)*
Es fuel-oil *(m)*
Fr mazout *(m)*
It petrolio da ardere *(m)*
Pt petróleo combustível *(m)*

**fuera de aduanas** Es
De verzollt
En ex bond
Fr à l'acquitté
It sdoganato
Pt livre de alfândega

**fuerte pérdida** *(f)* Es
De schwere Verluste *(m pl)*
En heavy loss
Fr lourde perte *(f)*
It forte perdita *(f)*
Pt perda avultada *(f)*

**fuerza** *(f)* *n* Es
De Gewalt *(f)*
En force
Fr force *(f)*

It forza *(f)*
Pt força *(f)*

**fuerzas armadas** *(f pl)* Es
De Streitkräfte *(f pl)*
En armed forces
Fr forces armées *(f pl)*
It forze armate *(f pl)*
Pt forças armadas *(f pl)*

**fuerzas del mercado** *(f pl)* Es
De Marktkräfte *(f pl)*
En market forces
Fr forces du marché *(f pl)*
It forze di mercato *(f pl)*
Pt forças de mercado *(f pl)*

**fuga a impostos** *(f)* Pt
De Steuerhinterziehung *(f)*
En evasion of tax
Es evasión de pago de impues-
   tos *(f)*
Fr fraude fiscale *(f)*
It evasione d'imposta *(f)*

**führende Marke** *(f)* De
En brand leader
Es marca directriz *(f)*
Fr marque de point *(f)*
It marca di punta *(f)*
Pt marca mais cotada *(f)*

**fuite** *(f)* *n* Fr
De Lecken *(n)*
En leakage
Es escape *(m)*
It colaggio *(m)*
Pt escape; fuga *(m f)*

**fulfil** *vb* En
De erfüllen
Es cumplir
Fr remplir
It adempiere
Pt comprir

**fulfilment** *n* En
De Erfüllung *(f)*
Es cumplimiento *(m)*
Fr accomplissement *(m)*
It adempimento *(m)*
Pt cumprimento *(m)*

**full** *adj* En
De voll
Es lleno
Fr plein

It pieno
Pt cheio

**full cover** En
De Vollwertdeckung *(f)*
Es garantía total *(f)*
Fr garantie totale *(f)*
It garanzia totale *(f)*
Pt cobertura total *(f)*

**full employment** En
De Vollbeschäftigung *(f)*
Es pleno empleo *(m)*
Fr plein emploi *(m)*
It piena occupazione *(f)*
Pt pleno emprego *(m)*

**fully subscribed** En
De vollgezeichnet
Es plenamente suscrito
Fr intégralement souscrit
It interamente sottoscritto
Pt totalmente subscrito

**fulmine** *(m)* *n* It
De Blitz *m*
En lightning
Es relámpago *(m)*
Fr foudre *(f)*
Pt relâmpago *(m)*

**função** *(f)* *n* Pt
De Aufgabe *(f)*
En function
Es función *(f)*
Fr fonction *(f)*
It funzione *(f)*

**función** *(f)* *n* Es
De Aufgabe *(f)*
En function
Fr fonction *(f)*
It funzione *(f)*
Pt função *(f)*

**funcional** *adj* Es, Pt
De sachlich
En functional
Fr fonctionnel
It funzionale

**funcionario del gobierno** *(m)*
   Es
De Beamte(r) *(m)*
En civil servant
Am government employee
Fr fonctionnaire *(m)*

It impiegato statale *(m)*
Pt foncionário público *(m)*

**function** *n* En
De Aufgabe *(f)*
Es función *(f)*
Fr fonction *(f)*
It fúnzione *(f)*
Pt função *(f)*

**functional** *adj* En
De sachlich
Es funcional
Fr fonctionnel
It funzionale
Pt funcional

**fund** *vb* En
De fundieren
Es fundar; consolidar
Fr fonder; consolider
It consolidare
Pt dotar de fundos

**fund** *n* En
De Fonds *(m)*
Es fondo *(m)*
Fr fonds *(m)*
It fondo *(m)*
Pt fundos *(m pl)*

**fundação discricionária** *(f)* Pt
De unumschränkte Treuhand *(f)*
En discretionary trust
Es fideicomiso discrecional *(m)*
Fr fidéicommis à appréciation *(m)*
It fondo fiduciario discrezionale *(m)*

**fundação fiduciária** *(f)* Pt
De Treuhandfonds *(m)*
En trust fund
Es fondo fiduciario *(m)*
Fr fonds fiduciaire *(m)*
It fondo fiduciario *(m)*

**fundador** *(m)* *n* Es, Pt
De Gründer *(m)*
En founder
Fr fondateur *(m)*
It fondatore *(m)*

**fundar** *vb* Es, Pt
De einrichten; gründen
En establish; found

Fr fonder; établir
It fondare; istituire

**fundar** (una deuda) *vb* Es
De fundieren
En fund
Fr fonder; consolider
It consolidare
Pt dotar de fundos

**fundieren** *vb* De
En fund
Es fundar; consolidar
Fr fonder; consolider
It consolidare
Pt dotar de fundos

**fundo de amortização** *(m)* Pt
De Tilgungsfonds *(m)*
En sinking fund
Es fondo de amortización *(m)*
Fr fonds d´amortissement *(m)*
It fondo di ammortamento *(m)*

**fundo de compensação** *(m)* Pt
De Ausgleichsfonds *(m)*
En equalization fund
Fr fonds de régularisation *(m)*
It cassa di compensazione *(f)*

**fundo de reserva** *(m)* Pt
De Reservefonds *(m)*
En reserve fund
Es fondo de reserva *(m)*
Fr fonds de réserve *(m)*
It fondo di riserva *(m)*

**Fundo Europeu** *(m)* Pt
De Europäische Fonds *(m)*
En European Fund
Es Fondo Europeo *(m)*
Fr Fonds Européen *(m)*
It Fondo Europeo *(m)*

**Fundo Monetário Internacional** *(m)* Pt
De Internationaler Währungsfonds *(m)*
En International Monetary Fund (IMF)
Es Fondo Monetario Internacional *(m)*
Fr Fonds Monétaire International *(m)*
It Fondo Monetario Internazionale *(m)*

**fundos** *(m pl)* *n* Pt
De Fonds *(m)*
En fund
Es fondo *(m)*
Fr fonds *(m)*
It fondo *(m)*

**fundos à ordem** *(m.pl)* Pt
De Barbestand *(m)*
En cash in hand
Es efectivo en caja *(m)*
Fr espèces en caisse *(f pl)*
It pronti contanti *(m pl)*

**fundos disponíveis** *(m pl)* Pt
De flüssige Mittel *(n pl)*
En funds available
Es fondos disponibles *(m pl)*
Fr disponibilités *(f pl)*
It fondi disponibili *(m pl)*

**fundos renováveis** *(m pl)* Pt
De Umlaufkapital *(n)*
En revolving fund
Es fondo circulante *(m)*
Fr fonds renouvelable *(m)*
It fondo rotativo *(m)*

**funds available** En
De flüssige Mittel *(n pl)*
Es fondos disponibles *(m pl)*
Fr disponibilités *(f pl)*
It fondi disponibili *(m pl)*
Pt fundos disponíveis *(m pl)*

**funzionale** *adj* It
De sachlich
En functional
Es funcional
Fr fonctionnel
Pt funcional

**funzione** *(f)* *n* It
De Aufgabe *(f)*
En function
Es función *(f)*
Fr fonction *(f)*
Pt função *(f)*

**furgón** *(m)* Es
De Packwagen *(m)*
En guard´s van
Fr fourgon *(m)*
It bagagliaio *(m)*
Pt carruagem do guarda *(f)*

# 291 — gagner

**furnished flat** En
Am furnished apartment
De möblierte Mietwohnung *(f)*
Es piso amueblado *(m)*
Fr appartement meublé *(m)*
It appartamento ammobigliato *(m)*
Pt andar mobilado *(m)*

**furniture** *n* En
De Möbel *(n pl)*
Es meubles *(m pl)*
Fr meubles *(m pl)*
It mobilia *(f)*
Pt mobília *(f)*

**further consideration** En
De Weiterüberlegung *(f)*
Es examen más detallado *(m)*
Fr examen plus attentif *(m)*
It esame più attento *(m)*
Pt consideração posterior mais detalhada *(f)*

**further information** En
De weitere Auskunft *(f)*
Es más detalles *(m pl)*
Fr renseignements complémentaires *(m pl)*
It ulteriori informazioni *(f pl)*
Pt informação adicional *(f)*

**further particulars** En
De nähere Umstände *(m pl)*
Es más detalles *(m pl)*
Fr plus amples renseignements *(m pl)*
It ulteriori particolari *(m pl)*
Pt pormenores adicionais *(m pl)*

**further reason** En
De weitere Gründe *(m pl)*
Es rasones adicionales *(f pl)*
Fr raison supplémentaire *(f)*
It ulteriori motivi *(m pl)*
Pt rasões adicionais *(f pl)*

**furto** *(m)* *n* It, Pt
De Diebstahl *(m)*
En theft
Es robo *(m)*
Fr vol *(m)*

**furto con scasso** *(m)* It
De Einbruchdiebstahl *(m)*
En burglary
Es robo *(m)*

Fr vol avec effraction *(m)*
Pt roubo *(m)*

**fusão** *(f)* *n* Pt
De Verschmelzung *(f)*
En merger
Es fusión *(f)*
Fr fusion *(f)*
It fusione *(f)*

**fusión** *(f)* *n* Es
De Verschmelzung *(f)*
En merger
Fr fusion *(f)*
It fusione *(f)*
Pt fusão *(f)*

**fusion** *(f)* *n* Fr
De Verschmelzung *(f)*
En merger
Es fusión *(f)*
It fusione *(f)*
Pt fusão *(f)*

**Fusion** *(f)* *n* De
En amalgamation
Am merger
Es amalgamación *(f)*
Fr fusion *(f)*
It fusione *(f)*
Pt amalgamento *(m)*

**fusione** *(f)* *n* It
De Verschmelzung *(f)*
En merger
Es fusión *(f)*
Fr fusion *(f)*
Pt fusão *(f)*

**fusionieren** *vb* De
En amalgamate
Am merge
Es amalgamar
Fr fusionner
It fondersi
Pt amalgamar

**fusionner** *vb* Fr
De fusionieren
En amalgamate
Am merge
Es amalgamar
It fondersi
Pt amalgamar

**Fussnote** *(f)* *n* De
En footnote
Es apostilla *(f)*

Fr apostille *(f)*
It postilla *(f)*
Pt nota de rodapé *(f)*

**futur** *adj* Fr
De künftig
En future
Es futuro
It futuro; avvenire
Pt futuro

**futura entrega** *(f)* Es, Pt
De zukünftige Lieferung *(f)*
En future delivery
Fr livraison à terme *(f)*
It consegna a termine *(f)*

**future** *adj* En
De künftig
Es futuro
Fr futur
It futuro; avvenire
Pt futuro

**future delivery** En
De zukünftige Lieferung *(f)*
Es futura entrega *(f)*
Fr livraison à terme *(f)*
It consegna a termine *(f)*
Pt futura entrega *(f)*

**futures market** En
De Terminmarkt *(m)*
Es mercado de futuros *(m)*
Fr marché du terme *(m)*
It mercato a termine *(m)*
Pt mercado de futuros *(m)*

**futuro** *adj* Es, It, Pt
De künftig
En future
Fr futur

**futuro proprietário** *(m)* Pt
De gutgläubiger Besitzer *(m)*
En holder in due course
Es tenedor en buena fe *(m)*
Fr porteur de bonne foi *(m)*
It titolare in buena fede *(m)*

# G

**gagner** *vb* Fr
De verdienen
En earn

Es ganar
It guadagnare
Pt ganhar

**gain** n En, Fr (m)
De Gewinn (m)
Es ganancia (f)
It guadagno (m)
Pt ganhos (m pl)

**gains en capital** (m pl) Fr
De Kapitalgewinn (n)
En capital gains
Es beneficios sobre capital (m pl)
It plusvalore di capitale (m pl)
Pt lucros de capital (m pl)

**gamble** vb En
De um Geld spielen; spekulieren
Es jugar; especular
Fr jouer de l'argent; spéculer
It speculare; arrischiare
Pt jogar; especular

**gamble on the stock exchange** En
De die Börse spielen
Es jugar a la Bolsa
Fr jouer à la Bourse
It giocare in Borsa
Pt jogar na Bolsa

**ganancia** (f) n Es
De Gewinn (m)
En gain; profit
Fr gain; profit (m)
It guadagno; profitto (m)
Pt ganhos; lucro (m pl; m)

**ganancia bruta** (f) Es
De Bruttogewinn (m)
En gross profit
Fr bénéfice brut (m)
It utile lordo (m)
Pt lucro bruto (m)

**ganancia neta** (f) Es
De Reingewinn (m)
En net profit
Fr bénéfice net (m)
It utile netto (m)
Pt lucro líquido (m)

**ganancia por realizar** (f) Es
De imaginärer Gewinn (m)
En paper profit

Fr profit fictif (m)
It utile sulla carta (m)
Pt lucros no papel (m)

**ganar** vb Es
De verdienen
En earn
Fr gagner
It guadagnare
Pt ganhar

**ganga** (f) n Es
De Gelegenheitskauf (m)
En bargain
Fr occasion (f)
It occasione (f)
Pt pechincha (f)

**ganhar** vb Pt
De verdienen
En earn
Es ganar
Fr gagner
It guadagnare

**ganhos** (m pl) n Pt
De Gewinn (m)
En gain
Es ganancia (f)
Fr gain (m)
It guadagno (m)

**ganz havariefrei** De
En free of all averages
Es franco de toda avería
Fr franc de toutes avaries
It franco d'ogni avaria
Pt franco de todas as avarías

**garage** n En, Fr (m)
De Garage (f)
Es garaje (m)
It autorimessa (f)
Pt garagem (f)

**Garage** (f) n De
En garage
Es garaje (m)
Fr garage (m)
It autorimessa (f)
Pt garagem (f)

**garagem** (f) n Pt
De Garage (f)
En garage
Es garaje (m)
Fr garage (m)
It autorimessa (f)

**garaje** (m) n Es
De Garage (f)
En garage
Fr garage (m)
It autorimessa (f)
Pt garagem (f)

**garant** (m) n Fr
De Bürge (m)
En guarantor
Es garante; fiador (m)
It garante; avallante (m)
Pt fiador; avalizador (m)

**garante** (m) n Es, It
De Bürge (m)
En guarantor
Fr garant; avaliste (m)
Pt fiador; avalizador (m)

**garantía** (f) n Es
De Garantie (f)
En guarantee; warranty
Fr garantie (f)
It garanzia (f)
Pt garantia (f)

**garantia** (f) n Pt
De Garantie (f)
En guarantee; warranty
Es garantía (f)
Fr garantie (f)
It garanzia (f)

**garantía bancaria** (f) Es
De Bankgarantie (f)
En banker's indemnity
Am banker's guarantee
Fr garantie de banque (f)
It garanzia bancaria (f)
Pt garantia bancária (f)

**garantia bancária** (f) Pt
De Bankgarantie (f)
En banker's indemnity
Am banker's guarantee
Es garantía bancaria (f)
Fr garantie de banque (f)
It garanzia bancaria (f)

**garantía colateral** (f) Es
De Sicherheit (f)
En collateral
Fr nantissement (m)
It garanzia collaterale (f)
Pt colateral (f)

**garantía total** *(f)* Es
De Vollwertdeckung *(f)*
En full cover
Fr garantie totale *(f)*
It garanzia totale *(f)*
Pt cobertura total *(f)*

**garantie** *(f)* n Fr
De Garantie *(f)*
En guarantee; warranty
Es garantía *(f)*
It garanzia *(f)*
Pt garantía *(f)*

**Garantie** *(f)* n De
En guarantee; warranty
Es garantía *(f)*
Fr garantie *(f)*
It garanzia *(f)*
Pt garantía *(f)*

**garantie d'assurance** *(f)* Fr
De Versicherungsdeckung *(f)*
En insurance cover
Es cobertura de la póliza de
  seguro *(f)*
It copertura assicurativa *(f)*
Pt cobertura de seguro *(f)*

**garantie de banque** *(f)* Fr
De Bankgarantie *(f)*
En banker's indemnity
Am banker's guarantee
Es garantía bancaria *(f)*.
It garanzia bancaria *(f)*
Pt garantía bancária *(f)*

**garantie totale** *(f)* Fr
De Vollwertdeckung *(f)*
En full cover
Es garantía total *(f)*
It garanzia totale *(f)*
Pt cobertura total *(f)*

**garantir** *vb* Fr, Pt
De Bürgschaft leisten; ge-
  währleisten
En guarantee
Es garantizar; avalar
It garantire; avallare

**garantire** *vb* It
De Bürgschaft leisten; ge-
  währleisten
En guarantee
Es garantizar; avalar
Fr garantir; avaliser
Pt garantir; assegurar

**garantizar** *vb* Es
De Bürgschaft leisten; ge-
  währleisten
En guarantee
Fr garantir; avaliser
It garantire; avallare
Pt garantir; assegurar

**garanzia** *(f)* n It
De Garantie *(f)*
En guarantee; warranty
Es garantía *(f)*
Fr garantie *(f)*
Pt garantía *(f)*

**garanzia bancaria** *(f)* It
De Bankgarantie *(f)*
En banker's indemnity
Am banker's guarantee
Es garantía bancaria *(f)*
Er garantie de banque *(f)*
Pt garantia bancária *(f)*

**garanzia collaterale** *(f)* It
De Sicherheit *(f)*
En collateral
Es garantía colateral *(f)*
Fr nantissement *(m)*
Pt colateral *(f)*

**garanzia totale** *(f)* It
De Vollwertdeckung *(f)*
En full cover
Es garantía total *(f)*
Fr garantie totale *(f)*
Pt cobertura total *(f)*.

**garder en stock** Fr
De vorrätig halten
En keep in stock
Es guardar en almacén
It tenere in magazzino
Pt reter em armazém

**gardien de nuit** *(m)* Fr
De Nachtwächter *(m)*
En nightwatchman
Es guarda de noche *(m)*
It guardiano notturno *(m)*
Pt guarda de noite *(m)*

**gas** *n* En; Es, It *(m)*
De Gas *(n)*
Fr gaz *(m)*
Pt gás *(m)*

**gás** *(m)* n Pt
De Gas *(n)*
En gas
Es gas *(m)*
Fr gaz *(m)*
It gas *(m)*

**Gas** *(n)* n De
En gas
Es gas *(m)*
Fr gaz *(m)*
It gas *(m)*
Pt gás *(m)*

**gas de ciudad** *(m)* Es
De Stadtgas *(n)*
En town gas
Fr gaz de ville *(m)*
It gas di carbon fossile *(m)*
Pt gás urbano *(m)*

**gas di carbon fossile** *(m)* It
De Stadtgas *(n)*
En town gas
Es gas de ciudad *(m)*
Fr gaz de ville *(m)*
Pt gás urbano *(m)*

**gas natural** *(m)* Es
De Erdgas *(n)*
En natural gas
Fr gaz naturel *(m)*
It gas naturale *(m)*
Pt gás natural *(m)*

**gás natural** *(m)* Pt
De Erdgas *(n)*
En natural gas
Es gas natural *(m)*
Fr gaz naturel *(m)*
It gas naturale *(m)*

**gas naturale** *(m)* It
De Erdgas *(n)*
En natural gas
Es gas natural *(m)*
Fr gaz naturel *(m)*
Pt gás natural *(m)*

**gasto** *(m)* n Es
De Kosten *(pl)*
En expense
Fr frais *(m pl)*
It spesa *(f)*
Pt despesa *(f)*

gastos

**gastos de almacenaje** (m pl)
Es
De Lagergeld (n)
En storage charges
Fr frais de magasinage (m pl)
It spese di magazzinaggio (f pl)
Pt encargos de armazenamento (m pl)

**gastos de banco** (m pl) Es
De Bankspesen (f pl)
En bank charges
Fr frais bancaires (m pl)
It spese di banca (f pl)
Pt taxas bancárias (f pl)

**gastos de cobrança** (m pl) Pt
De Einzugskosten (pl)
En collection charges
Es gastos de cobranza (m pl)
Fr frais d'encaissement (m pl)
It spese di riscossione (f pl)

**gastos de cobranza** (m pl) Es
De Einzugskosten (pl)
En collection charges
Fr frais d'encaissement (m pl)
It spese di riscossione (f pl)
Pt gastos de cobrança (m pl)

**gastos deducibles** (m pl) Es
De abziehbare Unkosten (pl)
En allowable expense
Fr dépense déductible (f)
It spesa permessa (f)
Pt despesas deduzíveis (f)

**gastos de los negocios** (m pl)
Es
De Geschäftskosten (pl)
En business expenses
Fr frais commerciaux (m pl)
It spese generali (f pl)
Pt despesas do exercício (f pl)

**gastos de manutención** (m pl)
Es
De Manipulationsgebühr (f)
En handling charges
Fr frais de manutention (m pl)
It spese di gestione (f pl)
Pt custas de manejo (f pl)

**gastos de representación** (m pl) Es
De Repräsentationskosten (pl)
En entertainment expenses

Fr frais de représentation (m pl)
It spese di rappresentanza (f pl)
Pt despesas de representação (f pl)

**gastos directos** (m pl) Es
De Einzelkosten (pl)
En direct expenses
Fr frais directs (m pl)
It spese dirette (f pl)
Pt despesas directas (f pl)

**gastos fuertes** (m pl) Es
De drückende Spesen (f pl)
En heavy charges
Fr charges lourdes (f pl)
It forti spese (f pl)
Pt encargos pesados (m pl)

**gastos generales** (m pl) Es
De allgemeine Unkosten; Generalunkosten (pl)
En general expenses; overheads
Fr frais généraux (m pl)
It spese generali (f pl)
Pt despesas gerais (f pl)

**gastos imprevistos** (m pl) Es
De Nebenkosten (pl)
En incidental expenses
Fr faux frais (m pl)
It spese impreviste (f pl)
Pt despesas ocasionais (f pl)

**gastos publicitarios** (m pl) Es
De Werbekosten (pl)
En advertising expenditure
Fr dépenses de publicité (f pl)
It spese di pubblicità (f pl)
Pt despesa com publicidade (f)

**gastos varios** (m pl) Es
De verschiedene Ausgaben (f pl)
En sundry expenses
Fr frais divers (m pl)
It spese varie (f pl)
Pt despesas diversas (f pl)

**gás urbano** (m) Pt
De Stadtgas (n)
En town gas
Es gas de ciudad (m)

Fr gaz de ville (m)
It gas di carbon fossile (m)

**gaz** (m) n Fr
De Gas (n)
En gas
Es gas (m)
It gas (m)
Pt gás (m)

**gaz de ville** (m) Fr
De Stadtgas (n)
En town gas
Es gas de ciudad (m)
It gas di carbon fossile (m)
Pt gás urbano (m)

**gaz naturel** (m) Fr
De Erdgas (n)
En natural gas
Es gas natural (m)
It gas naturale (m)
Pt gás natural (m)

**gearing** n En
De Getriebe (n)
Es engranaje (m)
Fr engrenage (m)
It ingranaggio (m)
Pt engrenagem (f)

**Geben und Nehmen** (n) De
En give and take
Es concesión recíproca (f)
Fr concessions mutuelles (f pl)
It concessione reciproca (f)
Pt concessão mútua (f)

**Gebrauchsanleitung** (f) n De
En instructions for use
Es modo de empleo (m)
Fr mode d'emploi (f)
It istruzioni per l'uso (f pl)
Pt instruções para uso (f pl)

**Gebühr** (f) n De
En duty; tax
Es derechos; impuesto (m)
Fr taxe; impôt (f m)
It tassa; imposta (f)
Pt taxa; imposto (f m)

**Gefahr** (f) n De
En peril
Es peligro (m)
Fr péril (m)

It    pericolo *(m)*
Pt   perigo *(m)*

**Gefahrenzulage** *(f)* n De
En  danger money
Es  suma para riesgos *(f)*
Fr   prime de risque *(f)*
It    compenso per il rischio *(m)*
Pt   prémio de risco *(m)*

**gefährliche Waren** *(f pl)* De
En  dangerous goods
Es  mercancías peligrosas *(f pl)*
Fr   marchandises dangereuses *(f pl)*
It    merce pericolosa *(f)*
Pt   mercadorias perigosas *(f pl)*

**Gefälligkeitswechsel** *(m)* n De
En  accommodation bill
Es  pagaré de favor *(m)*
Fr   billet de complaisance *(m)*
It    cambiale di favore *(f)*
Pt   letra de favor *(f)*

**gefälscht** *adj* De
En  fake; forged
Es  falso; falsificado
Fr   faux; contrefait
It    falso; falsificato
Pt   falso; falsificado

**gefälschter Scheck** *(m)* De
En  forged cheque
Es  cheque falsificado *(m)*
Fr   faux chèque *(m)*
It    assegno falsificato *(m)*
Pt   cheque falsificado *(m)*

**gefragt** *adj* De
En  in demand
Es  solicitado
Fr   demandé
It    ricercato
Pt   procurado

**(ein) Gegenangebot abgeben** De
En  make a counteroffer
Es  hacer una contraoferta
Fr   faire une contre-offre
It    fare una controfferta
Pt   fazer uma contra-proposta

**gegen Barzahlung** De
En  cash with order
Es  pagadero con el pedido

Fr   payable à la commande
It    pagamento con l'ordine
Pt   pagamento no acto de requisição

**gegen Haftkaution freigeben** De
En  grant bail
Es  conceder fianza
Fr   admettre une caution
It    concedere la libertà provvisoria su cauzione
Pt   autorizar caução

**Gegenkonto** *(n)* n De
En  contra account
Es  contracuenta *(f)*
Fr   compte contrepartie *(m)*
It    conto d'ordine *(m)*
Pt   contra-conta *(f)*

**gegenseitiges Einvernehmen** *(n)* De
En  mutual agreement
Es  acuerdo común *(m)*
Fr   accord mutuel *(m)*
It    comune accordo *(m)*
Pt   acordo mútuo *(m)*

**gegenzeichnen** *vb* De
En  back; countersign
Es  avalar; refrendar
Fr   avaliser; contresigner
It    avallare; controfirmare
Pt   avalizar; validar por assinatura

**Gegenzeichner** *(m)* n De
En  backer
Es  avalista *(m)*
Fr   avaliste *(m)*
It    avallante *(m)*
Pt   avalista *(m)*

**Gehalt** *(n)* n De
En  salary
Es  sueldo *(m)*
Fr   traitement *(m)*
It    stipendio *(m)*
Pt   ordenado *(m)*

**Geheimvertrag** *(m)* n De
En  secret agreement
Es  acuerdo secreto *(m)*
Fr   accord occulte *(m)*
It    accordo segreto *(m)*
Pt   acordo secreto *(m)*

**Geld** *(n)* n De
En  money
Es  dinero *(m)*
Fr   argent *(m)*
It    denaro *(m)*
Pt   dinheiro *(m)*

**Geldabwertung** *(f)* n De
En  depreciation of money
Es  desvalorización de la moneda *(f)*
Fr   dépréciation de la monnaie *(f)*
It    svalutazione della moneta *(f)*
Pt   desvalorização da moeda *(f)*

**Geldgeber** *(m)* n De
En  investor
Es  inversionista *(m)*
Fr   investisseur *(m)*
It    capitalista *(m)*
Pt   capitalista *(m)*

**Geldkassette** *(f)* n De
En  cash-box
Es  caja *(f)*
Fr   caisse *(f)*
It    cassetta *(f)*
Pt   caixa *(f)*

**Geldmarkt** *(m)* n De
En  money market
Es  mercado de dinero *(m)*
Fr   marché monétaire *(m)*
It    mercato di denaro *(m)*
Pt   mercado da moeda *(m)*

**Geldschrank** *(m)* n De
En  safe
Es  caja fuerte *(f)*
Fr   coffre-fort *(m)*
It    cassaforte *(f)*
Pt   cofre *(m)*

**Geldstrafe** *(f)* n De
En  fine
Es  sanción; multa *(f)*
Fr   amende *(f)*
It    multa *(f)*
Pt   multa *(f)*

**Geldverleiher** *(m)* n De
En  moneylender
Es  prestamista *(m)*
Fr   prêteur d'argent *(m)*

It usuraio *(m)*
Pt prestamista *(m)*

**Gelegenheitskauf** *(m)* n De
En bargain
Es ganga *(f)*
Fr occasion *(f)*
It occasione *(f)*
Pt pechincha *(f)*

**Gemeindesteuer** *(f)* n De
En rates
Am realty tax
Es contribución municipal *(f)*
Fr taxes municipales *(f pl)*
It tassa comunale *(f)*
Pt contribuições *(f pl)*

**Gemeinkosten** *(pl)* n De
En indirect costs
Es costes indirectos *(m pl)*
Fr frais indirects *(m pl)*
It costi indiretti *(m pl)*
Pt custos indirectos *(m pl)*

**gemeinnütziges Unternehmen**
*(n)* De
En utility company
Es empresa de servicios públi-
cos *(f)*
Fr entreprise d'utilité publique
*(f)*
It società di servizi pubblici *(f)*
Pt empresa de utilidade pú-
blica *(f)*

**gemeinsame Agrarpolitik** *(f)*
De
En Common Agricultural Policy
Es política agrícola común *(f)*
Fr politique agricole commune
*(f)*
It politica agricola comune *(f)*
Pt política agrícola comum *(f)*

**gemeinsame Handelspolitik**
*(f)* De
En Common Commercial Pol-
icy
Es política comercial común
*(f)*
Fr politique commerciale
commu–ne *(f)*
It politica commerciale comune *(f)*
Pt política comercial comum
*(f)*

**gemeinsamer Aussentariff** *(m)*
De
En common external tariff
Es tarifa exterior común *(f)*
Fr tarif extérieur commun *(m)*
It tariffa estera comune *(f)*
Pt tarifa externa comum *(f)*

**gemeinsamer Markt** *(m)* De
En Common Market
Es mercado común *(m)*
Fr marché commun *(m)*
It mercato comune *(m)*
Pt mercado comum *(m)*

**Gemeinschaft** *(f)* n De
En community
Es comunidad *(f)*
Fr communauté *(f)*
It comunità *(f)*
Pt comunidade *(f)*

**Gemeinschaftsgründung** *(f)* n
De
En joint venture
Es empresa en común *(f)*
Fr entreprise en participation
*(f)*
It impresa in comparteci-
pazione *(f)*
Pt iniciativa em comum *(f)*

**Gemeinschaftskonto** *(n)* n De
En joint account
Es cuenta común *(f)*
Fr compte joint *(m)*
It conto in comune *(m)*
Pt conta conjunta *(f)*

**Gemeinschuldner** *(m)* n De
En bankrupt
Es quebrado *(m)*
Fr failli *(m)*
It fallito *(m)*
Pt falido *(m)*

**Gemischtwirtschaft** *(f)* n De
En mixed economy
Es economía mixta *(f)*
Fr économie mixte *(f)*
It economia mista *(f)*
Pt economia mixta *(f)*

**genehmigtes Kapital** *(n)* De
En authorized capital
Es capital autorizado *(m)*
Fr capital autorisé *(m)*

It capitale autorizzato *(m)*
Pt capital autorizado *(m)*

**General Agreement on Tariffs
and Trade** (GATT) En
De Allgemeines Zoll- und Han-
delsabkommen *(n)*
Es Acuerdo General sobre
Tarifas Aduaneras y Comer-
cio *(m)*
Fr Accord Général sur les
Tarifs Douaniers et le
Commerce *(m)*
It Accordo Generale sulle
Tariffe Doganali e sul
Commercio *(m)*
Pt Acordo geral de Tarifas e
Comércio *(m)*

**general average** (G.A.) En
De grosse Havarie *(f)*
Es avería general *(f)*
Fr avaries communes *(f pl)*
It avaria generale *(f)*
Pt avaria grossa *(f)*

**general expenses** En
De allgemeine Unkosten *(pl)*
Es gastos generales *(m pl)*
Fr frais généraux *(m pl)*
It spese generali *(f pl)*
Pt despesas gerais *(f pl)*

**general ledger** En
De allgemeines Hauptbuch *(n)*
Es libro mayor general *(m)*
Fr journal général *(m)*
It libro mastro generale *(m)*
Pt livro-mestre geral *(m)*

**general lien** En
De allgemeines Pfandrecht *(n)*
Es privilegio general *(m)*
Fr privilège général *(m)*
It privilegio generale *(m)*
Pt privilégio geral *(m)*

**general meeting** En
De Hauptversammlung *(f)*
Es asamblea general *(f)*
Fr assemblée générale *(f)*
It assemblea generale *(f)*
Pt assembleia geral *(f)*

**general public** En
De Öffentlichkeit *(f)*
Es público en general *(m)*
Fr grand public *(m)*

It pubblico in genere (m)
Pt público em geral (m)

**Generalstreik** (m) n De
En general strike
Es huelga general (f)
Fr grève générale (f)
It sciopero generale (m)
Pt greve geral (f)

**general strike** En
De Generalstreik (m)
Es huelga general (f)
Fr grève générale (f)
It sciopero generale (m)
Pt greve geral (f)

**Generalunkosten** (pl) n De
En overhead costs
Es gastos generales (m pl)
Fr frais généraux (m pl)
It spese generali (f pl)
Pt despesas gerais (f pl)

**generi alimentari** (m pl) It
De Esswaren (f pl)
En foodstuffs
Es comestibles (m pl)
Fr alimentation (f)
Pt géneros alimentícios (m pl)

**géneros alimentícios** (m pl) Pt
De Esswaren (f pl)
En foodstuffs
Es comestibles (m pl)
Fr alimentation (f)
It generi alimentari (m pl)

**géneros de punto** (m pl) Es
De Strickwaren (f pl)
En knitted goods
Fr bonneterie (f)
It maglieria (f)
Pt artigos de malha de lã (m pl)

**génie** (m) n Fr
De Maschinenbau (m)
En engineering
Es ingeniería (f)
It ingegneria (f)
Pt engenharia (f)

**génie chimique** (m) Fr
De Industriechemie (f)
En chemical engineering
Es ingeniería química (f)

It ingegneria chimica (f)
Pt engenharia química (f)

**génie civil** (m) Fr
De Ingenieurbau (m)
En civil engineering
Es ingeniería civil (f)
It ingegneria civile (f)
Pt engenharia civil (f)

**Genossenschaft** (f) n De
En cooperative
Es cooperativa (f)
Fr société coopérative (f)
It cooperativa (f)
Pt cooperativa (f)

**gentleman's agreement** En
De Kavaliersabkommen (n)
Es acuerdo sobre palabra (m)
Fr convention verbale (f)
It accordo sulla parola (f)
Pt pacto de honra (m)

**Gepäckschliessfach** (n) n De
En luggage locker
Es casilla de equipaje (f)
Fr coffre de bagages (m)
It cassetta bagaglio (f)
Pt depósito de bagagem individualizado (m)

**gepfändete Güter** (n pl) De
En distressed goods
Es mercancías embargadas (f pl)
Fr biens saisis (m pl)
It merce sequestrata (f)
Pt mercadorias embargadas (f)

**geprüfte Geschäftsbücher** (n pl) De
En audited accounts
Es cuentas revisadas (f pl)
Fr comptes vérifiés et certifiés (m pl)
It conti verificati e certificati (m pl)
Pt contas fiscalizadas (f pl)

**geral de contas-correntes** (m) Pt
De allgemeines Hauptbuch (n)
En general ledger
Es libro mayor general (m)
Fr journal général (m)
It libro mastro generale (m)

**gérant d'affaires** (m) Fr
De Geschäftsführer (m)
En business manager
Es gerente de negocios (m)
It direttore commerciale (m)
Pt gerente de negócios (m)

**gerechtfertigt** adj De
En justifiable
Es justificable; legítimo
Fr légitime
It giustificabile; legittimo
Pt justificavel

**Gerechtigkeit** (f) n De
En justice
Es justicia (f)
Fr justice (f)
It giustizia (f)
Pt justiça (f)

**gerência** (f) n Pt
De Vorstand (m)
En management
Es dirección (f)
Fr administration (f)
It direzione; amministrazione (f)

**gerência superior** (f) Pt
De Direktion (f)
En top management
Es dirección superior (f)
Fr haute direction (f)
It direzione superiore (f)

**gerenta de negocios** (m) Es
De Geschäftsführer (m)
En business manager
Fr gérant d'affaires (m)
It direttore commerciale (m)
Pt gerente de negócios (m)

**gerente** (m) n Pt
De Geschäftsleiter (m)
En manager
Es director (m)
Fr directeur (m)
It direttore (m)

**gerente de exportações** (m) Pt
De Exportabteilungsleiter (m)
En export manager
Es jefe de exportación (m)
Fr chef du service exportation (m)
It direttore esportazione (m)

**gerente de negocios** *(m)* Es
De Geschäftsführer *(m)*
En business manager
Fr gérant d'affaires
It direttore commerciale *(m)*
Pt gerente de negócios *(m)*

**gerente de negócios** *(m)* Pt
De Geschäftsführer *(m)*
En business manager
Es gerente de negocios *(m)*
Fr gérant d'affaires *(m)*
It direttore commerciale *(m)*

**Gericht** *(n)* n De
En court of law
Es tribunal *(m)*
Fr tribunal *(m)*
It tribunale *(m)*
Pt tribunal *(m)*

**gerichtlich entscheiden** De
En adjudicate
Es adjudicar
Fr juger
It aggiudicare
Pt adjudicar

**gerichtliche Verfügung** *(f)* De
En injunction
Es entredicho *(m)*
Fr injonction; arrêt de suspension *(f m)*
It ingiunzione *(f)*
Pt interdição *(f)*

**gerichtlich vorgehen gegen** De
En institute proceedings against
Es iniciar un proceso contra
Fr intenter un procès à
It intentare un'azione legale contro
Pt instituir processo contra

**gesamt** *adj* De
En aggregate
Es total
Fr global
It complessivo
Pt total

**gesamtschuldnerisch** De
En jointly and severally
Es en conjunto y separadamente

Fr conjointement et solidairement
It solidalmente e individualmente
Pt em conjunto e por vários

**Geschäft** *(n)* n De
En business
Es negocios *(m pl)*
Fr affaires *(f pl)*
It affari *(m pl)*
Pt negócios *(m pl)*

**Geschäftsbereich** (eines Ministers) *(m)* n De
En portfolio
Es cartera *(f)*
Fr portefeuille *(f)*
It portafoglio *(m)*
Pt pasta *(f)*

**Geschäftsbücher** *(n pl)* n De
En books of account
Es libros de cuentas *(m pl)*
Fr livres comptables *(m pl)*
It libri contabili *(m pl)*
Pt livros de contabilidade *(m pl)*

**Geschäftsfaktur** *(f)* n De
En commercial invoice
Es factura comercial *(f)*
Fr facture commerciale *(f)*
It fattura commerciale *(f)*
Pt factura comercial *(f)*

**Geschäftsführer** *(m)* n De
En chief executive
Es jefe ejecutivo *(m)*
Fr directeur général *(m)*
It direttore generale *(m)*
Pt chefe de gerência *(m)*

**Geschäftsführungsberater** *(m)* n De
En management consultant
Es asesor administrativo *(m)*
Fr ingénieur-conseil en organisation *(m)*
It consulente di direzione aziendale *(m)*
Pt perito de administração *(m)*

**Geschäftsjahr** *(n)* n De
En financial year
Es año económico *(m)*
Fr exercice *(m)*

It esercizio *(m)*
Pt ano financeiro *(m)*

**Geschäftskosten** *(pl)* n De
En business expenses
Es gastos de los negocios *(m pl)*
Fr frais commerciaux *(m pl)*
It spese generali *(f pl)*
Pt despesas do exercício *(f pl)*

**Geschäftsleiter** *(m)* n De
En manager
Es director *(m)*
Fr directeur *(m)*
It direttore *(m)*
Pt gerente; diretor *(m)*

**Geschäftsmann** *(m)* n De
En businessman
Es hombre de negocios *(m)*
Fr homme d'affaires *(m)*
It uomo d'affari *(m)*
Pt homem de negócios *(m)*

**Geschäftsreisende(r)** *(m)* n De
En (commercial) traveller
Es viajante *(m)*
Fr commis-voyageur *(m)*
It viaggiatore di commercio *(m)*
Pt viajante *(m)*

**Geschäftsstunden** *(f pl)* n De
En office hours
Es horario de oficina *(m)*
Fr heures de bureau *(f pl)*
It orario d'ufficio *(m)*
Pt horário do escritório *(m)*

**Geschäftswert** *(m)* n De
En goodwill
Es valor de la clientela *(m)*
Fr bon vouloir *(m)*
It avviamento *(m)*
Pt boa vontade *(f)*

**Geschäftszeit** *(f)* n De
En business hours
Es horario de comercio *(m)*
Fr heures d'ouverture *(f pl)*
It orario d'apertura *(m)*
Pt horas de funcionamento *(f pl)*

**Geschäftszentrum** *(n)* n De
En shopping centre
Es centro de negocios *(m)*

Fr centre commercial *(m)*
It zona degli acquisti *(f)*
Pt centro de comércio *(m)*

**Geschenk** *(n)* n De
En gift
Es regalo *(m)*
Fr don; cadeau *(m)*
It dono: donazione *(m f)*
Pt prenda; presente *(f m)*

**(die) Geschworenen** *(pl)* n De
En jury
Es jurado *(m)*
Fr jury *(m)*
It giuria *(f)*
Pt juri *(m)*

**Gesellschaft** *(f)* n De
En company
Es compañía; empresa *(f)*
Fr société; entreprise *(f)*
It società *(f)*
Pt companhia *(f)*

**(eine) Gesellschaft gründen**
De
En float a company
Es lanzar una compañia
Fr lancer une entreprise
It lanciare una società
Pt lançar uma empresa

**Gesellschaft mit beschränkter
Haftung (GmbH)** *(f)* De
En private limited company
Es Compañía privada de responsabilidad limitada *(f)*
Fr Société à responsabilité limitée (SARL) *(f)*
It Società a responsabilità limitata (Sarl) *(f)*
Pt Sociedade por quotas de responsabilidade limitada *(f)*

**Gesellschaft mit Kontrollbefugnis** *(f)* De
En controlling company
Es compañía directriz *(f)*
Fr société directrice *(f)*
It società direttrice *(f)*
Pt companhia controladora *(f)*

**Gesellschaft notiert an der
Börse** *(f)* De
En quoted company

Es compañía cotizada en bolsa *(f)*
Fr société cotée à la Bourse *(f)*
It società quotata in borsa *(f)*
Pt companhia cotizada *(f)*

**Gesellschaftsvertrag** *(m)* n De
En articles of association
Am articles of incorporation
Es artículos de asociación *(m pl)*
Fr contrat de société *(m)*
It statuto sociale *(m)*
Pt escritura de sociedade *(f)*

**Gesetz** *(n)* n De
En statute
Es estatuto *(m)*
Fr statut *(m)*
It statuto *(m)*
Pt estatuto *(m)*

**Gesetzgebung** *(f)* n De
En legislation
Es legislación *(f)*
Fr législation *(f)*
It legislazione *(f)*
Pt legislação *(f)*

**gesetzlich** *adj* De
En statutory; lawful
Es estatutario; legitimo
Fr statutaire; légal
It statuario; legittimo
Pt estatutário; legitimo

**gesetzlicher Feiertag** *(m)* De
En public holiday
Es día de fiesta *(m)*
Fr jour férié *(m)*
It giorno di festa *(m)*
Pt feriado *(m)*

**gesicherte Schuldverschreibung** *(f)* De
En secured debenture
Es obligación garantizada *(f)*
Fr obligation garantie *(f)*
It obbligazione garantita *(f)*
Pt obrigação com garantia *(f)*

**gesperrte Einlagen** *(f pl)* De
En blocked deposits
Es depósitos bloqueados *(m pl)*
Fr dépôts bloqués *(m pl)*

It deposito con vincolo bloccato *(m)*
Pt depósitos bloqueados *(m pl)*

**gesperrter Markt** *(m)* De
En closed market
Es mercado cerrado *(m)*
Fr marché fermé *(m)*
It mercato chiuso *(m)*
Pt mercado fechado *(m)*

**gesperrtes Konto** *(n)* De
En blocked account
Es cuenta bloqueada *(f)*
Fr compte bloqué *(m)*
It conto bloccato *(m)*
Pt conta bloqueada *(f)*

**gestão** *(f)* n Pt
De Verwaltung *(f)*
En administration
Es administración *(f)*
Fr gestion *(f)*
It gestione *(f)*

**Gestehungskosten** *(m pl)* n De
En actual cost
Es precio verdadero *(m)*
Fr prix de revient effectif *(m)*
It costo effettivo *(m)*
Pt custo verdadeiro *(m)*

**gestern** *adv* De
En yesterday
Es ayer
Fr hier
It ieri
Pt ontem

**gestion** *(f)* n Fr
De Verwaltung *(f)*
En administration
Es administración *(f)*
It gestione *(f)*
Pt gestão *(f)*

**gestione** *(f)* n It
De Verwaltung *(f)*
En administration
Es administración *(f)*
Fr gestion *(f)*
Pt gestão *(f)*

**gestundete Zahlung** *(f)* De
En deferred payment
Es pago aplazado *(m)*
Fr paiement différé *(m)*

It pagamento differito *(m)*
Pt pagamento adiado *(m)*

**Gesundheitsbrief** *(m)* n De
En pratique
Es libre plática *(f)*
Fr libre pratique *(f)*
It libera pratica *(f)*
Pt livre prática *(f)*

**Gesundheitsdienst** *(m)* n De
En health service
Es servicio de sanidad *(m)*
Fr service de la santé *(m)*
It servizio sanitario *(m)*
Pt serviço de saúde *(m)*

**Getriebe** *(n)* n De
En gearing
Es engranaje *(m)*
Fr engrenage *(m)*
It ingranaggio *(m)*
Pt engrenagem *(f)*

**gewähren (einen Rabatt)** De
En allow (a discount)
Es conceder (un descuento)
Fr consentir (une remise)
It concedere (uno sconto)
Pt conceder (um desconto)

**Gewahrsaminhaber** *(m)* n De
En bailee
Es depositario *(m)*
Fr dépositaire *(m)*
It depositario *(m)*
Pt caucionado *(m)*

**Gewalt** *(f)* n De
En force
Es fuerza *(f)*
Fr force *(f)*
It forza *(f)*
Pt força *(f)*

**Gewerbe** *(n)* n De
En industry
Es industria *(f)*
Fr industrie *(f)*
It industria *(f)*
Pt indústria *(f)*

**Gewerbe-** De
En industrial
Es industrial
Fr industriel
It industriale
Pt industrial

**Gewerbearbeiter** *(m)* n De
En factory worker
Es obrero; operario *(m)*
Fr ouvrier *(m)*
It operaio *(m)*
Pt operário *(m)*

**Gewerbeaufsichtsbeamte(r)** *(m)* n De
En factory inspector
Es inspector de fábrica *(m)*
Fr inspecteur du travail *(m)*
It ispettore di fabbrica *(m)*
Pt inspector de fábrica *(m)*

**Gewerkschaft** *(f)* n De
En trade union
Es sindicato *(m)*
Fr syndicat *(m)*
It sindacato *(m)*
Pt sindicato *(m)*

**Gewicht** *(n)* n De
En weight
Es peso *(m)*
Fr poids *(m)*
It peso *(m)*
Pt peso *(m)*

**Gewinn** *(m)* n De
En profit; gain
Es ganancia; beneficio *(f m)*
Fr bénéfice; profit *(m)*
It utile; profitto *(m)*
Pt lucro; benefício *(m)*

**Gewinnanalyse** *(f)* n De
En cost benefit analysis
Es análisis de costes y beneficios *(m)*
Fr analyse des coûts et rendements *(f)*
It analisi dei costi e benefici *(f)*
Pt análise de custo e benefício *(f)*

**Gewinnanteilschein** *(m)* n De
En dividend warrant
Es cupón de dividendos *(m)*
Fr dividende-warrant *(m)*
It cedola di dividendo *(f)*
Pt cédula de dividendo *(f)*

**Gewinnausfall** *(m)* n De
En loss of profits

Es lucro cesante *(m)*
Fr perte de bénéfices *(f)*
It perdita di utili *(f)*
Pt perda de lucros *(f)*

**Gewinnbeteiligung** *(f)* n De
En profit-sharing
Es participación en los beneficios *(f)*
Fr participation aux bénéfices *(f)*
It partecipazione agli utili *(f)*
Pt repartição dos lucros *(f)*

**Gewinnler** *(m)* n De
En profiteer
Es acaparador *(m)*
Fr profiteur *(m)*
It profittatore *(m)*
Pt especulador *(m)*

**Gewinn pro Aktie** *(n)* De
En earnings per share
Es beneficios por acción *(m pl)*
Fr bénéfice par titre *(m)*
It profitti per azione *(m pl)*
Pt proventos por acção *(m pl)*

**Gewinnrealisation** *(f)* n De
En profit-taking
Es realización de utilidades *(f)*
Fr prise de bénéfices *(f)*
It realizzazione del utile *(f)*
Pt realização dos lucros *(m)*

**Gewinn- und Verlustkonto** *(n)* De
En profit and loss account
Es cuenta de ganancias y pérdidas *(f)*
Fr compte profits et pertes *(m)*
It conto profitti e perdite *(f)*
Pt conta de lucros e perdas *(f)*

**gewogener Durchschnitt** *(m)* De
En weighted average
Es media ponderada *(f)*
Fr moyenne pondérée *(f)*
It media ponderata *(f)*
Pt média ponderada *(f)*

**gezeichnetes Kapital** *(n)* De
En subscribed capital
Es capital subscrito *(m)*
Fr capital souscrit *(m)*

It    capitale sottoscritto *(m)*
Pt    capital subscrito *(m)*

**ghisa** *(f) n* It
De    Gusseisen *(n)*
En    cast iron
Es    hierro colado *(m)*
Fr    fer de fonte *(m)*
Pt    ferro fundido *(m)*

**giacimento petrolifero** *(m)* It
De    Ölfeld *(n)*
En    oilfield
Es    yacimiento de petróleo *(m)*
Fr    gisement petrolifère *(m)*
Pt    jazigo de petróleo *(m)*

**gift** *n* En
De    Geschenk *(n)*
Es    regalo *(m)*
Fr    don; cadeau *(m)*
It    dono; donazione *(m f)*
Pt    prenda; presente *(f m)*

**giftiger Abfall** *(m)* De
En    toxic waste
Es    efluentes tóxicos *(m pl)*
Fr    déchets toxiques *(m pl)*
It    rifiuti tossici *(m pl)*
Pt    despejos tóxicos *(m pl)*

**gilt-edged securities** En
De    mündelsichere Wertpapiere *(n pl)*
Es    valores de toda confianza *(m pl)*
Fr    valeurs de tout repos *(f pl)*
It    titoli di assoluta fiducia *(m pl)*
Pt    valores de todo a confiança *(m pl)*

**giocare in Borsa** It
De    die Börse spielen
En    gamble on the stock exchange
Es    jugar a la Bolsa
Fr    jouer à la Bourse
Pt    jogar na Bolsa

**giornale** *(m) n* It
De    Tagebuch *(n)*
En    day-book
Es    diario *(m)*
Fr    journal *(m)*
Pt    diário *(m)*

**giornata lavorativa** *(f)* It
De    Arbeitstag *(m)*
En    working day
Es    día laborable *(m)*
Fr    jour ouvrable *(m)*
Pt    dia de trabalho *(m)*

**giorni di grazia** *(m pl)* It
De    Nachfrist *(f)*
En    days of grace
Es    días de gracia *(f pl)*
Fr    délai supplémentaire *(m)*
Pt    dias de tolerância *(m pl)*

**giorno** *(m) n* It
De    Tag *(m)*
En    day
Es    día *(m)*
Fr    jour *(m)*
Pt    dia *(m)*

**giorno della pigione** *(m)* It
De    Quartalstag *(m)*
En    quarter day
Es    primer día del trimestre *(m)*
Fr    jour du terme *(m)*
Pt    dia de vencimento trimestral *(m)*

**giorno di borsa** *(m)* It
De    Börsentag *(m)*
En    (financial) market day
Es    día de bolsa *(m)*
Fr    jour de bourse *(m)*
Pt    dia de bolsa *(m)*

**giorno di festa** *(m)* It
De    gesetzlicher Feiertag *(m)*
En    public holiday
Es    día de fiesta *(m)*
Fr    jour férié *(m)*
Pt    feriado *(m)*

**giorno di liquidazione** *(m)* It
De    Abrechnungstag *(m)*
En    account day
Am    settlement day
Es    día de liquidación *(m)*
Fr    jour de liquidation *(m)*
Pt    dia de liquidação *(m)*

**giorno di mercato** *(m)* It
De    Markttag *(m)*
En    (local) market day
Es    día de mercado *(m)*
Fr    jour de place *(m)*
Pt    dia de mercado *(m)*

**giorno di paga** *(m)* It
De    Zahltag; Abrechnungstag *(m)*
En    pay day
Es    día de pago *(m)*
Fr    jour de paiement *(m)*
Pt    dia de recebimento *(m)*

**giorno di riposo** *(m)* It
De    dienstfreier Tag *(m)*
En    day off
Es    día libre *(m)*
Fr    jour de congé *(m)*
Pt    dia de folga *(m)*

**girare** *vb* It
De    indossieren
En    endorse
Es    endosar
Fr    endosser
Pt    endossar

**girar en descubierto** Es
De    überziehen
En    overdraw
Fr    mettre à découvert
It    trarre alla scoperto
Pt    levantar a descoberto

**girata** *(f) n* It
De    Indossament *(n)*
En    endorsement
Es    endoso *(m)*
Fr    endossement; endos *(m)*
Pt    endosse *(m)*

**girata in bianco** *(f)* It
De    Blankoindossament *(n)*
En    blank-endorsement
Es    endoso en blanco *(m)*
Fr    endossement en blanc *(m)*
Pt    endosse em branco *(m)*

**girata restrittiva** *(f)* It
De    Rektaindossement *(n)*
En    restrictive endorsement
Es    endoso restringido *(m)*
Fr    endossement restrictif *(m)*
Pt    endosse restritivo *(m)*

**giro bancario** *(m)* Es
De    Banktratte *(f)*
En    banker's draft
Fr    traite bancaire *(f)*
It    tratta bancaria *(f)*
Pt    letra de banco *(f)*

**Girobank** *(f)* n De
En clearing-bank
Es banco de compensación
*(m)*
Fr banque de virement *(f)*
It banca associata alla stanza
di compensazione *(f)*
Pt banco de compensação e
rateio *(m)*

**giro d'affari** *(m)* It
De Umsatz *(m)*
En turnover
Es volumen de ventas *(m)*
Fr chiffre d'affaires *(m)*
Pt movimento de dinheiro *(m)*

**giro postal** *(m)* Es
De Postanweisung *(f)*
En postal order
Fr mandat-poste *(m)*
It vaglia postale *(f)*
Pt vale postal *(m)*

**giro telegráfico** *(m)* Es
De Kabelauszahlung *(f)*
En telegraphic transfer
Fr virement télégraphique *(m)*
It rimessa telegrafica *(f)*
Pt transferência telegráfica *(f)*

**gisement petrolifère** *(m)* Fr
De Ölfeld *(n)*
En oilfield
Es yacimiento de petróleo *(m)*
It giacimento petrolifero *(m)*
Pt jazigo de petróleo *(m)*

**giudicare** *vb* It
De urteilen
En judge
Es juzgar
Fr juger
Pt julgar

**giudice** *(m)* n It
De Richter *(m)*
En judge
Es juez *(m)*
Fr juge *(m)*
Pt juiz *(m)*

**giudizio** *(m)* n It
De Urteil *(n)*
En judgment
Es juicio; adjudicación *(m f)*
Fr jugement; arrêt *(m)*
Pt julgamento *(m)*

**giuria** *(f)* n It
De die Geschworenen; Jury
*(pl; f)*
En jury
Es jurado *(m)*
Fr jury *(m)*
Pt juri *(m)*

**giurisdizione** *(f)* n It
De Rechtsprechung; Gerichts-
barkeit *(f)*
En jurisdiction
Es jurisdicción *(f)*
Fr juridiction *(f)*
Pt jurisdição *(f)*

**giustificabile** *adj* It
De gerechtfertigt
En justifiable
Es justificable; legítimo
Fr légitime
Pt justificavel

**giustizia** *(f)* n It
De Gerechtigkeit *(f)*
En justice
Es justicia *(f)*
Fr justice *(f)*
Pt justiça *(f)*

**give and take** En
De Geben und Nehmen *(n)*
Es concesión recíproca *(f)*
Fr concessions mutuelles *(f
pl)*
It concessione reciproca *(f)*
Pt concessão mútua *(f)*

**give a week's notice** En
De einwöchig kündigen
Es dar una semana de aviso
Fr donner ses huit jours
It dare una settimana di
preavviso
Pt dar um prazo de uma
semana para despedimento

**give up** En
De aufgeben
Es renunciar
Fr céder
It cedere
Pt desistir

**Glas** *(n)* n De
En glass
Es vidrio *(m)*
Fr verre *(m)*

It vetro *(m)*
Pt vidro *(m)*

**glass** n En
De Glas *(n)*
Es vidrio *(m)*
Fr verre *(m)*
It vetro *(m)*
Pt vidro *(m)*

**Gläubiger** *(m)* n De
En creditor
Es acreedor *(m)*
Fr créancier; créditeur *(m)*
It creditore *(m)*
Pt credor *(m)*

**Gläubigerversammlung** *(f)* n
De
En meeting of creditors
Es reunión de acreedores *(f)*
Fr assemblée de créanciers *(f)*
It assemblea dei creditori *(f)*
Pt assembleia de credores *(f)*

**Gleichgewicht** *(n)* n De
En equilibrium
Es equilibrio *(m)*
Fr équilibre *(m)*
It equilibrio *(m)*
Pt equilíbrio *(m)*

**Gleichordnung** *(f)* n De
En coordination
Es coordinación *(f)*
Fr coordination *(f)*
It coordinamento *(m)*
Pt coordenação *(f)*

**Gleichstrom** *(m)* n De
En direct current (d.c.)
Es corriente continua *(f)*
Fr courant continu *(m)*
It corrente continua *(f)*
Pt corrente continua *(f)*

**gleitende Skala** *(f)* De
En sliding scale
Es escala móvil *(f)*
Fr échelle mobile *(f)*
It scala mobile *(f)*
Pt escala móvel *(f)*

**Gleitklausel** *(f)* n De
En escalator clause
Es cláusula de revisión de
precios *(f)*
Fr échelle mobile *(f)*

It    scala mobile *(f)*
Pt    cláusula de actualização de
      preços *(f)*

**global** *adj* En, Es, Fr, Pt
De    Global-
It    globale

**Global-** De
En    global
Es    global
Fr    global
It    globale
Pt    global

**globale** *adj* It
De    Global-
En    global
Es    global
Fr    global
Pt    global

**Globalgeschäft** *(n) n* De
En    package deal
Es    contrato global *(m)*
Fr    marché global *(m)*
It    contratto globale *(m)*
Pt    contrato global *(m)*

**goal** *n* En
De    Ziel *(n)*
Es    meta; objetivo *(f m)*
Fr    bout *(m)*
It    scopo; traguardo *(m)*
Pt    meta; objectivo *(f m)*

**go bail for** En
De    Haftkaution geben
Es    salir fiados por
Fr    se porter garant de
It    rendersi garante di
Pt    prestar caução a favor de

**go bankrupt** En
De    Konkurs anmelden
Es    caer en quiebra
Fr    faire faillite
It    fallire
Pt    falir

**gobierno** *(m) n* Es
De    Regierung *(f)*
En    government
Fr    gouvernement *(m)*
It    governo *(m)*
Pt    governo *(m)*

**going concern** En
De    gewinnbringendes Unter-
      nehmen *(n)*
Es    negocio en marcha *(m)*
Fr    affaire qui marche *(f)*
It    azienda in piena attività *(f)*
Pt    negócio que vinga *(m)*

**gold** *n* En
De    Gold *(n)*
Es    oro *(m)*
Fr    or *(m)*
It    oro *(m)*
Pt    ouro *(m)*

**Gold** *(n) n* De
En    gold
Es    oro *(m)*
Fr    or *(m)*
It    oro *(m)*
Pt    ouro *(m)*

**gold fields** En
De    Goldgrube *(f)*
Es    yacimiento aurífero *(m)*
Fr    régions aurifères *(f pl)*
It    terreni auriferi *(m pl)*
Pt    jazigos de ouro *(m pl)*

**Goldgrube** *(f) n* De
En    gold fields
Es    yacimiento aurífero *(m)*
Fr    régions aurifères *(f pl)*
It    terreni auriferi *(m pl)*
Pt    jazigos de ouro *(m pl)*

**Goldobligation** *(f) n* De
En    gold standard
Es    patrón oro *(m)*
Fr    étalon or *(m)*
It    base aurea *(f)*
Pt    ouro-padrão *(m)*

**gold-plated** *adj* En
De    vergoldet
Es    chapado en oro
Fr    plaqué d'or
It    placcato in oro
Pt    laminado a ouro

**gold shares** En
De    Aktien von Goldbergwerken
      *(f pl)*
Es    acciones auríferas *(f pl)*
Fr    valeurs aurifères *(f pl)*
It    azioni aurifere *(f pl)*
Pt    acções de ouro *(f pl)*

**gold standard** En
De    Goldobligation *(f)*
Es    patrón oro *(m)*
Fr    étalon or *(m)*
It    base aurea *(f)*
Pt    ouro-padrão *(m)*

**good** *adj* En
De    gut
Es    bueno
Fr    bon
It    buono
Pt    bom

**good (for)** *adj* En
De    gut (für)
Es    válido
Fr    valable
It    valido
Pt    válido

**good offices** En
De    Liebesdienste *(m pl)*
Es    buenos servicios *(m pl)*
Fr    bons offices *(m pl)*
It    buoni uffici *(m pl)*
Pt    bons serviços *(m pl)*

**goods** *pl n* En
De    Güter *(n pl)*
Es    mercancías *(f pl)*
Fr    marchandises *(f pl)*
It    merce *(f)*
Pt    mercadorias *(f pl)*

**goods on approval** En
De    Probegüter *(n pl)*
Es    mercancías sujetas a apro-
      bación *(f pl)*
Fr    marchandises à condition
      *(f pl)*
It    merce soggetta ad appro-
      vazione *(f)*
Pt    artigos sujeitos a apro-
      vacão *(m pl)*

**goods on consignment** En
De    Kommissionsgüter *(n pl)*
Es    mercancías en consigna-
      ción *(f pl)*
Fr    marchandises en consigna-
      tion *(f pl)*
It    merce in conto deposito *(f)*
Pt    artigos à consignação *(m
      pl)*

**goods train** En
  Am freight train
  De Güterzug (m)
  Es tren de mercancías (m)
  Fr train de marchandises (m)
  It treno merci (m)
  Pt comboio de mercadorías (m)

**goodwill** n En
  De Geschäftswert (m)
  Es valor de la clientela (m)
  Fr bon vouloir (m)
  It avviamento (m)
  Pt boa vontade (f)

**gorjeta** (f) n Pt
  De Trinkgeld (n)
  En tip; gratuity
  Es propina (f)
  Fr pourboire (m)
  It mancia (f)

**go-slow strike** En
  Am slow down
  De Bummelstreik (m)
  Es huelga de producción lenta (f)
  Fr grève perlée (f)
  It sciopero a singhiozzo (m)
  Pt greve de abrandamento do ritmo de produção (f)

**goulot d'étranglement** (m) Fr
  De Engpass (m)
  En bottle-neck
  Es embotellamiento (m)
  It strozzatura (f)
  Pt engarrafamento (m)

**gouvernement** (m) n Fr
  De Regierung (f)
  En government
  Es gobierno (m)
  It governo (m)
  Pt governo (m)

**government** n En
  De Regierung (f)
  Es gobierno (m)
  Fr gouvernement (m)
  It governo (m)
  Pt governo (m)

**government bond** En
  De Staatsobligation (f)
  Es obligación del Estado (f)
  Fr obligation d'État (f)

  It obbligazione dello Stato (f)
  Pt obrigação do Tesouro (f)

**government employee** Am
  En civil servant
  De Beamte(r) (m)
  Es funcionario del gobierno (m)
  Fr fonctionnaire (m)
  It impiegato statale (m)
  Pt foncionário público (m)

**government loan** En
  De Staatsanleihe (f)
  Es empréstito público (m)
  Fr emprunt public (m)
  It prestito pubblico (m)
  Pt empréstimo do governo (m)

**government securities** En
  De Regierungsschuldverschrei-bungen (f pl)
  Es títulos públicos (m pl)
  Fr titres d'État (m pl)
  It titoli di Stato (m pl)
  Pt títulos do Tesouro (m pl)

**government subsidy** En
  De Staatszuschuss (m)
  Es subvención del Estado (f)
  Fr subvention de l'État (f)
  It sovvenzione dello Stato (f)
  Pt subvenções do Estado (f pl)

**governo** (m) n It, Pt
  De Regierung (f)
  En government
  Es gobierno (m)
  Fr gouvernement (m)

**Grad** (m) n De
  En grade
  Es grado (m)
  Fr grade (m)
  It grado (m)
  Pt grau (m)

**grade** n En, Fr (m)
  De Grad (m)
  Es grado (m)
  It grado (m)
  Pt grau (m)

**grado** (m) n Es, It
  De Grad (m)
  En grade

  Fr grade (m)
  Pt grau (m)

**gráfico** (m) n Es, Pt
  De Tabelle; graphische Dar-stellung (f)
  En chart; graph
  Fr graphique (m)
  It grafico (m)

**grafico** (m) n It
  De Tabelle; graphische Dar-stellung (f)
  En chart; graph
  Es gráfico (m)
  Fr graphique (m)
  Pt gráfico (m)

**gráfico de operação** (m) Pt
  De Flussplan (m)
  En flow chart
  Es diagrama de flujo (m)
  Fr ordinogramme (m)
  It diagramma di flusso (m)

**grampo** (m) n Pt
  De Büroklammer (f)
  En paper clip
  Es sujetapapeles (m)
  Fr attache-papiers (m)
  It fermacarte (m)

**grande magazzino** (m) It
  De Warenhaus; Kaufhaus (n)
  En department store
  Es grandes almacenes (m pl)
  Fr grand magasin (m)
  Pt armazém (m)

**grandes almacenes** (m pl) Es
  De Warenhaus; Kaufhaus (n)
  En department store
  Fr grand magasin (m)
  It grande magazzino (m)
  Pt armazém (m)

**grand livre** (m) Fr
  De Hauptbuch (n)
  En ledger
  Es libro mayor (m)
  It libro mastro (m)
  Pt livro-mestre (m)

**grand livre d'achats** (m) Fr
  De Einkaufsbuch (n)
  En bought ledger
  Am purchase book

Es libro mayor de compras *(m)*
It mastro acquisti *(m)*
Pt livro-mestre de compras *(m)*

**grand livre des ventes** *(m)* Fr
De Verkaufskontenbuch *(n)*
En sales ledger
Es libro mayor de ventas *(m)*
It partitario delle vendite *(m)*
Pt livro-mestre de vendas *(m)*

**grand magasin** *(m)* Fr
De Warenhaus; Kaufhaus *(n)*
En department store
Es grandes almacenes *(m pl)*
It grande magazzino *(m)*
Pt armazém *(m)*

**grand public** *(m)* Fr
De Öffentlichkeit *(f)*
En general public
Es público en general *(m)*
It pubblico in genere *(m)*
Pt público em geral *(m)*

**grant** (of a patent) *n* En
De Erteilung (eines Patentes) *(f)*
Es concesión (de una patente) *(f)*
Fr délivrance (d'un brevet) *(f)*
It concessione (di brevetto) *(f)*
Pt concessão (de uma patente) *(f)*

**grant** *n* En
De Unterstützung *(f)*
Es subvención *(f)*
Fr subvention *(f)*
It sovvenzione *(f)*
Pt subvenção *(f)*

**grant bail** En
De gegen Haftkaution freigeben
Es conceder fianza
Fr admettre une caution
It concedere la libertà provvisoria su cauzione
Pt autorizar caução

**graph** *n* En
De graphische Darstellung *(f)*
Es gráfico *(m)*
Fr graphique *(m)*

It grafico *(m)*
Pt gráfico *(m)*

**graphique** *(m)* *n* Fr
De Tabelle; graphische Darstellung *(f)*
En chart; graph
Es gráfico *(m)*
It grafico *(m)*
Pt gráfico *(m)*

**graphische Darstellung** *(f)* De
En diagram; graph
Es diagrama; gráfico *(m)*
Fr diagramme; graphique *(m)*
It diagramma; grafico *(m)*
Pt diagrama; gráfico *(m)*

**graph paper** En
De Millimeterpapier *(n)*
Es papel milimetrado *(m)*
Fr papier quadrillé *(m)*
It carta millimetrata *(f)*
Pt papel milimétrico *(m)*

**gratifica** *(f)* *n* It
De Gratifikation *(f)*
En gratuity
Es gratificación *(f)*
Fr gratification *(f)*
Pt gratificação *(f)*

**gratificação** *(f)* *n* Pt
De Gratifikation *(f)*
En gratuity
Es gratificación *(f)*
Fr gratification *(f)*
It gratifica *(f)*

**gratificación** *(f)* *n* Es
De Gratifikation *(f)*
En gratuity
Fr gratification *(f)*
It gratifica *(f)*
Pt gratificação *(f)*

**gratification** *(f)* *n* Fr
De Gratifikation *(f)*
En gratuity
Es gratificación *(f)*
It gratifica *(f)*
Pt gratificação *(f)*

**gratificazione** *(f)* *n* It
De Prämie *(f)*
En bonus
Es prima; gratificación *(f)*

Fr prime; gratification *(f)*
Pt bonus; gratificação *(m f)*

**Gratifikation** *(f)* *n* De
En gratuity
Es gratificación *(f)*
Fr gratification *(f)*
It gratifica *(f)*
Pt gratificação *(f)*

**Gratisaktien** *(f pl)* *n* De
En bonus shares
Am stock dividend
Es acciones dadas como primas *(f pl)*
Fr actions d'attribution *(f pl)*
It azioni di godimento *(f pl)*
Pt acções de prémio *(f pl)*

**gratuity** *n* En
De Gratifikation *(f)*
Es gratificación *(f)*
Fr gratification *(f)*
It gratifica *(f)*
Pt gratificação *(f)*

**grau** *(m)* *n* Pt
De Grad *(m)*
En grade
Es grado *(m)*
Fr grade *(m)*
It grado *(m)*

**graving dock** En
De Trockendock *(n)*
Es dique de carenas *(m)*
Fr bassin de radoub *(m)*
It bacino di raddobbo *(m)*
Pt doca de querenas *(f)*

**green pound** En
De grünes Pfund *(n)*
Es esterlina verde *(f)*
Fr livre sterling verte *(f)*
It sterlina verde *(f)*
Pt libra esterlina verde *(f)*

**greifbare Aktiven** *(n pl)* De
En tangible assets
Es activo tangible *(m)*
Fr biens immobiliers *(m pl)*
It beni materiali *(m pl)*
Pt bens visíveis *(m pl)*

**Grenze** *(f)* *n* De
En limit; frontier
Es límite; frontera *(m f)*
Fr limite; frontière *(f)*

It limite; frontiera (m f)
Pt limite; frontiera (m f)

**grève** (f) n Fr
De Streik (m)
En strike
Es huelga (f)
It sciopero (m)
Pt greve (f)

**greve** (f) n Pt
De Streik (m)
En strike
Es huelga (f)
Fr grève (f)
It sciopero (m)

**grève avec occupation des lieux** (f) Fr
De Sitzstreik (m)
En sit-down strike
Es huelga de brazos caídos (f)
It sciopero bianco (m)
Pt greve de braços caídos (f)

**greve de braços caídos** (f) Pt
De Sitzstreik (m)
En sit-down strike
Es huelga de brazos caídos (f)
Fr grève avec occupation des lieux (f)
It sciopero bianco (m)

**grève des dockers** (f) Fr
De Hafenarbeiterstreik (m)
En dock strike
Es huelga de obreros de muelle (f)
It sciopero portuale (m)
Pt greve na doca (f)

**grève générale** (f) Fr
De Generalstreik (m)
En general strike
Es huelga general (f)
It sciopero generale (m)
Pt greve geral (f)

**greve geral** (f) Pt
De Generalstreik (m)
En general strike
Es huelga general (f)
Fr grève générale (f)
It sciopero generale (m)

**grève na doca** (f) Pt
De Hafenarbeiterstreik (m)
En dock strike

Es huelga de obreros de muelle (f)
Fr grève des dockers (f)
It sciopero portuale (m)

**greve não oficializada** (f) Pt
De unanerkannter Streik (m)
En unofficial strike
Es huelga no-oficial (f)
Fr grève non reconnue (f)
It sciopero non ufficiale (m)

**grève non reconnue** (f) Fr
De unanerkannter Streik (m)
En unofficial strike
Es huelga no-oficial (f)
It sciopero non ufficiale (m)
Pt greve não oficializada (f)

**grève officielle** (f) Fr
De anerkannter Streik (m)
En official strike
Es huelga oficial (f)
It sciopero ufficiale (m)
Pt greve oficial (f)

**greve oficial** (f) Pt
De anerkannter Streik (m)
En official strike
Es huelga oficial (f)
Fr grève officielle (f)
It sciopero ufficiale (m)

**grève perlée** (f) Fr
De Bummelstreik (m)
En go-slow strike
Am slow down
Es huelga de producción lenta (f)
It sciopero a singhiozzo (m)
Pt greve de abrandamento do ritmo de produção (f)

**grève sauvage** (f) Fr
De wilder Streik (m)
En wildcat strike
Es huelga espontánea (f)
It sciopero selvaggio (m)
Pt greve não oficializada (f)

**grevista** (m) n Pt
De Streikende(r) (m)
En striker
Es huelguista (m)
Fr gréviste (m)
It scioperante (m)

**gréviste** (m) n Fr
De Streikende(r) (m)
En striker
Es huelguista (m)
It scioperante (m)
Pt grevista (m)

**grief** (m) n Fr
De Beschwerde (f)
En grievance
Es agravio (m)
It lagnanza (f)
Pt agravo (m)

**grievance** n En
De Beschwerde (f)
Es agravio (m)
Fr grief (m)
It lagnanza (f)
Pt agravo (m)

**gross** adj En
De brutto
Es bruto
Fr brut; gros
It lordo
Pt bruto

**gross amount** En
De Bruttobetrag (m)
Es importe bruto (m)
Fr montant brut (m)
It importo lordo (m)
Pt importância total (m)

**gross domestic product** (GDP) En
De Bruttoinlandprodukt (n)
Es producto interior bruto (m)
Fr produit intérieur brut (m)
It prodotto interno lordo (m)
Pt produto interno bruto (m)

**grosse Havarie** (f) De
En general average (G.A.)
Es avería general (f)
Fr avaries communes (f pl)
It avaria generale (f)
Pt avaria grossa (f)

**Grosshandel** (m) n De
En wholesale trade
Es comercio al por mayor (m)
Fr commerce en gros (m)
It commercio all'ingrosso (m)
Pt comércio por atacado (m)

**Grosshändler** *(m)* n De
En wholesaler
Es mayorista *(m)*
Fr grossiste *(m)*
It grossista *(m)*
Pt grossista *(m)*

**gross income** En
De Bruttoeinkommen *(n)*
Es ingreso bruto *(m)*
Fr rendement brut *(m)*
It reddito lordo *(m)*
Pt receita bruta *(f)*

**gross interest** En
De Bruttozins *(m)*
Es interés bruto *(m)*
Fr intérêts bruts *(m pl)*
It interesse lordo *(m)*
Pt juro bruto *(m)*

**grossista** *(m)* n It, Pt
De Grosshändler; Grossist *(m)*
En wholesaler
Es mayorista *(m)*
Fr grossiste *(m)*

**grossiste** *(m)* n Fr
De Grosshändler; Grossist *(m)*
En wholesaler
Es mayorista *(m)*
It grossista *(m)*
Pt grossista *(m)*

**gross margin** En
De Bruttoverdienstspanne *(f)*
Es márgen bruto *(m)*
Fr marge brute de bénéfices *(f)*
It margine lordo *(m)*
Pt margem bruta *(f)*

**gross national product** (GNP) En
De Bruttosozialprodukt *(n)*
Es producto nacional bruto *(m)*
Fr produit national brut *(m)*
It prodotto nazionale lordo *(m)*
Pt produto nacional bruto *(m)*

**gross premium** En
De Bruttoprämie *(f)*
Es prima bruta *(f)*
Fr prime brute *(f)*
It premio lordo *(m)*
Pt prémio bruto *(m)*

**gross profit** En
De Bruttogewinn *(m)*
Es ganancia bruta *(f)*
Fr bénéfice brut *(m)*
It utile lordo *(m)*
Pt lucro bruto *(m)*

**Grossraumbüro** *(n)* n De
En open-plan office
Es oficina sin particiones *(f)*
Fr bureau sans cloisons *(m)*
It ufficio senza divisioni *(m)*
Pt escritório sem divisões *(m)*

**gross register ton** En
De Brutto-Registertonne *(f)*
Es tonelada de registro bruto *(f)*
Fr tonneau de jauge brute *(m)*
It tonnellaggio lordo di registro *(m)*
Pt tonelada de registo bruto *(f)*

**gross ton** En
De Brutto-Tonne *(f)*
Es tonelada bruta *(f)*
Fr tonne forte *(f)*
It tonnellata lorda *(f)*
Pt tonelada de peso bruto *(f)*

**gross tonnage** En
De Brutto-Tonnage *(f)*
Es tonelaje bruto *(m)*
Fr tonnage brut *(m)*
It tonnellaggio lordo *(m)*
Pt tonelagem de peso bruto *(f)*

**gross weight** En
De Bruttogewicht *(n)*
Es peso bruto *(m)*
Fr poids brut *(m)*
It peso lordo *(m)*
Pt peso bruto *(m)*

**ground floor** En
De Erdgeschoss *(n)*
Es planta baja *(f)*
Fr rez-de-chaussée *(m)*
It pianterreno *(m)*
Pt rés-do-chão *(m)*

**ground glass** En
De Mattscheibe *(f)*
Es cristal deslustrado *(m)*
Fr verre dépoli *(m)*

It vetro smerigliato *(m)*
Pt vidro esmerilado *(m)*

**ground-landlord** n En
De Grundbesitzer *(m)*
Es propietario del terreno *(m)*
Fr propriétaire foncier *(m)*
It proprietario del terreno *(m)*
Pt proprietário do terreno *(m)*

**ground-rent** n En
De Grundpacht *(f)*
Es renta del terreno *(f)*
Fr rente foncière *(f)*
It affitto di terreno *(m)*
Pt renda sobre o terreno *(f)*

**Groupagedienst** *(m)* n De
En groupage service
Es servicio de agrupación *(m)*
Fr service de groupage *(m)*
It trasporto a collettame *(m)*
Pt serviço de agrupamento *(m)*

**groupage service** En
De Groupagedienst *(m)*
Es servicio de agrupación *(m)*
Fr service de groupage *(m)*
It trasporto a collettame *(m)*
Pt serviço de agrupamento *(m)*

**groupe consommateur** *(m)* Fr
De Abnehmerverein *(m)*
En consumer group
Es grupo de consumidores *(m)*
It gruppo di consumatori *(m)*
Pt grupo de consumidores *(m)*

**Groupe des Dix** *(m)* Fr
De Zehnerklub *(m)*
En Group of Ten
Es Grupo de los Diez *(m)*
It Gruppo dei Dieci *(m)*
Pt Grupo dos Dez *(m)*

**group insurance** En
De Gruppenversicherung *(f)*
Es seguro de grupo *(m)*
Fr assurance de groupe *(f)*
It assicurazione di gruppo *(f)*
Pt seguro de grupo *(m)*

**Group of Ten** En
De Zehnerklub *(m)*
Es Grupo de los Diez *(m)*
Fr Groupe des Dix *(m)*

It Gruppo dei Dieci *(m)*
Pt Grupo dos Dez *(m)*

**growth** *n* En
De Entwicklung *(f)*
Es crecimiento *(m)*
Fr croissance *(f)*
It crescita; sviluppo *(f; m)*
Pt crescimento *(m)*

**growth stocks** En
De wachstumorientierte Wert-papiere *(n pl)*
Es títulos de crecimiento *(m pl)*
Fr titres avec perspectives de croissance *(m pl)*
It titoli di sviluppo *(m pl)*
Pt acções de acréscimo de capital *(f pl)*

**grúa** *(f)* *n* Es, Pt
De Kran *(m)*
En crane
Fr grue *(f)*
It grue *(f)*

**grúa flotante** *(f)* Es
De Pontonkran *(m)*
En floating crane
Fr ponton-grue *(m)*
It grue galleggiante *(f)*
Pt guindaste flutuante *(m)*

**grue** *(f)* *n* Fr, It
De Kran *(m)*
En crane
Es grúa *(f)*
Pt grúa *(f)*

**grue galleggiante** *(f)* It
De Pontonkran *(m)*
En floating crane
Es grúa flotante *(f)*
Fr ponton-grue *(m)*
Pt guindaste flutuante *(m)*

**Grundbesitzer** *(m)* *n* De
En ground-landlord
Es propietario del terreno *(m)*
Fr propriétaire foncier *(m)*
It proprietario del terreno *(m)*
Pt proprietário do terreno *(m)*

**gründen** *vb* De
En found; establish
Es fundar; establecer
Fr fonder; établir

It fondare; stabilire
Pt fundar; estabelecer

**Gründer** *(m)* *n* De
En founder
Es fundador *(m)*
Fr fondateur *(m)*
It fondatore *(m)*
Pt fundador *(m)*

**Gründeraktien** *(f pl)* *n* De
En founder's shares
Es acciones del fundador *(f pl)*
Fr actions de fondateur *(f pl)*
It azioni del fondatore *(f pl)*
Pt acções de fundador *(f pl)*

**Gründermitglied** *(m)* *n* De
En founder member
Es miembro fundador *(m)*
Fr membre fondateur *(m)*
It socio fondatore *(m)*
Pt membro fondador *(m)*

**Grundjahr** *(n)* *n* De
En base year
Es año de base *(m)*
Fr année de base *(f)*
It anno di base *(m)*
Pt ano base *(m)*

**Grundlohn** *(m)* *n* De
En basic pay
Am base pay
Es salario-base *(m)*
Fr salaire de base *(m)*
It salario fondamentale *(m)*
Pt salário-base *(m)*

**Grundpacht** *(f)* *n* De
En ground-rent
Es renta del terreno *(f)*
Fr rente foncière *(f)*
It affitto di terreno *(m)*
Pt renda sobre o terreno *(f)*

**Grundsteuer** *(f)* *n* De
En property tax
Es impuesto sobre la pro-piedad *(m)*
Fr impôt foncier *(m)*
It imposta fondiaria *(f)*
Pt imposto sobre propriedade *(m)*

**grünes Pfund** *(n)* De
En green pound
Es esterlina verde *(f)*

Fr livre sterling verte *(f)*
It sterlina verde *(f)*
Pt libra esterlina verde *(f)*

**grupo de consumidores** *(m)* Es, Pt
De Abnehmerverein *(m)*
En consumer group
Fr groupe consommateur *(m)*
It gruppo di consumatori *(m)*

**Grupo de los Diez** *(m)* Es
De Zehnerklub *(m)*
En Group of Ten
Fr Groupe des Dix *(m)*
It Gruppo dei Dieci *(m)*
Pt Grupo dos Dez *(m)*

**grupo de suscriptores** *(m)* Es
De Emissionssyndikat *(n)*
En underwriting syndicate
Fr syndicat de garantie *(m)*
It consorzio finanziario *(m)*
Pt consórcio de subscritores *(m)*

**Grupo dos Dez** *(m)* Pt
De Zehnerklub *(m)*
En Group of Ten
Es Grupo de los Diez *(m)*
Fr Groupe des Dix *(m)*
It Gruppo dei Dieci *(m)*

**Gruppenversicherung** *(f)* *n* De
En group insurance
Es seguro de grupo *(m)*
Fr assurance de groupe *(f)*
It assicurazione di gruppo *(f)*
Pt seguro de grupo *(m)*

**Gruppo dei Dieci** *(m)* It
De Zehnerklub *(m)*
En Group of Ten
Es Grupo de los Diez *(m)*
Fr Groupe des Dix *(m)*
Pt Grupo dos Dez *(m)*

**gruppo di consumatori** *(m)* It
De Abnehmerverein *(m)*
En consumer group
Es grupo de consumidores *(m)*
Fr groupe consommateur *(m)*
Pt grupo de consumidores *(m)*

**guadagnare** *vb* It
De verdienen
En earn
Es ganar

Fr gagner
Pt ganhar

**guadagno** *(m) n* It
De Gewinn *(m)*
En gain
Es ganancia *(f)*
Fr gain *(m)*
Pt ganhos *(m pl)*

**guarantee** *vb* En
De Bürgschaft leisten; gewährleisten
Es garantizar; avalar
Fr garantir; avaliser
It garantire; avallare
Pt garantir; assegurar

**guarantee** *n* En
De Garantie *(f)*
Es garantía *(f)*
Fr garantie *(f)*
It garanzia *(f)*
Pt garantia *(f)*

**guarantor** *n* En
De Bürge *(m)*
Es garante; fiador *(m)*
Fr garant; avaliste *(m)*
It garante; avallante *(m)*
Pt fiador; avalizador *(m)*

**guarda de noche** *(m)* Es
De Nachtwächter *(m)*
En nightwatchman
Fr gardien de nuit *(m)*
It guardiano notturno *(m)*
Pt guarda de noite *(m)*

**guarda de noite** *(m)* Pt
De Nachtwächter *(m)*
En nightwatchman
Es guarda de noche *(m)*
Fr gardien de nuit *(m)*
It guardiano notturno *(m)*

**guarda-livros diplomado** *(m)* Pt
De Wirtschaftsprüfer *(m)*
En qualified accountant
Es contador habilitado *(m)*
Fr expert comptable *(m)*
It ragioniere diplomato *(m)*

**guardar** *vb* Pt, Es
De halten
En hold

Fr tenir; détenir
It tenere

**guardar en almacén** Es
De vorrätig halten
En keep in stock
Fr garder en stock
It tenere in magazzino
Pt reter em armazém

**guardar in fideicomiso** Es
De zu treuen Händen halten
En hold in trust
Fr tenir par fidéicommis
It tenere in fedecommesso
Pt reter em custódia

**guardian** (of a minor, etc.) *n* En
De Vormund *(m)*
Es tutor *(m)*
Fr tuteur *(m)*
It tutore *(m)*
Pt tutor *(m)*

**guardiano notturno** *(m)* It
De Nachtwächter *(m)*
En nightwatchman
Es guarda de noche *(m)*
Fr gardien de nuit *(m)*
Pt guarda de noite *(m)*

**guard's van** En
De Packwagen *(m)*
Es furgón *(m)*
Fr fourgon *(m)*
It bagagliaio *(m)*
Pt carruagem do guarda *(f)*

**guerra** *(f) n* Es, It, Pt
De Krieg *(m)*
En war
Fr guerre *(f)*

**guerra dei prezzi** *(f)* It
De Preiskrieg *(m)*
En price war
Es guerra de precios *(f)*
Fr guerre des prix *(f)*
Pt guerra de preços *(f)*

**guerra de precios** *(f)* Es
De Preiskrieg *(m)*
En price war
Fr guerre des prix *(f)*
It guerra dei prezzi *(f)*
Pt guerra de preços *(f)*

**guerra de preços** *(f)* Pt
De Preiskrieg *(m)*
En price war
Es guerra de precios *(f)*
Fr guerre des prix *(f)*
It guerra dei prezzi *(f)*

**guerre** *(f) n* Fr
De Krieg *(m)*
En war
Es guerra *(f)*
It guerra *(f)*
Pt guerra *(f)*

**guerre des prix** *(f)* Fr
De Preiskrieg *(m)*
En price war
Es guerra de precios *(f)*
It guerra dei prezzi *(f)*
Pt guerra de preços *(f)*

**guess-work** *n* En
De Mutmassung *(f)*
Es conjetura *(f)*
Fr conjecture *(f)*
It congettura *(f)*
Pt conjectura *(f)*

**guía** *(f) n* Es
De Adressbuch *(n)*
En directory
Fr répertoire *(m)*
It guida *(f)*
Pt guia *(m)*

**guia** *(m) n* Pt
De Adressbuch *(n)*
En directory
Es guía *(f)*
Fr répertoire *(m)*
It guida *(f)*

**guía comercial** *(f)* Es
De Handelsadressbuch *(n)*
En trade directory
Fr guide de commerce *(m)*
It guida commerciale *(f)*
Pt guia comercial *(m)*

**guia comercial** *(m)* Pt
De Handelsadressbuch *(n)*
En trade directory
Es guía comercial *(f)*
Fr guide de commerce *(m)*
It guida commerciale *(f)*

**guía de carga** (f) Es
De Frachtbrief (m)
En waybill
Fr lettre de voiture (f)
It lettera di vettura (f)
Pt guia de marcha (m)

**guia de consignação** (m) Pt
De Frachtbrief (m)
En consignment note
Es nota de consignación (f)
Fr lettre de voiture (f)
It nota di spedizione (f)

**guia de entrega** (m) Pt
De Lieferschein (m)
En delivery note
Es aviso de entrega (m)
Fr bordereau de livraison (m)
It nota di consegna (f)

**guia de marcha** (m) Pt
De Frachtbrief (m)
En waybill
Es guía de carga (f)
Fr lettre de voiture (f)
It lettera di vettura (f)

**guia de porte aéreo** (m) Pt
De Luftfrachtbrief (m)
En air waybill
Es carta de porte aéreo (f)
Fr lettre de transport aérien (f)
It nota di spedizione aerea (f)

**guia de remessa** (m) Pt
De Anzeige (f)
En advice note
Es aviso (m)
Fr lettre d'avis (f)
It lettera d'avviso (f)

**guía de teléfonos** (f) Es
De Fernsprechbuch (n)
En telephone directory
Fr annuaire des téléphones (m)
It elenco telefonico (m)
Pt lista telefónica (f)

**guida** (f) n It
De Adressbuch (n)
En directory
Es guía (f)
Fr répertoire (m)
Pt guia (m)

**guida commerciale** (f) It
De Handelsadressbuch (n)
En trade directory
Es guía comercial (f)
Fr guide de commerce (m)
Pt guia comercial (m)

**guide de commerce** (m) Fr
De Handelsadressbuch (n)
En trade directory
Es guía comercial (f)
It guida commerciale (f)
Pt guia comercial (m)

**guindaste flutuante** (m) Pt
De Pontonkran (m)
En floating crane
Es grúa flotante (f)
Fr ponton-grue (m)
It grue galleggiante (f)

**gültig** adj De
En valid
Es válido
Fr valable
It valido
Pt válido

**Gummistempel** (m) n De
En rubber stamp
Es estampilla de goma (f)
Fr tampon (m)
It stampino di gomma (m)
Pt carimbo (m)

**Gusseisen** (n) n De
En cast iron
Es hierro colado (m)
Fr fer de fonte (m)
It ghisa (f)
Pt ferro fundido (m)

**gut** adj De
En good
Es bueno
Fr bon
It buono
Pt bom

**Gut** (n) n De
En commodity
Es mercadería (f)
Fr marchandise (f)
It merce (f)
Pt mercadoria (f)

**gute Durchschnittsqualität** (f) De
En fair average quality (faq)
Es calidad media razonable (f)
Fr qualité commerciale moyenne (f)
It buona qualità media (f)
Pt qualidade media razoável (f)

**Güter** (n pl) n De
En goods
Es mercancías (f pl)
Fr marchandises (f pl)
It merce (f)
Pt mercadorias (f pl)

**Güterbeförderer** (m) n De
En common carrier
Es empresa de transportes (f)
Fr voiturier public (m)
It vettore (m)
Pt empresa de transportes (f)

**Güterzug** (m) n De
En goods train
Am freight train
Es tren de mercancías (m)
Fr train de marchandises (m)
It treno merci (m)
Pt comboio de mercadorías (m)

**gutgläubiger Besitzer** (m) De
En holder in due course
Es tenedor en buena fe (m)
Fr porteur de bonne foi (m)
It titolare in buona fede (m)
Pt futuro proprietário (m)

**Gutschriftanzeige** (f) n De
En credit note
Es nota de crédito (f)
Fr avis de crédit (m)
It nota di credito (f)
Pt aviso de crédito (m)

# H

**hacer efectivo** Es
De bewerkstelligen; ausführen
En implement
Fr exécuter
It attuare; effettuare
Pt executar

**hacer una cita** Es
De eine Verabredung treffen
En make an appointment
Fr prendre un rendez-vous
It fissare un appuntamento
Pt marcar um encontro

**hacer una contraoferta** Es
De ein Gegenangebot abgeben
En make a counteroffer
Fr faire une contre-offre
It fare una controfferta
Pt fazer uma contra-proposta

**hacer una oferta** Es
De eine Offerte machen
En make an offer
Fr faire une offre
It fare una offerta
Pt fazer uma oferta

**hacer un depósito** Es
De hinterlegen
En pay a deposit
Fr donner des arrhès
It versare un deposito
Pt pagar depósito

**hacer un pedido** Es
De bestellen
En order
Fr passer une commande
It ordinare
Pt encomendar

**hacienda** (f) n Es
De Schatzamt (n)
En exchequer
Am treasury
Fr trésorerie (f)
It tesoro (m)
Pt tesouro (m)

**Hafen** (m) n De
En port; harbour
Es puerto (m)
Fr port (m)
It porto (m)
Pt porto (m)

**Hafenanlagen** (f pl) n De
En harbour installations
Es instalaciones portuarias (f pl)
Fr installations portuaires (f pl)
It impianti portuali (m pl)
Pt instalações portuárias (f pl)

**Hafenarbeiter** (m) n De
En docker
Am longshoreman
Es cargador de muelle (m)
Fr docker (m)
It lavoratore del porto (m)
Pt trabalhador das docas (m)

**Hafenarbeiterstreik** (m) n De
En dock strike
Es huelga de obreros de muelle (f)
Fr grève des dockers (f)
It sciopero portuale (m)
Pt greve na doca (f)

**Hafengebühren** (f pl) n De
En port charges
Es derechos portuarios (m pl)
Fr droits de port (m pl)
It diritti portuali (m pl)
Pt direitos portuários (m pl)

**Hafenkonnossement** (n) n De
En shipped bill of lading
Es conocimiento de embarque a bordo (m)
Fr connaissement de marchandises à bord (m)
It polizza di carico con merce a bordo (f)
Pt conhecimento de carga embarcada (m)

**Hafenmeister** (m) n De
En harbour-master
Es capitán de puerto (m)
Fr capitaine de port (m)
It capitano di porto (m)
Pt capitão de porto (m)

**Haftkaution** (f) n De
En bail
Es fianza (f)
Fr caution (f)
It cauzione (f)
Pt caução (f)

**Haftkaution geben** De
En go bail for
Es salir fiados por
Fr se porter garant de
It rendersi garante di
Pt prestar caução a favor de

**Haftpflichtversicherung** (f) n De
En third-party insurance
Es seguro contra responsabilidad civil (m)
Fr assurance responsabilité civile (RC) (f)
It assicurazione contro terzi (f)
Pt seguro contra terceiros (m)

**haggle** vb En
Am bargain
De feilschen
Es regatear
Fr marchander; chipoter
It mercanteggiare; cavillare
Pt regatear

**halb** adj De
En half
Es medio
Fr à moitié; demi
It mezzo
Pt meio

**(zum) halben Preise** De
En half price
Es a mitad de precio
Fr à moitié prix
It metà prezzo
Pt metade do preço

**halbjährlich** adj De
En half-yearly
Es semestral
Fr semestriel
It semestrale
Pt semestral

**halbjährliche Dividende** (f) De
En half-yearly dividend
Es dividendo semestral (m)
Fr dividende semestrielle (f)
It dividendo semestrale (m)
Pt dividendo semi-anual (m)

**Halbsold** (m) n De
En half-pay
Es medio salario (m)
Fr demi-salaire (m)
It mezza paga (f)
Pt meio-salário (m)

**half** adj En
De halb
Es medio
Fr à moitié; demi
It mezzo
Pt meio

**half-pay** n En
De Halbsold (m)
Es medio salario (m)
Fr demi-salaire (m)
It mezza paga (f)
Pt meio-salário (m)

**half price** En
De zum halben Preise
Es a mitad de precio
Fr à moitié prix
It metà prezzo
Pt metade do preço

**half-year** n En
De Semester (n)
Es semestre (m)
Fr semestre (m)
It semestre (m)
Pt semestre (m)

**half-yearly** adj En
De halbjährlich
Es semestral
Fr semestriel
It semestrale
Pt semestral

**half-yearly dividend** En
De halbjährliche Dividende (f)
Es dividendo semestral (m)
Fr dividende semestrielle (f)
It dividendo semestrale (m)
Pt dividendo semi-anual (m)

**hall-mark** n En
De Feingehaltsstempel (m)
Es punzón de garantía (m)
Fr poinçon (m)
It punzonatura di garanzia (f)
Pt marca de garantia (f)

**hall-porter** n En
De Hausmeister (m)
Es conserje (m)
Fr concierge (m)
It portiere (m)
Pt porteiro (m)

**halten** vb De
En hold
Es tener
Fr tenir; détenir
It tenere
Pt guardar; conservar

**Hand-** De
En manual
Es manual
Fr manuel
It manuale
Pt manual

**handbook** n En
De Handbuch (n)
Es manual (m)
Fr manuel (m)
It manuale (m)
Pt manual (m)

**Handbuch** (n) n De
En handbook
Es manual (m)
Fr manuel (m)
It manuale (m)
Pt manual (m)

**Handel** (m) n De
En commerce; trade
Es comercio (m)
Fr commerce (m)
It commercio (m)
Pt comércio (m)

**Handels-** De
En mercantile
Es mercantil
Fr mercantile
It mercantile
Pt mercantil

**Handelsadressbuch** (n) n De
En trade directory
Es guía comercial (f)
Fr guide de commerce (m)
It guida commerciale (f)
Pt guia comercial (m)

**Handelsakzept** (n) n De
En trade acceptance
Es acceptación comercial (f)
Fr acceptation de commerce (f)
It accettazione commerciale (f)
Pt aceitação comercial (f)

**Handelsbank** (f) n De
En merchant bank
Es banco mercantil (m)
Fr banque commerciale (f)
It banca commerciale (f)
Pt banco comercial (m)

**Handelsbeschränkung** (f) n De
En restraint of trade
Es restricción del commercio (f)
Fr restriction au commerce (f)
It restrizione del commercio (f)
Pt restrição de comércio (f)

**Handelsbevollmächtigte(r)** (m) n De
En accredited agent
Es agente acreditudo (m)
Fr agent accrédité (m)
It agente accreditato (m)
Pt agente acreditado (m)

**Handelsbilanz** (f) n De
En balance of trade
Es balanza comercial (f)
Fr balance commerciale (f)
It bilancia commerciale (f)
Pt balança comercial (f)

**Handelsblock** (m) n De
En trade bloc
Es bloque comercial (m)
Fr bloc commercial (m)
It unione commerciale (f)
Pt bloque comercial (m)

**Handelsflotte** (f) n De
En merchant fleet
Es flota mercanto (f)
Fr flotte marchande (f)
It flotta mercantile (f)
Pt frota mercante (f)

**Handelsgebrauch** (m) n De
En custom of the trade
Es uso comercial (m)
Fr usage commercial (m)
It uso commerciale (m)
Pt uso comercial (m)

**Handelskammer** (f) n De
En chamber of commerce
Es cámara de comercio (f)
Fr chambre de commerce (f)
It camera di commercio (f)
Pt câmara de comércio (f)

**Handelskonto** (n) n De
En trade account
Es cuenta comercial (f)
Fr compte commercial (m)
It conto commerciale (m)
Pt conta comercial (f)

**Handelsmarke** *(f)* n De
  En brand
  Es marca (de fábrica) *(f)*
  Fr marque *(f)*
  It marca (di fabbrica) *(f)*
  Pt marca de fabrico *(f)*

**Handelsmesse** *(f)* n De
  En trade fair
  Es feria de muestras *(f)*
  Fr foire commerciale *(f)*
  It fiera commerciale *(f)*
  Pt feira comercial *(f)*

**Handelspreis** *(m)* n De
  En trade price
  Es precio al comerciante *(m)*
  Fr prix marchand *(m)*
  It prezzo al commerciante *(m)*
  Pt preço para comerciantes *(m)*

**Handelsschiff** *(n)* n De
  En merchant ship
  Es barco mercante *(m)*
  Fr navire marchand *(m)*
  It nave mercantile *(f)*
  Pt navio mercante *(m)*

**Handelsschranke** *(f)* n De
  En trade barrier
  Es barrera comercial *(f)*
  Fr barrière commerciale *(f)*
  It barriera commerciale *(f)*
  Pt barreira comercial *(f)*

**Handelstonne** *(f)* n De
  En freight ton
  Es tonelada de flete *(f)*
  Fr tonneau de fret *(m)*
  It tonnellata di nolo *(f)*
  Pt tonelada de frete *(f)*

**Handelsvertreter** *(m)* n De
  En mercantile agent
  Am sales agent
  Es agente mercantil *(m)*
  Fr agent de commerce *(m)*
  It agente di commercio *(m)*
  Pt agente comercial *(m)*

**Handelszyklus** *(m)* n De
  En trade cycle
  Es ciclo del negocio *(m)*
  Fr cycle de commerce *(m)*
  It cyclo degli affari *(m)*
  Pt ciclo comercial *(m)*

**Handgepäck** *(n)* n De
  En hand-luggage
  Es equipaje de mano *(m)*
  Fr bagages à main *(m pl)*
  It bagaglio a mano *(m)*
  Pt bagagem de mão *(f)*

**hand in one's resignation** En
  De den Rücktritt einreichen
  Es presentar la dimisión
  Fr remettre sa démission
  It rassegnare le dimissioni
  Pt apresentar demissão

**Händler** *(m)* n De
  En dealer
  Es comerciante *(m)*
  Fr négociant *(m)*
  It negoziante; commerciante *(m)*
  Pt negociante *(m)*

**Händlerrabatt** *(m)* n De
  En trade discount
  Es descuento comercial *(m)*
  Fr rabais de demi-gros *(m)*
  It sconto di revendita *(m)*
  Pt desconto à praça *(m)*

**handle with care!** En
  De Vorsicht!
  Es frágil!
  Fr fragile!
  It fragile!
  Pt frágil!

**handling charges** En
  De Manipulationsgebühr *(f)*
  Es gastos de manutención *(m pl)*
  Fr frais de manutention *(m pl)*
  It spese di gestione *(f pl)*
  Pt custas de manejo *(f pl)*

**hand-luggage** n En
  De Handgepäck *(n)*
  Es equipaje de mano *(m)*
  Fr bagages à main *(m pl)*
  It bagaglio a mano *(m)*
  Pt bagagem de mão *(f)*

**harbour** n En
  De Hafen *(m)*
  Es puerto *(m)*
  Fr port *(m)*
  It porto *(m)*
  Pt porto *(m)*

**harbour dues** En
  De Hafengebühren *(f pl)*
  Es derechos de puerto *(m pl)*
  Fr droits de port *(m pl)*
  It diritti portuali *(m pl)*
  Pt direitos portuários *(m pl)*

**harbour installations** En
  De Hafenanlagen *(f pl)*
  Es instalaciones portuarias *(f pl)*
  Fr installations portuaires *(f pl)*
  It impianti portuali *(m pl)*
  Pt instalações portuárias *(f pl)*

**harbour-master** n En
  De Hafenmeister *(m)*
  Es capitán de puerto *(m)*
  Fr capitaine de port *(m)*
  It capitano di porto *(m)*
  Pt capitão de porto *(m)*

**hard currency** En
  De harte Währung *(f)*
  Es moneda fuerta *(f)*
  Fr monnaie forte *(f)*
  It valuta forte *(f)*
  Pt moeda forte *(f)*

**hard sell** En
  De aufdrängliches Verkaufen *(n)*
  Es venta insistente *(f)*
  Fr vente débrouillarde *(f)*
  It vendita facendo sforzo *(f)*
  Pt venda insistente *(f)*

**hardware** (ironmongery) n En
  De Eisenwaren *(f pl)*
  Es ferretería; quincallería *(f)*
  Fr quincaillerie *(f)*
  It ferramenta *(f)*
  Pt ferragens *(f pl)*

**hardware** (computers) n En
  De Maschinenausrüstung; Hardware *(f)*
  Es mecánica de la máquina; hardware *(f m)*
  Fr hardware *(m)*
  It componenti di macchina calcolatore; hardware *(m pl; m)*
  Pt sistema fisico; hardware *(m)*

**harte Währung** (f) De
En hard currency
Es moneda fuerta (f)
Fr monnaie forte (f)
It valuta forte (f)
Pt moeda forte (f)

**harvest** n En
De Ernte (f)
Es cosecha (f)
Fr moisson; récolte (f)
It raccolto (m)
Pt colheita (f)

**hasard** (m) n Fr
De Wagnis (n)
En hazard
Es azar; riesgo (m)
It rischio (m)
Pt risco; azar (m)

**hasarder** vb Fr
De wagen
En hazard
Es arriesgar
It arrischiare
Pt arriscar

**Häufigkeit** (f) n De
En frequency
Es frecuencia (f)
Fr fréquence (f)
It frequenza (f)
Pt frequência (f)

**Häufigkeitsverteilung** (f) n De
En frequency distribution
Es distribución de las frecuencias (f)
Fr distribution de fréquences (f)
It distribuzione delle frequenze (f)
Pt distribuição de frequência (f)

**haulage** n En
Am trucking
De Transport (m)
Es transporte (m)
Fr camionnage; transport (m)
It trasporto (m)
Pt transporte (m)

**haulage contractor** En
Am trucking company
De Transportunternehmer (m)

Es contratista de transportes (m)
Fr entrepreneur de camionnage (m)
It imprenditore di trasporti (m)
Pt empreiteiro de transportes (m)

**Hauptanstalt** (f) n De
En head office
Es oficina central (f)
Fr siège; bureau principal (m)
It sede; ufficio centrale (f m)
Pt sede; escritório central (f m)

**Hauptbuch** (n) n De
En ledger
Es libro mayor (m)
Fr grand livre (m)
It libro mastro (m)
Pt livro-mestre (m)

**Haupteinkäufer** (m) n De
En head buyer
Es jefe del departamento de compras (m)
Fr chef du service des achats (m)
It capo servizio acquisti (m)
Pt chefe de compras (m)

**Hauptversammlung** (f) n De
En general meeting
Es asamblea general (f)
Fr assemblée générale (f)
It assemblea generale (f)
Pt assembleia geral (f)

**Haus** (n) n De
En house
Es casa (f)
Fr maison (f)
It casa (f)
Pt casa (f)

**Hausfrau** (f) n De
En housewife
Es ama de casa (f)
Fr ménagère (f)
It massaia (f)
Pt dona de casa (f)

**Haushalt** (m) n De
En household
Es hogar (m)
Fr ménage; domesticité (m f)

It famiglia (f)
Pt casa (f)

**Haushaltskontrolle** (f) n De
En budgetary control
Es control presupuestario (m)
Fr contrôle budgétaire (m)
It controllo a bilancio preventivo (m)
Pt controlo orçamental (m)

**Haushaltsplan** (m) n De
En budget
Es presupuesto (m)
Fr budget (m)
It bilancio preventivo (m)
Pt orçamento (m)

**(einen) Haushaltsplan ins Gleichgewicht bringen** De
En balance a budget
Es balancear el presupuesto
Fr équilibrer un budget
It pareggiare un bilancio
Pt equilibrar um orçamento

**Hausherr** (m) n De
En householder
Es jefe de familia (m)
Fr chef de famille (m)
It capo-famiglia (m)
Pt dono da casa (m)

**Hausmeister** (m) n De
En hall-porter
Es conserje (m)
Fr concierge (m)
It portiere (m)
Pt porteiro (m)

**hausse** (f) n Fr
De Steigen; Zunahme (n f)
En increase; rise
Es incremento; aumento (m)
It incremento; crescita (m f)
Pt aumento; incremento (m)

**Hausse** (f) n De
En boom
Es bonanza (f)
Fr haute conjoncture (f)
It rialzo (m)
Pt bonança (f)

**Haussemarkt** (m) n De
En bull market
Es mercado alcista (m)

Fr marché orienté à la hausse
   *(m)*
It mercato tendente al rialzo
   *(m)*
Pt mercado de tendência
   altista *(m)*


**Haussespekulant** *(m) n* De
En bull
Es alcista *(m)*
Fr haussier *(m)*
It rialzista *(m)*
Pt altista *(f)*


**haussier** *(m) n* Fr
De Haussespekulant *(m)*
En bull
Es alcista *(m)*
It rialzista *(m)*
Pt altista *(f)*


**haussier** *adj* Fr
De steigend
En bullish
Es alcista
It rialzista
Pt altista


**Haus-zu-Hausverkauf** *(m) n*
   De
En door-to-door selling
Es venta a domicilio *(f)*
Fr vente à domicile *(f)*
It vendita a domicilio *(f)*
Pt venda de porta-a-porta *(f)*


**haut** *adj* Fr
De hoch
En high
Es alto; elevado
It alto; elevato
Pt elevado


**haute conjoncture** *(f)* Fr
De Hausse *(f)*
En boom
Es bonanza *(f)*
It rialzo *(m)*
Pt bonança *(f)*


**haute direction** *(f)* Fr
De Direktion *(f)*
En top management
Es dirección superior *(f)*
It direzione superiore *(f)*
Pt gerência superior *(f)*


**hautes mers** *(f pl)* Fr
De hohe See *(f)*
En high seas
Es altamar *(f)*
It alto mare *(m)*
Pt alto-mar *(m)*


**Havarie** *(f) n* De
En average
Es avería *(f)*
Fr avarie *(f)*
It avaria *(f)*
Pt avaria *(f)*


**havariert** *adj* De
En with average (WA)
Es con avería
Fr avarié
It con avaria
Pt com avaria


**Havarieschein** *(m) n* De
En average bond
Es fianza de avería *(f)*
Fr compromis d'avarie *(m)*
It compromesso d'avaria *(m)*
Pt fiança de avaria *(f)*


**hazard** *vb* En
De wagen
Es arriesgar
Fr hasarder
It arrischiare
Pt arriscar


**hazard** *n* En
De Wagnis *(n)*
Es azar; riesgo *(m)*
Fr hasard; risque *(m)*
It rischio *(m)*
Pt risco; azar *(m)*


**head buyer** En
De Haupteinkäufer *(m)*
Es jefe del departamento de
   compras *(m)*
Fr chef du service des achats
   *(m)*
It capo servizio acquisti *(m)*
Pt chefe de compras *(m)*


**head foreman** En
De Werkmeister *(m)*
Es capataz jefe *(m)*
Fr chef d'atelier *(m)*
It capo officina *(m)*
Pt encarregado-chefe *(m)*


**head of department** En
De Abteilungsleiter *(m)*
Es jefe de departamento *(m)*
Fr chef de service *(m)*
It capo reparto *(m)*
Pt chefe de departamento *(m)*


**head office** En
De Hauptanstalt *(f)*
Es oficina central *(f)*
Fr siège; bureau principal *(m)*
It sede; ufficio centrale *(f m)*
Pt sede; escritório central *(f
   m)*


**health insurance** En
De Krankenversicherung *(f)*
Es seguro de enfermedad *(m)*
Fr assurance maladie *(f)*
It assicurazione malattia *(f)*
Pt seguro de obença *(m)*


**health service** En
De Gesundheitsdienst *(m)*
Es servicio de sanidad *(m)*
Fr service de la santé *(f)*
It servizio sanitario *(m)*
Pt serviço de saúde *(m)*


**heavy** *adj* En
De schwer
Es pesado; fuerte
Fr lourd; fort
It pesante; forte
Pt pesado


**heavy charges** En
De drückende Spesen *(f pl)*
Es gastos fuertes *(m pl)*
Fr charges lourdes *(f pl)*
It forti spese *(f pl)*
Pt encargos pesados *(m pl)*


**heavy fine** En
De schwere Busse *(f)*
Es sanción elevada *(f)*
Fr forte amende *(f)*
It forte multa *(f)*
Pt multa pesada *(f)*


**heavy industry** En
De Schwerindustrie *(f)*
Es industria pesada *(f)*
Fr industrie lourde *(f)*
It industria pesante *(f)*
Pt indústria pesada *(f)*

**heavy loss** En
De schwere Verluste *(m pl)*
Es fuerte pérdida; pérdida sensible *(f)*
Fr lourde perte *(f)*
It forte perdita *(f)*
Pt perda avultada *(f)*

**hecho** *(m) n* Es
De Tatsache *(f)*
En fact
Fr fait *(m)*
It fatto *(m)*
Pt facto *(m)*

**hedge** *vb* En
De sich decken
Es cubrirse
Fr arbitrager
It coprirsi
Pt cobrir-se

**Heimathafen** *(m) n* De
En port of registration
Es puerto de matrícula *(m)*
Fr port d'attache *(m)*
It porto d'immatricolazione *(m)*
Pt porto de matrícula *(m)*

**heir** *n* En
De Erbe *(m)*
Es heredero *(m)*
Fr héritier *(m)*
It erede *(m)*
Pt herdeiro *(m)*

**Heizöl** *(n) n* De
En fuel oil
Es fuel-oil *(m)*
Fr mazout *(m)*
It petrolio da ardere *(m)*
Pt petróleo combustível *(m)*

**help** *n* En
De Hilfe *(f)*
Es ayuda *(f)*
Fr secours *(m)*
It ainto *(m)*
Pt ajuda *(f)*

**herança** *(f) n* Pt
De Erbschaft *(f)*
En inheritance
Es herencia *(f)*
Fr succession *(f)*
It eredità *(f)*

**herdeiro** *(m) n* Pt
De Erbe *(m)*
En heir
Es heredero *(m)*
Fr héritier *(m)*
It erede *(m)*

**hereby** *adv* En
De hiermit
Es por esto
Fr par la présente acte
It col presente; con questo
Pt pelo presente

**heredero** *(m) n* Es
De Erbe *(m)*
En heir
Fr héritier *(m)*
It erede *(m)*
Pt herdeiro *(m)*

**herencia** *(f) n* Es
De Erbschaft; Nachlass *(f m)*
En inheritance; estate
Fr succession *(f)*
It eredità; successione *(f)*
Pt herança; património *(f m)*

**herewith** *adv* En
De hiermit
Es con esto; adjunto
Fr ci-joint; sous ce pli
It qui unito; con la presente
Pt incluso; junto

**héritier** *(m) n* Fr
De Erbe *(m)*
En heir
Es heredero *(m)*
It erede *(m)*
Pt herdeiro *(m)*

**Herkunftsland** *(n) n* De
En country of origin
Es pais de origen *(m)*
Fr pays de provenance *(m)*
It paese di origine *(m)*
Pt país de origem *(m)*

**heure** *(f) n* Fr
De Stunde *(f)*
En hour
Es hora *(f)*
It ora *(f)*
Pt hora *(f)*

**heure d'affluence** *(f)* Fr
De Verkehrsspitze *(f)*
En rush hour
Es hora punta *(f)*
It ora di punta *(f)*
Pt hora de ponta *(f)*

**heure du déjeuner** *(f)* Fr
De Mittagspause *(f)*
En lunch-hour
Es hora del almuerzo *(f)*
It ora di colazione *(f)*
Pt hora do almoço *(f)*

**heure légale** *(f)* Fr
De Normalzeit *(f)*
En standard time
Es hora oficial *(f)*
It ora legale *(f)*
Pt hora normal *(f)*

**heures de bureau** *(f pl)* Fr
De Geschäftsstunden *(f pl)*
En office hours
Es horario de oficina *(m)*
It orario d'ufficio *(m)*
Pt horário do escritório *(m)*

**heures de pointe** *(f pl)* Fr
De Spitzzeit *(f)*
En peak hours
Es horas punta *(f pl)*
It ore di punta *(f pl)*
Pt horas de ponta *(f pl)*

**heures d'ouverture** *(f pl)* Fr
De Geschäftszeit *(f)*
En business hours
Es horario de comercio *(m)*
It orario d'apertura *(m)*
Pt horas de funcionamento *(f pl)*

**heures-homme** *(f pl) n* Fr
De Arbeitsstunde pro Mann
En man-hours
Es horas-hombre *(f pl)*
It ore-uomo *(f pl)*
Pt horas-homem *(f pl)*

**heures supplémentaires** *(f pl)* Fr
De Überstunden *(f pl)*
En overtime
Es horas extraordinarias *(f pl)*
It lavoro straordinario *(m)*
Pt horas extraordinárias *(f pl)*

**hidden reserve** En
De stille Reserve *(f)*
Es reserva latente *(f)*
Fr réserve cachée *(f)*
It riserva occulta *(f)*
Pt reserva oculta *(f)*

**hidden tax** En
De versteckte Belastung *(f)*
Es impuesto latente *(m)*
Fr imposition latente *(f)*
It tassa invisibile *(f)*
Pt imposto ocultado *(m)*

**hier** *adv* Fr
De gestern
En yesterday
Es ayer
It ieri
Pt ontem

**hiermit** *adv* De
En hereby; herewith
Es por esto; con esto
Fr par la présente; ci-joint
It col presente; con questo
Pt pelo presente; incluso

**hierro** *(m) n* Es
De Eisen *(n)*
En iron
Fr fer *(m)*
It ferro *(m)*
Pt ferro *(m)*

**hierro bruto** *(m)* Es
De Roheisen *(n)*
En pig-iron
Fr fer en gueuse *(m)*
It pane di ghisa *(m)*
Pt ferro em bruto *(m)*

**hierro colado** *(m)* Es
De Gusseisen *(n)*
En cast iron
Fr fer de fonte *(m)*
It ghisa *(f)*
Pt ferro fundido *(m)*

**high** *adj* En
De hoch
Es alto; elevado
Fr haut; élevé
It alto; elevato
Pt elevado

**higher education** En
De Fortbildung *(f)*
Es enseñanza superior *(f)*
Fr enseignement supérieur *(m)*
It insegnamento superiore *(m)*
Pt instrução superior *(f)*

**highest bidder** En
De Meistbietende(r) *(m)*
Es ofertante más alto *(m)*
Fr plus offrant enchérisseur *(m)*
It miglior offerente *(m)*
Pt proponente mais elevado *(m)*

**high-grade** *adj* En
De erstklassig
Es alta calidad
Fr à haute teneur
It di qualità superiore
Pt alto-nível

**high seas** En
De hohe See *(f)*
Es altamar *(f)*
Fr hautes mers *(f pl)*
It alto mare *(m)*
Pt alto-mar *(m)*

**Hilfe** *(f) n* De
En help
Es ayuda *(f)*
Fr secours *(m)*
It ainto *(m)*
Pt ajuda *(f)*

**hinauslaufend auf** De
En amounting to
Es ascendiendo a
Fr à concurrence de
It ammontante a
Pt no montante de

**Hinderung** *(f) n* De
En hindrance
Es impedimento *(m)*
Fr empêchement *(m)*
It impedimento *(m)*
Pt impedimento *(m)*

**hindrance** *n* En
De Hinderung *(f)*
Es impedimento *(m)*
Fr empêchement *(m)*

It impedimento *(m)*
Pt impedimento *(m)*

**hinterlegen** *vb* De
En deposit
Es depositar
Fr déposer
It depositare
Pt depositar

**hinzufügen** *vb* De
En add
Es añadir
Fr ajouter
It aggiungere
Pt adicionar

**hinzuwählen** *vb* De
En co-opt
Es cooptar
Fr coopter
It cooptare
Pt cooptar

**hipoteca** *(f) n* Es, Pt
De Hypothek *(f)*
En mortgage; hypothecation
Fr hypothèque; nantissement *(f m)*
It ipoteca *(f)*

**hipotecar** *vb* Es, Pt
De verpfänden
En hypothecate
Fr hypothéquer
It ipotecare

**hipótese** *(f) n* Pt
De Hypothese *(f)*
En hypothesis
Es hipótesis *(f)*
Fr hypothèse *(f)*
It ipotesi *(f)*

**hipótesis** *(f) n* Es
De Hypothese *(f)*
En hypothesis
Fr hypothèse *(f)*
It ipotesi *(f)*
Pt hipótese *(f)*

**hire** (personnel) *vb* En
De anstellen
Es apalabrar
Fr engager
It fissare
Pt empregar

**hire** vb En
De mieten
Es alquilar
Fr louer
It noleggiare; affittare
Pt alugar

**hire-purchase** n En
De Ratenkauf (m)
Es compra a plazos (f)
Fr location-vente; vente à temperament (f)
It vendita a rate (f)
Pt venda a prestações (f)

**hirer** n En
De Mieter (m)
Es alquilador; arrendador (m)
Fr locataire (m)
It noleggiatore (m)
Pt alugador (m)

**histogram** n En
De Histogramm (n)
Es histograma (m)
Fr histogramme (m)
It istogramma (m)
Pt histograma (m)

**histograma** (m) n Es, Pt
De Histogramm (n)
En histogram
Fr histogramme (m)
It istogramma (m)

**Histogramm** (n) n De
En histogram
Es histograma (m)
Fr histogramme (m)
It istogramma (m)
Pt histograma (m)

**histogramme** (m) n Fr
De Histogramm (n)
En histogram
Es histograma (m)
It istogramma (m)
Pt histograma (m)

**historic cost** En
De Anschaffungskosten (pl)
Es coste primitivo (m)
Fr coût d'acquisition primitif (m)
It costo primitivo (m)
Pt custo original (m)

**hoard** n En
De Hort (m)
Es atesoramiento (m)
Fr thésaurisation (f)
It ammasso (m)
Pt acumulação (f)

**hoch** adj De
En high
Es alto; elevado
Fr haut; élevé
It alto; elevato
Pt elevado

**hochwertig** adj De
En top quality
Es de primera calidad
Fr de première qualité
It di qualità superiore
Pt de classe superior

**hogar** (m) n Es
De Haushalt (m)
En household
Fr ménage; domesticité (m f)
It famiglia (f)
Pt casa (f)

**Hoheitsgewässer** (n pl) De
En territorial waters
Es aguas territoriales (f pl)
Fr eaux territoriales (f pl)
It acque territoriali (f pl)
Pt águas territoriais (f pl)

**hohe See** (f) De
En high seas
Es altamar (f)
Fr hautes mers (f pl)
It alto mare (m)
Pt alto-mar (m)

**hold** (of a ship) n En
De Laderaum (m)
Es bodega (f)
Fr cale (f)
It stiva (f)
Pt porão (m)

**hold** vb En
De halten
Es tener
Fr tenir; détenir
It tenere
Pt guardar; conservar

**hold a meeting** En
De eine Versammlung abhalten
Es celebrar una reunión
Fr tenir une assemblée
It tenere una riunione
Pt fazer uma reunião

**holder** n En
De Inhaber (m)
Es titular (m)
Fr détenteur (m)
It titolare (m)
Pt titular (m)

**holder for value** En
De entgeltigter Besitzer (m)
Es tenedor legítimo (m)
Fr porteur à titre onéreux (m)
It detentore legittimo (m)
Pt proprietário legítimo (m)

**holder in due course** En
De gutgläubiger Besitzer (m)
Es tenedor en buena fe (m)
Fr porteur de bonne foi (m)
It titolare in buona fede (m)
Pt futuro proprietário (m)

**holding company** En
De Dachgesellschaft (f)
Es compañía tenedora (f)
Fr société holding (f)
It società holding (f)
Pt companhia proprietária (f)

**hold in trust** En
De zu treuen Händen halten
Es guardar in fideicomiso
Fr tenir par fidéicommis
It tenere in fedecommesso
Pt reter em custódia

**hold over** En
De aufschieben
Es aplazar; diferir
Fr différer
It differire
Pt conservar; adiar

**hold shares** En
De beteiligt sein; Aktien besitzen
Es tener acciones
Fr détenir des actions
It tenere azioni
Pt reter acções

**hold the line!** En
De am Apparat bleiben, bitte!
Es espere al aparato!
Fr ne quittez pas!
It resta in linea!
Pt aguarde!

**holiday** n En
Am vacation
De Ferien; Urlaub (pl: m)
Es vacaciones (f pl)
Fr vacances (f pl)
It vacanza (f)
Pt férias (f pl)

**holidays with pay** En
De bezahlter Urlaub (m)
Es vacaciones retribuidas (f pl)
Fr congés payés (m pl)
It vacanze retribuite (f pl)
Pt férias pagas (f pl)

**hombre de negocios** (m) Es
De Geschäftsmann (m)
En businessman
Fr homme d'affaires (m)
It uomo d'affari (m)
Pt homem de negócios (m)

**homem de negócios** (m) Pt
De Geschäftsmann (m)
En businessman
Es hombre de negocios (m)
Fr homme d'affaires (m)
It uomo d'affari (m)

**home trade** En
Am domestic sales
De Binnenhandel (m)
Es comercio interior (m)
Fr commerce intérieur (m)
It commercio interno (m)
Pt comércio interno (m)

**homme d'affaires** (m) Fr
De Geschäftsmann (m)
En businessman
Es hombre de negocios (m)
It uomo d'affari (m)
Pt homem de negócios (m)

**homologation d'un testament**
(f) Fr
De Testamentseröffnung; Bestätigung (f)
En probate
Es validación de los testamentos (f)

It omologazione di testamento (f)
Pt validação testamentária (f)

**honest** adj En
De ehrlich
Es honesto
Fr honnête
It onesto
Pt honesto

**honesto** adj Es, Pt
De ehrlich
En honest
Fr honnête
It onesto

**honnête** adj Fr
De ehrlich
En honest
Es honesto
It onesto
Pt honesto

**honneur** (f) n Fr
De Ehre (f)
En honour
Es honor (m)
It onore (m)
Pt honra (f)

**honor** (m) n Es
De Ehre (f)
En honour
Fr honneur (f)
It onore (m)
Pt honra (f)

**honoraire** adj Fr
De ehrenamtlich
En honorary
Es honorario
It onorario
Pt honorário

**honoraires** (m pl) n Fr
De Vergütung; Honorar (f n)
En fee
Es honorario (m)
It onorario (m)
Pt honorários (m pl)

**Honorar** (n) n De
En fee
Es honorario (m)
Fr honoraires (m pl)
It onorario (m)
Pt honorários (m pl)

**honorario** (m) n Es
De Vergütung; Honorar (f n)
En fee
Fr honoraires (m pl)
It onorario (m)
Pt honorários (m pl)

**honorario** adj Es
De ehrenamtlich
En honorary
Fr honoraire
It onorario
Pt honorário

**honorário** adj Pt
De ehrenamtlich
En honorary
Es honorario
Fr honoraire
It onorario

**honorários** (m pl) n Pt
De Vergütung; Honorar (f n)
En fee
Es honorario (m)
Fr honoraires (m pl)
It onorario (m)

**honorary** adj En
De ehrenamtlich
Es honorario
Fr honoraire
It onorario
Pt honorário

**honorer** vb Fr
De honorieren
En honour
Es honrar
It onorare
Pt honrar

**honorieren** vb De
En honour
Es honrar
Fr honorer
It onorare
Pt honrar

**honour** vb En
De honorieren
Es honrar
Fr honorer
It onorare
Pt honrar

**honour** n En
De Ehre (f)
Es honor (m)
Fr honneur (f)
It onore (m)
Pt honra (f)

**honra** (f) n Pt
De Ehre (f)
En honour
Es honor (m)
Fr honneur (f)
It onore (m)

**honrar** vb Es, Pt
De honorieren
En honour
Fr honorer
It onorare

**hora** (f) n Es, Pt
De Stunde (f)
En hour
Fr heure (f)
It ora (f)

**hora del almuerzo** (f) Es
De Mittagspause (f)
En lunch-hour
Fr heure du déjeuner (f)
It ora di colazione (f)
Pt hora do almoço (f)

**hora de ponta** (f) Pt
De Verkehrsspitze (f)
En rush hour
Es hora punta (f)
Fr heure d'affluence (f)
It ora di punta (f)

**hora do almoço** (f) Pt
De Mittagspause (f)
En lunch-hour
Es hora del almuerzo (f)
Fr heure du déjeuner (f)
It ora di colazione (f)

**hora normal** (f) Pt
De Normalzeit (f)
En standard time
Es hora oficial (f)
Fr heure légale (f)
It ora legale (f)

**hora oficial** (f) Es
De Normalzeit (f)
En standard time
Fr heure légale (f)

It ora legale (f)
Pt hora normal (f)

**hora punta** (f) Es
De Verkehrsspitze (f)
En rush hour
Fr heure d'affluence (f)
It ora di punta (f)
Pt hora de ponta (f)

**horário de caminhos de ferro** (m) Pt
De Eisenbahnfahrplan (m)
En railway timetable
Es horario de trenes (m)
Fr indicateur des chemins de fer (m)
It orario ferroviario (m)

**horario de comercio** (m) Es
De Geschäftszeit (f)
En business hours
Fr heures d'ouverture (f pl)
It orario d'apertura (m)
Pt horas de funcionamento (f pl)

**horario de oficina** (m) Es
De Geschäftsstunden (f pl)
En office hours
Fr heures de bureau (f pl)
It orario d'ufficio (m)
Pt horário do escritório (m)

**horario de trenes** (m) Es
De Eisenbahnfahrplan (m)
En railway timetable
Fr indicateur des chemins de fer (m)
It orario ferroviario (m)
Pt horário de caminhos de ferro (m)

**horário do escritório** (m) Pt
De Geschäftsstunden (f pl)
En office hours
Es horario de oficina (m)
Fr heures de bureau (f pl)
It orario d'ufficio (m)

**horas de funcionamento** (f pl) Pt
De Geschäftszeit (f)
En business hours
Es horario de comercio (m)
Fr heures d'ouverture (f pl)
It orario d'apertura (m)

**horas de ponta** (f pl) Pt
De Spitzzeit (f)
En peak hours
Es horas punta (f pl)
Fr heures de pointe (f pl)
It ore di punta (f pl)

**horas de trabalho** (f pl) Pt
De Arbeitszeit (f)
En hours of work
Es jornada laboral (f)
Fr durée du travail (f)
It ore lavorative (f pl)

**horas extraordinarias** (f pl) Es
De Überstunden (f pl)
En overtime
Fr heures supplémentaires (f pl)
It lavoro straordinario (m)
Pt horas extraordinárias (f pl)

**horas extraordinárias** (f pl) Pt
De Überstunden (f pl)
En overtime
Es horas extraordinarias (f pl)
Fr heures supplémentaires (f pl)
It lavoro straordinario (m)

**horas-hombre** (f pl) Es
De Arbeitsstunde pro Mann (f)
En man-hours
Fr heures-homme (f pl)
It ore-uomo (f pl)
Pt horas-homem (f pl)

**horas-homem** (f pl) Pt
De Arbeitsstunde pro Mann (f)
En man-hours
Es horas-hombre (f pl)
Fr heures-homme (f pl)
It ore-uomo (f pl)

**horas punta** (f pl) Es
De Spitzzeit (f)
En peak hours
Fr heures de pointe (f pl)
It ore di punta (f pl)
Pt horas de ponta (f pl)

**horizontaler Zusammenschluss** De
En horizontal integration
Es integración horizontal (f)
Fr intégration horizontale (f)
It integrazione orizzontale (f)
Pt integração horizontal (f)

**horizontal integration** En
De horizontaler Zusammen-
schluss
Es integración horizontal (f)
Fr intégration horizontale (f)
It integrazione orizzontale (f)
Pt integração horizontal (f)

**horse-power** (hp) n En
De Pferdestärke (PS) (f)
Es caballo de vapor (cv) (m)
Fr cheval-vapeur (ch-v) (m)
It cavallo (m)
Pt cavalo-vapor (m)

**hors taxe** (HT) Fr
De ausser Steuer
En excluding tax
Es impuesto no incluido
It tassa esclusa
Pt impostos excluidos

**Hort** (m) n De
En hoard
Es atesoramiento (m)
Fr thésaurisation (f)
It ammasso (m)
Pt acumulação (f)

**hotel** n En; Es, Pt (m)
De Hotel (n)
Fr hôtel (m)
It albergo (m)

**hôtel** (m) n Fr
De Hotel (n)
En hotel
Es hotel (m)
It albergo (m)
Pt hotel (m)

**Hotel** (n) n De
En hotel
Es hotel (m)
Fr hôtel (m)
It albergo (m)
Pt hotel (m)

**houille** (f) n Fr
De Kohle (f)
En coal
Es carbón (m)
It carbone (m)
Pt carvão (m)

**hour** n En
De Stunde (f)
Es hora (f)

Fr heure (f)
It ora (f)
Pt hora (f)

**hours of work** En
De Arbeitszeit (f)
Es jornada laboral (f)
Fr durée du travail (f)
It ore lavorative (f pl)
Pt horas de trabalho (f pl)

**house** n En
De Haus (n)
Es casa (f)
Fr maison (f)
It casa (f)
Pt casa (f)

**household** n En
De Haushalt (m)
Es hogar (m)
Fr ménage; domesticité (m f)
It famiglia (f)
Pt casa (f)

**household electrical goods** En
De elektrische Haushaltsgüter
(n pl)
Es aparatos eléctricos de casa
(m pl)
Fr electro-ménager (m)
It elettrodomestici (m pl)
Pt electro-domésticos (m pl)

**householder** n En
De Hausherr (m)
Es jefe de familia (m)
Fr chef de famille (m)
It capo-famiglia (m)
Pt dono da casa (m)

**household insurance** En
De Wohnungsversicherung (f)
Es seguro de casa (m)
Fr assurance ménagère (f)
It assicurazione domestica (f)
Pt seguro de casa (m)

**housewife** n En
De Hausfrau (f)
Es ama de casa (f)
Fr ménagère (f)
It massaia (f)
Pt dona de casa (f)

**Hubraum** (m) n De
En cubic capacity
Es cilindrada (f)

Fr cylindrée (f)
It cilindrata (f)
Pt cilindrada (f)

**huelga** (f) n Es
De Streik (m)
En strike
Fr grève (f)
It sciopero (m)
Pt greve (f)

**huelga de brazos caídos** (f) Es
De Sitzstreik (m)
En sit-down strike
Fr grève avec occupation des
lieux (f)
It sciopero bianco (m)
Pt greve de braços caídos (f)

**huelga de obreros de muelle**
(f) Es
De Hafenarbeiterstreik (m)
En dock strike
Fr grève des dockers (f)
It sciopero portuale (m)
Pt greve na doca (f)

**huelga de producción lenta** (f)
Es
De Bummelstreik (m)
En go-slow strike
Am slow down
Fr grève perlée (f)
It sciopero a singhiozzo (m)
Pt greve de abrandamento do
ritmo de produção (f)

**huelga espontánea** (f) Es
De wilder Streik (m)
En wildcat strike
Fr grève sauvage (f)
It sciopero selvaggio (m)
Pt greve não oficializada (f)

**huelga general** (f) Es
De Generalstreik (m)
En general strike
Fr grève générale (f)
It sciopero generale (m)
Pt greve geral (f)

**huelga no-oficial** (f) Es
De unanerkannter Streik (m)
En unofficial strike
Fr grève non reconnue (f)
It sciopero non ufficiale (m)
Pt greve não oficializada (f)

**huelga oficial** (f) Es
De anerkannter Streik (m)
En official strike
Fr grève officielle (f)
It sciopero ufficiale (m)
Pt greve oficial (f)

**huelguista** (m) n Es
De Streikende(r) (m)
En striker
Fr gréviste (m)
It scioperante (m)
Pt grevista (m)

**hull insurance** En
De Kaskoversicherung (f)
Es seguro del casco (m)
Fr assurance sur le corps (f)
It assicurazione corpo (m)
Pt seguro do casco (m)

**human relations** En
De zwischenmenschliche Be-
ziehungen (f pl)
Es relaciones humanas (f pl)
Fr relations humaines (f pl)
It relazioni umane (f pl)
Pt relações humanas (f pl)

**Hundertsatz** (m) n De
En percentage
Es porcentaje (m)
Fr pourcentage (m)
It percentuale (f)
Pt percentagem (f)

**hypothecate** vb En
De verpfänden
Es hipotecar
Fr hypothéquer
It ipotecare
Pt hipotecar

**hypothecation** n En
De Hypothek (f)
Es hipoteca (f)
Fr nantissement (m)
It ipoteca (f)
Pt hipoteca (f)

**Hypothek** (f) n De
En mortgage; hypothecation
Es hipoteca (f)
Fr hypothèque; nantissement
(f m)
It ipoteca (f)
Pt hipoteca (f)

**hypothekarisch gesicherte
Schuldverschreibung** (f)
De
En mortgage debenture
Es obligación hipotecaria (f)
Fr obligation hypothécaire (f)
It obbligazione ipotecaria (f)
Pt obrigação hipotecária (f)

**hypothèque** (f) n Fr
De Hypothek (f)
En mortgage
Es hipoteca (f)
It ipoteca (f)
Pt hipoteca (f)

**hypothéquer** vb Fr
De verpfänden
En hypothecate
Es hipotecar
It ipotecare
Pt hipotecar

**hypothèse** (f) n Fr
De Hypothese (f)
En hypothesis
Es hipótesis (f)
It ipotesi (f)
Pt hipótese (f)

**Hypothese** (f) n De
En hypothesis
Es hipótesis (f)
Fr hypothèse (f)
It ipotesi (f)
Pt hipótese (f)

**hypothesis** n En
De Hypothese (f)
Es hipótesis (f)
Fr hypothèse (f)
It ipotesi (f)
Pt hipótese (f)

## I

**I.O.U.** (I owe you) En
De Schuldschein (m)
Es pagaré (m)
Fr reconnaissance de dette (f)
It pagherò (m)
Pt vale (m)

**idea** n En; Es, It (f)
De Idee (f)
Fr idée (f)
Pt ideia (f)

**idée** (f) n Fr
De Idee (f)
En idea
Es idea (f)
It idea (f)
Pt ideia (f)

**Idee** (f) n De
En idea
Es idea (f)
Fr idée (f)
It idea (f)
Pt ideia (f)

**ideia** (f) n Pt
De Idee (f)
En idea
Es idea (f)
Fr idée (f)
It idea (f)

**identificar** vb Es, Pt
De identifizieren
En identify
Fr identifier
It identificare

**identificare** vb It
De identifizieren
En identify
Es identificar
Fr identifier
Pt identificar

**identifier** vb Fr
De identifizieren
En identify
Es identificar
It identificare
Pt identificar

**identifizieren** vb De
En identify
Es identificar
Fr identifier
It identificare
Pt identificar

**identify** vb En
De identifizieren
Es identificar
Fr identifier

It identificare
Pt identificar

**identity card** En
De Personalausweis (m)
Es carnet de identidad (m)
Fr carte d'identité (f)
It carta d'identità (f)
Pt bilhete de identidade (m)

**idle capacity** En
De unbenutzte Ladefähigkeit (f)
Es potencial no utilizado (m)
Fr potentiel non utilisé (m)
It potenziale non utilizzato (m)
Pt potencial não utilizado (m)

**idle money** En
De totes Kapital (n)
Es dinero sin invertir (m)
Fr capital oisif (m)
It denaro inattivo (m)
Pt dinheiro paralizado (m)

**idle time** En
De unbeschäftigte Zeit (f)
Es tiempo libre (m)
Fr temps improductif (m)
It tempo passivo (m)
Pt tempo improdutivo (m)

**ieri** adv It
De gestern
En yesterday
Es ayer
Fr hier
Pt ontem

**ilegal** adj Es, Pt
De ungesetzlich
En illegal
Fr illégal
It illegale

**ilegible** adj Es
De unleserlich
En illegible
Fr illisible
It illeggibile
Pt ilegível

**ilegível** adj Pt
De unleserlich
En illegible
Es ilegible
Fr illisible
It illeggibile

**ilíquido de impostos** Pt
De steuerabsetzbar
En tax-deductible
Es deducible de impuestos
Fr déductible à l'impôt
It deducibile da tassa

**illegal** adj En
De ungesetzlich
Es ilegal
Fr illégal
It illegale
Pt ilegal

**illégal** adj Fr
De ungesetzlich
En illegal
Es ilegal
It illegale
Pt ilegal

**illegale** adj It
De ungesetzlich
En illegal
Es ilegal
Fr illégal
Pt ilegal

**illeggibile** adj It
De unleserlich
En illegible
Es ilegible
Fr illisible
Pt ilegível

**illegible** adj En
De unleserlich
Es ilegible
Fr illisible
It illeggibile
Pt ilegível

**illisible** adj Fr
De unleserlich
En illegible
Es ilegible
It illeggibile
Pt ilegível

**imaginärer Gewinn** (m) De
En paper profit
Es ganancia por realizar (f)
Fr profit fictif (m)
It utile sulla carta (m)
Pt lucros no papel (m)

**imaginärer Verlust** (m) De
En paper loss
Es pérdida por realizar (f)
Fr perte fictive (f)
It perdita sulla carta (f)
Pt perdas no papel (f)

**im Ausland** De
En abroad
Es en el extranjero
Fr à l'étranger
It all'estero
Pt no estrangeiro

**imballaggio** (m) n It
De Verpackung (f)
En packing
Es embalaje; envase (m)
Fr emballage (m)
Pt embalagem;
empacotamento (m)

**imballaggio a perdere** (m) It
De wegwerfbare Verpackung (f)
En disposable wrapping
Es envoltura desechable (f)
Fr emballage perdu (m)
Pt embalagem a destruir (f)

**imballaggio incluso** It
De Verpackung einbegriffen
En including packing
Es franco embalaje
Fr franco d'emballage
Pt incluindo embalagem

**imbarcare** vb It
De verschiffen; sich einschiffen
En ship; embark
Es embarcar
Fr embarquer; s'embarquer
Pt embarcar

**imbarco** (m) n It
De Verladung; Einschiffung (f)
En shipment; embarcation
Es embarque; embarco (m)
Fr embarquement (m)
Pt embarque; embarcação (m f)

**im Durchgangsverkehr** De
En in transit
Es en tránsito
Fr en transit
It in transito
Pt em trânsito

**imediato** *(m)* *n* Pt
 De Maat *(m)*
 En mate
 Es primer oficial *(m)*
 Fr second *(m)*
 It primo ufficiale *(m)*

**im Einvernehmen mit** De
 En in agreement with
 Es de acuerdo con
 Fr d'accord avec
 It d'accordo con
 Pt de acordo com

**imigração** *(f)* *n* Pt
 De Einwanderung *(f)*
 En immigration
 Es inmigración *(f)*
 Fr immigration *(f)*
 It immigrazione *(f)*

**imitação** *(f)* *n* Pt
 De Nachahmung *(f)*
 En imitation
 Es imitación *(f)*
 Fr imitation *(f)*
 It imitazione *(f)*

**imitación** *(f)* *n* Es
 De Nachahmung *(f)*
 En imitation
 Fr imitation *(f)*
 It imitazione *(f)*
 Pt imitação *(f)*

**imitation** *n* En, Fr *(f)*
 De Nachahmung *(f)*
 Es imitación *(f)*
 It imitazione *(f)*
 Pt imitação *(f)*

**imitation gold** En
 De Kunstgold *(n)*
 Es oro de imitación *(m)*
 Fr similor *(m)*
 It similoro *(m)*
 Pt ouro de imitação *(m)*

**imitation leather** En
 De Kunstleder *(n)*
 Es piel de imitación *(f)*
 Fr similicuir *(m)*
 It finta pelle *(f)*
 Pt cabedal de imitação *(m)*

**imitazione** *(f)* *n* It
 De Nachahmung *(f)*
 En imitation

 Es imitación *(f)*
 Fr imitation *(f)*
 Pt imitação *(f)*

**immagazzinare** *vb* It
 De lagern
 En store
 Es almacenar
 Fr emmagasiner
 Pt armazenar

**immaterieller Schaden** *(m)* De
 En consequential damages
 Es daños indirectos *(m pl)*
 Fr dommages indirects *(m pl)*
 It danni indiretti *(m pl)*
 Pt danos decorrentes *(m pl)*

**immeuble** *(m)* *n* Fr
 De Wohnungsgebäude *(n)*
 En block of flats
 Am apartment house
 Es bloque de pisos *(m)*
 It fabbricato di appartamenti *(m)*
 Pt edifício de andares *(m)*

**immigration** *n* En, Fr *(f)*
 De Einwanderung *(f)*
 Es inmigración *(f)*
 It immigrazione *(f)*
 Pt imigração *(f)*

**immigrazione** *(f)* *n* It
 De Einwanderung *(f)*
 En immigration
 Es inmigración *(f)*
 Fr immigration *(f)*
 Pt imigração *(f)*

**Immobilienbüro** *(n)* *n* De
 En estate agency
 Am real estate agency
 Es correduría de fincas *(f)*
 Fr agence immobilière *(f)*
 It agenzia immobiliare *(f)*
 Pt agência de propriedades *(f)*

**immobilisations** *(f pl)* *n* Fr
 De Anlagevermögen *(n)*
 En fixed assets
 Es activo fijo *(m)*
 It immobilizzazioni; attivo fisso *(f pl; m)*
 Pt bens fixos *(m pl)*

**immobilizzazioni** *(f pl)* *n* It
 De Anlagevermögen *(n)*
 En fixed assets
 Es activo fijo *(m)*
 Fr immobilisations *(f pl)*
 Pt bens fixos *(m pl)*

**imparcial** *adj* Es, Pt
 De unparteiisch
 En impartial
 Fr impartial
 It imparziale

**impartial** *adj* En, Fr
 De unparteiisch
 Es imparcial
 It imparziale
 Pt imparcial

**imparziale** *adj* It
 De unparteiisch
 En impartial
 Es imparcial
 Fr impartial
 Pt imparcial

**impedimento** *(m)* *n* Es, It, Pt
 De Hinderung *(f)*
 En hindrance
 Fr empêchement *(m)*

**impersonal account** En
 De Firmenkonto *(n)*
 Es cuenta simulada *(f)*
 Fr compte impersonnel *(m)*
 It conto d'ordine *(m)*
 Pt conta impessoal *(f)*

**impianti portuali** *(m pl)* It
 De Hafenanlagen *(f pl)*
 En harbour installations
 Es instalaciones portuarias *(f pl)*
 Fr installations portuaires *(f pl)*
 Pt instalações portuárias *(f pl)*

**impianto** *(m)* *n* It
 De Anlage *(f)*
 En plant; installation
 Es planta; instalación *(f)*
 Fr appareil; installation *(m f)*
 Pt instalação *(f)*

**impianto piloto** *(m)* It
 De Musteranlage *(f)*
 En pilot plant
 Es instalación piloto *(f)*

Fr  installation témoine *(f)*
Pt  instalação piloto *(f)*


**impiegare** *vb* It
De  beschäftigen
En  employ
Es  emplear
Fr  employer
Pt  empregar


**impiegato** *(m) n* It
De  Angestellte(r);  Arbeitneh-
    mer *(m)*
En  employee; clerk
Es  empleado; oficinista *(m)*
Fr  employé; commis *(m)*
Pt  empregado; empregado de
    escritorio *(m)*


**impiegato statale** *(m)* It
De  Beamte(r) *(m)*
En  civil servant
Am  government employee
Es  funcionario del gobierno
    *(m)*
Fr  fonctionnaire *(m)*
Pt  foncionário público *(m)*


**impiego** *(m) n* It
De  Beschäftigung; Stellung *(f)*
En  employment; post
Es  empleo *(m)*
Fr  emploi *(m)*
Pt  emprego *(m)*


**implement** *vb* En
De  bewerkstelligen; ausführen
Es  hacer efectivo; ejecutar
Fr  exécuter
It  attuare; effettuare
Pt  executar


**implicar** *vb* Es
De  andeuten
En  imply
Fr  impliquer
It  implicare
Pt  significar


**implicare** *vb* It
De  andeuten
En  imply
Es  implicar
Fr  impliquer
Pt  significar


**implicit** *adj* En
De  stillschweigend
Es  implícito
Fr  implicite
It  implicito
Pt  implícito


**implicite** *adj* Fr
De  stillschweigend
En  implicit
Es  implícito
It  implicito
Pt  implícito


**implícito** *adj* Es, Pt
De  stillschweigend
En  implicit
Fr  implicite
It  implicito


**implicito** *adj* It
De  stillschweigend
En  implicit
Es  implícito
Fr  implicite
Pt  implícito


**implied terms** En
De  stillschweigende Bedingun-
    gen *(f pl)*
Es  condiciones implícitas *(f pl)*
Fr  conditions implicites *(f pl)*
It  condizioni implicite *(f pl)*
Pt  condições implícitas *(f pl)*


**impliquer** *vb* Fr
De  andeuten
En  imply
Es  implicar
It  implicare
Pt  significar


**imply** *vb* En
De  andeuten
Es  implicar
Fr  impliquer
It  implicare
Pt  significar


**import** *n* En
De  Einfuhr *(f)*
Es  importación *(f)*
Fr  importation *(f)*
It  importazione *(f)*
Pt  importação *(f)*


**importação** *(f) n* Pt
De  Einfuhr *(f)*
En  import
Es  importación *(f)*
Fr  importation *(f)*
It  importazione *(f)*


**importación** *(f) n* Es
De  Einfuhr *(f)*
En  import
Fr  importation *(f)*
It  importazione *(f)*
Pt  importação *(f)*


**importador** *(m) n* Es, Pt
De  Importeur *(m)*
En  importer
Fr  importateur *(m)*
It  importatore *(m)*


**importância líquida** *(f)* Pt
De  Nettobetrag *(m)*
En  net amount
Es  importe neto *(m)*
Fr  montant net *(m)*
It  importo netto *(m)*


**importância total** *(m)* Pt
De  Bruttobetrag *(m)*
En  gross amount
Es  importe bruto *(m)*
Fr  montant brut *(m)*
It  importo lordo *(m)*


**importância transportada** *(f)*
    Pt
De  Übertrag *(m)*
En  amount carried forward
Am  carry forward amount
Es  suma y sigue *(f)*
Fr  report à nouveau *(m)*
It  ammontare da riportare *(m)*


**importateur** *(m) n* Fr
De  Importeur *(m)*
En  importer
Es  importador *(m)*
It  importatore *(m)*
Pt  importador *(m)*


**importation** *n* En, Fr *(f)*
De  Einfuhr *(f)*
Es  importación *(f)*
It  importazione *(f)*
Pt  importação *(f)*

**importatore** *(m) n* It
De Importeur *(m)*
En importer
Es importador *(m)*
Fr importateur *(m)*
Pt importador *(m)*

**importazione** *(f) n* It
De Einfuhr *(f)*
En import
Es importación *(f)*
Fr importation *(f)*
Pt importação *(f)*

**import ban** En
De Einfuhrverbot *(n)*
Es prohibición de importación *(f)*
Fr prohibition d'entrée *(f)*
It divieto d'importazione *(m)*
Pt proibição de importação *(f)*

**import duty** En
De Einfuhrzoll *(m)*
Es derechos de importación *(m pl)*
Fr droits d'entrée *(m pl)*
It dazio d'importazione *(m)*
Pt direitos de importação *(m pl)*

**importe bruto** *(m)* Es
De Bruttobetrag *(m)*
En gross amount
Fr montant brut *(m)*
It importo lordo *(m)*
Pt importância total *(m)*

**importe neto** *(m)* Es
De Nettobetrag *(m)*
En net amount
Fr montant net *(m)*
It importo netto *(m)*
Pt importância líquida *(f)*

**importer** *n* En
De Importeur *(m)*
Es importador *(m)*
Fr importateur *(m)*
It importatore *(m)*
Pt importador *(m)*

**Importeur** *(m) n* De
En importer
Es importador *(m)*
Fr importateur *(m)*
It importatore *(m)*
Pt importador *(m)*

**import licence** En
De Importlizenz; Einfuhrerlaubnis *(f)*
Es permiso de importación *(m)*
Fr licence d'importation *(f)*
It permesso d'importazione *(m)*
Pt licença de importação *(f)*

**Importlizenz** *(f) n* De
En import licence
Es permiso de importación *(m)*
Fr licence d'importation *(f)*
It permesso d'importazione *(m)*
Pt licença de importação *(f)*

**importo lordo** *(m)* It
De Bruttobetrag *(m)*
En gross amount
Es importe bruto *(m)*
Fr montant brut *(m)*
Pt importância total *(m)*

**importo netto** *(m)* It
De Nettobetrag *(m)*
En net amount
Es importe neto *(m)*
Fr montant net *(m)*
Pt importância líquida *(f)*

**importo nominale** *(m)* It
De Nominalbetrag *(m)*
En nominal amount
Es suma nominal *(f)*
Fr montant nominal *(m)*
Pt quantia nominal *(f)*

**import quota** En
De Einfuhrkontingent *(n)*
Es cupo de importación *(m)*
Fr contingent d'importation *(m)*
It contingente d'importazione *(m)*
Pt quota de importação *(f)*

**import restrictions** En
De Einfuhrbeschränkungen *(f pl)*
Es restricciones de importación *(f pl)*
Fr restrictions d'importation *(f pl)*
It restrizioni delle importazioni *(f pl)*
Pt restricções de importação *(f pl)*

**imposible** *adj* Es
De unmöglich
En impossible
Fr impossible
It impossibile
Pt impossível

**imposition** *(f) n* Fr
De Besteuerung *(f)*
En taxation
Es tributación *(f)*
It tassazione *(f)*
Pt tributação *(f)*

**imposition différée** *(f)* Fr
De latente Steuerpflicht *(f)*
En deferred taxation
Es tasación diferida *(f)*
It tassazione differita *(f)*
Pt tributação diferida *(f)*

**imposition latente** *(f)* Fr
De versteckte Belastung *(f)*
En hidden tax
Es impuesto latente *(m)*
It tassa invisibile *(f)*
Pt imposto ocultado *(m)*

**impossibile** *adj* It
De unmöglich
En impossible
Es imposible
Fr impossible
Pt impossível

**impossible** *adj* En, Fr
De unmöglich
Es imposible
It impossibile
Pt impossível

**impossível** *adj* Pt
De unmöglich
En impossible
Es imposible
Fr impossible
It impossibile

**imposta** *(f) n* It
De Steuer; Erhebung *(f)*
En tax; levy
Es impuesto *(m)*
Fr impôt; prélèvement *(m)*
Pt imposto *(m)*

**imposta fondiaria** *(f)* It
De Grundsteuer *(f)*
En property tax

Es impuesto sobre la pro-
piedad (m)
Fr impôt foncier (m)
Pt imposto sobre propriedade
(m)

**imposta negativa sul reddito**
(f) It
De negative Einkommenssteuer (f)
En negative income tax
Es impuesto negativo sobre
renta (m)
Fr impôt négatif sur le revenu
(m)
Pt imposto negativo sobre
receita (m)

**imposta sui proventi delle
società** (f) It
De Körperschaftsteuer (f)
En corporation tax
Es impuesto sobre renta de la
sociedad (m)
Fr impôt sur le revenu des
sociétés (m)
Pt imposto sobre corporação
(m)

**imposta sui sopraprofitti** (f) It
De Übergewinnsteuer (f)
En excess profits tax
Es impuesto sobre beneficios
extraordinarios (m pl)
Fr impôts sur les superbéné-
fices (m pl)
Pt imposto sobre lucros exce-
ssivos (m)

**imposta sul consumo** (f) It
De Verbrauchsabgabe (f)
En excise duty
Es impuesto de consumos (m)
Fr droit sur la consommation
(m)
Pt imposto indirecto (m)

**imposta sulle vendite** (f) It
De Warenumsatzsteuer (f)
En sales tax
Es impuesto sobre la venta
(m)
Fr taxe de vente (f)
Pt imposto sobre vendas (m)

**imposta sull'impiego** (f) It
De Lohnsummensteuer (f)

En employment tax
Es impuesto por empleado (m)
Fr taxe sur l'emploi (f)
Pt imposto sobre emprego (m)

**imposta sul plusvalore di
capitale** (f) It
De Kapitalertragsteuer (f)
En capital gains tax
Es impuesto sobre las ganan-
cias de capital (m)
Fr impôt sur les plus-values
en capital (m)
Pt imposto sobre lucros de
capital (m)

**imposta sul reddito** (f) It
De Einkommensteuer (f)
En income tax
Es impuesto sobre la renta
(m)
Fr impôt sur le revenu (m)
Pt imposto de receitas (m)

**imposta sul valore aggiunto
(IVA)** (f) It
De Mehrwertsteuer (f)
En value added tax (VAT)
Es impuesto sobre valor aña-
dido (m)
Fr taxe sur la valeur ajoutée
(TVA) (f)
Pt imposto sobre valor aduzi-
do (m)

**imposte dirette** (f pl) It
De direkte Steuern (f pl)
En direct taxation
Es contribuciones directas (f
pl)
Fr contributions directes (f pl)
Pt tributação directa (f)

**imposte indirette** (f pl) It
De indirekte Steuern (f pl)
En indirect taxation; excise
Es contribuciones indirectas (f
pl)
Fr contributions indirectes (f
pl)
Pt tributação indirecta (f)

**imposto** (m) n Pt
De Steuer; Erhebung (f)
En tax; levy
Es impuesto (m)
Fr impôt (m)
It imposta (f)

**imposto de luxo** (m) Pt
De Luxussteuer (f)
En luxury tax
Es impuesto de lujo (m)
Fr impôt de luxe (m)
It tassa sugli articoli di lusso
(f)

**imposto de receitas** (m) Pt
De Einkommensteuer (f)
En income tax
Es impuesto sobre la renta
(m)
Fr impôt sur le revenu (m)
It imposta sul reddito (f)

**imposto de selo** (m) Pt
De Stempelgebühr (f)
En stamp duty
Es impuesto del timbre (m)
Fr droit de timbre (m)
It tassa di bollo (f)

**imposto indirecto** (m) Pt
De Verbrauchsabgabe (f)
En excise duty
Es impuesto de consumos (m)
Fr droit sur la consommation
(m)
It imposta sul consumo (f)

**imposto negativo sobre
receita** (m) Pt
De negative Einkommenssteuer (f)
En negative income tax
Es impuesto negativo sobre
renta (m)
Fr impôt négatif sur le revenu
(m)
It imposta negativa sul reddito (f)

**imposto ocultado** (m) Pt
De versteckte Belastung (f)
En hidden tax
Es impuesto latente (m)
Fr imposition latente (f)
It tassa invisibile (f)

**impostos de sucessão** (m pl)
Pt
De Erbschaftssteuern (f pl)
En death duties
Am estate taxes
Es derechos sucesorios (m pl)
Fr droits de succession (m pl)
It diritti di successione (m pl)

**impostos excluidos** Pt
De ausser Steuer
En excluding tax
Es impuesto no incluido
Fr hors taxe (HT)
It tassa esclusa

**imposto sobre corporação** (m)
Pt
De Körperschaftsteuer (f)
En corporation tax
Es impuesto sobre renta de la
sociedad (m)
Fr impôt sur le revenu des
sociétés (m)
It imposta sui proventi delle
società (f)

**imposto sobre emprego** (m) Pt
De Lohnsummensteuer (f)
En employment tax
Es impuesto por empleado (m)
Fr taxe sur l'emploi (f)
It imposta sull'impiego (f)

**imposto sobre lucros de
capital** (m) Pt
De Kapitalertragsteuer (f)
En capital gains tax
Es impuesto sobre las ganan-
cias de capital (m)
Fr impôt sur les plus-values
en capital (m)
It imposta sul plusvalore di
capitale (f)

**imposto sobre lucros exces-
sivos** (m) Pt
De Übergewinnsteuer (f)
En excess profits tax
Es impuesto sobre beneficios
extraordinarios (m pl)
Fr impôts sur les superbéné-
fices (m pl)
It imposta sui sopraprofitti (f)

**imposto sobre propriedade**
(m) Pt
De Grundsteuer (f)
En property tax
Es impuesto sobre la pro-
piedad (m)
Fr impôt foncier (m)
It imposta fondiaria (f)

**imposto sobre valor aduzido**
(m) Pt
De Mehrwertsteuer (f)

En value added tax (VAT)
Es impuesto sobre valor aña-
dido (m)
Fr taxe sur la valeur ajoutée
(TVA) (f)
It imposta sul valore aggiunto
(IVA) (f)

**imposto sobre vendas** (m) Pt
De Warenumsatzsteuer (f)
En sales tax
Es impuesto sobre la venta
(m)
Fr taxe de vente (f)
It imposta sulle vendite (f)

**impôt** (m) n Fr
De Steuer (f)
En tax
Es impuesto (m)
It imposta (f)
Pt imposto (m)

**impôt de luxe** (m) Fr
De Luxussteuer (f)
En luxury tax
Es impuesto de lujo (m)
It tassa sugli articoli di lusso
(f)
Pt imposto de luxo (m)

**impôt foncier** (m) Fr
De Grundsteuer (f)
En property tax
Es impuesto sobre la pro-
piedad (m)
It imposta fondiaria (f)
Pt imposto sobre propriedade
(m)

**impôt négatif sur le revenu**
(m) Fr
De negative Einkommenssteuer (f)
En negative income tax
Es impuesto negativo sobre
renta (m)
It imposta negativa sul reddito (f)
Pt imposto negativo sobre
receita (m)

**impôt sur le revenu** (m) Fr
De Einkommensteuer (f)
En income tax
Es impuesto sobre la renta
(m)

It imposta sul reddito (f)
Pt imposto de receitas (m)

**impôt sur le revenu des
sociétés** (m) Fr
De Körperschaftsteuer (f)
En corporation tax
Es impuesto sobre renta de la
sociedad (m)
It imposta sui proventi delle
società (f)
Pt imposto sobre corporação
(m)

**impôt sur les plus-values en
capital** (m) Fr
De Kapitalertragsteuer (f)
En capital gains tax
Es impuesto sobre las ganan-
cias de capital (m)
It imposta sul plusvalore di
capitale (f)
Pt imposto sobre lucros de
capital (m)

**imprenditore di trasporti** (m)
It
De Transportunternehmer (m)
En haulage contractor
Am trucking company
Es contratista de transportes
(m)
Fr entrepreneur de camion-
nage (m)
Pt empreiteiro de transportes
(m)

**impresa** (f) n It
De Unternehmen (n)
En enterprise
Es negocio (m)
Fr entreprise (f)
Pt empresa (f)

**impresa edile** (f) It
De Bauunternehmer (m)
En building contractor
Es contratista de obras (m)
Fr entrepreneur de bâtiment
(m)
Pt constructor de obras (m)

**impresa privata** (f) It
De Privatunternehmen (n)
En private enterprise
Es empresa privada (f)
Fr entreprise privée (f)
Pt empresa privada (f)

**impresario** *(m)* n It
De Unternehmer *(m)*
En contractor
Es contratista *(m)*
Fr entrepreneur *(m)*
Pt contractador *(m)*

**impresión** *(f)* n Es
De Ausgabedruck *(m)*
En computer printout
Fr sortie sur imprimante *(f)*
It stampato d'uscita del-l'elaboratore *(m)*
Pt informe impresso pelo computador *(m)*

**impresso** *(m)* n Pt
De Vordruck *(m)*
En printed form
Es formulario; impreso *(m)*
Fr formulaire *(m)*
It modulo stampato *(m)*

**impresso de admissão** *(m)* Pt
De Antragsformular *(n)*
En entry-form
Es solicitud de inscripción *(f)*
Fr feuille d'inscription *(f)*
It bolletta d'entrata *(f)*

**impresso de encomenda** *(m)* Pt
De Bestellformular *(n)*
En order-form
Es solicitud de pedido *(f)*
Fr bulletin de commande *(m)*
It foglio d'ordinazione *(m)*

**impresso em branco** *(m)* Pt
De Blankoformular *(n)*
En blank form
Es formulario en blanco *(m)*
Fr formulaire en blanc *(m)*
It modulo in bianco *(m)*

**improductif** *adj* Fr
De unproduktif
En unproductive
Es improductivo
It improduttivo
Pt improdutivo

**improductivo** *adj* Es
De unproduktif
En unproductive
Fr improductif
It improduttivo
Pt improdutivo

**improdutivo** *adj* Pt
De unproduktif
En unproductive
Es improductivo
Fr improductif
It improduttivo

**improduttivo** *adj* It
De unproduktif
En unproductive
Es improductivo
Fr improductif
Pt improdutivo

**improvement** n En
De Verbesserung *(f)*
Es mejora *(f)*
Fr amélioration *(f)*
It miglioramento *(m)*
Pt melhoramento *(m)*

**impuesto** *(m)* n Es
De Steuer; Erhebung *(f)*
En tax; levy
Fr impôt *(m)*
It imposta *(f)*
Pt imposto *(m)*

**impuesto de consumos** *(m)* Es
De Verbrauchsabgabe *(f)*
En excise duty
Fr droit sur la consommation *(m)*
It imposta sul consumo *(f)*
Pt imposto indirecto *(m)*

**impuesto del timbre** *(m)* Es
De Stempelgebühr *(f)*
En stamp duty
Fr droit de timbre *(m)*
It tassa di bollo *(f)*
Pt imposto de selo *(m)*

**impuesto de lujo** *(m)* Es
De Luxussteuer *(f)*
En luxury tax
Fr impôt de luxe *(m)*
It tassa sugli articoli di lusso *(f)*
Pt imposto de luxo *(m)*

**impuesto latente** *(m)* Es
De versteckte Belastung *(f)*
En hidden tax
Fr imposition latente *(f)*
It tassa invisibile *(f)*
Pt imposto ocultado *(m)*

**impuesto no incluido** Es
De ausser Steuer
En excluding tax
Fr hors taxe (HT)
It tassa esclusa
Pt impostos excluidos

**impuesto por empleado** *(m)* Es
De Lohnsummensteuer *(f)*
En employment tax
Fr taxe sur l'emploi *(f)*
It imposta sull'impiego *(f)*
Pt imposto sobre emprego *(m)*

**impuesto sobre beneficios extraordinarios** *(m pl)* Es
De Übergewinnsteuer *(f)*
En excess profits tax
Fr impôts sur les superbénéfices *(m pl)*
It imposta sui sopraprofitti *(f)*
Pt imposto sobre lucros excessivos *(m)*

**impuesto sobre la propiedad** *(m)* Es
De Grundsteuer *(f)*
En property tax
Fr impôt foncier *(m)*
It imposta fondiaria *(f)*
Pt imposto sobre propriedade *(m)*

**impuesto sobre la renta** *(m)* Es
De Einkommensteuer *(f)*
En income tax
Fr impôt sur le revenu *(m)*
It imposta sul reddito *(f)*
Pt imposto de receitas *(m)*

**impuesto sobre las ganancias de capital** *(m)* Es
De Kapitalertragsteuer *(f)*
En capital gains tax
Fr impôt sur les plus-values en capital *(m)*
It imposta sul plusvalore di capitale *(f)*
Pt imposto sobre lucros de capital *(m)*

**impuesto sobre la venta** *(m)* Es
De Warenumsatzsteuer *(f)*
En sales tax
Fr taxe de vente *(f)*

It imposta sulle vendite (f)
Pt imposto sobre vendas (m)

**impuesto sobre renta de la sociedad** (m) Es
De Körperschaftsteuer (f)
En corporation tax
Fr impôt sur le revenu des sociétés (m)
It imposta sui proventi delle società (f)
Pt imposto sobre corporação (m)

**impuesto sobre valor añadido** (m) Es
De Mehrwertsteuer (f)
En value added tax (VAT)
Fr taxe sur la valeur ajoutée (TVA) (f)
It imposta sul valore aggiunto (IVA) (f)
Pt imposto sobre valor aduzido (m)

**impulse buying** En
De Impulskaufen (n)
Es compra espontánea (f)
Fr achat sur l'entrainement du moment (m)
It compra sullo stimolo del momento (f)
Pt compra impulsiva (f)

**Impulskaufen** (n) n De
En impulse buying
Es compra espontánea (f)
Fr achat sur l'entrainement du moment (m)
It compra sullo stimolo del momento (f)
Pt compra impulsiva (f)

**imputabile** adj It
De anrechenbar
En chargeable
Es imputable; a cobrar
Fr imputable; imposable
Pt a cobrar

**imputable** adj Es, Fr
De anrechenbar
En chargeable
It imputabile; imponibile
Pt a cobrar

**im Wert steigen** De
En appreciate (in value)
Es subir (en valor)
Fr apprécier
It aumentare (di valore)
Pt aumentar; subir

**in abeyance** En
De in der Schwebe; unentschlossen
Es en suspenso
Fr en suspens
It in sospeso
Pt pendente

**in acconto** It
De a conto; auf Abschlag
En on account
Es a cuenta
Fr à valoir
Pt por conta

**in accordance with** En
De in Übereinstimmung mit
Es en conformidad con
Fr conforme à
It in conformità con
Pt em conformidade com

**inadempienza** (f) n It
De Nichterfüllung (f)
En nonfulfilment
Es incumplimiento (m)
Fr non-exécution (f)
Pt não cumprimento (m)

**in agreement with** En
De im Einvernehmen mit
Es de acuerdo con
Fr d'accord avec
It d'accordo con
Pt de acordo com

**in Ausführung begriffene Arbeit** (f) De
En work on hand
Es trabajo en curso (m)
Fr travail en cours (m)
It lavoro in corso (m)
Pt trabalho em mão (m)

**inautorizado** adj Es
De unbefugt
En unauthorized
Fr non autorisé
It non autorizzato
Pt não autorizado

**in bond** En
De unter Zollverschluss
Es en aduanas
Fr en entrepôt
It sotto vincolo doganale
Pt à ordem da alfândega

**in bulk** En
De in grosser Menge
Es a granel
Fr en vrac
It alla rinfusa
Pt a granel

**in buona fede** It
De auf Treu und Glauben
En in good faith
Es de buena fé
Fr de bonne foi
Pt de boa fé

**in buono stato** It
De in gutem Zustand
En in good repair
Es en buen estado
Fr en bon état
Pt em bom estado

**in case of default** En
De bei Nichterfüllung
Es en caso de incumplimiento
Fr en cas de défaillance
It in caso di inadempienza
Pt em caso de não cumprimento

**in caso di inadempienza** It
De bei Nichterfüllung
En in case of default
Es en caso de incumplimiento
Fr en cas de défaillance
Pt em caso de não cumprimento

**incassare** vb It
De einkassieren
En cash
Es cobrar
Fr encaisser
Pt cobrar

**incassare un assegno** It
De einen Scheck einlösen
En cash a cheque
Es cobrar un cheque
Fr toucher un chèque
Pt cobrar um cheque

**incassare un credito** It
De Schulden eintreiben
En collect a debt
Es recaudar una deuda
Fr recouvrer une créance
Pt cobrar uma dívida

**incendie** (f) n Fr
De Brand (m)
En fire
Es fuego; incendio (m)
It incendio (m)
Pt fogo; incêndio (m)

**incendio** (m) n It
De Brand (m)
En fire
Es fuego; incendio (m)
Fr incendie (f)
Pt fogo; incêndio (m)

**incentive** n En
De Anreiz (m)
Es estímulo; incentivo (m)
Fr incitation; stimulant (f m)
It incentivo (m)
Pt incentivo (m)

**incentivo** (m) n Es, It, Pt
De Anreiz (m)
En incentive
Fr incitation; stimulant (f m)

**incentivo alla esportazione**
(m) It
De Ausfuhranreiz (m)
En export incentive
Es estímulo de exportación (m)
Fr motif d'exportation (m)
Pt incentivo para a exportação
(m)

**incentivo de inversión** (m) Es
De Investierungsanreiz (m)
En investment incentive
Fr stimulant de l'investisse-
ment (m)
It incentivo d'investimento
(m)
Pt incentivo de investimento
(m)

**incentivo de investimento** (m)
Pt
De Investierungsanreiz (m)
En investment incentive
Es incentivo de inversión (m)

Fr stimulant de l'investissement (m)
It incentivo d'investimento
(m)

**incentivo d'investimento** (m)
It
De Investierungsanreiz (m)
En investment incentive
Es incentivo de inversión (m)
Fr stimulant de l'investisse-
ment (m)
Pt incentivo de investimento
(m)

**incentivo para a exportação**
(m) Pt
De Ausfuhranreiz (m)
En export incentive
Es estímulo de exportación (m)
Fr motif d'exportation (m)
It incentivo alla esportazione
(m)

**inch** n En
De Zoll (m)
Es pulgada (f)
Fr pouce (m)
It pollice (m)
Pt polegada (m)

**inchiesta** (f) n It
De Untersuchung (f)
En investigation; inquiry
Es investigación; encuesta (f)
Fr investigation; enquête (f)
Pt investigação; inquérito (f
m)

**incidental charges** En
De Nebenkosten (pl)
Es cargos imprevistos (m pl)
Fr charges annexes (f pl)
It spese accessorie (f pl)
Pt encargos ocasionais (m pl)

**incidental expenses** En
De Nebenkosten (pl)
Es gastos imprevistos (m pl)
Fr faux frais (m pl)
It spese impreviste (f pl)
Pt despesas ocasionais (f pl)

**incitation** (f) n Fr
De Anreiz (m)
En incentive
Es estímulo; incentivo (m)

It incentivo (m)
Pt incentivo (m)

**including packing** En
De Verpackung einbegriffen
Es franco embalaje
Fr franco d'emballage
It imballaggio incluso
Pt incluindo embalagem

**incluido** adj Es
De einschliesslich
En inclusive
Fr inclus; compris
It incluso; compreso
Pt incluindo; incluso

**incluindo** adj Pt
De einschliesslich
En inclusive
Es incluido
Fr inclus; compris
It incluso; compreso

**incluindo embalagem** Pt
De Verpackung einbegriffen
En including packing
Es franco embalaje
Fr franco d'emballage
It imballaggio incluso

**inclus** adj Fr
De einschliesslich
En inclusive
Es incluido; inclusive
It incluso; compreso
Pt incluindo; incluso

**inclusive** adj En
De einschliesslich
Es incluido; inclusive
Fr inclus; compris
It incluso; compreso
Pt incluindo

**incluso** adj Pt
De beiliegend
En enclosed
Es adjunto
Fr ci-joint; ci-inclus
It accluso

**incluso** adj It
De einschliesslich
En inclusive
Es incluido; inclusive
Fr inclus; compris
Pt incluindo

**income** n En
De Einkommen (n)
Es ingresos; renta (m pl; f)
Fr revenu (m)
It reddito (m)
Pt receita (f)

**income and expenditure account** En
De Ausgaben- und Ertragskonto (n)
Es cuenta de ingresos y gastos (f)
Fr compte de revenus et dépenses (m)
It conto proventi e spese (m)
Pt conta de receitas e despesas (f)

**incomes policy** En
De Lohnpolitik (f)
Es plan de renta (m)
Fr politique des salaires (f)
It politica dei redditi (f)
Pt programa salários (f)

**income tax** En
De Einkommensteuer (f)
Es impuesto sobre la renta (m)
Fr impôt sur le revenu (m)
It imposta sul reddito (f)
Pt imposto de receitas (m)

**income-tax return** En
De Einkommensteuererklärung (f)
Es declaración fiscal (f)
Fr déclaration de revenu (f)
It dichiarazione del reddito (f)
Pt declaração fiscal (f)

**income-tax year** En
De Einkommensteuerjahr (n)
Es año fiscal (m)
Fr exercice fiscal (m)
It anno fiscale (m)
Pt ano fiscal (m)

**incompetencia** (f) n Es
De Unfähigkeit (f)
En inefficiency
Fr inefficacité (f)
It inefficienza (f)
Pt ineficiência (f)

**incomplet** adj Fr
De unvollständig
En incomplete
Es incompleto
It incompleto
Pt incompleto

**incomplete** adj En
De unvollständig
Es incompleto
Fr incomplet
It incompleto
Pt incompleto

**incompleto** adj Es, It, Pt
De unvollständig
En incomplete
Fr incomplet

**in concorrenza** It
De wetteifernd
En competitive
Es competidor
Fr compétitif
Pt competitivo

**in conformità con** It
De in Übereinstimmung mit
En in accordance with
Es en conformidad con
Fr conforme à
Pt em conformidade com

**in conto deposito** It
De in Kommission
En on consignment
Es en consignación
Fr en consignation
Pt à consignação

**in contropartita** It
De als Gegenrechnung
En per contra
Es en contrapartida
Fr en contrepartie; par contre
Pt em contrapartida

**incorporação** (f) n Pt
De Eintragung (einer Gesellschaft) (f)
En incorporation
Es incorporación (f)
Fr incorporation (f)
It costituzione (f)

**incorporación** (f) n Es
De Eintragung (einer Gesellschaft) (f)

En incorporation
Fr incorporation (f)
It costituzione (f)
Pt incorporação (f)

**incorporation** n En, Fr (f)
De Eintragung (einer Gesellschaft) (f)
Es incorporación (f)
It costituzione (f)
Pt incorporação (f)

**increase** vb En
De steigen; zunehmen
Es aumentar; alzar
Fr augmenter; hausser
It aumentare; crescere
Pt aumentar

**increase** n En
De Steigen; Zunahme (n f)
Es incremento; aumento (m)
Fr hausse; augmentation (f)
It incremento; crescita (m f)
Pt aumento; incremento (m)

**increased cost of living** En
De erhöhte Lebenshaltungskosten (pl)
Es coste de vida más alto (m)
Fr renchérissement du coût de la vie (m)
It aumentato costo della vita (m)
Pt custo de vida mais elevado (m)

**increased costs** En
De erhöhte Kosten (pl)
Es costes incrementados (m pl)
Fr accroissement des coûts (m)
It costi aumentati (m pl)
Pt custos aumentados (m pl)

**increase of capital** En
De Kapitalerhöhung (f)
Es aumento de capital (m)
Fr augmentation de capital (f)
It aumento di capitale (m)
Pt aumento de capital (m)

**increment** n En
De Wertzuwachs (m)
Es aumento; incremento (m)

Fr accroissement; plus-value *(m f)*
It incremento *(m)*
Pt aumento; incremento *(m)*

**incremento** *(m) n* Es, It, Pt
De Steigen; Wertzuwachs *(n m)*
En increase; increment
Fr hausse; accroissement *(f m)*

**incumplimiento** *(m) n* Es
De Nichterfüllung *(f)*
En nonfulfilment
Fr non-exécution *(f)*
It inadempienza *(f)*
Pt não cumprimento *(m)*

**incumplimiento del contrato** *(m)* Es
De Vertragsverletzung *(f)*
En breach of contract
Fr rupture de contrat *(f)*
It rottura di contratto *(f)*
Pt rotura de contrato *(f)*

**indagine di mercato** *(f)* It
De Marktforschung *(f)*
En market research
Es investigación del mercado *(f)*
Fr étude du marché *(f)*
Pt pesquisa de mercado *(f)*

**indagine sul funzionamento** *(f)* It
De Unternehmensforschung *(f)*
En operational research (OR)
Es investigación operacional *(f)*
Fr recherche opérationnelle *(f)*
Pt investigação operacional *(f)*

**indagine sulle motivazioni** *(f)* It
De Motivforschung *(f)*
En motivational research
Es investigación de motivación *(f)*
Fr étude de motivation *(f)*
Pt investigação sobre motivação *(f)*

**indebitato** *adj* It
De verschuldet
En indebted
Es endeudado

Fr endetté
Pt endividado; em dívida

**indebted** *adj* En
De verschuldet
Es endeudado
Fr endetté
It indebitato
Pt endividado; em dívida

**in demand** En
De gefragt
Es solicitado
Fr demandé
It ricercato
Pt procurado

**indemnify** *vb* En
De entschädigen
Es indemnizar; resarcir
Fr dédommager; indemniser
It indennizzare; risarcire
Pt indemnizar

**indemnité** *(f) n* Fr
De Entschädigung *(f)*
En indemnity
Es indemnización *(f)*
It indennità; garanzia *(f)*
Pt indemnização *(f)*

**indemnité d'assurance** *(f)* Fr
De Versicherungsanspruch *(m)*
En insurance claim
Es reclamación de seguro *(f)*
It sinistro; reclamo d'indennizzo *(m)*
Pt reclamação de seguro *(f)*

**indemnité de principe** *(f)* Fr
De Ordnungsentschädigung *(f)*
En nominal damages
Es daños nominales *(m pl)*
It danni nominali *(m pl)*
Pt danos nominais *(m pl)*

**indemnité de sauvetage** *(f)* Fr
De Bergegeld *(n)*
En salvage charges
Es cargos de salvamento *(m pl)*
It spese di salvataggio *(f pl)*
Pt encargos de salvamento *(m pl)*

**indemnity** *n* En
De Entschädigung *(f)*
Es indemnización *(f)*

Fr indemnité; garantie *(f)*
It indennità; garanzia *(f)*
Pt indemnização *(f)*

**indemnização** *(f) n* Pt
De Entschädigung *(f)*
En indemnity
Es indemnización *(f)*
Fr indemnité *(f)*
It indennità *(f)*

**indemnização especial** *(f)* Pt
De Ersatz immateriellen Schadens *(m)*
En special damages
Es daños especiales *(m pl)*
Fr dommages indirects *(m pl)*
It danni particolari *(m pl)*

**indemnización** *(f) n* Es
De Entschädigung *(f)*
En indemnity
Fr indemnité; garantie *(f)*
It indennità; garanzia *(f)*
Pt garantia; caução *(f)*

**indemnizar** *vb* Es, Pt
De entschädigen
En indemnify
Fr dédommager; indemniser
It indennizzare; risarcire

**indennità** *(f) n* It
De Entschädigung *(f)*
En indemnity
Es indemnización *(f)*
Fr indemnité *(f)*
Pt indemnização *(f)*

**indennità di disoccupazione** *(f)* It
De Arbeitslosenunterstützung *(f)*
En unemployment benefit
Es subsidio de paro *(m)*
Fr secours de chômage *(m)*
Pt subsidio de desemprego *(m)*

**indennizzare** *vb* It
De entschädigen
En indemnify
Es indemnizar; resarcir
Fr dédommager; indemniser
Pt indemnizar

**independant** adj Fr
De selbständig
En independent
Es independiente
It indipendente
Pt independente

**independent** adj En
De selbständig
Es independiente
Fr independant
It indipendente
Pt independente

**independente** adj Pt
De selbständig
En independent
Es independiente
Fr independant
It indipendente

**independiente** adj Es
De selbständig
En independent
Fr independant
It indipendente
Pt independente

**in deposito** It
De auf Lager
En at warehouse
Es en almacén
Fr en dépôt
Pt em armazém

**in der Schwebe** De
En in abeyance
Es in suspenso
Fr en suspens
It in sospeso
Pt pendente

**index** n En, Fr (m)
De Index (m)
Es índice (m)
It indice (m)
Pt índice (m)

**Index** (m) n De
En index
Es índice (m)
Fr indice; index (m)
It indice (m)
Pt índice (m)

**index card** En
De Indexkarte (f)
Es ficha (f)

Fr fiche (f)
It scheda (f)
Pt ficha (f)

**Indexkarte** (f) n De
En index card
Es ficha (f)
Fr fiche (f)
It scheda (f)
Pt ficha (f)

**indicateur des chemins de fer** (m) Fr
De Eisenbahnfahrplan (m)
En railway timetable
Es horario de trenes (m)
It orario ferroviario (m)
Pt horário de caminhos de ferro (m)

**indicatif postal** (m) Fr
De Postleitzahl (f)
En postcode
Am zip code
Es designación postal (f)
It codice postale (m)
Pt designação postal (f)

**índice** (m) n Es, Pt
De Index (m)
En index
Fr indice; index (m)
It indice (m)

**indice** (m) n Fr, It
De Index (m)
En index
Es índice (m)
Pt índice (m)

**índice das acções** (m) Pt
De Aktienindex (m)
En share index
Es índice de las acciones (m)
Fr indice des actions (m)
It indice delle azioni (m)

**indice dei fallimenti** (m) It
De Durchfallquote (f)
En failure rate
Es proporción de fracasos (f)
Fr taux de défaillance (f)
Pt proporção de fracassos (f)

**índice de las acciones** (m) Es
De Aktienindex (m)
En share index
Fr indice des actions (m)

It indice delle azioni (m)
Pt índice das acções (m)

**indice delle azioni** (m) It
De Aktienindex (m)
En share index
Es índice de las acciones (m)
Fr indice des actions (m)
Pt índice das acções (m)

**indice des actions** (m) Fr
De Aktienindex (m)
En share index
Es índice de las acciones (m)
It indice delle azioni (m)
Pt índice das acções (m)

**indipendente** adj It
De selbständig
En independent
Es independiente
Fr independant
Pt independente

**indirect costs** En
De Gemeinkosten (pl)
Es costes indirectos (m pl)
Fr frais indirects (m pl)
It costi indiretti (m pl)
Pt custos indirectos (m pl)

**indirect taxation** En
De indirekte Steuern (f pl)
Es contribuciones indirectas (f pl)
Fr contributions indirectes (f pl)
It imposte indirette (f pl)
Pt tributação indirecta (f)

**indirekter Schaden** (m) De
En consequential damage
Es daños indirectos (m pl)
Fr dommage indirect (m)
It danno indiretti (m)
Pt dano por consequência (m)

**indirekte Steuern** (f pl) De
En indirect taxation
Es contribuciones indirectas (f pl)
Fr contributions indirectes (f pl)
It imposte indirette (f pl)
Pt tributação indirecta (f)

**indirizzo** *(m) n* It
De Adresse *(f)*
En address
Es dirección *(f)*
Fr adresse *(f)*
Pt endereço *(m)*

**indirizzo telegrafico** *(m)* It
De Telegrammadresse *(f)*
En telegraphic address
Es dirección telegráfica *(f)*
Fr adresse télégraphique *(f)*
Pt endereço telegráfico *(m)*

**Indossament** *(n) n* De
En endorsement
Es endoso *(m)*
Fr endossement; endos *(m)*
It girata *(f)*
Pt endosse *(m)*

**indossieren** *vb* De
En endorse
Es endosar
Fr endosser
It girare
Pt endossar

**in duplicate** En
De Duplikat-; zweifach
Es par duplicado
Fr en double
It in duplice copia
Pt em duplicado

**in duplice copia** It
De Duplikat-; zweifach
En in duplicate
Es par duplicado
Fr en double
Pt em duplicado

**industria** *(f) n* Es, It
De Industrie; Gewerbe *(f n)*
En industry
Fr industrie *(f)*
Pt indústria *(f)*

**indústria** *(f) n* Pt
De Industrie; Gewerbe *(f n)*
En industry
Es industria *(f)*
Fr industrie *(f)*
It industria *(f)*

**indústria chave** *(f)* Pt
De Schlüsselindustrie *(f)*
En key industry

Es industria clave *(f)*
Fr industrie-clef *(f)*
It industria chiave *(f)*

**industria chiave** *(f)* It
De Schlüsselindustrie *(f)*
En key industry
Es industria clave *(f)*
Fr industrie-clef *(f)*
Pt indústria chave *(f)*

**industria clave** *(f)* Es
De Schlüsselindustrie *(f)*
En key industry
Fr industrie-clef *(f)*
It industria chiave *(f)*
Pt indústria chave *(f)*

**industria del turismo** *(f)* Es
De Reisegewerbe *(n)*
En tourist trade
Fr commerce de tourisme *(m)*
It commercio turistico *(m)*
Pt indústria do turismo *(f)*

**indústria do turismo** *(f)* Pt
De Reisegewerbe *(n)*
En tourist trade
Es industria del turismo *(f)*
Fr commerce de tourisme *(m)*
It commercio turistico *(m)*

**industrial** *(m) n* Es, Pt
De Industrielle(r) *(m)*
En industrialist
Fr industriel *(m)*
It industriale *(m)*

**industrial** *adj* En, Es, Pt
De industriell; Gewerbe-
Fr industriel
It industriale

**industrial accident** En
De Arbeitsunfall *(m)*
Es accidente de trabajo *(m)*
Fr accident du travail *(m)*
It infortunio sul lavoro *(m)*
Pt acidente de trabalho *(m)*

**industrial dispute** En
De Arbeitskonflikt *(m)*
Es conflicto laboral *(m)*
Fr conflit ouvrier *(m)*
It vertenza operaia *(f)*
Pt conflito de trabalho *(m)*

**industriale** *(m) n* It
De Industrielle(r) *(m)*
En industrialist
Es industrial *(m)*
Fr industriel *(m)*
Pt industrial *(m)*

**industriale** *adj* It
De industriell; Gewerbe-
En industrial
Es industrial
Fr industriel
Pt industrial

**industrial espionage** En
De Wirtschaftsspionage *(f)*
Es espionaje industrial *(m)*
Fr espionage industriel *(m)*
It spionaggio industriale *(m)*
Pt espionagem industrial *(m)*

**industrial estate** En
Am industrial park
De Industriegebiet *(n)*
Es precinto industrial *(m)*
Fr domaine industriel *(m)*
It centro industriale *(m)*
Pt centro fabril *(m)*

**industrialist** *n* En
De Industrielle(r) *(m)*
Es industrial *(m)*
Fr industriel *(m)*
It industriale *(m)*
Pt industrial *(m)*

**industrial park** Am
En industrial estate
De Industriegebiet *(n)*
Es precinto industrial *(m)*
Fr domaine industriel *(m)*
It centro industriale *(m)*
Pt centro fabril *(m)*

**industrial psychology** En
De Arbeitspsychologie *(f)*
Es psicología industrial *(f)*
Fr psychotechnique *(f)*
It psicologia industriale *(f)*
Pt psicologia industrial *(f)*

**industrial relations** En
De Arbeitsbeziehungen *(f pl)*
Es relaciones humanas indus-
triales *(f pl)*
Fr relations humaines dans
l'entreprise *(f pl)*

It  relazioni nell'industria *(f pl)*
Pt  relações industriais *(f pl)*

**industria nacionalizada** *(f)* Es
De  verstaatlichte Industrie *(f)*
En  nationalized industry
Fr  industrie nationalisée *(f)*
It  industria nazionalizzata *(f)*
Pt  indústria nacionalizada *(f)*

**indústria nacionalizada** *(f)* Pt
De  verstaatlichte Industrie *(f)*
En  nationalized industry
Es  industria nacionalizada *(f)*
Fr  industrie nationalisée *(f)*
It  industria nazionalizzata *(f)*

**industria nazionalizzata** *(f)* It
De  verstaatlichte Industrie *(f)*
En  nationalized industry
Es  industria nacionalizada *(f)*
Fr  industrie nationalisée *(f)*
Pt  indústria nacionalizada *(f)*

**industria pesada** *(f)* Es
De  Schwerindustrie *(f)*
En  heavy industry
Fr  industrie lourde *(f)*
It  industria pesante *(f)*
Pt  indústria pesada *(f)*

**indústria pesada** *(f)* Pt
De  Schwerindustrie *(f)*
En  heavy industry
Es  industria pesada *(f)*
Fr  industrie lourde *(f)*
It  industria pesante *(f)*

**industria pesante** *(f)* It
De  Schwerindustrie *(f)*
En  heavy industry
Es  industria pesada *(f)*
Fr  industrie lourde *(f)*
Pt  indústria pesada *(f)*

**industrie** *(f)* n Fr
De  Industrie; Gewerbe *(f n)*
En  industry
Es  industria *(f)*
It  industria *(f)*
Pt  indústria *(f)*

**Industrie** *(f)* n De
En  industry
Es  industria *(f)*
Fr  industrie *(f)*
It  industria *(f)*
Pt  indústria *(f)*

**Industriechemie** *(f)* n De
En  chemical engineering
Es  ingeniería química *(f)*
Fr  génie chimique *(m)*
It  ingegneria chimica *(f)*
Pt  engenharia química *(f)*

**industrie-clef** *(f)* n Fr
De  Schlüsselindustrie *(f)*
En  key industry
Es  industria clave *(f)*
It  industria chiave *(f)*
Pt  indústria chave *(f)*

**Industriegebiet** *(n)* n De
En  industrial estate
Am  industrial park
Es  precinto industrial *(m)*
Fr  domaine industriel *(m)*
It  centro industriale *(m)*
Pt  centro fabril *(m)*

**industriel** *(m)* n Fr
De  Industrielle(r) *(m)*
En  industrialist
Es  industrial *(m)*
It  industriale *(m)*
Pt  industrial *(m)*

**industriel** *adj* Fr
De  industriell; Gewerbe-
En  industrial
Es  industrial
It  industriale
Pt  industrial

**industriell** *adj* De
En  industrial
Es  industrial
Fr  industriel
It  industriale
Pt  industrial

**Industrielle(r)** *(m)* n De
En  industrialist
Es  industrial *(m)*
Fr  industrie! *(m)*
It  industriale *(m)*
Pt  industrial *(m)*

**industrie lourde** *(f)* Fr
De  Schwerindustrie *(f)*
En  heavy industry
Es  industria pesada *(f)*
It  industria pesante *(f)*
Pt  indústria pesada *(f)*

**industrie nationalisée** *(f)* Fr
De  verstaatlichte Industrie *(f)*
En  nationalized industry
Es  industria nacionalizada *(f)*
It  industria nazionalizzata *(f)*
Pt  indústria nacionalizada *(f)*

**industry** n En
De  Industrie; Gewerbe *(f n)*
Es  industria *(f)*
Fr  industrie *(f)*
It  industria *(f)*
Pt  indústria *(f)*

**inefficacité** *(f)* n Fr
De  Unfähigkeit *(f)*
En  inefficiency
Es  incompetencia *(f)*
It  inefficienza *(f)*
Pt  ineficiência *(f)*

**inefficiency** n En
De  Unfähigkeit *(f)*
Es  incompetencia *(f)*
Fr  inefficacité *(f)*
It  inefficienza *(f)*
Pt  ineficiência *(f)*

**inefficienza** *(f)* n It
De  Unfähigkeit *(f)*
En  inefficiency
Es  incompetencia *(f)*
Fr  inefficacité *(f)*
Pt  ineficiência *(f)*

**ineficiência** *(f)* n Pt
De  Unfähigkeit *(f)*
En  inefficiency
Es  incompetencia *(f)*
Fr  inefficacité *(f)*
It  inefficienza *(f)*

**inesperienza** *(f)* n It
De  Unerfahrenheit *(f)*
En  inexperience
Es  falta de experiencia *(f)*
Fr  manque de pratique *(m)*
Pt  inexperiência *(f)*

**inexperience** n En
De  Unerfahrenheit *(f)*
Es  falta de experiencia *(f)*
Fr  manque de pratique *(m)*
It  inesperienza *(f)*
Pt  inexperiência *(f)*

**inexperiência** (f) n Pt
De  Unerfahrenheit (f)
En  inexperience
Es  falta de experiencia (f)
Fr  manque de pratique (m)
It  inesperienza (f)

**ínfiltração no mercado** (f) Pt
De  Markteindringen (n)
En  market penetration
Es  penetración en el mercado (f)
Fr  pénétration du marché (f)
It  penetrazione nel mercato (f)

**inflação** (f) n Pt
De  Inflation (f)
En  inflation
Es  inflación (f)
Fr  inflation (f)
It  inflazione (f)

**inflación** (f) n Es
De  Inflation (f)
En  inflation
Fr  inflation (f)
It  inflazione (f)
Pt  inflação (f)

**inflation** n En, Fr (f)
De  Inflation (f)
Es  inflación (f)
It  inflazione (f)
Pt  inflação (f)

**Inflation** (f) n De
En  inflation
Es  inflación (f)
Fr  inflation (f)
It  inflazione (f)
Pt  inflação (f)

**inflationary spiral** En
De  Inflationsspirale (f)
Es  espiral de inflación (f)
Fr  spirale inflationniste (f)
It  inflazione a spirale (f)
Pt  espiral inflacionária (f)

**Inflationsspirale** (f) n De
En  inflationary spiral
Es  espiral de inflación (f)
Fr  spirale inflationniste (f)
It  inflazione a spirale (f)
Pt  espiral inflacionária (f)

**inflazione** (f) n It
De  Inflation (f)
En  inflation
Es  inflación (f)
Fr  inflation (f)
Pt  inflação (f)

**inflazione a spirale** (f) It
De  Inflationsspirale (f)
En  inflationary spiral
Es  espiral de inflación (f)
Fr  spirale inflationniste (f)
Pt  espiral inflacionária (f)

**in force** En
De  in Kraft
Es  en vigor
Fr  en vigueur
It  in vigore
Pt  vigente

**inform** vb En
De  benachrichtigen
Es  informar; avisar
Fr  informer; renseigner
It  informare
Pt  informar

**informação** (f) n Pt
De  Auskunft (f)
En  information
Es  información (f)
Fr  information; renseignement (f m)
It  informazione (f)

**informação adicional** (f) Pt
De  weitere Auskunft (f)
En  further information
Es  más detalles (m pl)
Fr  renseignements complémentaires (m pl)
It  ulteriori informazioni (f pl)

**informação do mercado** (f) Pt
De  Marktbericht (m)
En  market report
Es  informe del mercado (m)
Fr  revue du marché (f)
It  relazione sul mercato (f)

**información** (f) n Es
De  Auskunft (f)
En  information
Fr  information; renseignement (f m)
It  informazione (f)
Pt  informação (f)

**informal** adj En
De  formlos; nicht formell
Es  sin ceremonia
Fr  sans formalités
It  senza formalità
Pt  sem formalidade

**informar** vb Es, Pt
De  benachrichtigen
En  inform
Fr  informer; renseigner
It  informare

**informare** vb It
De  benachrichtigen
En  inform
Es  informar; avisar
Fr  informer; renseigner
Pt  informar

**information** n En, Fr (f)
De  Auskunft (f)
Es  información (f)
It  informazione (f)
Pt  informação (f)

**information retrieval** En
De  Informationswiedergewinnung (f)
Es  rebusca de información (f)
Fr  récupération de données (f)
It  ricupero d'informazioni (m)
Pt  recuperação de informação (f)

**Informationswiedergewinnung** (f) n De
En  information retrieval
Es  rebusca de información (f)
Fr  récupération de données (f)
It  ricupero d'informazioni (m)
Pt  recuperação de informação (f)

**informazione** (f) n It
De  Auskunft (f)
En  information
Es  información (f)
Fr  information; renseignement (f m)
Pt  informação (f)

**informe** (m) n Es
De  Bericht; Meldung (m f)
En  report
Fr  rapport; compte-rendu (m)

It   relazione; rapporto *(f m)*
Pt   relatório *(m)*


**informe de la administración**
*(m)* Es
De   Vorstandsbericht *(m)*
En   directors' report
Fr   rapport des administrateurs
     *(m)*
It   relazione degli amminis-
     tratori *(f)*
Pt   relatório de directores *(m)*


**informe del especialista** *(m)*
Es
De   Sachverständigengutachten
     *(n)*
En   expert's report
Fr   expertise *(f)*
It   perizia *(f)*
Pt   relatório do perito *(m)*


**informe del mercado** *(m)* Es
De   Marktbericht *(m)*
En   market report
Fr   revue du marché *(f)*
It   relazione sul mercato *(f)*
Pt   informação do mercado *(f)*


**informe de los interventores**
*(m)* Es
De   Bericht des Abschluss-
     prüfers *(m)*
En   auditor's report
Fr   rapport des vérificateurs
     des comptes *(m)*
It   relazione dei sindaci *(f)*
Pt   relatório do fiscal de contas
     *(m)*


**informe impresso pelo com-
putador** *(m)* Pt
De   Ausgabedruck *(m)*
En   computer printout
Es   impresión *(f)*
Fr   sortie sur imprimante *(f)*
It   stampato d'uscita del-
     l'elaboratore *(m)*


**informer** *vb* Fr
De   benachrichtigen
En   inform
Es   informar; avisar
It   informare
Pt   informar


**infortunio sul lavoro** *(m)* It
De   Arbeitsunfall *(m)*
En   industrial accident
Es   accidente de trabajo *(m)*
Fr   accident du travail *(m)*
Pt   acidente de trabalho *(m)*


**infracção** *(f) n* Pt
De   Verletzung *(f)*
En   infringement
Es   infracción *(f)*
Fr   infraction *(f)*
It   infrazione *(f)*


**infracción** *(f) n* Es
De   Verletzung *(f)*
En   infringement
Fr   infraction *(f)*
It   infrazione *(f)*
Pt   infracção *(f)*


**infracción de los derechos de
autor** *(f)* Es
De   Urheberrechtsverletzung *(f)*
En   infringement of copyright
Fr   contrefaçon littéraire *(f)*
It   infrazione dei diritti d'auto-
     re *(f)*
Pt   infracção de direitos de
     autor *(f)*


**infraction** *(f) n* Fr
De   Verletzung *(f)*
En   infringement
Es   infracción *(f)*
It   infrazione *(f)*
Pt   infracção *(f)*


**infrazione** *(f) n* It
De   Verletzung *(f)*
En   infringement
Es   infracción *(f)*
Fr   infraction *(f)*
Pt   infracção *(f)*


**infrazione dei diritti d'autore**
*(f)* It
De   Urheberrechtsverletzung *(f)*
En   infringement of copyright
Es   infracción de los derechos
     de autor *(f)*
Fr   contrefaçon littéraire *(f)*
Pt   infracção de direitos de
     autor *(f)*


**infringement** *n* En
De   Verletzung *(f)*
Es   infracción *(f)*


Fr   infraction *(f)*
It   infrazione *(f)*
Pt   infracção *(f)*


**infringement of copyright** En
De   Urheberrechtsverletzung *(f)*
Es   infracción de los derechos
     de autor *(f)*
Fr   contrefaçon littéraire *(f)*
It   infrazione dei diritti d'auto-
     re *(f)*
Pt   infracção de direitos de
     autor *(f)*


**ingegnere** *(m) n* It
De   Ingenieur *(m)*
En   engineer
Es   ingeniero *(m)*
Fr   ingénieur *(m)*
Pt   engenheiro *(m)*


**ingegneria** *(f) n* It
De   Maschinenbau *(m)*
En   engineering
Es   ingeniería *(f)*
Fr   génie *(m)*
Pt   engenharia *(f)*


**ingegneria chimica** *(f)* It
De   Industriechemie *(f)*
En   chemical engineering
Es   ingeniería química *(f)*
Fr   génie chimique *(m)*
Pt   engenharia química *(f)*


**ingegneria civile** *(f)* It
De   Ingenieurbau *(m)*
En   civil engineering
Es   ingeniería civil *(f)*
Fr   génie civil *(m)*
Pt   engenharia civil *(f)*


**ingegneria meccanica** *(f)* It
De   Maschinenbau *(m)*
En   mechanical engineering
Es   ingeniería mecánica *(f)*
Fr   construction mécanique *(f)*
Pt   engenharia mecânica *(f)*


**ingeniería** *(f) n* Es
De   Maschinenbau *(m)*
En   engineering
Fr   génie *(m)*
It   ingegneria *(f)*
Pt   engenharia *(f)*

**ingeniería civil** *(f)* Es
De Ingenieurbau *(m)*
En civil engineering
Fr génie civil *(m)*
It ingegneria civile *(f)*
Pt engenharia civil *(f)*

**ingeniería eléctrica** *(f)* Es
De Elektrotechnik *(f)*
En electrical engineering
Fr construction électrique *(f)*
It elettrotecnica *(f)*
Pt engenharia electrotécnica *(f)*

**ingeniería mecánica** *(f)* Es
De Maschinenbau *(m)*
En mechanical engineering
Fr construction mécanique *(f)*
It ingegneria meccanica *(f)*
Pt engenharia mecânica *(f)*

**ingeniería química** *(f)* Es
De Industriechemie *(f)*
En chemical engineering
Fr génie chimique *(m)*
It ingegneria chimica *(f)*
Pt engenharia química *(f)*

**ingeniero** *(m)* n Es
De Ingenieur *(m)*
En engineer
Fr ingénieur *(m)*
It ingegnere *(m)*
Pt engenheiro *(m)*

**ingénieur** *(m)* n Fr
De Ingenieur *(m)*
En engineer
Es ingeniero *(m)*
It ingegnere *(m)*
Pt engenheiro *(m)*

**Ingenieur** *(m)* n De
En engineer
Es ingeniero *(m)*
Fr ingénieur *(m)*
It ingegnere *(m)*
Pt engenheiro *(m)*

**Ingenieurbau** *(m)* n De
En civil engineering
Es ingeniería civil *(f)*
Fr génie civil *(m)*
It ingegneria civile *(f)*
Pt engenharia civil *(f)*

**ingénieur-conseil en organi-
 sation** *(m)* Fr
De Geschäftsführungsberater *(m)*
En management consultant
Es asesor administrativo *(m)*
It consulente di direzione aziendale *(m)*
Pt perito de administração *(m)*

**ingiunzione** *(f)* n It
De gerichtliche Verfügung *(f)*
En injunction
Es entredicho *(m)*
Fr injonction; arrêt de suspension *(f m)*
Pt interdição *(f)*

**in good faith** En
De auf Treu und Glauben
Es de buena fé
Fr de bonne foi
It in buona fede
Pt de boa fé

**in good repair** En
De in gutem Zustand
Es en buen estado
Fr en bon état
It in buono stato
Pt em bom estado

**ingorgo stradale** *(m)* It
De Verkehrsstockung *(f)*
En traffic jam
Es embotellamiento de tráfico *(m)*
Fr encombrement de circulation *(m)*
Pt engarrafamento de tráfico *(m)*

**ingot** n En
De Barren *(m)*
Es lingote *(m)*
Fr lingot; barre *(m f)*
It lingotto *(m)*
Pt lingote *(m)*

**ingranaggio** *(m)* n It
De Getriebe *(n)*
En gearing
Es engranaje *(m)*
Fr engrenage *(m)*
Pt engrenagem *(f)*

**ingreso bruto** *(m)* Es
De Bruttoeinkommen *(n)*
En gross income
Fr rendement brut *(m)*
It reddito lordo *(m)*
Pt receita bruta *(f)*

**ingreso neto** *(f)* Es
De Nettoeinkommen *(n)*
En net income
Fr revenu net *(m)*
It reddito netto *(m)*
Pt receita líquida *(f)*

**ingresos** *(m pl)* n Es
De Einkommen; Einkünfte *(n; f pl)*
En revenue; income
Fr revenu; rentes *(m; f pl)*
It entrata; reddito *(f m)*
Pt rendimento; receita *(m f)*

**ingresos netos** *(m pl)* Es
De Nettoeinnahmen *(f pl)*
En net revenue
Fr recettes nettes *(f pl)*
It entrata netta *(f)*
Pt receita líquida *(f)*

**ingresos no imponibles** *(m pl)* Es
De steuerfreies Einkommen *(n)*
En nontaxable income
Fr revenu non imposable *(m)*
It reddito non tassabile *(m)*
Pt receita não tributável *(f)*

**ingresso gratuito** *(m)* It
De Eintritt frei *(m)*
En admission free
Es entrada gratuita *(f)*
Fr entrée gratuite *(f)*
Pt entrada gratis *(f)*

**in grosser Menge** De
En in bulk
Es a granel
Fr en vrac
It alla rinfusa
Pt a granel

**in gutem Zustand** De
En in good repair
Es en buen estado
Fr en bon état
It in buono stato
Pt em bom estado

**Inhaber** *(m)* n De
En holder
Es titular *(m)*
Fr détenteur *(m)*
It titolare *(m)*
Pt titular *(m)*

**Inhabereffekten** *(n pl)* n De
En bearer securities
Es valores al portador *(m pl)*
Fr valeurs au porteur *(f pl)*
It valori al portatore *(f pl)*
Pt valores ao portador *(m pl)*

**Inhaberobligation** *(f)* n De
En bearer debenture
Es obligación al portador *(f)*
Fr obligation au porteur *(f)*
It obbligazione al portatore *(f)*
Pt obrigação ao portador *(f)*

**Inhaberscheck** *(m)* n De
En cheque payable to bearer
Es cheque al portador *(m)*
Fr chèque payable au porteur *(m)*
It assegno al portatore *(m)*
Pt cheque ao portador *(m)*

**(an den) Inhaber zahlbar** De
En payable to bearer
Es pagadero al portador
Fr payable au porteur
It pagabile al portatore
Pt pagável ao portador

**Inhalt** *(m)* n De
En contents
Es contenido *(m)*
Fr contenu *(m)*
It contenuto *(m)*
Pt conteúdo *(m)*

**inheritance** n En
De Erbschaft *(f)*
Es herencia *(f)*
Fr succession *(f)*
It eredità *(f)*
Pt herança *(f)*

**inicial** *adj* Es, Pt
De Anfangs-
En initial
Fr initial; premier
It iniziale

**iniciar un proceso contra** Es
De gerichtlich vorgehen gegen
En institute proceedings a-gainst
Fr intenter un procès à
It intentare un'azione legale contro
Pt instituir processo contra

**iniciativa em comum** *(f)* Pt
De Gemeinschaftsgründung *(f)*
En joint venture
Es empresa en común *(f)*
Fr entreprise en participation *(f)*
It impresa in compartecipazione *(f)*

**inimigo** *(m)* n Pt
De Feind *(m)*
En enemy
Es enemigo *(m)*
Fr ennemi *(m)*
It nemico *(m)*

**initial** *vb* En
De paraphieren
Es rubricar; poner iniciales a
Fr parapher; viser
It siglare
Pt rubricar

**initial** *adj* En, Fr
De Anfangs-
Es inicial; primario
It iniziale
Pt inicial

**iniziale** *adj* It
De Anfangs-
En initial
Es inicial; primario
Fr initial; premier
Pt inicial

**inizio scarico** *(m)* It
De Löschen der Ladung *(n)*
En breaking bulk
Es fraccionamiento de la carga *(m)*
Fr rupture de charge *(f)*
Pt retalhar a carga *(f)*

**injonction** *(f)* n Fr
De gerichtliche Verfügung *(f)*
En injunction
Es entredicho *(m)*

It ingiunzione *(f)*
Pt interdição *(f)*

**injunction** n En
De gerichtliche Verfügung *(f)*
Es entredicho *(m)*
Fr injonction; arrêt de suspension *(f m)*
It ingiunzione *(f)*
Pt interdição *(f)*

**injured party** En
De Verletzte(r) *(m)*
Es parte lesionada *(f)*
Fr partie lésée *(f)*
It parte lesa *(f)*
Pt parte lesada *(f)*

**injury** n En
De Schaden *(m)*
Es daño *(m)*
Fr dommage; avarie *(m f)*
It danno *(m)*
Pt dano; injúria *(m f)*

**Inkassobeauftragte(r)** *(m)* n De
En debt collector
Es agente recaudador *(m)*
Fr agent de recouvrement *(m)*
It agente di ricupero crediti *(m)*
Pt cobrador *(m)*

**in kind** En
De in Waren
Es en especie
Fr en nature
It in natura
Pt em espécie

**in Kommission** De
En on consignment
Es en consignación
Fr en consignation
It in conto deposito
Pt à consignação

**in Kraft** De
En in force
Es en vigor
Fr en vigueur
It in vigore
Pt vigente

**in magazzino** It
De vorrätig
En in stock

**Es** en almacén
**Fr** en magasin
**Pt** em reserva

**inmigración** *(f)* *n* Es
**De** Einwanderung *(f)*
**En** immigration
**Fr** immigration *(f)*
**It** immigrazione *(f)*
**Pt** imigração *(f)*

**inmovilizaciones** *(f pl)* *n* Es
**De** Kapitalauslagen *(f pl)*
**En** capital expenditure
**Fr** immobilisations *(f pl)*
**It** immobilizzazioni *(f pl)*
**Pt** despesas em termos de capital *(f pl)*

**in natura** It
**De** in Waren
**En** in kind
**Es** en especie
**Fr** en nature
**Pt** em espécie

**innerlich** *adj* De
**En** internal; intrinsic
**Es** interno; intrínseco
**Fr** interne; intrinsèque
**It** interno; intrinsico
**Pt** interno; intrínseco

**innerlicher Wert** *(m)* De
**En** intrinsic value
**Es** valor intrínseco *(m)*
**Fr** valeur intrinsèque *(f)*
**It** valore intrinsico *(m)*
**Pt** valor intrínseco *(m)*

**innovación** *(f)* *n* Es
**De** Neuerung *(f)*
**En** innovation
**Fr** innovation *(f)*
**It** innovazione *(f)*
**Pt** inovação *(f)*

**innovation** *n* En, Fr *(f)*
**De** Neuerung *(f)*
**Es** innovación *(f)*
**It** innovazione *(f)*
**Pt** inovação *(f)*

**innovazione** *(f)* *n* It
**De** Neuerung *(f)*
**En** innovation
**Es** innovación *(f)*

**Fr** innovation *(f)*
**Pt** inovação *(f)*

**inovação** *(f)* *n* Pt
**De** Neuerung *(f)*
**En** innovation
**Es** innovación *(f)*
**Fr** innovation *(f)*
**It** innovazione *(f)*

**in piego a parte** It
**De** mit getrennter Post
**En** under separate cover
**Es** por correo aparte
**Fr** sous pli séparé
**Pt** por correio separado

**in prestito** It
**De** darlehensweise
**En** on loan
**Es** en préstamo
**Fr** sous forme de prêt
**Pt** por empréstimo

**inquérito** *(m)* *n* Pt
**De** Untersuchung *(f)*
**En** inquiry
**Es** encuesta *(f)*
**Fr** enquête *(f)*
**It** inchiesta *(f)*

**inquilino** *(m)* *n* Es, Pt
**De** Mieter *(m)*
**En** tenant
**Fr** locataire *(m)*
**It** affittuario; locatario *(m)*

**inquiry** (for information, etc.) *n* En
**De** Nachfrage *(f)*
**Es** demanda *(f)*
**Fr** demande *(f)*
**It** domanda *(f)*
**Pt** pergunta *(f)*

**inquiry** (legal) *n* En
**De** Untersuchung *(f)*
**Es** encuesta *(f)*
**Fr** enquête *(f)*
**It** inchiesta *(f)*
**Pt** inquérito *(m)*

**inscription** *(f)* *n* Fr
**De** Eintragung *(f)*
**En** entry
**Es** asiento *(m)*
**It** registrazione *(f)*
**Pt** lançamento *(m)*

**insegnamento superiore** *(m)* It
**De** Fortbildung *(f)*
**En** higher education
**Es** enseñanza superior *(f)*
**Fr** enseignement supérieur *(m)*
**Pt** instrução superior *(f)*

**insérer** *vb* Fr
**De** einsetzen
**En** insert
**Es** insertar
**It** inserire
**Pt** inserir

**inserir** *vb* Pt
**De** einsetzen
**En** insert
**Es** insertar
**Fr** insérer
**It** inserire

**inserire** *vb* It
**De** einsetzen
**En** insert
**Es** insertar
**Fr** insérer
**Pt** inserir

**insert** *vb* En
**De** einsetzen
**Es** insertar
**Fr** insérer
**It** inserire
**Pt** inserir

**insertar** *vb* Es
**De** einsetzen
**En** insert
**Fr** insérer
**It** inserire
**Pt** inserir

**inserzionista** *(m)* *n* It
**De** Anzeiger *(m)*
**En** advertiser
**Es** anunciante *(m)*
**Fr** annonceur *(m)*
**Pt** anunciante *(m)*

**insolvable** *adj* Fr
**De** zum Zahlen unfähig
**En** insolvent
**Es** insolvente; quebrado
**It** insolvente
**Pt** insolvente

**insolvencia** (f) n Es
De Zahlungsunfähigkeit (f)
En insolvency
Fr faillite; déconfiture (f)
It insolvenza (f)
Pt insolvência (f)

**insolvência** (f) n Pt
De Zahlungsunfähigkeit (f)
En insolvency
Es insolvencia; quiebra (f)
Fr faillite; déconfiture (f)
It insolvenza (f)

**insolvency** n En
De Zahlungsunfähigkeit (f)
Es insolvencia; quiebra (f)
Fr faillite; déconfiture (f)
It insolvenza (f)
Pt insolvência (f)

**insolvent** adj En
De zum Zahlen unfähig
Es insolvente; quebrado
Fr insolvable
It insolvente
Pt insolvente

**insolvente** adj Es, It, Pt
De zum Zahlen unfähig
En insolvent
Fr insolvable

**insolvenza** (f) n It
De Zahlungsunfähigkeit (f)
En insolvency
Es insolvencia; quiebra (f)
Fr faillite; déconfiture (f)
Pt insolvência (f)

**in sospeso** It
De in der Schwebe; unent-
schlossen
En in abeyance
Es en suspenso
Fr en suspens
Pt pendente

**inspecção** (f) n Pt
De Einsichtnahme (f)
En inspection
Es inspección; examen (f m)
Fr inspection; vérification (f)
It ispezione (f)

**inspecção médica** (f) Pt
De ärztliche Untersuchung (f)
En medical examination

Es examen médico (m)
Fr examen médical (m)
It visita medica (f)

**inspección** (f) n Es
De Einsichtnahme (f)
En inspection
Fr inspection; vérification (f)
It ispezione (f)
Pt inspecção (f)

**inspecteur** (m) n Fr
De Aufsichtsbeamte(r) (m)
En inspector
Es inspector (m)
It ispettore (m)
Pt inspector (m)

**inspecteur du travail** (m) Fr
De Gewerbeaufsichtsbeamte(r)
(m)
En factory inspector
Es inspector de fábrica (m)
It ispettore di fabbrica (m)
Pt inspector de fábrica (m)

**inspection** n En, Fr (f)
De Einsichtnahme (f)
Es inspección; examen (f m)
It ispezione (f)
Pt inspecção (f)

**inspector** n En; Es, Pt (m)
De Aufsichtsbeamte(r) (m)
Fr inspecteur; vérificateur (m)
It ispettore (m)

**inspector de fábrica** (m) Es, Pt
De Gewerbeaufsichtsbeamte(r)
(m)
En factory inspector
Fr inspecteur du travail (m)
It ispettore di fabbrica (m)

**instalação** (f) n Pt
De Anlage (f)
En installation
Es instalación (f)
Fr installation (f)
It impianto (m)

**instalação fabril** (f) Pt
De Anlage (f)
En plant
Es planta; instalación (f)
Fr appareil; installation (m f)
It impianto; macchinario (m)

**instalação piloto** (f) Pt
De Musteranlage (f)
En pilot plant
Es instalación piloto (f)
Fr installation témoine (f)
It impianto piloto (m)

**instalación** (f) n Es
De Anlage (f)
En installation
Fr installation (f)
It impianto; installazione (m f)
Pt instalação (f)

**instalaciones portuarias** (f pl)
Es
De Hafenanlagen (f pl)
En harbour installations
Fr installations portuaires (f
pl)
It impianti portuali (m pl)
Pt instalações portuárias (f pl)

**instalación piloto** (f) Es
De Musteranlage (f)
En pilot plant
Fr installation témoine (f)
It impianto piloto (m)
Pt instalação piloto (f)

**instalações portuárias** (f pl) Pt
De Hafenanlagen (f pl)
En harbour installations
Es instalaciones portuarias (f
pl)
Fr installations portuaires (f
pl)
It impianti portuali (m pl)

**installation** n En, Fr (f)
De Anlage (f)
Es instalación (f)
It impianto; installazione (m f)
Pt instalação (f)

**installations portuaires** (f pl)
Fr
De Hafenanlagen (f pl)
En harbour installations
Es instalaciones portuarias (f
pl)
It impianti portuali (m pl)
Pt instalações portuárias (f pl)

**installation témoine** (f) Fr
De Musteranlage (f)
En pilot plant
Es instalación piloto (f)

It  impianto piloto *(m)*
Pt  instalação piloto *(f)*

**instalment** *n* En
De  Rate *(f)*
Es  plazo *(m)*
Fr  acompte *(m)*
It  rata *(f)*
Pt  prestação *(f)*

**instalment plan** En
De  Ratenverkauf *(m)*
Es  pago a plazos *(m)*
Fr  vente à tempérament *(f)*
It  sistema di pagamento a rate *(f)*
Pt  plano de prestações *(m)*

**Instandhaltung** *(f) n* De
En  maintenance
Es  mantenimiento *(m)*
Fr  entretien *(m)*
It  manutenzione *(f)*
Pt  manutenção *(f)*

**instigar** *vb* Es, Pt
De  anstiften
En  instigate
Fr  provoquer
It  provocare; istigare

**instigate** *vb* En
De  anstiften
Es  instigar; provocar
Fr  provoquer
It  provocare; istigare
Pt  instigar

**institución** *(f) n* Es
De  Institut; Anstalt *(n f)*
En  institution
Fr  institut *(m)*
It  istituzione; istituto *(f m)*
Pt  instituição *(f)*

**instituição** *(f) n* Pt
De  Institut; Anstalt *(n f)*
En  institution
Es  institución; instituto *(f m)*
Fr  institut *(m)*
It  istituzione; istituto *(f m)*

**instituição de investimentos** *(f)* Pt
De  Investment-Trust *(m)*
En  investment trust
Es  fideicomiso de inversiones *(m)*

Fr  société fiduciaire de placements *(f)*
It  consorzio per investimenti *(m)*

**instituir processo contra** Pt
De  gerichtlich vorgehen gegen
En  institute proceedings against
Es  iniciar un proceso contra
Fr  intenter un procès à
It  intentare un'azione legale contro

**institut** *(m) n* Fr
De  Institut; Anstalt *(n f)*
En  institution
Es  institución; instituto *(f m)*
It  istituzione; istituto *(f m)*
Pt  instituição *(f)*

**Institut** *(n) n* De
En  institution
Es  institución; instituto *(f m)*
Fr  institut *(m)*
It  istituzione; istituto *(f m)*
Pt  instituição *(f)*

**institute proceedings against** En
De  gerichtlich vorgehen gegen
Es  iniciar un proceso contra
Fr  intenter un procès à
It  intentare un'azione legale contro
Pt  instituir processo contra

**institution** *n* En
De  Institut; Anstalt *(n f)*
Es  institución; instituto *(f m)*
Fr  institut *(m)*
It  istituzione; istituto *(f m)*
Pt  instituição *(f)*

**in stock** En
De  vorrätig
Es  en almacén
Fr  en magasin
It  in magazzino
Pt  em reserva

**instrução** *(f) n* Pt
De  Anleitung *(f)*
En  instruction
Es  instrucción *(f)*
Fr  instruction *(f)*
It  istruzione *(f)*

**instrução superior** *(f)* Pt
De  Fortbildung *(f)*
En  higher education
Es  enseñanza superior *(f)*
Fr  enseignement supérieur *(m)*
It  insegnamento superiore *(m)*

**instrucción** *(f) n* Es
De  Anleitung *(f)*
En  instruction
Fr  instruction *(f)*
It  istruzione *(f)*
Pt  instrução *(f)*

**instrucciones para uso** *(f pl)* Pt
De  Gebrauchsanweisung *(f)*
En  instructions for use
Es  modo de empleo *(m)*
Fr  mode d'emploi *(f)*
It  istruzioni per l'uso *(f pl)*

**instruction** *n* En, Fr *(f)*
De  Anleitung *(f)*
Es  instrucción *(f)*
It  istruzione *(f)*
Pt  instrução *(f)*

**instructions for use** En
De  Gebrauchsanleitung *(f)*
Es  modo de empleo *(m)*
Fr  mode d'emploi *(f)*
It  istruzioni per l'uso *(f pl)*
Pt  instruções para uso *(f pl)*

**instrument** *n* En, Fr *(m)*
De  Instrument *(n)*
Es  instrumento *(m)*
It  strumento *(m)*
Pt  instrumento *(m)*

**Instrument** *(n) n* De
En  instrument
Es  instrumento *(m)*
Fr  instrument *(m)*
It  strumento *(m)*
Pt  instrumento *(m)*

**instrument d'analyse** *(m)* Fr
De  Analysenwerkzeug *(n)*
En  analytical tool
Es  instrumento de análisis *(m)*
It  strumento d'analisi *(m)*
Pt  instrumento de análise *(m)*

**instrumento** *(m)* n Es, Pt
De Instrument *(n)*
En instrument
Fr instrument *(m)*
It strumento *(m)*

**instrumento de análise** *(m)* Pt
De Analysenwerkzeug *(n)*
En analytical tool
Es instrumento de análisis *(m)*
Fr instrument d'analyse *(m)*
It strumento d'analisi *(m)*

**instrumento de análisis** *(m)* Es
De Analysenwerkzeug *(n)*
En analytical tool
Fr instrument d'analyse *(m)*
It strumento d'analisi *(m)*
Pt instrumento de análise *(m)*

**insurable** *adj* En
De versicherbar
Es asegurable
Fr assurable
It assicurabile
Pt susceptível de ser objecto de seguro

**insurance** n En
De Versicherung *(f)*
Es seguro *(m)*
Fr assurance *(f)*
It assicurazione *(f)*
Pt seguro *(m)*

**insurance agent** En
De Versicherungsvertreter *(m)*
Es agente de seguros *(m)*
Fr agent d'assurances *(m)*
It agenzia d'assicurazioni *(f)*
Pt agente de seguros *(m)*

**insurance broker** En
De Versicherungsmakler *(m)*
Es corredor de seguros *(m)*
Fr courtier d'assurance *(m)*
It mediatore di assicurazioni *(m)*
Pt corretor de seguros *(m)*

**insurance certificate** En
De Versicherungsschein *(m)*
Es certificado de seguro *(m)*
Fr certificat d'assurance *(m)*
It certificato di assicurazione *(m)*
Pt certificado de seguro *(m)*

**insurance claim** En
De Versicherungsanspruch *(m)*
Es reclamación de seguro *(f)*
Fr indemnité d'assurance *(f)*
It sinistro; reclamo d'indennizzo *(m)*
Pt reclamação de seguro *(f)*

**insurance company** En
De Versicherungsgesellschaft *(f)*
Es compañía de seguros *(f)*
Fr compagnie d'assurance *(f)*
It compagnia di assicurazione *(f)*
Pt companhia de seguros *(f)*

**insurance cover** En
De Versicherungsdeckung *(f)*
Es cobertura de la póliza de seguro *(f)*
Fr garantie d'assurance *(f)*
It copertura assicurativa *(f)*
Pt cobertura de seguro *(f)*

**insurance policy** En
De Versicherungspolice *(f)*
Es póliza de seguro *(f)*
Fr police d'assurance *(f)*
It polizza di assicurazione *(f)*
Pt apólice de seguros *(f)*

**insurance premium** En
De Versicherungsprämie *(f)*
Es prima de póliza de seguro *(f)*
Fr prime d'assurance *(f)*
It premio di assicurazione *(m)*
Pt prémio de seguro *(m)*

**insure** *vb* En
De versichern
Es asegurar
Fr assurer
It assicurare
Pt segurar

**insured** n En
De Versicherte(r) *(m)*
Es asegurado *(m)*
Fr assuré *(m)*
It assicurato *(m)*
Pt titular de seguro *(m)*

**insurer** n En
De Versicherer *(m)*
Es asegurador *(m)*
Fr assureur *(m)*

It assicuratore *(m)*
Pt segurador *(m)*

**intangible assets** En
De nicht greifbare Aktiven *(n pl)*
Es activo intangible *(m)*
Fr actif incorporel *(m)*
It beni incorporali *(m pl)*
Pt bens intocáveis *(m pl)*

**integração** *(f)* n Pt
De Eingliederung *(f)*
En integration
Es integración *(f)*
Fr intégration *(f)*
It integrazione *(f)*

**integração horizontal** *(f)* Pt
De horizontaler Zusammenschluss
En horizontal integration
Es integración horizontal *(f)*
Fr intégration horizontale *(f)*
It integrazione orizzontale *(f)*

**integração vertical** *(f)* Pt
De vertikaler Zusammenschluss *(m)*
En vertical integration
Es integración vertical *(f)*
Fr integration verticale *(f)*
It integrazione verticale *(f)*

**integración** *(f)* n Es
De Eingliederung *(f)*
En integration
Fr intégration *(f)*
It integrazione *(f)*
Pt integração *(f)*

**integración horizontal** *(f)* Es
De horizontaler Zusammenschluss
En horizontal integration
Fr intégration horizontale *(f)*
It integrazione orizzontale *(f)*
Pt integração horizontal *(f)*

**integración vertical** *(f)* Es
De vertikaler Zusammenschluss *(m)*
En vertical integration
Fr integration verticale *(f)*
It integrazione verticale *(f)*
Pt integração vertical *(f)*

**intégralement souscrit** Fr
De vollgezeichnet
En fully subscribed
Es plenamente suscrito
It interamente sottoscritto
Pt totalmente subscrito

**integration** n En
De Eingliederung (f)
Es integración (f)
Fr intégration (f)
It integrazione (f)
Pt integração (f)

**intégration** (f) n Fr
De Eingliederung (f)
En integration
Es integración (f)
It integrazione (f)
Pt integração (f)

**intégration horizontale** (f) Fr
De horizontaler    Zusammen-
    schluss
En horizontal integration
Es integración horizontal (f)
It integrazione orizzontale (f)
Pt integração horizontal (f)

**integration verticale** (f) Fr
De vertikaler Zusammenschluss
    (m)
En vertical integration
Es integración vertical (f)
It integrazione verticale (f)
Pt integração vertical (f)

**integrazione** (f) n It
De Eingliederung (f)
En integration
Es integración (f)
Fr intégration (f)
Pt integração (f)

**integrazione orizzontale** (f) It
De horizontaler    Zusammen-
    schluss
En horizontal integration
Es integración horizontal (f)
Fr intégration horizontale (f)
Pt integração horizontal (f)

**integrazione verticale** (f) It
De vertikaler Zusammenschluss
    (m)
En vertical integration
Es integración vertical (f)

Fr integration verticale (f)
Pt integração vertical (f)

**intensif de capital** Fr
De kapitalintensiv
En capital-intensive
Es intensivo de capital
It concentrato sul capitale
Pt intensivo em termos de
    capital

**intensivo de capital** Es
De kapitalintensiv
En capital-intensive
Fr intensif de capital
It concentrato sul capitale
Pt intensivo em termos de
    capital

**intentare   un'azione   legale
    contro** It
De gerichtlich vorgehen gegen
En institute   proceedings   a-
    gainst
Es iniciar un proceso contra
Fr intenter un procès à
Pt instituir processo contra

**intenter un procès à** Fr
De gerichtlich vorgehen gegen
En institute   proceedings   a-
    gainst
Es iniciar un proceso contra
It intentare un'azione legale
    contro
Pt instituir processo contra

**interamente sottoscritto** It
De vollgezeichnet
En fully subscribed
Es plenamente suscrito
Fr intégralement souscrit
Pt totalmente subscrito

**interés** (m) n Es
De Zinsen (m pl)
En interest
Fr intérêt; prime (m f)
It interesse (m)
Pt juro (m)

**interés acumulado** (m) Es
De aufgelaufene Zinsen (m pl)
En accrued interest
Fr intérêts accumulés (m pl)
It interesse maturato (m)
Pt juro acumulado (m)

**interés bruto** (m) Es
De Bruttozins (m)
En gross interest
Fr intérêts bruts (m pl)
It interesse lordo (m)
Pt juro bruto (m)

**interés compuesto** (m) Es
De Zinsezinsen (m pl)
En compound interest
Fr intérêts composés (m pl)
It interesse composto (m)
Pt juro composto (m)

**interés creado** (m) Es
De festbegründetes Recht (n)
En vested interest
Fr droit acquis (m)
It diritto acquisito (m)
Pt interesse adquirido (m)

**interés mayoritario** (m) Es
De Mehrheitsbeteiligung (f)
En controlling interest
Fr participation   donnant   le
    contrôle (f)
It interesse della parte mag-
    gioritaria (m)
Pt interesse maioritário (m)

**interesse** (m) n It
De Zinsen (m pl)
En interest
Es interés (m)
Fr intérêt; prime (m f)
Pt juro (m)

**interesse adquirido** (m) Pt
De festbegründetes Recht (n)
En vested interest
Es interés creado (m)
Fr droit acquis (m)
It diritto acquisito (m)

**interesse composto** (m) It
De Zinsezinsen (m pl)
En compound interest
Es interés compuesto (m)
Fr intérêts composés (m pl)
Pt juro composto (m)

**interesse   della   parte   mag-
    gioritaria** (m) It
De Mehrheitsbeteiligung (f)
En controlling interest
Es interés mayoritario (m)

Fr participation donnant le
contrôle (f)
Pt interesse maioritário (m)

**interesse lordo** (m) It
De Bruttozins (m)
En gross interest
Es interés bruto (m)
Fr intérêts bruts (m pl)
Pt juro bruto (m)

**interesse maioritário** (m) Pt
De Mehrheitsbeteiligung (f)
En controlling interest
Es interés mayoritario (m)
Fr participation donnant le
contrôle (f)
It interesse della parte mag-
gioritaria (m)

**interesse maturato** (m) It
De aufgelaufene Zinsen (m pl)
En accrued interest
Es interés acumulado (m)
Fr intérêts accumulés (m pl)
Pt juro acumulado (m)

**interessenza a cambio marit-
timo** (f) It
De Bodmereidarlehenszinsen
(m pl)
En bottomry interest
Es interés de préstamo a la
gruesa (m)
Fr prôfit maritime (m)
Pt juro de bodemeria (m)

**interessenza di minoranza** (f)
It
De Minoritätsbeteiligung (f)
En minority interest
Es participación de la minoría
(f)
Fr participation de la minorité
(f)
Pt interesse representado pela
minoria (m)

**interesse representado pela
minoria** (m) Pt
De Minoritätsbeteiligung (f)
En minority interest
Es participación de la minoría
(f)
Fr participation de la minorité
(f)
It interessenza di minoranza
(f)

**interesse semplice** (m) It
De einfache Zinsen (m pl)
En simple interest
Es interés simple (m)
Fr intérêts simples (m pl)
Pt juro simples (m)

**interés simple** (m) Es
De einfache Zinsen (m pl)
En simple interest
Fr intérêts simples (m pl)
It interesse semplice (m)
Pt juro simples (m)

**interest** n En
De Zinsen (m pl)
Es interés (m)
Fr intérêt; prime (m f)
It interesse (m)
Pt juro (m)

**interest-bearing account** Am
En deposit account
De Depositenkonto (n)
Es cuenta de ahorras (f)
Fr compte de dépôt (m)
It conto di deposito (m)
Pt conta de depósito (m)

**interest rates** En
De Zinssätze (m pl)
Es tasas de interés (f pl)
Fr taux d'intérêt (m pl)
It tassi d'interesse (m pl)
Pt taxas de juro (m pl)

**intérêt** (m) n Fr
De Zinsen (m pl)
En interest
Es interés (m)
It interesse (m)
Pt juro (m)

**intérêts accumulés** (m pl) Fr
De aufgelaufene Zinsen (m pl)
En accrued interest
Es interés acumulado (m)
It interesse maturato (m)
Pt juro acumulado (m)

**intérêts bruts** (m pl) Fr
De Bruttozins (m)
En gross interest
Es interés bruto (m)
It interesse lordo (m)
Pt juro bruto (m)

**intérêts composés** (m pl) Fr
De Zinsezinsen (m pl)
En compound interest
Es interés compuesto (m)
It interesse composto (m)
Pt juro composto (m)

**intérêts simples** (m pl) Fr
De einfache Zinsen (m pl)
En simple interest
Es interés simple (m)
It interesse semplice (m)
Pt juro simples (m)

**interim dividend** En
De vorläufige Dividende (f)
Es dividendo provisional (m)
Fr dividende intérimaire (m)
It acconto di dividendo (m)
Pt dividendo interino (m)

**interim financial statement** En
De Zwischenbilanz (f)
Es extracto financiero pro-
visional (m)
Fr bilan intérimaire (m)
It rendiconto finanziario prov-
visorio (m)
Pt extracto financeiro interino
(m)

**intermediação** (f) n Pt
De Vermittlung (f)
En mediation
Es intermediación (f)
Fr médiation (f)
It mediazione (f)

**intermediación** (f) n Es
De Zwischenhändler (m)
En mediation
Fr médiation (f)
It mediazione (f)
Pt intermediação (f)

**intermédiaire** (m) n Fr
De Zwischenhändler (m)
En middle man
Es intermediario (m)
It intermediario (m)
Pt intermediário (m)

**intermediar** vb Es, Pt
De vermitteln
En mediate
Fr s'entremettre
It fare da intermediario

**intermediario** *(m) n* Es, It
De Zwischenhändler *(m)*
En middle man
Fr intermédiaire *(m)*
Pt intermediário *(m)*

**intermediário** *(m) n* Pt
De Zwischenhändler *(m)*
En middle man
Es intermediario *(m)*
Fr intermédiaire *(m)*
It intermediario *(m)*

**internácional** *adj* Es
De international
En international
Fr international
It internazionale
Pt internacional

**internacional** *adj* Pt
De international
En international
Es internácional
Fr international
It internazionale

**internal** *adj* En
De innerlich; inländisch
Es interno; interior
Fr interne
It interno
Pt interno

**internal audit** En
De interne Revision *(f)*
Es verificación contable interna *(f)*
Fr vérification interne *(f)*
It verifica contabile interna *(f)*
Pt fiscalização contabilística interna *(f)*

**international** *adj* De, En, Fr
Es internácional
It internazionale
Pt internacional

**International Bank for Reconstruction and Development** En
De Internationale Bank für Wiederaufbau und Wirtschaftsförderung *(f)*
Es Banco Internacional para Reconstruccion y Desarrollo *(m)*

Fr Banque Internationale pour la reconstruction et le développement *(f)*
It Banca Internazionale per la Ricostruzione e lo Sviluppo *(f)*
Pt Banco Internacional de Reconstrução e Desenvolvimento *(m)*

**International Chamber of Commerce** En
De Internationale Handelskammer *(f)*
Es Cámara Internacional de Comercio *(f)*
Fr Chambre de Commerce Internationale *(f)*
It Camera di Commercio Internazionale *(f)*
Pt Câmara Internacional do Comércio *(f)*

**Internationale Arbeitsorganisation** *(f)* De
En International Labour Organization (ILO)
Es Organisación Laboral Internacional *(f)*
Fr Organisation Internationale du Travail *(f)*
It Organizzazione Internazionale del Lavoro *(f)*
Pt Organização Internacional do Trabalho *(f)*

**Internationale Bank für Wiederaufbau und Wirtschaftsförderung** *(f)* De
En International Bank for Reconstruction and Development
Es Banco Internacional para Reconstrucción y Desarrollo *(m)*
Fr Banque Internationale pour la reconstruction et le développement *(f)*
It Banca Internazionale per la Ricostruzione e lo Sviluppo *(f)*
Pt Banco Internacional de Reconstrução e Desenvolvimento *(m)*

**Internationale Finanzkorporation** *(f)* De

En International Finance Corporation
Es Corporación Internacional de Finanzas *(f)*
Fr Société Financière Internationale *(f)*
It Corporazione Finanziaria Internazionale *(f)*
Pt Corporação Internacional de Finanças *(f)*

**Internationale Handelskammer** *(f)* De
En International Chamber of Commerce
Es Cámara Internacional de Comercio *(f)*
Fr Chambre de Commerce Internationale *(f)*
It Camera di Commercio Internazionale *(f)*
Pt Câmara Internacional do Comércio *(f)*

**Internationaler Währungsfonds** *(m)* De
En International Monetary Fund (IMF)
Es Fondo Monetario Internacional *(m)*
Fr Fonds Monétaire International *(m)*
It Fondo Monetario Internazionale *(m)*
Pt Fundo Monetário Internacional *(m)*

**International Finance Corporation** En
De Internationale Finanzkorporation *(f)*
Es Corporación Internacional de Finanzas *(f)*
Fr Société Financière Internationale *(f)*
It Corporazione Finanziaria Internazionale *(f)*
Pt Corporação Internacional de Finanças *(f)*

**International Labour Organization** (ILO) En
De Internationale Arbeitsorganisation *(f)*
Es Organisación Laboral Internacional *(f)*
Fr Organisation Internationale du Travail *(f)*

It  Organizzazione Internazionale del Lavoro *(f)*
Pt  Organização Internacional do Trabalho *(f)*

**International Monetary Fund** (IMF) En
De  Internationaler Währungsfonds *(m)*
Es  Fondo Monetario Internacional *(m)*
Fr  Fonds Monétaire International *(m)*
It  Fondo Monetario Internazionale *(m)*
Pt  Fundo Monetário Internacional *(m)*

**internazionale** *adj* It
De  international
En  international
Es  internácional
Fr  international
Pt  internacional

**interne** *adj* Fr
De  innerlich; inländisch
En  internal
Es  interno; interior
It  interno
Pt  interno

**interne Revision** *(f)* De
En  internal audit
Es  verificación contable interna *(f)*
Fr  vérification interne *(f)*
It  verifica contabile interna *(f)*
Pt  fiscalização contabilística interna *(f)*

**interno** *adj* Es, It, Pt
De  innerlich; inländisch
En  internal
Fr  interne

**interpolação** *(f)* n Pt
De  Einschaltung *(f)*
En  interpolation
Es  interpolación *(f)*
Fr  interpolation *(f)*
It  interpolazione *(f)*

**interpolación** *(f)* n Es
De  Einschaltung *(f)*
En  interpolation
Fr  interpolation *(f)*
It  interpolazione *(f)*.
Pt  interpolação *(f)*

**interpolation** n En, Fr *(f)*
De  Einschaltung *(f)*
Es  interpolación *(f)*
It  interpolazione *(f)*
Pt  interpolação *(f)*

**interpolazione** *(f)* n It
De  Einschaltung *(f)*
En  interpolation
Es  interpolación *(f)*
Fr  interpolation *(f)*
Pt  interpolação *(f)*

**interponer** *vb* Es
De  einlegen
En  file; lodge
Fr  déposer
It  depositare
Pt  registar

**interpretação** *(f)* n Pt
De  Auslegung *(f)*
En  interpretation
Es  interpretación *(f)*
Fr  interprétation *(f)*
It  interpretazione *(f)*

**interpretación** *(f)* n Es
De  Auslegung *(f)*
En  interpretation
Fr  interprétation *(f)*
It  interpretazione *(f)*
Pt  interpretação *(f)*

**interpretation** n En
De  Auslegung *(f)*
Es  interpretación *(f)*
Fr  interprétation *(f)*
It  interpretazione *(f)*
Pt  interpretação *(f)*

**interprétation** *(f)* n Fr
De  Auslegung *(f)*
En  interpretation
Es  interpretación *(f)*
It  interpretazione *(f)*
Pt  interpretação *(f)*

**interpretazione** *(f)* n It
De  Auslegung *(f)*
En  interpretation

Es  interpretación *(f)*
Fr  interprétation *(f)*
Pt  interpretação *(f)*

**intervalle d'acceptation** *(f)* Fr
De  Akzeptfrist *(f)*
En  acceptance interval
Es  intervalo de aceptación *(m)*
It  intervallo dell'accettazione *(m)*
Pt  intervalo de aceitação *(m)*

**intervallo dell'accettazione** *(m)* It
De  Akzeptfrist *(f)*
En  acceptance interval
Es  intervalo de aceptación *(m)*
Fr  intervalle d'acceptation *(f)*
Pt  intervalo de aceitação *(m)*

**intervalo de aceitação** *(m)* Pt
De  Akzeptfrist *(f)*
En  acceptance interval
Es  intervalo de aceptación *(m)*
Fr  intervalle d'acceptation *(f)*
It  intervallo dell'accettazione *(m)*

**intervalo de aceptación** *(m)* Es
De  Akzeptfrist *(f)*
En  acceptance interval
Fr  intervalle d'acceptation *(f)*
It  intervallo dell'accettazione *(m)*
Pt  intervalo de aceitação *(m)*

**Intervention (bei Wechselakzept)** *(f)* De
En  acceptance for honour
Es  aceptación por intervención *(f)*
Fr  acceptation par intervention *(f)*
It  accettazione per intervento *(f)*
Pt  aceitação por intervenção *(f)*

**intervention price** En
De  Interventionspreis *(m)*
Es  precio de intervención *(m)*
Fr  prix d'intervention *(m)*
It  prezzo d'intervento *(m)*
Pt  preço de intervenção *(m)*

**Interventionspreis** *(m)* n De
En  intervention price
Es  precio de intervención *(m)*

Fr prix d'intervention *(m)*
It prezzo d'intervento *(m)*
Pt preço de intervenção *(m)*

**interventor** *(m) n* Es
De Rechnungsprüfer *(m)*
En comptroller
Fr vérificateur des comptes *(m)*
It controllore *(m)*
Pt controlador *(m)*

**interview** *n* En, Fr *(f)*
De Interview *(n)*
Es entrevista *(f)*
It intervista; abboccamento *(f m)*
Pt entrevista; encontro *(f m)*

**Interview** *(n) n* De
En interview
Es entrevista *(f)*
Fr interview; entrevue *(f)*
It intervista; abboccamento *(f m)*
Pt entrevista; encontro *(f m)*

**interviewee** *n* En
De Befragte(r) *(m)*
Es persona entrevistada *(f)*
Fr personne interrogée *(f)*
It intervistato *(m)*
Pt entrevistado *(m)*

**interviewer** *n* En
De Interviewer *(m)*
Es entrevistador *(m)*
Fr intervieweur; enquêteur *(m)*
It intervistatore *(m)*
Pt entrevistador *(m)*

**Interviewer** *(m) n* De
En interviewer
Es entrevistador *(m)*
Fr intervieweur; enquêteur *(m)*
It intervistatore *(m)*
Pt entrevistador *(m)*

**intervieweur** *(m) n* Fr
De Interviewer *(m)*
En interviewer
Es entrevistador *(m)*
It intervistatore *(m)*
Pt entrevistador *(m)*

**intervista** *(f) n* It
De Interview *(n)*
En interview

Es entrevista *(f)*
Fr interview; entrevue *(f)*
Pt entrevista; encontro *(f m)*

**intervistato** *(m) n* It
De Befragte(r) *(m)*
En interviewee
Es persona entrevistada *(f)*
Fr personne interrogée *(f)*
Pt entrevistado *(m)*

**intervistatore** *(m) n* It
De Interviewer *(m)*
En interviewer
Es entrevistador *(m)*
Fr intervieweur; enquêteur *(m)*
Pt entrevistador *(m)*

**intestazione** *(f) n* It
De Briefkopf *(m)*
En letterhead
Es membrete *(m)*
Fr en-tête *(m)*
Pt cabeçalho *(m)*

**intimazione** *(f) n* It
De Inverzugsetzung *(f)*
En formal notice
Es aviso oficial *(m)*
Fr mise en demeure *(f)*
Pt notificação formal *(f)*

**in transit** En
De im Durchgangsverkehr
Es en tránsito
Fr en transit
It in transito
Pt em trânsito

**in transito** It
De im Durchgangsverkehr
En in transit
Es en tránsito
Fr en transit
Pt em trânsito

**intraprenditore** *(m) n* It
De Unternehmer *(m)*
En entrepreneur
Es empresario *(m)*
Fr entrepreneur *(m)*
Pt empresário *(m)*

**intrínseco** *adj* Es, Pt
De innerlich; wahr
En intrinsic
Fr intrinsèque
It intrinsico

**intrinsèque** *adj* Fr
De innerlich; wahr
En intrinsic
Es intrínseco
It intrinsico
Pt intrínseco

**intrinsic** *adj* En
De innerlich; wahr
Es intrínseco
Fr intrinsèque
It intrinsico
Pt intrínseco

**intrinsico** *adj* It
De innerlich; wahr
En intrinsic
Es intrínseco
Fr intrinsèque
Pt intrínseco

**intrinsic value** En
De innerlicher Wert *(m)*
Es valor intrínseco *(m)*
Fr valeur intrinsèque *(f)*
It valore intrinsico *(m)*
Pt valor intrínseco *(m)*

**in Übereinstimmung mit** De
En in accordance with
Es en conformidad con
Fr conforme à
It in conformità con
Pt em conformidade com

**inundación de mercancía barata** *(f)* Es
De Dumping *(n)*
En dumping
Fr dumping *(m)*
It dumping *(m)*
Pt saturação (de mercadorias baratas); descarga *(f)*

**invalid** *adj* En
De ungültig
Es inválido
Fr invalide
It invalido
Pt inválido

**invalide** *adj* Fr
De ungültig
En invalid
Es inválido
It invalido
Pt inválido

**inválido** adj Es, Pt
De ungültig
En invalid
Fr invalide
It invalido

**invalido** adj It
De ungültig
En invalid
Es inválido
Fr invalide
Pt inválido

**invenção** (f) n Pt
De Erfindung (f)
En invention
Es invento; invención (m f)
Fr invention (f)
It invenzione (f)

**inventaire** (m) n Fr
De Inventar (n)
En inventory
Es inventario (m)
It inventario (m)
Pt inventário (m)

**Inventar** (n) n De
En inventory
Es inventario (m)
Fr inventaire (m)
It inventario (m)
Pt inventário (m)

**inventario** (m) n Es, It
De Inventar (n)
En inventory
Fr inventaire (m)
Pt inventário (m)

**inventário** (m) n Pt
De Inventar (n)
En inventory
Es inventario (m)
Fr inventaire (m)
It inventario (m)

**invention** n En, Fr (f)
De Erfindung (f)
Es invento; invención (m f)
It invenzione (f)
Pt invenção (f)

**invento** (m) n Es
De Erfindung (f)
En invention
Fr invention (f)

It invenzione (f)
Pt invenção (f)

**inventory** n En
De Inventar (n)
Es inventario (m)
Fr inventaire (m)
It inventario (m)
Pt inventário (m)

**invenzione** (f) n It
De Erfindung (f)
En invention
Es invento; invención (m f)
Fr invention (f)
Pt invenção (f)

**inversión** (f) n Es
De Kapitalanlage; Investierung (f)
En investment
Fr investissement; placement (m)
It investimento (m)
Pt investimento (m)

**inversionista** (m) n Es
De Geldgeber (m)
En investor
Fr investisseur (m)
It capitalista (m)
Pt capitalista (m)

**invertir** vb Es
De anlegen
En invest
Fr investir; placer
It investire
Pt investir

**Inverzugsetzung** (f) n De
En formal notice
Es aviso oficial (m)
Fr mise en demeure (f)
It intimazione (f)
Pt notificação formal (f)

**invest** vb En
De anlegen; investieren
Es invertir
Fr investir; placer
It investire
Pt investir

**investieren** vb De
En invest
Es invertir
Fr investir; placer

It investire
Pt investir

**Investierung** (f) n De
En investment
Es inversión (f)
Fr investissement (m)
It investimento (m)
Pt investimento (m)

**Investierungsanreiz** (m) n De
En investment incentive
Es incentivo de inversión (m)
Fr stimulant de l'investissement (m)
It incentivo d'investimento (m)
Pt incentivo de investimento (m)

**Investierungsgesellschaft** n De
En investment company
Es compañía inversionista (f)
Fr société de placement (f)
It società per investimenti (f)
Pt companhia de investimentos (f)

**investigação** (f) n Pt
De Untersuchung; Forschung (f)
En investigation; research
Es investigación (f)
Fr investigation; recherche (f)
It investigazione; ricerca (f)

**investigação e desenvolvimento** Pt
De Zweckforschung; Entwicklung (f)
En research and development (R & D)
Es investigación y desarrollo
Fr recherche industrielle (f)
It studi e sviluppi

**investigação operacional** (f) Pt
De Unternehmensforschung (f)
En operational research (OR)
Es investigación operacional (f)
Fr recherche opérationnelle (f)
It indagine sul funzionamento

**investigación** (f) n Es
De Untersuchung; Forschung (f)

En investigation; research
Fr investigation; rècherche *(f)*
It investigazione; ricerca *(f)*
Pt investigação; pesquisa *(f)*


**investigación del mercado** *(f)*
   Es
De Marktforschung *(f)*
En market research
Fr étude du marché *(f)*
It indagine di mercato *(f)*
Pt pesquisa de mercado *(f)*


**investigación de motivación**
   *(f)* Es
De Motivforschung *(f)*
En motivational research
Fr étude de motivation *(f)*
It indagine sulle motivazioni
   *(f)*
Pt investigação sobre moti-
   vação *(f)*


**investigación operacional** *(f)*
   Es
De Unternehmensforschung *(f)*
En operational research (OR)
Fr recherche opérationnelle *(f)*
It indagine sul funzionamento
   *(f)*
Pt investigação operacional *(f)*


**investigación y desarrollo** Es
De Zweckforschung; Entwick-
   lung *(f)*
En research and development
   (R & D)
Fr recherche industrielle *(f)*
It studi e sviluppi
Pt investigação e desenvol-
   vimento


**investigation** *n* En, Fr *(f)*
De Untersuchung *(f)*
Es investigación *(f)*
It inchiesta; investigazione *(f)*
Pt investigação; pesquisa *(f)*


**investimento** *(m) n* It, Pt
De Kapitalanlage; Inyestierung
   *(f)*
En investment
Es inversión *(f)*
Fr investissement; placement
   *(m)*


**investir** *vb* Fr, Pt
De anlegen; investieren
En invest
Es invertir
It investire


**investire** *vb* It
De anlegen; investieren
En invest
Es invertir
Fr investir; placer
Pt investir


**investissement** *(m) n* Fr
De Kapitalanlage; Investierung
   *(f)*
En investment
Es inversión *(f)*
It investimento *(m)*
Pt investimento *(m)*


**investisseur** *(m) n* Fr
De Geldgeber *(m)*
En investor
Es inversionista *(m)*
It capitalista *(m)*
Pt capitalista *(m)*


**Investitionsanalyst** *(m) n* De
En investment analyst
Es analizador de inversiones
   *(m)*
Fr analyste d'investissements
   *(m)*
It analizzatore d'investimenti
   *(m)*
Pt analizador de investimen-
   tos *(m)*


**Investitionsportefeuille** *(n) n*
   De
En investment portfolio
Es cartera de inversiones *(f)*
Fr portefeuille d'investisse-
   ments *(m)*
It portafoglio titoli *(m)*
Pt carteira de investimentos
   *(f)*


**investment** *n* En
De Kapitalanlage; Investierung
   *(f)*
Es inversión *(f)*
Fr investissement; placement
   *(m)*
It investimento *(m)*
Pt investimento *(m)*


**investment analyst** En
De Investitionsanalyst *(m)*
Es analizador de inversiones
   *(m)*
Fr analyste d'investissements
   *(m)*
It analizzatore d'investimenti
   *(m)*
Pt analizador de investimen-
   tos *(m)*


**investment bank** En
De Finanzbank *(f)*
Es banco de inversiones *(m)*
Fr banque d'affaires *(f)*
It banca d'investimenti *(f)*
Pt banco de investimentos *(m)*


**investment company** En
De Investierungsgesellschaft *(f)*
Es compañía inversionista *(f)*
Fr société de placement *(f)*
It società per investimenti *(f)*
Pt companhia de investimen-
   tos *(f)*


**investment incentive** En
De Investierungsanreiz *(m)*
Es incentivo de inversión *(m)*
Fr stimulant de l'investisse-
   ment *(m)*
It incentivo d'investimento
   *(m)*
Pt incentivo de investimento
   *(m)*


**investment income** En
De Einkommen aus Kapitalan-
   lagen *(n)*
Es renta de inversiones *(f)*
Fr revenu de placements *(m)*
It reddito degli investimenti
   *(m)*
Pt rendimento de capitais
   investidos *(m)*


**investment portfolio** En
De Investitionsportefeuille *(n)*
Es cartera de inversiones *(f)*
Fr portefeuille d'investisse-
   ments *(m)*
It portafoglio titoli *(m)*
Pt carteira de investimentos
   *(f)*


**investment trust** En
De Investment-Trust *(m)*

Es fideicomiso de inversiones
*(m)*
Fr société fiduciaire de placements *(f)*
It consorzio per investimenti
*(m)*
Pt instituição de investimentos *(f)*

**Investment-Trust** *(m) n* De
En investment trust
Es fideicomiso de inversiones
*(m)*
Fr société fiduciaire de place-
ments *(f)*
It consorzio per investimenti
*(m)*
Pt instituição de investimen-
tos *(f)*

**investor** *n* En
De Geldgeber *(m)*
Es inversionista *(m)*
Fr investisseur *(m)*
It capitalista *(m)*
Pt capitalista *(m)*

**in vigore** It
De in Kraft
En in force
Es en vigor
Fr en vigueur
Pt vigente

**invisible exports** En
De unsichtbare Exporte *(m pl)*
Es exportaciones invisibles *(f
pl)*
Fr exportations invisibles *(f pl)*
It esportazioni invisibili *(f pl)*
Pt exportações invisíveis *(f pl)*

**invitación** *(f) n* Es
De Einladung; Aufforderung *(f)*
En invitation
Fr invitation; appel *(f m)*
It invito *(m)*
Pt convite *(m)*

**invitar** *vb* Es
De einladen; auffordern
En invite
Fr inviter
It invitare
Pt convidar

**invitare** *vb* It
De einladen; auffordern
En invite
Es invitar
Fr inviter
Pt convidar

**invitation** *n* En, Fr *(f)*
De Einladung; Aufforderung *(f)*
Es invitación *(f)*
It invito *(m)*
Pt convite *(m)*

**invite** *vb* En
De einladen; auffordern
Es invitar
Fr inviter
It invitare
Pt convidar

**inviter** *vb* Fr
De einladen; auffordern
En invite
Es invitar
It invitare
Pt convidar

**invito** *(m) n* It
De Einladung; Aufforderung *(f)*
En invitation
Es invitación *(f)*
Fr invitation; appel *(f m)*
Pt convite *(m)*

**invoice** *vb* En
De fakturieren
Es facturar
Fr facturer
It fatturare
Pt facturar

**invoice** *n* En
De Faktura; Rechnung *(f)*
Es factura *(f)*
Fr facture *(f)*
It fattura *(f)*
Pt factura *(f)*

**invoice price** En
De fakturierter Preis *(m)*
Es precio facturado *(m)*
Fr prix facturé *(m)*
It prezzo di fattura *(m)*
Pt preço de factura *(m)*

**in Waren** De
En in kind
Es en especie

Fr en nature
It in natura
Pt em espécie

**ipoteca** *(f) n* It
De Hypothek *(f)*
En mortgage; hypothecation
Es hipoteca *(f)*
Fr hypothèque; nantissement
*(f m)*
Pt hipoteca *(f)*

**ipotecare** *vb* It
De verpfänden
En hypothecate
Es hipotecar
Fr hypothéquer
Pt hipotecar

**ipotesi** *(f) n* It
De Hypothese *(f)*
En hypothesis
Es hipótesis *(f)*
Fr hypothèse *(f)*
Pt hipótese *(f)*

**iron** *n* En
De Eisen *(n)*
Es hierro *(m)*
Fr fer *(m)*
It ferro *(m)*
Pt ferro *(m)*

**iron ore** En
De Eisenerz *(n)*
Es mineral de hierro *(m)*
Fr minerai de fer *(m)*
It minerale di ferro *(m)*
Pt minério de ferro *(m)*

**irrécouvrable** *adj* Fr
De unersetzlich; uneinbringlich
En irrecoverable
Es irrecuperable
It irrecuperabile
Pt irrecuperável

**irrecoverable** *adj* En
De unersetzlich; uneinbringlich
Es irrecuperable
Fr irrécouvrable
It irrecuperabile
Pt irrecuperável

**irrecuperabile** *adj* It
De unersetzlich; uneinbringlich
En irrecoverable
Es irrecuperable

Fr  irrécouvrable
Pt  irrecuperável

**irrecuperable** adj Es
De  unersetzlich; uneinbringlich
En  irrecoverable
Fr  irrécouvrable
It  irrecuperabile
Pt  irrecuperável

**irrecuperável** adj Pt
De  unersetzlich
En  irrecoverable
Es  irrecuperable
Fr  irrécouvrable
It  irrecuperabile

**irredeemable debenture** En
De  uneinlösbare        Schuldver-
    schreibung (f)
Es  obligación no amortizable
    (f)
Fr  obligation irremboursable
    (f)
It  obbligazione irredimibile (f)
Pt  obrigação não amortizável

**irrevocable letter of credit** En
De  unwiderruflicher Kreditbrief
    (m)
Es  carta de crédito irrevocable
    (f)
Fr  lettre de crédit irrévocable
    (f)
It  lettera  di  credito  irre-
    vocabile (f)
Pt  carta de crédito irrevogável
    (f)

**Irrtum vorbehalten** De
En  errors and omissions ex-
    cepted
Es  salvo error u omisión
Fr  sauf erreur ou omission
It  salvo errori ed omissioni
Pt  salvo erro e omissão

**isenção** (f) n Pt
De  Befreiung (f)
En  exemption
Es  exención (f)
Fr  exemption (f)
It  esenzione (f)

**isenção de imposto** (f) Pt
De  Steuerbefreiung (f)
En  tax relief

Es  desgravación (f)
Fr  dégrèvement (m)
It  sgravio fiscale (m)

**isenção de tributação dupla**
    (f) Pt
De  Doppelbesteuerungserleich-
    terung (f)
En  double taxation relief
Es  desgravación de tributación
    doble (f)
Fr  dégrèvement de charges
    fiscales doubles (m)
It  sgravio per doppia tas-
    sazione (m)

**isento de comissão** Pt
De  maklergebührenfrei
En  free of commission
Es  franco-comisión
Fr  franco courtage
It  franco mediazione

**isento de impostos** Pt
De  abgabenfrei
En  duty-free
Es  exento de impuestos
Fr  exempt de douane
It  esente da dazio

**isento de impostos** Pt
De  steuerfrei
En  tax-free
Es  exento de impuestos
Fr  exempt d'impôts
It  esente di tassa

**ispettore** (m) n It
De  Aufsichtsbeamte(r) (m)
En  inspector
Es  inspector (m)
Fr  inspecteur; vérificateur (m)
Pt  inspector (m)

**ispettore di fabbrica** (m) It
De  Gewerbeaufsichtsbeamte(r)
    (m)
En  factory inspector
Es  inspector de fábrica (m)
Fr  inspecteur du travail (m)
Pt  inspector de fábrica (m)

**ispezione** (f) n It
De  Einsichtnahme (f)
En  inspection
Es  inspección; examen (f m)
Fr  inspection; vérification (f)
Pt  inspecção (f)

**issue** vb En
De  ausgeben
Es  emitir
Fr  émettre
It  emettere
Pt  emitir

**issued capital** En
De  ausgegebenes Kapital (n)
Es  capital emitido (m)
Fr  capital versé (m)
It  capitale emesso (m)
Pt  capital emitido (m)

**issuing bank** En
De  Notenbank (f)
Es  banco emisor (m)
Fr  banque d'émission (f)
It  banca di emissione (f)
Pt  banco emissor (m)

**istituzione** (f) n It
De  Institut; Anstalt (n f)
En  institution
Es  institución; instituto (f m)
Fr  institut (m)
Pt  instituição (f)

**istogramma** (m) n It
De  Histogramm (n)
En  histogram
Es  histograma (m)
Fr  histogramme (m)
Pt  histograma (m)

**istruzione** (f) n It
De  Anleitung (f)
En  instruction
Es  instrucción (f)
Fr  instruction (f)
Pt  instrução (f)

**istruzioni per l'uso** (f pl) It
De  Gebrauchsanweisung (f)
En  directions for use
Es  modo de empleo (m)
Fr  mode d'emploi (f)
Pt  instruções para uso (f pl)

**itemized** adj En
De  postenmässig dargestellt
Es  detallado
Fr  détaillé
It  dettagliato
Pt  pormenorizado

**items of expenditure** En
De Aufwendungsposten *(f pl)*
Es artículos de gasto *(m pl)*
Fr postes de dépense *(m pl)*
It articoli di spesa *(m pl)*
Pt itens de despesa *(m pl)*

**itens de despesa** *(m pl)* Pt
De Aufwendungsposten *(f pl)*
En items of expenditure
Es artículos de gasto *(m pl)*
Fr postes de dépense *(m pl)*
It articoli di spesa *(m pl)*

# J

**Jahresabschluss** *(m)* n De
En annual accounts
Es balance anual *(m)*
Fr bilan annuel *(m)*
It bilancio annuale *(m)*
Pt balancete anual *(m)*

**Jahresbericht** *(m)* n De
En annual report
Es memoria anual *(f)*
Fr rapport annuel *(m)*
It relazione annuale *(f)*
Pt relatório anual *(m)*

**Jahreshauptversammlung** *(f)*
De
En annual general meeting
Am stockholders' meeting
Es asamblea general anual *(f)*
Fr assemblée d'actionnaires
annuelle *(f)*
It assemblea generale annu-
ale *(f)*
Pt assembleia geral anual *(f)*

**Jahreskurs** *(m)* n De
En annual rate
Es tasa anual *(f)*
Fr taux annuel *(m)*
It tasso annuale *(m)*
Pt taxa anual *(f)*

**Jahreszeit** *(f)* n De
En season
Es estación *(f)*
Fr saison *(f)*
It stagione *(f)*
Pt estação *(f)*

**jahreszeitlich bedingte Ar-
beitslosigkeit** *(f)* De
En seasonal unemployment
Es paro de temporada *(m)*
Fr chômage saisonnier *(m)*
It disoccupazione stagionale
*(f)*
Pt desemprego de estação
*(m)*

**jährlich** *adj* De
En annual
Es anual
Fr annuel
It annuale
Pt anual

**jazigo de carvão** *(m)* Pt
De Kohlenrevier *(n)*
En coal field
Es yacimiento de carbón *(m)*
Fr bassin houiller *(m)*
It bacino carbonifero *(m)*

**jazigo de petróleo** *(m)* Pt
De Ölfeld *(n)*
En oilfield
Es yacimiento de petróleo *(m)*
Fr gisement petrolifère *(m)*
It giacimento petrolifero *(m)*

**jazigos de ouro** *(m pl)* Pt
De Goldgrube *(f)*
En gold fields
Es yacimiento aurífero *(m)*
Fr régions aurifères *(f pl)*
It terreni auriferi *(m pl)*

**jefe de contabilidad** *(m)* Es
De Oberbuchhalter *(m)*
En chief accountant
Fr chef comptable *(m)*
It ragioniere capo *(m)*
Pt chefe contabilista *(m)*

**jefe de departamento** *(m)* Es
De Abteilungsleiter *(m)*
En head of department
Fr chef de service *(m)*
It capo reparto *(m)*
Pt chefe de departamento *(m)*

**jefe de exportación** *(m)* Es
De Exportabteilungsleiter *(m)*
En export manager
Fr chef du service exportation
*(m)*

It direttore esportazione *(m)*
Pt gerente de exportações *(m)*

**jefe de familia** *(m)* Es
De Hausherr *(m)*
En householder
Fr chef de famille *(m)*
It capo-famiglia *(m)*
Pt dono da casa *(m)*

**jefe del departamento de
compras** *(m)* Es
De Haupteinkäufer *(m)*
En head buyer
Fr chef du service des achats
*(m)*
It capo servizio acquisti *(m)*
Pt chefe de compras *(m)*

**jefe de oficina** *(m)* Es
De Bürovorsteher *(m)*
En office manager
Fr chef de bureau *(m)*
It capo ufficio *(m)*
Pt chefe de escritório *(m)*

**jefe de personal** *(m)* Es
De Personalchef *(m)*
En personnel manager
Fr chef du personnel *(m)*
It direttore del personale *(m)*
Pt chefe do pessoal *(m)*

**jefe de ventas** *(m)* Es
De Verkaufsleiter *(m)*
En sales manager
Fr directeur commercial *(m)*
It direttore commerciale *(m)*
Pt chefe de vendas *(m)*

**jefe ejecutivo** *(m)* Es
De Geschäftsführer *(m)*
En chief executive
Fr directeur général *(m)*
It direttore generale *(m)*
Pt chefe de gerência *(m)*

**jerque note** En
De Eintrittsdeklarationsschein
*(m)*
Es certificado de declaración
de entrada *(m)*
Fr certificat d'entrée autorisée
*(m)*
It certificato di dichiarazione
d'entrata *(m)*
Pt certificado de verificação
alfandegária *(m)*

**jet aircraft** En
De Düsenflugzeug (n)
Es avión jet (m)
Fr avion à réaction (m)
It aviogetto (m)
Pt avião a jacto (m)

**jetée** (f) n Fr
De Mole (f)
En jetty
Es digue (m)
It molo (m)
Pt pontão; cais (m)

**jet engine** En
De Düsenmotor (m)
Es motor de propulsión a chorro (m)
Fr réacteur (m)
It motore a reazione (m)
Pt motor a jacto

**jeter à la mer** (la cargaison) Fr
De über Bord werfen
En jettison
Es echar al mar
It fare gettito
Pt alijar

**jettison** vb En
De über Bord werfen
Es echar al mar
Fr jeter à la mer
It fare gettito
Pt alijar

**jetty** n En
De Mole (f)
Es digue (m)
Fr jetée; digue (f)
It molo (m)
Pt pontão; cais (m)

**job** (post, situation, etc.) n En
De Stellung (f)
Es empleo (m)
Fr emploi (m)
It impiego (m)
Pt emprego (m)

**job** (occupation) n En
De Beruf (m)
Es trabajo (m)
Fr occupation (f)
It lavoro (m)
Pt ocupação (f)

**job** vb En
De spekulieren
Es especular
Fr spéculer
It speculare; trafficare
Pt especular

**job costing** En
De Kostenstellenrechnung (f)
Es evaluación del trabajo (f)
Fr évaluation du coût de tache (f)
It valutazione dei lavori durante la fabbricazione (f)
Pt cálculo do custo de obra (m)

**job description** En
De Arbeitsbeschreibung (f)
Es descripción del trabajo (f)
Fr description du travail (f)
It descrizione del lavoro (f)
Pt descrição da tarefa (f)

**job evaluation** En
De Arbeitsbewertung (f)
Es valoracion del trabajo (f)
Fr évaluation du travail (f)
It valutazione del lavoro (f)
Pt avaliação de tarefa (f)

**job specification** En
De Arbeitsaufgabe (f)
Es especificación del trabajo (f)
Fr donnée d'exécution (f)
It specifica del lavoro (f)
Pt especificação de obra (f)

**jogar na Bolsa** Pt
De die Börse spielen
En gamble on the stock exchange
Es jugar a la Bolsa
Fr jouer à la Bourse
It giocare in Borsa

**jogo limpo** (m) Pt
De anständige Handlungsweise (f)
En fair play
Es juego limpio (m)
Fr traitement juste (m)
It condotta leale (f)

**joint account** En
De Gemeinschaftskonto (n)
Es cuenta común (f)

Fr compte joint (m)
It conto in comune (m)
Pt conta conjunta (f)

**joint and several bond** En
De Solidarobligation (f)
Es obligación solidaria e indivisa (f)
Fr obligation conjointe et solidaire (f)
It obbligazione solidale (f)
Pt título solidário de diversos (m)

**jointly and severally** En
De gesamtschuldnerisch
Es en conjunto y separadamente
Fr conjointement et solidairement
It solidalmente e individualmente
Pt em conjunto e por vários

**joint ownership** En
De Miteigentum (n)
Es copropiedad (f)
Fr copropriété (f)
It comproprietà (f)
Pt copropriedade (f)

**joint venture** En
De Gemeinschaftsgründung (f)
Es empresa en común (f)
Fr entreprise en participation (f)
It impresa in compartecipazione (f)
Pt iniciativa em comum (f)

**jornada laboral** (f) Es
De Arbeitszeit (f)
En hours of work
Fr durée du travail (f)
It ore lavorative (f pl)
Pt horas de trabalho (f pl)

**jouer à la Bourse** Fr
De die Börse spielen
En gamble on the stock exchange
Es jugar a la Bolsa
It giocare in Borsa
Pt jogar na Bolsa

**jour** (m) n Fr
De Tag (m)
En day

Es día *(m)*
It giorno *(m)*
Pt dia *(m)*

**jour de bourse** *(m)* Fr
De Börsentag *(m)*
En (financial) market day
Es día de bolsa *(m)*
It giorno di borsa *(m)*
Pt dia de bolsa *(m)*

**jour de congé** *(m)* Fr
De dienstfreier Tag *(m)*
En day off
Es día libre *(m)*
It giorno di riposo *(m)*
Pt dia de folga *(m)*

**jour de liquidation** *(m)* Fr
De Abrechnungstag *(m)*
En account day
Am settlement date
Es día de liquidación *(m)*
It giorno di liquidazione *(m)*
Pt dia de liquidação *(m)*

**jour de paiement** *(m)* Fr
De Zahltag; Abrechnungstag *(m)*
En pay day
Es día de pago *(m)*
It giorno di paga *(m)*
Pt dia de recebimento *(m)*

**jour de place** *(m)* Fr
De Markttag *(m)*
En (local) market day
Es día de mercado *(m)*
It giorno di mercato *(m)*
Pt dia de mercado *(m)*

**jour de règlement** *(m)* Fr
De Abrechnungstag *(m)*
En settlement day
Am due date
Es día de liquidación *(m)*
It giorno della liquidazione *(m)*
Pt dia de liquidação *(m)*

**jour du terme** *(m)* Fr
De Quartalstag *(m)*
En quarter day
Es primer día del trimestre *(m)*
It giorno della pigione *(m)*
Pt dia de vencimento trimestral *(m)*

**jour férié** *(m)* Fr
De gesetzlicher Feiertag *(m)*
En public holiday
Es día de fiesta *(m)*
It giorno di festa *(m)*
Pt feriado *(m)*

**journal** *n* En, Fr *(m)*
De Tagebuch *(n)*
Es diario *(m)*
It giornale *(m)*
Pt diário *(m)*

**journal de navigation** *(m)* Fr
De Log *(n)*
En (ship's) log
Es diario de navegación *(m)*
It solcometro *(m)*
Pt diário de bordo *(m)*

**journal-entry** *n* En
De Tagebuchsposten *(m)*
Es asiento en el libro diario *(m)*
Fr article d'un livre journal *(m)*
It registrazione a giornale *(f)*
Pt anotação de diário *(f)*

**journal général** *(m)* Fr
De allgemeines Hauptbuch *(n)*
En general ledger
Es libro mayor general *(m)*
It libro mastro generale *(m)*
Pt livro-mestre geral *(m)*

**jour ouvrable** *(m)* Fr
De Arbeitstag *(m)*
En working day
Es día laborable *(m)*
It giornata lavorativa *(f)*
Pt dia de trabalho *(m)*

**judge** *vb* En
De urteilen
Es juzgar
Fr juger
It giudicare
Pt julgar

**judge** *n* En
De Richter *(m)*
Es juez *(m)*
Fr juge *(m)*
It giudice *(m)*
Pt juiz *(m)*

**judgment** *n* En
De Urteil *(n)*
Es juicio; adjudicación *(m f)*
Fr jugement; arrêt *(m)*
It giudizio *(m)*
Pt julgamento *(m)*

**juego limpio** *(m)* Es
De anständige Handlungsweise *(f)*
En fair play
Fr traitement juste *(m)*
It condotta leale *(f)*
Pt jogo limpo *(m)*

**juez** *(m)* *n* Es
De Richter *(m)*
En judge
Fr. juge *(m)*
It giudice *(m)*
Pt juiz *(m)*

**juez árbitro** *(m)* Es
De Schiedsobmann *(m)*
En umpire
Fr surarbitre *(m)*
It terzo arbitro *(m)*
Pt juiz árbitro *(m)*

**jugar a la Bolsa** Es
De die Börse spielen
En gamble on the stock exchange
Fr jouer à la Bourse
It giocare in Borsa
Pt jogar na Bolsa

**juge** *(m)* *n* Fr
De Richter *(m)*
En judge
Es juez *(m)*
It giudice *(m)*
Pt juiz *(m)*

**jugement** *(m)* *n* Fr
De Urteil *(n)*
En judgment
Es juicio; adjudicación *(m f)*
It giudizio *(m)*
Pt julgamento *(m)*

**juger** *vb* Fr
De urteilen
En judge
Es juzgar
It giudicare
Pt julgar

**juicio** *(m)* n Es
De Urteil *(n)*
En judgment
Fr jugement; arrêt *(m)*
It giudizio *(m)*
Pt julgamento *(m)*

**juiz** *(m)* n Pt
De Richter *(m)*
En judge
Es juez *(m)*
Fr juge *(m)*
It giudice *(m)*

**juiz árbitro** *(m)* Pt
De Schiedsobmann *(m)*
En umpire
Es juez árbitro *(m)*
Fr surarbitre *(m)*
It terzo arbitro *(m)*

**julgamento** *(m)* n Pt
De Urteil *(n)*
En judgment
Es juicio; adjudicación *(m f)*
Fr jugement; arrêt *(m)*
It giudizio *(m)*

**julgar** *vb* Pt
De urteilen
En judge
Es juzgar
Fr juger
It giudicare

**jüngerer Teilhaber** *(m)* De
En junior partner
Es segundo asociado *(m)*
Fr associé en second *(m)*
It socio giovane *(m)*
Pt sócio junior *(m)*

**junior partner** En
De jüngerer Teilhaber *(m)*
Es segundo asociado *(m)*
Fr associé en second *(m)*
It socio giovane *(m)*
Pt sócio junior *(m)*

**jurado** *(m)* n Es
De die Geschworenen; Jury
*(pl; f)*
En jury
Fr jury *(m)*
It giuria *(f)*
Pt juri *(m)*

**juri** *(m)* n Pt
De die Geschworenen; Jury
*(pl; f)*
En jury
Es tribunal de jurados *(m)*
Fr jury *(m)*
It giuria *(f)*

**juridiction** *(f)* n Fr
De Rechtsprechung; Gerichts-
barkeit *(f)*
En jurisdiction
Es jurisdicción *(f)*
It giurisdizione *(f)*
Pt jurisdição *(f)*

**jurisdição** *(f)* n Pt
De Rechtsprechung; Gerichts-
barkeit *(f)*
En jurisdiction
Es jurisdicción *(f)*
Fr juridiction *(f)*
It giurisdizione *(f)*

**jurisdicción** *(f)* n Es
De Rechtsprechung; Gerichts-
barkeit *(f)*
En jurisdiction
Fr juridiction *(f)*
It giurisdizione *(f)*
Pt jurisdição *(f)*

**jurisdiction** n En
De Rechtsprechung; Gerichts-
barkeit *(f)*
Es jurisdicción *(f)*
Fr juridiction *(f)*
It giurisdizione *(f)*
Pt jurisdição *(f)*

**juro** *(m)* n Pt
De Zinsen *(m pl)*
En interest
Es interés *(m)*
Fr intérêt; prime *(m f)*
It interesse *(m)*

**juro acumulado** *(m)* Pt
De aufgelaufene Zinsen *(m pl)*
En accrued interest
Es interés acumulado *(m)*
Fr intérêts accumulés *(m pl)*
It interesse maturato *(m)*

**juro composto** *(m)* Pt
De Zinsezinsen *(m pl)*
En compound interest
Es interés compuesto *(m)*

Fr intérêts composés *(m pl)*
It interesse composto *(m)*

**juro de bodemeria** *(m)* Pt
De Bodmereidarlehenszinsen
*(m pl)*
En bottomry interest
Es interés de préstamo a la
gruesa *(m)*
Fr profit maritime *(m)*
It interessenza a cambio ma-
rittimo *(f)*

**juro de mora** *(m)* Pt
De Kursabschlag *(m)*
En backwardation
Es prima de aplazamiento *(f)*
Fr déport *(m)*
It deporto *(m)*

**juro simples** *(m)* Pt
De einfache Zinsen *(m pl)*
En simple interest
Es interés simple *(m)*
Fr intérêts simples *(m pl)*
It interesse semplice *(m)*

**jury** n En, Fr *(m)*
De die Geschworenen; Jury
*(pl; f)*
Es jurado *(m)*
It giuria *(f)*
Pt juri *(m)*

**justiça** *(f)* n Pt
De Gerechtigkeit *(f)*
En justice
Es justicia *(f)*
Fr justice *(f)*
It giustizia *(f)*

**justice** n En, Fr *(f)*
De Gerechtigkeit *(f)*
Es justicia *(f)*
It giustizia *(f)*
Pt justiça *(f)*

**justicia** *(f)* n Es
De Gerechtigkeit *(f)*
En justice
Fr justice *(f)*
It giustizia *(f)*
Pt justiça *(f)*

**justifiable** *adj* En
De gerechtfertigt
Es justificable; legítimo
Fr légitime

It  giustificabile; legittimo
Pt  justificável

**justificable** *adj* Es
De  gerechtfertigt
En  justifiable
Fr  légitime
It  giustificabile; legittimo
Pt  justificável

**justificável** *adj* Pt
De  gerechtfertigt
En  justifiable
Es  justificable; legítimo
Fr  légitime
It  giustificabile; legittimo

**juzgar** *vb* Es
De  urteilen
En  judge
Fr  juger
It  giudicare
Pt  julgar

# K

**Kabelauszahlung** *(f)* n De
En  telegraphic transfer
Es  giro telegráfico *(m)*
Fr  virement télégraphique *(m)*
It  rimessa telegrafica *(f)*
Pt  transferência telegráfica *(f)*

**Kaffee** *(m)* n De
En  coffee
Es  café *(m)*
Fr  café *(m)*
It  caffè *(m)*
Pt  café *(m)*

**Kai** *(m)* n De
En  quay; wharf
Es  muelle *(m)*
Fr  quai *(m)*
It  banchina; scalo *(f m)*
Pt  cais *(m)*

**Kaigeld** *(n)* n De
En  wharfage
Es  muellaje *(m)*
Fr  quayage *(m)*
It  diritto di sosta *(m)*
Pt  atracagem *(m)*

**Kalender** *(m)* n De
En  calendar
Es  calendario *(m)*
Fr  calendrier *(m)*
It  calendario *(m)*
Pt  calendário *(m)*

**Kalenderjahr** *(n)* n De
En  calendar year
Es  año civil *(m)*
Fr  année civile *(f)*
It  anno solare *(m)*
Pt  ano civil *(m)*

**Kalkulator** *(m)* n De
En  cost accountant
Es  contable de costes *(m)*
Fr  comptable de prix de
     revient *(m)*
It  contabile dei costi di
     produzione *(m)*
Pt  calculador de custos *(m)*

**Kampagne** *(f)* n De
En  campaign
Es  campaña *(f)*
Fr  campagne *(f)*
It  campagna *(f)*
Pt  campanha *(f)*

**Kanal** *(m)* n De
En  canal
Es  canal *(m)*
Fr  canal *(m)*
It  canale *(m)*
Pt  canal *(m)*

**Kapital** *(n)* n De
En  capital; principal
Es  capital; principal *(m)*
Fr  capital; principal *(m)*
It  capitale *(m)*
Pt  capital *(m)*

**Kapitalanlage** *(f)* n De
En  investment
Es  inversión *(f)*
Fr  investissement; placement
     *(m)*
It  investimento *(m)*
Pt  investimento *(m)*

**Kapitalauslagen** *(f pl)* n De
En  capital expenditure
Es  inmovilizaciones *(f pl)*
Fr  immobilisations *(f pl)*
It  immobilizzazioni *(f pl)*

Pt  despesas em termos de
     capital *(f pl)*

**Kapitaleinkommen** *(n)* n De
En  unearned income
Es  rentas *(f pl)*
Fr  rente *(f)*
It  reddito di capitale *(m)*
Pt  rendimento do capital *(m)*

**Kapitalerhöhung** *(f)* n De
En  increase of capital
Es  aumento de capital *(m)*
Fr  augmentation de capital *(f)*
It  aumento di capitale *(m)*
Pt  aumento de capital *(m)*

**Kapitalertrag** *(m)* n De
En  return on capital
Es  beneficio sobre capital *(m)*
Fr  rémunération du capital *(f)*
It  reddito del capitale *(m)*
Pt  juro sobre o capital *(m)*

**Kapitalertragsteuer** *(f)* n De
En  capital gains tax
Es  impuesto sobre las ganan-
     cias de capital *(m)*
Fr  impôt sur les plus-values
     en capital *(m)*
It  imposta sul plusvalore di
     capitale *(f)*
Pt  imposto sobre lucros de
     capital *(m)*

**Kapitalgewinn** *(n)* n De
En  capital gains
Es  beneficios sobre capital *(m
     pl)*
Fr  gains en capital *(m pl)*
It  plusvalore di capitale *(m pl)*
Pt  lucros de capital *(m pl)*

**Kapitalherabsetzung** *(f)* n De
En  reduction of capital
Es  reducción de capital *(f)*
Fr  réduction du capital *(f)*
It  riduzione del capitale *(f)*
Pt  redução de capital *(f)*

**Kapitalhilfe** *(f)* n De
En  capital grants
Es  subvención de capital *(f)*
Fr  subventions en capital *(f pl)*
It  sovvenzioni di capitale *(f pl)*
Pt  subvenções de capital *(f pl)*

**kapitalintensiv** *adj* De
En capital-intensive
Es intensivo de capital
Fr intensif de capital
It concentrato sul capitale
Pt intensivo em termos de capital

**kapitalisieren** *vb* De
En capitalize
Es capitalizar
Fr capitaliser
It capitalizzare
Pt capitalizar

**kapitalisierter Wert** *(m)* De
En capitalized value
Es valor capitalizado *(m)*
Fr valeur capitalisée *(f)*
It valore capitalizzato *(m)*
Pt valor capitalizado *(m)*

**Kapitalisierung** *(f)* n De
En capitalization
Es capitalización *(f)*
Fr capitalisation *(f)*
It capitalizzazione *(f)*
Pt capitalização *(f)*

**Kapitalismus** *(m)* n De
En capitalism
Es capitalismo *(m)*
Fr capitalisme *(m)*
It capitalismo *(m)*
Pt capitalismo *(m)*

**Kapitalkonto** *(n)* n De
En capital account
Es cuenta de capital *(f)*
Fr compte capital *(m)*
It conto capitale *(m)*
Pt conta de capital *(f)*

**Kapitalreserve** *(f)* n De
En capital reserves
Es reserva de capital *(f)*
Fr réserve de capitaux *(f)*
It riserva di capitale *(f)*
Pt reservas de capital *(f pl)*

**Kapitalverlust** *(m)* n De
En capital loss
Es pérdida de capital *(f)*
Fr perte de capital *(f)*
It perdita di capitale *(f)*
Pt perdas de capital *(f pl)*

**Kapitän** *(m)* n De
En master of a ship
Es capitán de navío *(m)*
Fr capitaine *(m)*
It capitano di nave *(m)*
Pt capitão de navio *(m)*

**Karte** *(f)* n De
En card
Es tarjeta *(f)*
Fr carte *(f)*
It scheda *(f)*
Pt cartão *(m)*

**Kartei** *(f)* n De
En card-index file
Es archivo de fichas *(m)*
Fr fichier *(m)*
It schedario *(m)*
Pt ficheiro com indice *(m)*

**Kartell** *(n)* n De
En cartel
Es cartel *(m)*
Fr cartel *(m)*
It cartello *(m)*
Pt cartel *(m)*

**Karton** *(m)* n De
En carton
Es cartón *(m)*
Fr carton *(m)*
It cartone *(m)*
Pt caixa de cartão *(f)*

**Kartothek** *(f)* n De
En card index
Es fichero *(m)*
Fr fichier *(m)*
It schedario *(m)*
Pt ficheiro *(m)*

**Kaskoversicherung** *(f)* n De
En hull insurance
Es seguro del casco *(m)*
Fr assurance sur le corps *(f)*
It assicurazione corpo *(m)*
Pt seguro do casco *(m)*

**Kassageschäft** *(n)* n De
En cash sale
Es venta al conta *(f)*
Fr vente au comptant *(f)*
It vendita a contanti *(f)*
Pt venda a dinheiro *(f)*

**Kasse** *(f)* n De
En cash-desk
Es caja *(f)*
Fr caisse *(f)*
It cassa *(f)*
Pt caixa *(f)*

**Kassenbuch** *(n)* n De
En cash book
Es libro de caja *(m)*
Fr livre de caisse *(m)*
It libro cassa *(m)*
Pt livro de caixa *(m)*

**Kassenpension** *(f)* n De
En contributory pension
Es retiro contributivo *(m)*
Fr retraite de régime à cotisations *(f)*
It pensione a contributi *(f)*
Pt reforma de contribuição prévia *(f)*

**Kassenreserve** *(f)* n De
En cash reserve
Es reserva en efectivo *(f)*
Fr réserve en espèces *(f)*
It riserva in contanti *(f)*
Pt reserva em dinheiro *(f)*

**Kassensaldo** *(m)* n De
En cash balance
Es resto en efectivo *(m)*
Fr solde de caisse *(m)*
It residuo di cassa *(m)*
Pt saldo em dinheiro *(m)*

**Kassierer** *(m)* n De
En cashier
Am teller
Es cajero *(m)*
Fr caissier *(m)*
It cassiere *(m)*
Pt caixa *(m)*

**Katalog** *(m)* n De
En catalogue
Es catálogo *(m)*
Fr catalogue *(m)*
It catalogo *(m)*
Pt catálogo *(m)*

**Kauf** *(m)* n De
En purchase
Es compra *(f)*
Fr achat *(m)*
It compra *(f)*
Pt compra *(f)*

**Kaufabneigung** *(f)* n De
En sales resistance
Es dificultades de ventas *(f pl)*
Fr résistance à la vente *(f)*
It difficoltà di vendita *(f)*
Pt resistência contra vendas *(f)*

**kaufen** *vb* De
En buy
Es comprar
Fr acheter
It comprare
Pt comprar

**Käufer** *(m)* n De
En buyer
Es comprador *(m)*
Fr acheteur *(m)*
It compratore *(m)*
Pt comprador *(m)*

**Kaufkraft** *(f)* n De
En purchasing power
Es poder de compra *(m)*
Fr pouvoir d'achat *(m)*
It potere d'acquisto *(m)*
Pt poder de compra *(m)*

**Kaufmann** *(m)* n De
En merchant
Es comerciante *(m)*
Fr négociant *(m)*
It commerciante *(m)*
Pt comerciante *(m)*

**Kaufoption** *(f)* n De
En call option
Es opción de compras *(f)*
Fr option *(f)*
It premio d'acquisto *(m)*
Pt opção de compra *(f)*

**Kaufpreis** *(m)* n De
En purchase price
Es precio de compra *(m)*
Fr prix d'achat *(m)*
It prezzo d'acquisto *(m)*
Pt preço de compra *(m)*

**Kaufvertrag** *(m)* n De
En bill of sale
Es escritura de venta *(f)*
Fr acte de vente *(f)*
It contratto di vendita *(m)*
Pt escritura de venda *(f)*

**Kavaliersabkommen** *(n)* n De
En gentleman's agreement
Es acuerdo sobre palabra *(m)*
Fr convention verbale *(f)*
It accordo sulla parola *(m)*
Pt pacto de honra *(m)*

**keep** *vb* En
De behalten; unterhalten
Es tener; conservar
Fr tenir; maintenir
It tenere; mantenere
Pt manter; reter

**keep in stock** En
De vorrätig halten
Es guardar en almacén
Fr garder en stock
It tenere in magazzino
Pt reter em armazém

**keep the accounts** En
De Konto führen
Es llevar la contabilidad
Fr tenir la comptabilité
It tenere la contabilità
Pt fazer a contabilidade

**Kenntnis** *(f)* n De
En knowledge
Es conocimientos *(m pl)*
Fr connaissance *(f)*
It conoscenza *(f)*
Pt conhecimento *(m)*

**Kettengeschäft** *(n)* n De
En chain store
Es sucursal de cadena de almacenes *(f)*
Fr magasin à succursales multiples *(m)*
It negozio a catena *(m)*
Pt sucursal de cadeia de armazéns *(f)*

**key** (for locks, etc.) n En
De Schlüssel *(m)*
Es llave *(f)*
Fr clef *(f)*
It chiave *(f)*
Pt chave *(f)*

**key** (of typewriter, etc.) n En
De Taste *(f)*
Es tecla *(f)*
Fr touche *(f)*
It tasto *(m)*
Pt tecla *(f)*

**key industry** En
De Schlüsselindustrie *(f)*
Es industria clave *(f)*
Fr industrie-clef *(f)*
It industria chiave *(f)*
Pt indústria chave *(f)*

**key-punch** n En
De manueller Locher *(m)*
Es perforación en clave *(f)*
Fr perforatrice à clavier *(f)*
It perforatore *(f)*
Pt perforador *(m)*

**Klausel** *(f)* n De
En clause
Es cláusula *(f)*
Fr clause *(f)*
It clausola *(f)*
Pt cláusula *(f)*

**Kleinanzeige** *(f)* n De
En classified advertisement
Es anuncio por palabras *(m)*
Fr petite annonce *(f)*
It piccola pubblicità *(f)*
Pt anúncios classificados *(m pl)*

**kleine Kasse** *(f)* De
En petty cash
Es caja menor *(f)*
Fr petite caisse *(f)*
It piccola cassa *(f)*
Pt despesas de caixa *(f pl)*

**Kleingeld** *(n)* n De
En small change
Es moneda suelta *(f)*
Fr petite monnaie *(f)*
It spiccioli *(m pl)*
Pt troco miúdo *(m)*

**Klimatisierung** *(f)* n De
En air-conditioning
Es acondicionamiento de aire *(m)*
Fr climatisation *(f)*
It condizionamento dell'aria *(m)*
Pt condicionamento do ar *(m)*

**Knappheit** *(f)* n De
En short supply
Es escasez *(f)*
Fr disette *(f)*
It scarsezza *(f)*
Pt escassez *(f)*

**knitted goods** En
De Strickwaren *(f pl)*
Es géneros de punto *(m pl)*
Fr bonneterie *(f)*
It maglieria *(f)*
Pt artigos de malha de lã *(m pl)*

**knot** *n* En
De Knoten *(m)*
Es nudo *(m)*
Fr nœud *(m)*
It nodo *(m)*
Pt nó *(m)*

**Knoten** *(m)* n De
En knot
Es nudo *(m)*
Fr nœud *(m)*
It nodo *(m)*
Pt nó *(m)*

**knowledge** *n* En
De Kenntnis *(f)*
Es conocimientos *(m pl)*
Fr connaissance *(f)*
It conoscenza *(f)*
Pt conhecimento *(m)*

**Kohle** *(f)* n De
En coal
Es carbón *(m)*
Fr charbon; houille *(m f)*
It carbone *(m)*
Pt carvão *(m)*

**Kohlenrevier** *(n)* n De
En coal field
Es yacimiento de carbón *(m)*
Fr bassin houiller *(m)*
It bacino carbonifero *(m)*
Pt jazigo de carvão *(m)*

**Kohlepapier** *(n)* n De
En carbon paper
Es papel carbón *(m)*
Fr papier carbone *(m)*
It carta carbone *(f)*
Pt papel químico *(m)*

**kombinierte Versicherung** *(f)* De
En comprehensive insurance
Es seguro combinado *(m)*
Fr assurance combinée *(f)*
It assicurazione mista *(f)*
Pt seguro compreensivo *(m)*

**Kommanditgesellschaft** *(f)* n De
En limited partnership
Es sociedad en comandita *(f)*
Fr société en commandité *(f)*
It società in accomandita semplice *(f)*
Pt sociedade em comandita *(f)*

**Kommission** *(f)* n De
En committee
Es comité *(m)*
Fr comité *(f)*
It comitato *(m)*
Pt comité *(m)*

**Kommissionär** *(m)* n De
En commission agent
Es comisionista *(m)*
Fr commissionnaire en marchandises *(m)*
It commissionario *(m)*
Pt comissionista *(m)*

**Kommissionsgüter** *(n pl)* n De
En goods on consignment
Es mercancías en consignación *(f pl)*
Fr marchandises en consignation *(f pl)*
It merce in conto deposito *(f)*
Pt artigos à consignação *(m pl)*

**Kommunal-** De
En municipal
Es municipal
Fr communal
It municipale
Pt municipal

**Konflikt** *(m)* n De
En conflict
Es conflicto *(m)*
Fr cõnflit *(m)*
It conflitto *(m)*
Pt conflito *(m)*

**Kongress** *(m)* n De
En conference
Es conferencia *(f)*
Fr conférence *(f)*
It conferenza *(f)*
Pt conferência *(f)*

**Konjunkturzyklus** *(m)* n De
En business cycle
Es ciclo económico *(m)*
Fr cycle économique *(m)*
It ciclo d'affari *(m)*
Pt ciclo económico *(m)*

**Konkurrenz machen** De
En compete
Es competir
Fr concurrencer
It competere
Pt competir

**Konkurs** *(m)* n De
En bankruptcy
Es quiebra *(f)*
Fr faillite *(f)*
It fallimento *(m)*
Pt falência *(f)*

**Konkurs anmelden** De
En go bankrupt
Es caer en quiebra
Fr faire faillite
It fallire
Pt falir

**Konkursverwalter** *(m)* n De
En (official) receiver
Es sindico *(m)*
Fr syndic de faillite *(m)*
It curatore *(m)*
Pt sindico *(m)*

**Konnossement** *(n)* n De
En bill of lading
Es conocimiento (de embarque) *(m)*
Fr connaissement *(m)*
It polizza di carico *(f)*
Pt conhecimento *(m)*

**konsignieren** *vb* De
En consign
Es consignar
Fr consigner
It consegnare
Pt consignar

**konsolidiert** *adj* De
En consolidated
Es consolidado
Fr consolidé
It consolidato
Pt consolidado

**konsolidierter Kontenab-schluss** *(m)* De
En consolidated accounts
Es cuentas consolidadas *(f pl)*
Fr comptes consolidés *(m pl)*
It conti consolidati *(m pl)*
Pt contas consolidadas *(f pl)*

**Konsortium** *(n)* n De
En consortium
Es consorcio *(m)*
Fr consortium *(m)*
It consorzio *(m)*
Pt consórcio *(m)*

**Konsul** *(m)* n De
En consul
Es cónsul *(m)*
Fr consul *(m)*
It console *(m)*
Pt cônsul *(m)*

**Konsulat** *(n)* n De
En consulate
Es consulado *(m)*
Fr consulat *(m)*
It consolato *(m)*
Pt consulado *(m)*

**Konsulatsfaktura** *(f)* n De
En consular invoice
Es factura consular *(f)*
Fr facture consulaire *(f)*
It fattura consolare *(f)*
Pt factura consular *(f)*

**Konsumgüter** *(n pl)* n De
En consumer goods
Es bienes de consumo *(m pl)*
Fr biens de consommation *(m pl)*
It beni di consumo *(m pl)*
Pt bens de consumo *(m pl)*

**Kontaktgruppenleiter** *(m)* n De
En account executive
Es ejecutivo de cuenta *(m)*
Fr chef de comptes client *(m)*
It direttore conto cliente *(m)*
Pt chefe de conta de cliente *(m)*

**Konto** *(n)* n De
En account
Es cuenta *(f)*
Fr compte *(m)*
It conto *(m)*
Pt conta *(f)*

**Kontoauszug** *(m)* n De
En statement of account
Es extracto de cuenta *(m)*
Fr relevé de compte *(m)*
It estratto conto *(m)*
Pt extracto de conta *(m)*

**Kontobuch** *(n)* n De
En account book
Es libro de cuentas *(m)*
Fr livre de compte *(m)*
It libro di conti *(m)*
Pt livro de contas *(m)*

**Konto führen** De
En keep the accounts
Es llevar la contabilidad
Fr tenir la comptabilité
It tenere la contabilità
Pt fazer a contabilidade

**Kontokorrent** *(n)* n De
En current account
Am checking account
Es cuenta corriente *(f)*
Fr compte courant *(m)*
It conto corrente *(m)*
Pt conta corrente *(f)*

**Konto übergezogen** De
En account overdrawn
Es cuenta en descubierto *(f)*
Fr compte découvert *(m)*
It conto scoperto *(m)*
Pt conta a descoberto *(f)*

**Kontrolleur** *(m)* n De
En controller
Es interventor *(m)*
Fr contrôleur *(m)*
It controllore *(m)*
Pt controlador *(m)*

**Kontrollkonto** *(n)* n De
En control account
Es cuenta de control *(f)*
Fr compte de contrôle *(m)*
It conto di controllo *(m)*
Pt conta de controlo *(f)*

**Kontrollziffer** *(f)* n De
En check digit
Es número de control *(m)*
Fr digit de contrôle *(m)*
It cifra di controllo *(f)*
Pt dígito de controle *(m)*

**Konventionalstrafe** *(f)* n De
En liquidated damages
Es daños liquidados *(m pl)*
Fr dommages-intérêts fixés en argent *(m pl)*
It danni liquidati *(m pl)*
Pt danos liquidados *(m pl)*

**Konversion** *(f)* n De
En conversion
Es conversión *(f)*
Fr conversion *(f)*
It conversione *(f)*
Pt conversão *(f)*

**konvertierbar** *adj* De
En convertible
Es convertible
Fr convertible
It convertibile
Pt convertível

**konvertieren** *vb* De
En convert
Es convertir
Fr convertir
It convertire
Pt convertir

**Konzept** *(n)* n De
En draft
Es borrador *(m)*
Fr projet *(m)*
It bozza *(f)*
Pt rascunho *(m)*

**Konzession** *(f)* n De
En concession; franchise
Es concesión *(f)*
Fr concession *(f)*
It concessione *(f)*
Pt concessão *(f)*

**kopieren** *vb* De
En copy
Es copiar
Fr transcrire
It copiare
Pt copiar

**Körperschaft** *(f)* n De
En corporation
Es corporación *(f)*
Fr corporation *(f)*
It corporazione *(f)*
Pt corporação *(f)*

**körperschaftlich** *adj* De
En corporate
Es corporativo
Fr corporatif
It corporativo
Pt corporativo

**Körperschaftsteuer** *(f) n* De
En corporation tax
Es impuesto sobre renta de la sociedad *(m)*
Fr impôt sur le revenu des sociétés *(m)*
It imposta sui proventi delle società *(f)*
Pt imposto sobre corporação *(m)*

**korrigieren** *vb* De
En correct
Es corregir
Fr corriger
It correggere
Pt corrigir

**kosten** *vb* De
En cost
Es costar
Fr coûter
It costare
Pt custear

**Kosten** *(pl) n* De
En cost; charges
Es coste; gastos *(m; m pl)*
Fr coût; frais *(m; m pl)*
It costo; spese *(m; f pl)*
Pt custo; despesas *(m; f pl)*

**Kostenanalyse** *(f) n* De
En cost analysis
Es análisis de costes *(m)*
Fr analyse des coûts *(f)*
It analisi dei costi *(f)*
Pt análise de custo *(f)*

**Kostenanschlag** *(m) n* De
En quotation
Es cotización *(f)*
Fr cotation *(f)*
It quotazione *(f)*
Pt cotação *(f)*

**kostenlose Probe** *(f)* De
En free sample
Es muestra gratuita *(f)*
Fr échantillon gratuit *(m)*

It campione gratuito *(m)*
Pt amostra gratis *(f)*

**Kosten und Fracht** De
En cost and freight (c. & f.)
Es coste y flete
Fr coût et fret
It costo e nolo
Pt custo e frete

**Kosten und Vertrag** De
En cost-plus contract
Es contrato al costo más beneficio *(m)*
Fr contrat en régie *(m)*
It contratto in economia *(m)*
Pt contrato de custo e adicionais *(m)*

**kostspielig** *adj* De
En expensive
Es caro
Fr cher
It caro
Pt caro

**krach d'une banque** *(m)* Fr
De Bankkrach *(m)*
En bank crash
Es quiebra de banco *(f)*
It crollo di banca *(m)*
Pt falência bancária *(f)*

**Kran** *(m) n* De
En crane
Es grúa *(f)*
Fr grue *(f)*
It gru *(f)*
Pt grúa *(f)*

**Krankenversicherung** *(f) n* De
En health insurance
Es seguro de enfermedad *(m)*
Fr assurance maladie *(f)*
It assicurazione malattia *(f)*
Pt seguro de obença *(m)*

**Kredit** *(m) n* De
En credit
Es crédito *(m)*
Fr crédit *(m)*
It credito *(m)*
Pt crédito *(m)*

**Kreditbank** *(f) n* De
En lending bank
Es banco de préstamos *(m)*
Fr banque de prêts *(f)*

It banca di prestiti *(f)*
Pt banco de empréstimos *(m)*

**Kreditbrief** *(m) n* De
En letter of credit
Es carta de crédito *(f)*
Fr lettre de crédit *(f)*
It lettera di credito *(f)*
Pt carta de crédito *(f)*

**Kreditfähigkeit** *(f) n* De
En borrowing power
Es facultad de crédito *(f)*
Fr capacité à avoir du crédit *(f)*
It capacità creditizia *(f)*
Pt potencial de obtenção de crédito *(m)*

**Kreditkarte** *(f) n* De
En credit card
Es tarjeta de crédito *(f)*
Fr carte de crédit *(f)*
It carta di credito *(f)*
Pt cartão de crédito *(m)*

**Kreditklemme** *(f) n* De
En credit squeeze
Es escasez de créditos *(f)*
Fr resserrement de crédit *(m)*
It restrizione di credito *(f)*
Pt restrição de crédito *(f)*

**Kreditnehmer** *(m) n* De
En borrower
Es prestatario *(m)*
Fr emprunteur *(m)*
It accattatore *(m)*
Pt beneficiário de empréstimo *(m)*

**Kreditoren** *(m pl) n* De
En accounts payable
Es cuentas a pagar *(f pl)*
Fr comptes à payer *(m pl)*
It conti passivi *(m pl)*
Pt contas a pagar *(f pl)*

**Kreditsaldo** *(m) n* De
En credit balance
Es saldo acreedor *(m)*
Fr solde créditeur *(m)*
It saldo creditore *(m)*
Pt saldo credor *(m)*

**Kreditversicherung** *(f) n* De
En credit insurance
Es seguro crediticio *(m)*

**Fr** assurance crédit *(f)*
**It** assicurazione credito *(f)*
**Pt** seguro de crédito *(m)*


**Kreditwürdigkeit** *(f) n* De
**En** credit rating
**Es** límite de crédito *(m)*
**Fr** degré de solvabilité *(m)*
**It** stima del credito *(f)*
**Pt** nível de crédito *(m)*


**Krieg** *(m) n* De
**En** war
**Es** guerra *(f)*
**Fr** guerre *(f)*
**It** guerra *(f)*
**Pt** guerra *(f)*


**Kriegsrisikoversicherung** *(f) n*
De
**En** war-risk insurance
**Es** seguro contra riesgo de
guerra *(m)*
**Fr** assurance du risque de
guerre *(f)*
**It** assicurazione contro i rischi
di guerra *(f)*
**Pt** seguro contra risco de
guerra *(m)*


**Kubikinhalt** *(m) n* De
**En** cubic capacity
**Es** capacidad cúbica *(f)*
**Fr** volume *(m)*
**It** volume *(m)*
**Pt** capacidade cúbica *(f)*


**kumulativ** *adj* De
**En** cumulative
**Es** acumulativo
**Fr** cumulatif
**It** cumulativo
**Pt** cumulativo


**kumulative Vorzugsaktien** *(f
pl)* De
**En** cumulative preference
shares
**Es** valores privilegiados cumulativos *(m pl)*
**Fr** actions de priorité cumulatives *(f pl)*
**It** azioni preferenziali cumulative *(f pl)*
**Pt** acções preferenciais cumulativas *(f pl)*


**kündbare Obligation** *(f)* De
**En** redeemable bond
**Es** obligación reembolsable *(f)*
**Fr** obligation amortissable *(f)*
**It** obbligazione redimibile *(f)*
**Pt** obrigação reembolsável *(f)*


**Kunde** *(m) n* De
**En** customer
**Es** cliente *(m)*
**Fr** client *(m)*
**It** cliente *(m)*
**Pt** cliente *(m)*


**Kundenkonto** *(n) n* De
**En** charge account
**Es** cuenta personal *(f)*
**Fr** compte personnel *(m)*
**It** conto personale *(m)*
**Pt** conta pessoal *(f)*


**kündigen (vorläufig)** De
**En** lay off
**Es** despedir
**Fr** licencier
**It** licenziare
**Pt** despedir


**Kündigung (von Geldern)** *(f)*
De
**En** call (for funds)
**Es** llamada (de fondos) *(f)*
**Fr** appel (de fonds) *(m)*
**It** richiesta (di fondi) *(f)*
**Pt** chamada (de fundos) *(f)*


**Kundschaft** *(f) n* De
**En** custom; clientele
**Es** clientela *(f)*
**Fr** clientèle *(f)*
**It** clientela *(f)*
**Pt** clientela *(f)*


**künftig** *adj* De
**En** future
**Es** futuro
**Fr** futur
**It** futuro; avvenire
**Pt** futuro


**Kunstgold** *(n) n* De
**En** imitation gold
**Es** oro de imitación *(m)*
**Fr** similor *(m)*
**It** similoro *(m)*
**Pt** ouro de imitação *(m)*


**Kunstleder** *(n) n* De
**En** imitation leather
**Es** piel de imitación *(f)*
**Fr** similicuir *(m)*
**It** finta pelle *(f)*
**Pt** cabedal de imitação *(m)*


**Kupon** *(m) n* De
**En** coupon
**Es** cupón *(m)*
**Fr** coupon *(m)*
**It** cedola *(f)*
**Pt** cupão *(m)*


**Kursabschlag** *(m) n* De
**En** backwardation
**Es** prima de aplazamiento *(f)*
**Fr** déport *(m)*
**It** deporto *(m)*
**Pt** juro de mora *(m)*


**Kursvergleich** *(m) n* De
**En** arbitrage
**Es** arbitraje *(m)*
**Fr** arbitrage *(m)*
**It** arbitraggio *(m)*
**Pt** arbitragem *(f)*


**kurzfristig** *adj* De
**En** short-term
**Es** a corto plazo
**Fr** à court terme
**It** a breve termine
**Pt** a curto prazo


**kurzfristiger Effekt** *(m)* De
**En** short-dated security
**Es** título a corto plazo *(m)*
**Fr** titre à court terme *(m)*
**It** titolo a breve scadenza *(m)*
**Pt** título a curto prazo *(m)*


**kurzfristiges Kapital** *(n)* De
**En** short-term capital
**Es** capital a corto plazo *(m)*
**Fr** capitaux à court terme *(m
pl)*
**It** capitale a breve termine
*(m)*
**Pt** capital a curto prazo *(m)*


**kurzlebige Aktiva** *(n pl)* De
**En** wasting assets
**Am** depleting assets
**Es** activo gastable *(m)*
**Fr** actifs défectibles *(m pl)*
**It** attività in esaurimento *(f pl)*

Pt bens em uso ou deteriora-
  ção *(m pl)*

**Kurzschrift** *(f)* n De
En shorthand
Es taquigrafía *(f)*
Fr sténographie *(f)*
It stenografia *(f)*
Pt estenografia *(f)*

**Küstenschiffahrt** *(f)* n De
En cabotage
Es cabotaje *(m)*
Fr cabotage *(m)*
It cabotaggio *(m)*
Pt cabotagem *(f)*

**Kybernetik** *(f)* n De
En cybernetics
Es cibernética *(f)*
Fr cybernétique *(f)*
It cibernetica *(f)*
Pt cibernética *(f)*


# L


**label** n En
De Etikett *(n)*
Es etiqueta *(f)*
Fr étiquette *(f)*
It etichetta *(f)*
Pt rótulo; etiqueta *(m f)*

**laboratoire de langues** *(m)* Fr
De Sprachlabor *(n)*
En language laboratory
Es laboratorio de idiomas *(m)*
It laboratorio di linguaggio
  *(m)*
Pt laboratório de línguas *(m)*

**laboratorio de idiomas** *(m)* Es
De Sprachlabor *(n)*
En language laboratory
Fr laboratoire de langues *(m)*
It laboratorio di linguaggio
  *(m)*
Pt laboratório de línguas *(m)*

**laboratório de línguas** *(m)* Pt
De Sprachlabor *(n)*
En language laboratory
Es laboratorio de idiomas *(m)*
Fr laboratoire de langues *(m)*

It laboratorio di linguaggio
  *(m)*

**laboratorio di linguaggio** *(m)*
  It
De Sprachlabor *(n)*
En language laboratory
Es laboratorio de idiomas *(m)*
Fr laboratoire de langues *(m)*
Pt laboratório de línguas *(m)*

**labour force** En
De Arbeitskräfte *(f pl)*
Es mano de obra *(f)*
Fr main d'œuvre *(m)*
It mano d'opera *(f)*
Pt trabalhadores; mão de obra
  *(m f)*

**labour market** En
De Arbeitsmarkt *(m)*
Es mercado de mano de obra
  *(m)*
Fr marché du travail *(m)*
It mercato della mano
  d'opera *(m)*
Pt mercado de mão de obra
  *(m)*

**labour relations** En
De Arbeitsverhältnisse *(n pl)*
Es relaciones patrón-obrero *(f
  pl)*
Fr rapports du travail *(m pl)*
It relazioni con la mano
  d'opera *(f pl)*
Pt relações de trabalho *(f pl)*

**labour turnover** En
De Arbeitsumsatz *(m)*
Es movimiento de la mano de
  obra *(m)*
Fr fluctuations de personnel *(f
  pl)*
It movimento della mano
  d'opera *(m)*
Pt movimento de trabalha-
  dores *(m)*

**labour union** En
De Gewerkschaft *(f)*
Es sindicato obrero *(m)*
Fr syndicat *(m)*
It sindacato operaio *(m)*
Pt sindicato *(m)*

**Ladelinie** *(f)* n De
En loadline
Es linea de carga *(f)*
Fr ligne de charge *(f)*
It linea di carico *(f)*
Pt linha limite de carga *(f)*

**Laden** *(m)* n De
En shop
Es tienda *(f)*
Fr magasin *(m)*
It bottega *(f)*
Pt loja *(f)*

**Ladeplan** *(m)* n De
En stowage plan
Es plan de estiba *(m)*
Fr plan d'arrimage *(m)*
It piano di stivaggio *(m)*
Pt plano de estiva *(m)*

**Laderaum** *(m)* n De
En hold
Es bodega *(f)*
Fr cale *(f)*
It stiva *(f)*
Pt porão *(m)*

**Ladung** *(f)* n De
En cargo; loading
Es carga *(f)*
Fr cargaison; chargement *(f
  m)*
It carico; caricamento *(m)*
Pt carga; carregamento *(f m)*

**Ladungsverzeichnis** *(n)* n De
En manifest
Es manifiesto *(m)*
Fr manifeste *(m)*
It manifesto *(m)*
Pt manifesto *(m)*

**Lager** *(n)* n De
En store
Es almacén *(m)*
Fr magasin *(m)*
It magazzino *(m)*
Pt armazém *(m)*

**Lagergeld** *(n)* n De
En storage charges
Es gastos de almacenaje *(m
  pl)*
Fr frais de magasinage *(m pl)*
It spese di magazzinaggio *(f
  pl)*

Pt encargos de armazena-
   mento *(m pl)*

**lagern** *vb* De
En store
Es almacenar
Fr emmagasiner
It immagazzinare
Pt armazenar

**Lagerschein** *(m) n* De
En warrant
Es certificado *(m)*
Fr certificat *(m)*
It certificato *(m)*
Pt certificado *(m)*

**Lagerung** *(f) n* De
En storage
Es almacenamiento *(m)*
Fr emmagasinage *(m)*
It maggazzinaggio *(m)*
Pt armazenamento *(m)*

**Lager unter Zollverschluss** *(n)*
   De
En bonded warehouse
Es almacén de aduanas *(m)*
Fr entrepôt *(m)*
It magazzino doganale *(m)*
Pt armazém alfandegário *(m)*

**Lagerverwaltung** *(f) n* De
En stock control
Es fiscalización de las existen-
   cias *(f)*
Fr contrôle des stocks *(m)*
It controllo scorte *(m)*
Pt controlo de existências *(m)*

**lagnanza** *(f) n* It
De Beschwerde *(f)*
En grievance
Es agravio *(m)*
Fr grief *(m)*
Pt agravo *(m)*

**laminado a ouro** Pt
De vergoldet
En gold-plated
Es chapado en oro
Fr plaqué d'or
It placcato in oro

**lançamento** *(m) n* Pt
De Eintragung *(f)*
En entry
Es asiento *(m)*

Fr inscription *(f)*
It registrazione *(f)*

**lançamento duplo** *(m)* Pt
De doppelte Buchführung *(f)*
En double entry book-keeping
Es partida doble *(f)*
Fr partie double *(f)*
It partita doppia *(f)*

**lançar** (um produto) *vb* Pt
De auf den Markt bringen
En launch
Es lanzar
Fr lancer sur le marché
It lanciare

**lançar uma empresa** Pt
De eine Gesellschaft gründen
En float a company
Es lanzar una compañía
Fr lancer une entreprise
It lanciare una società

**lançar um empréstimo** Pt
De eine Anleihe begeben
En float a loan
Am raise a loan
Es emitir un empréstito
Fr émettre un emprunt
It lanciare un prestito

**lancer sur le marché** Fr
De auf den Markt bringen
En launch
Es lanzar
It lanciare
Pt lançar

**lancer une entreprise** Fr
De eine Gesellschaft gründen
En float a company
Es lanzar una compañía
It lanciare una società
Pt lançar uma empresa

**lanciare** (un prodotto) *vb* It
De auf den Markt bringen
En launch
Es lanzar
Fr lancer sur le marché
Pt lançar

**lanciare una società** It
De eine Gesellschaft gründen
En float a company
Es lanzar una compañía

Fr lancer une entreprise
Pt lançar uma empresa

**lanciare un prestito** It
De eine Anleihe begeben
En float a loan
Am raise a loan
Es emitir un empréstito
Fr émettre un emprunt
Pt lançar um empréstimo

**Land** *(n) n* De
En country
Es país *(m)*
Fr pays *(m)*
It paese *(m)*
Pt país *(m)*

**land bank** En
De Landbank *(f)*
Es banco agrícola *(m)*
Fr banque agricole *(f)*
It banca agricola *(f)*
Pt banca d'agricultura *(f)*

**Landbank** *(f) n* De
En land bank
Es banco agrícola *(m)*
Fr banque agricole *(f)*
It banca agricola *(f)*
Pt banca d'agricultura *(f)*

**landing account** En
De Löschungskonto *(n)*
Es cuenta de desembarque *(f)*
Fr compte de mise à terre *(m)*
It conto di sbarco *(m)*
Pt conta de descargas *(f)*

**landlord** (of property) *n* En
De Vermieter *(m)*
Es propietario; arrendador *(m)*
Fr propriétaire *(m)*
It proprietario; locatore *(m)*
Pt proprietário; senhorio *(m)*

**Landwirtschaft** *(f) n* De
En agriculture
Es agricultura *(f)*
Fr agriculture *(f)*
It agricoltura *(f)*
Pt agricultura *(f)*

**langage-machine** *(m) n* Fr
De Maschinensprache *(f)*
En machine language
Es lenguaje de máquina *(m)*

It linguaggio di macchina *(m)*
Pt linguagem da máquina *(f)*

**langfristig** *adj* De
En long-term
Es a largo plazo
Fr à long terme
It a lunga scadenza
Pt a longo prazo

**langfristiges Kapital** *(n)* n De
En long-term capital
Es capital a largo plazo *(m)*
Fr capitaux à long terme *(m pl)*
It capitale consolidato a lunga scadenza *(m)*
Pt capital a longo prazo *(m)*

**langlebige Güter** *(n pl)* De
En durable goods
Es mercancías no perecederas *(f pl)*
Fr biens durables *(m pl)*
It beni durevoli *(m pl)*
Pt mercadorias imperecíveis *(f pl)*

**language** n En
De Sprache *(f)*
Es lingua; lenguaje *(f m)*
Fr langue *(f)*
It lingua; linguaggio *(f m)*
Pt língua *(f)*

**language laboratory** En
De Sprachlabor *(n)*
Es laboratorio de idiomas *(m)*
Fr laboratoire de langues *(m)*
It laboratorio di linguaggio *(m)*
Pt laboratório de línguas *(m)*

**langue** *(f)* n Fr
De Sprache *(f)*
En language
Es lingua *(f)*
It lingua *(f)*
Pt língua *(f)*

**lanzar** (un producto) *vb* Es
De auf den Markt bringen
En launch
Fr lancer sur le marché
It lanciare
Pt lançar

**lanzar una compañía** Es
De eine Gesellschaft gründen
En float a company
Fr lancer une entreprise
It lanciare una società
Pt lançar uma empresa

**last in, first out** (LIFO) En
De LIFO
Es última entrada, primera salida
Fr LIFO
It ultimo a entrare, primo a uscire
Pt último a entrar, primeiro a saír

**Lastkahn** *(m)* n De
En barge
Es barcaza *(f)*
Fr péniche *(f)*
It chiatta *(f)*
Pt barcaça *(f)*

**lastre** *(m)* n Es
De Ballast *(m)*
En ballast
Fr lest *(m)*
It zavorra *(f)*
Pt lastro *(m)*

**lastro** *(m)* n Pt
De Ballast *(m)*
En ballast
Es lastre *(m)*
Fr lest *(m)*
It zavorra *(f)*

**Lastschrift** *(f)* n De
En debit note
Es nota de débito *(f)*
Fr avis de débit *(m)*
It nota di addebito *(f)*
Pt aviso de débito *(m)*

**Lateinamerikanische Freihandelszone** *(f)* De
En Latin American Free Trade Association (LAFTA)
Es Asociación de Mercado Libre de América Latina *(f)*
Fr Association Latine-Américaine de Libre-Échange *(f)*
It Associazione di Libero Scambio dell'America Latine *(f)*
Pt Associação do Comércio Livre da América Latina *(f)*

**latent defect** En
De versteckter Mangel *(m)*
Es defecto latente *(m)*
Fr vice caché *(m)*
It difetto latente *(m)*
Pt defeito latente *(m)*

**latente Steuerpflicht** *(f)* De
En deferred taxation
Es tasación diferida *(f)*
Fr imposition différée *(f)*
It tassazione differita *(f)*
Pt tributação diferida *(f)*

**Latin American Free Trade Association** (LAFTA) En
De Lateinamerikanische Freihandelszone *(f)*
Es Asociación de Mercado Libre de América Latina *(f)*
Fr Association Latine-Américaine de Libre-Échange *(f)*
It Associazione di Libero Scambio dell'America Latine *(f)*
Pt Associação do Comércio Livre da América Latina *(f)*

**laufend** *adj* De
En current
Es corriente
Fr courant; en cours
It corrente
Pt corrente

**laufende Polizze** *(f)* De
En floating policy
Es póliza flotante *(f)*
Fr police flottante *(f)*
It polizza flottante *(f)*
Pt apólice flutuante *(f)*

**laufendes Jahr** *(n)* De
En current year
Es año en curso *(m)*
Fr année en cours *(f)*
It anno in corso *(m)*
Pt ano corrente *(m)*

**laufende Verbindlichkeiten** *(f pl)* De
En current liabilities
Es pasivo exigible *(m)*
Fr passif exigible *(m)*
It passività esigibili *(f pl)*
Pt passivo actual *(m)*

**Laufzeit** (f) n De
En tenor
Es tenor (m)
Fr teneur (f)
It tenore (m)
Pt tenor (m)

**launch** (a product) vb En
De auf den Markt bringen
Es lanzar
Fr lancer sur le marché
It lanciare
Pt lançar

**lavoratore** (m) n It
De Arbeiter (m)
En worker
Es trabajador (m)
Fr ouvrier (m)
Pt trabalhador (m)

**lavoratore del porto** (m) It
De Hafenarbeiter (m)
En docker
Am longshoreman
Es cargador de muelle (m)
Fr docker (m)
Pt trabalhador das docas (m)

**lavoratore indipendente** (m) It
De selbständig Arbeitende(r) (m)
En self-employed person
Es trabajador por cuenta propia (m)
Fr travailleur indépendant (m)
Pt empregado por conta-própria (m)

**lavoro** (m) n It
De Arbeit; Beruf (f m)
En work; occupation
Es trabajo (m)
Fr travail; occupation (m f)
Pt trabalho; ocupação (m f)

**lavoro a cottimo** (m) It
De Akkordarbeit (f)
En piecework
Es trabajo a destajo (m)
Fr travail à la tâche (m)
Pt trabalho por peça (m)

**lavoro a turno** (m) It
De Schichtarbeit (f)
En shiftwork
Es trabajo por torno (m)

Fr travail par équipes (m)
Pt trabalho por turno (m)

**lavoro in corso** (m) It
De Arbeit in der Ausführung (f)
En work in progress
Am work in process
Es trabajo en curso (m)
Fr travaux en cours (m pl)
Pt trabalho em curso (m)

**lavoro in economia** (m) It
De produktive Arbeitskräfte (f pl)
En direct labour
Es jornales directos (m pl)
Fr travail en régie (m)
Pt trabalho directamente produtivo (m)

**lavoro notturno** (m) It
De Nachtarbeit (f)
En nightwork
Es trabajo nocturno (m)
Fr travail de nuit (m)
Pt trabalho nocturno (m)

**lavoro straordinario** (m) It
De Überstunden (f pl)
En overtime
Es horas extraordinarias (f pl)
Fr heures supplémentaires (f pl)
Pt horas extraordinárias (f pl)

**law** n En
De Recht (n)
Es ley (f)
Fr loi (f)
It legge (f)
Pt lei (f)

**lawful** adj En
De gesetzlich; rechtlich
Es lícito; legítimo
Fr licite; légal
It lecito; legittimo
Pt legítimo; legal

**lay days** En
De Liegezeit (f)
Es estadía (f)
Fr staries (f pl)
It stallie (f pl)
Pt estadía (f)

**lay off** En
De (vorläufig) kündigen
Es despedir
Fr licencier
It (temporaneamente) licenziare
Pt despedir

**lay up** (a ship) vb En
De auflegen
Es desarmar
Fr désarmer
It disarmare
Pt desarmar

**lazer** (m) n Pt
De Freizeit (f)
En leisure
Es descanso (m)
Fr loisir (m)
It svago (m)

**leakage** n En
De Lecken (n)
Es escape (m)
Fr fuite (f)
It colaggio (m)
Pt escape; fuga (m f)

**lease** n En
De Verpachtung (f)
Es alquiler (m)
Fr bail (m)
It affitto (m)
Pt aluguer; arrendamento (m)

**leasehold** n En
De Pachtung (f)
Es arrendamiento (m)
Fr tenure à bail (f)
It proprietà fondiaria in affitto (f)
Pt título de arrendamento (m)

**leasing company** En
De Leasinggesellschaft (f)
Es compañía arrendataria (f)
Fr société de leasing (f)
It società di leasing (f)
Pt companhia arrendatária (f)

**Leasinggesellschaft** (f) n De
En leasing company
Es compañía arrendataria (f)
Fr société de leasing (f)
It società di leasing (f)
Pt companhia arrendatária (f)

**leather goods** En
De Lederwaren *(f pl)*
Es marroquinería *(f)*
Fr maroquinerie *(f)*
It pelletterie *(f pl)*
Pt artigos de cabedal *(m pl)*

**Lebenshaltung** *(f)* n De
En standard of living
Es nivel de vida *(m)*
Fr niveau de vie *(m)*
It tenore di vita *(m)*
Pt nível de vida *(m)*

**Lebenshaltungskosten** *(pl)* n
De
En cost of living
Es coste de vida *(m)*
Fr coût de la vie *(m)*
It costo della vita *(m)*
Pt custo de vida *(m)*

**lebenslängliche Nutzniessung**
*(f)* De
En life-interest
Es usufructo vitalicio *(m)*
Fr usufruit viager *(m)*
It usufrutto vitalizio *(m)*
Pt usufruto vitalício *(m)*

**Lebensversicherung** *(f)* n De
En life insurance
Es seguro de vida *(m)*
Fr assurance sur la vie *(f)*
It assicurazione sulla vita *(f)*
Pt seguro de vida *(m)*

**lecito** *adj* It
De gesetzlich
En lawful
Es lícito
Fr licite
Pt legitimo

**Lecken** *(n)* n De
En leakage
Es escape *(m)*
Fr fuite *(f)*
It colaggio *(m)*
Pt escape; fuga *(m f)*

**Lederwaren** *(f pl)* n De
En leather goods
Es marroquinería *(f)*
Fr maroquinerie *(f)*
It pelletterie *(f pl)*
Pt artigos de cabedal *(m pl)*

**ledger** *n* En
De Hauptbuch *(n)*
Es libro mayor *(m)*
Fr grand livre *(m)*
It libro mastro *(m)*
Pt livro-mestre *(m)*

**ledger clerk** En
Am bookkeeper
De Buchhalter *(m)*
Es contable *(m)*
Fr commis-contable *(m)*
It contabile *(m)*
Pt empregado de contabili-
dade *(m)*

**Leerlaufzeit** *(f)* n De
En down time
Es tiempo improductivo *(m)*
Fr temps d'arrêt *(m)*
It tempo improduttivo *(m)*
Pt tempo improdutivo *(m)*

**legal** *adj* De, En, Es, Pt
Fr légal; judiciaire
It legale; giuridico

**légal** *adj* Fr
De rechtsgültig; legal
En legal
Es legal; juridico
It legale; giuridico
Pt legal

**legal action** En
De Prozess; Klage *(m f)*
Es pleito *(m)*
Fr action juridique *(f)*
It processo *(m)*
Pt acção judicial *(f)*

**legale** *adj* It
De rechtsgültig; legal
En legal
Es legal; juridico
Fr légal; judiciaire
Pt legal

**legal holiday** Am
En Bank Holiday
De gesetzlicher Feiertag *(m)*
Es día de fiesta *(m)*
Fr jour férié *(m)*
It festività legali *(f)*
Pt feriado *(m)*

**legal liability** En
De Rechtshaftung *(f)*
Es responsabilidad legal *(f)*
Fr responsabilité légale *(f)*
It responsabilità legale *(f)*
Pt responsabilidade legal *(f)*

**legal representative** En
De Rechtsvertreter *(m)*
Es representante legal *(m)*
Fr représentant mandaté *(m)*
It mandatario *(m)*
Pt representante legal *(m)*

**legal tender** En
De gesetzliches Zahlungsmittel
*(n)*
Es moneda legal *(f)*
Fr monnaie légale *(f)*
It denaro a corso legale *(m)*
Pt moeda legal *(m)*

**legge** *(f)* n It
De Recht *(n)*
En law
Es ley *(f)*
Fr loi *(f)*
Pt lei *(f)*

**legislação** *(f)* n Pt
De Gesetzgebung *(f)*
En legislation
Es legislación *(f)*
Fr législation *(f)*
It legislazione *(f)*

**legislación** *(f)* n Es
De Gesetzgebung *(f)*
En legislation
Fr législation *(f)*
It legislazione *(f)*
Pt legislação *(f)*

**legislation** *n* En
De Gesetzgebung *(f)*
Es legislación *(f)*
Fr législation *(f)*
It legislazione *(f)*
Pt legislação *(f)*

**législation** *(f)* n Fr
De Gesetzgebung *(f)*
En legislation
Es legislación *(f)*
It legislazione *(f)*
Pt legislação *(f)*

**legislazione** (f) n It
De Gesetzgebung (f)
En legislation
Es legislación (f)
Fr législation (f)
Pt legislação (f)

**légitime** adj Fr
De gerechtfertigt; gesetzlich
En justifiable; lawful
Es justificable; legítimo
It giustificabile; legittimo
Pt justificavel; legitimo

**legitimo** adj Es, Pt
De gesetzlich; rechtlich
En lawful; legal
Fr licite; légal
It lecito; legittimo

**Lehre** (Lehrzeit) (f) n De
En apprenticeship
Am trainee period
Es aprendizaje (m)
Fr apprentissage (m)
It tirocinio (m)
Pt aprendizagem (f)

**Lehrling** (m) n De
En apprentice
Am trainee
Es aprendiz (m)
Fr apprenti (m)
It apprendista (m)
Pt aprendiz (m)

**lei** (f) n Pt
De Recht (n)
En law
Es ley (f)
Fr loi (f)
It legge (f)

**Leichter** (m) n De
En lighter
Es barcaza; gabarra (f)
Fr allège (f)
It chiatta (f)
Pt barcaça (f)

**leihen** vb De
En lend
Es prestar
Fr prêter
It prestare
Pt emprestar

**leilão** (m) n Pt
De Versteigerung (f)
En auction
Es subasta (f)
Fr vente aux enchères (f)
It asta (f)

**leiloeiro** (m) n Pt
De Versteigerer (m)
En auctioneer
Es subastador (m)
Fr commissaire-priseur (m)
It venditore all'asta (m)

**Leistungsfähigkeit** (f) n De
En efficiency
Es eficiencia (f)
Fr efficacité (f)
It efficienza (f)
Pt eficiência (f)

**Leistungslohn** (m) n De
En payment by results
Es pago por resultados (m)
Fr salaire au rendement (m)
It pagamento secondo i risultati (m)
Pt pagamento relativo as resultados (m)

**leisure** n En
De Freizeit (f)
Es descanso (m)
Fr loisir (m)
It svago (m)
Pt lazer (m)

**Leitung** (Telefon) (f) n De
En (telephone) line
Es línea (telefónica) (f)
Fr ligne (téléphone) (f)
It linea (telefonica) (f)
Pt linha (telefónica) (f)

**lend** vb En
De leihen
Es prestar
Fr prêter
It prestare
Pt emprestar

**lending bank** En
De Kreditbank (f)
Es banco de préstamos (m)
Fr banque de prêts (f)
It banca di prestiti (f)
Pt banco de empréstimos (m)

**lenguaje de máquina** (m) Es
De Maschinensprache (f)
En machine language
Fr langage-machine (m)
It linguaggio di macchina (m)
Pt linguagem da máquina (f)

**lessee** n En
De Mieter (m)
Es arrendatario (m)
Fr locataire (m)
It locatario (m)
Pt locatário; arrendatário (m)

**lessor** n En
De Vermieter (m)
Es arrendador (m)
Fr bailleur (m)
It locatore (m)
Pt senhorio; arrendador (m)

**lest** (m) n Fr
De Ballast (m)
En ballast
Es lastre (m)
It zavorra (f)
Pt lastro (m)

**letra** (f) n Es, Pt
De Tratte (f)
En draft
Fr traite (f)
It tratta (f)

**letra a la vista** (f) Es
De Sichttratte (f)
En sight draft
Fr traite à vue (f)
It tratta a vista (f)
Pt letra à vista (f)

**letra à vista** (f) Pt
De Sichttratte (f)
En sight draft
Es letra a la vista (f)
Fr traite à vue (f)
It tratta a vista (f)

**letra de adjudicación** (f) Es
De Verteilungsbrief (m)
En allotment letter
Fr avis d'attribution (m)
It lettera da ripartizione (f)
Pt aviso de aporcionamento (m)

**letra de cambio** *(f)* Es
De Wechsel; Tratte *(m f)*
En bill of exchange
Fr lettre de change *(f)*
It tratta cambiale *(f)*
Pt letra de câmbio *(f)*

**letra de câmbio** *(f)* Pt
De Wechsel; Tratte *(m f)*
En bill of exchange
Es letra de cambio *(f)*
Fr lettre de change *(f)*
It tratta cambiale *(f)*

**letra de favor** *(f)* Pt
De Gefälligkeitswechsel *(m)*
En accommodation bill
Es pagaré de favor *(m)*
Fr billet de complaisance *(m)*
It cambiale di favore *(f)*

**letra de país a país (cambial)** *(f)* Pt
De Auslandswechsel *(m)*
En foreign bill
Es letra sobre el exterior *(f)*
Fr lettre de change sur l'étranger *(f)*
It cambiale sull'estero *(f)*

**letra descontada** *(f)* Pt
De Diskontwechsel *(m)*
En discounted bill
Es efecto descontado *(m)*
Fr effet escompté *(m)*
It cambiale scontata *(f)*

**letra em branco** *(f)* Pt
De Blankowechsel *(m)*
En blank bill
Es letra en blanco *(f)*
Fr traite en blanc *(f)*
It effetto in bianco *(m)*

**letra en blanco** *(f)* Es
De Blankowechsel *(m)*
En blank bill
Fr traite en blanc *(f)*
It effetto in bianco *(m)*
Pt letra em branco *(f)*

**letras a cobrar** *(f pl)* Es, Pt
De Wechselforderungen *(f pl)*
En bills receivable
Fr effets à recevoir *(m pl)*
It effetti attivi *(m pl)*

**letras a descontar** *(f pl)* Pt
De fällige Wechsel *(m pl)*
En bills for collection
Es efectos a cobrar *(m pl)*
Fr effets en recouvrement *(m pl)*
It effetti all'incasso *(m pl)*

**letras a pagar** *(f pl)* Pt
De Wechselschulden *(f pl)*
En bills payable
Es letras pagaderas *(f pl)*
Fr effets à payer *(m pl)*
It effetti passivi *(m pl)*

**letras descontadas** *(f pl)* Pt
De diskontierte Wechsel *(m pl)*
En bills discounted
Es efectos descontados *(m pl)*
Fr effets escomptés *(m pl)*
It effetti scontati *(m pl)*

**letra sobre el exterior** *(f)* Es
De Auslandswechsel *(m)*
En foreign bill
Fr lettre de change sur l'étranger *(f)*
It cambiale sull' estero *(f)*
Pt letra de país a país (cambial) *(f)*

**letras pagaderas** *(f pl)* Es
De Wechselschulden *(f pl)*
En bills payable
Fr effets à payer *(m pl)*
It effetti passivi *(m pl)*
Pt letras a pagar *(f pl)*

**letter** *n* En
De Brief *(m)*
Es carta; letra *(f)*
Fr lettre *(f)*
It lettera *(f)*
Pt carta *(f)*

**lettera** *(f)* *n* It
De Brief *(m)*
En letter
Es carta; letra *(f)*
Fr lettre *(f)*
Pt carta *(f)*

**lettera aerea** *(f)* It
De Luftpostbrief *(m)*
En air letter
Es carta por avión *(f)*
Fr aérogramme *(m)*
Pt carta de avião *(f)*

**lettera da ripartizione** *(f)* It
De Verteilungsbrief *(m)*
En allotment letter
Es letra de adjudicación *(f)*
Fr avis d'attribution *(m)*
Pt aviso de aporcionamento *(m)*

**lettera d'avviso** *(f)* It
De Anzeige *(f)*
En advice note
Es aviso *(m)*
Fr lettre d'avis *(f)*
Pt guia de remessa *(f)*

**lettera di credito** *(f)* It
De Kreditbrief *(m)*
En letter of credit
Es carta de crédito *(f)*
Fr lettre de crédit *(f)*
Pt carta de crédito *(f)*

**lettera di credito confermata e irrevocabile** *(f)* It
De bestätigter unwiderruflicher Kreditbrief *(m)*
En confirmed irrevocable letter of credit
Es carta de crédito irrevocable confirmada *(f)*
Fr lettre de crédit irrévocable confirmée *(f)*
Pt carta de crédito irrevogável confirmada *(f)*

**lettera di credito irrevocabile** *(f)* It
De unwiderruflicher Kreditbrief *(m)*
En irrevocable letter of credit
Es carta de crédito irrevocable *(f)*
Fr lettre de crédit irrévocable *(f)*
Pt carta de crédito irrevogável *(f)*

**lettera di garanzia** *(f)* It
De Ausfallbürgschaft *(f)*
En letter of indemnity
Es carta de indemnización *(f)*
Fr cautionnement *(m)*
Pt documento de garantia *(m)*

**lettera di vettura** *(f)* It
De Frachtbrief *(m)*
En waybill
Es guía de carga *(f)*

Fr lettre de voiture (f)
Pt guia de marcha (f)

**lettera espresso** (f) It
De Eilbrief (m)
En express letter
Am special delivery
Es carta urgente (f)
Fr lettre par exprès (f)
Pt carta expresso (f)

**lettera raccomandata** (f) It
De eingeschriebener Brief (m)
En registered letter
Es carta certificada (f)
Fr lettre recommandée (f)
Pt carta registada (f)

**letter-box** n En
Am mail-box
De Briefkasten (m)
Es buzón (m)
Fr boîte aux lettres (f)
It cassetta postale (f)
Pt caixa do correio (f)

**letterhead** n En
De Briefkopf (m)
Es membrete (m)
Fr en-tête (m)
It intestazione (f)
Pt cabeçalho (m)

**letter of credit** En
De Kreditbrief (m)
Es carta de crédito (f)
Fr lettre de crédit (f)
It lettera di credito (f)
Pt carta de crédito (f)

**letter of hypothecation** En
De Verpfändungsurkunde (f)
Es carta de hipoteca (f)
Fr lettre hypothécaire (f)
It atto ipotecario (m)
Pt carta de hipoteca (f)

**letter of indemnity** En
De Ausfallbürgschaft (f)
Es carta de indemnización (f)
Fr cautionnement (m)
It lettera di garanzia (f)
Pt documento de garantia (m)

**letters patent** En
Am patent
De Patenturkunde (f)
Es patente de invención (f)

Fr brevet (m)
It brevetto (m)
Pt patente de invenção (f)

**lettre** (f) n Fr
De Brief (m)
En letter
Es carta; letra (f)
It* lettera (f)
Pt carta (f)

**lettre d'avis** (f) Fr
De Anzeige (f)
En advice note
Es aviso (m)
It lettera d'avviso (f)
Pt guia de remessa (f)

**lettre de change** (f) Fr
De Wechsel; Tratte (m f)
En bill of exchange
Es letra de cambio (f)
It tratta cambiale (f)
Pt letra de câmbio (f)

**lettre de change sur l'étranger**
(f) Fr
De Auslandswechsel (m)
En foreign bill
Es letra sobre el exterior (f)
It cambiale sull' estero (f)
Pt letra de país a país
(cambial) (f)

**lettre de couverture** (f) Fr
De Deckungszusage (f)
En cover note
Es aviso de seguro del riesgo
(m)
It nota di copertura (f)
Pt nota de cobertura (f)

**lettre de crédit** (f) Fr
De Kreditbrief (m)
En letter of credit
Es carta de crédito (f)
It lettera di credito (f)
Pt carta de crédito (f)

**lettre de crédit confirmée** (f)
Fr
De bestätigter Kreditbrief (m)
En confirmed letter of credit
Es carta de crédito confirmada
It lettera di credito confer-
mata (f)

Pt carta de crédito confirmada
(f)

**lettre de crédit irrévocable** (f)
Fr
De unwiderruflicher Kreditbrief
(m)
En irrevocable letter of credit
Es carta de crédito irrevocable
(f)
It lettera di credito irre-
vocabile (f)
Pt carta de crédito irrevogável
(f)

**lettre de crédit irrévocable
confirmée** (f) Fr
De bestätigter unwiderruflicher
Kreditbrief (m)
En confirmed irrevocable letter
of credit
Es carta de crédito irrevocable
confirmada (f)
It lettera di credito confer-
mata e irrevocabile (f)
Pt carta de crédito irrevogável
confirmada (f)

**lettre de transport aérien** (f)
Fr
De Luftfrachtbrief (m)
En air waybill
Es carta de porte aéreo (f)
It nota di spedizione aerea (f)
Pt guia de porte aéreo (m)

**lettre de voiture** (f) Fr
De Frachtbrief (m)
En waybill
Es guía de carga (f)
It lettera di vettura (f)
Pt guia de marcha (f)

**lettre hypothécaire** (f) Fr
De Verpfändungsurkunde (f)
En letter of hypothecation
Es carta de hipoteca (f)
It atto ipotecario (m)
Pt carta de hipoteca (f)

**lettre par exprès** (f) Fr
De Eilbrief (m)
En express letter
Am special delivery
Es carta urgente (f)
It lettera espresso (f)
Pt carta expresso (f)

**lettre recommandée** *(f)* Fr
De  eingeschriebener Brief *(m)*
En  registered letter
Es  carta certificada *(f)*
It  lettera raccomandata *(f)*
Pt  carta registada *(f)*

**letzte Rate** *(f)* De
En  final instalment
Es  último plazo *(m)*
Fr  dernier versement *(m)*
It  ultima rata *(f)*
Pt  última prestação *(f)*

**levantar a descoberto** Pt
De  überziehen
En  overdraw
Es  girar en descubierto
Fr  mettre à découvert
It  trarre alla scoperto

**levée d'inventaire** *(f)* Fr
De  Bestandaufnahme *(f)*
En  stocktaking
Es  inventario; balance *(m)*
It  compilazione dell'inventario
    *(f)*
Pt  inventário de existências
    *(m)*

**levy** *n* En
De  Erhebung *(f)*
Es  impuesto *(m)*
Fr  prélèvement *(m)*
It  imposta *(f)*
Pt  imposto *(m)*

**ley** *(f)* *n* Es
De  Recht *(n)*
En  law
Fr  loi *(f)*
It  legge *(f)*
Pt  lei *(f)*

**liability** *n* En
De  Verpflichtung *(f)*
Es  responsabilidad *(f)*
Fr  responsabilité *(f)*
It  responsabilità *(f)*
Pt  responsabilidade *(f)*

**liable for damages** En ·
De  schadenersatzpflichtig
Es  responsable por daños
Fr  passible de dommages-
    intérêts
It  responsabile per i danni
Pt  responsavel por danos

**libera pratica** *(f)* It
De  Gesundheitsbrief *(m)*
En  pratique
Es  libre plática *(f)*
Fr  libre pratique *(f)*
Pt  livre prática *(f)*

**liberar** *vb* Es
De  befreien
En  free
Fr  libérer; affranchir
It  liberare
Pt  libertar; livrar

**liberare** *vb* It
De  befreien
En  free
Es  liberar
Fr  libérer; affranchir
Pt  libertar; livrar

**libération intégrale** *(f)* Fr
De  volle Zahlung *(f)*
En  payment in full
Es  pago en pleno *(m)*
It  pagamento in pieno *(m)*
Pt  pagamento completo *(m)*

**libérer** *vb* Fr
De  befreien
En  free
'Es  liberar
It  liberare
Pt  libertar; livrar

**libero** *adj* It
De  frei
En  free
Es  libre
Fr  libre
Pt  livre

**libero d'ipoteca** It
De  von Hypothek befreit
En  free from mortgage
Es  deshipotecado
Fr  déshypothéqué
Pt  livre de hipoteca

**libero scambio** *(m)* It
De  Freihandel *(m)*
En  free trade
Es  comercio libre *(m)*
Fr  libre-échange *(m)*
Pt  comércio franco *(m)*

**libertà d'iniziativa** *(f)* It
De  freie Wirtschaft *(f)*
En  free enterprise
Es  libre empresa *(f)*
Fr  libre entreprise *(f)*
Pt  livre-empreendimento *(m)*

**libertar** *vb* Pt
De  befreien
En  free
Es  liberar
Fr  libérer; affranchir
It  liberare

**librado** *(m)* *n* Es
De  Bezogene(r) *(m)*
En  drawee
Fr  tiré *(m)*
It  trattario *(m)*
Pt  sacado *(m)*

**librador** *(m)* *n* Es
De  Aussteller *(m)*
En  drawer
Fr  tireur *(m)*
It  traente *(m)*
Pt  sacador *(m)*

**libra esterlina** *(f)* Es
De  Pfund sterling *(n)*
En  pound sterling
Fr  livre sterling *(f)*
It  lira sterlina *(f)*
Pt  libra esterlina *(f)*

**libra esterlina** *(f)* Pt
De  Pfund sterling *(n)*
En  pound sterling
Es  libra esterlina *(f)*
Fr  livre sterling *(f)*
It  lira sterlina *(f)*

**libra esterlina verde** *(f)* Pt
De  grünes Pfund *(n)*
En  green pound
Es  esterlina verde *(f)*
Fr  livre sterling verte *(f)*
It  sterlina verde *(f)*

**libre** *adj* Es, Fr
De  frei
En  free
It  libero
Pt  livre

**libre-échange** *(m)* Fr
De  Freihandel *(m)*
En  free trade

Es comercio libre (m)
It libero scambio (m)
Pt comércio franco (m)

**libre empresa** (f) Es
De freie Wirtschaft (f)
En free enterprise
Fr libre entreprise (f)
It libertà d'iniziativa (f)
Pt livre-empreendimento (m)

**libre entrega** Es
De portofreie Lieferung
En delivery free
Fr livré franco
It consegna franco
Pt remessa gratuita

**libre entreprise** (f) Fr
De freie Wirtschaft (f)
En free enterprise
Es libre empresa (f)
It libertà d'iniziativa (f)
Pt livre-empreendimento (m)

**libre plática** (f) Es
De Gesundheitsbrief (m)
En pratique
Fr libre pratique (f)
It libera pratica (f)
Pt livre prática (f)

**libre pratique** (f) Fr
De Gesundheitsbrief (m)
En pratique
Es libre plática (f)
It libera pratica (f)
Pt livre prática (f)

**libre service** (m) Fr
De Selbstbedienung (f)
En self-service
Es auto-servicio (m)
It servirsi da sè (m)
Pt self-service (m)

**libreta de banco** (f) Es
De Bankbuch; Sparbuch (n)
En passbook
Am bankbook
Fr livret de compte (m)
It libretto di conto (m)
Pt livrete de conta (f)

**libretto assegni** (m) It
De Scheckheft (n)
En cheque book
Am check book

Es libro de cheques (m)
Fr carnet de chèques; chéquier (m)
Pt livro de cheques (m)

**libretto di conto** (m) It
De Bankbuch; Sparbuch (n)
En passbook
Am bankbook
Es libreta de banco (f)
Fr livret de compte (m)
Pt livrete de conta (f)

**libri contabili** (m pl) It
De Geschäftsbücher (n pl)
En books of account
Es libros de cuentas (m pl)
Fr livres comptables (m pl)
Pt livros de contabilidade (m pl)

**libro cassa** (m) It
De Kassenbuch (n)
En cash book
Es libro de caja (m)
Fr livre de caisse (m)
Pt livro de caixa (m)

**libro de caja** (m) Es
De Kassenbuch (n)
En cash book
Fr livre de caisse (m)
It libro cassa (m)
Pt livro de caixa (m)

**libro de cheques** (m) Es
De Scheckheft (n)
En cheque book
Am check book
Fr carnet de chèques; chéquier (m)
It libretto assegni (m)
Pt livro de cheques (m)

**libro de consulta** (m) Es
De Nachschlagebuch (n)
En reference book
Fr ouvrage de référence (m)
It libro di consultazione (m)
Pt livro de consulta (m)

**libro de cuentas** (m) Es
De Kontobuch (n)
En account book
Fr livre de compte (m)
It libro di conti (m)
Pt livro de contas (m)

**libro degli ordini** (m) It
De Auftragsbuch (n)
En order book
Es libro de pedidos (m)
Fr livre de commandes (m)
Pt livro de encomendas (m)

**libro de pedidos** (m) Es
De Auftragsbuch (n)
En order book
Fr livre de commandes (m)
It libro degli ordini (m)
Pt livro de encomendas (m)

**libro diario** (m) Es
De Tagebuch (n)
En journal
Fr journal (m)
It libro giornale (m)
Pt diário (m)

**libro di consultazione** (m) It
De Nachschlagebuch (n)
En reference book
Es libro de consulta (m)
Fr ouvrage de référence (m)
Pt livro de consulta (m)

**libro di conti** (m) It
De Kontobuch (n)
En account book
Es libro de cuentas (m)
Fr livre de compte (m)
Pt livro de contas (m)

**libro giornale** (m) It
De Tagebuch (n)
En journal
Es libro diario (m)
Fr journal (m)
Pt diário (m)

**libro mastro** (m) It
De Hauptbuch (n)
En ledger
Es libre mayor (m)
Fr grand livre (m)
Pt livro-mestre (m)

**libro mastro generale** (m) It
De allgemeines Hauptbuch (n)
En general ledger
Es libro mayor general (m)
Fr journal général (m)
Pt livro-mestre geral (m)

**libro mayor** *(m)* Es
De Hauptbuch *(n)*
En ledger
Fr grand livre *(m)*
It libro mastro *(m)*
Pt livro-mestre *(m)*

**libro mayor de compras** *(m)*
Es
De Einkaufsbuch *(n)*
En bought ledger
Am purchase book
Fr grand livre d'achats *(m)*
It mastro acquisti *(m)*
Pt livro de compras *(m)*

**libro mayor de ventas** *(m)* Es
De Verkaufskontenbuch *(n)*
En sales ledger
Fr grand livre des ventes *(m)*
It partitario delle vendite *(m)*
Pt livro de vendas *(m)*

**libro mayor general** *(m)* Es
De allgemeines Hauptbuch *(n)*
En general ledger
Fr journal général *(m)*
It libro mastro generale *(m)*
Pt livro-mestre geral *(m)*

**libro paga** *(m)* It
De Lohnbuch *(n)*
En payroll
Es nómina de pago *(f)*
Fr feuille de paie *(f)*
Pt folha de salários *(f)*

**libros de cuentas** *(m pl)* Es
De Geschäftsbücher *(n pl)*
En books of account
Fr livres comptables *(m pl)*
It libri contabili *(m pl)*
Pt livros de contabilidade *(m pl)*

**licença** *(f)* n Pt
De Erlaubnis *(f)*
En licence
Es licencia; permiso *(f m)*
Fr licence *(f)*
It licenza; permesso *(f m)*

**licença de exportação** *(f)* Pt
De Ausfuhrgenehmigung *(f)*
En export permit
Es permiso de exportación *(m)*
Fr autorisation d'exporter *(f)*

It permesso d'esportazione *(m)*

**licença de importação** *(f)* Pt
De Einfuhrerlaubnis *(f)*
En import licence
Es permiso de importación *(m)*
Fr licence d'importation *(f)*
It permesso d'importazione *(m)*

**licence** n En, Fr *(f)*
De Erlaubnis *(f)*
Es licencia; permiso *(f m)*
It licenza; permesso *(f m)*
Pt licença *(f)*

**licence d'importation** *(f)* Fr
De Einfuhrerlaubnis *(f)*
En import licence
Es permiso de importación *(m)*
It permesso d'importazione *(m)*
Pt licença de importação *(f)*

**licencia** *(f)* n Es
De Erlaubnis *(f)*
En licence
Fr licence *(f)*
It licenza; permesso *(f m)*
Pt licença *(f)*

**licencier** vb Fr
De kündigen
En dismiss; fire
Es despedir
It licenziare
Pt despedir

**licenza** *(f)* n It
De Erlaubnis *(f)*
En licence
Es licencia; permiso *(f m)*
Fr licence *(f)*
Pt licença *(f)*

**licenziamento** *(m)* n It
De Entlassung *(f)*
En firing; dismissal
Es despido *(m)*
Fr congédiement *(m)*
Pt despedimento *(m)*

**licenziare** vb It
De entlassen
En dismiss; fire
Es despedir

Fr congédier; licencier
Pt despedir

**licite** adj Fr
De gesetzlich; rechtlich
En lawful; legal
Es licito; legitimo
It lecito; legittimo
Pt legitimo; legal

**licito** adj Es
De gesetzlich; rechtlich
En lawful; legal
Fr licite; légal
It lecito; legittimo
Pt legitimo; legal

**Liebesdienste** *(m pl)* n De
En good offices
Es buenos servicios *(m pl)*
Fr bons offices *(m pl)*
It buoni uffici *(m pl)*
Pt bons serviços *(m pl)*

**Lieferant** *(m)* n De
En supplier
Es proveedor *(m)*
Fr fournisseur *(m)*
It fornitore *(m)*
Pt fornecedor *(m)*

**Lieferhafen** *(m)* n De
En port of discharge
Es puerto de descarga *(m)*
Fr port de livraison *(m)*
It porto di scarico *(m)*
Pt porto de descarga *(m)*

**liefern** vb De
En deliver; supply
Es entregar; provecer
Fr livrer; fournir
It consegnare; fornire
Pt entregar; fornecer

**Lieferpreis** *(m)* n De
En delivered price
Es precio incluida entrega *(m)*
Fr prix livraison inclus *(m)*
It prezzo incluso consegna *(m)*
Pt preço incluindo portes *(m)*

**Lieferschein** *(m)* n De
En delivery note
Es aviso de entrega *(m)*
Fr bordereau de livraison *(m)*

It  nota di consegna (f)
Pt  guia de entrega (f)

**Liefertermin** (m) n De
En  delivery date
Es  fecha de entrega (f)
Fr  date de livraison (f)
It  data di consegna (f)
Pt  data de entrega (f)

**Lieferung** (f) n De
En  delivery
Es  entrega (f)
Fr  livraison (f)
It  consegna (f)
Pt  entrega (f)

**Lieferung gegen Nachnahme**
De
En  cash on delivery (c.o.d.)
Es  entrega contra reembolso
Fr  paiement à la livraison
It  pagamento alla consegna
Pt  entrega contra reembolso

**Liegezeit** (f) n De
En  lay days
Es  estadía (f)
Fr  staries (f pl)
It  stallie (f pl)
Pt  estadía (f)

**lien** n En
De  Pfandrecht (n)
Es  derecho de retencíon (m)
Fr  droit de retention (m)
It  diritto di sequestro (m)
Pt  direito de retenção (m)

**life assurance** En
Am  life insurance
De  Lebensversicherung (f)
Es  seguro de vida (m)
Fr  assurance sur la vie (f)
It  assicurazione sulla vita (f)
Pt  seguro de vida (m)

**life-interest** n En
De  lebenslängliche Nutzniessung (f)
Es  usufructo vitalicio (m)
Fr  usufruit viager (m)
It  usufrutto vitalizio (m)
Pt  usufruto vitalício (m)

**LIFO** En, Fr, De
Es  última entrada, primera
salida

It  ultimo a entrare, primo a
uscire
Pt  último a entrar, primeiro a
saír

**lift** n En
Am  elevator
De  Aufzug (m)
Es  ascensor (m)
Fr  ascenseur (m)
It  ascensore (m)
Pt  ascensor (m)

**lighter** n En
De  Leichter (m)
Es  barcaza; gabarra (f)
Fr  allège (f)
It  chiatta (f)
Pt  barcaça (f)

**lightning** n En
De  Blitz m
Es  relámpago (m)
Fr  foudre (f)
It  fulmine (m)
Pt  relâmpago (m)

**ligne** (de chemin de fer) (f) n Fr
De  Linie; Eisenbahnlinie (f)
En  (railway) line
Es  línea (ferroviaria) (f)
It  linea (ferroviario) (f)
Pt  linha (de caminho de ferro)
(f)

**ligne** (de téléphone) (f) n Fr
De  Leitung (f)
En  (telephone) line
Es  línea (telefónica) (f)
It  linea (telefonica) (f)
Pt  linha (telefónica) (f)

**ligne de charge** (f) Fr
De  Ladelinie (f)
En  loadline
Es  línea de carga (f)
It  linea di carico (f)
Pt  linha limite de carga (f)

**limit** n En
De  Grenze (f)
Es  límite (m)
Fr  limite (f)
It  limite (m)
Pt  limite (m)

**limitação de dividendos** (f) Pt
De  Dividendenstop (m)
En  dividend limitation
Es  bloqueo de dividendos (m)
Fr  blocage des dividendes (m)
It  blocco dei dividendi (m)

**limitado** adj Es, Pt
De  beschränkt
En  limited
Fr  limité
It  limitato

**limitato** adj It
De  beschränkt
En  limited
Es  limitado
Fr  limité
Pt  limitado

**límite** (m) n Es
De  Grenze (f)
En  limit
Fr  limite (f)
It  limite (m)
Pt  limite (m)

**limite** n Fr (f); It, Pt (m)
De  Grenze (f)
En  limit
Es  límite (m)

**limité** adj Fr
De  beschränkt
En  limited
Es  limitado
It  limitato
Pt  limitado

**limited** adj En
De  beschränkt
Es  limitado
Fr  limité
It  limitato
Pt  limitado

**límite de crédito** (m) Es
De  Kreditwürdigkeit (f)
En  credit rating
Fr  degré de solvabilité (f)
It  stima del credito (f)
Pt  nível de crédito (m)

**limited partnership** En
De  Kommanditgesellschaft (f)
Es  sociedad en comandita (f)
Fr  société en commandité (f)

It società in accomandita
   semplice *(f)*
Pt sociedade en comandita *(f)*


**line** (railway) *n* En
De Linie; Eisenbahnlinie *(f)*
Es línea (ferroviaria) *(f)*
Fr ligne (de chemin de fer) *(f)*
It linea (ferroviario) *(f)*
Pt linha (de caminho de ferro)
   *(f)*


**line** (telephone) *n* En
De Leitung *(f)*
Es línea (telefónica) *(f)*
Fr ligne (de téléphone) *(f)*
It linea (telefonica) *(f)*
Pt linha (telefónica) *(f)*


**línea** (ferroviaria) *(f) n* Es
De Linie; Eisenbahnlinie *(f)*
En (railway) line
Fr ligne (de chemin de fer) *(f)*
It linea (ferroviario) *(f)*
Pt linha (de caminho de ferro)
   *(f)*


**linea** (ferroviario) *(f) n* It
De Linie; Eisenbahnlinie *(f)*
En (railway) line
Es línea (ferroviaria) *(f)*
Fr ligne (de chemin de fer) *(f)*
Pt linha (de caminho de ferro)
   *(f)*


**línea** (telefónica) *(f) n* Es
De Leitung *(f)*
En (telephone) line
Fr ligne (de téléphone) *(f)*
It linea (telefonica) *(f)*
Pt linha (telefónica) *(f)*


**linea** (telefonica) *(f) n* It
De Leitung *(f)*
En (telephone) line
Es línea (telefónica) *(f)*
Fr ligne (de téléphone) *(f)*
Pt linha (telefónica) *(f)*


**línea aérea** *(f)* Es
De Fluggesellschaft *(f)*
En air line
Fr compagnie aérienne *(f)*
It linea aerea *(f)*
Pt companhia de aviação *(f)*


**linea aerea** *(f)* It
De Fluggesellschaft *(f)*
En air line
Es línea aérea *(f)*
Fr compagnie aérienne *(f)*
Pt companhia de aviação *(f)*


**línea de carga** *(f)* Es
De Ladelinie *(f)*
En loadline
Fr ligne de charge *(f)*
It linea di carico *(f)*
Pt linha limite de carga *(f)*


**línea de montaje** *(f)* Es
De Montageband *(n)*
En assembly line
Fr chaîne de montage *(f)*
It catena di montaggio *(f)*
Pt cadeia de montagem *(f)*


**linea di carico** *(f)* It
De Ladelinie *(f)*
En loadline
Es línea de carga *(f)*
Fr ligne de charge *(f)*
Pt linha limite de carga *(f)*


**liner** *n* En
De Linienschiff *(n)*
Es vapor de línea *(m)*
Fr paquebot *(m)*
It nave di linea *(f)*
Pt paquete *(m)*


**lingot** *(m) n* Fr
De Barren *(m)*
En ingot
Es lingote *(m)*
It lingotto *(m)*
Pt lingote *(m)*


**lingote** *(m) n* Es, Pt
De Barren *(m)*
En ingot
Fr lingot; barre *(m f)*
It lingotto *(m)*


**lingotto** *(m) n* It
De Barren *(m)*
En ingot
Es lingote *(m)*
Fr lingot; barre *(m f)*
Pt lingote *(m)*


**lingua** *(f) n* Es, It
De Sprache *(f)*
En language

Fr langue *(f)*
Pt língua *(f)*


**língua** *(f) n* Pt
De Sprache *(f)*
En language
Es lingua *(f)*
Fr langue *(f)*
It lingua *(f)*


**linguagem da máquina** *(f)* Pt
De Maschinensprache *(f)*
En machine language
Es lenguaje de máquina *(m)*
Fr langage-machine *(m)*
It linguaggio di macchina *(m)*


**linguaggio di macchina** *(m)* It
De Maschinensprache *(f)*
En machine language
Es lenguaje de máquina *(m)*
Fr langage-machine *(m)*
Pt linguagem da máquina *(f)*


**linha** (de caminho de ferro) *(f) n*
   Pt
De Linie; Eisenbahnlinie *(f)*
En (railway) line
Es línea (ferroviaria) *(f)*
Fr ligne (de chemin de fer) *(f)*
It linea (ferroviario) *(f)*


**linha** (telefónica) *(f) n* Pt
De Leitung *(f)*
En line (telephone)
Es línea (telefónica) *(f)*
Fr ligne (de téléphone) *(f)*
It linea (telefonica) *(f)*


**linha limite de carga** *(f)* Pt
De Ladelinie *(f)*
En loadline
Es línea de carga *(f)*
Fr ligne de charge *(f)*
It linea di carico *(f)*


**Linie** (Eisenbahn) *(f) n* De
En (railway) line
Es línea (ferroviaria) *(f)*
Fr ligne (de chemin de fer) *(f)*
It linea (ferroviario) *(f)*
Pt linha (de caminho de ferro)
   *(f)*


**Linienschiff** *(n) n* De
En liner
Es vapor de línea *(m)*
Fr paquebot *(m)*

It   nave di linea *(f)*
Pt  paquete *(m)*

**liquidação** *(f)* n Pt
De  Liquidation; Auflösung *(f)*
En  liquidation
Es  liquidación *(f)*
Fr  liquidation *(f)*
It   liquidazione *(f)*

**liquidação forçada** *(f)* Pt
De  Zwangsliquidation *(f)*
En  compulsory winding-up
Am  forced liquidation
Es  liquidación forzosa *(f)*
Fr  liquidation forcée *(f)*
It   liquidazione forzata *(f)*

**liquidación** *(f)* n Es
De  Liquidation; Auflösung *(f)*
En  liquidation
Fr  liquidation *(f)*
It   liquidazione *(f)*
Pt  liquidação *(f)*

**liquidación forzosa** *(f)* Es
De  Zwangsliquidation *(f)*
En  compulsory winding-up
Am  forced liquidation
Fr  liquidation forcée *(f)*
It   liquidazione forzata *(f)*
Pt  liquidação forçada *(f)*

**liquidador** *(m)* n Es
De  Masseverwalter; Sachwalter *(m)*
En  liquidator
Fr  liquidateur *(m)*
It   liquidatore *(m)*
Pt  executor da liquidação *(m)*

**liquidare una azienda** It
De  ein Unternehmen abwickeln
En  wind up a business
Es  liquidar un negocio
Fr  liquider une entreprise
Pt  liquidar um negócio

**liquidar um negócio** Pt
De  ein Unternehmen abwickeln
En  wind up a business
Es  liquidar un negocio
Fr  liquider une entreprise
It   liquidare una azienda

**liquidar un negocio** Es
De  ein Unternehmen abwickeln
En  wind up a business
Fr  liquider une entreprise
It   liquidare una azienda
Pt  liquidar um negócio

**liquid assets** En
De  flüssige Aktiven *(n pl)*
Es  activo líquido *(m)*
Fr  actif liquide *(m)*
It   disponibilità; attività liquida *(f)*
Pt  bens de activo líquidos *(m pl)*

**liquidated damages** En
De  Konventionalstrafe *(f)*
Es  daños liquidados *(m pl)*
Fr  dommages-intérêts fixés en argent *(m pl)*
It   danni liquidati *(m pl)*
Pt  danos liquidados *(m pl)*

**liquidateur** *(m)* n Fr
De  Masseverwalter; Sachwalter *(m)*
En  liquidator
Es  liquidador *(m)*
It   liquidatore *(m)*
Pt  executor da liquidação *(m)*

**liquidation** n En
De  Liquidation; Auflösung *(f)*
Es  liquidación *(f)*
Fr  liquidation *(f)*
It   liquidazione *(f)*
Pt  liquidação *(f)*

**liquidation** *(f)* n Fr
De  Liquidation; Auflösung *(f)*
En  liquidation
Es  liquidación *(f)*
It   liquidazione *(f)*
Pt  liquidação *(f)*

**Liquidation** *(f)* n De
En  liquidation
Es  liquidación *(f)*
Fr  liquidation *(f)*
It   liquidazione *(f)*
Pt  liquidação *(f)*

**liquidation forcée** *(f)* Fr
De  Zwangsliquidation *(f)*
En  compulsory winding-up
Am  forced liquidation

Es  liquidación forzosa *(f)*
It   liquidazione forzata *(f)*
Pt  liquidação forçada *(f)*

**liquidator** n En
De  Masseverwalter; Sachwalter *(m)*
Es  liquidador *(m)*
Fr  liquidateur *(m)*
It   liquidatore *(m)*
Pt  executor da liquidação *(m)*

**liquidatore** *(m)* n It
De  Masseverwalter; Sachwalter *(m)*
En  liquidator
Es  liquidador *(m)*
Fr  liquidateur *(m)*
Pt  executor da liquidação *(m)*

**liquidazione** *(f)* n It
De  Liquidation; Auflösung *(f)*
En  liquidation
Es  liquidación *(f)*
Fr  liquidation *(f)*
Pt  liquidação *(f)*

**liquidazione forzata** *(f)* It
De  Zwangsliquidation *(f)*
En  compulsory winding-up
Am  forced liquidation
Es  liquidación forzosa *(f)*
Fr  liquidation forcée *(f)*
Pt  liquidação forçada *(f)*

**liquider une entreprise** Fr
De  ein Unternehmen abwickeln
En  wind up a business
Es  liquidar un negocio
It   liquidare una azienda
Pt  liquidar um negócio

**liquidez** *(f)* n Es, Pt
De  Liquidität *(f)*
En  liquidity
Fr  liquidité *(f)*
It   liquidità *(f)*

**liquidità** *(f)* n It
De  Liquidität *(f)*
En  liquidity
Es  liquidez *(f)*
Fr  liquidité *(f)*
Pt  liquidez *(f)*

**Liquidität** *(f)* n De
  En liquidity
  Es liquidez *(f)*
  Fr liquidité *(f)*
  It liquidità *(f)*
  Pt liquidez *(f)*

**liquidité** *(f)* n Fr
  De Liquidität *(f)*
  En liquidity
  Es liquidez *(f)*
  It liquidità *(f)*
  Pt liquidez *(f)*

**liquidity** n En
  De Liquidität *(f)*
  Es liquidez *(f)*
  Fr liquidité *(f)*
  It liquidità *(f)*
  Pt liquidez *(f)*

**líquido** *adj* Pt
  De Netto-; Rein-
  En net
  Es neto
  Fr net
  It netto

**lira sterlina** *(f)* It
  De Pfund sterling *(n)*
  En pound sterling
  Es libra esterlina *(f)*
  Fr livre sterling *(f)*
  Pt libra esterlina *(f)*

**lista** *(f)* n Es, It, Pt
  De Liste; Tabelle *(f)*
  En schedule; list
  Fr liste; tableau *(f m)*

**lista de espera** *(f)* Es, Pt
  De Warteliste *(f)*
  En waiting list
  Fr liste d´attente *(f)*
  It elenco delle prenotazioni *(m)*

**lista negra** *(f)* Es, Pt
  De schwarze Liste *(f)*
  En black list
  Fr liste noire *(f)*
  It lista nera *(f)*

**lista nera** *(f)* It
  De schwarze Liste *(f)*
  En black list
  Es lista negra *(f)*

  Fr liste noire *(f)*
  Pt lista negra *(f)*

**lista telefónica** *(f)* Pt
  De Fernsprechbuch *(n)*
  En telephone directory
  Es guía de teléfonos *(f)*
  Fr annuaire des téléphones *(m)*
  It elenco telefonico *(m)*

**liste** *(f)* n Fr
  De Liste; Tabelle *(f)*
  En list; schedule
  Es lista; cuadro *(f m)*
  It lista; tabella *(f)*
  Pt lista; tabela *(f)*

**Liste** *(f)* n De
  En list; schedule
  Es lista; cuadro *(f m)*
  Fr liste; tableau *(f m)*
  It lista; tabella *(f)*
  Pt lista; tabela *(f)*

**liste d'attente** *(f)* Fr
  De Warteliste *(f)*
  En waiting list
  Es lista de espera *(f)*
  It elenco delle prenotazioni *(m)*
  Pt lista de espera *(f)*

**Liste der Aktionäre** *(f)* De
  En share register
  Es registro de las acciones *(m)*
  Fr registre des actionnaires *(m)*
  It registro delle azioni *(m)*
  Pt registo de acções *(m)*

**listed security** En
  De an der Börse notierte Wertpapiere *(n pl)*
  Es valores cotizables *(m pl)*
  Fr valeurs admises à la Bourse *(f pl)*
  It titoli quotati in Borsa *(m pl)*
  Pt valor de Bolsa com cotação oficial *(m)*

**liste noire** *(f)* Fr
  De schwarze Liste *(f)*
  En black list
  Es lista negra *(f)*
  It lista nera *(f)*
  Pt lista negra *(f)*

**Listenpreis** *(m)* n De
  En list price
  Es precio de tarifa *(m)*
  Fr prix courant *(m)*
  It prezzo di listino *(m)*
  Pt preço de tabela *(m)*

**list price** En
  De Listenpreis *(m)*
  Es precio de tarifa *(m)*
  Fr prix courant *(m)*
  It prezzo di listino *(m)*
  Pt preço de tabela *(m)*

**livello dei prezzi** *(m)* It
  De Preisebene *(f)*
  En price level
  Es nivel de precios *(m)*
  Fr niveau des prix *(m)*
  Pt nível de preços *(m)*

**livraison** *(f)* n Fr
  De Lieferung *(f)*
  En delivery
  Es entrega *(f)*
  It consegna *(f)*
  Pt entrega *(f)*

**livraison à terme** *(f)* Fr
  De Terminlieferung *(f)*
  En forward delivery
  Es entrega futura *(f)*
  It consegna a termine *(f)*
  Pt entrega futura *(f)*

**livraison immédiate** *(f)* Fr
  De sofortige Lieferung *(f)*
  En prompt delivery
  Es entrega inmediata *(f)*
  It pronta consegna *(f)*
  Pt entrega imediata *(f)*

**livraison incomplète** *(f)* Fr
  De mangelhafte Lieferung *(f)*
  En short delivery
  Es entrega deficiente *(f)*
  It consegna deficiente *(f)*
  Pt entrega insuficiente *(f)*

**livre** *adj* Pt
  De frei
  En free
  Es libre
  Fr libre
  It libero

**livre de alfândega** Pt
De verzollt
En ex bond
Es fuera de aduanas
Fr à l'acquitté
It sdoganato

**livre de caisse** (m) Fr
De Kassenbuch (n)
En cash book
Es libro de caja (m)
It libro cassa (m)
Pt livro de caixa (m)

**livre de commandes** (m) Fr
De Auftragsbuch (n)
En order book
Es libro de pedidos (m)
It libro degli ordini (m)
Pt livro de encomendas (m)

**livre de compte** (m) Fr
De Kontobuch (n)
En account book
Es libro de cuentas (m)
It libro di conti (m)
Pt livro de contas (m)

**livre de hipoteca** Pt
De von Hypothek befreit
En free from mortgage
Es deshipotecado
Fr déshypothéqué
It libero d'ipoteca

**livre-empreendimento** (m) Pt
De freie Wirtschaft (f)
En free enterprise
Es libre empresa (f)
Fr libre entreprise (f)
It libertà d'iniziativa (f)

**livré franco** Fr
De portofreie Lieferung
En delivery free
Es libre entrega
It consegna franco
Pt remessa gratuita

**livre prática** (f) Pt
De Gesundheitsbrief (m)
En pratique
Es libre plática (f)
Fr libre pratique (f)
It libera pratica (f)

**livres comptables** (m pl) Fr
De Geschäftsbücher (n pl)
En books of account
Es libros de cuentas (m pl)
It libri contabili (m pl)
Pt livros de contabilidade (m pl)

**livre sterling** (f) Fr
De Pfund sterling (n)
En pound sterling
Es libra esterlina (f)
It lira sterlina (f)
Pt libra esterlina (f)

**livre sterling verte** (f) Fr
De grünes Pfund (n)
En green pound
Es esterlina verde (f)
It sterlina verde (f)
Pt libra esterlina verde (f)

**livret de compte** (m) Fr
De Bankbuch; Sparbuch (n)
En passbook
Am bankbook
Es libreta de banco (f)
It libretto di conto (m)
Pt livrete de conta (f)

**livrete de conta** (f) Pt
De Bankbuch; Sparbuch (n)
En passbook
Am bankbook
Es libreta de banco (f)
Fr livret de compte (m)
It libretto di conto (m)

**livro de caixa** (m) Pt
De Kassenbuch (n)
En cash book
Es libro de caja (m)
Fr livre de caisse (m)
It libro cassa (m)

**livro de cheques** (m) Pt
De Scheckheft (n)
En cheque book
Am check book
Es libro de cheques (m)
Fr carnet de chèques; chéquier (m)
It libretto assegni (m)

**livro de consulta** (m) Pt
De Nachschlagebuch (n)
En reference book
Es libro de consulta (m)

Fr ouvrage de référence (m)
It libro di consultazione (m)

**livro de contas** (m) Pt
De Kontobuch (n)
En account book
Es libro de cuentas (m)
Fr livre de compte (m)
It libro di conti (m)

**livro de encomendas** (m) Pt
De Auftragsbuch (n)
En order book
Es libro de pedidos (m)
Fr livre de commandes (m)
It libro degli ordini (m)

**livro-mestre** (m) Pt
De Hauptbuch (n)
En ledger
Es libro mayor (m)
Fr grand livre (m)
It libro mastro (m)

**livro-mestre de compras** (m) Pt
De Einkaufsbuch (n)
En bought ledger
Am purchase book
Es libro mayor de compras (m)
Fr grand livre d'achats (m)
It mastro acquisti (m)

**livro-mestre de vendas** (m) Pt
De Verkaufskontenbuch (n)
En sales ledger
Es libro mayor de ventas (m)
Fr grand livre des ventes (m)
It partitario delle vendite (m)

**livros de contabilidade** (m pl) Pt
De Geschäftsbücher (n pl)
En books of account
Es libros de cuentas (m pl)
Fr livres comptables (m pl)
It libri contabili (m pl)

**llamada** (de fondos) (f) n Es
De Kündigung (von Geldern) (f)
En call (for funds)
Fr appel (de fonds) (m)
It richiesta (di fondi) (f)
Pt chamada (de fundos) (f)

**llamada interurbana** *(f)* Es
De Ferngespräch *(n)*
En trunk call
Am long distance call
Fr appel téléphonique interurbain *(m)*
It comunicazione interurbana *(f)*
Pt chamada inter-urbana (troncas) *(f)*

**llamada telefónica** *(f)* Es
De Anruf *(m)*
En telephone call
Fr appel téléphonique *(m)*
It chiamata telefonica *(f)*
Pt chamada telefónica *(f)*

**llano** *adj* Es
De flach
En flat
Fr plat; uniforme
It piatto
Pt plano; liso

**llave** *(f)* *n* Es
De Schlüssel *(m)*
En key
Fr clef *(f)*
It chiave *(f)*
Pt chave *(f)*

**llegada** *(f)* *n* Es
De Ankunft *(f)*
En arrival
Fr arrivée *(f)*
It arrivo *(m)*
Pt chegada *(f)*

**lleno** *adj* Es
De voll
En full
Fr plein
It pieno
Pt cheio

**llevar la contabilidad** Es
De Konto führen
En keep the accounts
Fr tenir la comptabilité
It tenere la contabilità
Pt fazer a contabilidade

**loading** *n* En
De Ladung *(f)*
Es carga *(f)*
Fr chargement *(m)*

It caricamento *(m)*
Pt carregamento *(m)*

**loadline** *n* En
De Ladelinie *(f)*
Es línea de carga *(f)*
Fr ligne de charge *(f)*
It linea di carico *(f)*
Pt linha limite de carga *(f)*

**loan** *n* En
De Anleihe *(f)*
Es empréstito *(m)*
Fr emprunt *(m)*
It prestito *(m)*
Pt empréstime *(m)*

**loan account** En
De Anleihekonto *(n)*
Es cuenta de préstamos *(f)*
Fr compte des prêts *(m)*
It conto anticipazioni *(m)*
Pt conta de empréstimos *(f)*

**loan stock** En
De Anleihewerte *(m pl)*
Es títulos de préstamo *(m pl)*
Fr titres d'emprunt *(m pl)*
It titoli di prestito *(m pl)*
Pt títulos de empréstimo *(m pl)*

**locataire** *(m)* *n* Fr
De Mieter *(m)*
En tenant; hirer; lessee
Es inquilino; alquilador; arrendatario *(m)*
It affittuario; locatario; noleggiatore *(m)*
Pt inquilino; alugador; arrendatário *(m)*

**locatario** *(m)* *n* It
De Mieter *(m)*
En lessee
Es arrendatario *(m)*
Fr locataire *(m)*
Pt locatário; arrendatário *(m)*

**locatário** *(m)* *n* Pt
De Mieter *(m)*
En lessee
Es arrendatario *(m)*
Fr locataire *(m)*
It locatario *(m)*

**location-vente** *(f)* *n* Fr
De Ratenkauf *(m)*
En hire-purchase
Es compra a plazos *(f)*
It vendita a rate *(f)*
Pt venda a prestações *(f)*

**locatore** *(m)* *n* It
De Vermieter *(m)*
En lessor
Es arrendador *(m)*
Fr bailleur *(m)*
Pt senhorio; arrendador *(m)*

**Lochkarte** *(f)* *n* De
En punched card
Es tarjeta perforada *(f)*
Fr carte perforée
It scheda perforata *(f)*
Pt ficha perforada *(f)*

**lock-out** *n* En, Fr *(m)*
De Aussperrung *(f)*
Es cierre *(m)*
It serrata *(f)*
Pt lockout *(m)*

**lockout** *(m)* *n* Pt
De Aussperrung *(f)*
En lock-out
Es cierre *(m)*
Fr lock-out *(m)*
It serrata *(f)*

**lodge** *n* Am
En friendly society
De Versicherungsverein auf Gegenseitigkeit *(m)*
Es sociedad de socorro mutuo *(f)*
Fr société de secours mutuel *(f)*
It società di mutuo soccorso *(f)*
Pt mutualidade *(f)*

**lodo arbitrale** *(m)* It
De Schiedsspruch *(m)*
En arbitration award
Es sentencia arbitral *(f)*
Fr sentence arbitrale *(f)*
Pt decisão de arbitragem *(f)*

**log** (ship's) *n* En
De Log *(n)*
Es diario de navegación *(m)*
Fr journal de navigation *(m)*

It   solcometro *(m)*
Pt  diário de bordo *(m)*

**Log** *(n)* n De
En  log
Es  diario de navegación *(m)*
Fr  journal de navigation *(m)*
It   solcometro *(m)*
Pt  diário de bordo *(m)*

**logic** n En
De  Logik *(f)*
Es  lógica *(f)*
Fr  logique *(f)*
It   logica *(f)*
Pt  lógica *(f)*

**lógica** *(f)* n Es, Pt
De  Logik *(f)*
En  logic
Fr  logique *(f)*
It   logica *(f)*

**logica** *(f)* n It
De  Logik *(f)*
En  logic
Es  lógica *(f)*
Fr  logique *(f)*
Pt  lógica *(f)*

**Logik** *(f)* n De
En  logic
Es  lógica *(f)*
Fr  logique *(f)*
It   logica *(f)*
Pt  lógica *(f)*

**logique** *(f)* n Fr
De  Logik *(f)*
En  logic
Es  lógica *(f)*
It   logica *(f)*
Pt  lógica *(f)*

**logística** *(f)* n Es, Pt
De  Logistik *(f)*
En  logistics
Fr  logistique *(f)*
It   logistica *(f)*

**logistica** *(f)* n It
De  Logistik *(f)*
En  logistics
Es  logística *(f)*
Fr  logistique *(f)*
Pt  logística *(f)*

**logistics** n En
De  Logistik *(f)*
Es  logística *(f)*
Fr  logistique *(f)*
It   logistica *(f)*
Pt  logística *(f)*

**Logistik** *(f)* n De
En  logistics
Es  logística *(f)*
Fr  logistique *(f)*
It   logistica *(f)*
Pt  logística *(f)*

**logistique** *(f)* n Fr
De  Logistik *(f)*
En  logistics
Es  logística *(f)*
It   logistica *(f)*
Pt  logística *(f)*

**logorio naturale** *(m)* It
De  natürliche Abnützung *(f)*
En  wear and tear
Es  desgaste natural *(m)*
Fr  usure normale *(f)*
Pt  desgaste *(m)*

**Lohn** *(m)* n De
En  wage
Es  salario *(m)*
Fr  salaire *(m)*
It   salario *(m)*
Pt  salario *(m)*

**Lohnbeschränkung** *(f)* n De
En  wage restraint
Es  restricción de salario *(f)*
Fr  contrainte sur les salaires *(f)*
It   restrizioni sui salari *(f pl)*
Pt  restrição de salários *(f)*

**Lohnbuch** *(n)* n De
En  payroll
Es  nómina de pago *(f)*
Fr  feuille de paie *(f)*
It   libro paga *(m)*
Pt  folha de salários *(f)*

**Lohnempfänger** *(m)* n De
En  wage earner
Es  asalariado *(m)*
Fr  salarié *(m)*
It   salariato *(m)*
Pt  assalariado *(m)*

**Lohnforderung** *(f)* n De
En  wage claim
Es  reclamación de salario *(f)*
Fr  revendication de salaire *(f)*
It   rivendicazione salariale *(f)*
Pt  demanda de salário *(f)*

**Lohnkosten** *(pl)* n De
En  cost of labour
Es  coste de la mano de obra *(m)*
Fr  coût de la main-d'œuvre *(m)*
It   costo di mano d'opera *(m)*
Pt  custo da mão de obra *(m)*

**Lohnnachzahlung** *(f)* n De
En  back pay
Es  pago atrasado *(m)*
Fr  rappel de traitement *(m)*
It   arretrati di paga *(m pl)*
Pt  vencimento atrasado *(m)*

**Lohnpolitik** *(f)* n De
En  incomes policy
Es  plan de renta *(m)*
Fr  politique des salaires *(f)*
It   politica dei redditi *(f)*
Pt  programa salários *(f)*

**Lohnsatz** *(m)* n De
En  wage rate
Es  tarifa de salarios *(f)*
Fr  taux des salaires *(m)*
It   tariffa salariale *(f)*
Pt  base salarial *(f)*

**Lohnstopp** *(m)* n De
En  wage-freeze
Es  bloqueo de salarios *(m)*
Fr  blocage des salaires *(m)*
It   blocco dei salari *(m)*
Pt  congelação de salários *(f)*

**Lohnsummensteuer** *(f)* n De
En  employment tax
Es  impuesto por empleado *(m)*
Fr  taxe sur l'emploi *(f)*
It   imposta sull'impiego *(f)*
Pt  imposto sobre emprego *(m)*

**Lohnvereinbarung** *(f)* n De
En  wages agreement
Es  acuerdo sobre salarios *(m)*
Fr  convention des salaires *(f)*
It   accordo sui salari *(m)*
Pt  acordo sobre salários *(m)*

**loi** *(f)* n Fr
De Recht *(n)*
En law
Es ley *(f)*
It legge *(f)*
Pt lei *(f)*

**loisir** *(m)* n Fr
De Freizeit *(f)*
En leisure
Es descanso *(m)*
It svago *(m)*
Pt lazer *(m)*

**loja** *(f)* n Pt
De Laden *(m)*
En shop
Es tienda *(f)*
Fr magasin *(m)*
It bottega *(f)*

**long-dated** *adj* En
De langfristig
Es a largo plazo
Fr à longue échéance
It a lunga scadenza
Pt a longo prazo

**long distance call** Am
En trunk call
De Ferngespräch *(n)*
Es llamada interurbana *(f)*
Fr appel téléphonique interur-
   bain *(m)*
It comunicazione interurbana
   *(f)*
Pt chamada inter-urbana *(f)*

**longshoreman** n Am
En docker
De Hafenarbeiter *(m)*
Es cargador de muelle *(m)*
Fr docker *(m)*
It lavoratore del porto *(m)*
Pt trabalhador das docas *(m)*

**long-term** *adj* En
De langfristig
Es a largo plazo
Fr à long terme
It a lunga scadenza
Pt a longo prazo

**long-term capital** En
De langfristiges Kapital *(n)*
Es capital a largo plazo *(m)*
Fr capitaux à long terme *(m
   pl)*

It capitale consolidato a lunga
   scadenza *(m)*
Pt capital a longo prazo *(m)*

**long ton** En
De schwere Tonne *(f)*
Es tonelada inglesa *(f)*
Fr tonne forte *(f)*
It tonnellata inglese *(f)*
Pt tonelada inglesa *(f)*

**lordo** *adj* It
De brutto
En gross
Es bruto
Fr brut; gros
Pt bruto

**Löschen der Ladung** *(n)* De
En breaking bulk
Es fraccionamiento de la carga
   *(m)*
Fr rupture de charge *(f)*
It inizio scarico *(m)*
Pt retalhar a carga *(f)*

**Löschpapier** *(n)* n De
En blotting paper
Es papel secante *(m)*
Fr papier buvard *(m)*
It carta assorbente *(f)*
Pt papel mata-borrão *(m)*

**Löschungskonto** *(n)* n De
En landing account
Es cuenta de desembarque *(f)*
Fr compte de mise à terre *(m)*
It conto di sbarco *(m)*
Pt conta de descargas *(f)*

**loss** n En
De Verlust *(m)*
Es pérdida *(f)*
Fr perte *(f)*
It perdita *(f)*
Pt perda *(f)*

**loss of profits** En
De Gewinnausfall *(m)*
Es lucro cesante *(m)*
Fr perte de bénéfices *(f)*
It perdita di utili *(f)*
Pt perda de lucros *(f)*

**lot** *(m)* n Fr
De Stoss *(m)*
En batch
Es lote *(m)*

It lotto *(m)*
Pt lote *(m)*

**lote** *(m)* n Es, Pt
De Stoss *(m)*
En batch
Fr lot *(m)*
It lotto *(m)*

**lote avulso** *(m)* Pt
De Restpartie *(f)*
En odd lot
Es lote suelto *(m)*
Fr solde *(m)*
It partita spaiata *(f)*

**lote suelto** *(m)* Es
De Restpartie *(f)*
En odd lot
Fr solde *(m)*
It partita spaiata *(f)*
Pt lote avulso *(m)*

**Lotse** *(m)* n De
En (maritime) pilot
Es piloto *(m)*
Fr pilote *(m)*
It pilota *(m)*
Pt piloto *(m)*

**lotto** *(m)* n It
De Stoss *(m)*
En batch
Es lote *(m)*
Fr lot *(m)*
Pt lote *(m)*

**louer** *vb* Fr
De mieten; vermieten
En hire; rent
Es alquilar
It noleggiare; affittare
Pt alugar

**lourd** *adj* Fr
De schwer
En heavy
Es pesado
It pesante
Pt pesado

**lourde perte** *(f)* Fr
De schwere Verluste *(m pl)*
En heavy loss
Es fuerte    pérdida;    pérdida
   sensible *(f)*
It forte perdita *(f)*
Pt perda avultada *(f)*

**low-grade** adj En
De minderwertig
Es baja calidad
Fr de qualité inférieure
It di qualità inferiore
Pt baixo-nível

**loyer** (m) n Fr
De Miete (f)
En rent
Es alquiler (m)
It pigione; affitto (f m)
Pt renda (f)

**lucratif** adj Fr
De einträglich; gewinnbrin-
   gend
En lucrative
Es lucrativo
It lucrativo
Pt lucrativo

**lucrative** adj En
De einträglich; gewinnbrin-
   gend
Es lucrativo
Fr lucratif
It lucrativo
Pt lucrativo

**lucrativo** adj Es, It, Pt
De einträglich; gewinnbrin-
   gend
En lucrative
Fr lucratif

**lucro** (m) n Es, Pt
De Gewinn (m)
En profit
Fr bénéfice; profit (m)
It utile; profitto (m)

**lucro bruto** (m) Pt
De Bruttogewinn (m)
En gross profit
Es ganancia bruta (f)
Fr bénéfice brut (m)
It utile lordo (m)

**lucro cesante** (m) Es
De Gewinnausfall (m)
En loss of profits
Fr perte de bénéfices (f)
It perdita di utili (f)
Pt perda de lucros (f)

**lucro líquido** (m) Pt
De Reingewinn (m)
En net profit
Es ganancia neta (f)
Fr bénéfice net (m)
It utile netto (m)

**lucros de capital** (m pl) Pt
De Kapitalgewinn (n)
En capital gains
Es beneficios sobre capital (m
   pl)
Fr gains en capital (m pl)
It plusvalore di capitale (m pl)

**lucros não distribuidos** (m pl)
   Pt
De unverteilte Gewinne (n pl)
En undistributed profits
Es beneficios no distribuidos
   (m pl)
Fr bénéfices non répartis (m
   pl)
It profitti non distribuiti (m pl)

**lucros no papel** (m) Pt
De imaginärer Gewinn (m)
En paper profit
Es ganancia por realizar (f)
Fr profit fictif (m)
It utile sulla carta (m)

**Luftfracht** (f) n De
En air freight
Es flete aéreo (m)
Fr fret aérien (m)
It trasporto aereo (m)
Pt frete aéreo (m)

**Luftfrachtbrief** (m) n De
En air waybill
Es carta de porte aéreo (f)
Fr lettre de transport aérien
   (f)
It nota di spedizione aerea (f)
Pt guia de porte aéreo (m)

**Lufthafen** (m) n De
En airport
Es aeropuerto (m)
Fr aéroport (m)
It aeroporto (m)
Pt aeroporto (m)

**Luftpost** (f) n De
En airmail
Es correo aéreo (m)
Fr poste aérienne (f)

It posta aerea (f)
Pt correio aéreo (m)

**Luftpostbrief** (m) n De
En air letter
Es carta por avión (f)
Fr aérogramme (m)
It lettera aerea (f)
Pt carta de avião (f)

**Luftpostempfangsbescheini-
   gung** (f) n De
En airmail receipt
Es recibo aeropostal (m)
Fr récépissé de poste aérien-
   ne (m)
It ricevimento per posta aerea
   (m)
Pt recibo de via aérea (m)

**Luftterminal** (n) n De
En air terminal
Es terminal de aeropuerto (f)
Fr aérogare (f)
It aerostazione (f)
Pt estação terminal aérea (f)

**Lufttransport** (m) n De
En air transport
Es transporte aéreo (m)
Fr transport aérien (m)
It trasporto aereo (m)
Pt transporte aéreo (m)

**Luftverkehr** (m) n De
En air traffic
Es tráfico aéreo (m)
Fr trafic aérien (m)
It traffico aereo (m)
Pt tráfego aéreo (m)

**luggage locker** En
De Gepäckschliessfach (n)
Es casilla de equipaje (f)
Fr coffre de bagages (m)
It cassetta bagaglio (f)
Pt depósito de bagagem indi-
   vidualizado (m)

**lump sum** En
De Pauschalbetrag (m)
Es suma global (f)
Fr somme globale (f)
It somma globale (f)
Pt soma por inteiro (f)

**lunch-hour** *n* En
De Mittagspause *(f)*
Es hora del almuerzo *(f)*
Fr heure du déjeuner *(f)*
It ora di colazione *(f)*
Pt hora do almoço *(f)*

**luxury goods** En
De Luxuswaren *(f pl)*
Es artículos de lujo *(m pl)*
Fr articles de luxe *(m pl)*
It articoli di lusso *(m pl)*
Pt artigos de luxo *(m pl)*

**luxury tax** En
De Luxussteuer *(f)*
Es impuesto de lujo *(m)*
Fr impôt de luxe *(m)*
It tassa sugli articoli di lusso *(f)*
Pt imposto de luxo *(m)*

**Luxussteuer** *(f) n* De
En luxury tax
Es impuesto de lujo *(m)*
Fr impôt de luxe *(m)*
It tassa sugli articoli di lusso *(f)*
Pt imposto de luxo *(m)*

**Luxuswaren** *(f pl) n* De
En luxury goods
Es artículos de lujo *(m pl)*
Fr articles de luxe *(m pl)*
It articoli di lusso *(m pl)*
Pt artigos de luxo *(m pl)*

**M**

**Maat** *(m) n* De
En mate
Es primer oficial *(m)*
Fr second *(m)*
It primo ufficiale *(m)*
Pt imediato *(m)*

**macchina** *(f) n* It
De Maschine *(f)*
En machine
Es máquina *(f)*
Fr machine *(f)*
Pt máquina *(f)*

**macchina da scrivere** *(f)* It
De Schreibmaschine *(f)*
En typewriter
Es máquina de escribir *(f)*
Fr machine à écrire *(f)*
Pt máquina de escrever *(f)*

**macchina per stampare indi-rizzi** *(f)* It
De Adressiermaschine *(f)*
En addressing machine
Es máquina de imprimir direc-ciones *(f)*
Fr machine à imprimer les adresses *(f)*
Pt máquina de endereços *(m)*

**macchinario** *(m) n* It
De Maschinerie *(f)*
En machinery
Es maquinaría *(f)*
Fr machinerie *(f)*
Pt maquinaria *(f)*

**macchina venditrice auto-matica** *(f)* It
De Verkaufsautomat *(m)*
En vending machine
Es máquina expendedora *(f)*
Fr distributeur automatique *(m)*
Pt máquina de vendas *(f)*

**machine** *n* En, Fr *(f)*
De Maschine *(f)*
Es máquina *(f)*
It macchina *(f)*
Pt máquina *(f)*

**machine à additionner** *(f)* Fr
De Addiermaschine *(f)*
En adding machine
Es máquina de sumar *(f)*
It addizionatrice *(f)*
Pt máquina de somar *(f)*

**machine à affranchir** *(f)* Fr
De Frankiermaschine *(f)*
En franking machine
Es máquina de franquear *(f)*
It affrancatrice postale *(f)*
Pt máquina de franquear *(f)*

**machine à calculer** *(f)* Fr
De Rechenmaschine *(f)*
En calculator
Es calculadora *(f)*

It calcolatrice *(f)*
Pt máquina de calcular *(f)*

**machine à dictée** *(f)* Fr
De Diktaphon *(n)*
En dictating machine
Es dictáfono *(m)*
It dittafono *(m)*
Pt máquina de dictar *(f)*

**machine à écrire** *(f)* Fr
De Schreibmaschine *(f)*
En typewriter
Es máquina de escribir *(f)*
It macchina da scrivere *(f)*
Pt máquina de escrever *(f)*

**machine à imprimer les adresses** *(f)* Fr
De Adressiermaschine *(f)*
En addressing machine
Es máquina de imprimir direc-ciones *(f)*
It macchina per stampare indirizzi *(f)*
Pt máquina de endereços *(m)*

**machine down-time** En
De Maschinenstillstandzeit *(f)*
Es tiempo improductivo de la máquina *(m)*
Fr temps de panne machine *(m)*
It tempo passivo di macchina *(m)*
Pt tempo-morto da máquina *(m)*

**machine language** En
De Maschinensprache *(f)*
Es lenguaje de máquina *(m)*
Fr langage-machine *(m)*
It linguaggio di macchina *(m)*
Pt linguagem da máquina *(m)*

**machinerie** *n (f)* Fr
De Maschinerie *(f)*
En machinery
Es maquinaría *(f)*
It macchinario *(m)*
Pt maquinaria *(f)*

**machinery** *n* En
De Maschinerie *(f)*
Es maquinaría *(f)*
Fr machinerie *(f)*
It macchinario *(m)*
Pt maquinaria *(f)*

**magasin** *(m)* n Fr
De Laden; Lager *(m n)*
En shop; store
Es tienda; almacén *(f m)*
It bottega; magazzino *(f m)*
Pt loja; armazém *(f m)*

**magasin à succursales multiples** *(m)* Fr
De Kettengeschäft *(n)*
En chain store
Es sucursal de cadena de almacenes *(f)*
It negozio a catena *(m)*
Pt sucursal de cadeia de armazéns *(f)*

**magazzino** *(m)* n It
De Lager; Warenlager *(n)*
En store; warehouse
Es almacén *(m)*
Fr magasin; entrepôt *(m)*
Pt armazém *(m)*

**magazzino doganale** *(m)* It
De Lager unter Zollverschluss *(n)*
En bonded warehouse
Es almacén de aduanas *(m)*
Fr entrepôt des douanes *(m)*
Pt armazém alfandegário *(m)*

**maggazzinaggio** *(m)* n It
De Lagerung *(f)*
En storage
Es almacenamiento *(m)*
Fr emmagasinage *(m)*
Pt armazenamento *(m)*

**maglieria** *(f)* n It
De Strickwaren *(f pl)*
En knitted goods
Es géneros de punto *(m pl)*
Fr bonneterie *(f)*
Pt artigos de malha de lã *(m pl)*

**Magnetband** *(n)* n De
En magnetic tape
Es cinta magnética *(f)*
Fr bande magnétique *(f)*
It nastro magnetico *(m)*
Pt fita magnética *(f)*

**magnetic tape** En
De Magnetband *(n)*
Es cinta magnética *(f)*
Fr bande magnétique *(f)*

It nastro magnetico *(m)*
Pt fita magnética *(f)*

**mail** n En
De Post *(f)*
Es correo *(m)*
Fr poste *(f)*
It posta *(f)*
Pt correio *(m)*

**mail-box** n Am
En letter-box
De Briefkasten *(m)*
Es buzón *(m)*
Fr boîte aux lettres *(f)*
It cassetta postale *(f)*
Pt caixa do correio *(f)*

**mail order** En
De Auftrag durch die Post *(m)*
Es pedido por correo *(m)*
Fr commande par lettre *(f)*
It ordine per corrispondenza *(f)*
Pt venda pelo correio *(f)*

**mail transfer** En
De Postüberweisung *(f)*
Es transferencia postal *(f)*
Fr virement postal *(m)*
It trasferimento per posta *(m)*
Pt transferência postal *(f)*

**main-d'œuvre** *(f)* n Fr
De Arbeitskräfte; Manneskraft *(f pl; f)*
En manpower; labour force
Es mano de obra *(f)*
It mano d'opera *(f)*
Pt mão-de-obra *(f)*

**main-d'œuvre étrangère** *(f)* Fr
De Fremdarbeiterschaft *(f)*
En foreign labour
Es mano de obra extranjera *(f)*
It mano d'opera straniera *(f)*
Pt mão-de-obra estrangeira *(f)*

**maintenance** n En
De Instandhaltung *(f)*
Es mantenimiento *(m)*
Fr entretien *(m)*
It manutenzione *(f)*
Pt manutenção *(f)*

**mais barato** Pt
De billiger
En cheaper

Es más barato
Fr meilleur marché
It meno caro

**maison** *(f)* n Fr
De Haus *(n)*
En house
Es casa *(f)*
It casa *(f)*
Pt casa *(f)*

**maison d'édition** *(f)* Fr
De Verlag *(m)*
En publishing house
Es casa editorial *(f)*
It casa editrice *(f)*
Pt casa editora *(f)*

**maison d'escompte** *(f)* Fr
De Diskontbank *(f)*
En discount house
Es casa de descuentos *(f)*
It banca di sconto *(f)*
Pt agência corretora de descontos *(f)*

**maison de commerce** *(f)* Fr
De Firma *(f)*
En business; firm
Es casa de comercio *(f)*
It casa commerciale *(f)*
Pt casa de comércio *(f)*

**maison solide** *(f)* Fr
De alteingeführtes Geschäft *(n)*
En old-established business
Es casa sólida *(f)*
It casa di vecchia fondazione *(f)*
Pt empresa de há muito estabelecida *(f)*

**majority holding** En
De Mehrheitsbeteiligung *(f)*
Es tenencia de acciones por mayoría *(f)*
Fr participation majoritaire *(f)*
It partecipazione maggioritaria *(f)*
Pt propriedade em maioria *(f)*

**make a counteroffer** En
De ein Gegenangebot abgeben
Es hacer una contraoferta
Fr faire une contre-offre
It fare una controfferta
Pt fazer uma contra-proposta

**make an appointment** En
De eine Verabredung treffen
Es hacer una cita
Fr prendre un rendez-vous
It fissare un appuntamento
Pt marcar um encontro

**make an offer** En
De eine Offerte machen
Es hacer una oferta
Fr faire offre
It fare una oferta
Pt fazer uma oferta

**Makler** (m) n De
En broker
Es corredor (m)
Fr courtier (m)
It sensale (m)
Pt corretor (m)

**Makler für Verbrauchsgüter**
(m) De
En commodity broker
Es corredor de mercaderías
(m)
Fr courtier en marchandises
(m)
It sensale di merci (m)
Pt corretor de mercadorias
(m)

**Maklergebühr** (f) n De
En brokerage
Es corretaje (m)
Fr courtage (m)
It senseria (f)
Pt corretagem (f)

**maklergebührenfrei** De
En free of commission
Es franco-comisión
Fr franco courtage
It franco mediazione
Pt isento de comissão

**malhonnête** adj Fr
De unehrlich
En dishonest
Es deshonesto
It disonesto
Pt deshonesto

**malversatore** (m) n It
De Veruntreuer (m)
En embezzler
Es defalcador (m)

Fr détourneur (m)
Pt desfalcador (m)

**management** n En
De Vorstand (m)
Es dirección (f)
Fr administration; gestion (f)
It direzione; amministrazione
(f)
Pt gerência; direcção (f)

**management consultant** En
De Geschäftsführungsbera—ter
(m)
Es asesor administrativo (m)
Fr ingénieur-conseil en org-
anisation (m)
It consulente di direzione
aziendale (m)
Pt perito de administração (m)

**manager** n En
De Geschäftsleiter (m)
Es director (m)
Fr directeur (m)
It direttore (m)
Pt gerente; director (m)

**managing director** En
Am president
De geschäftsleitender Direktor
(m)
Es director gerente (m)
Fr administrateur délégué (m)
It amministratore delegato
(m)
Pt director geral (m)

**mañana** adv Es
De morgen
En tomorrow
Fr demain
It domani
Pt amanhã

**mancanza** (f) n It
De Nichteinhaltung (f)
En default
Es falta (f)
Fr défaillance; défaut (f m)
Pt falta (f)

**mancare** vb It
De versagen; durchfallen
En fail
Es fallar; faltar
Fr échouer; faillir
Pt falhar; faltar

**mancata accettazione** (f) It
De Nichtannahme (f)
En nonacceptance
Es rechazo (m)
Fr non-acceptation (f)
Pt não-aceitação (f)

**mancato pagamento** (m) It
De Nichtzahlung (f)
En failure to pay
Es falta de pago (f)
Fr défaut de paiement (m)
Pt falta de pagamento (f)

**mancia** (f) n It
De Trinkgeld (n)
En tip; gratuity
Es propina (f)
Fr pourboire (m)
Pt gorjeta (f)

**mandant** (m) n Fr
De Vollmachtgeber (m)
En principal
Es mandante (m)
It mandante (m)
Pt mandante (m)

**mandante** (m) n Es, It, Pt
De Vollmachtgeber (m)
En principal
Fr mandant (m)

**mandante não divulgado** (m)
Pt
De nicht bekanntgegebener
Auftraggeber (m)
En undisclosed principal
Es mandante no nombrado
(m)
Fr mandant non divulgé (m)
It mandante non nominato
(m)

**mandante non nominato** (m) It
De nicht bekanntgegebener
Auftraggeber (m)
En undisclosed principal
Es mandante no nombrado
(m)
Fr mandant non divulgé (m)
Pt mandante não divulgado
(m)

**mandante no nombrado** (m)
Es
De nicht bekanntgegebener
Auftraggeber (m)

**En** undisclosed principal
**Fr** mandant non divulgé (m)
**It** mandante non nominato (m)
**Pt** mandante não divulgado (m)

**mandant non divulgé** (m) Fr
**De** nicht bekanntgegebener Auftraggeber (m)
**En** undisclosed principal
**Es** mandante no nombrado (m)
**It** mandante non nominato (m)
**Pt** mandante não divulgado (m)

**mandat** (m) n Fr
**De** Vollmacht; Vertretung (f)
**En** authority; agency
**Es** autoridad; mandato (f m)
**It** autorità; mandato (f m)
**Pt** autoridade; mandato (f m)

**mandataire** (m) n Fr
**De** Bevollmächtigte(r) (m)
**En** attorney
**Es** apoderado (m)
**It** mandatario (m)
**Pt** procurador (m)

**mandatario** (m) n It
**De** Bevollmächtigte(r) (m)
**En** attorney
**Es** apoderado (m)
**Fr** mandataire (m)
**Pt** procurador (m)

**mandato** (m) n Es, It, Pt
**De** Vertretung; Befugnis (f)
**En** legal agency; warrant
**Fr** mandat; ordonnance (m f)

**mandat-poste** (m) n Fr
**De** Postanweisung (f)
**En** postal order
**Es** giro postal (m)
**It** vaglia postale (f)
**Pt** vale postal (m)

**Mangel** (m) n De
**En** deficiency; defect
**Es** deficiencia; defecto (f m)
**Fr** manque; défaut (m)
**It** ammanco; difetto (m)
**Pt** deficiência; defeito (f m)

**mangelhafte Lieferung** (f) De
**En** short delivery
**Es** entrega deficiente (f)
**Fr** livraison incomplète (f)
**It** consegna deficiente (f)
**Pt** entrega insuficiente (f)

**man-hours** n pl En
**De** Arbeitsstunde pro Mann (f)
**Es** horas-hombre (f pl)
**Fr** heures-homme (f pl)
**It** ore-uomo (f pl)
**Pt** horas-homem (f pl)

**manifest** n En
**De** Ladungsverzeichnis (n)
**Es** manifiesto (m)
**Fr** manifeste (m)
**It** manifesto (m)
**Pt** manifesto (m)

**manifeste** (m) n Fr
**De** Ladungsverzeichnis (n)
**En** manifest
**Es** manifiesto (m)
**It** manifesto (m)
**Pt** manifesto (m)

**manifesto** (m) n It, Pt
**De** Ladungsverzeichnis (n)
**En** manifest
**Es** manifiesto (m)
**Fr** manifeste (m)

**manifiesto** (m) n Es
**De** Ladungsverzeichnis (n)
**En** manifest
**Fr** manifeste (m)
**It** manifesto (m)
**Pt** manifesto (m)

**manipolazione** (f) n It
**De** Schiebung (f)
**En** manipulation
**Es** manipulación (f)
**Fr** manipulation (f)
**Pt** manipulação (f)

**manipulação** (f) n Pt
**De** Schiebung (f)
**En** manipulation
**Es** manipulación (f)
**Fr** manipulation (f)
**It** manipolazione (f)

**manipulación** (f) n Es
**De** Schiebung (f)
**En** manipulation

**Fr** manipulation (f)
**It** manipolazione (f)
**Pt** manipulação (f)

**manipulation** n En, Fr (f)
**De** Schiebung (f)
**Es** manipulación (f)
**It** manipolazione (f)
**Pt** manipulação (f)

**Manipulationsgebühr** (f) n De
**En** handling charges
**Es** gastos de manutención (m pl)
**Fr** frais de manutention (m pl)
**It** spese di gestione (f pl)
**Pt** custas de manejo (f pl)

**Manneskraft** (f) n De
**En** manpower
**Es** mano de obra (f)
**Fr** main-d´œuvre (f)
**It** mano d´opera (f)
**Pt** mão-de-obra (f)

**Mannschaft** (eines Schiffes) (f) n De
**En** crew
**Es** tripulación (f)
**Fr** équipage (m)
**It** equipaggio (m)
**Pt** tripulação (f)

**mano de obra** (f) Es
**De** Arbeitskräfte; Manneskraft (f pl; f)
**En** manpower; labour force
**Fr** main-d´œuvre (f)
**It** mano d´opera (f)
**Pt** mão-de-obra (f)

**mano de obra extranjera** (f) Es
**De** Fremdarbeiterschaft (f)
**En** foreign labour
**Fr** main-d´œuvre étrangère (f)
**It** mano d´opera straniera (f)
**Pt** mão-de-obra estrangeira (f)

**mano d'opera** (f) It
**De** Arbeitskräfte; Manneskraft (f pl; f)
**En** manpower; labour force
**Es** mano de obra (f)
**Fr** main-d´œuvre (f)
**Pt** mão-de-obra (f)

**mano d'opera straniera** *(f)* It
De Fremdarbeiterschaft *(f)*
En foreign labour
Es mano de obra extranjera *(f)*
Fr main-d'œuvre étrangère *(f)*
Pt mão-de-obra estrangeira *(f)*

**manomètre** *(m)* n Fr
De Druckmesser *(m)*
En pressure gauge
Es manómetro *(m)*
It manometro *(m)*
Pt manómetro *(m)*

**manómetro** *(m)* n Es, Pt
De Druckmesser *(m)*
En pressure gauge
Fr manomètre; jauge de pression *(m f)*
It manometro *(m)*

**manometro** *(m)* n It
De Druckmesser *(m)*
En pressure gauge
Es manómetro *(m)*
Fr manomètre; jauge de pression *(m f)*
Pt manómetro *(m)*

**manpower** n En
De Manneskraft *(f)*
Es mano de obra *(f)*
Fr main-d'œuvre *(f)*
It mano d'opera *(f)*
Pt mão-de-obra *(f)*

**manquant** *(m)* n Fr
De Abwesende(r) *(m)*
En absentee
Es ausente *(m)*
It assente *(m)*
Pt ausente *(m)*

**manque** *(m)* n Fr
De Mangel *(m)*
En deficiency
Es deficiencia *(f)*
It ammanco; insufficienza *(m f)*
Pt deficiência *(f)*

**manque de pratique** *(m)* Fr
De Unerfahrenheit *(f)*
En inexperience
Es falta de experiencia *(f)*
It inesperienza *(f)*
Pt inexperiência *(f)*

**mantenimiento** *(m)* n Es
De Instandhaltung *(f)*
En maintenance
Fr entretien *(m)*
It manutenzione *(f)*
Pt manutenção *(f)*

**manter** vb Pt
De behalten; unterhalten
En keep; maintain
Es tener; conservar
Fr tenir; maintenir
It tenere; mantenere

**manual** n En; Es, Pt *(m)*
De Handbuch *(n)*
Fr manuel *(m)*
It manuale *(m)*

**manual** adj En, Es, Pt
De Hand-
Fr manuel
It manuale

**manuale** *(m)* n It
De Handbuch *(n)*
En handbook
Es manual *(m)*
Fr manuel *(m)*
Pt manual *(m)*

**manuale** adj It
De Hand-
En manual
Es manual
Fr manuel
Pt manual

**manuel** *(m)* n Fr
De Handbuch *(n)*
En handbook
Es manual *(m)*
It manuale *(m)*
Pt manual *(m)*

**manuel** adj Fr
De Hand-
En manual
Es manual
It manuale
Pt manual

**manueller Locher** *(m)* De
En key-punch
Es perforación en clave *(f)*
Fr perforatrice à clavier *(f)*
It perforatore *(f)*
Pt perforador *(m)*

**manufacturer** n En
De Erzeuger; Hersteller *(m)*
Es fabricante *(m)*
Fr fabricant *(m)*
It fabbricante *(m)*
Pt fabricante *(m)*

**manuscrit dactylographié** *(m)* Fr
De Maschinenschrift *(f)*
En typescript
Es texto mecanografiado *(m)*
It dattiloscritto *(m)*
Pt texto dactilografado *(m)*

**manutenção** *(f)* n Pt
De Instandhaltung *(f)*
En maintenance
Es mantenimiento *(m)*
Fr entretien *(m)*
It manutenzione *(f)*

**manutenzione** *(f)* n It
De Instandhaltung *(f)*
En maintenance
Es mantenimiento *(m)*
Fr entretien *(m)*
Pt manutenção *(f)*

**mão-de-obra** *(f)* n Pt
De Manneskraft *(f)*
En manpower
Es mano de obra *(f)*
Fr main-d'œuvre *(f)*
It mano d'opera *(f)*

**mão-de-obra estrangeira** *(f)* Pt
De Fremdarbeiterschaft *(f)*
En foreign labour
Es mano de obra extranjera *(f)*
Fr main-d'œuvre étrangère *(f)*
It mano d'opera straniera *(f)*

**Mappe** *(f)* n De
En folder
Es carpeta *(f)*
Fr chemise *(f)*
It cartella *(f)*
Pt pasta *(f)*

**máquina** *(f)* n Es, Pt
De Maschine *(f)*
En machine
Fr machine *(f)*
It macchina *(f)*

**máquina de calcular** *(f)* Pt
De Rechenmaschine *(f)*
En calculator
Es calculadora *(f)*
Fr machine à calculer *(f)*
It calcolatrice *(f)*

**máquina de dictar** *(f)* Pt
De Diktaphon *(n)*
En dictating machine
Es dictáfono *(m)*
Fr machine à dictée *(f)*
It dittafono *(m)*

**máquina de endereços** *(m)* Pt
De Adressiermaschine *(f)*
En addressing machine
Es máquina de imprimir direcciones *(f)*
Fr machine à imprimer les adresses *(f)*
It macchina per stampare indirizzi *(f)*

**máquina de escrever** *(f)* Pt
De Schreibmaschine *(f)*
En typewriter
Es máquina de escribir *(f)*
Fr machine à écrire *(f)*
It macchina da scrivere *(f)*

**máquina de escribir** *(f)* Es
De Schreibmaschine *(f)*
En typewriter
Fr machine à écrire *(f)*
It macchina da scrivere *(f)*
Pt máquina de escrever *(f)*

**máquina de franquear** *(f)* Es, Pt
De Frankiermaschine *(f)*
En franking machine
Fr machine à affranchir *(f)*
It affrancatrice postale *(f)*

**máquina de imprimir direcciones** *(f)* Es
De Adressiermaschine *(f)*
En addressing machine
Fr machine à imprimer les adresses *(f)*
It macchina per stampare indirizzi *(f)*
Pt máquina de endereços *(m)*

**máquina de somar** *(f)* Pt
De Addiermaschine *(f)*
En adding machine

Es máquina de sumar *(f)*
Fr machine à additionner *(f)*
It addizionatrice *(f)*

**máquina de sumar** *(f)* Es
De Addiermaschine *(f)*
En adding machine
Fr machine à additionner *(f)*
It addizionatrice *(f)*
Pt máquina de somar *(f)*

**máquina de vendas** *(f)* Pt
De Verkaufsautomat *(m)*
En vending machine
Es máquina expendedora *(f)*
Fr distributeur automatique *(m)*
It macchina venditrice automatica *(f)*

**máquina expendedora** *(f)* Es
De Verkaufsautomat *(m)*
En vending machine
Fr distributeur automatique *(m)*
It macchina venditrice automatica *(f)*
Pt máquina de vendas *(f)*

**maquinaría** *(f)* n Es
De Maschinerie *(f)*
En machinery
Fr machinerie *(f)*
It macchinario *(m)*
Pt maquinaria *(f)*

**maquinaria** *(f)* n Pt
De Maschinerie *(f)*
En machinery
Es maquinaría *(f)*
Fr machinerie *(f)*
It macchinario *(m)*

**mar** *(m)* n Es, Pt
De See *(f)*
En sea
Fr mer *(f)*
It mare *(m)*

**marca** *(f)* n Es, It, Pt
De Marke *(f)*
En brand
Fr marque *(f)*

**marca de destino** *(f)* Es
De Benennung des Bestimmungshafen *(f)*
En port mark

Fr marque de destination *(f)*
It marche di destinazione *(f pl)*
Pt marca de porto *(f)*

**marca de fábrica** *(f)* Es
De Warenzeichen *(n)*
En trademark
Fr marque de fabrique *(f)*
It marchio di fabbrica *(m)*
Pt marca de fabrico *(f)*

**marca de fabrico** *(f)* Pt
De Warenzeichen *(n)*
En trademark
Es marca de fábrica *(f)*
Fr marque de fabrique *(f)*
It marchio di fabbrica *(m)*

**marca de garantia** *(f)* Pt
De Feingehaltsstempel *(m)*
En hall-mark
Es punzón de garantía *(m)*
Fr poinçon *(m)*
It punzonatura di garanzia *(f)*

**marca de porto** *(f)* Pt
De Benennung des Bestimmungshafen *(f)*
En port mark
Es marca de destino *(f)*
Fr marque de destination *(f)*
It marche di destinazione *(f pl)*

**marca di punta** *(f)* It
De führende Marke *(f)*
En brand leader
Es marca directriz *(f)*
Fr marque de point *(f)*
Pt marca mais cotada *(f)*

**marca directriz** *(f)* Es
De führende Marke *(f)*
En brand leader
Fr marque de point *(f)*
It marca di punta *(f)*
Pt marca mais cotada *(f)*

**marca mais cotada** *(f)* Pt
De führende Marke *(f)*
En brand leader
Es marca directriz *(f)*
Fr marque de point *(f)*
It marca di punta *(f)*

**marcar um encontro** Pt
De  eine Verabredung treffen
En  make an appointment
Es  hacer una cita
Fr  prendre un rendez-vous
It  fissare un appuntamento


**marchand de titres** (m) Fr
De  Börsenhändler (m)
En  stockjobber
Es  agiotista (m)
It  aggiotatore (m)
Pt  agiota (m)


**marchander** vb Fr
De  feilschen
En  haggle
Am  bargain
Es  regatear
It  mercanteggiare; cavillare
Pt  regatear


**marchandise** (f) n Fr
De  Gut; Ware (n f)
En  commodity; merchandise
Es  mercadería; mercancía (f)
It  merce; prodotto (f m)
Pt  mercadoria; produto (f m)
En  merchandise


**marchandises** (f pl) n Fr
De  Güter (n pl)
En  goods
Es  mercancías (f pl)
It  merce (f)
Pt  mercadorias (f pl)


**marchandises à condition** (f
    pl) Fr
De  Probegüter (n pl)
En  goods on approval
Es  mercancías sujetas a apro-
    bación (f pl)
It  merce soggetta ad appro-
    vazione (f pl)
Pt  artigos sujeitos a apro-
    vação (m pl)


**marchandises avariées** (f pl)
    Fr
De  beschädigte Waren (f pl)
En  damaged goods
Es  mercancías averiadas (f pl)
It  merce avariata (f)
Pt  mercadorias danificadas (f
    pl)


**marchandises dangereuses** (f
    pl) Fr
De  gefährliche Waren (f pl)
En  dangerous goods
Es  mercancías peligrosas (f pl)
It  merce pericolosa (f)
Pt  mercadorias perigosas (f
    pl)


**marchandises de retour** (f pl)
    Fr
De  Retourware (f)
En  returned goods
Es  mercancías devueltas (f pl)
It  merce di ritorno (f pl)
Pt  mercadorias devoluidas (f)


**marchandises disponibles** (f
    pl) Fr
De  sofort lieferbare Waren (f
    pl)
En  spot goods
Es  mercancías prontas (f pl)
It  merce pronta (f)
Pt  mercadorias prontas (f pl)


**marchandises en douane** (f pl)
    Fr
De  Waren unter Zollverschluss
    (f pl)
En  bonded goods
Es  mercancías en aduana (f
    pl)
It  merci sotto vincolo doga-
    nale (f pl)
Pt  mercadorias à ordem da
    alfândega (f pl)


**marchandises en magasin** (f
    pl) Fr
De  Vorrat auf Lager (m)
En  stock in hand
Es  mercancías en almacén (f
    pl)
It  merce in magazzino (f)
Pt  mercadorias em existência
    (f)


**marchandises périssables** (f
    pl) Fr
De  leicht verderbliche Waren (f
    pl)
En  perishable goods
Es  mercancías perecederas (f
    pl)
It  merci deperibili (f pl)
Pt  mercadorias perecíveis (f
    pl)


**marché** (m) n Fr
De  Markt; Handel (m)
En  market; deal
Es  mercado; negócio (m)
It  mercato; affare (m)
Pt  mercado; negócio (m)


**marché commercial** (m) Fr
De  Warenmarkt (m)
En  produce market
Es  mercado de productos (m)
It  mercato commerciale (m)
Pt  mercado de produtos (m)


**marché commun** (m) Fr
De  gemeinsamer Markt (m)
En  Common Market
Es  mercado común (m)
It  mercato comune (m)
Pt  mercado comum (m)


**marché de l'escompte** (m) Fr
De  Diskontmarkt (m)
En  discount market
Es  mercado de descuentos
    (m)
It  mercato di sconto (m)
Pt  mercado de desconto (m)


**marché de matières premières**
    (m) Fr
De  Rohstoffmarkt (m)
En  commodity market
Es  mercado de materias pri-
    mas (m)
It  mercato di materie prime
    (m)
Pt  mercado de matérias pri-
    mas (m)


**marché des valeurs** (m) Fr
De  Aktienmarkt (m)
En  share market
Am  stock market
Es  mercado de valores (m)
It  mercato azionario (m)
Pt  mercado de acções (m)


**marche di destinazione** (f pl)
    It
De  Benennung des Bestim-
    mungshafen (f)
En  port mark
Es  marca de destino (f)
Fr  marque de destination (f)
Pt  marca de porto (f)

**marché du terme** *(m)* Fr
De  Terminmarkt *(m)*
En  futures market
Es  mercado de futuros *(m)*
It  mercato a termine *(m)*
Pt  mercado de futuros *(m)*

**marché du travail** *(m)* Fr
De  Arbeitsmarkt *(m)*
En  labour market
Es  mercado de mano de obra *(m)*
It  mercato della mano d'opera *(m)*
Pt  mercado de mão de obra *(m)*

**marché exclusif** *(m)* Fr
De  ausschliesslicher Markt *(m)*
En  exclusive market
Es  mercado exclusivo *(m)*
It  mercato esclusivo *(m)*
Pt  mercado exclusivo *(m)*

**marché fermé** *(m)* Fr
De  gesperrter Markt *(m)*
En  closed market
Es  mercado cerrado *(m)*
It  mercato chiuso *(m)*
Pt  mercado fechado *(m)*

**marché global** *(m)* Fr
De  Globalgeschäft *(n)*
En  package deal
Es  contrato global *(m)*
It  contratto globale *(m)*
Pt  contrato global *(m)*

**marché libre** *(m)* Fr
De  freier Markt *(m)*
En  open market
Es  mercado libre *(m)*
It  mercato libero *(m)*
Pt  mercado livre *(m)*

**marché monétaire** *(m)* Fr
De  Geldmarkt *(m)*
En  money market
Es  mercado de dinero *(m)*
It  mercato di denaro *(m)*
Pt  mercado da moeda *(m)*

**marché noir** *(m)* Fr
De  schwarzer Markt *(m)*
En  black market
Es  mercado negro *(m)*
It  mercato nero *(m)*
Pt  mercado negro *(m)*

**marché orienté à la baisse** *(m)* Fr
De  Baissemarkt *(m)*
En  bear market; falling market
Es  mercado bajista *(m)*
It  mercato tendente al ribasso *(m)*
Pt  mercado de tendência baixista *(m)*

**marché orienté à la hausse** *(m)* Fr
De  Haussemarkt *(m)*
En  bull market
Es  mercado alcista *(m)*
It  mercato tendente al rialzo *(m)*
Pt  mercado de tendência altista *(m)*

**marchio di fabbrica** *(m)* It
De  Warenzeichen *(n)*
En  trademark
Es  marca de fábrica *(f)*
Fr  marque de fabrique *(f)*
Pt  marca de fabrico *(f)*

**mare** *(m)* n It
De  See *(f)*
En  sea
Es  mar *(m)*
Fr  mer *(f)*
Pt  mar *(m)*

**marge** *(f)* n Fr
De  Spanne *(f)*
En  margin
Es  margen *(m)*
It  margine *(m)*
Pt  margem *(f)*

**marge brute de bénéfices** *(f)* Fr
De  Bruttoverdienstspanne *(f)*
En  gross margin
Es  márgen bruto *(m)*
It  margine lordo *(m)*
Pt  margem bruta *(f)*

**margem** *(f)* n Pt
De  Spanne *(f)*
En  margin
Es  margen *(m)*
Fr  marge *(f)*
It  margine *(m)*

**margem bruta** *(f)* Pt
De  Bruttoverdienstspanne *(f)*
En  gross margin
Es  márgen bruto *(m)*
Fr  marge brute de bénéfices *(f)*
It  margine lordo *(m)*

**margem de lucro líquido** *(f)* Pt
De  Reingewinnspanne *(f)*
En  net profit margin
Es  margen de beneficio neto *(m)*
Fr  marge nette de bénéfices *(f)*
It  margine di utile netto *(m)*

**margen** *(m)* n Es
De  Spanne *(f)*
En  margin
Fr  marge *(f)*
It  margine *(m)*
Pt  margem *(f)*

**márgen bruto** *(m)* Es
De  Bruttoverdienstspanne *(f)*
En  gross margin
Fr  marge brute de bénéfices *(f)*
It  margine lordo *(m)*
Pt  margem bruta *(f)*

**margen de beneficio neto** *(m)* Es
De  Reingewinnspanne *(f)*
En  net profit margin
Fr  marge nette de bénéfices *(f)*
It  margine di utile netto *(m)*
Pt  margem de lucro líquido *(m)*

**marge nette de bénéfices** *(f)* Fr
De  Reingewinnspanne *(f)*
En  net profit margin
Es  margen de beneficio neto *(m)*
It  margine di utile netto *(m)*
Pt  margem de lucro líquido *(f)*

**margin** n En
De  Spanne *(f)*
Es  margen *(m)*
Fr  marge *(f)*
It  margine *(m)*
Pt  margem *(f)*

**marginal analysis** En
  De Randanalyse *(f)*
  Es análisis marginal *(f)*
  Fr analyse marginale *(f)*
  It analisi marginale *(f)*
  Pt análise marginal *(f)*

**marginal cost** En
  De Randkosten *(pl)*
  Es coste marginal *(m)*
  Fr coût marginal *(m)*
  It costa marginale *(m)*
  Pt custo marginal *(m)*

**margine** *(m)* n It
  De Spanne *(f)*
  En margin
  Es margen *(m)*
  Fr marge *(f)*
  Pt margem *(f)*

**margine di utile netto** *(m)* It
  De Reingewinnspanne *(f)*
  En net profit margin
  Es margen de beneficio neto
    *(m)*
  Fr marge nette de bénéfices
    *(f)*
  Pt margem de lucro líquido *(f)*

**margine lordo** *(m)* It
  De Bruttoverdienstspanne *(f)*
  En gross margin
  Es márgen bruto *(m)*
  Fr marge brute de bénéfices
    *(f)*
  Pt margem bruta *(f)*

**marine** *adj* En
  De See-
  Es marítimo; marino
  Fr maritime
  It marino; marittimo
  Pt marinho; marítimo

**marine insurance broker** En
  De Seetransportversicherungs-
    makler *(m)*
  Es corredor de seguro marí-
    timo *(m)*
  Fr courtier d'assurances mari-
    times *(f)*
  It agente di assicurazioni
    marittime *(m)*
  Pt corretor de seguros maríti-
    mos *(m)*

**marinero** *adj* Es
  De seefest
  En seaworthy
  Fr en état de navigabilité
  It atto a tenere il mare
  Pt em condições de nave-
    gação

**marinho** *adj* Pt
  De See-
  En marine
  Es marítimo; marino
  Fr maritime
  It marino; marittimo

**marino** *adj* Es, It
  De See-
  En marine
  Fr maritime
  Pt marinho; marítimo

**maritime** *adj* En, Fr
  De See-
  Es marítimo
  It marittimo
  Pt marítimo

**marítimo** *adj* Es, Pt
  De See-
  En maritime
  Fr maritime
  It marittimo

**marittimo** *adj* It
  De See-
  En maritime
  Es marítimo
  Fr maritime
  Pt marítimo

**Marke** *(f)* n De
  En brand
  Es marca *(f)*
  Fr marque *(f)*
  It marca *(f)*
  Pt marca *(f)*

**Markenwaren** *(f pl)* n De
  En branded goods
  Es artículos de marca *(m pl)*
  Fr articles de marque *(m pl)*
  It articoli di marca *(m pl)*
  Pt artigos de marca *(m pl)*

**market** n En
  De Markt *(m)*
  Es mercado *(m)*
  Fr marché *(m)*

  It mercato *(m)*
  Pt mercado *(m)*

**marketable** *adj* En
  De marktfähig
  Es vendible
  Fr vendable
  It vendibile
  Pt comercializável

**market day** (local) En
  De Markttag *(m)*
  Es día de mercado *(m)*
  Fr jour de place *(m)*
  It giorno di mercato *(m)*
  Pt dia de mercado *(m)*

**market day** (financial) En
  De Börsentag *(m)*
  Es día de bolsa *(m)*
  Fr jour de bourse *(m)*
  It giorno di borsa *(m)*
  Pt dia de bolsa *(m)*

**market forces** En
  De Marktkräfte *(f pl)*
  Es fuerzas del mercado *(f pl)*
  Fr forces du marché *(f pl)*
  It forze di mercato *(f pl)*
  Pt forças de mercado *(f pl)*

**marketing agreement** En
  De Absatzübereinkommen *(n)*
  Es acuerdo mercantil *(m)*
  Fr accord de commerciali-
    sation *(m)*
  It accordo di mercato *(m)*
  Pt acordo sobre comerciali-
    zação *(m)*

**marketing director** En
  De Absatzdirektor *(m)*
  Es director mercantil *(m)*
  Fr administrateur chef d'écou-
    lement *(m)*
  It direttore di mercato *(m)*
  Pt director de comercialização
    *(m)*

**market penetration** En
  De Markteindringen *(n)*
  Es penetración en el mercado
    *(f)*
  Fr pénétration du marché *(f)*
  It penetrazione nel mercato
    *(f)*
  Pt ínfiltração no mercado *(f)*

**market price** En
De Marktpreis *(m)*
Es precio de mercado *(m)*
Fr cours du marché *(f)*
It prezzo del mercato *(m)*
Pt preço de mercado *(m)*

**market report** En
De Marktbericht *(m)*
Es informe del mercado *(m)*
Fr revue du marché *(f)*
It relazione sul mercato *(f)*
Pt informação do mercado *(f)*

**market research** En
De Marktforschung *(f)*
Es investigación del mercado *(f)*
Fr étude du marché *(f)*
It indagine di mercato *(f)*
Pt pesquisa de mercado *(f)*

**market share** En
De Marktanteil *(m)*
Es participación del mercado *(f)*
Fr participation au marché *(f)*
It quota del mercato *(f)*
Pt quota-parte no mercado *(f)*

**market value** En
De Marktwert *(m)*
Es valor de mercado *(m)*
Fr valeur marchande *(f)*
It valore di mercato *(m)*
Pt valor de mercado *(m)*

**Markt** *(m) n* De
En market
Es mercado *(m)*
Fr marché *(m)*
It mercato *(m)*
Pt mercado *(m)*

**Marktanteil** *(m) n* De
En market share
Es participación del mercado *(f)*
Fr participation au marché *(f)*
It quota del mercato *(f)*
Pt quota-parte no mercado *(f)*

**Marktbericht** *(m) n* De
En market report
Es informe del mercado *(m)*
Fr revue du marché *(f)*
It relazione sul mercato *(f)*
Pt informação do mercado *(f)*

**Markteindringen** *(n) n* De
En market penetration
Es penetración en el mercado *(f)*
Fr pénétration du marché *(f)*
It penetrazione nel mercato *(f)*
Pt ínfiltração no mercado *(f)*

**marktfähig** *adj* De
En marketable
Es vendible
Fr vendable
It vendibile
Pt comercializável

**Marktforschung** *(f) n* De
En market research
Es investigación del mercado *(f)*
Fr étude du marché *(f)*
It indagine di mercato *(f)*
Pt pesquisa de mercado *(f)*

**marktgängige Qualität** *(f)* De
En merchantable quality
Es calidad comerciable *(f)*
Fr qualité vendable *(f)*
It qualità commerciabile *(f)*
Pt qualidade comerciável *(f)*

**Marktkräfte** *(f pl) n* De
En market forces
Es fuerzas del mercado *(f pl)*
Fr forces du marché *(f pl)*
It forze di mercato *(f pl)*
Pt forças de mercado *(f pl)*

**Markt mit Baissetendenz** *(m)* De
En falling market
Es mercado en baja *(m)*
Fr marché orienté à la baisse *(m)*
It mercato in declino *(m)*
Pt mercado em decréscimo *(m)*

**Marktpreis** *(m) n* De
En market price
Es precio de mercado *(m)*
Fr cours du marché *(m)*
It prezzo del mercato *(m)*
Pt preço de mercado *(m)*

**Markttag** *(m) n* De
En market day
Es día de mercado *(m)*

Fr jour de place *(m)*
It giorno di mercato *(m)*
Pt dia de mercado *(m)*

**Marktumständen** *(m pl) n* De
En state of the market
Es condiciones del mercado *(f pl)*
Fr état du marché *(m)*
It condizioni del mercato *(f pl)*
Pt situação do mercado *(f)*

**Marktwert** *(m) n* De
En market value
Es valor de mercado *(m)*
Fr valeur marchande *(f)*
It valore di mercato *(m)*
Pt valor de mercado *(m)*

**maroquinerie** *(f) n* Fr
De Lederwaren *(f pl)*
En leather goods
Es marroquinería *(f)*
It pelletterie *(f pl)*
Pt artigos de cabedal *(m pl)*

**marque** *(f) n* Fr
De Handelsmarke *(f)*
En brand
Es marca *(f)*
It marca *(f)*
Pt marca *(f)*

**marque de destination** *(f)* Fr
De Benennung des Bestim-mungshafen *(f)*
En port mark
Es marca de destino *(f)*
It marche di destinazione *(f pl)*
Pt marca de porto *(f)*

**marque de fabrique** *(f)* Fr
De Warenzeichen *(n)*
En trademark
Es marca de fábrica *(f)*
It marchio di fabbrica *(m)*
Pt marca de fabrico *(f)*

**marque de point** *(f)* Fr
De führende Marke *(f)*
En brand leader
Es marca directriz *(f)*
It marca di punta *(f)*
Pt marca mais cotada *(f)*

**marroquinería** *(f)* n Es
- De  Lederwaren *(f pl)*
- En  leather goods
- Fr  maroquinerie *(f)*
- It  pelletterie *(f pl)*
- Pt  artigos de cabedal *(m pl)*

**masa obrera** *(f)* Es
- De  Belegschaft *(f)*
- En  work force
- Fr  effectifs *(m pl)*
- It  massa lavoratrice *(f)*
- Pt  massa trabalhadora *(f)*

**más barato** Es
- De  billiger
- En  cheaper
- Fr  meilleur marché
- It  meno caro
- Pt  mais barato

**Maschine** *(f)* n De
- En  machine
- Es  máquina *(f)*
- Fr  machine *(f)*
- It  macchina *(f)*
- Pt  máquina *(f)*

**Maschinenausrüstung** *(f)* n De
- En  computer hardware
- Es  mecánica de la máquina *(f)*
- Fr  hardware *(m)*
- It  componenti di macchina calcolatore *(m pl)*
- Pt  sistema físico *(m)*

**Maschinenbau** *(m)* n De
- En  mechanical engineering
- Es  ingeniería mecánica *(f)*
- Fr  construction mécanique *(f)*
- It  ingegneria meccanica *(f)*
- Pt  engenharia mecânica *(f)*

**Maschinenschrift** *(f)* n De
- En  typescript
- Es  texto mecanografiado *(m)*
- Fr  manuscrit dactylographié *(m)*
- It  dattiloscritto *(m)*
- Pt  texto dactilografado *(m)*

**Maschinensprache** *(f)* n De
- En  machine language
- Es  lenguaje de máquina *(m)*
- Fr  langage-machine *(m)*
- It  linguaggio di macchina *(m)*
- Pt  linguagem da máquina *(f)*

**Maschinenstillstandzeit** *(f)* n De
- En  machine down-time
- Es  tiempo improductivo de la máquina *(m)*
- Fr  temps de panne machine *(m)*
- It  tempo passivo di macchina *(m)*
- Pt  tempo-morto da máquina *(m)*

**Maschinerie** *(f)* n De
- En  machinery
- Es  maquinaría *(f)*
- Fr  machinerie *(f)*
- It  macchinario *(m)*
- Pt  maquinaria *(f)*

**más detalles** *(m pl)* Es
- De  weitere Auskunft *(f)*
- En  further information
- Fr  renseignements complémentaires *(m pl)*
- It  ulteriori informazioni *(f pl)*
- Pt  informação adicional *(f)*

**más detalles** *(m pl)* Es
- De  nähere Umstände *(m pl)*
- En  further particulars
- Fr  plus amples renseignements *(m pl)*
- It  ulteriori particolari *(m pl)*
- Pt  pormenores adicionais *(m pl)*

**Mass** *(n)* n De
- En  measure
- Es  medida *(f)*
- Fr  mesure *(f)*
- It  misura *(f)*
- Pt  medida *(f)*

**massaia** *(f)* n It
- De  Hausfrau *(f)*
- En  housewife
- Es  ama de casa *(f)*
- Fr  ménagère *(f)*
- Pt  dona de casa *(f)*

**massa lavoratrice** *(f)* It
- De  Belegschaft *(f)*
- En  work force
- Es  masa obrera *(f)*
- Fr  effectifs *(m pl)*
- Pt  massa trabalhadora *(f)*

**massa trabalhadora** *(f)* Pt
- De  Belegschaft *(f)*
- En  work force
- Es  masa obrera *(f)*
- Fr  effectifs *(m pl)*
- It  massa lavoratrice *(f)*

**Massenberechner** *(m)* n De
- En  quantity surveyor
- Es  medidor de contidades de obra *(m)*
- Fr  métreur-vérificateur *(m)*
- It  perito misuratore *(m)*
- Pt  perito na avaliação de quantidades *(m)*

**Massenfrachtführer** *(m)* n De
- En  bulk carrier
- Es  transportador a grand *(m)*
- Fr  transporteur de marchandises en vrac *(m)*
- It  trasportatore di merce alla rinfusa *(m)*
- Pt  transportador de carga geral *(m)*

**Massenherstellung** *(f)* n De
- En  mass production
- Es  producción en masa *(f)*
- Fr  production en masse *(f)*
- It  fabbricazione in massa *(f)*
- Pt  produção em massa *(f)*

**Masseverwalter** *(m)* n De
- En  liquidator
- Es  liquidador *(m)*
- Fr  liquidateur *(m)*
- It  liquidatore *(m)*
- Pt  executor da liquidação *(m)*

**massima buona fede** *(f)* It
- De  äusserst guter Glaube *(m)*
- En  utmost good faith
- Es  máxima buena fé *(f)*
- Fr  plus grande bonne foie *(f)*
- Pt  máxima boa-fé *(f)*

**massimo** *adj* It
- De  maximal
- En  maximum
- Es  máximo
- Fr  maximum
- Pt  máximo

**Mass oder Gewicht** De
- En  weight or measurement
- Es  peso o cubicaje
- Fr  poids ou mesure

It    peso o volume
Pt    peso ou medida

**mass production** En
De    Massenherstellung (f)
Es    producción en masa (f)
Fr    production en masse (f)
It    fabbricazione in massa (f)
Pt    produção em massa (f)

**Masstab** (m) n De
En    scale
Es    escala (f)
Fr    échelle (f)
It    scala (f)
Pt    escala (f)

**master of a ship** En
De    Kapitän (m)
Es    capitán de navío (m)
Fr    capitaine (m)
It    capitano di nave (m)
Pt    capitão de navio (m)

**mastro acquisti** (m) It
De    Einkaufsbuch (n)
En    bought ledger
Am    purchase book
Es    libro mayor de compras (m)
Fr    grand livre d'achats (m)
Pt    livro-mestre de compras (m)

**mate** (of a ship) n En
De    Maat (m)
Es    primer oficial (m)
Fr    second (m)
It    primo ufficiale (m)
Pt    imediato (m)

**mate's receipt** En
De    Übernahmebescheinigung (f)
Es    recibo de embarco (m)
Fr    billet de bord (m)
It    ricevuta d'imbarco (f)
Pt    recibo de embarque (m)

**materia** (f) n Es, It
De    Material (n)
En    material
Fr    matière (f)
Pt    matéria (f)

**matéria** (f) n Pt
De    Material (n)
En    material

Es    materia (f)
Fr    matière (f)
It    materia (f)

**material** (cloth) n En
De    Stoff (m)
Es    tejido (m)
Fr    étoffe; tissu (f m)
It    stoffa; tessuto (f m)
Pt    tecido (m)

**material** (substance) n En
De    Material (n)
Es    materia (f)
Fr    matière (f)
It    materia (f)
Pt    matéria (f)

**material** adj En, Es, Pt
De    wesentlich
Fr    essentiel
It    materiale

**Material** (n) n De
En    material
Es    materia (f)
Fr    matière (f)
It    materia (f)
Pt    matéria (f)

**materiale** adj It
De    wesentlich
En    material
Es    material
Fr    essentiel
Pt    material

**material publicitario** (m) Es
De    Werbetext (m)
En    advertising copy
Fr    copie publicitaire (f)
It    testo pubblicitario (m)
Pt    texto de publicidade (m)

**materia prima** (f) Es, It
De    Rohstoff (m)
En    raw material
Fr    matière première (f)
Pt    matéria prima (f)

**materia prima** (f) It
De    Rohstoff (m)
En    raw material
Es    materia prima (f)
Fr    matière première (f)
Pt    matéria prima (f)

**matéria prima** (f) Pt
De    Rohstoff (m)
En    raw material
Es    materia prima (f)
Fr    matière première (f)
It    materia prima (f)

**matière** (f) n Fr
De    Material (n)
En    material (substance)
Es    materia (f)
It    materia (f)
Pt    matéria (f)

**matière première** (f) Fr
De    Rohstoff (m)
En    raw material
Es    materia prima (f)
It    materia prima (f)
Pt    matéria prima (f)

**matrice** (f) n It
De    Talon (m)
En    counterfoil
Am    stub
Es    talón (m)
Fr    talon (m)
Pt    talão (m)

**Mattscheibe** (f) n De
En    ground glass
Es    cristal deslustrado (m)
Fr    verre dépoli (m)
It    vetro smerigliato (m)
Pt    vidro esmerilado (m)

**maturazione** (f) n It
De    Auflaufen (n)
En    accrual
Es    acumulación (f)
Fr    accumulation (f)
Pt    acumulação (f)

**maturity** n En
De    Fälligkeit (f)
Es    vencimiento (m)
Fr    échéance (f)
It    scadenza (f)
Pt    vencimento (m)

**mau-pagador** (m) n Pt
De    schlechter Zahler (m)
En    slow payer
Es    deudor moroso (m)
Fr    mauvais payeur (m)
It    cattivo pagatore (m)

**mauvais payeur** *(m)* Fr
De schlechter Zahler *(m)*
En slow payer
Es deudor moroso *(m)*
It cattivo pagatore *(m)*
Pt mau-pagador *(m)*

**máxima boa-fé** *(f)* Pt
De äusserst guter Glaube *(m)*
En utmost good faith
Es máxima buena fé *(f)*
Fr plus grande bonne foie *(f)*
It massima buona fede *(f)*

**máxima buena fé** *(f)* Es
De äusserst guter Glaube *(m)*
En utmost good faith
Fr plus grande bonne foie *(f)*
It massima buona fede *(f)*
Pt máxima boa-fé *(f)*

**maximal** *adj* De
En maximum
Es máximo
Fr maximum
It massimo
Pt máximo

**máximo** *adj* Es, Pt
De maximal
En maximum
Fr maximum
It massimo

**maximum** *adj* En, Fr
De maximal
Es máximo
It massimo
Pt máximo

**mayorista** *(m)* n Es
De Grosshändler; Grossist *(m)*
En wholesaler
Fr grossiste *(m)*
It grossista *(m)*
Pt vendedor por atacado *(m)*

**mazout** *(m)* n Fr
De Heizöl *(n)*
En fuel oil
Es fuel-oil *(m)*
It petrolio da ardere *(m)*
Pt petróleo combustível *(m)*

**mean price** En
De Mittelkurs *(m)*
Es precio medio *(m)*
Fr prix moyen *(m)*

It prezzo medio *(m)*
Pt preço médio *(m)*

**measure** n En
De Mass *(n)*
Es medida *(f)*
Fr mesure *(f)*
It misura *(f)*
Pt medida *(f)*

**measure** *vb* En
De messen
Es medir
Fr mesurer; mensurer
It misurare
Pt medir

**measurement** n En
De Messung *(f)*
Es medida; dimensión *(f)*
Fr mesurage *(m)*
It misura; dimensione *(f)*
Pt medida; dimensão *(f)*

**mecánica de la máquina** *(f)* Es
De Maschinenausrüstung *(f)*
En computer hardware
Fr hardware *(m)*
It componenti di macchina calcolatore *(m pl)*
Pt sistema fisico *(m)*

**mécanicien** *(m)* n Fr
De Mechaniker *(m)*
En mechanic
Es mecánico *(m)*
It meccanico *(m)*
Pt mecânico *(m)*

**mecánico** *(m)* n Es
De Mechaniker *(m)*
En mechanic
Fr mécanicien *(m)*
It meccanico *(m)*
Pt mecânico *(m)*

**mecânico** *(m)* n Pt
De Mechaniker *(m)*
En mechanic
Es mecánico *(m)*
Fr mécanicien *(m)*
It meccanico *(m)*

**mecanógrafa** *(f)* n Es
De Abschreibtypistin *(f)*
En copy typist
Am transcriber
Fr dactylo copiste *(f)*

It dattilografa *(f)*
Pt dactilógrafa *(f)*

**meccanico** *(m)* n It
De Mechaniker *(m)*
En mechanic
Es mecánico *(m)*
Fr mécanicien *(m)*
Pt mecânico *(m)*

**mechanic** n En
De Mechaniker *(m)*
Es mecánico *(m)*
Fr mécanicien *(m)*
It meccanico *(m)*
Pt mecânico *(m)*

**mechanical engineering** En
De Maschinenbau *(m)*
Es ingeniería mecánica *(f)*
Fr construction mécanique *(f)*
It ingegneria meccanica *(f)*
Pt engenharia mecânica *(f)*

**Mechaniker** *(m)* n De
En mechanic
Es mecánico *(m)*
Fr mécanicien *(m)*
It meccanico *(m)*
Pt mecânico *(m)*

**media** *(f)* n It
De Durchschnitt *(m)*
En average
Es promedio *(m)*
Fr moyenne *(f)*
Pt média *(f)*

**média** *(f)* n Pt
De Durchschnitt *(m)*
En average
Es promedio *(m)*
Fr moyenne *(f)*
It media *(f)*

**media** n En
De Werbeträger *(m pl)*
Es medios de información *(m pl)*
Fr supports *(m pl)*
It canali d'informazione *(m pl)*
Pt meios de informação *(m pl)*

**media aritmética** *(f)* Es
De arithmetisches Mittel *(n)*
En arithmetic mean
Fr moyenne arithmétique *(f)*

It    media aritmetica *(f)*
Pt    média aritmética *(f)*

**media aritmetica** *(f)* It
De    arithmetisches Mittel *(n)*
En    arithmetic mean
Es    media aritmética *(f)*
Fr    moyenne arithmétique *(f)*
Pt    média aritmética *(f)*

**média aritmética** *(f)* Pt
De    arithmetisches Mittel *(n)*
En    arithmetic mean
Es    media aritmética *(f)*
Fr    moyenne arithmétique *(f)*
It    media aritmetica *(f)*

**media ponderada** *(f)* Es
De    gewogener Durchschnitt *(m)*
En    weighted average
Fr    moyenne pondérée *(f)*
It    media ponderata *(f)*
Pt    média ponderada *(f)*

**média ponderada** *(f)* Pt
De    gewogener Durchschnitt *(m)*
En    weighted average
Es    media ponderada *(f)*
Fr    moyenne pondérée *(f)*
It    media ponderata *(f)*

**media ponderata** *(f)* It
De    gewogener Durchschnitt *(m)*
En    weighted average
Es    media ponderada *(f)*
Fr    moyenne pondérée *(f)*
Pt    média ponderada *(f)*

**mediate** *vb* En
De    vermitteln
Es    intermediar
Fr    s'entremettre
It    fare da intermediario
Pt    intermediar

**mediation** *n* En
De    Vermittlung *(f)*
Es    intermediación *(f)*
Fr    médiation *(f)*
It    mediazione *(f)*
Pt    intermediação *(f)*

**médiation** *(f)* Fr
De    Vermittlung *(f)*
En    mediation

Es    intermediación *(f)*
It    mediazione *(f)*
Pt    intermediação *(f)*

**mediatore di assicurazioni** *(m)* It
De    Versicherungsmakler *(m)*
En    insurance broker
Es    corredor de seguros *(m)*
Fr    courtier d'assurance *(m)*
Pt    corretor de seguros *(m)*

**mediazione** *(f)* n It
De    Vermittlung *(f)*
En    mediation
Es    intermediación *(f)*
Fr    médiation *(f)*
Pt    intermediação *(f)*

**medical examination** En
De    ärztliche Untersuchung *(f)*
Es    examen médico *(m)*
Fr    examen médical *(m)*
It    visita medica *(f)*
Pt    inspecção médica *(f)*

**medida** *(f)* n Es, Pt
De    Mass; Messung *(n f)*
En    measure; measurement
Fr    mesure; mesurage *(f m)*
It    misura *(f)*

**medidor de contidades de obra** *(m)* Es
De    Massenberechner *(m)*
En    quantity surveyor
Fr    métreur-vérificateur *(m)*
It    perito misuratore *(m)*
Pt    perito na avaliação de quantidades *(m)*

**medio** *adj* Es
De    halb
En    half
Fr    à moitié; demi
It    mezzo
Pt    meio

**medio de publicidad** *(m)* Es
De    Werbemittel *(n)*
En    advertising medium
Fr    support publicitaire *(m)*
It    mezzo pubblicitario *(m)*
Pt    meio publicitário *(m)*

**medio salario** *(m)* Es
De    Halbsold *(m)*
En    half-pay

Fr    demi-salaire *(m)*
It    mezza paga *(f)*
Pt    meio-salário *(m)*

**medios de información** *(m pl)* Es
De    Werbeträger *(m pl)*
En    media
Fr    supports *(m pl)*
It    canali d'informazione *(m pl)*
Pt    meios de informação *(m pl)*

**medir** *vb* Es, Pt
De    messen
En    measure
Fr    mesurer; mensurer
It    misurare

**meeting** *n* En
De    Versammlung *(f)*
Es    reunión *(f)*
Fr    réunion; assemblée *(f)*
It    riunione; assemblea *(f)*
Pt    reunião; assembleia *(f)*

**meeting of creditors** En
De    Gläubigerversammlung *(f)*
Es    concurso de acreedores *(m)*
Fr    assemblée de créanciers *(f)*
It    convocazione dei creditori *(f)*
Pt    reunião de credores *(f)*

**Mehrarbeit** *(f)* n De
En    overtime
Es    horas extraordinarias *(f pl)*
Fr    heures supplémentaires *(f pl)*
It    lavoro straordinario *(m)*

**Mehrheitsbeteiligung** *(f)* n De
En    majority holding
Es    tenencia de acciones por mayoría *(f)*
Fr    participation majoritaire *(f)*
It    partecipazione maggioritaria *(f)*
Pt    propriedade em maioria *(f)*

**mehrseitiges Handeln** *(n)* De
En    multilateral trade
Es    comercio multilateral *(m)*
Fr    commerce multilateral *(m)*
It    commercio multilaterale *(m)*
Pt    comércio multilateral *(m)*

**Mehrwert** *(f)* n De
En added value
Es valor agregado *(m)*
Fr valeur ajoutée *(f)*
It valore aggiunto *(m)*
Pt valor adicionado *(m)*

**Mehrwertsteuer** *(f)* n De
En value added tax (VAT)
Es impuesto sobre valor aña-
dido *(m)*
Fr taxe sur la valeur ajoutée
(TVA) *(f)*
It imposta sul valore aggiunto
(IVA) *(f)*
Pt imposto sobre valor aduzi-
do *(m)*

**meilleur marché** Fr
De billiger
En cheaper
Es más barato
It meno caro
Pt mais barato

**Meinung** *(f)* n De
En opinion
Es opinión *(f)*
Fr opinion *(f)*
It opinione *(f)*
Pt opinião *(f)*

**meio** *adj* Pt
De halb
En half
Es medio
Fr à moitié; demi
It mezzo

**meio publicitário** *(m)* Pt
De Werbemittel *(n)*
En advertising medium
Es medio de publicidad *(m)*
Fr support publicitaire *(m)*
It mezzo pubblicitario *(m)*

**meio-salário** *(m)* n Pt
De Halbsold *(m)*
En half-pay
Es medio salario *(m)*
Fr demi-salaire *(m)*
It mezza paga *(f)*

**meios de informação** *(m pl)* Pt
De Werbeträger *(m pl)*
En media
Es medios de información *(m
pl)*

Fr supports *(m pl)*
It canali d'informazione *(m
pl)*

**Meistbietende(r)** *(m)* n De
En highest bidder
Es ofertante más alto *(m)*
Fr plus offrant enchérisseur
*(m)*
It miglior offerente *(m)*
Pt proponente mais elevado
*(m)*

**mejora** *(f)* n Es
De Verbesserung *(f)*
En improvement
Fr amélioration *(f)*
It miglioramento *(m)*
Pt melhoramento *(m)*

**melhoramento** *(m)* n Pt
De Verbesserung *(f)*
En improvement
Es mejora *(f)*
Fr amélioration *(f)*
It miglioramento *(m)*

**melhoria** *(f)* n Pt
De Planungsgewinn *(m)*
En betterment
Es plusvalía *(f)*
Fr appréciation *(f)*
It plus-valore *(m)*

**member** n En
De Mitglied *(n)*
Es miembro; socio *(m)*
Fr membre *(m)*
It membro; socio *(m)*
Pt membro; sócio *(m)*

**membre** *(m)* n Fr
De Mitglied *(n)*
En member
Es miembro; socio *(m)*
It membro; socio *(m)*
Pt membro; sócio *(m)*

**membre fondateur** *(m)* Fr
De Gründermitglied *(m)*
En founder member
Es miembro fundador *(m)*
It socio fondatore *(m)*
Pt membro fondador *(m)*

**membrete** *(m)* n Es
De Briefkopf *(m)*
En letterhead

Fr en-tête *(m)*
It intestazione *(f)*
Pt cabeçalho *(m)*

**membro** *(m)* n It
De Mitglied *(n)*
En member
Es miembro; socio *(m)*
Fr membre *(m)*

**membro fondador** *(m)* Pt
De Gründermitglied *(m)*
En founder member
Es miembro fundador *(m)*
Fr membre fondateur *(m)*
It socio fondatore *(m)*

**memorando** *(m)* n Es, Pt
De Vermerk *(m)*
En memorandum
Fr note *(f)*
It promemoria *(f)*

**memorandum** n En
De Vermerk *(m)*
Es memorando; apunte *(m)*
Fr note *(f)*
It promemoria *(f)*
Pt memorando *(m)*

**Memorandum and Articles of
Association** En
Am articles of incorporation
De Statuten *(f pl)*
Es estatutos; carta orgánica
*(m pl; f)*
Fr statuts; acte constitutif *(m
pl; m)*
It atto costitutivo e statuto
sociale *(m)*
Pt estatuto de associação *(m)*

**memoria anual** *(f)* Es
De Jahresbericht *(m)*
En annual report
Fr rapport annuel *(m)*
It relazione annuale *(f)*
Pt relatório anual *(m)*

**ménage** *(m)* n Fr
De Haushalt *(m)*
En household
Es hogar *(m)*
It famiglia *(f)*
Pt casa *(f)*

**ménagère** (f) n Fr
De Hausfrau (f)
En housewife
Es ama de casa (f)
It massaia (f)
Pt dona de casa (f)

**Menge** (f) n De
En quantity
Es cantidad (f)
Fr quantité (f)
It quantità (f)
Pt quantidade (f)

**meno caro** It
De billiger
En cheaper
Es más barato
Fr meilleur marché
Pt mais barato

**mensilità** (f) n It
De Monatsrate (f)
En monthly instalment
Es mensualidad (f)
Fr mensualité (f)
Pt prestação mensal (f)

**mensualidad** (f) n Es
De Monatsrate (f)
En monthly instalment
Fr mensualité (f)
It mensilità (f)
Pt prestação mensal (f)

**mensualité** (f) n Fr
De Monatsrate (f)
En monthly instalment
Es mensualidad (f)
It mensilità (f)
Pt prestação mensal (f)

**mer** (f) n Fr
De See (f)
En sea
Es mar (m)
It mare (m)
Pt mar (m)

**mercadería** (f) n Es
De Gut; Ware (n f)
En commodity
Fr marchandise; produit (f m)
It merce; prodotto (f m)
Pt mercadoria; produto (f m)

**mercado** (m) n Es, Pt
De Markt (m)
En market
Fr marché (m)
It mercato (m)

**mercado alcista** (m) Es
De Haussemarkt (m)
En bull market
Fr marché orienté à la hausse (m)
It mercato tendente al rialzo (m)
Pt mercado de tendência altista (m)

**mercado bajista** (m) Es
De Baissemarkt (m)
En bear market
Fr marché orienté à la baisse (m)
It mercato tendente al ribasso (m)
Pt mercado de tendência baixista (m)

**mercado cerrado** (m) Es
De gesperrter Markt (m)
En closed market
Fr marché fermé (m)
It mercato chiuso (m)
Pt mercado fechado (m)

**mercado comum** (m) Pt
De gemeinsamer Markt (m)
En Common Market
Es mercado común (m)
Fr marché commun (m)
It mercato comune (m)

**mercado común** (m) Es
De gemeinsamer Markt (m)
En Common Market
Fr marché commun (m)
It mercato comune (m)
Pt mercado comum (m)

**mercado da moeda** (m) Pt
De Geldmarkt (m)
En money market
Es mercado de dinero (m)
Fr marché monétaire (m)
It mercato di denaro (m)

**mercado de acções** (m) Pt
De Aktienmarkt (m)
En share market
Am stock market

Es mercado de valores (m)
Fr marché des valeurs (m)
It mercato azionario (m)

**mercado de desconto** (m) Pt
De Diskontmarkt (m)
En discount market
Es mercado de descuentos (m)
Fr marché de l'escompte (m)
It mercato di sconto (m)

**mercado de descuentos** (m) Es
De Diskontmarkt (m)
En discount market
Fr marché de l'escompte (m)
It mercato di sconto (m)
Pt mercado de desconto (m)

**mercado de dinero** (m) Es
De Geldmarkt (m)
En money market
Fr marché monétaire (m)
It mercato di denaro (m)
Pt mercado da moeda (m)

**mercado de futuros** (m) Es, Pt
De Terminmarkt (m)
En futures market
Fr marché du terme (m)
It mercato a termine (m)

**mercado de mano de obra** (m) Es
De Arbeitsmarkt (m)
En labour market
Fr marché du travail (m)
It mercato della mano d'opera (m)
Pt mercado de mão de obra (m)

**mercado de mão de obra** (m) Pt
De Arbeitsmarkt (m)
En labour market
Es mercado de mano de obra (m)
Fr marché du travail (m)
It mercato della mano d'opera (m)

**mercado de materias primas** (m) Es
De Rohstoffmarkt (m)
En commodity market

Fr marché de matières premières (m)
It mercato di materie prime
(m)
Pt mercado de matérias primas (m)

**mercado de matérias primas**
(m) Pt
De Rohstoffmarkt (m)
En commodity market
Es mercado de materias pri-
mas (m)
Fr marché de matières pre-
mières (m)
It mercato di materie prime
(m)

**mercado de productos** (m) Es
De Warenmarkt (m)
En produce market
Fr marché commercial (m)
It mercato commerciale (m)
Pt mercado de produtos (m)

**mercado de produtos** (m) Pt
De Warenmarkt (m)
En produce market
Es mercado de productos (m)
Fr marché commercial (m)
It mercato commerciale (m)

**mercado de tendência altista**
(m) Pt
De Haussemarkt (m)
En bull market
Es mercado alcista (m)
Fr marché orienté à la hausse
(m)
It mercato tendente al rialzo
(m)

**mercado de valores** (m) Es
De Aktienmarkt (m)
En share market
Am stock market
Fr marché des valeurs (m)
It mercato azionario (m)
Pt mercado de acções (m)

**mercado em decréscimo** (m)
Pt
De Markt mit Baissetendenz
(m)
En falling market
Es mercado en baja (m)

Fr marché orienté à la baisse
(m)
It mercato in declino (m)

**mercado en baja** (m) Es
De Markt mit Baissetendenz
(m)
En falling market
Fr marché orienté à la baisse
(m)
It mercato in declino (m)
Pt mercado em decréscimo
(m)

**mercado exclusivo** (m) Es, Pt
De ausschliesslicher Markt (m)
En exclusive market
Fr marché exclusif (m)
It mercato esclusivo (m)

**mercado fechado** (m) Pt
De gesperrter Markt (m)
En closed market
Es mercado cerrado (m)
Fr marché fermé (m)
It mercato chiuso (m)

**mercado libre** (m) Es
De freier Markt (m)
En open market
Fr marché libre (m)
It mercato libero (m)
Pt mercado livre (m)

**mercado livre** (m) Pt
De freier Markt (m)
En open market
Es mercado libre (m)
Fr marché libre (m)
It mercato libero (m)

**mercado negro** (m) Es, Pt
De schwarzer Markt (m)
En black market
Fr marché noir (m)
It mercato nero (m)

**mercadoria** (f) n Pt
De Gut; Ware (n f)
En commodity; merchandise
Es mercadería; producto (f m)
Fr marchandise; produit (f m)
It merce; prodotto (f m)

**mercadorias** (f pl) n Pt
De Güter (n pl)
En goods
Es mercancías (f pl)

Fr marchandises (f pl)
It merce (f)

**mercadorias à ordem da alfân-
dega** (f pl) Pt
De Waren unter Zollverschluss
(f pl)
En bonded goods
Es mercancías en aduana (f
pl)
Fr marchandises en douane (f
pl)
It merci sotto vincolo doganale (f pl)

**mercadorias danificadas** (f pl)
Pt
De beschädigte Waren (f pl)
En damaged goods
Es mercancías averiadas (f pl)
Fr marchandises avariées (f
pl)
It merce avariata (f)

**mercadorias de capital** (f pl)
Pt
De Anlagegüter (n pl)
En capital goods
Es bienes de producción (m
pl)
Fr biens d'équipement (m pl)
It beni strumentali (m pl)

**mercadorias devoluidas** (f) Pt
De Retourware (f)
En returned goods
Es mercancías devueltas (f pl)
Fr marchandises de retour (f
pl)
It merce di ritorno (f pl)

**mercadorias embargadas** (f)
Pt
De gepfändete Güter (n pl)
En distressed goods
Es mercancías embargadas (f
pl)
Fr biens saisis (m pl)
It merce sequestrata (f)

**mercadorias em existência** (f)
Pt
De Vorrat auf Lager (m)
En stock in hand
Es mercancías en almacén (f
pl)

Fr marchandises en magasin *(f pl)*
It merce in magazzino *(f)*

**mercadorias imperecíveis** *(f pl)* Pt
De langlebige Güter *(n pl)*
En durable goods
Es mercancías no perecederas *(f pl)*
Fr biens durables *(m pl)*
It beni durevoli *(m pl)*

**mercadorias perecíveis** *(f pl)* Pt
De leicht verderbliche Waren *(f pl)*
En perishable goods
Es mercancías perecederas *(f pl)*
Fr marchandises périssables *(f pl)*
It merci deperibili *(f pl)*

**mercadorias perigosas** *(f pl)* Pt
De gefährliche Waren *(f pl)*
En dangerous goods
Es mercancías peligrosas *(f pl)*
Fr marchandises dangereuses *(f pl)*
It merce pericolosa *(f)*

**mercadorias prontas** *(f pl)* Pt
De sofort lieferbare Waren *(f pl)*
En spot goods
Es mercancías prontas *(f pl)*
Fr marchandises disponibles *(f pl)*
It merce pronta *(f)*

**mercancía** *(f)* n Es
De Ware *(f)*
En merchandise
Fr marchandise *(f)*
It merce *(f)*
Pt mercadoria *(f)*

**mercancías** *(f pl)* n Es
De Güter *(n pl)*
En goods
Fr marchandises *(f pl)*
It merce *(f)*
Pt mercadorias *(f pl)*

**mercancías averiadas** *(f pl)* Es
De beschädigte Waren *(f pl)*
En damaged goods

Fr marchandises avariées *(f pl)*
It merce avariata *(f)*
Pt mercadorias danificadas *(f pl)*

**mercancías devueltas** *(f pl)* Es
De Retourware *(f)*
En returned goods
Fr marchandises de retour *(f pl)*
It merce di ritorno *(f pl)*
Pt mercadorias devoluidas *(f)*

**mercancías embargadas** *(f pl)* Es
De gepfändete Güter *(n pl)*
En distressed goods
Fr biens saisis *(m pl)*
It merce sequestrata *(f)*
Pt mercadorias embargadas *(f)*

**mercancías en aduana** *(f pl)* Es
De Waren unter Zollverschluss *(f pl)*
En bonded goods
Fr marchandises en douane *(f pl)*
It merci sotto vincolo doganale *(f pl)*
Pt mercadorias à ordem da alfândega *(f pl)*

**mercancías en almacén** *(f pl)* Es
De Vorrat auf Lager *(m)*
En stock in hand
Fr marchandises en magasin *(f pl)*
It merce in magazzino *(f)*
Pt mercadorias em existência *(f)*

**mercancías en consignación** *(f pl)* Es
De Kommissionsgüter *(n pl)*
En goods on consignment
Fr marchandises en consignation *(f pl)*
It merce in conto deposito *(f)*
Pt artigos à consignação *(m pl)*

**mercancías no perecederas** *(f pl)* Es
De langlebige Güter *(n pl)*
En durable goods

Fr biens durables *(m pl)*
It beni durevoli *(m pl)*
Pt mercadorias imperecíveis *(f pl)*

**mercancías peligrosas** *(f pl)* Es
De gefährliche Waren *(f pl)*
En dangerous goods
Fr marchandises dangereuses *(f pl)*
It merce pericolosa *(f)*
Pt mercadorias perigosas *(f pl)*

**mercancías perecederas** *(f pl)* Es
De leicht verderbliche Waren *(f pl)*
En perishable goods
Fr marchandises périssables *(f pl)*
It merci deperibili *(f pl)*
Pt mercadorias perecíveis *(f pl)*

**mercancías prontas** *(f pl)* Es
De sofort lieferbare Waren *(f pl)*
En spot goods
Fr marchandises disponibles *(f pl)*
It merce pronta *(f)*
Pt mercadorias prontas *(f pl)*

**mercancías sujetas a aprobación** *(f pl)* Es
De Probegüter *(n pl)*
En goods on approval
Fr marchandises à condition *(f pl)*
It merce soggetta ad approvazione *(f)*
Pt artigos sujeitos a aprovação *(m pl)*

**mercanteggiare** *vb* It
De feilschen
En haggle
Am bargain
Es regatear
Fr marchander; chipoter
Pt regatear

**mercantil** *adj* Es, Pt
De Handels-
En mercantile
Fr mercantile
It mercantile

**mercantile** *adj* En, Fr, It
De Handels-
Es mercantil
Pt mercantil

**mercantile agent** En
Am sales agent
De Handelsvertreter *(m)*
Es agente mercantil *(m)*
Fr agent de commerce *(m)*
It agente di commercio *(m)*
Pt agente comercial *(m)*

**mercato** *(m) n* It
De Markt *(m)*
En market
Es mercado *(m)*
Fr marché *(m)*
Pt mercado *(m)*

**mercato a termine** *(m)* It
De Terminmarkt *(m)*
En futures market
Es mercado de futuros *(m)*
Fr marché du terme *(m)*
Pt mercado de futuros *(m)*

**mercato azionario** *(m)* It
De Aktienmarkt *(m)*
En share market
Am stock market
Es mercado de valores *(m)*
Fr marché des valeurs *(m)*
Pt mercado de acções *(m)*

**mercato chiuso** *(m)* It
De gesperrter Markt *(m)*
En closed market
Es mercado cerrado *(m)*
Fr marché fermé *(m)*
Pt mercado fechado *(m)*

**mercato commerciale** *(m)* It
De Warenmarkt *(m)*
En produce market
Es mercado de productos *(m)*
Fr marché commercial *(m)*
Pt mercado de produtos *(m)*

**mercato comune** *(m)* It
De gemeinsamer Markt *(m)*
En Common Market
Es mercado común *(m)*
Fr marché commun *(m)*
Pt mercado comum *(m)*

**mercato della mano d'opera**
*(m)* It
De Arbeitsmarkt *(m)*
En labour market
Es mercado de mano de obra
*(m)*
Fr marché du travail *(m)*
Pt mercado de mão de obra
*(m)*

**mercato di denaro** *(m)* It
De Geldmarkt *(m)*
En money market
Es mercado de dinero *(m)*
Fr marché monétaire *(m)*
Pt mercado da moeda *(m)*

**mercato di materie prime** *(m)*
It
De Rohstoffmarkt *(m)*
En commodity market
Es mercado de materias pri-
mas *(m)*
Fr marché de matières pre-
mières *(m)*
Pt mercado de matérias pri-
mas *(m)*

**mercato di sconto** *(m)* It
De Diskontmarkt *(m)*
En discount market
Es mercado de descuentos
*(m)*
Fr marché de l'escompte *(m)*
Pt mercado de desconto *(m)*

**mercato esclusivo** *(m)* It
De ausschliesslicher Markt *(m)*
En exclusive market
Es mercado exclusivo *(m)*
Fr marché exclusif *(m)*
Pt mercado exclusivo *(m)*

**mercato in declino** *(m)* It
De Markt mit Baissetendenz
*(m)*
En falling market
Es mercado en baja *(m)*
Fr marché orienté à la baisse
*(m)*
Pt mercado em decréscimo
*(m)*

**mercato libero** *(m)* It
De freier Markt *(m)*
En open market
Es mercado libre *(m)*

Fr marché libre *(m)*
Pt mercado livre *(m)*

**mercato nero** *(m)* It
De schwarzer Markt *(m)*
En black market
Es mercado negro *(m)*
Fr marché noir *(m)*
Pt mercado negro *(m)*

**mercato tendente al rialzo** *(m)*
It
De Haussemarkt *(m)*
En bull market
Es mercado alcista *(m)*
Fr marché orienté à la hausse
*(m)*
Pt mercado de tendência
altista *(m)*

**mercato tendente al ribasso**
*(m)* It
De Baissemarkt *(m)*
En bear market
Es mercado bajista *(m)*
Fr marché orienté à la baisse
*(m)*
Pt mercado de tendência
baixista *(m)*

**merce** *(f) n* It
De Güter; Waren *(n pl; f pl)*
En goods; merchandise
Es mercancías *(f pl)*
Fr marchandises *(f pl)*
Pt mercadorias *(f pl)*

**merce avariata** *(f)* It
De beschädigte Waren *(f pl)*
En damaged goods
Es mercancías averiadas *(f pl)*
Fr marchandises avariées *(f
pl)*
Pt mercadorias danificadas *(f
pl)*

**merce di ritorno** *(f pl)* It
De Retourware *(f)*
En returned goods
Es mercancías devueltas *(f pl)*
Fr marchandises de retour *(f
pl)*
Pt mercadorias devoluidas *(f)*

**merce in conto deposito** *(f)* It
De Kommissionsgüter *(n pl)*
En goods on consignment

Es mercancías en consignación *(f pl)*
Fr marchandises en consignation *(f pl)*
Pt artigos à consignação *(m
pl)*

**merce in magazzino** *(f)* It
De Vorrat auf Lager *(m)*
En stock in hand
Es mercancías en almacén *(f
pl)*
Fr marchandises en magasin
*(f pl)*
Pt mercadorias em existência
*(f)*

**merce pericolosa** *(f)* It
De gefährliche Waren *(f pl)*
En dangerous goods
Es mercancías peligrosas *(f pl)*
Fr marchandises dangereuses
*(f pl)*
Pt mercadorias perigosas *(f
pl)*

**merce pronta** *(f)* It
De sofort lieferbare Waren *(f
pl)*
En spot goods
Es mercancías prontas *(f pl)*
Fr marchandises disponibles
*(f pl)*
Pt mercadorias prontas *(f pl)*

**merce sequestrata** *(f)* It
De gepfändete Güter *(n pl)*
En distressed goods
Es mercancías embargadas *(f
pl)*
Fr biens saisis *(m pl)*
Pt mercadorias embargadas
*(f)*

**merce soggetta ad appro-
vazione** *(f)* It
De Probegüter *(n pl)*
En goods on approval
Es mercancías sujetas a apro-
bación *(f pl)*
Fr marchandises à condition
*(f pl)*
Pt artigos sujeitos a apro-
vação *(m pl)*

**merchandise** *n* En
De Waren; Güter *(f pl; n pl)*
Es mercancías *(f pl)*

Fr marchandises *(f pl)*
It merce *(f)*
Pt mercadorias *(f pl)*

**merchant** *n* En
De Kaufmann *(m)*
Es comerciante *(m)*
Fr négociant *(m)*
It commerciante *(m)*
Pt comerciante *(m)*

**merchantable quality** En
De marktgängige Qualität *(f)*
Es calidad comerciable *(f)*
Fr qualité vendable *(f)*
It qualità commerciabile *(f)*
Pt qualidade comerciável *(f)*

**merchant bank** En
De Handelsbank *(f)*
Es banco mercantil *(m)*
Fr banque commerciale *(f)*
It banca commerciale *(f)*
Pt banco comercial *(m)*

**merchant fleet** En
De Handelsflotte *(f)*
Es flota mercanto *(f)*
Fr flotte marchande *(f)*
It flotta mercantile *(f)*
Pt frota mercante *(f)*

**merchant ship** En
De Handelsschiff *(n)*
Es barco mercante *(m)*
Fr navire marchand *(m)*
It nave mercantile *(f)*
Pt navio mercante *(m)*

**merci deperibili** *(f pl)* It
De leicht verderbliche Waren *(f
pl)*
En perishable goods
Es mercancías perecederas *(f
pl)*
Fr marchandises périssables
*(f pl)*
Pt mercadorias perecíveis *(f
pl)*

**merci sotto vincolo doganale**
*(f pl)* It
De Waren unter Zollverschluss
*(f pl)*
En bonded goods
Es mercancías en aduana *(f
pl)*

Fr marchandises en douane *(f
pl)*
Pt mercadorias à ordem da
alfândega *(f pl)*

**merge** *vb* En
De fusionieren
Es amalgamar
Fr fusionner
It fondersi
Pt amalgamar

**merger** *n* En
De Fusion *(f)*
Es fusión *(f)*
Fr fusion *(f)*
It fusione *(f)*
Pt fusão *(f)*

**Merkmal** *(n)* *n* De
En feature
Es característica *(f)*
Fr particularité *(f)*
It caratteristica *(f)*
Pt característica *(f)*

**merma natural** *(f)* Es
De natürlicher Abgang *(m)*
En natural wastage
Fr déperdition naturelle *(f)*
It consumo naturale *(m)*
Pt desperdício natural *(m)*

**mesa** *(f)* *n* Es
De Schreibtisch *(m)*
En desk
Fr bureau *(m)*
It scrittoio *(m)*
Pt secretária *(f)*

**Messe** *(f)* *n* De
En fair
Es feria *(f)*
Fr foire *(f)*
It fiera *(f)*
Pt feira *(f)*

**messen** *vb* De
En measure
Es medir
Fr mesurer; mensurer
It misurare
Pt medir

**Messung** *(f)* *n* De
En measurement
Es medida *(f)*
Fr mesurage *(m)*

It    misura *(f)*
Pt   medida *(f)*

**mesurage** *(m)* n Fr
De   Messung *(f)*
En   measurement
Es   medida *(f)*
It    misura *(f)*
Pt   medida *(f)*

**mesure** *(f)* n Fr
De   Mass *(n)*
En   measure
Es   medida *(f)*
It    misura *(f)*
Pt   medida *(f)*

**mesurer** *vb* Fr
De   messen
En   measure
Es   medir
It    misurare
Pt   medir

**meta** *(f)* n Es, Pt
De   Ziel *(n)*
En   goal
Fr   bout *(m)*
It    scopo *(m)*

**metade do preço** Pt
De   zum halben Preise
En   half price
Es   a mitad de precio
Fr   à moitié prix
It    metà prezzo

**metal no noble** *(m)* Es
De   unedles Metall *(n)*
En   base metal
Fr   métal vil *(m)*
It    basso metallo *(m)*
Pt   metal pobre *(m)*

**metal pobre** *(m)* Pt
De   unedles Metall *(n)*
En   base metal
Es   metal no noble *(m)*
Fr   métal vil *(m)*
It    basso metallo *(m)*

**métal vil** *(m)* Fr
De   unedles Metall *(n)*
En   base metal
Es   metal no noble *(m)*
It    basso metallo *(m)*
Pt   metal pobre *(m)*

**metà prezzo** It
De   zum halben Preise
En   half price
Es   a mitad de precio
Fr   à moitié prix
Pt   metade do preço

**métreur-vérificateur** *(m)* n Fr
De   Massenberechner *(m)*
En   quantity surveyor
Es   medidor de contidades de
       obra *(m)*
It    perito misuratore *(m)*
Pt   perito na avaliação de
       quantidades *(m)*

**metrication** En
De   Einführung des metrischen
       Systems *(f)*
Es   adopción del sistema mé-
       trico *(f)*
Fr   introduction du système
       métrique *(f)*
It    adozione del sistema me-
       trico *(f)*
Pt   adopção do sistema mé-
       trico *(f)*

**metric system** En
De   metrisches System *(n)*
Es   sistema métrico *(m)*
Fr   système métrique *(m)*
It    sistema metrico *(m)*
Pt   sistema métrico *(m)*

**metric ton** (tonne) En
De   metrische Tonne *(f)*
Es   tonelada métrica *(f)*
Fr   tonne métrique *(f)*
It    tonnellata metrica *(f)*
Pt   tonelada métrica *(f)*

**metrisches System** *(n)* De
En   metric system
Es   sistema métrico *(m)*
Fr   système métrique *(m)*
It    sistema metrico *(m)*
Pt   sistema métrico *(m)*

**meubles** *(m pl)* n Fr
De   Möbel *(n pl)*
En   furniture
Es   muebles *(m pl)*
It    mobilia *(f)*
Pt   mobília *(f)*

**mezza paga** *(f)* It
De   Halbsold *(m)*
En   half-pay
Es   medio salario *(m)*
Fr   demi-salaire *(m)*
Pt   meio-salário *(m)*

**mezzo** *adj* It
De   halb
En   half
Es   medio
Fr   à moitié; demi
Pt   meio

**mezzo pubblicitario** *(m)* It
De   Werbemittel *(n)*
En   advertising medium
Es   medio de publicidad *(m)*
Fr   support publicitaire *(m)*
Pt   meio publicitário *(m)*

**microficha** *(f)* n Es, Pt
De   Mikrofilmkarte *(f)*
En   microfiche
Fr   microfiche *(f)*
It    microscheda *(f)*

**microfiche** n En, Fr *(f)*
De   Mikrofilmkarte *(f)*
Es   microficha *(f)*
It    microscheda *(f)*
Pt   microficha *(f)*

**microscheda** *(f)* n It
De   Mikrofilmkarte *(f)*
En   microfiche
Es   microficha *(f)*
Fr   microfiche *(f)*
Pt   microficha *(f)*

**middle man** En
De   Mittelsperson; Zwischen-
       händler *(m f)*
Es   intermediario *(m)*
Fr   intermédiaire *(m)*
It    intermediario *(m)*
Pt   intermediário *(m)*

**middle price** En
De   Mittelpreis; Mittelkurs *(m)*
Es   precio medio *(m)*
Fr   cours moyen *(m)*
It    prezzo medio *(m)*
Pt   preço médio *(m)*

**miembro** *(m)* n Es
De   Mitglied *(n)*
En   member
Fr   membre *(m)*

It   membro: socio *(m)*
Pt   membro: sócio *(m)*

**miembro fundador** *(m)* Es
De   Gründermitglied *(m)*
En   founder member
Fr   membre fondateur *(m)*
It   socio fondatore *(m)*
Pt   membro fondador *(m)*

**Miete** *(f)* n De
En   rent
Es   alquiler *(m)*
Fr   loyer *(m)*
It   pigione; affitto *(f m)*
Pt   renda *(f)*

**mieten** *vb* De
En   hire: rent
Es   alquilar
Fr   louer
It   noleggiare; affittare
Pt   alugar

**Mieter** *(m)* n De
En   hirer; tenant; lessee
Es   alquilador;     arrendatario;
      inquilino *(m)*
Fr   locataire *(m)*
It   noleggiatore; locatario *(m)*
Pt   alugador; locatário; inqui-
      lino *(m)*

**(einen) Mieter entfernen** De
En   evict a tenant
Es   desalojar un inquilino
Fr   expulser un locataire
It   sfrattare un locatario
Pt   desalojar um inquilino

**Mietzinskontrolle** *(f)* n De
En   rent control
Es   control de alquileres *(m)*
Fr   contrôle des loyers *(m)*
It   blocco degli affitti *(m)*
Pt   controlo de rendas *(m)*

**miglioramento** *(m)* n It
De   Verbesserung *(f)*
En   improvement
Es   mejora *(f)*
Fr   amélioration *(f)*
Pt   melhoramento *(m)*

**miglior offerente** *(m)* It
De   Meistbietende(r) *(m)*
En   highest bidder
Es   ofertante más alto *(m)*

Fr   plus offrant enchérisseur
      *(m)*
Pt   proponente mais elevado
      *(m)*

**Mikrofilmkarte** *(f)* n De
En   microfiche
Es   microficha *(f)*
Fr   microfiche *(f)*
It   microscheda *(f)*
Pt   microficha *(f)*

**Millimeterpapier** *(n)* n De
En   graph paper
Es   papel milimetrado *(m)*
Fr   papier quadrillé *(m)*
It   carta millimetrata *(f)*
Pt   papel milimétrico *(m)*

**mina** *(f)* n Es, Pt
De   Bergwerk *(n)*
En   mine
Fr   mine *(f)*
It   miniera *(f)*

**minderwertig** *adj* De
En   low-grade
Es   baja calidad
Fr   de qualité inférieure
It   di qualità inferiore
Pt   baixo-nível

**Mindestpreis** *(m)* n De
En   reserve price
Es   precio mínimo fijado *(m)*
Fr   mise à prix *(f)*
It   prezzo minimo *(m)*
Pt   preço de reserva *(m)*

**mine** n En, Fr *(f)*
De   Bergwerk *(n)*
Es   mina *(f)*
It   miniera *(f)*
Pt   mina *(f)*

**minerai de fer** *(m)* Fr
De   Eisenerz *(n)*
En   iron ore
Es   mineral de hierro *(m)*
It   minerale di ferro *(m)*
Pt   minério de ferro *(m)*

**mineral** n En, Es, Pt
De   Mineral *(n)*
Fr   minéral *(m)*
It   minerale *(m)*

**minéral** *(m)* n Fr
De   Mineral *(n)*
En   mineral
Es   minéral *(m)*
It   minerale *(m)*
Pt   mineral *(m)*

**Mineral** *(n)* n De
En   mineral
Es   mineral *(m)*
Fr   minéral *(m)*
It   minerale *(m)*
Pt   mineral *(m)*

**mineral concession** En
De   Bergwerkskonzession *(f)*
Es   concesión minera *(f)*
Fr   concession minière *(f)*
It   concessione mineraria *(f)*
Pt   concessão mineira *(f)*

**mineral de hierro** *(m)* Es
De   Eisenerz *(n)*
En   iron ore
Fr   minerai de fer *(m)*
It   minerale di ferro *(m)*
Pt   minério de ferro *(m)*

**minerale** *(m)* n It
De   Mineral *(n)*
En   mineral
Es   mineral *(m)*
Fr   minéral *(m)*
Pt   mineral *(m)*

**minerale di ferro** *(m)* It
De   Eisenerz *(n)*
En   iron ore
Es   mineral de hierro *(m)*
Fr   minerai de fer *(m)*
Pt   minério de ferro *(m)*

**Mineralgewinnungsrechte** *(n
      pl)* n De
En   mineral rights
Es   derechos mineros *(m pl)*
Fr   droits miniers *(m pl)*
It   diritti minerari *(m pl)*
Pt   direitos mineiros *(m pl)*

**mineral rights** En
De   Mineralgewinnungsrechte
      *(n pl)*
Es   derechos mineros *(m pl)*
Fr   droits miniers *(m pl)*
It   diritti minerari *(m pl)*
Pt   direitos mineiros *(m pl)*

**minério de ferro** *(m)* Pt
De  Eisenerz *(n)*
En  iron ore
Es  mineral de hierro *(m)*
Fr  minerai de fer *(m)*
It  minerale di ferro *(m)*

**miniera** *(f)* n It
De  Bergwerk *(n)*
En  mine
Es  mina *(f)*
Fr  mine *(f)*
Pt  mina *(f)*

**minimal** *adj* De
En  minimum
Es  mínimo
Fr  minimum
It  minimo
Pt  mínimo

**mínimo** *adj* Es, Pt
De  minimal
En  minimum
Fr  minimum
It  minimo

**minimo** *adj* It
De  minimal
En  minimum
Es  mínimo
Fr  minimum
Pt  mínimo

**minimum** *adj* En, Fr
De  minimal
Es  mínimo
It  minimo
Pt  mínimo

**ministère** *(m)* n Fr
De  Ministerium *(n)*
En  ministry
Es  ministerio *(m)*
It  ministero *(m)*
Pt  ministério *(m)*

**ministerio** *(m)* n Es
De  Ministerium *(n)*
En  ministry
Fr  ministère *(m)*
It  ministero *(m)*
Pt  ministério *(m)*

**ministério** *(m)* n Pt
De  Ministerium *(n)*
En  ministry
Es  ministerio *(m)*

Fr  ministère *(m)*
It  ministero *(m)*

**Ministerium** *(n)* n De
En  ministry
Es  ministerio *(m)*
Fr  ministère *(m)*
It  ministero *(m)*
Pt  ministério *(m)*

**ministero** *(m)* n It
De  Ministerium *(n)*
En  ministry
Es  ministerio *(m)*
Fr  ministère *(m)*
Pt  ministério *(m)*

**ministry** n En
De  Ministerium *(n)*
Es  ministerio *(m)*
Fr  ministère *(m)*
It  ministero *(m)*
Pt  ministério *(m)*

**Minoritätsbeteiligung** *(f)* n De
En  minority interest
Es  participación de la minoría *(f)*
Fr  participation de la minorité *(f)*
It  interessenza di minoranza *(f)*
Pt  interesse representado pela minoria *(m)*

**minority interest** En
De  Minoritätsbeteiligung *(f)*
Es  participación de la minoría *(f)*
Fr  participation de la minorité *(f)*
It  interessenza di minoranza *(f)*
Pt  interesse representado pela minoria *(m)*

**mint** n En
De  Münze *(f)*
Es  casa de la moneda *(f)*
Fr  la Monnaie
It  zecca *(f)*
Pt  casa da moeda *(f)*

**minuta de contrato** *(f)* Pt
De  Vertragsentwurf *(m)*
En  draft contract
Es  proyecto de contrato *(m)*

Fr  projet de contrat *(m)*
It  progetto di contratto *(m)*

**minutas de acta** *(f pl)* Pt
De  Protokoll *(n)*
En  minutes
Es  actas *(f pl)*
Fr  procès-verbal *(m)*
It  verbale *(m)*

**minutes** (of a meeting) n En
De  Protokoll *(n)*
Es  actas *(f pl)*
Fr  procès-verbal *(m)*
It  verbale *(m)*
Pt  minutas de acta *(f pl)*

**miscalculation** n En
De  Rechenfehler *(m)*
Es  cálculo erróneo *(m)*
Fr  erreur de calcul *(f)*
It  calcolo errato *(m)*
Pt  erro de cálculo *(m)*

**mise à prix** *(f)* Fr
De  Mindestpreis *(m)*
En  reserve price
Es  precio mínimo fijado *(m)*
It  prezzo minimo *(m)*
Pt  preço de reserva *(m)*

**mise en demeure** *(f)* Fr
De  Inverzugsetzung *(f)*
En  formal notice
Es  aviso oficial *(m)*
It  intimazione *(f)*
Pt  notificação formal *(f)*

**misrepresentation** n En
De  Verdrehung *(f)*
Es  declaración falsa *(f)*
Fr  déclaration inexacte *(f)*
It  dichiarazione falsa *(f)*
Pt  deturpação *(f)*

**misura** *(f)* n It
De  Mass; Messung *(n f)*
En  measure; measurement
Es  medida *(f)*
Fr  mesure; mesurage *(f m)*
Pt  medida *(f)*

**misurare** *vb* It
De  messen
En  measure
Es  medir
Fr  mesurer; mensurer
Pt  medir

**mitarbeiten** *vb* De
En collaborate
Es colaborar
Fr collaborer
It collaborare
Pt colaborar

**mit Dividende** De
En cum dividend
Es con dividendo
Fr droit attaché
It con dividendo
Pt com dividendo

**Miteigentum** *(n)* n De
En co-ownership; joint owner-
   ship
Es copropiedad *(f)*
Fr copropriété *(f)*
It condominio; comproprietà
   *(m f)*
Pt copropriedade *(f)*

**mit getrennter Post** De
En under separate cover
Es por correo aparte
Fr sous pli séparé
It in piego a parte
Pt por correio separado

**Mitglied** *(n)* n De
En member
Es miembro; socio *(m)*
Fr membre *(m)*
It membro; socio *(m)*
Pt membro; sócio *(m)*

**mit Rückgriff** De
En with recourse
Es con recurso
Fr avec droit de recours
It con ricorso
Pt com recurso

**Mittagspause** *(f)* n De
En lunch-hour
Es hora del almuerzo *(f)*
Fr heure du déjeuner *(f)*
It ora di colazione *(f)*
Pt hora do almoço *(f)*

**Mitte** *(f)* n De
En centre
Am center
Es centro *(m)*
Fr centre *(m)*
It centro *(m)*
Pt centro *(m)*

**Mitteilung** *(f)* n De
En notification
Es notificación *(f)*
Fr notification *(f)*
It notifica *(f)*
Pt notificação *(f)*

**Mittelkurs** *(m)* n De
En middle price
Es precio medio *(m)*
Fr cours moyen *(m)*
It prezzo medio *(m)*
Pt preço médio *(m)*

**mixed economy** En
De Gemischtwirtschaft *(f)*
Es economía mixta *(f)*
Fr économie mixte *(f)*
It economia mista *(f)*
Pt economia mixta *(f)*

**Möbel** *(n pl)* n De
En furniture
Es muebles *(m pl)*
Fr meubles *(m pl)*
It mobilia *(f)*
Pt mobília *(f)*

**mobilia** *(f)* n It
De Möbel *(n pl)*
En furniture
Es muebles *(m pl)*
Fr meubles *(m pl)*
Pt mobília *(f)*

**mobília** *(f)* n Pt
De Möbel *(n pl)*
En furniture
Es muebles *(m pl)*
Fr meubles *(m pl)*
It mobilia *(f)*

**mobiliario** *(m)* n Es
De bewegliche Güter *(n pl)*
En movable assets
Fr biens mobiliers *(m pl)*
It proprietà mobiliare *(f)*
Pt bens mobiliários *(m pl)*

**mobilidade** *(f)* n Pt
De Beweglichkeit *(f)*
En mobility
Es movilidad *(f)*
Fr mobilité *(f)*
It mobilità *(f)*

**mobilità** *(f)* n It
De Beweglichkeit *(f)*
En mobility
Es movilidad *(f)*
Fr mobilité *(f)*
Pt mobilidade *(f)*

**mobilité** *(f)* n Fr
De Beweglichkeit *(f)*
En mobility
Es movilidad *(f)*
It mobilità *(f)*
Pt mobilidade *(f)*

**mobility** n En
De Beweglichkeit *(f)*
Es movilidad *(f)*
Fr mobilité *(f)*
It mobilità *(f)*
Pt mobilidade *(f)*

**möblierte Mietwohnung** *(f)* De
En furnished flat
Am furnished apartment
Es piso amueblado *(m)*
Fr appartement meublé *(m)*
It appartamento ammobigli-
   ato *(m)*
Pt andar mobilado *(m)*

**moção** *(f)* n Pt
De Antrag *(m)*
En motion
Es moción *(f)*
Fr motion *(f)*
It mozione *(f)*

**moción** *(f)* n Es
De Antrag *(m)*
En motion
Fr motion *(f)*
It mozione *(f)*
Pt moção *(f)*

**Modeartikel** *(m pl)* n De
En fancy goods
Es artículos de fantasía *(m pl)*
Fr nouveautés *(f pl)*
It articoli fantasia *(m pl)*
Pt artigos de fantasia *(m pl)*

**mode d'emploi** *(m)* Fr
De Gebrauchsanweisung *(f)*
En directions for use
Es modo de empleo *(m)*
It istruzioni per l'uso *(f pl)*
Pt instruções para uso *(f pl)*

**modificações** *(f pl) n* Pt
De Umbau *(m)*
En alterations
Es reformas *(f pl)*
Fr travaux de transformation *(m pl)*
It modifiche *(f pl)*

**modificações e renovações** Pt
De Änderungen und Erneuerungen
En alterations and renewals
Es reformas y renovaciones
Fr réfections et améliorations
It modifiche e rinnovamenti

**modificações e reparações** Pt
De Änderungen und Reparaturen
En alterations and repairs
Es reformas y reparaciones
Fr transformations et réparations
It modifiche e riparazioni

**modifiche** *(f pl) n* It
De Umbau *(m)*
En alterations
Es reformas *(f pl)*
Fr travaux de transformation *(m pl)*
Pt modificações *(f pl)*

**modifiche e rinnovamenti** It
De Änderungen und Erneuerungen
En alterations and renewals
Es reformas y renovaciones
Fr réfections et améliorations
Pt modificações e renovações

**modifiche e riparazioni** It
De Änderungen und Reparaturen
En alterations and repairs
Es reformas y reparaciones
Fr transformations et réparations
Pt modificações e reparações

**modo de empleo** *(m)* Es
De Gebrauchsanweisung *(f)*
En directions for use
Fr mode d'emploi *(f)*
It istruzioni per l'uso *(f pl)*
Pt instruções para uso *(f pl)*

**modulo** *(m) n* It
De Formular *(n)*
En form
Es formulario *(m)*
Fr formule *(f)*
Pt formulário *(m)*

**modulo di domanda** *(m)* It
De Antragsformular *(n)*
En application form
Es formulario de solicitud *(m)*
Fr formulaire de demande *(m)*
Pt formulário de requisição *(m)*

**modulo in bianco** *(m)* It
De Blankoformular *(n)*
En blank form
Es formulario en blanco *(m)*
Fr formulaire en blanc *(m)*
Pt impresso em branco *(m)*

**modulo stampato** *(m)* It
De Vordruck *(m)*
En printed form
Es formulario; impreso *(m)*
Fr formulaire *(m)*
Pt impresso *(m)*

**moeda** *(f) n* Pt
De Währung; Münze *(f)*
En currency; coin
Es moneda *(f)*
Fr monnaie; pièce *(f)*
It valuta; moneta *(f)*

**moeda de reserva** *(f)* Pt
De Reservewährung *(f)*
En reserve currency
Es moneda de reserva *(f)*
Fr monnaie de réserve *(f)*
It valuta di riserva *(f)*

**moeda estrangeira** *(f)* Pt
De Devisen *(f pl)*
En foreign currency
Es divisas extranjeras *(f pl)*
Fr devises *(f pl)*
It valuta estera *(f)*

**moeda forte** *(f)* Pt
De harte Währung *(f)*
En hard currency
Es moneda fuerta *(f)*
Fr monnaie forte *(f)*
It valuta forte *(f)*

**moeda fraca** *(f)* Pt
De schwache Währung *(f)*
En soft currency
Es moneda débil *(f)*
Fr monnaie faible *(f)*
It valuta debole *(f)*

**moeda legal** *(m)* Pt
De gesetzliches Zahlungsmittel *(n)*
En legal tender
Es moneda legal *(f)*
Fr monnaie légale *(f)*
It denaro a corso legale *(m)*

**möglich** *adj* De
En possible; potential
Es posible; potencial
Fr possible; potentiel
It possibile; potenziale
Pt possível; potencial

**moisson** *(f) n* Fr
De Ernte *(f)*
En harvest
Es cosecha *(f)*
It raccolto *(m)*
Pt colheita *(f)*

**Mole** *(f) n* De
En jetty
Es digue *(m)*
Fr jetée; digue *(f)*
It molo *(m)*
Pt pontão; cais *(m)*

**molo** *(m) n* It
De Mole *(f)*
En jetty
Es digue *(m)*
Fr jetée; digue *(f)*
Pt pontão; cais *(m)*

**moltiplicare** *vb* It
De vervielfältigen
En multiply
Es multiplicar
Fr multipliquer
Pt multiplicar

**moltiplicatore** *(m) n* It
De Vervielfältiger *(m)*
En multiplier
Es multiplicador *(m)*
Fr multiplicateur *(m)*
Pt multiplicador *(m)*

**Monatsrate** (f) n De
En monthly instalment
Es mensualidad (f)
Fr mensualité (f)
It mensilità (f)
Pt prestação mensal (f)

**moneda** (f) n Es
De Währung; Münze (f)
En currency; coin
Fr monnaie; pièce (f)
It valuta; moneta (f)
Pt moeda (f)

**moneda débil** (f) Es
De schwache Währung (f)
En soft currency
Fr monnaie faible (f)
It valuta debole (f)
Pt moeda fraca (f)

**moneda de reserva** (f) Es
De Reservewährung (f)
En reserve currency
Fr monnaie de réserve (f)
It valuta di riserva (f)
Pt moeda de reserva (f)

**moneda fuerta** (f) Es
De harte Währung (f)
En hard currency
Fr monnaie forte (f)
It valuta forte (f)
Pt moeda forte (f)

**moneda legal** (f) Es
De gesetzliches Zahlungsmittel
(n)
En legal tender
Fr monnaie légale (f)
It denaro a corso legale (m)
Pt moeda legal (m)

**moneda suelta** (f) Es
De Kleingeld (n)
En small change
Fr petite monnaie (f)
It spiccioli (m pl)
Pt troco miúdo (m)

**moneta** (f) n It
De Münze (f)
En coin
Es moneda (f)
Fr pièce de monnaie (f)
Pt moeda (f)

**monetary policy** En
De Währungspolitik (f)
Es politica monetaria (f)
Fr politique monétaire (f)
It politica monetaria (f)
Pt política monetária (f)

**monetary reform** En
De Währungsreform (f)
Es reforma monetaria (f)
Fr réforme monétaire (f)
It riforma monetaria (f)
Pt reforma monetária (f)

**money** n En
De Geld (n)
Es dinero (m)
Fr argent (m)
It denaro (m)
Pt dinheiro (m)

**moneylender** n En
De Geldverleiher (m)
Es prestamista (m)
Fr prêteur d'argent (m)
It usuraio (m)
Pt prestamista (m)

**money market** En
De Geldmarkt (m)
Es mercado de dinero (m)
Fr marché monétaire (m)
It mercato di denaro (m)
Pt mercado da moeda (m)

**money on call** En
De Sichtgelder (n pl)
Es dinero a la vista (m)
Fr argent à vue (m)
It denaro a vista (m)
Pt dinheiro à ordem (m)

**monnaie** (f) n Fr
De Währung (f)
En currency
Es moneda (f)
It valuta (f)
Pt moeda (f)

**(la) Monnaie** (f) n Fr
De Münze (f)
En mint
Es casa de la moneda (f)
It zecca (f)
Pt casa da moeda (f)

**monnaie de réserve** (f) Fr
De Reservewährung (f)
En reserve currency
Es moneda de reserva (f)
It valuta di riserva (f)
Pt moeda de reserva (f)

**monnaie faible** (f) Fr
De schwache Währung (f)
En soft currency
Es moneda débil (f)
It valuta debole (f)
Pt moeda fraca (f)

**monnaie forte** (f) Fr
De harte Währung (f)
En hard currency
Es moneda fuerta (f)
It valuta forte (f)
Pt moeda forte (f)

**monnaie légale** (f) Fr
De gesetzliches Zahlungsmittel
(n)
En legal tender
Es moneda legal (f)
It denaro a corso legale (m)
Pt moeda legal (m)

**Monopol** (n) n De
En monopoly
Es monopolio (m)
Fr monopole (m)
It monopolio (m)
Pt monopólio (m)

**monopole** (m) n Fr
De Monopol (n)
En monopoly
Es monopolio (m)
It monopolio (m)
Pt monopólio (m)

**monopolio** (m) n Es, It
De Monopol (n)
En monopoly
Fr monopole (m)
Pt monopólio (m)

**monopólio** (m) n Pt
De Monopol (n)
En monopoly
Es monopolio (m)
Fr monopole (m)
It monopolio (m)

**monopoly** n En
De Monopol (n)
Es monopolio (m)
Fr monopole (m)
It monopolio (m)
Pt monopólio (m)

**Montageband** (n) n De
En assembly line
Es línea de montaje (f)
Fr chaîne de montage (f)
It catena di montaggio (f)
Pt cadeia de montagem (f)

**montant brut** (m) Fr
De Bruttobetrag (m)
En gross amount
Es importe bruto (m)
It importo lordo (m)
Pt importância total (m)

**montant net** (m) Fr
De Nettobetrag (m)
En net amount
Es importe neto (m)
It importo netto (m)
Pt importância líquida (f)

**montant nominal** (m) Fr
De Nominalbetrag (m)
En nominal amount
Es suma nominal (f)
It importo nominale (m)
Pt quantia nominal (f)

**monthly instalment** En
De Monatsrate (f)
Es mensualidad (f)
Fr mensualité (f)
It mensilità (f)
Pt prestação mensal (f)

**montra** (f) n Pt
De Schaukasten (m)
En display unit
Es presentación (f)
Fr présentoir (m)
It mostra (f)

**moratoire** (m) n Fr
De Zahlungsaufschub (m)
En moratorium
Es moratorio (m)
It moratoria (f)
Pt moratória (f)

**moratória** (f) n It
De Zahlungsaufschub (m)
En moratorium
Es moratorio (m)
Fr moratoire (m)
Pt moratória (f)

**moratória** (f) n Pt
De Zahlungsaufschub (m)
En moratorium
Es moratorio (m)
Fr moratoire (m)
It moratoria (f)

**moratorio** (m) n Es
De Zahlungsaufschub (m)
En moratorium
Fr moratoire (m)
It moratoria (f)
Pt moratória (f)

**moratorium** n En
De Zahlungsaufschub (m)
Es moratorio (m)
Fr moratoire (m)
It moratoria (f)
Pt moratória (f)

**morgen** adv De
En tomorrow
Es mañana
Fr demain
It domani
Pt amanhã

**mort** (f) n Fr
De Tod (m)
En death
Es muerte (m)
It morte (f)
Pt morte (f)

**mortalidad** (f) n Es
De Sterblichkeitsziffer (f)
En death rate
Fr taux de mortalité (m)
It tasso di mortalità (m)
Pt taxa de mortalidade (f)

**morte** (f) n It, Pt
De Tod (m)
En death
Es muerte (m)
Fr mort (f)

**mortgage** n En
De Hypothek (f)
Es hipoteca (f)

Fr hypothèque (f)
It ipoteca (f)
Pt hipoteca (f)

**mortgage debenture** En
De hypothekarisch gesicherte
    Schuldverschreibung (f)
Es obligación hipotecaria (f)
Fr obligation hypothécaire (f)
It obbligazione ipotecaria (f)
Pt obrigação hipotecária (f)

**mostra** (f) n It
De Schaustellung (f)
En display
Es presentación (f)
Fr présentation (f)
Pt exposição (f)

**mostra in vetrina** (f) It
De Fensterauslegung (f)
En window-display
Es exhibición en vitrina (f)
Fr étalage (m)
Pt exposição de montra (f)

**motif d'exportation** (m) Fr
De Ausfuhranreiz (m)
En export incentive
Es estímulo de exportación (m)
It incentivo alla esportazione
    (m)
Pt incentivo para a exportação
    (m)

**motins e perturbações civis**
    Pt
De Aufruhr und innere Unru-
    hen
En riot and civil commotion
Es revueltas y conmociones
    civiles
Fr émeutes et désordres
It rivolte e moti civili

**motion** n En, Fr (f)
De Antrag (m)
Es moción (f)
It mozione (f)
Pt moção (f)

**motivational research** En
De Motivforschung (f)
Es investigación de motivación
    (f)
Fr étude de motivation (f)
It indagine sulle motivazioni
    (f)

Pt investigação sobre motivação (f)

**Motivforschung** (f) n De
En motivational research
Es investigación de motivación (f)
Fr étude de motivation (f)
It indagine sulle motivazioni (f)
Pt investigação sobre motivação (f)

**motor a jacto** Pt
De Düsenmotor (m)
En jet engine
Es motor de propulsión a chorro (m)
Fr réacteur (m)
It motore a reazione (m)

**motor de propulsión a chorro** (m) Es
De Düsenmotor (m)
En jet engine
Fr réacteur (m)
It motore a reazione (m)
Pt motor a jacto

**motore a reazione** (m) It
De Düsenmotor (m)
En jet engine
Es motor de propulsión a chorro (m)
Fr réacteur (m)
Pt motor a jacto

**movable assets** En
De bewegliche Güter (n pl)
Es mobiliario (m)
Fr biens mobiliers (m pl)
It proprietà mobiliare (f)
Pt bens mobiliários (m pl)

**móvel ficheiro** (m) Pt
De Aktenschrank (m)
En filing cabinet
Es fichero (m)
Fr classeur (m)
It schedario (m)

**movilidad** (f) n Es
De Beweglichkeit (f)
En mobility
Fr mobilité (f)
It mobilità (f)
Pt mobilidade (f)

**movimento de dinheiro** (m) Pt
De Umsatz (m)
En turnover
Es volumen de ventas (m)
Fr chiffre d'affaires (m)
It giro d'affari (m)

**movimento della mano d'opera** (m) It
De Arbeitsumsatz (m)
En labour turnover
Es movimiento de la mano de obra (m)
Fr fluctuations de personnel (f pl)
Pt movimento de trabalhadores (m)

**movimento de trabalhadores** (m) Pt
De Arbeitsumsatz (m)
En labour turnover
Es movimiento de la mano de obra (m)
Fr fluctuations de personnel (f pl)
It movimento della mano d'opera (m)

**movimento em dinheiro** (m) Pt
De Cash-flow (n)
En cash flow
Es flujo de caja (m)
Fr cash flow (m)
It flusso di cassa (m)

**movimiento de la mano de obra** (m) Es
De Arbeitsumsatz (m)
En labour turnover
Fr fluctuations de personnel (f pl)
It movimento della mano d'opera (m)
Pt movimento de trabalhadores (m)

**moyenne** (f) n Fr
De Durchschnitt (m)
En average
Es promedio (m)
It media (f)
Pt média (f)

**moyenne arithmétique** (f) Fr
De arithmetisches Mittel (n)
En arithmetic mean

Es media aritmética (f)
It media aritmetica (f)
Pt média aritmética (f)

**moyenne pondérée** (f) Fr
De gewogener Durchschnitt (m)
En weighted average
Es media ponderada (f)
It media ponderata (f)
Pt média ponderada (f)

**mozione** (f) n It
De Antrag (m)
En motion
Es moción (f)
Fr motion (f)
Pt moção (f)

**muebles** (m pl) n Es
De Möbel (n pl)
En furniture
Fr meubles (m pl)
It mobilia (f)
Pt mobília (f)

**muellaje** (m) n Es
De Kaigeld (n)
En wharfage
Fr quayage (m)
It diritto di sosta (m)
Pt atracagem (m)

**muelle** (m) n Es
De Kai; Dock (m n)
En quay; wharf; dock
Fr quai; dock (m)
It banchina; dock (f m)
Pt cais; doca (m f)

**muerte** (m) n Es
De Tod (m)
En death
Fr mort (f)
It morte (f)
Pt morte (f)

**muestra** (f) n Es
De Probe; Muster (f n)
En sample
Fr échantillon (m)
It campione (m)
Pt amostra (f)

**muestra aleatoria** (f) Es
De Stichprobe (f)
En random sample
Fr épreuve au hasard (f)

It   campione a casaccio *(m)*
Pt   amostra avulso *(f)*


**muestra gratuita** *(f)* Es
De   kostenlose Probe *(f)*
En   free sample
Fr   échantillon gratuit *(m)*
It   campione gratuito *(m)*
Pt   amostra gratis *(f)*


**muestra sin valor** *(f)* Es
De   Muster ohne Wert *(n)*
En   sample of no value
Fr   échantillon sans valeur *(m)*
It   campione senza valore *(m)*
Pt   amostra sem valor *(f)*


**multa** *(f)* *n* Es, It, Pt
De   Geldstrafe *(f)*
En   fine
Fr   amende *(f)*


**multa pesada** *(f)* Pt
De   schwere Busse *(f)*
En   heavy fine
Es   sanción elevada *(f)*
Fr   forte amende *(f)*
It   forte multa *(f)*


**multilateral trade** En
De   mehrseitiges Handeln *(n)*
Es   comercio multilateral *(m)*
Fr   commerce multilatéral *(m)*
It   commercio multila–terale *(m)*
Pt   comércio multilateral *(m)*


**multiplicador** *(m)* *n* Es, Pt
De   Vervielfältiger *(m)*
En   multiplier
Fr   multiplicateur *(m)*
It   moltiplicatore *(m)*


**multiplicar** *vb* Es, Pt
De   vervielfältigen
En   multiply
Fr   multipliquer
It   moltiplicare


**multiplicateur** *(m)* *n* Fr
De   Vervielfältiger *(m)*
En   multiplier
Es   multiplicador *(m)*
It   moltiplicatore *(m)*
Pt   multiplicador *(m)*


**multiplier** *n* En
De   Vervielfältiger *(m)*
Es   multiplicador *(m)*
Fr   multiplicateur *(m)*
It   moltiplicatore *(m)*
Pt   multiplicador *(m)*


**multipliquer** *vb* Fr
De   vervielfältigen
En   multiply
Es   multiplicar
It   moltiplicare
Pt   multiplicar


**multiply** *vb* En
De   vervielfältigen
Es   multiplicar
Fr   multipliquer
It   moltiplicare
Pt   multiplicar


**mündelsichere Wertpapiere** *(n pl)* De
En   gilt-edged securities
Es   valores de toda confianza *(m pl)*
Fr   valeurs de tout repos *(f pl)*
It   titoli di assoluta fiducia *(m pl)*
Pt   valores de todo a confiança *(m pl)*


**municipal** *adj* En, Es, Pt
De   Kommunal-
Fr   communal
It   municipale


**municipale** *adj* It
De   Kommunal-
En   municipal
Es   municipal
Fr   communal
Pt   municipal


**Münze** *(f)* *n* De
En   coin
Es   moneda *(f)*
Fr   pièce de monnaie *(f)*
It   moneta *(f)*
Pt   moeda *(f)*


**Münze** (Münzanstalt) *(f)* *n* De
En   mint
Es   casa de la moneda *(f)*
Fr   la Monnaie
It   zecca *(f)*
Pt   casa da moeda *(f)*


**Musteranlage** *(f)* *n* De
En   pilot plant
Es   instalación piloto *(f)*
Fr   installation témoine *(f)*
It   impianto piloto *(m)*
Pt   instalação piloto *(f)*


**Muster ohne Wert** *(n)* De
En   sample of no value
Es   muestra sin valor *(f)*
Fr   échantillon sans valeur *(m)*
It   campione senza valore *(m)*
Pt   amostra sem valor *(f)*


**Mutmassung** *(f)* *n* De
En   guess-work
Es   conjetura *(f)*
Fr   conjecture *(f)*
It   congettura *(f)*
Pt   conjectura *(f)*


**Muttergesellschaft** *(f)* *n* De
En   parent company
Es   compañía matriz *(f)*
Fr   société mère *(f)*
It   società madre *(f)*
Pt   empresa matriz *(f)*


**mutua assicurazione** *(f)* It
De   Versicherung auf Gegenseitigkeit *(f)*
En   mutual insurance
Es   coaseguro *(m)*
Fr   assurance mutuelle *(f)*
Pt   seguro mútuo *(m)*


**mutual agreement** En
De   gegenseitiges Einvernehmen *(n)*
Es   acuerdo común *(m)*
Fr   accord mutuel *(m)*
It   comune accordo *(m)*
Pt   acordo mútuo *(m)*


**mutualidade** *(f)* *n* Pt
De   Versicherungsverein auf Gegenseitigkeit *(m)*
En   friendly society
Am   lodge
Es   sociedad de socorro mutuo
Fr   société de secours mutuel *(f)*
It   società di mutuo soccorso *(f)*

**mutual insurance** En
- De Versicherung auf Gegenseitigkeit (f)
- Es coaseguro (m)
- Fr assurance mutuelle (f)
- It mutua assicurazione (f)
- Pt seguro mútuo (m)

# N

**Nachahmung** (f) n De
- En imitation
- Es imitación (f)
- Fr imitation (f)
- It imitazione (f)
- Pt imitação (f)

**nachdatierter Scheck** (m) De
- En postdated cheque
- Es cheque a fecha retrasada (m)
- Fr chèque postdaté (m)
- It assegno postdatato (m)
- Pt cheque post-datado (m)

**Nachfrage** (f) n De
- En demand; inquiry
- Es demanda (f)
- Fr demande (f)
- It domanda (f)
- Pt procura; pergunta (f)

**Nachfragekurve** (f) n De
- En demand curve
- Es curva de relación demanda (f)
- Fr courbe de la demande (f)
- It curva della domanda (f)
- Pt curva de procura (f)

**Nachfrist** (f) n De
- En days of grace
- Es días de gracia (f pl)
- Fr délai supplémentaire (m)
- It giorni di grazia (m pl)
- Pt dias de tolerância (m pl)

**Nachlass** (Erbschaft) (m) n De
- En estate
- Es herencia (f)
- Fr succession (f)
- It patrimonio; successione (m f)
- Pt patrimônio; herança (m f)

**Nachlass** (Rabatt) (m) n De
- En rebate
- Es rebaja (f)
- Fr rabais (m)
- It ribasso; sconto (m)
- Pt desconto (m)

**nachlassen** vb De
- En fall off; decrease
- Es bajar de valor; disminuir
- Fr ralentir; baisser de valeur
- It diminuire
- Pt diminuir; decrescer

**Nachlasssteuer** (f) n De
- En estate duty; estate tax
- Es derechos de sucesión (m pl)
- Fr droits de succession (m pl)
- It diritti di successione (m pl)
- Pt direitos de sucessão (m pl)

**Nachlassverwalter** (m) n De
- En administrator
- Es administrador (m)
- Fr curateur (m)
- It curatore (m)
- Pt curador (m)

**nachprüfen** vb De
- En verify
- Es verificar
- Fr vérifier
- It verificare
- Pt verificar

**Nachrichtenbüro** (n) n De
- En news agency
- Es agencia de prensa (f)
- Fr agence de presse (f)
- It agenzia d'informazioni (f)
- Pt agência de notícias (f)

**Nachschätzung** (f) n De
- En supplementary estimate
- Es cálculo suplementario (m)
- Fr devis supplémentaire (f)
- It preventivo supplementare (m)
- Pt estimativa suplementar (f)

**Nachschlagebuch** (n) n De
- En reference book
- Es libro de consulta (m)
- Fr ouvrage de référence (m)
- It libro di consultazione (m)
- Pt livro de consulta (m)

**Nachschrift** (f) n De
- En postscript (PS)
- Es posdata (f)
- Fr post-scriptum; postface (m f)
- It poscritto (PS) (m)
- Pt pós-escrito; post-scriptum (PS) (m)

**Nachtarbeit** (f) n De
- En nightwork
- Es trabajo nocturno (m)
- Fr travail de nuit (m)
- It lavoro notturno (m)
- Pt trabalho nocturno (m)

**Nachteil** (m) n De
- En prejudice
- Es prejuicio; perjuicio (m)
- Fr préjudice (m)
- It pregiudizio (m)
- Pt preconceito; prejuízo (m)

**nachträglicher Umsatzbonus** (m) De
- En deferred rebate
- Es descuento diferido (m)
- Fr rabais différé (m)
- It sconto differito (m)
- Pt dedução adiada (f)

**Nachtschicht** (f) n De
- En night shift
- Es turno de noche (m)
- Fr équipe de nuit (f)
- It turno di notte (m)
- Pt turno da noite (m)

**Nachttresor** (m) n De
- En night safe
- Es caja de seguridad nocturna (f)
- Fr coffre de nuit (m)
- It deposito notturno (m)
- Pt cofre nocturno (m)

**Nachtwächter** (m) n De
- En nightwatchman
- Es guarda de noche (m)
- Fr gardien de nuit (m)
- It guardiano notturno (m)
- Pt guarda de noite (m)

**Nachzugsaktien** (f pl) n De
- En deferred shares
- Es acciones aplazadas (f pl)
- Fr actions différées (f pl)

It  azioni postergate *(f pl)*
Pt  acções diferidas *(f pl)*

**nacional** *adj* Es, Pt
De  national
En  national
Fr  national
It  nazionale

**nacionalidad** *(f) n* Es
De  Staatsangehörigkeit *(f)*
En  nationality
Fr  nationalité *(f)*
It  nazionalità *(f)*
Pt  nacionalidade *(f)*

**nacionalidade** *(f) n* Pt
De  Staatsangehörigkeit *(f)*
En  nationality
Es  nacionalidad *(f)*
Fr  nationalité *(f)*
It  nazionalità *(f)*

**nacionalização** *(f) n* Pt
De  Verstaatlichung *(f)*
En  nationalization
Es  nacionalización *(f)*
Fr  nationalisation *(f)*
It  nazionalizzazione *(f)*

**nacionalización** *(f) n* Es
De  Verstaatlichung *(f)*
En  nationalization
Fr  nationalisation *(f)*
It  nazionalizzazione *(f)*
Pt  nacionalização *(f)*

**nada lucrativo** Es
De  unvorteilhaft
En  unprofitable
Fr  sans profit
It  poco proficuo
Pt  não lucrativo

**na fábrica** Pt
De  ab Fabrik
En  ex factory
Es  de fábrica
Fr  prise usine
It  franco fabbrica

**nähere Umstände** *(m pl)* De
En  further particulars
Es  más detalles *(m pl)*
Fr  plus amples renseigne-
    ments *(m pl)*
It  ulteriori particolari *(m pl)*

Pt  pormenores adicionais *(m
    pl)*

**naked bond** Am
En  unsecured debenture
De  ungesicherte    Schuldver-
    schreibung *(f)*
Es  obligación no garantizada
    *(f)*
Fr  obligation sans garantie *(f)*
It  obbligazione non garantita
    *(f)*
Pt  obrigação sem garantia *(f)*

**nantissement** *(m) n* Fr
De  Nebenbürgschaft;  Hypo-
    thek *(f)*
En  security; hypothecation
Es  fianza; hipoteca *(f)*
It  pegno; ipoteca *(m f)*
Pt  fiança; hipoteca *(f)*

**não-aceitação** *(f) n* Pt
De  Nichtannahme *(f)*
En  nonacceptance
Es  rechazo *(m)*
Fr  non-acceptation *(f)*
It  mancata accettazione *(f)*

**não autorizado** Pt
De  unbefugt
En  unauthorized
Es  inautorizado
Fr  non autorisé
It  non autorizzato

**não-cumprimento** *(m) n* Pt
De  Nichterfüllung *(f)*
En  nonfulfilment
Es  incumplimiento *(m)*
Fr  non-exécution *(f)*
It  inadempienza *(f)*

**não lucrativo** Pt
De  unvorteilhaft
En  unprofitable
Es  nada lucrativo
Fr  sans profit
It  poco proficuo

**não transaccionavel por ter-
ceiros** Pt
De  nicht übertragbar
En  not negotiable
Es  no negociable
Fr  non négociable
It  non negoziabile

**nascondersi** *vb* It
De  sich heimlich davonmachen
En  abscond
Es  esconderse
Fr  s'enfuir; décamper
Pt  ausentar-se  para  parte
    incerta

**nastro magnetico** *(m)* It
De  Magnetband *(n)*
En  magnetic tape
Es  cinta magnética *(f)*
Fr  bande magnétique *(f)*
Pt  fita magnética *(f)*

**national** *adj* De, En, Fr
Es  nacional
It  nazionale
Pt  nacional

**national debt** En
De  Staatsschuld *(f)*
Es  deuda pública *(f)*
Fr  dette publique *(f)*
It  debito pubblico *(m)*
Pt  dívida pública *(f)*

**Nationaleinkommen** *(n) n* De
En  national income
Es  renta nacional *(f)*
Fr  revenu national *(m)*
It  reddito nazionale *(m)*
Pt  receita pública *(m)*

**national income** En
De  Nationaleinkommen *(n)*
Es  renta nacional *(f)*
Fr  revenu national *(m)*
It  reddito nazionale *(m)*
Pt  receita pública *(m)*

**national insurance** En
Am  social security
De  staatliche Versicherung *(f)*
Es  seguridad social *(f)*
Fr  assurance d'état *(f)*
It  assicurazione obbligatoria
    *(f)*
Pt  seguro nacional *(m)*

**nationalisation** *(f) n* Fr
De  Verstaatlichung *(f)*
En  nationalization
Es  nacionalización *(f)*
It  nazionalizzazione *(f)*
Pt  nacionalização *(f)*

**nationalité** (f) n Fr
De Staatsangehörigkeit (f)
En nationality
Es nacionalidad (f)
It nazionalità (f)
Pt nacionalidade (f)

**nationality** n En
De Staatsangehörigkeit (f)
Es nacionalidad (f)
Fr nationalité (f)
It nazionalità (f)
Pt nacionalidade (f)

**nationalization** n En
De Verstaatlichung (f)
Es nacionalización (f)
Fr nationalisation (f)
It nazionalizzazione (f)
Pt nacionalização (f)

**nationalized industry** En
De verstaatlichte Industrie (f)
Es industria nacionalizada (f)
Fr industrie nationalisée (f)
It industria nazionalizzata (f)
Pt indústria nacionalizada (f)

**natural gas** En
De Erdgas (n)
Es gas natural (m)
Fr gaz naturel (m)
It gas naturale (m)
Pt gás natural (m)

**natural wastage** En
De natürlicher Abgang (m)
Es merma natural (f)
Fr déperdition naturelle (f)
It consumo naturale (m)
Pt desperdício natural (m)

**natürliche Abnützung** (f) De
En wear and tear
Es desgaste natural (m)
Fr usure normale (f)
It logorio naturale (m)
Pt desgaste (m)

**natürlicher Abgang** (m) De
En natural wastage
Es merma natural (f)
Fr déperdition naturelle (f)
It consumo naturale (m)
Pt desperdício natural (m)

**nautical** adj En
De nautisch
Es náutico
Fr nautique
It nautico
Pt náutico

**náutico** adj Es, Pt
De nautisch
En nautical
Fr nautique
It nautico

**nautico** adj It
De nautisch
En nautical
Es náutico
Fr nautique
Pt náutico

**nautique** adj Fr
De nautisch
En nautical
Es náutico
It nautico
Pt náutico

**nautisch** adj De
En nautical
Es náutico
Fr nautique
It nautico
Pt náutico

**nave** (f) n It
De Schiff (n)
En ship
Es barco (m)
Fr navire (m)
Pt navio (m)

**nave da carico** (f) It
De Frachtschiff (n)
En cargo boat
Es buque de carga (m)
Fr cargo (m)
Pt barco de carga (m)

**nave da contenitori** (f) It
De Containerschiff (n)
En container ship
Es barco de contenedores (m)
Fr navire porte-containers (m)
Pt navio de contentres (m)

**nave di linea** (f) It
De Linienschiff (n)
En liner

Es vapor de línea (m)
Fr paquebot (m)
Pt paquete (m)

**navegable** adj Es
De schiffbar
En navigable
Fr navigable
It navigabile
Pt navegável

**navegação** (f) n Pt
De Schiffahrt (f)
En navigation
Es navegación (f)
Fr navigation (f)
It navigazione (f)

**navegación** (f) n Es
De Schiffahrt (f)
En navigation
Fr navigation (f)
It navigazione (f)
Pt navegação (f)

**navegável** adj Pt
De schiffbar
En navigable
Es navegable
Fr navigable
It navigabile

**nave mercantile** (f) It
De Handelsschiff (n)
En merchant ship
Es barco mercante (m)
Fr navire marchand (m)
Pt navio mercante (m)

**nave traghetto** (f) It
De Fährboot (n)
En ferry-boat
Es transbordador (m)
Fr bac (m)
Pt barco de travessia (m)

**navigabile** adj It
De schiffbar
En navigable
Es navegable
Fr navigable
Pt navegável

**navigable** adj En, Fr
De schiffbar
Es navegable
It navigabile
Pt navegável

**navigation** n En, Fr (f)
De Schiffahrt (f)
Es navegación (f)
It navigazione (f)
Pt navegação (f)

**navigazione** (f) n It
De Schiffahrt (f)
En navigation
Es navegación (f)
Fr navigation (f)
Pt navegação (f)

**navio** (m) n Pt
De Schiff (n)
En ship
Es barco (m)
Fr navire (m)
It nave (f)

**navio de contentres** (m) Pt
De Containerschiff (n)
En container ship
Es barco de contenedores (m)
Fr navire porte-containers (m)
It nave da contenitori (f)

**navio mercante** (m) Pt
De Handelsschiff (n)
En merchant ship
Es barco mercante (m)
Fr navire marchand (m)
It nave mercantile (f)

**navire** (m) n Fr
De Schiff (n)
En ship
Es barco (m)
It nave (f)
Pt navio (m)

**navire de tramping** (m) Fr
De Trampschiff (n)
En tramp steamer
Es vapor volandero (m)
It carretta (f)
Pt vapor de serviço autónomo (m)

**navire marchand** (m) Fr
De Handelsschiff (n)
En merchant ship
Es barco mercante (m)
It nave mercantile (f)
Pt navio mercante (m)

**navire porte-containers** (m) Fr
De Containerschiff (n)
En container ship
Es barco de contenedores (m)
It nave da contenitori (f)
Pt navio de contentres (m)

**nazionale** adj It
De national
En national
Es nacional
Fr national
Pt nacional

**nazionalità** (f) n It
De Staatsangehörigkeit (f)
En nationality
Es nacionalidad (f)
Fr nationalité (f)
Pt nacionalidade (f)

**nazionalizzazione** (f) n It
De Verstaatlichung (f)
En nationalization
Es nacionalización (f)
Fr nationalisation (f)
Pt nacionalização (f)

**Nebenbürgschaft** (f) n De
En security
Es fianza (f)
Fr nantissement (m)
It pegno (m)
Pt fiança (f)

**Nebenkosten** (pl) n De
En incidental expenses
Es gastos imprevistos (m pl)
Fr faux frais (m pl)
It spese impreviste (f pl)
Pt despesas ocasionais (f pl)

**Nebenprodukt** (n) n De
En by-product
Es producto derivado (m)
Fr sous-produit (m)
It sottoprodotto (m)
Pt produto derivado (m)

**negative balance** Am
En adverse balance
De Passivsaldo (m)
Es saldo adverso (m)
Fr balance déficitaire (f)
It saldo passivo (m)
Pt saldo negativo (m)

**negative Einkommenssteuer** (f) De
En negative income tax
Es impuesto negativo sobre renta (m)
Fr impôt négatif sur le revenu (m)
It imposta negativa sul reddito (f)
Pt imposto negativo sobre receita (m)

**negative income tax** En
De negative Einkommenssteuer (f)
Es impuesto negativo sobre renta (m)
Fr impôt négatif sur le revenu (m)
It imposta negativa sul reddito (f)
Pt imposto negativo sobre receita (m)

**negligence** n En
De Fahrlässigkeit (f)
Es negligencia (f)
Fr négligence (f)
It negligenza (f)
Pt negligência (f)

**négligence** (f) n Fr
De Fahrlässigkeit (f)
En negligence
Es negligencia (f)
It negligenza (f)
Pt negligência (f)

**negligencia** (f) n Es
De Fahrlässigkeit (f)
En negligence
Fr négligence (f)
It negligenza (f)
Pt negligência (f)

**negligência** (f) n Pt
De Fahrlässigkeit (f)
En negligence
Es negligencia (f)
Fr négligence (f)
It negligenza (f)

**negligenza** (f) n It
De Fahrlässigkeit (f)
En negligence
Es negligencia (f)
Fr négligence (f)
Pt negligência (f)

**negociable** adj Es
De begebbar
En negotiable
Fr négotiable
It negoziabile
Pt negociável

**negociação** (f) n Pt
De Verhandlung (f)
En negotiation
Es negociación (f)
Fr négotiation (f)
It trattativa (f)

**negociación** (f) n Es
De Verhandlung (f)
En negotiation
Fr négotiation (f)
It trattativa (f)
Pt negociação (f)

**negociaciones a término** (f pl)
Es
De Zeitgeschäfte (n pl)
En forward dealings
Fr opérations à terme (f pl)
It operazioni a termine (f pl)
Pt transacções adiantadas (f
pl)

**négociant** (m) n Fr
De Händler; Kaufmann (m)
En dealer; merchant
Es comerciante (m)
It negoziante; commerciante
(m)
Pt negociante; comerciante
(m)

**negociante** (m) n Es, Pt
De Händler (m)
En dealer
Fr négociant (m)
It negoziante; commerciante
(m)

**negociar** vb Es, Pt
De verhandeln
En negotiate
Fr négocier
It negoziare

**négociations de conventions**
**collectives** (f pl) Fr
De Tarifvertragsverhandlung (f)
En collective bargaining
Es contratación collectiva (f)

It contrattazione collettiva (f)
Pt regateio colectivo (m)

**negociável** adj Pt
De begebbar
En negotiable
Es negociable
Fr négotiable
It negoziabile

**négocier** vb Fr
De verhandeln
En negotiate
Es negociar
It negoziare
Pt negociar

**negocio** (m) n Es
De Handel; Geschäft (m n)
En trade; deal
Fr affaires; affaire (f pl; f)
It negozio; affare (m)
Pt negócio (m)

**negócio** (m) n Pt
De Handel; Geschäft (m n)
En trade; deal
Es negocio (m)
Fr affaires; affaire (f pl; f)
It negozio; affare (m)

**negócio em dinheiro** (m) Pt
De Bargeschäft (n)
En cash deal
Es trato al contado (m)
Fr transaction au comptant (f)
It operazione a contanti (f)

**negocios** (m pl) n Es
De Geschäft (n)
En business
Fr affaires (f pl)
It affari (m pl)
Pt negócios (m pl)

**negócios** (m pl) n Pt
De Geschäft (n)
En business
Es negocios (m pl)
Fr affaires (f pl)
It affari (m pl)

**negotiable** adj En
De begebbar
Es negociable
Fr négotiable
It negoziabile
Pt negociável

**négotiable** adj Fr
De begebbar
En negotiable
Es negociable
It negoziabile
Pt negociável

**negotiable instrument** En
De begebbares Wertpapier (n)
Es título negociable (m)
Fr effet de commerce (m)
It titolo negoziabile (m)
Pt título negociável (m)

**negotiate** vb En
De verhandeln
Es negociar
Fr négocier
It negoziare
Pt negociar

**negotiation** n En
De Verhandlung (f)
Es negociación (f)
Fr négotiation (f)
It trattativa (f)
Pt negociação (f)

**négotiation** (f) n Fr
De Verhandlung (f)
En negotiation
Es negociación (f)
It trattativa (f)
Pt negociação (f)

**negoziabile** adj It
De begebbar
En negotiable
Es negociable
Fr négotiable
Pt negociável

**negoziante** (m) n It
De Händler (m)
En dealer
Es comerciante (m)
Fr négociant (m)
Pt negociante (m)

**negoziare** vb It
De verhandeln
En negotiate
Es negociar
Fr négocier
Pt negociar

**negozio** *(m)* n It
De Handel; Geschäft *(m n)*
En trade; business
Es negocio *(m)*
Fr affaires; affaire *(f pl; f)*
Pt negócio *(m)*

**negozio a catena** *(m)* It
De Kettengeschäft *(n)*
En chain store
Es sucursal de cadena de almacenes *(f)*
Fr magasin à succursales multiples *(m)*
Pt sucursal de cadeia de armazéns *(f)*

**nemico** *(m)* n It
De Feind *(m)*
En enemy
Es enemigo *(m)*
Fr ennemi *(m)*
Pt inimigo *(m)*

**Nennkapital** *(m)* n De
En nominal capital
Es capital nominal *(m)*
Fr capital nominal *(m)*
It capitale nominale *(m)*
Pt capital nominal *(m)*

**Nennpreis** *(m)* n De
En nominal price
Es precio nominal *(m)*
Fr prix nominal *(m)*
It prezzo nominale *(m)*
Pt preço nominal *(m)*

**Nennwert** *(m)* n De
En nominal value
Es valor nominal *(m)*
Fr valeur nominale *(f)*
It valore nominale *(m)*
Pt valor nominal *(m)*

**ne pas honorer un effet** Fr
De einen Wechsel nicht akzeptieren
En dishonour a bill
Es protestar una letra
It non onorare un effetto
Pt protestar uma letra

**ne quittez pas!** Fr
De am Apparat bleiben
En hold the line
Es espere al aparato

It resta in linea
Pt aguarde

**net** *adj* En, Fr
De Netto-; Rein-
Es neto
It netto
Pt líquido

**net amount** En
De Nettobetrag *(m)*
Es importe neto *(m)*
Fr montant net *(m)*
It importo netto *(m)*
Pt importância líquida *(f)*

**net assets** En
De Reinvermögen *(n)*
Es activo neto *(m)*
Fr actif net *(m)*
It attivo netto *(m)*
Pt bens líquidos *(m pl)*

**net income** En
De Nettoeinkommen *(n)*
Es ingreso neto *(f)*
Fr revenu net *(m)*
It reddito netto *(m)*
Pt receita líquida *(f)*

**neto** *adj* Es
De Netto-; Rein-
En net
Fr net
It netto
Pt líquido

**net price** En
De Nettopreis; Nettokurs *(m)*
Es precio neto *(m)*
Fr prix net *(m)*
It prezzo netto *(m)*
Pt preço líquido *(m)*

**net proceeds** En
De Reinerlös *(m)*
Es rédito neto *(m)*
Fr produit net *(m)*
It ricavo netto *(m)*
Pt proventos líquidos *(m pl)*

**net profit** En
De Reingewinn *(m)*
Es ganancia neta *(f)*
Fr bénéfice net *(m)*
It utile netto *(m)*
Pt lucro líquido *(m)*

**net profit margin** En
De Reingewinnspanne *(f)*
Es margen de beneficio neto *(m)*
Fr marge nette de bénéfices *(f)*
It margine di utile netto *(m)*
Pt margem de lucro líquido *(f)*

**net revenue** En
De Nettoeinnahmen *(f pl)*
Es ingresos netos *(m pl)*
Fr recettes nettes *(f pl)*
It entrata netta *(f)*
Pt receita líquida *(f)*

**netto** *adj* It
De Netto-; Rein-
En net
Es neto
Fr net
Pt líquido

**Netto-** De
En net
Es neto
Fr net
It netto
Pt líquido

**Nettobetrag** *(m)* n De
En net amount
Es importe neto *(m)*
Fr montant net *(m)*
It importo netto *(m)*
Pt importância líquida *(f)*

**Nettoeinkommen** *(n)* n De
En net income
Es ingreso neto *(f)*
Fr revenu net *(m)*
It reddito netto *(m)*
Pt receita líquida *(f)*

**Nettoeinnahmen** *(f pl)* n De
En net revenue
Es ingresos netos *(m pl)*
Fr recettes nettes *(f pl)*
It entrata netta *(f)*
Pt receita líquida *(f)*

**Nettoertrag** *(m)* n De
En net yield
Es rendimiento neto *(m)*
Fr rendement net *(m)*
It reddito netto *(m)*
Pt rendimento líquido *(m)*

**Nettolohn** *(m)* n De
En  take-home pay
Es  paga neta *(f)*
Fr  salaire nette *(f)*
It  paga netta *(f)*
Pt  salário líquido *(m)*

**Nettopreis** *(m)* n De
En  net price
Es  precio neto *(m)*
Fr  prix net *(m)*
It  prezzo netto *(m)*
Pt  preço líquido *(m)*

**net weight** En
De  Reingewicht *(n)*
Es  peso neto *(m)*
Fr  poids net *(m)*
It  peso netto *(m)*
Pt  peso líquido *(m)*

**network** n En
De  Netz *(n)*
Es  red *(f)*
Fr  réseau *(m)*
It  rete *(f)*
Pt  rede *(f)*

**net yield** En
De  Nettoertrag *(m)*
Es  rendimiento neto *(m)*
Fr  rendement net *(m)*
It  reddito netto *(m)*
Pt  rendimento líquido *(m)*

**Netz** *(n)* n De
En  network
Es  red *(f)*
Fr  réseau *(m)*
It  rete *(f)*
Pt  rede *(f)*

**Netzplantechnik** *(f)* n De
En  critical   path   analysis
    (c.p.a.)
Es  análisis de recorrido crítico
    *(m)*
Fr  analyse du chemin critique
    *(m)*
It  analisi della linea critica *(f)*
Pt  análise de transcurso crí-
    tico *(f)*

**Neuerung** *(f)* n De
En  innovation
Es  innovación *(f)*
Fr  innovation *(f)*

It  innovazione *(f)*
Pt  inovação *(f)*

**new issue** En
De  Ausgabe junger Aktien *(f)*
Es  nueva emisión *(f)*
Fr  émission d'actions nouvel-
    les *(f)*
It  nuova emissione *(f)*
Pt  emissão nova *(f)*

**news agency** En
De  Nachrichtenbüro *(n)*
Es  agencia de prensa *(f)*
Fr  agence de presse *(f)*
It  agenzia d'informazioni *(f)*
Pt  agência de notícias *(f)*

**Nichtannahme** *(f)* n De
En  nonacceptance
Es  rechazo *(m)*
Fr  non-acceptation *(f)*
It  mancata accettazione *(f)*
Pt  não-aceitação *(f)*

**nicht ausgegebenes Kapital**
*(n)* De
En  unissued capital
Es  capital no emitido *(m)*
Fr  capitaux pas encore émis
    *(m pl)*
It  capitale non emesso *(m)*
Pt  capital não emitido *(m)*

**nicht bekanntgegebener Auf-**
**traggeber** *(m)* De
En  undisclosed principal
Es  mandante  no  nombrado
    *(m)*
Fr  mandant non divulgé *(m)*
It  mandante  non  nominato
    *(m)*
Pt  mandante não divulgado
    *(m)*

**nicht dauerhafte Verbrauchs-**
**güter** *(n pl)* De
En  consumer non-durables
Es  bienes de consumo pere-
    cederos *(m pl)*
Fr  biens de consommation
    non-durables *(m pl)*
It  beni di consumo non dure-
    voli *(m pl)*
Pt  bens de consumo não
    duráveis *(m pl)*

**nicht eingerufenes Kapital** *(n)*
De
En  uncalled capital
Es  capital de reserva *(m)*
Fr  capital non appelé *(m)*
It  capitale non richiamato *(m)*
Pt  capital irrealizado *(m)*

**Nichteinhaltung** *(f)* n De
En  default
Es  falta *(f)*
Fr  défaillance; défaut *(f m)*
It  mancanza *(f)*
Pt  falta *(f)*

**Nichterfüllung** *(f)* n De
En  nonfulfilment
Es  incumplimiento *(m)*
Fr  non-exécution *(f)*
It  inadempienza *(f)*
Pt  não cumprimento *(m)*

**nicht fest anbieten** De
En  quote not firm
Es  cotizar sin compromiso
Fr  coter sans obligation
It  quotare senza impegno
Pt  cotizar sem fixação de valor

**nicht gesicherter Gläubiger**
*(m)* De
En  unsecured creditor
Es  acreedor  no  garantizado
    *(m)*
Fr  créancier   chirographaire
    *(m)*
It  creditore non garantito *(m)*
Pt  credor sem garantia *(m)*

**nicht greifbare Aktiven** *(n pl)*
De
En  intangible assets
Es  activo intangible *(m)*
Fr  actif incorporel *(m)*
It  beni incorporali *(m pl)*
Pt  bens intocáveis *(m pl)*

**nichtig** *adj* De
En  void
Es  nulo
Fr  nul
It  nullo
Pt  nulo

**nicht notierte Werte** *(m pl)* De
En  unquoted securities
Es  títulos no cotizados *(m pl)*
Fr  valeurs non cotées *(f pl)*

It    titoli non quotati *(m pl)*
Pt    títulos não cotados *(m pl)*

**nicht rückzahlbare Schuldver-schreibung** *(f)* De
En    undated debenture
Es    obligación sin fecha *(f)*
Fr    obligation non amortissable *(f)*
It    obbligazione senza data *(f)*
Pt    obrigação sem data *(f)*

**nicht übereinstimmen** De
En    disagree
Es    no estar de acuerdo
Fr    être en désaccord
It    essere in disaccordo
Pt    discordar

**nicht übertragbar** De
En    not negotiable
Es    no negociable
Fr    non négociable
It    non negoziabile
Pt    não transaccionavel por terceiros

**Nichtzahlung** *(f)* n De
En    failure to pay
Es    falta de pago *(f)*
Fr    défaut de paiement *(m)*
It    mancato pagamento *(m)*
Pt    falta de pagamento *(f)*

**Niessbrauchnutzer** *(m)* n De
En    beneficial owner
Es    usufructuario *(m)*
Fr    usufruitier *(m)*
It    usufruttuario *(m)*
Pt    usufrutuário *(m)*

**Niessbrauchsrecht** *(n)* n De
En    usufruct; beneficial interest
Es    usufructo *(m)*
Fr    usufruit *(m)*
It    usufrutto *(m)*
Pt    usufruto *(m)*

**night safe** En
De    Nachttresor *(m)*
Es    caja de seguridad nocturna *(f)*
Fr    coffre de nuit *(m)*
It    deposito notturno *(m)*
Pt    cofre nocturno *(m)*

**night shift** En
De    Nachtschicht *(f)*
Es    turno de noche *(m)*
Fr    équipe de nuit *(m)*
It    turno di notte *(m)*
Pt    turno da noite *(m)*

**nightwatchman** n En
De    Nachtwächter *(m)*
Es    guarda de noche *(m)*
Fr    gardien de nuit *(m)*
It    guardiano notturno *(m)*
Pt    guarda de noite *(m)*

**nightwork** n En
De    Nachtarbeit *(f)*
Es    trabajo nocturno *(m)*
Fr    travail de nuit *(m)*
It    lavoro notturno *(m)*
Pt    trabalho nocturno *(m)*

**nil balance** En
Am    zero balance
De    Nullsaldo *(m)*
Es    saldo nulo *(m)*
Fr    solde nul *(m)*
It    saldo nullo *(m)*
Pt    saldo nulo *(m)*

**niveau des prix** *(m)* Fr
De    Preisebene *(f)*
En    price level
Es    nivel de precios *(m)*
It    livello dei prezzi *(m)*
Pt    nível de preços *(m)*

**niveau de vie** *(m)* Fr
De    Lebenshaltung *(f)*
En    standard of living
Es    nivel de vida *(m)*
It    tenore di vita *(m)*
Pt    nível de vida *(m)*

**nível de crédito** *(m)* Pt
De    Kreditwürdigkeit *(f)*
En    credit rating
Es    límite de crédito *(m)*
Fr    degré de solvabilité *(m)*
It    stima del credito *(f)*

**nivel de precios** *(m)* Es
De    Preisebene *(f)*
En    price level
Fr    niveau des prix *(m)*
It    livello dei prezzi *(m)*
Pt    nível de preços *(m)*

**nível de preços** *(m)* Pt
De    Preisebene *(f)*
En    price level
Es    nivel de precios *(m)*
Fr    niveau des prix *(m)*
It    livello dei prezzi *(m)*

**nivel de vida** *(m)* Es
De    Lebenshaltung *(f)*
En    standard of living
Fr    niveau de vie *(m)*
It    tenore di vita *(m)*
Pt    nível de vida *(m)*

**nível de vida** *(m)* Pt
De    Lebenshaltung *(f)*
En    standard of living
Es    nivel de vida *(m)*
Fr    niveau de vie *(m)*
It    tenore di vita *(m)*

**nó** *(m)* n Pt
De    Knoten *(m)*
En    knot
Es    nudo *(m)*
Fr    nœud *(m)*
It    nodo *(m)*

**no armazém** Pt
De    an Zollfreilager
En    ex warehouse
Es    puesto en almacén
Fr    à prendre en entrepôt
It    franco magazzino

**noch nicht entlasteter Gemeinschuldner** *(m)* De
En    undischarged bankrupt
Es    fallido no rehabilitado *(m)*
Fr    failli non réhabilité *(m)*
It    fallito non riabilitato *(m)*
Pt    falido insolvente *(m)*

**no-claims discount (bonus)** En
De    Schadenfreiheitsrabatt *(m)*
Es    bonificación por no-reclamación *(f)*
Fr    bonification pour non sinistre *(f)*
It    sconto per assenza di sinistri *(m)*
Pt    disconto por ausência de reclamações *(m)*

**nodo** *(m)* n It
De    Knoten *(m)*
En    knot

Es nudo *(m)*
Fr nœud *(m)*
Pt nó *(m)*

**no estar de acuerdo** Es
De nicht übereinstimmen
En disagree
Fr être en désaccord
It essere in disaccordo
Pt discordar

**no estrangeiro** Pt
De im Ausland
En abroad
Es en el extranjero
Fr à l'étranger
It all'estero

**nœud** *(m)* n Fr
De Knoten *(m)*
En knot
Es nudo *(m)*
It nodo *(m)*
Pt nó *(m)*

**noleggiare** *vb* It
De mieten
En hire
Es alquilar
Fr louer
Pt alugar

**noleggiatore** *(m)* n It
De Mieter; Befrachter *(m)*
En hirer; charterer
Es alquilador; fletador *(m)*
Fr locataire; affréteur *(m)*
Pt alugador; fretador *(m)*

**noleggio** *(m)* n It
De Befrachtung *(f)*
En chartering
Es fletamento *(m)*
Fr affrètement *(m)*
Pt fretamento *(m)*

**nolo** *(m)* n It
De Fracht *(f)*
En freight
Es flete *(m)*
Fr fret *(m)*
Pt frete *(m)*

**nolo prepagato** It
De Fracht vorausbezahlt
En freight pre-paid
Es flete pagado

Fr fret payé d'avance
Pt frete pago

**nombrar** *vb* Es
De ernennen
En appoint
Fr nommer
It nominare
Pt nomear

**nombre comercial** *(m)* Es
De Markenbezeichnung *(f)*
En brand name
Fr marque de fabrique *(f)*
It marca *(f)*
Pt marca *(f)*

**nomeado** *(m)* n Pt
De Benannte(r); Vorgeschlagene(r) *(m)*
En nominee
Es nominatario *(m)*
Fr personne dénommée *(f)*
It persona nominata *(f)*

**nomear** *vb* Pt
De ernennen
En appoint
Es nombrar
Fr nommer
It nominare

**Nomenclatura de Bruselas** *(f)*
Es
De Brüsseler Verzeichnis *(n)*
En Brussels Nomenclature
Fr Nomenclature de Bruxelles
(N.D.B.) *(f)*
It Nomenclatura di Bruxelles
*(f)*
Pt Nomenclatura de Bruxelas
*(f)*

**Nomenclatura de Bruxelas** *(f)*
Pt
De Brüsseler Verzeichnis *(n)*
En Brussels Nomenclature
Es Nomenclatura de Bruselas
*(f)*
Fr Nomenclature de Bruxelles
(N.D.B.) *(f)*
It Nomenclatura di Bruxelles
*(f)*

**Nomenclatura di Bruxelles** *(f)*
It
De Brüsseler Verzeichnis *(n)*
En Brussels Nomenclature

Es Nomenclatura de Bruselas
*(f)*
Fr Nomenclature de Bruxelles
(N.D.B.) *(f)*
Pt Nomenclatura de Bruxelas
*(f)*

**Nomenclature de Bruxelles**
**(N.D.B.)** *(f)* Fr
De Brüsseler Verzeichnis *(n)*
En Brussels Nomenclature
Es Nomenclatura de Bruselas
*(f)*
It Nomenclatura di Bruxelles
*(f)*
Pt Nomenclatura de Bruxelas
*(f)*

**nómina de pago** *(f)* Es
De Lohnbuch *(n)*
En payroll
Fr feuille de paie *(f)*
It libro paga *(m)*
Pt folha de salários *(f)*

**nominal** *adj* En, Es, Fr, Pt
De nominell
It nominale

**nominal account** En
De Firmenkonto *(n)*
Es cuenta de resultado *(f)*
Fr compte nominal *(m)*
It conto d'ordine *(m)*
Pt conta nominal *(f)*

**nominal amount** En
De Nominalbetrag *(m)*
Es suma nominal *(f)*
Fr montant nominal *(m)*
It importo nominale *(m)*
Pt quantia nominal *(f)*

**Nominalbetrag** *(m)* n De
En nominal amount
Es suma nominal *(f)*
Fr montant nominal *(m)*
It importo nominale *(m)*
Pt quantia nominal *(f)*

**nominal capital** En
De Nennkapital *(m)*
Es capital nominal *(m)*
Fr capital nominal *(m)*
It capitale nominale *(m)*
Pt capital nominal *(m)*

**nominal damages** En
  De Ordnungsentschädigung *(f)*
  Es daños nominales *(m pl)*
  Fr indemnité de principe *(f)*
  It danni nominali *(m pl)*
  Pt danos nominais *(m pl)*

**nominale** *adj* It
  De nominell
  En nominal
  Es nominal
  Fr nominal
  Pt nominal

**nominal price** En
  De Nennpreis *(m)*
  Es precio nominal *(m)*
  Fr prix nominal *(m)*
  It prezzo nominale *(m)*
  Pt preço nominal *(m)*

**nominal value** En
  De Nennwert *(m)*
  Es valor nominal *(m)*
  Fr valeur nominale *(f)*
  It valore nominale *(m)*
  Pt valor nominal *(m)*

**nominare** *vb* It
  De ernennen
  En appoint
  Es nombrar
  Fr nommer
  Pt nomear

**nominatario** *(m) n* Es
  De Benannte(r); Vorgeschla-
    gene(r) *(m)*
  En nominee
  Fr personne dénommée *(f)*
  It persona nominata *(f)*
  Pt nomeado *(m)*

**nominee** *n* En
  De Benannte(r); Vorgeschla-
    gene(r) *(m)*
  Es nominatario *(m)*
  Fr personne dénommée *(f)*
  It persona nominata *(f)*
  Pt nomeado *(m)*

**nominell** *adj* De
  En nominal
  Es nominal
  Fr nominal
  It nominale
  Pt nominal

**nommer** *vb* Fr
  De ernennen
  En appoint
  Es nombrar
  It nominare
  Pt nomear

**no montante de** Pt
  De hinauslaufend auf
  En amounting to
  Es ascendiendo a
  Fr à concurrence de
  It ammontare a

**nonacceptance** *n* En
  De Nichtannahme *(f)*
  Es rechazo *(m)*
  Fr non-acceptation *(f)*
  It mancata accettazione *(f)*
  Pt não-aceitação *(f)*

**non-acceptation** *(f) n* Fr
  De Nichtannahme *(f)*
  En nonacceptance
  Es rechazo *(m)*
  It mancata accettazione *(f)*
  Pt não-aceitação *(f)*

**non autorisé** Fr
  De unbefugt
  En unauthorized
  Es inautorizado
  It non autorizzato
  Pt não autorizado

**non autorizzato** It
  De unbefugt
  En unauthorized
  Es inautorizado
  Fr non autorisé
  Pt não autorizado

**noncontributory pension** En
  De Pension ohne Beitrags-
    pflicht *(f)*
  Es pensión sin entregas del
    beneficiario *(f)*
  Fr pension non-contribuable
    *(f)*
  It pensione senza contributi
    *(f)*
  Pt pensão sem contribuição
    prévia *(f)*

**no negociable** Es
  De nicht übertragbar
  En not negotiable
  Fr non négociable

  It non negoziabile
  Pt não transaccionavel por
    terceiros

**non-exécution** *(f) n* Fr
  De Nichterfüllung *(f)*
  En nonfulfilment
  Es incumplimiento *(m)*
  It inadempienza *(f)*
  Pt não cumprimento *(m)*

**nonfulfilment** *n* En
  De Nichterfüllung *(f)*
  Es incumplimiento *(m)*
  Fr non-exécution *(f)*
  It inadempienza *(f)*
  Pt não cumprimento *(m)*

**non négociable** Fr
  De nicht übertragbar
  En not negotiable
  Es no negociable
  It non negoziabile
  Pt não transaccionavel por
    terceiros

**non negoziabile** It
  De nicht übertragbar
  En not negotiable
  Es no negociable
  Fr non négociable
  Pt não transaccionavel por
    terceiros

**non onorare un effetto** It
  De einen Wechsel nicht akzep-
    tieren
  En dishonour a bill
  Es protestar una letra
  Fr ne pas honorer un effet
  Pt protestar uma letra

**nonprofitmaking** *adj* En
  De ohne Gewinnabsicht
  Es sin finos lucrativos
  Fr sans but lucratif
  It senza scopo di lucro
  Pt sem fins lucrativos

**nontaxable income** En
  De steuerfreies Einkommen *(n)*
  Es ingresos no imponibles *(m pl)*
  Fr revenu non imposable *(m)*
  It reddito non tassabile *(m)*
  Pt receita não tributavel *(f)*

**nonvoting shares** En
De Aktien ohne Stimmrecht (f
    pl)
Es acciones sin derecho a voto
    (f pl)
Fr actions sans droit de vote
    (f pl)
It azioni senza diritto a voto (f
    pl)
Pt acções sem direito a voto
    (f)

**norm** n En
De Norm (f)
Es norma (f)
Fr norme (f)
It norma (f)
Pt norma (f)

**Norm** (f) n De
En norm
Es norma (f)
Fr norme (f)
It norma (f)
Pt norma (f)

**norma** (f) n Es, It, Pt
De Norm; Standard (f m)
En norm; standard
Fr norme; étalon (f m)

**normale Abweichung** (f) De
En standard deviation
Es desviación normal (f)
Fr déviation normale (f)
It deviazione normale (f)
Pt desvio normal (m)

**Normalmass** (n) n De
En standard gauge
Es calibre patrón (m)
Fr écartement normal (m)
It scartamento normale (m)
Pt calibre padrão (m)

**Normalzeit** (f) n De
En standard time
Es hora oficial (f)
Fr heure légale (f)
It ora legale (f)
Pt hora normal (f)

**norme** (f) n Fr
De Standard; Norm (m f)
En standard; norm
Es norma; standard (f m)
It norma (f)
Pt padrão; norma (m f)

**nota** (f) n Es, It, Pt
De Rechnung (f)
En bill; account
Fr note; compte (f m)

**nota-contrato** (f) n Pt
De Schlusschein (m)
En contract note
Es nota de contrato (f)
Fr bordereau d'achat (m)
It nota di contratto (f)

**nota de banco** (f) Pt
De Banknote (f)
En banknote; bill
Es billete de banco (m)
Fr billet de banque (m)
It biglietto di banca (m)

**nota de cobertura** (f) Pt
De Deckungszusage (f)
En cover note
Es aviso de seguro del riesgo
    (m)
Fr lettre de couverture (f)
It nota di copertura (f)

**nota de consignación** (f) Es
De Frachtbrief (m)
En consignment note
Fr lettre de voiture (f)
It nota di spedizione (f)
Pt guia de consignação (f)

**nota de contrato** (f) Es
De Schlusschein (m)
En contract note
Fr bordereau d'achat (m)
It nota di contratto (f)
Pt nota-contrato (f)

**nota de crédito** (f) Es
De Gutschriftanzeige (f)
En credit note
Fr avis de crédit (m)
It nota di credito (f)
Pt aviso de crédito (m)

**nota de débito** (f) Es
De Lastschrift (f)
En debit note
Fr avis de débit (m)
It nota di addebito (f)
Pt aviso de débito (m)

**nota de rodapé** (f) Pt
De Fussnote (f)
En footnote

Es apostilla (f)
Fr apostille (f)
It postilla (f)

**nota di addebito** (f) It
De Lastschrift (f)
En debit note
Es nota de débito (f)
Fr avis de débit (m)
Pt aviso de débito (m)

**nota di consegna** (f) It
De Lieferschein (m)
En delivery note
Es aviso de entrega (m)
Fr bordereau de livraison (m)
Pt guia de entrega (f)

**nota di contratto** (f) It
De Schlusschein (m)
En contract note
Es nota de contrato (f)
Fr bordereau d'achat (m)
Pt nota-contrato (f)

**nota di copertura** (f) It
De Deckungszusage (f)
En cover note
Es aviso de seguro del riesgo
    (m)
Fr lettre de couverture (f)
Pt nota de cobertura (f)

**nota di credito** (f) It
De Gutschriftanzeige (f)
En credit note
Es nota de crédito (f)
Fr avis de crédit (m)
Pt aviso de crédito (m)

**nota di spedizione** (f) It
De Frachtbrief (m)
En consignment note
Es nota de consignación (f)
Fr lettre de voiture (f)
Pt guia de consignação (f)

**nota di spedizione aerea** (f) It
De Luftfrachtbrief (m)
En air waybill
Es carta de porte aéreo (f)
Fr lettre de transport aérien
    (f)
Pt guia de porte aéreo (m)

**notaio pubblico** (m) It
De Notar (m)
En notary public

Es notario público *(m)*
Fr notaire *(m)*
Pt notário público *(m)*

**notaire** *(m)* n Fr
De Notar *(m)*
En notary public
Es notario público *(m)*
It notaio pubblico *(m)*
Pt notário público *(m)*

**Notar** *(m)* n De
En notary public
Es notario público *(m)*
Fr notaire *(m)*
It notaio pubblico *(m)*
Pt notário público *(m)*

**notario público** *(m)* Es
De Notar *(m)*
En notary public
Fr notaire *(m)*
It notaio pubblico *(m)*
Pt notário público *(m)*

**notário público** *(m)* Pt
De Notar *(m)*
En notary public
Es notario público *(m)*
Fr notaire *(m)*
It notaio pubblico *(m)*

**notary public** En
De Notar *(m)*
Es notario público *(m)*
Fr notaire *(m)*
It notaio pubblico *(m)*
Pt notário público *(m)*

**not binding** Am
En without prejudice
De ohne Verbindlichkeit
Es sin prejuicio
Fr sous toutes réserves
It senza pregiudizio
Pt sem prejuízo

**note** *(f)* n Fr
De Rechnung *(f)*
En bill; account
Es cuenta; nota *(f)*
It conto; nota *(m f)*
Pt conta; nota *(f)*

**note de poids** *(f)* Fr
De Wiegeschein *(m)*
En weight note
Es certificado de pesaje *(m)*

It distinta pesi *(f)*
Pt certidão de peso *(f)*

**Notenbank** *(f)* n De
En issuing bank
Es banco emisor *(m)*
Fr banque d'émission *(f)*
It banca di emissione *(f)*
Pt banco emissor *(m)*

**notice** n En
De Benachrichtigung *(f)*
Es aviso *(m)*
Fr avis; préavis *(m)*
It avviso; preavviso *(m)*
Pt aviso *(m)*

**notifica** *(f)* n It
De Mitteilung *(f)*
En notification
Es notificación *(f)*
Fr notification *(f)*
Pt notificação *(f)*

**notificação** *(f)* n Pt
De Mitteilung *(f)*
En notification
Es notificación *(f)*
Fr notification *(f)*
It notifica *(f)*

**notificação formal** *(f)* Pt
De Inverzugsetzung *(f)*
En formal notice
Es aviso oficial *(m)*
Fr mise en demeure *(f)*
It intimazione *(f)*

**notificación** *(f)* n Es
De Mitteilung *(f)*
En notification
Fr notification *(f)*
It notifica *(f)*
Pt notificação *(f)*

**notification** n En, Fr *(f)*
De Mitteilung *(f)*
Es notificación *(f)*
It notifica *(f)*
Pt notificação *(f)*

**not negotiable** En
De nicht übertragbar
Es no negociable
Fr non négociable
It non negoziabile
Pt não transaccionavel por terceiros

**Notstandsgebiet** *(n)* n De
En distressed area
Es región deprimida *(f)*
Fr région déprimée *(f)*
It area indigente *(f)*
Pt zona deprimida *(f)*

**Notvereinbarung** *(f)* n De
En stand-by agreement
Es contrato de reserva *(m)*
Fr accord en réserve *(m)*
It accordo di riserva *(m)*
Pt acordo a postos *(m)*

**nouveautés** *(f pl)* n Fr
De Modeartikel *(m pl)*
En fancy goods
Es artículos de fantasía *(m pl)*
It articoli fantasia *(m pl)*
Pt artigos de fantasia *(m pl)*

**nudo** *(m)* n Es
De Knoten *(m)*
En knot
Fr nœud *(m)*
It nodo *(m)*
Pt nó *(m)*

**nueva emisión** *(f)* Es
De Ausgabe junger Aktien *(f)*
En new issue
Fr émission d'actions nouvelles *(f)*
It nuova emissione *(f)*
Pt emissão nova *(f)*

**nul** *adj* Fr
De nichtig
En void
Es nulo
It nullo
Pt nulo

**nul et non avenu** Fr
De null und nichtig
En null and void
Es nulo y sin valor
It nullo e senza effetto
Pt nulo e sem valor

**null and void** En
De null und nichtig
Es nulo y sin valor
Fr nul et non avenu
It nullo e senza effetto
Pt nulo e sem valor

**nullo** *adj* It
De nichtig
En void
Es nulo
Fr nul
Pt nulo

**nullo e senza effetto** It
De null und nichtig
En null and void
Es nulo y sin valor
Fr nul et non avenu
Pt nulo e sem valor

**Nullsaldo** *(m)* *n* De
En nil balance
Am zero balance
Es saldo nulo *(m)*
Fr solde nul *(m)*
It saldo nullo *(m)*
Pt saldo nulo *(m)*

**null und nichtig** De
En null and void
Es nulo y sin valor
Fr nul et non avenu
It nullo e senza effetto
Pt nulo e sem valor

**nulo** *adj* Es, Pt
De nichtig
En void
Fr nul
It nullo

**nulo e sem valor** Pt
De null und nichtig
En null and void
Es nulo y sin valor
Fr nul et non avenu
It nullo e senza effetto

**nulo y sin valor** Es
De null und nichtig
En null and void
Fr nul et non avenu
It nullo e senza effetto
Pt nulo e sem valor

**number** *n* En
De Nummer; Anzahl *(f)*
Es número *(m)*
Fr numéro *(m)*
It numero *(m)*
Pt número *(m)*

**numbered account** En
De numeriertes Konto *(n)*
Es cuenta identificada con número *(f)*
Fr compte identifié par numéro *(m)*
It conto identificato da numero *(m)*
Pt conta numerada *(f)*

**numeriertes Konto** *(n)* De
En numbered account
Es cuenta identificada con número *(f)*
Fr compte identifié par numéro *(m)*
It conto identificato da numero *(m)*
Pt conta numerada *(f)*

**número** *(m)* *n* Es, Pt
De Nummer; Anzahl *(f)*
En number
Fr numéro *(m)*
It numero *(m)*

**numéro** *(m)* *n* Fr
De Nummer; Anzahl *(f)*
En number
Es número *(m)*
It numero *(m)*
Pt número *(m)*

**numero** *(m)* *n* It
De Nummer; Anzahl *(f)*
En number
Es número *(m)*
Fr numéro *(m)*
Pt número *(m)*

**número de control** *(m)* Es
De Kontrollziffer *(f)*
En check digit
Fr digit de contrôle *(m)*
It cifra di controllo *(f)*
Pt dígito de controle *(m)*

**número de telefone** *(m)* Pt
De Telephonnummer *(f)*
En telephone number
Es número de teléfono *(m)*
Fr numéro de téléphone *(m)*
It numero di telefono *(m)*

**número de teléfono** *(m)* Es
De Telephonnummer *(f)*
En telephone number
Fr numéro de téléphone *(m)*

It numero di telefono *(m)*
Pt número de telefone *(m)*

**numéro de téléphone** *(m)* Fr
De Telephonnummer *(f)*
En telephone number
Es número de teléfono *(m)*
It numero di telefono *(m)*
Pt número de telefone *(m)*

**numero di telefono** *(m)* It
De Telephonnummer *(f)*
En telephone number
Es número de teléfono *(m)*
Fr numéro de téléphone *(m)*
Pt número de telefone *(m)*

**Nummer** *(f)* *n* De
En number
Es número *(m)*
Fr numéro *(m)*
It numero *(m)*
Pt número *(m)*

**nuova emissione** *(f)* It
De Ausgabe junger Aktien *(f)*
En new issue
Es nueva emisión *(f)*
Fr émission d'actions nouvelles *(f)*
Pt emissão nová *(f)*

**Nutzfahrzeug** *(n)* *n* De
En commercial vehicle
Es vehículo comercial *(m)*
Fr véhicule commerciale *(m)*
It veicolo commerciale *(m)*
Pt veículo comercial *(m)*

# O

**obbligatorio** *adj* It
De verbindlich
En compulsory
Es obligatorio
Fr obligatoire
Pt obrigatório

**obbligazione** *(f)* *n* It
De Obligation; Schuldverschreibung *(f)*
En debenture
Es obligación *(f)*
Fr obligation *(f)*
Pt obrigação *(f)*

**obbligazione al portatore** *(f)* It
De Inhaberobligation *(f)*
En bearer debenture
Es obligación al portador *(f)*
Fr obligation au porteur *(f)*
Pt obrigação ao portador *(f)*

**obbligazione dello Stato** *(f)* It
De Staatsobligation *(f)*
En government bond
Es obligación del Estado *(f)*
Fr obligation d'État *(f)*
Pt obrigação do Tesouro *(f)*

**obbligazione fondiaria** *(f)* It
De Grund- und Gebäudeobli-
gation *(f)*
En property bond
Es cédula hipotecaria *(f)*
Fr obligation foncière *(f)*
Pt título de investimento imo-
biliário *(m)*

**obbligazione garantita** *(f)* It
De gesicherte Schuldversch-
reibung *(f)*
En secured debenture
Es obligación garantizada *(f)*
Fr obligation garantie *(f)*
Pt obrigação com garantia *(f)*

**obbligazione ipotecaria** *(f)* It
De hypothekarisch gesicherte
Schuldschreibung *(f)*
En mortgage debenture
Es obligación hipotecaria *(f)*
Fr obligation hypothécaire *(f)*
Pt obrigação hipotecária *(f)*

**obbligazione irredimibile** *(f)* It
De uneinlösbare Schuldvers-
chreibung *(f)*
En irredeemable debenture
Es obligación no amortizable
*(f)*
Fr obligation irremboursable
*(f)*
Pt obrigação não amortizável
*(f)*

**obbligazione non garantita** *(f)*
It
De ungesicherte Schuldvers-
chreibung *(f)*
En unsecured debenture
Am naked bond

Es obligación no garantizada
*(f)*
Fr obligation sans garantie *(f)*
Pt obrigação sem garantia *(f)*

**obbligazione perpetua** *(f)* It
De Dauerschuldverschreibung
*(f)*
En perpetual debenture
Es obligación a perpetuidad *(f)*
Fr obligation perpétuelle *(f)*
Pt obrigação de perenidade *(f)*

**obbligazione redimibile** *(f)* It
De kündbare Obligation *(f)*
En redeemable bond
Es obligación reembolsable *(f)*
Fr obligation amortissable *(f)*
Pt obrigação reembolsável *(f)*

**obbligazione senza data** *(f)* It
De unbefristete Obligation *(f)*
En undated debenture
Es obligación sin fecha *(f)*
Fr obligation non amortissable
*(f)*
Pt obrigação sem data *(f)*

**obbligazione solidale** *(f)* It
De Solidarobligation *(f)*
En joint and several bond
Es obligación solidaria e indi-
visa *(f)*
Fr obligation conjointe et
solidaire *(f)*
Pt título solidário de diversos
*(m)*

**obbligazionista** *(f)* n It
De Obligationsinhaber *(m)*
En debenture holder
Es obligacionista *(m)*
Fr porteur d'obligations; obli-
gataire *(m)*
Pt titular de obrigação *(m)*

**obenerwähnt** *adj* De
En above-mentioned
Es susodicho
Fr susmentionné
It suddetto
Pt supracitado

**Oberbuchhalter** *(m)* n De
En chief accountant

Es jefe de contabilidad *(m)*
Fr chef comptable *(m)*
It ragioniere capo *(m)*
Pt chefe contabilista *(m)*

**objectivo** *(m)* n Pt
De Ziel *(n)*
En target
Es objetivo *(m)*
Fr but *(m)*
It bersaglio *(m)*

**objetivo** *(m)* n Es
De Ziel *(n)*
En target
Fr but *(m)*
It bersaglio *(m)*
Pt objectivo *(m)*

**obligación** *(f)* n Es
De Obligation; Schuldversch-
reibung *(f)*
En debenture
Fr obligation *(f)*
It obbligazione *(f)*
Pt obrigação *(f)*

**obligación a interés fijo** *(f)* Es
De festverzinsliches Wertpa-
pier *(n)*
En fixed-interest security
Fr valeur à revenu fixe *(f)*
It titolo a interesse fisso *(f)*
Pt obrigação de juro fixo *(f)*

**obligación al portador** *(f)* Es
De Inhaberobligation *(f)*
En bearer debenture
Fr obligation au porteur *(f)*
It obbligazione al portatore *(f)*
Pt obrigação ao portador *(f)*

**obligación a perpetuidad** *(f)*
Es
De Dauerschuldverschreibung
*(f)*
En perpetual debenture
Fr obligation perpétuelle *(f)*
It obbligazione perpetua *(f)*
Pt obrigação de perenidade *(f)*

**obligación del Estado** *(f)* Es
De Staatsobligation *(f)*
En government bond
Fr obligation d'État *(f)*

It obbligazione dello Stato *(f)*
Pt obrigação do Tesouro *(f)*

**obligación garantizada** *(f)* Es
De gesicherte Schuldversch-
reibung *(f)*
En secured debenture
Fr obligation garantie *(f)*
It obbligazione garantita *(f)*
Pt obrigação com garantia *(f)*

**obligación hipotecaria** *(f)* Es
De hypothekarisch gesicherte
Schuldverschreibung *(f)*
En mortgage debenture
Fr obligation hypothécaire *(f)*
It obbligazione ipotecaria *(f)*
Pt obrigação hipotecária *(f)*

**obligación irrevocable** *(f)* Es
De bindender Vertrag *(m)*
En binding agreement
Fr convention irrévocable *(f)*
It contratto vincolante *(m)*
Pt acordo irrevogável *(m)*

**obligacionista** *(m)* n Es
De Obligationär *(m)*
En bondholder; debenture hol-
der
Fr obligataire *(f)*
It obbligazionista *(m)*
Pt titular de obrigações *(m)*

**obligación no amortizable** *(f)*
Es
De uneinlösbare Schuldvers-
chreibung *(f)*
En irredeemable debenture
Fr obligation irremboursable
*(f)*
It obbligazione irredimibile *(f)*
Pt obrigação não amortizável
*(f)*

**obligación no garantizada** *(f)*
Es
De ungesicherte Schuldvers-
chreibung *(f)*
En unsecured debenture
Am naked bond
Fr obligation sans garantie *(f)*
It obbligazione non garantita
*(f)*
Pt obrigação sem garantia *(f)*

**obligación reembolsable** *(f)* Es
De kündbare Obligation *(f)*
En redeemable bond
Fr obligation amortissable *(f)*
It obbligazione redimibile *(f)*
Pt obrigação reembolsável *(f)*

**obligación sin fecha de ven-
cimiento** *(f)* Es
De Schuldverschreibung ohne
Fälligkeitsdatum *(f)*
En undated debenture
Fr obligation sans date d'éch-
éance *(f)*
It obbligazione senza data di
scadenza *(f)*
Pt obrigação sem data de
vencimento *(f)*

**obligación solidaria e indivisa**
*(f)* Es
De Solidarobligation *(f)*
En joint and several bond
Fr obligation conjointe et
solidaire *(f)*
It obbligazione solidale *(f)*
Pt título solidário de diversos
*(m)*

**obligataire** *(m)* n Fr
De Obligationär *(m)*
En bondholder
Es obligacionista *(m)*
It portatore di obbligazioni
*(m)*
Pt titular de obrigações *(m)*

**obligation** *(f)* n Fr
De Obligation; Schuldversch-
reibung *(f)*
En debenture; bond
Es obligación *(f)*
It obbligazione *(f)*
Pt obrigação *(f)*

**Obligation** *(f)* n De
En debenture; bond
Es obligación *(f)*
Fr obligation *(f)*
It obbligazione *(f)*
Pt obrigação *(f)*

**obligation amortissable** *(f)* Fr
De kündbare Obligation *(f)*
En redeemable bond
Es obligación reembolsable *(f)*
It obbligazione redimibile *(f)*
Pt obrigação reembolsável *(f)*

**Obligationär** *(m)* n De
En bondholder
Es obligacionista *(m)*
Fr obligataire *(m)*
It portatore di obbligazioni
*(m)*
Pt titular de obrigações *(m)*

**obligation au porteur** *(f)* Fr
De Inhaberobligation *(f)*
En bearer debenture
Es obligación al portador *(f)*
It obbligazione al portatore *(f)*
Pt obrigação ao portador *(f)*

**obligation conjointe et soli-
daire** *(f)* Fr
De Solidarobligation *(f)*
En joint and several bond
Es obligación solidaria e indi-
visa *(f)*
It obbligazione solidale *(f)*
Pt título solidário de diversos
*(m)*

**obligation d'État** *(f)* Fr
De Staatsobligation *(f)*
En government bond
Es obligación del Estado *(f)*
It obbligazione dello Stato *(f)*
Pt obrigação do Tesouro *(f)*

**obligation éventuelle** *(f)* Fr
De Eventualverpflichtung *(f)*
En contingent liability
Es responsabilidad contingen-
te *(f)*
It sopravvenienza passiva *(f)*
Pt responsabilidade
contingente *(f)*

**obligation foncière** *(f)* Fr
De Grund- und Gebäudeobli-
gation *(f)*
En property bond
Es cédula hipotecaria *(f)*
It obbligazione fondiaria *(f)*
Pt título de investimento imo-
biliário *(m)*

**obligation garantie** *(f)* Fr
De gesicherte Schuldversch-
reibung *(f)*
En secured debenture
Es obligación garantizada *(f)*
It obbligazione garantita *(f)*
Pt obrigação com garantia *(f)*

**obligation hypothécaire** *(f)* Fr
De hypothekarisch gesicherte Schuldverschreibung *(f)*
En mortgage debenture
Es obligación hipotecaria *(f)*
It obbligazione ipotecaria *(f)*
Pt obrigação hipotecária *(f)*

**obligation irremboursable** *(f)* Fr
De uneinlösbare Schuldverschreibung *(f)*
En irredeemable debenture
Es obligación no amortizable *(f)*
It obbligazione irredimibile *(f)*
Pt obrigação não amortizável *(f)*

**obligation perpétuelle** *(f)* Fr
De Dauerschuldverschreibung *(f)*
En perpetual debenture
Es obligación a perpetuidad *(f)*
It obbligazione perpetua *(f)*
Pt obrigação de perenidade *(f)*

**obligation sans date d'échéance** *(f)* Fr
De unbefristete Obligation *(f)*
En undated bond
Es obligación sin fecha de vencimiento *(f)*
It obbligazione senza data di scadenza *(f)*
Pt obrigação sem data de vencimento *(f)*

**obligation sans garantie** *(f)* Fr
De ungesicherte Schuldverschreibung *(f)*
En unsecured debenture
Am naked bond
Es obligación no garantizada *(f)*
It obbligazione non garantita *(f)*
Pt obrigação sem garantia *(f)*

**Obligationsinhaber** *(m)* n De
En debenture holder
Es obligacionista *(m)*
Fr porteur d'obligations; obligataire *(m)*
It obbligazionista *(f)*
Pt titular de obrigação *(m)*

**obligatoire** *adj* Fr
De verbindlich
En compulsory
Es obligatorio
It obbligatorio
Pt obrigatório

**obligatorio** *adj* Es
De verbindlich
En compulsory
Fr obligatoire
It obbligatorio
Pt obrigatório

**obrero** *(m)* n Es
De Arbeiter *(m)*
En worker; workman
Fr ouvrier *(m)*
It operaio *(m)*
Pt operário *(m)*

**obrigação** *(f)* n Pt
De Obligation; Schuldverschreibung *(f)*
En debenture
Es obligación *(f)*
Fr obligation *(f)*
It obbligazione *(f)*

**obrigação ao portador** *(f)* Pt
De Inhaberobligation *(f)*
En bearer debenture
Es obligación al portador *(f)*
Fr obligation au porteur *(f)*
It obbligazione al portatore *(f)*

**obrigação com garantia** *(f)* Pt
De gesicherte Schuldverschreibung *(f)*
En secured debenture
Es obligación garantizada *(f)*
Fr obligation garantie *(f)*
It obbligazione garantita *(f)*

**obrigação de juro fixo** *(f)* Pt
De festverzinsliches Wertpapier *(n)*
En fixed-interest security
Es obligación a interés fijo *(f)*
Fr valeur à revenu fixe *(f)*
It titolo a interesse fisso *(m)*

**obrigação de perenidade** *(f)* Pt
De Dauerschuldverschreibung *(f)*
En perpetual debenture
Es obligación a perpetuidad *(f)*

Fr obligation perpétuelle *(f)*
It obbligazione perpetua *(f)*

**obrigação do Tesouro** *(f)* Pt
De Staatsobligation *(f)*
En government bond
Es obligación del Estado *(f)*
Fr obligation d'État *(f)*
It obbligazione dello Stato *(f)*

**obrigação hipotecária** *(f)* Pt
De hypothekarisch gesicherte Schuldverschreibung *(f)*
En mortgage debenture
Es obligación hipotecaria *(f)*
Fr obligation hypothécaire *(f)*
It obbligazione ipotecaria *(f)*

**obrigação não amortizável** *(f)* Pt
De uneinlösbare Schuldverschreibung *(f)*
En irredeemable debenture
Es obligación no amortizable *(f)*
Fr obligation irremboursable *(f)*
It obbligazione irredimibile *(f)*

**obrigação reembolsável** *(f)* Pt
De kündbare Obligation *(f)*
En redeemable bond
Es obligación reembolsable *(f)*
Fr obligation amortissable *(f)*
It obbligazione redimibile *(f)*

**obrigação restritiva** *(f)* Pt
De einschränkende Bestimmung *(f)*
En restrictive covenant
Es convenio restrictivo *(m)*
Fr accord restrictif *(m)*
It accordo restrittivo *(m)*

**obrigação sem data de vencimento** *(f)* Pt
De Schuldverschreibung ohne Fälligkeitsdatum *(f)*
En undated debenture
Es obligación sin fecha de vencimiento *(f)*
Fr obligation sans date d'échéance *(f)*
It obbligazione senza data di scadenza *(f)*

**obrigação sem garantia** *(f)* Pt
De ungesicherte Schuldver-
   schreibung *(f)*
En unsecured debenture
Am naked bond
Es obligación no garantizada
   *(f)*
Fr obligation sans garantie *(f)*
It obbligazione non garantita
   *(f)*

**obrigatório** *adj* Pt
De verbindlich
En compulsory
Es obligatorio
Fr obligatoire
It obbligatorio

**obsolência pre-incorporada** *(f)*
   Pt
De eingebautes Veralten *(n)*
En built-in obsolescence
Es decaimiento incorporado
   *(m)*
Fr désuétude incorporée *(f)*
It decadimento incorporato
   *(m)*

**occasion** *(f)* n Fr
De Gelegenheitskauf *(m)*
En bargain
Es ganga *(f)*
It occasione *(f)*
Pt pechincha *(f)*

**occasione** *(f)* n It
De Gelegenheitskauf *(m)*
En bargain
Es ganga *(f)*
Fr occasion *(f)*
Pt pechincha *(f)*

**occupation** n En
De Beschäftigung *(f)*
Es ocupación; empleo *(f m)*
Fr occupation; emploi *(f m)*
It occupazione; impiego *(f m)*
Pt ocupação *(f)*

**occupation** *(f)* n Fr
De Beschäftigung *(f)*
En occupation; job
Es ocupación; empleo *(f m)*
It occupazione; impiego *(f m)*
Pt ocupação *(f)*

**occupational hazard** En
De Berufsrisiko *(n)*
Es riesgo profesional *(m)*
Fr risque professionnel *(m)*
It rischio del lavoro *(m)*
Pt acidente próprio da profis-
   são *(m)*

**occupazione** *(f)* n It
De Beschäftigung *(f)*
En occupation; job
Es ocupación; empleo *(f m)*
Fr occupation; emploi *(f m)*
Pt ocupação *(f)*

**ocupação** *(f)* n Pt
De Beschäftigung *(f)*
En occupation; job
Es ocupación; empleo *(f m)*
Fr occupation; emploi *(f m)*
It occupazione; impiego *(f m)*

**ocupación** *(f)* n Es
De Beschäftigung *(f)*
En occupation; job
Fr occupation; emploi *(f m)*
It occupazione; impiego *(f m)*
Pt ocupação *(f)*

**odd lot** En
De Restpartie *(f)*
Es lote suelto *(m)*
Fr solde *(m)*
It partita spaiata *(f)*
Pt lote avulso *(m)*

**oferecer** vb Pt
De anbieten
En offer
Es ofrecer
Fr offrir
It offrire

**oferta** *(f)* n Es, Pt
De Angebot; Offerte *(n f)*
En bid; offer
Fr offre *(f)*
It offerta *(f)*

**oferta a preço excepcional** *(f)*
   Pt
De Sonderangebot *(n)*
En bargain offer
Es oferta de ocasión *(f)*
Fr offre exceptionelle *(f)*
It offerta di occasione *(f)*

**oferta a prima** *(f)* Es
De Verkauf mit Zugaben *(m)*
En premium offer
Fr offre à prime *(f)*
It offerta sopra la pari *(f)*
Pt oferta-prémio *(f)*

**oferta de adquisición** *(f)* Es
De Übernahmeangebot *(n)*
En take-over bid
Fr offre de rachat *(f)*
It offerta di acquisto *(f)*
Pt proposta de apropriação *(f)*

**oferta de ocasión** *(f)* Es
De Sonderangebot *(n)*
En bargain offer
Fr offre exceptionelle *(f)*
It offerta di occasione *(f)*
Pt oferta a preço excepcional
   *(f)*

**oferta en firme** *(f)* Es
De festes Angebot *(n)*
En firm offer
Fr offre ferme *(f)*
It offerta ferma *(f)*
Pt oferta firme *(f)*

**oferta e procura** Pt
De Angebot und Nachfrage
En supply and demand
Es oferta y demanda
Fr offre et demande
It offerta e domanda

**oferta especial** *(f)* Es, Pt
De Sonderangebot *(m)*
En special offer
Fr offre spéciale *(f)*
It offerta speciale *(f)*

**oferta firme** *(f)* Pt
De festes Angebot *(n)*
En firm offer
Es oferta en firme *(f)*
Fr offre ferme *(f)*
It offerta ferma *(f)*

**ofertante** *(m)* n Es
De Bietende(r) *(m)*
En bidder
Fr enchérisseur *(m)*
It offerente *(m)*
Pt proponente *(m)*

**ofertante más alto** *(m)* Es
De Meistbietende(r) *(m)*
En highest bidder
Fr plus offrant enchérisseur *(m)*
It miglior offerente *(m)*
Pt proponente mais elevado *(m)*

**oferta-prémio** *(f) n* Pt
De Verkauf mit Zugaben *(m)*
En premium offer
Es oferta a prima *(f)*
Fr offre à prime *(f)*
It offerta sopra la pari *(f)*

**oferta y demanda** Es
De Angebot und Nachfrage
En supply and demand
Fr offre et demande
It offerta e domanda
Pt oferta e procura

**offene Handelsgesellschaft (OHG)** *(f)* De
En partnership
Es sociedad regular colectiva (SRC) *(f)*
Fr société en nom collectif *(f)*
It società *(f)*
Pt sociedade em nome colectivo *(f)*

**offene Position** *(f)* De
En open position
Es posición descubierta *(f)*
Fr position ouverte *(f)*
It posizione aperta *(f)*
Pt posição em aberto *(f)*

**offener Kredit** *(m)* De
En open credit
Es crédito en descubierto *(m)*
Fr crédit à découvert *(m)*
It credito allo scoperto *(m)*
Pt crédito em aberto *(m)*

**offene Versicherung** *(f)* De
En open cover
Es cobertura flotante *(f)*
Fr police à aliment *(f)*
It polizza flottante *(f)*
Pt cobertura ilimitada *(f)*

**Offenlegung** *(f) n* De
En disclosure
Es revelación *(f)*
Fr révélation; divulgation *(f)*

It rivelazione *(f)*
Pt revelação; divulgação *(f)*

**öffentlich** *adj* De
En public
Es público
Fr public
It pubblico
Pt público

**öffentliche Hand** *(f)* De
En public sector
Es sector público *(m)*
Fr secteur public *(m)*
It settore statale *(m)*
Pt sector público *(m)*

**Öffentlichkeit** *(f) n* De
En (general) public
Es público *(m)*
Fr grand public *(m)*
It pubblico *(m)*
Pt público *(m)*

**offer** *n* En
De Offerte *(f)*
Es oferta *(f)*
Fr offre *(f)*
It offerta *(f)*
Pt oferta *(f)*

**offer** *vb* En
De anbieten
Es ofrecer
Fr offrir
It offrire
Pt oferecer

**offerente** *(m) n* It
De Bietende(r) *(m)*
En bidder
Es ofertante *(m)*
Fr enchérisseur *(m)*
Pt proponente *(m)*

**offer for sale** En
De zum Verkauf anbieten
Es ofrecer en venta
Fr offrir en vente
It offrire in vendita
Pt pôr à venda

**offerta** *(f) n* It
De Angebot; Offerte *(n f)*
En bid; offer
Es oferta *(f)*
Fr offre *(f)*
Pt oferta *(f)*

**offerta di acquisto** *(f)* It
De Übernahmeangebot *(n)*
En take-over bid
Es oferta de adquisición *(f)*
Fr offre de rachat *(f)*
Pt proposta de apropriação *(f)*

**offerta di occasione** *(f)* It
De Sonderangebot *(n)*
En bargain offer
Es oferta de ocasión *(f)*
Fr offre exceptionelle *(f)*
Pt oferta a preço excepcional *(f)*

**offerta e domanda** It
De Angebot und Nachfrage
En supply and demand
Es oferta y demanda
Fr offre et demande
Pt oferta e procura

**offerta ferma** *(f)* It
De festes Angebot *(n)*
En firm offer
Es oferta en firme *(f)*
Fr offre ferme *(f)*
Pt oferta firme *(f)*

**offerta sopra la pari** *(f)* It
De Verkauf mit Zugaben *(m)*
En premium offer
Es oferta a prima *(f)*
Fr offre à prime *(f)*
Pt oferta-prémio *(f)*

**offerta speciale** *(f)* It
De Sonderangebot *(m)*
En special offer
Es oferta especial *(f)*
Fr offre spéciale *(f)*
Pt oferta especial *(f)*

**Offerte** *(f) n* De
En offer
Es oferta *(f)*
Fr offre *(f)*
It offerta *(f)*
Pt oferta *(f)*

**office** *n* En
De Büro *(n)*
Es oficina *(f)*
Fr bureau *(m)*
It ufficio *(m)*
Pt escritório *(m)*

**office hours** En
- De Geschäftsstunden *(f pl)*
- Es horario de oficina *(m)*
- Fr heures de bureau *(f pl)*
- It orario d´ufficio *(m)*
- Pt horário do escritório *(m)*

**office manager** En
- De Bürovorsteher *(m)*
- Es jefe de oficina *(m)*
- Fr chef de bureau *(m)*
- It capo ufficio *(m)*
- Pt chefe de escritório *(m)*

**official** *adj* En
- De amtlich
- Es oficial
- Fr officiel
- It ufficiale
- Pt oficial

**official strike** En
- De anerkannter Streik *(m)*
- Es huelga oficial *(f)*
- Fr grève officielle *(f)*
- It sciopero ufficiale *(m)*
- Pt greve oficial *(f)*

**officiel** *adj* Fr
- De amtlich
- En official
- Es oficial
- It ufficiale
- Pt oficial

**offre** *(f) n* Fr
- De Angebot; Offerte *(n f)*
- En bid; offer
- Es oferta *(f)*
- It offerta *(f)*
- Pt oferta *(f)*

**offre à prime** *(f)* Fr
- De Verkauf mit Zugaben *(m)*
- En premium offer
- Es oferta a prima *(f)*
- It offerta sopra la pari *(f)*
- Pt oferta-prémio *(f)*

**offre de rachat** *(f)* Fr
- De Übernahmeangebot *(n)*
- En take-over bid
- Es oferta de adquisición *(f)*
- It offerta di acquisto *(f)*
- Pt proposta de apropriação *(f)*

**offre et demande** Fr
- De Angebot und Nachfrage
- En supply and demand
- Es oferta y demanda
- It offerta e domanda
- Pt oferta e procura

**offre exceptionelle** *(f)* Fr
- De Sonderangebot *(n)*
- En bargain offer
- Es oferta de ocasión *(f)*
- It offerta di occasione *(f)*
- Pt oferta a preço excepcional *(f)*

**offre ferme** *(f)* Fr
- De festes Angebot *(n)*
- En firm offer
- Es oferta en firme *(f)*
- It offerta ferma *(f)*
- Pt oferta firme *(f)*

**offre spéciale** *(f)* Fr
- De Sonderangebot *(m)*
- En special offer
- Es oferta especial *(f)*
- It offerta speciale *(f)*
- Pt oferta especial *(f)*

**offrir** *vb* Fr
- De anbieten
- En offer
- Es ofrecer
- It offrire
- Pt oferecer

**offrire** *vb* It
- De anbieten
- En offer
- Es ofrecer
- Fr offrir
- Pt oferecer

**offrire in vendita** It
- De zum Verkauf anbieten
- En offer for sale
- Es ofrecer en venta
- Fr offrir en vente
- Pt pôr à venda

**offrir en vente** Fr
- De zum Verkauf anbieten
- En offer for sale
- Es ofrecer en venta
- It offrire in vendita
- Pt pôr à venda

**oficial** *adj* Es, Pt
- De amtlich
- En official
- Fr officiel
- It ufficiale

**oficina** *(f) n* Es
- De Büro *(n)*
- En office
- Fr bureau *(m)*
- It ufficio *(m)*
- Pt escritório *(m)*

**oficina central** *(f)* Es
- De Hauptanstalt *(f)*
- En head office
- Fr siège; bureau principal *(m)*
- It sede; ufficio centrale *(f m)*
- Pt sede; escritório central *(f m)*

**oficina central de compras** *(f)* Es
- De Einkaufszentrale *(f)*
- En central buying office
- Fr centrale d´achats *(f)*
- It ufficio centrale d´acquisti *(m)*
- Pt escritório central de compras *(m)*

**oficina de correos** *(f)* Es
- De Postamt *(n)*
- En post office
- Fr bureau de poste *(m)*
- It ufficio postale *(m)*
- Pt estação de correios *(f)*

**oficinista** *(m) n* Es
- De Angestellte(r) *(m)*
- En clerk
- Fr commis *(m)*
- It impiegato *(m)*
- Pt empregado de escritório

**ofrecer** *vb* Es
- De anbieten
- En offer
- Fr offrir
- It offrire
- Pt oferecer

**ofrecer en venta** Es
- De zum Verkauf anbieten
- En offer for sale
- Fr offrir en vente

It   offrire in vendita
Pt   pôr à venda

**ohne Bezugsrechte** De
En   ex rights
Es   sin privilegio
Fr   ex-droits
It   senza diritti
Pt   privilégios excluidos

**ohne Coupon** De
En   ex coupon
Es   sin cupón
Fr   ex coupon
It   senza cedola
Pt   talão excluido

**ohne Dividende** De
En   ex dividend
Es   sin dividendo
Fr   ex-dividende
It   senza dividendo
Pt   dividendo excluido

**ohne Gewinnabsicht** De
En   nonprofitmaking
Es   sin finos lucrativos
Fr   sans but lucratif
It   senza scopo di lucro
Pt   sem fins lucrativos

**ohne Rückgriff** De
En   without recourse
Es   sin recurso
Fr   sans droit de recours
It   senza ricorso
Pt   sem recurso

**ohne Verbindlichkeit** De
En   without prejudice
Am   not binding
Es   sin prejuicio
Fr   sous toutes réserves
It   senza pregiudizio
Pt   sem prejuízo

**oilfield** n En
De   Ölfeld (f)
Es   yacimiento de petróleo (m)
Fr   gisement petrolifère (m)
It   giacimento petrolifero (m)
Pt   jazigo de petróleo (m)

**Ökonometrik** (f) n De
En   econometrics
Es   econometría (f)
Fr   économétrie (f)

It   econometria (f)
Pt   econometria (f)

**old-age pension** En
De   Altersversorgung; Rente (f)
Es   retiro de vejez (m)
Fr   pension de retraite (f)
It   pensione per la vecchiaia
     (f)
Pt   pensão (f)

**old-established business** En
De   alteingeführtes Geschäft (n)
Es   casa sólida (f)
Fr   maison solide (f)
It   casa di vecchia fondazione
     (f)
Pt   empresa de há muito
     estabelecida (f)

**Öldollar** (m) n De
En   petrodollar
Es   petrodólar (m)
Fr   dollar pétrolier (m)
It   petrodollaro (m)
Pt   petrodólar (m)

**Ölfeld** (n) n De
En   oilfield
Es   yacimiento de petróleo (m)
Fr   gisement petrolifère (m)
It   giacimento petrolifero (m)
Pt   jazigo de petróleo (m)

**Oligopol** (n) n De
En   oligopoly
Es   oligopolio (m)
Fr   oligopole (m)
It   oligopolio (m)
Pt   oligopólio (m)

**oligopole** (m) n Fr
De   Oligopol (n)
En   oligopoly
Es   oligopolio (m)
It   oligopolio (m)
Pt   oligopólio (m)

**oligopolio** (m) n Es, It
De   Oligopol (n)
En   oligopoly
Fr   oligopole (m)
Pt   oligopólio (m)

**oligopólio** (m) n Pt
De   Oligopol (n)
En   oligopoly
Es   oligopolio (m)

Fr   oligopole (m)
It   oligopolio (m)

**oligopoly** n En
De   Oligopol (n)
Es   oligopolio (m)
Fr   oligopole (m)
It   oligopolio (m)
Pt   oligopólio (m)

**omisión** (f) n Es
De   Auslassung; Unterlassung
     (f)
En   omission
Fr   omission (f)
It   omissione (f)
Pt   omissão (f)

**omissão** (f) n Pt
De   Auslassung; Unterlassung
     (f)
En   omission
Es   omisión (f)
Fr   omission (f)
It   omissione (f)

**omission** n En, Fr (f)
De   Auslassung; Unterlassung
     (f)
Es   omisión (f)
It   omissione (f)
Pt   omissão (f)

**omissione** (f) n It
De   Auslassung; Unterlassung
     (f)
En   omission
Es   omisión (f)
Fr   omission (f)
Pt   omissão (f)

**omologazione di testamento**
     (f) It
De   Testamentseröffnung; Be-
     stätigung (f)
En   probate
Es   validación de los testamen-
     tos (f)
Fr   homologation d'un testa-
     ment (f)
Pt   validação testamentária (f)

**on account** En
De   a conto; auf Abschlag
Es   a cuenta
Fr   à valoir
It   in acconto
Pt   por conta

**on condition** En
De vorausgesetzt
Es a condición
Fr sous réserve
It a condizione
Pt sob condição de

**on consignment** En
De in Kommission
Es en consignación
Fr en consignation
It in conto deposito
Pt à consignação

**on demand** En
De auf Verlangen
Es a vista
Fr sur demande
It a vista
Pt à vista; sob demanda

**onesto** adj It
De ehrlich
En honest
Es honesto
Fr honnête
Pt honesto

**one way fare** Am
En single fare
De einfache Fahrkarte (f)
Es pasaje de ida (m)
Fr billet d'aller (m)
It biglietto d'andata (m)
Pt passagem de ida (f)

**on hand** En
De vorrätig
Es disponible
Fr disponible
It disponibile
Pt à mão; ao dispôr

**on loan** En
De darlehensweise
Es en préstamo
Fr sous forme de prêt
It in prestito
Pt por empréstimo

**onorare** vb It
De honorieren
En honour
Es honrar
Fr honorer
Pt honrar

**onorario** (m) n It
De Vergütung; Honorar (f n)
En fee
Es honorario (m)
Fr honoraires (m pl)
Pt honorários (m pl)

**onorario** adj It
De ehrenamtlich
En honorary
Es honorario
Fr honoraire
Pt honorário

**onore** (m) n It
De Ehre (f)
En honour
Es honor (m)
Fr honneur (f)
Pt honra (f)

**ontem** adv Pt
De gestern
En yesterday
Es ayer
Fr hier
It ieri

**opção** (f) n Pt
De Option (f)
En option
Es opción (f)
Fr option (f)
It opzione (f)

**opção de compra** (f) Pt
De Kaufoption (f)
En call option
Es opción de compras (f)
Fr option (f)
It premio d'acquisto (m)

**opção de venda** (f) Pt
De Verkaufsoption (f)
En put option
Es opción de venta (f)
Fr option à vendre (f)
It premio a vendere (m)

**opção dupla** (f) Pt
De Stellgeschäft (n)
En double option
Es opción doble (f)
Fr double option (f)
It opzione doppia (f)

**opción** (f) n Es
De Option (f)
En option
Fr option (f)
It opzione (f)
Pt opção (f)

**opción de compras** (f) Es
De Kaufoption (f)
En call option
Fr option (f)
It premio d'acquisto (m)
Pt opção de compra (f)

**opción de venta** (f) Es
De Verkaufsoption (f)
En put option
Fr option à vendre (f)
It premio a vendere (m)
Pt opção de venda (f)

**opción doble** (f) Es
De Stellgeschäft (n)
En double option
Fr double option (f)
It opzione doppia (f)
Pt opção dupla (f)

**open cheque** En
De Inhaberscheck (m)
Es cheque abierto (m)
Fr chèque ouvert (m)
It assegno aperto (m)
Pt cheque em branco (m)

**open cover** En
De offene Versicherung (f)
Es cobertura flotante (f)
Fr police à aliment (f)
It polizza flottante (f)
Pt cobertura ilimitada (f)

**open credit** En
De offener Kredit (m)
Es crédito en descubierto (m)
Fr crédit à découvert (m)
It credito allo scoperto (m)
Pt crédito em aberto (m)

**open market** En
De freier Markt (m)
Es mercado libre (m)
Fr marché libre (m)
It mercato libero (m)
Pt mercado livre (m)

**open-plan office** En
De Grossraumbüro (n)
Es oficina sin particiones (f)
Fr bureau sans cloisons (m)
It ufficio senza divisioni (m)
Pt escritório sem divisões (m)

**open position** En
De offene Position (f)
Es posición descubierta (f)
Fr position ouverte (f)
It posizione aperta (f)
Pt posição em aberto (f)

**operación anterior** (f) Es
De Leistung in der Vergangen-
   heit (f)
En past performance
Fr comportement antérieur
   (m)
It comportamento preceden-
   te (m)
Pt desempenho anterior (m)

**operación (mercantil)** (f) Es
De Transaktion; Abschluss (f
   m)
En transaction
Fr opération (f)
It operazione (f)
Pt transacção (f)

**operador a prima** (m) Es
De Terminmakler (m)
En option dealer
Fr opérateur à prime (m)
It operatore in contratti a
   premio (m)
Pt corretor de opções (m)

**operaio** (m) It
De Arbeiter (m)
En worker
Es obrero; operario (m)
Fr ouvrier (m)
Pt operário (m)

**operário** (m) Pt
De Arbeiter (m)
En worker
Es obrero; operario (m)
Fr ouvrier (m)
It operaio (m)

**opérateur à prime** (m) Fr
De Terminmakler (m)
En option dealer
Es operador a prima (m)

It operatore in contratti a
   premio (m)
Pt corretor de opções (m)

**operating costs** En
De Betriebsausgaben (f pl)
Es costes operacionales (m pl)
Fr frais d'exploitation (m pl)
It spese di gestione (f pl)
Pt custos de exercício (m pl)

**opération** (affaire) (f) n Fr
De Transaktion; Abschluss (f
   m)
En transaction
Es operación (mercantil) (f)
It operazione (f)
Pt transacção (f)

**operational research** (OR) En
De Unternehmensforschung (f)
Es investigación operacional (f)
Fr recherche opérationnelle (f)
It indagine sul funzionamento
   (f)
Pt investigação operacional (f)

**opérations à terme** (f pl) Fr
De Zeitgeschäfte (n pl)
En forward dealings
Es negociaciones a término (f
   pl)
It operazioni a termine (f pl)
Pt transacções adiantadas (f
   pl)

**operative** adj En
De wirksam
Es operativo; activo
Fr actif
It attivo; operativo
Pt efectivo; em vigor

**operativo** adj Es, It
De wirksam
En operative
Fr actif
Pt efectivo; em vigor

**operatore in contratti a pre-
   mio** (m) It
De Terminmakler (m)
En option dealer
Es operador a prima (m)
Fr opérateur à prime (m)
Pt corretor de opções (m)

**operazione** (f) n It
De Transaktion; Abschluss (f
   m)
En transaction
Es operación mercantil (f)
Fr opération (f)
Pt transacção (f)

**operazione a contanti** (f) It
De Bargeschäft (n)
En cash deal
Es trato al contado (m)
Fr transaction au comptant (f)
Pt negócio em dinheiro (m)

**operazioni a termine** (f pl) It
De Zeitgeschäfte (n pl)
En forward dealings
Es negociaciones a término (f
   pl)
Fr opérations à terme (f pl)
Pt transacções adiantadas (f
   pl)

**opinião** (f) n Pt
De Meinung (f)
En opinion
Es opinión (f)
Fr opinion (f)
It opinione (f)

**opinion** n En, Fr (f)
De Meinung (f)
Es opinión (f)
It opinione (f)
Pt opinião (f)

**opinión** (f) n Es
De Meinung (f)
En opinion
Fr opinion (f)
It opinione (f)
Pt opinião (f)

**opinione** (f) n It
De Meinung (f)
En opinion
Es opinión (f)
Fr opinion (f)
Pt opinião (f)

**opposition d'intérêts** (f) Fr
De widerstreitende Interessen
   (n pl)
En conflict of interest
Es pugna de intereses (f)
It conflitto d'interessi (m)
Pt conflito de interesses (m)

**option** *n* En, Fr *(f)*
De Option *(f)*
Es opción *(f)*
It opzione *(f)*
Pt opção *(f)*

**Option** *(f) n* De
En option
Es opción *(f)*
Fr option *(f)*
It opzione *(f)*
Pt opção *(f)*

**option à vendre** *(f)* Fr
De Verkaufsoption *(f)*
En put option
Es opción de venta *(f)*
It premio a vendere *(m)*
Pt opção de venda *(f)*

**option dealer** En
De Terminmakler *(m)*
Es operador a prima *(m)*
Fr opérateur à prime *(m)*
It operatore in contratti a premio *(m)*
Pt corretor de opções *(m)*

**opuscolo pubblicitario** *(m)* It
De Werbeschrift *(f)*
En advertising brochure
Es folleto publicitario *(m)*
Fr prospectus publicitaire *(m)*
Pt folheto publicitário *(m)*

**opzione** *(f) n* It
De Option *(f)*
En option
Es opción *(f)*
Fr option *(f)*
Pt opção *(f)*

**opzione doppia** *(f)* It
De Stellgeschäft *(n)*
En double option
Es opción doble *(f)*
Fr double option *(f)*
Pt opção dupla *(f)*

**or** *(m) n* Fr
De Gold *(n)*
En gold
Es oro *(m)*
It oro *(m)*
Pt ouro *(m)*

**ora** *(f) n* It
De Stunde *(f)*
En hour
Es hora *(f)*
Fr heure *(f)*
Pt hora *(f)*

**ora di colazione** *(f)* It
De Mittagspause *(f)*
En lunch-hour
Es hora del almuerzo *(f)*
Fr heure du déjeuner *(f)*
Pt hora do almoço *(f)*

**ora di punta** *(f)* It
De Verkehrsspitze *(f)*
En rush hour
Es hora punta *(f)*
Fr heure d'affluence *(f)*
Pt hora de ponta *(f)*

**ora legale** *(f)* It
De Normalzeit *(f)*
En standard time
Es hora oficial *(f)*
Fr heure légale *(f)*
Pt hora normal *(f)*

**orario d'apertura** *(m)* It
De Geschäftszeit *(f)*
En business hours
Es horario de comercio *(m)*
Fr heures d'ouverture *(f pl)*
Pt horas de funcionamento *(f pl)*

**orario d'ufficio** *(m)* It
De Geschäftsstunden *(f pl)*
En office hours
Es horario de oficina *(m)*
Fr heures de bureau *(f pl)*
Pt horário do escritório *(m)*

**orario ferroviario** *(m)* It
De Eisenbahnfahrplan *(m)*
En railway timetable
Es horario de trenes *(m)*
Fr indicateur des chemins de fer *(m)*
Pt horário de caminhos de ferro *(m)*

**orçamento** *(m) n* Pt
De Haushaltsplan *(m)*
En budget
Es presupuesto *(m)*
Fr budget *(m)*
It bilancio preventivo *(m)*

**ordem bancária** *(f)* Pt
De Bankauftrag *(m)*
En banker's order
Es orden bancaria *(f)*
Fr ordre bancaire *(m)*
It ordine bancario *(m)*

**ordem de serviço** *(f)* Pt
De Verordnung *(f)*
En directive
Es directiva *(f)*
Fr directive *(f)*
It direttivo *(m)*

**ordenado** *(m) n* Pt
De Gehalt *(n)*
En salary
Es sueldo *(m)*
Fr traitement *(m)*
It stipendio *(m)*

**orden bancaria** *(f)* Es
De Bankauftrag *(m)*
En banker's order
Fr ordre bancaire *(m)*
It ordine bancario *(m)*
Pt ordem bancária *(f)*

**orden del día** *(m)* Es
De Tagesordnung *(f)*
En agenda
Fr ordre du jour *(m)*
It ordine del giorno *(m)*
Pt agenda *(f)*

**ordentliche Generalversammlung** *(f)* De
En ordinary general meeting
Am stockholders' meeting
Es asamblea general ordinaria *(f)*
Fr assemblée générale *(f)*
It assemblea generale ordinaria *(f)*
Pt assembleia geral ordinária *(f)*

**ordentliche Versammlung** *(f)* De
En statutory meeting
Es asamblea general *(f)*
Fr assemblée ordinaire *(f)*
It assemblea generale *(f)*
Pt assembleia estatutária *(f)*

**order** n En
De Bestellung (f)
Es pedido (m)
Fr commande (f)
It ordine (m)
Pt encomenda (f)

**order** vb En
De bestellen
Es hacer un pedido
Fr passer une commande
It ordinare
Pt encomendar

**order book** En
De Auftragsbuch (n)
Es libro de pedidos (m)
Fr livre de commandes (m)
It libro degli ordini (m)
Pt livro de encomendas (m)

**order-form** n En
De Bestellformular (n)
Es solicitud de pedido (f)
Fr bulletin de commande (m)
It foglio d'ordinazione (m)
Pt impresso de encomenda (m)

**ordinare** vb It
De bestellen
En order
Es hacer un pedido
Fr passer une commande
Pt encomendar

**ordinary general meeting** En
De ordentliche General-versammlung (f)
Es asamblea general ordinaria (f)
Fr assemblée générale (f)
It assemblea generale ordinaria (f)
Pt assembleia geral ordinária (f)

**ordinary share** En
De Stammaktie (f)
Es acción ordinaria (f)
Fr action ordinaire (f)
It azione ordinaria (f)
Pt acção ordinária (f)

**ordinary share certificate** En
Am stock certificate
De Aktie (f)
Es certificado de acción (m)

Fr certificat d'action (m)
It certificato azionario (m)
Pt título de acções ordinárias (m)

**ordinateur** (m) n Fr
De Rechner; Computer (m)
En computer
Es computadora (f)
It elaboratore; calcolatore (m)
Pt computador (m)

**ordine** (m) n It
De Bestellung (f)
En order
Es pedido (m)
Fr commande (f)
Pt encomenda (f)

**ordine bancario** (m) It
De Bankauftrag (m)
En banker's order
Es orden bancaria (f)
Fr ordre bancaire (m)
Pt ordem bancária (f)

**ordine del giorno** (m) It
De Tagesordnung (f)
En agenda
Es orden del día (m)
Fr ordre du jour (m)
Pt agenda (f)

**ordine per corrispondenza** (f) It
De Auftrag durch die Post (m)
En mail order
Es pedido por correo (m)
Fr commande par lettre (f)
Pt venda pelo correio (f)

**ordine per esportazione** (m) It
De Exportauftrag (m)
En export order
Es pedido de exportación (m)
Fr commande d'exportation (f)
Pt encomenda de exportação (f)

**ordinogramme** (m) n Fr
De Flussplan (m)
En flow chart
Es diagrama de flujo (m)
It diagramma di flusso (m)
Pt gráfico de operação (m)

**Ordnung** (f) n De
En (legal) code
Es código (m)
Fr code (m)
It codice (m)
Pt código (m)

**Ordnungsentschädigung** (f) n De
En nominal damages
Es daños nominales (m pl)
Fr indemnité de principe (f)
It danni nominali (m pl)
Pt danos nominais (m pl)

**ordonnance** (f) n Fr
De Befugnis (f)
En warrant
Es mandato (m)
It mandato (m)
Pt mandato (m)

**ordonner une grève** Fr
De zum Streik auffordern
En call a strike
Es declararse en huelga
It proclamare uno sciopero
Pt declarar greve

**ordre bancaire** (m) Fr
De Bankauftrag (m)
En banker's order
Es orden bancaria (f)
It ordine bancario (m)
Pt ordem bancária (f)

**ordre du jour** (m) Fr
De Tagesordnung (f)
En agenda
Es orden del día (m)
It ordine del giorno (m)
Pt agenda (f)

**ore di punta** (f pl) It
De Spitzeit (f)
En peak hours
Es horas punta (f pl)
Fr heures de pointe (f pl)
Pt horas de ponta (f pl)

**ore lavorative** (f pl) It
De Arbeitszeit (f)
En hours of work
Es jornada laboral (f)
Fr durée du travail (f)
Pt horas de trabalho (f pl)

**ore-uomo** *(f pl) n* It
De Arbeitsstunde pro Mann *(f)*
En man-hours
Es horas-hombre *(f pl)*
Fr heures-homme *(f pl)*
Pt horas-homem *(f pl)*

**organigrama** *(m)* Pt
De Säulendiagramm *(m)*
En block diagram
Es diagrama de bloque *(m)*
Fr ordinogramme *(m)*
It schema a blocchi *(m)*

**Organisación Laboral Internacional** *(f)* Es
De Internationale Arbeitsorganisation *(f)*
En International Labour Organization (ILO)
Fr Organisation Internationale du Travail *(f)*
It Organizzazione Internazionale del Lavoro *(f)*
Pt Organização Internacional do Trabalho *(f)*

**organisation** *(f) n* Fr
De Organisation *(f)*
En organization
Es organización *(f)*
It organizzazione *(f)*
Pt organização *(f)*

**Organisation** *(f) n* De
En organization
Es organización *(f)*
Fr organisation *(f)*
It organizzazione *(f)*
Pt organização *(f)*

**Organisation de Coopération et de Développement Économiques** *(f)* Fr
De Organisation für Wirtschaftliche Zusammenarbeit und Entwicklung *(f)*
En Organization for Economic Cooperation and Development (OECD)
Es Organización para Cooperacion y Desarrollo Economico *(f)*
It Organizzazione per la Cooperazione e lo Sviluppo Economico *(f)*
Pt Organização para a Cooperação e o Desenvolvimento Econômico *(f)*

**Organisation für Wirtschaftliche Zusammenarbeit und Entwicklung** *(f)* De
En Organization for Economic Cooperation and Development (OECD)
Es Organización para Cooperacion y Desarrollo Economico *(f)*
Fr Organisation de Coopération et de Développement Économiques *(f)*
It Organizzazione per la Cooperazione e lo Sviluppo Economico *(f)*
Pt Organização para a Cooperação e o Desenvolvimento Econômico *(f)*

**Organisation Internationale du Travail** *(f)* Fr
De Internationale Arbeitsorganisation *(f)*
En International Labour Organization (ILO)
Es Organisación Laboral Internacional *(f)*
It Organizzazione Internazionale del Lavoro *(f)*
Pt Organização Internacional do Trabalho *(f)*

**Organisation Mondiale de la Santé (OMS)** Fr
De Weltgesundheitsorganisation (WGO) *(f)*
En World Health Organization (WHO)
Es Organización Mundial de la Salud (OMS) *(f)*
It Organizzazione Mondiale della Sanità (OMS) *(f)*
Pt Organização Mondial da Saúde (OMS) *(f)*

**organização** *(f) n* Pt
De Organisation *(f)*
En organization
Es organización *(f)*
Fr organisation *(f)*
It organizzazione *(f)*

**Organização Internacional do Trabalho** *(f)* Pt
De Internationale Arbeitsorganisation *(f)*
En International Labour Organization (ILO)
Es Organisación Laboral Internacional *(f)*
Fr Organisation Internationale du Travail *(f)*
It Organizzazione Internazionale del Lavoro *(f)*

**Organização Mondial da Saúde (OMS)** *(f)* Pt
De Weltgesundheitsorganisation (WGO) *(f)*
En World Health Organization (WHO)
Es Organización Mundial de la Salud (OMS) *(f)*
Fr Organisation Mondiale de la Santé (OMS)
It Organizzazione Mondiale della Sanità (OMS) *(f)*

**Organização para a Cooperação e o Desenvolvimento Econômico** *(f)* Pt
De Organisation für Wirtschaftliche Zusammenarbeit und Entwicklung *(f)*
En Organization for Economic Cooperation and Development (OECD)
Es Organización para Cooperacion y Desarrollo Economico *(f)*
Fr Organisation de Coopération et de Développement Économiques *(f)*
It Organizzazione per la Cooperazione e lo Sviluppo Economico *(f)*

**organización** *(f) n* Es
De Organisation *(f)*
En organization
Fr organisation *(f)*
It organizzazione *(f)*
Pt organização *(f)*

**Organización Mundial de la Salud (OMS)** *(f)* Es
De Weltgesundheitsorganisation (WGO) *(f)*

En World Health Organization (WHO)
Fr Organisation Mondiale de la Santé (OMS)
It Organizzazione Mondiale della Sanità (OMS) *(f)*
Pt Organização Mondial da Saúde (OMS) *(f)*

**Organización para Coopera-
cion y Desarrollo
Economico** *(f)* Es
De Organisation für Wirtschaftliche Zusammenarbeit und Entwicklung *(f)*
En Organization for Economic Cooperation and Development (OECD)
Fr Organisation de Coopéra-
tion et de Développement Économiques *(f)*
It Organizzazione per la Cooperazione e lo Sviluppo Economico *(f)*
Pt Organização para a Cooperação e o Desenvol-
vimento Económico *(f)*

**organization** *n* En
De Organisation *(f)*
Es organización *(f)*
Fr organisation *(f)*
It organizzazione *(f)*
Pt organização *(f)*

**Organization for Economic
Cooperation and Deve-
lopment** (OECD) En
De Organisation für Wirt-
schaftliche Zusammenar-
beit und Entwicklung *(f)*
Es Organización para Coo-
peracion y Desarrollo Economico *(f)*
Fr Organisation de Coopéra-
tion et de Développement Économiques *(f)*
It Organizzazione per la Cooperazione e lo Sviluppo Economico *(f)*
Pt Organização para a Cooperação e o Desenvol-
vimento Económico *(f)*

**organizzazione** *(f)* *n* It
De Organisation *(f)*
En organization
Es organización *(f)*

Fr organisation *(f)*
Pt organização *(f)*

**Organizzazione Internazionale
del Lavoro** *(f)* It
De Internationale Arbeitsor-
ganisation *(f)*
En International Labour Org-
anization (ILO)
Es Organisación Laboral Inter-
nacional *(f)*
Fr Organisation Internationale du Travail *(f)*
Pt Organização Internacional do Trabalho *(f)*

**Organizzazione Mondiale
della Sanità (OMS)** *(f)* It
De Weltgesundheitsorganisation (WGO) *(f)*
En World Health Organization (WHO)
Es Organización Mundial de la Salud (OMS) *(f)*
Fr Organisation Mondiale de la Santé (OMS)
Pt Organização Mondial da Saúde (OMS) *(f)*

**Organizzazione per la Coo-
perazione e lo Sviluppo
Economico** *(f)* It
De Organisation für Wirtschaftliche Zusammenarbeit und Entwicklung *(f)*
En Organization for Economic Cooperation and Development (OECD)
Es Organización para Coo-
peracion y Desarrollo Economico *(f)*
Fr Organisation de Coopéra-
tion et de Développement Économiques *(f)*
Pt Organização para a Coo-
peração e o Desenvol-
vimento Económico *(f)*

**orienté à la baisse** Fr
De flau
En bearish
Es bajista
It ribassista
Pt baixista

**origem** *(f)* *n* Pt
De Ursprung *(m)*
En origin

Es origen *(m)*
Fr origine *(f)*
It origine *(f)*

**origen** *(m)* *n* Es
De Ursprung *(m)*
En origin
Fr origine *(f)*
It origine *(f)*
Pt origem *(f)*

**origin** *n* En
De Ursprung *(m)*
Es origen *(m)*
Fr origine *(f)*
It origine *(f)*
Pt origem *(f)*

**original** *(m)* *n* Es, Fr, Pt
De Original *(n)*
En top copy
It originale *(m)*

**Original** *(n)* *n* De
En top copy
Es original *(m)*
Fr original *(m)*
It originale *(m)*
Pt original *(m)*

**originale** *(m)* It
De Original *(n)*
En top copy
Es original *(m)*
Fr original *(m)*
Pt original *(m)*

**origine** *(f)* *n* Fr, It
De Ursprung *(m)*
En origin
Es origen *(m)*
Pt origem *(f)*

**oro** *(m)* *n* Es, It
De Gold *(n)*
En gold
Fr or *(m)*
Pt ouro *(m)*

**oro de imitación** *(m)* Es
De Kunstgold *(n)*
En imitation gold
Fr similor *(m)*
It similoro *(m)*
Pt ouro de imitação *(m)*

**Ortsplanungsgebiet** (n) n De
En development area
Es zona de desarrollo (f)
Fr zone de développement (f)
It zona di sviluppo (f)
Pt zona de desenvolvimento (f)

**ostracismo** (m) n It
De Boykott (m)
En blacking
Am boycott
Es boicoteo (m)
Fr boycottage (m)
Pt boicote (m)

**otorgar poder notarial** Es
De eine Vollmacht erteilen
En execute a power of attorney
Fr conférer des pleins pouvoirs
It conferire una procura
Pt dar execução a poderes de procuração

**ouro** (m) n Pt
De Gold (n)
En gold
Es oro (m)
Fr or (m)
It oro (m)

**ouro de imitação** (m) Pt
De Kunstgold (n)
En imitation gold
Es oro de imitación (m)
Fr similor (m)
It similoro (m)

**ouro-padrão** (m) n Pt
De Goldobligation (f)
En gold standard
Es patrón oro (m)
Fr étalon or (m)
It base aurea (f)

**outer harbour** En
De Aussenhafen (m)
Es antepuerto (m)
Fr avant-port (m)
It avamporto (m)
Pt anteporto (m)

**out of bond** En
De verzollt
Es despachado de aduanas
Fr dédouané

It sdoganato
Pt despachado alfândega

**out of date** En
De verfallen
Es vencido
Fr périmé
It scaduto
Pt vencido

**out of stock** En
De ausverkauft
Es stock agotado
Fr tout vendu
It esaurito
Pt esgotado

**out of work** En
De arbeitslos
Es parado; sin trabajo
Fr en chômage
It disoccupato
Pt desempregado

**output** n En
De Erzeugung (f)
Es rendimiento (m)
Fr rendement (m)
It produzione (f)
Pt rendimento; produção (m f)

**outstanding accounts** En
De ausstehende Schulden (m pl)
Es cuentas pendientes (f pl)
Fr comptes à percevoir (m pl)
It conti aperti (m pl)
Pt contas por saldar (f pl)

**ouvrage de référence** (m) Fr
De Nachschlagebuch (n)
En reference book
Es libro de consulta (m)
It libro di consultazione (m)
Pt livro de consulta (m)

**ouvrier** (m) n Fr
De Arbeiter (m)
En worker; workman
Es obrero; trabajador (m)
It operaio; lavoratore (m)
Pt operário; trabalhador (m)

**overcapacity** n En
De Überkapazität (f)
Es exceso de capacidad (m)
Fr surcapacité (f)

It capacità in eccedenza (f)
Pt capacidade excessiva (f)

**overdraft** n En
De Überziehung (f)
Es sobregiro; saldo deudor (m)
Fr découvert; solde débiteur (m)
It scoperto (m)
Pt conta a descoberto (f)

**overdraft facilities** En
Am overdraw facility
De Überziehungsdisposition (f)
Es facilidades de descubierto (f pl)
Fr facilités de caisse (f pl)
It facilitazione di scoperto (f)
Pt disponibilidades de crédito sem cabertura (f pl)

**overdraw** (an account) vb En
De überziehen
Es girar en descubierto
Fr mettre à découvert
It trarre alla scoperto
Pt levantar a descoberto

**overdue** adj En
De rückständig
Es vencido
Fr arriéré
It scaduto
Pt vencido

**over-estimate** n En
De Überschätzung (f)
Es presupuesto por exceso (m)
Fr surestimation (f)
It valutazione eccessiva (f)
Pt avaliação excessiva (f)

**overheads** pl n En
De Generalunkosten (pl)
Es gastos generales (m pl)
Fr frais généraux (m pl)
It spese generali (f pl)
Pt gastos gerais (m pl)

**overproduction** n En
De Überproduktion (f)
Es exceso de producción (m)
Fr surproduction (f)
It sovraproduzione (f)
Pt produção excessiva (f)

**overtime** n En
De Überstunden (f pl)
Es horas extraordinarias (f pl)
Fr heures supplémentaires (f pl)
It lavoro straordinario (m)
Pt horas extraordinárias (f pl)

**overweight** n En
De Übergewicht (n)
Es exceso de peso (m)
Fr excédent (m)
It sovrappeso (m)
Pt peso excessivo (m)

**owner** n En
De Eigentümer (m)
Es propietario; dueño (m)
Fr propriétaire (m)
It proprietario (m)
Pt proprietário; dono (m)

**ownership** n En
De Eigentum (n)
Es propiedad (f)
Fr propriété (f)
It proprietà (f)
Pt propriedade (f)

# P

**pacco** (m) n It
De Paket (n)
En parcel; package
Es paquete (m)
Fr paquet (m)
Pt pacote (m)

**package** n En
De Paket (n)
Es paquete (m)
Fr paquet (m)
It pacco; collo (m)
Pt pacote (m)

**package deal** En
De Globalgeschäft (n)
Es contrato global (m)
Fr marché global (m)
It contratto globale (m)
Pt contrato global (m)

**packing** n En
De Verpackung (f)
Es embalaje; envase (m)

Fr emballage (m)
It imballaggio (m)
Pt embalagem;
    empacotamento (m)

**Packwagen** (m) n De
En guard's van
Es furgón (m)
Fr fourgon (m)
It bagagliaio (m)
Pt carruagem do guarda (f)

**pacote** (m) n Pt
De Paket (n)
En parcel; package
Es paquete (m)
Fr paquet (m)
It pacco; collo (m)

**pacte** (m) n Fr
De Pakt (m)
En deed of covenant
Es pacto (m)
It patto (m)
Pt pacto (m)

**pacto** (m) n Es, Pt
De Abkommen; Pakt (m)
En covenant; deed of covenant
Fr convention; pacte (f m)
It convenzione; patto (f m)

**pacto de honra** (m) Pt
De Kavaliersabkommen (n)
En gentleman's agreement
Es acuerdo sobre palabra (m)
Fr convention verbale (f)
It accordo sulla parola (m)

**padrão** (m) n Pt
De Standard; Norm (m f)
En standard
Es norma; standard (f m)
Fr norme; étalon (f m)
It norma (f)

**padrone** (m) n It
De Arbeitgeber; Chef (m)
En employer; principal
Es patrono; principal (m)
Fr patron; employeur (m)
Pt patrão; director (m)

**paese** (m) n It
De Land (n)
En country
Es país (m)

Fr pays (m)
Pt país (m)

**paese di origine** (m) It
De Herkunftsland (n)
En country of origin
Es pais de origen (m)
Fr pays de provenance (m)
Pt país de origem (m)

**paese in via di sviluppo** (m) It
De Entwicklungsland (n)
En developing country
Es pais en desarrollo (m)
Fr pays en voie de dévelop-
    pement (m)
Pt país em desenvolvimento
    (m)

**paesi sottosviluppati** (m pl) It
De unterentwickelte Länder (n pl)
En underdeveloped countries
Es países en desarrollo (m pl)
Fr pays sous-développés (m pl)
Pt países subdesenvolvido (m pl)

**pagabile** adj It
De zahlbar
En payable
Es pagadero; pagable
Fr payable
Pt pagável

**pagabile al portatore** It
De an den Inhaber zahlbar
En payable to bearer
Es pagadero al portador
Fr payable au porteur
Pt pagável ao portador

**pagabile a vista** It
De zahlbar bei Sicht
En payable at sight
Es pagadero a la vista
Fr payable à vue
Pt pagável à vista

**pagadero** adj Es
De zahlbar
En payable
Fr payable
It pagabile
Pt pagável

**pagadero a la vista** Es
De zahlbar bei Sicht
En payable at sight
Fr payable à vue
It pagabile a vista
Pt pagável à vista

**pagadero al portador** Es
De an den Inhaber zahlbar
En payable to bearer
Fr payable au porteur
It pagabile al portatore
Pt pagável ao portador

**pagadero a presentación** Es
De zahlbar bei Vorlage
En payable on demand
Fr payable sur demande
It pagabile a vista
Pt pagável à vista

**pagadero con el pedido** Es
De gegen Barzahlung
En cash with order
Fr payable à la commande
It pagamento con l'ordine
Pt pagamento no acto de
   requisição

**pagado por adelantado** Es
De vorausbezahlt
En prepaid
Fr payé d'avance
It pagato in anticipo
Pt pago adiantadamente

**pagamenti trimestrali** *(m pl)* It
De vierteljährliche Zahlungen *(f pl)*
En quarterly payments
Es pagos trimestrales *(m pl)*
Fr paiements trimestriels *(m pl)*
Pt pagamentos trimestrais *(m pl)*

**pagamento** *(m)* n It, Pt
De Zahlung *(f)*
En payment
Es pago *(m)*
Fr paiement *(m)*

**pagamento a completa tacitazione** *(m)* It
De Zahlung zum vollen Ausgleich *(f)*
En payment in full discharge
Es pago de liberación *(m)*

Fr paiement libératoire *(m)*
Pt pagamento contra execução completa *(m)*

**pagamento adiado** *(m)* Pt
De gestundete Zahlung *(f)*
En deferred payment
Es pago aplazado *(m)*
Fr paiement différé
It pagamento differito *(m)*

**pagamento adiantado** *(m)* Pt
De Vorauszahlung *(f)*
En prepayment; payment in advance
Es pago andelantado *(m)*
Fr paiement anticipé *(m)*
It pagamento anticipato *(m)*

**pagamento alla consegna** It
De Lieferung gegen Nachnahme
En cash on delivery (c.o.d.)
Es entrega contra reembolso
Fr paiement à la livraison
Pt entrega contra reembolso

**pagamento anticipato** *(m)* It
De Vorauszahlung *(f)*
En prepayment; advance payment
Es pago andelantado *(m)*
Fr paiement anticipé *(m)*
Pt pagamento adiantado *(m)*

**pagamento completo** *(m)* Pt
De volle Zahlung *(f)*
En payment in full
Es pago en pleno *(m)*
Fr libération intégrale *(f)*
It pagamento in pieno *(m)*

**pagamento con l'ordine** It
De gegen Barzahlung
En cash with order
Es pagadero con el pedido
Fr payable à la commande
Pt pagamento no acto de requisição

**pagamento contra execução completa** *(m)* Pt
De Zahlung zum vollen Ausgleich *(f)*
En payment in full discharge
Es pago de liberación *(m)*
Fr paiement libératoire *(m)*

It pagamento a completa tacitazione *(m)*

**pagamento differito** *(m)* It
De gestundete Zahlung *(f)*
En deferred payment
Es pago aplazado *(m)*
Fr paiement différé
Pt pagamento adiado *(m)*

**pagamento in anticipo** *(m)* It
De Vorauszahlung *(f)*
En payment in advance
Es pago por adelantado *(m)*
Fr paiement anticipé *(m)*
Pt pagamento adiantado *(m)*

**pagamento in conto** *(m)* It
De Anzahlung *(f)*
En payment on account
Es pago a cuenta *(m)*
Fr versement à compte *(m)*
Pt pagamento por conta *(m)*

**pagamento inicial** *(m)* Pt
De Sofortzahlung *(f)*
En down-payment
Es pago de entrada *(m)*
Fr acompte *(m)*
It acconto *(m)*

**pagamento in pieno** *(m)* It
De volle Zahlung *(f)*
En payment in full
Es pago en pleno *(m)*
Fr libération intégrale *(f)*
Pt pagamento completo *(m)*

**pagamento no acto de requisição** Pt
De gegen Barzahlung
En cash with order
Es pagadero con el pedido
Fr payable à la commande
It pagamento con l'ordine

**pagamento parcial** *(m)* Pt
De Ratenzahlung *(f)*
En part payment
Es pago parcial *(m)*
Fr paiement partiel *(m)*
It pagamento parziale *(m)*

**pagamento parziale** *(m)* It
De Ratenzahlung *(f)*
En part payment
Es pago parcial *(m)*

Fr  paiement partiel *(m)*
Pt  pagamento parcial *(m)*

**pagamento por conta** *(m)* Pt
De  Anzahlung *(f)*
En  payment on account
Es  pago a cuenta *(m)*
Fr  versement à compte *(m)*
It  pagamento in conto *(m)*

**pagamento sob protesto** *(m)* Pt
De  Protestzahlung *(f)*
En  payment under protest
Es  pago sobre protesta *(m)*
Fr  paiement sous protêt *(m)*
It  pagamento sotto protesta *(m)*

**pagamento sotto protesta** *(m)* It
De  Protestzahlung *(f)*
En  payment under protest
Es  pago sobre protesta *(m)*
Fr  paiement sous protêt *(m)*
Pt  pagamento sob protesto *(m)*

**pagamentos trimestrais** *(m pl)* Pt
De  vierteljährliche Zahlungen *(f pl)*
En  quarterly payments
Es  pagos trimestrales *(m pl)*
Fr  paiements trimestriels *(m pl)*
It  pagamenti trimestrali *(m pl)*

**paga neta** *(f)* Es
De  Nettolohn *(m)*
En  take-home pay
Fr  salaire nette *(f)*
It  paga netta *(f)*
Pt  salário líquido de descontos *(m)*

**paga netta** *(f)* It
De  Nettolohn *(m)*
En  take-home pay
Es  paga neta *(f)*
Fr  salaire nette *(f)*
Pt  salário líquido de descontos *(m)*

**pagar** *vb* Es, Pt
De  zahlen
En  pay

Fr  payer
It  pagare

**pagar ao portador** Pt
De  zahlen bei Vorlage
En  pay to bearer
Es  páguese al portador
Fr  payez au porteur
It  pagare al portatore

**pagar a plazos mensuales (semanales)** Es
De  monatlich (wochentlich) in Raten zahlen
En  pay by monthly (weekly) instalments
Fr  payer par termes mensuels (hebdomadaires)
It  pagare a rate mensili (settimanali)
Pt  pagar a prestações mensais (semanais)

**pagar a prestações mensais (semanais)** Pt
De  monatlich (wochentlich) in Raten zahlen
En  pay by monthly (weekly) instalments
Es  pagar a plazos mensuales (semanales)
Fr  payer par termes mensuels (hebdomadaires)
It  pagare a rate mensili (settimanali)

**pagar depósito** Pt
De  hinterlegen
En  pay a deposit
Es  hacer un depósito
Fr  donner des arrhès
It  versare un deposito

**pagaré** *(m)* *n* Es
De  Schuldschein *(m)*
En  promissory note; I.O.U.
Fr  billet à ordre; reconnaissance de dette *(m f)*
It  pagherò *(m)*
Pt  promissória; vale *(f m)*

**pagare** *vb* It
De  zahlen
En  pay
Es  pagar
Fr  payer
Pt  pagar

**pagare al portatore** It
De  zahlen bei Vorlage
En  pay to bearer
Es  páguese al portador
Fr  payez au porteur
Pt  pagar ao portador

**pagare a rate mensili (settimanali)** It
De  monatlich (wochentlich) in Raten zahlen
En  pay by monthly (weekly) instalments
Es  pagar a plazos mensuales (semanales)
Fr  payer par termes mensuels (hebdomadaires)
Pt  pagar a prestações mensais (semanais)

**pagaré de favor** *(m)* Es
De  Gefälligkeitswechsel *(m)*
En  accommodation bill
Fr  billet de complaisance *(m)*
It  cambiale di favore *(f)*
Pt  letra de favor *(f)*

**pagato in anticipo** It
De  vorausbezahlt
En  prepaid
Es  pagado por adelantado
Fr  payé d'avance
Pt  pago adiantamente

**pagável** *adj* Pt
De  zahlbar
En  payable
Es  pagadero; pagable
Fr  payable
It  pagabile

**pagável ao portador** Pt
De  an den Inhaber zahlbar
En  payable to bearer
Es  pagadero al portador
Fr  payable au porteur
It  pagabile al portatore

**pagável à vista** Pt
De  zahlbar bei Sicht
En  payable at sight
Es  pagadero a la vista
Fr  payable à vue
It  pagabile a vista

**pagherò** *(m)* *n* It
De  Schuldschein *(m)*
En  promissory note; I.O.U.

Es pagaré *(m)*
Fr billet à ordre; reconnaissance de dette *(m f)*
Pt promissória; vale *(f m)*

**pago** *(m) n* Es
De Zahlung *(f)*
En payment
Fr versement *(m)*
It pagamento *(m)*
Pt pagamento *(m)*

**pago a cuenta** *(m)* Es
De Anzahlung *(f)*
En payment on account
Fr versement à compte *(m)*
It pagamento in conto *(m)*
Pt pagamento por conta *(m)*

**pago adiantadamente** Pt
De vorausbezahlt
En prepaid
Es pagado por adelantado
Fr payé d'avance
It pagato in anticipo

**pago andelantado** *(m)* Es
De Vorauszahlung *(f)*
En prepayment
Fr paiement anticipé *(m)*
It pagamento anticipato *(m)*
Pt pagamento adiantado *(m)*

**pago aplazado** *(m)* Es
De gestundete Zahlung *(f)*
En deferred payment
Fr paiement différé
It pagamento differito *(m)*
Pt pagamento adiado *(m)*

**pago a plazos** *(m)* Es
De Ratenzahlung *(f)*
En payment by instalments
Fr paiement à temperament *(m)*
It pagamento a rate *(m)*
Pt pagamento a prestações *(m)*

**pago atrasado** *(m)* Es
De Lohnnachzahlung *(f)*
En back pay
Fr rappel de traitement *(m)*
It arretrati di paga *(m pl)*
Pt vencimento atrasado *(m)*

**pago de entrada** *(m)* Es
De Sofortzahlung *(f)*
En down-payment
Fr acompte *(m)*
It acconto *(m)*
Pt pagamento inicial *(m)*

**pago de liberación** *(m)* Es
De Zahlung zum vollen Ausgleich *(f)*
En payment in full discharge
Fr paiement libératoire *(m)*
It pagamento a completa tacitazione *(m)*
Pt pagamento contra execução completa *(m)*

**pago en pleno** *(m)* Es
De volle Zahlung *(f)*
En payment in full
Fr libération intégrale *(f)*
It pagamento in pieno *(m)*
Pt pagamento completo *(m)*

**pago parcial** *(m)* Es
De Ratenzahlung *(f)*
En part payment
Fr paiement partiel *(m)*
It pagamento parziale *(m)*
Pt pagamento parcial *(m)*

**pago por adelantado** *(m)* Es
De Vorauszahlung *(f)*
En payment in advance
Fr paiement anticipé *(m)*
It pagamento in anticipo *(m)*
Pt pagamento adiantado *(m)*

**pago por resultados** *(m)* Es
De Leistungslohn *(m)*
En payment by results
Fr salaire au rendement *(m)*
It pagamento secondo i risultati *(m)*
Pt pagamento relativo as resultados *(m)*

**pago sobre protesta** *(m)* Es
De Protestzahlung *(f)*
En payment under protest
Fr paiement sous protêt *(m)*
It pagamento sotto protesta *(m)*
Pt pagamento sob protesto *(m)*

**pagos trimestrales** *(m pl)* Es
De vierteljährliche Zahlungen *(f pl)*
En quarterly payments
Fr paiements trimestriels *(m pl)*
It pagamenti trimestrali *(m pl)*
Pt pagamentos trimestrais *(m pl)*

**páguese al portador** Es
De zahlen bei Vorlage
En pay to bearer
Fr payez au porteur
It pagare al portatore
Pt pagar ao portador

**paid-up capital** En
De eingezahltes Kapital *(n)*
Es capital desembolsado *(m)*
Fr capital versé *(m)*
It capitale versato *(m)*
Pt capital realizado *(m)*

**paid-up policy** En
De beitragsfreie Police *(f)*
Es póliza liberada *(f)*
Fr assurance libérée *(f)*
It polizza interamente pagata *(f)*
Pt apólice liquidada *(f)*

**paiement à la livraison** Fr
De Lieferung gegen Nachnahme
En cash on delivery (c.o.d.)
Es entrega contra reembolso
It pagamento alla consegna
Pt entrega contra reembolso

**paiement anticipé** *(m)* Fr
De Vorauszahlung *(f)*
En prepayment
Es pago andelantado *(m)*
It pagamento anticipato *(m)*
Pt pagamento adiantado *(m)*

**paiement différé** Fr
De gestundete Zahlung *(f)*
En deferred payment
Es pago aplazado *(m)*
It pagamento differito *(m)*
Pt pagamento adiado *(m)*

**paiement libératoire** *(m)* Fr
De Zahlung zum vollen Ausgleich *(f)*

En payment in full discharge
Es pago de liberación (m)
It pagamento a completa tacitazione (m)
Pt pagamento contra execução completa (m)

**paiement par anticipation** (m) Fr
De Vorauszahlung (f)
En advance payment
Es anticipo (m)
It pagamento anticipato (m)
Pt pagamento adiantado (m)

**paiement partiel** (m) Fr
De Ratenzahlung (f)
En part payment
Es pago parcial (m)
It pagamento parziale (m)
Pt pagamento parcial (m)

**paiement sous protêt** (m) Fr
De Protestzahlung (f)
En payment under protest
Es pago sobre protesta (m)
It pagamento sotto protesta (m)
Pt pagamento sob protesto (m)

**paiements trimestriels** (m pl) Fr
De vierteljährliche Zahlungen (f pl)
En quarterly payments
Es pagos trimestrales (m pl)
It pagamenti trimestrali (m pl)
Pt pagamentos trimestrais (m pl)

**país** (m) n Es, Pt
De Land (n)
En country
Fr pays (m)
It paese (m)

**país de origem** (m) Pt
De Herkunftsland (n)
En country of origin
Es país de origen (m)
Fr pays de provenance (m)
It paese di origine (m)

**país de origen** (m) Es
De Herkunftsland (n)
En country of origin

Fr pays de provenance (m)
It paese di origine (m)
Pt país de origem (m)

**país em desenvolvimento** (m) Pt
De Entwicklungsland (n)
En developing country
Es país en desarrollo (m)
Fr pays en voie de développement (m)
It paese in via di sviluppo (m)

**país en desarrollo** (m) Es
De Entwicklungsland (n)
En developing country
Fr pays en voie de développement (m)
It paese in via di sviluppo (m)
Pt país em desenvolvimento (m)

**países subdesenvolvido** (m pl) Pt
De unterentwickelte Länder (n pl)
En underdeveloped countries
Es países en desarrollo (m pl)
Fr pays sous-développés (m pl)
It paesi sottosviluppati (m pl)

**Paket** (n) n De
En parcel; package
Es paquete (m)
Fr paquet (m)
It pacco; collo (m)
Pt pacote (m)

**Paketpost** (f) De
En parcel post
Es servicio de paquete postal (m)
Fr service des colis postaux (m)
It servizio dei pacchi postali (m)
Pt serviço de encomendas postais (m)

**Pakt** (m) n De
En deed of covenant
Es pacto (m)
Fr pacte (m)
It patto (m)
Pt escritura de compromisso (m)

**paleta** (f) n Pt
De Palette (f)
En pallet
Es bandeja (f)
Fr palette (f)
It paletta (f)

**paletisation** (f) n Fr
De Paletisierung (f)
En palletization
Es paletización (f)
It palettizzazione (f)
Pt paletização (f)

**Paletisierung** (f) n De
En palletization
Es paletización (f)
Fr paletisation (f)
It palettizzazione (f)
Pt paletização (f)

**paletização** (f) n Pt
De Paletisierung (f)
En palletization
Es paletización (f)
Fr paletisation (f)
It palettizzazione (f)

**paletización** (f) n Es
De Paletisierung (f)
En palletization
Fr paletisation (f)
It palettizzazione (f)
Pt paletização (f)

**paletta** (f) n It
De Palette (f)
En pallet
Es bandeja (f)
Fr palette (f)
Pt paleta (f)

**palette** (f) n Fr
De Palette (f)
En pallet
Es bandeja (f)
It paletta (f)
Pt paleta (f)

**Palette** (f) n De
En pallet
Es bandeja (f)
Fr palette (f)
It paletta (f)
Pt paleta (f)

**palettizzazione** *(f)* n It
De Paletisierung *(f)*
En palletization
Es paletización *(f)*
Fr paletisation *(f)*
Pt paletização *(f)*

**pallet** n En
De Palette *(f)*
Es bandeja *(f)*
Fr palette *(f)*
It paletta *(f)*
Pt paleta *(f)*

**palletization** n En
De Paletisierung *(f)*
Es paletización *(f)*
Fr paletisation *(f)*
It palettizzazione *(f)*
Pt paletização *(f)*

**pane di ghisa** *(m)* It
De Roheisen *(n)*
En pig-iron
Es hierro bruto *(m)*
Fr fer en gueuse *(m)*
Pt ferro em bruto *(m)*

**papel carbón** *(m)* Es
De Kohlepapier *(n)*
En carbon paper
Fr papier carbone *(m)*
It carta carbone *(f)*
Pt papel químico *(m)*

**papel mata-borrão** *(m)* Pt
De Löschpapier *(n)*
En blotting paper
Es papel secante *(m)*
It carta assorbente *(f)*

**papel milimetrado** *(m)* Es
De Millimeterpapier *(n)*
En graph paper
Fr papier quadrillé *(m)*
It carta millimetrata *(f)*
Pt papel milimétrico *(m)*

**papel milimétrico** *(m)* Pt
De Millimeterpapier *(n)*
En graph paper
Es papel milimetrado *(m)*
Fr papier quadrillé *(m)*
It carta millimetrata *(f)*

**papel-moeda** *(m)* n Pt
De Papiergeld *(n)*
En paper money

Es papel monetario *(m)*
Fr papier-monnaie *(m)*
It carta moneta *(f)*

**papel monetario** *(m)* Es
De Papiergeld *(n)*
En paper money
Fr papier-monnaie *(m)*
It carta moneta *(f)*
Pt papel-moeda *(m)*

**papel químico** *(m)* Pt
De Kohlepapier *(n)*
En carbon paper
Es papel carbón *(m)*
Fr papier carbone *(m)*
It carta carbone *(f)*

**papel secante** *(m)* Es
De Löschpapier *(n)*
En blotting paper
Fr papier buvard *(m)*
It carta assorbente *(f)*
Pt papel mata-borrão *(m)*

**paper clip** En
De Büroklammer *(f)*
Es sujetapapeles *(m)*
Fr attache-papiers *(m)*
It fermacarte *(m)*
Pt grampo *(m)*

**paper loss** En
De imaginärer Verlust *(m)*
Es pérdida por realizar *(f)*
Fr perte fictive *(f)*
It perdita sulla carta *(f)*
Pt perdas no papel *(f)*

**paper money** En
De Papiergeld *(n)*
Es papel monetario *(m)*
Fr papier-monnaie *(m)*
It carta moneta *(f)*
Pt papel-moeda *(m)*

**paper profit** En
De imaginärer Gewinn *(m)*
Es ganancia por realizar *(f)*
Fr profit fictif *(m)*
It utile sulla carta *(m)*
Pt lucros no papel *(m)*

**papier bancable** *(m)* Fr
De diskontierbare Wechsel *(m pl)*
En bankable bills
Es efectos negociables *(m pl)*

It effetti scontabili *(m pl)*
Pt valores transaccionáveis pelo banco *(m pl)*

**papier buvard** *(m)* Fr
De Löschpapier *(n)*
En blotting paper
Es papel secante *(m)*
It carta assorbente *(f)*
Pt papel mata-borrão *(m)*

**papier carbone** *(m)* Fr
De Kohlepapier *(n)*
En carbon paper
Es papel carbón *(m)*
It carta carbone *(f)*
Pt papel químico *(m)*

**papier de haut commerce** *(m)* Fr
De erstklassiger Handelswechsel *(m)*
En prime trade bill
Es carta comercial de primera orden *(f)*
It carta commerciale di primo ordine *(f)*
Pt estatuto de comercialização de primeira ordem *(m)*

**Papiergeld** *(n)* n De
En paper money
Es papel monetario *(m)*
Fr papier-monnaie *(m)*
It carta moneta *(f)*
Pt papel-moeda *(m)*

**papier-monnaie** *(m)* n Fr
De Papiergeld *(n)*
En paper money
Es papel monetario *(m)*
It carta moneta *(f)*
Pt papel-moeda *(m)*

**papier quadrillé** *(m)* Fr
De Millimeterpapier *(n)*
En graph paper
Es papel milimetrado *(m)*
It carta millimetrata *(f)*
Pt papel milimétrico *(m)*

**papiers de bord** *(m pl)* Fr
De Schiffspapiere *(n pl)*
En ship's papers
Es documentación marítima *(f)*
It carte di bordo *(f pl)*
Pt documentação do navio *(f)*

**paquebot** *(m)* n Fr
De Linienschiff *(n)*
En liner
Es vapor de línea *(m)*
It nave di linea *(f)*
Pt paquete *(m)*

**paquet** *(m)* n Fr
De Paket *(n)*
En parcel; package
Es paquete *(m)*
It pacco; collo *(m)*
Pt pacote *(m)*

**paquete** *(m)* n Pt
De Linienschiff *(n)*
En liner
Es vapor de línea *(m)*
Fr paquebot *(m)*
It nave di linea *(f)*

**paquete** *(m)* n Es
De Paket *(n)*
En parcel; package
Fr paquet *(m)*
It pacco; collo *(m)*
Pt pacote *(m)*

**parado** Es
De arbeitslos
En out of work
Fr en chômage
It disoccupato
Pt desempregado

**parapher** *vb* Fr
De paraphieren
En initial
Es rubricar; poner iniciales a
It siglare
Pt rubricar

**paraphieren** *vb* De
En initial
Es rubricar; poner iniciales a
Fr parapher; viser
It siglare
Pt rubricar

**par avion** Fr
De per Flugpost
En by air
Es por avión
It per via aerea
Pt por avião

**parcel** (package) n En
De Paket *(n)*
Es paquete *(m)*
Fr paquet *(m)*
It pacco; collo *(m)*
Pt pacote *(m)*

**parcel** (of land) n En
Am plot
De Parzelle *(f)*
Es parcela *(f)*
Fr parcelle *(f)*
It pezzo; lotto *(m)*
Pt parcela *(f)*

**parcela** *(f)* n Es, Pt
De Parzelle *(f)*
En parcel (of land)
Am plot
Fr parcelle *(f)*
It pezzo; lotto *(m)*

**parcelle** *(f)* n Fr
De Parzelle *(f)*
En parcel (of land)
Am plot
Es parcela *(f)*
It pezzo; lotto *(m)*
Pt parcela *(f)*

**parcel post** En
De Paketpost *(f)*
Es servicio de paquete postal *(m)*
Fr service des colis postaux *(m)*
It servizio dei pacchi postali *(m)*
Pt serviço de encomendas postais *(m)*

**par duplicado** Es
De Duplikat-; zweifach
En in duplicate
Fr en double
It in duplice copia
Pt em duplicado

**pareggiare un bilancio** It
De einen Haushaltsplan ins Gleichgewicht bringen
En balance a budget
Es balancear el presupuesto
Fr équilibrer un budget
Pt equilibrar um orçamento

**pareggiare un conto** It
De eine Rechnung ausgleichen
En balance an account
Es saldar una cuenta
Fr balancer un compte
Pt equilibrar uma conta

**parent company** En
De Muttergesellschaft *(f)*
Es compañía matriz *(f)*
Fr société mère *(f)*
It società madre *(f)*
Pt empresa matriz *(f)*

**paridad** *(f)* n Es
De Parität *(f)*
En parity
Fr parité *(f)*
It parità *(f)*
Pt paridade *(f)*

**paridade** *(f)* n Pt
De Parität *(f)*
En parity
Es paridad *(f)*
Fr parité *(f)*
It parità *(f)*

**paridade fixa** *(f)* Pt
De feste Parität *(f)*
En fixed parity
Es paridad fija *(f)*
Fr parité fixe *(f)*
It parità fissa *(f)*

**paridad fija** *(f)* Es
De feste Parität *(f)*
En fixed parity
Fr parité fixe *(f)*
It parità fissa *(f)*
Pt paridade fixa *(f)*

**parità** *(f)* n It
De Parität *(f)*
En parity
Es paridad *(f)*
Fr parité *(f)*
Pt paridade *(f)*

**parità fissa** *(f)* It
De feste Parität *(f)*
En fixed parity
Es paridad fija *(f)*
Fr parité fixe *(f)*
Pt paridade fixa *(f)*

**Parität** (f) n De
En parity
Es paridad (f)
Fr parité (f)
It parità (f)
Pt paridade (f)

**parité** (f) n Fr
De Parität (f)
En parity
Es paridad (f)
It parità (f)
Pt paridade (f)

**parité fixe** (f) Fr
De feste Parität (f)
En fixed parity
Es paridad fija (f)
It parità fissa (f)
Pt paridade fixa (f)

**parity** n En
De Parität (f)
Es paridad (f)
Fr parité (f)
It parità (f)
Pt paridade (f)

**par la présente** Fr
De hiermit
En hereby
Es por esto
It col presente; con questo
Pt pelo presente

**paro de temporada** (m) Es
De jahreszeitlich bedingte Arbeitslosigkeit (f)
En seasonal unemployment
Fr chômage saisonnier (m)
It disoccupazione stagionale (f)
Pt desemprego de estação (m)

**part** (f) n Fr
De Teil (m)
En share
Es parte (f)
It parte (f)
Pt quota (f)

**partager** vb Fr
De teilen
En share
Es repartir
It dividere
Pt repartir

**partager la différence** Fr
De einen strittigen Preisunterschied teilen
En split the difference
Es repartir la diferencia
It dividere a metà la differenza
Pt dividir a meio a diferença

**parte** (f) n Es, It
De Teil (m)
En share
Fr part (f)
Pt quota (f)

**partecipare** vb It
De beteiligen
En participate
Es participar
Fr participer
Pt participar

**partecipazione agli utili** (f) It
De Gewinnbeteiligung (f)
En profit-sharing
Es participación en los beneficios (f)
Fr participation aux bénéfices (f)
Pt repartição dos lucros (f)

**partecipazione maggioritaria** (f) It
De Mehrheitsbeteiligung (f)
En majority holding
Es tenencia de acciones por mayoría (f)
Fr participation majoritaire (f)
Pt propriedade em maioria (f)

**parte lesa** (f) It
De Verletzte(r) (m)
En injured party
Es parte lesionada (f)
Fr partie lésée (f)
Pt parte lesada (f)

**parte lesada** (f) Pt
De Verletzte(r) (m)
En injured party
Es parte lesionada (f)
Fr partie lésée (f)
It parte lesa (f)

**parte lesionada** (f) Es
De Verletzte(r) (m)
En injured party
Fr partie lésée (f)

It parte lesa (f)
Pt parte lesada (f)

**par tête** Fr
De pro Kopf
En per capita
Es por cabeza
It per testa
Pt per capita

**participación de la minoría** (f) Es
De Minoritätsbeteiligung (f)
En minority interest
Fr participation de la minorité (f)
It interessenza di minoranza (f)
Pt interesse representado pela minoria (m)

**participación del mercado** (f) Es
De Marktanteil (m)
En market share
Fr participation au marché (f)
It quota del mercato (f)
Pt quota-parte no mercado (f)

**participación en los beneficios** (f) Es
De Gewinnbeteiligung (f)
En profit-sharing
Fr participation aux bénéfices (f)
It partecipazione agli utili (f)
Pt repartição dos lucros (f)

**participar** vb Es, Pt
De beteiligen
En participate
Fr participer
It partecipare

**participate** vb En
De beteiligen
Es participar
Fr participer
It partecipare
Pt participar

**participating policy** Am
En with-profits policy
De Police mit Gewinnberechtigung (f)
Es póliza con beneficios (f)
Fr police avec participation aux bénéfices (f)

It    polizza con profitti *(f)*
Pt    apólice com participação
      nos lucros *(f)*

**participation au marché** *(f)* Fr
De    Marktanteil *(m)*
En    market share
Es    participación del mercado
      *(f)*
It    quota del mercato *(f)*
Pt    quota-parte no mercado *(f)*

**participation aux bénéfices** *(f)*
      Fr
De    Gewinnbeteiligung *(f)*
En    profit-sharing
Es    participación en los bene-
      ficios *(f)*
It    partecipazione agli utili *(f)*
Pt    repartição dos lucros *(f)*

**participation de la minorité** *(f)*
      Fr
De    Minoritätsbeteiligung *(f)*
En    minority interest
Es    participación de la minoría
      *(f)*
It    interessenza di minoranza
      *(f)*
Pt    interesse representado pela
      minoria *(m)*

**participation donnant le con-
trôle** *(f)* Fr
De    Mehrheitsbeteiligung *(f)*
En    controlling interest
Es    interés mayoritario *(m)*
It    interesse della parte mag-
      gioritaria *(m)*
Pt    interesse maioritário *(m)*

**participation majoritaire** *(f)* Fr
De    Mehrheitsbeteiligung *(f)*
En    majority holding
Es    tenencia de acciones por
      mayoría *(f)*
It    partecipazione maggiori-
      taria *(f)*
Pt    propriedade em maioria *(f)*

**participer** *vb* Fr
De    beteiligen
En    participate
Es    participar
It    partecipare
Pt    participar

**particolari** *(m pl)* n It
De    Einzelheiten; Angaben *(f pl)*
En    particulars
Es    detalles *(m pl)*
Fr    détails *(m pl)*
Pt    pormenores *(m pl)*

**particular average** En
De    besondere Havarie *(f)*
Es    avería particular *(f)*
Fr    avarie particulière *(f)*
It    avaria particolare *(f)*
Pt    avaria particular *(f)*

**particularité** *(f)* n Fr
De    Merkmal *(n)*
En    feature
Es    característica *(f)*
It    caratteristica *(f)*
Pt    característica *(f)*

**particulars** *pl* n En
De    Einzelheiten; Angaben *(f pl)*
Es    detalles *(m pl)*
Fr    détails *(m pl)*
It    particolari *(m pl)*
Pt    pormenores *(m pl)*

**partida de defunción** *(f)* Es
De    Totenschein *(m)*
En    death certificate
Fr    extrait d'acte de décès *(m)*
It    certificato di morte *(m)*
Pt    certidão de óbito *(f)*

**partida doble** *(f)* Es
De    doppelte Buchführung *(f)*
En    double entry book-keeping
Fr    partie double *(f)*
It    partita doppia *(f)*
Pt    lançamento duplo *(m)*

**partie double** *(f)* Fr
De    doppelte Buchführung *(f)*
En    double entry book-keeping
Es    partida doble *(f)*
It    partita doppia *(f)*
Pt    lançamento duplo *(m)*

**partie lésée** *(f)* Fr
De    Verletzte(r) *(m)*
En    injured party
Es    parte lesionada *(f)*
It    parte lesa *(f)*
Pt    parte lesada *(f)*

**partita doppia** *(f)* It
De    doppelte Buchführung *(f)*
En    double entry book-keeping
Es    partida doble *(f)*
Fr    partie double *(f)*
Pt    lançamento duplo *(m)*

**partitario delle vendite** *(m)* It
De    Verkaufskontenbuch *(n)*
En    sales ledger
Es    libro mayor de ventas *(m)*
Fr    grand livre des ventes *(m)*
Pt    livro-mestre de vendas *(m)*

**partita spaiata** *(f)* It
De    Restpartie *(f)*
En    odd lot
Es    lote suelto *(m)*
Fr    solde *(m)*
Pt    lote avulso *(m)*

**partner** n En
De    Teilhaber *(m)*
Es    socio *(m)*
Fr    associé *(m)*
It    socio *(m)*
Pt    sócio *(m)*

**partnership** n En
De    offene Handelsgesellschaft
      (OHG) *(f)*
Es    sociedad regular colectiva
      (SRC) *(f)*
Fr    société en nom collectif *(f)*
It    società *(f)*
Pt    sociedade *(f)*

**part payment** En
De    Ratenzahlung *(f)*
Es    pago parcial *(m)*
Fr    paiement partiel *(m)*
It    pagamento parziale *(m)*
Pt    pagamento parcial *(m)*

**Parzelle** *(f)* n De
En    parcel (of land)
Am    plot
Es    parcela *(f)*
Fr    parcelle *(f)*
It    pezzo; lotto *(m)*
Pt    parcela *(f)*

**pasado mañana** Es
De    übermorgen
En    day after tomorrow
Fr    après demain
It    dopodomani
Pt    depois de amanhã

**pasaje** *(m) n* Es
De  Fahrgeld *(n)*
En  fare
Fr  prix du voyage *(m)*
It  prezzo di viaggio *(m)*
Pt  preço de passagem *(m)*

**pasaje de ida** *(m)* Es
De  einfache Fahrkarte *(f)*
En  single fare
Am  one way fare
Fr  billet d´aller *(m)*
It  biglietto d´andata *(m)*
Pt  passagem de ida *(f)*

**pasaje de ida y vuelta** *(m)* Es
De  Rückfahrkarte *(f)*
En  return fare
Am  roundtrip fare
Fr  billet d´aller et retour *(m)*
It  biglietto di andata e ritorno *(m)*
Pt  passagem de ida e volta *(f)*

**pasajero** *(m) n* Es
De  Reisende(r) *(m)*
En  passenger
Fr  passager *(m)*
It  passeggero *(m)*
Pt  passageiro *(m)*

**pasar de contrabando** Es
De  schmuggeln
En  smuggle
Fr  faire la contrebande
It  contrabbandare
Pt  passar por contrabando

**pasivo exigible** *(m)* Es
De  laufende Verbindlichkeiten *(f pl)*
En  current liabilities
Fr  passif exigible *(m)*
It  passività esigibili *(f pl)*
Pt  passivo actual *(m)*

**pasivo transitorio** *(m)* Es
De  aufgeschobene Schulden *(f pl)*
En  deferred liabilities
Fr  passif différé *(m)*
It  passività differite *(f pl)*
Pt  passivo adiado- *(m)*

**paso de aduanas** *(f)* Es
De  Zollabfertigung *(f)*
En  customs clearance
Fr  dédouanement *(m)*

It  sdoganamento *(m)*
Pt  despacho alfandegário *(m)*

**passageiro** *(m) n* Pt
De  Reisende(r) *(m)*
En  passenger
Es  pasajero *(m)*
Fr  passager *(m)*
It  passeggero *(m)*

**passagem de ida** *(f)* Pt
De  einfache Fahrkarte *(f)*
En  single fare
Am  one way fare
Es  pasaje de ida *(m)*
Fr  billet d´aller *(m)*
It  biglietto d´andata *(m)*

**passagem de ida e volta** *(f)* Pt
De  Rückfahrkarte *(f)*
En  return fare
Am  roundtrip fare
Es  pasaje de ida y vuelta *(m)*
Fr  billet d´aller et retour *(m)*
It  biglietto di andata e ritorno *(m)*

**passager** *(m) n* Fr
De  Reisende(r) *(m)*
En  passenger
Es  pasajero *(m)*
It  passeggero *(m)*
Pt  passageiro *(m)*

**passar por contrabando** Pt
De  schmuggeln
En  smuggle
Es  pasar de contrabando
Fr  faire la contrebande
It  contrabbandare

**passar um cheque** Pt
De  einen Scheck ausstellen
En  draw a cheque
Es  extender un cheque
Fr  tirer un chèque
It  emettere un assegno

**passbook** *n* En
Am  bankbook
De  Bankbuch; Sparbuch *(n)*
Es  libreta de banco *(f)*
Fr  livret de compte *(m)*
It  libretto di conto *(m)*
Pt  livrete de conta *(f)*

**passeggero** *(m) n* It
De  Reisende(r) *(m)*
En  passenger
Es  pasajero *(m)*
Fr  passager *(m)*
Pt  passageiro *(m)*

**passenger** *n* En
De  Reisende(r) *(m)*
Es  pasajero *(m)*
Fr  passager *(m)*
It  passeggero *(m)*
Pt  passageiro *(m)*

**passer un acte** Fr
De  eine Urkunde unterzeichnen
En  execute a deed
Es  firmar una escritura
It  perfezionare un atto
Pt  dar execução a um título legal

**passer une commande** Fr
De  bestellen
En  order
Es  hacer un pedido
It  ordinare
Pt  encomendar

**passif différé** *(m)* Fr
De  aufgeschobene Schulden *(m pl)*
En  deferred liabilities
Es  pasivo transitorio *(m)*
It  passività differite *(f pl)*
Pt  passivo adiado *(m)*

**passif exigible** *(m)* Fr
De  laufende Verbindlichkeiten *(f pl)*
En  current liabilities
Es  pasivo exigible *(m)*
It  passività esigibili *(f pl)*
Pt  passivo actual *(m)*

**passività differite** *(f pl)* It
De  aufgeschobene Schulden *(f pl)*
En  deferred liabilities
Es  pasivo transitorio *(m)*
Fr  passif différé *(m)*
Pt  passivo adiado *(m)*

**passività esigibili** *(f pl)* It
De  laufende Verbindlichkeiten *(f pl)*
En  current liabilities
Es  pasivo exigible *(m)*

Fr passif exigible (m)
Pt passivo actual (m)

**passivo actual** (m) Pt
De laufende Verbindlichkeiten
(f pl)
En current liabilities
Es pasivo exigible (m)
Fr passif exigible (m)
It passività esigibili (f pl)

**passivo adiado** (m) Pt
De aufgeschobene Schulden
(m pl)
En deferred liabilities
Es pasivo transitorio (m)
Fr passif différé (m)
It passività differite (f pl)

**Passivsaldo** (m) n De
En adverse balance
Am negative balance
Es saldo adverso (m)
Fr balance déficitaire (f)
It saldo passivo (m)
Pt saldo negativo (m)

**pasta** (ministerial) (f) n Pt
De Portefeuille; Geschäftsbe-
reich (n m)
En portfolio
Es cartera (f)
Fr portefeuille (f)
It portafoglio (m)

**past performance** En
De Leistung in der Vergangen-
heit (f)
Es operación anterior (f)
Fr comportement antérieur
(m)
It comportamento precede-
nte (m)
Pt desempenho anterior (m)

**patent** n En
De Erfindungspatent (n)
Es patente (f)
Fr brevet d'invention (m)
It brevetto (m)
Pt patente (f)

**patent agent** En
De Patentanwalt (m)
Es agente de patentes (m)
Fr conseil en brevets (m)
It agente di brevetti (m)
Pt agente de patentes (m)

**Patentanwalt** (m) n De
En patent agent
Es agente de patentes (m)
Fr conseil en brevets (m)
It agente di brevetti (m)
Pt agente de patentes (m)

**patente** (f) n Es, Pt
De Erfindungspatent (n)
En patent
Fr brevet d'invention (m)
It brevetto (m)

**Patenturkunde** (f) n De
En letters patent
Am patent
Es patente de invención (f)
Fr brevet (m)
It brevetto (m)
Pt patente de invenção (f)

**patrão** (m) n Pt
De Arbeitgeber; Chef (m)
En employer; principal
Es patrono; principal (m)
Fr employeur; patron (m)
It datore di lavoro; padrone
(m)

**patrimonio** (m) n It
De Nachlass (m)
En estate
Es herencia (f)
Fr succession (f)
Pt património; herança (m f)

**património** (m) n Pt
De Nachlass (m)
En estate
Es herencia (f)
Fr succession (f)
It patrimonio; successione (m
f)

**patron** (m) n Fr
De Arbeitgeber; Chef (m)
En employer; principal
Es patrono; principal (m)
It padrone; principale (m)
Pt patrão; director (m)

**patrono** (m) n Es
De Arbeitgeber; Chef (m)
En employer; principal
Fr employeur; patron (m)
It datore di lavoro; padrone
(m)
Pt patrão; director (m)

**patrón oro** (m) Es
De Goldobligation (f)
En gold standard
Fr étalon or (m)
It base aurea (f)
Pt ouro-padrão (m)

**patto** (m) n It
De Pakt (m)
En deed of covenant
Es pacto (m)
Fr pacte (m)
Pt pacto (m)

**Pauschalbetrag** (m) n De
En lump sum
Es suma global (f)
Fr somme globale (f)
It somma globale (f)
Pt soma por inteiro (f)

**pavillon** (drapeau) (m) n Fr
De Flagge (f)
En flag
Es bandera (f)
It bandiera (f)
Pt bandeira (f)

**pawnbroker** n En
De Pfandleiher (m)
Es prestamista (m)
Fr prêteur sur gage (m)
It prestatore su pegno (m)
Pt prestamista (m)

**pay** vb En
De zahlen
Es pagar
Fr payer
It pagare
Pt pagar

**payable** adj En, Fr
De zahlbar
Es pagadero; pagable
It pagabile
Pt pagável

**payable à la commande** Fr
De gegen Barzahlung
En cash with order
Es pagadero con el pedido
It pagamento con l'ordine
Pt pagamento no acto de
requisição

**payable at sight** En
De zahlbar bei Sicht
Es pagadero a la vista
Fr payable à vue
It pagabile a vista
Pt pagável à vista

**payable au porteur** Fr
De an den Inhaber zahlbar
En payable to bearer
Es pagadero al portador
It pagabile al portatore
Pt pagável ao portador

**payable à vue** Fr
De zahlbar bei Sicht
En payable at sight
Es pagadero a la vista
It pagabile a vista
Pt pagável à vista

**payable on demand** En
De zahlbar bei Vorlage
Es pagadero a presentación
Fr payable sur demande
It pagabile a vista
Pt pagável à vista

**payables** pl n En
De fällige Wechsel; Wechsel-
schulden (m pl; f pl)
Es efectos a pagar (m pl)
Fr effets à payer (m pl)
It passività esigibili (f)
Pt contas a pagar (f pl)

**payable sur demande** Fr
De zahlbar bei Vorlage
En payable on demand
Es pagadero a presentación
It pagabile a vista
Pt pagável à vista

**payable to bearer** En
De an den Inhaber zahlbar
Es pagadero al portador
Fr payable au porteur
It pagabile al portatore
Pt pagável ao portador

**pay a deposit** En
De hinterlegen
Es hacer un depósito
Fr donner des arrhès
It versare un deposito
Pt pagar depósito

**pay by monthly (weekly) instalments** En
De monatlich (wochentlich) in Raten zahlen
Es pagar a plazos mensuales (semanales)
Fr payer par termes mensuels (hebdomadaires)
It pagare a rate mensili (setti- manali)
Pt pagar a prestações men- sais (semanais)

**pay day** En
De Zahltag; Abrechnungstag (m)
Es día de pago (m)
Fr jour de paiement (m)
It giorno di paga (m)
Pt dia de recebimento (m)

**payé d'avance** Fr
De vorausbezahlt
En prepaid
Es pagado por adelantado
It pagato in anticipo
Pt pago adiantadamente

**payee** n En
De Zahlungsberechtigte(r) (m)
Es beneficiario (m)
Fr bénéficiaire (m)
It beneficiario (m)
Pt beneficiário de pagamento (m)

**payer** vb Fr
De zahlen
En pay
Es pagar
It pagare
Pt pagar

**payer par termes mensuels (hebdomadaires)** Fr
De monatlich (wochentlich) in Raten zahlen
En pay by monthly (weekly) instalments
Es pagar a plazos mensuales (semanales)
It pagare a rate mensili (setti- manali)
Pt pagar a prestações men- sais (semanais)

**payer une lettre de change** Fr
De einen Wechsel einlösen
En retire a bill
Es recoger una letra
It ritirare un effetto
Pt recuperar uma letra

**payez au porteur** Fr
De zahlen bei Vorlage
En pay to bearer
Es páguese al portador
It pagare al portatore
Pt pagar ao portador

**payment** n En
De Zahlung (f)
Es pago (m)
Fr versement (m)
It pagamento (m)
Pt pagamento (m)

**payment by results** En
De Leistungslohn (m)
Es pago por resultados (m)
Fr salaire au rendement (m)
It pagamento secondo i risul- tati (m)
Pt pagamento relativo as re- sultados (m)

**payment in advance** En
De Vorauszahlung (f)
Es pago por adelantado (m)
Fr paiement anticipé (m)
It pagamento in anticipo (m)
Pt pagamento adiantado (m)

**payment in full** En
De volle Zahlung (f)
Es pago en pleno (m)
Fr libération intégrale (f)
It pagamento in pieno (m)
Pt pagamento completo (m)

**payment in full discharge** En
De Zahlung zum vollen Aus- gleich (f)
Es pago de liberación (m)
Fr paiement libératoire (m)
It pagamento a completa tacitazione (m)
Pt pagamento contra execu- ção completa (m)

**payment on account** En
De Anzahlung (f)
Es pago a cuenta (m)
Fr versement à compte (m)

It   pagamento in conto *(m)*
Pt   pagamento por conta *(m)*

**payment terms** En
De   Zahlungsbedingungen *(f pl)*
Es   condiciones de pago *(f pl)*
Fr   conditions de paiement *(f pl)*
It   condizioni di pagamento *(f pl)*
Pt   condições de pagamento *(f pl)*

**payment under protest** En
De   Protestzahlung *(f)*
Es   pago sobre protesta *(m)*
Fr   paiement sous protêt *(m)*
It   pagamento sotto protesta *(m)*
Pt   pagamento sob protesto *(m)*

**payroll** *n* En
De   Lohnbuch *(n)*
Es   nómina de pago *(f)*
Fr   feuille de paie *(f)*
It   libro paga *(m)*
Pt   folha de salários *(f)*

**pays** *(m) n* Fr
De   Land *(n)*
En   country
Es   país *(m)*
It   paese *(m)*
Pt   país *(m)*

**pays de provenance** *(m)* Fr
De   Herkunftsland *(n)*
En   country of origin
Es   pais de origen *(m)*
It   paese di origine *(m)*
Pt   país de origem *(m)*

**pays en voie de développement** *(m)* Fr
De   Entwicklungsland *(n)*
En   developing country
Es   pais en desarrollo *(m)*
It   paese in via di sviluppo *(m)*
Pt   país em desenvolvimento *(m)*

**pays sous-développés** *(m pl)* Fr
De   unterentwickelte Länder *(n pl)*
En   underdeveloped countries
Es   países en desarrollo *(m pl)*

It   paesi sottosviluppati *(m pl)*
Pt   países subdesenvolvido *(m pl)*

**pay to bearer** En
De   zahlen bei Vorlage
Es   páguese al portador
Fr   payez au porteur
It   pagare al portatore
Pt   pagar ao portador

**peak hours** En
De   Spitzzeit *(f)*
Es   horas punta *(f pl)*
Fr   heures de pointe *(f pl)*
It   ore di punta *(f pl)*
Pt   horas de ponta *(f pl)*

**pechincha** *(f) n* Pt
De   Gelegenheitskauf *(m)*
En   bargain
Es   ganga *(f)*
Fr   occasion *(f)*
It   occasione *(f)*

**pedido** *(m) n* Es, Pt
De   Bestellung; Anforderung *(f)*
En   order; requisition
Fr   commande; demande *(f)*
It   ordine; requisizione *(m f)*

**pedido de exportación** *(m)* Es
De   Exportauftrag *(m)*
En   export order
Fr   commande d'exportation *(f)*
It   ordine per esportazione *(m)*
Pt   encomenda de exportação *(f)*

**pedido por correo** *(m)* Es
De   Auftrag durch die Post *(m)*
En   mail order
Fr   commande par lettre *(f)*
It   ordine per corrispondenza *(f)*
Pt   venda pelo correio *(f)*

**pedir un préstamo** Es
De   entleihen
En   borrow
Fr   emprunter
It   prestire
Pt   contrair empréstimo

**pegno** *(m) n* It
De   Nebenbürgschaft *(f)*
En   security; pledge
Es   fianza *(f)*

Fr   nantissement *(m)*
Pt   fiança *(f)*

**peligro** *(m) n* Es
De   Gefahr *(f)*
En   peril
Fr   péril *(m)*
It   pericolo *(m)*
Pt   perigo *(m)*

**pelletterie** *(f pl) n* It
De   Lederwaren *(f pl)*
En   leather goods
Es   marroquinería *(f)*
Fr   maroquinerie *(f)*
Pt   artigos de cabedal *(m pl)*

**pelo presente** Pt
De   hiermit
En   hereby
Es   por esto
Fr   par la présente
It   col presente; con questo

**penalidade** *(f) n* Pt
De   Strafe *(f)*
En   penalty
Es   multa *(f)*
Fr   pénalité *(f)*
It   penalità *(f)*

**penalità** *(f) n* It
De   Strafe *(f)*
En   penalty
Es   multa *(f)*
Fr   pénalité *(f)*
Pt   penalidade *(f)*

**pénalité** *(f) n* Fr
De   Strafe *(f)*
En   penalty
Es   multa *(f)*
It   penalità *(f)*
Pt   penalidade *(f)*

**penalty** *n* En
De   Strafe *(f)*
Es   multa *(f)*
Fr   pénalité *(f)*
It   penalità *(f)*
Pt   penalidade *(f)*

**penalty clause** En
De   Strafklausel *(f)*
Es   cláusula de multa *(f)*
Fr   clause pénale *(f)*
It   clausola penale *(f)*
Pt   cláusula de penalidade *(f)*

**pendant** *adj* Fr
  De  schwebend
  En  pending
  Es  pendiente
  It  pendente
  Pt  pendente

**pendente** *adj* It, Pt
  De  schwebend
  En  pending
  Es  pendiente
  Fr  pendant

**pendiente** *adj* Es
  De  schwebend
  En  pending
  Fr  pendant
  It  pendente
  Pt  pendente

**pending** *adj* En
  De  schwebend
  Es  pendiente
  Fr  pendant
  It  pendente
  Pt  pendente

**penetración en el mercado** *(f)*
       Es
  De  Markteindringen *(n)*
  En  market penetration
  Fr  pénétration du marché *(f)*
  It  penetrazione nel mercato
       *(f)*
  Pt  ínfiltração no mercado *(f)*

**pénétration du marché** *(f)* Fr
  De  Markteindringen *(n)*
  En  market penetration
  Es  penetración en el mercado
       *(f)*
  It  penetrazione nel mercato
       *(f)*
  Pt  ínfiltração no mercado *(f)*

**penetrazione nel mercato** *(f)* It
  De  Markteindringen *(n)*
  En  market penetration
  Es  penetración en el mercado
       *(f)*
  Fr  pénétration du marché *(f)*
  Pt  ínfiltração no mercado *(f)*

**péniche** *(f)* n Fr
  De  Lastkahn *(m)*
  En  barge
  Es  barcaza *(f)*

  It  chiatta *(f)*
  Pt  barcaça *(f)*

**pensão** *(f)* n Pt
  De  Pension; Rente *(f)*
  En  pension
  Es  pensión *(f)*
  Fr  pension *(f)*
  It  pensione *(f)*

**pensão sem contribuição pré-
       via** *(f)* Pt
  De  Pension ohne Beitrags-
       pflicht *(f)*
  En  noncontributory pension
  Es  pensión sin entregas del
       beneficiario *(f)*
  Fr  pension non-contribuable
       *(f)*
  It  pensione senza contributi
       *(f)*

**pension** *n* En, Fr *(f)*
  De  Pension; Rente *(f)*
  Es  pensión *(f)*
  It  pensione *(f)*
  Pt  pensão *(f)*

**pensión** *(f)* n Es
  De  Pension; Rente *(f)*
  En  pension
  Fr  pension *(f)*
  It  pensione *(f)*
  Pt  pensão *(f)*

**Pension** *(f)* n De
  En  pension
  Es  pensión *(f)*
  Fr  pension *(f)*
  It  pensione *(f)*
  Pt  pensão *(f)*

**pensionado** *(m)* n Es
  De  Rentner *(m)*
  En  pensioner
  Fr  pensionnaire *(m)*
  It  pensionato *(m)*
  Pt  pensionista *(m)*

**pensionato** *(m)* n It
  De  Rentner *(m)*
  En  pensioner
  Es  pensionado; pensionista
       *(m)*
  Fr  pensionnaire *(m)*
  Pt  pensionista *(m)*

**pensione** *(f)* n It
  De  Pension; Rente *(f)*
  En  pension
  Es  pensión *(f)*
  Fr  pension *(f)*
  Pt  pensão *(f)*

**pensione a contributi** *(f)* It
  De  Kassenpension *(f)*
  En  contributory pension
  Es  retiro contributivo *(m)*
  Fr  retraite de régime à cotisa-
       tions *(f)*
  Pt  reforma de contribuição
       prévia *(f)*

**pensioner** *n* En
  De  Rentner *(m)*
  Es  pensionado; pensionista
       *(m)*
  Fr  pensionnaire *(m)*
  It  pensionato *(m)*
  Pt  pensionista *(m)*

**pensione senza contributi** *(f)*
       It
  De  Pension ohne Beitrags-
       pflicht *(f)*
  En  noncontributory pension
  Es  pensión sin entregas del
       beneficiario *(f)*
  Fr  pension non-contribuable
       *(f)*
  Pt  pensão sem contribuição
       prévia *(f)*

**pensionista** *(m)* n Es, Pt
  De  Rentner *(m)*
  En  pensioner
  Fr  pensionnaire *(m)*
  It  pensionato *(m)*

**pensionnaire** *(m)* n Fr
  De  Rentner *(m)*
  En  pensioner
  Es  pensionado; pensionista
       *(m)*
  It  pensionato *(m)*
  Pt  pensionista *(m)*

**pension non-contribuable** *(f)*
       Fr
  De  Pension ohne Beitrags-
       pflicht *(f)*
  En  noncontributory pension
  Es  pensión sin entregas del
       beneficiario *(f)*

It    pensione senza contributi
      (f)
Pt    pensão sem contribuição
      prévia (f)

**pensión sin entregas del
beneficiario** (f) Es
De    Pension ohne Beitrags-
      pflicht (f)
En    noncontributory pension
Fr    pension non-contribuable
      (f)
It    pensione senza contributi
      (f)
Pt    pensão sem contribuição
      prévia (f)

**per capita** En, Pt
De    pro Kopf
Es    por cabeza
Fr    par tête
It    per testa

**per cent** En
De    prozent
Es    por ciento
Fr    pour cent
It    per cento
Pt    por cento

**percentage** n En
De    Prozentsatz (m)
Es    porcentaje (m)
Fr    pourcentage (m)
It    percentuale (f)
Pt    percentagem (f)

**percentagem** (f) n Pt
De    Prozentsatz (m)
En    percentage
Es    porcentaje (m)
Fr    pourcentage (m)
It    percentuale (f)

**per cento** It
De    prozent
En    per cent
Es    por ciento
Fr    pour cent
Pt    por cento

**percentuale** (f) n It
De    Prozentsatz (m)
En    percentage
Es    porcentaje (m)
Fr    pourcentage (m)
Pt    percentagem (f)

**percepteur** (des impôts) (m) Fr
De    Steuereinnehmer (m)
En    tax collector
Es    recaudador de impuestos
      (m)
It    esattore delle imposte (m)
Pt    cobrador de impostos (m)

**per contra** En
De    als Gegenrechnung
Es    en contrapartida
Fr    en contrepartie; par contre
It    in contropartita
Pt    em contrapartida

**perda** (f) n Pt
De    Verlust (m)
En    loss
Es    pérdida (f)
Fr    perte (f)
It    perdita (f)

**perda avultada** (f) Pt
De    schwere Verluste (m pl)
En    heavy loss
Es    fuerte pérdida; pérdida
      sensible (f)
Fr    lourde perte (f)
It    forte perdita (f)

**perda de capital** (f) Pt
De    Kapitalverlust (m)
En    capital loss
Es    pérdida de capital (f)
Fr    perte de capital (f)
It    perdita di capitale (f)

**perda de lucros** (f) Pt
De    Gewinnausfall (m)
En    loss of profits
Es    lucro cesante (m)
Fr    perte de bénéfices (f)
It    perdita di utili (f)

**perda em impostos** (f) Pt
De    Steuerverlust (m)
En    tax loss
Es    pérdida fiscal (f)
Fr    perte fiscale (f)
It    perdita a scopi fiscali (f)

**perda no papel** (f) Pt
De    imaginärer Verlust (m)
En    paper loss
Es    pérdida por realizar (f)
Fr    perte fictive (f)
It    perdita sulla carta (f)

**perda por consequência** (f) Pt
De    Folgeschaden (m)
En    consequential loss
Es    pérdida indirecta (f)
Fr    perte indirect (f)
It    perdita indiretta (f)

**perda total construtiva** (f) Pt
De    angenommener Totalver-
      lust (m)
En    constructive total loss
Es    pérdida total constructiva
      (f)
Fr    perte réputée totale (f)
It    perdita presunta totale (f)

**perda total efectiva** (f) Pt
De    wirklicher Totalverlust (m)
En    actual total loss
Es    pérdida total efectiva (f)
Fr    perte totale effective (f)
It    perdita totale assoluta (f)

**pérdida** (f) n Es
De    Verlust (m)
En    loss
Fr    perte (f)
It    perdita (f)
Pt    perda (f)

**pérdida de capital** (f) Es
De    Kapitalverlust (m)
En    capital loss
Fr    perte de capital (f)
It    perdita di capitale (f)
Pt    perda de capital (f)

**pérdida fiscal** (f) Es
De    Steuerverlust (m)
En    tax loss
Fr    perte fiscale (f)
It    perdita a scopi fiscali (f)
Pt    perda em impostos (f)

**pérdida indirecta** (f) Es
De    Folgeschaden (m)
En    consequential loss
Fr    perte indirect (f)
It    perdita indiretta (f)
Pt    perda por consequência (f)

**pérdida por realizar** (f) Es
De    imaginärer Verlust (m)
En    paper loss
Fr    perte fictive (f)
It    perdita sulla carta (f)
Pt    perda no papel (f)

**pérdida total constructiva** *(f)*
Es
De angenommener Totalver-
   lust *(m)*
En constructive total loss
Fr perte réputée totale *(f)*
It perdita presunta totale *(f)*
Pt perda total construtiva *(f)*

**pérdida total efectiva** *(f)* Es
De wirklicher Totalverlust *(m)*
En actual total loss
Fr perte totale effective *(f)*
It perdita totale assoluta *(f)*
Pt perda total efectiva *(f)*

**perdita** *(f)* n It
De Verlust *(m)*
En loss
Es pérdida *(f)*
Fr perte *(f)*
Pt perda *(f)*

**perdita a scopi fiscali** *(f)* It
De Steuerverlust *(m)*
En tax loss
Es pérdida fiscal *(f)*
Fr perte fiscale *(f)*
Pt perda em impostos *(f)*

**perdita di capitale** *(f)* It
De Kapitalverlust *(m)*
En capital loss
Es pérdida de capital *(f)*
Fr perte de capital *(f)*
Pt perda de capital *(f)*

**perdita di utili** *(f)* It
De Gewinnausfall *(m)*
En loss of profits
Es lucro cesante *(m)*
Fr perte de bénéfices *(f)*
Pt perda de lucros *(f)*

**perdita indiretta** *(f)* It
De Folgeschaden *(m)*
En consequential loss
Es pérdida indirecta *(f)*
Fr perte indirect *(f)*
Pt perda por consequência *(f)*

**perdita presunta totale** *(f)* It
De angenommener Totalver-
   lust *(m)*
En constructive total loss
Es pérdida total constructiva
   *(f)*

Fr perte réputée totale *(f)*
Pt perda total construtiva *(f)*

**perdita sulla carta** *(f)* It
De imaginärer Verlust *(m)*
En paper loss
Es pérdida por realizar *(f)*
Fr perte fictive *(f)*
Pt perda no papel *(f)*

**perdita totale assoluta** *(f)* It
De wirklicher Totalverlust *(m)*
En actual total loss
Es pérdida total efectiva *(f)*
Fr perte totale effective *(f)*
Pt perda total efectiva *(f)*

**perfezionare un atto** It
De eine Urkunde unterzeichnen
En execute a deed
Es firmar una escritura
Fr passer un acte
Pt dar execução a um título
   legal

**per Flugpost** De
En by air
Es por avión
Fr par avion
It per via aerea
Pt por avião

**perforación en clave** *(f)* Es
De manueller Locher *(m)*
En key-punch
Fr perforatrice à clavier *(f)*
It perforatore *(f)*
Pt perforador *(m)*

**perforador** *(m)* Pt
De manueller Locher *(m)*
En key-punch
Es perforación en clave *(f)*
Fr perforatrice à clavier *(f)*
It perforatore *(f)*

**perforatore** *(f)* It
De manueller Locher *(m)*
En key-punch
Es perforación en clave *(f)*
Fr perforatrice à clavier *(f)*
Pt perforador *(m)*

**perforatrice à clavier** *(f)* Fr
De manueller Locher *(m)*
En key-punch
Es perforación en clave *(f)*

It perforatore *(f)*
Pt perforador *(m)*

**performance** n En
De Erfüllung; Vollstreckung *(f)*
Es ejecución *(f)*
Fr exécution *(f)*
It esecuzione *(f)*
Pt desempenho *(m)*

**pergunta** *(f)* n Pt
De Nachfrage *(f)*
En inquiry
Es demanda *(f)*
Fr demande *(f)*
It domanda *(f)*

**pericolo** *(m)* n It
De Gefahr *(f)*
En peril
Es peligro *(m)*
Fr péril *(m)*
Pt perigo *(m)*

**perigo** *(m)* n Pt
De Gefahr *(f)*
En peril
Es peligro *(m)*
Fr péril *(m)*
It pericolo *(m)*

**peril** n En
De Gefahr *(f)*
Es peligro *(m)*
Fr péril *(m)*
It pericolo *(m)*
Pt perigo *(m)*

**péril** *(m)* n Fr
De Gefahr *(f)*
En peril
Es peligro *(m)*
It pericolo *(m)*
Pt perigo *(m)*

**périmé** Fr
De verfallen
En out of date; expired
Es vencido
It scaduto
Pt vencido

**perishable goods** En
De leicht verderbliche Waren *(f*
   *pl)*
Es mercancías perecederas *(f*
   *pl)*

Fr marchandises périssables (f pl)
It merci deperibili (f pl)
Pt mercadorias perecíveis (f pl)

**erito** (m) n Es, It, Pt
De Sachverständige(r); Fachmann (m)
En expert; specialist
Fr spécialiste; expert (m)

**erito de administração** (m) Pt
De Geschäftsführungsberater (m)
En management consultant
Es asesor administrativo (m)
Fr ingénieur-conseil en organisation (m)
It consulente di direzione aziendale (m)

**erito de publicidade** (m) Pt
De Werbeberater (m)
En advertising consultant
Es consultor de publicidad (m)
Fr conseil en publicité (m)
It consulente di pubblicità (m)

**erito misuratore** (m) It
De Massenberechner (m)
En quantity surveyor
Es medidor de contidades de obra (m)
Fr métreur-vérificateur (m)
Pt perito na avaliação de quantidades (m)

**erito na avaliação de quantidades** (m) Pt
De Massenberechner (m)
En quantity surveyor
Es medidor de contidades de obra (m)
Fr métreur-vérificateur (m)
It perito misuratore (m)

**perizia** (f) n It
De Sachverständigengutachten (n)
En expert's report
Es informe del especialista (m)
Fr expertise (f)
Pt relatório do perito (m)

**permesso** (m) n It
De Erlaubnis; Genehmigung (f)
En permit

Es permiso (m)
Fr permis (m)
Pt autorização (f)

**permesso d'esportazione** (m) It
De Ausfuhrgenehmigung (f)
En export permit
Es permiso de exportación (m)
Fr autorisation d'exporter (f)
Pt licença de exportação (f)

**permesso d'importazione** (m) It
De Einfuhrgenehmigung (f)
En import licence
Es permiso de importación (m)
Fr licence d'importation (f)
Pt licença de importação (f)

**permesso di lavoro** (m) It
De Arbeitserlaubnis (f)
En work permit
Es permiso de trabajo (m)
Fr permis de travail (m)
Pt carta de trabalho (f)

**permis** (m) n Fr
De Erlaubnis; Genehmigung (f)
En permit
Es permiso (m)
It permesso (m)
Pt autorização (f)

**permis de travail** (m) Fr
De Arbeitserlaubnis (f)
En work permit
Es permiso de trabajo (m)
It permesso di lavoro (m)
Pt carta de trabalho (f)

**permiso** (m) n Es
De Erlaubnis; Genehmigung (f)
En permit
Fr permis (m)
It permesso (m)
Pt autorização (f)

**permiso de exportación** (m) Es
De Ausfuhrgenehmigung (f)
En export permit
Fr autorisation d'exporter (f)
It permesso d'esportazione (m)
Pt licença de exportação (f)

**permiso de importación** (m) Es
De Einfuhrgenehmigung (f)
En import licence
Fr licence d'importation (f)
It permesso d'importazione (m)
Pt licença de importação (f)

**permiso de trabajo** (m) Es
De Arbeitserlaubnis (f)
En work permit
Fr permis de travail (m)
It permesso di lavoro (m)
Pt carta de trabalho (f)

**permit** n En
De Erlaubnis; Genehmigung (f)
Es permiso (m)
Fr permis (m)
It permesso (m)
Pt autorização (f)

**per Nachnahme** De
En charges forward; cash on delivery
Es entrega contra reembolso
Fr frais à percevoir à la livraison
It spese assegnate; pagamento alla consegna
Pt entrega contra reembolso

**perpetual debenture** En
De Dauerschuldverschreibung (f)
Es obligación a perpetuidad (f)
Fr obligation perpétuelle (f)
It obbligazione perpetua (f)
Pt obrigação de perenidade (f)

**perseguir** vb Es, Pt
De weiterverfolgen
En follow up
Fr poursuivre
It seguitare

**personal** (m) n Es
De Personal (n)
En personnel
Fr personnel (m)
It personale (m)
Pt pessoal (m)

**Personal** (n) n De
En personnel
Es personal (m)
Fr personnel (m)

It  personale *(m)*
Pt  pessoal *(m)*

**personal assistant** (PA) En
Am administrative assistant
De  persönlicher Assistent *(m)*
Es  asistente privado *(m)*
Fr  fonctionnel *(m)*
It  assistente privato *(m)*
Pt  secretário *(m)*

**Personalausweis** *(m) n* De
En  identity card
Es  carnet de identidad *(m)*
Fr  carte d'identité *(f)*
It  carta d'identità *(f)*
Pt  bilhete de identidade *(m)*

**Personalchef** *(m) n* De
En  personnel manager
Es  jefe de personal *(m)*
Fr  chef du personnel *(m)*
It  direttore del personale *(m)*
Pt  chefe do pessoal *(m)*

**personal de ventas** *(m)* Es
De  Verkaufspersonal *(n)*
En  sales force
Fr  personnel de vente *(m)*
It  forze di vendita *(f pl)*
Pt  pessoal de vendas *(m)*

**personale** *(m) n* It
De  Personal *(n)*
En  personnel
Es  personal *(m)*
Fr  personnel *(m)*
Pt  pessoal *(m)*

**persönlicher Assistent** *(m)* De
En  personal assistant (PA)
Am administrative assistant
Es  asistente privado *(m)*
Fr  fonctionnel *(m)*
It  assistente privato *(m)*
Pt  secretário *(m)*

**personnel** *n* En, Fr *(m)*
De  Personal *(n)*
Es  personal *(m)*
It  personale *(m)*
Pt  pessoal *(m)*

**personnel de vente** *(m)* Fr
De  Verkaufspersonal *(n)*
En  sales force
Es  personal de ventas *(m)*

It  forze di vendita *(f pl)*
Pt  pessoal de vendas *(m)*

**personnel manager** En
De  Personalchef *(m)*
Es  jefe de personal *(m)*
Fr  chef du personnel *(m)*
It  direttore del personale *(m)*
Pt  chefe do pessoal *(m)*

**perte** *(f) n* Fr
De  Verlust *(m)*
En  loss
Es  pérdida *(f)*
It  perdita *(f)*
Pt  perda *(f)*

**perte de bénéfices** *(f)* Fr
De  Gewinnausfall *(m)*
En  loss of profits
Es  lucro cesante *(m)*
It  perdita di utili *(f)*
Pt  perda de lucros *(f)*

**perte de capital** *(f)* Fr
De  Kapitalverlust *(m)*
En  capital loss
Es  pérdida de capital *(f)*
It  perdita di capitale *(f)*
Pt  perda de capital *(f)*

**perte fictive** *(f)* Fr
De  imaginärer Verlust *(m)*
En  paper loss
Es  pérdida por realizar *(f)*
It  perdita sulla carta *(f)*
Pt  perda no papel *(f)*

**perte fiscale** *(f)* Fr
De  Steuerverlust *(m)*
En  tax loss
Es  pérdida fiscal *(f)*
It  perdita a scopi fiscali *(f)*
Pt  perda em impostos *(f)*

**perte indirect** *(f)* Fr
De  Folgeschaden *(m)*
En  consequential loss
Es  pérdida indirecta *(f)*
It  perdita indiretta *(f)*
Pt  perda por consequência *(f)*

**perte réputée totale** *(f)* Fr
De  angenommener Totalverlust *(m)*
En  constructive total loss
Es  pérdida total constructiva *(f)*

It  perdita presunta totale *(f)*
Pt  perda total construtiva *(f)*

**per testa** It
De  pro Kopf
En  per capita
Es  por cabeza
Fr  par tête
Pt  per capita

**perte totale effective** *(f)* Fr
De  wirklicher Totalverlust *(m)*
En  actual total loss
Es  pérdida total efectiva *(f)*
It  perdita totale assoluta *(f)*
Pt  perda total efectiva *(f)*

**per via aerea** It
De  per Flugpost
En  by air
Es  por avión
Fr  par avion
Pt  por avião

**pesado** *adj* Es, Pt
De  schwer
En  heavy
Fr  lourd; fort
It  pesante; forte

**pesante** *adj* It
De  schwer
En  heavy
Es  pesado; fuerte
Fr  lourd; fort
Pt  pesado

**pesar** *vb* Es, Pt
De  wiegen
En  weigh
Fr  peser
It  pesare

**pesare** *vb* It
De  wiegen
En  weigh
Es  pesar
Fr  peser
Pt  pesar

**pescaggio** *(m) n* It
De  Tiefgang *(m)*
En  draught
Es  calado *(m)*
Fr  tirant d'eau *(m)*
Pt  calado *(m)*

**peser** *vb* Fr
  De wiegen
  En weigh
  Es pesar
  It pesare
  Pt pesar

**peso** *(m) n* Es, It, Pt
  De Gewicht *(n)*
  En weight
  Fr poids *(m)*

**peso bruto** *(m)* Es, Pt
  De Bruttogewicht *(n)*
  En gross weight
  Fr poids brut *(m)*
  It peso lordo *(m)*

**peso excedente** *(m)* Es
  De Übergewicht *(n)*
  En excess weight
  Fr excédent de poids *(m)*
  It eccedenza di peso *(f)*
  Pt excesso de peso *(m)*

**peso líquido** *(m)* Pt
  De Reingewicht *(n)*
  En net weight
  Es peso neto *(m)*
  Fr poids net *(m)*
  It peso netto *(m)*

**peso lordo** *(m)* It
  De Bruttogewicht *(n)*
  En gross weight
  Es peso bruto *(m)*
  Fr poids brut *(m)*
  Pt peso bruto *(m)*

**peso morto** *(m)* It, Pt
  De Tragfähigkeit *(f)*
  En deadweight
  Es peso muerto *(m)*
  Fr port en lourd *(m)*

**peso muerto** *(m)* Es
  De Tragfähigkeit *(f)*
  En deadweight
  Fr port en lourd *(m)*
  It peso morto *(m)*
  Pt peso morto *(m)*

**peso neto** *(m)* Es
  De Reingewicht *(n)*
  En net weight
  Fr poids net *(m)*
  It peso netto *(m)*
  Pt peso líquido *(m)*

**peso netto** *(m)* It
  De Reingewicht *(n)*
  En net weight
  Es peso neto *(m)*
  Fr poids net *(m)*
  Pt peso líquido *(m)*

**peso o cubicaje** Es
  De Mass oder Gewicht
  En weight or measurement
  Fr poids ou mesure
  It peso o volume
  Pt peso ou medida

**peso ou medida** Pt
  De Mass oder Gewicht
  En weight or measurement
  Es peso o cubicaje
  Fr poids ou mesure
  It peso o volume

**peso o volume** It
  De Mass oder Gewicht
  En weight or measurement
  Es peso o cubicaje
  Fr poids ou mesure
  Pt peso ou medida

**pesquisa de mercado** *(f)* Pt
  De Marktforschung *(f)*
  En market research
  Es investigación del mercado *(f)*
  Fr étude du marché *(f)*
  It indagine di mercato *(f)*

**pessoal** *(m) n* Pt
  De Personal *(n)*
  En personnel
  Es personal *(m)*
  Fr personnel *(m)*
  It personale *(m)*

**pessoal de vendas** *(m)* Pt
  De Verkaufspersonal *(n)*
  En sales force
  Es personal de ventas *(m)*
  Fr personnel de vente *(m)*
  It forze di vendita *(f pl)*

**petite annonce** *(f)* Fr
  De Kleinanzeige *(f)*
  En classified advertisement
  Es anuncio por palabras *(m)*
  It piccola pubblicità *(f)*
  Pt anúncios classificados *(m pl)*

**petite caisse** *(f)* Fr
  De kleine Kasse *(f)*
  En petty cash
  Es caja menor *(f)*
  It piccola cassa *(f)*
  Pt despesas de caixa *(f pl)*

**petite monnaie** *(f)* Fr
  De Kleingeld *(n)*
  En small change
  Es moneda suelta *(f)*
  It spiccioli *(m pl)*
  Pt troco miúdo *(m)*

**petrodólares** *(m pl) n* Es
  De Öldollar *(m pl)*
  En petrodollars
  Fr dollars pétroliers *(m pl)*
  It petrodollari *(m pl)*
  Pt petrodólares *(m pl)*

**petrodólares** *(m pl) n* Pt
  De Öldollar *(m pl)*
  En petrodollars
  Es petrodólares *(m pl)*
  Fr dollars pétroliers *(m pl)*
  It petrodollari *(m pl)*

**petrodollari** *(m pl) n* It
  De Öldollar *(m pl)*
  En petrodollars
  Es petrodólares *(m pl)*
  Fr dollars pétroliers *(m pl)*
  Pt petrodólares *(m pl)*

**petrodollars** *pl n* En
  De Öldollar *(m pl)*
  Es petrodólares *(m pl)*
  Fr dollars pétroliers *(m pl)*
  It petrodollari *(m pl)*
  Pt petrodólares *(m pl)*

**petróleo combustível** *(m)* Pt
  De Heizöl *(n)*
  En fuel oil
  Es fuel-oil *(m)*
  Fr mazout *(m)*
  It petrolio da ardere *(m)*

**petrolio da ardere** *(m)* It
  De Heizöl *(n)*
  En fuel oil
  Es fuel-oil *(m)*
  Fr mazout *(m)*
  Pt petróleo combustível *(m)*

**petty cash** En
De kleine Kasse *(f)*
Es caja menor *(f)*
Fr petite caisse *(f)*
It piccola cassa *(f)*
Pt despesas de caixa *(f pl)*

**pezza d'appoggio** *(f)* It
De Belegstück *(n)*
En voucher
Es pieza justificativa *(f)*
Fr pièce justificative; fiche *(f)*
Pt vale *(m)*

**pezzo** *(m)* n It
De Parzelle *(f)*
En parcel (of land)
Am plot
Es parcela *(f)*
Fr parcelle *(f)*
Pt parcela *(f)*

**Pfandleiher** *(m)* n De
En pawnbroker
Es prestamista *(m)*
Fr prêteur sur gage *(m)*
It prestatore su pegno *(m)*
Pt prestamista *(m)*

**Pfandrecht** *(n)* n De
En lien
Es derecho de retencíon *(m)*
Fr droit de retention *(m)*
It diritto de sequestro *(m)*
Pt direito de retençáo *(m)*

**Pferdestärke** (PS) *(f)* n De
En horse-power (hp)
Es caballo de vapor (cv) *(m)*
Fr cheval-vapeur (ch-v) *(m)*
It cavallo *(m)*
Pt cavalo-vapor *(m)*

**Pfund sterling** *(n)* De
En pound sterling
Es libra esterlina *(f)*
Fr livre sterling *(f)*
It lira sterlina *(f)*
Pt libra esterlina *(f)*

**phantom operation** Am
En bogus company
De Schwindelgesellschaft *(f)*
Es sociedad fantasma *(f)*
Fr société fantôme *(f)*
It società fasulla *(f)*
Pt sociedade fantasma *(f)*

**piano di stivaggio** *(m)* It
De Ladeplan *(m)*
En stowage plan
Es plan de estiba *(m)*
Fr plan d'arrimage *(m)*
Pt plano de estiva *(m)*

**pianterreno** *(m)* n It
De Erdgeschoss *(n)*
En ground floor
Es planta baja *(f)*
Fr rez-de-chaussée *(m)*
Pt rés-do-chão *(m)*

**piatto** *adj* It
De flach
En flat
Es llano; plano
Fr plat; uniforme
Pt plano; liso

**picchetto** *(m)* n It
De Posten *(m)*
En picket
Es piquete *(m)*
Fr piquet *(m)*
Pt piquete *(m)*

**piccola cassa** *(f)* It
De kleine Kasse *(f)*
En petty cash
Es caja menor *(f)*
Fr petite caisse *(f)*
Pt despesas de caixa *(f pl)*

**piccola pubblicità** *(f)* It
De Kleinanzeige *(f)*
En classified advertisement
Es anuncio por palabras *(m)*
Fr petite annonce *(f)*
Pt anúncios classificados *(m pl)*

**picket** n En
De Posten *(m)*
Es piquete *(m)*
Fr piquet *(m)*
It picchetto *(m)*
Pt piquete *(m)*

**pièce** (de monnaie) *(f)* Fr
De Münze *(f)*
En coin
Es moneda *(f)*
It moneta *(f)*
Pt moeda *(f)*

**pièce justificative** *(f)* Fr
De Belegstück *(n)*
En voucher
Es pieza justificativa *(f)*
It pezza d'appoggio *(f)*
Pt vale *(m)*

**piecework** n En
De Akkordarbeit *(f)*
Es trabajo a destajo *(m)*
Fr travail à la tâche *(m)*
It lavoro a cottimo *(m)*
Pt trabalho por peça *(m)*

**piel de imitación** *(f)* Es
De Kunstleder *(n)*
En imitation leather
Fr similicuir *(m)*
It finta pelle *(f)*
Pt cabedal de imitação *(m)*

**piena occupazione** *(f)* It
De Vollbeschäftigung *(f)*
En full employment
Es pleno empleo *(m)*
Fr plein emploi *(m)*
Pt pleno emprego *(m)*

**pieno** *adj* It
De voll
En full
Es lleno
Fr plein
Pt cheio

**pier** n Am
En quay
De Kai *(m)*
Es muelle *(m)*
Fr quai *(m)*
It banchina *(f)*
Pt cais *(m)*

**pieza justificativa** *(f)* Es
De Belegstück *(n)*
En voucher
Fr pièce justificative; fiche *(f)*
It pezza d'appoggio *(f)*
Pt vale *(m)*

**pigione** *(f)* n It
De Miete *(f)*
En rent
Es alquiler *(m)*
Fr loyer *(m)*
Pt renda *(f)*

**pig-iron** *n* En
De Roheisen *(n)*
Es hierro bruto *(m)*
Fr fer en gueuse *(m)*
It pane di ghisa *(m)*
Pt ferro em bruto *(m)*

**pilot** (sea) *n* En
De Lotse *(m)*
Es piloto *(m)*
Fr pilote *(m)*
It pilota *(m)*
Pt piloto *(m)*

**pilota** *(m)* *n* It
De Lotse *(m)*
En (sea) pilot
Es piloto *(m)*
Fr pilote *(m)*
Pt piloto *(m)*

**pilote** *(m)* *n* Fr
De Lotse *(m)*
En (sea) pilot
Es piloto *(m)*
It pilota *(m)*
Pt piloto *(m)*

**piloto** *(m)* *n* Es, Pt
De Lotse *(m)*
En (sea) pilot
Fr pilote *(m)*
It pilota *(m)*

**pilot plant** En
De Musteranlage *(f)*
Es instalación piloto *(f)*
Fr installation témoine *(f)*
It impianto piloto *(m)*
Pt instalação piloto *(f)*

**piquet** *(m)* *n* Fr
De Posten *(m)*
En picket
Es piquete *(m)*
It picchetto *(m)*
Pt piquete *(m)*

**piquete** *(m)* *n* Es, Pt
De Posten *(m)*
En picket
Fr piquet *(m)*
It picchetto *(m)*

**piso amueblado** *(m)* Es
De möblierte Mietwohnung *(f)*
En furnished flat
Am furnished apartment

Fr appartement meublé *(m)*
It appartamento ammobigliato *(m)*
Pt andar mobilado *(m)*

**piso con servicio incluido** *(m)* Es
De Etagenwohnung mit Bedienung *(f)*
En service flat
Fr appartement avec service *(m)*
It appartamento con servizio *(m)*
Pt andar com serviço incluido *(m)*

**piso independiente completo** *(m)* Es
De Einfamilienwohnung *(f)*
En self-contained flat
Fr appartement indépendant *(m)*
It appartamento indipendente *(m)*
Pt andar independente *(m)*

**placcato in oro** It
De vergoldet
En gold-plated
Es chapado en oro
Fr plaqué d'or
Pt laminado a ouro

**plan** *n* En; Es, Fr *(m)*
De Plan *(m)*
It progetto; piano *(m)*
Pt plano *(m)*

**Plan** *(m)* *n* De
En plan
Es plan *(m)*
Fr projet; plan *(m)*
It progetto; piano *(m)*
Pt plano *(m)*

**plan d'arrimage** *(m)* Fr
De Ladeplan *(m)*
En stowage plan
Es plan de estiba *(m)*
It piano di stivaggio *(m)*
Pt plano de estiva *(m)*

**plan de estiba** *(m)* Es
De Ladeplan *(m)*
En stowage plan
Fr plan d'arrimage *(m)*

It piano di stivaggio *(m)*
Pt plano de estiva *(m)*

**plan de propaganda** *(m)* Es
De Werbeplan *(m)*
En advertising schedule
Fr programme des annonces *(m)*
It programma delle inserzioni *(m)*
Pt plano de campanha publicitária *(m)*

**plan de renta** *(m)* Es
De Lohnpolitik *(f)*
En incomes policy
Fr politique des salaires *(f)*
It politica dei redditi *(f)*
Pt programa salários *(f)*

**planned economy** En
De Planwirtschaft *(f)*
Es economía planificada *(f)*
Fr économie planifiée *(f)*
It economia pianificata *(f)*
Pt economia planeada *(f)*

**plano** *adj* Es, Pt
De flach
En flat
Fr plat; uniforme
It piatto

**plano** *(m)* *n* Pt
De Plan *(m)*
En plan
Es plan *(m)*
Fr plan; projet *(m)*
It piano; progetto *(m)*

**plano de campanha publicitária** *(m)* Pt
De Werbeplan *(m)*
En advertising schedule
Es plan de propaganda *(m)*
Fr programme des annonces *(m)*
It programma delle inserzioni *(m)*

**plano de estiva** *(m)* Pt
De Ladeplan *(m)*
En stowage plan
Es plan de estiba *(m)*
Fr plan d'arrimage *(m)*
It piano di stivaggio *(m)*

**plant** (industrial) n En
De Anlage (f)
Es planta; instalación (f)
Fr appareil; installation (m f)
It impianto; macchinario (m)
Pt instalação fabril (f)

**planta** (f) n Es
De Anlage (f)
En plant
Fr appareil; installation (m f)
It impianto; macchinario (m)
Pt instalação fabril (f)

**planta baja** (f) Es
De Erdgeschoss (n)
En ground floor
Fr rez-de-chaussée (m)
It pianterreno (m)
Pt rés-do-chão (m)

**Planungsgewinn** (m) n De
En betterment
Es plusvalía (f)
Fr appréciation (f)
It plus-valore (m)
Pt melhoria (f)

**Planwirtschaft** (f) n De
En planned economy
Es economía planificada (f)
Fr économie planifiée (f)
It economia pianificata (f)
Pt economia planeada (f)

**plaqué d'or** Fr
De vergoldet
En gold-plated
Es chapado en oro
It placcato in oro
Pt laminado a ouro

**plat** adj Fr
De flach
En flat
Es llano; plano
It piatto
Pt plano; liso

**plate glass** En
De Spiegelglas (n)
Es vidrio plano pulido (m)
Fr verre à glaces; glace de vitrage (m f)
It cristallo (m)
Pt chapa de vidro (f)

**plazo** (m) n Es
De Rate (f)
En instalment
Fr acompte (m)
It rata (f)
Pt prestação (f)

**please forward** En
De bitte nachsenden
Es se ruega hacer seguir
Fr prière de faire suivre
It far proseguire
Pt é favor enviar

**plein** adj Fr
De voll
En full
Es lleno
It pieno
Pt cheio

**plein emploi** (m) Fr
De Vollbeschäftigung (f)
En full employment
Es pleno empleo (m)
It piena occupazione (f)
Pt pleno emprego (m)

**pleito** (m) n Es
De Prozess; Klage (m f)
En legal action; lawsuit
Fr action juridique; procès (f m)
It processo (m)
Pt acção judicial (f)

**plenamente suscrito** Es
De vollgezeichnet
En fully subscribed
Fr intégralement souscrit
It interamènte sottoscritto
Pt totalmente subscrito

**pleno empleo** (m) Es
De Vollbeschäftigung (f)
En full employment
Fr plein emploi (m)
It piena occupazione (f)
Pt pleno emprego (m)

**pleno emprego** (m) Pt
De Vollbeschäftigung (f)
En full employment
Es pleno empleo (m)
Fr plein emploi (m)
It piena occupazione (f)

**plot** n Am
En parcel (of land)
De Parzelle (f)
Es parcela (f)
Fr parcelle (f)
It pezzo; lotto (m)
Pt parcela (f)

**plus amples renseignements**
(m pl) Fr
De nähere Umstände (m pl)
En further particulars
Es más detalles (m pl)
It ulteriori particolari (m pl)
Pt pormenores adicionais (m pl)

**plus grande bonne foie** (f) Fr
De äusserst guter Glaube (m)
En utmost good faith
Es máxima buena fé (f)
It massima buona fede (f)
Pt máxima boa-fé (f)

**plus offrant enchérisseur** (m) Fr
De Meistbietende(r) (m)
En highest bidder
Es ofertante más alto (m)
It miglior offerente (m)
Pt proponente mais elevado (m)

**plusvalía** (f) n Es
De Planungsgewinn (m)
En betterment
Fr appréciation (f)
It plus-valore (m)
Pt melhoria (f)

**plus-valore** (m) n It
De Planungsgewinn (m)
En betterment
Es plusvalía (f)
Fr appréciation (f)
Pt melhoria (f)

**plusvalore di capitale** (m pl) It
De Kapitalgewinn (n)
En capital gains
Es beneficios sobre capital (m pl)
Fr gains en capital (m pl)
Pt lucros de capital (m pl)

**población** (f) n Es
De Bevölkerung (f)
En population

Fr population *(f)*
It popolazione *(f)*
Pt população *(f)*

**poco proficuo** It
De unvorteilhaft
En unprofitable
Es nada lucrátivo
Fr sans profit
Pt não lucrativo

**poder** *(m) n* Es
De Vollmacht *(f)*
En power of attorney
Fr pouvoirs; procuration *(m pl; f)*
It procura *(f)*
Pt poderes de procuração *(m pl)*

**poder de compra** *(m)* Es, Pt
De Kaufkraft *(f)*
En purchasing power
Fr pouvoir d´achat *(m)*
It potere d´acquisto *(m)*

**poder de negociación** *(m)* Es
De Verhandlungsposition *(f)*
En bargaining power
Fr pouvoir de négociation *(m)*
It potere di contrattare *(m)*
Pt poder de regateio *(m)*

**poder de regateio** *(m)* Pt
De Verhandlungsposition *(f)*
En bargaining power
Es poder de negociación *(m)*
Fr pouvoir de négociation *(m)*
It potere di contrattare *(m)*

**poderes de procuração** *(m pl)* Pt
De Vollmacht *(f)*
En power of attorney
Es poder *(m)*
Fr pouvoirs; procuration *(m pl; f)*
It procura *(f)*

**poder procuración** *(m)* Es
De Stellvertretung *(f)*
En proxy
Fr procuration *(f)*
It procura *(f)*
Pt procuração *(f)*

**poids** *(m) n* Fr
De Gewicht *(n)*
En weight
Es peso *(m)*
It peso *(m)*
Pt peso *(m)*

**poids brut** *(m)* Fr
De Bruttogewicht *(n)*
En gross weight
Es peso bruto *(m)*
It peso lordo *(m)*
Pt peso bruto *(m)*

**poids net** *(m)* Fr
De Reingewicht *(n)*
En net weight
Es peso neto *(m)*
It peso netto *(m)*
Pt peso líquido *(m)*

**poids ou mesure** Fr
De Mass oder Gewicht
En weight or measurement
Es peso o cubicaje
It peso o volume
Pt peso ou medida

**poinçon** *(m) n* Fr
De Feingehaltsstempel *(m)*
En hall-mark
Es punzón de garantía *(m)*
It punzonatura di garanzia *(f)*
Pt marca de garantia *(f)*

**point de seuil** *(m)* Fr
De Rentabilitätsgrenze *(f)*
En break-even point
Es punto de igualdad de ingresos y gastos *(m)*
It punto di pareggio *(m)*
Pt ponto de acerto *(m)*

**Police** (Versicherung) *(f) n* De
En policy
Es póliza *(f)*
Fr police *(f)*
It polizza *(f)*
Pt apólice *(f)*

**police** (d´assurance) *(f)* Fr
De Police *(f)*
En policy
Es póliza *(f)*
It polizza *(f)*
Pt apólice *(f)*

**police à aliment** *(f)* Fr
De offene Versicherung *(f)*
En open cover
Es cobertura flotante *(f)*
It polizza flottante *(f)*
Pt cobertura ilimitada *(f)*

**police avec participation aux bénéfices** *(f)* Fr
De Police mit Gewinnberechtigung *(f)*
En with-profits policy
Am participating policy
Es póliza con beneficios *(f)*
It polizza con profitti *(f)*
Pt apólice com participação nos lucros *(f)*

**police d'assurance** *(f)* Fr
De Versicherungspolice *(f)*
En insurance policy
Es póliza de seguro *(f)*
It polizza di assicurazione *(f)*
Pt apólice de seguros *(f)*

**police flottante** *(f)* Fr
De laufende Polizze *(f)*
En floating policy
Es póliza flotante *(f)*
It polizza flottante *(f)*
Pt apólice flutuante *(f)*

**police incendie** *(f)* Fr
De Feuerversicherungspolice *(f)*
En fire insurance policy
Es póliza de seguro de incendios *(f)*
It polizza d´assicurazione incendio *(f)*
Pt apólice de seguro de incêndio *(f)*

**Police mit Gewinnberechtigung** *(f)* De
En with-profits policy
Am participating policy
Es póliza con beneficios *(f)*
Fr police avec participation aux bénéfices *(f)*
It polizza con profitti *(f)*
Pt apólice com participação nos lucros *(f)*

**policy** (insurance) *n* En
De Police *(f)*
Es póliza *(f)*
Fr police *(f)*

It   polizza (f)
Pt   apólice (f)

**policy** (plan) n En
De   Politik (f)
Es   política (f)
Fr   politique (f)
It   politica (f)
Pt   política (f)

**política** (f) n Es, Pt
De   Politik (f)
En   policy
Fr   politique (f)
It   politica (f)

**politica** (f) n It
De   Politik (f)
En   policy
Es   política (f)
Fr   politique (f)
Pt   política (f)

**política agrícola comum** (f) Pt
De   gemeinsame Agrarpolitik (f)
En   Common Agricultural Policy
Es   política agricola común (f)
Fr   politique agricole commune (f)
It   politica agricola comune (f)

**política agricola común** (f) Es
De   gemeinsame Agrarpolitik (f)
En   Common Agricultural Policy
Fr   politique agricole commune (f)
It   politica agricola comune (f)
Pt   política agrícola comum (f)

**politica agricola comune** (f) It
De   gemeinsame Agrarpolitik (f)
En   Common Agricultural Policy
Es   política agricola común (f)
Fr   politique agricole commune (f)
Pt   política agrícola comum (f)

**política comercial comum** (f) Pt
De   gemeinsame Handelspolitik (f)
En   Common Commercial Policy
Es   política comercial común (f)
Fr   politique commerciale commune (f)

It   politica commerciale comune (f)

**política comercial común** (f) Es
De   gemeinsame Handelspolitik (f)
En   Common Commercial Policy
Fr   politique commerciale commune (f)
It   politica commerciale comune (f)
Pt   política comercial comum (f)

**politica commerciale comune** (f) It
De   gemeinsame Handelspolitik (f)
En   Common Commercial Policy
Es   política comercial común (f)
Fr   politique commerciale commune (f)
Pt   política comercial comum (f)

**política comum da pesca** (f) Pt
De   gemeinsame Fischereipolitik (f)
En   Common Fisheries Policy
Es   política común de la pesca (f)
Fr   politique commune de la pêche (f)
It   politica comune della pesca (f)

**política común de la pesca** (f) Es
De   gemeinsame Fischereipolitik (f) '
En   Common Fisheries Policy
Fr   politique commune de la pêche (f)
It   politica comune della pesca (f)
Pt   política comum da pesca (f)

**politica comune della pesca** (f) It
De   gemeinsame Fischereipolitik (f)
En   Common Fisheries Policy

Es   política común de la pesca (f)
Fr   politique commune de la pêche (f)
Pt   política comum da pesca (f)

**politica dei redditi** (f) It
De   Lohnpolitik (f)
En   incomes policy
Es   plan de renta (m)
Fr   politique des salaires (f)
Pt   programa salários (f)

**política monetaria** (f) Es
De   Währungspolitik (f)
En   monetary policy
Fr   politique monétaire (f)
It   politica monetaria (f)
Pt   política monetária (f)

**politica monetaria** (f) It
De   Währungspolitik (f)
En   monetary policy
Es   política monetaria (f)
Fr   politique monétaire (f)
Pt   política monetária (f)

**política monetária** (f) Pt
De   Währungspolitik (f)
En   monetary policy
Es   política monetaria (f)
Fr   politique monétaire (f)
It   politica monetaria (f)

**Politik** (f) n De
En   policy
Es   política (f)
Fr   politique (f)
It   politica (f)
Pt   política (f)

**politique** (f) n Fr
De   Politik (f)
En   policy
Es   política (f)
It   politica (f)
Pt   política (f)

**politique agricole commune** (f) Fr
De   gemeinsame Agrarpolitik (f)
En   Common Agricultural Policy
Es   política agricola común (f)
It   politica agricola comune (f)
Pt   política agrícola comum (f)

**politique commerciale commune** *(f)* Fr
De gemeinsame Handelspolitik *(f)*
En Common Commercial Policy
Es política comercial común *(f)*
It politica commerciale comune *(f)*
Pt política comercial comum *(f)*

**politique commune de la pêche** *(f)* Fr
De gemeinsame Fischereipolitik *(f)*
En Common Fisheries Policy
Es política común de la pesca *(f)*
It politica comune della pesca *(f)*
Pt política comum da pesca *(f)*

**politique des salaires** *(f)* Fr
De Lohnpolitik *(f)*
En incomes policy
Es plan de renta *(m)*
It politica dei redditi *(f)*
Pt programa salários *(f)*

**politique monétaire** *(f)* Fr
De Währungspolitik *(f)*
En monetary policy
Es política monetaria *(f)*
It politica monetaria *(f)*
Pt política monetária *(f)*

**póliza (de seguros)** *(f)* Es
De Police *(f)*
En policy
Fr police *(f)*
It polizza *(f)*
Pt apólice *(f)*

**póliza con beneficios** *(f)* Es
De Police mit Gewinnberechtigung *(f)*
En with-profits policy
Am participating policy
Fr police avec participation aux bénéfices *(f)*
It polizza con profitti *(f)*
Pt apólice com participação nos lucros *(f)*

**póliza de seguro** *(f)* Es
De Versicherungspolice *(f)*
En insurance policy
Fr police d'assurance *(f)*
It polizza di assicurazione *(f)*
Pt apólice de seguros *(f)*

**póliza de seguro de incendios** *(f)* Es
De Feuerversicherungsschein *(m)*
En fire insurance policy
Fr police incendie *(f)*
It polizza d'assicurazione incendio *(f)*
Pt apólice de seguro de incêndio *(f)*

**póliza de seguro sobre la vida** *(f)* Es
De Versicherungspolice *(f)*
En life assurance policy
Fr police d'assurance *(f)*
It polizza d'assicurazione *(f)*
Pt apólice de seguro de vida *(f)*

**póliza dotal** *(f)* Es
De Erlebensversicherung *(f)*
En endowment policy
Fr assurance à terme fixe *(f)*
It assicurazione dotale *(f)*
Pt título de doação *(m)*

**póliza flotante** *(f)* Es
De laufende Polizze *(f)*
En floating policy
Fr police flottante *(f)*
It polizza flottante *(f)*
Pt apólice flutuante *(f)*

**póliza liberada** *(f)* Es
De beitragsfreie Police *(f)*
En paid-up policy
Fr assurance libérée *(f)*
It polizza interamente pagata *(f)*
Pt apólice liquidada *(f)*

**polizza (di assicurazione)** *(f)* It
De Police *(f)*
En policy
Es póliza *(f)*
Fr police *(f)*
Pt apólice *(f)*

**polizza con profitti** *(f)* It
De Police mit Gewinnberechtigung *(f)*
En with-profits policy
Am participating policy
Es póliza con beneficios *(f)*
Fr police avec participation aux bénéfices *(f)*
Pt apólice com participação nos lucros *(f)*

**polizza de carico** *(f)* It
De Konnossement *(n)*
En bill of lading
Es conocimiento (de embarque) *(m)*
Fr connaissement *(m)*
Pt conhecimento *(m)*

**polizza di assicurazione** *(f)* It
De Versicherungspolizze *(f)*
En insurance policy
Es póliza de seguro *(f)*
Fr police d'assurance *(f)*
Pt apólice de seguros *(f)*

**polizza di assicurazione incendio** *(f)* It
De Feuerversicherungsschein *(m)*
En fire insurance policy
Es póliza de seguro de incendios *(f)*
Fr police incendie *(f)*
Pt apólice de seguro de incêndio *(f)*

**polizza di carico con merce a bordo** *(f)* It
De Hafenkonnossement *(n)*
En shipped bill of lading
Es conocimiento de embarque a bordo *(m)*
Fr connaissement de marchandises à bord *(m)*
Pt conhecimento de carga embarcada *(m)*

**polizza di carico con riserve** *(f)* It
De einschränkendes Konnossement *(n)*
En foul (dirty) bill of lading
Es conocimiento de embarque con objecciones *(m)*
Fr connaissement avec réserve *(m)*

Pt conhecimento com embargos *(m)*

**polizza di carico senza riserve** *(f)* It
De echtes Konnossement *(n)*
En clean bill of lading
Es conocimiento de embarque sin objecciones *(m)*
Fr connaissement sans réserve *(m)*
Pt conhecimento sem embargos *(m)*

**polizza flottante** *(f)* It
De laufende Polizze *(f)*
En floating policy
Es póliza flotante *(f)*
Fr police flottante *(f)*
Pt apólice flutuante *(f)*

**polizza interamente pagata** *(f)* It
De beitragsfreie Police *(f)*
En paid-up policy
Es póliza liberada *(f)*
Fr assurance libérée *(f)*
Pt apólice liquidada *(f)*

**pont** *(m)* n Fr
De Deck *(n)*
En deck
Es cubierta *(f)*
It coperta; ponte *(f m)*
Pt convés *(m)*

**pontão** *(m)* n Pt
De Mole *(f)*
En jetty
Es digue *(m)*
Fr jetée; digue *(f)*
It molo *(m)*

**ponto de acerto** *(m)* Pt
De Rentabilitätsgrenze *(f)*
En break-even point
Es punto de igualdad de ingresos y gastos *(m)*
Fr point de seuil *(m)*
It punto di pareggio *(m)*

**ponton-grue** *(m)* n Fr
De Pontonkran *(m)*
En floating crane
Es grúa flotante *(f)*
It grue galleggiante *(f)*
Pt guindaste flutuante *(m)*

**Pontonkran** *(m)* n De
En floating crane
Es grúa flotante *(f)*
Fr ponton-grue *(m)*
It grue galleggiante *(f)*
Pt guindaste flutuante *(m)*

**popolazione** *(f)* n It
De Bevölkerung *(f)*
En population
Es población *(f)*
Fr population *(f)*
Pt população *(f)*

**população** *(f)* n Pt
De Bevölkerung *(f)*
En population
Es población *(f)*
Fr population *(f)*
It popolazione *(f)*

**population** n En, Fr *(f)*
De Bevölkerung *(f)*
Es población *(f)*
It popolazione *(f)*
Pt população *(f)*

**porão** *(m)* n Pt
De Laderaum *(m)*
En (ship´s) hold
Es bodega *(f)*
Fr cale *(f)*
It stiva *(f)*

**pôr à venda** Pt
De zum Verkauf anbieten
En offer for sale
Es ofrecer en venta
Fr offrir en vente
It offrire in vendita

**por avião** Pt
De per Flugpost
En by air
Es por avión
Fr par avion
It per via aerea

**por avión** Es
De per Flugpost
En by air
Fr par avion
It per via aerea
Pt por avião

**por cabeza** Es
De pro Kopf
En per capita

Fr par tête
It per testa
Pt per capita

**porcentaje** *(m)* n Es
De Prozentsatz *(m)*
En percentage
Fr pourcentage *(m)*
It percentuale *(f)*
Pt percentagem *(f)*

**por cento** Pt
De prozent
En per cent
Es por ciento
Fr pour cent
It per cento

**por ciento** Es
De prozent
En per cent
Fr pour cent
It per cento
Pt por cento

**por conta** Pt
De a conto; auf Abschlag
En on account
Es a cuenta
Fr à valoir
It in acconto

**por correio separado** Pt
De mit getrennter Post
En under separate cover
Es por correo aparte
Fr sous pli séparé
It in piego a parte

**por correo aparte** Es
De mit getrennter Post
En under separate cover
Fr sous pli séparé
It in piego a parte
Pt por correio separado

**por empréstimo** Pt
De darlehensweise
En on loan
Es en préstamo
Fr sous forme de prêt
It in prestito

**por esto** Es
De hiermit
En hereby
Fr par la présente

It    col presente; con questo
Pt    pelo presente


**pormenores** (m pl) Pt
De    Einzelheiten; Angaben (f pl)
En    particulars
Es    detalles (m pl)
Fr    détails (m pl)
It    particolari (m pl)


**pormenores adicionais** (m pl)
      Pt
De    nähere Umstände (m pl)
En    further particulars
Es    más detalles (m pl)
Fr    plus amples renseigne-
      ments (m pl)
It    ulteriori particolari (m pl)


**pormenorizado** adj Pt
De    postenmässig dargestellt
En    itemized
Es    detallado
Fr    détaillé
It    dettagliato


**por separado** Es
De    getrennt
En    under separate cover
Fr    sous pli séparé
It    con plico a parte
Pt    em separado


**port** n En, Fr (m)
De    Hafen (m)
Es    puerto (m)
It    porto (m)
Pt    porto (m)


**portafoglio** (di un ministro) (m)
      n It
De    Portefeuille; Geschäftsbe-
      reich (n m)
En    portfolio
Es    cartera (f)
Fr    portefeuille (f)
Pt    pasta (f)


**portafoglio titoli** (m) It
De    Investitionsportefeuille (n)
En    investment portfolio
Es    cartera de inversiones (f)
Fr    portefeuille d'investisse-
      ments (m)
Pt    carteira de investimentos
      (f)


**portatore di obbligazioni** (m)
      It
De    Obligationär (m)
En    bondholder
Es    obligacionista (m)
Fr    obligataire (m)
Pt    titular de obrigações (m)


**port charges** En
De    Hafengebühren (f pl)
Es    derechos portuarios (m pl)
Fr    droits de port (m pl)
It    diritti portuali (m pl)
Pt    direitos portuários (m pl)


**port d'attache** (m) Fr
De    Heimathafen (m)
En    port of registration
Es    puerto de matrícula (m)
It    porto d'immatricolazione
      (m)
Pt    porto de matrícula (m)


**port d'escale** (m) Fr
De    Anlaufhafen (m)
En    port of call
Es    puerto de escala (m)
It    porto di scalo (m)
Pt    porto de escala (m)


**port de destination** (m) Fr
De    Bestimmungshafen (m)
En    port of destination
Es    puerto de destino (m)
It    porto di destinazione (m)
Pt    porto de destino (m)


**port de livraison** (m) Fr
De    Lieferhafen (m)
En    port of discharge
Es    puerto de descarga (m)
It    porto di scarico (m)
Pt    porto de descarga (m)


**portefeuille** (d'un ministre) (f)
      n Fr
De    Portefeuille; Geschäftsbe-
      reich (n m)
En    portfolio
Es    cartera (f)
It    portafoglio (m)
Pt    pasta (f)


**Portefeuille** (eines Ministers)
      (n) n De
En    portfolio
Es    cartera (f)
Fr    portefeuille (f)


It    portafoglio (m)
Pt    pasta (f)


**portefeuille d'investisse-
      ments** (m) Fr
De    Investitionsportefeuille (n)
En    investment portfolio
Es    cartera de inversiones (f)
It    portafoglio titoli (m)
Pt    carteira de investimentos
      (f)


**porte gratis** Pt
De    frachtfrei
En    carriage free
Am    F.O.B. destination
Es    franco de porte
Fr    franco
It    porto franco


**porteiro** (m) n Pt
De    Hausmeister (m)
En    hall-porter
Es    conserje (m)
Fr    concierge (m)
It    portiere (m)


**port en lourd** (m) Fr
De    Tragfähigkeit (f)
En    deadweight
Es    peso muerto (m)
It    peso morto (m)
Pt    peso morto (m)


**porte pago** Pt
De    franko
En    carriage paid
Am    freight charges paid
Es    a porte pagado
Fr    port payé
It    franco di porto


**portes pagos** Pt
De    portofrei
En    postage paid
Es    franco de porte
Fr    port-payé
It    porto pagato


**porteur à titre onéreux** (m) Fr
De    entgeltigter Besitzer (m)
En    holder for value
Es    tenedor legítimo (m)
It    detentore legittimo (m)
Pt    proprietário legítimo (m)

**porteur d'obligations** (m) Fr
De Obligationsinhaber (m)
En debenture holder
Es obligacionista (m)
It obbligazionista (f)
Pt titular de obrigação (m)

**porteur de bonne foi** (m) Fr
De gutgläubiger Besitzer (m)
En holder in due course
Es tenedor en buena fe (m)
It titolare in buona fede (m)
Pt futuro proprietário (m)

**portfolio** (of a minister) n En
De Portefeuille; Geschäftsbe-
reich (n m)
Es cartera (f)
Fr portefeuille (f)
It portafoglio (m)
Pt pasta (f)

**port franc** (m) Fr
De Freihafen (m)
En free port
Es puerto libre (m)
It porto franco (m)
Pt porto franco (m)

**portiere** (m) n It
De Hausmeister (m)
En hall-porter
Es conserje (m)
Fr concierge (m)
Pt porteiro (m)

**port mark** En
De Benennung des Bestim-
mungshafen (f)
Es marca de destino (f)
Fr marque de destination (f)
It marche di destinazione (f
pl)
Pt marca de porto (f)

**porto** (m) n It, Pt
De Hafen (m)
En harbour; port
Es puerto (m)
Fr port (m)

**porto assegnato** It
De Portonachnahme
En carriage forward
Am F.O.B. shipping point
Es a porte debido
Fr en port dû
Pt transporte a pagar

**porto de descarga** (m) Pt
De Lieferhafen (m)
En port of discharge
Es puerto de descarga (m)
Fr port de livraison (m)
It porto di scarico (m)

**porto de destino** (m) Pt
De Bestimmungshafen (m)
En port of destination
Es puerto de destino (m)
Fr port de destination (m)
It porto di destinazione (m)

**porto de escala** (m) Pt
De Anlaufhafen (m)
En port of call
Es puerto de escala (m)
Fr port d'escale (m)
It porto di scalo (m)

**porto de matrícula** (m) Pt
De Heimathafen (m)
En port of registration
Es puerto de matrícula (m)
Fr port d'attache (m)
It porto d'immatricolazione
(m)

**porto di destinazione** (m) It
De Bestimmungshafen (m)
En port of destination
Es puerto de destino (m)
Fr port de destination (m)
Pt porto de destino (m)

**porto d'immatricolazione** (m)
It
De Heimathafen (m)
En port of registration
Es puerto de matrícula (m)
Fr port d'attache (m)
Pt porto de matrícula (m)

**porto di scalo** (m) It
De Anlaufhafen (m)
En port of call
Es puerto de escala (m)
Fr port d'escale (m)
Pt porto de escala (m)

**porto di scarico** (m) It
De Lieferhafen (m)
En port of discharge
Es puerto de descarga (m)
Fr port de livraison (m)
Pt porto de descarga (m)

**port of call** En
De Anlaufhafen (m)
Es puerto de escala (m)
Fr port d'escale (m)
It porto di scalo (m)
Pt porto de escala (m)

**port of destination** En
De Bestimmungshafen (m)
Es puerto de destino (m)
Fr port de destination (m)
It porto di destinazione (m)
Pt porto de destino (m)

**port of discharge** En
De Lieferhafen (m)
Es puerto de descarga (m)
Fr port de livraison (m)
It porto di scarico (m)
Pt porto de descarga (m)

**porto franco** It
De frachtfrei
En carriage free
Am F.O.B. destination
Es franco de porte
Fr franco
Pt porte gratis

**porto franco** (m) It, Pt
De Freihafen (m)
En free port
Es puerto libre (m)
Fr port franc (m)

**port of registration** En
De Heimathafen (m)
Es puerto de matrícula (m)
Fr port d'attache (m)
It porto d'immatricolazione
(m)
Pt porto de matrícula (m)

**portofrei** De
En postage paid
Es franco de porte
Fr port payé
It porto pagato
Pt portes pagos

**portofreie Lieferung** De
En delivery free
Es libre entrega
Fr livré franco
It consegna franco
Pt remessa gratuita

**Portonachnahme** De
  En  carriage forward
  Am  F.O.B. shipping point
  Es  a porte debido
  Fr  en port dû
  It  porto assegnato
  Pt  transporte a pagar

**porto pagato** It
  De  portofrei
  En  postage paid
  Es  franco de porte
  Fr  port-payé
  Pt  portes pagos

**port payé** Fr
  De  franko; portofrei
  En  carriage paid; postage paid
  Es  a porte pagado; franco de
      porte
  It  franco di porto; porto
      pagato
  Pt  porte pago

**poscritto (PS)** *(m)* It
  De  Nachschrift *(f)*
  En  postscript (PS)
  Es  posdata *(f)*
  Fr  post-scriptum; postface *(m
      f)*
  Pt  pós-escrito; post-scriptum
      (PS) *(m)*

**posdata** *(f)* n Es
  De  Nachschrift *(f)*
  En  postscript (PS)
  Fr  post-scriptum; postface *(m
      f)*
  It  poscritto (PS) *(m)*
  Pt  pós-escrito; post-scriptum
      (PS) *(m)*

**pós-escrito** *(m)* n Pt
  De  Nachschrift *(f)*
  En  postscript (PS)
  Es  posdata *(f)*
  Fr  post-scriptum; postface *(m
      f)*
  It  poscritto (PS) *(m)*

**posição em aberto** *(f)* Pt
  De  offene Position *(f)*
  En  open position
  Es  posición descubierta *(f)*
  Fr  position ouverte *(f)*
  It  posizione aperta *(f)*

**posición descubierta** *(f)* Es
  De  offene Position *(f)*
  En  open position
  Fr  position ouverte *(f)*
  It  posizione aperta *(f)*
  Pt  posição em aberto *(f)*

**position ouverte** *(f)* Fr
  De  offene Position *(f)*
  En  open position
  Es  posición descubierta *(f)*
  It  posizione aperta *(f)*
  Pt  posição em aberto *(f)*

**posizione aperta** *(f)* It
  De  offene Position *(f)*
  En  open position
  Es  posición descubierta *(f)*
  Fr  position ouverte *(f)* .
  Pt  posição em aberto *(f)*

**Post** *(f)* n De
  En  mail
  Es  correo *(m)*
  Fr  poste *(f)*
  It  posta *(f)*
  Pt  correio *(m)*

**posta** *(f)* n It
  De  Post *(f)*
  En  mail
  Es  correo *(m)*
  Fr  poste *(f)*
  Pt  correio *(m)*

**posta aerea** *(f)* It
  De  Luftpost *(f)*
  En  airmail
  Es  correo aéreo *(m)*
  Fr  poste aérienne *(f)*
  Pt  correio aéreo *(m)*

**postage** n En
  De  Postgebühr *(f)*
  Es  tarifa postal; franqueo *(f m)*
  Fr  frais de poste *(m pl)*
  It  tariffa postale; affrancatura
      *(f)*
  Pt  tarifa postal *(f)*

**postage paid** En
  De  portofrei
  Es  franco de porte
  Fr  port payé
  It  porto pagato
  Pt  portes pagos

**postage stamp** En
  De  Briefmarke *(f)*
  Es  sello de correos *(m)*
  Fr  timbre-poste *(m)*
  It  francobollo *(m)*
  Pt  selo postal *(m)*

**postal order** En
  De  Postanweisung *(f)*
  Es  giro postal *(m)*
  Fr  mandat-poste *(m)*
  It  vaglia postale *(f)*
  Pt  vale postal *(m)*

**Postamt** *(n)* n De
  En  post office
  Es  oficina de correos *(f)*
  Fr  bureau de poste *(m)*
  It  ufficio postale *(m)*
  Pt  estação de correios *(f)*

**Postanweisung** *(f)* n De
  En  postal order
  Es  giro postal *(m)*
  Fr  mandat-poste *(m)*
  It  vaglia postale *(f)*
  Pt  vale postal *(m)*

**postcode** n En
  Am  zip code
  De  Postleitzahl *(f)*
  Es  designación postal *(f)*
  Fr  indicatif postal *(m)*
  It  codice postale *(m)*
  Pt  designação postal *(f)*

**postdated cheque** En
  De  nachdatierter Scheck *(m)*
  Es  cheque a fecha retrasada
      *(m)*
  Fr  chèque postdaté *(m)*
  It  assegno postdatato *(m)*
  Pt  cheque post-datado *(m)*

**poste** *(f)* n Fr
  De  Post *(f)*
  En  mail
  Es  correo *(m)*
  It  posta *(f)*
  Pt  correio *(m)*

**poste aérienne** *(f)* Fr
  De  Luftpost *(f)*
  En  airmail
  Es  correo aéreo *(m)*
  It  posta aerea *(f)*
  Pt  correio aéreo *(m)*

**Posten** *(m)* *n* De
En picket
Es piquete *(m)*
Fr piquet *(m)*
It picchetto *(m)*
Pt piquete *(m)*

**postenmässig dargestellt** De
En itemized
Es detallado
Fr détaillé
It dettagliato
Pt pormenorizado

**postes de dépense** *(m pl)* Fr
De Aufwendungsposten *(f pl)*
En items of expenditure
Es artículos de gasto *(m pl)*
It articoli di spesa *(m pl)*
Pt itens de despesa *(m pl)*

**postes rééquilibrants** *(m pl)* Fr
De Ausgleichsposten *(m pl)*
En balancing items
Es asientos saldados *(m pl)*
It voci di pareggio *(f pl)*
Pt valores de equilíbrio *(m pl)*

**Postgebühr** *(f)* *n* De
En postage
Es tarifa postal; franqueo *(f m)*
Fr frais de poste *(m pl)*
It tariffa postale; affrancatura *(f)*
Pt tarifa postal *(f)*

**postilla** *(f)* *n* It
De Fussnote *(f)*
En footnote
Es apostilla *(f)*
Fr apostille *(f)*
Pt nota de rodapé *(f)*

**Postleitzahl** *(f)* *n* De
En postcode
Am zip code
Es designación postal *(f)*
Fr indicatif postal *(m)*
It codice postale *(m)*
Pt designação postal *(f)*

**post office** En
De Postamt *(n)*
Es oficina de correos *(f)*
Fr bureau de poste *(m)*
It ufficio postale *(m)*
Pt estação de correios *(f)*

**Post Office Savings Bank** En
De Postsparkasse *(f)*
Es caja postal de ahorros *(f)*
Fr caisse d'épargne postale *(f)*
It cassa di risparmio postale *(f)*
Pt caixa económica postal *(f)*

**postscript** (PS) *n* En
De Nachschrift *(f)*
Es posdata *(f)*
Fr post-scriptum; postface *(m f)*
It poscritto (PS) *(m)*
Pt pós-escrito; post-scriptum (PS) *(m)*

**post-scriptum** *(m)* *n* Fr
De Nachschrift *(f)*
En postscript (PS)
Es posdata *(f)*
It poscritto (PS) *(m)*
Pt pós-escrito; post-scriptum (PS) *(m)*

**Postsparkasse** *(f)* *n* De
En Post Office Savings Bank
Es caja postal de ahorros *(f)*
Fr caisse d'épargne postale *(f)*
It cassa di risparmio postale *(f)*
Pt caixa económica postal *(f)*

**Postüberweisung** *(f)* *n* De
En mail transfer
Es transferencia postal *(f)*
Fr virement postal *(m)*
It trasferimento per posta *(m)*
Pt transferência postal *(f)*

**Postversandwerbung** *(f)* *n* De
En direct mail
Es propaganda directa por correo *(f)*
Fr publicité directe *(f)*
It pubblicità diretta *(f)*
Pt publicidade por correio ao domicílio *(f)*

**pot-de-vin** *(m)* *n* Fr
De Bestechungsgeld *(n)*
En bribe
Es soborno *(m)*
It dono per corrompere *(m)*
Pt soborno *(m)*

**potencial** *adj* Es, Pt
De möglich; potentiell
En potential
Fr potentiel
It potenziale

**potencial não utilizado** *(m)* Pt
De unbenutzte Ladefähigkeit *(f)*
En idle capacity
Es potencial no utilizado *(m)*
Fr potentiel non utilisé *(m)*
It potenziale non utilizzato *(m)*

**potencial no utilizado** *(m)* Es
De unbenutzte Ladefähigkeit *(f)*
En idle capacity
Fr potentiel non utilisé *(m)*
It potenziale non utilizzato *(m)*
Pt potencial não utilizado *(m)*

**potential** *adj* En
De möglich; potentiell
Es potencial
Fr potentiel
It potenziale
Pt potencial

**potentiel** *adj* Fr
De möglich; potentiell
En potential
Es potencial
It potenziale
Pt potencial

**potentiell** *adj* De
En potential
Es potencial
Fr potentiel
It potenziale
Pt potencial

**potentiel non utilisé** *(m)* Fr
De unbenutzte Ladefähigkeit *(f)*
En idle capacity
Es potencial no utilizado *(m)*
It potenziale non utilizzato *(m)*
Pt potencial não utilizado *(m)*

**potenziale** *adj* It
De möglich; potentiell
En potential
Es potencial
Fr potentiel
Pt potencial

**potenziale non utilizzato** *(m)* It
De unbenutzte Ladefähigkeit *(f)*

En idle capacity
Es potencial no utilizado (m)
Fr potentiel non utilisé (m)
Pt potencial não utilizado (m)

**potere d'acquisto** (m) It
De Kaufkraft (f)
En purchasing power
Es poder de compra (m)
Fr pouvoir d'achat (m)
Pt poder de compra (m)

**potere di contrattare** (m) It
De Verhandlungsposition (f)
En bargaining power
Es poder de negociación (m)
Fr pouvoir de négociation (m)
Pt poder de regateio (m)

**pound sterling** En
De Pfund sterling (n)
Es libra esterlina (f)
Fr livre sterling (f)
It lira sterlina (f)
Pt libra esterlina (f)

**poupar** vb Pt
De aufsparen
En save
Es ahorrar
Fr épargner
It risparmiare

**pourboire** (m) n Fr
De Trinkgeld (n)
En tip; gratuity
Es propina (f)
It mancia (f)
Pt gorjeta (f)

**pour cent** Fr
De prozent
En per cent
Es por ciento
It per cento
Pt por cento

**pourcentage** (m) n Fr
De Prozentsatz (m)
En percentage
Es porcentaje (m)
It percentuale (f)
Pt percentagem (f)

**poursuivre** vb Fr
De weiterverfolgen
En follow up
Es perseguir

It seguitare
Pt perseguir

**pouvoir d'achat** (m) Fr
De Kaufkraft (f)
En purchasing power
Es poder de compra (m)
It potere d'acquisto (m)
Pt poder de compra (m)

**pouvoir de négociation** (m) Fr
De Verhandlungsposition (f)
En bargaining power
Es poder de negociación (m)
It potere di contrattare (m)
Pt poder de regateio (m)

**pouvoirs** (m pl) Fr
De Vollmacht (f)
En power of attorney
Es poder (m)
It procura (f)
Pt poderes de procuração (m pl)

**power of attorney** En
De Vollmacht (f)
Es poder (m)
Fr pouvoirs; procuration (m pl; f)
It procura (f)
Pt poderes de procuração (m pl)

**practicabilidad** (f) n Es
De Durchführbarkeit (f)
En feasibility
Fr practicabilité (f)
It fattibilità (f)
Pt viabilidade (f)

**practicabilité** (f) n Fr
De Durchführbarkeit (f)
En feasibility
Es practicabilidad (f)
It fattibilità (f)
Pt viabilidade (f)

**práctica comercial desleal** (f) Es
De unlautere Handelspraktik (f)
En unfair trade practice
Fr pratique de commerce déloyale (f)
It pratica commerciale sleale (f)
Pt prática comercial imprópria (f)

**Prämie** (f) n De
En premium; bonus
Es prima; premio (f m)
Fr prime (f)
It premio (m)
Pt prêmio (m)

**prática comercial imprópria** (f) Pt
De unlautere Handelspraktik (f)
En unfair trade practice
Es práctica comercial desleal (f)
Fr pratique de commerce déloyale (f)
It pratica commerciale sleale (f)

**pratica commerciale sleale** (f) It
De unlautere Handelspraktik (f)
En unfair trade practice
Es práctica comercial desleal (f)
Fr pratique de commerce déloyale (f)
Pt prática comercial imprópria (f)

**pratique** n En
De Gesundheitsbrief (m)
Es libre plática (f)
Fr libre pratique (f)
It libera pratica (f)
Pt livre prática (f)

**precinto industrial** (m) Es
De Industriegebiet (n)
En industrial estate
Am industrial park
Fr domaine industriel (m)
It centro industriale (m)
Pt centro fabril (m)

**precio** (m) n Es
De Preis (m)
En price
Fr prix (m)
It prezzo (m)
Pt preço (m)

**precio al comerciante** (m) Es
De Handelspreis (m)
En trade price
Fr prix marchand (m)
It prezzo al commerciante (m)
Pt preço para comerciantes (m)

**precio al por menor** *(m)* Es
De Einzelhandelspreis *(m)*
En retail price
Fr prix de détail *(m)*
It prezzo al minuto *(m)*
Pt preço a retalho *(m)*

**precio a término** *(m)* Es
De Terminnotierung *(f)*
En forward price
Fr cours à terme *(m)*
It prezzo per futura consegna *(m)*
Pt preço adiantado *(m)*

**precio contractual** *(m)* Es
De Vertragspreis *(m)*
En contract price
Fr prix contractuel *(m)*
It prezzo contrattuale *(m)*
Pt preço contractual *(m)*

**precio cotizado** *(m)* Es
De angegebener Preis *(m)*
En quoted price
Fr prix coté *(m)*
It prezzo quotato *(m)*
Pt preço cotizado *(m)*

**precio de catálogo** *(m)* Es
De Listenpreis *(m)*
En catalogue price
Fr prix de catalogue *(m)*
It prezzo di catalogo *(m)*
Pt preço de catálogo *(m)*

**precio de cierre** *(m)* Es
De Schlussnotierung *(f)*
En closing price
Fr cours de clôture *(m)*
It prezzo di chiusura *(m)*
Pt último preço *(m)*

**precio de compra** *(m)* Es
De Kaufpreis (m)
En purchase price
Fr prix d'achat *(m)*
It prezzo d'acquisto *(m)*
Pt preço de compra *(m)*

**precio de coste** *(m)* Es
De Einstandspreis *(m)*
En cost price
Fr prix de revient *(m)*
It prezzo di costo *(m)*
Pt preço de custo *(m)*

**precio de intervención** *(m)* Es
De Interventionspreis *(m)*
En intervention price
Fr prix d'intervention *(m)*
It prezzo d'intervento *(m)*
Pt preço de intervenção *(m)*

**precio de mercado** *(m)* Es
De Marktpreis *(m)*
En market price
Fr cours du marché *(m)*
It prezzo del mercato *(m)*
Pt preço de mercado *(m)*

**precio de ocasión** *(m)* Es
De Spottpreis *(m)*
En bargain price
Fr prix de solde *(m)*
It prezzo d'occasione *(m)*
Pt preço excepcional *(m)*

**precio de reventa** *(m)* Es
De Wiederverkaufspreis *(m)*
En resale price
Fr prix de revente *(m)*
It prezzo di rivendita *(m)*
Pt preço de revenda *(m)*

**precio detallista recomendado** *(m)* Es
De empfohlener Ladenpreis *(m)*
En recommended retail selling price
Fr prix de détail racommandé *(m)*
It prezzo al minuto indicativo *(m)*
Pt preço de venda a retalho recomendado *(m)*

**precio de tarifa** *(m)* Es
De Listenpreis *(m)*
En list price
Fr prix courant *(m)*
It prezzo di listino *(m)*
Pt preço de tabela *(m)*

**precio de umbral** *(m)* Es
De Schwellenpreis *(m)*
En threshold price
Fr prix de seuil *(m)*
It prezzo soglia *(m)*
Pt preço convencionado *(m)*

**precio facturado** *(m)* Es
De fakturierter Preis *(m)*
En invoice price

Fr prix facturé *(m)*
It prezzo di fattura *(m)*
Pt preço de factura *(m)*

**precio incluida entrega** *(m)* Es
De Lieferpreis *(m)*
En delivered price
Fr prix livraison inclus *(m)*
It prezzo incluso consegna *(m)*
Pt preço incluindo portes *(m)*

**precio medio** *(m)* Es
De Mittelkurs *(m)*
En mean price
Fr prix moyen *(m)*
It prezzo medio *(m)*
Pt preço médio *(m)*

**precio mínimo fijado** *(m)* Es
De Mindestpreis *(m)*
En reserve price
Fr mise à prix *(f)*
It prezzo minimo *(m)*
Pt preço de reserva *(m)*

**precio neto** *(m)* Es
De Nettopreis; Nettokurs *(m)*
En net price
Fr prix net *(m)*
It prezzo netto *(m)*
Pt preço líquido *(m)*

**precio nominal** *(m)* Es
De Nennpreis *(m)*
En nominal price
Fr prix nominal *(m)*
It prezzo nominale *(m)*
Pt preço nominal *(m)*

**precio razonable** *(m)* Es
De angemessener Preis *(m)*
En fair price
Fr prix raisonnable *(m)*
It prezzo equo *(m)*
Pt preço razoável *(m)*

**precio verdadero** *(m)* Es
De Gestehungskosten *(pl)*
En actual cost
Fr prix de revient effectif *(m)*
It costo effettivo *(m)*
Pt custo verdadeiro *(m)*

**preço** *(m)* n Pt
De Preis; Kurs *(m)*
En price
Es precio *(m)*

Fr  prix *(m)*
It  prezzo *(m)*

**preço adiantado** *(m)* Pt
De  Terminnotierung *(f)*
En  forward price
Es  precio a término *(m)*
Fr  cours à terme *(m)*
It  prezzo per futura consegna
     *(m)*

**preço a retalho** *(m)* Pt
De  Einzelhandelspreis *(m)*
En  retail price
Es  precio al por menor *(m)*
Fr  prix de détail *(m)*
It  prezzo al minuto *(m)*

**preço contractual** *(m)* Pt
De  Vertragspreis *(m)*
En  contract price
Es  precio contractual *(m)*
Fr  prix contractuel *(m)*
It  prezzo contrattuale *(m)*

**preço convencionado** *(m)* Pt
De  Schwellenpreis *(m)*
En  threshold price
Es  precio de umbral *(m)*
Fr  prix de seuil *(m)*
It  prezzo soglia *(m)*

**preço cotizado** *(m)* Pt
De  angegebener Preis *(m)*
En  quoted price
Es  precio cotizado *(m)*
Fr  prix coté *(m)*
It  prezzo quotato *(m)*

**preço de catálogo** *(m)* Pt
De  Listenpreis *(m)*
En  catalogue price
Es  precio de catálogo *(m)*
Fr  prix de catalogue *(m)*
It  prezzo di catalogo *(m)*

**preço de compra** *(m)* Pt
De  Kaufpreis *(m)*
En  purchase price
Es  precio de compra *(m)*
Fr  prix d'achat *(m)*
It  prezzo d'acquisto *(m)*

**preço de custo** *(m)* Pt
De  Einstandspreis *(m)*
En  cost price
Es  precio de coste *(m)*

Fr  prix de revient *(m)*
It  prezzo di costo *(m)*

**preço de factura** *(m)* Pt
De  fakturierter Preis *(m)*
En  invoice price
Es  precio facturado *(m)*
Fr  prix facturé *(m)*
It  prezzo di fattura *(m)*

**preço de intervenção** *(m)* Pt
De  Interventionspreis *(m)*
En  intervention price
Es  precio de intervención *(m)*
Fr  prix d'intervention *(m)*
It  prezzo d'intervento *(m)*

**preço de mercado** *(m)* Pt
De  Marktpreis *(m)*
En  market price
Es  precio de mercado *(m)*
Fr  cours du marché *(m)*
It  prezzo del mercato *(m)*

**preço de passagem** *(m)* Pt
De  Fahrgeld *(n)*
En  fare
Es  pasaje *(m)*
Fr  prix du voyage *(m)*
It  prezzo di viaggio *(m)*

**preço de reserva** *(m)* Pt
De  Mindestpreis *(m)*
En  reserve price
Es  precio mínimo fijado *(m)*
Fr  mise à prix *(f)*
It  prezzo minimo *(m)*

**preço de revenda** *(m)* Pt
De  Wiederverkaufspreis *(m)*
En  resale price
Es  precio de reventa *(m)*
Fr  prix de revente *(m)*
It  prezzo di rivendita *(m)*

**preço de tabela** *(m)* Pt
De  Listenpreis *(m)*
En  list price
Es  precio de tarifa *(m)*
Fr  prix courant *(m)*
It  prezzo di listino *(m)*

**preço de venda a retalho
recomendado** *(m)* Pt
De  empfohlener Ladenpreis
     *(m)*
En  recommended retail selling
     price

Es  precio detallista recomen-
     dado *(m)*
Fr  prix de détail racommandé
     *(m)*
It  prezzo al minuto indicativo
     *(m)*

**preço excepcional** *(m)* Pt
De  Spottpreis *(m)*
En  bargain price
Es  precio de ocasión *(m)*
Fr  prix de solde *(m)*
It  prezzo d'occasione *(m)*

**preço incluindo portes** *(m)* Pt
De  Lieferpreis *(m)*
En  delivered price
Es  precio incluida entrega *(m)*
Fr  prix livraison inclus *(m)*
It  prezzo  incluso  consegna
     *(m)*

**preço líquido** *(m)* Pt
De  Nettopreis; Nettokurs *(m)*
En  net price
Es  precio neto *(m)*
Fr  prix net *(m)*
It  prezzo netto *(m)*

**preço médio** *(m)* Pt
De  Mittelkurs *(m)*
En  mean price
Es  precio medio *(m)*
Fr  prix moyen *(m)*
It  prezzo medio *(m)*

**preço nominal** *(m)* Pt
De  Nennpreis *(m)*
En  nominal price
Es  precio nominal *(m)*
Fr  prix nominal *(m)*
It  prezzo nominale *(m)*

**preço para comerciantes** *(m)*
     Pt
De  Handelspreis *(m)*
En  trade price
Es  precio al comerciante *(m)*
Fr  prix marchand *(m)*
It  prezzo al commerciante *(m)*

**preço razoável** *(m)* Pt
De  angemessener Preis *(m)*
En  fair price
Es  precio razonable *(m)*
Fr  prix raisonnable *(m)*
It  prezzo equo *(m)*

**prefabbricare** vb It
De vorfabrizieren
En prefabricate
Es prefabricar
Fr préfabriquer
Pt pre-fabricar

**prefabricar** vb Es
De vorfabrizieren
En prefabricate
Fr préfabriquer
It prefabbricare
Pt pre-fabricar

**pre-fabricar** vb Pt
De vorfabrizieren
En prefabricate
Es prefabricar
Fr préfabriquer
It prefabbricare

**prefabricate** vb En
De vorfabrizieren
Es prefabricar
Fr préfabriquer
It prefabbricare
Pt pre-fabricar

**préfabriquer** vb Fr
De vorfabrizieren
En prefabricate
Es prefabricar
It prefabbricare
Pt pre-fabricar

**preference share** En
De Vorzugsaktie (f)
Es acción preferente (f)
Fr action privilégiée (f)
It azione privilegiata (f)
Pt acção preferencial (f)

**preferential creditor** En
De bevorrechtigter Gläubiger (m)
Es acreedor privilegiado (m)
Fr créancier privilégié (m)
It creditore privilegiato (m)
Pt credor preferencial (m)

**preferential duty** En
De Vorzugssatz (m)
Es derechos preferenciales (m pl)
Fr tarif de faveur (m)
It tariffa preferenziale (f)
Pt direito preferencial (m)

**pregiudizio** (m) n It
De Nachteil (m)
En prejudice
Es prejuicio; perjuicio (m)
Fr préjudice (m)
Pt prejuízo (m)

**Preis** (m) n De
En price
Es precio (m)
Fr prix (m)
It prezzo (m)
Pt preço (m)

**Preisabsprache** (f) n De
En price ring
Es coalición de vendedores (f)
Fr coalition de vendeurs (f)
It sindacato dei prezzi (m)
Pt convénio de preços (m)

**Preisdehnbarkeit** (f) n De
En price-elasticity
Es elasticidad de precio (f)
Fr élasticité-prix (f)
It elasticità di prezzo (f)
Pt flexibilidade de preços (f)

**Preisebene** (f) n De
En price level
Es nivel de precios (m)
Fr niveau des prix (m)
It livello dei prezzi (m)
Pt nível de preços (m)

**Preiserhöhung** (f) n De
En advance in price
Es encarecimiento (m)
Fr renchérissement (m)
It rialzo
Pt encarecimento (m)

**Preisherabsetzung** (f) n De
En price-cutting
Es reducción de precios (f)
Fr rabais des prix (m)
It riduzione dei prezzi (f)
Pt redução de preços (f)

**Preiskatalog** (m) n De
En trade catalogue
Es catálogo comercial (m)
Fr tarif-album (m)
It catalogo commerciale (m)
Pt catálogo comercial (m)

**Preiskontrolle** (f) n De
En price control
Es control de precios (m)
Fr contrôle des prix (m)
It controllo sui prezzi (m)
Pt controlo de preços (m)

**Preiskrieg** (m) n De
En price war
Es guerra de precios (f)
Fr guerre des prix (f)
It guerra dei prezzi (f)
Pt guerra de preços (f)

**Preisunterschied** (m) n De
En difference in price
Es diferencia de precio (f)
Fr écart de prix (m)
It differenza di prezzo (f)
Pt diferença de preço (f)

**prejudice** n En
De Nachteil (m)
Es prejuicio; perjuicio (m)
Fr préjudice (m)
It pregiudizio (m)
Pt prejuízo (m)

**préjudice** (m) n Fr
De Nachteil (m)
En prejudice
Es prejuicio; perjuicio (m)
It pregiudizio (m)
Pt prejuízo (m)

**prejuicio** (m) n Es
De Nachteil (m)
En prejudice
Fr préjudice (m)
It pregiudizio (m)
Pt prejuízo (m)

**prejuízo** (m) n Pt
De Nachteil (m)
En prejudice
Es prejuicio (m)
Fr préjudice (m)
It pregiudizio (m)

**prelevare dalle riserve** It
De die Reserven angreifen
En draw on reserves
Es sacar reservas
Fr prélever sur les réserves
Pt recorrer a reservas

**prélèvement** (m) n Fr
De Erhebung (f)
En levy
Es impuesto (m)
It imposta (f)
Pt imposto (m)

**prélever sur les réserves** Fr
De die Reserven angreifen
En draw on reserves
Es sacar reservas
It prelevare dalle riserve
Pt recorrer a reservas

**préliminaire** adj Fr
De vorläufig; einleitend
En preliminary
Es preliminar
It preliminare
Pt preliminar

**preliminar** adj Es, Pt
De vorläufig; einleitend
En preliminary
Fr préliminaire; préalable
It preliminare

**preliminare** adj It
De vorläufig; einleitend
En preliminary
Es preliminar
Fr préliminaire; préalable
Pt preliminar

**preliminary** adj En
De vorläufig; einleitend
Es preliminar
Fr préliminaire; préalable
It preliminare
Pt preliminar

**première classe** (f) Fr
De erste Klasse (f)
En first class
Es primera clase (f)
It prima classe (f)
Pt primeira classe (f)

**première de change** (f) Fr
De Primawechsel (m)
En first of exchange
Es primera de cambio (f)
It prima di cambio (f)
Pt primeira de câmbio (f)

**premio** (m) n It, Es
De Prämie (f)
En premium

Fr prime (f)
Pt prémio (m)

**prémio** (m) n Pt
De Prämie (f)
En premium
Es prima; premio (f m)
Fr prime (f)
It premio (m)

**premio a vendere** (m) It
De Verkaufsoption (f)
En put option
Es opción de venta (f)
Fr option à vendre (f)
Pt opção de venda (f)

**prémio bruto** (m) Pt
De Bruttoprämie (f)
En gross premium
Es prima bruta (f)
Fr prime brute (f)
It premio lordo (m)

**premio d'acquisto** (m) It
De Kaufoption (f)
En call option
Es opción de compras (f)
Fr option (f)
Pt opção de compra (f)

**prémio de risco** (m) Pt
De Gefahrenzulage (f)
En danger money
Es suma para riesgos (f)
Fr prime de risque (f)
It compenso per il rischio (m)

**prémio de seguro** (m) Pt
De Versicherungsprämie (f)
En insurance premium
Es prima de póliza de seguro (f)
Fr prime d'assurance (f)
It premio di assicurazione (m)

**premio d'esportazione** (m) It
De Ausfuhrprämie (f)
En export bonus
Es subsidio a las exportaciones (m)
Fr prime à l'exportation (f)
Pt subsídio de exportação (m)

**premio di assicurazione** (m) It
De Versicherungsprämie (f)
En insurance premium

Es prima de póliza de seguro (f)
Fr prime d'assurance (f)
Pt prémio de seguro (m)

**premio lordo** (m) It
De Bruttoprämie (f)
En gross premium
Es prima bruta (f)
Fr prime brute (f)
Pt prémio bruto (m)

**premium** n En
De Prämie (f)
Es prima; premio (f m)
Fr prime (f)
It premio (m)
Pt prémio (m)

**premium offer** En
De Verkauf mit Zugaben (m)
Es oferta a prima (f)
Fr offre à prime (f)
It offerta sopra la pari (f)
Pt oferta-prémio (f)

**prenda** (f) n Pt
De Geschenk (n)
En gift
Es regalo (m)
Fr don; cadeau (m)
It dono (m)

**prendre un rendez-vous** Fr
De eine Verabredung treffen
En make an appointment
Es hacer una cita
It fissare un appuntamento
Pt marcar um encontro

**prepaid** adj En
De vorausbezahlt
Es pagado por adelantado
Fr payé d'avance
It pagato in anticipo
Pt pago adiantamente

**preparação de montras** (f) Pt
De Schaufensterdekoration (f)
En window-dressing
Es preparación de escaparates (f)
Fr art de l'étalage (m)
It allestimento delle vetrine (m)

**preparación de escaparates** (f) Es
De Schaufensterdekoration (f)
En window-dressing
Fr art de l'étalage (m)
It allestimento delle vetrine (m)
Pt preparação de montras (f)

**prepayment** n En
De Vorauszahlung (f)
Es pago andelantado (m)
Fr paiement anticipé (m)
It pagamento anticipato (m)
Pt pagamento adiantado (m)

**present a bill for acceptance** En
De einen Wechsel vorlegen
Es presentar una letra para aceptación
Fr présenter une traite à l'acceptation
It presentare una cambiale per accettazione
Pt apresentar letra para aceite

**presentare una cambiale per accettazione** It
De einen Wechsel vorlegen
En present a bill for acceptance
Es presentar una letra para aceptación
Fr présenter une traite à l'acceptation
Pt apresentar letra para aceite

**presentar la dimisión** Es
De den Rücktritt einreichen
En hand in one's resignation
Fr remettre sa démission
It rassegnare le dimissioni
Pt apresentar demissão

**presentar una letra para aceptación** Es
De einen Wechsel vorlegen
En present a bill for acceptance
Fr présenter une traite à l'acceptation
It presentare una cambiale per accettazione
Pt apresentar letra para aceite

**présenter une traite à l'acceptation** Fr
De einen Wechsel vorlegen
En present a bill for acceptance
Es presentar una letra para aceptación
It presentare una cambiale per accettazione
Pt apresentar letra para aceite

**présentoir** (m) n Fr
De Schaukasten (m)
En display unit
Es presentación (f)
It mostra (f)
Pt montra (f)

**président** (m) n Fr
De Vorsitzende(r) (m)
En chairman
Es presidente (m)
It presidente (m)
Pt presidente (m)

**presidente** (m) n Es, It, Pt
De Vorsitzende(r) (m)
En chairman
Fr président (m)

**pressure gauge** En
De Druckmesser (m)
Es manómetro (m)
Fr manomètre: jauge de pression (m f)
It manometro (m)
Pt manómetro (m)

**prestação** (f) n Pt
De Rate (f)
En instalment
Es plazo (m)
Fr acompte (m)
It rata (f)

**prestação mensal** (f) Pt
De Monatsrate (f)
En monthly instalment
Es mensualidad (f)
Fr mensualité (f)
It mensilità (f)

**prestamista** (m) n Es, Pt
De Geldverleiher; Pfandleiher (m)
En moneylender; pawnbroker
Fr prêteur d'argent; prêteur sur gage (m)

It usuraio; prestatore su pegno (m)

**préstamo bancario** (m) Es
De Bankdarlehen (n)
En bank loan
Fr prêt bancaire (m)
It prestito bancario (m)
Pt empréstimo bancário (m)

**préstamo exterior** (m) Es
De Auslandsanleihe (f)
En external loan
Fr emprunt extérieur (m)
It prestito esterno (m)
Pt empréstimo externo (m)

**prestar** vb Es
De leihen
En lend
Fr prêter
It prestare
Pt emprestar

**prestar caución a favor de** Pt
De Haftkaution geben
En go bail for
Es salir fiados por
Fr se porter garant de
It rendersi garante di

**prestare** vb It
De leihen
En lend
Es prestar
Fr prêter
Pt emprestar

**prestatario** (m) n Es
De Kreditnehmer (m)
En borrower
Fr emprunteur (m)
It accattatore (m)
Pt beneficiário de empréstimo (m)

**prestatore su pegno** (m) It
De Pfandleiher (m)
En pawnbroker
Es prestamista (m)
Fr prêteur sur gage (m)
Pt prestamista (m)

**prestire** vb It
De entleihen
En borrow
Es pedir un préstamo

Fr  emprunter
Pt  contrair empréstimo

**prestito** (m) n It
De  Anleihe (f)
En  loan
Es  empréstito (m)
Fr  emprunt (m)
Pt  empréstime (m)

**prestito bancario** (m) It
De  Bankdarlehen (n)
En  bank loan
Es  préstamo bancario (m)
Fr  prêt bancaire (m)
Pt  empréstimo bancário (m)

**prestito esterno** (m) It
De  Auslandsanleihe (f)
En  external loan
Es  préstamo exterior (m)
Fr  emprunt extérieur (m)
Pt  empréstimo externo (m)

**prestito immobiliare** (m) It
De  Baukredit (m)
En  building loan
Es  crédito de construcción (m)
Fr  crédit de construction (m)
Pt  empréstimo para constru-
    ção (m)

**prestito pubblico** (m) It
De  Staatsanleihe (f)
En  government loan
Es  empréstito público (m)
Fr  emprunt public (m)
Pt  empréstimo do governo (m)

**presupuesto** (m) n Es
De  Haushaltsplan; Voranschlag
    (m)
En  budget; estimate
Fr  budget; devis (m)
It  bilancio preventivo; preven-
    tivo (m)
Pt  orçamento; previsão (m f)

**presupuesto aproximado** (m)
    Es
De  rohe Schätzung (f)
En  rough estimate
Fr  estimation approximative (f)
It  valutazione approssimativa
    (f)
Pt  avaliação aproximada (f)

**presupuesto por defecto** (m)
    Es
De  Unterschätzung (f)
En  under-estimate
Fr  sous-estimation (f)
It  sottovalutazione (f)
Pt  avaliação insuficiente (f)

**presupuesto por exceso** (m)
    Es
De  Überschätzung (f)
En  over-estimate
Fr  surestimation (f)
It  valutazione eccessiva (f)
Pt  avaliação excessiva (f)

**presupuesto prudente** (m) Es
De  vorsichtige Schätzung (f)
En  conservative estimate
Fr  évaluation prudente (f)
It  valutazione prudente (f)
Pt  avaliação cautelosa (f)

**prêt bancaire** (m) Fr
De  Bankdarlehen (n)
En  bank loan
Es  préstamo bancario (m)
It  prestito bancario (m)
Pt  empréstimo bancário (m)

**prêter** vb Fr
De  leihen
En  lend
Es  prestar
It  prestare
Pt  emprestar

**prêteur d'argent** (m) Fr
De  Geldverleiher (m)
En  moneylender
Es  prestamista (m)
It  usuraio (m)
Pt  prestamista (m)

**prêteur sur gage** (m) Fr
De  Pfandleiher (m)
En  pawnbroker
Es  prestamista (m)
It  prestatore su pegno (m)
Pt  prestamista (m)

**preuve** (f) n Fr
De  Beweis (m)
En  evidence
Es  evidencia (f)
It  prova (f)
Pt  prova (f)

**preuve écrite** (f) Fr
De  Urkundenbeweis (m)
En  documentary evidence
Es  prueba documental (f)
It  prova scritta (f)
Pt  prova documental (f)

**preventivo** (m) n It
De  Voranschlag (m)
En  estimate
Es  presupuesto (m)
Fr  devis (m)
Pt  previsão (f)

**preventivo riveduto** (m) It
De  überarbeitete Schätzung (f)
En  revised estimate
Es  cálculo revisado (m)
Fr  devis rectifié (m)
Pt  estimativa revista (f)

**preventivo supplementare** (m)
    It
De  Nachschätzung (f)
En  supplementary estimate
Es  cálculo suplementario (m)
Fr  devis supplémentaire (f)
Pt  estimativa suplementar (f)

**previa condición** (f) Es
De  aufschiebende Bedingung
    (f)
En  condition precedent
Fr  condition suspensive (f)
It  condizione sospensiva (f)
Pt  condição prévia (f)

**previsão** (f) n Pt
De  Voranschlag; Voraussagen
    (m n)
En  estimate; forecast
Es  presupuesto; pronóstico
    (m)
Fr  devis; prévision (m f)
It  preventivo; previsione (m f)

**previsão de fundos** (f) Pt
De  Bargeldvoraussage (f)
En  cash forecast
Es  previsión de fondos (f)
Fr  prévision comptant (f)
It  previsione contanti (f)

**previsão de vendas** (f) Pt
De  Verkaufsvoraussage (f)
En  sales forecast
Es  pronóstico de ventas (m)

Fr prévision de ventes *(f)*
It previsione delle vendite *(f)*

**prévision** *(f) n* Fr
De Voraussagen *(n)*
En forecasting
Es pronóstico *(m)*
It previsione *(f)*
Pt previsão *(f)* ·

**prévision comptant** *(f)* Fr
De Bargeldvoraussage *(f)*
En cash forecast
Es previsión de fondos *(f)*
It previsione contanti *(f)*
Pt previsão de fundos (em dinheiro) *(f)*

**previsión de fondos** *(f)* Es
De Bargeldvoraussage *(f)*
En cash forecast
Fr prévision comptant *(f)*
It previsione contanti *(f)*
Pt previsão de fundos *(f)*

**prévision de ventes** *(f)* Fr
De Verkaufsvoraussage *(f)*
En sales forecast
Es pronóstico de ventas *(m)*
It previsione delle vendite *(f)*
Pt previsão de vendas *(f)*

**previsione** *(f) n* It
De Voraussagen *(n)*
En forecasting
Es pronóstico *(m)*
Fr prévision *(f)*
Pt previsão *(f)*

**previsione contanti** *(f)* It
De Bargeldvoraussage *(f)*
En cash forecast
Es previsión de fondos *(f)*
Fr prévision comptant *(f)*
Pt previsão de fundos *(f)*

**previsione delle vendite** *(f)* It
De Verkaufsvoraussage *(f)*
En sales forecast
Es pronóstico de ventas *(m)*
Fr prévision de ventes *(f)*
Pt previsão de vendas *(f)*

**prévoir** *vb* Fr
De vorhersehen
En forecast
Es pronosticar

It pronosticare
Pt prognosticar

**prezzo** *(m) n* It
De Preis; Kurs *(m)*
En price
Es precio *(m)*
Fr prix *(m)*
Pt preço *(m)*

**prezzo al commerciante** *(m)* It
De Handelspreis *(m)*
En trade price
Es precio al comerciante *(m)*
Fr prix marchand *(m)*
Pt preço para comerciantes *(m)*

**prezzo al minuto** *(m)* It
De Einzelhandelspreis *(m)*
En retail price
Es precio al por menor *(m)*
Fr prix de détail *(m)*
Pt preço a retalho *(m)*

**prezzo al minuto indicativo** *(m)* It
De empfohlener Ladenpreis *(m)*
En recommended retail selling price
Es precio detallista recomendado *(m)*
Fr prix de détail racommandé *(m)*
Pt preço de venda a retalho recomendado *(m)*

**prezzo contrattuale** *(m)* It
De Vertragspreis *(m)*
En contract price
Es precio contractual *(m)*
Fr prix contractuel *(m)*
Pt preço contractual *(m)*

**prezzo d'acquisto** *(m)* It
De Kaufpreis *(m)*
En purchase price
Es precio de compra *(m)*
Fr prix d'achat *(m)*
Pt preço de compra *(m)*

**prezzo del mercato** *(m)* It
De Marktpreis *(m)*
En market price
Es precio de mercado *(m)*
Fr cours du marché *(m)*
Pt preço de mercado *(m)*

**prezzo di catalogo** *(m)* It
De Listenpreis *(m)*
En catalogue price
Es precio de catálogo *(m)*
Fr prix de catalogue *(m)*
Pt preço de catálogo *(m)* ·

**prezzo di chiusura** *(m)* It
De Schlussnotierung *(f)*
En closing price
Es precio de cierre *(m)*
Fr cours de clôture *(m)*
Pt último preço *(m)*

**prezzo di costo** *(m)* It
De Einstandspreis *(m)*
En cost price
Es precio de coste *(m)*
Fr prix de revient *(m)*
Pt preço de custo *(m)*

**prezzo di fattura** *(m)* It
De fakturierter Preis *(m)*
En invoice price
Es precio facturado *(m)*
Fr prix facturé *(m)*
Pt preço de factura *(m)*

**prezzo di listino** *(m)* It
De Listenpreis *(m)*
En list price
Es precio de tarifa *(m)*
Fr prix courant *(m)*
Pt preço de tabela *(m)*

**prezzo d'intervento** *(m)* It
De Interventionspreis *(m)*
En intervention price
Es precio de intervención *(m)*
Fr prix d'intervention *(m)*
Pt preço de intervenção *(m)*

**prezzo di rivendita** *(m)* It
De Wiederverkaufspreis *(m)*
En resale price
Es precio de reventa *(m)*
Fr prix de revente *(m)*
Pt preço de revenda *(m)*

**prezzo di viaggio** *(m)* It
De Fahrgeld *(n)*
En fare
Es pasaje *(m)*
Fr prix du voyage *(m)*
Pt preço de passagem *(m)*

**prezzo d'occasione** *(m)* It
De Spottpreis *(m)*
En bargain price
Es precio de ocasión *(m)*
Fr prix de solde *(m)*
Pt preço excepcional *(m)*

**prezzo equo** *(m)* It
De angemessener Preis *(m)*
En fair price
Es precio razonable *(m)*
Fr prix raisonnable *(m)*
Pt preço razoável *(m)*

**prezzo incluso consegna** *(m)* It
De Lieferpreis *(m)*
En delivered price
Es precio incluida entrega *(m)*
Fr prix livraison inclus *(m)*
Pt preço incluindo portes *(m)*

**prezzo medio** *(m)* It
De Mittelkurs *(m)*
En mean price
Es precio medio *(m)*
Fr prix moyen *(m)*
Pt preço médio *(m)*

**prezzo minimo** *(m)* It
De Mindestpreis *(m)*
En reserve price
Es precio mínimo fijado *(m)*
Fr mise à prix *(f)*
Pt preço de reserva *(m)*

**prezzo netto** *(m)* It
De Nettopreis; Nettokurs *(m)*
En net price
Es precio neto *(m)*
Fr prix net *(m)*
Pt preço líquido *(m)*

**prezzo nominale** *(m)* It
De Nennpreis *(m)*
En nominal price
Es precio nominal *(m)*
Fr prix nominal *(m)*
Pt preço nominal *(m)*

**prezzo per futura consegna** *(m)* It
De Terminnotierung *(f)*
En forward price
Es precio a término *(m)*
Fr cours à terme *(m)*
Pt preço adiantado *(m)*

**prezzo quotato** *(m)* It
De angegebener Preis *(m)*
En quoted price
Es precio cotizado *(m)*
Fr prix coté *(m)*
Pt preço cotizado *(m)*

**prezzo soglia** *(m)* It
De Schwellenpreis *(m)*
En threshold price
Es precio de umbral *(m)*
Fr prix de seuil *(m)*
Pt preço convencionado *(m)*

**price** *n* En
De Preis; Kurs *(m)*
Es precio *(m)*
Fr prix *(m)*
It prezzo *(m)*
Pt preço *(m)*

**price control** En
De Preiskontrolle *(f)*
Es control de precios *(m)*
Fr contrôle des prix *(m)*
It controllo sui prezzi *(m)*
Pt controlo de preços *(m)*

**price-cutting** *n* En
De Preisherabsetzung *(f)*
Es reducción de precios *(f)*
Fr rabais des prix *(m)*
It riduzione dei prezzi *(f)*
Pt redução de preços *(f)*

**price-earnings ratio** (P/E) En
De Verhältnis des Aktienkurses zum Reingewinn *(n)*
Es proporción precio-ingresos *(f)*
Fr quotient cours-bénéfice *(m)*
It rapporto prezzo-utile *(m)*
Pt taxa custo-ganhos *(f)*

**price-elasticity** *n* En
De Preisdehnbarkeit *(f)*
Es elasticidad de precio *(f)*
Fr élasticité-prix *(f)*
It elasticità di prezzo *(f)*
Pt flexibilidade de preços *(f)*

**price level** En
De Preisebene *(f)*
Es nivel de precios *(m)*
Fr niveau des prix *(m)*
It livello dei prezzi *(m)*
Pt nível de preços *(m)*

**price ring** En
De Preisabsprache *(f)*
Es coalición de vendedores *(f)*
Fr coalition de vendeurs *(f)*
It sindacato dei prezzi *(m)*
Pt convénio de preços *(m)*

**price war** En
De Preiskrieg *(m)*
Es guerra de precios *(f)*
Fr guerre des prix *(f)*
It guerra dei prezzi *(f)*
Pt guerra de preços *(f)*

**prière de faire suivre** Fr
De bitte nachsenden
En please forward
Es se ruega hacer seguir
It far proseguire
Pt é favor enviar

**prima** *(f)* n Es
De Prämie *(f)*
En premium; bonus
Fr prime *(f)*
It premio *(m)*
Pt prémio *(m)*

**prima bruta** *(f)* Es
De Bruttoprämie *(f)*
En gross premium
Fr prime brute *(f)*
It premio lordo *(m)*
Pt prémio bruto *(m)*

**prima classe** *(f)* It
De erste Klasse *(f)*
En first class
Es primera clase *(f)*
Fr première classe *(f)*
Pt primeira classe *(f)*

**prima de aplazamiento** *(f)* Es
De Kursabschlag *(m)*
En backwardation
Fr déport *(m)*
It deporto *(m)*
Pt juro de mora *(m)*

**prima de póliza de seguro** *(f)* Es
De Versicherungsprämie *(f)*
En insurance premium
Fr prime d'assurance *(f)*
It premio di assicurazione *(m)*
Pt prémio de seguro *(m)*

**prima di cambio** *(f)* It
De Primawechsel *(m)*
En first of exchange
Es primera de cambio *(f)*
Fr première de change *(f)*
Pt primeira de câmbio *(f)*

**Primawechsel** *(m)* n De
En first of exchange
Es primera de cambio *(f)*
Fr première de change *(f)*
It prima di cambio *(f)*
Pt primeira de câmbio *(f)*

**prime** *(f)* n Fr
De Prämie *(f)*
En premium; bonus
Es prima; premio *(f m)*
It premio *(m)*
Pt prémio *(m)*

**prime à l'exportation** *(f)* Fr
De Ausfuhrprämie *(f)*
En export bonus
Es subsidio a las exportaciones *(m)*
It premio d'esportazione *(m)*
Pt subsídio de exportação *(m)*

**prime brute** *(f)* Fr
De Bruttoprämie *(f)*
En gross premium
Es prima bruta *(f)*
It premio lordo *(m)*
Pt prémio bruto *(m)*

**prime cost** En
De Selbstkosten *(pl)*
Es precio de coste *(m)*
Fr prix de revient *(m)*
It prezzo di costo *(m)*
Pt preço de custo *(m)*

**prime d'assurance** *(f)* Fr
De Versicherungsprämie *(f)*
En insurance premium
Es prima de póliza de seguro *(f)*
It premio di assicurazione *(m)*
Pt prémio de seguro *(m)*

**prime de risque** *(f)* Fr
De Gefahrenzulage *(f)*
En danger money
Es suma para riesgos *(f)*
It compenso per il rischio *(m)*
Pt prémio de risco *(m)*

**primeira classe** *(f)* Pt
De erste Klasse *(f)*
En first class
Es primera clase *(f)*
Fr première classe *(f)*
It prima classe *(f)*

**primeira de câmbio** *(f)* Pt
De Primawechsel *(m)*
En first of exchange
Es primera de cambio *(f)*
Fr première de change *(f)*
It prima di cambio *(f)*

**primera clase** *(f)* Es
De erste Klasse *(f)*
En first class
Fr première classe *(f)*
It prima classe *(f)*
Pt primeira classe *(f)*

**primera de cambio** *(f)* Es
De Primawechsel *(m)*
En first of exchange
Fr première de change *(f)*
It prima di cambio *(f)*
Pt primeira de câmbio *(f)*

**primer día del trimestre** *(m)* Es
De Quartalstag *(m)*
En quarter day
Fr jour du terme *(m)*
It giorno della pigione *(m)*
Pt dia de vencimento trimestral *(m)*

**primer oficial** *(m)* Es
De Maat *(m)*
En (ship's) mate
Fr second *(m)*
It primo ufficiale *(m)*
Pt imediato *(m)*

**prime trade bill** En
De erstklassiger Handelswechsel *(m)*
Es carta comercial de primera orden *(f)*
Fr papier de haut commerce *(m)*
It carta commerciale di primo ordine *(f)*
Pt estatuto de comercialização de primeira ordem *(m)*

**primo ufficiale** *(m)* It
De Maat *(m)*
En (ship's) mate

**primer oficial** *(m)* Es
Fr second *(m)*
Pt imediato *(m)*

**principal** (head) n En
De Prinzipal; Direktor *(m)*
Es principal; jefe *(m)*
Fr patron; directeur *(m)*
It principale; direttore *(m)*
Pt director; reitor *(m)*

**principal** (capital) n En; Es, Fr *(m)*
Am capital
De Kapital *(n)*
It capitale *(m)*
Pt capital *(m)*

**principal** (to a contract) n En
De Vollmachtgeber *(m)*
Es mandante *(m)*
Fr mandant *(m)*
It mandante *(m)*
Pt mandante *(m)*

**principal** (jefe) *(m)* n Es
De Prinzipal; Direktor *(m)*
En principal; head
Fr patron; directeur *(m)*
It principale; direttore *(m)*
Pt director; reitor *(m)*

**principale** *(m)* n It
De Prinzipal; Direktor *(m)*
En principal; head
Es principal; jefe *(m)*
Fr patron; directeur *(m)*
Pt director; reitor *(m)*

**printed form** En
De Vordruck *(m)*
Es formulario; impreso *(m)*
Fr formulaire *(m)*
It modulo stampato *(m)*
Pt impresso *(m)*

**Prinzipal** *(m)* n De
En principal; head
Es principal; jefe *(m)*
Fr patron; directeur *(m)*
It principale; direttore *(m)*
Pt director; reitor *(m)*

**prioridad** *(f)* n Es
De Vorrecht *(n)*
En priority
Fr priorité *(f)*

It   priorità *(f)*
Pt   prioridade *(f)*

**prioridade** *(f)* n Pt
De   Vorrecht *(n)*
En   priority
Es   prioridad *(f)*
Fr   priorité *(f)*
It   priorità *(f)*

**priorità** *(f)* n It
De   Vorrecht *(n)*
En   priority
Es   prioridad *(f)*
Fr   priorité *(f)*
Pt   prioridade *(f)*

**priorité** *(f)* n Fr
De   Vorrecht *(n)*
En   priority
Es   prioridad *(f)*
It   priorità *(f)*
Pt   prioridade *(f)*

**priority** n En
De   Vorrecht *(n)*
Es   prioridad *(f)*
Fr   priorité *(f)*
It   priorità *(f)*
Pt   prioridade *(f)*

**prise de bénéfices** *(f)* Fr
De   Gewinnrealisation *(f)*
En   profit-taking
Es   realización de utilidades *(f)*
It   realizzazione del utile *(f)*
Pt   realização dos lucros *(m)*

**prise usine** Fr
De   ab Werk
En   ex works
Es   de fábrica
It   franco fabbrica
Pt   na fábrica

**Privatbank** *(f)* n De
En   private bank
Es   banco privado *(m)*
Fr   bánque privée *(f)*
It   banca privata *(f)*
Pt   banco privado *(m)*

**private bank** En
De   Privatbank *(f)*
Es   banco privado *(m)*
Fr   banque privée *(f)*
It   banca privata *(f)*
Pt   banco privado *(m)*

**private enterprise** En
De   Privatunternehmen *(n)*
Es   empresa privada *(f)*
Fr   entreprise privée *(f)*
It   impresa privata *(f)*
Pt   empresa privada *(f)*

**private limited company** En
De   Gesellschaft mit beschränk-
      ter Haftung (GmbH) *(f)*
Es   Companía privada de res-
      ponsabilidad limitada *(f)*
Fr   Société à responsabilité
      limitée (SARL) *(f)*
It   Società a responsabilità
      limitata (Sarl) *(f)*
Pt   Sociedade por quotas de
      responsabilidade limitada
      *(f)*

**private sector** En
De   freie Marktwirtschaft *(f)*
Es   sector privado *(m)*
Fr   secteur privé *(m)*
It   settore privato *(m)*
Pt   sector privado *(m)*

**Privatunternehmen** *(n)* n De
En   private enterprise
Es   empresa privada *(f)*
Fr   entreprise privée *(f)*
It   impresa privata *(f)*
Pt   empresa privada *(f)*

**privilège général** *(m)* Fr
De   allgemeines Pfandrecht *(n)*
En   general lien
Es   privilegio general *(m)*
It   privilegio generale *(m)*
Pt   privilégio geral *(m)*

**privilegio general** *(m)* Es
De   allgemeines Pfandrecht *(n)*
En   general lien
Fr   privilège général *(m)*
It   privilegio generale *(m)*
Pt   privilégio geral *(m)*

**privilegio generale** *(m)* It
De   allgemeines Pfandrecht *(n)*
En   general lien
Es   privilegio general *(m)*
Fr   privilège général *(m)*
Pt   privilégio geral *(m)*

**privilégio geral** *(m)* Pt
De   allgemeines Pfandrecht *(n)*
En   general lien

Es   privilegio general *(m)*
Fr   privilège général *(m)*
It   privilegio generale *(m)*

**privilégios excluidos** Pt
De   ohne Bezugsrechte
En   ex rights
Es   sin privilegio
Fr   ex-droits
It   senza diritti

**prix** *(m)* n Fr
De   Preis; Kurs *(m)*
En   price
Es   precio *(m)*
It   prezzo *(m)*
Pt   preço *(m)*

**prix contractuel** *(m)* Fr
De   Vertragspreis *(m)*
En   contract price
Es   precio contractual *(m)*
It   prezzo contrattuale *(m)*
Pt   preço contractual *(m)*

**prix coté** *(m)* Fr
De   angegebener Preis *(m)*
En   quoted price
Es   precio cotizado *(m)*
It   prezzo quotato *(m)*
Pt   preço cotizado *(m)*

**prix courant** *(m)* Fr
De   Listenpreis *(m)*
En   list price
Es   precio de tarifa *(m)*
It   prezzo di listino *(m)*
Pt   preço de tabela *(m)*

**prix coûtant unitaire** *(m)* Fr
De   Einheitskosten *(f pl)*
En   unit cost
Es   coste unitario *(m)*
It   costo unitario *(m)*
Pt   custo por unidade *(m)*

**prix d'achat** *(m)* Fr
De   Kaufpreis *(m)*
En   purchase price
Es   precio de compra *(m)*
It   prezzo d'acquisto *(m)*
Pt   preço de compra *(m)*

**prix de catalogue** *(m)* Fr
De   Listenpreis *(m)*
En   catalogue price
Es   precio de catálogo *(m)*

It    prezzo di catalogo *(m)*
Pt    preço de catálogo *(m)*

**prix de détail** *(m)* Fr
De    Einzelhandelspreis *(m)*
En    retail price
Es    precio al por menor *(m)*
It    prezzo al minuto *(m)*
Pt    preço a retalho *(m)*

**prix de détail racommandé**
      *(m)* Fr
De    empfohlener    Ladenpreis
      *(m)*
En    recommended retail selling
      price
Es    precio detallista recomen-
      dado *(m)*
It    prezzo al minuto indicativo
      *(m)*
Pt    preço de venda a retalho
      recomendado *(m)*

**prix de revente** *(m)* Fr
De    Wiederverkaufspreis *(m)*
En    resale price
Es    precio de reventa *(m)*
It    prezzo di rivendita *(m)*
Pt    preço de revenda *(m)*

**prix de revient** *(m)* Fr
De    Einstandspreis *(m)*
En    cost price
Es    precio de coste *(m)*
It    prezzo di costo *(m)*
Pt    preço de custo *(m)*

**prix de revient comptable** *(m)*
      Fr
De    Buchwert der Einkäufe *(m)*
En    book cost
Es    coste contàble *(m)*
It    costo contabile *(m)*
Pt    custo contabilizado *(m)*

**prix de revient effectif** *(m)* Fr
De    Gestehungskosten *(pl)*
En    actual cost
Es    precio verdadero *(m)*
It    costo effettivo *(m)*
Pt    custo verdadeiro *(m)*

**prix de seuil** *(m)* Fr
De    Schwellenpreis *(m)*
En    threshold price
Es    precio de umbral *(m)*
It    prezzo soglia *(m)*
Pt    preço convencionado *(m)*

**prix de solde** *(m)* Fr
De    Spottpreis *(m)*
En    bargain price
Es    precio de ocasión *(m)*
It    prezzo d'occasione *(m)*
Pt    preço excepcional *(m)*

**prix d'intervention** *(m)* Fr
De    Interventionspreis *(m)*
En    intervention price
Es    precio de intervención *(m)*
It    prezzo d'intervento *(m)*
Pt    preço de intervenção *(m)*

**prix direct de revient** *(m)* Fr
De    direkte Kosten *(pl)*
En    direct cost
Es    coste directo *(m)*
It    costo diretto *(m)*
Pt    custo directo *(m)*

**prix du voyage** *(m)* Fr
De    Fahrgeld *(n)*
En    fare
Es    pasaje *(m)*
It    prezzo di viaggio *(m)*
Pt    preço de passagem *(m)*

**prix facturé** *(m)* Fr
De    fakturierter Preis *(m)*
En    invoice price
Es    precio facturado *(m)*
It    prezzo di fattura *(m)*
Pt    preço de factura *(m)*

**prix livraison inclus** *(m)* Fr
De    Lieferpreis *(m)*
En    delivered price
Es    precio incluida entrega *(m)*
It    prezzo incluso consegna
      *(m)*
Pt    preço incluindo portes *(m)*

**prix marchand** *(m)* Fr
De    Handelspreis *(m)*
En    trade price
Es    precio al comerciante *(m)*
It    prezzo al commerciante *(m)*
Pt    preço para comerciantes
      *(m)*

**prix moyen** *(m)* Fr
De    Mittelkurs *(m)*
En    mean price
Es    precio medio *(m)*
It    prezzo medio *(m)*
Pt    preço médio *(m)*

**prix net** *(m)* Fr
De    Nettopreis: Nettokurs *(m)*
En    net price
Es    precio neto *(m)*
It    prezzo netto *(m)*
Pt    preço líquido *(m)*

**prix nominal** *(m)* Fr
De    Nennpreis *(m)*
En    nominal price
Es    precio nominal *(m)*
It    prezzo nominale *(m)*
Pt    preço nominal *(m)*

**prix raisonnable** *(m)* Fr
De    angemessener Preis *(m)*
En    fair price
Es    precio razonable *(m)*
It    prezzo equo *(m)*
Pt    preço razoável *(m)*

**probabilidad** *(f)* n Es
De    Wahrscheinlichkeit *(f)*
En    probability
Fr    probabilité *(f)*
It    probabilità *(f)*
Pt    probabilidade *(f)*

**probabilidade** *(f)* n Pt
De    Wahrscheinlichkeit *(f)*
En    probability
Es    probabilidad *(f)*
Fr    probabilité *(f)*
It    probabilità *(f)*

**probabilità** *(f)* n It
De    Wahrscheinlichkeit *(f)*
En    probability
Es    probabilidad *(f)*
Fr    probabilité *(f)*
Pt    probabilidade *(f)*

**probabilité** *(f)* n Fr
De    Wahrscheinlichkeit *(f)*
En    probability
Es    probabilidad *(f)*
It    probabilità *(f)*
Pt    probabilidade *(f)*

**probability** n En
De    Wahrscheinlichkeit *(f)*
Es    probabilidad *(f)*
Fr    probabilité *(f)*
It    probabilità *(f)*
Pt    probabilidade *(f)*

**probate** n En
De Testamentseröffnung; Bestätigung (f)
Es validación de los testamentos (f)
Fr homologation d'un testament (f)
It omologazione di testamento (f)
Pt validação testamentária (f)

**Probe** (f) n De
En test; sample
Es ensayo; muestra (m f)
Fr épreuve; échantillon (f m)
It prova; campione (f m)
Pt prova; amostra (f)

**Probebilanz** (f) n De
En trial balance
Es balance de comprobación de saldos (m)
Fr bilan de vérification (m)
It bilancio di verifica (m)
Pt balancete de verificação (m)

**Probegüter** (n pl) n De
En goods on approval
Es mercancías sujetas a aprobación (f pl)
Fr marchandises à condition (f pl)
It merce soggetta ad approvazione (f)
Pt artigos sujeitos a aprovação (m pl)

**pro capite** It
De pro Kopf
En per capita
Es por cabeza
Fr par tête
Pt per capita; por unidade

**procedimento** (m) n Pt
De Verfahren (n)
En procedure
Es procedimiento (m)
Fr procédure (f)
It procedura (f)

**procedimiento** (m) n Es
De Verfahren (n)
En procedure
Fr procédure (f)
It procedura (f)
Pt procedimento (m)

**procedura** (f) n It
De Verfahren (n)
En procedure
Es procedimiento (m)
Fr procédure (f)
Pt procedimento (m)

**procedure** n En
De Verfahren (n)
Es procedimiento (m)
Fr procédure (f)
It procedura (f)
Pt procedimento (m)

**procédure** (f) n Fr
De Verfahren (n)
En procedure
Es procedimiento (m)
It procedura (f)
Pt procedimento (m)

**procès** (m) n Fr
De Rechtsfall; Prozess (m)
En lawsuit; trial
Es proceso; causa (m f)
It processo; causa (m f)
Pt processo; causa (m f)

**proceso** (m) n Es
De Rechtsfall; Prozess (m)
En lawsuit; trial
Fr procès (m)
It processo; causa (m f)
Pt processo; causa (m f)

**processamento de dados** (m) Pt
De Datenverarbeitung (f)
En data processing
Es tratamiento de datos (m)
Fr traitement d'informatique (m)
It elaborazione dei dati (f)

**processamento por danos** (m) Pt
De Schadenersatzklage (f)
En action for damages
Es acción por daños (f)
Fr action en dommages et intérêts (f)
It processo per risarcimento (m)

**processo** (m) It, Pt
De Rechtsfall; Prozess (m)
En lawsuit; trial

Es proceso; causa (m f)
Fr procès (m)

**processo per risarcimento** (m) It
De Schadenersatzklage (f)
En action for damages
Es acción por daños (f)
Fr action en dommages et intérêts (f)
Pt processamento por danos (m)

**procès-verbal** (m) n Fr
De Protokoll (n)
En minutes
Es actas (f pl)
It verbale (m)
Pt minutas de acta (f pl)

**proclamare uno sciopero** It
De zum Streik auffordern
En call a strike
Es declararse en huelga
Fr ordonner une grève
Pt declarar greve

**procura** (f) n It
De Vollmacht; Stellvertretung (f)
En power of attorney; proxy
Es poder; procuración (m f)
Fr pouvoirs; procuration (m pl; f)
Pt procuração (f)

**procuração** (f) n Pt
De Vollmacht; Stellvertretung (f)
En power of attorney; proxy
Es poder; procuración (m f)
Fr pouvoirs; procuration (m pl; f)
It procura (f)

**procuración** (f) n Es
De Vollmacht; Stellvertretung (f)
En power of attorney; proxy
Fr pouvoirs; procuration (m pl; f)
It procura (f)
Pt procuração (f)

**procurado** Pt
De gefragt
En in demand
Es solicitado

Fr demandé
It ricercato

**procurador** (m) n Es, Pt
De Bevollmächtigte(r); Stellvertreter (m)
En attorney; proxy
Fr mandataire (m)
It procuratore; mandatario (m)

**procuration** (f) n Fr
De Vollmacht; Stellvertretung (f)
En power of attorney; proxy
Es poder; procuración (m f)
It procura (f)
Pt procuração (f)

**procuratore** (m) n It
De Bevollmächtigte(r); Stellvertreter (m)
En attorney; proxy
Es procurador; apoderado (m)
Fr mandataire (m)
Pt procurador (m)

**prodotti di rifiuto** (m) It
De Abfallprodukt (n)
En waste products
Es desperdicios (m pl)
Fr déchets (m pl)
Pt desperdicios (m pl)

**prodotto** (m) n It
De Produkt (n)
En product
Es producto (m)
Fr produit (m)
Pt resultado (m)

**prodotto finale** (m) It
De Endprodukt (n)
En end-product
Es producto final (m)
Fr produit final (m)
Pt produto final (m)

**prodotto interno lordo** (m) It
De Bruttoinlandprodukt (n)
En gross domestic product (GDP)
Es producto interior bruto (m)
Fr produit intérieur brut (m)
Pt produto interno bruto (m)

**prodotto nazionale lordo** (m)
It
De Bruttosozialprodukt (n)
En gross national product (GNP)
Es producto nacional bruto (m)
Fr produit national brut (m)
Pt produto nacional bruto (m)

**produção** (f) n Pt
De Erzeugung (f)
En production
Es producción (f)
Fr production (f)
It produzione (f)

**produção em massa** (f) Pt
De Massenherstellung (f)
En mass production
Es producción en masa (f)
Fr production en masse (f)
It fabbricazione in massa (f)

**produção excessiva** (f) Pt
De Uberproduktion (f)
En overproduction
Es exceso de producción (m)
Fr surproduction (f)
It sovraproduzione (f)

**producción** (f) n Es
De Erzeugung (f)
En production
Fr production (f)
It produzione (f)
Pt produção (f)

**producción en masa** (f) Es
De Massenherstellung (f)
En mass production
Fr production en masse (f)
It fabbricazione in massa (f)
Pt produção em massa (f)

**produce** n En
De Erzeugnis (n)
Es productos (m pl)
Fr produit (m)
It prodotti (m pl)
Pt produtos (m pl)

**produce market** En
De Warenmarkt (m)
Es mercado de productos (m)
Fr marché commercial (m)
It mercato commerciale (m)
Pt mercado de produtos (m)

**product** n En
De Produkt (n)
Es producto (m)
Fr produit (m)
It prodotto (m)
Pt produto (m)

**production** n En, Fr (f)
De Erzeugung (f)
Es producción (f)
It produzione (f)
Pt produção (f)

**production control** En
De Produktionskontrolle (f)
Es control de producción (m)
Fr contrôle de production (m)
It controllo della produzione (m)
Pt controlo da produção (m)

**production en masse** (f) Fr
De Massenherstellung (f)
En mass production
Es producción en masa (f)
It fabbricazione in massa (f)
Pt produção em massa (f)

**productividad** (f) n Es
De Produktivität (f)
En productivity
Fr productivité (f)
It produttività (f)
Pt produtividade (f)

**productivité** (f) n Fr
De Produktivität (f)
En productivity
Es productividad (f)
It produttività (f)
Pt produtividade (f)

**productivity** n En
De Produktivität (f)
Es productividad (f)
Fr productivité (f)
It produttività (f)
Pt produtividade (f)

**producto** (m) n Es
De Produkt (n)
En product
Fr produit (m)
It prodotto (m)
Pt produto (m)

**producto derivado** *(m)* Es
De Nebenprodukt *(n)*
En by-product
Fr sous-produit *(m)*
It sottoprodotto *(m)*
Pt produto derivado *(m)*

**producto final** *(m)* Es
De Endprodukt *(n)*
En end-product
Fr produit final *(m)*
It prodotto finale *(m)*
Pt produto final *(m)*

**producto interior bruto** *(m)* Es
De Bruttoinlandprodukt *(n)*
En gross domestic product (GDP)
Fr produit intérieur brut *(m)*
It prodotto interno lordo *(m)*
Pt produto interno bruto *(m)*

**producto nacional bruto** *(m)* Es
De Bruttosozialprodukt *(n)*
En gross national product (GNP)
Fr produit national brut *(m)*
It prodotto nazionale lordo *(m)*
Pt produto nacional bruto *(m)*

**produit** *(m)* n Fr
De Produkt *(n)*
En product
Es producto *(m)*
It prodotto *(m)*
Pt produto *(m)*

**produit final** *(m)* Fr
De Endprodukt *(n)*
En end-product
Es producto final *(m)*
It prodotto finale *(m)*
Pt produto final *(m)*

**produit intérieur brut** *(m)* Fr
De Bruttoinlandprodukt *(n)*
En gross domestic product (GDP)
Es producto interior bruto *(m)*
It prodotto interno lordo *(m)*
Pt produto interno bruto *(m)*

**produit national brut** *(m)* Fr
De Bruttosozialprodukt *(n)*
En gross national product (GNP)

Es producto nacional bruto *(m)*
It prodotto nazionale lordo *(m)*
Pt produto nacional bruto *(m)*

**produit net** *(m)* Fr
De Reinerlös *(m)*
En net proceeds
Es rédito neto *(m)*
It ricavo netto *(m)*
Pt proventos líquidos *(m pl)*

**Produkt** *(n)* n De
En product
Es producto *(m)*
Fr produit *(m)*
It prodotto *(m)*
Pt produto *(m)*

**Produktionskontrolle** *(f)* n De
En production control
Es control de producción *(m)*
Fr contrôle de production *(m)*
It controllo della produzione *(m)*
Pt controlo da produção *(m)*

**produktive Arbeitskräfte** *(f pl)* De
En direct labour
Es jornales directos *(m pl)*
Fr travail en régie *(m)*
It lavoro in economia *(m)*
Pt trabalho directamente produtivo *(m)*

**Produktivität** *(f)* n De
En productivity
Es productividad *(f)*
Fr productivité *(f)*
It produttività *(f)*
Pt produtividade *(f)*

**produtividade** *(f)* n Pt
De Produktivität *(f)*
En productivity
Es productividad *(f)*
Fr productivité *(f)*
It produttività *(f)*

**produto** *(m)* n Pt
De Produkt *(n)*
En product
Es producto *(m)*
Fr produit *(m)*
It prodotto *(m)*

**produto derivado** *(m)* Pt
De Nebenprodukt *(n)*
En by-product
Es producto derivado *(m)*
Fr sous-produit *(m)*
It sottoprodotto *(m)*

**produto final** *(m)* Pt
De Endprodukt *(n)*
En end-product
Es producto final *(m)*
Fr produit final *(m)*
It prodotto finale *(m)*

**produto interno bruto** *(m)* Pt
De Bruttoinlandprodukt *(n)*
En gross domestic product (GDP)
Es producto interior bruto *(m)*
Fr produit intérieur brut *(m)*
It prodotto interno lordo *(m)*

**produto nacional bruto** *(m)* Pt
De Bruttosozialprodukt *(n)*.
En gross national product (GNP)
Es producto nacional bruto *(m)*
Fr produit national brut *(m)*
It prodotto nazionale lordo *(m)*

**produttività** *(f)* n It
De Produktivität *(f)*
En productivity
Es productividad *(f)*
Fr productivité *(f)*
Pt produtividade *(f)*

**produzione** *(f)* n It
De Erzeugung *(f)*
En production; output
Es producción; rendimiento *(f m)*
Fr production; rendement *(f m)*
Pt produção; rendimento *(f m)*

**profit** n En, Fr *(m)*
De Gewinn; Profit *(m)*
Es ganancia; beneficio *(f m)*
It utile; profitto *(m)*
Pt lucro; benefício *(m)*

**Profit** *(m)* n De
En profit
Es ganancia; beneficio *(f m)*
Fr profit; bénéfice *(m)*

It utile; profitto *(m)*
Pt lucro; benefício *(m)*

**profitability** *n* En
De Rentabilität *(f)*
Es rentabilidad *(f)*
Fr rentabilité *(f)*
It redditività *(f)*
Pt rentabilidade *(f)*

**profit and loss account** En
De Gewinn- und Verlustkonto *(n)*
Es cuenta de ganancias y pérdidas *(f)*
Fr compte profits et pertes *(m)*
It conto profitti e perdite *(m)*
Pt conta de lucros e perdas *(f)*

**profiteer** *n* En
De Gewinnler *(m)*
Es acaparador *(m)*
Fr profiteur *(m)*
It profittatore *(m)*
Pt especulador *(m)*

**profiteur** *(m) n* Fr
De Gewinnler *(m)*
En profiteer
Es acaparador *(m)*
It profittatore *(m)*
Pt especulador *(m)*

**profit fictif** *(m)* Fr
De imaginärer Gewinn *(m)*
En paper profit
Es ganancia por realizar *(f)*
It utile sulla carta *(m)*
Pt lucros no papel *(m)*

**profit maritime** *(m)* Fr
De Bodmereidarlehenszinsen *(m pl)*
En bottomry interest
Es interés de préstamo a la gruesa *(m)*
It interessenza a cambio marittimo *(f)*
Pt juro de bodemeria *(m)*

**profit-sharing** *n* En
De Gewinnbeteiligung *(f)*
Es participación en los beneficios *(f)*
Fr participation aux bénéfices *(f)*

It partecipazione agli utili *(f)*
Pt repartição dos lucros *(f)*

**profit-taking** *n* En
De Gewinnrealisation *(f)*
Es realización de utilidades *(f)*
Fr prise de bénéfices *(f)*
It realizzazione del utile *(f)*
Pt realização dos lucros *(m)*

**profittatore** *(m) n* It
De Gewinnler *(m)*
En profiteer
Es acaparador *(m)*
Fr profiteur *(m)*
Pt especulador *(m)*

**profitti non distribuiti** *(m pl)* It
De unverteilte Gewinne *(n pl)*
En undistributed profits
Es beneficios no distribuidos *(m pl)*
Fr bénéfices non répartis *(m pl)*
Pt lucros não distribuidos *(m pl)*

**profitti per azione** *(m pl)* It
De Gewinn pro Aktie *(n)*
En earnings per share
Es beneficios por acción *(m pl)*
Fr bénéfice par titre *(m)*
Pt proventos por acção *(m pl)*

**profitto** *(m) n* It
De Gewinn; Profit *(m)*
En profit
Es ganancia; beneficio *(f m)*
Fr bénéfice; profit *(m)*
Pt lucro; benefício *(m)*

**pró-forma de accordo** *(m)* Pt
De Entwurf eines Übereinkommens *(m)*
En draft agreement
Es proyecto de convenio *(m)*
Fr projet de convention *(m)*
It schema di contratto *(m)*

**proforma invoice** En
De Proformarechnung *(f)*
Es factura proforma *(f)*
Fr facture fictive *(f)*
It fattura proforma *(f)*
Pt factura proforma *(f)*

**Proformarechnung** *(f) n* De
En proforma invoice
Es factura proforma *(f)*
Fr facture fictive *(f)*
It fattura proforma *(f)*
Pt factura proforma *(f)*

**progetto** *(m) n* It
De Entwurf; Plan *(m)*
En plan; project
Es plan; proyecto *(m)*
Fr projet; plan *(m)*
Pt plano; projecto *(m)*

**progetto di contratto** *(m)* It
De Vertragsentwurf *(m)*
En draft contract
Es proyecto de contrato *(m)*
Fr projet de contrat *(m)*
Pt minuta de contrato *(f)*

**prognosticar** *vb* Pt
De vorhersehen
En forecast
Es pronosticar
Fr prévoir
It pronosticare

**program** *vb* En
De programmieren
Es programar
Fr programmer
It programmare
Pt programar

**programa de computador** *(m)* Pt
De Computerprogramm *(n)*
En computer program
Es programa de computadora *(m)*
Fr programme d'ordinateur *(m)*
It programma di elaboratore *(m)*

**programa de computadora** *(m)* Es
De Computerprogramm *(n)*
En computer program
Fr programme d'ordinateur *(m)*
It programma di elaboratore *(m)*
Pt programa de computador *(m)*

**programar** vb Es, Pt
De programmieren
En program
Fr programmer
It programmare

**programa salários** (f) Pt
De Lohnpolitik (f)
En incomes policy
Es plan de renta (m)
Fr politique des salaires (f)
It politica dei redditi (f)

**programma delle inserzioni** (m) It
De Werbeplan (m)
En advertising schedule
Es plan de propaganda (m)
Fr programme des annonces (m)
Pt plano de campanha publicitária (m)

**programma di elaboratore** (m) It
De Computerprogramm (n)
En computer program
Es programa de computadora (m)
Fr programme d'ordinateur (m)
Pt programa de computador (m)

**programmare** vb It
De programmieren
En program
Es programar
Fr programmer
Pt programar

**programmatura** (f) n It
De Programmausrüstung (f)
En (computer) software
Es conjunto de rutinas; software (m)
Fr software (m)
Pt sistema lógico; software (m)

**Programmausrüstung** (f) n De
En (computer) software
Es conjunto de rutinas; software (m)
Fr software (m)
It programmatura; software (f m)

Pt sistema lógico; software (m)

**programme des annonces** (m) Fr
De Werbeplan (m)
En advertising schedule
Es plan de propaganda (m)
It programma delle inserzioni (m)
Pt plano de campanha publicitária (m)

**programme d'ordinateur** (m) Fr
De Computerprogramm (n)
En computer program
Es programa de computadora (m)
It programma di elaboratore (m)
Pt programa de computador (m)

**programmer** vb Fr
De programmieren
En program
Es programar
It programmare
Pt programar

**programmieren** vb De
En program
Es programar
Fr programmer
It programmare
Pt programar

**prohibición de importación** (f) Es
De Einfuhrverbot (n)
En import ban
Fr prohibition d'entrée (f)
It divieto d'importazione (m)
Pt proibição de importação (f)

**prohibition d'entrée** (f) Fr
De Einfuhrverbot (n)
En import ban
Es prohibición de importación (f)
It divieto d'importazione (m)
Pt proibição de importação (f)

**proibição de importação** (f) Pt
De Einfuhrverbot (n)
En import ban

Es prohibición de importación (f)
Fr prohibition d'entrée (f)
It divieto d'importazione (m)

**projet** (m) n Fr
De Konzept; Plan (n m)
En draft; plan
Es borrador; plan (m)
It bozza; progetto (f m)
Pt rascunho; plano (m)

**projet de contrat** (m) Fr
De Vertragsentwurf (m)
En draft contract
Es proyecto de contrato (m)
It progetto di contratto (m)
Pt minuta de contrato (f)

**projet de convention** (m) Fr
De Entwurf eines Übereinkommens (m)
En draft agreement
Es proyecto de convenio (m)
It schema di contratto (m)
Pt pró-forma de accordo (m)

**pro Kopf** De
En per capita
Es por cabeza
Fr par tête
It per testa
Pt per capita

**prolongation d'un crédit** (f) Fr
De Verlängerung eines Kredites (f)
En extension of credit
Es prórroga de crédito (f)
It proroga di credito (f)
Pt prorrogação de crédito (f)

**promedio** (m) n Es
De Durchschnitt (m)
En average
Fr moyenne (f)
It media (f)
Pt média (f)

**promemoria** (f) n It
De Vermerk (m)
En memorandum
Es memorando; apunte (m)
Fr note (f)
Pt memorando (m)

**promissória** (f) n Pt
De Schuldschein (m)
En promissory note
Es pagaré (m)
Fr billet à ordre (m)
It pagherò (m)

**promissory note** En
De Schuldschein (m)
Es pagaré (m)
Fr billet à ordre (m)
It pagherò (m)
Pt promissória (f)

**promoção** (f) n Pt
De Beförderung; Förderung (f)
En promotion; advancement
Es promoción; ascenso (f m)
Fr promotion; avancement (f m)
It promozione; avanzamento (f m)

**promoção de vendas** (f) Pt
De Werbung; Verkaufsbeförderung (f)
En sales promotion
Es promoción de ventas (f)
Fr promotion des ventes (f)
It sviluppo delle vendite (m)

**promoción** (f) n Es
De Beförderung; Förderung (f)
En promotion; advancement
Fr promotion; avancement (f m)
It promozione; avanzamento (f m)
Pt promoção; fomento (f m)

**promoción de ventas** (f) Es
De Werbung; Verkaufsbeförderung (f)
En sales promotion
Fr promotion des ventes (f)
It sviluppo delle vendite (m)
Pt promoção de vendas (f)

**promote** vb En
De fördern; befördern
Es promover; ascender
Fr promouvoir; donner de l'avancement à
It dare impulso a; promuovere
Pt promover

**promotion** n En, Fr (f)
De Beförderung; Förderung (f)
Es promoción; ascenso (f m)
It promozione; avanzamento (f m)
Pt promoção; fomento (f m)

**promotion des ventes** (f) Fr
De Werbung; Verkaufsbeförderung (f)
En sales promotion
Es promoción de ventas (f)
It sviluppo delle vendite (m)
Pt promoção de vendas (f)

**promouvoir** vb Fr
De befördern; fördern
En promote
Es promover; ascender
It promuovere; dare impulso a
Pt promover

**promover** vb Es, Pt
De befördern; fördern
En promote
Fr promouvoir; donner de l'avancement à
It promuovere; dare impulso a

**promozione** (f) n It
De Beförderung; Förderung (f)
En promotion
Es promoción; ascenso (f m)
Fr promotion; avancement (f m)
Pt promoção; fomento (f m)

**prompt delivery** En
De sofortige Lieferung (f)
Es entrega inmediata (f)
Fr livraison immédiate (f)
It pronta consegna (f)
Pt entrega imediata (f)

**promuovere** vb It
De befördern; fördern
En promote
Es promover; ascender
Fr promouvoir; donner de l'avancement à
Pt promover

**pronosticar** vb Es
De vorhersehen
En forecast
Fr prévoir

It pronosticare
Pt prognosticar

**pronosticare** vb It
De vorhersehen
En forecast
Es pronosticar
Fr prévoir
Pt prognosticar

**pronóstico** (m) n Es
De Voraussagen (n)
En forecasting
Fr prévision (f)
It previsione (f)
Pt previsão (f)

**pronóstico de ventas** (m) Es
De Verkaufsvoraussage (f)
En sales forecast
Fr prévision de ventes (f)
It previsione delle vendite (f)
Pt previsão de vendas (f)

**pronta consegna** (f) It
De sofortige Lieferung (f)
En prompt delivery
Es entrega inmediata (f)
Fr livraison immédiate (f)
Pt entrega imediata (f)

**pronti contanti** (m pl) It
De Barbestand (m)
En cash in hand
Es efectivo en caja (m)
Fr espèces en caisse (f pl)
Pt fundos à ordem (m pl)

**property bond** En
De Grund- und Gebäudeobligation (f)
Es cédula hipotecaria (f)
Fr obligation foncière (f)
It obbligazione fondiaria (f)
Pt título de investimento imobiliário (m)

**property tax** En
De Grundsteuer (f)
Es impuesto sobre la propiedad (m)
Fr impôt foncier (m)
It imposta fondiaria (f)
Pt imposto sobre propriedade (m)

**propiedad** (f) n Es
De Eigentum (n)
En ownership; property
Fr propriété (f)
It proprietà (f)
Pt propriedade (f)

**propiedad estatal** (f) Es
De Staatsbesitz (m)
En public ownership
Fr propriété publique (f)
It proprietà statale (f)
Pt propriedade pública (f)

**propietario** (m) n Es
De Eigentümer; Vermieter (m)
En owner; landlord
Fr propriétaire (m)
It proprietario; locatore (m)
Pt proprietário; senhorio (m)

**propietario del terreno** (m) Es
De Grundbesitzer (m)
En ground-landlord
Fr propriétaire foncier (m)
It proprietario del terreno (m)
Pt proprietário do terreno (m)

**propina** (f) n Es
De Trinkgeld (n)
En tip; gratuity
Fr pourboire (m)
It mancia (f)
Pt gorjeta (f)

**proponente** (m) n Pt
De Bietende(r) (m)
En bidder
Es ofertante (m)
Fr enchérisseur (m)
It offerente (m)

**proponente mais elevado** (m) Pt
De Meistbietende(r) (m)
En highest bidder
Es ofertante más alto (m)
Fr plus offrant enchérisseur (m)
It miglior offerente (m)

**proporção** (f) n Pt
De Verhältnis; Anteil (n m)
En proportion
Es proporción (f)
Fr proportion (f)
It proporzione (f)

**proporção de fracassos** (f) Pt
De Durchfallquote (f)
En failure rate
Es proporción de fracasos (f)
Fr taux de défaillance (m)
It indice dei fallimenti (m)

**proporción** (f) n Es
De Verhältnis; Anteil (n m)
En proportion
Fr proportion (f)
It proporzione (f)
Pt proporção (f)

**proporción de fracasos** (f) Es
De Durchfallquote (f)
En failure rate
Fr taux de défaillance (m)
It indice dei fallimenti (m)
Pt proporção de fracassos (f)

**proporción precio-ingresos** (f) Es
De Verhältnis des Aktienkurses zum Reingewinn (n)
En price-earnings ratio (P/E)
Fr quotient cours-bénéfice (m)
It rapporto prezzo-utile (m)
Pt taxa custo-ganhos (f)

**proportion** n En, Fr (f)
De Verhältnis; Anteil (n m)
Es proporción (f)
It proporzione (f)
Pt proporção (f)

**proporzione** (f) n It
De Verhältnis; Anteil (n m)
En proportion
Es proporción
Fr proportion (f)
Pt proporcão (f)

**proposal** n En
De Vorschlag (m)
Es propuesta (f)
Fr proposition (f)
It proposta (f)
Pt proposta (f)

**proposition** (f) n Fr
De Vorschlag (m)
En proposal
Es propuesta (f)
It proposta (f)
Pt proposta (f)

**proposta** (f) n It, Pt
De Vorschlag; Angebot (m n)
En proposal; offer
Es propuesta; oferta (f)
Fr proposition; offre (f)

**proposta de apropriação** (f) Pt
De Übernahmeangebot (n)
En take-over bid
Es oferta de adquisición (f)
Fr offre de rachat (f)
It offerta di acquisto (f)

**propriedade** (f) n Pt
De Eigentum (n)
En property; ownership
Es propiedad (f)
Fr propriété (f)
It proprietà (f)

**propriedade em maioria** (f) Pt
De Mehrheitsbeteiligung (f)
En majority holding
Es tenencia de acciones por mayoría (f)
Fr participation majoritaire (f)
It partecipazione maggioritaria (f)

**propriedade imobiliária** (f) Pt
De unbewegliches Vermögen; Immobilien (n; f pl)
En real estate
Es bienes inmuebles (m pl)
Fr biens immeubles (m pl)
It beni immobili (m pl)

**propriedade pública** (f) Pt
De Staatsbesitz (m)
En public ownership
Es propiedad estatal (f)
Fr propriété publique (f)
It proprietà statale (f)

**proprietà** (f) n It
De Eigentum (n)
En property; ownership
Es propiedad (f)
Fr propriété (f)
Pt propriedade (f)

**propriétaire** (m) n Fr
De Eigentümer; Vermieter (m)
En owner; landlord
Es propietario; arrendador (m)
It proprietario; locatore (m)
Pt proprietário; senhorio (m)

**propriétaire foncier** (m) Fr
De  Grundbesitzer (m)
En  ground-landlord
Es  propietario del terreno (m)
It  proprietario del terreno (m)
Pt  proprietário do terreno (m)


**proprietà mobiliare** (f) It
De  bewegliche Güter (n pl)
En  movable assets
Es  mobiliario (m)
Fr  biens mobiliers (m pl)
Pt  bens mobiliários (m pl)


**proprietario** (m) n It
De  Eigentümer; Vermieter (m)
En  owner; landlord
Es  propietario; arrendador (m)
Fr  propriétaire (m)
Pt  proprietário; senhorio (m)


**proprietário** (m) n Pt
De  Eigentümer; Vermieter (m)
En  owner; landlord
Es  propietario; arrendador (m)
Fr  propriétaire (m)
It  proprietario; locatore (m)


**proprietario del terreno** (m) It
De  Grundbesitzer (m)
En  ground-landlord
Es  propietario del terreno (m)
Fr  propriétaire foncier (m)
Pt  proprietário do terreno (m)


**proprietário do terreno** (m) Pt
De  Grundbesitzer (m)
En  ground-landlord
Es  propietario del terreno (m)
Fr  propriétaire foncier (m)
It  proprietario del terreno (m)


**proprietário legítimo** (m) Pt
De  entgeltigter Besitzer (m)
En  holder for value
Es  tenedor legítimo (m)
Fr  porteur à titre onéreux (m)
It  detentore legittimo (m)


**proprietà statale** (f) It
De  Staatsbesitz (m)
En  public ownership
Es  propiedad estatal (f)
Fr  propriété publique (f)
Pt  propriedade pública (f)


**propriété** (f) n Fr
De  Eigentum (n)
En  property; ownership
Es  propiedad (f)
It  proprietà (f)
Pt  propriedade (f)


**propriété publique** (f) Fr
De  Staatsbesitz (m)
En  public ownership
Es  propiedad estatal (f)
It  proprietà statale (f)
Pt  propriedade pública (f)


**propuesta** (f) n Es
De  Vorschlag (m)
En  proposal
Fr  proposition (f)
It  proposta (f)
Pt  proposta (f)


**pro rata** En
De  anteilsmässig; pro rata
Es  proporcionalmente; a pror-
      rata
Fr  proportionnellement;  au
      prorata
It  proporzionalmente; pro rata
Pt  proporcionalmente;   pro
      rata


**proroga di credito** (f) It
De  Verlängerung  eines  Kre-
      dites (f)
En  extension of credit
Es  prórroga de crédito (f)
Fr  prolongation d'un crédit (f)
Pt  prorrogação de crédito (f)


**proroga di pagamento** (f) It
De  Verlängerungszeitraum (m)
En  extension of payment time
Es  prórroga de pago (f)
Fr  delai de paiement (m)
Pt  prorrogação de pagamento
      (f)


**prorrogação de crédito** (f) Pt
De  Verlängerung  eines  Kre-
      dites (f)
En  extension of credit
Es  prórroga de crédito (f)
Fr  prolongation d'un crédit (f)
It  proroga di credito (f)


**prorrogação de pagamento** (f)
      Pt
De  Verlängerungszeitraum (m)


En  extension of payment time
Es  prórroga de pago (f)
Fr  délai de paiement (m)
It  proroga di pagamento (f)


**prórroga de crédito** (f) Es
De  Verlängerung  eines  Kre-
      dites (f)
En  extension of credit
Fr  prolongation d'un crédit (f)
It  proroga di credito (f)
Pt  prorrogação de crédito (f)


**prórroga de pago** (f) Es
De  Verlängerungszeitraum (m)
En  extension of payment time
Fr  délai de paiement (m)
It  proroga di pagamento (f)
Pt  prorrogação de pagamento
      (f)


**prospecto** (m) n Es, Pt
De  Prospekt (m)
En  prospectus
Fr  prospectus (m)
It  prospetto; programma (m)


**prospectus** n En, Fr (m)
De  Prospekt (m)
Es  prospecto (m)
It  prospetto; programma (m)
Pt  prospecto (m)


**prospectus publicitaire** (m) Fr
De  Werbeschrift (f)
En  advertising brochure
Es  folleto publicitario (m)
It  opuscolo pubblicitario (m)
Pt  folheto publicitário (m)


**Prospekt** (m) n De
En  prospectus
Es  prospecto (m)
Fr  prospectus (m)
It  prospetto; programma (m)
Pt  prospecto (m)


**prospetto** (m) n It
De  Prospekt (m)
En  prospectus
Es  prospecto (m)
Fr  prospectus (m)
Pt  prospecto (m)


**protest** n En
De  Protest (m)
Es  protesta (f)
Fr  protêt (m)

It   protesto *(m)*
Pt   protesto *(m)*

**protest** (a bill) *vb* En
De  protestieren
Es  protestar
Fr  faire protester
It   protestare .
Pt  protestar

**Protest** *(m) n* De
En  protest
Es  protesta *(f)*
Fr  protêt *(m)*
It   protesto *(m)*
Pt  protesto *(m)*

**protesta** *(f) n* Es
De  Protest *(m)*
En  protest
Fr  protêt *(m)*
It   protesto *(m)*
Pt  protesto *(m)*

**protestar** (uma letra) Pt
De  protestieren
En  protest
Es  protestar
Fr  faire protester
It   protestare

**protestar** (una letra) Es
De  protestieren
En  protest
Fr  faire protester
It   protestare
Pt  protestar

**protestare** (una cambiale) It
De  protestieren
En  protest
Es  protestar
Fr  faire protester
Pt  protestar

**protestieren** (einen Wechsel)
    De
En  protest
Es  protestar
Fr  faire protester
It   protestare
Pt  protestar

**protesto** *(m) n* It, Pt
De  Protest *(m)*
En  protest
Es  protesta *(f)*
Fr  protêt *(m)*

**Protestzahlung** *(f) n* De
En  payment under protest
Es  pago sobre protesta *(m)*
Fr  paiement sous protêt *(m)*
It   pagamento sotto protesta *(m)*
Pt  pagamento sob protesto *(m)*

**protêt** *(m) n* Fr
De  Protest *(m)*
En  protest
Es  protesta *(f)*
It   protesto *(m)*
Pt  protesto *(m)*

**Protokoll** *(n) n* De
En  minutes
Es  actas *(f pl)*
Fr  procès-verbal *(m)*
It   verbale *(m)*
Pt  minutas de acta *(f pl)*

**prototipo** *(m) n* Es, It
De  Prototyp *(m)*
En  prototype
Fr  prototype *(m)*
Pt  protótipo *(m)*

**protótipo** *(m) n* Pt
De  Prototyp *(m)*
En  prototype
Es  prototipo *(m)*
Fr  prototype *(m)*
It   prototipo *(m)*

**Prototyp** *(m) n* De
En  prototype
Es  prototipo *(m)*
Fr  prototype *(m)*
It   prototipo *(m)*
Pt  protótipo *(m)*

**prototype** *n* En, Fr *(m)*
De  Prototyp *(m)*
Es  prototipo *(m)*
It   prototipo *(m)*
Pt  protótipo *(m)*

**prova** *(f) n* It, Pt
De  Probe; Beweis *(f m)*
En  test; evidence
Es  prueba; evidencia *(f)*
Fr  épreuve; preuve *(f)*

**prova documental** *(f)* Pt
De  Urkundenbeweis *(m)*
En  documentary evidence

Es  prueba documental *(f)*
Fr  preuve écrite *(f)*
It   prova scritta *(f)*

**prova gratuita** *(f)* It, Pt
De  kostenlose Probe *(f)*
En  free trial
Es  prueba gratuita *(f)*
Fr  essai gratuit *(m)*

**prova scritta** *(f)* It
De  Urkundenbeweis *(m)*
En  documentary evidence
Es  prueba documental *(f)*
Fr  preuve écrite *(f)*
Pt  prova documental *(f)*

**proveedor** *(m) n* Es
De  Lieferant *(m)*
En  supplier
Fr  fournisseur *(m)*
It   fornitore *(m)*
Pt  fornecedor *(m)*

**proventi decrescenti** *(m pl)* It
De  abnehmender Ertrag *(m)*
En  diminishing returns
Es  rendimientos decrecientes *(m pl)*
Fr  rendements décroissants *(m pl)*
Pt  rendimentos decrescentes *(m pl)*

**proventos líquidos** *(m pl)* Pt
De  Reinerlös *(m)*
En  net proceeds
Es  rédito neto *(m)*
Fr  produit net *(m)*
It   ricavo netto *(m)*

**proventos por acção** *(m pl)* Pt
De  Gewinn pro Aktie *(n)*
En  earnings per share
Es  beneficios por acción *(m pl)*
Fr  bénéfice par titre *(m)*
It   profitti per azione *(m pl)*

**provisão** *(f) n* Pt
De  Rabatt *(m)*
En  allowance
Es  bonificación *(f)*
Fr  rabais *(m)*
It   abbuono *(m)*

**provisão para amortização** (f)
Pt
De Abschreibung für Abnutzung (f)
En depreciation allowance
Es provisión para amortización (f)
Fr provision pour amortissement (f)
It quota di ammortamento (f)

**Provision** (f) n De
En commission
Es comisión (f)
Fr commission (f)
It provvigione (f)
Pt comissão (f)

**provisiones existentes** (f pl)
Es
De lieferfertiges Angebot (n)
En supplies on hand
Fr ressources existantes (f pl)
It forniture esistenti (f pl)
Pt fornecimentos em existência (m pl)

**provisión para amortización** (f) Es
De Abschreibung für Abnützung (AfA) (f)
En depreciation allowance
Fr provision pour amortissement (f)
It quota di ammortamento (f)
Pt provisão para amortização (f)

**provision pour amortissement** (f) Fr
De Abschreibung für Abnützung (AfA) (f)
En depreciation allowance
Es provisión para amortización (f)
It quota di ammortamento (f)
Pt provisão para amortização (f)

**provision pour créances douteuses** (f) Fr
De Dubiosenreserve (f)
En bad debt reserve
Es reserva para deudas incobrables (f)
It riserva per crediti inesigibili (f)

Pt reserva para dividas incobráveis (f)

**provisoire** adj Fr
De einstweilig
En temporary
Es temporal
It temporaneo
Pt temporário

**provocare** vb It
De anstiften
En instigate
Es instigar; provocar
Fr provoquer
Pt instigar

**provoquer** vb Fr
De anstiften
En instigate
Es instigar; provocar
It provocare; istigare
Pt instigar

**provvigione** (f) n It
De Provision (f)
En commission
Es comisión (f)
Fr commission (f)
Pt comissão (f)

**proxy** (power) n En
De Stellvertretung (f)
Es procuración (f)
Fr procuration (f)
It procura (f)
Pt procuração (f)

**proxy** (person) n En
De Stellvertreter (m)
Es apoderado (m)
Fr mandataire (m)
It procuratore (m)
Pt procurador (m)

**proyecto de contrato** (m) Es
De Vertragsentwurf (m)
En draft contract
Fr projet de contrat (m)
It progetto di contratto (m)
Pt minuta de contrato (f)

**proyecto de convenio** (m) Es
De Entwurf eines Übereinkommens (m)
En draft agreement
Fr projet de convention (m)

It schema di contratto (m)
Pt pró-forma de accordo (m)

**prozent** De
En per cent
Es por ciento
Fr pour cent
It per cento
Pt por cento

**Prozentsatz** (m) n De
En percentage
Es porcentaje (m)
Fr pourcentage (m)
It percentuale (f)
Pt percentagem (f)

**Prozess** (m) n De
En lawsuit; trial
Es proceso; causa (m f)
Fr procès (m)
It processo; causa (m f)
Pt processo; causa (m f)

**prueba** (f) n Es
De Probe; Beweis (f m)
En test; evidence
Fr épreuve; preuve (f)
It prova (f)
Pt prova (f)

**prueba documental** (f) Es
De Urkundenbeweis (m)
En documentary evidence
Fr preuve écrite (f)
It prova scritta (f)
Pt prova documental (f)

**prueba gratuita** (f) Es
De kostenlose Probe (f)
En free trial
Fr essai gratuit (m)
It prova gratuita (f)
Pt prova gratuita (f)

**prüfen** vb De
En examine; audit
Es verificar; revisar
Fr examiner; vérifier et certifier
It verificare; rivedere
Pt verificar; fiscalizar

**psicología industrial** (f) Es
De Arbeitspsychologie (f)
En industrial psychology
Fr psychotechnique (f)

It  psicologia industriale *(f)*
Pt  psicologia industrial *(f)*

**psicologia industrial** *(f)* Pt
De  Arbeitspsychologie *(f)*
En  industrial psychology
Es  psicología industrial *(f)*
Fr  psychotechnique *(f)*
It  psicologia industriale *(f)*

**psicologia industriale** *(f)* It
De  Arbeitspsychologie *(f)*
En  industrial psychology
Es  psicología industrial *(f)*
Fr  psychotechnique *(f)*
Pt  psicologia industrial *(f)*

**psychotechnique** *(f)* n Fr
De  Arbeitspsychologie *(f)*
En  industrial psychology
Es  psicología industrial *(f)*
It  psicologia industriale *(f)*
Pt  psicologia industrial *(f)*

**pubbliche relazioni** *(f pl)* It
De  Public-Relations *(n pl)*
En  public relations (PR)
Es  relaciones públicas *(f pl)*
Fr  relations publiques *(f pl)*
Pt  relações públicas *(f pl)*

**pubblicità** *(f)* n It
De  Reklame; Werbung *(f)*
En  advertising; publicity
Es  publicidad *(f)*
Fr  publicité *(f)*
Pt  publicidade *(f)*

**pubblicità diretta** *(f)* It
De  Postversandwerbung *(f)*
En  direct mail
Es  propaganda directa por
    correo *(f)*
Fr  publicité directe *(f)*
Pt  publicidade por correio ao
    domicílio *(f)*

**pubblico** *adj* It
De  öffentlich
En  public
Es  público
Fr  public
Pt  público

**pubblico** *(m)* n It
De  Öffentlichkeit *(f)*
En  (general) public
Es  público *(m)*

Fr  public *(m)*
Pt  público *(m)*

**public** *adj* En, Fr
De  öffentlich
Es  público
It  pubblico
Pt  público

**public** n En, Fr *(m)*
· De  Öffentlichkeit *(f)*
Es  público *(m)*
It  pubblico *(m)*
Pt  público *(m)*

**public holiday** En
De  gesetzlicher Feiertag *(m)*
Es  día de fiesta *(m)*
Fr  jour férié *(m)*
It  giorno di festa *(m)*
Pt  feriado *(m)*

**publicidad** *(f)* n Es
De  Reklame; Werbung *(f)*
En  advertising; publicity
Fr  publicité *(f)*
It  pubblicità *(f)*
Pt  publicidade *(f)*

**publicidade** *(f)* n Pt
De  Reklame; Werbung *(f)*
En  advertising; publicity
Es  publicidad *(f)*
Fr  publicité *(f)*
It  pubblicità *(f)*

**publicidade por correio ao
domicílio** *(f)* Pt
De  Postversandwerbung *(f)*
En  direct mail
Es  propaganda directa por
    correo *(f)*
Fr  publicité directe *(f)*
It  pubblicità diretta *(f)*

**publicité** *(f)* n Fr
De  Reklame; Werbung *(f)*
En  advertising; publicity
Es  publicidad *(f)*
It  pubblicità *(f)*
Pt  publicidade *(f)*

**publicité directe** *(f)* Fr
De  Postversandwerbung *(f)*
En  direct mail

Es  propaganda directa por
    correo *(f)*
It  pubblicità diretta *(f)*
Pt  publicidade por correio ao
    domicílio *(f)*

**publicity** n En
De  Werbung *(f)*
Es  publicidad *(f)*
Fr  publicité *(f)*
It  pubblicità *(f)*
Pt  publicidade *(f)*

**publicity campaign** En
De  Werbefeldzug *(m)*
Es  campaña publicitaria *(f)*
Fr  campagne de publicité *(f)*
It  campagna pubblicitaria *(f)*
Pt  campanha publicitária *(f)*

**public limited company** En
De  Aktiengesellschaft (AG) *(f)*
Es  Sociedad anónima (SA) *(f)*
Fr  Société anonyme (SA) *(f)*
It  Società anonima (SA) *(f)*
Pt  Sociedade anónima (SA) *(f)*

**público** *adj* Es, Pt
De  öffentlich
En  public
Fr  public
It  pubblico

**público** *(m)* n Es, Pt
De  Öffentlichkeit *(f)*
En  (general) public
Fr  public *(m)*
It  pubblico *(m)*

**public ownership** En
De  Staatsbesitz *(m)*
Es  propiedad estatal *(f)*
Fr  propriété publique *(f)*
It  proprietà statale *(f)*
Pt  propriedade pública *(f)*

**public relations** (PR) En
De  Public-Relations *(n pl)*
Es  relaciones públicas *(f pl)*
Fr  relations publiques *(f pl)*
It  pubbliche relazioni *(f pl)*
Pt  relações públicas *(f pl)*

**Public-Relations** *(n pl)* n De
En  public relations (PR)
Es  relaciones públicas *(f pl)*
Fr  relations publiques *(f pl)*

It pubbliche relazioni *(f pl)*
Pt relações públicas *(f pl)*

**public sector** En
De öffentliche Hand *(f)*
Es sector público *(m)*
Fr secteur public *(m)*
It settore statale *(m)*
Pt sector público *(m)*

**publishing house** En
De Verlag *(m)*
Es casa editorial *(f)*
Fr maison d'édition *(f)*
It casa editrice *(f)*
Pt casa editora *(f)*

**puerto** *(m) n* Es
De Hafen *(m)*
En port; harbour
Fr port *(m)*
It porto *(m)*
Pt porto *(m)*

**puerto de descarga** *(m)* Es
De Lieferhafen *(m)*
En port of discharge
Fr port de livraison *(m)*
It porto di scarico *(m)*
Pt porto de descarga *(m)*

**puerto de destino** *(m)* Es
De Bestimmungshafen *(m)*
En port of destination
Fr port de destination *(m)*
It porto di destinazione *(m)*
Pt porto de destino *(m)*

**puerto de escala** *(m)* Es
De Anlaufhafen *(m)*
En port of call
Fr port d'escale *(m)*
It porto di scalo *(m)*
Pt porto de escala *(m)*

**puerto de matrícula** *(m)* Es
De Heimathafen *(m)*
En port of registration
Fr port d'attache *(m)*
It porto d'immatricolazione *(m)*
Pt porto de matrícula *(m)*

**puerto libre** *(m)* Es
De Freihafen *(m)*
En free port
Fr port franc *(m)*

It porto franco *(m)*
Pt porto franco *(m)*

**puesto en almacén** Es
De an Zollfreilager
En ex warehouse
Fr à prendre en entrepôt
It franco magazzino
Pt no armazzém

**pugna de intereses** *(f)* Es
De widerstreitende Interessen *(n pl)*
En conflict of interest
Fr opposition d'intérêts *(f)*
It conflitto d'interessi *(m)*
Pt conflito de interesses *(m)*

**punched card** En
De Lochkarte *(f)*
Es tarjeta perforada *(f)*
Fr carte perforée *(f)*
It scheda perforata *(f)*
Pt ficha perforada *(f)*

**punto de igualdad de ingresos y gastos** *(m)* Es
De Rentabilitätsgrenze *(f)*
En break-even point
Fr point de seuil *(m)*
It punto di pareggio *(m)*
Pt ponto de acerto *(m)*

**punto di pareggio** *(m)* It
De Rentabilitätsgrenze *(f)*
En break-even point
Es punto de igualdad de ingresos y gastos *(m)*
Fr point de seuil *(m)*
Pt ponto de acerto *(m)*

**punzonatura di garanzia** *(f)* It
De Feingehaltsstempel *(m)*
En hall-mark
Es punzón de garantía *(m)*
Fr poinçon *(m)*
Pt marca de garantia *(f)*

**punzón de garantía** *(m)* Es
De Feingehaltsstempel *(m)*
En hall-mark
Fr poinçon *(m)*
It punzonatura di garanzia *(f)*
Pt marca de garantia *(f)*

**purchase** *n* En
De Kauf; Anschaffung *(m f)*
Es compra *(f)*

Fr achat *(m)*
It compra *(f)*
Pt compra *(f)*

**purchase book** Am
En bought ledger
De Einkaufsbuch *(n)*
Es libro mayor de compras *(m)*
Fr grand livre d'achats *(m)*
It mastro acquisti *(m)*
Pt livro-mestre de compras *(m)*

**purchase price** En
De Kaufpreis *(m)*
Es precio de compra *(m)*
Fr prix d'achat *(m)*
It prezzo d'acquisto *(m)*
Pt preço de compra *(m)*

**purchases** (in balance sheet) *pl n* En
De Einkäufe *(m pl)*
Es adquisiciones *(f pl)*
Fr achats *(m pl)*
It acquisti *(m pl)*
Pt aquisições *(f pl)*

**purchase tax** En
De Kaufsteuer *(f)*
Es impuesto sobre las compras *(m)*
Fr impôt sur les acquisitions *(m)*
It tassa sugli acquisti *(f)*
Pt imposto sobre aquisições *(m)*

**purchasing power** En
De Kaufkraft *(f)*
Es poder de compra *(m)*
Fr pouvoir d'achat *(m)*
It potere d'acquisto *(m)*
Pt poder de compra *(m)*

**purser** *n* En
De Zahlmeister *(m)*
Es contador de navio *(m)*
Fr commissaire de la marine *(m)*
It commissario di bordo *(m)*
Pt commissário de bordo *(m)*

**put option** En
De Verkaufsoption *(f)*
Es opción de venta *(f)*
Fr option à vendre *(f)*

It   premio a vendere *(m)*
Pt   opção de venda *(f)*

**pyramid selling** En
De   Schneeball Verkauf *(m)*
Es   venta en pirámide *(f)*
Fr   vente en pyramide *(f)*
It   vendita a piramide *(f)*
Pt   vendas em pirâmide *(f)*


## Q

**quadro de distribuição** *(m)* Pt
De   Schalttafel *(f)*
En   switchboard
Es   cuadro de conexión *(m)*
Fr   tableau de distribution *(m)*
It   quadro di comando *(m)*

**quadro di comando** *(m)* It
De   Schalttafel *(f)*
En   switchboard
Es   cuadro de conexión *(m)*
Fr   tableau de distribution *(m)*
Pt   quadro de distribuição *(m)*

**quai** *(m)* n Fr
De   Kai *(m)*
En   quay; wharf
Es   muelle *(m)*
It   scalo *(m)*
Pt   cais *(m)*

**qualidade** *(f)* n Pt
De   Qualität *(f)*
En   quality
Es   calidad *(f)*
Fr   qualité *(f)*
It   qualità *(f)*

**qualidade comerciável** *(f)* Pt
De   marktgängige Qualität *(f)*
En   merchantable quality
Es   calidad comerciable *(f)*
Fr   qualité vendable *(f)*
It   qualità commerciabile *(f)*

**qualidade e conteúdo descon-
  hecidos** Pt
De   Qualität und Inhalt nicht
     bekannt
En   quality and contents un-
     known
Es   calidad del contenido des-
     conocida

Fr   qualité et contenu incon-
     nus
It   qualità e contenuto scono-
     sciuti

**qualidade media razoável** *(f)*
  Pt
De   gute Durchschnittsqualität
     *(f)*
En   fair average quality (faq)
Es   calidad media razonable *(f)*
Fr   qualité commerciale mo-
     yenne *(f)*
It   buona qualità media *(f)*

**qualifica** *(f)* n It
De   Qualifikation *(f)*
En   qualification
Es   requisito *(m)*
Fr   qualification; capacité *(f)*
Pt   qualificação *(f)*

**qualificação** *(f)* n Pt
De   Qualifikation *(f)*
En   qualification
Es   requisito *(m)*
Fr   qualification; capacité *(f)*
It   qualifica; requisito *(f m)*

**qualification** n En, Fr *(f)*
De   Qualifikation *(f)*
Es   requisito *(m)*
It   qualifica; requisito *(f m)*
Pt   qualificação *(f)*

**qualified acceptance** En
De   Annahme unter Vorbehalt
     *(f)*
Es   aceptación condicionada *(f)*
Fr   acceptation conditionnelle
     *(f)*
It   accettazione con riserva *(f)*
Pt   aceitação com reservas *(f)*

**qualified accountant** En
De   Wirtschaftsprüfer *(m)*
Es   contador habilitado *(m)*
Fr   expert comptable *(m)*
It   ragioniere diplomato *(m)*
Pt   guarda-livros    diplomado
     *(m)*

**Qualifikation** *(f)* n De
En   qualification
Es   requisito *(m)*
Fr   qualification; capacité *(f)*
It   qualifica; requisito *(f m)*
Pt   qualificação *(f)*

**qualità** *(f)* n It
De   Qualität *(f)*
En   quality
Es   calidad *(f)*
Fr   qualité *(f)*
Pt   qualidade *(f)*

**qualità commerciabile** *(f)* It
De   marktgängige Qualität *(f)*
En   merchantable quality
Es   calidad comerciable *(f)*
Fr   qualité vendable *(f)*
Pt   qualidade comerciável *(f)*

**qualità e contenuto scono-
  sciuti** It
De   Qualität und Inhalt nicht
     bekannt
En   quality and contents un-
     known
Es   calidad del contenido des-
     conocida
Fr   qualité et contenu incon-
     nus
Pt   qualidade e conteúdo des-
     conhecidos

**Qualität** *(f)* n De
En   quality
Es   calidad *(f)*
Fr   qualité *(f)*
It   qualità *(f)*
Pt   qualidade *(f)*

**Qualitätskontrolle** *(f)* n De
En   quality control
Es   control de calidad *(m)*
Fr   contrôle de qualité *(f)*
It   controllo di qualità *(m)*
Pt   controlo de qualidade *(m)*

**Qualität und Inhalt nicht
  bekannt** De
En   quality and contents un-
     known
Es   calidad del contenido des-
     conocida
Fr   qualité et contenu incon-
     nus
It   qualità e contenuto scono-
     sciuti
Pt   qualidade e conteúdo des-
     conhecidos

**qualité** *(f)* n Fr
De   Qualität *(f)*
En   quality
Es   calidad *(f)*

It qualità (f)
Pt qualidade (f)

**qualité commerciale moyenne**
(f) Fr
De gute Durchschnittsqualität
(f)
En fair average quality (faq)
Es calidad media razonable (f)
It buona qualità media (f)
Pt qualidade media razoável
(f)

**qualité et contenu inconnus**
Fr
De Qualität und Inhalt nicht
bekannt
En quality and contents un-
known
Es calidad del contenido des-
conocida
It qualità e contenuto scono-
sciuti
Pt qualidade e conteúdo des-
conhecidos

**qualité vendable** (f) Fr
De marktgängige Qualität (f)
En merchantable quality
Es calidad comerciable (f)
It qualità commerciabile (f)
Pt qualidade comerciável (f)

**quality** n En
De Qualität (f)
Es calidad (f)
Fr qualité (f)
It qualità (f)
Pt qualidade (f)

**quality and contents un-
known** En
De Qualität und Inhalt nicht
bekannt
Es calidad del contenido desconocida
Fr qualité et contenu inconnus
It qualità e contenuto sconosciuti
Pt qualidade e conteúdo desconhecidos

**quality control** En
De Qualitätskontrolle (f)
Es control de calidad (m)
Fr contrôle de qualité (m)

It controllo di qualità (m)
Pt controlo de qualidade (m)

**quantia** (f) n Pt
De Betrag (m)
En amount
Es suma (f)
Fr somme (f)
It ammontare (m)

**quantia nominal** (f) Pt
De Nominalbetrag (m)
En nominal amount
Es suma nominal (f)
Fr montant nominal (m)
It importo nominale (m)

**quantidade** (f) n Pt
De Menge (f)
En quantity
Es cantidad (f)
Fr quantité (f)
It quantità (f)

**quantità** (f) n It
De Menge (f)
En quantity
Es cantidad (f)
Fr quantité (f)
Pt quantidade (f)

**quantité** (f) n Fr
De Menge (f)
En quantity
Es cantidad (f)
It quantità (f)
Pt quantidade (f)

**quantity** n En
De Menge (f)
Es cantidad (f)
Fr quantité (f)
It quantità (f)
Pt quantidade (f)

**quantity surveyor** En
De Massenberechner (m)
Es medidor de contidades de
obra (m)
Fr métreur-vérificateur (m)
It perito misuratore (m)
Pt perito na avaliação de
quantidades (m)

**quarantaine** (f) n Fr
De Quarantäne (f)
En quarantine
Es cuarentena (f)

It quarantena (f)
Pt quarantena (f)

**Quarantäne** (f) n De
En quarantine
Es cuarentena (f)
Fr quarantaine (f)
It quarantena (f)
Pt quarantena (f)

**quarantena** (f) n It, Pt
De Quarantäne (f)
En quarantine
Es cuarentena (f)
Fr quarantaine (f)

**quarantine** n En
De Quarantäne (f)
Es cuarentena (f)
Fr quarantaine (f)
It quarantena (f)
Pt quarantena (f)

**Quartalstag** (m) n De
En quarter day
Es primer día del trimestre (m)
Fr jour du terme (m)
It giorno della pigione (m)
Pt dia de vencimento tri-
mestral (m)

**quarter day** En
De Quartalstag (m)
Es primer día del trimestre (m)
Fr jour du terme (m)
It giorno della pigione (m)
Pt dia de vencimento tri-
mestral (m)

**quarterly** adj En
De vierteljährlich
Es trimestral
Fr trimestriel
It trimestrale
Pt trimestral

**quarterly payments** En
De vierteljährliche Zahlungen (f
pl)
Es pagos trimestrales (m pl)
Fr paiements trimestriels (m
pl)
It pagamenti trimestrali (m
pl)
Pt pagamentos trimestrais (m
pl)

**quay** n En
  Am pier
  De Kai (m)
  Es muelle (m)
  Fr quai (m)
  It banchina (f)
  Pt cais (m)

**quayage** (m) n Fr
  De Kaigeld (n)
  En wharfage
  Es muellaje (m)
  It diritto di sosta (m)
  Pt atracagem (m)

**quebrado** (m) n Es
  De Gemeinschuldner (m)
  En bankrupt
  Fr failli (m)
  It fallito (m)
  Pt falido (m)

**questionario** (m) n It
  De Fragebogen (m)
  En questionnaire
  Es cuestionario (m)
  Fr questionnaire (m)
  Pt questionário (m)

**questionário** (m) n Pt
  De Fragebogen (m)
  En questionnaire
  Es cuestionario (m)
  Fr questionnaire (m)
  It questionario (m)

**questionnaire** n En, Fr (m)
  De Fragebogen (m)
  Es cuestionario (m)
  It questionario (m)
  Pt questionário (m)

**quiebra** (f) n Es
  De Konkurs (m)
  En bankruptcy
  Fr faillite (f)
  It fallimento (m)
  Pt falência (f)

**quiebra de banco** (f) Es
  De Bankkrach (m)
  En bank crash
  Fr krach d'une banque (m)
  It crollo di banca (m)
  Pt falência bancária (f)

**quietanza** (f) n It
  De Quittung (f)
  En receipt; acquittance
  Es recibo; satisfacción (m f)
  Fr quittance (f)
  Pt recibo; quitacão (m f)

**quietanza di darsena** (f) It
  De Dockempfangsschein (m)
  En dock receipt
  Es recibo de entrega en muelle
    (m)
  Fr quittance de dock (f)
  Pt recibo de doca (m)

**quietanza finale** (f) It
  De Rechnungsentlastung (f)
  En final discharge
  Es finiquito (m)
  Fr quitus (m)
  Pt cumprimento final (m)

**quincaillerie** (f) n Fr
  De Eisenwaren (f pl)
  En hardware; ironmongery
  Es ferretería; quincallería (f)
  It ferramenta (f)
  Pt ferragens (f pl)

**quitação** (f) n Pt
  De Quittung (f)
  En acquittance; discharge
  Es finiquito (m)
  Fr quittance (f)
  It quietanza (f)

**quittance** n En, Fr (f)
  De Quittung (f)
  Es recibo (m)
  It quietanza (f)
  Pt recibo; quitação (m f)

**quittance de dock** (f) Fr
  De Dockempfangsschein (m)
  En dock receipt
  Es recibo de entrega en muelle
    (m)
  It quietanza di darsena (f)
  Pt recibo de doca (m)

**Quittung** (f) n De
  En receipt; acquittance
  Es recibo; finiquito (m)
  Fr quittance; acquit (f m)
  It quietanza (f)
  Pt recibo; quitação (m f)

**quitus** (m) n Fr
  De Rechnungsentlastung (f)
  En final discharge
  Es finiquito (m)
  It quietanza finale (f)
  Pt cumprimento final (m)

**quorum** n En; Fr, It, Pt (m)
  De beschlussfähige Anzahl (f)
  Es quórum (m)

**quórum** (m) n Es
  De beschlussfähige Anzahl (f)
  En quorum
  Fr quorum (m)
  It quorum (m)
  Pt quorum (m)

**quota** n En; It, Pt (f)
  De Quote; Anteil (f m)
  Es cuota (f)
  Fr quote-part (f)

**quota de importação** (f) Pt
  De Einfuhrkontingent (n)
  En import quota
  Es cupo de importación (m)
  Fr contingent d'importation
    (m)
  It contingente d'importazione
    (m)

**quota del mercato** (f) It
  De Marktanteil (m)
  En market share
  Es participación del mercado
    (f)
  Fr participation au marché (f)
  Pt quota-parte no mercado (f)

**quota di ammortamento** (f) It
  De Abschreibung für Abnut-
    zung (f)
  En depreciation allowance
  Es provisión por depreciación
    (f)
  Fr provision pour amortis-
    sement (f)
  Pt provisão para amortização
    (f)

**quota-parte** (f) n Pt
  De Quote; Anteil (f m)
  En quota; share
  Es cuota; parte (f)
  Fr quote-part (f)
  It quota; parte (f)

**quota-parte no mercado** *(f)* Pt
De Marktanteil *(m)*
En market share
Es participación del mercado *(f)*
Fr participation au marché *(f)*
It quota del mercato *(f)*

**quotare** *vb* It
De (den Preis) angeben
En quote
Es cotizar
Fr coter
Pt cotizar

**quotare senza impegno** It
De nicht fest anbieten
En quote not firm
Es cotizar sin compromiso
Fr coter sans obligation
Pt cotizar sem fixação de valor

**quotation** *n* En
De Kostenanschlag *(m)*
Es cotización *(f)*
Fr cotation *(f)*
It quotazione *(f)*
Pt cotação *(f)*

**quotation di borsa** *(f)* It
De Börsenkurs *(m)*
En stock-exchange quotation
Es curso de bolsa *(m)*
Fr cours de bourse *(m)*
Pt cotação da bolsa *(f)*

**quotazione** *(f)* *n* It
De Kostenanschlag *(m)*
En quotation
Es cotización *(f)*
Fr cotation *(f)*
Pt cotação *(f)*

**quote** *vb* En
De (den Preis) angeben
Es cotizar
Fr coter
It quotare
Pt cotizar

**Quote** *(f)* *n* De
En quota
Es cuota *(f)*
Fr quote-part *(f)*
It quota *(f)*
Pt cota; quota-parte *(f)*

**quoted company** En
De Gesellschaft notiert an der Börse *(f)*
Es compañía cotizada en bolsa *(f)*
Fr société cotée à la Bourse *(f)*
It società quotata in borsa *(f)*
Pt companhia cotizada *(f)*

**quoted price** En
De angegebener Preis *(m)*
Es precio cotizado *(m)*
Fr prix coté *(m)*
It prezzo quotato *(m)*
Pt preço cotizado *(m)*

**quote not firm** En
De nicht fest anbieten
Es cotizar sin compromiso
Fr coter sans obligation
It quotare senza impegno
Pt cotizar sem fixação de valor

**quote-part** *(f)* *n* Fr
De Quote; Anteil *(f m)*
En quota; share
Es cuota; parte *(f)*
It quota; parte *(f)*
Pt cota; quota-parte *(f)*

**quotient cours-bénéfice** *(m)* Fr
De Verhältnis des Aktienkurses zum Reingewinn *(n)*
En price-earnings ratio (P/E)
Es proporción precio-ingresos *(f)*
It rapporto prezzo-utile *(m)*
Pt taxa custo-ganhos *(f)*

# R

**rabais** *(m)* *n* Fr
De Nachlass; Rabatt *(m)*
En rebate; allowance
Es rebaja; bonificación *(f)*
It ribasso; abbuono *(m)*
Pt desconto; provisão *(m f)*

**rabais de demi-gros** *(m)* Fr
De Händlerrabatt *(m)*
En trade discount
Es descuento comercial *(m)*
It sconto di revendita *(m)*
Pt desconto à praça *(m)*

**rabais des prix** *(m)* Fr
De Preisherabsetzung *(f)*
En price-cutting
Es reducción de precios *(f)*
It riduzione dei prezzi *(f)*
Pt redução de preços *(f)*

**rabais différé** *(m)* Fr
De nachträglicher Umsatzbonus *(m)*
En deferred rebate
Es descuento diferido *(m)*
It sconto differito *(m)*
Pt dedução adiada *(f)*

**Rabatt** *(m)* *n* De
En rebate; allowance
Es rebaja; bonificación *(f)*
Fr rabais *(m)*
It ribasso; abbuono *(m)*
Pt desconto; provisão *(m f)*

**ração** *(f)* *n* Pt
De Ration *(f)*
En ration
Es ración *(f)*
Fr ration *(f)*
It razione *(f)*

**raccolta dati** *(f)* It
De Datenerfassung *(f)*
En data capture
Es recogida de datos *(f)*
Fr saisie des données *(f)*
Pt recolha de dados *(f)*

**raccolto** *(m)* *n* It
De Ernte *(f)*
En harvest
Es cosecha *(f)*
Fr moisson; récolte *(f)*
Pt colheita *(f)*

**ración** *(f)* *n* Es
De Ration *(f)*
En ration
Fr ration *(f)*
It razione *(f)*
Pt ração *(f)*

**racionalização** *(f)* *n* Pt
De Rationalisierung *(f)*
En rationalization
Es racionalización *(f)*
Fr rationalisation *(f)*
It razionalizzazione *(f)*

**racionalización** *(f)* n Es
   De  Rationalisierung *(f)*
   En  rationalization
   Fr  rationalisation *(f)*
   It  razionalizzazione *(f)*
   Pt  racionalização *(f)*

**ragioniere capo** *(m)* It
   De  Oberbuchhalter *(m)*
   En  chief accountant
   Es  jefe de contabilidad *(m)*
   Fr  chef comptable *(m)*
   Pt  chefe contabilista *(m)*

**ragioniere diplomato** *(m)* It
   De  Wirtschaftsprüfer *(m)*
   En  qualified accountant
   Es  contador habilitado *(m)*
   Fr  expert comptable *(m)*
   Pt  guarda-livros  diplomado
      *(m)*

**railway** n En
   De  Eisenbahn *(f)*
   Es  ferrocarril *(m)*
   Fr  chemin de fer *(m)*
   It  ferrovia *(f)*
   Pt  caminho de ferro *(m)*

**railway carriage** En
   Am railroad car
   De  Eisenbahnwagen *(m)*
   Es  vagón de ferrocarril *(m)*
   Fr  wagon de chemin de fer
      *(m)*
   It  carrozza ferroviaria *(f)*
   Pt  vagão de caminhos de ferro
      *(m)*

**railway receipt** En
   De  Bahnfrachtbrief *(m)*
   Es  recibo ferroviario *(m)*
   Fr  bulletin de chargement *(m)*
   It  ricevuta ferroviaria *(f)*
   Pt  recibo ferroviário *(m)*

**railway timetable** En
   De  Eisenbahnfahrplan *(m)*
   Es  horario de trenes *(m)*
   Fr  indicateur des chemins de
      fer *(m)*
   It  orario ferroviario *(m)*
   Pt  horário de caminhos de
      ferro *(m)*

**raise a loan** Am
   En  float a loan
   De  eine Anleihe begeben

Es  emitir un empréstito
   Fr  émettre un emprunt
   It  lanciare un prestito
   Pt  lançar um empréstimo

**raison sociale** *(f)* Fr
   De  Firmenname *(m)*
   En  trade name
   Es  razón social *(f)*
   It  denominazione commercia-
      le *(f)*
   Pt  razão comercial *(f)*

**raisons supplémentaires** *(f pl)*
      Fr
   De  weitere Gründe *(m pl)*
   En  further reasons
   Es  rasones adicionales *(f pl)*
   It  ulteriori motivi *(m pl)*
   Pt  rasões adicionais *(f pl)*

**Randanalyse** *(f)* n De
   En  marginal analysis
   Es  análisis marginal *(m)*
   Fr  analyse marginale *(f)*
   It  analisi marginale *(f)*
   Pt  análise marginal *(f)*

**Randkosten** *(pl)* n De
   En  marginal cost
   Es  coste marginal *(m)*
   Fr  coût marginal *(m)*
   It  costa marginale *(m)*
   Pt  custo marginal *(m)*

**random sample** En
   De  Stichprobe *(f)*
   Es  muestra aleatoria *(f)*
   Fr  épreuve au hasard *(f)*
   It  campione a casaccio *(m)*
   Pt  amostra avulso *(f)*

**ranimer l'économie** Fr
   De  die Wirtschaft neu beleben
   En  reflate the economy
   Es  reanimar la economía
   It  reflaziare l'economia
   Pt  reflacionar a economia

**rappel de traitement** *(m)* Fr
   De  Lohnnachzahlung *(f)*
   En  back pay
   Es  pago atrasado *(m)*
   It  arretrati di paga *(m pl)*
   Pt  vencimento atrasado *(m)*

**rapport** *(m)* n Fr
   De  Bericht: Verhältnis *(m n)*
   En  report: relation
   Es  informe: relación *(m f)*
   It  relazione: rapporto *(f m)*
   Pt  relatório: razão *(m f)*

**rapport annuel** *(m)* Fr
   De  Jahresbericht *(m)*
   En  annual report
   Es  memoria anual *(f)*
   It  relazione annuale *(f)*
   Pt  relatório anual *(m)*

**rapport des administrateurs**
      *(m)* Fr
   De  Vorstandsbericht *(m)*
   En  directors' report
   Es  informe  de  la  admin-
      istración *(m)*
   It  relazione  degli  ammini-
      stratori *(f)*
   Pt  relatório de directores *(m)*

**rapport des vérificateurs des**
      **comptes** *(m)* Fr
   De  Bericht  des  Abschluss-
      prüfers *(m)*
   En  auditor's report
   Es  informe de los interventores
      *(m)*
   It  relazione dei sindaci *(f)*
   Pt  relatório do fiscal de contas
      *(m)*

**rapporto** *(m)* n It
   De  Verhältnis *(n)*
   En  ratio
   Es  razón: relación *(f)*
   Fr  rapport *(m)*
   Pt  razão *(f)*

**rapporto prezzo-utile** *(m)* It
   De  Verhältnis des Aktienkurses
      zum Reingewinn.*(n)*
   En  price-earnings ratio (P/E)
   Es  proporción  precio-ingresos
      *(f)*
   Fr  quotient cours-bénéfice *(m)*
   Pt  taxa custo-ganhos *(f)*

**rapports du travail** *(m pl)* Fr
   De  Arbeitsverhältnisse *(n pl)*
   En  labour relations
   Es  relaciones patrón-obrero *(f
      pl)*

It relazioni con-la mano
d'opera *(f pl)*
Pt relações de trabalho *(f pl)*

**rappresentante** *(m) n* It
De Vertreter *(m)*
En representative
Es representante *(m)*
Fr représentant *(m)*
Pt representante *(m)*

**rappresentante esclusivo** *(m)*
It
De Alleinvertreter *(m)*
En sole agent
Es agente exclusivo *(m)*
Fr agent exclusif *(m)*
Pt agente exclusivo *(m)*

**rappresentare** *vb* It
De vertreten
En represent
Es representar
Fr représenter
Pt representar

**rascunho** *(m) n* Pt
De Konzept *(n)*
En draft
Es borrador *(m)*
Fr projet *(m)*
It bozza *(f)*

**rasões adicionais** *(f pl)* Pt
De weitere Gründe *(m pl)*
En further reasons
Es rasones adicionales *(f pl)*
Fr raisons supplémentaires *(f
pl)*
It ulteriori motivi *(m pl)*

**rasones adicionales** *(f pl)* Es
De weitere Gründe *(m pl)*
En further reasons
Fr raisons supplémentaires *(f
pl)*
It ulteriori motivi *(m pl)*
Pt rasões adicionais *(f pl)*

**rassegnare le dimissioni** It
De den Rücktritt einreichen
En hand in one's resignation
Es presentar la dimisión
Fr remettre sa démission
Pt apresentar demissão

**rata** *(f) n* It
De Rate *(f)*
En instalment
Es plazo *(m)*
Fr acompte *(m)*
Pt prestação *(f)*

**rate** *n* En
De Satz; Kurs *(m)*
Es tasa; tipo *(f m)*
Fr taux; cours *(m)*
It tasso; tariffa *(m f)*
Pt taxa *(f)*

**Rate** *(f) n* De
En instalment
Es plazo *(m)*
Fr acompte *(m)*
It rata *(f)*
Pt prestação *(f)*

**Ratenkauf** *(m) n* De
En hire-purchase
Es compra a plazos *(f)*
Fr location-vente; vente à
tempérament *(f)*
It vendita a rate *(f)*
Pt venda a prestações *(f)*

**Ratenzahlung** *(f) n* De
En part payment
Es pago parcial *(m)*
Fr paiement partiel *(m)*
It pagamento parziale *(m)*
Pt pagamento parcial *(m)*

**rate of exchange** En
De Umrechnungskurs *(m)*
Es tipo de cambio *(m)*
Fr cours de change *(m)*
It corso del cambio *(m)*
Pt taxa de câmbio *(f)*

**rate of interest** En
De Zinsfuss *(m)*
Es tipo de interés *(m)*
Fr taux d'intérêt *(m)*
It tasso d'interesse *(m)*
Pt taxa de juro *(f)*

**rate of return** En
De Ertragsrate *(f)*
Es tipo de rédito *(m)*
Fr taux de rendement *(m)*
It tasso di reddito *(m)*
Pt taxa de rendimento *(f)*

**rates** *pl n* En
Am realty tax
De Gemeindesteuer *(f)*
Es contribución municipal *(f)*
Fr taxes municipales *(f pl)*
It tassa comunale *(f)*
Pt contribuições municipais *(f
pl)*

**ratifica** *(f) n* It
De Ratifizierung *(f)*
En ratification
Es ratificación *(f)*
Fr ratification *(f)*
Pt ratificação *(f)*

**ratificação** *(f) n* Pt
De Ratifizierung *(f)*
En ratification
Es ratificación *(f)*
Fr ratification *(f)*
It ratifica *(f)*

**ratificación** *(f) n* Es
De Ratifizierung *(f)*
En ratification
Fr ratification *(f)*
It ratifica *(f)*
Pt ratificação *(f)*

**ratificar** *vb* Es, Pt
De ratifizieren
En ratify
Fr ratifier
It ratificare

**ratificare** *vb* It
De ratifizieren
En ratify
Es ratificar
Fr ratifier
Pt ratificar

**ratification** *n* En, Fr *(f)*
De Ratifizierung *(f)*
Es ratificación *(f)*
It ratifica *(f)*
Pt ratificação *(f)*

**ratifier** *vb* Fr
De ratifizieren
En ratify
Es ratificar
It ratificare
Pt ratificar

**ratifizieren** *vb* De
  En ratify
  Es ratificar
  Fr ratifier
  It ratificare
  Pt ratificar

**Ratifizierung** *(f) n* De
  En ratification
  Es ratificación *(f)*
  Fr ratification *(f)*
  It ratifica *(f)*
  Pt ratificação *(f)*

**ratify** *vb* En
  De ratifizieren
  Es ratificar
  Fr ratifier
  It ratificare
  Pt ratificar

**ratio** *n* En
  De Verhältnis *(n)*
  Es razón; relación *(f)*
  Fr rapport *(m)*
  It rapporto *(m)*
  Pt razão *(f)*

**ration** *n* En, Fr *(f)*
  De Ration *(f)*
  Es ración *(f)*
  It razione *(f)*
  Pt ração *(f)*

**Ration** *(f) n* De
  En ration
  Es ración *(f)*
  Fr ration *(f)*
  It razione *(f)*
  Pt ração *(f)*

**rationalisation** *(f) n* Fr
  De Rationalisierung *(f)*
  En rationalization
  Es racionalización *(f)*
  It razionalizzazione *(f)*
  Pt racionalização *(f)*

**Rationalisierung** *(f) n* De
  En rationalization
  Es racionalización *(f)*
  Fr rationalisation *(f)*
  It razionalizzazione *(f)*
  Pt racionalização *(f)*

**rationalization** *n* En
  De Rationalisierung *(f)*
  Es racionalización *(f)*

  Fr rationalisation *(f)*
  It razionalizzazione *(f)*
  Pt racionalização *(f)*

**raw material** En
  De Rohstoff *(m)*
  Es materia prima *(f)*
  Fr matière première *(f)*
  It materia prima *(f)*
  Pt matéria prima *(f)*

**rayer** *vb* Fr
  De streichen
  En delete
  Es tachar; anular
  It cancellare
  Pt cortar; riscar

**razão** *(f) n* Pt
  De Grund; Verhältnis *(m n)*
  En reason; ratio
  Es razón; relación *(f)*
  Fr raison; rapport *(f m)*
  It ragione; rapporto *(f m)*

**razão comercial** *(f)* Pt
  De Firmenname *(m)*
  En trade name
  Es razón social *(f)*
  Fr raison sociale *(f)*
  It denominazione commerciale *(f)*

**razionalizzazione** *(f) n* It
  De Rationalisierung *(f)*
  En rationalization
  Es racionalización *(f)*
  Fr rationalisation *(f)*
  Pt racionalização *(f)*

**razione** *(f) n* It
  De Ration *(f)*
  En ration
  Es ración *(f)*
  Fr ration *(f)*
  Pt ração *(f)*

**razón** *(f) n* Es
  De Verhältnis *(n)*
  En ratio
  Fr proportion *(f)*
  It rapporto *(m)*
  Pt razão *(f)*

**razón social** *(f)* Es
  De Firmenname *(m)*
  En trade name
  Fr raison sociale *(f)*

  It denominazione commerciale *(f)*
  Pt razão comercial *(f)*

**reabrir discussões** Pt
  De Verhandlungen wiederaufnehmen
  En re-open discussions
  Es reabrir la discusión
  Fr rouvrir la discussion
  It riaprire la discussione

**reabrir la discusión** Es
  De Verhandlungen wiederaufnehmen
  En re-open discussions
  Fr rouvrir la discussion
  It riaprire la discussione
  Pt reabrir discussões

**réacteur** *(m) n* Fr
  De Düsenmotor *(m)*
  En jet engine
  Es motor de propulsión a chorro *(m)*
  It motore a reazione *(m)*
  Pt motor a jacto

**real estate** En
  De unbewegliches Vermögen; Immobilien *(n; f pl)*
  Es bienes inmuebles *(m pl)*
  Fr biens immeubles *(m pl)*
  It beni immobili *(m pl)*
  Pt propriedade imobiliária *(f)*

**real estate agency** Am
  En estate agency
  De Immobilienbüro *(n)*
  Es correduría de fincas *(f)*
  Fr agence immobilière *(f)*
  It agenzia immobiliare *(f)*
  Pt agência de propriedades *(f)*

**realização dos lucros** *(m)* Pt
  De Gewinnrealisation *(f)*
  En profit-taking
  Es realización de utilidades *(f)*
  Fr prise de bénéfices *(f)*
  It realizzazione del utile *(f)*

**realización de utilidades** *(f)* Es
  De Gewinnrealisation *(f)*
  En profit-taking
  Fr prise de bénéfices *(f)*
  It realizzazione del utile *(f)*
  Pt realização dos lucros *(m)*

**realizzazione del utile** (f) It
De Gewinnrealisation (f)
En profit-taking
Es realización de utilidades (f)
Fr prise de bénéfices (f)
Pt realização dos lucros (m)

**realty tax** Am
En rates
De Gemeindesteuer (f)
Es contribución municipal (f)
Fr taxes municipales (f pl)
It tassa comunale (f)
Pt contribuições municipais (f pl)

**reanimar la economía** Es
De die Wirtschaft neu beleben
En reflate the economy
Fr ranimer l´économie
It reflaziare l´economia
Pt reflacionar a economia

**reaseguro** (m) n Es
De Rückversicherung (f)
En reinsurance
Fr réassurance (f)
It riassicurazione (f)
Pt re-seguro (m)

**réassurance** (f) n Fr
De Rückversicherung (f)
En reinsurance
Es reaséguro (m)
It riassicurazione (f)
Pt re-seguro (m)

**rebaja** (f) n Es
De Nachlass (m)
En rebate
Fr rabais (m)
It ribasso; sconto (m)
Pt desconto (m)

**rebate** n En
De Nachlass (m)
Es rebaja (f)
Fr rabais (m)
It ribasso; sconto (m)
Pt desconto (m)

**rebocador** (m) n Pt
De Schleppdampfer (m)
En tug-boat
Es remolcador (m)
Fr remorqueur (m)
It rimorchiatore (m)

**rebusca de información** (f) Es
De Informationswiedergewin-
nung (f)
En information retrieval
Fr récupération de données (f)
It ricupero d´informazioni (m)
Pt recuperação de informação (f)

**recaudador de impuestos** (m) Es
De Steuereinnehmer (m)
En tax collector
Fr percepteur des impôts (m)
It esattore delle imposte (m)
Pt cobrador de impostos (m)

**recaudar** vb Es
De einkassieren
En collect
Fr encaisser
It incassare
Pt cobrar

**recaudar una deuda** Es
De Schulden eintreiben
En collect a debt
Fr recouvrer une créance
It incassare un credito
Pt cobrar uma dívida

**recebido para carregamento** Pt
De zur Absendung empfangen
En received for shipment
Es recibido para envío
Fr reçu pour envoi
It ricevuto per caricazione

**receipt** n En
De Quittung (f)
Es recibo (m)
Fr quittance; acquit (f m)
It ricevuta (f)
Pt recibo (m)

**receita** (f) n Pt
De Einkommen (n)
En income
Es ingresos; renta (m pl; f)
Fr revenu (m)
It reddito (m)

**receita bruta** (f) Pt
De Bruttoeinkommen (n)
En gross income
Es ingreso bruto (m)

Fr rendement brut (m)
It reddito lordo (m)

**receita de trabalho** (f) Pt
De Arbeitseinkommen (n)
En earned income
Es renta del trabajo (f)
Fr revenu du travail (m)
It reddito di lavoro (m)

**receita disponível** (f) Pt
De verfügbares Einkommen (n)
En disposable income
Es renta disponible (f)
Fr revenu disponible (m)
It reddito disponibile (m)

**receita líquida** (f) Pt
De Nettoeinkommen (n)
En net income
Es ingreso neto (f)
Fr revenu net (m)
It reddito netto (m)

**receita não tributável** (f) Pt
De steuerfreies Einkommen (n)
En nontaxable income
Es renta no imponible (f)
Fr revenu non imposable (m)
It reddito non tassabile (m)

**receita pública** (m) Pt
De Nationaleinkommen (n)
En national income
Es renta nacional (f)
Fr revenu national (m)
It reddito nazionale (m)

**receita tributável** (f) Pt
De steuerpflichtiges Einkom-
men (n)
En taxable income
Es renta imponible (f)
Fr revenu imposable (m)
It reddito tassabile (m)

**received for shipment** En
De zur Absendung empfangen
Es recibido para envío
Fr reçu pour envoi
It ricevuto per caricazione
Pt recebido para carrega-
mento

**receiver** (in bankruptcy) n En
De Konkursverwalter (m)
Es sindico (m)
Fr syndic de faillite (m)

It  curatore *(m)*
Pt  sindico *(m)*

**recensement** *(m) n* Fr
De  Volkszählung *(f)*
En  census
Es  censo *(m)*
It  censimento *(m)*
Pt  censo *(m)*

**récépissé de dépôt** *(m)* Fr
De  Depositenschein *(m)*
En  deposit receipt
Es  recibo de depósito *(m)*
It  certificato di deposito *(m)*
Pt  recibo de depósito *(m)*

**récépissé de poste aérienne**
  *(m)* Fr
De  Luftpostempfangsbescheini-
    gung *(f)*
En  airmail receipt
Es  recibo aeropostal *(m)*
It  ricevimento per posta aerea
    *(m)*
Pt  recibo de via aérea *(m)*

**recesión** *(f) n* Es
De  Rezession *(f)*
En  recession
Fr  récession *(f)*
It  recessione *(f)*
Pt  recessão *(f)*

**recessão** *(f) n* Pt
De  Rezession *(f)*
En  recession
Es  recesión *(f)*
Fr  récession *(f)*
It  recessione *(f)*

**recession** *n* En
De  Rezession *(f)*
Es  recesión *(f)*
Fr  récession *(f)*
It  recessione *(f)*
Pt  recessão *(f)*

**récession** *(f) n* Fr
De  Rezession *(f)*
En  recession
Es  recesión *(f)*
It  recessione *(f)*
Pt  recessão *(f)*

**recessione** *(f) n* It
De  Rezession *(f)*
En  recession

Es  recesión *(f)*
Fr  récession *(f)*
Pt  recessão *(f)*

**recettes nettes** *(f pl)* Fr
De  Nettoeinnahmen *(f pl)*
En  net revenue
Es  ingresos netos *(m pl)*
It  entrata netta *(f)*
Pt  receita líquida *(f)*

**rechazar una reclamación** Es
De  einen Ersatzanspruch nicht
    anerkennen
En  repudiate a claim
Fr  renier un sinistre
It  respingere un reclamo
Pt  repudiar uma reclamação

**rechazo** *(m) n* Es
De  Nichtannahme; Ablehnung
    *(f)*
En  nonacceptance; rejection
Fr  non-acceptation; refus *(f*
    *m)*
It  mancata accettazione; ri-
    fiuto *(f m)*
Pt  não-aceitação; rejeicão *(f)*

**Rechenfehler** *(m) n* De
En  miscalculation
Es  cálculo erróneo *(m)*
Fr  erreur de calcul *(f)*
It  calcolo errato *(m)*
Pt  erro de cálculo *(m)*

**Rechenmaschine** *(f) n* De
En  calculator
Es  calculadora *(f)*
Fr  machine à calculer *(f)*
It  calcolatrice *(f)*
Pt  máquina de calcular *(f)*

**recherche** *(f) n* Fr
De  Forschung *(f)*
En  research
Es  investigación *(f)*
It  ricerca *(f)*
Pt  investigação *(f)*

**recherche industrielle** *(f)* Fr
De  Zweckforschung; Entwick-
    lung *(f)*
En  research and development
    (R & D)
Es  investigación y desarrollo
It  studi e sviluppi

Es  recesión *(f)*
Fr  récession *(f)*
Pt  recessão *(f)*

**recherche opérationnelle** *(f)* Fr
De  Unternehmensforschung *(f)*
En  operational research (OR)
Es  investigación operacional *(f)*
It  indagine sul funzionamento
    *(f)*
Pt  investigação operacional *(f)*

**Rechner** *(m) n* De
En  computer
Es  computadora *(f)*
Fr  ordinateur *(m)*
It  elaboratore; calcolatore *(m)*
Pt  computador *(m)*

**Rechnersprache** *(f) n* De
En  computer language
Es  lenguaje de computadoras
    *(m)*
Fr  langage-machine *(m)*
It  linguaggio macchina *(m)*
Pt  linguagem de computador
    *(f)*

**Rechnung** *(f) n* De
En  bill; account
Es  cuenta, nota *(f)*
Fr  compte; note *(m f)*
It  conto; nota *(m f)*
Pt  conta *(f)*

**Rechnungsentlastung** *(f) n* De
En  final discharge
Es  finiquito *(m)*
Fr  quitus *(m)*
It  quietanza finale *(f)*
Pt  cumprimento final *(m)*

**Rechnungsprüfer** *(m) n* De
En  comptroller
Es  interventor *(m)*
Fr  vérificateur des comptes
    *(m)*
It  controllore *(m)*
Pt  controlador *(m)*

**Recht** *(n) n* De
En  law; right
Es  ley; derecho *(f m)*
Fr  loi; droit *(f m)*
It  legge; diritto *(f m)*
Pt  lei; direito *(f m)*

Es  recesión *(f)*
Fr  récession *(f)*
Pt  recessão *(f)*

Pt  investigação e desenvol-
    vimento

**Rechtsfall** (m) n De
En (legal) case
Es causa (f)
Fr procès (m)
It causa (f)
Pt causa (f)

**rechtsgültig** adj De
En legal
Es legal
Fr légal
It legale
Pt legal

**Rechtshaftung** (f) n De
En legal liability
Es responsabilidad legal (f)
Fr responsabilité légale (f)
It responsabilità legale (f)
Pt responsabilidade legal (f)

**Rechtsprechung** (f) n De
En jurisdiction
Es jurisdicción (f)
Fr juridiction (f)
It giurisdizione (f)
Pt jurisdição (f)

**Rechtsvertreter** (m) n De
En legal representative
Es representante legal (m)
Fr représentant mandaté (m)
It mandatario (m)
Pt representante legal (m)

**recht und billig** De
En fair
Es razonable
Fr équitable
It equo
Pt razoável

**recibido para envío** Es
De zur Absendung empfangen
En received for shipment
Fr reçu pour envoi
It ricevuto per caricazione
Pt recebido para carrega-
   mento

**recibo** (m) n Es, Pt
De Quittung (f)
En receipt
Fr quittance; acquit (f m)
It ricevuta (f)

**recibo aeropostal** (m) Es
De Luftpostempfangsbescheini-
   gung (f)
En airmail receipt
Fr récépissé de poste aé-
   rienne (m)
It ricevimento per posta aerea
   (m)
Pt recibo de via aérea (m)

**recibo de depósito** (m) Es, Pt
De Depositenschein (m)
En deposit receipt
Fr récépissé de dépôt (m)
It certificato di deposito (m)

**recibo de doca** (m) Pt
De Dockempfangsschein (m)
En dock receipt
Es recibo de entrega en muelle
   (m)
Fr quittance de dock (f)
It quietanza di darsena (f)

**recibo de embarco** (m) Es
De Übernahmebescheinigung
   (f)
En mate's receipt
Fr billet de bord (m)
It ricevuta d'imbarco (f)
Pt recibo de embarque (m)

**recibo de embarque** (m) Pt
De Übernahmebescheinigung
   (f)
En mate's receipt
Es recibo de embarco (m)
Fr billet de bord (m)
It ricevuta d'imbarco (f)

**recibo de entrega en muelle**
   (m) Es
De Dockempfangsschein (m)
En dock receipt
Fr quittance de dock (f)
It quietanza di darsena (f)
Pt recibo de doca (m)

**recibo de via aérea** (m) Pt
De Luftpostempfangsbescheini-
   gung (f)
En airmail receipt
Es recibo aeropostal (m)
Fr récépissé de poste aé-
   rienne (m)
It ricevimento per posta aerea
   (m)

**recibo ferroviario** (m) Es
De Bahnfrachtbrief (m)
En railway receipt
Fr bulletin de chargement (m)
It ricevuta ferroviaria (f)
Pt recibo ferroviário (m)

**recibo ferroviário** (m) Pt
De Bahnfrachtbrief (m)
En railway receipt
Es recibo ferroviario (m)
Fr bulletin de chargement (m)
It ricevuta ferroviaria (f)

**reclamação** (f) n Pt
De Anspruch (m)
En claim
Es reclamación (f)
Fr réclamation (f)
It reclamo (m)

**reclamação de seguro** (f) Pt
De Versicherungsanspruch (m)
En insurance claim
Es reclamación de seguro (f)
Fr indemnité d'assurance (f)
It sinistro; reclamo d'inden-
   nizzo (m)

**reclamación** (f) n Es
De Anspruch (m)
En claim
Fr réclamation (f)
It reclamo (m)
Pt reclamação (f)

**reclamación de salario** (f) Es
De Lohnforderung (f)
En wage claim
Fr revendication de salaire (f)
It rivendicazione salariale (f)
Pt demanda de salário (f)

**reclamación de seguro** (f) Es
De Versicherungsanspruch (m)
En insurance claim
Fr indemnité d'assurance (f)
It sinistro; reclamo d'inden-
   nizzo (m)
Pt reclamação de seguro (f)

**réclamation** (f) n Fr
De Anspruch (m)
En claim
Es reclamación (f)
It reclamo (m)
Pt reclamação (f)

**reclamo** *(m) n* It
De Anspruch *(m)*
En claim
Es reclamación *(f)*
Fr réclamation; créance *(f)*
Pt reclamação *(f)*

**recoger una letra** Es
De einen Wechsel einlösen
En retire a bill
Fr payer une lettre de change
It ritirare un effetto
Pt recuperar uma letra

**recogida de datos** *(f)* Es
De Datenerfassung *(f)*
En data capture
Fr saisie des données *(f)*
It raccolta dati *(f)*
Pt recolha de dados *(f)*

**recolha de dados** *(f)* Pt
De Datenerfassung *(f)*
En data capture
Es recogida de datos *(f)*
Fr saisie des données *(f)*
It raccolta dati *(f)*

**récolte** *(f) n* Fr
De Ernte *(f)*
En harvest
Es cosecha *(f)*
It raccolto *(m)*
Pt colheita *(f)*

**recommended retail selling price** En
De empfohlener Ladenpreis *(m)*
Es precio detallista recomendado *(m)*
Fr prix de détail racommandé *(m)*
It prezzo al minuto indicativo *(m)*
Pt preço de venda a retalho recomendado *(m)*

**reconnaissance de dette** *(f)* Fr
De Schuldschein *(m)*
En I.O.U. (I owe you)
Es pagaré *(m)*
It pagherò *(m)*
Pt vale *(m)*

**reconstrução** *(f) n* Pt
De Wiederaufbau *(m)*
En reconstruction

Es reconstrucción *(f)*
Fr reconstruction *(f)*
It ricostruzione *(f)*

**reconstrucción** *(f) n* Es
De Wiederaufbau *(m)*
En reconstruction
Fr reconstruction *(f)*
It ricostruzione *(f)*
Pt reconstrução *(f)*

**reconstruction** *n* En, Fr *(f)*
De Wiederaufbau *(m)*
Es reconstrucción *(f)*
It ricostruzione *(f)*
Pt reconstrução *(f)*

**recorrer a reservas** Pt
De die Reserven angreifen
En draw on reserves
Es sacar reservas
Fr prélever sur les réserves
It prelevare dalle riserve

**recouvrer une créance** Fr
De Schulden eintreiben
En collect a debt
Es recaudar una deuda
It incassare un credito
Pt cobrar uma dívida

**recuperação de informação** *(f)* Pt
De Informationswiedergewinnung *(f)*
En information retrieval
Es rebusca de información *(f)*
Fr récupération de données *(f)*
It ricupero d'informazioni *(m)*

**recuperar uma letra** Pt
De einen Wechsel einlösen
En retire a bill
Es recoger una letra
Fr payer une lettre de change
It ritirare un effetto

**récupération de données** *(f)* Fr
De Informationswiedergewinnung *(f)*
En information retrieval
Es rebusca de información *(f)*
It ricupero d'informazioni *(m)*
Pt recuperação de informação *(f)*

**reçu pour envoi** Fr
De zur Absendung empfangen
En received for shipment
Es recibido para envío
It ricevuto per caricazione
Pt recebido para carregamento

**red** *(f) n* Es
De Netz *(n)*
En network
Fr réseau *(m)*
It rete *(f)*
Pt rede *(f)*

**redactar un contrato** Es
De einen Vertrag formulieren
En draw up a contract
Fr rédiger un contrat
It redigere un contratto
Pt redigir um contrato

**redditività** *(f) n* It
De Rentabilität *(f)*
En profitability
Es rentabilidad *(f)*
Fr rentabilité *(f)*
Pt rentabilidade *(f)*

**reddito** *(m) n* It
De Einkommen; Rendite *(n f)*
En income; yield
Es ingresos; rédito *(m pl; m)*
Fr revenu *(m)*
Pt receita; rédito *(f m)*

**reddito degli investimenti** *(m)* It
De Einkommen aus Kapitalanlagen *(n)*
En investment income
Es renta de inversiones *(f)*
Fr revenu de placements *(m)*
Pt rendimento de capitais investidos *(m)*

**reddito del capitale** *(m)* It
De Kapitalertrag *(m)*
En return on capital; unearned income
Es beneficio sobre capital *(m)*
Fr rémunération du capital *(f)*
Pt juro sobre o capital *(m)*

**reddito di lavoro** *(m)* It
De Arbeitseinkommen *(n)*
En earned income
Es renta del trabajo *(f)*

Fr revenu du travail *(m)*
Pt receita de trabalho *(f)*

**reddito disponibile** *(m)* It
De verfügbares Einkommen *(n)*
En disposable income
Es renta disponible *(f)*
Fr revenu disponible *(m)*
Pt receita disponível *(f)*

**reddito lordo** *(m)* It
De Bruttoeinkommen *(n)*
En gross income
Es ingreso bruto *(m)*
Fr rendement brut *(m)*
Pt receita bruta *(f)*

**reddito nazionale** *(m)* It
De Nationaleinkommen *(n)*
En national income
Es renta nacional *(f)*
Fr revenu national *(m)*
Pt receita pública *(m)*

**reddito netto** *(m)* It
De Nettoeinkommen *(n)*
En net income
Es ingreso neto *(f)*
Fr revenu net *(m)*
Pt receita líquida *(f)*

**reddito non tassabile** *(m)* It
De steuerfreies Einkommen *(n)*
En nontaxable income
Es ingresos no imponibles *(m pl)*
Fr revenu non imposable *(m)*
Pt receita não tributavel *(f)*

**reddito tassabile** *(m)* It
De steuerpflichtiges Einkommen *(n)*
En taxable income
Es renta imponible *(f)*
Fr revenu imposable *(m)*
Pt receita tributável *(f)*

**rede** *(f)* n Pt
De Netz *(n)*
En network
Es red *(f)*
Fr réseau *(m)*
It rete *(f)*

**redeem** *vb* En
De tilgen; gutmachen
Es redimir; rescatar
Fr rembourser; dégager

It redimere; rimborsare
Pt remir; resgatar

**redeemable bond** En
De kündbare Obligation *(f)*
Es obligación reembolsable *(f)*
Fr obligation amortissable *(f)*
It obbligazione redimibile *(f)*
Pt obrigação reembolsável *(f)*

**redemption** n En
De Tilgung; Amortisation *(f)*
Es amortización *(f)*
Fr amortissement; rembourse-
ment *(m)*
It ammortamento *(m)*
Pt amortização *(f)*

**redemption date** En
De Einlösungstag *(m)*
Es fecha de reembolso *(f)*
Fr date du remboursement *(f)*
It data di rimborso *(f)*
Pt data de resgate *(f)*

**redemption yield** En
De Einlösungsertrag *(m)*
Es rédito de reembolso *(m)*
Fr rendement sur rembourse-
ment *(m)*
It rendita di rimborso *(f)*
Pt rendimento de resgate *(m)*

**redevable** *adj* Fr
De verbunden
En indebted
Es endeudado
It indebitato
Pt endividado

**redevance** *(f)* n Fr
De Tantieme; Miete *(f)*
En royalty; rental
Es derechos; alquiler *(m pl; m)*
It diritti; affitto *(m pl; m)*
Pt direitos; renda *(m pl; f)*

**redigere un contratto** It
De einen Vertrag formulieren
En draw up a contract
Es redactar un contrato
Fr rédiger un contrat
Pt redigir um contrato

**rédiger un contrat** Fr
De einen Vertrag formulieren
En draw up a contract

Es redactar un contrato
It redigere un contratto
Pt redigir um contrato

**redigir um contrato** Pt
De einen Vertrag formulieren
En draw up a contract
Es redactar un contrato
Fr rédiger un contrat
It redigere un contratto

**redimere** *vb* It
De tilgen; gutmachen
En redeem
Es redimir; rescatar
Fr rembourser; dégager
Pt remir; resgatar

**redimir** *vb* Es, Pt
De tilgen; gutmachen
En redeem
Fr rembourser; dégager
It redimere; rimborsare

**rédito** *(m)* n Es, Pt
De Rendite *(f)*
En yield; return
Fr revenu *(m)*
It reddito *(m)*

**rédito de reembolso** *(m)* Es
De Einlösungsertrag *(m)*
En redemption yield
Fr rendement sur rembourse-
ment *(m)*
It rendita di rimborso *(f)*
Pt rendimento de resgate *(m)*

**rédito neto** *(m)* Es
De Reinerlös *(m)*
En net proceeds
Fr produit net *(m)*
It ricavo netto *(m)*
Pt proventos líquidos *(m pl)*

**redução de capital** *(f)* Pt
De Kapitalherabsetzung *(f)*
En reduction of capital
Es reducción de capital *(f)*
Fr réduction du capital *(f)*
It riduzione del capitale *(f)*

**redução de preços** *(f)* Pt
De Preisherabsetzung *(f)*
En price-cutting
Es reducción de precios *(f)*
Fr rabais des prix *(m)*
It riduzione dei prezzi *(f)*

**reducción de capital** *(f)* Es
De Kapitalherabsetzung *(f)*
En reduction of capital
Fr réduction du capital *(f)*
It riduzione del capitale *(f)*
Pt redução de capital *(f)*

**reducción de precios** *(f)* Es
De Preisherabsetzung *(f)*
En price-cutting
Fr rabais des prix *(m)*
It riduzione dei prezzi *(f)*
Pt redução de preços *(f)*

**réduction du capital** *(f)* Fr
De Kapitalherabsetzung *(f)*
En reduction of capital
Es reducción de capital *(f)*
It riduzione del capitale *(f)*
Pt redução de capital *(f)*

**reduction of capital** En
De Kapitalherabsetzung *(f)*
Es reducción de capital *(f)*
Fr réduction du capital *(f)*
It riduzione del capitale *(f)*
Pt redução de capital *(f)*

**Reederei** *(f)* n De
En shipping line
Es compañia navièra *(f)*
Fr compagnie de navigation
   *(f)*
It società di navigazione *(f)*
Pt companhia de navegação
   *(f)*

**reembolso** *(m)* n Es, Pt
De Rückerstattung *(f)*
En refund
Fr remboursement *(m)*
It rimborso *(m)*

**reembolso de derechos de
aduana** *(m)* Es
De Zollrückvergütung *(f)*
En (customs) drawback
Fr remboursement des droits
   d'importation *(m)*
It rimborso d'esportazione
   *(m)*
Pt reimbolso de direitos alfan-
   degários *(m)*

**re-export** *vb* En
De wiederausführen
Es reexportar
Fr reexporter

It riesportare
Pt re-exportar

**reexportação** *(f)* n Pt
De Wiederausfuhr *(f)*
En re-exportation
Es reexportación *(f)*
Fr réexportation *(f)*
It riesporto *(m)*

**reexportación** *(f)* n Es
De Wiederausfuhr *(f)*
En re-exportation
Fr réexportation *(f)*
It riesporto *(m)*
Pt reexportação *(f)*

**reexportar** *vb* Es, Pt
De wiederausführen
En re-export
Fr reexporter
It riesportare

**re-exportation** n En
De Wiederausfuhr *(f)*
Es reexportación *(f)*
Fr réexportation *(f)*
It riesporto *(m)*
Pt reexportação *(f)*

**réexportation** *(f)* n Fr
De Wiederausfuhr *(f)*
En re-exportation
Es reexportación *(f)*
It riesporto *(m)*
Pt reexportação *(f)*

**reexporter** *vb* Fr
De wiederausführen
En re-export
Es reexportar
It riesportare
Pt reexportar

**réfections et améliorations** Fr
De Änderungen und Erneu-
   erungen
En alterations and renewals
Es reformas y renovaciones
It modifiche e rinnovamenti
Pt modificações e renovações

**refer a cheque to drawer** En
Am refer a check to drawer
De einen Scheck uneingelöst
   lassen
Es rehusar pago de un cheque

Fr refuser    d'honorer    un
   chèque
It rifiutare    di    pagare    un
   assegno
Pt devolver um cheque ao
   sacado

**reference** n En
De Referenz *(f)*
Es referencia *(f)*
Fr référence *(f)*
It referenza *(f)*
Pt referência *(f)*

**référence** *(f)* n Fr
De Referenz *(f)*
En reference
Es referencia *(f)*
It referenza *(f)*
Pt referência *(f)*

**reference book** En
De Nachschlagebuch *(n)*
Es libro de consulta *(m)*
Fr ouvrage de référence *(m)*
It libro di consultazione *(m)*
Pt livro de consulta *(m)*

**référence commerciale** *(f)* Fr
De Kreditauskunft *(f)*
En trade reference
Es referencia comercial *(f)*
It referenze commerciali *(f pl)*
Pt referência comercial *(f)*

**référence de banquier** *(f)* Fr
De Bankzeugnis *(n)*
En banker's reference
Es referencia bancaria *(f)*
It referenza bancaria *(f)*
Pt referência bancária *(f)*

**referencia** *(f)* n Es
De Referenz *(f)*
En reference
Fr référence *(f)*
It referenza *(f)*
Pt referência *(f)*

**referência** *(f)* n Pt
De Referenz *(f)*
En reference
Es referencia *(f)*
Fr référence *(f)*
It referenza *(f)*

**referencia bancaria** (f) Es
De Bankzeugnis (n)
En banker's reference
Fr référence de banquier (f)
It referenza bancaria (f)
Pt referência bancária (f)

**referência bancária** (f) Pt
De Bankzeugnis (n)
En banker's reference
Es referencia bancaria (f)
Fr référence de banquier (f)
It referenza bancaria (f)

**referencia comercial** (f) Es
De Kreditauskunft (f)
En trade reference
Fr référence commerciale (f)
It referenze commerciali (f pl)
Pt referência comercial (f)

**referência comercial** (f) Pt
De Kreditauskunft (f)
En trade reference
Es referencia comercial (f)
Fr référence commerciale (f)
It referenze commerciali (f pl)

**Referenz** (f) n De
En reference
Es referencia (f)
Fr référence (f)
It referenza (f)
Pt referência (f)

**referenza** (f) n It
De Referenz (f)
En reference
Es referencia (f)
Fr référence (f)
Pt referência (f)

**referenza bancaria** (f) It
De Bankzeugnis (n)
En banker's reference
Es referencia bancaria (f)
Fr référence de banquier (f)
Pt referência bancária (f)

**referenze commerciali** (f pl) It
De Kreditauskunft (f)
En trade reference
Es referencia comercial (f)
Fr référence de fournisseur (f)
Pt referência comercial (f)

**reflacionar a economia** Pt
De die Wirtschaft neu beleben
En reflate the economy
Es reanimar la economía
Fr ranimer l'économie
It reflaziare l'economia

**reflate the economy** En
De die Wirtschaft neu beleben
Es reanimar la economía
Fr ranimer l'économie
It reflaziare l'economia
Pt reflacionar a economia

**reflaziare l'economia** It
De die Wirtschaft neu beleben
En reflate the economy
Es reanimar la economía
Fr ranimer l'économie
Pt reflacionar a economia

**reforma de contribuição pré-via** (f) Pt
De Kassenpension (f)
En contributory pension
Es retiro contributivo (m)
Fr retraite de régime à cotisations (f)
It pensione a contributi (f)

**reforma monetaria** (f) Es
De Währungsreform (f)
En monetary reform
Fr réforme monétaire (f)
It riforma monetaria (f)
Pt reforma monetária (f)

**reforma monetária** (f) Pt
De Währungsreform (f)
En monetary reform
Es reforma monetaria (f)
Fr réforme monétaire (f)
It riforma monetaria (f)

**reformas** (f pl) Es
De Umbau (m)
En alterations
Fr travaux de transformation (m pl)
It modifiche (f pl)
Pt modificações (f pl)

**reformas y renovaciones** Es
De Änderungen und Erneuerungen
En alterations and renewals
Fr réfections et améliorations

It modifiche e rinnovamenti
Pt modificações e renovações

**reformas y reparaciones** Es
De Änderungen und Reparaturen
En alterations and repairs
Fr transformations et réparations
It modifiche e riparazioni
Pt modificações e reparações

**réforme monétaire** (f) Fr
De Währungsreform (f)
En monetary reform
Es reforma monetaria (f)
It riforma monetaria (f)
Pt reforma monetária (f)

**refrendar** vb Es
De gegenzeichnen
En countersign
Fr contresigner
It controfirmare
Pt validar por assinatura

**refuge fiscal** (m) Fr
De Steuerparadies (n)
En tax haven
Es refugio fiscal (m)
It rifugio fiscale (m)
Pt refúgio fiscal (m)

**refugio fiscal** (m) Es
De Steuerparadies (n)
En tax haven
Fr refuge fiscal (m)
It rifugio fiscale (m)
Pt refúgio fiscal (m)

**refúgio fiscal** (m) Pt
De Steuerparadies (n)
En tax haven
Es refugio fiscal (m)
Fr refuge fiscal (m)
It rifugio fiscale (m)

**refund** n En
De Rückerstattung (f)
Es reembolso (m)
Fr remboursement (m)
It rimborso (m)
Pt reembolso (m)

**refus** (m) n Fr
De Ablehnung (f)
En rejection
Es rechazo (m)

It rifiuto *(m)*
Pt rejeição *(f)*

**refuser d'honorer un chèque**
Fr
De einen Scheck uneingelöst lassen
En refer a cheque to drawer
Es rehusar pago de un cheque
It rifiutare di pagaré un assegno
Pt devolver um cheque ao sacado

**regalo** *(m) n* Es
De Geschenk *(n)*
En gift
Fr don; cadeau *(m)*
It dono; donazione *(m f)*
Pt prenda; presente *(f m)*

**regatear** *vb* Es, Pt
De feilschen
En haggle
Am bargain
Fr marchander; chipoter
It mercanteggiare; cavillare

**regateio colectivo** *(m)* Pt
De Tarifvertragsverhandlung *(f)*
En collective bargaining
Es contratación collectiva *(f)*
Fr négociations de conventions collectives *(f pl)*
It contrattazione collettiva *(f)*

**Regierung** *(f) n* De
En government
Es gobierno *(m)*
Fr gouvernement *(m)*
It governo *(m)*
Pt governo *(m)*

**Regierungsschuldverschreibungen** *(f pl) n* De
En Government securities
Es títulos públicos *(m pl)*
Fr titres d'État *(m pl)*
It titoli di Stato *(m pl)*
Pt títulos do Tesouro *(m pl)*

**région déprimée** *(f)* Fr
De Notstandsgebiet *(n)*
En distressed area
Es región deprimida *(f)*
It area indigente *(f)*
Pt zona deprimida *(f)*

**región deprimida** *(f)* Es
De Notstandsgebiet *(n)*
En distressed area
Fr région déprimée *(f)*
It area indigente *(f)*
Pt zona deprimida *(f)*

**régions aurifères** *(f pl)* Fr
De Goldgrube *(f)*
En gold fields
Es yacimiento aurífero *(m)*
It terreni auriferi *(m pl)*
Pt jazigos de ouro *(m pl)*

**registar** *vb* Pt
De registrieren; einlegen
En register; file
Es registrar; interponer
Fr enregistrer; déposer
It registrare; depositare

**register** *vb* En
De registrieren
Es registrar
Fr enregistrer
It registrare
Pt registar

**registered letter** En
De eingeschriebener Brief *(m)*
Es carta certificada *(f)*
Fr lettre recommandée *(f)*
It lettera raccomandata *(f)*
Pt carta registada *(f)*

**registo de acções** *(m)* Pt
De Liste der Aktionäre *(f)*
En share register
Es registro de las acciones *(m)*
Fr registre des actionnaires *(m)*
It registro delle azioni *(m)*

**registo do navio** *(m)* Pt
De Schiffsregister *(n)*
En ship's register
Es registro del barco *(m)*
Fr certificat d'immatriculation *(m)*
It atto di nazionalità *(m)*

**registrar** *vb* Es
De registrieren
En register
Fr enregistrer
It registrare
Pt registar

**registrare** *vb* It
De registrieren
En register
Es registrar
Fr enregistrer
Pt registar

**registration fee** En
De Anmeldegebühr *(f)*
Es derechos de registro *(m pl)*
Fr droit d'enregistrement *(m)*
It tassa di registrazione *(f)*
Pt custas de registo *(f pl)*

**registrazione** *(f) n* It
De Eintragung *(f)*
En entry
Es asiento *(m)*
Fr inscription *(f)*
Pt lançamento *(m)*

**registrazione a giornale** *(f)* It
De Tagebuchsposten *(m)*
En journal-entry
Es asiento en el libro diario *(m)*
Fr article d'un livre journal *(m)*
Pt anotação de diário *(f)*

**registre des actionnaires** *(m)* Fr
De Liste der Aktionäre *(f)*
En share register
Es registro de las acciones *(m)*
It registro delle azioni *(m)*
Pt registo de acções *(m)*

**registrieren** *vb* De
En register
Es registrar
Fr enregistrer
It registrare
Pt registar

**registro de las acciones** *(m)* Es
De Liste der Aktionäre *(f)*
En share register
Fr registre des actionnaires *(m)*
It registro delle azioni *(m)*
Pt registo de acções *(m)*

**registro del barco** *(m)* Es
De Schiffsregister *(n)*
En ship's register

Fr certificat d'immatriculation (m)
It atto di nazionalità (m)
Pt registo do navio (m)

**registro delle azioni** (m) It
De Liste der Aktionäre (f)
En share register
Es registro de las acciones (m)
Fr registre des actionnaires (m)
Pt registo de acções (m)

**reglamento** (m) n Es
De Verordnung (f)
En regulation
Fr règlement (m)
It regolamento (m)
Pt regulação (f)

**règlement** (m) n Fr
De Verordnung; Abrechnung (f)
En regulation; settlement
Es reglamento; ajuste (m)
It regolamento; quietanza (m f)
Pt ajuste; regulação (m f)

**regolamento** (m) n It
De Verordnung; Ausgleich (f m)
En regulation; settlement
Es reglamento; satisfacción (m f)
Fr règlement (m)
Pt regulação; satisfação (f)

**regulação** (f) n Pt
De Verordnung; Ausgleich (f m)
En regulation; settlement
Es reglamento; satisfacción (m f)
Fr règlement (m)
It regolamento (m)

**rehusar pago de un cheque** Es
De einen Scheck uneingelöst lassen
En refer a cheque to drawer
Fr refuser d'honorer un chèque
It rifiutare di pagare un assegno
Pt devolver um cheque ao sacado

**reimbolso de direitos alfande-gários** (m) Pt
De Zollrückvergütung (f)
En (customs) drawback
Es reembolso de derechos de aduana (m)
Fr remboursement des droits d'importation (m)
It rimborso d'esportazione (m)

**Reinerlös** (m) n De
En net proceeds
Es rédito neto (m)
Fr produit net (m)
It ricavo netto (m)
Pt proventos líquidos (m pl)

**Reingewicht** (n) n De
En net weight
Es peso neto (m)
Fr poids net (m)
It peso netto (m)
Pt peso líquido (m)

**Reingewinn** (m) n De
En net profit
Es ganancia neta (f)
Fr bénéfice net (m)
It utile netto (m)
Pt lucro líquido (m)

**Reingewinnspanne** (f) n De
En net profit margin
Es margen de beneficio neto (m)
Fr marge nette de bénéfices (f)
It margine di utile netto (m)
Pt margem de lucro líquido (f)

**reinsurance** n En
De Rückversicherung (f)
Es reaseguro (m)
Fr réassurance (f)
It riassicurazione (f)
Pt re-seguro (m)

**Reinvermögen** (n) n De
En net assets
Es activo neto (m)
Fr actif net (m)
It attivo netto (m)
Pt bens líquidos (m pl)

**Reisebüro** (n) n De
En travel agency
Es agencia de viajes (f)

Fr agence de voyages (f)
It agenzia di viaggi (f)
Pt agente de viagems (m)

**Reisegewerbe** (n) n De
En tourist trade
Es industria del turismo (f)
Fr commerce de tourisme (m)
It commercio turistico (m)
Pt indústria do turismo (f)

**Reisekosten** (pl) n De
En travelling expenses
Es dietas de viajes (f pl)
Fr frais de voyage (m pl)
It spese di viaggio (f pl)
Pt despesas de viagem (f pl)

**Reisende(r)** (m) n De
En passenger
Es pasajero (m)
Fr passager (m)
It passeggero (m)
Pt passageiro (m)

**Reisescheck** (m) n De
En traveller's cheque
Es cheque de viajero (m)
Fr chèque de voyage (m)
It assegno turistico (m)
Pt cheque de viajante (m)

**rejection** n En
De Ablehnung (f)
Es rechazo (m)
Fr refus (m)
It rifiuto (m)
Pt rejeição (f)

**rejeição** (f) n Pt
De Ablehnung (f)
En rejection
Es rechazo (m)
Fr refus (m)
It rifiuto (m)

**Reklame** (f) n De
En advertising
Es publicidad (f)
Fr publicité (f)
It pubblicità (f)
Pt publicidade (f)

**Rektaindossement** (n) n De
En restrictive endorsement
Es endoso restringido (m)
Fr endossement restrictif (m)

It  girata restrittiva *(f)*
Pt  endosse restritivo *(m)*

**relação de quantidades** *(f)* Pt
De  Baukostenvoranschlag *(m)*
En  bill of quantities
Es  cubicación de obra *(f)*
Fr  devis *(m)*
It  preventivo *(m)*

**relaciones humanas** *(f pl)* Es
De  zwischenmenschliche Be-
    ziehungen *(f pl)*
En  human relations
Fr  relations humaines *(f pl)*
It  relazioni umane *(f pl)*
Pt  relações humanas *(f pl)*

**relaciones humanas indus-
    triales** *(f pl)* Es
De  Arbeitsbeziehungen *(f pl)*
En  industrial relations
Fr  relations humaines dans
    l'entreprise *(f pl)*
It  relazioni nell'industria *(f pl)*
Pt  relações industriais *(f pl)*

**relaciones patrón-obrero** *(f pl)*
    Es
De  Arbeitsverhältnisse *(n pl)*
En  labour relations
Fr  rapports du travail *(m pl)*
It  relazioni con la mano
    d'opera *(f pl)*
Pt  relações de trabalho *(f pl)*

**relaciones públicas** *(f pl)* Es
De  Public-Relations *(n pl)*
En  public relations (PR)
Fr  relations publiques *(f pl)*
It  pubbliche relazioni *(f pl)*
Pt  relações públicas *(f pl)*

**relações de trabalho** *(f pl)* Pt
De  Arbeitsverhältnisse *(n pl)*
En  labour relations
Es  relaciones patrón-obrero *(f
    pl)*
Fr  rapports du travail *(m pl)*
It  relazioni con la mano
    d'opera *(f pl)*

**relações humanas** *(f pl)* Pt
De  zwischenmenschliche Be-
    ziehungen *(f pl)*
En  human relations
Es  relaciones humanas *(f pl)*

Fr  relations humaines *(f pl)*
It  relazioni umane *(f pl)*

**relações industriais** *(f pl)* Pt
De  Arbeitsbeziehungen *(f pl)*
En  industrial relations
Es  relaciones humanas indus-
    triales *(f pl)*
Fr  relations humaines dans
    l'entreprise *(f pl)*
It  relazioni nell'industria *(f pl)*

**relações públicas** *(f pl)* Pt
De  Public-Relations *(n pl)*
En  public relations (PR)
Es  relaciones públicas *(f pl)*
Fr  relations publiques *(f pl)*
It  pubbliche relazioni *(f pl)*

**relámpago** *(m)* n Es
De  Blitz *(m)*
En  lightning
Fr  foudre *(f)*
It  fulmine *(m)*
Pt  relâmpago *(m)*

**relâmpago** *(m)* n Pt
De  Blitz *(m)*
En  lightning
Es  relámpago *(m)*
Fr  foudre *(f)*
It  fulmine *(m)*

**relations humaines** *(f pl)* Fr
De  zwischenmenschliche Be-
    ziehungen *(f pl)*
En  human relations
Es  relaciones humanas *(f pl)*
It  relazioni umane *(f pl)*
Pt  relações humanas *(f pl)*

**relations    humaines    dans
    l'entreprise** *(f pl)* Fr
De  Arbeitsbeziehungen *(f pl)*
En  industrial relations
Es  relaciones humanas indus-
    triales *(f pl)*
It  relazioni nell'industria *(f pl)*
Pt  relações industriais *(f pl)*

**relations publiques** *(f pl)* Fr
De  Public-Relations *(n pl)*
En  public relations (PR)
Es  relaciones públicas *(f pl)*
It  pubbliche relazioni *(f pl)*
Pt  relações públicas *(f pl)*

**relatório** *(m)* n Pt
De  Bericht *(m)*
En  report
Es  informe *(m)*
Fr  rapport *(m)*
It  relazione *(m)*

**relatório anual** *(m)* Pt
De  Jahresbericht *(m)*
En  annual report
Es  memoria anual *(f)*
Fr  rapport annuel *(m)*
It  relazione annuale *(f)*

**relatório de directores** *(m)* Pt
De  Vorstandsbericht *(m)*
En  directors' report
Es  informe de la administra-
    ción *(m)*
Fr  rapport des administrateurs
    *(m)*
It  relazione degli amministra-
    tori *(f)*

**relatório do fiscal de contas**
    *(m)* Pt
De  Bericht des Abschluss-
    prüfers *(m)*
En  auditor's report
Es  informe de los interventores
    *(m)*
Fr  rapport des vérificateurs
    des comptes *(m)*
It  relazione dei sindaci *(f)*

**relatório do perito** *(m)* Pt
De  Sachverständigengutachten
    *(n)*
En  expert's report
Es  informe del especialista *(m)*
Fr  expertise *(f)*
It  perizia *(f)*

**relazione** *(f)* n It
De  Bericht *(m)*
En  report
Es  informe *(m)*
Fr  rapport *(m)*
Pt  relatório *(m)*

**relazione annuale** *(f)* It
De  Jahresbericht *(m)*
En  annual report
Es  memoria anual *(f)*
Fr  rapport annuel *(m)*
Pt  relatório anual *(m)*

**relazione degli amministratori**
*(f)* It
De Vorstandsbericht *(m)*
En directors' report
Es informe de la administración *(m)*
Fr rapport des administrateurs *(m)*
Pt relatório de directores *(m)*

**relazione dei sindaci** *(f)* It
De Bericht des Abschlussprüfers *(m)*
En auditor's report
Es informe de los interventores *(m)*
Fr rapport des vérificateurs des comptes *(m)*
Pt relatório do fiscal de contas *(m)*

**relazione finanziaria** *(f)* It
De Finanzausweis *(m)*
En financial statement
Es extracto financiero *(m)*
Fr état de finances *(m)*
Pt extracto financeiro *(m)*

**relazione sul mercato** *(f)* It
De Marktbericht *(m)*
En market report
Es informe del mercado *(m)*
Fr revue du marché *(f)*
Pt informação do mercado *(f)*

**relazioni con la mano d'opera**
*(f pl)* It
De Arbeitsverhältnisse *(n pl)*
En labour relations
Es relaciones patrón-obrero *(f pl)*
Fr rapports du travail *(m pl)*
Pt relações de trabalho *(f pl)*

**relazioni nell'industria** *(f pl)* It
De Arbeitsbeziehungen *(f pl)*
En industrial relations
Es relaciones humanas industriales *(f pl)*
Fr relations humaines dans l'entreprise *(f pl)*
Pt relações industriais *(f pl)*

**relazioni umane** *(f pl)* It
De zwischenmenschliche Beziehungen *(f pl)*
En human relations
Es relaciones humanas *(f pl)*

Fr relations humaines *(f pl)*
Pt relações humanas *(f pl)*

**relevé de compte** *(m)* Fr
De Kontoauszug *(m)*
En statement of account
Es extracto de cuenta *(m)*
It estratto conto *(m)*
Pt extracto de conta *(m)*

**reliable** *adj* En
De zuverlässig
Es digno de confianza
Fr digne de confiance
It fidato; attendibile
Pt digno de confiança

**remboursement** *(m)* n Fr
De Rückerstattung *(f)*
En refund
Es reembolso *(m)*
It rimborso *(m)*
Pt reembolso *(m)*

**remboursement des droits d'importation** *(m)* Fr
De Zollrückvergütung *(f)*
En (customs) drawback
Es reembolso de derechos de aduana *(m)*
It rimborso d'esportazione *(m)*
Pt reimbolso de direitos alfandegários *(m)*

**rembourser** *vb* Fr
De tilgen; zurückzahlen
En redeem; reimburse
Es redimir; reembolsar
It redimere; rimborsare
Pt remir; reembolsar

**remessa gratuita** Pt
De portofreie Lieferung
En delivery free
Es libre entrega
Fr livré franco
It consegna franco

**remettre sa démission** Fr
De den Rücktritt einreichen
En hand in one's resignation
Es presentar la dimisión
It rassegnare le dimissioni
Pt apresentar demissão

**remir** *vb* Pt
De tilgen; gutmachen
En redeem
Es redimir
Fr rembourser; dégager
It redimere; rimborsare

**remise sur les exports** *(f)* Fr
De Ausführsonderrabatt *(m)*
En export rebate
Es descuento por exportación *(m)*
It sconto d'esportazione *(m)*
Pt desconto de exportação *(m)*

**remolcador** *(m)* n Es
De Schleppdampfer *(m)*
En tug-boat
Fr remorqueur *(m)*
It rimorchiatore *(m)*
Pt rebocador *(m)*

**remorqueur** *(m)* n Fr
De Schleppdampfer *(m)*
En tug-boat
Es remolcador *(m)*
It rimorchiatore *(m)*
Pt rebocador *(m)*

**remplir** *vb* Fr
De erfüllen
En fulfil
Es cumplir
It adempiere
Pt comprir

**remuneração** *(f)* n Pt
De Vergütung *(f)*
En remuneration
Es remuneración *(f)*
Fr rémunération *(f)*
It rimunerazione *(f)*

**remuneración** *(f)* n Es
De Vergütung *(f)*
En remuneration
Fr rémunération *(f)*
It rimunerazione *(f)*
Pt remuneração *(f)*

**remuneration** n En
De Vergütung *(f)*
Es remuneración *(f)*
Fr rémunération *(f)*
It rimunerazione *(f)*
Pt remuneração *(f)*

**rémunération** (f) n Fr
De Vergütung (f)
En remuneration
Es remuneración (f)
It rimunerazione (f)
Pt remuneração (f)

**rémunération du capital** (f) Fr
De Kapitalertrag (m)
En return on capital
Es beneficio sobre capital (m)
It reddito del capitale (m)
Pt juro sobre o capital (m)

**renchérir** vb Fr
De teurer werden; steigen
En advance in price
Es encarecer
It aumentare di prezzo
Pt encarecer

**renchérissement** (m) n Fr
De Preiserhöhung (f)
En advance in price
Es encarecimiento (m)
It rialzo (m)
Pt encarecimento (m)

**renchérissement du coût de la vie** (m) Fr
De erhöhte Lebenshaltungskosten (pl)
En increased cost of living
Es coste de vida más alto (m)
It aumentato costo della vita (m)
Pt custo de vida mais elevado (m)

**renda** (f) n Pt
De Miete (f)
En rent
Es alquiler (m)
Fr loyer (m)
It pigione; affitto (f m)

**renda sobre o terreno** (f) Pt
De Grundpacht (f)
En ground-rent
Es renta del terreno (f)
Fr rente foncière (f)
It affitto di terreno (m)

**rendement** (m) n Fr
De Erzeugung; Rendite (f)
En output; yield
Es rendimiento; rédito (m)

It produzione; reddito (f m)
Pt rendimento; rédito (m)

**rendement brut** (m) Fr
De Bruttoeinkommen (n)
En gross income
Es ingreso bruto (m)
It reddito lordo (m)
Pt receita bruta (f)

**rendement équitable** (m) Fr
De angemessener Ertrag (m)
En fair return
Es beneficio razonable (m)
It discreto profitto (m)
Pt rendimento justo (m)

**rendement net** (m) Fr
De Nettoertrag (m)
En net yield
Es rendimiento neto (m)
It reddito netto (m)
Pt rendimento líquido (m)

**rendements décroissants** (m pl) Fr
De abnehmender Ertrag (m)
En diminishing returns
Es rendimientos decrecientes (m pl)
It proventi decrescenti (m pl)
Pt rendimentos decrescentes (m pl)

**rendement sur remboursement** (m) Fr
De Einlösungsertrag (m)
En redemption yield
Es rédito de reembolso (m)
It rendita di rimborso (f)
Pt rendimento de resgate (m)

**rendersi garante di** It
De Haftkaution geben
En go bail for
Es salir fiados por
Fr se porter garant de
Pt prestar caução a favor de

**rendiconto finanziario provvisorio** (m) It
De Zwischenbilanz (f)
En interim financial statement
Es extracto financiero provisional (m)
Fr bilan intérimaire (m)
Pt extracto financeiro interino (m)

**rendimento** (m) n Pt
De Erzeugung; Rendite (f)
En output; yield
Es rendimiento; rédito (m)
Fr rendement (m)
It produzione; reddito (f m)

**rendimento de capitais investidos** (m) Pt
De Einkommen aus Kapitalanlagen (n)
En investment income
Es renta de inversiones (f)
Fr revenu de placements (m)
It reddito degli investimenti (m)

**rendimento della spesa** (m) It
De Wirtschaftlichkeit (f)
En cost-effectiveness
Es efectividad de coste (f)
Fr coût et efficacité
Pt eficiência relativa ao custo (f)

**rendimento de resgate** (m) Pt
De Einlösungsertrag (m)
En redemption yield
Es rédito de reembolso (m)
Fr rendement sur remboursement (m)
It rendita di rimborso (f)

**rendimento do capital** (m) Pt
De Kapitaleinkommen (n)
En unearned income
Es rentas (f pl)
Fr rente (f)
It reddito di capitale (m)

**rendimento justo** (m) Pt
De angemessener Ertrag (m)
En fair return
Es beneficio razonable (m)
Fr rendement équitable (m)
It discreto profitto (m)

**rendimento líquido** (m) Pt
De Nettoertrag (m)
En net yield
Es rendimiento neto (m)
Fr rendement net (m)
It reddito netto (m)

**rendimentos decrescentes** (m pl) Pt
De abnehmender Ertrag (m)
En diminishing returns

Es rendimientos decrecientes
(m pl)
Fr rendements décroissants
(m pl)
It proventi decrescenti (m pl)

**rendimiento** (m) n Es
De Erzeugung; Rendite (f)
En output; yield
Fr rendement (m)
It produzione; reddito (f m)
Pt rendimento; rédito (m)

**rendimiento neto** (m) Es
De Nettoertrag (m)
En net yield
Fr rendement net (m)
It reddito netto (m)
Pt rendimento líquido (m)

**rendimientos decrecientes** (m
pl) Es
De abnehmender Ertrag (m)
En diminishing returns
Fr rendements décroissants
(m pl)
It proventi decrescenti (m pl)
Pt rendimentos decrescentes
(m pl)

**rendita di rimborso** (f) It
De Einlösungsertrag (m)
En redemption yield
Es rédito de reembolso (m)
Fr rendement sur rembourse-
ment (m)
Pt rendimento de resgate (m)

**rendita vitalizia differita** (f) It
De Anwartschaft auf Leibrente
(f)
En deferred annuity
Es anualidad aplazada (f)
Fr annuité différée (f)
Pt anuidade diferida (f)

**Rendite** (f) n De
En yield
Es rédito (m)
Fr revenu; rendement (m)
It reddito (m)
Pt rédito (m)

**renier un sinistre** Fr
De einen Ersatzanspruch nicht
anerkennen
En repudiate a claim
Es rechazar una reclamación

It respingere un reclamo
Pt repudiar uma reclamação

**renoncer** vb Fr
De verzichten auf
En renounce
Es renunciar
It rinunžiare
Pt renunciar

**renonciation** (f) n Fr
De Verzicht (m)
En renunciation
Es renuncia (f)
It rinunzia (f)
Pt renúncia (f)

**renounce** vb En
De verzichten auf
Es renunciar
Fr renoncer
It rinunziare
Pt renunciar

**renseignements complémen-
taires** (m pl) Fr
De weitere Auskunft (f)
En further information
Es más detalles (m pl)
It ulteriori informazioni (f pl)
Pt informação adicional (f)

**rent** n En
De Miete (f)
Es alquiler (m)
Fr loyer (m)
It pigione; affitto (f m)
Pt renda (f)

**rent** vb En
De vermieten
Es alquilar
Fr louer; affermer
It affittare; appigionare
Pt alugar

**rentabilidad** (f) n Es
De Rentabilität (f)
En profitability
Fr rentabilité (f)
It redditività (f)
Pt rentabilidade (f)

**rentabilidade** (f) n Pt
De Rentabilität (f)
En profitability
Es rentabilidad (f)

Fr rentabilité (f)
It redditività (f)

**Rentabilität** (f) n De
En profitability
Es rentabilidad (f)
Fr rentabilité (f)
It redditività (f)
Pt rentabilidade (f)

**Rentabilitätsgrenze** (f) n De
En break-even point
Es punto de igualdad de ingre-
sos y gastos (m)
Fr point de seuil (m)
It punto di pareggio (m)
Pt ponto de acerto (m)

**rentabilité** (f) n Fr
De Rentabilität (f)
En profitability
Es rentabilidad (f)
It redditività (f)
Pt rentabilidade (f)

**renta de inversiones** (f) Es
De Einkommen aus Kapitalan-
lagen (n)
En investment income
Fr revenu de placements (m)
It reddito degli investimenti
(m)
Pt rendimento de capitais
investidos (m)

**renta del terreno** (f) Es
De Grundpacht (f)
En ground-rent
Fr rente foncière (f)
It affitto di terreno (m)
Pt renda sobre o terreno (f)

**renta del trabajo** (f) Es
De Arbeitseinkommen (n)
En earned income
Fr revenu du travail (m)
It reddito di lavoro (m)
Pt receita de trabalho (f)

**renta disponible** (f) Es
De verfügbares Einkommen (n)
En disposable income
Fr revenu disponible (m)
It reddito disponibile (m)
Pt receita disponível (f)

**renta imponible** *(f)* Es
De  steuerpflichtiges Einkommen *(n)*
En  taxable income
Fr  revenu imposable *(m)*
It  reddito tassabile *(m)*
Pt  receita tributável *(f)*

**renta nacional** *(f)* Es
De  Nationaleinkommen *(n)*
En  national income
Fr  revenu national *(m)*
It  reddito nazionale *(m)*
Pt  receita pública *(m)*

**rentas** *(f pl)* Es
De  Kapitaleinkommen *(n)*
En  unearned income
Fr  rente *(f)*
It  reddito di capitale *(m)*
Pt  rendimento do capital *(m)*

**rent control** En
De  Mietzinskontrolle *(f)*
Es  control de alquileres *(m)*
Fr  contrôle des loyers *(m)*
It  blocco degli affitti *(m)*
Pt  controlo de rendas *(m)*

**Rente** *(f)* n De
En  pension
Es  pensión *(f)*
Fr  pension *(f)*
It  pensione *(f)*
Pt  pensão *(f)*

**rente foncière** *(f)* Fr
De  Grundpacht *(f)*
En  ground-rent
Es  renta del terreno *(f)*
It  affitto di terreno *(m)*
Pt  renda sobre o terreno *(f)*

**rentes** *(f pl)* n Fr
De  Kapitaleinkommen *(n)*
En  unearned income
Es  rentas *(f pl)*
It  reddito di capitale *(m)*
Pt  rendimento do capital *(m)*

**Rentner** *(m)* n De
En  pensioner
Es  pensionado *(m)*
Fr  pensionnaire *(m)*
It  pensionato *(m)*
Pt  pensionista *(m)*

**renuncia** *(f)* n Es
De  Verzicht *(m)*
En  renunciation
Fr  renonciation *(f)*
It  rinunzia *(f)*
Pt  renúncia *(f)*

**renúncia** *(f)* n Pt
De  Verzicht *(m)*
En  renunciation
Es  renuncia *(f)*
Fr  renonciation *(f)*
It  rinunzia *(f)*

**renunciar** Es, Pt
De  aufgeben; verzichten auf
En  give up; renounce
Fr  céder; renoncer
It  cedere; rinunziare

**renunciation** n En
De  Verzicht *(m)*
Es  renuncia *(f)*
Fr  renonciation *(f)*
It  rinunzia *(f)*
Pt  renúncia *(f)*

**re-open discussions** En
De  Verhandlungen wiederaufnehmen
Es  reabrir la discusión
Fr  rouvrir la discussion
It  riaprire la discussione
Pt  reabrir discussões

**repair** n En
De  Reparatur *(f)*
Es  reparación *(f)*
Fr  réparation *(f)*
It  riparazione *(f)*
Pt  reparação *(f)*

**repair** vb En
De  reparieren
Es  reparar; componer
Fr  réparer; réfectionner
It  riparare; rifare
Pt  consertar; reparar

**reparação** *(f)* n Pt
De  Reparatur *(f)*
En  repair
Es  reparación *(f)*
Fr  réparation *(f)*
It  riparazione *(f)*

**reparación** *(f)* n Es
De  Reparatur *(f)*
En  repair
Fr  réparation *(f)*
It  riparazione *(f)*
Pt  reparação *(f)*

**reparar** vb Es, Pt
De  reparieren
En  repair
Fr  réparer; réfectionner
It  riparare; rifare

**réparation** *(f)* n Fr
De  Reparatur *(f)*
En  repair
Es  reparación *(f)*
It  riparazione *(f)*
Pt  reparação *(f)*

**Reparatur** *(f)* n De
En  repair
Es  reparación *(f)*
Fr  réparation *(f)*
It  riparazione *(f)*
Pt  reparação *(f)*

**réparer** vb Fr
De  reparieren
En  repair
Es  reparar; componer
It  riparare; rifare
Pt  consertar; reparar

**reparieren** vb De
En  repair
Es  reparar; componer
Fr  réparer; réfectionner
It  riparare; rifare
Pt  consertar; reparar

**repartição dos lucros** *(f)* Pt
De  Gewinnbeteiligung *(f)*
En  profit-sharing
Es  participación en los beneficios *(f)*
Fr  participation aux bénéfices *(f)*
It  partecipazione agli utili *(f)*

**repartir** vb Es, Pt
De  verteilen; zuteilen
En  distribute; apportion
Fr  répartir
It  ripartire

**répartir** *vb* Fr
De verteilen; zuteilen
En distribute; apportion
Es repartir
It ripartire
Pt repartir

**reparto** *(m) n* Es
De Verteilung *(f)*
En distribution
Fr distribution *(f)*
It ripartizione *(f)*
Pt distribuição *(f)*

**répertoire** *(m) n* Fr
De Adressbuch *(n)*
En directory
Es guía *(f)*
It guida *(f)*
Pt guia *(m)*

**replacement cost** En
De Wiederanschaffungskosten *(pl)*
Es coste de repuesto *(m)*
Fr coût de remplacement *(m)*
It costo di rimpiazzo *(m)*
Pt custo de substituição *(m)*

**reply paid** En
Am post paid
De Rückantwort bezahlt
Es respuesta pagada
Fr réponse payée
It risposta pagata
Pt resposta paga

**réponse** *(f) n* Fr
De Antwort *(f)*
En answer
Es respuesta *(f)*
It risposta *(f)*
Pt resposta *(f)*

**réponse payée** Fr
De Rückantwort bezahlt
En reply paid
Am post paid
Es respuesta pagada
It risposta pagata
Pt resposta paga

**report** *n* En
De Bericht; Meldung *(m f)*
Es informe; reportaje *(m)*
Fr rapport; compte-rendu *(m)*
It relazione; rapporto *(f m)*
Pt relatório *(m)*

**report à nouveau** *(m)* Fr
De Saldovortrag *(m)*
En balance carried forward
Es saldo de entrada *(m)*
It saldo da riportare *(m)*
Pt saldo transportado *(m)*

**Repräsentationskosten** *(pl) n* De
En entertainment expenses
Es gastos de representación *(m pl)*
Fr frais de représentation *(m pl)*
It spese di rappresentanza *(f pl)*
Pt despesas de representação *(f pl)*

**represent** *vb* En
De vertreten
Es representar
Fr représenter
It rappresentare
Pt representar

**représentant** *(m) n* Fr
De Vertreter *(m)*
En representative
Es representante *(m)*
It rappresentante *(m)*
Pt representante *(m)*

**representante** *(m) n* Es, Pt
De Vertreter *(m)*
En representative
Fr représentant *(m)*
It rappresentante *(m)*

**representante legal** *(m)* Es, Pt
De Rechtsvertreter *(m)*
En legal representative
Fr représentant mandaté *(m)*
It mandatario *(m)*

**représentant mandaté** *(m)* Fr
De Rechtsvertreter *(m)*
En legal representative
Es representante legal *(m)*
It mandatario *(m)*
Pt representante legal *(m)*

**representar** *vb* Es, Pt
De vertreten
En represent
Fr représenter
It rappresentare

**representative** *n* En
De Vertreter *(m)*
Es representante *(m)*
Fr représentant *(m)*
It rappresentante *(m)*
Pt representante *(m)*

**représenter** *vb* Fr
De vertreten
En represent
Es representar
It rappresentare
Pt representar

**repudiar uma reclamação** Pt
De einen Ersatzanspruch nicht anerkennen
En repudiate a claim
Es rechazar una reclamación
Fr renier un sinistre
It respingere un reclamo

**repudiate a claim** En
De einen Ersatzanspruch nicht anerkennen
Es rechazar una reclamación
Fr renier un sinistre
It respingere un reclamo
Pt repudiar uma reclamação

**requisar** *vb* Es
De verlangen
En requisition
Fr réquisitionner
It requisire
Pt requisitar

**requisição** *(f) n* Pt
De Antrag *(m)*
En application
Es solicitud *(f)*
Fr demande *(f)*
It domanda *(f)*

**requisire** *vb* It
De verlangen
En requisition
Es requisar
Fr réquisitionner
Pt requisitar

**requisitar** *vb* Pt
De verlangen
En requisition
Es requisar
Fr réquisitionner
It requisire

**requisition** *vb* En
De verlangen
Es requisar
Fr réquisitionner
It requisire
Pt requisitar

**requisition** *n* En
De Anforderung *(f)*
Es pedido; solicitud *(m f)*
Fr demande *(f)*
It richiesta; requisizione *(f)*
Pt pedido *(m)*

**réquisitionner** *vb* Fr
De verlangen
En requisition
Es requisar
It requisire
Pt requisitar

**requisito** *(m) n* Es
De Qualifikation *(f)*
En qualification
Fr qualification; capacité *(f)*
It qualifica; requisito *(f m)*
Pt qualificação *(f)*

**resale price** En
De Wiederverkaufspreis *(m)*
Es precio de reventa *(m)*
Fr prix de revente *(m)*
It prezzo di rivendita *(m)*
Pt preço de revenda *(m)*

**rescisão de contrato** *(f)* Pt
De Vertragsbeendigung *(f)*
En determination of a contract
Es rescisión de un contrato *(f)*
Fr résolution d'un contrat *(f)*
It risoluzione di un contratto *(f)*

**rescisión de un contrato** *(f)* Es
De Vertragsbeendigung *(f)*
En determination of a contract
Fr résolution d'un contrat *(f)*
It risoluzione di un contratto *(f)*
Pt rescisão de contrato *(f)*

**rés-do-chão** *(m)* Pt
De Erdgeschoss *(n)*
En ground floor
Es planta baja *(f)*
Fr rez-de-chaussée *(m)*
It pianterreno *(m)*

**research** *n* En
De Forschung *(f)*
Es investigación *(f)*
Fr recherche *(f)*
It ricerca *(f)*
Pt investigação *(f)*

**research and development (R & D)** En
De Zweckforschung und Entwicklung *(f)*
Es investigación y desarrollo
Fr recherche industrielle *(f)*
It studi e sviluppi
Pt investigação e desenvolvimento

**réseau** *(m) n* Fr
De Netz *(n)*
En network
Es red *(f)*
It rete *(f)*
Pt rede *(f)*

**re-seguro** *(m) n* Pt
De Rückversicherung *(f)*
En reinsurance
Es reaseguro *(m)*
Fr réassurance *(f)*
It riassicurazione *(f)*

**reserva de capital** *(f)* Es
De Kapitalreserve *(f)*
En capital reserves
Fr réserve de capitaux *(f)*
It riserva di capitale *(f)*
Pt reservas de capital *(f pl)*

**reserva em dinheiro** *(f)* Pt
De Kassenreserve *(f)*
En cash reserve
Es reserva en efectivo *(f)*
Fr réserve en espèces *(f)*
It riserva in contanti *(f)*

**reserva en efectivo** *(f)* Es
De Kassenreserve *(f)*
En cash reserve
Fr réserve en espèces *(f)*
It riserva in contanti *(f)*
Pt reserva em dinheiro *(f)*

**reserva latente** *(f)* Es
De stille Reserve *(f)*
En hidden reserve
Fr réserve cachée *(f)*
It riserva occulta *(f)*
Pt reserva oculta *(f)*

**reserva oculta** *(f)* Pt
De stille Reserve *(f)*
En hidden reserve
Es reserva latente *(f)*
Fr réserve cachée *(f)*
It riserva occulta *(f)*

**reserva para deudas incobrables** *(f)* Es
De Dubiosenreserve *(f)*
En bad debt reserve
Fr provision pour créances douteuses *(f)*
It riserva per crediti inesigibili *(f)*
Pt reserva para dívidas incobráveis *(f)*

**reserva para dividas incobráveis** *(f)* Pt
De Dubiosenreserve *(f)*
En bad debt reserve
Es reserva para deudas incobrables *(f)*
Fr provision pour créances douteuses *(f)*
It riserva per crediti inesigibili *(f)*

**reserva para imprevistos** *(f)* Es
De Rückstellung für Eventualverbindlichkeiten *(f)*
En contingency reserve
Fr réserve de prévoyance *(f)*
It riserva di previdenza *(f)*
Pt reserva para as contingências *(f)*

**reservar** *vb* Es, Pt
De vorbehalten
En reserve
Fr réserver
It riservare

**reservas de capital** *(f pl)* Pt
De Kapitalreserve *(f)*
En capital reserves
Es reserva de capital *(f)*
Fr réserve de capitaux *(f)*
It riserva di capitale *(f)*

**reserve** *vb* En
De vorbehalten
Es reservar
Fr réserver
It riservare
Pt reservar

**réserve cachée** *(f)* Fr
De stille Reserve *(f)*
En hidden reserve
Es reserva latente *(f)*
It riserva occulta *(f)*
Pt reserva oculta *(f)*

**reserve currency** En
De Reservewährung *(f)*
Es moneda de reserva *(f)*
Fr monnaie de réserve *(f)*
It valuta di riserva *(f)*
Pt moeda de reserva *(f)*

**réserve de capitaux** *(f)* Fr
De Kapitalreserve *(f)*
En capital reserves
Es reserva de capital *(f)*
It riserva di capitale *(f)*
Pt reservas de capital *(f pl)*

**réserve de prévoyance** *(f)* Fr
De Rückstellung für Eventual-
verbindlichkeiten *(f)*
En contingency reserve
Es reserva para imprevistos *(f)*
It riserva di previdenza *(f)*
Pt reserva para as contingên-
cias *(f)*

**réserve en espèces** *(f)* Fr
De Kassenreserve *(f)*
En cash reserve
Es reserva en efectivo *(f)*
It riserva in contanti *(f)*
Pt reserva em dinheiro *(f)*

**Reservefonds** *(m)* n De
En reserve fund
Es fondo de reserva *(m)*
Fr fonds de réserve *(m)*
It fondo di riserva *(m)*
Pt fundo de reserva *(m)*

**reserve fund** En
De Reservefonds *(m)*
Es fondo de reserva *(m)*
Fr fonds de réserve *(m)*
It fondo di riserva *(m)*
Pt fundo de reserva *(m)*

**(die) Reserven angreifen** De
En draw on reserves
Es sacar reservas
Fr prélever sur les réserves
It prelevare dalle riserve
Pt recorrer a reservas

**reserve price** En
De Mindestpreis *(m)*
Es precio mínimo fijado *(m)*
Fr mise à prix *(f)*
It prezzo minimo *(m)*
Pt preço de reserva *(m)*

**réserver** *vb* Fr
De vorbehalten
En reserve
Es reservar
It riservare
Pt reservar

**Reservewährung** *(f)* n De
En reserve currency
Es moneda de reserva *(f)*
Fr monnaie de réserve *(f)*
It valuta di riserva *(f)*
Pt moeda de reserva *(f)*

**residuo di cassa** *(m)* It
De Kassensaldo *(m)*
En cash balance
Es resto en efectivo *(m)*
Fr solde de caisse *(m)*
Pt saldo em dinheiro *(m)*

**resign** *vb* En
De zurücktreten
Es dimitir
Fr se démettre
It dimettersi
Pt demitir-se

**résistance à la vente** *(f)* Fr
De Kaufabneigung *(f)*
En sales resistance
Es dificultades de ventas *(f pl)*
It difficoltà di vendita *(f)*
Pt resistência contra vendas
*(f)*

**resistência contra vendas** *(f)*
Pt
De Kaufabneigung *(f)*
En sales resistance
Es dificultades de ventas *(f pl)*
Fr résistance à la vente *(f)*
It difficoltà di vendita *(f)*

**resolução** *(f)* n Pt
De Beschluss *(m)*
En resolution
Es resolución *(f)*
Fr resolution *(f)*
It deliberazione *(f)*

**resolução extraordinária** *(f)* Pt
De Sonderentschluss *(m)*
En extraordinary resolution
Es resolución extraordinaria *(f)*
Fr résolution extraordinaire *(f)*
It deliberazione straordinaria
*(f)*

**resolución** *(f)* n Es
De Beschluss *(m)*
En resolution
Fr resolution *(f)*
It deliberazione *(f)*
Pt resolução *(f)*

**resolución extraordinaria** *(f)*
Es
De Sonderentschluss *(m)*
En extraordinary resolution
Fr résolution extraordinaire *(f)*
It deliberazione straordinaria
*(f)*
Pt resolução extraordinária *(f)*

**resolution** n En, Fr *(f)*
De Beschluss *(m)*
Es resolución *(f)*
It deliberazione *(f)*
Pt resolução *(f)*

**résolution d'un contrat** *(f)* Fr
De Vertragsbeendigung *(f)*
En determination of a contract
Es rescisión de un contrato *(f)*
It risoluzione di un contratto
*(f)*
Pt rescisão de contrato *(f)*

**résolution extraordinaire** *(f)* Fr
De Sonderentschluss *(m)*
En extraordinary resolution
Es resolución extraordinaria *(f)*
It deliberazione straordinaria
*(f)*
Pt resolução extraordinária *(f)*

**respingere un reclamo** It
De einen Ersatzanspruch nicht
anerkennen
En repudiate a claim
Es rechazar una reclamación
Fr renier un sinistre
Pt repudiar uma reclamação

**responsabile per i danni** It
De schadenersatzpflichtig
En liable for damages
Es responsable por daños

Fr passible de dommages-
   intérêts
Pt responsavel por danos

**responsabilidad** (f) n Es
De Verantwortlichkeit (f)
En responsibility; liability
Fr responsabilité (f)
It responsabilità (f)
Pt responsabilidade (f)

**responsabilidad del patrono**
   (f) Es
De Haftpflicht des Arbeitge-
   bers (f)
En employer's liability
Fr responsabilité patronale (f)
It responsabilità del datore di
   lavoro (f)
Pt responsabilidade do patrão
   (f)

**responsabilidade** (f) n Pt
De Verantwortlichkeit (f)
En responsibility; liability
Es responsabilidad (f)
Fr responsabilité (f)
It responsabilità (f)

**responsabilidade contingente**
   (f) Pt
De Eventualverpflichtung (f)
En contingent liability
Es responsabilidad continge-
   nte (f)
Fr obligation éventuelle (f)
It sopravvenienza passiva (f)

**responsabilidade do patrão** (f)
   Pt
De Haftpflicht des Arbeitge-
   bers (f)
En employer's liability
Es responsabilidad del patrono
   (f)
Fr responsabilité patronale (f)
It responsabilità del datore di
   lavoro (f)

**responsabilidade legal** (f) Pt
De Rechtshaftung (f)
En legal liability
Es responsabilidad legal (f)
Fr responsabilité légale (f)
It responsabilità legale (f)

**responsabilidad legal** (f) Es
De Rechtshaftung (f)
En legal liability
Fr responsabilité légale (f)
It responsabilità legale (f)
Pt responsabilidade legal (f)

**responsabilità** (f) n It
De Verantwortlichkeit (f)
En responsibility; liability
Es responsabilidad (f)
Fr responsabilité (f)
Pt responsabilidade (f)

**responsabilità del datore di**
   **lavoro** (f) It
De Haftpflicht des Arbeitge-
   bers (f)
En employer's liability
Es responsabilidad del patrono
   (f)
Fr responsabilité patronale (f)
Pt responsabilidade do patrão
   (f)

**responsabilità legale** (f) It
De Rechtshaftung (f)
En legal liability
Es responsabilidad legal (f)
Fr responsabilité légale (f)
Pt responsabilidade legal (f)

**responsabilité** (f) n Fr
De Verantwortlichkeit (f)
En responsibility; liability
Es responsabilidad (f)
It responsabilità (f)
Pt responsabilidade (f)

**responsabilité légale** (f) Fr
De Rechtshaftung (f)
En legal liability
Es responsabilidad legal (f)
It responsabilità legale (f)
Pt responsabilidade legal (f)

**responsabilité patronale** (f) Fr
De Haftpflicht des Arbeitge-
   bers (f)
En employer's liability
Es responsabilidad del patrono
   (f)
It responsabilità del datore di
   lavoro (f)
Pt responsabilidade do patrão
   (f)

**responsable por daños** Es
De schadenersatzpflichtig
En liable for damages
Fr passible de dommages-
   intérêts
It responsabile per i danni
Pt responsavel por danos

**responsavel por danos** Pt
De schadenersatzpflichtig
En liable for damages
Es responsable por daños
Fr passible de dommages-
   intérêts
It responsabile per i danni

**responsibility** n En
De Verantwortlichkeit (f)
Es responsabilidad (f)
Fr responsabilité (f)
It responsabilità (f)
Pt responsabilidade (f)

**resposta** (f) n Pt
De Antwort (f)
En answer
Es respuesta (f)
Fr réponse (f)
It risposta (f)

**resposta paga** Pt
De Rückantwort bezahlt
En reply paid
Am post paid
Es respuesta pagada
Fr réponse payée
It risposta pagata

**respuesta** (f) n Es
De Antwort (f)
En answer
Fr réponse (f)
It risposta (f)
Pt resposta (f)

**respuesta pagada** Es
De Rückantwort bezahlt
En reply paid
Am post paid
Fr réponse payée
It risposta pagata
Pt resposta paga

**resserrement de crédit** (m) Fr
De Kreditklemme (f)
En credit squeeze
Es escasez de créditos (f)

It restrizione di credito (f)
Pt restrição de crédito (f)

**ressources existantes** (f pl) Fr
De lieferfertiges Angebot (n)
En supplies on hand
Es provisiones existentes (f pl)
It forniture esistenti (f pl)
Pt fornecimentos em existência (m pl)

**resta in linea** It
De am Apparat bleiben
En hold the line
Es espere al aparato
Fr ne quittez pas
Pt aguarde

**resto en efectivo** (m) Es
De Kassensaldo (m)
En cash balance
Fr solde de caisse (m)
It residuo di cassa (m)
Pt saldo em dinheiro (m)

**Restpartie** (f) n De
En odd lot
Es lote suelto (m)
Fr solde (m)
It partita spaiata (f)
Pt lote avulso (m)

**restraint of trade** En
De Handelsbeschränkung (f)
Es restricción del commercio (f)
Fr restriction au commerce (f)
It restrizione del commercio (f)
Pt restrição de comércio (f)

**restrição de comércio** (f) Pt
De Handelsbeschränkung (f)
En restraint of trade
Es restricción del commercio (f)
Fr restriction au commerce (f)
It restrizione del commercio (f)

**restrição de crédito** (f) Pt
De Kreditklemme (f)
En credit squeeze
Es escasez de créditos (f)
Fr resserrement de crédit (m)
It restrizione di credito (f)

**restrição de salários** (f) Pt
De Lohnbeschränkung (f)
En wage restraint
Es restricción de salario (f)
Fr contrainte sur les salaires (f)
It restrizioni sui salari (f pl)

**restricción del commercio** (f) Es
De Handelsbeschränkung (f)
En restraint of trade
Fr restriction au commerce (f)
It restrizione del commercio (f)
Pt restrição de comércio (f)

**restricción de salario** (f) Es
De Lohnbeschränkung (f)
En wage restraint
Fr contrainte sur les salaires (f)
It restrizioni sui salari (f pl)
Pt restrição de salários (f)

**restricciones de importación** (f pl) Es
De Einfuhrbeschränkungen (f pl)
En import restrictions
Fr restrictions d'importation (f pl)
It restrizioni delle importazioni (f pl)
Pt restricções de importação (f pl)

**restricções de importação** (f pl) Pt
De Einfuhrbeschränkungen (f pl)
En import restrictions
Es restricciones de importación (f pl)
Fr restrictions d'importation (f pl)
It restrizioni delle importazioni (f pl)
Pt restricções de importação (f pl)

**restriction au commerce** (f) Fr
De Handelsbeschränkung (f)
En restraint of trade
Es restricción del commercio (f)
It restrizione del commercio (f)
Pt restrição de comércio (f)

**restrictions d'importation** (f pl) Fr
De Einfuhrbeschränkungen (f pl)
En import restrictions
Es restricciones de importación (f pl)
It restrizioni delle importazioni (f pl)
Pt restricções de importação (f pl)

**restrictive covenant** En
De einschränkende Bestimmung (f)
Es convenio restrictivo (m)
Fr accord restrictif (m)
It accordo restrittivo (m)
Pt obrigação restritiva (f)

**restrictive endorsement** En
De Rektaindossement (n)
Es endoso restringido (m)
Fr endossement restrictif (m)
It girata restrittiva (f)
Pt endosse restritivo (m)

**restrizione del commercio** (f) It
De Handelsbeschränkung (f)
En restraint of trade
Es restricción del commercio (f)
Fr restriction au commerce (f)
Pt restrição de comércio (f)

**restrizione di credito** (f) It
De Kreditklemme (f)
En credit squeeze
Es escasez de créditos (f)
Fr resserrement de crédit (m)
Pt restrição de crédito (f)

**restrizioni delle importazioni** (f pl) It
De Einfuhrbeschränkungen (f pl)
En import restrictions
Es restricciones de importación (f pl)
Fr restrictions d'importation (f pl)
Pt restricções de importação (f pl)

**restrizioni sui salari** (f pl) It
De Lohnbeschränkung (f)
En wage restraint

Es restricción de salario *(f)*
Fr contrainte sur les salaires *(f)*
Pt restrição de salários *(f)*

**résumé** *(m)* n Fr
De Abriss *(m)*
En abstract; summary
Es resumen *(m)*
It riassunto *(m)*
Pt resumo *(m)*

**resumen** *(m)* n Es
De Abriss *(m)*
En abstract; summary
Fr résumé *(m)*
It riassunto *(m)*
Pt resumo *(m)*

**resumo** *(m)* n Pt
De Abriss *(m)*
En abstract; summary
Es resumen *(m)*
Fr résumé *(m)*
It riassunto *(m)*

**retailer** n En
De Einzelhändler; Kleinhändler *(m)*
Es comerciante al por menor *(m)*
Fr commerçant au détail *(m)*
It commerciante al minuto *(m)*
Pt comerciante a retalho; retalhista *(m)*

**retail price** En
De Einzelhandelspreis *(m)*
Es precio al por menor *(m)*
Fr prix de détail *(m)*
It prezzo al minuto *(m)*
Pt preço a retalho *(m)*

**retail trade** En
De Einzelhandel *(m)*
Es comercio al por menor *(m)*
Fr commerce en détail *(m)*
It commercio al minuto *(m)*
Pt comércio a retalho *(m)*

**retalhar a carga** *(f)* Pt
De Löschen der Ladung *(n)*
En breaking bulk
Es fraccionamiento de la carga *(m)*
Fr rupture de charge *(f)*
It inizio scarico *(m)*

**retard** *(m)* n Fr
De Verzug *(m)*
En delay
Es retraso *(m)*
It ritardo *(m)*
Pt atrazo *(m)*

**rete** *(f)* n It
De Netz *(n)*
En network
Es red *(f)*
Fr réseau *(m)*
Pt rede *(f)*

**reter acções** Pt
De beteiligt sein; Aktien besitzen
En hold shares
Es tener acciones
Fr détenir des actions
It tenere azioni

**reter em armazém** Pt
De vorrätig halten
En keep in stock
Es guardar en almacén
Fr garder en stock
It tenere in magazzino

**reter em custódia** Pt
De zu treuen Händen halten
En hold in trust
Es guardar in fideicomiso
Fr tenir par fidéicommis
It tenere in fedecommesso

**retirar de aduanas** Es
De verzollen
En clear through customs
Fr dédouaner
It sdoganare
Pt despachar na alfândega

**retire a bill** En
De einen Wechsel einlösen
Es recoger una letra
Fr payer une lettre de change
It ritirare un effetto
Pt recuperar uma letra

**retirement** n En
De Rücktritt; Pensionierung *(m f)*
Es retiro *(m)*
Fr retraite *(f)*
It ritiro *(m)*
Pt aposentação *(f)*

**retiro** *(m)* n Es
De Rücktritt; Rente *(m f)*
En retirement; pension
Fr retraite; pension
It ritiro; pensione *(m f)*
Pt aposentação; pensão *(f)*

**retiro contributivo** *(m)* Es
De Kassenpension *(f)*
En contributory pension
Fr retraite de régime à cotisations *(f)*
It pensione a contributi *(f)*
Pt reforma de contribuição prévia *(f)*

**retiro de vejez** *(m)* Es
De Altersversorgung; Rente *(f)*
En old-age pension
Fr retraite pour la vieillesse *(f)*
It pensione per la vecchiaia *(f)*
Pt pensão *(f)*

**Retourware** *(f)* n De
En returned goods
Es mercancías devueltas *(f pl)*
Fr marchandises de retour *(f pl)*
It merce di ritorno *(f pl)*
Pt mercadorias devoluidas *(f)*

**retraite** *(f)* n Fr
De Rücktritt; Rente *(m f)*
En retirement; pension
Es retiro *(m)*
It ritiro; pensione *(m f)*
Pt aposentação; pensão *(f)*

**retraite de régime à cotisations** *(f)* Fr
De Kassenpension *(f)*
En contributory pension
Es retiro contributivo *(m)*
It pensione a contributi *(f)*
Pt reforma de contribuição prévia *(f)*

**retraite pour la vieillesse** *(f)* Fr
De Altersversorgung *(f)*
En old-age pension
Es retiro de vejez *(m)*
It pensione per la vecchiaia *(f)*
Pt pensão *(f)*

**retraso** *(m) n* Es
 De Verzug *(m)*
 En delay
 Fr retard; délai *(m)*
 It ritardo *(m)*
 Pt atrazo *(m)*

**rétroactif** *adj* Fr
 De rückwirkend
 En retroactive
 Es retroactivo
 It retroattivo
 Pt retroactivo

**retroactive** *adj* En
 De rückwirkend
 Es retroactivo
 Fr rétroactif
 It retroattivo
 Pt retroactivo

**retroactivo** *adj* Es, Pt
 De rückwirkend
 En retroactive
 Fr rétroactif
 It retroattivo

**retroattivo** *adj* It
 De rückwirkend
 En retroactive
 Es retroactivo
 Fr rétroactif
 Pt retroactivo

**retten** *vb* De
 En save
 Es salvar
 Fr sauver
 It salvare
 Pt salvar

**returned goods** En
 De Retourware *(f)*
 Es mercancías devueltas *(f pl)*
 Fr marchandises de retour *(f pl)*
 It merce di ritorno *(f pl)*
 Pt mercadorias devoluidas *(f)*

**return fare** En
 Am roundtrip fare
 De Rückfahrkarte *(f)*
 Es pasaje de ida y vuelta *(m)*
 Fr billet d'aller et retour *(m)*
 It biglietto di andata e ritorno *(m)*
 Pt passagem de ida e volta *(f)*

**return on capital** En
 De Kapitalertrag *(m)*
 Es beneficio sobre capital *(m)*
 Fr rémunération du capital *(f)*
 It reddito del capitale *(m)*
 Pt juro sobre o capital *(m)*

**reunião** *(f) n* Pt
 De Versammlung *(f)*
 En meeting
 Es reunión *(f)*
 Fr réunion; assemblée *(f)*
 It riunione; assemblea *(f)*

**reunião da administração** *(f)* Pt
 De Vorstandssitzung *(f)*
 En board meeting
 Es reunión del consejo de administración *(f)*
 Fr réunion du conseil d'administration *(f)*
 It riunione del consiglio d'amministrazione *(f)*

**reunião de credores** *(f)* Pt
 De Gläubigerversammlung *(f)*
 En meeting of creditors
 Es concurso de acreedores *(m)*
 Fr assemblée de créanciers *(f)*
 It convocazione dei creditori *(f)*

**reunión** *(f) n* Es
 De Versammlung *(f)*
 En meeting
 Fr réunion; assemblée *(f)*
 It riunione; assemblea *(f)*
 Pt reunião; assembleia *(f)*

**réunion** *(f) n* Fr
 De Versammlung *(f)*
 En meeting
 Es reunión *(f)*
 It riunione; assemblea *(f)*
 Pt reunião; assembleia *(f)*

**reunión de acreedores** *(f)* Es
 De Gläubigerversammlung *(f)*
 En meeting of creditors
 Fr assemblée de créanciers *(f)*
 It assemblea dei creditori *(f)*
 Pt assembleia de credores *(f)*

**reunión del consejo de administración** *(f)* Es
 De Vorstandssitzung *(f)*

En board meeting
 Fr réunion du conseil d'administration *(f)*
 It riunione del consiglio d'amministrazione *(f)*
 Pt reunião da administração *(f)*

**réunion du conseil d'administration** *(f)* Fr
 De Vorstandssitzung *(f)*
 En board meeting
 Es reunión del consejo de administración *(f)*
 It riunione del consiglio d'amministrazione *(f)*
 Pt reunião da administração *(f)*

**revalorisation** *(f) n* Fr
 De Aufwertung *(f)*
 En revaluation
 Es revalorización *(f)*
 It rivalutazione *(f)*
 Pt revalorização *(f)*

**revalorização** *(f) n* Pt
 De Aufwertung *(f)*
 En revaluation
 Es revalorización *(f)*
 Fr revalorisation *(f)*
 It rivalutazione *(f)*

**revalorización** *(f) n* Es
 De Aufwertung *(f)*
 En revaluation
 Fr revalorisation *(f)*
 It rivalutazione *(f)*
 Pt revalorização *(f)*

**revaluation** *n* En
 De Aufwertung *(f)*
 Es revalorización *(f)*
 Fr revalorisation *(f)*
 It rivalutazione *(f)*
 Pt revalorização *(f)*

**revelação** *(f) n* Pt
 De Offenlegung *(f)*
 En disclosure
 Es revelación *(f)*
 Fr révélation; divulgation *(f)*
 It rivelazione *(f)*

**revelación** *(f) n* Es
 De Offenlegung *(f)*
 En disclosure
 Fr révélation; divulgation *(f)*

It rivelazione (f)
Pt revelação; divulgação (f)

**révélation** (f) n Fr
De Offenlegung (f)
En disclosure
Es revelación (f)
It rivelazione (f)
Pt revelação; divulgação (f)

**revendication de salaire** (f) Fr
De Lohnforderung (f)
En wage claim
Es reclamación de salario (f)
It rivendicazione salariale (f)
Pt demanda de salário (f)

**revenu** (m) n Fr
De Einkommen; Einkünfte (n; f pl)
En income; revenue
Es ingresos; rédito (m pl; m)
It entrata; reddito (f m)
Pt receita; rendimento (f)

**revenu de placements** (m) Fr
De Einkommen aus Kapitalanlagen (n)
En investment income
Es renta de inversiones (f)
It reddito degli investimenti (m)
Pt rendimento de capitais investidos (m)

**revenu disponible** (m) Fr
De verfügbares Einkommen (n)
En disposable income
Es renta disponible (f)
It reddito disponibile (m)
Pt receita disponível (f)

**revenu du travail** (m) Fr
De Arbeitseinkommen (n)
En earned income
Es renta del trabajo (f)
It reddito di lavoro (m)
Pt receita de trabalho (f)

**revenue** n En
De Einkommen; Einkünfte (n; f pl)
Es ingresos; rédito (m pl; m)
Fr revenu; rentes (m; f pl)
It entrata; reddito (f m)
Pt rendimento (m)

**revenu imposable** (m) Fr
De steuerpflichtiges Einkommen (n)
En taxable income
Es renta imponible (f)
It reddito tassabile (m)
Pt receita tributável (f)

**revenu national** (m) Fr
De Nationaleinkommen (n)
En national income
Es renta nacional (f)
It reddito nazionale (m)
Pt receita pública (m)

**revenu net** (m) Fr
De Nettoeinkommen (n)
En net income
Es ingreso neto (f)
It reddito netto (m)
Pt receita líquida (f)

**revenu non imposable** (m) Fr
De steuerfreies Einkommen (n)
En nontaxable income
Es ingresos no imponibles (m pl)
It reddito non tassabile (m)
Pt receita não tributavel (f)

**revisar** (cuentas) vb Es
De prüfen
En audit
Fr vérifier et certifier
It rivedere
Pt fiscalizar

**revised estimate** En
De überarbeitete Schätzung (f)
Es cálculo revisado (m)
Fr devis rectifié (m)
It preventivo riveduto (m)
Pt estimativa revista (f)

**réviseur des comptes** (m) Fr
De Bücherrevisor (m)
En auditor
Es revisor de conti (m)
It sindaco (m)
Pt fiscal de contas (m)

**revisión de cuentas** (f) Es
De Bücherrevision (f)
En audit
Fr vérification comptable (f)
It revisione dei conti (f)
Pt fiscalização de contas (f)

**revisione dei conti** (f) It
De Bücherrevision (f)
En audit
Es revisión de cuentas (f)
Fr vérification comptable (f)
Pt fiscalização de contas (f)

**revisor de conti** (m) Es
De Bücherrevisor (m)
En auditor
Fr réviseur des comptes (m)
It sindaco (m)
Pt fiscal de contas (m)

**revoca** (f) n It
De Widerruf (m)
En revocation
Es revocación (f)
Fr révocation (f)
Pt revogação (f)

**revocación** (f) n Es
De Widerruf (m)
En revocation
Fr révocation (f)
It revoca (f)
Pt revogação (f)

**revocar** vb Es
De widerrufen
En revoke
Fr révoquer
It revocare
Pt revogar

**revocare** vb It
De widerrufen
En revoke
Es revocar
Fr révoquer
Pt revogar

**revocation** n En
De Widerruf (m)
Es revocación (f)
Fr révocation (f)
It revoca (f)
Pt revogação (f)

**révocation** (f) n Fr
De Widerruf (m)
En revocation
Es revocación (f)
It revoca (f)
Pt revogação (f)

**revogação** (f) n Pt
De Widerruf (m)
En revocation
Es revocación (f)
Fr révocation (f)
It revoca (f)

**revogar** vb Pt
De widerrufen
En revoke
Es revocar
Fr révoquer
It revocare

**revoke** vb En
De widerrufen
Es revocar
Fr révoquer
It revocare
Pt revogar

**revolving credit** En
De automatisch sich erneuen-
des Akkreditiv (n)
Es crédito reponible (m)
Fr accréditif automatiquement
renouvelable (m)
It credito rotativo (m)
Pt crédito renovável (m)

**revolving fund** En
De Umlaufkapital (n)
Es fondo circulante (m)
Fr fonds renouvelable (m)
It fondo rotativo (m)
Pt fundos renováveis (m pl)

**révoquer** vb Fr
De widerrufen
En revoke
Es revocar
It revocare
Pt revogar

**revue du marché** (f) Fr
De Marktbericht (m)
En market report
Es informe del mercado (m)
It relazione sul mercato (f)
Pt informação do mercado (f)

**revueltas y conmociones civi-
les** Es
De Aufruhr und innere Unru-
hen
En riot and civil commotion
Fr émeutes et désordres

It rivolte e moti civili
Pt motins e perturbações civis

**rez-de-chaussée** (m) Fr
De Erdgeschoss (n)
En ground floor
Es planta baja (f)
It pianterreno (m)
Pt rés-do-chão (m)

**Rezession** (f) n De
En recession
Es recesión (f)
Fr récession (f)
It recessione (f)
Pt recessão (f)

**rialzista** (m) n It
De Haussespekulant (m)
En bull
Es alcista (m)
Fr haussier (m)
Pt altista (f)

**rialzista** adj It
De steigend
En bullish
Es alcista
Fr haussier
Pt altista

**rialzo** (m) n It
De Hausse (f)
En boom
Es bonanza (f)
Fr haute conjoncture (f)
Pt bonança (f)

**rialzo** (di prezzo) (m) n It
De Preiserhöhung (f)
En advance in price
Es encarecimiento (m)
Fr renchérissement (m)
Pt encarecimento (m)

**riaprire la discussione** It
De Verhandlungen wiederauf-
nehmen
En re-open discussions
Es reabrir la discusión
Fr rouvrir la discussion
Pt reabrir discussões

**riassicurazione** (f) n It
De Rückversicherung (f)
En reinsurance
Es reaseguro (m)

Fr réassurance (f)
Pt re-seguro (m)

**riassunto** (m) n It
De Abriss (m)
En abstract; summary
Es resumen (m)
Fr résumé (m)
Pt resumo (m)

**ribassista** (m) n It
De Baissespekulant; Baissier
(m)
En bear
Es bajista (m)
Fr baissier (m)
Pt baixista (m)

**ribassista** adj It
De flau
En bearish
Es bajista
Fr orienté à la baisse
Pt baixista

**ribasso** (m) n It
De Nachlass (m)
En rebate
Es rebaja (f)
Fr rabais (m)
Pt desconto (m)

**ricavo netto** (m) It
De Reinerlös (m)
En net proceeds
Es rédito neto (m)
Fr produit net (m)
Pt proventos líquidos (m pl)

**ricchezza** (f) n It
De Wohlstand (m)
En wealth
Es riqueza (f)
Fr richesse (f)
Pt riqueza (f)

**ricerca** (f) n It
De Forschung (f)
En research
Es investigación (f)
Fr recherche (f)
Pt investigação (f)

**ricercato** It
De gefragt
En in demand
Es solicitado

Fr demandé
Pt procurado

**ricevimento per posta aerea** *(m)* It
De Luftpostempfangsbescheinigung *(f)*
En airmail receipt
Es recibo aeropostal *(m)*
Fr récépissé de poste aérienne *(m)*
Pt recibo de via aérea *(m)*

**ricevuta** *(f)* n It
De Quittung *(f)*
En receipt
Es recibo *(m)*
Fr quittance; acquit *(f m)*
Pt recibo *(m)*

**ricevuta d'imbarco** *(f)* It
De Übernahmebescheinigung *(f)*
En mate's receipt
Es recibo de embarco *(m)*
Fr billet de bord *(m)*
Pt recibo de embarque *(m)*

**ricevuta ferroviaria** *(f)* It
De Bahnfrachtbrief *(m)*
En railway receipt
Es recibo ferroviario *(m)*
Fr bulletin de chargement *(m)*
Pt recibo ferroviário *(m)*

**ricevuto per caricazione** It
De zur Absendung empfangen
En received for shipment
Es recibido para envío
Fr reçu pour envoi
Pt recebido para carregamento

**richesse** *(f)* n Fr
De Wohlstand *(m)*
En wealth
Es riqueza *(f)*
It ricchezza *(f)*
Pt riqueza *(f)*

**richiesta** *(f)* n It
De Anforderung *(f)*
En requisition
Es pedido; solicitud *(m f)*
Fr demande *(f)*
Pt pedido *(m)*

**richiesta (di fondi)** *(f)* It
De Kündigung (von Geldern) *(f)*
En call (for funds)
Es llamada (de fondos) *(f)*
Fr appel (de fonds) *(m)*
Pt chamada (de fundos) *(f)*

**Richter** *(m)* n De
En judge
Es juez *(m)*
Fr juge *(m)*
It giudice *(m)*
Pt juiz *(m)*

**ricostruzione** *(f)* n It
De Wiederaufbau *(m)*
En reconstruction
Es reconstrucción *(f)*
Fr reconstruction *(f)*
Pt reconstrução *(f)*

**ricupero d'informazioni** *(m)* It
De Informationswiedergewinnung *(f)*
En information retrieval
Es rebusca de información *(f)*
Fr récupération de données *(f)*
Pt recuperação de informação *(f)*

**riduzione dei prezzi** *(f)* It
De Preisherabsetzung *(f)*
En price-cutting
Es reducción de precios *(f)*
Fr rabais des prix *(m)*
Pt redução de preços *(f)*

**riduzione del capitale** *(f)* It
De Kapitalherabsetzung *(f)*
En reduction of capital
Es reducción de capital *(f)*
Fr réduction du capital *(f)*
Pt redução de capital *(f)*

**riesgo** *(m)* n Es
De Risiko *(n)*
En risk
Fr risque *(m)*
It rischio *(m)*
Pt risco *(m)*

**riesgo profesional** *(m)* Es
De Berufsrisiko *(n)*
En occupational hazard
Fr risque professionnel *(m)*
It rischio del lavoro *(m)*

Pt acidente próprio da profissão *(m)*

**riesportare** *vb* It
De wiederausführen
En re-export
Es reexportar
Fr reexporter
Pt reexportar

**riesporto** *(m)* n It
De Wiederausfuhr *(f)*
En re-exportation
Es reexportación *(f)*
Fr réexportation *(f)*
Pt reexportação *(f)*

**rifiuti tossici** *(m pl)* It
De giftiger Abfall *(m)*
En toxic waste
Es efluentes tóxicos *(m pl)*
Fr déchets toxiques *(m pl)*
Pt despejos tóxicos *(m pl)*

**rifiuto** *(m)* n It
De Ablehnung *(f)*
En rejection
Es rechazo *(m)*
Fr refus *(m)*
Pt rejeição *(f)*

**riforma monetaria** *(f)* It
De Währungsreform *(f)*
En monetary reform
Es reforma monetaria *(f)*
Fr réforme monétaire *(f)*
Pt reforma monetária *(f)*

**rifugio fiscale** *(m)* It
De Steuerparadies *(n)*
En tax haven
Es refugio fiscal *(m)*
Fr refuge fiscal *(m)*
Pt refúgio fiscal *(m)*

**rights** *pl* n En
De Rechte *(n pl)*
Es derechos *(m pl)*
Fr droits *(m pl)*
It diritti *(m pl)*
Pt direitos *(m pl)*

**rights issue** En
De Sonderemission gegen Bezugsrechte *(f)*
Es emisión de derechos *(f)*
Fr émission sous droit de souscription *(f)*

It emissione di diritti (f)
Pt emissão de direitos (f)

**rimborso** (m) n It
De Rückerstattung (f)
En refund
Es reembolso (m)
Fr remboursement (m)
Pt reembolso (m)

**rimborso d'esportazione** (m) It
De Zollrückvergütung (f)
En (customs) drawback
Es reembolso de derechos de
aduana (m)
Fr remboursement des droits
d'importation (m)
Pt reimbolso de direitos alfan-
degários (m)

**rimessa telegrafica** (f) It
De Kabelauszahlung (f)
En telegraphic transfer
Es giro telegráfico (m)
Fr virement télégraphique (m)
Pt transferência telegráfica (f)

**rimorchiatore** (m) n It
De Schleppdampfer (m)
En tug-boat
Es remolcador (m)
Fr remorqueur (m)
Pt rebocador (m)

**rimunerazione** (f) n It
De Vergütung (f)
En remuneration
Es remuneración (f)
Fr rémunération (f)
Pt remuneração (f)

**rinunzia** (f) n It
De Verzicht (m)
En renunciation
Es renuncia (f)
Fr renonciation (f)
Pt renúncia (f)

**rinunziare** vb It
De verzichten auf
En renounce
Es renunciar
Fr renoncer
Pt renunciar

**riot and civil commotion** En
De Aufruhr und innere Unruhen

Es revueltas y conmociones
civiles
Fr émeutes et désordres
It rivolte e moti civili
Pt motins e perturbações civis

**riparare** vb It
De reparieren
En repair
Es reparar; componer
Fr réparer; réfectionner
Pt consertar; reparar

**riparazione** (f) n It
De Reparatur (f)
En repair
Es reparación (f)
Fr réparation (f)
Pt reparação (f)

**ripartire** vb It
De verteilen; zuteilen
En distribute; apportion
Es repartir
Fr répartir
Pt repartir

**ripartizione** (f) n It
De Verteilung (f)
En distribution; allotment
Es reparto; adjudicación (f)
Fr distribution; attribution (f)
Pt distribuição; aporcionamen-
to (f m)

**ripartizione della tassazione**
(f) It
De Bemessungsgrundlage (f)
En tax base
Es base contributiva (f)
Fr assiette de l'impôt (f)
Pt base de imposto (f)

**riqueza** (f) n Es, Pt
De Wohlstand (m)
En wealth
Fr richesse (f)
It ricchezza (f)

**riscaldamento centrale** (m) It
De Zentralheizung (f)
En central heating
Es calefacción central (f)
Fr chauffage central (m)
Pt aquecimento central (m)

**rischio** (m) n It
De Wagnis; Risiko (n)
En hazard; risk
Es azar; riesgo (m)
Fr hasard; risque (m)
Pt risco; azar (m)

**rischio del lavoro** (m) It
De Berufsrisiko (n)
En occupational hazard
Es riesgo profesional (m)
Fr risque professionnel (m)
Pt acidente próprio da profis-
são (m)

**risco** (m) n Pt
De Wagnis; Risiko (n)
En hazard; risk
Es azar; riesgo (m)
Fr hasard; risque (m)
It rischio (m)

**riserva di capitale** (f) It
De Kapitalreserve (f)
En capital reserves
Es reserva de capital (f)
Fr réserve de capitaux (f)
Pt reservas de capital (f pl)

**riserva di previdenza** (f) It
De Rückstellung für Eventual-
verbindlichkeiten (f)
En contingency reserve
Es reserva para imprevistos (f)
Fr réserve de prévoyance (f)
Pt reserva para as contingên-
cias (f)

**riserva in contanti** (f) It
De Kassenreserve (f)
En cash reserve
Es reserva en efectivo (f)
Fr réserve en espèces (f)
Pt reserva em dinheiro (f)

**riserva occulta** (f) It
De stille Reserve (f)
En hidden reserve
Es reserva latente (f)
Fr réserve cachée (f)
Pt reserva oculta (f)

**riserva per crediti inesigibili**
(f) It
De Dubiosenreserve (f)
En bad debt reserve
Es reserva para deudas inco-
brables (f)

Fr provision pour créances douteuses *(f)*
Pt reserva para dividas incobráveis *(f)*

**riservare** *vb* It
De vorbehalten
En reserve
Es reservar
Fr réserver
Pt reservar

**Risiko** *(n) n* De
En risk
Es riesgo *(m)*
Fr risque *(m)*
It rischio *(m)*
Pt risco *(m)*

**risk** *n* En
De Risiko *(n)*
Es riesgo *(m)*
Fr risque *(m)*
It rischio *(m)*
Pt risco *(m)*

**risk capital** En
De Spekulationskapital *(n)*
Es capital de especulación *(m)*
Fr capitaux spéculatifs *(m pl)*
It capitale di speculazione *(m)*
Pt capital de especulação *(m)*

**risoluzione di un contratto** *(f)* It
De Vertragsbeendigung *(f)*
En determination of a contract
Es rescisión de un contrato *(f)*
Fr résolution d'un contrat *(f)*
Pt rescisão de contrato *(f)*

**risparmiare** *vb* It
De aufsparen
En save
Es ahorrar
Fr épargner
Pt poupar

**risposta** *(f) n* It
De Antwort *(f)*
En answer
Es respuesta *(f)*
Fr réponse *(f)*
Pt resposta *(f)*

**risposta pagata** It
De Rückantwort bezahlt
En reply paid

Am post paid
Es respuesta pagada
Fr réponse payée
Pt resposta paga

**risque** *(m) n* Fr
De Risiko *(n)*
En risk
Es riesgo *(m)*
It rischio *(m)*
Pt risco *(m)*

**risque professionnel** *(m)* Fr
De Berufsrisiko *(n)*
En occupational hazard
Es riesgo profesional *(m)*
It rischio del lavoro *(m)*
Pt acidente próprio da profissão *(m)*

**ritardo** *(m) n* It
De Verzug *(m)*
En delay
Es retraso *(m)*
Fr retard; délai *(m)*
Pt atrazo *(m)*

**ritirare un effetto** It
De einen Wechsel einlösen
En retire a bill
Es recoger una letra
Fr payer une lettre de change
Pt recuperar uma letra

**ritiro** *(m) n* It
De Rücktritt; Pensionierung *(m f)*
En retirement
Es retiro *(m)*
Fr retraite *(f)*
Pt aposentação *(f)*

**riunione** *(f) n* It
De Versammlung *(f)*
En meeting
Es reunión *(f)*
Fr réunion; assemblée *(f)*
Pt reunião; assembleia *(f)*

**riunione del consiglio d'amministrazione** *(f)* It
De Vorstandssitzung *(f)*
En board meeting
Es reunión del consejo de administración *(f)*
Fr réunion du conseil d'administration *(f)*

Pt reunião da administração *(f)*

**rival** *n* En; Es, Fr, Pt *(m)*
De Rivale *(m)*
It rivale *(m)*

**rivale** *(m) n* It
De Rivale *(m)*
En rival
Es rival *(m)*
Fr rival *(m)*
Pt rival *(m)*

**Rivale** *(m) n* De
En rival
Es rival *(m)*
Fr rival *(m)*
It rivale *(m)*
Pt rival *(m)*

**rivalutazione** *(f) n* It
De Aufwertung *(f)*
En revaluation
Es revalorización *(f)*
Fr revalorisation *(f)*
Pt revalorização *(f)*

**rivedere** (i conti) *vb* It
De prüfen
En audit
Es revisar
Fr vérifier et certifier
Pt fiscalizar as contas

**rivelazione** *(f) n* It
De Offenlegung *(f)*
En disclosure
Es revelación *(f)*
Fr révélation; divulgation *(f)*
Pt revelação; divulgação *(f)*

**rivendicazione salariale** *(f)* It
De Lohnforderung *(f)*
En wage claim
Es reclamación de salario *(f)*
Fr revendication de salaire *(f)*
Pt demanda de salário *(f)*

**rivolte e moti civili** It
De Aufruhr und innere Unruhen
En riot and civil commotion
Es revueltas y conmociones civiles
Fr émeutes et désordres
Pt motins e perturbações civis

**robo** *(m)* *n* Es
De Diebstahl *(m)*
En theft
Fr vol *(m)*
It furto *(m)*
Pt furto *(m)*

**Roheisen** *(n)* *n* De
En pig-iron
Es hierro bruto *(m)*
Fr fer en gueuse *(m)*
It pane di ghisa *(m)*
Pt ferro em bruto *(m)*

**rohe Schätzung** *(f)* De
En rough estimate
Es presupuesto aproximado *(m)*
Fr estimation approximative *(f)*
It valutazione approssimativa *(f)*
Pt avaliação aproximada *(f)*

**Rohstoff** *(m)* *n* De
En raw material
Es materia prima *(f)*
Fr matière première *(f)*
It materia prima *(f)*
Pt matéria prima *(f)*

**Rohstoffmarkt** *(m)* *n* De
En commodity market
Es mercado de materias primas *(m)*
Fr marché de matières premières *(m)*
It mercato di materie prime *(m)*
Pt mercado de matérias primas *(m)*

**rotação de culturas** *(f)* Pt
De Fruchtwechsel *(m)*
En rotation of crops
Es rotación de cultivos *(f)*
Fr rotation des cultures *(f)*
It rotazione delle coltivazioni *(f)*
Pt rotação de culturas *(f)*

**rotación de cultivos** *(f)* Es
De Fruchtwechsel *(m)*
En rotation of crops
Fr rotation des cultures *(f)*
It rotazione delle coltivazioni *(f)*
Pt rotação de culturas *(f)*

**rotation des cultures** *(f)* Fr
De Fruchtwechsel *(m)*
En rotation of crops
Es rotación de cultivos *(f)*
It rotazione delle coltivazioni *(f)*
Pt rotação de culturas *(f)*

**rotation of crops** En
De Fruchtwechsel *(m)*
Es rotación de cultivos *(f)*
Fr rotation des cultures *(f)*
It rotazione delle coltivazioni *(f)*
Pt rotação de culturas *(f)*

**rottura di contratto** *(f)* It
De Vertragsverletzung *(f)*
En breach of contract
Es incumplimiento del contrato *(m)*
Fr rupture de contrat *(f)*
Pt rotura de contrato *(f)*

**rótulo** *(m)* *n* Pt
De Etikett *(n)*
En label
Es etiqueta *(f)*
Fr étiquette *(f)*
It etichetta *(f)*

**rotura de contrato** *(f)* Pt
De Vertragsverletzung *(f)*
En breach of contract
Es incumplimiento del contrato *(m)*
Fr rupture de contrat *(f)*
It rottura di contratto *(f)*

**rough estimate** En
De rohe Schätzung *(f)*
Es presupuesto aproximado *(m)*
Fr estimation approximative *(f)*
It valutazione approssimativa *(f)*
Pt avaliação aproximada *(f)*

**roundtrip fare** Am
En return fare
De Rückfahrkarte *(f)*
Es pasaje de ida y vuelta *(m)*
Fr billet d'aller et retour *(m)*
It biglietto di andata e ritorno *(m)*
Pt passagem de ida e volta *(f)*

**rouvrir la discussion** Fr
De Verhandlungen wiederaufnehmen
En re-open discussions
Es reabrir la discusión
It riaprire la discussione
Pt reabrir discussões

**royalty** *n* En
De Tantieme; Gewinnanteil *(f m)*
Es derechos *(m pl)*
Fr redevance; droits *(f; m pl)*
It diritti *(m pl)*
Pt direitos *(m pl)*

**rubber stamp** En
De Gummistempel *(m)*
Es estampilla de goma *(f)*
Fr tampon *(m)*
It stampino di gomma *(m)*
Pt carimbo *(m)*

**rubricar** *vb* Es, Pt
De paraphieren
En initial
Fr parapher; viser
It siglare

**Rückantwort bezahlt** De
En reply paid
Am post paid
Es respuesta pagada
Fr réponse payée
It risposta pagata
Pt resposta paga

**Rückerstattung** *(f)* *n* De
En refund
Es reembolso *(m)*
Fr remboursement *(m)*
It rimborso *(m)*
Pt reembolso *(m)*

**Rückfahrkarte** *(f)* *n* De
En return fare
Am roundtrip fare
Es pasaje de ida y vuelta *(m)*
Fr billet d'aller et retour *(m)*
It biglietto di andata e ritorno *(m)*
Pt passagem de ida e volta *(f)*

**rückgängig machen** (ein Geschäft) De
En call off (a deal)
Es anular (un negocio)
Fr annuler (un marché)

It     annullare (un affare)
Pt    anular (uma transacção)

**Rückkaufswert** *(m)* n De
En    surrender value
Es    valor de rescate *(m)*
Fr    valeur de rachat *(f)*
It     valore di riscatto *(m)*
Pt    valor de resgate *(m)*

**Rücksendung wenn unverkauft** De
En    sale or return
Es    venta o devolución
Fr    vente avec faculté de retour
It     da vendere o rimandare
Pt    venda ou devolução

**Rückstand** *(m)* n De
En    arrears
Es    atrasos *(m pl)*
Fr    arrérages *(m pl)*
It     arretrati *(m pl)*
Pt    atrasos *(m pl)*

**rückständig** *adj* De
En    overdue
Es    vencido
Fr    arriéré
It     scaduto
Pt    vencido

**Rückstellung für Eventualverbindlichkeiten** *(f)* De
En    contingency reserve
Es    reserva para imprevistos *(f)*
Fr    réserve de prévoyance *(f)*
It     riserva di previdenza *(f)*
Pt    reserva para as contingências *(f)*

**Rückstellungskonto** *(n)* n De
En    appropriation account
Es    cuenta de apropiación *(f)*
Fr    compte d'affectation *(m)*
It     conto di stanziamento *(m)*
Pt    conta de apropriação *(f)*

**Rücktritt** *(m)* n De
En    retirement
Es    retiro *(m)*
Fr    retraite *(f)*
It     ritiro *(m)*
Pt    aposentação *(f)*

**(den) Rücktritt einreichen** De
En    hand in one's resignation
Es    presentar la dimisión

Fr     remettre sa démission
It     rassegnare le dimissioni
Pt    apresentar demissão

**Rücktrittsklausel** *(f)* n De
En    determination clause
Es    cláusula resolutiva *(f)*
Fr    clause résolutoire *(f)*
It     clausola risolutiva *(f)*
Pt    cláusula de rescisão *(f)*

**Rückversicherung** *(f)* n De
En    reinsurance
Es    reaseguro *(m)*
Fr    réassurance *(f)*
It     riassicurazione *(f)*
Pt    re-seguro *(m)*

**rückwirkend** *adj* De
En    retroactive
Es    retroactivo
Fr    rétroactif
It     retroattivo
Pt    retro-activo

**Ruhegeld** *(n)* n De
En    pension
Es    pensión *(f)*
Fr    pension *(f)*
It     pensione *(f)*
Pt    pensão *(f)*

**rupture de charge** *(f)* Fr
De    Löschen der Ladung *(n)*
En    breaking bulk
Es    fraccionamiento de la carga *(m)*
It     inizio scarico *(m)*
Pt    retalhar a carga *(f)*

**rupture de contrat** *(f)* Fr
De    Vertragsverletzung *(f)*
En    breach of contract
Es    incumplimiento del contrato *(m)*
It     rottura di contratto *(f)*
Pt    rotura de contrato *(f)*

**rupture de garantie** *(f)* Fr
De    Verletzung der Gewährleistungspflicht *(f)*
En    breach of warranty
Es    incumplimiento de la garantía *(m)*
It     violazione di garanzia *(f)*
Pt    violação de garantia *(f)*

**rush hour** En
De    Verkehrsspitze *(f)*
Es    hora punta *(f)*
Fr    heure d'affluence *(f)*
It     ora di punta *(f)*
Pt    hora de ponta *(f)*


# S

**sacado** *(m)* n Pt
De    Bezogene(r) *(m)*
En    drawee
Es    librado *(m)*
Fr    tiré *(m)*
It     trattario *(m)*

**sacador** *(m)* n Pt
De    Aussteller *(m)*
En    drawer
Es    librador *(m)*
Fr    tireur *(m)*
It     traente *(m)*

**sacar reservas** Es
De    die Reserven angreifen
En    draw on reserves
Fr    prélever sur les réserves
It     prelevare dalle riserve
Pt    recorrer a reservas

**Sachkundige(r)** *(m)* n De
En    expert
Es    experto *(m)*
Fr    expert *(m)*
It     competente *(m)*
Pt    experiente *(m)*

**Sachverständigengutachten** *(n)* n De
En    expert's report
Es    informe del especialista *(m)*
Fr    expertise *(f)*
It     perizia *(f)*
Pt    relatório do perito *(m)*

**Sachverständige(r)** *(m)* n De
En    expert; specialist
Es    especialista *(m)*
Fr    spécialiste; expert *(m)*
It     perito; specialista *(m)*
Pt    perito; especialista *(m)*

**safe** n En
De    Geldschrank *(m)*
Es    caja fuerte *(f)*

Fr coffre-fort *(m)*
It cassaforte *(f)*
Pt cofre *(m)*

**safe custody** En
De sichere Verwahrung *(f)*
Es custodia *(f)*
Fr bonne garde *(f)*
It custodia *(f)*
Pt custódia segura *(f)*

**safe deposit** En
De Verwahrung in Stahlfach *(f)*
Es depósito en caja fuerte *(m)*
Fr dépôt en coffre-fort *(m)*
It servizio di cassette di sicurezza *(m)*
Pt depósito em cofre forte *(m)*

**safety factor** En
De Sicherheitskoeffizient *(m)*
Es factor de seguridad *(m)*
Fr facteur de sécurité *(m)*
It coefficiente di sicurezza *(m)*
Pt factor de segurança *(m)*

**saggio** *(m) n* It
De Probe *(f)*
En assay; test
Es ensayo; prueba *(m f)*
Fr essai; épreuve *(m f)*
Pt ensaio; prova *(m f)*

**sailing date** En
De Abgangstag *(m)*
Es día de salida *(m)*
Fr date de départ *(f)*
It data di partenza *(f)*
Pt dia de saída *(f)*

**saisie des données** *(f)* Fr
De Datenerfassung *(f)*
En data capture
Es recogida de datos *(f)*
It raccolta dati *(f)*
Pt recolha de dados *(f)*

**saison** *(f) n* Fr
De Jahreszeit *(f)*
En season
Es estación *(f)*
It stagione *(f)*
Pt estação *(f)*

**salaire** *(m) n* Fr
De Lohn *(m)*
En wages; earnings
Es salario *(m)*

It guadagni *(m pl)*
Pt salario *(m)*

**salaire au rendement** *(m)* Fr
De Leistungslohn *(m)*
En payment by results
Es pago por resultados *(m)*
It pagamento secondo i risultati *(m)*
Pt pagamento relativo as resultados *(m)*

**salaire de base** *(f)* Fr
De Grundlohn *(m)*
En basic pay
Am base pay
Es salario-base *(m)*
It salario fondamentale *(m)*
Pt salário-base *(m)*

**salaire nette** *(f)* Fr
De Nettolohn *(m)*
En take-home pay
Es paga neta *(f)*
It paga netta *(f)*
Pt salário líquido *(m)*

**salariato** *(m) n* It
De Lohnempfänger *(m)*
En wage earner
Es asalariado *(m)*
Fr salarié *(m)*
Pt assalariado *(m)*

**salarié** *(m) n* Fr
De Lohnempfänger *(m)*
En wage earner
Es asalariado *(m)*
It salariato *(m)*
Pt assalariado *(m)*

**salaried employee** En
De Angestellte(r) *(m)*
Es empleado a sueldo *(m)*
Fr appointé *(m)*
It stipendiato *(m)*
Pt assalariado *(m)*

**salario** *(m) n* Es, Pt
De Lohn *(m)*
En wages; earnings
Fr salaire *(m)*
It guadagni *(m pl)*

**salario-base** *(m) n* Es
De Grundlohn *(m)*

En basic pay
Am base pay
Fr salaire de base *(f)*
It salario fondamentale *(m)*
Pt salário-base *(m)*

**salário-base** *(m) n* Pt
De Grundlohn *(m)*
En basic pay
Am base pay
Es salario-base *(m)*
Fr salaire de base *(f)*
It salario fondamentale *(m)*

**salario fondamentale** *(m)* It
De Grundlohn *(m)*
En basic pay
Am base pay
Es salario-base *(m)*
Fr salaire de base *(f)*
Pt salário-base *(m)*

**salário líquido** *(m)* Pt
De Nettolohn *(m)*
En take-home pay
Es paga neta *(f)*
Fr salaire nette *(f)*
It paga netta *(f)*

**salary** *n* En
De Gehalt *(n)*
Es sueldo *(m)*
Fr traitement *(m)*
It stipendio *(m)*
Pt ordenado *(m)*

**saldar una cuenta** Es
De eine Rechnung ausgleichen
En balance an account
Fr balancer un compte
It pareggiare un conto
Pt equilibrar uma conta

**saldo** *(m) n* Es, It, Pt
De Saldo *(m)*
En balance
Fr solde *(m)*

**Saldo** *(m) n* De
En balance
Es saldo *(m)*
Fr solde *(m)*
It saldo *(m)*
Pt saldo *(m)*

**saldo acreedor** *(m)* Es
De Kreditsaldo *(m)*
En credit balance
Fr solde créditeur *(m)*
It saldo creditore *(m)*
Pt saldo credor *(m)*

**saldo activo** *(m)* Es
De Aktivsaldo *(m)*
En active balance
Fr balance excédentaire *(f)*
It saldo attivo *(m)*
Pt saldo positivo *(m)*

**saldo adverso** *(m)* Es
De Passivsaldo *(m)*
En adverse balance
Am negative balance
Fr balance déficitaire *(f)*
It saldo passivo *(m)*
Pt saldo negativo *(m)*

**saldo attivo** *(m)* It
De Aktivsaldo *(m)*
En active balance
Es saldo activo *(m)*
Fr balance excédentaire *(f)*
Pt saldo positivo *(m)*

**saldo creditore** *(m)* It
De Kreditsaldo *(m)*
En credit balance
Es saldo acreedor *(m)*
Fr solde créditeur *(m)*
Pt saldo credor *(m)*

**saldo credor** *(m)* Pt
De Kreditsaldo *(m)*
En credit balance
Es saldo acreedor *(m)*
Fr solde créditeur *(m)*
It saldo creditore *(m)*

**saldo da riportare** *(m)* It
De Saldovortrag *(m)*
En balance carried forward
Es saldo de entrada *(m)*
Fr report à nouveau *(m)*
Pt saldo transportado *(m)*

**saldo de banco** *(m)* Es
De Bankguthaben *(n)*
En bank balance
Fr solde en banque *(m)*
It saldo in banca *(m)*
Pt saldo no banco *(m)*

**saldo debitore** *(m)* It
De Sollsaldo *(m)*
En debit balance
Es saldo en débito *(m)*
Fr solde débiteur *(m)*
Pt saldo devedor *(m)*

**saldo de entrada** *(m)* Es
De Saldovortrag *(m)*
En balance carried forward
Fr report à nouveau *(m)*
It saldo da riportare *(m)*
Pt saldo transportado *(m)*

**saldo del dividendo** *(m)* Es, It
De Schlussdividende *(f)*
En final dividend
Fr solde de dividende *(m)*
Pt dividendo final *(m)*

**saldo devedor** *(m)* Pt
De Sollsaldo *(m)*
En debit balance
Es saldo en débito *(m)*
Fr solde débiteur *(m)*
It saldo debitore *(m)*

**saldo dovuto** *(m)* It
De Ausgleichssaldo *(m)*
En balance due
Es balance vencido *(m)*
Fr solde dû *(m)*
Pt saldo em dívida *(m)*

**saldo em dinheiro** *(m)* Pt
De Kassensaldo *(m)*
En cash balance
Es resto en efectivo *(m)*
Fr solde de caisse *(m)*
It residuo di cassa *(m)*

**saldo em dívida** *(m)* Pt
De Ausgleichssaldo *(m)*
En balance due
Es balance vencido *(m)*
Fr solde dû *(m)*
It saldo dovuto *(m)*

**saldo em poder** *(m)* Pt
De verfügbarer Saldo *(m)*
En balance in hand
Es sobrante *(m)*
Fr solde en caisse *(m)*
It saldo in cassa *(m)*

**saldo en débito** *(m)* Es
De Sollsaldo *(m)*
En debit balance

**saldo debitore** *(m)* It
De Sollsaldo *(m)*
En debit balance
Pt saldo devedor *(m)*

**saldo final** *(m)* Es
De Schlussbilanz *(f)*
En final balance
Fr solde net *(m)*
It saldo finale *(m)*
Pt balanço final *(m)*

**saldo finale** *(m)* It
De Schlussbilanz *(f)*
En final balance
Es saldo final *(m)*
Fr solde net *(m)*
Pt balanço final *(m)*

**saldo in banca** *(m)* It
De Bankguthaben *(n)*
En bank balance
Es saldo de banco *(m)*
Fr solde en banque *(m)*
Pt saldo no banco *(m)*

**saldo in cassa** *(m)* It
De verfügbarer Saldo *(m)*
En balance in hand
Es sobrante *(m)*
Fr solde en caisse *(m)*
Pt saldo em poder *(m)*

**saldo negativo** *(m)* Pt
De Passivsaldo *(m)*
En adverse balance
Am negative balance
Es saldo adverso *(m)*
Fr balance déficitaire *(f)*
It saldo passivo *(m)*

**saldo no banco** *(m)* Pt
De Bankguthaben *(n)*
En bank balance
Es saldo de banco *(m)*
Fr solde en banque *(m)*
It saldo in banca *(m)*

**saldo nullo** *(m)* It
De Nullsaldo *(m)*
En nil balance
Am zero balance
Es saldo nulo *(m)*
Fr solde nul *(m)*
Pt saldo nulo *(m)*

**saldo nulo** *(m)* Es, Pt
De Nullsaldo *(m)*
En nil balance

**saldo**
Am zero balance
Fr solde nul (m)
It saldo nullo (m)

**saldo passivo** (m) It
De Passivsaldo (m)
En adverse balance
Am negative balance
Es saldo adverso (m)
Fr balance déficitaire (f)
Pt saldo negativo (m)

**saldo positivo** (m) Pt
De Kreditsaldo (m)
En credit balance
Es saldo activo (m)
Fr solde créditeur (m)
It saldo a credito (m)

**saldo transportado** (m) Pt
De Saldovortrag (m)
En balance carried forward
Es saldo de entrada (m)
Fr report à nouveau (m)
It saldo da riportare (m)

**Saldovortrag** (m) n De
En balance carried forward
Es saldo de entrada (m)
Fr report à nouveau (m)
It saldo da riportare (m)
Pt saldo transportado (m)

**sale** n En
De Verkauf (m)
Es venta (f)
Fr vente (f)
It vendita (f)
Pt venda (f)

**sale by auction** En
De Versteigerung (f)
Es venta a subasta (f)
Fr vente aux enchères (f)
It vendita all'asta (f)
Pt venda em leilão (f)

**sale or return** En
De Rücksendung wenn unver-
kauft
Es venta o devolución
Fr vente avec faculté de retour
It da vendere o rimandare
Pt venda ou devolução

**sales agent** Am
En mercantile agent
De Handelsvertreter (m)
Es agente mercantil (m)
Fr agent de commerce (m)
It agente di commercio (m)
Pt agente comercial (m)

**sales analysis** En
De Verkaufsanalyse (f)
Es análisis de ventas (m)
Fr analyse des ventes (f)
It analisi delle vendite (f)
Pt análise de vendas (f)

**sales department** En
De Verkaufsabteilung (f)
Es departamento de ventas
(m)
Fr service ventes (m)
It ufficio vendite (m)
Pt departamento de vendas
(m)

**sales figure** En
De Umsatz (m)
Es cifra de ventas (f)
Fr chiffre d'affaires (f)
It cifra di vendite (f)
Pt número de vendas (m)

**sales force** En
De Verkaufspersonal (n)
Es personal de ventas (m)
Fr personnel de vente (m)
It forze di vendita (f pl)
Pt pessoal de vendas (m)

**sales forecast** En
De Verkaufsvoraussage (f)
Es pronóstico de ventas (m)
Fr prévision de ventes (f)
It previsione delle vendite (f)
Pt previsão de vendas (f)

**sales ledger** En
De Verkaufskontenbuch (n)
Es libro mayor de ventas (m)
Fr grand livre des ventes (m)
It partitario delle vendite (m)
Pt livro-mestre de vendas (m)

**sales (publicity) letter** En
De Werbebrief (m)
Es carta de publicidad de
ventas (f)
Fr lettre de publicité ventes (f)
It lettera di pubblicità vendite
(f)
Pt carta de publicidade de
vendas (f)

**salesman** n En
De Verkäufer; Handelsvertreter
(m)
Es vendedor; viajante de co-
mercio (m)
Fr vendeur; commis-voyageur
(m)
It venditore; commesso (m)
Pt vendedor; caixeiro (m)

**sales manager** En
De Verkaufsleiter (m)
Es jefe de ventas (m)
Fr directeur commercial (m)
It direttore commerciale (m)
Pt chefe de vendas (m)

**salesmanship** n En
De Verkaufsgewandtheit (f)
Es arte de vender (m)
Fr art de vendre (m)
It arte della vendita (f)
Pt ciência de vender (f)

**sales promotion** En
De Werbung; Verkaufsbeförde-
rung (f)
Es promoción de ventas (f)
Fr promotion des ventes (f)
It sviluppo delle vendite (m)
Pt promoção de vendas (f)

**sales resistance** En
De Kaufabneigung (f)
Es dificultades de ventas (f pl)
Fr résistance à la vente (f)
It difficoltà di vendita (f)
Pt resistência contra vendas
(f)

**sales tax** En
De Warenumsatzsteuer (f)
Es impuesto sobre la venta
(m)
Fr taxe de vente (f)
It imposta sulle vendite (f)
Pt imposto sobre vendas (m)

**salir fiados por** Es
De Haftkaution geben
En go bail for
Fr se porter garant de
It rendersi garante di
Pt prestar caução a favor de

**salvage** n En
De Bergung (f)
Es salvamento (m)

Fr sauvetage *(m)*
It salvataggio *(m)*
Pt salvamento *(m)*

**salvage charges** En
De Bergegeld *(n)*
Es cargos de salvamento *(m pl)*
Fr indemnité de sauvetage *(f)*
It spese di salvataggio *(f pl)*
Pt encargos de salvamento *(m pl)*

**salvamento** *(m) n* Es, Pt
De Bergung *(f)*
En salvage
Fr sauvetage *(m)*
It salvataggio *(m)*

**salvar** *vb* Es, Pt
De retten
En save
Fr sauver
It salvare

**salvare** *vb* It
De retten
En save
Es salvar
Fr sauver
Pt salvar

**salvataggio** *(m) n* It
De Bergung *(f)*
En salvage
Es salvamento *(m)*
Fr sauvetage *(m)*
Pt salvamento *(m)*

**salvo erro e omissão** Pt
De Irrtum vorbehalten
En errors and omissions excepted (e & oe)
Es salvo error u omisión
Fr sauf erreur ou omission
It salvo errori ed omissioni

**salvo errori ed omissioni** It
De Irrtum vorbehalten
En errors and omissions excepted (e & oe)
Es salvo error u omisión
Fr sauf erreur ou omission
Pt salvo erro e omissão

**salvo error u omisión** Es
De Irrtum vorbehalten

En errors and omissions excepted (e & oe)
Fr sauf erreur ou omission
It salvo errori ed omissioni
Pt salvo erro e omissão

**sample** *n* En
De Probe; Muster *(f n)*
Es muestra *(f)*
Fr échantillon *(m)*
It campione *(m)*
Pt amostra *(f)*

**sample of no value** En
De Muster ohne Wert *(n)*
Es muestra sin valor *(f)*
Fr échantillon sans valeur *(m)*
It campione senza valore *(m)*
Pt amostra sem valor *(f)*

**sanción** *(f) n* Es
De Geldstrafe *(f)*
En fine
Fr amende *(f)*
It multa *(f)*
Pt multa *(f)*

**sanción elevada** *(f)* Es
De schwere Busse *(f)*
En heavy fine
Fr forte amende *(f)*
It forte multa *(f)*
Pt multa pesada *(f)*

**sanciones económicas** *(f pl)* Es
De wirtschaftliche Sanktionen *(f pl)*
En economic sanctions
Fr sanctions économiques *(f pl)*
It sanzioni economiche *(f pl)*
Pt sanções económicas *(f pl)*

**sanções económicas** *(f pl)* Pt
De wirtschaftliche Sanktionen *(f pl)*
En economic sanctions
Es sanciones económicas *(f pl)*
Fr sanctions économiques *(f pl)*
It sanzioni economiche *(f pl)*

**sanctions économiques** *(f pl)* Fr
De wirtschaftliche Sanktionen *(f pl)*

En economic sanctions
Es sanciones económicas *(f pl)*
It sanzioni economiche *(f pl)*
Pt sanções económicas *(f pl)*

**sans but lucratif** Fr
De ohne Gewinnabsicht
En nonprofitmaking
Es sin finos lucrativos
It senza scopo di lucro
Pt sem fins lucrativos

**sans droit de recours** Fr
De ohne Rückgriff
En without recourse
Es sin recurso
It senza ricorso
Pt sem recurso

**sans formalités** Fr
De formlos
En informal
Es sin ceremonia
It senza formalità
Pt sem formalidade

**sans profit** Fr
De unvorteilhaft
En unprofitable
Es nada lucrativo
It poco proficuo
Pt não lucrativo

**sanzioni economiche** *(f pl)* It
De wirtschaftliche Sanktionen *(f pl)*
En economic sanctions
Es sanciones económicas *(f pl)*
Fr sanctions économiques *(f pl)*
Pt sanções económicas *(f pl)*

**satisfação** *(f) n* Pt
De Zufriedenstellung; Ausgleich *(f m)*
En satisfaction; settlement
Es satisfacción *(f)*
Fr satisfaction; règlement *(f m)*
It soddisfazione; regolamento *(f m)*

**satisfacción** *(f) n* Es
De Zufriedenstellung; Ausgleich *(f m)*
En satisfaction; settlement

Fr satisfaction; règlement *(f m)*
It soddisfazione; regolamento *(f m)*
Pt satisfação *(f)*

**satisfaction** *n* En, Fr *(f)*
De Zufriedenstellung; Begleichung *(f)*
Es satisfacción *(f)*
It soddisfazione *(f)*
Pt satisfação *(f)*

**saturação** (de mercadorias baratas) *(f) n* Pt
De Dumping *(n)*
En dumping
Es inundación de mercancía barata *(f)*
Fr dumping *(m)*
It dumping *(m)*

**Satz** *(m) n* De
En rate
Es tasa; tipo *(f m)*
Fr taux; cours *(m)*
It tasso; tariffa *(m f)*
Pt taxa *(f)*

**sauf erreur ou omission** Fr
De Irrtum vorbehalten
En errors and omissions excepted (e & oe)
Es salvo error u omisión
It salvo errori ed omissioni
Pt salvo erro e omissão

**Säulendiagramm** *(m) n* De
En block diagram
Es diagrama de bloque *(m)*
Fr ordinogramme *(m)*
It schema a blocchi *(m)*
Pt organigrama *(m)*

**sauver** *vb* Fr
De retten
En save
Es salvar
It salvare
Pt salvar

**sauvetage** *(m) n* Fr
De Bergung *(f)*
En salvage
Es salvamento *(m)*
It salvataggio *(m)*
Pt salvamento *(m)*

**save** (appearances, situation, etc.) *vb* En
De retten
Es salvar
Fr sauver
It salvare
Pt salvar

**save** (money) *vb* En
De aufsparen
Es ahorrar; economizar
Fr épargner; économiser
It risparmiare; economizzare
Pt poupar; economizar

**savings bank** En
De Sparkasse *(f)*
Es caja de ahorros *(f)*
Fr caisse d'épargne *(f)*
It cassa di risparmio *(f)*
Pt caixa económica *(f)*

**scadenza** *(f) n* It
De Fälligkeit *(f)*
En maturity
Es vencimiento *(m)*
Fr échéance *(f)*
Pt vencimento *(m)*

**scadere** *vb* It
De fällig sein
En fall due
Es vencer
Fr échoir; venir à échéance
Pt vencer-se

**scaduto** *adj* It
De verfallen; rückständig
En expired; out of date; overdue
Es vencido
Fr expiré; perimé; arriéré
Pt vencido

**scala** *(f) n* It
De Skala; Masstab *(f m)*
En scale
Es escala *(f)*
Fr échelle *(f)*
Pt escala *(f)*

**scala mobile** *(f)* It
De gleitende Skala *(f)*
En sliding scale
Es escala móvil *(f)*
Fr échelle mobile *(f)*
Pt escala móvel *(f)*

**scale** (fees, charges, etc.) *n* En
De Tarif *(m)*
Es tarifa *(f)*
Fr barème *(m)*
It tariffa *(f)*
Pt tarifa *(f)*

**scale** (of a map, etc.) *n* En
De Masstab *(m)*
Es escala *(f)*
Fr échelle *(f)*
It scala *(f)*
Pt escala *(f)*

**scales** (weighing) *pl n* En
De Waagé *(f)*
Es balanza *(f)*
Fr balance *(f)*
It bilancia *(f)*
Pt balança *(f)*

**scalo** *(m) n* It
De Kai *(m)*
En wharf
Es muelle *(m)*
Fr quai *(m)*
Pt cais *(m)*

**scarsezza** *(f) n* It
De Knappheit *(f)*
En short supply
Es escasez *(f)*
Fr disette *(f)*
Pt escassez *(f)*

**scartamento normale** *(m)* It
De Normalmass *(n)*
En standard gauge
Es calibre patrón *(m)*
Fr écartement normal *(m)*
Pt calibre padrão *(m)*

**sceau** *(m) n* Fr
De Siegel *(n)*
En seal
Es sello *(m)*
It sigillo *(m)*
Pt selo *(m)*

**Schaden** *(m) n* De
En damage; injury
Es daño *(m)*
Fr dommage; avarie *(m f)*
It danno *(m)*
Pt dano *(m)*

**Schadenersatz** *(m)* n De
En damages
Es daños *(m pl)*
Fr dommages-intérêts *(m pl)*
It danni *(m pl)*
Pt danos *(m pl)*

**(den) Schadenersatzbetrag feststellen** De
En assess damages
Es evaluar daños
Fr fixer des dommages-intérêts
It valutare i danni
Pt avaliar os danos

**Schadenersatzklage** *(f)* n De
En action for damages
Es acción por daños *(f)*
Fr action en dommages et intérêts *(f)*
It processo per risarcimento *(m)*
Pt processamento por danos *(m)*

**schadenersatzpflichtig** *adj* De
En liable for damages
Es responsable por daños
Fr passible de dommages-intérêts
It responsabile per i danni
Pt responsavel por danos

**Schadenersatz zugestehen** De
En award damages
Es conceder daños
Fr adjuger des dommages-intérêts
It concedere i danni
Pt conceder compensação

**Schadenfreiheitsrabatt** *(m)* De
En no-claims discount (bonus)
Es bonificación por no-reclamación *(f)*
Fr bonification pour non sinistre *(f)*
It sconto per assenza di sinistri *(m)*
Pt disconto por ausência de reclamações *(m)*

**Schalttafel** *(f)* n De
En switchboard
Es cuadro de conexión *(m)*
Fr tableau de distribution *(m)*

It quadro di comando *(m)*
Pt quadro de distribuição *(m)*

**Schatzamt** *(n)* n De
En exchequer
Am treasury
Es hacienda *(f)*
Fr trésorerie *(f)*
It tesoro *(m)*
Pt tesouro *(m)*

**Schätzer** *(m)* n De
En assessor
Es asesor *(m)*
Fr appréciateur *(m)*
It agente delle imposte *(m)*
Pt avaliador *(m)*

**Schatzwechsel** *(m)* n De
En exchequer bond
Am treasury bond
Es bono de tesorería *(m)*
Fr bon du trésor *(m)*
It buono del tesoro *(m)*
Pt título do tesouro *(m)*

**Schaufensterdekoration** *(f)* n De
En window-dressing
Es preparación de escaparates *(f)*
Fr art de l'étalage *(m)*
It allestimento delle vetrine *(m)*
Pt preparação de montras *(f)*

**Schaukasten** *(m)* n De
En display unit
Es presentación *(f)*
Fr présentoir *(m)*
It mostra *(f)*
Pt montra *(f)*

**Schaustellung** *(f)* n De
En display
Es presentación *(f)*
Fr présentation *(f)*
It mostra *(f)*
Pt exposição *(f)*

**Scheck** *(m)* n De
En cheque
Am check
Es cheque *(m)*
Fr chèque *(m)*
It assegno *(m)*
Pt cheque *(m)*

**(einen) Scheck ausstellen** De
En draw a cheque
Es extender un cheque
Fr tirer un chèque
It emettere un assegno
Pt passar um cheque

**(einen) Scheck einlösen** De
En cash a cheque
Es cobrar un cheque
Fr toucher un chèque
It incassare un assegno
Pt cobrar um cheque

**Scheckheft** *(n)* n De
En cheque book
Am check book
Es libro de cheques *(m)*
Fr carnet de chèques: chéquier *(m)*
It libretto assegni *(m)*
Pt livro de cheques *(m)*

**Scheckkarte** *(f)* n De
En cheque card
Am bank credit card
Es tarjeta de cheque *(f)*
Fr carte de chèque *(f)*
It scheda per assegni *(f)*
Pt cartão de validação de cheques *(m)*

**Scheckkonto** *(n)* n De
En drawing account
Es cuenta corrienta *(f)*
Fr compte courant *(m)*
It conto corrente *(m)*
Pt conta corrente *(f)*

**(einen) Scheck rückgängig machen** De
En cancel a cheque
Es anular un cheque
Fr annuler un chèque
It annullare un assegno
Pt cancelar um cheque

**(einen) Scheck sperren** De
En stop a cheque
Es suspender el pago de un cheque
Fr bloquer un chèque
It fermare un assegno
Pt suspender o pagamento de um cheque

**scheda** (f) n It
De Karte; Indexkarte (f)
En card; index card
Es tarjeta; ficha (f)
Fr carte; fiche (f)
Pt cartão; ficha (m f)

**scheda per assegni** (f) It
De Scheckkarte (f)
En cheque card
Am bank credit card
Es tarjeta de cheque (f)
Fr carte de chèque (f)
Pt cartão de validação de cheques (m)

**scheda perforata** (f) It
De Lochkarte (f)
En punched card
Es tarjeta perforada (f)
Fr carte perforée
Pt ficha perforada (f)

**schedario** (m) n It
De Kartothek; Aktenschrank (f m)
En card index; filing cabinet
Es fichero (m)
Fr fichier; classeur (m)
Pt ficheiro (m)

**schedule** n En
De Plan; Programm (m n)
Es plano; programa (m)
Fr plan; programme (m)
It piano; programma (m)
Pt plano; programa (m)

**schedule** vb En
De planen; programmieren
Es programar
Fr programmer; planifier
It programmare
Pt programar

**schema a blocchi** (m) It
De Säulendiagramm (m)
En block diagram
Es diagrama de bloque (m)
Fr ordinogramme (m)
Pt organigrama (m)

**schema di contratto** (m) It
De Entwurf eines Übereinkommens (m)
En draft agreement
Es proyecto de convenio (m)

Fr projet de convention (m)
Pt pró-forma de accordo (m)

**Schicht** (f) n De
En shift
Es turno (m)
Fr équipe (f)
It turno (m)
Pt turno (m)

**Schiedsgericht** (n) n De
En court of arbitration
Es tribunal arbitral (m)
Fr cour d'arbitrage (m)
It corte arbitrale (f)
Pt tribunal de arbitragem (m)

**Schiedsgerichtverfahren** (n) n De
En arbitration
Es arbitramento (m)
Fr arbitrage (m)
It arbitrato (m)
Pt arbitragem (f)

**Schiedsobmann** (m) n De
En umpire
Es juez árbitro (m)
Fr surarbitre (m)
It terzo arbitro (m)
Pt juiz árbitro (m)

**Schiedsrichter** (m) n De
En arbitrator
Es arbitrador (m)
Fr arbitre (m)
It arbitro (m)
Pt árbitro (m)

**Schiedsspruch** (m) n De
En arbitration award
Es sentencia arbitral (f)
Fr sentence arbitrale (f)
It lodo arbitrale (m)
Pt decisão de arbitragem (f)

**Schiff** (n) n De
En ship
Es barco (m)
Fr navire (m)
It nave (f)
Pt navio (m)

**Schiffahrt** (f) n De
En navigation
Es navegación (f)
Fr navigation (f)

It navigazione (f)
Pt navegação (f)

**schiffbar** adj De
En navigable
Es navegable
Fr navigable
It navigabile
Pt navegável

**Schiffsmakler** (m) n De
En shipbroker
Es corredor marítimo (m)
Fr courtier maritime (m)
It sensale marittimo (m)
Pt corretor marítimo (m)

**Schiffspapiere** (n pl) n De
En ship's papers
Es documentación marítima (f)
Fr papiers de bord (m pl)
It carte di bordo (f pl)
Pt documentação do navio (f)

**Schiffsregister** (n) n De
En ship's register
Es registro del barco (m)
Fr certificat d'immatriculation (m)
It atto di nazionalità (m)
Pt registo do navio (m)

**Schiffswerft** (f) n De
En dockyard
Es astillero (m)
Fr chantier de construction de navires (m)
It cantiere (m)
Pt estaleiro (m)

**schlechter Zahler** (m) De
En slow payer
Es deudor moroso (m)
Fr mauvais payeur (m)
It cattivo pagatore (m)
Pt mau-pagador (m)

**Schleppdampfer** (m) n De
En tug-boat
Es remolcador (m)
Fr remorqueur (m)
It rimorchiatore (m)
Pt rebocador (m)

**Schlichtung** (f) n De
En conciliation
Es conciliación (f)
Fr conciliation (f)

It    conciliazione *(f)*
Pt   conciliação *(f)*

**Schlussbilanz** *(f) n* De
En   final balance
Es   saldo final *(m)*
Fr   solde net *(m)*
It    saldo finale *(m)*
Pt   balanço final *(m)*

**Schlusschein** *(m) n* De
En   contract note
Es   nota de contrato *(f)*
Fr   bordereau d'achat *(m)*
It    nota di contratto *(f)*
Pt   nota-contrato *(f)*

**Schlussdividende** *(f) n* De
En   final dividend
Es   saldo del dividendo *(m)*
Fr   solde de dividende *(m)*
It    saldo del dividendo *(m)*
Pt   dividendo final *(m)*

**Schlüssel** *(m) n* De
En   key; code
Es   llave; clave *(f)*
Fr   clef *(f)*
It    chiave; codice *(f m)*
Pt   chave; código *(f m)*

**Schlüsselindustrie** *(f) n* De
En   key industry
Es   industria clave *(f)*
Fr   industrie-clef *(f)*
It    industria chiave *(f)*
Pt   indústria chave *(f)*

**Schlussnotierung** *(f) n* De
En   closing price
Es   precio de cierre *(m)*
Fr   cours de clôture *(m)*
It    prezzo di chiusura *(m)*
Pt   último preço *(m)*

**Schlusstermin** *(m) n* De
En   closing date
Es   último día *(m)*
Fr   dernier jour *(m)*
It    ultima data *(f)*
Pt   último dia *(m)*

**schmuggeln** *vb* De
En   smuggle
Es   pasar de contrabando
Fr   faire la contrebande
It    contrabbandare
Pt   passar por contrabando

**Schmuggelware** *(f) n* De
En   contraband
Es   contrabando *(m)*
Fr   contrebande *(f)*
It    contrabbando *(m)*
Pt   contrabando *(m)*

**Schneeball Verkauf** *(m)* De
En   pyramid selling
Es   venta en pirámide *(f)*
Fr   vente en pyramide *(f)*
It    vendita a piramide *(f)*
Pt   vendas em pirâmide *(f)*

**Schreibmaschine** *(f) n* De
En   typewriter
Es   máquina de escribir *(f)*
Fr   machine à écrire *(f)*
It    macchina da scrivere *(f)*
Pt   máquina de escrever *(f)*

**(auf  der)  Schreibmaschine
       schreiben** De
En   type
Es   escribir a máquina
Fr   écrire à la machine
It    scrivere a macchina
Pt   escrever à máquina

**Schreibtisch** *(m) n* De
En   desk
Es   mesa *(f)*
Fr   bureau *(m)*
It    scrittoio *(m)*
Pt   secretária *(f)*

**schriftlich bestätigen** De
En   confirm in writing
Es   confirmar por escrito
Fr   confirmer par écrit
It    confermare per iscritto
Pt   confirmar por escrito

**Schuld** *(f) n* De
En   debt
Es   deuda *(f)*
Fr   créance *(f)*
It    debito *(m)*
Pt   dívida *(f)*

**(eine) Schuld begleichen** De
En   discharge a debt
Es   descargar una deuda
Fr   acquitter une dette
It    estinguere un debito
Pt   cancelar uma dívida

**(eine) Schuld eintreiben** De
En   collect a debt
Es   recaudar una deuda
Fr   recouvrer une créance
It    incassare un credito
Pt   cobrar uma dívida

**(eine) Schuld erlassen** De
En   write off a debt
Es   cancelar una deuda
Fr   amortir une créance
It    cancellare un credito
Pt   cancelar uma dívida

**Schuldner** *(m) n* De
En   debtor
Es   deudor *(m)*
Fr   débiteur *(m)*
It    debitore *(m)*
Pt   devedor *(m)*

**Schuldschein** *(m) n* De
En   promissory note; I.O.U.
Es   pagaré *(m)*
Fr   billet  à  ordre;  reconnais-
     sance de dette *(m f)*
It    pagherò *(m)*
Pt   promissória; vale *(f m)*

**Schuldverschreibung    ohne
      Fälligkeitsdatum** *(f)* De
En   undated debenture
Es   obligación sin fecha *(f)*
Fr   obigation perpétuelle *(f)*
It    obbligazione perpetua *(f)*
Pt   obrigação sem data *(f)*

**Schüttgut** *(n) n* De
En   bulk cargo
Es   carga en granel *(f)*
Fr   cargaison en vrac *(f)*
It    carico alla rinfusa *(m)*
Pt   carga geral *(f)*

**schwache Währung** *(f) n* De
En   soft currency
Es   moneda débil *(f)*
Fr   monnaie faible *(f)*
It    valuta debole *(f)*
Pt   moeda fraca *(f)*

**schwanken** *vb* De
En   fluctuate
Es   fluctuar
Fr   fluctuer
It    fluttuare
Pt   flutuar

**schwankend** adj De
En fluctuating
Es fluctuando
Fr fluctuant
It fluttuante
Pt flutuando

**schwankender Kurs** (m) De
En fluctuating rate
Es tipo oscilante (m)
Fr taux variable (m)
It tasso variabile (m)
Pt taxa variável (f)

**Schwankung** (f) n De
En fluctuation
Es fluctuación (f)
Fr fluctuation (f)
It fluttuazione (f)
Pt flutuação (f)

**schwarze Börse** (f) De
En (securities) black market
Es bolsa negra (f)
Fr bourse noire (f)
It borsa nera (f)
Pt bolsa negra (f)

**schwarze Liste** (f) De
En black list
Es lista negra (f)
Fr liste noire (f)
It lista nera (f)
Pt lista negra (f)

**schwarzer Markt** (m) De
En black market
Es mercado negro (m)
Fr marché noir (m)
It mercato nero (m)
Pt mercado negro (m)

**schwebend** adj De
En pending
Es pendiente
Fr pendant
It pendente
Pt pendente

**Schwellenpreis** (m) n De
En threshold price
Es precio de umbral (m)
Fr prix de seuil (m)
It prezzo soglia (m)
Pt preço convencionado (m)

**schwer** adj De
En heavy
Es pesado; fuerte
Fr lourd; fort
It pesante; forte
Pt pesado

**schwere Busse** (f) De
En heavy fine
Es sanción elevada (f)
Fr forte amende (f)
It forte multa (f)
Pt multa pesada (f)

**schwerer Verlust** (m) De
En heavy loss
Es fuerte pérdida; pérdida
  sensible (f)
Fr lourde perte (f)
It forte perdita (f)
Pt perda avultada (f)

**schwere Tonne** (f) De
En long ton
Es tonelada inglesa (f)
Fr tonne forte (f)
It tonnellata inglese (f)
Pt tonelada inglesa (f)

**Schwerindustrie** (f) n De
En heavy industry
Es industria pesada (f)
Fr industrie lourde (f)
It industria pesante (f)
Pt indústria pesada (f)

**Schwestergesellschaft** (f) n
  De
En sister company
Es compañía asociada (f)
Fr société sœur (f)
It società sorella (f)
Pt empresa gémea (f)

**schwierig** adj De
En difficult
Es difícil
Fr difficile
It difficile
Pt difícil

**Schwindelgesellschaft** (f) n
  De
En bogus company
Am phantom operation
Es sociedad fantasma (f)
Fr société fantôme (f)

It società fasulla (f)
Pt sociedade fantasma (f)

**schwindeln** vb De
En swindle
Es estafar
Fr filouter
It truffare
Pt enganar

**Schwindlertrick** (m) n De
En confidence trick
Am confidence game
Es timo (m)
Fr escroquerie (f)
It truffa all'americana (f)
Pt conto do vigário (m)

**scioglimento** (m) n It
De Auflösung (f)
En dissolution
Es disolución (f)
Fr dissolution (f)
Pt dissolução (f)

**scioperante** (m) n It
De Streikende(r) (m)
En striker
Es huelguista (m)
Fr gréviste (m)
Pt grevista (m)

**scioperare** vb It
De streiken
En strike
Es declarar huelga
Fr faire la grève
Pt fazer greve

**sciopero** (m) n It
De Streik (m)
En strike
Es huelga (f)
Fr grève (f)
Pt greve (f)

**sciopero a singhiozzo** (m) It
De Bummelstreik (m)
En go-slow strike
Am slow down
Es huelga de producción lenta
  (f)
Fr grève perlée (f)
Pt greve de abrandamento do
  ritmo de produção (f)

**sciopero bianco** *(m)* It
De Sitzstreik *(m)*
En sit-down strike
Es huelga de brazos caídos *(f)*
Fr grève avec occupation des lieux *(f)*
Pt greve de braços caídos *(f)*

**sciopero generale** *(m)* It
De Generalstreik *(m)*
En general strike
Es huelga general *(f)*
Fr grève générale *(f)*
Pt greve geral *(f)*

**sciopero non ufficiale** *(m)* It
De unanerkannter Streik *(m)*
En unofficial strike
Es huelga no-oficial *(f)*
Fr grève non reconnue *(f)*
Pt greve não oficializada *(f)*

**sciopero portuale** *(m)* It
De Hafenarbeiterstreik *(m)*
En dock strike
Es huelga de obreros de muelle *(f)*
Fr grève des dockers *(f)*
Pt greve na doca *(f)*

**sciopero selvaggio** *(m)* It
De wilder Streik *(m)*
En wildcat strike
Es huelga espontánea *(f)*
Fr grève sauvage *(f)*
Pt greve não oficializada *(f)*

**sciopero ufficiale** *(m)* It
De anerkannter Streik *(m)*
En official strike
Es huelga oficial *(f)*
Fr grève officielle *(f)*
Pt greve oficial *(f)*

**sconto** *(m)* n It
De Skonto *(m)*
En discount
Es descuento *(m)*
Fr escompte *(m)*
Pt desconto *(m)*

**sconto d'esportazione** *(m)* It
De Ausführsonderrabatt *(m)*
En export rebate
Es descuento por exportación *(m)*
Fr remise sur les exports *(f)*

**sconto di banca** *(m)* It
De Diskont *(m)*
En bank discount
Es descuento bancario *(m)*
Fr escompte en dehors *(m)*
Pt desconto bancário *(m)*

**sconto differito** *(m)* It
De nachträglicher Umsatzbonus *(m)*
En deferred rebate
Es descuento diferido *(m)*
Fr rabais différé *(m)*
Pt dedução adiada *(f)*

**sconto di revendita** *(m)* It
De Händlerrabatt *(m)*
En trade discount
Es descuento comercial *(m)*
Fr rabais de demi-gros *(m)*
Pt desconto à praça *(m)*

**sconto per assenza di sinistri** *(m)* It
De Schadenfreiheitsrabatt *(m)*
En no-claims discount or bonus
Es bonificación por no-reclamación *(f)*
Fr bonification pour non sinistre *(f)*
Pt disconto por ausência de reclamações *(m)*

**sconto per pagamento a contanti** *(m)* It
De Barrabatt *(m)*
En cash discount
Es descuento de caja *(m)*
Fr escompte de caisse *(m)*
Pt desconto de contado *(m)*

**scoperto** *(m)* n It
De Überziehung *(f)*
En overdraft
Es sobregiro; saldo deudor *(m)*
Fr découvert; solde débiteur *(m)*
Pt conta a descoberto *(f)*

**scopo** *(m)* n It
De Ziel *(n)*
En goal
Es meta; objetivo *(f m)*

Pt desconto de exportação *(m)*

**scopo dell'assemblea** *(m)* It
De Tagesordnung *(f)*
En business before the meeting
Am agenda
Es orden del día *(f)*
Fr ordre du jour *(m)*
Pt agenda da reunião *(f)*

**scorta** *(f)* n It
De Vorrat *(m)*
En stock
Es stock; existencias *(m; f pl)*
Fr stock; marchandises *(m; f pl)*
Pt existências *(f pl)*

**scorte di equilibrio** *(f pl)* It
De Buffer-stocks *(m pl)*
En buffer stocks
Es existencias de regularización *(f pl)*
Fr stocks de régularisation *(m pl)*
Pt existências de regularização *(f pl)*

**scrittoio** *(m)* n It
De Schreibtisch *(m)*
En desk
Es mesa *(f)*
Fr bureau *(m)*
Pt secretária *(f)*

**scrivere a macchina** It
De auf der Schreibmaschine schreiben
En type
Es escribir a máquina
Fr écrire à la machine
Pt escrever à máquina

**sdoganamento** *(m)* n It
De Zollabfertigung *(f)*
En customs clearance
Es paso de aduanas *(f)*
Fr dédouanement *(m)*
Pt despacho alfandegário *(m)*

**sdoganare** *vb* It
De verzollen
En clear through customs
Es retirar de aduanas
Fr dédouaner
Pt despachar na alfândega

**sdoganato** *adj* It
De verzollt
En ex bond; out of bond
Es fuera de aduanas; despachado de aduanas
Fr à l'acquitté; dédouané
Pt livre de alfândega; despachado alfândega

**sea** *n* En
De See *(f)*
Es mar *(m)*
Fr mer *(f)*
It mare *(m)*
Pt mar *(m)*

**seal** *n* En
De Siegel *(n)*
Es sello *(m)*
Fr sceau *(m)*
It sigillo *(m)*
Pt selo *(m)*

**season** *n* En
De Jahreszeit *(f)*
Es estación *(f)*
Fr saison *(f)*
It stagione *(f)*
Pt estação *(f)*

**seasonal fluctuations** En
De saisonbedingte Schwankungen *(f pl)*
Es fluctuaciones estacionales *(f pl)*
Fr variations saisonnières *(f pl)*
It fluttuazioni stagionali *(f pl)*
Pt flutuações de época *(f pl)*

**seasonal unemployment** En
De jahreszeitlich bedingte Arbeitslosigkeit *(f)*
Es paro de temporada *(m)*
Fr chômage saisonnier *(m)*
It disoccupazione stagionale *(f)*
Pt desemprego de estação *(m)*

**sea-water damage** En
De Seewasserschaden *(m)*
Es daño de agua de mar *(m)*
Fr dégâts d'eau de mer *(m pl)*
It danno d'acqua di mare *(m)*
Pt dano causado pela água do mar *(m)*

**seaworthy** *adj* En
De seefest
Es marinero
Fr en état de navigabilité
It atto a tenere il mare
Pt em condições de navegação

**secção** *(f)* *n* Pt
De Abteilung *(f)*
En division
Es sección *(f)*
Fr division *(f)*
It divisione *(f)*

**sección** *(f)* *n* Es
De Abteilung *(f)*
En division
Fr division *(f)*
It divisione *(f)*
Pt secção *(f)*

**second** *(m)* *n* Fr
De Maat *(m)*
En (ship's) mate
Es primer oficial *(m)*
It primo ufficiale *(m)*
Pt imediato *(m)*

**seconda di cambio** *(f)* It
De Sekundawechsel *(m)*
En second of exchange
Es segunda de cambio *(f)*
Fr seconde de change *(f)*
Pt segunda de câmbio *(f)*

**seconde de change** *(f)* Fr
De Sekundawechsel *(m)*
En second of exchange
Es segunda de cambio *(f)*
It seconda di cambio *(f)*
Pt segunda de câmbio *(f)*

**second-hand** *adj* En
De aus zweiter Hand; Gebraucht-
Es de segunda mano
Fr d'occasion
It di seconda mano
Pt de segunda mão

**second of exchange** En
De Sekundawechsel *(m)*
Es segunda de cambio *(f)*
Fr seconde de change *(f)*
It seconda di cambio *(f)*
Pt segunda de câmbio *(f)*

**secours** *(m)* *n* Fr
De Hilfe *(f)*
En help
Es ayuda *(f)*
It ainto *(m)*
Pt ajuda *(f)*

**secours de chômage** *(m)* Fr
De Arbeitslosenunterstützung *(f)*
En unemployment benefit
Es subsidio de paro *(m)*
It indennità di disoccupazione *(f)*
Pt subsidio de desemprego *(m)*

**secret agreement** En
De Geheimvertrag *(m)*
Es acuerdo secreto *(m)*
Fr accord occulte *(m)*
It accordo segreto *(m)*
Pt acordo secreto *(m)*

**secrétaire** *(m/f)* *n* Fr
De Sekretär; Sekretärin *(m f)*
En (male or female) secretary
Es secretario; secretaria *(m f)*
It segretario; segretaria *(m f)*
Pt secretário; secretária *(m f)*

**secretaria** *(f)* *n* Es
De Sekretärin *(f)*
En (female) secretary
Fr secrétaire *(f)*
It segretaria *(f)*
Pt secretária *(f)*

**secretária** *(f)* *n* Pt
De Sekretärin; Schreibtisch *(f m)*
En (female) secretary; desk
Es secretaria; mesa *(f)*
Fr secrétaire; bureau *(f m)*
It segretaria; scrittoio *(f m)*

**secretario** *(m)* *n* Es
De Sekretär *(m)*
En (male) secretary
Fr secrétaire *(m)*
It segretario *(m)*
Pt secretário *(m)*

**secretário** *(m)* *n* Pt
De Sekretär *(m)*
En (male) secretary
Es secretario *(m)*

Fr   secrétaire *(m)*
It   segretario *(m)*

**secretary** *n* En
De   Sekretär; Sekretärin *(m f)*
Es   secretario; secretaria *(m f)*
Fr   secrétaire *(m/f)*
It   segretario; segretaria *(m f)*
Pt   secretário; secretária *(m f)*

**secret industriel** *(m)* Fr
De   Betriebsgeheimnis *(n)*
En   trade secret
Es   secreto comercial *(m)*
It   segreto commerciale *(m)*
Pt   segredo comercial *(m)*

**secreto comercial** *(m)* Es
De   Betriebsgeheimnis *(n)*
En   trade secret
Fr   secret industriel *(m)*
It   segreto commerciale *(m)*
Pt   segredo comercial *(m)*

**secteur privé** *(m)* Fr
De   freie Marktwirtschaft *(f)*
En   private sector
Es   sector privado *(m)*
It   settore privato *(m)*
Pt   sector privado *(m)*

**secteur public** *(m)* Fr
De   öffentliche Hand *(f)*
En   public sector
Es   sector público *(m)*
It   settore statale *(m)*
Pt   sector público *(m)*

**sector privado** *(m)* Es, Pt
De   freie Marktwirtschaft *(f)*
En   private sector
Fr   secteur privé *(m)*
It   settore privato *(m)*

**sector público** *(m)* Es, Pt
De   öffentliche Hand *(f)*
En   public sector
Fr   secteur public *(m)*
It   settore statale *(m)*

**secured debenture** En
De   gesicherte Schuldverschrei-
     bung *(f)*
Es   obligación garantizada *(f)*
Fr   obligation garantie *(f)*
It   obbligazione garantita *(f)*
Pt   obrigação com garantia *(f)*

**sécurité** *(f)* n Fr
De   Sicherheit *(f)*
En   security; safety
Es   seguridad *(f)*
It   sicurezza *(f)*
Pt   segurança *(f)*

**sécurité sociale** *(f)* Fr
De   Sozialversicherung *(f)*
En   social security
Es   seguridad social *(f)*
It   sicurezza sociale *(f)*
Pt   segurança social *(f)*

**securities** *pl* n En
De   Effekten *(m pl)*
Es   títulos; valores *(m pl)*
Fr   titres; valeurs *(m pl; f pl)*
It   titoli; valori *(m pl)*
Pt   títulos; valores *(m pl)*

**security** (on loan, etc.) n En
De   Nebenbürgschaft *(f)*
Es   fianza *(f)*
Fr   nantissement *(m)*
It   pegno *(m)*
Pt   fiança *(f)*

**security** (protection) n En
De   Sicherheit *(f)*
Es   seguridad *(f)*
Fr   sécurité *(f)*
It   sicurezza *(f)*
Pt   segurança *(f)*

**sede** *(f)* n It, Pt
De   Hauptanstalt *(f)*
En   head office
Es   oficina central *(f)*
Fr   siège; bureau principal *(m)*

**See** *(f)* n De
En   sea
Es   mar *(m)*
Fr   mer *(f)*
It   mare *(m)*
Pt   mar *(m)*

**See-** De
En   marine; maritime
Es   marítimo; marino
Fr   maritime
It   marino; marittimo
Pt   marinho; marítimo

**seefest** *adj* De
En   seaworthy
Es   marinero

Fr   en état de navigabilité
It   atto a tenere il mare
Pt   em condições de nave-
     gação

**Seereise** *(f)* n De
En   voyage
Es   viaje *(m)*
Fr   voyage *(m)*
It   viaggio *(m)*
Pt   viagem *(f)*

**Seewasserschaden** *(m)* n De
En   sea-water damage
Es   daño de agua de mar *(m)*
Fr   dégâts d'eau de mer *(m pl)*
It   danno d'acqua di mare *(m)*
Pt   dano causado pela água
     do mar *(m)*

**segredo comercial** *(m)* Pt
De   Betriebsgeheimnis *(n)*
En   trade secret
Es   secreto comercial *(m)*
Fr   secret industriel *(m)*
It   segreto commerciale *(m)*

**segretaria** *(f)* n It
De   Sekretärin *(f)*
En   (female) secretary
Es   secretaria *(f)*
Fr   secrétaire *(f)*
Pt   secretária *(f)*

**segretario** *(m)* n It
De   Sekretär *(m)*
En   (male) secretary
Es   secretario *(m)*
Fr   secrétaire *(m)*
Pt   secretário *(m)*

**segreto commerciale** *(m)* It
De   Betriebsgeheimnis *(n)*
En   trade secret
Es   secreto comercial *(m)*
Fr   secret industriel *(m)*
Pt   segredo comercial *(m)*

**seguitare** *vb* It
De   weiterverfolgen
En   follow up
Es   perseguir
Fr   poursuivre
Pt   perseguir

**segunda de cambio** *(f)* Es
De   Sekundawechsel *(m)*
En   second of exchange

Fr seconde de change (f)
It seconda di cambio (f)
Pt segunda de câmbio (f)

**segunda de câmbio** (f) Pt
De Sekundawechsel (m)
En second of exchange
Es segunda de cambio (f)
Fr seconde de change (f)
It seconda di cambio (f)

**segundo asociado** (m) Es
De jüngerer Teilhaber (m)
En junior partner
Fr associé en second (m)
It socio giovane (m)
Pt sócio junior (m)

**segurador** (m) n Pt
De Versicherer (m)
En insurer
Es asegurador (m)
Fr assureur (m)
It assicuratore (m)

**segurança** (f) n Pt
De Sicherheit (f)
En security; safety
Es seguridad (f)
Fr sécurité (f)
It sicurezza (f)

**segurança social** (f) Pt
De Sozialversicherung (f)
En social security
Es seguridad social (f)
Fr sécurité sociale (f)
It sicurezza sociale (f)

**segurar** vb Pt
De versichern
En insure
Es asegurar
Fr assurer
It assicurare

**seguridad** (f) n Es
De Sicherheit (f)
En security; safety
Fr sécurité (f)
It sicurezza (f)
Pt segurança (f)

**seguridad social** (f) Es
De Sozialversicherung (f)
En social security
Fr sécurité sociale (f)

It sicurezza sociale (f)
Pt segurança social (f)

**seguro** (m) n Es, Pt
De Versicherung (f)
En insurance; assurance
Fr assurance (f)
It assicurazione (f)

**seguro combinado** (m) Es
De kombinierte Versicherung (f)
En comprehensive insurance
Fr assurance combinée (f)
It assicurazione mista (f)
Pt seguro compreensivo (m)

**seguro compreensivo** (m) Pt
De kombinierte Versicherung (f)
En comprehensive insurance
Es seguro combinado (m)
Fr assurance combinée (f)
It assicurazione mista (f)

**seguro contra responsabilidad civil** (m) Es
De Haftpflichtversicherung (f)
En third-party insurance
Fr assurance responsabilité civile (RC) (f)
It assicurazione contro terzi (f)
Pt seguro contra terceiros (m)

**seguro contra riesgo de guerra** (m) Es
De Kriegsrisikoversicherung (f)
En war-risk insurance
Fr assurance du risque de guerre (f)
It assicurazione contro i rischi di guerra (f)
Pt seguro contra risco di guerra (m)

**seguro contra risco de guerra** (m) Pt
De Kriegsrisikoversicherung (f)
En war-risk insurance
Es seguro contra riesgo de guerra (m)
Fr assurance du risque de guerre (f)
It assicurazione contro i rischi di guerra (f)

**seguro contra terceiros** (m) Pt
De Haftpflichtversicherung (f)
En third-party insurance
Es seguro contra responsabilidad civil (m)
Fr assurance responsabilité civile (RC) (f)
It assicurazione contro terzi (f)

**seguro creditício** (m) Es
De Kreditversicherung (f)
En credit insurance
Fr assurance crédit (f)
It assicurazione credito (f)
Pt seguro de crédito (m)

**seguro de casa** (m) Es, Pt
De Wohnungsversicherung (f)
En household insurance
Fr assurance ménagère (f)
It assicurazione domestica (f)

**seguro de crédito** (m) Pt
De Kreditversicherung (f)
En credit insurance
Es seguro creditício (m)
Fr assurance crédit (f)
It assicurazione credito (f)

**seguro de enfermedad** (m) Es
De Krankenversicherung (f)
En health insurance
Fr assurance maladie (f)
It assicurazione malattia (f)
Pt seguro de obença (m)

**seguro de grupo** (m) Es, Pt
De Gruppenversicherung (f)
En group insurance
Fr assurance de groupe (f)
It assicurazione di gruppo (f)

**seguro de incêndio** (m) Pt
De Feuerversicherung (f)
En fire insurance
Es seguro de incendios (m)
Fr assurance incendie (f)
It assicurazione incendio (f)

**seguro de incendios** (m) Es
De Feuerversicherung (f)
En fire insurance
Fr assurance incendie (f)
It assicurazione incendio (f)
Pt seguro de incêndio (m)

**seguro del casco** *(m)* Es
De Kaskoversicherung *(f)*
En hull insurance
Fr assurance sur le corps *(f)*
It assicurazione corpo *(m)*
Pt seguro do casco *(m)*

**seguro de obença** *(m)* Pt
De Krankenversicherung *(f)*
En health insurance
Es seguro de enfermedad *(m)*
Fr assurance maladie *(f)*
It assicurazione malattia *(f)*

**seguro de vida** *(m)* Es, Pt
De Lebensversicherung *(f)*
En life assurance
Am life insurance
Fr assurance sur la vie *(f)*
It assicurazione sulla vita *(f)*

**seguro do casco** *(m)* Pt
De Kaskoversicherung *(f)*
En hull insurance
Es seguro del casco *(m)*
Fr assurance sur le corps *(f)*
It assicurazione corpo *(m)*

**seguro mútuo** *(m)* Pt
De Versicherung auf Gegen-
seitigkeit *(f)*
En mutual insurance
Es coaseguro *(m)*
Fr assurance mutuelle *(f)*
It mutua assicurazione *(f)*

**seguro social** *(m)* Pt
De Sozialversicherung *(f)*
En social security
Es seguridad social *(f)*
Fr sécurité sociale *(f)*
It sicurezza sociale *(f)*

**Sekretär** *(m)* n De
En (male) secretary
Es secretario *(m)*
Fr secrétaire *(m)*
It segretario *(m)*
Pt secretário *(m)*

**Sekretärin** *(f)* n De
En (female) secretary
Es secretaria *(f)*
Fr secrétaire *(f)*
It segretaria *(f)*
Pt secretária *(f)*

**Sekundawechsel** *(m)* n De
En second of exchange
Es segunda de cambio *(f)*
Fr seconde de change *(f)*
It seconda di cambio *(f)*
Pt segunda de câmbio *(f)*

**selbständig** *adj* De
En independent
Es independiente
Fr independant
It indipendente
Pt independente

**Selbstbedienung** *(f)* n De
En self-service
Es auto-servicio *(m)*
Fr libre service *(m)*
It servirsi da sè *(m)*
Pt self-service *(m)*

**Selbstkosten** *(pl)* n De
En prime cost
Es precio de coste *(m)*
Fr prix de revient *(m)*
It prezzo di costo *(m)*
Pt preço de custo *(m)*

**self-contained flat** En
De Einfamilienwohnung *(f)*
Es piso independiente com-
pleto *(m)*
Fr appartement indépendant
*(m)*
It appartamento indipendente
*(m)*
Pt andar independente *(m)*

**self-employed person** En
De selbständig Arbeitende(r)
*(m)*
Es trabajador por cuenta pro-
pia *(m)*
Fr travailleur indépendant *(m)*
It lavoratore indipendente *(m)*
Pt empregado por conta-pró-
pria *(m)*

**self-service** *n* En, Pt *(m)*
De Selbstbedienung *(f)*
Es auto-servicio *(m)*
Fr libre service *(m)*
It servirsi da sè *(m)*

**sell** *vb* En
De verkaufen
Es vender
Fr vendre

It vendere
Pt vender

**selling cost** En
De Verkaufskosten *(pl)*
Es coste de venta *(m)*
Fr frais de vente *(m)*
It costo di vendita *(m)*
Pt custo de venda *(m)*

**sello** *(m)* n Es
De Stempel; Siegel *(m)*
En stamp; seal
Fr tampon; sceau *(m)*
It bollo; sigillo *(m)*
Pt selo; carimbo *(m)*

**sello de correos** *(m)* Es
De Briefmarke *(f)*
En postage stamp
Fr timbre-poste *(m)*
It francobollo *(m)*
Pt selo postal *(m)*

**sello de fecha** *(m)* Es
De Tagesstempel *(m)*
En date-stamp
Fr dateur *(m)*
It timbro a data *(m)*
Pt carimbo de datas *(m)*

**selo** *(m)* n Pt
De Marke; Siegel *(f m)*
En stamp; seal
Es sello *(m)*
Fr timbre; sceau *(m)*
It bollo; sigillo *(m)*

**selo postal** *(m)* Pt
De Briefmarke *(f)*
En postage stamp
Es sello de correos *(m)*
Fr timbre-poste *(m)*
It francobollo *(m)*

**Semester** *(n)* n De
En half-year
Es semestre *(m)*
Fr semestre *(m)*
It semestre *(m)*
Pt semestre *(m)*

**semestral** *adj* Es, Pt
De halbjährlich
En half-yearly
Fr semestriel
It semestrale

**semestrale** *adj* It
De halbjährlich
En half-yearly
Es semestral
Fr semestriel
Pt semestral

**semestre** *(m)* n Es, Fr, It, Pt
De Semester *(n)*
En half-year

**semestriel** *adj* Fr
De halbjährlich
En half-yearly
Es semestral
It semestrale
Pt semestral

**sem fins lucrativos** Pt
De ohne Gewinnabsicht
En nonprofitmaking
Es sin finos lucrativos
Fr sans but lucratif
It senza scopo di lucro

**sem formalidade** Pt
De formlos
En informal
Es sin ceremonia
Fr sans formalités
It senza formalità

**semidiestro** *adj* Es
De angelernt
En semi-skilled
Fr semi-qualifié
It semiprovetto
Pt semi-especializado

**semi-especializado** *adj* Pt
De angelernt
En semi-skilled
Es semidiestro
Fr semi-qualifié
It semiprovetto

**semiprovetto** *adj* It
De angelernt
En semi-skilled
Es semidiestro
Fr semi-qualifié
Pt semi-especializado

**semi-qualifié** *adj* Fr
De angelernt
En semi-skilled
Es semidiestro

It semiprovetto
Pt semi-especializado

**semi-skilled** *adj* En
De angelernt
Es semidiestro
Fr semi-qualifié
It semiprovetto
Pt semi-especializado

**sem prejuízo** Pt
De ohne Verbindlichkeit
En without prejudice
Am not binding
Es sin prejuicio
Fr sous toutes réserves
It senza pregiudizio

**sem recurso** Pt
De ohne Rückgriff
En without recourse
Es sin recurso
Fr sans droit de recours
It senza ricorso

**senhorio** *(m)* n Pt
De Eigentümer; Vermieter *(m)*
En landlord; lessor
Es propietario; arrendador *(m)*
Fr propriétaire; bailleur *(m)*
It proprietario; locatore *(m)*

**sensale** *(m)* n It
De Makler *(m)*
En broker
Es corredor *(m)*
Fr courtier *(m)*
Pt corretor *(m)*

**sensale di merci** *(m)* It
De Makler für Verbrauchsgüter *(m)*
En commodity broker
Es corredor de mercaderías *(m)*
Fr courtier en marchandises *(m)*
Pt corretor de mercadorias *(m)*

**sensale marittimo** *(m)* It
De Schiffsmakler *(m)*
En shipbroker
Es corredor marítimo *(m)*
Fr courtier maritime *(m)*
Pt corretor marítimo *(m)*

**senseria** *(f)* n It
De Maklergebühr *(f)*
En brokerage
Es corretaje *(m)*
Fr courtage *(m)*
Pt corretagem *(f)*

**sentence arbitrale** *(f)* Fr
De Schiedsspruch *(m)*
En arbitration award
Es sentencia arbitral *(f)*
It lodo arbitrale *(m)*
Pt decisão de arbitragem *(f)*

**sentencia arbitral** *(f)* Es
De Schiedsspruch *(m)*
En arbitration award
Fr sentence arbitrale *(f)*
It lodo arbitrale *(m)*
Pt decisão de arbitragem *(f)*

**senza cedola** It
De ohne Coupon
En ex coupon
Es sin cupón
Fr ex coupon
Pt talão excluido

**senza diritti** It
De ohne Bezugsrechte
En ex rights
Es sin privilegio
Fr ex-droits
Pt privilégios excluidos

**senza dividendo** It
De ohne Dividende
En ex dividend
Es sin dividendo
Fr ex-dividende
Pt dividendo excluido

**senza formalità** It
De formlos
En informal
Es sin ceremonia
Fr sans formalités
Pt sem formalidade

**senza lavoro** It
De arbeitslos
En out of a job
Es sin trabajo; parado
Fr en chômage
Pt desempregado

**senza pregiudizio** It
De ohne Verbindlichkeit
En without prejudice
Am not binding
Es sin prejuicio
Fr sous toutes réserves
Pt sem prejuízo

**senza ricorso** It
De ohne Rückgriff
En without recourse
Es sin recurso
Fr sans droit de recours
Pt sem recurso

**senza scopo di lucro** It
De ohne Gewinnabsicht
En nonprofitmaking
Es sin finos lucrativos
Fr sans but lucratif
Pt sem fins lucrativos

**se porter garant de** Fr
De Haftkaution geben
En go bail for
Es salir fiados por
It rendersi garante di
Pt prestar caução a favor de

**serrata** (f) n It
De Aussperrung (f)
En lock-out
Es cierre (m)
Fr lock-out (m)
Pt lockout (m)

**se ruega hacer seguir** Es
De bitte nachsenden
En please forward
Fr prière de faire suivre
It far proseguire
Pt é favor enviar

**service agreement** En
De Dienstvertrag (m)
Es contrato de servicio (m)
Fr contrat de service (m)
It accordo di servizio (m)
Pt contrato de serviço (m)

**service de groupage** (m) Fr
De Groupagedienst (m)
En groupage service
Es servicio de agrupación (m)
It trasporto a collettame (m)
Pt serviço de agrupamento
    (m)

**service de la comptabilité** (m)
    Fr
De Buchhaltung (f)
En accounts department
Am accounting department
Es departamento de contabili-
    dad (m)
It ufficio contabilità (m)
Pt departamento de contabili-
    dade (m)

**service de la santé** (m) Fr
De Gesundheitsdienst (m)
En health service
Es servicio de sanidad (m)
It servizio sanitario (m)
Pt serviço de saúde (m)

**service des colis postaux** (m)
    Fr
De Paketpost (f)
En parcel post
Es servicio de paquete postal
    (m)
It servizio dei pacchi postali
    (m)
Pt serviço de encomendas
    postais (m)

**service flat** En
De Etagenwohnung mit Be-
    dienung (f)
Es piso con servicio incluido
    (m)
Fr appartement avec service
    (m)
It appartamento con servizio
    (m)
Pt andar com serviço incluido
    (m)

**service ventes** (m) Fr
De Verkaufsabteilung (f)
En sales department
Es departamento de ventas
    (m)
It ufficio vendite (m)
Pt departamento de vendas
    (m)

**servicio de agrupación** (m) Es
De Groupagedienst (m)
En groupage service
Fr service de groupage (m)
It trasporto a collettame (m)
Pt serviço de agrupamento
    (m)

**servicio de paquete postal**
    (m) Es
De Paketpost (f)
En parcel post
Fr service des colis postaux
    (m)
It servizio dei pacchi postali
    (m)
Pt serviço de encomendas
    postais (m)

**servicio de sanidad** (m) Es
De Gesundheitsdienst (m)
En health service
Fr service de la santé (m)
It servizio sanitario (m)
Pt serviço de saúde (m)

**serviço de agrupamento** (m)
    Pt
De Groupagedienst (m)
En groupage service
Es servicio de agrupación (m)
Fr service de groupage (m)
It trasporto a collettame (m)

**serviço de encomendas pos-
    tais** (m) Pt
De Paketpost (f)
En parcel post
Es servicio de paquete postal
    (m)
Fr service des colis postaux
    (m)
It servizio dei pacchi postali
    (m)

**serviço de saúde** (m) Pt
De Gesundheitsdienst (m)
En health service
Es servicio de sanidad (m)
Fr service de la santé (m)
It servizio sanitario (m)

**servirsi da sè** (m) It
De Selbstbedienung (f)
En self-service
Es auto-servicio (m)
Fr libre service (m)
Pt self-service (m)

**servizio dei pacchi postali** (m)
    It
De Paketpost (f)
En parcel post
Es servicio de paquete postal
    (m)

Fr service des colis postaux (m)
Pt serviço de encomendas postais (m)

**servizio di cassette di sicurezza** (m) It
De Verwahrung in Stahlfach (f)
En safe deposit
Es depósito en caja fuerte (m)
Fr dépôt en coffre-fort (m)
Pt depósito em cofre forte (m)

**servizio sanitario** (m) It
De Gesundheitsdienst (m)
En health service
Es servicio de sanidad (m)
Fr service de la santé (m)
Pt serviço de saúde (m)

**settlement** (of claim) n En
De Ausgleich (m)
Es satisfacción (f)
Fr règlement (m)
It regolamento (m)
Pt satisfação (f)

**settlement** (of accounts) n En
De Abrechnung (f)
Es ajuste (m)
Fr règlement (m)
It quietanza (f)
Pt ajuste (m)

**settlement** (agreement) n En
De Vereinbarung (f)
Es acuerdo (m)
Fr accord (m)
It accordo (m)
Pt acordo (m)

**settlement day** En
Am due date
De Abrechnungstag (m)
Es día de liquidación (m)
Fr jour de règlement (m)
It giorno della liquidazione (m)
Pt dia de liquidação (m)

**settore privato** (m) It
De freie Marktwirtschaft (f)
En private sector
Es sector privado (m)
Fr secteur privé (m)
Pt sector privado (m)

**settore statale** (m) It
De öffentliche Hand (f)
En public sector
Es sector público (m)
Fr secteur public (m)
Pt sector público (m)

**severance pay** En
De Abfindungssumme (bei Entlassung) (f)
Es indemnización de despido (f)
Fr indemnité de licenciement (f)
It sussidio per rottura del rapporto d'impiego (m)
Pt indeminização por despedimento (f)

**sfrattare un locatario** It
De einen Mieter entfernen
En evict a tenant
Es desalojar un inquilino
Fr expulser un locataire
Pt desalojar um inquilino

**sfruttare** vb It
De ausbeuten
En exploit
Es explotar
Fr exploiter
Pt explorar

**sgravio fiscale** (m) It
De Steuerbefreiung (f)
En tax relief
Es desgravación (f)
Fr dégrèvement (m)
Pt isenção de imposto (f)

**share** vb En
De teilen
Es participar; repartir
Fr partager
It dividere; partecipare
Pt participar; repartir

**share** (in a private company) n En
De Teil (m)
Es parte (f)
Fr part (f)
It parte (f)
Pt quota (f)

**share** (in a public company) n En
De Aktie (f)

Es acción (f)
Fr action (f)
It azione (f)
Pt acção (f)

**share capital** En
Am stock capital
De Aktienkapital (n)
Es capital en acciones (m)
Fr capital social (m)
It capitale azionario (m)
Pt capital em acções (m)

**share certificate** En
Am certificate of stock
De Aktienzertifikat (n)
Es título de acción (m)
Fr certificat d'actions (m)
It certificato azionario (m)
Pt título de acções (m)

**shareholder** n En
Am stockholder
De Aktionär (m)
Es accionista (m)
Fr actionnaire (m)
It azionista (m)
Pt accionista (m)

**share index** En
De Aktienindex (m)
Es índice de las acciones (m)
Fr indice des actions (m)
It indice delle azioni (m)
Pt índice das acções (m)

**share market** En
Am stock market
De Aktienmarkt (m)
Es mercado de valores (m)
Fr marché des valeurs (m)
It mercato azionario (m)
Pt mercado de acções (m)

**share register** En
De Liste der Aktionäre (f)
Es registro de las acciones (m)
Fr registre des actionnaires (m)
It registro delle azioni (m)
Pt registo de acções (m)

**shift** (working) n En
De Schicht (f)
Es turno (m)
Fr équipe (f)

It  turno (m)
Pt  turno (m)

**shiftwork** n En
De  Schichtarbeit (f)
Es  trabajo por torno (m)
Fr  travail par équipes (m)
It  lavoro a turno (m)
Pt  trabalho por turno (m)

**ship** n En
De  Schiff (n)
Es  barco (m)
Fr  navire (m)
It  nave (f)
Pt  navio (m)

**ship** vb En
De  verschiffen
Es  embarcar
Fr  embarquer
It  imbarcare
Pt  embarcar

**shipbroker** n En
De  Schiffsmakler (m)
Es  corredor marítimo (m)
Fr  courtier maritime (m)
It  sensale marittimo (m)
Pt  corretor marítimo (m)

**shipment** n En
De  Verladung (f)
Es  embarque (m)
Fr  embarquement (m)
It  imbarco (m)
Pt  embarque (m)

**shipment from origin** En
De  Versendung vom Ursprungsort (f)
Es  envío desde el punto de origen (m)
Fr  envoi du lieu de départ (m)
It  spedizione dall'origine (f)
Pt  carregamento desde a origem (m)

**shipped bill of lading** En
De  Hafenkonnossement (n)
Es  conocimiento de embarque a bordo (m)
Fr  connaissement de marchandises à bord (m)
It  polizza di carico con merce a bordo (f)
Pt  conhecimento de carga embarcada (m)

**shipping clerk** En
De  Expedient (m)
Es  dependiente de muelle (m)
Fr  expéditionnaire (m)
It  commesso di spedizioniere (m)
Pt  despachante (m)

**shipping line** En
De  Reederei (f)
Es  compañia navièra (f)
Fr  compagnie de navigation (f)
It  società di navigazione (f)
Pt  companhia de navegação (f)

**ship's papers** En
De  Schiffspapiere (n pl)
Es  documentación marítima (f)
Fr  papiers de bord (m pl)
It  carte di bordo (f pl)
Pt  documentação do navio (f)

**ship's register** En
De  Schiffsregister (n)
Es  registro del barco (m)
Fr  certificat d'immatriculation (m)
It  atto di nazionalità (m)
Pt  registo do navio (m)

**shop** n En
De  Laden (m)
Es  tienda (f)
Fr  magasin (m)
It  bottega (f)
Pt  loja (f)

**shopping centre** En
De  Geschäftszentrum (n)
Es  centro de negocios (m)
Fr  centre commercial (m)
It  zona degli acquisti (f)
Pt  centro de comércio (m)

**short-dated** adj En
De  kurzfristig
Es  a corto plazo
Fr  à courte échéance
It  a breve scadenza
Pt  a curto prazo

**short-dated security** En
De  kurzfristiger Effekt (m)
Es  título a corto plazo (m)
Fr  titre à court terme (m)

It  titolo a breve scadenza (m)
Pt  título a curto prazo (m)

**short delivery** En
De  mangelhafte Lieferung (f)
Es  entrega deficiente (f)
Fr  livraison incomplète (f)
It  consegna deficiente (f)
Pt  entrega insuficiente (f)

**shorthand** n En
De  Kurzschrift (f)
Es  taquigrafía (f)
Fr  sténographie (f)
It  stenografia (f)
Pt  estenografia (f)

**shorthand typist** En
De  Stenotypistin (f)
Es  taquimecanógrafa (f)
Fr  sténodactylographe (f)
It  stenodattilografa (f)
Pt  estenodactilógrafa (f)

**short supply** En
De  Knappheit (f)
Es  escasez (f)
Fr  disette (f)
It  scarsezza (f)
Pt  escassez (f)

**short-term** adj En
De  kurzfristig
Es  a corto plazo
Fr  à court terme
It  a breve termine
Pt  a curto prazo

**short-term capital** En
De  kurzfristiges Kapital (n)
Es  capital a corto plazo (m)
Fr  capitaux à court terme (m pl)
It  capitale a breve termine (m)
Pt  capital a curto prazo (m)

**sich decken** De
En  hedge
Es  cubrirse
Fr  arbitrager
It  coprirsi
Pt  cobrir-se

**sich einschiffen** De
En  embark
Es  embarcar
Fr  s'embarquer

It imbarcare
Pt embarcar

**sichere Verwahrung** (f) De
En safe custody
Es custodia (f)
Fr bonne garde (f)
It custodia (f)
Pt custódia segura (f)

**Sicherheit** (f) n De
En security
Es seguridad (f)
Fr sécurité (f)
It sicurezza (f)
Pt segurança (f)

**Sicherheitskoeffizient** (m) n De
En safety factor
Es factor de seguridad (m)
Fr facteur de sécurité (m)
It coefficiente di sicurezza (m)
Pt factor de segurança (m)

**Sichtgelder** (n pl) n De
En money on call
Es dinero a la vista (m)
Fr argent à vue (m)
It denaro a vista (m)
Pt dinheiro à ordem (m)

**Sichttratte** (f) n De
En sight draft
Es letra a la vista (f)
Fr traite à vue (f)
It tratta a vista (f)
Pt letra à vista (f)

**sicurezza** (f) n It
De Sicherheit (f)
En security; safety
Es seguridad (f)
Fr sécurité (f)
Pt segurança (f)

**sicurezza sociale** (f) It
De Sozialversicherung (f)
En social security
Es seguridad social (f)
Fr sécurité sociale (f)
Pt segurança social (f)

**siège** (m) n Fr
De Hauptanstalt (f)
En head office
Es oficina central (f)
It sede; ufficio centrale (f m)

Pt sede; escritório central (f m)

**Siegel** (n) n De
En seal
Es sello (m)
Fr sceau (m)
It sigillo (m)
Pt selo (m)

**sight draft** En
De Sichttratte (f)
Es letra a la vista (f)
Fr traite à vue (f)
It tratta a vista (f)
Pt letra à vista (f)

**sigillo** (m) n It
De Siegel (n)
En seal
Es sello (m)
Fr sceau (m)
Pt selo (m)

**siglare** vb It
De paraphieren
En initial
Es rubricar; poner iniciales a
Fr parapher; viser
Pt rubricar

**signature** n En, Fr (f)
De Unterschrift (f)
Es firma (f)
It firma (f)
Pt assinatura (f)

**silent partner** Am
En sleeping partner
De stiller Gesellschafter (m)
Es socio comanditario (m)
Fr commanditaire (m)
It socio accomandante (m)
Pt sócio comanditário (m)

**símbolo** (m) n Es, Pt
De Symbol (n)
En symbol
Fr symbole (m)
It symbolo (m)
It symbolo (m)

**similicuir** (m) n Fr
De Kunstleder (n)
En imitation leather
Es piel de imitación (f)
It finta pelle (f)
Pt cabedal de imitação (m)

**similor** (m) n Fr
De Kunstgold (n)
En imitation gold
Es oro de imitación (m)
It similoro (m)
Pt ouro de imitação (m)

**similoro** (m) n It
De Kunstgold (n)
En imitation gold
Es oro de imitación (m)
Fr similor (m)
Pt ouro de imitação (m)

**simple interest** En
De einfache Zinsen (m pl)
Es interés simple (m)
Fr intérêts simples (m pl)
It interesse semplice (m)
Pt juro simples (m)

**simulação** (f) n Pt
De Simulation (f)
En simulation
Es simulación (f)
Fr simulation (f)
It simulazione (f)

**simulación** (f) n Es
De Simulation (f)
En simulation
Fr simulation (f)
It simulazione (f)
Pt simulação (f)

**simulation** n En, Fr (f)
De Simulation (f)
Es simulación (f)
It simulazione (f)
Pt simulação (f)

**Simulation** (f) n De
En simulation
Es simulación (f)
Fr simulation (f)
It simulazione (f)
Pt simulação (f)

**simulazione** (f) n It
De Simulation (f)
En simulation
Es simulación (f)
Fr simulation (f)
Pt simulação (f)

**sinal** (depósito) (m) n Pt
De Anzahlung (f)
En deposit

**Es** desembolso inicial *(m)*
**Fr** arrhes *(f pl)*
**It** caparra *(f)*


**sin ceremonia** Es
**De** formlos
**En** informal
**Fr** sans formalités
**It** senza formalità
**Pt** sem formalidade


**sin cupón** Es
**De** ohne Coupon
**En** ex coupon
**Fr** ex coupon
**It** senza cedola
**Pt** talão excluido


**sindacato** *(m)* n It
**De** Gewerkschaft *(f)*
**En** trade union
**Es** sindicato *(m)*
**Fr** syndicat *(m)*
**Pt** sindicato *(m)*


**sindacato dei prezzi** *(m)* It
**De** Preisabsprache *(f)*
**En** price ring
**Es** coalición de vendedores *(f)*
**Fr** coalition de vendeurs *(f)*
**Pt** convénio de preços *(m)*


**sindacato di assicuratori** *(m)* It
**De** Versicherungssyndikat *(n)*
**En** underwriting syndicate (insurance)
**Es** sindicato de seguros *(m)*
**Fr** syndicat d'assureurs *(m)*
**Pt** consórcio de seguradores *(m)*


**sindaco** *(m)* n It
**De** Bücherrevisor *(m)*
**En** auditor
**Es** revisor de conti *(m)*
**Fr** réviseur des comptes *(m)*
**Pt** fiscal de contas *(m)*


**sindicato** *(m)* n Es, Pt
**De** Gewerkschaft; Syndikat *(f n)*
**En** trade union; syndicate
**Fr** syndicat *(m)*
**It** sindacato; consorzio finanziario *(m)*


**sindicato de seguros** *(m)* Es
**De** Versicherungssyndikat *(n)*
**En** underwriting syndicate
**Fr** syndicat d'assureurs *(m)*
**It** sindacato di assicuratori *(m)*
**Pt** consórcio de seguradores *(m)*


**sindico** *(m)* n Es, Pt
**De** Konkursverwalter *(m)*
**En** (official) receiver
**Fr** syndic de faillite *(m)*
**It** curatore *(m)*


**sin finos lucrativos** Es
**De** ohne Gewinnabsicht
**En** nonprofitmaking
**Fr** sans but lucratif
**It** senza scopo di lucro
**Pt** sem fins lucrativos


**single-entry book-keeping** En
**De** einfache Buchführung *(f)*
**Es** contabilidad por partida sencilla *(f)*
**Fr** comptabilité en partie simple *(f)*
**It** contabilità in partita semplice *(f)*
**Pt** contabilização por lançamento simples *(f)*


**single fare** En
**Am** one way fare
**De** einfache Fahrkarte *(f)*
**Es** pasaje de ida *(m)*
**Fr** billet d'aller *(m)*
**It** biglietto d'andata *(m)*
**Pt** passagem de ida *(f)*


**sinking fund** En
**De** Tilgungsfonds *(m)*
**Es** fondo de amortización *(m)*
**Fr** fonds d'amortissement *(m)*
**It** fondo di ammortamento *(m)*
**Pt** fundo de amortização *(m)*


**sin prejuicio** Es
**De** ohne Verbindlichkeit
**En** without prejudice
**Am** not binding
**Fr** sous toutes réserves
**It** senza pregiudizio
**Pt** sem prejuízo


**sin privilegio** Es
**De** ohne Bezugsrechte
**En** ex rights
**Fr** ex-droits
**It** senza diritti
**Pt** privilégios excluidos


**sin recurso** Es
**De** ohne Rückgriff
**En** without recourse
**Fr** sans droit de recours
**It** senza ricorso
**Pt** sem recurso


**sin trabajo** Es
**De** arbeitslos
**En** out of a job
**Fr** en chômage
**It** senza lavoro
**Pt** desempregado


**sistema** *(m)* n Es, It, Pt
**De** System *(n)*
**En** system
**Fr** système *(m)*


**sistema fisico** *(m)* Pt
**De** Maschinenausrüstung *(f)*
**En** (computer) hardware
**Es** mecánica de la máquina *(f)*
**Fr** hardware *(m)*
**It** componenti di macchina calcolatore *(m pl)*


**sistema lógico** *(m)* Pt
**De** Programmausrüstung *(f)*
**En** (computer) software
**Es** conjunto de rutinas; software *(m)*
**Fr** software *(m)*
**It** programmatura; software *(f m)*


**sistema métrico** *(m)* Es, Pt
**De** metrisches System *(n)*
**En** metric system
**Fr** système métrique *(m)*
**It** sistema metrico *(m)*


**sistema metrico** *(m)* It
**De** metrisches System *(n)*
**En** metric system
**Es** sistema métrico *(m)*
**Fr** système métrique *(m)*
**Pt** sistema métrico *(m)*

**sister company** En
  De  Schwestergesellschaft *(f)*
  Es  compañía asociada *(f)*
  Fr  société sœur *(f)*
  It  società sorella *(f)*
  Pt  empresa gémea *(f)*

**sit-down strike** En
  De  Sitzstreik *(m)*
  Es  huelga de brazos caídos *(f)*
  Fr  grève avec occupation des
      lieux *(f)*
  It  sciopero bianco *(m)*
  Pt  greve de braços caídos *(f)*

**situação de regatear** *(f)* Pt
  De  Verhandlungslage *(f)*
  En  bargaining position
  Es  situación de negociar *(f)*
  Fr  situation permettant de
      négocier *(f)*
  It  situazione permettente di
      trattare *(f)*

**situação do mercado** *(f)* Pt
  De  Marktumständen *(m pl)*
  En  state of the market
  Es  condiciones del mercado *(f pl)*
  Fr  état du marché *(m)*
  It  condizioni del mercato *(f pl)*

**situación de negociar** *(f)* Es
  De  Verhandlungslage *(f)*
  En  bargaining position
  Fr  situation permettant de
      négocier *(f)*
  It  situazione permettente di
      trattare *(f)*
  Pt  situação de regatear *(f)*

**situation permettant de négocier** *(f)* Fr
  De  Verhandlungslage *(f)*
  En  bargaining position
  Es  situación de negociar *(f)*
  It  situazione permettente di
      trattare *(f)*
  Pt  situação de regatear *(f)*

**situazione permettente di trattare** *(f)* It
  De  Verhandlungslage *(f)*
  En  bargaining position
  Es  situación de negociar *(f)*

**Sitzstreik** *(m)* n De
  En  sit-down strike
  Es  huelga de brazos caídos *(f)*
  Fr  grève avec occupation des
      lieux *(f)*
  It  sciopero bianco *(m)*
  Pt  greve de braços caídos *(f)*

**Skonto** *(m)* n De
  En  discount
  Es  descuento *(m)*
  Fr  escompte *(m)*
  It  sconto; ribasso *(m)*
  Pt  desconto *(m)*

**sleeping partner** En
  Am  silent partner
  De  stiller Gesellschafter *(m)*
  Es  socio comanditario *(m)*
  Fr  commanditaire *(m)*
  It  socio accomandante *(m)*
  Pt  sócio comanditário *(m)*

**sliding scale** En
  De  gleitende Skala *(f)*
  Es  escala móvil *(f)*
  Fr  échelle mobile *(f)*
  It  scala mobile *(f)*
  Pt  escala móvel *(f)*

**slow down** Am
  En  go-slow strike
  De  Bummelstreik *(m)*
  Es  huelga de producción lenta *(f)*
  Fr  grève perlée *(f)*
  It  sciopero a singhiozzo *(m)*
  Pt  greve de abrandamento do ritmo de produção *(f)*

**slow payer** En
  De  schlechter Zahler *(m)*
  Es  deudor moroso *(m)*
  Fr  mauvais payeur *(m)*
  It  cattivo pagatore *(m)*
  Pt  mau-pagador *(m)*

**small change** En
  De  Kleingeld *(n)*
  Es  moneda suelta *(f)*
  Fr  petite monnaie *(f)*
  It  spiccioli *(m pl)*
  Pt  troco miúdo *(m)*

**smuggle** *vb* En
  De  schmuggeln
  Es  pasar de contrabando
  Fr  faire la contrebande
  It  contrabbandare
  Pt  passar por contrabando

**sob condição** Pt
  De  vorausgesetzt
  En  on condition
  Es  a condición
  Fr  sous réserve
  It  a condizione

**sobornar** *vb* Es, Pt
  De  bestechen
  En  bribe
  Fr  corrompre
  It  corrompere

**soborno** *(m)* n Es, Pt
  De  Bestechung; Bestechungs-
      geld *(f n)*
  En  bribery; bribe
  Fr  corruption; pot-de-vin *(f m)*
  It  corruzione; dono per cor-
      rompere *(f m)*

**sobrante** *(m)* n Es
  De  verfügbarer Saldo *(m)*
  En  balance in hand
  Fr  solde en caisse *(m)*
  It  saldo in cassa *(m)*
  Pt  saldo em poder *(m)*

**sobre** *(m)* n Es
  De  Umschlag *(m)*
  En  envelope
  Fr  enveloppe *(f)*
  It  busta *(f)*
  Pt  envelope *(m)*

**sobre de ventanilla** *(m)* Es
  De  Fensterbriefumschlag *(m)*
  En  window-envelope
  Fr  enveloppe à fenêtre *(f)*
  It  busta con finestra *(f)*
  Pt  envelope de endereço
      exposto *(m)*

**sobreestadía** *(f)* n Es, Pt
  De  Überliegezeit *(f)*
  En  demurrage
  Fr  surestarie *(f)*
  It  controstallia *(f)*

**sobregiro** *(m)* *n* Es
De Überziehung *(f)*
En overdraft
Fr découvert; solde débiteur *(m)*
It scoperto *(m)*
Pt conta a descoberto *(f)*

**sobre partida** Es
De in Konsignation
En on consignment
Fr en consignation
It in conto deposito
Pt à consignação

**sobretasa** *(f)* *n* Es
De Zuschlagssteuer *(f)*
En surtax
Fr surtaxe *(f)*
It sopratassa *(f)*
Pt sobretaxa *(f)*

**sobretaxa** *(f)* *n* Pt
De Zuschlagssteuer *(f)*
En surtax
Es sobretasa *(f)*
Fr surtaxe *(f)*
It sopratassa *(f)*

**social cost** En
De Sozialkosten *(pl)*
Es coste social *(m)*
Fr coût social *(m)*
It costo sociale *(m)*
Pt custo social *(m)*

**social security** En
De Sozialversicherung *(f)*
Es seguridad social *(f)*
Fr sécurité sociale *(f)*
It sicurezza sociale *(f)*
Pt segurança social *(f)*

**Sociedad anónima (SA)** *(f)* Es
De Aktiengesellschaft (AG) *(f)*
En public limited company
Fr Société anonyme (SA) *(f)*
It Società anonima (SA) *(f)*
Pt Sociedade anónima (SA) *(f)*

**sociedad de socorro mutuo** *(f)* Es
De Versicherungsverein auf Gegenseitigkeit *(m)*
En friendly society
Am lodge
Fr société de secours mutuel *(f)*

It società di mutuo soccorso *(f)* .
Pt mutualidade *(f)*

**sociedade** *(f)* *n* Pt
De Gesellschaft *(f)*
En company
Es sociedad *(f)*
Fr société *(f)*
It società *(f)*

**Sociedade anónima (SA)** *(f)* Pt
De Aktiengesellschaft (AG) *(f)*
En limited liability company
Es Sociedad anónima (SA) *(f)*
Fr Société anonyme (SA) *(f)*
It Società anonima (SA) *(f)*

**sociedade em comandita** *(f)* Pt
De Kommanditgesellschaft *(f)*
En limited partnership
Es sociedad en comandita *(f)*
Fr société en commandité *(f)*
It società in accomandita semplice *(f)*

**sociedade em nome colectivo** *(f)* Pt
De offene Handelsgesellschaft (OHG) *(f)*
En partnership
Es sociedad regular colectiva (SRC) *(f)*
Fr société en nom collectif *(f)*
It società *(f)*

**sociedade fantasma** *(f)* Pt
De Schwindelgesellschaft *(f)*
En bogus company
Am phantom operation
Es sociedad fantasma *(f)*
Fr société fantôme *(f)*
It società fasulla *(f)*

**sociedad en comandita** *(f)* Es
De Kommanditgesellschaft *(f)*
En limited partnership
Fr société en commandité *(f)*
It società in accomandita semplice *(f)*
Pt sociedade em comandita *(f)*

**Sociedade por quotas de responsabilidade limitada** *(f)* Pt
De Gesellschaft mit beschränkter Haftung (GmbH) *(f)*

En private limited company
Es Companía privada de responsabilidad limitada *(f)*
Fr Société à responsabilité limitée (SARL) *(f)*
It Società a responsabilità limitata (Sarl) *(f)*

**sociedad extinta** *(f)* Es
De erloschene Gesellschaft *(f)*
En defunct company
Fr société liquidée *(f)*
It società estinta *(f)*
Pt empresa extinta *(f)*

**sociedad fantasma** *(f)* Es
De Schwindelgesellschaft *(f)*
En bogus company
Am phantom operation
Fr société fantôme *(f)*
It società fasulla *(f)*
Pt sociedade fantasma *(f)*

**sociedad regular colectiva (SRC)** *(f)* Es
De Gesellschaft; offene Handelsgesellschaft (OHG) *(f)*
En company; partnership
Fr société; société en nom collectif *(f)*
It società *(f)*
Pt sociedade; sociedade em nome colectivo *(f)*

**società** *(f)* *n* It
De Gesellschaft *(f)*
En company; partnership
Es compañía; sociedad regular colectiva (SRC) *(f)*
Fr société; entreprise *(f)*
Pt sociedade; companhia *(f)*

**società affiliata** *(f)* It
De Schwestergesellschaft *(f)*
En affiliated company
Es compañía afiliada *(f)*
Fr société sœur *(f)*
Pt companhia subsidiária *(f)*

**Società anonima (SA)** *(f)* It
De Aktiengesellschaft (AG) *(f)*
En public limited company
Es Sociedad anónima (SA) *(f)*
Fr Société anonyme (SA) *(f)*
Pt Sociedade anónima (SA) *(f)*

**Società a responsabilità limitata (Sarl)** *(f)* It
De Gesellschaft mit beschränkter Haftung (GmbH) *(f)*
En private limited company
Es Companía privada de responsabilidad limitada *(f)*
Fr Société à responsabilité limitée (SARL) *(f)*
Pt Sociedade por quotas de responsabilidade limitada *(f)*

**società d'imprese** *(f)* It
De Erschliessungsgesellschaft *(f)*
En development company
Es compañía de explotación *(f)*
Fr société d'exploitation *(f)*
Pt empresa de exploração *(f)*

**società di leasing** *(f)* It
De Leasinggesellschaft *(f)*
En leasing company
Es compañía arrendataria *(f)*
Fr société de leasing *(f)*
Pt companhia arrendatária *(f)*

**società di mutuo soccorso** *(f)* It
De Versicherungsverein auf Gegenseitigkeit *(m)*
En friendly society
Am lodge
Es sociedad de socorro mutuo *(f)*
Fr société de secours mutuel *(f)*
Pt mutualidade *(f)*

**società di navigazione** *(f)* It
De Reederei *(f)*
En shipping line
Es compañía navièra *(f)*
Fr compagnie de navigation *(f)*
Pt companhia de navegação *(f)*

**società direttrice** *(f)* It
De Gesellschaft mit Kontrollbefugnis *(f)*
En controlling company
Es compañía directriz *(f)*
Fr société directrice *(f)*
Pt companhia controladora *(f)*

**società di servizi pubblici** *(f)* It
De gemeinnütziges Unternehmen *(n)*
En utility company
Es empresa de servicios públicos *(f)*
Fr entreprise d'utilité publique *(f)*
Pt empresa de utilidade pública *(f)*

**società estinta** *(f)* It
De erloschene Gesellschaft *(f)*
En defunct company
Es sociedad extinta *(f)*
Fr société liquidée *(f)*
Pt empresa extinta *(f)*

**società fasulla** *(f)* It
De Schwindelgesellschaft *(f)*
En bogus company
Am phantom operation
Es sociedad fantasma *(f)*
Fr société fantôme *(f)*
Pt sociedade fantasma *(f)*

**società fiduciaria** *(f)* It
De Treuhandgesellschaft *(f)*
En trust company
Es banco fideicomisario *(m)*
Fr société fiduciaire *(f)*
Pt empresa de investimentos *(f)*

**società finanziaria** *(f)* It
De Finanzierungsgesellschaft *(f)*
En finance company
Es compañía de crédito comercial *(f)*
Fr société de financement *(f)*
Pt empresa financeira *(f)*

**società holding** *(f)* It
De Dachgesellschaft *(f)*
En holding company
Es compañía tenedora *(f)*
Fr société holding *(f)*
Pt companhia proprietária *(f)*

**società in accomandita semplice** *(f)* It
De Kommanditgesellschaft *(f)*
En limited partnership
Es sociedad en comandita *(f)*
Fr société en commandité *(f)*
Pt sociedade em comandita *(f)*

**società in nome collettivo** *(f)* It
De offene Handelsgesellschaft *(f)*
En partnership
Es sociedad *(f)*
Fr société en nom collectif *(f)*
Pt sociedade em nome colectivo *(f)*

**società madre** *(f)* It
De Muttergesellschaft *(f)*
En parent company
Es compañía matriz *(f)*
Fr société mère *(f)*
Pt empresa matriz *(f)*

**società per investimenti** *(f)* It
De Investierungsgesellschaft *(f)*
En investment company
Es compañía inversionista *(f)*
Fr société de placement *(f)*
Pt companhia de investimentos *(f)*

**società quotata in borsa** *(f)* It
De Gesellschaft notiert an der Börse *(f)*
En quoted company
Es compañía cotizada en bolsa *(f)*
Fr société cotée à la Bourse *(f)*
Pt companhia cotizada *(f)*

**società sorella** *(f)* It
De Schwestergesellschaft *(f)*
En sister company
Es compañía asociada *(f)*
Fr société sœur *(f)*
Pt empresa gémea *(f)*

**société** *(f)* n Fr
De Gesellschaft *(f)*
En company
Es compañía; sociedad *(f)*
It società *(f)*
Pt sociedade; companhia *(f)*

**Société anonyme (SA)** *(f)* Fr
De Aktiengesellschaft (AG) *(f)*
En public limited company
Es Sociedad anónima (SA) *(f)*
It Società anonima (SA) *(f)*
Pt Sociedade anónima (SA) *(f)*

**Société à responsabilité limitée (SARL)** *(f)* Fr
De Gesellschaft mit beschränkter Haftung (GmbH) *(f)*
En private limited company
Es Compañía privada de responsabilidad limitada *(f)*
It Società a responsabilità limitata (Sarl) *(f)*
Pt Sociedade por quotas de responsabilidade limitada *(f)*

**société coopérative** *(f)* Fr
De Genossenschaft *(f)*
En cooperative
Es cooperativa *(f)*
It cooperativa *(f)*
Pt cooperativa *(f)*

**société cotée à la Bourse** *(f)* Fr
De Gesellschaft notiert an der Börse *(f)*
En quoted company
Es compañía cotizada en bolsa *(f)*
It società quotata in borsa *(f)*
Pt companhia cotizada *(f)*

**société de financement** *(f)* Fr
De Finanzierungsgesellschaft *(f)*
En finance company
Es compañía de crédito comercial *(f)*
It società finanziaria *(f)*
Pt empresa financeira *(f)*

**société de leasing** *(f)* Fr
De Leasinggesellschaft *(f)*
En leasing company
Es compañía arrendataria *(f)*
It società di leasing *(f)*
Pt companhia arrendatária *(f)*

**société de placement** *(f)* Fr
De Investierungsgesellschaft *(f)*
En investment company
Es compañía inversionista *(f)*
It società per investimenti *(f)*
Pt companhia de investimentos *(f)*

**société de secours mutuel** *(f)* Fr
De Versicherungsverein auf Gegenseitigkeit *(m)*

En friendly society
Am lodge
Es sociedad de socorro mutuo *(f)*
It società di mutuo soccorso *(f)*
Pt mutualidade *(f)*

**société d'exploitation** *(f)* Fr
De Erschliessungsgesellschaft *(f)*
En development company
Es compañía de explotación *(f)*
It società d'imprese *(f)*
Pt empresa de exploração *(f)*

**société directrice** *(f)* Fr
De Gesellschaft mit Kontrollbefugnis *(f)*
En controlling company
Es compañía directriz *(f)*
It società direttrice *(f)*
Pt companhia controladora *(f)*

**société en commandité** *(f)* Fr
De Kommanditgesellschaft *(f)*
En limited partnership
Es sociedad en comandita *(f)*
It società in accomandita semplice *(f)*
Pt sociedade em comandita *(f)*

**société en nom collectif** *(f)* Fr
De offene Handelsgesellschaft (OHG) *(f)*
En partnership
Es sociedad regular colectiva (SRC) *(f)*
It società in nome collettivo *(f)*
Pt sociedade em nome colectivo *(f)*

**société fantôme** *(f)* Fr
De Schwindelgesellschaft *(f)*
En bogus company
Am phantom operation
Es sociedad fantasma *(f)*
It società fasulla *(f)*
Pt sociedade fantasma *(f)*

**société fiduciaire** *(f)* Fr
De Treuhandgesellschaft *(f)*
En trust company
Es banco fideicomisario *(m)*
It società fiduciaria *(f)*

Pt empresa de investimentos *(f)*

**société fiduciaire de placements** *(f)* Fr
De Investment-Trust *(m)*
En investment trust
Es fideicomiso de inversiones *(m)*
It consorzio per investimenti *(m)*
Pt instituição de investimentos *(f)*

**Société Financière Internationale** *(f)* Fr
De Internationale Finanzkorporation *(f)*
En International Finance Corporation
Es Corporación Internacional de Finanzas *(f)*
It Corporazione Finanziaria Internazionale *(f)*
Pt Corporação Internacional de Finanças *(f)*

**société holding** *(f)* Fr
De Dachgesellschaft *(f)*
En holding company
Es compañía tenedora *(f)*
It società holding *(f)*
Pt companhia proprietária *(f)*

**société liquidée** *(f)* Fr
De erloschene Gesellschaft *(f)*
En defunct company
Es sociedad extinta *(f)*
It società estinta *(f)*
Pt empresa extinta *(f)*

**société mère** *(f)* Fr
De Muttergesellschaft *(f)*
En parent company
Es compañía matriz *(f)*
It società madre *(f)*
Pt empresa matriz *(f)*

**société sœur** *(f)* Fr
De Schwestergesellschaft *(f)*
En sister company
Es compañía asociada *(f)*
It società sorella *(f)*
Pt empresa gémea *(f)*

**socio** *(m)* n Es, It
De Teilhaber; Mitglied *(m)*
En partner; member

Fr associé; membre (m)
Pt sócio (m)

**sócio** (m) n Pt
De Teilhaber; Mitglied (m)
En partner; member
Es socio (m)
Fr associé; membre (m)
It socio (m)

**socio accomandante** (m) It
De stiller Gesellschafter (m)
En sleeping partner
Am silent partner
Es socio comanditario (m)
Fr commanditaire (m)
Pt sócio comanditário (m)

**socio activo** (m) Es
De aktiver Teilhaber (m)
En active partner
Fr associé en nom (m)
It socio attivo (m)
Pt sócio activo (m)

**sócio activo** (m) Pt
De aktiver Teilhaber (m)
En active partner
Es socio activo (m)
Fr associé en nom (m)
It socio attivo (m)

**socio attivo** (m) It
De aktiver Teilhaber (m)
En active partner
Es socio activo (m)
Fr associé en nom (m)
Pt sócio activo (m)

**socio comanditario** (m) Es
De stiller Gesellschafter (m)
En sleeping partner
Am silent partner
Fr commanditaire (m)
It socio accomandante (m)
Pt sócio comanditário (m)

**sócio comanditário** (m) Pt
De stiller Gesellschafter (m)
En sleeping partner
Am silent partner
Es socio comanditario (m)
Fr commanditaire (m)
It socio accomandante (m)

**socio fondatore** (m) It
De Gründermitglied (m)
En founder member

Es miembro fundador (m)
Fr membre fondateur (m)
Pt membro fondador (m)

**socio giovane** (m) It
De jüngerer Teilhaber (m)
En junior partner
Es segundo asociado (m)
Fr associé en second (m)
Pt sócio junior (m)

**sócio junior** (m) Pt
De jüngerer Teilhaber (m)
En junior partner
Es segundo asociado (m)
Fr associé en second (m)
It socio giovane (m)

**soddisfazione** (f) n It
De Zufriedenstellung; Begleichung (f)
En satisfaction
Es satisfacción (f)
Fr satisfaction (f)
Pt satisfação (f)

**sofortige Lieferung** (f) De
En prompt delivery
Es entrega inmediata (f)
Fr livraison immédiate (f)
It pronta consegna (f)
Pt entrega imediata (f)

**sofort lieferbare Waren** (f pl) De
En spot goods
Es mercancías prontas (f pl)
Fr marchandises disponibles (f pl)
It merce pronta (f)
Pt mercadorias prontas (f pl)

**Sofortzahlung** (f) n De
En down-payment
Es pago de entrada (m)
Fr acompte (m)
It acconto (m)
Pt pagamento inicial (m)

**soft currency** En
De schwache Währung (f)
Es moneda débil (f)
Fr monnaie faible (f)
It valuta debole (f)
Pt moeda fraca (f)

**soft sell** En
De Verkauf ohne Aufdringen (m)
Es venta sencilla (f)
Fr vente par des moyens discrets (f)
It vendere senza forzare (m)
Pt venda sobtil (f)

**software** (computer) n En
De Programmausrüstung; Software (f)
Es conjunto de rutinas; software (m)
Fr software (m)
It programmatura; software (f m)
Pt sistema lógico; software (m)

**solares** (m pl) n Es
De Bauland (n)
En building land
Fr terrain à bâtir (m)
It terreno edile (m)
Pt terreno para construção (m)

**solcometro** (m) n It
De Log (n)
En (ship's) log
Es diario de navegación (m)
Fr journal de navigation (m)
Pt diário de bordo (m)

**solde** (m) n Fr
De Saldo; Restpartie (m f)
En balance; odd lot
Es saldo; lote suelto (m)
It saldo; partita spaiata (m f)
Pt saldo; lote avulso (m)

**solde à reporter** (m) Fr
De Übertrag (m)
En balance carried forward
Es balance a cuenta nueva (m)
It bilancio riportato (m)
Pt saldo transportado (m)

**solde créditeur** (m) Fr
De Kreditsaldo (m)
En credit balance
Es saldo acreedor (m)
It saldo creditore (m)
Pt saldo credor (m)

**solde débiteur** *(m)* Fr
  De Sollsaldo *(m)*
  En debit balance
  Es saldo en débito *(m)*
  It saldo debitore *(m)*
  Pt saldo devedor *(m)*

**solde de caisse** *(m)* Fr
  De Kassensaldo *(m)*
  En cash balance
  Es resto en efectivo *(m)*
  It residuo di cassa *(m)*
  Pt saldo em dinheiro *(m)*

**solde de dividende** *(m)* Fr
  De Schlussdividende *(f)*
  En final dividend
  Es saldo del dividendo *(m)*
  It saldo del dividendo *(m)*
  Pt dividendo final *(m)*

**solde dû** *(m)* Fr
  De Ausgleichssaldo *(m)*
  En balance due
  Es balance vencido *(m)*
  It saldo dovuto *(m)*
  Pt saldo em dívida *(m)*

**solde en banque** *(m)* Fr
  De Bankguthaben *(n)*
  En bank balance
  Es saldo de banco *(m)*
  It saldo in banca *(m)*
  Pt saldo no banco *(m)*

**solde en caisse** *(m)* Fr
  De verfügbarer Saldo *(m)*
  En balance in hand
  Es sobrante *(m)*
  It saldo in cassa *(m)*
  Pt saldo em poder *(m)*

**solde net** *(m)* Fr
  De Schlussbilanz *(f)*
  En final balance
  Es saldo final *(m)*
  It saldo finale *(m)*
  Pt balanço final *(m)*

**solde nul** *(m)* Fr
  De Nullsaldo *(m)*
  En nil balance
  Am zero balance
  Es saldo nulo *(m)*
  It saldo nullo *(m)*
  Pt saldo nulo *(m)*

**sold out** En
  De ausverkauft
  Es agotado
  Fr tout vendu
  It tutto venduto
  Pt esgotado

**sole agent** En
  De Alleinvertreter *(m)*
  Es agente exclusivo *(m)*
  Fr agent exclusif *(m)*
  It rappresentante esclusivo *(m)*
  Pt agente exclusivo *(m)*

**solicitado** *adj* Es
  De gefragt
  En in demand
  Fr demandé
  It ricercato
  Pt procurado

**solicitud** *(f)* n Es
  De Antrag *(m)*
  En application
  Fr demande *(f)*
  It domanda *(f)*
  Pt requisição *(f)*

**solicitud de inscripción** *(f)* Es
  De Antragsformular *(n)*
  En entry-form
  Fr feuille d'inscription *(f)*
  It bolletta d'entrata *(f)*
  Pt impresso de admissão *(m)*

**solicitud de pedido** *(f)* Es
  De Bestellformular *(n)*
  En order-form
  Fr bulletin de commande *(m)*
  It foglio d'ordinazione *(m)*
  Pt impresso de encomenda *(m)*

**solidalmente e individual-
    mente** It
  De gesamtschuldnerisch
  En jointly and severally
  Es en conjunto y separada-
    mente
  Fr conjointement et solidaire-
    ment
  Pt em conjunto e por vários

**Solidarobligation** *(f)* n De
  En joint and several bond
  Es obligación solidaria e indi-
    visa *(f)*

  Fr obligation conjointe et
    solidaire *(f)*
  It obbligazione solidale *(f)*
  Pt título solidário de diversos
    *(m)*

**Sollsaldo** *(m)* n De
  En debit balance
  Es saldo en débito *(m)*
  Fr solde débiteur *(m)*
  It saldo debitore *(m)*
  Pt saldo devedor *(m)*

**solvable** *adj* Fr
  De zahlungsfähig
  En solvent
  Es solvente
  It solvibile
  Pt solvente

**solvent** *adj* En
  De zahlungsfähig
  Es solvente
  Fr solvable
  It solvibile
  Pt solvente

**solvente** *adj* Es, Pt
  De zahlungsfähig
  En solvent
  Fr solvable
  It solvibile

**solvibile** *adj* It
  De zahlungsfähig
  En solvent
  Es solvente
  Fr solvable
  Pt solvente

**soma** *(f)* n Pt
  De Summe *(f)*
  En sum; amount
  Es suma *(f)*
  Fr somme *(f)*
  It somma *(f)*

**soma por inteiro** *(f)* Pt
  De Pauschalbetrag *(m)*
  En lump sum
  Es suma global *(f)*
  Fr somme globale *(f)*
  It somma globale *(f)*

**somar** *vb* Pt
  De addieren
  En add up
  Es sumar

Fr totaliser; additioner
It sommare

**somma** *(f) n* It
De Summe *(f)*
En sum; amount
Es suma *(f)*
Fr somme *(f)*
Pt soma *(f)*

**somma globale** *(f)* It
De Pauschalbetrag *(m)*
En lump sum
Es suma global *(f)*
Fr somme globale *(f)*
Pt soma por inteiro *(f)*

**sommare** *vb* It
De addieren
En add up
Es sumar
Fr totaliser; additioner
Pt somar

**somme** *(f) n* Fr
De Betrag; Summe *(f)*
En amount; sum
Es suma *(f)*
It ammontare *(m)*
Pt quantia *(f)*

**somme globale** *(f)* Fr
De Pauschalbetrag *(m)*
En lump sum
Es suma global *(f)*
It somma globale *(f)*
Pt soma por inteiro *(f)*

**Sommerferien** *(pl) n* De
En summer holidays
Es vacaciones de verano; ve-
raneo *(f pl; m)*
Fr vacances d'été *(f pl)*
It vacanze estive *(f pl)*
Pt férias de verão *(f pl)*

**Sonderangebot** *(m) n* De
En special offer
Es oferta especial *(f)*
Fr offre spéciale *(f)*
It offerta speciale *(f)*
Pt oferta especial *(f)*

**Sonderemission gegen Be-
zugsrechte** *(f)* De
En rights issue
Es emisión de derechos *(f)*

Fr émission sous droit de
souscription *(f)*
It emissione di diritti *(f)*
Pt emissão de direitos *(f)*

**Sonderentschluss** *(m) n* De
En extraordinary resolution
Es resolución extraordinaria *(f)*
Fr résolution extraordinaire *(f)*
It deliberazione straordinaria
*(f)*
Pt resolução extraordinária *(f)*

**sopra la pari** It
De über Pari
En above par
Es a premio
Fr au-dessus du pair
Pt a prémio

**soprappeso** *(m) n* It
De Übergewicht *(n)*
En excess weight
Es peso excedente *(m)*
Fr excédent de poids *(m)*
Pt excesso de peso *(m)*

**sopratassa** *(f) n* It
De Zuschlagssteuer *(f)*
En surtax
Es sobretasa *(f)*
Fr surtaxe *(f)*
Pt sobretaxa *(f)*

**sopravvenienza passiva** *(f)* It
De Eventualverpflichtung *(f)*
En contingent liability
Es responsabilidad contingen-
te *(f)*
Fr obligation éventuelle *(f)*
Pt responsabilidade conting-
ente *(f)*

**sortie sur imprimante** *(f)* Fr
De Ausgabedruck *(m)*
En computer printout
Es impresión *(f)*
It stampato d'uscita del-
l'elaboratore *(m)*
Pt informe impresso pelo
computador *(m)*

**sottoprodotto** *(m) n* It
De Nebenprodukt *(n)*
En by-product
Es producto derivado *(m)*
Fr sous-produit *(m)*
Pt produto derivado *(m)*

**sottoscrizione** *(f) n* It
De Zeichnung *(f)*
En subscription
Es suscripción *(f)*
Fr souscription *(f)*
Pt subscrição *(f)*

**sottovalutazione** *(f) n* It
De Unterschätzung *(f)*
En under-estimate
Es presupuesto por defecto
*(m)*
Fr sous-estimation *(f)*
Pt avaliação insuficiente *(f)*

**sotto vincolo doganale** It
De unter Zollverschluss
En in bond
Es en aduanas
Fr en entrepôt
Pt à ordem da alfândega

**sottrazione** *(f) n* It
De Subtraktion *(f)*
En subtraction
Es substracción *(f)*
Fr soustraction *(f)*
Pt subtracção *(f)*

**soumission** *(f) n* Fr
De Angebot *(n)*
En bid; tender
Es oferta *(f)*
It offerta *(f)*
Pt proposta *(f)*

**sous-agent** *(m) n* Fr
De Untervertreter *(m)*
En sub-agent
Es sub-agente *(m)*
It sub-agente *(m)*
Pt sub-agente *(m)*

**souscription** *(f) n* Fr
De Zeichnung *(f)*
En subscription
Es suscripción *(f)*
It sottoscrizione *(f)*
Pt subscrição *(f)*

**sous-directeur** *(m) n* Fr
De Unterdirektor *(m)*
En assistant manager
Es sub-director *(m)*
It vice-direttore *(m)*
Pt sub-director *(m)*

**sous-estimation** *(f)* n Fr
De Unterschätzung *(f)*
En under-estimate
Es presupuesto por defecto *(m)*
It sottovalutazione *(f)*
Pt avaliação insuficiente *(f)*

**sous forme de prêt** Fr
De darlehensweise
En on loan
Es en préstamo
It in prestito
Pt por empréstimo

**sous-location** *(m)* n Fr
De Untervermietung *(f)*
En sub-letting
Es sub-alquiler *(m)*
It subaffitto *(m)*
Pt sub-aluguer *(m)*

**sous pli séparé** Fr
De mit getrennter Post
En under separate cover
Es por correo aparte
It in piego a parte
Pt por correio separado

**sous-produit** *(m)* n Fr
De Nebenprodukt *(n)*
En by-product
Es producto derivado *(m)*
It sottoprodotto *(m)*
Pt produto derivado *(m)*

**sous réserve** Fr
De vorausgesetzt
En on condition
Es a condición
It a condizione
Pt sob condição de

**sous toutes réserves** Fr
De ohne Verbindlichkeit
En without prejudice
Am not binding
Es sin prejuicio
It senza pregiudizio
Pt sem prejuízo

**soustraction** *(f)* n Fr
De Subtraktion *(f)*
En subtraction
Es substracción *(f)*
It sottrazione *(f)*
Pt subtracção *(f)*

**soute** *(f)* n Fr
De Bunker *(m)*
En bunker
Es carbonera *(f)*
It carbonile *(m)*
Pt carvoeira *(f)*

**sovraproduzione** *(f)* n It
De Uberproduktion *(f)*
En overproduction
Es exceso de producción *(m)*
Fr surproduction *(f)*
Pt produção excessiva *(f)*

**sovvenzione dello Stato** *(f)* It
De Staatszuschuss *(m)*
En government subsidy
Es subvención del Estado *(f)*
Fr subvention de l'État *(f)*
Pt subvenções do Estado *(f pl)*

**sovvenzioni di capitale** *(f pl)* It
De Kapitalhilfe *(f)*
En capital grants
Es subvención de capital *(f)*
Fr subventions en capital *(f pl)*
Pt subvenções de capital *(f pl)*

**Sozialkosten** *(pl)* n De
En social cost
Es coste social *(m)*
Fr coût social *(m)*
It costo sociale *(m)*
Pt custo social *(m)*

**Sozialleistungen** *(f pl)* n De
En fringe benefits
Es beneficios suplementarios *(m pl)*
Fr avantages accessoires *(m pl)*
It vantaggi accessori *(m pl)*
Pt benefícios extras *(m pl)*

**Sozialversicherung** *(f)* n De
En social security
Es seguridad social *(f)*
Fr sécurité sociale *(f)*
It sicurezza sociale *(f)*
Pt segurança social *(f)*

**Spalte** *(f)* n De
En column
Es columna *(f)*
Fr colonne *(f)*
It colonna *(f)*
Pt coluna *(f)*

**Spanne** *(f)* n De
En margin
Es margen *(m)*
Fr marge *(f)*
It margine *(m)*
Pt margem *(f)*

**Sparkasse** *(f)* n De
En savings bank
Es caja de ahorros *(f)*
Fr caisse d'épargne *(f)*
It cassa di risparmio *(f)*
Pt caixa económica *(f)*

**special damages** En
De Ersatz immateriellen Schadens *(m)*
Es daños especiales *(m pl)*
Fr dommages indirects *(m pl)*
It danni particolari *(m pl)*
Pt indemnização especial *(f)*

**special delivery** Am
En express letter
De Eilbrief *(m)*
Es carta urgente *(f)*
Fr lettre par exprès *(f)*
It lettera espresso *(f)*
Pt carta expresso *(f)*

**specialist** n En
De Sachverständige(r) *(m)*
Es especialista *(m)*
Fr spécialiste; expert *(m)*
It specialista *(m)*
Pt especialista *(m)*

**specialista** *(m)* n It
De Sachverständige(r) *(m)*
En specialist
Es especialista *(m)*
Fr spécialiste; expert *(m)*
Pt especialista *(m)*

**spécialiste** *(m)* n Fr
De Sachverständige(r) *(m)*
En specialist; expert
Es especialista *(m)*
It specialista *(m)*
Pt especialista *(m)*

**special offer** En
De Sonderangebot *(m)*
Es oferta especial *(f)*
Fr offre spéciale *(f)*
It offerta speciale *(f)*
Pt oferta especial *(f)*

**specifica del lavoro** *(f)* It
De Arbeitsaufgabe *(f)*
En job specification
Es especificación del trabajo *(f)*
Fr donnée d'exécution *(f)*
Pt especificação de obra *(f)*

**speculare** *vb* It
De spekulieren
En speculate; job
Es especular
Fr spéculer
Pt especular

**speculate** *vb* En
De spekulieren
Es especular
Fr spéculer
It speculare
Pt especular

**spéculer** *vb* Fr
De spekulieren
En speculate; job
Es especular
It speculare
Pt especular

**spedieren** *vb* De
En dispatch; forward
Es expedir
Fr expédier
It spedire
Pt expedir

**spedire** *vb* It
De expedieren; absenden
En forward; dispatch
Es expedir; remitir
Fr envoyer; expédier
Pt expedir; remeter

**Spediteur** *(m)* n De
En forwarding agent; carrier
Es agente expedidor; transportador *(m)*
Fr transitaire; expéditeur *(m)*
It spedizioniere; vettore *(m)*
Pt agente expedidor; transportador *(m)*

**speditore** *(m)* n It
De Absender *(m)*
En consignor
Es consignador *(m)*
Fr expéditeur *(m)*
Pt consignante *(m)*

**spedizione** *(f)* n It
De Versand; Spedition *(m f)*
En shipment; dispatch
Es despacho; expedición *(m f)*
Fr envoi; expédition *(m f)*
Pt despacho; expedição *(m f)*

**spedizione dall'origine** *(f)* It
De Versendung vom Ursprungsort *(f)*
En shipment from origin
Es envío desde el punto de origen *(m)*
Fr envoi du lieu de départ *(m)*
Pt carregamento desde a origem *(m)*

**spedizioniere** *(m)* n It
De Spediteur *(m)*
En forwarding agent
Es agente expedidor *(m)*
Fr transitaire *(m)*
Pt agente expedidor *(m)*

**Spekulationskapital** *(n)* n De
En risk capital
Es capital de especulación *(m)*
Fr capitaux spéculatifs *(m pl)*
It capitale di speculazione *(m)*
Pt capital de especulação *(m)*

**spekulieren** *vb* De
En speculate; job
Es especular
Fr spéculer
It speculare
Pt especular

**spesa** *(f)* n It
De Ausgaben; Kosten *(f pl; pl)*
En expenditure; expense
Es desembolso; gasto *(m)*
Fr frais *(m pl)*
Pt despesas *(f pl)*

**spesa permessa** *(f)* It
De abziehbare Unkosten *(f pl)*
En allowable expense
Es gastos deducibles *(m pl)*
Fr dépense déductible *(f)*
Pt despesas deduzíveis *(f)*

**spesa supplementare** *(f)* It
De Zuschlagsgebühr *(f)*
En extra charge
Es suplemento *(m)*
Fr supplément *(m)*
Pt encargo suplementar *(m)*

**spese accessorie** *(f pl)* It
De Nebenkosten *(pl)*
En incidental charges
Es cargos imprevistos *(m pl)*
Fr charges annexes *(f pl)*
Pt encargos ocasionais *(m pl)*

**spese assegnate** It
De per Nachnahme
En charges forward
Es costes a reembolso
Fr frais à percevoir à la livraison
Pt entrega contra reembolso

**spese di banca** *(f pl)* It
De Bankspesen *(f pl)*
En bank charges
Es gastos de banco *(m pl)*
Fr frais bancaires *(m pl)*
Pt taxas bancárias *(f pl)*

**spese di gestione** *(f pl)* It
De Betriebsausgaben *(f pl)*
En operating costs
Es costes operacionales *(m pl)*
Fr frais d'exploitation *(m pl)*
Pt custos de exercício *(m pl)*

**spese di magazzinaggio** *(f pl)* It
De Lagergeld *(n)*
En storage charges
Es gastos de almacenaje *(m pl)*
Fr frais de magasinage *(m pl)*
Pt encargos de armazenamento *(m pl)*

**spese di pubblicità** *(f pl)* It
De Werbekosten *(pl)*
En advertising expenditure
Es gastos publicitarios *(m pl)*
Fr dépenses de publicité *(f pl)*
Pt despesa com publicidade *(f)*

**spese di rappresentanza** *(f pl)* It
De Repräsentationskosten *(pl)*
En entertainment expenses
Es gastos de representación *(m pl)*
Fr frais de représentation *(m pl)*
Pt despesas de representação *(f pl)*

**spese dirette** *(f pl)* It
De  Einzelkosten *(pl)*
En  direct expenses
Es  gastos directos *(m pl)*
Fr  frais directs *(m pl)*
Pt  despesas directas *(f pl)*

**spese di riscossione** *(f pl)* It
De  Einzugskosten *(pl)*
En  collection charges
Es  gastos de cobranza *(m pl)*
Fr  frais d'encaissement *(m pl)*
Pt  gastos de cobrança *(m pl)*

**spese di salvataggio** *(f pl)* It
De  Bergegeld *(n)*
En  salvage charges
Es  cargos de salvamento *(m pl)*
Fr  indemnité de sauvetage *(f)*
Pt  encargos de salvamento *(m pl)*

**spese di viaggio** *(f pl)* It
De  Reisekosten *(pl)*
En  travelling expenses
Es  dietas de viajes *(f pl)*
Fr  frais de voyage *(m pl)*
Pt  despesas de viagem *(f pl)*

**spese generali** *(f pl)* It
De  allgemeine Unkosten; Generalunkosten *(pl)*
En  general expenses; overheads
Es  gastos generales *(m pl)*
Fr  frais généraux *(m pl)*
Pt  despesas gerais *(f pl)*

**spese impreviste** *(f pl)* It
De  Nebenkosten *(pl)*
En  incidental expenses
Es  gastos imprevistos *(m pl)*
Fr  faux frais *(m pl)*
Pt  despesas ocasionais *(f pl)*

**spese varie** *(f pl)* It
De  verschiedene Ausgaben *(f pl)*
En  sundry expenses
Es  gastos varios *(m pl)*
Fr  frais divers *(m pl)*
Pt  despesas diversas *(f pl)*

**spiccioli** *(m pl)* It
De  Kleingeld *(n)*
En  small change
Es  moneda suelta *(f)*

Fr  petite monnaie *(f)*
Pt  troco miúdo *(m)*

**Spiegelglas** *(n)* n De
En  plate glass
Es  vidrio plano pulido *(m)*
Fr  verre à glaces; glace de vitrage *(m f)*
It  cristallo *(m)*
Pt  chapa de vidro *(f)*

**spionaggio industriale** *(m)* It
De  Wirtschaftsspionage *(f)*
En  industrial espionage
Es  espionaje industrial *(m)*
Fr  espionage industriel *(m)*
Pt  espionagem industrial *(m)*

**spirale inflationniste** *(f)* Fr
De  Inflationsspirale *(f)*
En  inflationary spiral
Es  espiral de inflación *(f)*
It  inflazione a spirale *(f)*
Pt  espiral inflacionária *(f)*

**Spitzzeit** *(f)* n De
En  peak hours
Es  horas punta *(f pl)*
Fr  heures de pointe *(f pl)*
It  ore di punta *(f pl)*
Pt  horas de ponta *(f pl)*

**split the difference** En
De  einen strittigen Preisunterschied teilen
Es  repartir la diferencia
Fr  partager la différence
It  dividere a metà la differenza
Pt  dividir a meio a diferença

**spot check** En
De  Stichprobe *(f)*
Es  control al azar *(m)*
Fr  contrôle par sondage *(m)*
It  controllo saltuario *(m)*
Pt  controlo de ocasião *(m)*

**spot goods** En
De  sofort lieferbare Waren *(f pl)*
Es  mercancías prontas *(f pl)*
Fr  marchandises disponibles *(f pl)*
It  merce pronta *(f)*
Pt  mercadorias prontas *(f pl)*

**Spottpreis** *(m)* n De
En  bargain price
Es  precio de ocasión *(m)*
Fr  prix de solde *(m)*
It  prezzo d'occasione *(m)*
Pt  preço excepcional *(m)*

**Sprache** *(f)* n De
En  language
Es  lingua *(f)*
Fr  langue *(f)*
It  lingua *(f)*
Pt  língua *(f)*

**Sprachlabor** *(n)* n De
En  language laboratory
Es  laboratorio de idiomas *(m)*
Fr  laboratoire de langues *(m)*
It  laboratorio di linguaggio *(m)*
Pt  laboratório de línguas *(m)*

**Staatsangehörigkeit** *(f)* n De
En  nationality
Es  nacionalidad *(f)*
Fr  nationalité *(f)*
It  nazionalità *(f)*
Pt  nacionalidade *(f)*

**Staatsanleihe** *(f)* n De
En  government loan
Es  empréstito público *(m)*
Fr  emprunt public *(m)*
It  prestito pubblico *(m)*
Pt  empréstimo do governo *(m)*

**Staatsbesitz** *(m)* n De
En  public ownership
Es  propiedad estatal *(f)*
Fr  propriété publique *(f)*
It  proprietà statale *(f)*
Pt  propriedade pública *(f)*

**Staatsobligation** *(f)* n De
En  government bond
Es  obligación del Estado *(f)*
Fr  obligation d'État *(f)*
It  obbligazione dello Stato *(f)*
Pt  obrigação do Tesouro *(f)*

**Staatsschuld** *(f)* n De
En  national debt
Es  deuda pública *(f)*
Fr  dette publique *(f)*
It  debito pubblico *(m)*
Pt  dívida pública *(f)*

**Staatsverwaltung** (f) n De
En administration; government
Es gobierno; ministerio (m)
Fr gouvernement (m)
It governo (m)
Pt governo; administração (m f)

**Staatszuschuss** (m) n De
En government subsidy
Es subvención del Estado (f)
Fr subvention de l'État (f)
It sovvenzione dello Stato (f)
Pt subvenções do Estado (f pl)

**Stadtgas** (n) n De
En town gas
Es gas de ciudad (m)
Fr gaz de ville (m)
It gas di carbon fossile (m)
Pt gás urbano (m)

**staff** (personnel) n En
De Personal (n)
Es personal (m)
Fr personnel (m)
It personale (m)
Pt pessoal (m)

**stagione** (f) n It
De Jahreszeit (f)
En season
Es estación (f)
Fr saison (f)
Pt estação (f)

**stallie** (f pl) n It
De Liegezeit (f)
En lay days
Es estadía (f)
Fr staries (f pl)
Pt estadía (f)

**Stammaktie** (f) n De
En ordinary share
Es acción ordinaria (f)
Fr action ordinaire (f)
It azione ordinaria (f)
Pt acção ordinária (f)

**stamp** n En
De Marke; Stempel (f m)
Es sello; estampilla (m f)
Fr timbre; tampon (m)
It francobollo; stampiglia (m f)
Pt selo; carimbo (m)

**stampato d'uscita dell'elaboratore** (m) It
De Ausgabedruck (m)
En computer printout
Es impresión (f)
Fr sortie sur imprimante (f)
Pt informe impresso pelo computador (m)

**stamp duty** En
De Stempelgebühr (f)
Es impuesto del timbre (m)
Fr droit de timbre (m)
It tassa di bollo (f)
Pt imposto de selo (m)

**stampiglia** (f) n It
De Stempel (m)
En stamp
Es estampilla (f)
Fr tampon; timbre (m)
Pt carimbo (m)

**standard** n En
De Standard; Norm (m f)
Es norma; standard (f m)
Fr norme; étalon (f m)
It norma (f)
Pt padrão; norma (m f)

**Standard** (m) n De
En standard
Es norma; standard (f m)
Fr norme; étalon (f m)
It norma (f)
Pt padrão; norma (m f)

**Standardbedingungen** (f pl) n De
En standard conditions
Es condiciones normales (f pl)
Fr conditions courantes (f pl)
It condizioni normali (f pl)
Pt condições normais (f pl)

**standard conditions** En
De Standardbedingungen (f pl)
Es condiciones normales (f pl)
Fr conditions courantes (f pl)
It condizioni normali (f pl)
Pt condições normais (f pl)

**standard deviation** En
De normale Abweichung (f)
Es desviación normal (f)
Fr déviation normale (f)
It deviazione normale (f)
Pt desvio normal (m)

**standard gauge** En
De Normalmass (n)
Es calibre patrón (m)
Fr écartement normal (m)
It scartamento normale (m)
Pt calibre padrão (m)

**standard of living** En
De Lebenshaltung (f)
Es nivel de vida (m)
Fr niveau de vie (m)
It tenore di vita (m)
Pt nível de vida (m)

**standard time** En
De Normalzeit (f)
Es hora oficial (f)
Fr heure légale (f)
It ora legale (f)
Pt hora normal (f)

**stand-by agreement** En
De Notvereinbarung (f)
Es contrato de reserva (m)
Fr accord en réserve (m)
It accordo di riserva (m)
Pt acordo a postos (m)

**stanza di compensazione** (f) It
De Verrechnungsstelle (f)
En clearing house
Es cámara de compensaciones (f)
Fr chambre de compensation (f)
Pt câmara de compensações e rateio (f)

**stanziamento** (m) n It
De Zuführung (f)
En appropriation
Es apropiación (f)
Fr affectation (f)
Pt apropriação (f)

**Stapelkostenberechnung** (f) n De
En batch costing
Es fijación de precio por lotes (f)
Fr évaluation du coût des lots (f)
It valutazione del costo per partita (f)
Pt fixação do preço por lote (f)

**staries** *(f pl) n* Fr
De Liegezeit *(f)*
En lay days
Es estadía *(f)*
It stallie *(f pl)*
Pt estadía *(f)*

**state employment agency** Am
En employment exchange
De Arbeitsnachweisstelle *(f)*
Es bolsa de trabajo *(f)*
Fr bureau de placement *(m)*
It ufficio di collocamento *(m)*
Pt centro de serviços de emprego *(m)*

**statement of account** En
De Kontoauszug *(m)*
Es extracto de cuenta *(m)*
Fr relevé de compte *(m)*
It estratto conto *(m)*
Pt extracto de conta *(m)*

**state of the market** En
De Marktumständen *(m pl)*
Es condiciones del mercado *(f pl)*
Fr état du marché *(m)*
It condizioni del mercato *(f pl)*
Pt situação do mercado *(f)*

**statistica** *(f) n* It
De Statistik *(f)*
En statistics
Es estadística *(f)*
Fr statistique *(f)*
Pt estatística *(f)*

**statistics** *n* En
De Statistik *(f)*
Es estadística *(f)*
Fr statistique *(f)*
It statistica *(f)*
Pt estatística *(f)*

**Statistik** *(f) n* De
En statistics
Es estadística *(f)*
Fr statistique *(f)*
It statistica *(f)*
Pt estatística *(f)*

**statistique** *(f) n* Fr
De Statistik *(f)*
En statistics
Es estadística *(f)*

It statistica *(f)*
Pt estatística *(f)*

**statuario** *adj* It
De gesetzlich
En statutory
Es estatutario
Fr statutaire
Pt estatutário

**statut** *(m) n* Fr
De Gesetz *(n)*
En statute
Es estatuto *(m)*
It statuto *(m)*
Pt estatuto *(m)*

**statutaire** *adj* Fr
De gesetzlich
En statutory
Es estatutario
It statuario
Pt estatutário

**statute** *n* En
De Gesetz *(n)*
Es estatuto *(m)*
Fr statut *(m)*
It statuto *(m)*
Pt estatuto *(m)*

**Statuten** *(f pl) n* De
En Memorandum and Articles of Association
Am articles of incorporation
Es estatutos; carta orgánica *(m pl; f)*
Fr statuts; acte constitutif *(m pl; m)*
It atto costitutivo e statuto sociale *(m)*
Pt estatuto de associação *(m)*

**statuto** *(m) n* It
De Gesetz *(n)*
En statute
Es estatuto *(m)*
Fr statut *(m)*
Pt estatuto *(m)*

**statutory** *adj* En
De gesetzlich
Es estatutario
Fr statutaire
It statuario
Pt estatutário

**statutory meeting** En
De ordentliche Versammlung *(f)*
Es asamblea general *(f)*
Fr assemblée ordinaire *(f)*
It assemblea generale *(f)*
Pt assembleia estatutária *(f)*

**statuto sociale** *(m)* It
De Gesellschaftsvertrag *(m)*
En articles of association
Am articles of incorporation
Es artículos de asociación *(m pl)*
Fr contrat de société *(m)*
Pt escritura de sociedade *(f)*

**statuts** *(m pl) n* Fr
De Statuten *(f pl)*
En Memorandum and Articles of Association
Am articles of incorporation
Es estatutos; carta orgánica *(m pl; f)*
It atto costitutivo e statuto sociale *(m)*
Pt estatuto de associação *(m)*

**steamer** *n* En
De Dampfer *(m)*
Es buque de vapor *(m)*
Fr bateau à vapeur *(m)*
It vapore *(m)*
Pt vapor *(m)*

**steigen** *vb* De
En increase
Es aumentar; alzar
Fr augmenter; hausser
It aumentare; crescere
Pt aumentar

**Steigen** *(n) n* De
En increase; rise
Es incremento; aumento *(m)*
Fr hausse; augmentation *(f)*
It incremento; crescita *(m f)*
Pt aumento; incremento *(m)*

**steigend** *adj* De
En bullish
Es alcista
Fr haussier
It rialzista
Pt altista

**Stellenüberblick** *(m) n* De
En field study
Es estudio sobre el terreno *(m)*
Fr enquête sur les lieux *(f)*
It studio sul terreno *(m)*
Pt estudo de campo *(m)*

**Stellenvermittlungsbüro** *(n) n* De
En employment agency
Es agencia de colocaciones *(f)*
Fr agence de placement *(f)*
It agenzia di collocamento *(f)*
Pt agência de emprego *(f)*

**Stellgeschäft** *(n) n* De
En double option
Es opción doble *(f)*
Fr double option *(f)*
It opzione doppia *(f)*
Pt opção dupla *(f)*

**Stellung** *(f) n* De
En job; post
Es empleo *(m)*
Fr emploi *(m)*
It impiego *(m)*
Pt emprego *(m)*

**stellvertretender Vorsitzende(r)** *(m)* De
En vice-chairman
Es vice-presidente *(m)*
Fr vice-président *(m)*
It vicepresidente *(m)*
Pt vice-presidente *(m)*

**Stellvertreter** *(m) n* De
En proxy
Es apoderado *(m)*
Fr mandataire *(m)*
It procuratore *(m)*
Pt procurador *(m)*

**Stellvertretung** *(f) n* De
En proxy
Es poder procuración *(m)*
Fr procuration *(f)*
It procura *(f)*
Pt procuração *(f)*

**Stempel** *(m) n* De
En stamp
Es sello; estampilla *(m f)*
Fr tampon *(m)*
It stampo *(m)*
Pt carimbo *(m)*

**Stempelgebühr** *(f) n* De
En stamp duty
Es impuesto del timbre *(m)*
Fr droit de timbre *(m)*
It tassa di bollo *(f)*
Pt imposto de selo *(m)*

**sténodactylographe** *(f) n* Fr
De Stenotypistin *(f)*
En shorthand typist
Es taquimecanógrafa *(f)*
It stenodattilografa *(f)*
Pt estenodactilógrafa *(f)*

**stenodattilografa** *(f) n* It
De Stenotypistin *(f)*
En shorthand typist
Es taquimecanógrafa *(f)*
Fr sténodactylographe *(f)*
Pt estenodactilógrafa *(f)*

**stenografia** *(f) n* It
De Kurzschrift *(f)*
En shorthand
Es taquigrafía *(f)*
Fr sténographie *(f)*
Pt estenografia *(f)*

**sténographie** *(f) n* Fr
De Kurzschrift *(f)*
En shorthand
Es taquigrafía *(f)*
It stenografia *(f)*
Pt estenografia *(f)*

**Stenotypistin** *(f) n* De
En shorthand typist
Es taquimecanógrafa *(f)*
Fr sténodactylographe *(f)*
It stenodattilografa *(f)*
Pt estenodactilógrafa *(f)*

**Sterblichkeitsziffer** *(f) n* De
En death rate
Es mortalidad *(f)*
Fr taux de mortalité *(m)*
It tasso di mortalità *(m)*
Pt taxa de mortalidade *(f)*

**sterlina verde** *(f)* It
De grünes Pfund *(n)*
En green pound
Es esterlina verde *(f)*
Fr livre sterling verte *(f)*
Pt libra esterlina verde *(f)*

**sterling area** En
De Sterlinggebiet *(n)*
Es zona de la esterlina *(f)*
Fr zone sterling *(f)*
It zona della sterlina *(f)*
Pt zona esterlina *(f)*

**Sterlinggebiet** *(n) n* De
En sterling area
Es zona de la esterlina *(f)*
Fr zone sterling *(f)*
It zona della sterlina *(f)*
Pt zona esterlina *(f)*

**Steuer** *(f) n* De
En tax
Es impuesto *(m)*
Fr impôt *(m)*
It imposta *(f)*
Pt imposto *(m)*

**steuerabsetzbar** *adj* De
En tax deductible
Es deducible de impuestos
Fr déductible à l'impôt
It deducibile da tassa
Pt ilíquido de impostos

**Steuerbefreiung** *(f) n* De
En tax relief
Es desgravación *(f)*
Fr dégrèvement *(m)*
It sgravio fiscale *(m)*
Pt isenção de imposto *(f)*

**Steuerbegünstigung auf Anlagen** *(f)* De
En capital allowances
Es deducciones fiscales sobre inversiones *(f pl)*
Fr déductions fiscales sur les investissements *(f pl)*
It deduzioni fiscali sugli investimenti *(f pl)*
Pt concessões sobre capital *(f pl)*

**Steuereinnehmer** *(m) n* De
En tax collector
Es recaudador de impuestos *(m)*
Fr percepteur des impôts *(m)*
It esattore delle imposte *(m)*
Pt cobrador de impostos *(m)*

**Steuererklärung** *(f) n* De
En tax return
Es declaración de ingresos *(f)*

Fr déclaration de l'impôt *(f)*
It dichiarazione fiscale *(f)*
Pt declaração para efeitos de tributação *(f)*

**steuerfrei** *adj* De
En tax-free
Es exento de impuestos
Fr exempt d'impôts
It esente di tassa
Pt isento de impostos

**steuerfreies Einkommen** *(n)* De
En nontaxable income
Es ingresos no imponibles *(m pl)*
Fr revenu non imposable *(m)*
It reddito non tassabile *(m)*
Pt receita não tributável *(f)*

**Steuerhinterziehung** *(f)* n De
En evasion of tax
Es evasión de pago de impuestos *(f)*
Fr fraude fiscale *(f)*
It evasione d'imposta *(f)*
Pt fuga a impostos *(f)*

**Steuerjahr** *(n)* n De
En tax year
Es año fiscal *(m)*
Fr exercice fiscal *(m)*
It anno fiscale *(m)*
Pt ano fiscal *(m)*

**Steuerparadies** *(n)* n De
En tax haven
Es refugio fiscal *(m)*
Fr refuge fiscal *(m)*
It rifugio fiscale *(m)*
Pt refúgio fiscal *(m)*

**Steuerverlust** *(m)* n De
En tax loss
Es pérdida fiscal *(f)*
Fr perte fiscale *(f)*
It perdita a scopi fiscali *(f)*
Pt perda em impostos *(f)*

**Steuerzahler** *(m)* n De
En tax payer
Es contribuyente *(m)*
Fr contribuable *(m)*
It contribuente fiscale *(m)*
Pt contribuinte *(m)*

**Steureinnehmer** *(m)* n De
En tax-collector
Es recaudador de impuestos *(m)*
Fr percepteur *(m)*
It esattore delle imposte *(m)*
Pt cobrador de impostos *(m)*

**Stichprobe** *(f)* n De
En spot check
Es control al azar *(m)*
Fr contrôle par sondage *(m)*
It controllo saltuario *(m)*
Pt controlo de ocasião *(m)*

**stille Reserve** *(f)* De
En hidden reserve
Es reserva latente *(f)*
Fr réserve cachée *(f)*
It riserva occulta *(f)*
Pt reserva oculta *(f)*

**stiller Gesellschafter** *(m)* De
En sleeping partner
Am silent partner
Es socio comanditario *(m)*
Fr commanditaire *(m)*
It socio accomandante *(m)*
Pt sócio comanditário *(m)*

**stillschweigend** *adj* De
En implicit
Es implícito
Fr implicite
It implicito
Pt implícito

**stillschweigende Bedingungen** *(f pl)* De
En implied terms
Es condiciones implícitas *(f pl)*
Fr conditions implicites *(f pl)*
It condizioni implicite *(f pl)*
Pt condições implícitas *(f pl)*

**stillschweigendes Übereinkommen** *(n)* De
En tacit agreement
Es acuerdo tácito *(m)*
Fr convention tacite *(f)*
It accordo tacito *(m)*
Pt acordo tácito *(m)*

**stima del credito** *(f)* It
De Kreditwürdigkeit *(f)*
En credit rating
Es límite de crédito *(m)*

Fr degré de solvabilité *(m)*
Pt nível de crédito *(m)*

**stimare** *vb* It
De einschätzen
En estimate
Es estimar
Fr estimer
Pt avaliar

**stimmberechtigte Aktien** *(f pl)* De
En voting shares
Es acciones con derecho de voto *(f pl)*
Fr actions avec droit de vote *(f pl)*
It azioni con diritto a voto *(f pl)*
Pt acçoes com direito a voto *(f pl)*

**stimmen** *vb* De
En vote
Es votar
Fr voter
It votare
Pt votar

**stimulant de l'investissement** *(m)* Fr
De Investierungsanreiz *(m)*
En investment incentive
Es incentivo de inversión *(m)*
It incentivo d'investimento *(m)*
Pt incentivo de investimento *(m)*

**stipendiato** *(m)* n It
De Angestellte(r) *(m)*
En salaried employee
Es empleado a sueldo *(m)*
Fr appointé *(m)*
Pt assalariado *(m)*

**stipendio** *(m)* n It
De Gehalt *(n)*
En salary
Es sueldo *(m)*
Fr traitement *(m)*
Pt ordenado *(m)*

**stiva** *(f)* n It
De Laderaum *(m)*
En (ship's) hold
Es bodega *(f)*

Fr cale (f)
Pt porão (m)

**stivaggio** (m) n It
De Verstauung (f)
En stowage
Es estiba (f)
Fr arrimage (m)
Pt estiva (f)

**stivare** vb It
De verstauen
En stow
Es estibar
Fr arrimer
Pt estivar

**stock** (securities) n En
De Wertpapiere (n pl)
Es títulos; valores (m pl)
Fr titres; valeurs (m pl; f pl)
It titoli; valori (m pl)
Pt títulos; valores (m pl)

**stock** (of goods) n En
De Vorrat (m)
Es stock; existencias (m; f pl)
Fr stock; marchandises (m; f pl)
It stock; scorta (m f)
Pt existências (f pl)

**stock** (m) n Es, Fr, It
De Vorrat (m)
En stock
Pt existências (f pl)

**stock agotado** Es
De ausverkauft
En out of stock
Fr tout vendu
It esaurito
Pt esgotado

**stockbroker** n En
De Börsenmakler (m)
Es corredor de bolsa (m)
Fr courtier en bourse (m)
It agente di borsa (m)
Pt corretor da bolsa (m)

**stock capital** Am
En share capital
De Aktienkapital (n)
Es capital en acciones (m)
Fr capital social (m)
It capitale azionario (m)
Pt capital em acções (m)

**stock certificate** Am
En ordinary share certificate
De Aktie (f)
Es certificado de acción (m)
Fr certificat d'action (m)
It certificato azionario (m)
Pt título de acções ordinárias (m)

**stock control** En
De Lagerverwaltung (f)
Es fiscalización de las existencias (f)
Fr contrôle des stocks (m)
It controllo delle scorte (m)
Pt controlo de existências (m)

**stock dividend** Am
En bonus shares
De Gratisaktien (f pl)
Es acciones dadas como primas (f pl)
Fr actions d'attribution (f pl)
It azioni di godimento (f pl)
Pt acções de prémio (f pl)

**stocker** vb Fr
De Vorratslager anlegen
En stockpile
Es acumular existencias
It ammassare
Pt acumular existências

**stock exchange** En
De Börse (f)
Es bolsa (f)
Fr bourse (f)
It borsa (f)
Pt bolsa (f)

**stock-exchange quotation** En
De Börsenkurs (m)
Es curso de bolsa (m)
Fr cours de bourse (m)
It quotation di borsa (f)
Pt cotação da bolsa (f)

**stockholder** n En
De Aktionär (m)
Es accionista (m)
Fr actionnaire (m)
It azionista (m)
Pt accionista (m)

**stock in hand** En
De Vorrat auf Lager (m)
Es mercancías en almacén (f pl)

Fr marchandises en magasin (f pl)
It merce in magazzino (f)
Pt mercadorias em existência (f)

**stockjobber** n En
De Börsenhändler (m)
Es agiotista (m)
Fr marchand de titres (m)
It aggiotatore (m)
Pt agiota (m)

**stock market** Am
En share market
De Aktienmarkt (m)
Es mercado de valores (m)
Fr marché des valeurs (m)
It mercato azionario (m)
Pt mercado de acções (m)

**stockpile** vb En
De Vorratslager anlegen
Es acumular existencias
Fr stocker
It ammassare
Pt acumular existências

**stocks de régularisation** (m pl) Fr
De Buffer-stocks (m pl)
En buffer stocks
Es existencias de regularización (f pl)
It scorte di equilibrio (f pl)
Pt existências de regularização (f pl)

**stocktaking** n En
De Bestandaufnahme (f)
Es inventario; balance (m)
Fr levée d'inventaire (f)
It compilazione dell'inventario (f)
Pt inventário de existências (m)

**Stoff** (m) n De
En material; cloth
Es tejido (m)
Fr étoffe; tissu (f m)
It stoffa; tessuto (f m)
Pt tecido (m)

**stoffa** (f) n It
De Stoff (m)
En material; cloth
Es tejido (m)

Fr  étoffe; tissu *(f m)*
Pt  tecido *(m)*

**stop a cheque** En
Am  stop a check
De  einen Scheck sperren
Es  suspender el pago de un
    cheque
Fr  bloquer un chèque
It  fermare un assegno
Pt  suspender o pagamento de
    um cheque

**stop-gap** *n* En
De  Überbrückung *(f)*
Es  recurso provisional *(m)*
Fr  bouche-trou *(m)*
It  provvedimento temporaneo
    *(m)*
Pt  tapa-buracos *(m)*

**storage** *n* En
De  Lagerung *(f)*
Es  almacenamiento *(m)*
Fr  emmagasinage *(m)*
It  maggazzinaggio *(m)*
Pt  armazenamento *(m)*

**storage charges** En
De  Lagergeld *(n)*
Es  gastos de almacenaje *(m
    pl)*
Fr  frais de magasinage *(m pl)*
It  spese di magazzinaggio *(f
    pl)*
Pt  encargos de armazena-
    mento *(m pl)*

**store** *vb* En
De  lagern
Es  almacenar
Fr  emmagasiner
It  immagazzinare
Pt  armazenar

**store** *n* En
De  Lager *(n)*
Es  almacén *(m)*
Fr  màgasin *(m)*
It  magazzino *(m)*
Pt  armazém *(m)*

**storm** *n* En
De  Sturm *(m)*
Es  tormenta *(f)*
Fr  tempête *(f)*
It  tempesta *(f)*
Pt  temporal *(m)*

**Stoss** *(m)* *n* De
En  batch
Es  lote *(m)*
Fr  lot *(m)*
It  lotto *(m)*
Pt  lote *(m)*

**stow** *vb* En
De  verstauen
Es  estibar
Fr  arrimer
It  stivare
Pt  estivar

**stowage** *n* En
De  Verstauung *(f)*
Es  estiba *(f)*
Fr  arrimage *(m)*
It  stivaggio *(m)*
Pt  estiva *(f)*

**stowage plan** En
De  Ladeplan *(m)*
Es  plan de estiba *(m)*
Fr  plan d´arrimage *(m)*
It  piano di stivaggio *(m)*
Pt  plano de estiva *(m)*

**Strafe** *(f)* *n* De
En  penalty
Es  multa *(f)*
Fr  pénalité *(f)*
It  penalità *(f)*
Pt  penalidade *(f)*

**Strafklausel** *(f)* *n* De
En  penalty clause
Es  cláusula de multa *(f)*
Fr  clause pénale *(f)*
It  clausola penale *(f)*
Pt  cláusula de penalidade *(f)*

**straniero** *adj* It
De  ausländisch; fremd
En  foreign; alien
Es  extranjero
Fr  étranger
Pt  estrangeiro

**straniero** *(m)* *n* It
De  Ausländer *(m)*
En  foreigner
Es  extranjero *(m)*
Fr  étranger *(m)*
Pt  estrangeiro *(m)*

**streichen** *vb* De
En  delete
Es  tachar; anular
Fr  rayer; effacer
It  cancellare
Pt  cortar; riscar

**Streik** *(m)* *n* De
En  strike
Es  huelga *(f)*
Fr  grève *(f)*
It  sciopero *(m)*
Pt  greve *(f)*

**(zum) Streik auffordern** De
En  call a strike
Es  declararse en huelga
Fr  ordonner une grève
It  proclamare uno sciopero
Pt  declarar greve

**streiken** *vb* De
En  strike
Es  declarar huelga
Fr  faire la grève
It  scioperare
Pt  fazer greve

**Streikende(r)** *(m)* *n* De
En  striker
Es  huelguista *(m)*
Fr  gréviste *(m)*
It  scioperante *(m)*
Pt  grevista *(m)*

**Streit** *(m)* *n* De
En  dispute
Es  disputa *(f)*
Fr  contestation *(f)*
It  disputa *(f)*
Pt  disputa *(f)*

**Streitkräfte** *(f pl)* *n* De
En  armed forces
Es  fuerzas armadas *(f pl)*
Fr  forces armées *(f pl)*
It  forze armate *(f pl)*
Pt  forças armadas *(f pl)*

**Strickwaren** *(f pl)* *n* De
En  knitted goods
Es  géneros de punto *(m pl)*
Fr  bonneterie *(f)*
It  maglieria *(f)*
Pt  artigos de malha de lã *(m
    pl)*

**strike** n En
De Streik (m)
Es huelga (f)
Fr grève (f)
It sciopero (m)
Pt greve (f)

**strike** vb En
De streiken
Es declarar huelga
Fr faire la grève
It scioperare
Pt fazer greve

**striker** n En
De Streikende(r) (m)
Es huelguista (m)
Fr gréviste (m)
It scioperante (m)
Pt grevista (m)

**Strom** (m) n De
En flow
Es flujo (m)
Fr flux (m)
It flusso (m)
Pt circulação (f)

**strozzatura** (f) n It
De Engpass (m)
En bottle-neck
Es embotellamiento (m)
Fr goulot d'étranglement (m)
Pt engarrafamento (m)

**strumento** (m) n It
De Instrument (n)
En instrument
Es instrumento (m)
Fr instrument (m)
Pt instrumento (m)

**strumento d'analisi** (m) It
De Analysenwerkzeug (n)
En analytical tool
Es instrumento de análisis (m)
Fr instrument d'analyse (m)
Pt instrumento de análise (m)

**stub** n Am
En counterfoil
De Talon (m)
Es talón (m)
Fr talon (m)
It matrice (f)
Pt talão (m)

**Stückelung** (f) n De
En denomination
Es valor (m)
Fr valeur nominale (f)
It taglio (m)
Pt valor nominal (m)

**studi e sviluppi** It
De Zweckforschung; Entwicklung (f)
En research and development (R & D)
Es investigación y desarrollo
Fr recherche industrielle (f)
Pt investigação e desenvolvimento

**studio dei tempi e dei movimenti** (m) It
De Arbeitszeit- und Ablaufstudie (f)
En time and motion study
Es estudio de tiempo y progreso (m)
Fr étude du temps et mouvements (f)
Pt análise do tempo e progresso (f)

**studio delle possibilità** (m) It
De Durchführbarkeitanalyse (f)
En feasibility study
Es estudio de viabilidad (m)
Fr étude probatoire (f)
Pt estudo de viabilidade (m)

**studio di lavoro** (m) It
De Arbeitsstudium (n)
En work study
Es estudio del trabajo (m)
Fr étude du travail (f)
Pt estudo sobre trabalho (m)

**studio sul terreno** (m) It
De Stellenüberblick (m)
En field study
Es estudio sobre el terreno (m)
Fr enquête sur les lieux (f)
Pt estudo de campo (m)

**Stunde** (f) n De
En hour
Es hora (f)
Fr heure (f)
It ora (f)
Pt hora (f)

**Sturm** (m) n De
En storm
Es tormenta (f)
Fr tempête (f)
It tempesta (f)
Pt temporal (m)

**Sturz** (m) n De
En fall; drop
Es baja; caida (f)
Fr baisse; chute (f)
It caduta; ribasso (f; m)
Pt baixa; gueda (f)

**stürzen** vb De
En fall; drop
Es caer; bajar
Fr baisser; tomber
It cadere; ribassare
Pt cair; baixar

**subaffitto** (m) n It
De Untervermietung (f)
En sub-letting
Es sub-alquiler (m)
Fr sous-location (m)
Pt sub-aluguer (m)

**sub-agent** n En
De Untervertreter (m)
Es sub-agente (m)
Fr sous-agent (m)
It sub-agente (m)
Pt sub-agente (m)

**sub-agente** (m) n Es, It, Pt
De Untervertreter (m)
En sub-agent
Fr sous-agent (m)

**sub-alquiler** (m) n Es
De Untervermietung (f)
En sub-letting
Fr sous-location (m)
It subaffitto (m)
Pt sub-aluguer (m)

**subalterne** (m) n Fr
De Untergebene(r) (m)
En subordinate
Es subalterno (m)
It subalterno (m)
Pt subordinado (m)

**subalterno** (m) n Es, It
De Untergebene(r) (m)
En subordinate

Fr  subalterne *(m)*
Pt  subordinado *(m)*

**sub-aluguer** *(m) n* Pt
De  Untervermietung *(f)*
En  sub-letting
Es  sub-alquiler *(m)*
Fr  sous-location *(m)*
It  subaffitto *(m)*

**subasta** *(f) n* Es
De  Versteigerung *(f)*
En  auction
Fr  vente aux enchères *(f)*
It  asta *(f)*
Pt  leilão *(m)*

**subastador** *(m) n* Es
De  Versteigerer *(m)*
En  auctioneer
Fr  commissaire-priseur *(m)*
It  venditore all'asta *(m)*
Pt  leiloeiro *(m)*

**sub-director** *(m) n* Es, Pt
De  Unterdirektor *(m)*
En  assistant manager
Fr  sous-directeur *(m)*
It  vice-direttore *(m)*

**subida** (en valor) *(f) n* Es
De  Wertsteigerung *(f)*
En  appreciation
Fr  appréciation *(f)*
It  aumento *(m)*
Pt  aumento *(m)*

**subir** (en valor) *vb* Es
De  im Wert steigen
En  appreciate
Fr  apprécier
It  aumentare
Pt  aumentar

**sub-letting** *n* En
De  Untervermietung *(f)*
Es  sub-alquiler *(m)*
Fr  sous-location *(m)*
It  subaffitto *(m)*
Pt  sub-aluguer *(m)*

**subordinado** *(m) n* Pt
De  Untergebene(r) *(m)*
En  subordinate
Es  subalterno *(m)*
Fr  subalterne *(m)*
It  subalterno *(m)*

**subordinate** *n* En
De  Untergebene(r) *(m)*
Es  subalterno *(m)*
Fr  subalterne *(m)*
It  subalterno *(m)*
Pt  subordinado *(m)*

**sub-rogação** *(f) n* Pt
De  Ersetzung *(f)*
En  subrogation
Es  subrogación *(f)*
Fr  subrogation *(f)*
It  surrogazione *(f)*

**subrogación** *(f) n* Es
De  Ersetzung *(f)*
En  subrogation
Fr  subrogation *(f)*
It  surrogazione *(f)*
Pt  sub-rogação *(f)*

**subrogation** *n* En, Fr *(f)*
De  Ersetzung *(f)*
Es  subrogación *(f)*
It  surrogazione *(f)*
Pt  sub-rogação *(f)*

**subscribed capital** En
De  gezeichnetes Kapital *(n)*
Es  capital subscrito *(m)*
Fr  capital souscrit *(m)*
It  capitale sottoscritto *(m)*
Pt  capital subscrito *(m)*

**subscrição** *(f) n* Pt
De  Zeichnung *(f)*
En  subscription
Es  suscripción *(f)*
Fr  souscription *(f)*
It  sottoscrizione *(f)*

**subscription** (to shares, etc.) *n* En
De  Zeichnung *(f)*
Es  suscripción *(f)*
Fr  souscription *(f)*
It  sottoscrizione *(f)*
Pt  subscrição *(f)*

**subscription** (to a journal, etc.) *n* En
De  Abonnement *(n)*
Es  abono *(m)*
Fr  abonnement *(m)*
It  abbonamento *(m)*
Pt  assinatura *(f)*

**subsidiary company** En
De  Tochtergesellschaft *(f)*
Es  filial; empresa subsidiaría *(f)*
Fr  filiale *(f)*
It  ale *(f)*
Pt  companhia subsidiária *(f)*

**subsidio** *(m) n* Es
De  Subvention *(f)*
En  subsidy
Fr  subvention *(f)*
It  sussidio *(m)*
Pt  subsídio *(m)*

**subsídio** *(m) n* Pt
De  Subvention *(f)*
En  subsidy
Es  subsidio *(m)*
Fr  subvention *(f)*
It  sussidio *(m)*

**subsidio a las exportaciones** *(m)* Es
De  Ausfuhrprämie *(f)*
En  export bonus
Fr  prime à l'exportation *(f)*
It  premio d'esportazione *(m)*
Pt  subsídio de exportação *(m)*

**subsidio de desemprego** *(m)* Pt
De  Arbeitslosenunterstützung *(f)*
En  unemployment benefit
Es  subsidio de paro *(m)*
Fr  secours de chômage *(m)*
It  indennità di disoccupazione *(f)*

**subsídio de exportação** *(m)* Pt
De  Ausfuhrprämie *(f)*
En  export bonus
Es  subsidio a las exportaciones *(m)*
Fr  prime à l'exportation *(f)*
It  premio d'esportazione *(m)*

**subsidio de paro** *(m)* Es
De  Arbeitslosenunterstützung *(f)*
En  unemployment benefit
Fr  secours de chômage *(m)*
It  indennità di disoccupazione *(f)*
Pt  subsidio de desemprego *(m)*

**subsidy** n En
De Subvention (f)
Es subsidio (m)
Fr subvention (f)
It sussidio (m)
Pt subsídio (m)

**substracción** (f) n Es
De Subtraktion (f)
En subtraction
Fr soustraction (f)
It sottrazione (f)
Pt subtracção (f)

**subtracção** (f) n Pt
De Subtraktion (f)
En subtraction
Es substracción (f)
Fr soustraction (f)
It sottrazione (f)

**subtraction** n En
De Subtraktion (f)
Es substracción (f)
Fr soustraction (f)
It sottrazione (f)
Pt subtracção (f)

**Subtraktion** (f) n De
En subtraction
Es substracción (f)
Fr soustraction (f)
It sottrazione (f)
Pt subtracção (f)

**subvenção** (f) n Pt
De Unterstützung; Subvention
   (f)
En grant; subsidy
Es subvención (f)
Fr subvention (f)
It sovvenzione (f)

**subvención de capital** (f) Es
De Kapitalhilfe (f)
En capital grants
Fr subventions en capital (f pl)
It sovvenzioni di capitale (f pl)
Pt subvenções de capital (f pl)

**subvención del Estado** (f) Es
De Staatszuschuss (m)
En government subsidy
Fr subvention de l'État (f)
It sovvenzione dello Stato (f)
Pt subvenções do Estado (f
   pl)

**subvenções de capital** (f pl) Pt
De Kapitalhilfe (f)
En capital grants
Es subvención de capital (f pl)
Fr subventions en capital (f pl)
It sovvenzioni di capitale (f)

**subvenções do Estado** (f pl)
   Pt
De Staatszuschuss (m)
En government subsidy
Es subvención del Estado (f)
Fr subvention de l'État (f)
It sovvenzione dello Stato (f)

**subvention** (f) n Fr
De Subvention (f)
En subsidy
Es subsidio (m)
It sussidio (m)
Pt subsídio (m)

**Subvention** (f) n De
En subsidy
Es subsidio (m)
Fr subvention (f)
It sussidio (m)
Pt subsídio (m)

**subvention de l'État** (f) Fr
De Staatszuschuss (m)
En government subsidy
Es subvención del Estado (f)
It sovvenzione dello Stato (f)
Pt subvenções do Estado (f
   pl)

**subventions en capital** (f pl) Fr
De Kapitalhilfe (f)
En capital grants
Es subvención de capital (f)
It sovvenzioni di capitale (f pl)
Pt subvenções de capital (f pl)

**succession** (f) n Fr
De Erbschaft; Nachlass (f m)
En inheritance; estate
Es sucesión (f)
It successione (f)
Pt sucessão (f)

**successione** (f) n It
De Erbschaft; Nachlass (f m)
En inheritance; estate
Es sucesión (f)
Fr succession (f)
Pt sucessão (f)

**succursale** (f) n Fr, It
De Filiale; Zweigstelle (f)
En branch; branch office
Es sucursal; filial (f)
Pt sucursal; filial (f)

**sucesión** (f) n Es
De Erbschaft; Nachlass (f m)
En estate; inheritance
Fr succession (f)
It successione (f)
Pt sucessão (f)

**sucessão** (f) n Pt
De Erbschaft; Nachlass (f m)
En estate; inheritance
Es sucesión (f)
Fr succession (f)
It successione (f)

**Sucht nach Sonderangeboten**
   (f) De
En bargain-hunting
Es caza de rebajas (f)
Fr chasse aux soldes (f)
It caccia alle occasioni (f)
Pt caça aos saldos (f)

**sucursal** (f) n Es, Pt
De Filiale; Zweigstelle (f)
En branch; branch office
Fr succursale; filiale (f)
It succursale; filiale (f)

**sucursal de cadena de alma-
   cenes** (f) Es
De Kettengeschäft (n)
En chain store
Fr magasin à succursales
   multiples (f)
It negozio a catena (m)
Pt sucursal de cadeia de
   armazéns (f)

**sucursal del banco** (f) Es
De Filialbank; Zweigbank (f)
En branch bank
Fr banque succursale (f)
It banca succursale (f)
Pt filial de banco (f)

**suddetto** adj It
De obenerwähnt
En above-mentioned
Es susodicho
Fr susmentionné
Pt supracitado

**sueldo** *(m)* *n* Es
De Gehalt *(n)*
En salary
Fr traitement *(m)*
It stipendio *(m)*
Pt ordenado *(m)*

**sujetapapeles** *(m)* *n* Es
De Büroklammer *(f)*
En paper clip
Fr attache-papiers *(m)*
It fermacarte *(m)*
Pt grampo *(m)*

**sulla banchina** It
De ab Kai
En ex quay
Es en muelle
Fr à prendre sur quai
Pt ex-cais

**suma** *(f)* *n* Es
De Summe *(f)*
En sum
Fr somme *(f)*
It somma *(f)*
Pt soma *(f)*

**suma global** *(f)* Es
De Pauschalbetrag *(m)*
En lump sum
Fr somme globale *(f)*
It somma globale *(f)*
Pt soma por inteiro *(f)*

**suma nominal** *(f)* Es
De Nominalbetrag *(m)*
En nominal amount
Fr montant nominal *(m)*
It importo nominale *(m)*
Pt quantia nominal *(f)*

**suma para riesgos** *(f)* Es
De Gefahrenzulage *(f)*
En danger money
Fr prime de risque *(f)*
It compenso per il rischio *(m)*
Pt prémio de risco *(m)*

**sumar** *vb* Es
De addieren
En add up
Fr totaliser; additioner
It sommare
Pt somar

**suma y sigue** *(f)* Es
De Ubertrag *(m)*
En amount carried forward
Am carry forward amount
Fr report à nouveau *(m)*
It ammontare da riportare *(m)*
Pt importância transportada *(f)*

**Summe** *(f)* *n* De
En sum; amount
Es suma *(f)*
Fr somme *(f)*
It somma *(f)*
Pt soma *(f)*

**summer holidays** En
De Sommerferien *(pl)*
Es vacaciones de verano;
    veraneo *(f pl; m)*
Fr vacances d'été *(f pl)*
It vacanze estive *(f pl)*
Pt férias de verão *(f pl)*

**sundry creditors** En
De Kreditoren *(m pl)*
Es acreedores varios *(m pl)*
Fr créditeurs divers *(m pl)*
It creditori diversi *(m pl)*
Pt créditos diversos *(m pl)*

**sundry expenses** En
De verschiedene Ausgaben *(f pl)*
Es gastos varios *(m pl)*
Fr frais divers *(m pl)*
It spese varie *(f pl)*
Pt despesas diversas *(f pl)*

**superficie de piso** *(f)* Es
De Bodenfläche *(f)*
En floor space
Fr surface de plancher *(f)*
It superficie di pavimento *(f)*
Pt área de chão *(f)*

**superficie di pavimento** *(f)* It
De Bodenfläche *(f)*
En floor space
Es superficie de piso *(f)*
Fr surface de plancher *(f)*
Pt área de chão *(f)*

**supermarché** *(m)* *n* Fr
De Supermarkt *(m)*
En supermarket
Es supermercado *(m)*
It supermercato *(m)*
Pt supermercado *(m)*

**supermarket** *n* En
De Supermarkt *(m)*
Es supermercado *(m)*
Fr supermarché *(m)*
It supermercato *(m)*
Pt supermercado *(m)*

**Supermarkt** *(m)* *n* De
En supermarket
Es supermercado *(m)*
Fr supermarché *(m)*
It supermercato *(m)*
Pt supermercado *(m)*

**supermercado** *(m)* *n* Es, Pt
De Supermarkt *(m)*
En supermarket
Fr supermarché *(m)*
It supermercato *(m)*

**supermercato** *(m)* *n* It
De Supermarkt *(m)*
En supermarket
Es supermercado *(m)*
Fr supermarché *(m)*
Pt supermercado *(m)*

**supervisor** *n* En; Es, Pt *(m)*
De Aufseher *(m)*
Fr surveillant *(m)*
It supervisore *(m)*

**supervisore** *(m)* *n* It
De Aufseher *(m)*
En supervisor
Es supervisor *(m)*
Fr surveillant *(m)*
Pt supervisor *(m)*

**suplemento** *(m)* *n* Es
De Zuschlagsgebühr *(f)*
En extra charge
Fr supplément *(m)*
It spesa supplementare *(f)*
Pt encargo suplementar *(m)*

**supplément** *(m)* *n* Fr
De Zuschlagsgebühr *(f)*
En extra charge
Es suplemento *(m)*
It spesa supplementare *(f)*
Pt encargo suplementar *(m)*

**supplementary estimate** En
De Nachschätzung *(f)*
Es cálculo suplementario *(m)*
Fr devis supplémentaire *(f)*

It preventivo supplementare *(m)*

Pt estimativa suplementar *(f)*

**supplier** *n* En
De Lieferant *(m)*
Es proveedor *(m)*
Fr fournisseur *(m)*
It fornitore *(m)*
Pt fornecedor *(m)*

**supplies on hand** En
De lieferfertiges Angebot *(n)*
Es provisiones existentes *(f pl)*
Fr ressources existantes *(f pl)*
It forniture esistenti *(f pl)*
Pt fornecimentos em existência *(m pl)*

**supply** *vb* En
De beliefern
Es surtir
Fr fournir
It fornire
Pt fornecer

**supply and demand** En
De Angebot und Nachfrage
Es oferta y demanda
Fr offre et demande
It offerta e domanda
Pt oferta e procura

**support publicitaire** *(m)* Fr
De Werbemittel *(n)*
En advertising medium
Es medio de publicidad *(m)*
It mezzo pubblicitario *(m)*
Pt meio publicitário *(m)*

**supports** *(m pl)* n Fr
De Werbeträger *(m pl)*
En media
Es medios de información *(m pl)*
It canali d'informazione *(m pl)*
Pt meios de informação *(m pl)*

**supracitado** *adj* Pt
De obenerwähnt
En above-mentioned
Es susodicho
Fr susmentionné
It suddetto

**surarbitre** *(m)* n Fr
De Schiedsobmann *(m)*
En umpire
Es juez árbitro *(m)*
It terzo arbitro *(m)*
Pt juiz árbitro *(m)*

**surcapacité** *(f)* n Fr
De Überkapazität *(f)*
En overcapacity
Es exceso de capacidad *(m)*
It capacità in eccedenza *(f)*
Pt capacidade excessiva *(f)*

**sur demande** Fr
De auf Verlangen
En on demand
Es a vista
It a vista
Pt à vista; sob demanda

**surestarie** *(f)* n Fr
De Überliegezeit *(f)*
En demurrage
Es sobreestadía *(f)*
It controstallia *(f)*
Pt sobreestadía *(f)*

**surestimation** *(f)* n Fr
De Überschätzung *(f)*
En over-estimate
Es presupuesto por exceso *(m)*
It valutazione eccessiva *(f)*
Pt avaliação excessiva *(f)*

**surety** (money) *n* En
De Bürge *(m)*
Es fianza *(f)*
Fr cautionnement *(m)*
It cauzione *(f)*
Pt fiança *(f)*

**surety** (for a person) *n* En
De Bürgschaft *(f)*
Es fiador *(m)*
Fr caution *(f)*
It garante *(m)*
Pt fiador *(m)*

**surface de plancher** *(f)* Fr
De Bodenfläche *(f)*
En floor space
Es superficie de piso *(f)*
It superficie di pavimento *(f)*
Pt área de chão *(f)*

**surplus** *n* En, Fr *(m)*
De Überschuss *(m)*
Es excedente *(m)*
It eccesso *(m)*
Pt excedente *(m)*

**surproduction** *(f)* n Fr
De Überproduktion *(f)*
En overproduction
Es exceso de producción *(m)*
It sovraproduzione *(f)*
Pt produção excessiva *(f)*

**surrender value** En
De Rückkaufswert *(m)*
Es valor de rescate *(m)*
Fr valeur de rachat *(f)*
It valore di riscatto *(m)*
Pt valor de resgate *(m)*

**surrogazione** *(f)* n It
De Ersetzung *(f)*
En subrogation
Es subrogación *(f)*
Fr subrogation *(f)*
Pt sub-rogação *(f)*

**surtax** *n* En
De Zuschlagssteuer *(f)*
Es sobretasa *(f)*
Fr surtaxe *(f)*
It sopratassa *(f)*
Pt sobretaxa *(f)*

**surtaxe** *(f)* n Fr
De Zuschlagssteuer *(f)*
En surtax
Es sobretasa *(f)*
It sopratassa *(f)*
Pt sobretaxa *(f)*

**surtir** *vb* Es
De beliefern
En supply
Fr fournir
It fornire
Pt fornecer

**surveillant** *(m)* n Fr
De Aufseher *(m)*
En supervisor
Es supervisor *(m)*
It supervisore *(m)*
Pt supervisor *(m)*

**suscripción** *(f)* n Es
De Zeichnung *(f)*
En subscription

Fr souscription *(f)*
It sottoscrizione *(f)*
Pt subscrição *(f)*

**susmentionné** *adj* Fr
De obenerwähnt
En above-mentioned
Es susodicho
It suddetto
Pt supracitado

**susodicho** *adj* Es
De obenerwähnt
En above-mentioned
Fr susmentionné
It suddetto
Pt supracitado

**suspender el pago de un cheque** Es
De einen Scheck sperren
En stop a cheque
Fr bloquer un chèque
It fermare un assegno
Pt suspender o pagamento de um cheque

**suspender o pagamento de um cheque** Pt
De einen Scheck sperren
En stop a cheque
Es suspender el pago de un cheque
Fr bloquer un chèque
It fermare un assegno

**suspense account** En
De Übergangskonto *(n)*
Es cuenta suspensa *(f)*
Fr compte d'ordre *(m)*
It conto sospeso *(m)*
Pt conta pendente *(m)*

**sussidio** *(m) n* It
De Subvention *(f)*
En subsidy
Es subsidio *(m)*
Fr subvention *(f)*
Pt subsídio *(m)*

**Süsswasserschaden** *(m) n* De
En fresh-water damage
Es daño de agua dulce *(m)*
Fr dégâts d'eau douce *(m pl)*
It danno d'acqua dolce *(m)*
Pt dano causado por água doce *(m)*

**svago** *(m) n* It
De Freizeit *(f)*
En leisure
Es descanso *(m)*
Fr loisir *(m)*
Pt lazer *(m)*

**svalutazione** *(f) n* It
De Währungsabwertung *(f)*
En devaluation
Es devaluación *(f)*
Fr dévaluation *(f)*
Pt desvalorização *(f)*

**sviluppo delle vendite** *(m)* It
De Werbung; Verkaufsbeförderung *(f)*
En sales promotion
Es promoción de ventas *(f)*
Fr promotion des ventes *(f)*
Pt promoção de vendas *(f)*

**sviluppo economico** *(m)* It
De Wirtschaftswachstum *(m)*
En economic growth
Es crecimiento económico *(m)*
Fr croissance économique *(f)*
Pt crescimento económico *(m)*

**swindle** *vb* En
De schwindeln
Es estafar
Fr filouter
It truffare
Pt enganar

**switchboard** *n* En
De Schalttafel *(f)*
Es cuadro de conexión *(m)*
Fr tableau de distribution *(m)*
It quadro di comando *(m)*
Pt quadro de distribuição *(m)*

**symbol** *n* En
De Symbol *(n)*
Es símbolo *(m)*
Fr symbole *(m)*
It simbolo *(m)*
Pt símbolo *(m)*

**Symbol** *(n) n* De
En symbol
Es símbolo *(m)*
Fr symbole *(m)*
It simbolo *(m)*
Pt símbolo *(m)*

**symbole** *(m) n* Fr
De Symbol *(n)*
En symbol
Es símbolo *(m)*
It simbolo *(m)*
Pt símbolo *(m)*

**symbolo** *(m) n* It
De Symbol *(n)*
En symbol
Es símbolo *(m)*
Fr symbole *(m)*
Pt símbolo *(m)*

**syndicat** *(m) n* Fr
De Syndikat; Gewerkschaft *(n f)*
En syndicate; trade union
Es sindicato *(m)*
It sindacato *(m)*
Pt sindicato *(m)*

**syndicat d'assureurs** *(m)* Fr
De Versicherungssyndikat *(n)*
En underwriting syndicate (insurance)
Es sindicato de seguros *(m)*
It sindacato di assicuratori *(m)*
Pt consórcio de seguradores *(m)*

**syndicat de garantie** *(m)* Fr
De Emissionssyndikat *(n)*
En underwriting syndicate (new issues)
Es grupo de suscriptores *(m)*
It consorzio finanziario *(m)*
Pt consórcio de subscritores *(m)*

**syndicate** *n* En
De Syndikat *(n)*
Es sindicato *(m)*
Fr syndicat *(m)*
It consorzio finanziario *(m)*
Pt sindicato *(m)*

**syndic de faillite** *(m)* Fr
De Konkursverwalter *(m)*
En (official) receiver
Es sindico *(m)*
It curatore *(m)*
Pt sindico *(m)*

**Syndikat** *(n) n* De
En syndicate
Es sindicato *(m)*

Fr  syndicat *(m)*
It  sindacato *(m)*
Pt  sindicato *(m)*

**T**

**system** *n* En
De  System *(n)*
Es  sistema *(m)*
Fr  système *(m)*
It  sistema *(m)*
Pt  sistema *(m)*

**System** *(n) n* De
En  system
Es  sistema *(m)*
Fr  système *(m)*
It  sistema *(m)*
Pt  sistema *(m)*

**Systemanalyse** *(f) n* De
En  systems analysis
Es  análisis de sistemas *(m)*
Fr  analyse de systèmes *(f)*
It  analisi di sistemi *(f)*
Pt  análise de sistemas *(f)*

**système** *(m) n* Fr
De  System *(n)*
En  system
Es  sistema *(m)*
It  sistema *(m)*
Pt  sistema *(m)*

**système économique du mar-
ché libre** *(m)* Fr
De  freie Marktwirtschaft *(f)*
En  free economy
Es  economía del mercado libre
    *(f)*
It  economia di mercato libero
    *(f)*
Pt  economia de mercado livre
    *(f)*

**système métrique** *(m)* Fr
De  metrisches System *(n)*
En  metric system
Es  sistema métrico *(m)*
It  sistema metrico *(m)*
Pt  sistema métrico *(m)*

**systems analysis** En
De  Systemanalyse *(f)*
Es  análisis de sistemas *(m)*
Fr  analyse de systèmes *(f)*
It  analisi di sistemi *(f)*
Pt  análise de sistemas *(f)*

**tableau de distribution** *(m)* Fr
De  Schalttafel *(f)*
En  switchboard
Es  cuadro de conexión *(m)*
It  quadro di comando *(m)*
Pt  quadro de distribuição *(m)*

**tachar** *vb* Es
De  streichen
En  delete
Fr  rayer; effacer
It  cancellare
Pt  cortar; riscar

**tacit agreement** En
De  stillschweigendes  Über-
    einkommen *(n)*
Es  acuerdo tácito *(m)*
Fr  convention tacite *(f)*
It  accordo tacito *(m)*
Pt  acordo tácito *(m)*

**Tag** *(m) n* De
En  day
Es  día *(m)*
Fr  jour *(m)*
It  giorno *(m)*
Pt  dia *(m)*

**Tagebuch** *(n) n* De
En  journal; day-book
Es  libro diario *(m)*
Fr  journal *(m)*
It  libro giornale *(m)*
Pt  diário *(m)*

**Tagebuchsposten** *(m) n* De
En  journal-entry
Es  asiento en el libro diario
    *(m)*
Fr  article d'un livre journal *(m)*
It  registrazione a giornale *(f)*
Pt  anotação de diário *(f)*

**Tagesordnung** *(f) n* De
En  agenda
Es  orden del día *(m)*
Fr  ordre du jour *(m)*
It  ordine del giorno *(m)*
Pt  agenda *(f)*

**Tagesstempel** *(m) n* De
En  date-stamp
Es  sello de fecha *(m)*
Fr  dateur *(m)*
It  timbro a data *(m)*
Pt  carimbo de datas *(m)*

**täglich** *adj* De
En  daily
Es  cotidiano
Fr  cotidien
It  quotidiano
Pt  diário

**taglio** *(m) n* It
De  Stückelung *(f)*
En  denomination
Es  valor *(m)*
Fr  valeur nominale *(f)*
Pt  valor nominal *(m)*

**Tagschicht** *(f) n* De
En  day-shift
Es  turno de día *(m)*
Fr  équipe du jour *(f)*
It  turno di giorno *(m)*
Pt  turno de dia *(m)*

**take-home pay** En
De  Nettolohn *(m)*
Es  paga neta *(f)*
Fr  salaire nette *(f)*
It  paga netta *(f)*
Pt  salário líquido *(m)*

**take-over bid** En
De  Übernahmeangebot *(n)*
Es  oferta de adquisición *(f)*
Fr  offre de rachat *(f)*
It  offerta di acquisto *(f)*
Pt  proposta de apropriação *(f)*

**talão** *(m) n* Pt
De  Talon *(m)*
En  counterfoil
Am  stub
Es  talón *(m)*
Fr  talon *(m)*
It  matrice *(f)*

**talão excluido** Pt
De  ohne Coupon
En  ex coupon
Es  sin cupón
Fr  ex coupon
It  senza cedola

**talón** *(m) n* Es
De Talon *(m)*
En counterfoil
Am stub
Fr talon *(m)*
It matrice *(f)*
Pt talão *(m)*

**talon** *(m) n* Fr
De Talon *(m)*
En counterfoil
Am stub
Es talón *(m)*
It matrice *(f)*
Pt talão *(m)*

**Talon** *(m) n* De
En counterfoil
Am stub
Es talón *(m)*
Fr talon *(m)*
It matrice *(f)*
Pt talão *(m)*

**tampon** *(m) n* Fr
De Stempel *(m)*
En stamp
Es estampilla *(f)*
It stampiglia *(f)*
Pt carimbo *(m)*

**tangible assets** En
De greifbare Aktiven *(n pl)*
Es activo tangible *(m)*
Fr biens immobiliers *(m pl)*
It beni materiali *(m pl)*
Pt bens visíveis *(m pl)*

**Tantieme** *(f) n* De
En royalty
Es derechos *(m pl)*
Fr redevance; droits *(f; m pl)*
It diritti *(m pl)*
Pt direitos *(m pl)*

**tapa-buracos** *(m) n* Pt
De Überbrückung *(f)*
En stop-gap
Es recurso provisional *(m)*
Fr bouche-trou *(m)*
It provvedimento temporaneo *(m)*

**taquigrafía** *(f) n* Es
De Kurzschrift *(f)*
En shorthand
Fr sténographie *(f)*

It stenografia *(f)*
Pt estenografia *(f)*

**taquimecanógrafa** *(f) n* Es
De Stenotypistin *(f)*
En shorthand typist
Fr sténodactylographe *(f)*
It stenodattilografa *(f)*
Pt estenodactilógrafa *(f)*

**tara** *(f) n* Es, It, Pt
De Tara *(f)*
En tare
Fr tare *(f)*

**Tara** *(f) n* De
En tare
Es tara *(f)*
Fr tare *(f)*
It tara *(f)*
Pt tara *(f)*

**tare** *n* En, Fr *(f)*
De Tara *(f)*
Es tara *(f)*
It tara *(f)*
Pt tara *(f)*

**target** *n* En
De Ziel *(n)*
Es objetivo *(m)*
Fr but *(m)*
It bersaglio *(m)*
Pt objectivo *(m)*

**tarif** *(m) n* Fr
De Tarif *(m)*
En tariff
Es tarifa *(f)*
It tariffa *(f)*
Pt tarifa *(f)*

**Tarif** *(m) n* De
En tariff
Es tarifa *(f)*
Fr tarif *(m)*
It tariffa *(f)*
Pt tarifa *(f)*

**tarifa** *(f) n* Es, Pt
De Tarif *(m)*
En tariff
Fr tarif *(m)*
It tariffa *(f)*

**tarifa de salarios** *(f)* Es
De Lohnsatz *(m)*
En wage rate

Fr taux des salaires *(m)*
It tariffa salariale *(f)*
Pt base salarial *(f)*

**tarifa diferencial** *(f)* Es
De diskriminierender Tarif *(m)*
En discriminating tariff
Fr tarif discriminatoire *(m)*
It tariffa discriminante *(f)*
Pt tarifa discriminatória *(f)*

**tarifa discriminatória** *(f)* Pt
De diskriminierender Tarif *(m)*
En discriminating tariff
Es tarifa diferencial *(f)*
Fr tarif discriminatoire *(m)*
It tariffa discriminante *(f)*

**tarifa exterior común** *(f)* Es
De gemeinsamer Aussentarif *(m)*
En common external tariff
Fr tarif extérieur commun *(m)*
It tariffa estera comune *(f)*
Pt tarifa externa comum *(f)*

**tarifa externa comum** *(f)* Pt
De gemeinsamer Aussentarif *(m)*
En common external tariff
Es tarifa exterior común *(f)*
Fr tarif extérieur commun *(m)*
It tariffa estera comune *(f)*

**tarif-album** *(m) n* Fr
De Preiskatalog *(m)*
En trade catalogue
Es catálogo comercial *(m)*
It catalogo commerciale *(m)*
Pt catálogo comercial *(m)*

**tarifa para anuncios** *(f)* Es
De Werbetarif *(m)*
En advertising rates
Fr tarifs de publicité *(m pl)*
It tariffa delle inserzioni *(f)*
Pt taxas de publicidade *(f)*

**tarifa postal** *(f)* Es, Pt
De Postgebühr *(f)*
En postage
Fr frais de poste *(m pl)*
It tariffa postale *(f)*

**tarifa unificada** *(f)* Es
De Einheitssatz *(m)*
En flat rate
Fr tarif uniforme *(m)*

It   tariffa uniforme (f)
Pt   tarifa de base (f)

**tarif de faveur** (m) Fr
De   Vorzugssatz (m)
En   preferential duty
Es   derechos preferenciales (m pl)
It   tariffa preferenziale (f)
Pt   direito preferencial (m)

**tarif discriminatoire** (m) Fr
De   diskriminierender Tarif (m)
En   discriminating tariff
Es   tarifa diferencial (f)
It   tariffa discriminante (f)
Pt   tarifa discriminatória (f)

**tarif extérieur commun** (m) Fr
De   gemeinsamer Aussentarif (m)
En   common external tariff
Es   tarifa exterior común (f)
It   tariffa estera comune (f)
Pt   tarifa externa comum (f)

**tariff** n En
De   Tarif (m)
Es   tarifa (f)
Fr   tarif (m)
It   tariffa (f)
Pt   tarifa (f)

**tariffa** (f) n It
De   Tarif (m)
En   tariff
Es   tarifa (f)
Fr   tarif (m)
Pt   tarifa (f)

**tariffa delle inserzioni** (f) It
De   Werbetarif (m)
En   advertising rates
Es   tarifa para anuncios (f)
Fr   tarifs de publicité (m pl)
Pt   taxas de publicidade (f)

**tariffa discriminante** (f) It
De   diskriminierender Tarif (m)
En   discriminating tariff
Es   tarifa diferencial (f)
Fr   tarif discriminatoire (m)
Pt   tarifa discriminatória (f)

**tariffa estera comune** (f) It
De   gemeinsamer Aussentarif (m)
En   common external tariff

Es   tarifa exterior común (f)
Fr   tarif extérieur commun (m)
Pt   tarifa externa comum (f)

**tariff agreement** En
De   Zollabkommen (n)
Es   acuerdo tarifario (m)
Fr   accord tarifaire (m)
It   accordo tariffario (m)
Pt   acordo de tarifas (m)

**tariffa postale** (f) It
De   Postgebühr (f)
En   postage
Es   tarifa postal (f)
Fr   frais de poste (m pl)
Pt   tarifa postal (f)

**tariffa preferenziale** (f) It
De   Vorzugssatz (m)
En   preferential duty
Es   derechos preferenciales (m pl)
Fr   tarif de faveur (m)
Pt   direito preferencial (m)

**tariffa salariale** (f) It
De   Lohnsatz (m)
En   wage rate
Es   tarifa de salarios (f)
Fr   taux des salaires (m)
Pt   base salarial (f)

**tariffa uniforme** (f) It
De   Einheitssatz (m)
En   flat rate
Es   tarifa unificada (f)
Fr   tarif uniforme (m)
Pt   tarifa de base (f)

**tarifs de publicité** (m pl) Fr
De   Werbetarif (m)
En   advertising rates
Es   tarifa para anuncios (f)
It   tariffa delle inserzioni (f)
Pt   taxas de publicidade (f)

**tarif uniforme** (m) Fr
De   Einheitssatz (m)
En   flat rate
Es   tarifa unificada (f)
It   tariffa uniforme (f)
Pt   tarifa de base (f)

**Tarifvertragsverhandlung** (f) n De
En   collective bargaining
Es   contratación collectiva (f)

Fr   négociations de conventions collectives (f pl)
It   contrattazione collettiva (f)
Pt   regateio colectivo (m)

**tarjeta** (f) n Es
De   Karte (f)
En   card
Fr   carte (f)
It   scheda (f)
Pt   cartão (m)

**tarjeta de cheque** (f) Es
De   Scheckkarte (f)
En   cheque card
Am   bank credit card
Fr   carte de chèque (f)
It   scheda per assegni (f)
Pt   cartão de validação de cheques (m)

**tarjeta de crédito** (f) Es
De   Kreditkarte (f)
En   credit card
Fr   carte de crédit (f)
It   carta di credito (f)
Pt   cartão de crédito (m)

**tarjeta perforada** (f) Es
De   Lochkarte (f)
En   punched card
Fr   carte perforée
It   scheda perforata (f)
Pt   ficha perforada (f)

**tasa** (f) n Es
De   Satz; Kurs (m)
En   rate
Fr   taux; cours (m)
It   tasso; tariffa (m f)
Pt   taxa (f)

**tasa anual** (f) Es
De   Jahreskurs (m)
En   annual rate
Fr   taux annuel (m)
It   tasso annuale (m)
Pt   taxa anual (f)

**tasable** adj Es
De   abgabenpflichtig
En   dutiable
Fr   taxable
It   tassabile
Pt   tributável

**tasación diferida** *(f)* Es
  De  latente Steuerpflicht *(f)*
  En  deferred taxation
  Fr  imposition différée *(f)*
  It  tassazione differita *(f)*
  Pt  tributação diferida *(f)*

**tasa de descuento** *(f)* Es
  De  Diskontsatz *(m)*
  En  discount rate
  Fr  taux d'escompte *(m)*
  It  tasso di sconto *(m)*
  Pt  taxa de desconto *(f)*

**tasas de cambio exterior** *(f pl)*
      Es
  De  Devisenkurs *(m)*
  En  foreign exchange rates
  Fr  cours des changes *(m)*
  It  corso dei cambi *(m)*
  Pt  taxas de câmbio *(f pl)*

**tasas de interés** *(f pl)* Es
  De  Zinssätze *(m pl)*
  En  interest rates
  Fr  taux d'intérêt *(m pl)*
  It  tassi d'interesse *(m pl)*
  Pt  taxas de juro *(m pl)*

**tassa** *(f)* n It
  De  Gebühr; Abgabe *(f)*
  En  duty; tax
  Es  derechos; impuesto *(m)*
  Fr  taxe; impôt *(f m)*
  Pt  taxa; imposto *(f m)*

**tassabile** *adj* It
  De  abgabenpflichtig
  En  dutiable
  Es  tasable
  Fr  taxable
  Pt  tributável

**tassa comunale** *(f)* It
  De  Gemeindesteuer *(f)*
  En  rates
  Am  realty tax
  Es  contribución municipal *(f)*
  Fr  taxes municipales *(f pl)*
  Pt  contribuições municipais *(f pl)*

**tassa d'entrata** *(f)* It
  De  Eintrittsgebühr *(f)*
  En  entrance fee
  Es  derecho de entrada *(m)*
  Fr  droit d'entrée *(m)*
  Pt  taxa de admissão *(f)*

**tassa di bollo** *(f)* It
  De  Stempelgebühr *(f)*
  En  stamp duty
  Es  impuesto del timbre *(m)*
  Fr  droit de timbre *(m)*
  Pt  imposto de selo *(m)*

**tassa di registrazione** *(f)* It
  De  Anmeldegebühr *(f)*
  En  registration fee
  Es  derechos de registro *(m pl)*
  Fr  droit d'enregistrement *(m)*
  Pt  custas de registo *(f pl)*

**tassa esclusa** It
  De  ausser Steuer
  En  excluding tax
  Es  impuesto no incluido
  Fr  hors taxe (HT)
  Pt  impostos excluidos

**tassa invisibile** *(f)* It
  De  versteckte Belastung *(f)*
  En  hidden tax
  Es  impuesto latente *(m)*
  Fr  imposition latente *(f)*
  Pt  imposto ocultado *(m)*

**tassa sugli articoli di lusso** *(f)*
      It
  De  Luxussteuer *(f)*
  En  luxury tax
  Es  impuesto de lujo *(m)*
  Fr  impôt de luxe *(m)*
  Pt  imposto de luxo *(m)*

**tassazione** *(f)* n It
  De  Besteuerung *(f)*
  En  taxation
  Es  tributación *(f)*
  Fr  imposition *(f)*
  Pt  tributação *(f)*

**tassazione differita** *(f)* It
  De  latente Steuerpflicht *(f)*
  En  deferred taxation
  Es  tasación diferida *(f)*
  Fr  imposition différée *(f)*
  Pt  tributação diferida *(f)*

**tassì** *(m)* n It
  De  Taxi *(n)*
  En  taxi
  Es  taxi *(m)*
  Fr  taxi *(m)*
  Pt  taxi *(m)*

**tasso** *(m)* n It
  De  Satz; Kurs *(m)*
  En  rate
  Es  tasa; tipo *(f m)*
  Fr  taux; cours *(m)*
  Pt  taxa *(f)*

**tasso annuale** *(m)* It
  De  Jahreskurs *(m)*
  En  annual rate
  Es  tasa anual *(f)*
  Fr  taux annuel *(m)*
  Pt  taxa anual *(f)*

**tasso d'interesse** *(m)* It
  De  Zinsfuss *(m)*
  En  rate of interest
  Es  tipo de interés *(m)*
  Fr  taux d'intérêt *(m)*
  Pt  taxa de juro *(f)*

**tasso di mortalità** *(m)* It
  De  Sterblichkeitsziffer *(f)*
  En  death rate
  Es  mortalidad *(f)*
  Fr  taux de mortalité *(m)*
  Pt  taxa de mortalidade *(f)*

**tasso di reddito** *(m)* It
  De  Ertragsrate *(f)*
  En  rate of return
  Es  tipo de rédito *(m)*
  Fr  taux de rendement *(m)*
  Pt  taxa de rendimento *(f)*

**tasso di sconto** *(m)* It
  De  Diskontsatz *(m)*
  En  discount rate
  Es  tasa de descuento *(f)*
  Fr  taux d'escompte *(m)*
  Pt  taxa de desconto *(f)*

**tasso variabile** *(m)* It
  De  schwankender Kurs *(m)*
  En  fluctuating rate
  Es  tipo oscilante *(m)*
  Fr  taux variable *(m)*
  Pt  taxa variável *(f)*

**Taste** (Schreibmaschine) *(f)* n
  De
  En  key
  Es  tecla *(f)*
  Fr  touche *(f)*
  It  tasto *(m)*
  Pt  tecla *(f)*

**tasto** (di macchina da scrivere)
   (m) n It
  De Taste (f)
  En key
  Es tecla (f)
  Fr touche (f)
  Pt tecla (f)

**Tatsache** (f) n De
  En fact
  Es hecho (m)
  Fr fait (m)
  It fatto (m)
  Pt facto (m)

**Tausch** (m) n De
  En exchange
  Es cambio (m)
  Fr échange (m)
  It cambio (m)
  Pt câmbio (m)

**Tauschhandel treiben** De
  En barter
  Es trocar
  Fr troquer
  It barattare
  Pt trocar

**taux** (m) n Fr
  De Satz; Kurs (m)
  En rate
  Es tasa; tipo (f m)
  It tasso; tariffa (m f)
  Pt taxa (f)

**taux annuel** (m) Fr
  De Jahreskurs (m)
  En annual rate
  Es tasa anual (f)
  It tasso annuale (m)
  Pt taxa anual (f)

**taux de change** (m) Fr
  De Wechselkurs (m)
  En exchange rate
  Es tipo de cambio (m)
  It corso del cambio (m)
  Pt taxa de câmbio (f)

**taux de change flottant** (m) Fr
  De flexibler Wechselkurs (m)
  En floating exchange rate
  Es tipo de cambio flotante (m)
  It cambio fluttuante (m)
  Pt taxa de câmbio flutuante (f)

**taux de défaillance** (m) Fr
  De Durchfallquote (f)
  En failure rate
  Es proporción de fracasos (f)
  It indice dei fallimenti (m)
  Pt proporção de fracassos (f)

**taux de mortalité** (m) Fr
  De Sterblichkeitsziffer (f)
  En death rate
  Es mortalidad (f)
  It tasso di mortalità (m)
  Pt taxa de mortalidade (f)

**taux de rendement** (m) Fr
  De Ertragsrate (f)
  En rate of return
  Es tipo de rédito (m)
  It tasso di reddito (m)
  Pt taxa de rendimento (f)

**taux d'escompte** (m) Fr
  De Diskontsatz (m)
  En discount rate
  Es tasa de descuento (f)
  It tasso di sconto (m)
  Pt taxa de desconto

**taux des salaires** (m) Fr
  De Lohnsatz (m)
  En wage rate
  Es tarifa de salarios (f)
  It tariffa salariale (f)
  Pt base salarial (f)

**taux d'intérêt** (m) Fr
  De Zinsfuss (m)
  En interest rate
  Es tipo de interés (m)
  It tasso d'interesse (m)
  Pt taxa de juro (f)

**taux variable** (m) Fr
  De schwankender Kurs (m)
  En fluctuating rate
  Es tipo oscilante (m)
  It tasso variabile (m)
  Pt taxa variável (f)

**tax** n En
  De Steuer (f)
  Es impuesto (m)
  Fr impôt (m)
  It imposta (f)
  Pt imposto (m)

**taxa** (f) n Pt
  De Satz; Gebühr (m f)
  En rate; duty
  Es tasa; impuesto (f m)
  Fr taux; impôt (m)
  It tasso; imposta (m f)

**taxa anual** (f) Pt
  De Jahreskurs (m)
  En annual rate
  Es tasa anual (f)
  Fr taux annuel (m)
  It tasso annuale (m)

**taxable** adj Fr
  De abgabenpflichtig
  En dutiable
  Es tasable
  It tassabile
  Pt tributável

**taxable income** En
  De steuerpflichtiges Einkommen (n)
  Es renta imponible (f)
  Fr revenu imposable (m)
  It reddito tassabile (m)
  Pt receita tributável (f)

**taxa custo-ganhos** (f) Pt
  De Verhältnis des Aktienkurses zum Reingewinn (n)
  En price-earnings ratio (P/E)
  Es proporción precio-ingresos (f)
  Fr quotient cours-bénéfice (m)
  It rapporto prezzo-utile (m)

**taxa de admissão** (f) Pt
  De Eintrittsgebühr (f)
  En entrance fee
  Es derecho de entrada (m)
  Fr droit d'entrée (m)
  It tassa d'entrata (f)

**taxa de câmbio** (f) Pt
  De Wechselkurs (m)
  En exchange rate
  Es tipo de cambio (m)
  Fr taux de change (m)
  It corso del cambio (m)

**taxa de câmbio flutuante** (f) Pt
  De flexibler Wechselkurs (m)
  En floating exchange rate
  Es tipo de cambio flotante (m)

Fr  taux de change flottant *(m)*
It   cambio fluttuante *(m)*

**taxa de desconto** *(f)* Pt
De  Diskontsatz *(m)*
En  discount rate
Es  tasa de descuento *(f)*
Fr  taux d'escompte *(m)*
It   tasso di sconto *(m)*

**taxa de juro** *(f)* Pt
De  Zinsfuss *(m)*
En  rate of interest
Es  tipo de interés *(m)*
Fr  taux d'intérêt *(m)*
It   tasso d'interesse *(m)*

**taxa de mortalidade** *(f)* Pt
De  Sterblichkeitsziffer *(f)*
En  death rate
Es  mortalidad *(f)*
Fr  taux de mortalité *(m)*
It   tasso di mortalità *(m)*

**taxa de rendimento** *(f)* Pt
De  Ertragsrate *(f)*
En  rate of return
Es  tipo de rédito *(m)*
Fr  taux de rendement *(m)*
It   tasso di reddito *(m)*

**taxas bancárias** *(f pl)* Pt
De  Bankspesen *(f pl)*
En  bank charges
Es  gastos de banco *(m pl)*
Fr  frais bancaires *(m pl)*
It   spese di banca *(f pl)*

**taxas de publicidade** *(f)* Pt
De  Werbetarif *(m)*
En  advertising rates
Es  tarifa para anuncios *(f)*
Fr  tarifs de publicité *(m pl)*
It   tariffa delle inserzioni *(f)*

**taxation** *n* En
De  Besteuerung *(f)*
Es  tributación *(f)*
Fr  imposition *(f)*
It   tassazione *(f)*
Pt  tributação *(f)*

**taxa variável** *(f)* Pt
De  schwankender Kurs *(m)*
En  fluctuating rate
Es  tipo oscilante *(m)*
Fr  taux variable *(m)*
It   tasso variabile *(m)*

**tax base** En
De  Bemessungsgrundlage *(f)*
Es  base contributiva *(f)*
Fr  assiette de l'impôt *(f)*
It   ripartizione della tassazione *(f)*
Pt  base de imposto *(f)*

**tax collector** En
De  Steuereinnehmer *(m)*
Es  recaudador de impuestos *(m)*
Fr  percepteur des impôts *(m)*
It   esattore delle imposte *(m)*
Pt  cobrador de impostos *(m)*

**tax-deductible** *adj* En
De  steuerabsetzbar
Es  deducible de impuestos
Fr  déductible à l'impôt
It   deducibile da tassa
Pt  ilíquido de impostos

**taxe** *(f)* *n* Fr
De  Gebühr; Abgabe *(f)*
En  duty; tax
Es  derechos; impuesto *(m)*
It   tassa; imposta *(f)*
Pt  taxa; imposto *(f m)*

**taxe de vente** *(f)* Fr
De  Warenumsatzsteuer *(f)*
En  sales tax
Es  impuesto sobre la venta *(m)*
It   imposta sulle vendite *(f)*
Pt  imposto sobre vendas *(m)*

**taxes municipales** *(f pl)* Fr
De  Gemeindesteuer *(f)*
En  rates
Am  realty tax
Es  contribución municipal *(f)*
It   tassa comunale *(f)*
Pt  contribuições municipais *(f pl)*

**taxe sur la valeur ajoutée (TVA)** *(f)* Fr
De  Mehrwertsteuer *(f)*
En  value added tax (VAT)
Es  impuesto sobre valor añadido *(m)*
It   imposta sul valore aggiunto (IVA) *(f)*
Pt  imposto sobre valor aduzido *(m)*

**taxe sur l'emploi** *(f)* Fr
De  Lohnsummensteuer *(f)*
En  employment tax
Es  impuesto por empleado *(m)*
It   imposta sull'impiego *(f)*
Pt  imposto sobre emprego *(m)*

**tax-free** *adj* En
De  steuerfrei
Es  exento de impuestos
Fr  exempt d'impôts
It   esente di tassa
Pt  isento de impostos

**tax haven** En
De  Steuerparadies *(n)*
Es  refugio fiscal *(m)*
Fr  refuge fiscal *(m)*
It   rifugio fiscale *(m)*
Pt  refúgio fiscal *(m)*

**taxi** *n* En; Es, Fr, Pt *(m)*
De  Taxi *(n)*
It   tassì *(m)*

**Taxi** *(n)* *n* De
En  taxi
Es  taxi *(m)*
Fr  taxi *(m)*
It   tassì *(m)*
Pt  taxi *(m)*

**tax loss** En
De  Steuerverlust *(m)*
Es  pérdida fiscal *(f)*
Fr  perte fiscale *(f)*
It   perdita a scopi fiscali *(f)*
Pt  perda em impostos *(f)*

**tax payer** En
De  Steuerzahler *(m)*
Es  contribuyente *(m)*
Fr  contribuable *(m)*
It   contribuente fiscale *(m)*
Pt  contribuinte *(m)*

**tax relief** En
De  Steuerbefreiung *(f)*
Es  desgravación *(f)*
Fr  dégrèvement *(m)*
It   sgravio fiscale *(m)*
Pt  isenção de imposto *(f)*

**tax return** En
De  Steuererklärung *(f)*
Es  declaración de ingresos *(f)*
Fr  déclaration de l'impôt *(f)*
It   dichiarazione fiscale *(f)*

Pt declaração para efeitos de
  tributação (f)

**tax year** En
  De Steuerjahr (n)
  Es año fiscal (m)
  Fr exercice fiscal (m)
  It anno fiscale (m)
  Pt ano fiscal (m)

**Technik** (f) n De
  En technique
  Es técnica (f)
  Fr technique (f)
  It tecnica (f)
  Pt técnica (f)

**technique** n En, Fr (f)
  De Technik (f)
  Es técnica (f)
  It tecnica (f)
  Pt técnica (f)

**technologie** (f) n Fr
  De Technologie (f)
  En technology
  Es tecnología (f)
  It tecnologia (f)
  Pt tecnologia (f)

**Technologie** (f) n De
  En technology
  Es tecnología (f)
  Fr technologie (f)
  It tecnologia (f)
  Pt tecnologia (f)

**technology** n En
  De technisches Wissen (n)
  Es tecnología (f)
  Fr technologie (f)
  It tecnologia (f)
  Pt tecnologia (f)

**tecido** (m) n Pt
  De Stoff (m)
  En material; cloth
  Es tejido (m)
  Fr étoffe; tissu (f m)
  It stoffa; tessuto (f m)

**técnica** (f) n Es, Pt
  De Technik (f)
  En technique
  Fr technique (f)
  It tecnica (f)

**tecnica** (f) n It
  De Technik (f)
  En technique
  Es técnica (f)
  Fr technique (f)
  Pt técnica (f)

**tecnología** (f) n Es
  De Technologie (f)
  En technology
  Fr technologie (f)
  It tecnologia (f)
  Pt tecnologia (f)

**tecnologia** (f) n It, Pt
  De Technologie (f)
  En technology
  Es tecnología (f)
  Fr technologie (f)

**Teil** (m) n De
  En share
  Es parte (f)
  Fr part (f)
  It parte (f)
  Pt quota (f)

**teilen** vb De
  En share
  Es repartir
  Fr partager
  It dividere
  Pt repartir

**Teilhaber** (m) n De
  En partner
  Es socio (m)
  Fr associé (m)
  It socio (m)
  Pt sócio (m)

**Teilung** (f) n De
  En division
  Es división (f)
  Fr division (f)
  It divisione (f)
  Pt divisão (f)

**tejido** (m) n Es
  De Stoff (m)
  En material; cloth
  Fr étoffe; tissu (f m)
  It stoffa; tessuto (f m)
  Pt tecido (m)

**telefone** (m) n Pt
  De Fernsprecher; Telephon (m
    n)

  En telephone
  Es teléfono (m)
  Fr téléphone (m)
  It telefono (m)

**telefonista** (m/f) Es, It, Pt
  De Telephonist; Telephonistin
    (m f)
  En telephone operator
  Fr téléphoniste (m/f)

**teléfono** (m) n Es
  De Fernsprecher; Telephon (m
    n)
  En telephone
  Fr téléphone (m)
  It telefono (m)
  Pt telefone (m)

**telefono** (m) n It
  De Fernsprecher; Telephon (m
    n)
  En telephone
  Es teléfono (m)
  Fr téléphone (m)
  Pt telefone (m)

**telégrafar** vb Es
  De telegraphieren
  En telegraph
  Fr télégraphier
  It telegrafare
  Pt telegrafar

**telegrafar** vb Pt
  De telegraphieren
  En telegraph
  Es telégrafar
  Fr télégraphier
  It telegrafare

**telegrafare** vb It
  De telegraphieren
  En telegraph
  Es telégrafar
  Fr télégraphier
  Pt telegrafar

**telegram** n En
  De Telegramm (n)
  Es telegrama (m)
  Fr télégramme (m)
  It telegramma (m)
  Pt telegrama (m)

**telegrama** (m) n Es, Pt
  De Telegramm (n)
  En telegram

Fr télégramme *(m)*
It telegramma *(m)*

**Telegramm** *(n) n* De
En telegram
Es telegrama *(m)*
Fr télégramme *(m)*
It telegramma *(m)*
Pt telegrama *(m)*

**telegramma** *(m) n* It
De Telegramm *(n)*
En telegram
Es telegrama *(m)*
Fr télégramme *(m)*
Pt telegrama *(m)*

**Telegrammadresse** *(f) n* De
En telegraphic address
Es dirección telegráfica *(f)*
Fr adresse télégraphique *(f)*
It indirizzo telegrafico *(m)*
Pt endereço telegráfico *(m)*

**télégramme** *(m) n* Fr
De Telegramm *(n)*
En telegram
Es telegrama *(m)*
It telegramma *(m)*
Pt telegrama *(m)*

**telegraph** *vb* En
De telegraphieren
Es telegrafar
Fr télégraphier
It telegrafare
Pt telegrafar

**telegraphic address** En
De Telegrammadresse *(f)*
Es dirección telegráfica *(f)*
Fr adresse télégraphique *(f)*
It indirizzo telegrafico *(m)*
Pt endereço telegráfico *(m)*

**telegraphic transfer** En
De Kabelauszahlung *(f)*
Es giro telegráfico *(m)*
Fr virement télégraphique *(m)*
It rimessa telegrafica *(f)*
Pt transferência telegráfica *(f)*

**télégraphier** *vb* Fr
De telegraphieren
En telegraph
Es telegrafar
It telegrafare
Pt telegrafar

**telegraphieren** *vb* De
En telegraph
Es telegrafar
Fr télégraphier
It telegrafare
Pt telegrafar

**Telephon** *(n) n* De
En telephone
Es teléfono *(m)*
Fr téléphone *(m)*
It telefono *(m)*
Pt telefone *(m)*

**telephone** *n* En
De Fernsprecher; Telephon *(m n)*
Es teléfono *(m)*
Fr téléphone *(m)*
It telefono *(m)*
Pt telefone *(m)*

**téléphone** *(m) n* Fr
De Fernsprecher; Telephon *(m n)*
En telephone
Es teléfono *(m)*
It telefono *(m)*
Pt telefone *(m)*

**telephone call** En
De Anruf *(m)*
Es llamada telefónica *(f)*
Fr appel téléphonique *(m)*
It chiamata telefonica *(f)*
Pt chamada telefónica *(f)*

**telephone directory** En
De Fernsprechbuch *(n)*
Es guía de teléfonos *(f)*
Fr annuaire des téléphones *(m)*
It elenco telefonico *(m)*
Pt lista telefónica *(f)*

**telephone exchange** En
De Fernsprechamt *(n)*
Es central telefónica *(f)*
Fr central téléphonique *(m)*
It centrale telefonica *(f)*
Pt central telefónica *(f)*

**telephone number** En
De Telephonnummer *(f)*
Es número de teléfono *(m)*
Fr numéro de téléphone *(m)*
It numero di telefono *(m)*
Pt número de telefone *(m)*

**telephone operator** En
De Telephonist; Telephonistin *(m f)*
Es telefonista *(m/f)*
Fr téléphoniste *(m/f)*
It telefonista *(m/f)*
Pt telefonista *(m/f)*

**Telephonist** *(m) n* De
En telephone operator
Es telefonista *(m/f)*
Fr téléphoniste *(m/f)*
It telefonista *(m/f)*
Pt telefonista *(m/f)*

**téléphoniste** *(m/f) n* Fr
De Telephonist; Telephonistin *(m f)*
En telephone operator
Es telefonista *(m/f)*
It telefonista *(m/f)*
Pt telefonista *(m/f)*

**Telephonistin** *(f) n* De
En (female) telephone operator
Es telefonista *(f)*
Fr téléphoniste *(f)*
It telefonista *(f)*
Pt telefonista *(f)*

**Telephonnummer** *(f) n* De
En telephone number
Es número de teléfono *(m)*
Fr numéro de téléphone *(m)*
It numero di telefono *(m)*
Pt número de telefone *(m)*

**telex** *n* En; It, Pt *(m)*
De Fernschreiber *(m)*
Es télex *(m)*
Fr télex *(m)*

**télex** *(m) n* Es, Fr
De Fernschreiber *(m)*
En Telex
It telex *(m)*
Pt telex *(m)*

**teller** *n* Am
En cashier
De Kassierer *(m)*
Es cajero *(m)*
Fr caissier *(m)*
It cassiere *(m)*
Pt caixa *(m)*

**témoin** (m) n Fr
De Zeuge (m)
En witness
Es testigo (m)
It testimone (m)
Pt testemunha (f)

**tempesta** (f) n It
De Sturm (m)
En storm
Es tormenta (f)
Fr tempête (f)
Pt temporal (m)

**tempête** (f) n Fr
De Sturm (m)
En storm
Es tormenta (f)
It tempesta (f)
Pt temporal (m)

**tempo improdutivo** (m) Pt
De Leerlaufzeit (f)
En down time
Es tiempo improductivo (m)
Fr temps d'arrêt (m)
It tempo passivo (m)

**tempo-morto da máquina** (m) Pt
De Maschinenstillstandzeit (f)
En machine down-time
Es tiempo improductivo de la máquina (m)
Fr temps de panne machine (m)
It tempo passivo di macchina (m)

**tempo passivo** (m) It
De Leerlaufzeit (f)
En down time
Es tiempo improductivo (m)
Fr temps d'arrêt (m)
Pt tempo improdutivo (m)

**tempo passivo di macchina** (m) It
De Maschinenstillstandzeit (f)
En machine down-time
Es tiempo improductivo de la máquina (m)
Fr temps de panne machine (m)
Pt tempo-morto da máquina (m)

**temporal** (m) n Pt
De Sturm (m)
En storm
Es tormenta (f)
Fr tempête (f)
It tempesta (f)

**temporal** adj Es
De einstweilig
En temporary
Fr provisoire
It temporaneo
Pt temporário

**temporaneo** adj It
De einstweilig
En temporary
Es temporal
Fr provisoire
Pt temporário

**temporäre Deckung** (f) De
En temporary cover
Es cobertura provisional (f)
Fr couverture temporaire (m)
It copertura provvisoria (f)
Pt cobertura provisória (f)

**temporário** adj Pt
De einstweilig
En temporary
Es temporal
Fr provisoire
It temporaneo

**temporary** adj En
De einstweilig
Es temporal
Fr provisoire
It temporaneo
Pt temporário

**temporary cover** En
De temporäre Deckung (f)
Es cobertura provisional (f)
Fr couverture temporaire (m)
It copertura provvisoria (f)
Pt cobertura provisória (f)

**temps d'arrêt** (m) Fr
De Leerlaufzeit (f)
En down time
Es tiempo improductivo (m)
It tempo improduttivo (m)
Pt tempo passivo (m)

**temps de panne machine** (m) Fr
De Maschinenstillstandzeit (f)
En machine down-time
Es tiempo improductivo de la máquina (m)
It tempo passivo di macchina (m)
Pt tempo-morto da máquina (m)

**tenant** n En
De Mieter (m)
Es inquilino (m)
Fr locataire (m)
It affittuario; locatario (m)
Pt inquilino (m)

**tender** n En
De Angebot (n)
Es oferta (f)
Fr soumission (f)
It offerta (f)
Pt proposta (f)

**tenedor en buena fe** (m) Es
De gutgläubiger Besitzer (m)
En holder in due course
Fr porteur de bonne foi (m)
It titolare in buona fede (m)
Pt futuro proprietário (m)

**tenedor legítimo** (m) Es
De entgeltigter Besitzer (m)
En holder for value
Fr porteur à titre onéreux (m)
It detentore legittimo (m)
Pt proprietário legítimo (m)

**tenencia de acciones por mayoría** (f) Es
De Mehrheitsbeteiligung (f)
En majority holding
Fr participation majoritaire (f)
It partecipazione maggioritaria (f)
Pt propriedade em maioria (f)

**tener** vb Es
De halten
En hold
Fr tenir; détenir
It tenere
Pt reter

**tener acciones** Es
De beteiligt sein; Aktien besitzen

En hold shares
Fr détenir des actions
It tenere azioni
Pt reter acções

**tenere** *vb* It
De halten
En hold
Es tener
Fr tenir; détenir
Pt reter

**tenere azioni** It
De beteiligt sein; Aktien besitzen
En hold shares
Es tener acciones
Fr détenir des actions
Pt reter acções

**tenere in fedecommesso** It
De zu treuen Händen halten
En hold in trust
Es guardar in fideicomiso
Fr tenir par fidéicommis
Pt reter em custódia

**tenere in magazzino** It
De vorrätig halten
En keep in stock
Es guardar en almacén
Fr garder en stock
Pt reter em armazém

**tenere la contabilità** It
De Konto führen
En keep the accounts
Es llevar la contabilidad
Fr tenir la comptabilité
Pt fazer a contabilidade

**tenere una riunione** It
De eine Versammlung abhalten
En hold a meeting
Es celebrar una reunión
Fr tenir une assemblée
Pt fazer uma reunião

**teneur** *(f) n* Fr
De Laufzeit *(f)*
En tenor
Es tenor *(m)*
It tenore *(m)*
Pt tenor *(m)*

**tenir** *vb* Fr
De halten
En hold
Es tener
It tenere
Pt reter

**tenir la comptabilité** Fr
De Konto führen
En keep the accounts
Es llevar la contabilidad
It tenere la contabilità
Pt fazer a contabilidade

**tenir par fidéicommis** Fr
De zu treuen Händen halten
En hold in trust
Es guardar in fideicomiso
It tenere in fedecommesso
Pt reter em custódia

**tenir une assemblée** Fr
De eine Versammlung abhalten
En hold a meeting
Es celebrar una reunión
It tenere una riunione
Pt fazer uma reunião

**tenor** *n* En; Es, Pt *(m)*
De Laufzeit *(f)*
Fr teneur *(f)*
It tenore *(m)*

**tenore** *(m) n* It
De Laufzeit *(f)*
En tenor
Es tenor *(m)*
Fr teneur *(f)*
Pt tenor *(m)*

**tenore di vita** *(m)* It
De Lebenshaltung *(f)*
En standard of living
Es nivel de vida *(m)*
Fr niveau de vie *(m)*
Pt nível de vida *(m)*

**teoria de decisão** *(f)* Pt
De Entscheidungslehre *(f)*
En decision theory
Es teoría de la decisión *(f)*
Fr théorie de la décision *(f)*
It teoria della decisione *(f)*

**teoría de la decisión** *(f)* Es
De Entscheidungslehre *(f)*
En decision theory

Fr théorie de la décision *(f)*
It teoria della decisione *(f)*
Pt teoria de decisão *(f)*

**teoria della decisione** *(f)* It
De Entscheidungslehre *(f)*
En decision theory
Es teoría de la decisión *(f)*
Fr théorie de la décision *(f)*
Pt teoria de decisão *(f)*

**terceiros** *(m pl) n* Pt
De Dritte(r) *(m)*
En third party
Es tercero *(m)*
Fr tiers *(m)*
It terzi *(m pl)*

**tercero** *(m) n* Es
De Dritte(r) *(m)*
En third party
Fr tiers *(m)*
It terzi *(m pl)*
Pt terceiros *(m pl)*

**Termin-** De
En forward
Es a término
Fr en avant; à terme
It a termine
Pt adiante

**terminal de aeropuerto** *(f)* Es
De Luftterminal *(n)*
En air terminal
Fr aérogare *(f)*
It aerostazione *(f)*
Pt estação terminal aérea *(f)*

**Termindevisen** *(f pl) n* De
En forward exchange
Es divisas a término *(f pl)*
Fr change à terme *(m)*
It cambio a termine *(m)*
Pt divisas adiantada *(f pl)*

**termine** *(m) n* It
De Ablauf *(m)*
En expiry
Es expiración *(f)*
Fr expiration *(f)*
Pt expiração *(f)*

**Terminlieferung** *(f) n* De
En forward delivery
Es entrega futura *(f)*
Fr livraison à terme *(f)*

It  consegna a termine *(f)*
Pt  entrega futura *(f)*

**Terminmakler** *(m) n* De
En  option dealer
Es  operador a prima *(m)*
Fr  opérateur à prime *(m)*
It  operatore in contratti a premio *(m)*
Pt  corretor de opções *(m)*

**Terminmarkt** *(m) n* De
En  futures market
Es  mercado de futuros *(m)*
Fr  marché du terme *(m)*
It  mercato a termine *(m)*
Pt  mercado de futuros *(m)*

**Terminnotierung** *(f) n* De
En  forward price
Es  precio a término *(m)*
Fr  cours à terme *(m)*
It  prezzo per futura consegna *(m)*
Pt  preço adiantado *(m)*

**terms** *pl n* En
De  Bedingungen *(f pl)*
Es  condiciones *(f pl)*
Fr  conditions *(f pl)*
It  condizioni *(f pl)*
Pt  condições *(f pl)*

**terrain à bâtir** *(m)* Fr
De  Bauland *(n)*
En  building land
Es  solares *(m pl)*
It  terreno edile *(m)*
Pt  terreno para construção *(m)*

**terreni auriferi** *(m pl)* It
De  Goldgrube *(f)*
En  gold fields
Es  yacimiento aurífero *(m)*
Fr  régions aurifères *(f pl)*
Pt  jazigos de ouro *(m pl)*

**terreno edile** *(m)* It
De  Bauland *(n)*
En  building land
Es  solares *(m pl)*
Fr  terrain à bâtir *(m)*
Pt  terreno para construção *(m)*

**terreno para construção** *(m)* Pt
De  Bauland *(n)*
En  building land
Es  solares *(m pl)*
Fr  terrain à bâtir *(m)*
It  terreno edile *(m)*

**territorial waters** En
De  Hoheitsgewässer *(n pl)*
Es  aguas territoriales *(f pl)*
Fr  eaux territoriales *(f pl)*
It  acque territoriali *(f pl)*
Pt  águas territoriais *(f pl)*

**terzi** *(m pl) n* It
De  Dritte(r) *(m)*
En  third party
Es  tercero *(m)*
Fr  tiers *(m)*
Pt  terceiros *(m pl)*

**terzo arbitro** *(m)* It
De  Schiedsobmann *(m)*
En  umpire
Es  juez árbitro *(m)*
Fr  surarbitre *(m)*
Pt  juiz árbitro *(m)*

**tesoro** *(m) n* It
De  Schatzamt *(n)*
En  exchequer
Am  treasury
Es  hacienda *(f)*
Fr  trésorerie *(f)*
Pt  tesouro *(m)*

**tesouro** *(m) n* Pt
De  Schatzamt *(n)*
En  exchequer
Am  treasury
Es  hacienda *(f)*
Fr  trésorerie *(f)*
It  tesoro *(m)*

**tessile** *(m) n* It
De  Webware *(f)*
En  textile
Es  textil *(m)*
Fr  textile *(m)*
Pt  textil *(m)*

**Testamentseröffnung** *(f) n* De
En  probate
Es  validación de los testamentos *(f)*
Fr  homologation d'un testament *(f)*

It  omologazione di testamento *(f)*
Pt  validação testamentária *(f)*

**testemunha** *(f) n* Pt
De  Zeuge *(m)*
En  witness
Es  testigo *(m)*
Fr  témoin *(m)*
It  testimone *(m)*

**testigo** *(m) n* Es
De  Zeuge *(m)*
En  witness
Fr  témoin *(m)*
It  testimone *(m)*
Pt  testemunha *(f)*

**testimone** *(m) n* It
De  Zeuge *(m)*
En  witness
Es  testigo *(m)*
Fr  témoin *(m)*
Pt  testemunha *(f)*

**testo pubblicitario** *(m)* It
De  Werbetext *(m)*
En  advertising copy
Es  material publicitario *(m)*
Fr  copie publicitaire *(f)*
Pt  texto de publicidade *(m)*

**teuer** *adj* De
En  expensive
Es  caro
Fr  cher
It  caro
Pt  caro

**teueres Geld** *(n)* De
En  dear money
Es  dinero caro *(m)*
Fr  argent cher *(m)*
It  denaro ad alto interesse *(m)*
Pt  dinheiro caro *(m)*

**teurer werden** *vb* De
En  advance in price; go up
Es  encarecer
Fr  renchérir
It  aumentare di prezzo
Pt  encarecer

**textil** *(m) n* Es, Pt
De  Webware *(f)*
En  textile

Fr textile *(m)*
It tessile *(m)*

**textile** *n* En, Fr *(m)*
De Webware *(f)*
Es textil *(m)*
It tessile *(m)*
Pt textil *(m)*

**texto dactilografado** *(m)* Pt
De Maschinenschrift *(f)*
En typescript
Es texto mecanografiado *(m)*
Fr manuscrit dactylographié *(m)*
It dattiloscritto *(m)*

**texto de publicidade** *(m)* Pt
De Werbetext *(m)*
En advertising copy
Es material publicitario *(m)*
Fr copie publicitaire *(f)*
It testo pubblicitario *(m)*

**texto mecanografiado** *(m)* Es
De Maschinenschrift *(f)*
En typescript
Fr manuscrit dactylographié *(m)*
It dattiloscritto *(m)*
Pt texto dactilografado *(m)*

**Textverfasser** *(m)* *n* De
En copywriter
Es redactor publicitario *(m)*
Fr concepteur-rédacteur *(m)*
It redattore publicitario *(m)*
Pt redactor de publicidade *(m)*

**theft** *n* En
De Diebstahl *(m)*
Es robo *(m)*
Fr vol *(m)*
It furto *(m)*
Pt furto *(m)*

**théorie de la décision** *(f)* Fr
De Entscheidungslehre *(f)*
En decision theory
Es teoría de la decisión *(f)*
It teoria della decisione *(f)*
Pt teoria de decisão *(f)*

**thésaurisation** *(f)* *n* Fr
De Hort *(m)*
En hoard
Es atesoramiento *(m)*

It ammasso *(m)*
Pt acumulação *(f)*

**third party** En
De Dritte(r) *(m)*
Es tercero *(m)*
Fr tiers *(m)*
It terzi *(m pl)*
Pt terceiros *(m pl)*

**third-party insurance** En
De Haftpflichtversicherung *(f)*
Es seguro contra responsabilidad civil *(m)*
Fr assurance responsabilité civile (RC) *(f)*
It assicurazione contro terzi *(f)*
Pt seguro contra terceiros *(m)*

**threshold price** En
De Schwellenpreis *(m)*
Es precio de umbral *(m)*
Fr prix de seuil *(m)*
It prezzo soglia *(m)*
Pt preço convencionado *(m)*

**Tiefgang** *(m)* *n* De
En draught (of a ship)
Es calado *(m)*
Fr tirant d'eau *(m)*
It pescaggio *(m)*
Pt calado *(m)*

**tiempo improductivo** *(m)* Es
De Leerlaufzeit *(f)*
En down time
Fr temps d'arrêt *(m)*
It tempo passivo *(m)*
Pt tempo improdutivo *(m)*

**tiempo improductivo de la máquina** *(m)* Es
De Maschinenstillstandzeit *(f)*
En machine down-time
Fr temps de panne machine *(m)*
It tempo passivo di macchina *(m)*
Pt tempo-morto da máquina *(m)*

**tienda** *(f)* *n* Es
De Laden *(m)*
En shop
Fr magasin *(m)*
It bottega *(f)*
Pt loja *(f)*

**tiers** *(m)* *n* Fr
De Dritte(r) *(m)*
En third party
Es tercero *(m)*
It terzi *(m pl)*
Pt terceiros *(m pl)*

**tilgen** *vb* De
En redeem
Es redimir
Fr rembourser; dégager
It redimere; rimborsare
Pt remir; resgatar

**Tilgung** *(f)* *n* De
En redemption
Es amortización *(f)*
Fr amortissement *(m)*
It ammortamento *(m)*
Pt amortização *(f)*

**Tilgungsfonds** *(m)* *n* De
En sinking fund
Es fondo de amortización *(m)*
Fr fonds d'amortissement *(m)*
It fondo di ammortamento *(m)*
Pt fundo de amortização *(m)*

**timbre** *(m)* *n* Fr
De Stempel; Marke *(m f)*
En stamp
Es sello *(m)*
It timbro; francobollo *(m)*
Pt selo; carimbo *(m)*

**timbre-poste** *(m)* *n* Fr
De Briefmarke *(f)*
En postage stamp
Es sello de correos *(m)*
It francobollo *(m)*
Pt selo postal *(m)*

**timbro a data** *(m)* It
De Tagesstempel *(m)*
En date-stamp
Es sello de fecha *(m)*
Fr dateur *(m)*
Pt carimbo de datas *(m)*

**time and motion study** En
De Arbeitszeit- und Ablaufstudie *(f)*
Es estudio de tiempo y progreso *(m)*
Fr étude du temps et mouvements *(f)*

It studio dei tempi e dei movimenti *(m)*

Pt análise do tempo e progresso *(f)*

**time charter** En
De Zeitcharter *(f)*
Es fletamento de tiempo *(m)*
Fr affrètement à temps *(m)*
It contratto di noleggio a tempo *(m)*
Pt fretamento de tempo *(m)*

**timo** *(m) n* Es
De Schwindlertrick *(m)*
En confidence trick
Am confidence game
Fr vol à l´américaine *(m)*
It truffa all´americana *(f)*
Pt conto do vigário *(m)*

**tip** *n* En
De Trinkgeld *(n)*
Es propina *(f)*
Fr pourboire *(m)*
It mancia *(f)*
Pt gorjeta *(f)*

**tipo de cambio** *(m)* Es
De Wechselkurs *(m)*
En exchange rate
Fr taux de change *(m)*
It corso del cambio *(m)*
Pt taxa de câmbio *(m)*

**tipo de cambio flotante** *(m)* Es
De flexibler Wechselkurs *(m)*
En floating exchange rate
Fr taux de change flottant *(m)*
It cambio fluttuante *(m)*
Pt taxa de câmbio flutuante *(f)*

**tipo de interés** *(m)* Es
De Zinsfuss *(m)*
En rate of interest
Fr taux d´intérêt *(m)*
It tasso d´interesse *(m)*
Pt taxa de juro *(f)*

**tipo de rédito** *(m)* Es
De Ertragsrate *(f)*
En rate of return
Fr taux de rendement *(m)*
It tasso di reddito *(m)*
Pt taxa de rendimento *(f)*

**tipo oscilante** *(m)* Es
De schwankender Kurs *(m)*
En fluctuating rate
Fr taux variable *(m)*
It tasso variabile *(m)*
Pt taxa variável *(f)*

**tirant d'eau** *(m)* Fr
De Tiefgang *(m)*
En (ship´s) draught
Es calado *(m)*
It pescaggio *(m)*
Pt calado *(m)*

**tiré** *(m) n* Fr
De Bezogene(r) *(m)*
En drawee
Es librado *(m)*
It trattario *(m)*
Pt sacado *(m)*

**tirer un chèque** Fr
De einen Scheck ausstellen
En draw a cheque
Es extender un cheque
It emettere un assegno
Pt passar um cheque

**tireur** *(m) n* Fr
De Aussteller *(m)*
En drawer
Es librador *(m)*
It traente *(m)*
Pt sacador *(m)*

**tirocinio** *(m) n* It
De Lehre *(f)*
En apprenticeship
Am trainee period
Es aprendizaje *(m)*
Fr apprentissage *(m)*
Pt aprendizagem *(f)*

**title** (legal) *n* En
De Anspruch; Titel *(m)*
Es título *(m)*
Fr titre; droit *(m)*
It titolo; diritto *(m)*
Pt título *(m)*

**title deed** En
De Eigentumstitel *(m)*
Es título de propiedad *(m)*
Fr titre de propriété *(m)*
It titolo di proprietà *(m)*
Pt título de propriedade *(m)*

**titolare** *(m) n* It
De Inhaber *(m)*
En holder
Es titular *(m)*
Fr détenteur *(m)*
Pt titular *(m)*

**titolare in buona fede** *(m)* It
De gutgläubiger Besitzer *(m)*
En holder in due course
Es tenedor en buena fe *(m)*
Fr porteur de bonne foi *(m)*
Pt futuro proprietário *(m)*

**titoli** *(m pl) n* It
De Wertpapiere; Effekten *(n pl; m pl)*
En stock; securities
Es títulos; valores *(m pl)*
Fr titres; valeurs *(m pl; f pl)*.
Pt títulos; valores *(m pl)*

**titoli di assoluta fiducia** *(m pl)* It
De mündelsichere Wertpapiere *(n pl)*
En gilt-edged securities
Es valores de toda confianza *(m pl)*
Fr valeurs de tout repos *(f pl)*
Pt valores de todo a confiança *(m pl)*

**titoli di prestito** *(m pl)* It
De Anleihewerte *(m pl)*
En loan stock
Es títulos de préstamo *(m pl)*
Fr titres d´emprunt *(m pl)*
Pt títulos de empréstimo *(m pl)*

**titoli di Stato** *(m pl)* It
De Regierungsschuldverschreibungen *(f pl)*
En Government securities
Es títulos públicos *(m pl)*
Fr titres d´État *(m pl)*
Pt títulos do Tesouro *(m pl)*

**titoli non quotati** *(m pl)* It
De nicht notierte Werte *(m pl)*
En unquoted securities
Es títulos no cotizados *(m pl)*
Fr valeurs non cotées *(f pl)*
Pt títulos não cotados *(m pl)*

**titoli quotati (in borsa)** *(m pl)*
It
De an der Börse notierte Wert-
papiere *(n pl)*
En listed security
Es valores cotizables *(m pl)*
Fr valeurs admises à la Bourse
*(f pl)*
Pt valor de Bolsa com cotação
oficial *(m)*

**titolo** *(m)* n It
De Titel; Wertpapier *(m n)*
En (legal) title; security
Es título *(m)*
Fr titre *(m)*
Pt título *(m)*

**titolo a breve scadenza** *(m)* It
De kurzfristiger Effekt *(m)*
En short-dated security
Es título a corto plazo *(m)*
Fr titre à court terme *(m)*
Pt título a curto prazo *(m)*

**titolo a interesse fisso** *(m)* It
De festverzinsliches Wertpa-
pier *(n)*
En fixed-interest security
Es obligación a interés fijo *(f)*
Fr valeur à revenu fixe *(f)*
Pt obrigação de juro fixo *(f)*

**titolo al portatore** *(m)* It
De Inhaberobligation *(f)*
En bearer bond
Es título al portador *(m)*
Fr bon au porteur *(m)*
Pt título ao portador *(m)*

**titolo di proprietà** *(m)* It
De Eigentumstitel *(m)*
En title deed
Es título de propiedad *(m)*
Fr titre de propriété *(m)*
Pt título de propriedade *(m)*

**titolo negoziabile** *(m)* It
De begebbares Wertpapier *(n)*
En negotiable instrument
Es título negociable *(m)*
Fr effet de commerce *(m)*
Pt título negociável *(m)*

**titre** *(m)* n Fr
De Titel; Wertpapier *(m n)*
En (legal) title; security
Es título *(m)*

It titolo *(m)*
Pt título *(m)*

**titre à court terme** *(m)* Fr
De kurzfristiger Effekt *(m)*
En short-dated security
Es título a corto plazo *(m)*
It titolo a breve scadenza *(m)*
Pt título a curto prazo *(m)*

**titre de propriété** *(m)* Fr
De Eigentumstitel *(m)*
En title deed
Es título de propiedad *(m)*
It titolo di proprietà *(m)*
Pt título de propriedade *(m)*

**titres** *(m pl)* n Fr
De Wertpapiere; Effekten *(n pl;
m pl)*
En stock; securities
Es títulos; valores *(m pl)*
It titoli; valori *(m pl)*
Pt títulos; valores *(m pl)*

**titres avec perspectives de
croissance** *(m pl)* Fr
De wachstumorientierte Wert-
papiere *(n pl)*
En growth stocks
Es títulos de crecimiento *(m
pl)*
It titoli di sviluppo *(m pl)*
Pt acções de acréscimo de
capital *(f pl)*

**titres d'emprunt** *(m pl)* Fr
De Anleihewerte *(m pl)*
En loan stock
Es títulos de préstamo *(m pl)*
It titoli di prestito *(m pl)*
Pt títulos de empréstimo *(m
pl)*

**titres d'État** *(m pl)* Fr
De Regierungsschuldverschrei-
bungen *(f pl)*
En Government securities
Es títulos públicos *(m pl)*
It titoli di Stato *(m pl)*
Pt títulos do Tesouro *(m pl)*

**titular** *(m)* n Es, Pt
De Inhaber *(m)*
En holder
Fr détenteur *(m)*
It titolare *(m)*

**titular de obrigação** *(m)* Pt
De Obligationsinhaber *(m)*
En debenture holder; bond-
holder
Es obligacionista *(m)*
Fr porteur d'obligations; obli-
gataire *(m)*
It obbligazionista *(f)*

**titular de seguro** *(m)* Pt
De Versicherte(r) *(m)*
En insured
Es asegurado *(m)*
Fr assuré *(m)*
It assicurato *(m)*

**título** *(m)* n Es, Pt
De Titel; Wertpapier; Urkunde
*(m n f)*
En (legal) title; stock; deed
Fr titre; droit; acte *(m)*
It titolo; diritto; atto *(m)*

**título a corto plazo** *(m)* Es
De kurzfristiger Effekt *(m)*
En short-dated security
Fr titre à court terme *(m)*
It titolo a breve scadenza *(m)*
Pt título a curto prazo *(m)*

**título a curto prazo** *(m)* Pt
De kurzfristiger Effekt *(m)*
En short-dated security
Es título a corto plazo *(m)*
Fr titre à court terme *(m)*
It titolo a breve scadenza *(m)*

**título al portador** *(m)* Es
De Inhaberobligation *(f)*
En bearer bond
Fr bon au porteur *(m)*
It titolo al portatore *(m)*
Pt título ao portador *(m)*

**título ao portador** *(m)* Pt
De Inhaberobligation *(f)*
En bearer bond
Es título al portador *(m)*
Fr bon au porteur *(m)*
It titolo al portatore *(m)*

**título de acción** *(m)* Es
De Aktienzertifikat *(n)*
En share certificate
Am certificate of stock
Fr certificat d'actions *(m)*
It certificato azionario *(m)*
Pt título de acções *(m)*

**título de acções** *(m)* Pt
De Aktienzertifikat *(n)*
En share certificate
Am certificate of stock
Es título de acción *(m)*
Fr certificat d'actions *(m)*
It certificato azionario *(m)*

**título de asignación** *(m)* Es
De Abtretungsvertrag *(m)*
En deed of assignment
Fr acte attributif *(m)*
It atto di cessione *(m)*
Pt título de consignação *(m)*

**título de bodemeria** *(m)* Pt
De Bodmereibrief *(m)*
En bottomry bond
Es contrato de préstamo a la gruesa *(m)*
Fr contrat à la grosse aventure *(m)*
It contratto di prestito a cambio marittimo *(m)*

**título de consignação** *(m)* Pt
De Abtretungsvertrag *(m)*
En deed of assignment
Es título de asignación *(m)*
Fr acte attributif *(m)*
It atto di cessione *(m)*

**título de doação** *(m)* Pt
De Erlebensversicherung *(f)*
En endowment policy
Es póliza dotal *(f)*
Fr assurance à terme fixe *(f)*
It assicurazione dotale *(f)*

**título de investimento imobiliário** *(m)* Pt
De Grund- und Gebäudeobligation *(f)*
En property bond
Es cédula hipotecaria *(f)*
Fr obligation foncière *(f)*
It obbligazione fondiaria *(f)*

**título de propiedad** *(m)* Es
De Eigentumstitel *(m)*
En title deed
Fr titre de propriété *(m)*
It titolo di proprietà *(m)*
Pt título de propriedade *(m)*

**título de propriedade** *(m)* Pt
De Eigentumstitel *(m)*
En title deed

Es título de propiedad *(m)*
Fr titre de propriété *(m)*
It titolo di proprietà *(m)*

**título de transferência** *(m)* Pt
De Übertragungsvertrag *(m)*
En transfer deed
Es escritura de transferencia *(f)*
Fr acte de cession *(m)*
It atto di trapasso *(m)*

**título documental** *(m)* Pt
De Dokumentenwechsel *(m)*
En documentary bill
Es efecto documentario *(m)*
Fr traite documentaire *(f)*
It tratta documentaria *(f)*

**título do tesouro** *(m)* Pt
De Schatzwechsel *(m)*
En exchequer bond
Am treasury bond
Es bono de tesorería *(m)*
Fr bon du trésor *(m)*
It buono del tesoro *(m)*

**título negociable** *(m)* Es
De begebbares Wertpapier *(n)*
En negotiable instrument
Fr effet de commerce *(m)*
It titolo negoziabile *(m)*
Pt título negociável *(m)*

**título negociável** *(m)* Pt
De begebbares Wertpapier *(n)*
En negotiable instrument
Es título negociable *(m)*
Fr effet de commerce *(m)*
It titolo negoziabile *(m)*

**títulos** *(m pl)* n Es, Pt
De Wertpapiere; Effekten *(n pl; m pl)*
En stocks; securities
Fr titres; valeurs *(m pl; f pl)*
It titoli; valori *(m pl)*

**títulos de crecimiento** *(m pl)* Es
De wachstumorientierte Wertpapiere *(n pl)*
En growth stocks
Fr titres avec perspectives de croissance
It bitoli di sviluppo *(m pl)*
Pt acções de acréscimo de capital *(f pl)*

**títulos de empréstimo** *(m pl)* Pt
De Anleihewerte *(m pl)*
En loan stock
Es títulos de préstamo *(m pl)*
Fr titres d'emprunt *(m pl)*
It titoli di prestito *(m pl)*

**títulos de préstamo** *(m pl)* Es
De Anleihewerte *(m pl)*
En loan stock
Fr titres d'emprunt *(m pl)*
It titoli di prestito *(m pl)*
Pt títulos de empréstimo *(m pl)*

**títulos do Tesouro** *(m pl)* Pt
De Regierungsschuldverschreibungen *(f pl)*
En Government securities
Es títulos públicos *(m pl)*
Fr titres d'État *(m pl)*
It titoli di Stato *(m pl)*

**títulos não cotados** *(m pl)* Pt
De nicht notierte Werte *(m pl)*
En unquoted securities
Es títulos no cotizados *(m pl)*
Fr valeurs non cotées *(f pl)*
It titoli non quotati *(m pl)*

**títulos no cotizados** *(m pl)* Es
De nicht notierte Werte *(m pl)*
En unquoted securities
Fr valeurs non cotées *(f pl)*
It titoli non quotati *(m pl)*
Pt títulos não cotados *(m pl)*

**título solidário de diversos** *(m)* Pt
De Solidarobligation *(f)*
En joint and several bond
Es obligación solidaria e indivisa *(f)*
Fr obligation conjointe et solidaire *(f)*
It obbligazione solidale *(f)*

**títulos públicos** *(m pl)* Es
De Regierungsschuldverschreibungen *(f pl)*
En Government securities
Fr titres d'État *(m pl)*
It titoli di Stato *(m pl)*
Pt títulos do Tesouro *(m pl)*

**Tochtergesellschaft** *(f) n* De
En subsidiary company
Es filial; empresa subsidiaría
    *(f)*
Fr filiale *(f)*
It filiale *(f)*
Pt companhia subsidiária *(f)*

**Tod** *(m) n* De
En death
Es muerte *(m)*
Fr mort *(f)*
It morte *(f)*
Pt morte *(f)*

**todos los riesgos** *(m pl)* Es
De alle Gefahren *(f pl)*
En all risks
Fr tous risques *(m pl)*
It tutti i rischi *(m pl)*
Pt todos os riscos *(m pl)*

**todos os riscos** *(m pl)* Pt
De alle Gefahren *(f pl)*
En all risks
Es todos los riesgos *(m pl)*
Fr tous risques *(m pl)*
It tutti i rischi *(m pl)*

**tomorrow** *adv* En
De morgen
Es mañana
Fr demain
It domani
Pt amanhã

**tonelada** *(f) n* Es, Pt
De Tonne *(f)*
En tonne
Fr tonne *(f)*
It tonnellata *(f)*

**tonelada bruta** *(f)* Es
De Brutto-Tonne *(f)*
En gross ton
Fr tonne forte *(f)*
It tonnellata lorda *(f)*
Pt tonelada de peso bruto *(f)*

**tonelada de deslocação** *(f)* Pt
De Verdrängungstonne *(f)*
En displacement-ton
Es tonelada de desplazami-
    ento *(f)*
Fr tonneau de déplacement
    *(m)*
It tonnellata di dislocamento
    *(f)*

**tonelada de desplazamiento**
    *(f)* Es
De Verdrängungstonne *(f)*
En displacement-ton
Fr tonneau de déplacement
    *(m)*
It tonnellata di dislocamento
    *(f)*
Pt tonelada de deslocação *(f)*

**tonelada de flete** *(f)* Es
De Handelstonne *(f)*
En freight ton
Fr tonneau de fret *(m)*
It tonnellata di nolo *(f)*
Pt tonelada de frete *(f)*

**tonelada de frete** *(f)* Pt
De Handelstonne *(f)*
En freight ton
Es tonelada de flete *(f)*
Fr tonneau de fret *(m)*
It tonnellata di nolo *(f)*

**tonelada de peso bruto** *(f)* Pt
De Brutto-Tonne *(f)*
En gross ton
Es tonelada bruta *(f)*
Fr tonne forte *(f)*
It tonnellata lorda *(f)*

**tonelada de registo bruto** *(f)*
    Pt
De Brutto-Registertonne *(f)*
En gross register ton
Es tonelada de registro bruto
    *(f)*
Fr tonneau de jauge brute *(m)*
It tonnellaggio lordo di regi-
    stro *(m)*

**tonelada de registro bruto** *(f)*
    Es
De Brutto-Registertonne *(f)*
En gross register ton
Fr tonneau de jauge brute *(m)*
It tonnellaggio lordo di regi-
    stro *(m)*
Pt tonelada de registo bruto
    *(f)*

**tonelada inglesa** *(f)* Es, Pt
De schwere Tonne *(f)*
En long ton
Fr tonne forte *(f)*
It tonnellata inglese *(f)*

**tonelagem** *(f) n* Pt
De Tonnengehalt *(m)*
En tonnage
Es tonelaje *(m)*
Fr tonnage *(m)*
It tonnellaggio *(m)*

**tonelagem de peso bruto** *(f)*
    Pt
De Brutto-Tonnage *(f)*
En gross tonnage
Es tonelaje bruto *(m)*
Fr tonnage brut *(m)*
It tonnellaggio lordo *(m)*

**tonelaje** *(m) n* Es
De Tonnengehalt *(m)*
En tonnage
Fr tonnage *(m)*
It tonnellaggio *(m)*
Pt tonelagem *(f)*

**tonelaje bruto** *(m)* Es
De Brutto-Tonnage *(f)*
En gross tonnage
Fr tonnage brut *(m)*
It tonnellaggio lordo *(m)*
Pt tonelagem de peso bruto
    *(f)*

**tonnage** *n* En, Fr *(m)*
De Tonnengehalt *(m)*
Es tonelaje *(m)*
It tonnellaggio *(m)*
Pt tonelagem *(f)*

**tonnage brut** *(m)* Fr
De Brutto-Tonnage *(f)*
En gross tonnage
Es tonelaje bruto *(m)*
It tonnellaggio lordo *(m)*
Pt tonelagem de peso bruto
    *(f)*

**tonne** *n* En, Fr *(f)*
De Tonne *(f)*
Es tonelada *(f)*
It tonnellata *(f)*
Pt tonelada *(f)*

**Tonne** *(f) n* De
En tonne
Es tonelada *(f)*
Fr tonne *(f)*
It tonnellata *(f)*
Pt tonelada *(f)*

**tonneau** (m) n Fr
De Fass (n)
En barrel
Es barril (m)
It botte (f)
Pt barril (m)

**tonneau de déplacement** (m) Fr
De Verdrängungstonne (f)
En displacement-ton
Es tonelada de desplazamiento (f)
It tonnellata di dislocamento (f)
Pt tonelada de deslocação (f)

**tonneau de fret** (m) Fr
De Handelstonne (f)
En freight ton
Es tonelada de flete (f)
It tonnellata di nolo (f)
Pt tonelada de frete (f)

**tonneau de jauge brute** (m) Fr
De Brutto-Registertonne (f)
En gross register ton
Es tonelada de registro bruto (f)
It tonnellaggio lordo di registro (m)
Pt tonelada de registo bruto (f)

**tonne forte** (f) Fr
De Brutto-Tonne (f)
En gross ton
Es tonelada bruta (f)
It tonnellata lorda (f)
Pt tonelada de peso bruto (f)

**tonnellaggio** (m) n It
De Tonnengehalt (m)
En tonnage
Es tonelaje (m)
Fr tonnage (m)
Pt tonelagem (m)

**tonnellaggio lordo** (m) It
De Brutto-Tonnage (f)
En gross tonnage
Es tonelaje bruto (m)
Fr tonnage brut (m)
Pt tonelagem de peso bruto (f)

**tonnellaggio lordo di registro** (m) It
De Brutto-Registertonne (f)
En gross register ton
Es tonelada de registro bruto (f)
Fr tonneau de jauge brute (m)
Pt tonelada de registo bruto (f)

**tonnellata** (f) n It
De Tonne (f)
En tonne
Es tonelada (f)
Fr tonne (f)
Pt tonelada (f)

**tonnellata di dislocamento** (f) It
De Verdrängungstonne (f)
En displacement-ton
Es tonelada de desplazamiento (f)
Fr tonneau de déplacement (m)
Pt tonelada de deslocação (f)

**tonnellata di nolo** (f) It
De Handelstonne (f)
En freight ton
Es tonelada de flete (f)
Fr tonneau de fret (m)
Pt tonelada de frete (f)

**tonnellata inglese** (f) It
De schwere Tonne (f)
En long ton
Es tonelada inglesa (f)
Fr tonne forte (f)
Pt tonelada inglesa (f)

**tonnellata lorda** (f) It
De Brutto-Tonne (f)
En gross ton
Es tonelada bruta (f9
Fr tonne forte (f)
Pt tonelada de peso bruto (f)

**Tonnengehalt** (m) n De
En tonnage
Es tonelaje (m)
Fr tonnage (m)
It tonnellaggio (m)
Pt tonelagem (f)

**top copy** En
De Original (n)
Es original (m)
Fr original (m)
It originale (m)
Pt original (m)

**top management** En
De Direktion (f)
Es dirección superior (f)
Fr haute direction (f)
It direzione superiore (f)
Pt gerência superior (f)

**top quality** En
De hochwertig
Es de primera calidad
Fr de première qualité
It di qualità superiore
Pt de classe superior

**tormenta** (f) n Es
De Sturm (m)
En storm
Fr tempête (f)
It tempesta (f)
Pt temporal (m)

**tort** n En
De unerlaubte Handlung (f)
Es agravio (m)
Fr acte dommageable (m)
It torto (m)
Pt agravo (m)

**torto** (m) n It
De unerlaubte Handlung (f)
En tort
Es agravio (m)
Fr acte dommageable (m)
Pt agravo (m)

**totaliser** vb Fr
De addieren
En add up
Es sumar
It sommare
Pt somar

**totalmente pago** Pt
De voll bezahlt
En fully paid up
Es completamente pagado
Fr entièrement versé
It interamente pagato

**totalmente subscrito** Pt
De vollgezeichnet
En fully subscribed
Es plenamente suscrito

Fr   intégralement souscrit
It   interamente sottoscritto

**Totenschein** *(m) n* De
En   death certificate
Es   partida de defunción *(f)*
Fr   extrait d´acte de décès *(m)*
It   certificato di morte *(m)*
Pt   certidão de óbito *(f)*

**totes Kapital** *(n)* De
En   idle money
Es   dinero sin invertır *(m)*
Fr   capital oisif *(m)*
It   denaro inattivo *(m)*
Pt   dinheiro paralizado *(m)*

**touche** (de machine à écrire) *(f)*
        *n* Fr
De   Taste *(f)*
En   key
Es   tecla *(f)*
It   tasto *(m)*
Pt   tecla *(f)*

**toucher un chèque** Fr
De   einen Scheck einlösen
En   cash a cheque
Am  cash a check
Es   cobrar un cheque
It   incassare un assegno
Pt   cobrar um cheque

**tourist trade** En
De   Reisegewerbe *(n)*
Es   industria del turismo *(f)*
Fr   commerce de tourisme *(m)*
It   commercio turistico *(m)*
Pt   indústria do turismo *(f)*

**tous risques** *(m pl)* Fr
De   alle Gefahren *(f pl)*
En   all risks
Es   todos los riesgos *(m pl)*
It   tutti i rischi *(m pl)*
Pt   todos os riscos *(m pl)*

**tout vendu** Fr
De   ausverkauft
En   sold out
Es   agotado
It   tutto venduto
Pt   esgotado

**to whom it may concern** En
De   an alle, die es angeht
Es   a quien concierna
Fr   à qui de droit

It   a tutti gli interessati
Pt   a quem disser respeito

**town gas** En
De   Stadtgas *(n)*
Es   gas de ciudad *(m)*
Fr   gaz de ville *(m)*
It   gas di carbon fossile *(m)*
Pt   gás urbano *(m)*

**toxic waste** En
De   giftiger Abfall *(m)*
Es   efluentes tóxicos *(m pl)*
Fr   déchets toxiques *(m pl)*
It   rifiuti tossici *(m pl)*
Pt   despejos tóxicos *(m pl)*

**trabajador** *(m) n* Es
De   Arbeiter *(m)*
En   worker
Fr   ouvrier *(m)*
It   lavoratore *(m)*
Pt   trabalhador *(m)*

**trabajador por cuenta propia**
        *(m)* Es
De   selbständig  Arbeitende(r)
        *(m)*
En   self-employed person
Fr   travailleur indépendant *(m)*
It   lavoratore indipendente *(m)*
Pt   empregado por conta-pró-
        pria *(m)*

**trabajo** *(m) n* Es
De   Arbeit; Beruf *(f m)*
En   work; job
Fr   travail; emploi *(m)*
It   lavoro *(m)*
Pt   trabalho *(m)*

**trabajo a destajo** *(m)* Es
De   Akkordarbeit *(f)*
En   piecework
Fr   travail à la tâche *(m)*
It   lavoro a cottimo *(m)*
Pt   trabalho por peça *(m)*

**trabajo en curso** *(m)* Es
De   Arbeit in der Ausführung *(f)*
En   work-in-progress
Am  work in process
Fr   travaux en cours *(m pl)*
It   lavoro in corso *(m)*
Pt   trabalho em curso *(m)*

**trabajo nocturno** *(m)* Es
De   Nachtarbeit *(f)*
En   nightwork
Fr   travail de nuit *(m)*
It   lavoro notturno *(m)*
Pt   trabalho nocturno *(m)*

**trabajo por torno** *(m)* Es
De   Arbeitsschicht *(f)*
En   shiftwork
Fr   travail par équipes *(m)*
It   lavoro a turno *(m)*
Pt   trabalho por turno *(m)*

**trabalhador** *(m) n* Pt
De   Arbeiter *(m)*
En   worker
Es   trabajador *(m)*
Fr   ouvrier *(m)*
It   lavoratore *(m)*

**trabalhador das docas** *(m)* Pt
De   Hafenarbeiter *(m)*
En   docker
Am  longshoreman
Es   cargador de muelle *(m)*
Fr   docker *(m)*
It   lavoratore del porto *(m)*

**trabalho** *(m) n* Pt
De   Arbeit *(f)*
En   work
Es   trabajo *(m)*
Fr   travail *(m)*
It   lavoro *(m)*

**trabalho  directamente  pro-
        dutivo** *(m)* Pt
De   produktive Arbeitskräfte *(f
        pl)*
En   direct labour
Es   jornales directos *(m pl)*
Fr   travail en régie *(m)*
It   lavoro in economia *(m)*

**trabalho em curso** *(m)* Pt
De   Arbeit in der Ausführung *(f)*
En   work-in-progress
Am  work in process
Es   trabajo en curso *(m)*
Fr   travaux en cours *(m pl)*
It   lavoro in corso *(m)*

**trabalho por peça** *(m)* Pt
De   Akkordarbeit *(f)*
En   piecework
Es   trabajo a destajo *(m)*

Fr travail à la tâche *(m)*
It lavoro a cottimo *(m)*

**trabalho nocturno** *(m)* Pt
De Nachtarbeit *(f)*
En nightwork
Es trabajo nocturno *(m)*
Fr travail de nuit *(m)*
It lavoro notturno *(m)*

**trabalho por turno** *(m)* Pt
De Arbeitsschicht *(f)*
En shiftwork
Es trabajo por torno *(m)*
Fr travail par équipes *(m)*
It lavoro a turno *(m)*

**trade** *n* En
De Handel *(m)*
Es comercio *(m)*
Fr commerce *(m)*
It commercio *(m)*
Pt comércio *(m)*

**trade acceptance** En
De Handelsakzept *(n)*
Es acceptación comercial *(f)*
Fr acceptation de commerce *(f)*
It accettazione commerciale *(f)*
Pt aceitação comercial *(f)*

**trade account** En
De Handelskonto *(n)*
Es cuenta comercial *(f)*
Fr compte commercial *(m)*
It conto commerciale *(m)*
Pt conta comercial *(f)*

**trade association** En
De Unternehmerverband *(m)*
Es asociación comercial *(f)*
Fr association professionnelle *(f)*
It associazione commerciale *(f)*
Pt associação comercial *(f)*

**trade balance** En
De Handelsbilanz *(f)*
Es balanza comercial *(f)*
Fr balance commerciale *(f)*
It bilancia commerciale *(f)*
Pt balança comercial *(f)*

**trade barrier** En
De Handelsschranke *(f)*
Es barrera comercial *(f)*
Fr barrière commerciale *(f)*
It barriera commerciale *(f)*
Pt barreira comercial *(f)*

**trade bloc** En
De Handelsblock *(m)*
Es bloque comercial *(m)*
Fr bloc commercial *(m)*
It unione commerciale *(f)*
Pt bloque comercial *(m)*

**trade catalogue** En
De Preiskatalog *(m)*
Es catálogo comercial *(m)*
Fr tarif-album *(m)*
It catalogo commerciale *(m)*
Pt catálogo comercial *(m)*

**trade cycle** En
De Handelszyklus *(m)*
Es ciclo del negocio *(m)*
Fr cycle de commerce *(m)*
It cyclo degli affari *(m)*
Pt ciclo comercial *(m)*

**trade directory** En
De Handelsadressbuch *(n)*
Es guía comercial *(f)*
Fr guide de commerce *(m)*
It guida commerciale *(f)*
Pt guia comercial *(m)*

**trade discount** En
De Händlerrabatt *(m)*
Es descuento comercial *(m)*
Fr rabais de demi-gros *(m)*
It sconto di revendita *(m)*
Pt desconto à praça *(m)*

**trade dispute** En
De Arbeitsstreitigkeit *(f)*
Es conflicto laboral *(m)*
Fr conflit du travail *(m)*
It vertenza di lavoro *(m)*
Pt conflito comercial *(m)*

**trade fair** En
De Handelsmesse *(f)*
Es feria de muestras *(f)*
Fr foire commerciale *(f)*
It fiera commerciale *(f)*
Pt feira comercial *(f)*

**trade gap** En
De Aussenhandelsdefizit *(n)*
Es vacío comercial *(m)*
Fr déficit du commerce extérieur *(m)*
It disavanzo della bilancia commerciale *(m)*
Pt vazio comercial *(m)*

**trademark** *n* En
De Warenzeichen *(n)*
Es marca de fábrica *(f)*
Fr marque de fabrique *(f)*
It marchio di fabbrica *(m)*
Pt marca de fabrico *(f)*

**trade name** En
De Firmenname *(m)*
Es razón social *(f)*
Fr raison sociale *(f)*
It denominazione commerciale *(f)*
Pt razão comercial *(f)*

**trade price** En
De Handelspreis *(m)*
Es precio al comerciante *(m)*
Fr prix marchand *(m)*
It prezzo al commerciante *(m)*
Pt preço para comerciantes *(m)*

**trade reference** En
De Kreditauskunft *(f)*
Es referencia comercial *(f)*
Fr référence de fournisseur *(f)*
It referenze commerciali *(f pl)*
Pt referência comercial *(f)*

**trade secret** En
De Betriebsgeheimnis *(n)*
Es secreto comercial *(m)*
Fr secret industriel *(m)*
It segreto commerciale *(m)*
Pt segredo comercial *(m)*

**trade union** En
De Gewerkschaft *(f)*
Es sindicato *(m)*
Fr syndicat ouvrier *(m)*
It sindacato *(m)*
Pt sindicato *(m)*

**trading capital** En
De Betriebskapital *(n)*
Es capital de explotación *(m)*
Fr fonds de roulement *(m)*

It capitale d'esercizio *(m)*
Pt capital de exploração *(m)*

**traente** *(m)* n It
De Aussteller *(m)*
En drawer
Es librador *(m)*
Fr tireur *(m)*
Pt sacador *(m)*

**tráfego aéreo** *(m)* Pt
De Luftverkehr *(m)*
En air traffic
Es tráfico aéreo *(m)*
Fr trafic aérien *(m)*
It traffico aereo *(m)*

**traffic jam** En
De Verkehrsstockung *(f)*
Es embotellamiento de tráfico *(m)*
Fr encombrement de circu-lation *(m)*
It ingorgo stradale *(m)*
Pt engarrafamento de tráfico *(m)*

**traffico aereo** *(m)* It
De Luftverkehr *(m)*
En air traffic
Es tráfico aéreo *(m)*
Fr trafic aérien *(m)*
Pt tráfego aéreo *(m)*

**trafic aérien** *(m)* Fr
De Luftverkehr *(m)*
En air traffic
Es tráfico aéreo *(m)*
It traffico aereo *(m)*
Pt tráfego aéreo *(m)*

**tráfico aéreo** *(m)* Es
De Luftverkehr *(m)*
En air traffic
Fr trafic aérien *(m)*
It traffico aereo *(m)*
Pt tráfego aéreo *(m)*

**Tragfähigkeit** *(f)* n De
En deadweight
Es peso muerto *(m)*
Fr port en lourd *(m)*
It peso morto *(m)*
Pt peso morto *(m)*

**train de marchandises** *(m)* Fr
De Güterzug *(m)*
En goods train

Am freight train
Es tren de mercancías *(m)*
It treno merci *(m)*
Pt comboio de mercadorías *(m)*

**train express** *(m)* Fr
De D-Zug; Schnellzug *(m)*
En express train
Es tren expreso *(m)*
It direttissimo; rapido *(m)*
Pt comboio rápido *(m)*

**traite** *(f)* n Fr
De Tratte *(f)*
En draft
Es letra *(f)*
It tratta *(f)*
Pt letra *(f)*

**traite à vue** *(f)* Fr
De Sichttratte *(f)*
En sight draft
Es letra a la vista *(f)*
It tratta a vista *(f)*
Pt letra à vista *(f)*

**traite bancaire** *(f)* Fr
De Banktratte *(f)*
En banker's draft
Es giro bancario *(m)*
It tratta bancaria *(f)*
Pt letra de banco *(f)*

**traite documentaire** *(f)* Fr
De Dokumentenwechsel *(m)*
En documentary bill
Es efecto documentario *(m)*
It tratta documentaria *(f)*
Pt título documental *(m)*

**traite en blanc** *(f)* Fr
De Blankowechsel *(m)*
En blank bill
Es letra en blanco *(f)*
It effetto in bianco *(m)*
Pt letra em branco *(f)*

**traitement** *(m)* n Fr
De Gehalt *(n)*
En salary
Es sueldo *(m)*
It stipendio *(m)*
Pt ordenado *(m)*

**traitement d'informatique** *(m)* Fr
De Datenverarbeitung *(f)*

En data processing
Es tratamiento de datos *(m)*
It elaborazione dei dati *(f)*
Pt processamento de dados *(m)*

**traitement juste** *(m)* Fr
De anständige Handlungs-weise *(f)*
En fair play
Es juego limpio *(m)*
It condotta leale *(f)*
Pt jogo limpo *(m)*

**Trampschiff** *(n)* n De
En tramp steamer
Es vapor volandero *(m)*
Fr navire de tramping *(m)*
It carretta *(f)*
Pt vapor de serviço autónomo *(m)*

**tramp steamer** En
De Trampschiff *(n)*
Es vapor volandero *(m)*
Fr navire de tramping *(m)*
It carretta *(f)*
Pt vapor de serviço autónomo *(m)*

**transacção** *(f)* n Pt
De Transaktion *(f)*
En transaction
Es transacción *(f)*
Fr transaction *(f)*
It transazione *(f)*

**transacção razoável** *(f)* Pt
De anständige Abmachung *(f)*
En fair deal
Es trato equitativo *(m)*
Fr affaire équitable *(f)*
It affare giusto *(m)*

**transacción** *(f)* n Es
De Transaktion *(f)*
En transaction
Fr transaction *(f)*
It transazione *(f)*
Pt transacção *(f)*

**transacções adiantadas** *(f pl)* Pt
De Zeitgeschäfte *(n pl)*
En forward dealings
Es negociaciones a término *(f pl)*

Fr  opérations à terme *(f pl)*
It  operazioni a termine *(f pl)*

**transaction** *n* En, Fr *(f)*
De  Transaktion *(f)*
Es  transacción *(f)*
It  transazione *(f)*
Pt  transacção *(f)*

**transaction au comptant** *(f)* Fr
De  Bargeschäft *(n)*
En  cash deal
Es  trato al contado *(m)*
It  operazione a contanti *(f)*
Pt  negócio em dinheiro *(m)*

**Transaktion** *(f) n* De
En  transaction
Es  transacción *(f)*
Fr  transaction *(f)*
It  transazione *(f)*
Pt  transacção *(f)*

**transatlántico** *(m) n* Es
De  Linienschiff *(n)*
En  liner
Fr  paquebot *(m)*
It  nave di linea *(f)*
Pt  paquete *(m)*

**transazione** *(f) n* It
De  Transaktion *(f)*
En  transaction
Es  transacción *(f)*
Fr  transaction *(f)*
Pt  transacção *(f)*

**transbordador** *(m) n* Es
De  Fährboot *(n)*
En  ferry-boat
Fr  bac *(m)*
It  nave traghetto *(f)*
Pt  barco de travessia *(m)*

**transbordement** *(m) n* Fr
De  Umladung *(f)*
En  transhipment
Es  transbordo *(m)*
It  trasbordo *(m)*
Pt  transbordo *(m)*

**transbordo** *(m) n* Es, Pt
De  Umladung *(f)*
En  transhipment
Fr  transbordement *(m)*
It  trasbordo *(m)*

**transcriber** *n* Am
En  copy typist
De  Abschreibtypistin *(f)*
Es  mecanógrafa *(f)*
Fr  dactylo copiste *(f)*
It  dattilografa *(f)*
Pt  dactilógrafa *(f)*

**transcrire** *vb* Fr
De  kopieren
En  copy
Es  copiar
It  copiare
Pt  copiar

**transfer** (of ownership) *n* En
De  Überweisung *(f)*
Es  cesión *(f)*
Fr  transfert; cession *(m f)*
It  cessione *(f)*
Pt  trespasse *(m)*

**transfer** (property, etc.) *vb* En
De  überweisen
Es  transferir
Fr  céder; transférer
It  trasferire
Pt  transferir

**transfer deed** En
De  Übertragungsvertrag *(m)*
Es  escritura de transferencia *(f)*
Fr  acte de cession *(m)*
It  atto di trapasso *(m)*
Pt  título de transferência *(m)*

**transferee** *n* En
De  Zessionär *(m)*
Es  cesionario *(m)*
Fr  cessionnaire *(m)*
It  cessionario *(m)*
Pt  cessionário *(m)*

**transferencia bancaria** *(f)* Es
De  Banküberweisung *(f)*
En  bank transfer
Fr  virement bancaire *(m)*
It  trasferimento bancario *(m)*
Pt  transferência bancária *(f)*

**transferência bancária** *(f)* Pt
De  Banküberweisung *(f)*
En  bank transfer
Es  transferencia bancaria *(f)*
Fr  virement bancaire *(m)*
It  trasferimento bancario *(m)*

**transferencia postal** *(f)* Es
De  Postüberweisung *(f)*
En  mail transfer
Fr  virement postal *(m)*
It  trasferimento per posta *(m)*
Pt  transferência postal *(f)*

**transferência postal** *(f)* Pt
De  Postüberweisung *(f)*
En  mail transfer
Es  transferencia postal *(f)*
Fr  virement postal *(m)*
It  trasferimento per posta *(m)*

**transferência telegráfica** *(f)* Pt
De  Kabelauszahlung *(f)*
En  telegraphic transfer
Es  giro telegráfico *(m)*
Fr  virement télégraphique *(m)*
It  rimessa telegrafica *(f)*

**transférer** *vb* Fr
De  überweisen
En  transfer
Es  transferir
It  trasferire
Pt  transferir

**transferir** *vb* Es, Pt
De  überweisen
En  transfer
Fr  céder; transférer
It  trasferire

**transferor** *n* En
De  Zedent *(m)*
Es  cesionista *(m)*
Fr  cédant *(m)*
It  cedente *(m)*
Pt  cessionista *(m)*

**transfert** *(m) n* Fr
De  Überweisung *(f)*
En  transfer
Es  cesión *(f)*
It  cessione *(f)*
Pt  trespasse *(m)*

**transformations et réparations** Fr
De  Änderungen und Reparaturen
En  alterations and repairs
Es  reformas y reparaciones
It  modifiche e riparazioni
Pt  modificações e reparações

**transhipment** *n* En
De Umladung *(f)*
Es transbordo *(m)*
Fr transbordement *(m)*
It trasbordo *(m)*
Pt transbordo *(m)*

**transitaire** *(m) n* Fr
De Spediteur *(m)*
En forwarding agent
Es agente expedidor *(m)*
It spedizioniere *(m)*
Pt agente expedidor *(m)*

**transmission de biens** *(f)* Fr
De Übertragung *(f)*
En conveyance of property
Es traspaso de propiedad *(m)*
It trasferimento di beni *(m)*
Pt trespasse de propriedade *(m)*

**transport** *n* En, Fr *(m)*
De Beförderung; Transport *(f m)*
Es transporte *(m)*
It trasporto *(m)*
Pt transporte *(m)*

**Transport** *(m) n* De
En transport
Es transporte *(m)*
Fr transport *(m)*
It trasporto *(m)*
Pt transporte *(m)*

**transportador** *(m) n* Es, Pt
De Spediteur *(m)*
En carrier
Am conveyer
Fr expéditeur *(m)*
It vettore *(m)*

**transportador a grand** *(m)* Es
De Massenfrachtführer *(m)*
En bulk carrier
Fr transporteur de marchandises en vrac *(m)*
It trasportatore di merce alla rinfusa *(m)*
Pt transportador de carga geral *(m)*

**transportador de carga geral** *(m)* Pt
De Massenfrachtführer *(m)*
En bulk carrier
Es transportador a grand *(m)*

Fr transporteur de marchandises en vrac *(m)*
It trasportatore di merce alla rinfusa *(m)*

**transport aérien** *(m)* Fr
De Lufttransport *(m)*
En air transport
Es transporte aéreo *(m)*
It trasporto aereo *(m)*
Pt transporte aéreo *(m)*

**transporte** *(m) n* Es, Pt
De Beförderung; Transport *(f m)*
En transport
Fr transport *(m)*
It trasporto *(m)*

**transporte aéreo** *(m)* Es, Pt
De Lufttransport *(m)*
En air transport
Fr transport aérien *(m)*
It trasporto aereo *(m)*

**transporte a pagar (pelo destinatário)** Pt
De Portonachnahme
En carriage forward
Am F.O.B. shipping point
Es a porte debido
Fr en port dû
It porto assegnato

**transporteur de marchandises en vrac** *(m)* Fr
De Massenfrachtführer *(m)*
En bulk carrier
Es transportador a grand *(m)*
It trasportatore di merce alla rinfusa *(m)*
Pt transportador de carga geral *(m)*

**Transportunternehmer** *(m) n* De
En haulage contractor
Am trucking company
Es contratista de transportes *(m)*
Fr entrepreneur de camionnage *(m)*
It imprenditore di trasporti *(m)*
Pt empreiteiro de transportes *(m)*

**trarre alla scoperto** It
De überziehen
En overdraw
Es girar en descubierto
Fr mettre à découvert
Pt levantar a descoberto

**trasbordo** *(m) n* It
De Umladung *(f)*
En transhipment
Es transbordo *(m)*
Fr transbordement *(m)*
Pt transbordo *(m)*

**trasferimento bancario** *(m)* It
De Banküberweisung *(f)*
En bank transfer
Es transferencia bancaria *(f)*
Fr virement bancaire *(m)*
Pt transferência bancária *(f)*

**trasferimento di beni** *(m)* It
De Übertragung *(f)*
En conveyance of property
Es traspaso de propiedad *(m)*
Fr transmission de biens *(f)*
Pt trespasse de propriedade *(m)*

**trasferimento per posta** *(m)* It
De Postüberweisung *(f)*
En mail transfer
Es transferencia postal *(f)*
Fr virement postal *(m)*
Pt transferência postal *(f)*

**trasferire** *vb* It
De überweisen
En transfer
Es transferir
Fr transférer
Pt transferir

**traspaso de propiedad** *(m)* Es
De Übertragung *(f)*
En conveyance of property
Fr transmission de biens *(f)*
It trasferimento di beni *(m)*
Pt trespasse de propriedade *(m)*

**trasportatore di merce alla rinfusa** *(m)* It
De Massenfrachtführer *(m)*
En bulk carrier
Es transportador a grand *(m)*
Fr transporteur de marchandises en vrac *(m)*

Pt transportador de carga geral *(m)*

**trasporto** *(m) n* It
De Beförderung; Transport *(f m)*
En transport
Es transporte *(m)*
Fr transport *(m)*
Pt transporte *(m)*

**trasporto a collettame** *(m)* It
De Groupagedienst *(m)*
En groupage service
Es servicio de agrupación *(m)*
Fr service de groupage *(m)*
Pt serviço de agrupamento *(m)*

**trasporto aereo** *(m)* It
De Lufttransport *(m)*
En air transport
Es transporte aéreo *(m)*
Fr transport aérien *(m)*
Pt transporte aéreo *(m)*

**tratamiento de datos** *(m)* Es
De Datenverarbeitung *(f)*
En data processing
Fr traitement d'informatique *(m)*
It elaborazione dei dati *(f)*
Pt processamento de dados *(m)*

**trato al contado** *(m)* Es
De Bargeschäft *(n)*
En cash deal
Fr transaction au comptant *(f)*
It operazione a contanti *(f)*
Pt negócio em dinheiro *(m)*

**trato equitativo** *(m)* Es
De anständige Abmachung *(f)*
En fair deal
Fr affaire équitable *(f)*
It affare giusto *(m)*
Pt transacção razoável *(f)*

**tratta** *(f) n* It
De Tratte *(f)*
En draft
Es letra *(f)*
Fr traite *(f)*
Pt letra *(f)*

**tratta a vista** *(f)* It
De Sichttratte *(f)*
En sight draft
Es letra a la vista *(f)*
Fr traite à vue *(f)*
Pt letra à vista *(f)*

**tratta bancaria** *(f)* It
De Banktratte *(f)*
En banker's draft
Es giro bancario *(m)*
Fr traite bancaire *(f)*
Pt letra de banco *(f)*

**tratta cambiale** *(f)* It
De Wechsel; Tratte *(m f)*
En bill of exchange
Es letra de cambio *(f)*
Fr lettre de change *(f)*
Pt letra de câmbio *(f)*

**tratta documentaria** *(f)* It
De Dokumentenwechsel *(m)*
En documentary bill
Es efecto documentario *(m)*
Fr traite documentaire *(f)*
Pt título documental *(m)*

**trattario** *(m) n* It
De Bezogene(r) *(m)*
En drawee
Es librado *(m)*
Fr tiré *(m)*
Pt sacado *(m)*

**trattativa** *(f) n* It
De Verhandlung *(f)*
En negotiation
Es negociación *(f)*
Fr négotiation *(f)*
Pt negociação *(f)*

**Tratte** *(f) n* De
En draft
Es letra *(f)*
Fr traite *(f)*
It tratta *(f)*
Pt letra *(f)*

**travail** *(m) n* Fr
De Arbeit *(f)*
En work
Es trabajo *(m)*
It lavoro *(m)*
Pt trabalho *(m)*

**travail à la tâche** *(m)* Fr
De Akkordarbeit *(f)*
En piecework
Es trabajo a destajo *(m)*
It lavoro a cottimo *(m)*
Pt trabalho por peça *(m)*

**travail de nuit** *(m)* Fr
De Nachtarbeit *(f)*
En nightwork
Es trabajo nocturno *(m)*
It lavoro notturno *(m)*
Pt trabalho nocturno *(m)*

**travail en régie** *(m)* Fr
De produktive Arbeitskräfte *(f pl)*
En direct labour
Es jornales directos *(m pl)*
It lavoro in economia *(m)*
Pt trabalho directamente produtivo *(m)*

**travailleur indépendant** *(m)* Fr
De selbständig Arbeitende(r) *(m)*
En self-employed person
Es trabajador por cuenta propia *(m)*
It lavoratore indipendente *(m)*
Pt empregado por conta-própria *(m)*

**travail par équipes** *(m)* Fr
De Arbeitsschicht *(f)*
En shiftwork
Es trabajo por torno *(m)*
It lavoro a turno *(m)*
Pt trabalho por turno *(m)*

**travaux de transformation** *(m pl)* Fr
De Umbau *(m)*
En alterations -
Es reformas *(f pl)*
It modifiche *(f pl)*
Pt modificações *(f pl)*

**travaux en cours** *(m pl)* Fr
De Arbeit in der Ausführung *(f)*
En work-in-progress
Am work in process
Es trabajo en curso *(m)*
It lavoro in corso *(m)*
Pt trabalho em curso *(m)*

**travel agent** En
De  Reisebüro *(n)*
Es  agencia de viajes *(f)*
Fr  agence de voyages *(f)*
It  agenzia di viaggi *(f)*
Pt  agente de viagems *(m)*


**traveller's cheque** En
Am  traveler's check
De  Reisescheck *(m)*
Es  cheque de viajero *(m)*
Fr  chèque de voyage *(m)*
It  assegno turistico *(m)*
Pt  cheque de viajante *(m)*


**travelling expenses** En
De  Reisekosten *(pl)*
Es  dietas de viajes *(f pl)*
Fr  frais de voyage *(m pl)*
It  spese di viaggio *(f pl)*
Pt  despesas de viagem *(f pl)*


**treasury** *n* Am
En  exchequer
De  Schatzamt *(n)*
Es  hacienda *(f)*
Fr  trésorerie *(f)*
It  tesoro *(m)*
Pt  tesouro *(m)*


**treasury bond** Am
En  exchequer bond
De  Schatzwechsel *(m)*
Es  bono de tesorería *(m)*
Fr  bon du trésor *(m)*
It  buono del tesoro *(m)*
Pt  título do tesouro *(m)*


**treino vocacional** *(m)* Pt
De  Berufsausbildung *(f)*
En  vocational training
Es  formación profesional *(f)*
Fr  formation professionnelle *(f)*
It  addestramento professionale *(m)*


**tren de mercancías** *(m)* Es
De  Güterzug *(m)*
En  goods train
Am  freight train
Fr  train de marchandises *(m)*
It  treno merci *(m)*
Pt  comboio de mercadorías *(m)*


**tren expreso** *(m)* Es
De  D-Zug; Schnellzug *(m)*
En  express train
Fr  train express *(m)*
It  direttissimo; rapido *(m)*
Pt  comboio rápido *(m)*


**treno merci** *(m)* It
De  Güterzug *(m)*
En  goods train
Am  freight train
Es  tren de mercancías *(m)*
Fr  train de marchandises *(m)*
Pt  comboio de mercadorías *(m)*


**trésorerie** *(f)* n Fr
De  Schatzamt *(n)*
En  exchequer
Am  treasury
Es  hacienda *(f)*
It  tesoro *(m)*
Pt  tesouro *(m)*


**trespasse de propriedade** *(m)* Pt
De  Übertragung *(f)*
En  conveyance of property
Es  traspaso de propiedad *(m)*
Fr  transmission de biens *(f)*
It  trasferimento di beni *(m)*


**Treue** *(f)* n De
En  fidelity
Es  fidelidad *(f)*
Fr  fidélité *(f)*
It  fedeltà *(f)*
Pt  fidelidade *(f)*


**(zu) treuen Händen halten** De
En  hold in trust
Es  guardar in fideicomiso
Fr  tenir par fidéicommis
It  tenere in fedecommesso
Pt  guardar


**Treuhänder** *(m)* n De
En  trustee
Es  fideicomisario *(m)*
Fr  fidéicommissaire *(m)*
It  fidecommissario *(m)*
Pt  fiduciário *(m)*


**treuhänderisch** *adj* De
En  fiduciary
Es  fiduciario
Fr  fiduciaire


It  fiduciario
Pt  fiduciário


**Treuhandfonds** *(m)* n De
En  trust fund
Es  fondo fiduciario *(m)*
Fr  fonds fiduciaire *(m)*
It  fondo fiduciario *(m)*
Pt  fundação fiduciária *(f)*


**Treuhandgesellschaft** *(f)* n De
En  trust company
Es  banco fideicomisario *(m)*
Fr  société fiduciaire *(f)*
It  società fiduciaria *(f)*
Pt  empresa de investimentos *(f)*


**trial balance** En
De  Probebilanz *(f)*
Es  balance de comprobación de saldos *(m)*
Fr  bilan de vérification *(m)*
It  bilancio di verifica *(m)*
Pt  balancete de verificação *(m)*


**tribunal** *(m)* n Es, Fr, Pt
De  Gericht *(n)*
En  court (of law)
It  tribunale *(m)*


**tribunal arbitral** *(m)* Es
De  Schiedsgericht *(n)*
En  court of arbitration
Fr  cour d'arbitrage *(f)*
It  tribunale arbitrale *(m)*
Pt  tribunal de arbitragem *(m)*


**tribunal de apelação** *(m)* Pt
De  Berufungsgericht *(n)*
En  court of appeal
Es  tribunal de apelación *(m)*
Fr  cour d'appel *(m)*
It  corte d'appello *(f)*


**tribunal de apelación** *(m)* Es
De  Berufungsgericht *(n)*
En  court of appeal
Fr  cour d'appel *(m)*
It  corte d'appello *(f)*
Pt  tribunal de apelação *(m)*


**tribunal de arbitragem** *(m)* Pt
De  Schiedsgericht *(n)*
En  court of arbitration
Es  tribunal arbitral *(m)*

Fr  cour d'arbitrage *(m)*
It  tribunale arbitrale *(f)*

**tribunale** *(m)* n It
De  Gericht *(n)*
En  court (of law)
Es  tribunal *(m)*
Fr  tribunal *(m)*
Pt  tribunal *(m)*

**tribunale arbitrale** *(m)* It
De  Schiedsgericht *(n)*
En  court of arbitration
Es  tribunal arbitral *(m)*
Fr  cour d'arbitrage *(m)*
Pt  tribunal de arbitragem *(m)*

**tributação** *(f)* n Pt
De  Besteuerung *(f)*
En  taxation
Es  tributación *(f)*
Fr  imposition *(f)*
It  tassazione *(f)*

**tributação diferida** *(f)* Pt
De  latente Steuerpflicht *(f)*
En  deferred taxation
Es  tasación diferida *(f)*
Fr  imposition différée *(f)*
It  tassazione differita *(f)*

**tributação directa** *(f)* Pt
De  direkte Steuern *(f pl)*
En  direct taxation
Es  contribuciones directas *(f pl)*
Fr  contributions directes *(f pl)*
It  imposte dirette *(f pl)*

**tributação indirecta** *(f)* Pt
De  indirekte Steuern *(f pl)*
En  indirect taxation
Es  contribuciones indirectas *(f pl)*
Fr  contributions indirectes *(f pl)*
It  imposte indirette *(f pl)*

**tributación** *(f)* n Es
De  Besteuerung *(f)*
En  taxation
Fr  imposition *(f)*
It  tassazione *(f)*
Pt  tributação *(f)*

**tributável** *adj* Pt
De  abgabenpflichtig
En  dutiable

Es  tasable
Fr  taxable
It  tassabile

**tricher** *vb* Fr
De  betrügen
En  cheat
Es  engañar
It  truffare
Pt  enganar

**trimestral** *adj* Es, Pt
De  vierteljährlich
En  quarterly
Fr  trimestriel
It  trimestrale

**trimestrale** *adj* It
De  vierteljährlich
En  quarterly
Es  trimestral
Fr  trimestriel
Pt  trimestral

**trimestriel** *adj* Fr
De  vierteljährlich
En  quarterly
Es  trimestral
It  trimestrale
Pt  trimestral

**Trinkgeld** *(n)* n De
En  tip
Es  propina *(f)*
Fr  pourboire *(m)*
It  mancia *(f)*
Pt  gorjeta *(f)*

**tripulação** *(f)* n Pt
De  Mannschaft *(f)*
En  crew
Es  tripulación *(f)*
Fr  équipage *(m)*
It  equipaggio *(m)*

**tripulación** *(f)* n Es
De  Mannschaft *(f)*
En  crew
Fr  équipage *(m)*
It  equipaggio *(m)*
Pt  tripulação *(f)*

**trocar** *vb* Es, Pt
De  Tauschhandel treiben
En  barter
Fr  troquer
It  barattare

**Trockendock** *(n)* n De
En  dry dock
Es  dique seco *(m)*
Fr  cale sèche *(f)*
It  bacino di carenaggio *(m)*
Pt  doca-seca *(f)*

**troco miúdo** *(m)* Pt
De  Kleingeld *(n)*
En  small change
Es  moneda suelta *(f)*
Fr  petite monnaie *(f)*
It  spiccioli *(m pl)*

**troquer** *vb* Fr
De  Tauschhandel treiben
En  barter
Es  trocar
It  barattare
Pt  trocar

**trucking** n Am
En  haulage
De  Transport *(m)*
Es  transporte *(m)*
Fr  camionnage; transport *(m)*
It  trasporto *(m)*
Pt  transporte *(m)*

**trucking company** Am
En  haulage contractor
De  Transportunternehmer *(m)*
Es  contratista de transportes *(m)*
Fr  entrepreneur de camionnage *(m)*
It  imprenditore di trasporti *(m)*
Pt  empreiteiro de transportes *(m)*

**truffa all'americana** *(f)* It
De  Schwindlertrick *(m)*
En  confidence trick
Am  confidence game
Es  timo *(m)*
Fr  vol à l'américaine *(m)*
Pt  conto do vigário *(m)*

**truffare** *vb* It
De  betrügen
En  cheat
Es  engañar
Fr  tricher
Pt  enganar

**trunk call** En
Am long distance call
De Ferngespräch (n)
Es llamada interurbana (f)
Fr appel téléphonique interurbain (m)
It comunicazione interurbana (f)
Pt chamada inter-urbana (f)

**truqué** adj Fr
De gefälscht
En fake
Es falso
It falso
Pt falsificado

**trust company** En
De Treuhandgesellschaft (f)
Es banco fideicomisario (m)
Fr société fiduciaire (f)
It società fiduciaria (f)
Pt empresa de investimentos (f)

**trustee** n En
De Treuhänder (m)
Es fideicomisario (m)
Fr fidéicommissaire (m)
It fidecommissario (m)
Pt fiduciário (m)

**trust fund** En
De Treuhandfonds (m)
Es fondo fiduciario (m)
Fr fonds fiduciaire (m)
It fondo fiduciario (m)
Pt fundação fiduciária (f)

**tug-boat** n En
De Schleppdampfer (m)
Es remolcador (m)
Fr remorqueur (m)
It rimorchiatore (m)
Pt rebocador (m)

**turno** (m) n Es, It, Pt
De Schicht (f)
En shift
Fr équipe (f)

**turno da noite** (m) Pt
De Nachtschicht (f)
En night shift
Es turno de noche (m)
Fr équipe de nuit (m)
It turno di notte (m)

**turno de día** (m) Es
De Tagschicht (f)
En day shift
Fr équipe du jour (f)
It turno di giorno (m)
Pt turno de dia (m)

**turno de dia** (m) Pt
De Tagschicht (f)
En day shift
Es turno de día (m)
Fr équipe du jour (f)
It turno di giorno (m)

**turno de noche** (m) Es
De Nachtschicht (f)
En night shift
Fr équipe de nuit (m)
It turno di notte (m)
Pt turno da noite (m)

**turno di giorno** (m) It
De Tagschicht (f)
En day-shift
Es turno de día (m)
Fr équipe du jour (f)
Pt turno de dia (m)

**turno di notte** (m) It
De Nachtschicht (f)
En night shift
Es turno de noche (m)
Fr équipe de nuit (m)
Pt turno da noite (m)

**turnover** n En
De Umsatz (m)
Es volumen de ventas (m)
Fr chiffre d'affaires (m)
It giro d'affari (m)
Pt movimento de dinheiro (m)

**tuteur** (d'un mineur) (m) n Fr
De Vormund (m)
En guardian
Es tutor (m)
It tutore (m)
Pt tutor (m)

**tutor** (m) n Es, Pt
De Vormund (m)
En guardian
Fr tuteur (m)
It tutore (m)

**tutore** (m) n It
De Vormund (m)
En guardian

Es tutor (m)
Fr tuteur (m)
Pt tutor (m)

**tutti i rischi** (m pl) It
De alle Gefahren (f pl)
En all risks
Es todos los riesgos (m pl)
Fr tous risques (m pl)
Pt todos os riscos (m pl)

**tutto venduto** It
De ausverkauft
En sold out
Es agotado
Fr tout vendu
Pt esgotado

**type** vb En
De auf der Schreibmaschine schreiben
Es escribir a máquina
Fr écrire à la machine
It scrivere a macchina
Pt escrever à máquina

**typescript** n En
De Maschinenschrift (f)
Es texto mecanografiado (m)
Fr manuscrit dactylographié (m)
It dattiloscritto (m)
Pt texto dactilografado (m)

**typewriter** n En
De Schreibmaschine (f)
Es máquina de escribir (f)
Fr machine à écrire (f)
It macchina da scrivere (f)
Pt máquina de escrever (f)

# U

**überarbeitete Schätzung** (f) De
En revised estimate
Es cálculo revisado (m)
Fr devis rectifié (m)
It preventivo riveduto (m)
Pt estimativa revista (f)

**über Bord werfen** De
En jettison
Es echar al mar
Fr jeter à la mer

It  fare gettito
Pt  alijar

**Überbrückung** *(f) n* De
En  stop-gap
Es  recurso provisional *(m)*
Fr  bouche-trou *(m)*
It  provvedimento temporaneo *(m)*
Pt  tapa-buracos *(m)*

**Übergangskonto** *(n) n* De
En  suspense account
Es  cuenta suspensa *(f)*
Fr  compte d ordre *(m)*
It  conto sospeso *(m)*
Pt  conta pendente *(m)*

**Übergepäck** *(n) n* De
En  excess luggage (baggage)
Es  exceso de equipaje *(m)*
Fr  excédent de bagages *(m)*
It  bagaglio eccedente *(m)*
Pt  excesso de bagagem *(m)*

**Übergewicht** *(n) n* De
En  excess weight
Es  peso excedente *(m)*
Fr  excédent de poids *(m)*
It  eccedenza di peso *(f)*
Pt  excesso de peso *(m)*

**Übergewicht** *(n) n* De
En  overweight
Es  exceso de peso *(m)*
Fr  excédent *(m)*
It  sovrappeso *(m)*
Pt  peso excessivo *(m)*

**Übergewinnsteuer** *(f) n* De
En  excess profits tax
Es  impuesto sobre beneficios extraordinarios *(m pl)*
Fr  impôts sur les superbénéfices *(m pl)*
It  imposta sui sopraprofitti *(f)*
Pt  imposto sobre lucros excessivos *(m)*

**Überkapazität** *(f) n* De
En  overcapacity
Es  exceso de capacidad *(m)*
Fr  surcapacité *(f)*
It  capacità in eccedenza *(f)*
Pt  capacidade excessiva *(f)*

**Überliegezeit** *(f) n* De
En  demurrage
Es  sobreestadía *(f)*
Fr  surestarie *(f)*
It  controstallia *(f)*
Pt  sobreestadía *(f)*

**übermässig** *adj* De
En  excessive
Es  excesivo
Fr  excessif
It  eccessivo
Pt  excessivo

**übermorgen** *adv* De
En  day after tomorrow
Es  pasado mañana
Fr  après demain
It  dopodomani
Pt  depois de amanhã

**Übernahmeangebot** *(n) n* De
En  take-over bid
Es  oferta de adquisición *(f)*
Fr  offre de rachat *(f)*
It  offerta di acquisto *(f)*
Pt  proposta de apropriação *(f)*

**Übernahmebescheinigung** *(f) n* De
En  mate's receipt
Es  recibo de embarco *(m)*
Fr  billet de bord *(m)*
It  ricevuta d'imbarco *(f)*
Pt  recibo de embarque *(m)*

**über Pari** De
En  above par
Es  a premio
Fr  au-dessus du pair
It  sopra la pari
Pt  a prémio

**Überproduktion** *(f) n* De
En  overproduction
Es  exceso de producción *(m)*
Fr  surproduction *(f)*
It  sovraproduzione *(f)*
Pt  produção excessiva *(f)*

**Überschätzung** *(f) n* De
En  over-estimate
Es  presupuesto por exceso *(m)*
Fr  surestimation *(f)*
It  valutazione eccessiva *(f)*
Pt  avaliação excessiva *(f)*

**Überschuss** *(m) n* De
En  surplus; excess
Es  excedente; exceso *(m)*
Fr  surplus; excédent *(m)*
It  eccesso; soprappeso *(m)*
Pt  excedente; excesso *(m)*

**Überstunden** *(f pl) n* De
En  overtime
Es  horas extraordinarias *(f pl)*
It  lavoro straordinario *(m)*
Pt  horas extraordinárias *(f pl)*

**Übertrag** *(m) n* De
En  balance brought down
Am  balance carried forward
Es  balance a cuenta nueva *(m)*
Fr  solde à reporter *(m)*
It  bilancio riportato *(m)*
Pt  saldo transportado *(m)*

**Übertrager** *(m) n* De
En  assignor
Es  cesionista *(m)*
Fr  cédant *(m)*
It  cedente *(m)*
Pt  cessionista *(m)*

**Übertragung** *(f) n* De
En  assignment; conveyance of property
Es  cesión; traspaso de propiedad *(f m)*
Fr  cession; transmission de biens *(f)*
It  cessione; trasferimento di beni *(f m)*
Pt  consignação; trespasse de propriedade *(f m)*

**Übertragungsvertrag** *(m) n* De
En  transfer deed
Es  escritura de transferencia *(f)*
Fr  acte de cession *(m)*
It  atto di trapasso *(m)*
Pt  título de transferência *(m)*

**überweisen** *vb* De
En  transfer
Es  transferir
Fr  transférer
It  trasferire
Pt  transferir

**Überweisung** *(f)* n De
En transfer
Es cesión *(f)*
Fr transfert; cession *(m f)*
It cessione *(f)*
Pt trespasse *(m)*

**überziehen** *vb* De
En overdraw
Es girar en descubierto
Fr mettre à découvert
It trarre alla scoperto
Pt levantar a descoberto

**Überziehung** *(f)* n De
En overdraft
Es sobregiro; saldo deudor *(m)*
Fr découvert; solde débiteur *(m)*
It scoperto *(m)*
Pt conta a descoberto *(f)*

**Überziehungsdisposition** *(f)* n De
En overdraft facilities
Am overdraw facility
Es facilidades de descubierto *(f pl)*
Fr facilités de caisse *(f pl)*
It facilitazione di scoperto *(f)*
Pt disponibilidades de crédito sem cabertura *(f pl)*

**übliche Abnützung** *(f)* De
En fair wear and tear
Es uso y desgaste razonable *(m)*
Fr usure normale *(f)*
It usura normale *(f)*
Pt uso e desgase razoável *(m)*

**ufficiale** *adj* It
De amtlich
En official
Es oficial
Fr officiel
Pt oficial

**ufficio** *(m)* n It
De Büro *(n)*
En office
Es oficina *(f)*
Fr bureau *(m)*
Pt escritório *(m)*

**ufficio centrale d'acquisti** *(m)* It
De Einkaufszentrale *(f)*

En central buying office
Es oficina central de compras *(f)*
Fr centrale d'achats *(f)*
Pt escritório central de compras *(m)*

**ufficio contabilità** *(m)* It
De Buchhaltung *(f)*
En accounts department
Am accounting department
Es departamento de contabilidad *(m)*
Fr service de la comptabilité *(m)*
Pt departamento de contabilidade *(m)*

**ufficio di collocamento** *(m)* It
De Arbeitsnachweisstelle *(f)*
En employment exchange
Am state employment agency
Es bolsa de trabajo *(f)*
Fr bureau de placement *(m)*
Pt centro de serviços de emprego *(m)*

**ufficio postale** *(m)* It
De Postamt *(n)*
En post office
Es oficina de correos *(f)*
Fr bureau de poste *(m)*
Pt estação de correios *(f)*

**ufficio senza divisioni** *(m)* It
De Grossraumbüro *(n)*
En open-plan office
Es oficina sin particiones *(f)*
Fr bureau sans cloisons *(m)*
Pt escritório sem divisões *(m)*

**ufficio vendite** *(m)* It
De Verkaufsabteilung *(f)*
En sales department
Es departamento de ventas *(m)*
Fr service ventes *(m)*
Pt departamento de vendas *(m)*

**ulteriori informazioni** *(f pl)* It
De weitere Auskunft *(f)*
En further information
Es más detalles *(m pl)*
Fr renseignements complémentaires *(m pl)*
Pt informação adicional *(f)*

**ulteriori motivi** *(m pl)* It
De weitere Gründe *(m pl)*
En further reasons
Es rasones adicionales *(f pl)*
Fr raisons supplémentaires *(f pl)*
Pt rasões adicionais *(f pl)* '

**ulteriori particolari** *(m pl)* It
De nähere Umstände *(m pl)*
En further particulars
Es más detalles *(m pl)*
Fr plus amples renseignements *(m pl)*
Pt pormenores adicionais *(m pl)*

**ultima data** *(f)* It
De Schlusstermin *(m)*
En closing date
Es último día *(m)*
Fr dernier jour *(m)*
Pt último dia *(m)*

**última entrad· ·rimera salida** Es
De LIFO
En last in, first out (LIFO)
Fr LIFO
It ultimo a entrare, primo a uscire
Pt último a entrar, primeiro a saír

**última prestação** *(f)* Pt
De letzte Rate *(f)*
En final instalment
Es último plazo *(m)*
Fr dernier versement *(m)*
It ultima rata *(f)*

**ultima rata** *(f)* It
De letzte Rate *(f)*
En final instalment
Es último plazo *(m)*
Fr dernier versement *(m)*
Pt última prestação *(f)*

**último a entrar, primeiro a saír** Pt
De LIFO
En last in, first out (LIFO)
Es última entrada, primera salida
Fr LIFO
It ultimo a entrare, primo a uscire

**ultimo a entrare, primo a uscire** It
De LIFO
En last in, first out (LIFO)
Es última entrada, primera salida
Fr LIFO
Pt último a entrar, primeiro a saír

**último día** *(m)* Es
De Schlusstermin *(m)*
En closing date
Fr dernier jour *(m)*
It ultima data *(f)*
Pt último dia *(m)*

**último dia** *(m)* Pt
De Schlusstermin *(m)*
En closing date
Es último día *(m)*
Fr dernier jour *(m)*
It ultima data *(f)*

**último plazo** *(m)* Es
De letzte Rate *(f)*
En final instalment
Fr dernier versement *(m)*
It ultima rata *(f)*
Pt última prestação *(f)*

**último preço** *(m)* Pt
De Schlussnotierung *(f)*
En closing price
Es precio de cierre *(m)*
Fr cours de clôture *(m)*
It prezzo di chiusura *(m)*

**Umbau** *(m)* n De
En alterations
Es reformas *(f pl)*
Fr travaux de transformation *(m pl)*
It modifiche *(f pl)*
Pt modificações *(f pl)*

**umfassend** *adj* De
En comprehensive
Es completo
Fr exhaustif; complet
It comprensivo
Pt compreensivo

**Umladung** *(f)* n De
En transhipment
Es transbordo *(m)*
Fr transbordement *(m)*

It trasbordo *(m)*
Pt transbordo *(m)*

**Umlaufkapital** *(n)* n De
En revolving fund
Es fondo circulante *(m)*
Fr fonds renouvelable *(m)*
It fondo rotativo *(m)*
Pt fundos renováveis *(m pl)*

**Umlaufsvermögen** *(n)* n De
En current assets
Es activo realizable *(m)*
Fr actif courant *(m)*
It attivo liquido *(m)*
Pt bens no activo actual *(m pl)*

**umpire** n En
De Schiedsobmann *(m)*
Es juez árbitro *(m)*
Fr surarbitre *(m)*
It terzo arbitro *(m)*
Pt juiz árbitro *(m)*

**Umrechnungskoeffizient** *(m)* n De
En conversion factor
Es factor de conversión *(m)*
Fr facteur de conversion *(m)*
It fattore di conversion *(m)*
Pt factor de conversão *(m)*

**Umrechnungskurs** *(m)* n De
En rate of exchange
Es tipo de cambio *(m)*
Fr cours de change *(m)*
It corso del cambio *(m)*
Pt taxa de câmbio *(f)*

**Umsatz** *(m)* n De
En turnover
Es volumen de ventas *(m)*
Fr chiffre d'affaires *(m)*
It giro d'affari *(m)*
Pt movimento de dinheiro *(m)*

**Umschlag** *(m)* n De
En envelope
Es sobre *(m)*
Fr enveloppe *(f)*
It busta *(f)*
Pt envelope *(m)*

**Umstand** *(m)* n De
En factor
Es factor *(m)*
Fr facteur *(m)*

It fattore *(m)*
Pt factor *(m)*

**unanerkannter Streik** *(m)* De
En unofficial strike
Es huelga no-oficial *(f)*
Fr grève non reconnue *(f)*
It sciopero non ufficiale *(m)*
Pt greve não oficializada *(f)*

**unauthorized** *adj* En
De unbefugt
Es inautorizado
Fr non autorisé
It non autorizzato
Pt não autorizado

**unbefristete Obligation** *(f)* De
En undated bond
Es obligación sin fecha de vencimiento *(f)*
Fr obligation sans date d'échéance *(f)*
It obbligazione senza data di scadenza *(f)*
Pt obrigação sem data de vencimento *(f)*

**unbefugt** *adj* De
En unauthorized
Es inautorizado
Fr non autorisé
It non autorizzato
Pt não autorizado

**unbenutzte Ladefähigkeit** *(f)* De
En idle capacity
Es potencial no utilizado *(m)*
Fr potentiel non utilisé *(m)*
It potenziale non utilizzato *(m)*
Pt potencial não utilizado *(m)*

**unbeschäftigte Zeit** *(f)* De
En idle time
Es tiempo libre *(m)*
Fr temps improductif *(m)*
It tempo passivo *(m)*
Pt tempo improdutivo *(m)*

**unbewegliches Vermögen** *(n)* De
En real estate
Es bienes inmuebles *(m pl)*
Fr biens immeubles *(m pl)*
It beni immobili *(m pl)*
Pt propriedade imobiliária *(f)*

**uncalled capital** En
De nicht eingerufenes Kapital (n)
Es capital de reserva (m)
Fr capital non appelé (m)
It capitale non richiamato (m)
Pt capital irrealizado (m)

**undated bond** En
De unbefristete Obligation (f)
Es obligación sin fecha de vencimiento (f)
Fr obligation sans date d'échéance (f)
It obbligazione senza data di scadenza (f)
Pt obrigação sem data de vencimento (f)

**undated debenture** En
De Schuldverschreibung ohne Fälligkeitsdatum (f)
Es obligación sin fecha (f)
Fr obigation perpétuelle (f)
It obbligazione perpetua (f)
Pt obrigação sem data (f)

**under-estimate** n En
De Unterschätzung (f)
Es presupuesto por defecto (m)
Fr sous-estimation (f)
It sottovalutazione (f)
Pt avaliação insuficiente (f)

**underdeveloped countries** En
De unterentwickelte Länder (n pl)
Es países en desarrollo (m pl)
Fr pays sous-développés (m pl)
It paesi sottosviluppati (m pl)
Pt países subdesenvolvido (m pl)

**under separate cover** En
De mit getrennter Post
Es por correo aparte
Fr sous pli séparé
It in piego a parte
Pt por correio separado

**undersubscribed issue** En
De nicht in voller Höhe gezeichnete Emission (f)
Es emisión no totalmente subscrita (f)
Fr émission non couverte (f)

It emissione non interamente sottoscritta (f)
Pt emissão não subscrita na totalidade (f)

**underwriter** n En
De Versicherer (m)
Es asegurador (m)
Fr assureur (m)
It assicuratore (m)
Pt segurador (m)

**underwriting syndicate** (insurance) En
De Versicherungssyndikat (n)
Es sindicato de seguros (m)
Fr syndicat d'assureurs (m)
It sindacato di assicuratori (m)
Pt consórcio de seguradores (m)

**underwriting syndicate** (new issues) En
De Emissionssyndikat (n)
Es grupo de suscriptores (m)
Fr syndicat de garantie (m)
It consorzio finanziario (m)
Pt consórcio de subscritores (m)

**undischarged bankrupt** En
De noch nicht entlasteter Gemeinschuldner (m)
Es fallido no rehabilitado (m)
Fr failli non réhabilité (m)
It fallito non riabilitato (m)
Pt falido insolvente (m)

**undisclosed principal** En
De nicht bekanntgegebener Auftraggeber (m)
Es mandante no nombrado (m)
Fr mandant non divulgé (m)
It mandante non nominato (m)
Pt mandante não divulgado (m)

**undistributed profits** En
De unverteilte Gewinne (n pl)
Es beneficios no distribuidos (m pl)
Fr bénéfices non répartis (m pl)
It profitti non distribuiti (m pl)

Pt lucros não distribuidos (m pl)

**unearned income** En
De Kapitaleinkommen (n)
Es rentas (f pl)
Fr rente (f)
It reddito di capitale (m)
Pt rendimento do capital (m)

**unedles Metall** (n) De
En base metal
Es metal no noble (m)
Fr métal vil (m)
It basso metallo (m)
Pt metal pobre (m)

**unehrlich** adj De
En dishonest
Es deshonesto
Fr malhonnête
It disonesto
Pt deshonesto

**uneinbringliche Schuld** (f) De
En bad debt
Es deuda incobrable (f)
Fr créance irrécouvrable (f)
It credito inesigibile (m)
Pt dívida incobrável (f)

**uneinlösbare Schuldverschreibung** (f) De
En irredeemable debenture
Es obligación no amortizable (f)
Fr obligation irremboursable (f)
It obbligazione irredimibile (f)
Pt obrigação não amortizável (f)

**unemployment** n En
De Arbeitslosigkeit (f)
Es desempleo (m)
Fr chômage (m)
It disoccupazione (f)
Pt desemprego (m)

**unemployment benefit** En
De Arbeitslosenunterstützung (f)
Es subsidio de paro (m)
Fr secours de chômage (m)
It indennità di disoccupazione (f)
Pt subsidio de desemprego (m)

**Unerfahrenheit** *(f)* *n* De
En inexperience
Es falta de experiencia *(f)*
Fr manque de pratique *(m)*
It inesperienza *(f)*
Pt inexperiência *(f)*

**unerlaubte Abwesenheit** *(f)* De
En absenteeism
Es ausentismo *(m)*
Fr absentéisme *(m)*
It assenteismo *(m)*
Pt absentismo *(m)*

**unerlaubte Handlung** *(f)* De
En tort
Es agravio *(m)*
Fr acte dommageable *(m)*
It torto *(m)*
Pt agravo *(m)*

**unersetzlich** (Verlust usw.) *adj* De
En irrecoverable
Es irrecuperable
Fr irrécouvrable
It irrecuperabile
Pt irrecuperável

**Unfähigkeit** *(f)* *n* De
En inability, inefficiency
Es incapacidad; incompetencia *(f)*
Fr incapacité; inefficacité *(f)*
It incapacità; inefficienza *(f)*
Pt incapacidade; ineficiência *(f)*

**unfair trade practice** En
De unlautere Handelspraktik *(f)*
Es práctica comercial desleal *(f)*
Fr pratique de commerce déloyale *(f)*
It pratica commerciale sleale *(f)*
Pt prática comercial imprópria *(f)*

**ungebildet** *adj* De
En uneducated; illiterate
Es ignorante; analfabeto
Fr ignorant; illettré
It incolto; analfabeta
Pt inculto analfabeto

**ungedecktes Geld** *(n)* De
En fiduciary issue
Es emisión fiduciaria *(f)*
Fr émission fiduciaire *(f)*
It emissione fiduciaria *(f)*
Pt emissão fiduciária *(f)*

**ungesetzlich** *adj* De
En illegal
Es ilegal
Fr illégal
It illegale
Pt ilegal

**ungesicherte Schuldverschreibung** *(f)* De
En unsecured debenture
Am naked bond
Es obligación no garantizada *(f)*
Fr obligation sans garantie *(f)*
It obbligazione non garantita *(f)*
Pt obrigação sem garantia *(f)*

**ungültig** *adj* De
En invalid
Es inválido
Fr invalide
It invalido
Pt inválido

**união aduaneira** *(f)* Pt
De Zollunion *(f)*
En customs union
Es unión aduanera *(f)*
Fr union douanière *(f)*
It unione doganale *(f)*

**unidad de visualización** *(f)* Es
De Bildschirmeinheit *(f)*
En visual-display unit (vdu)
Fr unité de visualisation *(f)*
It unità di visualizzazione *(f)*
Pt móvel-montra de exposição de visuais *(f)*

**unión aduanera** *(f)* Es
De Zollunion *(f)*
En customs union
Fr union douanière *(f)*
It unione doganale *(f)*
Pt união aduaneira *(f)*

**union douanière** *(f)* Fr
De Zollunion *(f)*
En customs union
Es unión aduanera *(f)*

**unione doganale** *(f)*
Pt união aduaneira *(f)*

**unione commerciale** *(f)* It
De Handelsblock *(m)*
En trade bloc
Es bloque comercial *(m)*
Fr bloc commercial *(m)*
Pt bloque comercial *(m)*

**unione doganale** *(f)* It
De Zollunion *(f)*
En customs union
Es unión aduanera *(f)*
Fr union douanière *(f)*
Pt união aduaneira *(f)*

**unissued capital** En
De nicht ausgegebenes Kapital *(n)*
Es capital no emitido *(m)*
Fr capitaux pas encore émis *(m pl)*
It capitale non emesso *(m)*
Pt capital não emitido *(m)*

**unità di visualizzazione** *(f)* It
De Bildschirmeinheit *(f)*
En visual-display unit (vdu)
Es unidad de visualización *(f)*
Fr unité de visualisation *(f)*
Pt móvel-montra de exposição de visuais *(f)*

**unit cost** En
De Einheitskosten *(pl)*
Es coste por unidad *(m)*
Fr coût de l'unité *(m)*
It costo unitario *(m)*
Pt custo por unidade *(m)*

**unité de visualisation** *(f)* Fr
De Bildschirmeinheit *(f)*
En visual-display unit (vdu)
Es unidad de visualización *(f)*
It unità di visualizzazione *(f)*
Pt móvel-montra de exposição de visuais *(f)*

**unlautere Handelspraktik** *(f)* De
En unfair trade practice
Es práctica comercial desleal *(f)*
Fr pratique de commerce déloyale *(f)*
It pratica commerciale sleale *(f)*

Pt prática comercial imprópria
(f)

**unleserlich** adj De
En illegible
Es ilegible
Fr illisible
It illeggibile
Pt ilegível

**unmässig** adj De
En exorbitant
Es exorbitante
Fr exorbitant
It esorbitante
Pt exorbitante

**unmöglich** adj De
En impossible
Es imposible
Fr impossible
It impossibile
Pt impossível

**unofficial strike** En
De unanerkannter Streik (m)
Es huelga no-oficial (f)
Fr grève non reconnue (f)
It sciopero non ufficiale (m)
Pt greve não oficializada (f)

**unparteiisch** adj De
En impartial
Es imparcial
Fr impartial
It imparziale
Pt imparcial

**unproductive** adj En
De unproduktif
Es improductivo
Fr improductif
It improduttivo
Pt improdutivo

**unproduktif** adj De
En unproductive
Es improductivo
Fr improductif
It improduttivo
Pt improdutivo

**unprofitable** adj En
De unvorteilhaft
Es nada lucrativo
Fr sans profit
It poco proficuo
Pt não lucrativo

**unquoted securities** En
De nicht notierte Werte (m pl)
Es títulos no cotizados (m pl)
Fr valeurs non cotées (f pl)
It titoli non quotati (m pl)
Pt títulos não cotados (m pl)

**unsecured creditor** En
De nicht gesicherter Gläubiger
(m)
Es acreedor no garantizado
(m)
Fr créancier chirographaire
(m)
It creditore non garantito (m)
Pt credor sem garantia (m)

**unsecured debenture** En
Am naked bond
De ungesicherte Schuldver-
schreibung (f)
Es obligación no garantizada
(f)
Fr obligation sans garantie (f)
It obbligazione non garantita
(f)
Pt obrigação sem garantia (f)

**unsichtbare Exporte** (m pl) De
En invisible exports
Es exportaciones invisibles (f
pl)
Fr exportations invisibles (f pl)
It esportazioni invisibili (f pl)
Pt exportações invisíveis (f pl)

**Unterdirektor** (m) De
En assistant manager
Es sub-director (m)
Fr sous-directeur (m)
It vice-direttore (m)
Pt sub-director (m)

**unterentwickelte Länder** (n
pl) De
En underdeveloped countries
Es países en desarrollo (m pl)
Fr pays sous-développés (m
pl)
It paesi sottosviluppati (m pl)
Pt países subdesenvolvido (m
pl)

**Untergebene(r)** (m) n De
En subordinate
Es subalterno (m)
Fr subalterne (m)

It subalterno (m)
Pt subordinado (m)

**Unternehmen** (n) n De
En enterprise
Es negocio (m)
Fr entreprise (f)
It impresa (f)
Pt empresa (f)

**Unternehmensforschung** (f) n
De
En operational research (OR)
Es investigación operacional (f)
Fr recherche opérationnelle (f)
It indagine sul funzionamento
(f)
Pt investigação operacional (f)

**Unternehmer** (m) n De
En contractor; entrepreneur
Es contratista; empresario (m)
Fr entrepreneur (m)
It impresario; intraprenditore
(m)
Pt contractador; empresário
(m)

**Unternehmerverband** (m) n De
En trade association
Es asociación comercial (f)
Fr association professionnelle
(f)
It associazione commerciale
(f)
Pt associação comercial (f)

**Unterschätzung** (f) n De
En under-estimate
Es presupuesto por defecto
(m)
Fr sous-estimation (f)
It sottovalutazione (f)
Pt avaliação insuficiente (f)

**Unterschied** (m) n De
En difference
Es diferencia (f)
Fr différence (f)
It differenza (f)
Pt diferença (f)

**unterschiedlich** (Behandlung
usw.) adj De
En discriminatory
Es discriminatorio
Fr discriminatoire

It discriminatorio
Pt discriminatório

**unterschlagen** *vb* De
En embezzle
Es defalcar
Fr détourner
It appropriarsi indebitamente
Pt desfalcar

**Unterschlagung** *(f)* *n* De
En embezzlement
Es defalco *(m)*
Fr détournement de fonds *(m)*
It appropriazione indebita *(f)*
Pt desfalque *(m)*

**Unterschrift** *(f)* *n* De
En signature
Es firma *(f)*
Fr signature *(f)*
It firma *(f)*
Pt assinatura *(f)*

**Unterstützung** (geldlich) *(f)* *n* De
En grant; subsidy
Es subvención *(f)*
Fr subvention *(f)*
It sovvenzione *(f)*
Pt subvenção *(f)*

**untersuchen** *vb* De
En examine
Es examinar
Fr examiner
It esaminare
Pt examinar

**Untersuchung** *(f)* *n* De
En investigation; legal inquiry
Es investigación; encuesta *(f)*
Fr investigation; enquête *(f)*
It inchiesta; investigazione *(f)*
Pt investigação; inquérito *(f m)*

**Untervermietung** *(f)* *n* De
En sub-letting
Es sub-alquiler *(m)*
Fr sous-location *(m)*
It subaffitto *(m)*
Pt sub-aluguer *(m)*

**Untervertreter** *(m)* *n* De
En sub-agent
Es sub-agente *(m)*
Fr sous-agent *(m)*

It sub-agente *(m)*
Pt sub-agente *(m)*

**unter Zollverschluss** De
En in bond
Es en aduanas
Fr en entrepôt
It sotto vincolo doganale
Pt à ordem da alfândega

**unumschränkte Treuhand** *(f)* De
En discretionary trust
Es fideicomiso discrecional *(m)*
Fr fidéicommis à appréciation *(m)*
It fondo fiduciario discrezionale *(m)*
Pt fundação discricionária *(f)*

**unverteilte Gewinne** *(n pl)* De
En undistributed profits
Es beneficios no distribuidos *(m pl)*
Fr bénéfices non répartis *(m pl)*
It profitti non distribuiti *(m pl)*
Pt lucros não distribuidos *(m pl)*

**unvollständig** *adj* De
En incomplete
Es incompleto
Fr incomplet
It incompleto
Pt incompleto

**unvorteilhaft** *adj* De
En unprofitable
Es nada lucrativo
Fr sans profit
It poco proficuo
Pt não lucrativo

**unwiderruflicher Kreditbrief** *(m)* De
En irrevocable letter of credit
Es carta de crédito irrevocable *(f)*
Fr lettre de crédit irrévocable *(f)*
It lettera di credito irrevocabile *(f)*
Pt carta de crédito irrevogável *(f)*

**uomo d'affari** *(m)* It
De Geschäftsmann *(m)*
En businessman
Es hombre de negocios *(m)*
Fr homme d'affaires *(m)*
Pt homem de negócios *(m)*

**Urheberrecht** *(n)* *n* De
En copyright
Es derechos de autor *(m pl)*
Fr droit d'auteur *(m)*
It diritto d'autore *(m)*
Pt direitos de autor *(m pl)*

**Urheberrechtsverletzung** *(f)* *n* De
En infringement of copyright
Es infracción de los derechos de autor *(f)*
Fr contrefaçon littéraire *(f)*
It infrazione dei diritti d'autore *(f)*
Pt infracção de direitos de autor *(f)*

**Urkunde** *(f)* *n* De
En deed; document
Es título; documento *(m)*
Fr titre; document *(m)*
It atto; documento *(m)*
Pt título; documento *(m)*

**Urkundenbeweis** *(m)* *n* De
En documentary evidence
Es prueba documental *(f)*
Fr preuve écrite *(f)*
It prova scritta *(f)*
Pt prova documental *(f)*

**Ursprung** *(m)* *n* De
En origin
Es origen *(m)*
Fr origine *(f)*
It origine *(f)*
Pt origem *(f)*

**Ursprungszeugnis** *(n)* *n* De
En certificate of origin
Es certificado de origen *(m)*
Fr certificat d'origine *(m)*
It certificato d'origine *(m)*
Pt certificado de origem *(m)*

**Urteil** *(n)* *n* De
En judgment
Es juicio; adjudicación *(m f)*
Fr jugement; arrêt *(m)*

It giudizio *(m)*
Pt julgamento *(m)*

**urteilen** *vb* De
En judge
Es juzgar
Fr juger
It giudicare
Pt julgar

**usage commercial** *(m)* Fr
De Handelsgebrauch *(m)*
En custom of the trade
Es uso comercial *(m)*
It uso commerciale *(m)*
Pt uso comercial *(m)*

**usança** *(f)* *n* Pt
De Usance *(f)*
En usance
Es usanza *(f)*
Fr usance *(f)*
It usanza *(f)*

**usance** *n* En, Fr *(f)*
De Usance *(f)*
Es usanza *(f)*
It usanza *(f)*
Pt usança *(f)*

**Usance** *(f)* *n* De
En usance
Es usanza *(f)*
Fr usance *(f)*
It usanza *(f)*
Pt usança *(f)*

**usanza** *(f)* *n* Es, It
De Usance *(f)*
En usance
Fr usance *(f)*
Pt usança *(f)*

**uso comercial** *(m)* Es, Pt
De Handelsgebrauch *(m)*
En custom of the trade
Fr usage commercial *(m)*
It uso commerciale *(m)*

**uso commerciale** *(m)* It
De Handelsgebrauch *(m)*
En custom of the trade
Es uso comercial *(m)*
Fr usage commercial *(m)*
Pt uso comercial *(m)*

**uso e desgaste razoável** *(m)*
Pt
De übliche Abnützung *(f)*
En fair wear and tear
Es uso y desgaste razonable
*(m)*
Fr usure normale *(f)*
It usura normale *(f)*

**uso y desgaste razonable** *(m)*
Es
De übliche Abnützung *(f)*
En fair wear and tear
Fr usure normale *(f)*
It usura normale *(f)*
Pt uso e desgaste razoável
*(m)*

**usufruct** *n* En
De Niessbrauchsrecht *(n)*
Es usufructo *(m)*
Fr usufruit *(m)*
It usufrutto *(m)*
Pt usufruto *(m)*

**usufructo** *(m)* *n* Es
De Niessbrauchsrecht *(n)*
En usufruct; beneficial interest
Fr usufruit *(m)*
It usufrutto *(m)*
Pt usufruto *(m)*

**usufructo vitalicio** *(m)* Es
De lebenslängliche Nutznies-
sung *(f)*
En life-interest
Fr usufruit viager *(m)*
It usufrutto vitalizio *(m)*
Pt usufruto vitalício *(m)*

**usufructuario** *(m)* *n* Es
De Niessbrauchnutzer *(m)*
En beneficial owner
Fr usufruitier *(m)*
It usufruttuario *(m)*
Pt usufrutuário *(m)*

**usufruit** *(m)* *n* Fr
De Niessbrauchsrecht *(n)*
En usufruct; beneficial interest
Es usufructo *(m)*
It usufrutto *(m)*
Pt usufruto *(m)*

**usufruitier** *(m)* *n* Fr
De Niessbrauchnutzer *(m)*
En beneficial owner
Es usufructuario *(m)*

It usufruttuario *(m)*
Pt usufrutuário *(m)*

**usufruit viager** *(m)* Fr
De lebenslängliche Nutznies-
sung *(f)*
En life-interest
Es usufructo vitalicio *(m)*
It usufrutto vitalizio *(m)*
Pt usufruto vitalício *(m)*

**usufruto** *(m)* *n* Pt
De Niessbrauchsrecht *(n)*
En usufruct; beneficial interest
Es usufructo *(m)*
Fr usufruit *(m)*
It usufrutto *(m)*

**usufruto vitalício** *(m)* Pt
De lebenslängliche Nutznies-
sung *(f)*
En life-interest
Es usufructo vitalicio *(m)*
Fr usufruit viager *(m)*
It usufrutto vitalizio *(m)*

**usufrutto** *(m)* *n* It
De Niessbrauchsrecht *(n)*
En usufruct; beneficial interest
Es usufructo *(m)*
Fr usufruit *(m)*
Pt usufruto *(m)*

**usufrutto vitalizio** *(m)* *n* It
De lebenslängliche Nutznies-
sung *(f)*
En life-interest
Es usufructo vitalicio *(m)*
Fr usufruit viager *(m)*
Pt usufruto vitalício *(m)*

**usufruttuario** *(m)* *n* It
De Niessbrauchnutzer *(m)*
En beneficial owner
Es usufructuario *(m)*
Fr usufruitier *(m)*
Pt usufrutuário *(m)*

**usufrutuário** *(m)* *n* Pt
De Niessbrauchnutzer *(m)*
En beneficial owner
Es usufructuario *(m)*
Fr usufruitier *(m)*
It usufruttuario *(m)*

**usura** *(f)* *n* Es, It, Pt
De Wucher *(m)*

En usury
Fr usure (f)

**usuraio** (m) n It
De Geldverleiher (m)
En moneylender
Es prestamista (m)
Fr prêteur d'argent (m)
Pt prestamista (m)

**usura normale** (f) It
De übliche Abnützung (f)
En fair wear and tear
Es uso y desgaste razonable (m)
Fr usure normale (f)
Pt uso e desgaste razoável (m)

**usure** (f) n Fr
De Wucher (m)
En usury
Es usura (f)
It usura (f)
Pt usura (f)

**usure normale** (f) Fr
De übliche Abnützung (f)
En fair wear and tear
Es uso y desgaste razonable (m)
It usura normale (f)
Pt uso e desgaste razoável (m)

**usury** n En
De Wucher (m)
Es usura (f)
Fr usure (f)
It usura (f)
Pt usura (f)

**utile** (m) n It
De Gewinn (m)
En profit
Es ganancia; beneficio (f m)
Fr bénéfice; profit (m)
Pt lucro; benefício (m)

**utile lordo** (m) It
De Bruttogewinn (m)
En gross profit
Es ganancia bruta (f)
Fr bénéfice brut (m)
Pt lucro bruto (m)

**utile netto** (m) It
De Reingewinn (m)
En net profit
Es ganancia neta (f)
Fr bénéfice net (m)
Pt lucro líquido (m)

**utile sulla carta** (m) It
De imaginärer Gewinn (m)
En paper profit
Es ganancia por realizar (f)
Fr profit fictif (m)
Pt lucros no papel (m)

**utility company** En
De gemeinnütziges Unternehmen (n)
Es empresa de servicios públicos (f)
Fr entreprise d'utilité publique (f)
It società di servizi pubblici (f)
Pt empresa de utilidade pública (f)

**utmost good faith** En
De äusserst guter Glaube (m)
Es máxima buena fé (f)
Fr plus grande bonne foie (f)
It massima buona fede (f)
Pt máxima boa-fé (f)

# V

**vacación** (f) n Es
De Ferien; Urlaub (pl; m)
En vacation; holiday
Fr vacances (f pl)
It vacanza (f)
Pt férias (f pl)

**vacaciones de verano** (f pl) Es
De Sommerferien (pl)
En summer holidays
Fr vacances d'été (f pl)
It vacanze estive (f pl)
Pt férias de verão (f pl)

**vacaciones retribuidas** (f pl) Es
De bezahlter Urlaub (m)
En holidays with pay
Fr congés payés (m pl)
It vacanze retribuite (f pl)
Pt férias pagas (f pl)

**vacances** (f pl) n Fr
De Ferien; Urlaub (pl; m)
En vacation; holiday
Es vacación (f)
It vacanza (f)
Pt férias (f pl)

**vacances d'été** (f pl) Fr
De Sommerferien (pl)
En summer holidays
Es vacaciones de verano; veraneo (f pl; m)
It vacanze estive (f pl)
Pt férias de verão (f pl)

**vacanza** (f) n It
De Ferien; Urlaub (pl; m)
En vacation; holiday
Es vacación (f)
Fr vacances (f pl)
Pt férias (f pl)

**vacanze estive** (f pl) It
De Sommerferien (pl)
En summer holidays
Es vacaciones de verano; veraneo (f pl; m)
Fr vacances d'été (f pl)
Pt férias de verão (f pl)

**vacanze retribuite** (f pl) It
De bezahlter Urlaub (m)
En holidays with pay
Es vacaciones retribuidas (f pl)
Fr congés payés (m pl)
Pt férias pagas (f pl)

**vacation** n En
De Ferien; Urlaub (pl; m)
Es vacación (f)
Fr vacances (f pl)
It vacanza (f)
Pt férias (f pl)

**vacío comercial** (m) Es
De Aussenhandelsdefizit (n)
En trade gap
Fr déficit du commerce extérieur (m)
It disavanzo della bilancia commerciale (m)
Pt vazio comercial (m)

**vagão de caminhos de ferro** (m) Pt
De Eisenbahnwagen (m)
En railway carriage
Am railroad car

Es vagón de ferrocarril *(m)*
Fr wagon de chemin de fer *(m)*
It carrozza ferroviaria *(f)*

**vaglia postale** *(f)* It
De Postanweisung *(f)*
En postal order
Es giro postal *(m)*
Fr mandat-poste *(m)*
Pt vale postal *(m)*

**vagón de ferrocarril** *(m)* Es
De Eisenbahnwagen *(m)*
En railway carriage
Am railroad car
Fr wagon de chemin de fer *(m)*
It carrozza ferroviaria *(f)*
Pt vagão de caminhos de ferro *(m)*

**valable** *adj* Fr
De gültig; gut (für)
En valid; good (for)
Es válido
It valido
Pt válido

**vale** *(m)* n Pt
De Belegstück; Schuldschein *(n m)*
En voucher; I.O.U.
Es pieza justificativa; pagaré *(f m)*
Fr pièce justificative; fiche *(f)*
It pezza d'appoggio; pagherò *(m f)*

**vale postal** *(m)* Pt
De Postanweisung *(f)*
En postal order
Es giro postal *(m)*
Fr mandat-poste *(m)*
It vaglia postale *(f)*

**valeur** *(f)* n Fr
De Wert *(m)*
En value
Es valor *(m)*
It valore *(m)*
Pt valor *(m)*

**valeur ajoutée** *(f)* Fr
De Mehrwert *(f)*
En added value
Es valor agregado *(m)*

It valore aggiunto *(m)*
Pt valor adicionado *(m)*

**valeur à revenu fixe** *(f)* Fr
De festverzinsliches Wertpapier *(n)*
En fixed-interest security
Es obligación a interés fijo *(f)*
It titolo a interesse fisso *(m)*
Pt obrigação de juro fixo *(f)*

**valeur au porteur** *(f)* Fr
De Inhabereffekten *(n pl)*
En bearer security
Es valor al portador *(m)*
It valore al portatore *(f)*
Pt título ao portador *(m)*

**valeur capitalisée** *(f)* Fr
De kapitalisierter Wert *(m)*
En capitalized value
Es valor capitalizado *(m)*
It valore capitalizzato *(m)*
Pt valor capitalizado *(m)*

**valeur comptable** *(f)* Fr
De Buchwert *(m)*
En book value
Es valor contable *(m)*
It valore d'inventario *(m)*
Pt valor contabilizado *(m)*

**valeur déclarée** *(f)* Fr
De angegebener Zollwert *(m)*
En declared value
Es valor declarado *(m)*
It valore dichiarato *(m)*
Pt valor declarado *(m)*

**valeur de l'actif** *(f)* Fr
De Aktivwert *(m)*
En asset value
Es valor en activo *(m)*
It valore in attivo *(m)*
Pt valor do activo *(m)*

**valeur de rachat** *(f)* Fr
De Rückkaufswert *(m)*
En surrender value
Es valor de rescate *(m)*
It valore di riscatto *(m)*
Pt valor de resgate *(m)*

**valeurs de tout repos** *(f pl)* Fr
De mündelsichere Wertpapiere *(n pl)*
En gilt-edged securities

Es valores de toda confianza *(m pl)*
It titoli di assoluta fiducia *(m pl)*
Pt valores de todo a confiança *(m pl)*

**valeur intrinsèque** *(f)* Fr
De innerlicher Wert *(m)*
En intrinsic value
Es valor intrínseco *(m)*
It valore intrinsico *(m)*
Pt valor intrínseco *(m)*

**valeur marchande** *(f)* Fr
De Marktwert *(m)*
En market value
Es valor de mercado *(m)*
It valore di mercato *(m)*
Pt valor de mercado *(m)*

**valeur nominale** *(f)* Fr
De Nennwert; Stückelung *(m f)*
En nominal value; face value; denomination
Es valor; valor nominal *(m)*
It valore nominale; taglio *(m)*
Pt valor nominal *(m)*

**valeurs admises à la Bourse** *(f pl)* Fr
De an der Börse notierte Wertpapiere *(n pl)*
En listed security
Es valores cotizables *(m pl)*
It titoli quotati (in borsa) *(m pl)*
Pt valor de Bolsa com cotação oficial *(m)*

**valeurs aurifères** *(f pl)* Fr
De Aktien von Goldbergwerken *(f pl)*
En gold shares
Es acciones auríferas *(f pl)*
It azioni aurifere *(f pl)*
Pt acções de ouro *(f pl)*

**valeurs non cotées** *(f pl)* Fr
De nicht notierte Werte *(m pl)*
En unquoted securities
Es títulos no cotizados *(m pl)*
It titoli non quotati *(m pl)*
Pt títulos não cotados *(m pl)*

**valid** *adj* En
De gültig
Es válido
Fr valable
It valido
Pt válido

**validação testamentária** *(f)* Pt
De Testamentseröffnung; Bestätigung *(f)*
En probate
Es validación de los testamentos *(f)*
Fr homologation d'un testament *(f)*
It omologazione di testamento *(f)*

**validar por assinatura** Pt
De gegenzeichnen
En countersign
Es refrendar
Fr contresigner
It controfirmare

**valido** *adj* It
De gültig; gut (für)
En valid; good (for)
Es válido
Fr valable
Pt válido

**válido** *adj* Es, Pt
De gültig; gut (für)
En valid; good (for)
Fr valable
It valido

**valioso** *adj* Es, Pt
De wertvoll
En valuable
Fr de valeur
It di valore

**valor** *(m)* *n* Es, Pt
De Wert; Aktivposten *(m)*
En value; asset
Fr valeur; actif *(f m)*
It valore; attivo *(m)*

**valoracion del trabajo** *(f)* Es
De Arbeitsbewertung *(f)*
En job evaluation
Fr évaluation du travail *(f)*
It valutazione del lavoro *(f)*
Pt avaliação de tarefa *(f)*

**valor adicionado** *(m)* Pt
De Mehrwert *(f)*
En added value
Es valor agregado *(m)*
Fr valeur ajoutée *(f)*
It valore aggiunto *(m)*

**valor agregado** *(m)* Es
De Mehrwert *(f)*
En added value
Fr valeur ajoutée *(f)*
It valore aggiunto *(m)*
Pt valor adicionado *(m)*

**valor al portador** *(m)* Es
De Inhabereffekten *(n pl)*
En bearer security
Fr valeur au porteur *(f)*
It valore al portatore *(f)*
Pt título ao portador *(m)*

**valor capitalizado** *(m)* Es, Pt
De kapitalisierter Wert *(m)*
En capitalized value
Fr valeur capitalisée *(f)*
It valore capitalizzato *(m)*

**valor contabilizado** *(m)* Pt
De Buchwert *(m)*
En book value
Es valor contable *(m)*
Fr valeur comptable *(f)*
It valore d'inventario *(m)*

**valor contable** *(m)* Es
De Buchwert *(m)*
En book value
Fr valeur comptable *(f)*
It valore d'inventario *(m)*
Pt valor contabilizado *(m)*

**valor de Bolsa com cotação oficial** *(m)* Pt
De an der Börse notierte Wertpapiere *(n pl)*
En listed security
Es valores cotizables *(m pl)*
Fr valeurs admises à la Bourse *(f pl)*
It titoli quotati (in borsa) *(m pl)*

**valor declarado** *(m)* Es, Pt
De angegebener Zollwert *(m)*
En declared value
Fr valeur déclarée *(f)*
It valore dichiarato *(m)*

**valor de la clientela** *(m)* Es
De Geschäftswert *(m)*
En goodwill
Fr bon vouloir *(m)*
It avviamento *(m)*
Pt boa vontade *(f)*

**valor de mercado** *(m)* Es, Pt
De Marktwert *(m)*
En market value
Fr valeur marchande *(f)*
It valore di mercato *(m)*

**valor de rescate** *(m)* Es
De Rückkaufswert *(m)*
En surrender value
Fr valeur de rachat *(f)*
It valore di riscatto *(m)*
Pt valor de resgate *(m)*

**valor de resgate** *(m)* Pt
De Rückkaufswert *(m)*
En surrender value
Es valor de rescate *(m)*
Fr valeur de rachat *(f)*
It valore di riscatto *(m)*

**valor do activo** *(m)* Pt
De Aktivwert *(m)*
En asset value
Es valor en activo *(m)*
Fr valeur de l'actif *(f)*
It valore in attivo *(m)*

**valore** *(m)* *n* It
De Wert *(m)*
En value
Es valor *(m)*
Fr valeur *(f)*
Pt valor *(m)*

**valore aggiunto** *(m)* It
De Mehrwert *(f)*
En added value
Es valor agregado *(m)*
Fr valeur ajoutée *(f)*
Pt valor adicionado *(m)*

**valore al portatore** *(f)* It
De Inhabereffekten *(n pl)*
En bearer security
Es valor al portador *(m)*
Fr valeur au porteur *(f)*
Pt título ao portador *(m)*

**valore capitalizzato** *(m)* It
De kapitalisierter Wert *(m)*
En capitalized value

Es  valor capitalizado *(m)*
Fr  valeur capitalisée *(f)*
Pt  valor capitalizado *(m)*

**valore dichiarato** *(m)* It
De  angegebener Zollwert *(m)*
En  declared value
Es  valor declarado *(m)*
Fr  valeur déclarée *(f)*
Pt  valor declarado *(m)*

**valore d'inventario** *(m)* It
De  Buchwert *(m)*
En  book value
Es  valor contable *(m)*
Fr  valeur comptable *(f)*
Pt  valor contabilizado *(m)*

**valore di mercato** *(m)* It
De  Marktwert *(m)*
En  market value
Es  valor de mercado *(m)*
Fr  valeur marchande *(f)*
Pt  valor de mercado *(m)*

**valore di riscatto** *(m)* It
De  Rückkaufswert *(m)*
En  surrender value
Es  valor de rescate *(m)*
Fr  valeur de rachat *(f)*
Pt  valor de resgate *(m)*

**valore in attivo** *(m)* It
De  Aktivwert *(m)*
En  asset value
Es  valor en activo *(m)*
Fr  valeur de l'actif *(f)*
Pt  valor do activo *(m)*

**valore intrinsico** *(m)* It
De  innerlicher Wert *(m)*
En  intrinsic value
Es  valor intrínseco *(m)*
Fr  valeur intrinsèque *(f)*
Pt  valor intrínseco *(m)*

**valor en activo** *(m)* Es
De  Aktivwert *(m)*
En  asset value
Fr  valeur de l'actif *(f)*
It  valore in attivo *(m)*
Pt  valor do activo *(m)*

**valore nominale** *(m)* It
De  Nennwert *(m)*
En  face value; nominal value
Es  valor nominal *(m)*

Fr  valeur nominale *(f)*
Pt  valor nominal *(m)*

**valores cotizables** *(m pl)* Es
De  an der Börse notierte Wertpapiere *(n pl)*
En  listed security
Fr  valeurs admises à la Bourse *(f pl)*
It  titoli quotati (in borsa) *(m pl)*
Pt  valor de Bolsa com cotação oficial *(m)*

**valores de equilíbrio** *(m pl)* Pt
De  Ausgleichsposten *(m pl)*
En  balancing items
Es  asientos saldados *(m pl)*
Fr  postes rééquilibrants *(m pl)*
It  voci di pareggio *(f pl)*

**valores de toda confianza** *(m pl)* Es
De  mündelsichere Wertpapiere *(n pl)*
En  gilt-edged securities
Fr  valeurs de tout repos *(f pl)*
It  titoli di assoluta fiducia *(m pl)*
Pt  valores de todo a confiança *(m pl)*

**valores de todo a confiança** *(m pl)* Pt
De  mündelsichere Wertpapiere *(n pl)*
En  gilt-edged securities
Es  valores de toda confianza *(m pl)*
Fr  valeurs de tout repos *(f pl)*
It  titoli di assoluta fiducia *(m pl)*

**valores privilegiados cumulativos** *(m pl)* Es
De  kumulative Vorzugsaktien *(f pl)*
En  cumulative preference shares
Fr  actions de priorité cumulatives *(f pl)*
It  azioni preferenziali cumulative *(f pl)*
Pt  acções preferenciais cumulativas *(f pl)*

**valores transaccionáveis pelo banco** *(m pl)* Pt
De  diskontierbare Wechsel *(m pl)*
En  bankable bills
Es  efectos negociables *(m pl)*
Fr  papier bancable *(m)*
It  effetti scontabili *(m pl)*

**valor intrínseco** *(m)* Es, Pt
De  innerlicher Wert *(m)*
En  intrinsic value
Fr  valeur intrinsèque *(f)*
It  valore intrinsico *(m)*

**valorizzazione** *(f)* n It
De  Erschliessung *(f)*
En  development
Es  explotación *(f)*
Fr  exploitation; lotissement *(f m)*
Pt  exploração *(f)*

**valor nominal** *(m)* Es, Pt
De  Nennwert; Stückelung *(m f)*
En  nominal value; face value
Fr  valeur nominale *(f)*
It  valore nominale; taglio *(m)*

**valuable** *adj* En
De  wertvoll
Es  valioso
Fr  de valeur
It  di valore
Pt  valioso

**valuación** *(f)* n Es
De  Wertbestimmung *(f)*
En  valuation
Fr  évaluation *(f)*
It  valutazione *(f)*
Pt  avaliação *(f)*

**valuation** (of assets) n En
De  Wertbestimmung *(f)*
Es  valuación *(f)*
Fr  évaluation *(f)*
It  valutazione *(f)*
Pt  avaliação *(f)*

**value** n En
De  Wert *(m)*
Es  valor *(m)*
Fr  valeur *(f)*
It  valore *(m)*
Pt  valor *(m)*

**value added tax** (VAT) En
De Mehrwertsteuer *(f)*
Es impuesto sobre valor aña-
dido *(m)*
Fr taxe sur la valeur ajoutée
(TVA) *(f)*
It imposta sul valore aggiunto
(IVA) *(f)*
Pt imposto sobre valor adu-
zido *(m)*

**valuta** *(f) n* It
De Währung *(f)*
En currency
Es moneda *(f)*
Fr monnaie *(f)*
Pt moeda *(f)*

**valuta debole** *(f)* It
De schwache Währung *(f)*
En soft currency
Es moneda débil *(f)*
Fr monnaie faible *(f)*
Pt moeda fraca *(f)*

**valuta di riserva** *(f)* It
De Reservewährung *(f)*
En reserve currency
Es moneda de reserva *(f)*
Fr monnaie de réserve *(f)*
Pt moeda de reserva *(f)*

**valuta estera** *(f)* It
De Devisen *(f pl)*
En foreign currency; foreign
exchange
Es divisas extranjeras *(f pl)*
Fr devises *(f pl)*
Pt moeda estrangeira *(f)*

**valuta forte** *(f)* It
De harte Währung *(f)*
En hard currency
Es moneda fuerta *(f)*
Fr monnaie forte *(f)*
Pt moeda forte *(f)*

**valutare** *vb* It
De bewerten
En evaluate
Es evaluar
Fr évaluer
Pt avaliar

**valutare i danni** It
De den Schadenersatzbetrag
feststellen
En assess damages

Es evaluar daños
Fr fixer des dommages-intér-
êts
Pt avaliar os danos

**valutazione** *(f) n* It
De Wertbestimmung; Ab-
schätzung *(f)*
En valuation; appraisal
Es evaluación; valuación *(f)*
Fr évaluation *(f)*
Pt avaliação *(f)*

**valutazione approssimativa** *(f)*
It
De rohe Schätzung *(f)*
En rough estimate
Es presupuesto aproximado
*(m)*
Fr estimation approximative *(f)*
Pt avaliação aproximada *(f)*

**valutazione del costo per
partita** *(f)* It
De Stapelkostenberechnung *(f)*
En batch costing
Es fijación de precio por lotes
*(f)*
Fr évaluation du coût des lots
*(f)*
Pt fixação do preço por lote
*(f)*

**valutazione del lavoro** *(f)* It
De Arbeitsbewertung *(f)*
En job evaluation
Es valoracion del trabajo *(f)*
Fr évaluation du travail *(f)*
Pt avaliação de tarefa *(f)*

**valutazione eccessiva** *(f)* It
De Überschätzung *(f)*
En over-estimate
Es presupuesto por exceso *(m)*
Fr surestimation *(f)*
Pt avaliação excessiva *(f)*

**valutazione prudente** *(f)* It
De vorsichtige Schätzung *(f)*
En conservative estimate
Es presupuesto prudente *(m)*
Fr évaluation prudente *(f)*
Pt avaliação cautelosa *(f)*

**valute bloccate** *(f pl)* It
De blockierte Devisen *(f pl)*
En blocked exchange
Es divisas bloqueadas *(f pl)*

Fr devises bloquées *(f pl)*
Pt câmbio bloqueado *(m)*

**vantaggi accessori** *(m pl)* It
De Sozialleistungen *(f pl)*
En fringe benefits
Es beneficios suplementarios
*(m pl)*
Fr avantages accessoires *(m
pl)*
Pt benefícios extras *(m pl)*

**vapor** *(m) n* Pt
De Dampfer *(m)*
En steamer
Es buque de vapor *(m)*
Fr bateau à vapeur *(m)*
It vapore *(m)*

**vapor de serviço autónomo**
*(m)* Pt
De Trampschiff *(n)*
En tramp steamer
Es vapor volandero *(m)*
Fr navire de tramping *(m)*
It carretta *(f)*

**vapore** *(m) n* It
De Dampfer *(m)*
En steamer
Es buque de vapor *(m)*
Fr bateau à vapeur *(m)*
Pt vapor *(m)*

**vapor volandero** *(m)* Es
De Trampschiff *(n)*
En tramp steamer
Fr navire de tramping *(m)*
It carretta *(f)*
Pt vapor de serviço autónomo
*(m)*

**variable cost** En
De variable Kosten *(pl)*
Es coste variable *(m)*
Fr coût variable *(m)*
It costo variabile *(m)*
Pt custo variavel *(m)*

**variable Kosten** *(pl) n* De
En variable cost
Es coste variable *(m)*
Fr coût variable *(m)*
It costo variabile *(m)*
Pt custo variavel *(m)*

**variance analysis** En
De Varianzanalyse (f)
Es análisis de variaciones (m)
Fr analyse de la variance (f)
It analisi della variazione (f)
Pt análise de variação (f)

**Varianzanalyse** (f) n De
En variance analysis
Es análisis de variaciones (m)
Fr analyse de la variance (f)
It analisi della variazione (f)
Pt análise de variação (f)

**variations saisonnières** (f pl)
Fr
De saisonbedingte Schwankungen (f pl)
En seasonal fluctuations
Es fluctuaciones estacionales (f pl)
It fluttuazioni stagionali (f pl)
Pt flutuações de época (f pl)

**vazio comercial** (m) Pt
De Aussenhandelsdefizit (n)
En trade gap
Es vacío comercial (m)
Fr déficit du commerce extérieur (m)
It disavanzo della bilancia commerciale (m)

**véhicule commerciale** (f) Fr
De Nutzfahrzeug (n)
En commercial vehicle
Es vehículo comercial (m)
It veicolo commerciale (m)
Pt veículo comercial (m)

**vehículo comercial** (m) Es
De Nutzfahrzeug (n)
En commercial vehicle
Fr véhicule commerciale (f)
It veicolo commerciale (m)
Pt veículo comercial (m)

**veicolo commerciale** (m) It
De Nutzfahrzeug (n)
En commercial vehicle
Es vehículo comercial (m)
Fr véhicule commerciale (f)
Pt veículo comercial (m)

**veículo comercial** (m) Pt
De Nutzfahrzeug (n)
En commercial vehicle
Es vehículo comercial (m)

Fr véhicule commerciale (f)
It veicolo commerciale (m)

**vencer** vb Es
De fällig sein
En fall due
Fr échoir; venir à échéance
It scadere; essere pagabile
Pt vencer-se

**vencer-se** vb Pt
De fällig sein
En fall due
Es vencer
Fr échoir; venir à échéance
It scadere; essere pagabile

**vencido** adj Es; Pt
De rückständig; verfallen
En overdue; expired
Fr arriéré; expiré
It scaduto

**vencimento** (m) n Pt
De Fälligkeit (f)
En maturity
Es vencimiento (m)
Fr échéance (f)
It scadenza (f)

**vencimento atrasado** (m) Pt
De Lohnnachzahlung (f)
En back pay
Es pago atrasado (m)
Fr rappel de traitement (m)
It arretrati di paga (m pl)

**vencimiento** (m) n Es
De Fälligkeit (f)
En maturity
Fr échéance (f)
It scadenza (f)
Pt vencimento (m)

**venda** (f) n Pt
De Verkauf (m)
En sale
Es venta (f)
Fr vente (f)
It vendita (f)

**venda a dinheiro** (f) Pt
De Kassageschäft (n)
En cash sale
Es venta al conta (f)
Fr vente au comptant (f)
It vendita a contanti (f)

**venda a prestações** (f) Pt
De Ratenkauf (m)
En hire-purchase
Es compra a plazos (f)
Fr vente à tempérament (f)
It vendita a rate (f)

**vendable** adj Fr
De marktfähig
En marketable
Es vendible
It vendibile
Pt comercializável

**venda de porta-a-porta** (f) Pt
De Haus-zu-Hausverkauf (m)
En door-to-door selling
Es venta a domicilio (f)
Fr vente à domicile (f)
It vendita a domicilio (f)

**venda directa ao consumidor** (f) Pt
De Direktverkauf (m)
En direct selling
Es venta directa (f)
Fr vente directe (f)
It vendita diretta (f)

**venda em leilão** (f) Pt
De Versteigerung (f)
En sale by auction
Es venta a subasta (f)
Fr vente aux enchères (f)
It vendita all'asta (f)

**venda forçada** (f) Pt
De Zwangsverkauf (m)
En forced sale
Es venta forzosa (f)
Fr vente forcée (f)
It vendita sforzosa (f)

**venda insistente** (f) Pt
De aufdrängliches Verkaufen (n)
En hard sell
Es venta insistente (f)
Fr vente débrouillarde (f)
It vendita facendo sforzo (f)

**venda ou devolução** Pt
De Rücksendung wenn unverkauft
En sale or return
Es venta o devolución
Fr vente avec faculté de retour
It da vendere o rimandare

**venda pelo correio** *(f)* Pt
De Auftrag durch die Post *(m)*
En mail order
Es pedido por correo *(m)*
Fr commande par lettre *(f)*
It ordine per corrispondenza *(f)*

**vendas de exportação** *(f pl)* Pt
De Ausfuhrverkäufe *(m pl)*
En export sales
Es ventas de exportación *(f pl)*
Fr ventes d'exportation *(f pl)*
It vendite per esportazione *(f pl)*

**vendas em pirâmide** *(f)* Pt
De Schneeball Verkauf *(m)*
En pyramid selling
Es venta en pirámide *(f)*
Fr vente en pyramide *(f)*
It vendita a piramide *(f)*

**venda sobtil** *(f)* Pt
De Verkauf ohne Aufdringen *(m)*
En soft sell
Es venta sencilla *(f)*
Fr vente par des moyens discrets *(f)*
It vendere senza forzare

**vendedor** *(m)* n Es, Pt
De Verkäufer *(m)*
En salesman; vender
Fr vendeur *(m)*
It venditore; commesso *(m)*

**vendedor por atacado** *(m)* Pt
De Grosshändler; Grossist *(m)*
En wholesaler
Es mayorista *(m)*
Fr grossiste *(m)*
It grossista *(m)*

**vender** vb Es, Pt
De verkaufen
En sell
Fr vendre
It vendere

**vender** n En
De Verkäufer *(m)*
Es vendedor *(m)*
Fr vendeur *(m)*
It venditore *(m)*
Pt vendedor *(m)*

**vendere** vb It
De verkaufen
En sell
Es vender
Fr vendre
Pt vender

**vendeur** *(m)* n Fr
De Verkäufer *(m)*
En salesman; vender
Es vendedor *(m)*
It venditore; commesso *(m)*
Pt vendedor; caixeiro *(m)*

**vendibile** adj It
De marktfähig
En marketable
Es vendible
Fr vendable
Pt comercializável

**vendible** adj Es
De marktfähig
En marketable
Fr vendable
It vendibile
Pt comercializável

**vending machine** En
De Verkaufsautomat *(m)*
Es máquina expendedora *(f)*
Fr distributeur automatique *(m)*
It macchina venditrice automatica *(f)*
Pt máquina de vendas *(f)*

**vendita** *(f)* n It
De Verkauf *(m)*
En sale
Es venta *(f)*
Fr vente *(f)*
Pt venda *(f)*

**vendita a contanti** *(f)* It
De Kassageschäft *(n)*
En cash sale
Es venta al conta *(f)*
Fr vente au comptant *(f)*
Pt venda a dinheiro *(f)*

**vendita a domicilio** *(f)* It
De Haus-zu-Hausverkauf *(m)*
En door-to-door selling
Es venta a domicilio *(f)*
Fr vente à domicile *(f)*
Pt venda de porta-a-porta *(f)*

**vendita all'asta** *(f)* It
De Versteigerung *(f)*
En sale by auction
Es venta a subasta *(f)*
Fr vente aux enchères *(f)*
Pt venda em leilão *(f)*

**vendita a piramide** *(f)* It
De Schneeball Verkauf *(m)*
En pyramid selling
Es venta en pirámide *(f)*
Fr vente en pyramide *(f)*
Pt vendas em pirâmide *(f)*

**vendita a rate** *(f)* It
De Ratenkauf *(m)*
En hire-purchase
Es compra a plazos *(f)*
Fr location-vente *(f)*
Pt compras a prestações *(f pl)*

**vendita diretta** *(f)* It
De Direktverkauf *(m)*
En direct selling
Es venta directa *(f)*
Fr vente directe *(f)*
Pt venda directa ao consumidor *(f)*

**vendita facendo sforzo** *(f)* It
De aufdrängliches Verkaufen *(n)*
En hard sell
Es venta insistente *(f)*
Fr vente débrouillarde *(f)*
Pt venda insistente *(f)*

**vendita per giudizio ipotecario** *(f)* It
De Zwangsvollstreckung *(f)*
En foreclosure
Es venta por juicio hipotecario *(f)*
Fr vente de l'immeuble hypothéqué *(f)*
Pt execução judicial a uma hipoteca *(f)*

**vendita sforzosa** *(f)* It
De Zwangsverkauf *(m)*
En forced sale
Es venta forzosa *(f)*
Fr vente forcée *(f)*
Pt venda forçada *(f)*

**vendite per esportazione** *(f pl)* It
De Ausfuhrverkäufe *(m pl)*

En export sales
Es ventas de exportación (f pl)
Fr ventes d'exportation (f pl)
Pt vendas de exportação (f pl)

**venditore** (m) n It
De Verkäufer (m)
En salesman; vender
Es vendedor (m)
Fr vendeur (m)
Pt vendedor; caixeiro (m)

**venditore all'asta** (m) It
De Versteigerer (m)
En auctioneer
Es subastador (m)
Fr commissaire-priseur (m)
Pt leiloeiro (m)

**vendre** vb Fr
De verkaufen
En sell
Es vender
It vendere
Pt vender

**venta** (f) n Es
De Verkauf (m)
En sale
Fr vente (f)
It vendita (f)
Pt venda (f)

**venta a domicilio** (f) Es
De Haus-zu-Hausverkauf (m)
En door-to-door selling
Fr vente à domicile (f)
It vendita a domicilio (f)
Pt venda de porta-a-porta (f)

**venta al conta** (f) Es
De Kassageschäft (n)
En cash sale
Fr vente au comptant (f)
It vendita a contanti (f)
Pt venda a dinheiro (f)

**venta a subasta** (f) Es
De Versteigerung (f)
En sale by auction
Fr vente aux enchères (f)
It vendita all'asta (f)
Pt venda em leilão (f)

**venta directa** (f) Es
De Direktverkauf (m)
En direct selling
Fr vente directe (f)

It vendita diretta (f)
Pt venda directa ao con-
sumidor (f)

**venta en pirámide** (f) Es
De Schneeball Verkauf (m)
En pyramid selling
Fr vente en pyramide (f)
It vendita a piramide (f)
Pt vendas em pirâmide (f)

**venta forzosa** (f) Es
De Zwangsverkauf (m)
En forced sale
Fr vente forcée (f)
It vendita sforzosa (f)
Pt venda forçada (f)

**venta insistente** (f) Es
De aufdrängliches Verkaufen
(n)
En hard sell
Fr vente débrouillarde (f)
It vendita facendo sforzo (f)
Pt venda insistente (f)

**venta o devolución** Es
De Rücksendung wenn unver-
kauft
En sale or return
Fr vente avec faculté de retour
It da vendere o rimandare
Pt venda ou devolução

**venta por juicio hipotecario**
(f) Es
De Zwangsvollstreckung (f)
En foreclosure
Fr vente de l'immeuble hypo-
théqué (f)
It vendita per giudizio ipo-
tecario (f)
Pt execução judicial a uma
hipoteca (f)

**ventas de exportación** (f pl) Es
De Ausfuhrverkäufe (m pl)
En export sales
Fr ventes d'exportation (f pl)
It vendite per esportazione (f
pl)
Pt vendas de exportação (f pl)

**venta sencilla** (f) Es
De Verkauf ohne Aufdringen
(m)
En soft sell

Fr vente par des moyens
discrets (f)
It vendere senza forzare
Pt venda sobtil (f)

**vente** (f) n Fr
De Verkauf (m)
En sale
Es venta (f)
It vendita (f)
Pt venda (f)

**vente à domicile** (f) Fr
De Haus-zu-Hausverkauf (m)
En door-to-door selling
Es venta a domicilio (f)
It vendita a domicilio (f)
Pt venda de porta-a-porta (f)

**vente à tempérament** (f) Fr
De Ratenverkauf (m)
En hire-purchase
Es compra a plazos (f)
It vendita a rate (f)
Pt venda a prestações (f)

**vente au comptant** (f) Fr
De Kassageschäft (n)
En cash sale
Es venta al conta (f)
It vendita a contanti (f)
Pt venda a dinheiro (f)

**vente aux enchères** (f) Fr
De Versteigerung (f)
En sale by auction
Es venta a subasta (f)
It vendita all'asta (f)
Pt venda em leilão (f)

**vente avec faculté de retour**
Fr
De Rücksendung wenn unver-
kauft
En sale or return
Es venta o devolución
It da vendere o rimandare
Pt venda ou devolução

**vente débrouillarde** (f) Fr
De aufdrängliches Verkaufen
(n)
En hard sell
Es venta insistente (f)
It vendita facendo sforzo (f)
Pt venda insistente (f)

**vente de l'immeuble hypothé-qué** *(f)* Fr
De Zwangsvollstreckung *(f)*
En foreclosure
Es venta por juicio hipotecario *(f)*
It vendita per giudizio ipotecario *(f)*
Pt execução judicial a uma hipoteca *(f)*

**vente directe** *(f)* Fr
De Direktverkauf *(m)*
En direct selling
Es venta directa *(f)*
It vendita diretta *(f)*
Pt venda directa ao consumidor *(f)*

**vente en pyramide** *(f)* Fr
De Schneeball Verkauf *(m)*
En pyramid selling
Es venta en pirámide *(f)*
It vendita a piramide *(f)*
Pt vendas em pirâmide *(f)*

**vente forcée** *(f)* Fr
De Zwangsverkauf *(m)*
En forced sale
Es venta forzosa *(f)*
It vendita sforzosa *(f)*
Pt venda forçada *(f)*

**vente par des moyens discrets** *(f)* Fr
De Verkauf ohne Aufdringen *(m)*
En soft sell
Es venta sencilla *(f)*
It vendere senza forzare
Pt venda sobtil *(f)*

**ventes d'exportation** *(f pl)* Fr
De Ausfuhrverkäufe *(m pl)*
En export sales
Es ventas de exportación *(f pl)*
It vendite per esportazione *(f pl)*
Pt vendas de exportação *(f pl)*

**Verabredung** *(f)* n De
En appointment
Es entrevista *(f)*
Fr entrevue *(f)*
It appuntamento *(m)*
Pt encontro *(m)*

**Verantwortlichkeit** *(f)* n De
En accountability; responsibility
Es responsabilidad *(f)*
Fr responsabilité *(f)*
It responsabilità *(f)*
Pt responsabilidade *(f)*

**verbale** *(m)* n It
De Protokoll *(n)*
En minutes (of a meeting)
Es actas *(f pl)*
Fr procès-verbal *(m)*
Pt minutas de acta *(f pl)*

**Verband** *(m)* n De
En association
Es asociación *(f)*
Fr association *(f)*
It associazione *(f)*
Pt associação *(f)*

**Verbesserung** *(f)* n De
En improvement
Es mejora *(f)*
Fr amélioration *(f)*
It miglioramento *(m)*
Pt melhoramento *(m)*

**verbindlich** adj De
En compulsory
Es obligatorio
Fr obligatoire
It obbligatorio
Pt obrigatório

**Verbrauch** *(m)* n De
En consumption
Es consumición *(f)*
Fr consommation *(f)*
It consumo *(m)*
Pt consumo *(m)*

**Verbraucher** *(m)* n De
En consumer
Es consumidor *(m)*
Fr consommateur *(m)*
It consumatore *(m)*
Pt consumidor *(m)*

**Verbrauchsabgabe** *(f)* De
En excise duty
Es impuesto de consumos *(m)*
Fr droit sur la consommation *(m)*
It imposta sul consumo *(f)*
Pt imposto indirecto *(m)*

**verderbliche Waren** *(f pl)* De
En perishable goods
Es mercancías perecederas *(f pl)*
Fr marchandises périssables *(f pl)*
It merci deperibili *(f pl)*
Pt mercadorias perecíveis *(f pl)*

**verdienen** vb De
En earn
Es ganar
Fr gagner
It guadagnare
Pt ganhar

**Verdrängungstonne** *(f)* n De
En displacement-ton
Es tonelada de desplazamiento *(f)*
Fr tonneau de déplacement *(m)*
It tonnellata di dislocamento *(f)*
Pt tonelada de deslocação *(f)*

**Verdrehung** *(f)* n De
En misrepresentation
Es declaración falsa *(f)*
Fr déclaration inexacte *(f)*
It dichiarazione falsa *(f)*
Pt deturpação *(f)*

**Vereinbarung** *(f)* n De
En settlement
Es acuerdo *(m)*
Fr accord *(m)*
It accordo *(m)*
Pt acordo *(m)*

**Verfahren** *(n)* n De
En procedure
Es procedimiento *(m)*
Fr procédure *(f)*
It procedura *(f)*
Pt procedimento *(m)*

**verfallen** adj De
En expired; out of date
Es vencido
Fr expiré; périmé
It scaduto
Pt vencido

**Verfalltermin** *(m)* n De
En deadline
Es fecha tope *(f)*

Fr  date limite *(f)*
It  ultima data o ora possibile *(f)*
Pt  data de vencimento *(f)*

**verfügbar** *adj* De
En  available
Es  disponible
Fr  disponible
It  disponibile
Pt  disponível

**verfügbarer Saldo** *(m)* De
En  balance in hand
Es  sobrante *(m)*
Fr  solde en caisse *(m)*
It  saldo in cassa *(m)*
Pt  saldo em poder *(m)*

**verfügbares Einkommen** *(n)* De
En  disposable income
Es  renta disponible *(f)*
Fr  revenu disponible *(m)*
It  reddito disponibile *(m)*
Pt  receita disponível *(f)*

**Verfügung** *(f)* n De
En  disposal
Es  disposición *(f)*
Fr  disposition *(f)*
It  disposizione *(f)*
Pt  disposição *(f)*

**Vergleichsabkommen** *(n)* n De
En  deed of arrangement; deed of composition
Es  acta de disposición; concordato *(m f)*
Fr  contrat d´arrangement; concordat *(m)*
It  atto di accordo; atto di concordato *(m)*
Pt  escritura de acordo; concordata (por escrito) *(f)*

**vergoldet** *adj* De
En  gold-plated
Es  chapado en oro
Fr  plaqué d´or
It  placcato in oro
Pt  laminado a ouro

**vergüten** *vb* De
En  compensate
Es  compensar
Fr  compenser

It  compensare
Pt  compensar

**Vergütung** *(f)* n De
En  remuneration
Es  remuneración *(f)*
Fr  rémunération *(f)*
It  rimunerazione *(f)*
Pt  remuneração *(f)*

**Verhältnis** *(n)* n De
En  ratio; proportion
Es  razón; relación; proporción *(f)*
Fr  rapport; proportion *(m f)*
It  rapporto; proporzione *(m f)*
Pt  razão; proporção *(f)*

**Verhältnis des Aktienkurses zum Reingewinn** De
En  price-earnings ratio (P/E)
Es  proporción precio-ingresos *(f)*
Fr  quotient cours-bénéfice *(m)*
It  rapporto prezzo-utile *(m)*
Pt  taxa custo-ganhos *(f)*

**verhandeln** *vb* De
En  negotiate
Es  negociar
Fr  négocier
It  negoziare
Pt  negociar

**Verhandlung** *(f)* n De
En  negotiation
Es  negociación *(f)*
Fr  négotiation *(f)*
It  trattativa *(f)*
Pt  negociação *(f)*

**Verhandlungen wiederaufnehmen** De
En  re-open discussions
Es  reabrir la discusión
Fr  rouvrir la discussion
It  riaprire la discussione
Pt  reabrir discussões

**Verhandlungslage** *(f)* De
En  bargaining position
Es  situación de negociar *(f)*
Fr  situation permettant de négocier *(f)*
It  situazione permettente di trattare *(f)*
Pt  situação de regatear *(f)*

**Verhandlungsposition** *(f)* De
En  bargaining power
Es  poder de negociación *(m)*
Fr  pouvoir de négociation *(m)*
It  potere di contrattare *(m)*
Pt  poder de regateio *(m)*

**verificação** *(f)* n Pt
De  Untersuchung *(f)*
En  examination; verification
Es  verificación *(f)*
Fr  vérification *(f)*
It  verifica *(f)*

**verificação alfandegária** *(f)* Pt
De  zollamtliche Untersuchung *(f)*
En  customs examination
Es  control de aduanas *(m)*
Fr  visite douanière *(f)*
It  visita doganale *(f)*

**verificación contable interna** *(f)* Es
De  interne Revision *(f)*
En  internal audit
Fr  vérification interne *(f)*
It  verifica contabile interna *(f)*
Pt  fiscalização contabilística interna *(f)*

**verifica contabile interna** *(f)* It
De  interne Revision *(f)*
En  internal audit
Es  verificación contable interna *(f)*
Fr  vérification interne *(f)*
Pt  fiscalização contabilística interna *(f)*

**verificar** *vb* Es
De  nachprüfen
En  verify
Fr  vérifier
It  verificare
Pt  verificar

**verificar** *vb* Pt
De  nachprüfen
En  verify
Es  verificar
Fr  vérifier
It  verificare

**verificare** *vb* It
De  nachprüfen
En  verify
Es  verificar

Fr   vérifier
Pt   verificar

**vérificateur des comptes** (m)
     Fr
De   Rechnungsprüfer (m)
En   comptroller
Es   interventor (m)
It   controllore (m)
Pt   controlador (m)

**vérification comptable** (f) Fr
De   Bücherrevision (f)
En   audit
Es   revisión (examen) de cuen-
     tas (f)
It   revisione dei conti (f)
Pt   fiscalização de contas (f)

**vérification interne** (f) Fr
De   interne Revision (f)
En   internal audit
Es   verificación contable in-
     terna (f)
It   verifica contabile interna
     (f)
Pt   fiscalização contabilística
     interna (f)

**vérifier** vb Fr
De   nachprüfen
En   verify
Es   verificar
It   verificare
Pt   verificar

**vérifier et certifier** Fr
De   prüfen
En   audit
Es   revisar
It   rivedere
Pt   fiscalizar as contas

**verify** vb En
De   nachprüfen
Es   verificar
Fr   vérifier
It   verificare
Pt   verificar

**Verkauf** (m) n De
En   sale
Es   venta (f)
Fr   vente (f)
It   vendita (f)
Pt   venda (f)

**(zum) Verkauf anbieten** De
En   offer for sale
Es   ofrecer en venta
Fr   offrir en vente
It   offrire in vendita
Pt   pôr à venda

**verkaufen** vb De
En   sell
Es   vender
Fr   vendre
It   vendere
Pt   vender

**Verkäufer** (m) n De
En   salesman; vender
Es   vendedor (m)
Fr   vendeur (m)
It   venditore; commesso (m)
Pt   vendedor; caixeiro (m)

**Verkauf mit Zugaben** (m) De
En   premium offer
Es   oferta a prima (f)
Fr   offre à prime (f)
It   offerta sopra la pari (f)
Pt   oferta-prémio (f)

**Verkauf ohne Aufdringen** (m)
     De
En   soft sell
Es   venta sencilla (f)
Fr   vente par des moyens
     discrets (f)
It   vendere senza forzare
Pt   venda sobtil (f)

**Verkaufsabteilung** (f) n De
En   sales department
Es   departamento de ventas
     (m)
Fr   service ventes (m)
It   ufficio vendite (m)
Pt   departamento de vendas
     (m)

**Verkaufsagent** (m) n De
En   distributor
Es   distribuidor; concesionario
     (m)
Fr   distributeur; concession-
     naire (m)
It   distributore; concessionario
     (m)
Pt   distribuidor; concessionário
     (m)

**Verkaufsanalyse** (f) n De
En   sales analysis
Es   análisis de ventas (m)
Fr   analyse des ventes (f)
It   analisi delle vendite (f)
Pt   análise de vendas (f)

**Verkaufsautomat** (m) n De
En   vending machine
Es   máquina expendedora (f)
Fr   distributeur automatique
     (m)
It   macchina venditrice auto-
     matica (f)
Pt   máquina de vendas (f)

**Verkaufsgewandtheit** (f) n De
En   salesmanship
Es   arte de vender (m)
Fr   art de vendre (m)
It   arte della vendita (f)
Pt   ciência de vender (f)

**Verkaufskontenbuch** (n) n De
En   sales ledger
Es   libro mayor de ventas (m)
Fr   grand livre des ventes (m)
It   partitario delle vendite (m)
Pt   livro-mestre de vendas (m)

**Verkaufskosten** (pl) n De
En   selling cost
Es   coste de venta (m)
Fr   frais de vente (m)
It   costo di vendita (m)
Pt   custo de venda (m)

**Verkaufsleiter** (m) n De
En   sales manager
Es   jefe de ventas (m)
Fr   directeur commercial (m)
It   direttore commerciale (m)
Pt   chefe de vendas (m)

**Verkaufsoption** (f) n De
En   put option
Es   opción de venta (f)
Fr   option à vendre (f)
It   premio a vendere (m)
Pt   opção de venda (f)

**Verkaufspersonal** (n) n De
En   sales force
Es   personal de ventas (m)
Fr   personnel de vente (m)
It   forze di vendita (f pl)
Pt   pessoal de vendas (m)

**Verkaufsvoraussage** *(f)* n De
En sales forecast
Es pronóstico de ventas *(m)*
Fr prévision de ventes *(f)*
It previsione delle vendite *(f)*
Pt previsão de vendas *(f)*

**Verkehrsspitze** *(f)* n De
En rush hour
Es hora punta *(f)*
Fr heure d'affluence *(f)*
It ora di punta *(f)*
Pt hora de ponta *(f)*

**Verkehrsstockung** *(f)* n De
En traffic jam
Es embotellamiento de tráfico *(m)*
Fr encombrement de circulation *(m)*
It ingorgo stradale *(m)*
Pt engarrafamento de tráfico *(m)*

**Verladung** *(f)* n De
En shipment
Es embarque *(m)*
Fr embarquement *(m)*
It imbarco *(m)*
Pt embarque *(m)*

**Verlag** *(m)* n De
En publishing house
Es casa editorial *(f)*
Fr maison d'édition *(f)*
It casa editrice *(f)*
Pt casa editora *(f)*

**verlangen** *vb* De
En requisition
Es requisar
Fr réquisitionner
It requisire
Pt requisitar

**Verlängerung eines Kredites** *(f)* De
En extension of credit
Es prórroga de crédito *(f)*
Fr prolongation d'un crédit *(f)*
It proroga di credito *(f)*
Pt prorrogação de crédito *(f)*

**Verlängerungszeitraum** *(m)* n De
En extension of payment time
Es prórroga de pago *(f)*
Fr délai de paiement *(m)*

It proroga di pagamento *(f)*
Pt prorrogação de pagamento *(f)*

**Verletzte(r)** *(m)* n De
En injured party
Es parte lesionada *(f)*
Fr partie lésée *(f)*
It parte lesa *(f)*
Pt parte lesada *(f)*

**Verletzung** (eines Rechtes, usw.) *(f)* n De
En infringement
Es infracción *(f)*
Fr infraction *(f)*
It infrazione *(f)*
Pt infracção *(f)*

**Verletzung der Gewährleistungspflicht** *(f)* De
En breach of warranty
Es incumplimiento de la garantía *(m)*
Fr rupture de garantie *(f)*
It violazione di garanzia *(f)*
Pt violação de garantia *(f)*

**Verlust** *(m)* n De
En loss
Es pérdida *(f)*
Fr perte *(f)*
It perdita *(f)*
Pt perda *(f)*

**(einen) Verlust abschreiben** De
En write off a loss
Es cancelar una pérdida
Fr amortir une perte
It cancellare una perdita
Pt anular um prejuízo

**Vermerk** *(m)* n De
En memorandum
Es memorando; apunte *(m)*
Fr note *(f)*
It promemoria *(f)*
Pt memorando *(m)*

**vermieten** *vb* De
En rent
Es alquilar
Fr louer; affermer
It affittare; appigionare
Pt alugar

**Vermieter** *(m)* n De
En landlord; lessor
Es propietario; arrendador *(m)*
Fr propriétaire; bailleur *(m)*
It proprietario; locatore *(m)*
Pt proprietário; arrendador *(m)*

**vermitteln** *vb* De
En mediate
Es intermediar
Fr s'entremettre
It fare da intermediario
Pt intermediar

**Vermittlung** *(f)* n De
En mediation
Es intermediación *(f)*
Fr médiation *(f)*
It mediazione *(f)*
Pt intermediação *(f)*

**Vermögen** *(n)* n De
En estate
Es finca *(f)*
Fr bien; propriété *(m f)*
It proprietà *(f)*
Pt bens; propriedade *(m pl; m)*

**Vermögensanlage** *(f)* n De
En capital asset
Am fixed asset
Es activo fijo *(m)*
Fr actif immobilisé *(m)*
It capitale fisso *(m)*
Pt bens de capital *(m pl)*

**Verordnung** *(f)* n De
En directive
Es directiva *(f)*
Fr directive *(f)*
It direttivo *(m)*
Pt ordem de serviço *(f)*

**Verpachtung** *(f)* n De
En lease
Es alquiler *(m)*
Fr bail *(m)*
It affitto *(m)*
Pt aluguer; arrendamento *(m)*

**Verpackung** *(f)* n De
En packing
Es embalaje; envase *(m)*
Fr emballage *(m)*
It imballaggio *(m)*
Pt embalagem; empacotamento *(m)*

**Verpackung einbegriffen** De
En including packing
Es franco embalaje
Fr franco d'emballage
It imballaggio incluso
Pt incluindo embalagem

**verpfänden** vb De
En hypothecate
Es hipotecar
Fr hypothéquer
It ipotecare
Pt hipotecar

**Verpfändungsurkunde** (f) n De
En letter of hypothecation
Es carta de hipoteca (f)
Fr lettre hypothécaire (f)
It atto ipotecario (m)
Pt carta de hipoteca (f)

**Verpflichtung** (f) n De
En obligation; liability
Es obligación; responsabilidad (f)
Fr obligation; responsabilité (f)
It obbligazione; responsabilità (f)
Pt obrigação; responsabilidade (f)

**verre** (m) n Fr
De Glas (n)
En glass
Es vidrio (m)
It vetro (m)
Pt vidro (m)

**verre à glaces** (m) Fr
De Spiegelglas (n)
En plate glass
Es vidrio plano pulido (m)
It cristallo (m)
Pt chapa de vidro (f)

**verre à vitres** (m) Fr
De Fensterglas (n)
En window glass
Es cristal de ventana (m)
It vetro da finestre (m)
Pt vidro de montra (m)

**Verrechnungsscheck** (m) n De
En crossed cheque
Es cheque cruzado (m)
Fr chèque barré (m)
It assegno sbarrato (m)
Pt cheque cruzado (m)

**Verrechnungsstelle** (f) n De
En clearing house
Es cámara de compensaciones (f)
Fr chambre de compensation (f)
It stanza di compensazione (f)
Pt câmara de compensações e rateio (f)

**verre dépoli** (m) Fr
De Mattscheibe (f)
En ground glass
Es cristal deslustrado (m)
It vetro smerigliato (m)
Pt vidro esmerilado (m)

**versagen** vb De
En fail
Es fallar; faltar
Fr échouer; faillir
It mancare; fallire
Pt falhar; faltar

**Versammlung** (f) n De
En meeting
Es reunión (f)
Fr réunion; assemblée (f)
It riunione; assemblea (f)
Pt reunião; assembleia (f)

**(eine) Versammlung abhalten** De
En hold a meeting
Es celebrar una reunión
Fr tenir une assemblée
It tenere una riunione
Pt fazer uma reunião

**Versand** (m) n De
En despatch; dispatch
Es despacho; expedición (m f)
Fr envoi (m)
It spedizione; dispaccio (f m)
Pt despacho; remessa (m f)

**Versandschein** (m) De
En despatch note
Es aviso de expedición (m)
Fr bordereau d'expédition; bulletin d'envoi (m)
It bollettino di spedizione (m)
Pt aviso de despacho (m)

**versare un deposito** It
De hinterlegen
En pay a deposit
Es hacer un depósito

Fr donner des arrhès
Pt pagar depósito

**verschiedene Ausgaben** (f pl) De
En sundry expenses
Es gastos varios (m pl)
Fr frais divers (m pl)
It spese varie (f pl)
Pt despesas diversas (f pl)

**verschiffen** vb De
En ship
Es embarcar
Fr embarquer
It imbarcare
Pt embarcar

**Verschmelzung** (f) n De
En merger
Es fusión (f)
Fr fusion (f)
It fusione (f)
Pt fusão (f)

**versement** (m) n Fr
De Zahlung (f)
En payment
Es pago (m)
It pagamento (m)
Pt pagamento (m)

**versement à compte** (m) Fr
De Anzahlung (f)
En payment on account
Es pago a cuenta (m)
It pagamento in conto (m)
Pt pagamento por conta (m)

**Versendung** (f) n De
En consignment
Es consignación (f)
Fr envoi; expédition (m f)
It consegna; spedizione (f)
Pt consignação (f)

**Versendung vom Ursprungsort** (f) De
En shipment from origin
Es envío desde el punto de origen (m)
Fr envoi du lieu de départ (m)
It spedizione dall'origine (f)
Pt carregamento desde a origem (m)

**versicherbar** *adj* De
En insurable
Es asegurable
Fr assurable
It assicurabile
Pt susceptível de ser objecto de seguro

**Versicherer** *(m) n* De
En insurer; underwriter
Es asegurador *(m)*
Fr assureur *(m)*
It assicuratore *(m)*
Pt segurador *(m)*

**versichern** *vb* De
En insure
Es asegurar
Fr assurer
It assicurare
Pt segurar

**Versicherte(r)** *(m) n* De
En insured
Es asegurado *(m)*
Fr assuré *(m)*
It assicurato *(m)*
Pt titular de seguro *(m)*

**Versicherung** *(f) n* De
En insurance; assurance
Es seguro *(m)*
Fr assurance *(f)*
It assicurazione *(f)*
Pt seguro *(m)*

**Versicherung auf Gegensei-tigkeit** *(f)* De
En mutual insurance
Es coaseguro *(m)*
Fr assurance mutuelle *(f)*
It mutua assicurazione *(f)*
Pt seguro mútuo *(m)*

**Versicherungsdeckung** *(f) n* De
En insurance cover
Es cobertura de la póliza de seguro *(f)*
Fr garantie d'assurance *(f)*
It copertura assicurativa *(f)*
Pt cobertura de seguro *(f)*

**Versicherungsgesellschaft** *(f) n* De
En insurance company
Es compañía de seguros *(f)*
Fr compagnie d'assurance *(f)*

It compagnia di assicurazione *(f)*
Pt companhia de seguros *(f)*

**Versicherungsmakler** *(m) n* De
En insurance broker
Es corredor de seguros *(m)*
Fr courtier d'assurance *(m)*
It mediatore di assicurazioni *(m)*
Pt corretor de seguros *(m)*

**versicherungsmathematisch** *adj* De
En actuarial
Es actuarial
Fr actuariel
It attuariale
Pt actuarial

**Versicherungspolice** *(f) n* De
En insurance policy
Es póliza de seguro *(f)*
Fr police d'assurance *(f)*
It polizza di assicurazione *(f)*
Pt apólice de seguro *(f)*

**Versicherungsprämie** *(f) n* De
En insurance premium
Es prima de póliza de seguro *(f)*
Fr prime d'assurance *(f)*
It premio di assicurazione *(m)*
Pt prémio de seguro *(m)*

**Versicherungsschein** *(m) n* De
En insurance certificate
Es certificado de seguro *(m)*
Fr certificat d'assurance *(m)*
It certificato di assicurazione *(m)*
Pt certificado de seguro *(m)*

**Versicherungssyndikat** *(n) n* De
En underwriting syndicate (in-surance)
Es sindicato de seguros *(m)*
Fr syndicat d'assureurs *(m)*
It sindacato di assicuratori *(m)*
Pt consórcio de seguradores *(m)*

**Versicherungsverein auf Ge-genseitigkeit** *(m)* De
En friendly society
Am lodge

Es sociedad de socorro mutuo *(f)*
Fr société de secours mutuel *(f)*
It società di mutuo soccorso *(f)*
Pt mutualidade *(f)*

**Versicherungsvertreter** *(m) n* De
En insurance agent
Es agente de seguros *(m)*
Fr agent d'assurances *(m)*
It agenzia di assicurazioni *(f)*
Pt agente de seguros *(m)*

**verstaatlichte Industrie** *(f)* De
En nationalized industry
Es industria nacionalizada *(f)*
Fr industrie nationalisée *(f)*
It industria nazionalizzata *(f)*
Pt indústria nacionalizada *(f)*

**Verstaatlichung** *(f) n* De
En nationalization
Es nacionalización *(f)*
Fr nationalisation *(f)*
It nazionalizzazione *(f)*
Pt nacionalização *(f)*

**verstauen** *vb* De
En stow
Es estibar
Fr arrimer
It stivare
Pt estivar

**Verstauung** *(f) n* De
En stowage
Es estiba *(f)*
Fr arrimage *(m)*
It stivaggio *(m)*
Pt estiva *(f)*

**versteckte Belastung** *(f)* De
En hidden tax
Es impuesto latente *(m)*
Fr imposition latente *(f)*
It tassa invisibile *(f)*
Pt imposto ocultado *(m)*

**versteckter Mangel** *(m)* De
En latent defect
Es defecto latente *(m)*
Fr vice caché *(m)*
It difetto latente *(m)*
Pt defeito latente *(m)*

**Versteigerer** *(m)* n De
En auctioneer
Es subastador *(m)*
Fr commissaire-priseur *(m)*
It venditore all'asta *(m)*
Pt leiloeiro *(m)*

**Versteigerung** *(f)* n De
En auction; sale by auction
Es subasta; venta a subasta
 *(f)*
Fr vente aux enchères *(f)*
It asta; vendita all'asta *(f)*
Pt leilão; venda em leilão *(m f)*

**vertagen** *vb* De
En adjourn
Es aplazar
Fr ajourner
It aggiornare
Pt adiar

**Vertagung** *(f)* n De
En adjournment
Es aplazamiento *(m)*
Fr ajournement *(m)*
It aggiornamento *(m)*
Pt adiamento *(m)*

**verteilen** *vb* De
En distribute; allot
Es repartir; asignar
Fr répartir; attribuer
It repartire; assegnare
Pt repartir; atribuir

**Verteilung** *(f)* n De
En distribution; allotment
Es reparto; adjudicación *(m f)*
Fr distribution; attribution *(f)*
It ripartizione *(f)*
Pt distribuição; aporcionamen-
 to *(f m)*

**Verteilungsbrief** *(m)* n De
En allotment letter
Es letra de adjudicación *(f)*
Fr avis d'attribution *(m)*
It lettera da ripartizione *(f)*
Pt aviso de aporcionamento
 *(m)*

**vertenza di lavoro** *(f)* It
De Arbeitsstreitigkeit *(f)*
En trade dispute
Es conflicto laboral *(m)*

Fr conflit du travail *(m)*
Pt conflito comercial *(m)*

**vertenza operaia** *(f)* It
De Arbeitskonflikt *(m)*
En industrial dispute
Es conflicto laboral *(m)*
Fr conflit ouvrier *(m)*
Pt conflito de trabalho *(m)*

**vertical integration** En
De vertikaler Zusammenschluss
 *(m)*
Es integración vertical *(f)*
Fr integration verticale *(f)*
It integrazione verticale *(f)*
Pt integração vertical *(f)*

**vertikaler Zusammenschluss**
 *(m)* De
En vertical integration
Es integración vertical *(f)*
Fr integration verticale *(f)*
It integrazione verticale *(f)*
Pt integração vertical *(f)*

**Vertrag** *(m)* n De
En contract
Es contrato *(m)*
Fr contrat *(m)*
It contratto *(m)*
Pt contrato *(m)*

**(einen) Vertrag formulieren**
 De
En draw up a contract
Es redactar un contrato
Fr rédiger un contrat
It redigere un contratto
Pt redigir um contrato

**vertraglich** *adj* De
En contractual
Es contractual
Fr contractuel
It contrattuale
Pt contractual

**Vertragsbeendigung** *(f)* n De
En determination of a contract
Es rescisión de un contrato *(f)*
Fr résolution d'un contrat *(f)*
It risoluzione di un contratto
 *(f)*
Pt rescisão de contrato *(f)*

**Vertragsentwurf** *(m)* n De
En draft contract
Es proyecto de contrato *(m)*
Fr projet de contrat *(m)*
It progetto di contratto *(m)*
Pt minuta de contrato *(f)*

**Vertragspreis** *(m)* n De
En contract price
Es precio contractual *(m)*
Fr prix contractuel *(m)*
It prezzo contrattuale *(m)*
Pt preço contractual *(m)*

**Vertragsverletzung** *(f)* n De
En breach of contract
Es incumplimiento del con-
 trato *(m)*
Fr rupture de contrat *(f)*
It rottura di contratto *(f)*
Pt rotura de contrato *(f)*

**vertreiben** (Waren, usw.) *vb* De
En distribute
Es distribuir
Fr distribuer
It distribuire
Pt distribuir

**vertreten** *vb* De
En represent
Es representar
Fr représenter
It rappresentare
Pt representar

**Vertreter** *(m)* n De
En representative
Es representante *(m)*
Fr représentant *(m)*
It rappresentante *(m)*
Pt representante *(m)*

**Vertrieb** *(m)* n De
En distribution (of goods)
Es distribución *(f)*
Fr distribution *(f)*
It distribuzione *(f)*
Pt distribuição *(f)*

**Veruntreuer** *(m)* n De
En embezzler
Es desfalcador *(m)*
Fr détourneur *(m)*
It malversatore *(m)*
Pt desfalcador *(m)*

**vervielfältigen** vb De
En multiply
Es multiplicar
Fr multipliquer
It moltiplicare
Pt multiplicar

**Vervielfältiger** (m) n De
En multiplier
Es multiplicador (m)
Fr multiplicateur (m)
It moltiplicatore (m)
Pt multiplicador (m)

**Vervielfältigung der Produkte**
(f) De
En diversification
Es diversificación (f)
Fr diversification (f)
It diversificazione (f)
Pt diversificação (f)

**Verwahrer** (m) n De
En depositary
Es depositario (m)
Fr dépositaire (m)
It depositario (m)
Pt depositário (m)

**Verwahrung in Stahlfach** (f)
De
En safe deposit
Es depósito en caja fuerte (m)
Fr dépôt en coffre-fort (m)
It servizio di cassette di
sicurezza (m)
Pt depósito em cofre forte (m)

**verwalten** vb De
En administer
Es administrar
Fr administrer
It amministrare
Pt administrar

**Verwalter** (m) n De
En administrator
Es administrador (m)
Fr administrateur (m)
It amministratore (m)
Pt administrador (m)

**Verwaltung** (f) n De
En administration
Es administración (f)
Fr gestion (f)
It gestione (f)
Pt gestão (f)

**Verwaltungsrat** (m) n De
En director
Es director (m)
Fr administrateur (m)
It amministratore (m)
Pt director (m)

**Verzicht** (m) n De
En renunciation; waiver
Es renuncia (f)
Fr renonciation (f)
It rinunzia (f)
Pt renúncia (f)

**verzollen** vb De
En clear through customs
Es retirar de aduanas
Fr dédouaner
It sdoganare
Pt despachar na alfândega

**verzollt** adj De
En duty-paid; out of bond; ex
bond
Es derechos pagados; des-
pachado de aduanas; fuera
de aduanas
Fr acquitté; dédouané; à
l'acquitté
It dazio pagato; sdoganato
Pt direitos pagos; despachado
alfândega

**Verzollung** (f) n De
En customs clearance
Es despacho de aduana (m)
Fr formalités douanières (f pl)
It sdoganamento (m)
Pt despacho de alfândega (m)

**Verzug** (m) n De
En delay
Es retraso (m)
Fr retard; délai (m)
It ritardo (m)
Pt atrazo (m)

**vested interest** En
De festbegründetes Recht (n)
Es interés creado (m)
Fr droit acquis (m)
It diritto acquisito (m)
Pt interesse adquirido (m)

**vetro** (m) n It
De Glas (n)
En glass
Es vidrio (m)

Fr verre (m)
Pt vidro (m)

**vetro da finestre** (m) It
De Fensterglas (n)
En window glass
Es cristal de ventana (m)
Fr verre à vitres (m)
Pt vidro de montra (m)

**vetro smerigliato** (m) It
De Mattscheibe (f)
En ground glass
Es cristal deslustrado (m)
Fr verre dépoli (m)
Pt vidro esmerilado (m)

**vettore** (m) n It
De Spediteur (m)
En carrier
Am conveyer
Es transportador (m)
Fr expéditeur (m)
Pt transportador (m)

**viabilidade** (f) n Pt
De Durchführbarkeit (f)
En feasibility
Es practicabilidad (f)
Fr practicabilité (f)
It fattibilità (f)

**viagem** (f) n Pt
De Seereise (f)
En voyage
Es viaje (m)
Fr voyage (m)
It viaggio (m)

**viaggiatore di commercio** (m)
It
De Geschäftsreisende(r); Han-
delsvertreter (m)
En commercial traveller
Es viajante de comercio (m)
Fr commis-voyageur (m)
Pt caixeiro viajante (m)

**viaggio** (m) n It
De Seereise (f)
En voyage
Es viaje (m)
Fr voyage (m)
Pt viagem (f)

**viajante de comercio** (m) Es
De Handelsvertreter; Geschäfts-
reisende(r) (m)

En commercial traveller
Am salesman
Fr commis-voyageur *(m)*
It viaggiatore di commercio *(m)*
Pt caixeiro viajante *(m)*

**viaje** *(m)* n Es
De Seereise *(f)*
En voyage
Fr voyage *(m)*
It viaggio *(m)*
Pt viagem *(f)*

**vice caché** *(m)* Fr
De versteckter Mangel *(m)*
En latent defect
Es defecto latente *(m)*
It difetto latente *(m)*
Pt defeito latente *(m)*

**vice-chairman** n En
De stellvertretender Vorsitzende(r) *(m)*
Es vice-presidente *(m)*
Fr vice-président *(m)*
It vicepresidente *(m)*
Pt vice-presidente *(m)*

**vice-direttore** *(m)* n It
De Unterdirektor *(m)*
En assistant manager
Es sub-director *(m)*
Fr sous-directeur *(m)*
Pt sub-director *(m)*

**vice-président** *(m)* n Fr
De stellvertretender Vorsitzende(r) *(m)*
En vice-chairman
Es vice-presidente *(m)*
It vicepresidente *(m)*
Pt vice-presidente *(m)*

**vice-presidente** *(m)* n Es, Pt
De stellvertretender Vorsitzende(r) *(m)*
En vice-chairman
Fr vice-président *(m)*
It vicepresidente *(m)*

**vicepresidente** *(m)* n It
De stellvertretender Vorsitzende(r) *(m)*
En vice-chairman
Es vice-presidente *(m)*
Fr vice-président *(m)*
Pt vice-presidente *(m)*

**vidrio** *(m)* n Es
De Glas *(n)*
En glass
Fr verre *(m)*
It vetro *(m)*
Pt vidro *(m)*

**vidrio plano pulido** *(m)* Es
De Spiegelglas *(n)*
En plate glass
Fr verre à glaces: glace de vitrage *(m f)*
It cristallo *(m)*
Pt chapa de vidro *(f)*

**vidro** *(m)* n Pt
De Glas *(n)*
En glass
Es vidrio *(m)*
Fr verre *(m)*
It vetro *(m)*

**vidro de montra** *(m)* Pt
De Fensterglas *(n)*
En window glass
Es cristal de ventana *(m)*
Fr verre à vitres *(m)*
It vetro da finestre *(m)*

**vidro esmerilado** *(m)* Pt
De Mattscheibe *(f)*
En ground glass
Es cristal deslustrado *(m)*
Fr verre dépoli *(m)*
It vetro smerigliato *(m)*

**vierteljährlich** adj De
En quarterly
Es trimestral
Fr trimestriel
It trimestrale
Pt trimestral

**vierteljährliche Zahlungen** *(f pl)* De
En quarterly payments
Es pagos trimestrales *(m pl)*
Fr paiements trimestriels *(m pl)*
It pagamenti trimestrali *(m pl)*
Pt pagamentos trimestrais *(m pl)*

**vigente** adj Pt
De in Kraft
En in force
Es en vigor

Fr en vigueur
It in vigore

**violação de garantia** *(f)* Pt
De Verletzung der Gewährleistungspflicht *(f)*
En breach of warranty
Es incumplimiento de la garantía *(m)*
Fr rupture de garantie *(f)*
It violazione di garanzia *(f)*

**violazione di garanzia** *(f)* It
De Verletzung der Gewährleistungspflicht *(f)*
En breach of warranty
Es incumplimiento de la garantía *(m)*
Fr rupture de garantie *(f)*
Pt violação de garantia *(f)*

**virement bancaire** *(m)* Fr
De Banküberweisung *(f)*
En bank transfer
Es transferencia bancaria *(m)*
It trasferimento bancario *(m)*
Pt transferência bancária *(f)*

**virement postal** *(m)* Fr
De Postüberweisung *(f)*
En mail transfer
Es transferencia postal *(f)*
It trasferimento per posta *(m)*
Pt transferência postal *(f)*

**virement télégraphique** *(m)* Fr
De Kabelauszahlúng *(f)*
En telegraphic transfer
Es giro telegráfico *(m)*
It rimessa telegrafica *(f)*
Pt transferência telegráfica *(f)*

**visa** n En; Es *(f)*, Fr *(m)*
De Visum *(n)*
It visto *(m)*
Pt visto *(m)*

**visita doganale** *(f)* It
De zollamtliche Untersuchung *(f)*
En customs examination
Es control de aduanas *(m)*
Fr visite douanière *(f)*
Pt verificação alfandegária *(f)*

**visita medica** *(f)* It
De ärztliche Untersuchung *(f)*
En medical examination

Es examen médico (m)
Fr examen médical (m)
Pt inspecção médica (f)

**visite douanière** (f) Fr
De zollamtliche Untersuchung (f)
En customs examination
Es control de aduanas (m)
It visita doganale (f)
Pt verificação alfandegária (f)

**visto** (m) n It, Pt
De Visum (n)
En visa
Es visa (f)
Fr visa (m)

**visual-display unit** (vdu) En
De Bildschirmeinheit (f)
Es unidad de visualización (f)
Fr unité de visualisation (f)
It unità di visualizzazione (f)
Pt móvel-montra de exposição de visuais (f)

**Visum** (n) n De
En visa
Es visa (f)
Fr visa (m)
It visto (m)
Pt visto (m)

**vocational training** En
De Berufsausbildung (f)
Es formación profesional (f)
Fr formation professionnelle (f)
It addestramento professionale (m)
Pt treino vocacional (m)

**voci di pareggio** (f pl) It
De Ausgleichsposten (m pl)
En balancing items
Es asientos saldados (m pl)
Fr postes rééquilibrants (m pl)
Pt valores de equilíbrio (m pl)

**void** (of a contract, etc.) adj En
De nichtig
Es nulo
Fr nul
It nullo
Pt nulo

**voiture** (f) n Fr
De Auto; Wagen (n m)
En car
Es coche (m)
It automobile; macchina (f)
Pt carro; automóvel (m)

**voiturier public** (m) Fr
De Güterbeförderer (m)
En common carrier
Es empresa de transportes (f)
It vettore (m)
Pt empresa de transportes (f)

**voix prépondérante** (f) Fr
De entscheidende Stimme (f)
En casting vote
Es voto decisivo (m)
It voto decisivo (m)
Pt voto decisivo (m)

**vol** (m) n Fr
De Diebstahl; Flucht (m f)
En theft; flight
Es robo; vuelo (m)
It furto; volo (m)
Pt furto; voo (m)

**vol avec effraction** (m) Fr
De Einbruchdiebstahl (m)
En burglary
Es robo (m)
It furto con scasso (m)
Pt roubo (m)

**Volkswirtschaftslehre** (f) n De
En economics
Es economía (f)
Fr économie (f)
It economia (f)
Pt economia (f pl)

**Volkszählung** (f) n De
En census
Es censo (m)
Fr recensement (m)
It censimento (m)
Pt censo (m)

**voll** adj De
En full
Es lleno
Fr plein
It pieno
Pt cheio

**Vollbeschäftigung** (f) n De
En full employment
Es pleno empleo (m)
Fr plein emploi (m)
It piena occupazione (f)
Pt pleno emprego (m)

**volle Zahlung** (f) De
En payment in full
Es pago en pleno (m)
Fr libération intégrale (f)
It pagamento in pieno (m)
Pt pagamento completo (m)

**vollgezeichnet** adj De
En fully subscribed
Es plenamente suscrito
Fr intégralement souscrit
It interamente sottoscritto
Pt totalmente subscrito

**Vollmacht** (f) n De
En authority; power of attorney
Es autoridad; poder (f m)
Fr mandat; procuration (m f)
It autorità; procura (f)
Pt autoridade; poderes de procuração (f; m pl)

**(eine) Vollmacht erteilen** De
En execute a power of attorney
Es otorgar poder notarial
Fr conférer des pleins pouvoirs
It conferire una procura
Pt dar execução a poderes de procuração

**Vollmachtgeber** (m) n De
En principal
Es mandante (m)
Fr mandant (m)
It mandante (m)
Pt mandante (m)

**vollstrecken** vb De
En execute
Es ejecutar; legalizar
Fr exécuter; réaliser
It eseguire; effettuare
Pt executar

**Vollstrecker** (m) n De
En executor
Es albacea (m)
Fr exécuteur (m)

It   esecutore (m)
Pt   executor (m)

**Vollwertdeckung** (f) n De
En   full cover
Es   garantía total (f)
Fr   garantie totale (f)
It   garanzia totale (f)
Pt   cobertura total (f)

**volo** (m) n It
De   Flucht (f)
En   flight
Es   vuelo (m)
Fr   vol (m)
Pt   voo (m)

**volontaire** adj Fr
De   freiwillig
En   voluntary
Es   voluntario
It   volontario
Pt   voluntário

**volontario** adj It
De   freiwillig
En   voluntary
Es   voluntario
Fr   volontaire
Pt   voluntário

**volume** (m) Fr, It
De   Kubikinhalt (m)
En   cubic capacity
Es   capacidad cúbica (f)
Pt   capacidade cúbica (f)

**volumen de ventas** (m) Es
De   Umsatz (m)
En   turnover
Fr   chiffre d'affaires (m)
It   giro d'affari (m)
Pt   movimento de dinheiro (m)

**voluntario** adj Es
De   freiwillig
En   voluntary
Fr   volontaire
It   volontario
Pt   voluntário

**voluntário** adj Pt
De   freiwillig
En   voluntary
Es   voluntario
Fr   volontaire
It   volontario

**voluntary** adj En
De   freiwillig
Es   voluntario
Fr   volontaire
It   volontario
Pt   voluntário

**von Hypothek befreit** De
En   free from mortgage
Es   deshipotecado
Fr   déshypothéqué
It   libero d'ipoteca
Pt   livre de hipoteca

**voo** (m) n Pt
De   Flucht (f)
En   flight
Es   vuelo (m)
Fr   vol (m)
It   volo (m)

**Voranschlag** (m) n De
En   estimate
Es   presupuesto (m)
Fr   devis (m)
It   preventivo (m)
Pt   previsão (f)

**Vorarbeiter** (m) n De
En   foreman
Es   capataz (m)
Fr   contremaître; chef d'équipe (m)
It   capo operaio; capo squadra (m)
Pt   encarregado; capataz (m)

**vorausbezahlt** adj De
En   prepaid
Es   pagado por adelantado
Fr   payé d'avance
It   pagato in anticipo
Pt   pago adiantamente

**vorausgesetzt** De
En   on condition
Es   a condición
Fr   sous réserve
It   a condizione
Pt   sob condição de

**Voraussagen** (n) n De
En   forecasting
Es   pronóstico (m)
Fr   prévision (f)
It   previsione (f)
Pt   previsão (f)

**Vorauszahlung** (f) De
En   advance payment; prepayment
Es   anticipo (m)
Fr   paiement par anticipation (m)
It   pagamento anticipato (m)
Pt   pagamento adiantado (m)

**vorbehalten** vb De
En   reserve
Es   reservar
Fr   réserver
It   riservare
Pt   reservar

**Vorderfront** (f) n De
En   frontage
Es   fachada (f)
Fr   façade (f)
It   facciata (f)
Pt   fachada (f)

**Vordruck** (m) De
En   printed form
Es   formulario; impreso (m)
Fr   formulaire (m)
It   modulo stampato (m)
Pt   impresso (m)

**vorfabrizieren** vb De
En   prefabricate
Es   prefabricar
Fr   préfabriquer
It   prefabbricare
Pt   pre-fabricar

**vorgestern** adv De
En   day before yesterday
Es   anteayer
Fr   avant-hier
It   avantieri
Pt   anteontem

**vorhersehen** vb De
En   forecast
Es   pronosticar
Fr   prévoir
It   pronosticare
Pt   prognosticar

**Vorladung** (f) n De
En   writ
Es   auto; orden (m f)
Fr   assignation (f)
It   citazione (f)
Pt   citação; ordem (f m)

votar

**vorläufig** *adj* De
En preliminary
Es preliminar
Fr préliminaire; préalable
It preliminare
Pt preliminar

**vorläufige Dividende** *(f)* De
En interim dividend
Es dividendo provisional *(m)*
Fr dividende intérimaire *(m)*
It acconto di dividendo *(m)*
Pt dividendo interino *(m)* ·

**Vormund** (eines Minderjährigen) *(m)* n De
En guardian
Es tutor *(m)*
Fr tuteur *(m)*
It tutore *(m)*
Pt tutor *(m)*

**Vorrat** *(m)* n De
En stock
Es stock; existencias *(m; f pl)*
Fr stock; marchandises *(m; f pl)*
It stock; scorta *(m f)*
Pt existências *(f pl)*

**Vorrat auf Lager** *(m)* De
En stock in hand
Es mercancías en almacén *(f pl)*
Fr marchandises en magasin *(f pl)*
It merce in magazzino *(f)*
Pt mercadorias em existência *(f)*

**vorrätig** De
En in stock; on hand
Es en almacén; disponible
Fr en magasin; disponible
It in magazzino; disponibile
Pt à mão; ao dispôr

**vorrätig halten** De
En keep in stock
Es guardar en almacén
Fr garder en stock
It tenere in magazzino
Pt reter em armazém

**Vorratslager anlegen** De
En stockpile
Es acumular existencias
Fr stocker

It ammassare
Pt acumular existências

**Vorrecht** *(n)* n De
En. priority
Es prioridad *(f)*
Fr priorité *(f)*
It priorità *(f)*
Pt prioridade *(f)*

**vorschiessen** *vb* De
En advance (money)
Am prepay
Es anticipar
Fr avancer (de l'argent)
It anticipare
Pt adiantar

**Vorschlag** *(m)* n De
En proposal
Es propuesta *(f)*
Fr proposition *(f)*
It proposta *(f)*
Pt proposta *(f)*

**Vorschuss** *(m)* n De
En advance
Am prepayment
Es adelanto *(m)*
Fr avance *(f)*
It anticipazione *(f)*
Pt adiantamento *(m)*

**Vorschusskredit** *(m)* n De
En bridging loan
Am bridge-over
Es crédito provisional *(m)*
Fr crédit provisoire *(m)*
It credito provvisorio *(m)*
Pt crédito provisório *(m)*

**vorsichtige Schätzung** *(f)* De
En conservative estimate
Es presupuesto prudente *(m)*
Fr évaluation prudente *(f)*
It valutazione prudente *(f)*
Pt avaliação cautelosa *(f)*

**Vorsitzende(r)** *(m)* n De
En chairman
Es presidente *(m)*
Fr président *(m)*
It presidente *(m)*
Pt presidente *(m)*

**Vorstand** *(m)* n De
En management; board of directors

Es dirección; consejo de administración *(f m)*
Fr administration; conseil d'administration *(f m)*
It direzione; consiglio d'amministrazione *(m f)*
Pt gerência; direcção *(f)*

**Vorstandsbericht** *(m)* n De
En directors' report
Es informe de la administración *(m)*
Fr rapport des administrateurs *(m)*
It relazione degli amministratori *(f)*
Pt relatório de directores *(m)*

**Vorstandssitzung** *(f)* n De
En board meeting
Es reunión del consejo de administración *(f)*
Fr réunion du conseil d'administration *(f)*
It riunione del consiglio d'amministrazione *(f)*
Pt reunião da administração *(f)*

**vorzeitig (bezahlt)** De
En anticipated
Es anticipado
Fr anticipé
It anticipato
Pt antecipado

**Vorzugsaktie** *(f)* n De
En preference share
Es acción preferente *(f)*
Fr action privilégiée *(f)*
It azione privilegiata *(f)*
Pt acção preferencial *(f)*

**Vorzugssatz** *(m)* n De
En preferential duty
Es derechos preferenciales *(m pl)*
Fr tarif de faveur *(m)*
It tariffa preferenziale *(f)*
Pt direito preferencial *(m)*

**votar** *vb* Es, Pt
De stimmen
En vote
Fr voter
It votare

# W

**votare** *vb* It
De stimmen
En vote
Es votar
Fr voter
Pt votar

**vote** *vb* En
De stimmen
Es votar
Fr voter
It votare
Pt votar

**voter** *vb* Fr
De stimmen
En vote
Es votar
It votare
Pt votar

**voting shares** En
De stimmberechtigte Aktien *(f pl)*
Es acciones con derecho de voto *(f pl)*
Fr actions avec droit de vote *(f pl)*
It azioni con diritto a voto *(f pl)*
Pt acçoes com direito a voto *(f pl)*

**voto decisivo** *(m)* Es, It, Pt
De entscheidende Stimme *(f)*
En casting vote
Fr voix prépondérante *(f)*

**voucher** *n* En
De Belegstück *(n)*
Es pieza justificativa *(f)*
Fr pièce justificative; fiche *(f)*
It pezza d'appoggio *(f)*
Pt vale *(m)*

**voyage** *n* En, Fr *(m)*
De Seereise *(f)*
Es viaje *(m)*
It viaggio *(m)*
Pt viagem *(f)*

**vuelo** *(m)* *n* Es
De Flucht *(f)*
En flight
Fr vol *(m)*
It volo *(m)*
Pt voo *(m)*

**Waage** *(f)* *n* De
En scales
Es balanza *(f)*
Fr balance *(f)*
It bilancia *(f)*
Pt balança *(f)*

**wachstumorientierte Wertpapiere** *(n pl)* De
En growth stocks
Es títulos de crecimiento *(m pl)*
Fr titres avec perspectives de croissance
It titoli di sviluppo *(m pl)*
Pt acções de acréscimo de capital *(f pl)*

**wage** *n* En
De Lohn *(m)*
Es salario *(m)*
Fr salaire *(m)*
It salario *(m)*
Pt salário *(m)*

**wage claim** En
De Lohnforderung *(f)*
Es reclamación de salario *(f)*
Fr revendication de salaire *(f)*
It rivendicazione salariale *(f)*
Pt demanda de salário *(f)*

**wage earner** En
De Lohnempfänger *(m)*
Es asalariado *(m)*
Fr salarié *(m)*
It salariato *(m)*
Pt assalariado *(m)*

**wage freeze** En
De Lohnstopp *(m)*
Es bloqueo de salarios *(m)*
Fr blocage des salaires *(m)*
It blocco dei salari *(m)*
Pt congelação de salários *(m)*

**wage rate** En
De Lohnsatz *(m)*
Es tarifa de salarios *(f)*
Fr taux des salaires *(m)*
It tariffa salariale *(f)*
Pt base salarial *(f)*

**wage restraint** En
De Lohnbeschränkung *(f)*
Es restricción de salario *(f)*
Fr contrainte sur les salaires *(f)*
It restrizioni sui salari *(f pl)*
Pt restrição de salários *(f)*

**wages agreement** En
De Lohnvereinbarung *(f)*
Es acuerdo sobre salarios *(m)*
Fr convention des salaires *(f)*
It accordo sui salari *(m)*
Pt acordo sobre salários *(m)*

**wagon de chemin de fer** *(m)* Fr
De Eisenbahnwagen *(m)*
En railway carriage
Am railroad car
Es vagón de ferrocarril *(m)*
It carrozza ferroviaria *(f)*
Pt vagão de caminhos de ferro *(m)*

**Wahrscheinlichkeit** *(f)* *n* De
En probability
Es probabilidad *(f)*
Fr probabilité *(f)*
It probabilità *(f)*
Pt probabilidade *(f)*

**Währung** *(f)* *n* De
En currency
Es moneda *(f)*
Fr monnaie *(f)*
It valuta *(f)*
Pt moeda *(f)*

**Währungsabwertung** *(f)* *n* De
En devaluation
Es devaluación *(f)*
Fr dévaluation *(f)*
It svalutazione *(f)*
Pt desvalorização *(f)*

**Währungsausgleichsfonds** *(m)* *n* De
En exchange equalization account
Es cuenta de compensación de cambio *(f)*
Fr fonds de stabilisation des changes *(m pl)*
It conto per la stabilizzazione dei cambi *(m)*
Pt conta de compensação de transacções *(f)*

**Währungsgebiet** *(n)* n De
En currency area
Es zona monetaria *(f)*
Fr zone monétaire *(f)*
It zona monetaria *(f)*
Pt zona monetária *(f)*

**Währungspolitik** *(f)* n De
En monetary policy
Es politica monetaria *(f)*
Fr politique monétaire *(f)*
It politica monetaria *(f)*
Pt política monetária *(f)*

**Währungsreform** *(f)* n De
En monetary reform
Es reforma monetaria *(f)*
Fr réforme monétaire *(f)*
It riforma monetaria *(f)*
Pt reforma monetária *(f)*

**waiting list** En
De Warteliste *(f)*
Es lista de espera *(f)*
Fr liste d´attente *(f)*
It elenco delle prenotazioni *(m)*
Pt lista de espera *(f)*

**waiver** n En
De Verzicht *(m)*
Es renuncia *(f)*
Fr renonciation *(f)*
It rinunzia *(f)*
Pt renúncia *(f)*

**war** n En
De Krieg *(m)*
Es guerra *(f)*
Fr guerre *(f)*
It guerra *(f)*
Pt guerra *(f)*

**war-risk insurance** En
De Kriegsrisikoversicherung *(f)*
Es seguro contra riesgo de guerra *(m)*
Fr assurance du risque de guerre *(f)*
It assicurazione contro i rischi di guerra *(f)*
Pt seguro contra risco de guerra *(m)*

**warehouse** n En
De Warenlager *(n)*
Es almacén *(m)*
Fr magasin; entrepôt *(m)*

It magazzino *(m)*
Pt armazém *(m)*

**Waren** *(f pl)* n De
En merchandise
Es mercancía *(f)*
Fr marchandise *(f)*
It merce *(f)*
Pt mercadoria *(f)*

**Warenhaus** *(n)* n De
En department store
Es grandes almacenes *(m pl)*
Fr grand magasin *(m)*
It grande magazzino *(m)*
Pt armazém *(m)*

**Warenlager** *(n)* n De
En warehouse
Es almacén *(m)*
Fr magasin; entrepôt *(m)*
It magazzino *(m)*
Pt armazém *(m)*

**Warenmarkt** *(m)* n De
En produce market
Es mercado de productos *(m)*
Fr marché commercial *(m)*
It mercato commerciale *(m)*
Pt mercado de produtos *(m)*

**Warenumsatzsteuer** *(f)* n De
En sales tax
Es impuesto sobre la venta *(m)*
Fr taxe de vente *(f)*
It imposta sulle vendite *(f)*
Pt imposto sobre vendas *(m)*

**Waren unter Zollverschluss** *(f pl)* De
En bonded goods
Es mercancías en aduana *(f pl)*
Fr marchandises en douane *(f pl)*
It merci sotto vincolo doganale *(f pl)*
Pt mercadorias à ordem da alfândega *(f pl)*

**Warenzeichen** *(n)* n De
En trademark
Es marca de fábrica *(f)*
Fr marque de fabrique *(f)*
It marchio di fabbrica *(m)*
Pt marca de fabrico *(f)*

**warrant** (for payment) n En
De Befugnis *(f)*
Es mandato *(m)*
Fr ordonnance *(f)*
It mandato *(m)*
Pt mandato *(m)*

**warrant** (for goods) n En
De Lagerschein *(m)*
Es certificado *(m)*
Fr certificat *(m)*
It certificato *(m)*
Pt certificado *(m)*

**warranty** n En
De Garantie *(f)*
Es garantía *(f)*
Fr garantie *(f)*
It garanzia *(f)*
Pt garantia *(f)*

**Warteliste** *(f)* n De
En waiting list
Es lista de espera *(f)*
Fr liste d´attente *(f)*
It elenco delle prenotazioni *(m)*
Pt lista de espera *(f)*

**Wasserschaden** *(m)* n De
En water damage
Es daño causado por el agua *(m)*
Fr dégâts des eaux *(m pl)*
It danno causato dall´acqua *(m)*
Pt dano causado por água *(m)*

**waste products** En
De Abfallprodukte *(n pl)*
Es desperdicios *(m pl)*
Fr déchets *(m pl)*
It produtto di rifiuto *(m)*
Pt desperdicios *(m pl)*

**wasting assets** En
Am depleting assets
De kurzlebige Aktiva *(n pl)*
Es activo gastable *(m)*
Fr actifs défectibles *(m pl)*
It attività in esaurimento *(f pl)*
Pt bens em uso ou deterioração *(m pl)*

**water damage** En
De Wasserschaden *(m)*
Es daño causado por el agua *(m)*

Fr dégâts des eaux *(m pl)*
It danno causato dall'acqua *(m)*
Pt dano causado por água *(m)*

**waybill** *n* En
De Frachtbrief *(m)*
Es guía de carga *(f)*
Fr lettre de voiture *(f)*
It lettera di vettura *(f)*
Pt guia de marcha *(f)*

**wealth** *n* En
De Wohlstand *(m)*
Es riqueza *(f)*
Fr richesse *(f)*
It ricchezza *(f)*
Pt riqueza *(f)*

**wear and tear** En
De natürliche Abnützung *(f)*
Es desgaste natural *(m)*
Fr usure normale *(f)*
It logorio naturale *(m)*
Pt desgaste *(m)*

**Webware** *(f) n* De
En textile
Es textil *(m)*
Fr textile *(m)*
It tessile *(m)*
Pt textil *(m)*

**Wechsel** *(m)* De
En bill of exchange
Es letra de cambio *(f)*
Fr lettre de change *(f)*
It tratta cambiale *(f)*
Pt letra de câmbio *(f)*

**(einen) Wechsel einlösen** De
En retire a bill
Es recoger una letra
Fr payer une lettre de change
It ritirare un effetto
Pt recuperar uma letra

**(einen) Wechsel nicht akzeptieren** De
En dishonour a bill
Es protestar una letra
Fr ne pas honorer un effet
It non onorare un effetto
Pt protestar uma letra

**(einen) Wechsel vorlegen** De
En present a bill for acceptance

Es presentar una letra para aceptación
Fr présenter une traite à l'acceptation
It presentare una cambiale per accettazione
Pt apresentar uma letra para aceite

**Wechselforderungen** *(f pl) n* De
En bills receivable
Es letras a cobrar *(f pl)*
Fr effets à recevoir *(m pl)*
It effetti attivi *(m pl)*
Pt letras a cobrar *(f pl)*

**Wechselkurs** *(m) n* De
En exchange rate
Es tipo de cambio *(m)*
Fr cours de change *(f)*
It corso del cambio *(m)*
Pt câmbio *(m)*

**Wechselmakler** *(m) n* De
En bill broker
Es corredor de cambios *(m)*
Fr courtier de bons *(m)*
It agente di sconto *(m)*
Pt corretor de câmbios *(m)*

**Wechselschulden** *(f pl) n* De
En bills payable
Es letras pagaderas *(f pl)*
Fr effets à payer *(m pl)*
It effetti passivi *(m pl)*
Pt letras a pagar *(f pl)*

**wegwerfbare Verpackung** *(f)* De
En disposable wrapping
Es envoltura desechable *(f)*
Fr emballage perdu *(m)*
It imballaggio a perdere *(m)*
Pt embalagem a destruir *(f)*

**weigh** *vb* En
De wiegen
Es pesar
Fr peser
It pesare
Pt pesar

**weight** *n* En
De Gewicht *(n)*
Es peso *(m)*
Fr poids *(m)*

It peso *(m)*
Pt peso *(m)*

**weighted average** En
De gewogener Durchschnitt *(m)*
Es media ponderada *(f)*
Fr moyenne pondérée *(f)*
It media ponderata *(f)*
Pt média ponderada *(f)*

**weight note** En
De Wiegeschein *(m)*
Es certificado de pesaje *(m)*
Fr note de poids *(f)*
It distinta pesi *(f)*
Pt certidão de peso *(f)*

**weight or measurement** En
De Mass oder Gewicht
Es peso o cubicaje
Fr poids ou mesure
It peso o volume
Pt peso ou medida

**weitere Auskunft** *(f)* De
En further information
Es más detalles *(m pl)*
Fr renseignements complémentaires *(m pl)*
It ulteriori informazioni *(f pl)*
Pt informação adicional *(f)*

**weitere Gründe** *(m pl)* De
En further reasons
Es rasones adicionales *(f pl)*
Fr raisons supplémentaires *(f pl)*
It ulteriori motivi *(m pl)*
Pt rasões adicionais *(f pl)*

**Weiterüberlegung** *(f) n* De
En further consideration
Es examen más detallado *(m)*
Fr examen plus attentif *(m)*
It esame più attento *(m)*
Pt consideração posterior mais detalhada *(f)*

**weiterverfolgen** *vb* De
En follow up
Es perseguir
Fr poursuivre
It seguitare
Pt perseguir

**Weltgesundheitsorganisation (WGO)** *(f) n* De
En World Health Organization (WHO)
Es Organización Mundial de la Salud (OMS) *(f)*
Fr Organisation Mondiale de la Santé (OMS) *(f)*
It Organizzazione Mondiale della Sanità (OMS) *(f)*
Pt Organização Mondial da Saúde (OMS) *(f)*

**Werbeberater** *(m)* De
En advertising consultant
Es consultor de publicidad *(m)*
Fr conseil en publicité *(m)*
It consulente di pubblicità *(m)*
Pt perito de publicidade *(m)*

**Werbebrief** *(m) n* De
En sales letter
Es carta de publicidad de ventas *(f)*
Fr lettre de publicité ventes *(f)*
It lettera di pubblicità vendite *(f)*
Pt carta de publicidade de vendas *(f)*

**Werbebüro** *(n) n* De
En advertising agency
Es agencia de publicidad *(f)*
Fr agence de publicité *(f)*
It agenzia pubblicitaria *(f)*
Pt agência de publicidade *(f)*

**Werbefeldzug** *(m) n* De
En advertising campaign
Es campaña publicitaria *(f)*
Fr campagne de publicité *(f)*
It campagna pubblicitaria *(f)*
Pt campanha publicitária *(f)*

**Werbekosten** *(pl) n* De
En advertising expenditure
Es gastos publicitarios *(m pl)*
Fr dépenses de publicité *(f pl)*
It spese di pubblicità *(f pl)*
Pt despesa com publicidade *(f)*

**Werbemittel** *(n) n* De
En advertising medium
Es medio de publicidad *(m)*
Fr support publicitaire *(m)*
It mezzo pubblicitario *(m)*
Pt meio publicitário *(m)*

**Werbeplan** *(m) n* De
En advertising schedule
Es plan de propaganda *(m)*
Fr programme des annonces *(m)*
It programma delle inserzioni *(m)*
Pt plano de campanha publicitária *(m)*

**Werbeschrift** *(f) n* De
En advertising brochure
Es folleto publicitario *(m)*
Fr prospectus publicitaire *(m)*
It opuscolo pubblicitario *(m)*
Pt folheto publicitário *(m)*

**Werbetarif** *(m) n* De
En advertising rates
Es tarifa para anuncios *(f)*
Fr tarifs de publicité *(m pl)*
It tariffa delle inserzioni *(f)*
Pt taxas de publicidade *(f)*

**Werbetext** *(m) n* De
En advertising copy
Es material publicitario *(m)*
Fr copie publicitaire *(f)*
It testo pubblicitario *(m)*
Pt texto de publicidade *(m)*

**Werbeträger** *(m pl) n* De
En media
Es medios de información *(m pl)*
Fr supports *(m pl)*
It canali d'informazione *(m pl)*
Pt meios de informação *(m pl)*

**Werbung** *(f) n* De
En publicity; advertising
Es publicidad *(f)*
Fr publicité *(f)*
It pubblicità *(f)*
Pt publicidade *(f)*

**Werkmeister** *(m) n* De
En head foreman
Es capataz jefe *(m)*
Fr chef d'atelier *(m)*
It capo officina *(m)*
Pt encarregado-chefe *(m)*

**Wert** *(m) n* De
En value
Es valor *(m)*
Fr valeur *(f)*

It valore *(m)*
Pt valor *(m)*

**Wertbestimmung** *(f) n* De
En valuation
Es valuación *(f)*
Fr évaluation *(f)*
It valutazione *(f)*
Pt avaliação *(f)*

**Wertpapiere** *(n pl) n* De
En stock; securities
Es títulos; valores *(m pl)*
Fr titres; valeurs *(m pl; f pl)*
It titoli; valori *(m pl)*
Pt títulos; valores *(m pl)*

**Wertsteigerung** *(f) n* De
En appreciation
Es subida *(f)*
Fr appréciation *(f)*
It aumento *(m)*
Pt aumento *(m)*

**wertvoll** *adj* De
En valuable
Es valioso
Fr de valeur
It di valore
Pt valioso

**Wertzuwachs** *(m) n* De
En increment
Es aumento; incremento *(m)*
Fr accroissement; plus-value *(m f)*
It incremento *(m)*
Pt aumento; incremento *(m)*

**Wettbewerb** *(m) n* De
En competition
Es competición *(f)*
Fr concurrence *(f)*
It concorrenza *(f)*
Pt competição *(f)*

**wetteifernd** *adj* De
En competitive
Es competidor
Fr compétitif
It in concorrenza
Pt competitivo

**wharf** *n* En
De Kai *(m)*
Es muelle *(m)*
Fr quai *(m)*

It   scalo *(m)*
Pt   cais *(m)*

**wharfage** *n* En
De   Kaigeld *(n)*
Es   muellaje *(m)*
Fr   quayage *(m)*
It   diritto di sosta *(m)*
Pt   atracagem *(m)*

**wholesaler** *n* En
De   Grosshändler; Grossist *(m)*
Es   mayorista *(m)*
Fr   grossiste *(m)*
It   grossista *(m)*
Pt   grossista *(m)*

**wholesale trade** En
De   Grosshandel *(m)*
Es   comercio al por mayor *(m)*
Fr   commerce en gros *(m)*
It   commercio all'ingrosso *(m)*
Pt   comércio por atacado *(m)*

**Widerruf** *(m) n* De
En   revocation
Es   revocación *(f)*
Fr   révocation *(f)*
It   revoca *(f)*
Pt   revogação *(f)*

**widerrufen** *vb* De
En   revoke
Es   revocar
Fr   révoquer
It   revocare
Pt   revogar

**widerstreitende Interessen** *(n pl)* De
En   conflict of interest
Es   pugna de intereses *(f)*
Fr   opposition d'intérêts *(f)*
It   conflitto d'interessi *(m)*
Pt   conflito de interesses *(m)*

**Wiederanschaffungskosten** *(pl) n* De
En   replacement cost
Es   coste de repuesto *(m)*
Fr   coût de remplacement *(m)*
It   costo di rimpiazzo *(m)*
Pt   custo de substituição *(m)*

**Wiederaufbau** *(m) n* De
En   reconstruction
Es   reconstrucción *(f)*
Fr   reconstruction *(f)*

It   ricostruzione *(f)*
Pt   reconstrução *(f)*

**Wiederausfuhr** *(f) n* De
En   re-exportation
Es   reexportación *(f)*
Fr   réexportation *(f)*
It   riesporto *(m)*
Pt   reexportação *(f)*

**wiederausführen** *vb* De
En   re-export
Es   reexportar
Fr   reexporter
It   riesportare
Pt   reexportar

**Wiederverkaufspreis** *(m) n* De
En   resale price
Es   precio de reventa *(m)*
Fr   prix de revente *(m)*
It   prezzo di rivendita *(m)*
Pt   preço de revenda *(m)*

**wiegen** *vb* De
En   weigh
Es   pesar
Fr   peser
It   pesare
Pt   pesar

**Wiegeschein** *(m) n* De
En   weight note
Es   certificado de pesaje *(m)*
Fr   note de poids *(f)*
It   distinta pesi *(f)*
Pt   certidão de peso *(f)*

**wildcat strike** En
De   wilder Streik *(m)*
Es   huelga espontánea *(f)*
Fr   grève sauvage *(f)*
It   sciopero selvaggio *(m)*
Pt   greve não oficializada *(f)*

**wilder Streik** *(m)* De
En   wildcat strike
Es   huelga espontánea *(f)*
Fr   grève sauvage *(f)*
It   sciopero selvaggio *(m)*
Pt   greve não oficializada *(f)*

**Willenserklärung** *(f) n* De
En   declaration of intent
Es   declaración de intención *(f)*
Fr   déclaration d'intention *(f)*

It   dichiarazione d'intenzione *(f)*
Pt   declaração de propósito *(f)*

**window display** En
De   Fensterauslegung *(f)*
Es   exhibición en vitrina *(f)*
Fr   étalage *(m)*
It   mostra in vetrina *(f)*
Pt   exposição de montra *(f)*

**window dressing** En
De   Schaufensterdekoration *(f)*
Es   preparación de escaparates *(f)*
Fr   art de l'étalage *(m)*
It   allestimento delle vetrine *(m)*
Pt   preparação de montras *(f)*

**window envelope** En
De   Fensterbriefumschlag *(m)*
Es   sobre de ventanilla *(m)*
Fr   enveloppe à fenêtre *(f)*
It   busta con finestra *(f)*
Pt   envelope de endereço exposto *(m)*

**window glass** En
De   Fensterglas *(n)*
Es   cristal de ventana *(m)*
Fr   verre à vitres *(m)*
It   vetro da finestre *(m)*
Pt   vidro de montra *(m)*

**wind up a business** En
De   ein Unternehmen abwickeln
Es   liquidar un negocio
Fr   liquider une entreprise
It   liquidare una azienda
Pt   liquidar um negócio

**wirklicher Totalverlust** *(m)* De
En   actual total loss
Es   pérdida total efectiva *(f)*
Fr   perte totale effective *(f)*
It   perdita totale assoluta *(f)*
Pt   perda total efectiva *(f)*

**wirksam** *adj* De
En   effective; operative
Es   efectivo; eficaz
Fr   effectif; actif
It   efficace; operativo
Pt   efectivo; eficaz

631

**Wirksamkeit** (f) n De
En effectiveness
Es eficacia (f)
Fr efficacité (f)
It efficacia (f)
Pt eficácia (f)

**wirksam werden** De
En become operative
Es entrar en vigor
Fr entrer en vigueur
It entrare in vigore
Pt entrar em vigor

**Wirtschaft** (f) n De
En (the) economy
Es economía (f)
Fr économie (f)
It economia (f)
Pt economia (f)

**(die) Wirtschaft neu beleben** De
En reflate the economy
Es reanimar la economía
Fr ranimer l'économie
It reflaziare l'economia
Pt reflacionar a ecónomia

**wirtschaftlich** adj De
En economic
Es económico
Fr économique
It economico
Pt económico

**wirtschaftliche Sanktionen** (f pl) De
En economic sanctions
Es sanciones económicas (f pl)
Fr sanctions économiques (f pl)
It sanzioni economiche (f pl)
Pt sanções económicas (f pl)

**Wirtschaftlichkeit** (f) n De
En cost-effectiveness
Es efectividad de coste (f)
Fr coût et efficacité
It rendimento della spesa (m)
Pt eficiência relativa ao custo (f)

**Wirtschaftskrise** (f) n De
En depression
Es crisis económica (f)
Fr crise économique (f)
It crisi (f)
Pt depressão (f)

**Wirtschaftsprüfer** (m) n De
En qualified accountant
Es contador habilitado (m)
Fr expert comptable (m)
It ragioniere diplomato (m)
Pt guarda-livros diplomado (m)

**Wirtschaftsspionage** (f) n De
En industrial espionage
Es espionaje industrial (m)
Fr espionage industriel (m)
It spionaggio industriale (m)
Pt espionagem industrial (m)

**Wirtschaftswachstum** (m) n De
En economic growth
Es crecimiento económico (m)
Fr croissance économique (f)
It sviluppo economico (m)
Pt crescimento económico (m)

**with average** (WA) En
De havariert
Es con avería
Fr avarié
It con avaria
Pt com avaria

**without prejudice** En
Am not binding
De ohne Verbindlichkeit
Es sin prejuicio
Fr sous toutes réserves
It senza pregiudizio
Pt sem prejuízo

**without recourse** En
De ohne Rückgriff
Es sin recurso
Fr sans droit de recours
It senza ricorso
Pt sem recurso

**with-profits policy** En
Am participating policy
De Police mit Gewinnberechtigung (f)
Es póliza con beneficios (f)
Fr police avec participation aux bénéfices (f)
It polizza con profitti (f)
Pt apólice com participação nos lucros (f)

**with recourse** En
De mit Rückgriff
Es con recurso
Fr avec droit de recours
It con ricorso
Pt com recurso

**witness** n En
De Zeuge (m)
Es testigo (m)
Fr témoin (m)
It testimone (m)
Pt testemunha (f)

**Wohlstand** (m) n De
En wealth
Es riqueza (f)
Fr richesse (f)
It ricchezza (f)
Pt riqueza (f)

**Wohnungsgebäude** (n) n De
En block of flats
Am apartment house
Es bloque de pisos (m)
Fr immeuble (m)
It fabbricato di appartamenti (m)
Pt edifício de andares (m)

**Wohnungsversicherung** (f) n De
En household insurance
Es seguro de casa (m)
Fr assurance ménagère (f)
It assicurazione domestica (f)
Pt seguro de casa (m)

**work** n En
De Arbeit (f)
Es trabajo (m)
Fr travail (m)
It lavoro (m)
Pt trabalho (m)

**worker** n En
De Arbeiter (m)
Es trabajador (m)
Fr ouvrier (m)
It lavoratore (m)
Pt trabalhador (m)

**work force** En
De Belegschaft (f)
Es masa obrera (f)

Fr effectifs *(m pl)*
It massa lavoratrice *(f)*
Pt massa trabalhadora *(f)*


**working capital** En
De Betriebskapital *(n)*
Es capital circulante *(m)*
Fr fonds de roulement *(m pl)*
It capitale d'esercizio *(m)*
Pt capital para movimentação *(m)*


**working conditions** En
De Arbeitsbedingungen *(f pl)*
Es condiciones de trabajo *(f pl)*
Fr conditions de travail *(f pl)*
It condizioni di lavoro *(f pl)*
Pt condições de trabalho *(f pl)*


**working day** En
De Arbeitstag *(m)*
Es día laborable *(m)*
Fr jour ouvrable *(m)*
It giornata lavorativa *(f)*
Pt dia de trabalho *(m)*


**working partner** En
De aktiver Teilhaber *(m)*
Es socio activo *(m)*
Fr associé actif *(m)*
It socio attivo *(m)*
Pt sócio actuante *(m)*


**working week** En
De Arbeitswoche *(f)*
Es semana laboral *(f)*
Fr semaine de travail *(f)*
It settimana lavorativa *(f)*
Pt semana de trabalho *(f)*


**work in progress** En
Am work in process
De Arbeit in der Ausführung *(f)*
Es trabajo en curso *(m)*
Fr travaux en cours *(m pl)*
It lavoro in corso *(m)*
Pt trabalho em curso *(m)*


**work on hand** En
De in Ausführung begriffene Arbeit *(f)*
Es trabajo en curso *(m)*
Fr travail en cours *(m)*
It lavoro in corso *(m)*
Pt trabalho em mão *(m)*


**work permit** En
De Arbeitserlaubnis *(n)*
Es permiso de trabajo *(m)*
Fr permis de travail *(m)*
It permesso di lavoro *(m)*
Pt carta de trabalho *(f)*


**work study** En
De Arbeitsstudium *(n)*
Es estudio del trabajo *(m)*
Fr étude du travail *(f)*
It studio di lavoro *(m)*
Pt estudo sobre trabalho *(m)*


**World Health Organization** (WHO) En
De Weltgesundheitsorganisation (WGO) *(f)*
Es Organización Mundial de la Salud (OMS) *(f)*
Fr Organisation Mondiale de la Santé (OMS) *(f)*
It Organizzazione Mondiale della Sanità (OMS) *(f)*
Pt Organização Mundial da Saúde (OMS) *(f)*


**writ** *n* En
De Vorladung *(f)*
Es auto; orden *(m f)*
Fr assignation *(f)*
It citazione *(f)*
Pt citação; ordem *(f m)*


**write off a debt** En
De eine Schuld erlassen
Es cancelar una deuda
Fr amortir une créance
It cancellare un credito
Pt cancelar um débito


**write off a loss** En
De einen Verlust abschreiben
Es cancelar una pérdida
Fr amortir une perte
It cancellare una perdita
Pt anular um prejuízo


**Wucher** *(m) n* De
En usury
Es usura *(f)*
Fr usure *(f)*
It usura *(f)*
Pt usura *(f)*


# Y

**yacimiento aurífero** *(m)* Es
De Goldgrube *(f)*
En gold fields
Fr régions aurifères *(f pl)*
It terreni auriferi *(m pl)*
Pt jazigos de ouro *(m pl)*


**yacimiento de carbón** *(m)* Es
De Kohlenrevier *(n)*
En coal field
Fr bassin houiller *(m)*
It bacino carbonifero *(m)*
Pt jazigo de carvão *(m)*


**yacimiento de petróleo** *(m)* Es
De Ölfeld *(n)*
En oilfield
Fr gisement petrolifère *(m)*
It giacimento petrolifero *(m)*
Pt jazigo de petróleo *(m)*


**yesterday** *adv* En
De gestern
Es ayer
Fr hier
It ieri
Pt ontem


**yield** (on capital, etc.) *n* En
De Rendite *(f)*
Es rédito *(m)*
Fr revenu *(m)*
It reddito *(m)*
Pt rédito *(m)*


# Z

**Zahl** *(f) n* De
En number; figure
Es número; cifra *(m f)*
Fr nombre; chiffre *(m)*
It numero; cifra *(m f)*
Pt número *(m)*


**zahlbar** *adj* De
En payable
Es pagadero; pagable
Fr payable; remboursable
It pagabile
Pt pagável

**zahlbar bei Sicht** De
En  payable at sight
Es  pagadero a la vista
Fr  payable à vue
It  pagabile a vista
Pt  pagável à vista

**zahlbar bei Vorlage** De
En  payable on demand
Es  pagadero a presentación
Fr  payable sur demande
It  pagabile a vista
Pt  pagável à vista

**zahlen** vb De
En  pay
Es  pagar
Fr  payer
It  pagare
Pt  pagar

**Zahlmeister** (m) n De
En  purser
Es  contador de navio (m)
Fr  commissaire de la marine
    (m)
It  commissario di bordo (m)
Pt  commissário de bordo (m)

**Zahltag** (m) n De
En  pay day
Es  día de pago (m)
Fr  jour de paiement (m)
It  giorno di paga (m)
Pt  dia de recebimento (m)

**Zahlung** (f) n De
En  payment
Es  pago (m)
Fr  paiement (m)
It  pagamento (m)
Pt  pagamento (m)

**Zahlungsaufschub** (m) n De
En  moratorium
Es  moratorio (m)
Fr  moratoire (m)
It  moratoria (f)
Pt  moratória (f)

**Zahlungsbedingungen** (f pl) n
    De
En  payment terms
Es  condiciones de pago (f pl)
Fr  conditions de paiement (f
    pl)
It  condizioni di pagamento (f
    pl)

Pt  condições de pagamento (f
    pl)

**Zahlungsberechtigte(r)** (m) n
    De
En  payee
Es  beneficiario (m)
Fr  bénéficiaire (m)
It  beneficiario (m)
Pt  beneficiário (m)

**Zahlungsbilanz** (f) n De
En  balance of payments
Es  balanza de pagos (f)
Fr  balance des paiements (f)
It  bilancia dei pagamenti (f)
Pt  balança de pagamentos (f)

**zahlungsfähig** adj De
En  solvent
Es  solvente
Fr  solvable
It  solvibile
Pt  solvente

**zahlungsunfähig** adj De
En  insolvent
Es  insolvente
Fr  insolvable
It  insolvente
Pt  insolvente

**Zahlungsunfähigkeit** (f) n De
En  insolvency
Es  insolvencia; quiebra (f)
Fr  faillite; déconfiture (f)
It  insolvenza (f)
Pt  insolvência (f)

**Zahlung zum vollen Ausgleich**
    (f) De
En  payment in full discharge
Es  pago de liberación (m)
Fr  paiement libératoire (m)
It  pagamento a completa
    tacitazione (m)
Pt  pagamento contra execu-
    ção completa (m)

**zavorra** (f) n It
De  Ballast (m)
En  ballast
Es  lastre (m)
Fr  lest (m)
Pt  lastro (m)

**zecca** (f) n It
De  Münze (f)
En  mint
Es  casa de la moneda (f)
Fr  la Monnaie
Pt  casa da moeda (f)

**Zedent** (m) n De
En  transferor
Es  cesionista (m)
Fr  cédant (m)
It  cedente (m)
Pt  cessionista (m)

**Zehnerklub** (m) n De
En  Group of Ten (Paris Club)
Es  Grupo de los Diez (m)
Fr  Groupe des Dix (m)
It  Gruppo dei Dieci (m)
Pt  Grupo dos Dez (m)

**Zeichner** (m) n De
En  designer
Es  diseñador (m)
Fr  dessinateur (m)
It  disegnatore (m)
Pt  desenhador (m)

**Zeichnung** (f) n De
En  design
Es  diseño (m)
Fr  dessein (m)
It  disegno (m)
Pt  desenho (f)

**Zeichnung** (einer Anleihe) (f) n
    De
En  subscription
Es  suscripción (f)
Fr  souscription (f)
It  sottoscrizione (f)
Pt  subscrição (f)

**Zeitcharter** (f) n De
En  time charter
Es  fletamento de tiempo (m)
Fr  affrètement à temps (m)
It  contratto di noleggio a
    tempo (m)
Pt  fretamento de tempo (m)

**Zeitgeschäfte** (n pl) n De
En  forward dealings
Es  negociaciones a término (f
    pl)
Fr  opérations à terme (f pl)
It  operazioni a termine (f pl)

Pt transacções adiantadas (f pl)

**Zentralheizung** (f) n De
En central heating
Es calefacción central (f)
Fr chauffage central (m)
It riscaldamento centrale (m)
Pt aquecimento central (m)

**Zentralisierung** (f) n De
En centralization
Es centralización (f)
Fr centralisation (f)
It centralizzazione (f)
Pt centralização (f)

**zerbrechlich** adj De
En fragile
Es frágil
Fr fragile
It fragile
Pt frágil

**zero balance** Am
En nil balance
De Nullsaldo (m)
Es saldo nulo (m)
Fr solde nul (m)
It saldo nullo (m)
Pt saldo nulo (m)

**Zessionär** (m) n De
En transferee; assignee
Es cesionario (m)
Fr cessionnaire (m)
It cessionario (m)
Pt cessionário (m)

**Zeuge** (m) n De
En witness
Es testigo (m)
Fr témoin (m)
It testimone (m)
Pt testemunha (f)

**Ziel** (n) n De
En goal; target
Es meta; objetivo (f m)
Fr bout; but (m)
It scopo; traguardo (m)
Pt meta; objectivo (f m)

**Zinsen** (m pl) n De
En interest
Es interés (m)
Fr intérêt; prime (m f)

It interesse (m)
Pt juro (m)

**Zinsezinsen** (m pl) n De
En compound interest
Es interés compuesto (m)
Fr intérêts composés (m pl)
It interesse composto (m)
Pt juro composto (m)

**Zinsfuss** (m) n De
En interest rate
Es tipo de interés (m)
Fr taux d'intérêt (m)
It tasso d'interesse (m)
Pt taxa de juro (f)

**Zinssatz** (m) n De
En interest rate
Es tipo de interés (m)
Fr taux d'intérêt (m)
It tasso d'interesse (m)
Pt taxa de juro (f)

**zip code** Am
En postcode
De Postleitzahl (f)
Es designación postal (f)
Fr indicatif postal (m)
It codice postale (m)
Pt designação postal (f)

**Zoll** (m) n De
En customs; customs duty
Es aduana; derechos de aduanas (f; m pl)
Fr douane; droit de douane (f m)
It dogana; diritto doganale (f m)
Pt alfândega; direitos alfandegários (f; m pl)

**Zollabfertigung** (f) n De
En customs clearance
Es paso de aduanas (f)
Fr dédouanement (m)
It sdoganamento (m)
Pt despacho alfandegário (m)

**Zollabkommen** (n) n De
En tariff agreement
Es acuerdo tarifario (m)
Fr accord tarifaire (m)
It accordo tariffario (m)
Pt acordo de tarifas (m)

**zollamtliche Untersuchung** (f) De
En customs examination
Es control de aduanas (m)
Fr visite douanière (f)
It visita doganale (f)
Pt verificação alfandegária (f)

**Zolleinfuhrschein** (m) n De
En bill of entry
Es declaración de aduana (f)
Fr déclaration en douane (f)
It bolletta di entrata (f)
Pt declaração alfandegária (f)

**Zollerklärung** (f) n De
En customs declaration
Es declaración de aduana (f)
Fr déclaration en douane (f)
It dichiarazione doganale (f)
Pt declaração alfandegária (f)

**zollfreie Einfuhr** (f) De
En duty-free admission
Es admisión libre de impuestos (f)
Fr admission en franchise (f)
It ammissione in franchigia doganale (f)
Pt admissão livre de impostos (f)

**Zollrückvergütung** (f) n De
En (customs) drawback
Es reembolso de derechos de aduana (m)
Fr remboursement des droits d'importation (m)
It rimborso d'esportazione (m)
Pt reimbolso de direitos alfandegários (m)

**Zollschranke** (f) n De
En customs barrier
Es barrera aduanera (f)
Fr barrière douanière (f)
It barriera doganale (f)
Pt barreira alfandegária (f)

**Zollunion** (f) n De
En customs union
Es unión aduanera (f)
Fr union douanière (f)
It unione doganale (f)
Pt união aduaneira (f)

**zona** (f) n Es, It, Pt
De Zone (f)
En zone
Fr zone (f)

**zona de desarrollo** (f) Es
De Ortsplanungsgebiet (n)
En development area
Fr zone de développement (f)
It zona di sviluppo (f)
Pt zona de desenvolvimento
(f)

**zona de desenvolvimento** (f)
Pt
De Ortsplanungsgebiet (n)
En development area
Es zona de desarrollo (f)
Fr zone de développement (f)
It zona di sviluppo (f)

**zona degli acquisti** (f) It
De Geschäftszentrum (n)
En shopping centre
Es centro de negocios (m)
Fr centre commercial (m)
Pt centro de comércio (m)

**zona de la esterlina** (f) Es
De Sterlinggebiet (n)
En sterling area
Fr zone sterling (f)
It zona della sterlina (f)
Pt zona esterlina (f)

**zona della sterlina** (f) It
De Sterlinggebiet (n)
En sterling area
Es zona de la esterlina (f)
Fr zone sterling (f)
Pt zona esterlina (f)

**zona deprimida** (f) Pt
De Notstandsgebiet (n)
En distressed area
Es región deprimida (f)
Fr région déprimée (f)
It area indigente (f)

**zona di sviluppo** (f) It
De Ortsplanungsgebiet (n)
En development area
Es zona de desarrollo (f)
Fr zone de développement (f)
Pt zona de desenvolvimento
(f)

**zona esterlina** (f) Pt
De Sterlinggebiet (n)
En sterling area
Es zona de la esterlina (f)
Fr zone sterling (f)
It zona della sterlina (f)

**Zona Europea de Comercio
Libre** (f) Es
De Europäische Freihandels-
zone (f)
En European Free Trade Area
(EFTA)
Fr Zone Européenne de Libre
Échange (f)
It Zona Europea di Libero
Scambio (f)
Pt Zona Europeia de Comér-
cio Livre (f)

**Zona Europea di Libero Scam-
bio** (f) It
De Europäische Freihandels-
zone (f)
En European Free Trade Area
(EFTA)
Es Zona Europea de Comercio
Libre (f)
Fr Zone Européenne de Libre
Échange (f)
Pt Zona Europeia de Comér-
cio Livre (f)

**Zona Europeia de Comércio
Livre** (f) Pt
De Europäische Freihandels-
zone (f)
En European Free Trade Area
(EFTA)
Es Zona Europea de Comercio
Libre (f)
Fr Zone Européenne de Libre
Échange (f)
It Zona Europea di Libero
Scambio (f)

**zona monetaria** (f) Es, It
De Währungsgebiet (n)
En currency area
Fr zone monétaire (f)
Pt zona monetária (f)

**zona monetária** (f) Pt
De Währungsgebiet (n)
En currency area
Es zona monetaria (f)
Fr zone monétaire (f)
It zona monetaria (f)

**zone** n En, Fr (f)
De Zone (f)
Es zona (f)
It zona (f)
Pt zona (f)

**Zone** (f) n De
En zone
Es zona (f)
Fr zone (f)
It zona (f)
Pt zona (f)

**zone de développement** (f) Fr
De Ortsplanungsgebiet (n)
En development area
Es zona de desarrollo (f)
It zona di sviluppo (f)
Pt zona de desenvolvimento
(f)

**Zone Européenne de Libre
Échange** (f) Fr
De Europäische Freihandels-
zone (f)
En European Free Trade Area
(EFTA)
Es Zona Europea de Comercio
Libre (f)
It Zona Europea di Libero
Scambio (f)
Pt Zona Europeia de Comér-
cio Livre (f)

**zone monétaire** (f) Fr
De Währungsgebiet (n)
En currency area
Es zona monetaria (f)
It zona monetaria (f)
Pt zona monetária (f)

**zone sterling** (f) Fr
De Sterlinggebiet (n)
En sterling area
Es zona de la esterlina (f)
It zona della sterlina (f)
Pt zona esterlina (f)

**Zufriedenstellung** (f) n De
En satisfaction
Es satisfacción (f)
Fr satisfaction (f)
It soddisfazione (f)
Pt satisfação (f)

**Zuführung** (f) n De
En appropriation
Es apropiación (f)

Fr affectation *(f)*
It stanziamento *(m)*
Pt apropriação *(f)*

**Zugang** *(m)* n De
En accrual
Es incremento *(m)*
Fr augmentation *(f)*
It incremento *(m)*
Pt acréscimo *(m)*

**zukünftige Lieferung** *(f)* De
En future delivery
Es futura entrega *(f)*
Fr livraison à terme *(f)*
It consegna a termine *(f)*
Pt futura remessa ou entrega *(f)*

**zurückstellen** *vb* De
En defer
Es aplazar
Fr différer; ajourner
It differire
Pt adiar

**zurücktreten** *vb* De
En resign
Es dimitir
Fr se démettre
It dimettersi
Pt demitir-se

**Zusammenarbeit** *(f)* n De
En cooperation
Es cooperación *(f)*
Fr coopération *(f)*
It cooperazione *(f)*
Pt cooperação *(f)*

**Zuschlagsgebühr** *(f)* n De
En extra charge
Es suplemento *(m)*
Fr supplément *(m)*
It spesa supplementare *(f)*
Pt encargo suplementar *(m)*

**Zuschlagssteuer** *(f)* n De
En surtax
Es sobretasa *(f)*
Fr surtaxe *(f)*
It sopratassa *(f)*
Pt sobretaxa *(f)*

**zuteilen** *vb* De
En apportion
Es repartir
Fr répartir

It ripartire
Pt atribuir

**zu treuen Händen halten** De
En hold in trust
Es quardar in fideicomiso
Fr tenir par fidéicommis
It tenere in fedecommesso
Pt reter em custódia

**zuverlässig** *adj* De
En reliable
Es digno de confianza
Fr digne de confiance
It fidato; attendibile
Pt digno de confiança

**Zwang** *(m)* n De
En duress
Es compulsión *(f)*
Fr contrainte *(f)*
It costrizione *(f)*
Pt coerção *(f)*

**Zwangs-** De
En forced
Es forzado
Fr forcé
It forzato
Pt forçado

**Zwangsliquidation** *(f)* n De
En compulsory winding-up
Am forced liquidation
Es liquidación forzosa *(f)*
Fr liquidation forcée *(f)*
It liquidazione forzata *(f)*
Pt liquidação forçada *(f)*

**Zwangsverkauf** *(m)* n De
En forced sale
Es venta forzosa *(f)*
Fr vente forcée *(f)*
It vendita sforzosa *(f)*
Pt venda forçada *(f)*

**Zwangsvollstreckung** *(f)* n De
En foreclosure
Es venta por juicio hipotecario *(f)*
Fr vente de l'immeuble hypothéqué *(f)*
It vendita per giudizio ipotecario *(f)*
Pt execução judicial a uma hipoteca *(f)*

**Zweckforschung** *(f)* n De
En research and development (R & D)
Es investigación y desarrollo
Fr recherche industrielle *(f)*
It studi e sviluppi
Pt investigação e desenvolvimento

**zweifelhafte Forderung** *(f)* De
En doubtful debt
Es deuda de pago dudoso *(f)*
Fr créance douteuse *(f)*
It credito dubbio *(m)*
Pt dívida duvidosa *(f)*

**Zweigbüro** *(n)* n De
En branch office
Es sucursal *(f)*
Fr succursale *(f)*
It sucursale *(f)*
Pt sucursal *(f)*

**Zwischenbilanz** *(f)* n De
En interim financial statement
Es extracto financiero provisional *(m)*
Fr bilan intérimaire *(m)*
It rendiconto finanziario provvisorio *(m)*
Pt extracto financeiro interino *(m)*

**Zwischenhändler** *(m)* n De
En middle man
Es intermediario *(m)*
Fr intermédiaire *(f)*
It intermediario *(m)*
Pt intermediário *(m)*

**zwischenmenschliche Beziehungen** *(f pl)* De
En human relations
Es relaciones humanas *(f pl)*
Fr relations humaines *(f pl)*
It relazioni umane *(f pl)*
Pt relações humanas *(f pl)*